# HORTICULTURAL SOILS

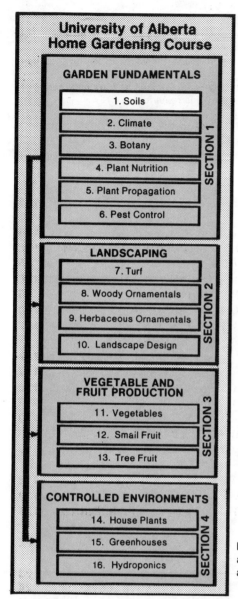

## University of Alberta Home Gardening Course

### GARDEN FUNDAMENTALS
1. Soils
2. Climate
3. Botany
4. Plant Nutrition
5. Plant Propagation
6. Pest Control

SECTION 1

### LANDSCAPING
7. Turf
8. Woody Ornamentals
9. Herbaceous Ornamentals
10. Landscape Design

SECTION 2

### VEGETABLE AND FRUIT PRODUCTION
11. Vegetables
12. Small Fruit
13. Tree Fruit

SECTION 3

### CONTROLLED ENVIRONMENTS
14. House Plants
15. Greenhouses
16. Hydroponics

SECTION 4

# SELF-STUDY LESSON FEATURES

Self-study is an educational approach which allows you to study a subject where and when you want. The course is designed to allow you to study efficiently and incorporates the following features:

**OBJECTIVES** — are found at the beginning of each lesson and allow you to determine what you can expect to learn in the lesson.

**LESSON MATERIAL** — is logically organized and broken down into fundamental components by ordered headings to assist you to comprehend the subject.

**REFERENCING** — between lessons and within lessons allows you to integrate course material.

The last two digits of the page number identify the page and the digits preceding these identify the lesson number (eg., 107: Lesson 1, page 7 or 1227: Lesson 12, page 27).

Referencing:

> sections within the same lesson (eg., see OSMOSIS)

> sections in other lessons (eg., see Botany lesson, OSMOSIS)

> figures and tables (eg., see Figure 7-3)

**FIGURES AND TABLES** — are found in abundance throughout the lessons and are designed to convey useful information in an easy to understand form.

**SIDEBARS** — are those areas in the lesson which are boxed and toned. They present information supplementary to the core content of the lesson.

**PRACTICAL PROJECTS** — are integrated within the lesson material and are included to allow you to apply principles and practices.

**SELF-CHECK QUIZ** — is provided at the end of each lesson and allows you to test your comprehension of the lesson material. Answers to the questions and references to the sections dealing with the questions are provided in the answer section. You should review any questions that you are unable to answer.

**GLOSSARY** — is provided at the end of each lesson and alphabetically lists the definitions of key concepts and terms.

**RESOURCE MATERIALS** — are provided at the end of each lesson and comprise a list of recommended learning materials for further study of the subject. Also included are author's comments on the potential application of each publication.

**INDEX** — alphabetically lists useful topics and their location within the lesson.

---

© 1986 University of Alberta Faculty of Extension

**Written by: John Harapiak**

Technical Reviewers:        Don Laverty    Pam North

THE PRODUCTION TEAM

| | |
|---|---|
| Managing Editor | Thom Shaw |
| Editor | Frank Procter |
| Production Coordinator | Frank Procter |
| Graphic Artist | Melanie Eastley Harbourne |
| Data Entry | Joan Geisterfer |

ISBN 0-88864-852-9

(Book 1, Lesson 1)

Published by the University of Alberta
Faculty of Extension Corbett Hall
Edmonton, Alberta, T6G 2G4

## LEARNING OBJECTIVES

After completing this lesson, the student should be able to:

1. Understand how soils are formed.
2. Identify the components of soil.
3. Understand how the texture of a soil influences its suitability for gardening.
4. Determine the role organic matter plays in creating a suitable garden soil.
5. Understand the role of soil water and soil air in creating a productive garden soil.
6. Recognize the importance of soil testing in identifying and overcoming deficiencies in soil.
7. Identify methods that can be used to improve garden soils.
8. Appreciate the uniqueness of soils and the importance of maintaining this precious resource.

## TABLE OF CONTENTS

## WHAT IS SOIL?

Basically, soil is the outer portion of the earth's crust that provides a medium for plant growth. Soils physically support plants and act as reservoirs for the water and nutrients needed to sustain plant growth and development. This seemingly insignificant segment of the earth's crust is extremely important to the soil-plant-animal food chain. Without soil, there would be no plants; without plants, there would be no food; without food, animals could not survive. Mankind is clearly very dependent on the maintenance of the earth's thin layer of soil.

Soil forms the very basis of man's existence on earth. In fact, the earliest of the great civilizations were founded on pockets of naturally fertile soils. Today, the productive partnership between the farmer and his land forms the very essence of our complex social structure. Life on earth would be quite different if we spent all our time in gathering the food we require to feed ourselves and our families. Today, the efforts of one farmer can produce enough food to easily feed another 70 people.

Soils are extremely complex and some researchers can spend a lifetime attempting to provide a better understanding of one specific aspect of soil behaviour (e.g., characterizing the behaviour of one specific portion of the soil organic matter pool). However, the purpose of this lesson is not to deal with all of the complexities of soil and its behaviour. Rather, it is to provide the home gardener with sufficient background knowledge to gain a better understanding of the uniqueness of soil and its limitations, as well as methods that can be employed for improving soils so that they are made more productive and the efforts of the home gardener made more rewarding.

## HOW SOILS ARE FORMED

Soil is a naturally occurring product of the environment. In many respects, the soil that forms in a given region is a distinctive fingerprint of the soil forming conditions that were active in that area. To the trained soils specialist, an examination of the soil reveals a great deal about the climate and the vegetation that was prevalent in the region.

The development of soils is a long-term process, starting with native mineral materials and involving both physical and chemical weathering, as well as biological activity. Key soil forming factors are:

- **Parent Material** — the material from which the soils were formed.

- **Climate** — temperature and water supply.

- **Vegetation** — type of plants that normally grow in the region, as well as the associated chemical, physical, and microbial processes involved in the decomposition of the plant residues.

- **Topography** — shape and position of land surfaces.

- **Time** — period of time during which the parent materials have been subjected to the processes involved in soil formation.

## PARENT MATERIALS

In many parts of the world, soils formed from the weathering of the original bedrock. On the Canadian prairies, most of the parent materials have been modified and transported by some action associated with glaciation. Materials transported by the movement of glaciers are termed **glacial**. Where water was the transporting agent, the parent materials are referred to as **alluvial** (stream deposited), **marine** (sea deposited), or **lacustrine** (lake deposited). Wind deposited materials are called **aeolian**. Materials moved as a result of gravity, as is the case at the base of a mountain slope, are called **colluvial**.

The majority of prairie soils are formed on glacial parent materials (usually referred to as **glacial till**). These soils are typically associated with a rolling topography and are (usually) somewhat stoney. Problem soils in the prairie region are usually associated with glacially modified marine deposits. The best agricultural soils are associated with the lacustrine deposits that settled out of fresh water lakes formed from glacial melt waters. These soils are fairly level and relatively stone-free.

## SOIL ZONES

In the three prairie provinces, the varying degree to which the different soil forming processes have been active has resulted in the formation of several broad soil zones. These soil zones are categorized on the basis of several characteristics, including surface color (see Figure 1-1).

Travelling across the various soil zones reveals that climate is one of the most influential of the soil forming factors. To a large extent, climate determines the type and the amount of native vegetation that grew in a region over the 10,000 to 13,000 year period during which it is estimated that prairie soils have been developing. Young soils (e.g., those that may have been subjected to erosion) are poorly developed because the regional soil forming factors have not had an opportunity to be fully expressed.

Under the lower rainfall and the higher temperatures of the more southern regions of the prairies, the sparse, short grasses dominated the landscape. As a result, the relatively shallow, low organic matter containing brown soils of the arid southern prairies developed. Proceeding northward, moisture conditions improve somewhat. The more dense stands of short grasses of the dark brown soil zone resulted in the formation of soils that are slightly deeper and higher in organic matter content. The next soil zone consists of the black soils that contain the highest organic matter content. These soils are generally the deepest and the most productive of the prairie soils. Black soils formed under a mixed prairie type of vegetation (i.e., mixture of tall grasses, shrubs, and aspen groves). The reduced temperatures and improved moisture conditions of the more northern areas favored the growth of heavy and continuous stands of trees (such as poplar and spruce) rather than grasses. Under forested conditions, a different form of organic matter decomposition resulted in the formation of degraded or grey soils that are low in organic matter content. Grey soils have the least desirable physical characteristics for the production of many common crops.

Within a given soil zone, climatic conditions tend to be similar, but not necessarily identical. For example, a slightly lower rainfall within a given soil

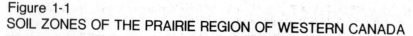

Figure 1-1
## SOIL ZONES OF THE PRAIRIE REGION OF WESTERN CANADA

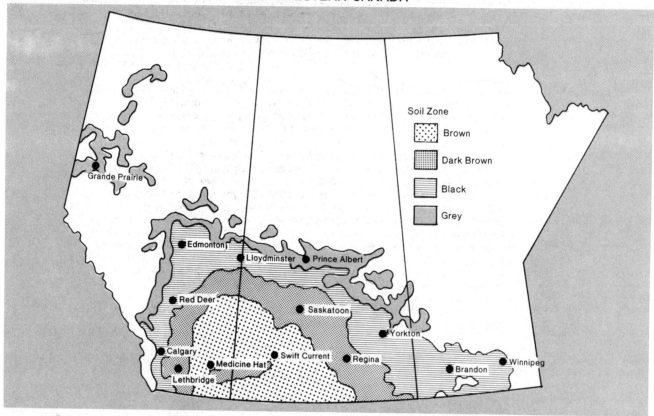

zone can be balanced by fewer hot, drying winds. Therefore, a reduced evaporative demand on soil stored moisture can result in very similar vegetation and soils, although the regions may be quite widely separated and experience significantly different precipitation patterns. For example, the soils of the Lloydminster region are classed as black soils although this region routinely receives less rainfall than the Olds, Melfort, and Winnipeg regions. However, the lower rainfall of the Lloydminster region is compensated for by lower temperatures and a reduced frequency of hot, drying winds, resulting in more efficient soil moisture utilization.

Soils can also differ a great deal within a relatively short distance as a result of the influence of topography (i.e., slope and aspect). For example, in the dark brown soil zone, the north-facing slopes of a river valley or a knoll often supports much more vegetation than the corresponding warmer, south-facing slopes that absorb much more of the energy from the sun and tend to dry out more rapidly. As a result, the soils on the south-facing slope more closely

resemble those of the more arid brown soil zone, while the soils associated with the north-facing slopes may more closely resemble those of the black soil zone, despite the fact that both slopes receive equal amounts of rainfall.

## ZONAL AND AZONAL SOILS

Soils that reflect the normal, regional soil forming factors (i.e., predominantly climate and its associated natural vegetative cover) are referred to as **zonal** soils. If some other soil forming factors are dominant (e.g., parent materials with a high sodium and/or salt content), then the influence of the regional climate in soil development cannot be fully expressed. These are referred to as **azonal** soils. Azonal soils usually tend to be the unproductive, problem soils of the prairie region.

## SOIL CLASSIFICATION

Soil is a natural body that consists of various layers or horizons that differ in appearance and composition from the underlying material. The arrangement of soil layers is called the soil profile (see

SOIL PROFILES), and the recognition of different profiles forms the basis of modern soil classification and mapping (see Figure 1-1).

The most important agricultural soils located in the three prairie provinces are those zonal soils that formed under prairie grassland vegetation or in the parkland region. Typically, the surface layer of these soils are enriched in organic matter. The subsoils of these soils feature good structure and unrestricted internal drainage. These soils are classified as **chernozemic**.

The zonal soils associated with the forested region are characterized by a leached, acidic, poorly structured, low organic matter containing surface soil that is low in natural fertility. The associated subsoil is quite compact and enriched in clay content. These soils are classified as **luvisolic**.

The most important azonal soils in the prairie region are associated with parent materials that are strongly alkaline in reaction (pH values of 8.5-9.0 or more) and contain excessive amounts of sodium based salts. The subsoil can be extremely compact, resulting in very poor root penetration. Crop growth on these soils is often extremely variable. These soils are classified as **solonetzic** and should be avoided for gardening purposes.

Azonal soils that are poorly developed due to erosion or the presence of excessive amounts of salts in the parent material are classified as **regosolic**. Soils whose development is strongly influenced by poor internal drainage are classified as **gleysolic**.

Many parts of the prairies are plagued by a short frost-free season and/or less than desirable soils for gardening. Although the application of amendments (see IMPROVING SOIL STRUCTURE) to improve the quality of a garden soil can be considered for a home garden, such considerations are usually prohibitively expensive for a commercial gardening operation. Therefore, initial selection of a suitable location is of utmost importance. It is strongly recommended

that anyone considering gardening on a large (commercial) scale should visit their regional agricultural extension office to obtain the appropriate soil and climatic maps to determine if the location selected is suitable for such an enterprise.

## SOIL PROFILES

A vertical cross-section through a soil exposes a layered pattern that is somewhat unique to the types of soils that developed in a given area. This cross-section is called a **profile** and the individual layers are referred to as **horizons**. Most soils have three major horizons that can easily be detected. These soil horizons can be differentiated on the basis of color and structural characteristics, as well as physical and chemical properties. Figure 1-2 shows typical cross-sections of the major zonal soils that developed in the prairie region. Soil profiles vary greatly in depth, but frequently extend to about 1 m (3 ft).

The uppermost horizon includes the topsoil and is referred to as the **A-horizon**. This layer of surface soil is the most subject to climatic and biological influences. Most of the organic matter accumulates in the A-horizon and gives it a darker color than the underlying horizons. The darker color indicates higher organic matter accumulations and a more productive soil.

Very little organic matter accumulates in the surface layer of forested soils. The chemical composition of the organic matter returned to the soil under tree cover is quite different than in the grasslands. As a result, forested soils have a very shallow topsoil layer which is often acidic and overlain by leaf litter. Once these soils are cultivated, they are characterized by a grey surface color and poor structure that lends itself to crusting after rain. On these soils, crusting can frequently restrict crop emergence and development. This problem is directly related to the low organic content of these soils.

The subsoil (**B-horizon**) is usually a brownish-colored layer in which leached materials (from the A-horizon) accumulate. Therefore, the B-horizon is usually enriched in clay minerals. As a result, this layer has a more compact structure. In extreme cases, the compaction can result in reduced movement of moisture and air within this layer, as well as restricted root growth. Subsoil compaction is usually not a factor in the zonal soils found within the grassland regions. The A- and B-horizons are often collectively referred to as the **solum**, which is the active rooting zone for most plants.

Underlying the B-horizon is the parent material or **C-horizon**. This layer is least affected by physical, chemical, and biological factors involved in soil formation. Because this horizon contains little or no organic matter, parent materials are a poor medium in which to grow plants.

### URBAN SOIL PROFILE

Because of the strong influence of climate on soil profile development, certain general characteristics of soils formed in areas of different climatic patterns can be readily described. For the urban home gardener, a discussion of soil profile formation under natural soil forming conditions may very well be

## Figure 1-2
## TYPICAL SOIL PROFILE DEVELOPMENT IN MAJOR SOIL ZONES

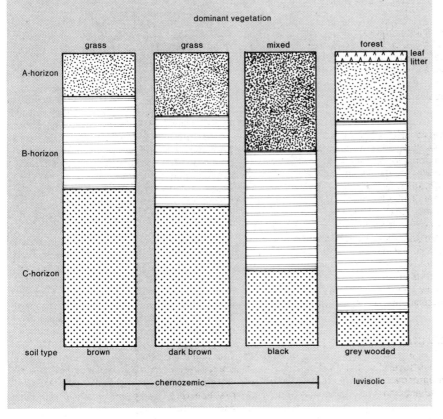

academic. Nonetheless, a knowledge of the soil forming processes and how soil profiles are developed may help the home gardener to understand some of the soil conditions that exist in the garden.

Topsoil is routinely stripped by developers. As a result, most urban soils have been severely disturbed and subsequently reformed. Thus, the type of soil profile present in an urban lot will bear very little, if any, relationship to the kind of soil that existed there prior to development taking place.

The soil profile normally desired in most urban sites is a relatively uniform, thick layer of topsoil over reworked material that probably most closely resembles the original parent material (C-horizon). Problems arise when little emphasis is placed on establishing the desired grade before the topsoil is placed back in the yard. The topsoil, therefore, must be used to accomplish the final slope when landscaping. As a result, the depth of topsoil within the yard can easily vary from 5-30 cm (2-12in.). Since no effort is made to preserve the B-horizon, a thick and uniform depth of topsoil (30 cm) is most desirable to ensure uniform growing conditions across the entire yard. Often, topsoil can be added to improve growth in garden and flower-bed areas.

## SOIL COMPONENTS

The four principal components of soil are organic matter, mineral particles, water, and air. The relative proportions of these components can vary significantly, depending on the soil type and its moisture content. The soil volume occupied by each component in a typical loam topsoil is illustrated in Figure 1-3. Basically, the soil consists of approximately one-half solids (minerals and organic matter) and one-half voids (air and water). In a prairie loam topsoil, organic matter content most frequently ranges from 2-8 per cent by volume. The corresponding mineral content (sand, silt, and clay) amounts to 48-42 per cent. At the ideal moisture content for this typical loam soil, one-half of the pore space (i.e., 25% of the total soil volume) contains water, and the remaining pore space contains air.

## Figure 1-3
## SOIL COMPONENTS (BY VOLUME) OF AN IDEAL GARDEN SOIL

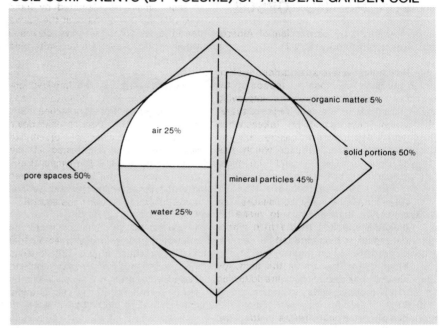

## ORGANIC MATTER

Plants growing on soils provide the main source of soil organic matter. As plants die, leaves, stems, and root materials are added to the soil. These materials are decomposed through the action of various soil microbes. The rate of decay varies, depending on the type of organic material added. Upon death of the various soil microbes, the products of their decomposition also contribute to the pool of soil organic matter.

The end product of decomposition is a material called **humus**. Humus is a dark-colored, odorless, uniform, and relatively stable product that has a high capacity to store the nutrients and moisture required for plant growth. Despite the fact that it usually forms a relatively small proportion of the total solids contained in soil, it has a major positive impact on improving many of the physical soil properties that determine the suitability of a soil for gardening. These include improved soil structure and aeration, as well as the water retention capacity of the soil. Soils with a high organic matter content are more friable and are less likely to compact and cake than are soils that are low in organic matter content. Organic matter favorably influences the structure and tilth of soils which contributes to good

seedling development and root penetration (see SOIL STRUCTURE AND TILTH). Given a choice, an experienced gardener or farmer would prefer to grow his crop in **a rich dark soil**; that is, a soil containing a generous amount of well decomposed organic matter.

The range in organic matter content of some typical prairie region soils is shown in Table 1-1. A loam topsoil from the thick black soil zone is most suited to gardening purposes because of its high content of natural organic matter. However, it should be pointed out that not all thick black soils are loams (see SOIL TEXTURE). Soils containing greater than 20 per cent organic matter are considered to be non-mineral soils. Some organic muck soils can contain as much as 80 per cent organic matter in the surface layer.

Gardening does not lend itself to maintaining or increasing soil organic matter levels because plant residues produced in the garden are not normally worked into the soil. For this reason, the addition of organic matter to garden soils is recommended (see IMPROVING SOIL STRUCTURE). Under farm conditions, returning the residue of an annual, high yielding crop of grain to the soil is one method of ensuring the soil system is well fueled with the raw

# PURCHASING TOPSOIL

reproduced by permission of Alberta Agriculture: Agdex 525-1

New homeowners and gardeners often require additional topsoil for landscaping their yard or improving gardens and flower beds. Several precautions should be taken when purchasing topsoil to ensure that you are obtaining a product which has desirable physical and chemical properties.

Often, the only way to ensure the suitability of topsoil is to make an on-site inspection of the field where the topsoil is being loaded.

When inspecting soil in the field, you should consider each of the following soil characteristics:

**Texture**: This refers to the percentage of sand, silt, and clay in a soil. A medium-textured soil (loam), containing approximately equal parts of sand, silt, and clay is the most desirable for landscaping and gardening purposes. Of lesser quality would be the heavy texture soils which contain too much clay, making the soil hard and difficult to work into a fine seedbed. Also of lower quality are the light texture soils which contain too much sand, making the soil loose and low in moisture-holding capacity (droughty).

A rough estimate of soil texture can be made by wetting a small handful of soil with water and rubbing it between the thumb and forefinger. The different particle size fractions can be identified by feel as follows:

'gritty' - this is the individual sand particles which do not break down on wetting.

'soapy' or 'silky' - this indicates the presence of intermediate-size silt particles.

'sticky' - this is the fine clay particles which adhere to one another.

A loam would be identified by hand texturing as having each of the above features, whereas a heavy clay soil would be very sticky with no grittiness.

**Structure**: 'Friable' and 'mellow' are words describing desirable soil structure or physical condition. Soil clods (lumps) should break down easily into granular or crumb-like aggregates when squeezed in the hand. Large, compacted lumps of soil could indicate that the soil was stripped too deep and heavy subsoil material was mixed with the topsoil.

**Organic Matter**: Soil color is an indication of the kind and amount of organic matter in soil. Black soils have high organic matter content, whereas a light grey color indicates low organic matter content. Organic materials such as peat, manure, or compost can be added to the existing topsoil to increase its porosity and generally improve the physical condition of the soil. Use of these organic amendments may replace the need for trucking in additional topsoil.

**Salts**: Excess amounts of salts in soil are not wanted. White crystals on the surface of dried soil particles could indicate the presence of free salts in soil, which can be harmful to plants when present in high concentrations. Excess amounts of salts in a recently delivered load of topsoil will not be visible to you until the soil has had time to dry and then it will be too late to reject the soil. For this reason, it is a good idea to check for salt crusting in the field before purchase of topsoil is arranged.

**Weeds**: Although not a soil characteristic as such, the presence of weed seeds (e.g. quackgrass or other seeds) in topsoil is an undesirable feature. Stripping of topsoil from land close to urban centres often occurs in fields which have been abandoned or poorly managed for a number of years prior to development, resulting in weed infestation in the field. Annual grasses and broadleaf weeds pose less of a problem in establishment and maintenance of a lawn than do the perennial grasses such as quackgrass. For this reason, an on-site inspection of the field should be made before purchasing topsoil in order to determine the types of weeds present.

From the above description of soil characteristics, it is apparent that the best topsoil for landscaping and gardening is a weed and salt-free black loam. Often, however, a trade-off has to be made between the more desirable and less desirable characteristics of available supplies of topsoil in order to obtain the soil which will best meet your individual needs. There are numerous reputable dealers in all areas supplying suitable topsoil and you would be well advised to deal with those firms which have proven customer satisfaction.

More stringent laws are being imposed which restrict the stripping of topsoil from agricultural land. This limits the number of dealers supplying suitable topsoil and often results in material of low quality being offered for sale. Reputable dealers should be willing to tell you the location of the field where they are loading topsoil and, with this information, you should make an on-sight inspection of the field to determine suitability of soil.

Table 1-1
## ORGANIC MATTER CONTENTS OF SOME TYPICAL PRAIRIE SOILS

| Soil Zone | Per Cent Organic Matter Content* | |
| --- | --- | --- |
| | Usual Range | Most Typical |
| brown | 1-3 | 2 |
| dark brown | 2-5 | 3 |
| black | 4-8 | 5 |
| thick black | 6-10 | 8 |
| grey black | 4-8 | 5 |
| grey | 1-3 | 2 |

*Expressed on a dry weight basis.

Table 1-2
## SIZE LIMITS OF SOIL MINERAL PARTICLES

| Textural Component | Size Range (mm) |
| --- | --- |
| very coarse sand | 2.0 - 1.0 |
| coarse sand | 1.0 - 0.5 |
| medium sand | 0.5 - 0.25 |
| fine sand | 0.25 - 0.10 |
| very fine sand | 0.10 - 0.05 |
| silt | 0.05 - 0.002 |
| clay | less than 0.002 |

organic matter required to maintain a productive soil. If manure is available, relatively high rates can be applied to help improve localized problem soils. The most harmful practise is that of keeping the soil idle and uncropped for a year (i.e., summerfallowing) because without the annual addition of raw organic matter, the soil microbes attack some of the more stable soil organic matter (humus) to provide them with required energy. The long-term net result of summerfallowing is reduced soil organic matter levels and a decline in soil fertility. Farmers often deliberately choose to grow a crop that can be worked into the soil while it is still green (i.e., green manuring) for the purpose of increasing soil organic matter.

## MINERAL MATTER

The mineral portion of a loam soil usually accounts for about 45 per cent of the soil **volume**. On a **weight** basis, however, it accounts for more than 90 per cent of the solid materials in most loam soils because of the higher density of minerals compared to organic matter. The mineral portion of soils consist of major fractions based on particle size (i.e., sand, silt, and clay). The relative proportion of these mineral fractions has a major impact on the soil properties of a garden soil and how it should be managed (see SOIL MANAGEMENT and PHYSICAL ASPECTS OF SOIL). Table 1-2 defines the relative size of the various soil mineral particles. Figure 1-4 illustrates the relative differences between sand (fine), silt, and clay sized particles. Although size differences are quite significant, the impact of textural category is much more striking in terms of actual surface area. For example, one gram of clay has 10 times more surface than one gram of silt. Compared to very fine sand particles, clay has an effective surface that is 50 times as large.

The importance of the large difference in surface area between clay and even the finest sand fraction can be grasped in the fact that water and many nutrients are held and stored on the surface of soil minerals. That means, for example, that the same weight of clay can retain 50 times as much soil water as very fine sand particles. Although a soil composed completely of clay is undesireable, a certain percentage of clay is very beneficial in the creation of a productive soil. In this respect, soil organic matter (humus) also serves a similar role to clay in terms of water and nutrient retention.

The more predominant one size particle is in a soil, the less versatile that soil becomes for many crops, and the more exacting are the management requirements to ensure that the soils are productive. If a soil contains a significant amount of sand, it feels gritty when rubbed between the fingers. In fact, the finest sand particles are the smallest that can be detected in this manner and the smallest that can be detected by the naked eye.

## SOIL WATER

Soil solids (mineral particles and organic matter) account for approximately one-half of the total soil volume. The remainder of the soil volume is composed of pore space. The size of the pore spaces is dramatically influenced by the distribution of mineral

Figure 1-4
## RELATIVE SIZE OF SOIL MINERAL PARTICLES

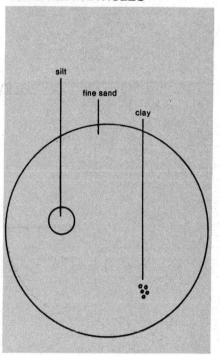

Table 1-3
## MOISTURE-CAPACITY OF SEVERAL TYPICAL SOILS AND PEAT MOSS

| Soil Texture | Water-Holding Capacity (%)* |
|---|---|
| sandy loam | 12-18 |
| silt loam | 24-32 |
| clay loam | 32-48 |
| peat | 100+ |

*As a percentage of the dry soil weight.

particles and the organic matter content of the soil. The smaller the pores, the greater the ability of the soil to store water. Conversely, the larger the pores, the lower the water-holding capacity and the greater the volume of air. For a loam soil under ideal growing conditions, one-half of the void or pore space is filled with water and an equal amount (25%) of the total soil volume is filled with soil air.

Water available for plant growth comes from two sources; precipitation (or irrigation) and soil storage. Precipitation can be quite variable and its effectiveness depends on both the

Figure 1-5
## RELATIVE SOIL COMPONENTS AT THREE MOISTURE CONTENTS

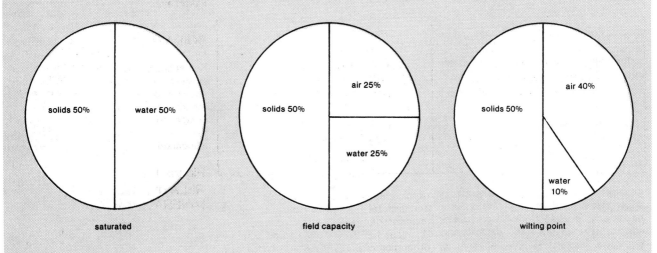

Figure 1-6
## RELATIVE VOLUMES OF SOLIDS, WATER, AND AIR AT FIELD CAPACITY AS INFLUENCED BY SOIL TEXTURE

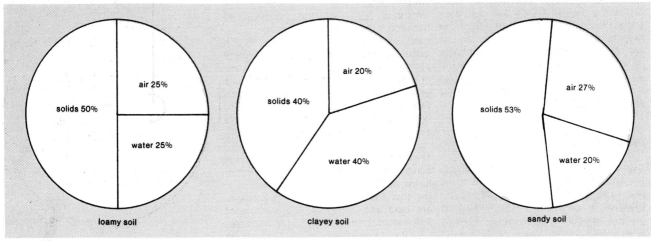

amount and its timing, as well as the ability of the soil to store the infiltrating water. The amount of available water that can be stored in the soil is a fixed property of that soil. A deficit occurs if the moisture supplied by precipitation plus soil storage is less than the water requirements of the crop.

The capacity of a soil to store water is strongly influenced by soil texture (i.e., relative proportion of sand, silt, and clay sized mineral particles) as well as the organic matter (humus) content of the soil. The finer sized particles (clay and humus) are much more effective at retaining soil moisture than are the sand particles (see Table 1-3). This is due to the relatively large surface area of these fine particles which attract and hold a thin layer of water against drainage (the downward movement of water in response to the force of gravity).

If all of the pore space is filled with water, the soil is considered to be **saturated**. Providing a soil has adequate internal drainage, this amount of water (i.e., pores full of water) simply cannot be retained against the force of gravity in the soil profile (see Figure 1-5). The amount of water that stabilizes after drainage has ceased and before plant uptake has been initiated is a fixed characteristic of the soil that is called the **field capacity** or moisture-holding capacity. The moisture-holding capacity of a 'clayey' soil is higher than for a sandy soil because of the much greater surface area of the finer textured clay soil (see Figure 1-6). The presence of soil organic matter (humus) also has a very positive impact on increasing the water-holding capacity of a soil. Peat moss, for example, has the ability to retain more than 100 per cent of its weight in water (see Table 1-3).

Plants cannot extract all of the water that is held in the thin layer on the surface of soil particles. As plant roots extract moisture from the soil, it becomes more and more difficult to remove. If water is not replenished by rainfall or irrigation, plants start to wilt (lack sufficient water to maintain plant growth). The point at which the plants cannot remove sufficient additional water from the soil to maintain plant growth is called the **wilting point**. Water remaining at the wilting point is considered to be unavailable water because it cannot be removed by plants. Although clayey soils have a greater water-holding capacity than sandy soils, they also hold more

unavailable water at the wilting point. The characteristic water-holding capacity and wilting point for some typical textural groups is shown in Figure 1-7.

The difference in soil water content between field capacity and the wilting point is the amount of water available to sustain plant growth. Available water is generally highest in those soils with a high organic matter content and/or a high clay content (see Figure 1-8).

The actual amount of water required to replenish a soil depends on the type of soil being watered, as well as its water content at the time of watering. A sandy loam soil requires almost 2.5 cm (1 in.) of water to replenish it to a depth of 30 cm (12 in.), while a loam soil requires about 4 cm (1½ in.) and a clay soil about 5 cm (2 in.).

## SOIL AIR

The portion of soil pore space that is not filled with water is occupied by air. During growth, plant roots require oxygen and give off carbon dioxide. The composition of the air in surface soil is similar to that of the atmosphere, except that the oxygen content is lower and the carbon dioxide content is higher in the soil. An adequate supply of oxygen in the soil air is essential for plant roots to function properly. A productive soil is a well aerated or ventilated soil in which there is a good exchange of air from the atmosphere with air from the soil.

The amount and size of the pore spaces (porosity) varies widely in soils, depending on the relative proportion of sand, silt, and clay, and the amount of organic matter that the soil contains. Besides providing channels through which water can move downward, the soil pores are necessary for providing

## Figure 1-7
## WATER-HOLDING CAPACITY AND WILTING POINT AS INFLUENCED BY SOIL TEXTURE

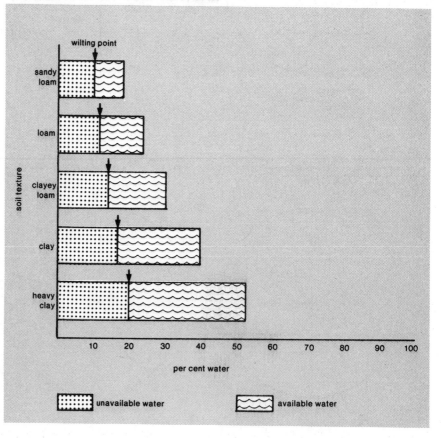

## Figure 1-8
## WATER-HOLDING CAPACITY AND WILTING POINT AS INFLUENCED BY ORGANIC MATTER

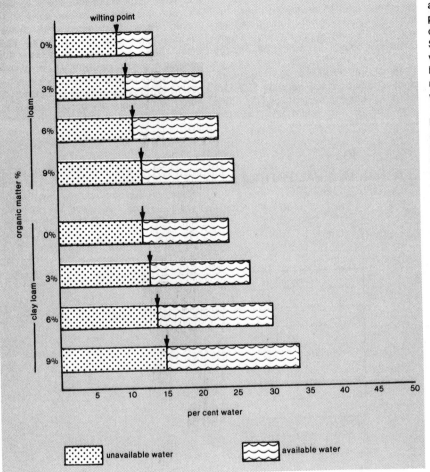

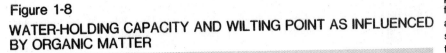

wilting point

organic matter %

loam — 0% 3% 6% 9%

clay loam — 0% 3% 6% 9%

per cent water

5 10 15 20 25 30 35 40 45 50

unavailable water          available water

## Figure 1-9
## RELATIVE SOIL COMPONENTS IN A HIGHLY ORGANIC LOAM AND A COMPACTED CLAYEY SOIL

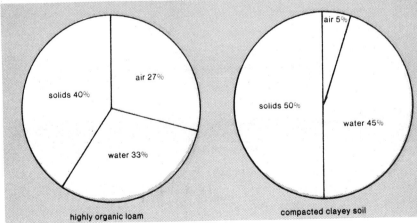

air 27%

solids 40%

water 33%

highly organic loam

air 5%

solids 50%

water 45%

compacted clayey soil

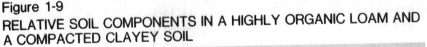

plant roots with a continual supply of fresh air (oxygen) from the atmosphere above the soil surface. In a well aerated soil, plants root to a greater depth, thereby taking advantage of nutrients and moisture stored deeper in the soil. In poorly aerated soils, the plant roots are confined to the surface layer of soil. Shallow rooted plants are more vulnerable to periods of moisture stress because they can only tap into a relatively small percentage of the total water reserve stored in the soil.

In a dry soil, air occupies a high percentage of the total pore space. Following a heavy rainfall or watering, water occupies a higher percentage of the pore space (see Figure 1-5). When the soil water content is above field capacity, some water initially drains out of the soil pores in response to the downward force of gravity and is replaced with air (i.e., until the soil pore volume is filled with approximately equal amounts of air and water for a loam soil). Beyond this stage, removal of additional water from the pores depends on uptake by the roots of actively growing plants. As the crop removes more of the available water and the soil dries out, progressively less of the pore space is occupied by soil water and more by soil air. During this stage, the plant receives water from the finer pores and air from the larger pores.

When a soil is flooded, anaerobic (absence of air) conditions develop and the lack of oxygen dramatically reduces root growth and the development of most crops. A well structured soil contains larger pore spaces between soil aggregates that drain water quickly. When the water is drained, these channels serve as major pathways through which the soil can discard the carbon dioxide given off by the plant roots and take in oxygen from the atmosphere (i.e., aerobic conditions) to allow roots to function normally.

A well structured soil has large and small pore spaces that allow for storage of water and movement of air and water. Such a soil is also the most productive. Coarse textured soils tend to have a high proportion of large pores filled with air and a low water-holding capacity. Fine textured soils are dominated by small pores and have poor air circulation. A lack of larger pores can particularly be a problem with the clayey soils that are dominated by the smaller pore spaces (see Figures 1-6 and 1-9).

In these soils, proper surface drainage is essential. In extreme cases, sub-surface drainage may also be required to maintain adequate aeration. The incorporation of organic matter may also be beneficial in terms of increasing the larger pore spaces in clayey soils.

## PHYSICAL ASPECTS OF SOIL

### SOIL TEXTURE

Soil texture refers to the relative percentage of sand, silt, and clay in a soil. Soil is classified into one of fourteen textural groups, depending on the proportion of these three components that are present. Typical sand, silt, and clay contents of some of the most important textural groups are illustrated in Figure 1-10. Soil texture is important because it has a major influence on soil structure and other physical properties. Within a given textural class, there is room for some variation in the amount of the three particle sizes that can be present. This fact is illustrated in Figure 1-11, where some of the extremes in sand, silt, and clay contents that are tolerated within the loam textural group are contrasted with the typical or median mineral composition of a loam texture. A loam is a soil containing a certain proportion of sand, silt, and clay and, therefore, classifying a soil as a loam has nothing to do with its color or organic matter content, since a loam can easily contain anywhere between 0-8 per cent organic matter. Furthermore, a surface soil that has a loam texture may have a very dark or a very light color.

It should be emphasized that the scientific use of the word loam is not in keeping with common usage in the landscaping industry. In many cases, this term is used to denote a mechanical mixture of topsoil and peat moss that is dark in color, uniform in appearance, and is light and crumbly to handle (at least initially). In other cases, it is simply a dark-colored soil of unknown texture that may be wind-blown dirt collected from some fenceline, or pulverized B-horizon material.

### TEXTURE INFLUENCES PHYSICAL PROPERTIES

Physical properties of soils, such as water-holding capacity and whether they are loose, compact, hard, or friable, are primarily determined by the texture of the soil.

Clay soils tend to be sticky when they are wet and contain very small pores into which water penetrates very slowly. Under wet conditions, a high percentage of soil pores are filled with water and, as a result, these soils are frequently plagued with poor soil aeration. The fact that clay soils are subject to compaction can lead to an aggravation of this problem. If 'clayey' soils are worked while wet, they tend to compact and become lumpy after drying. On the other hand, sandy soils feel gritty and have too many large pores that are filled with air. For this reason, sandy soils allow faster water percolation and better aeration than the finer textured clay soils. Although sandy soils are the easiest to cultivate, they have a low ability to hold water and supply nutrients. Loams are usually crumbly by nature, not sticky, and do not dry out as quickly as sandy soils.

## Figure 1-10

### TYPICAL MINERAL PARTICLE CONTENT OF SELECTED TEXTURAL GROUPS

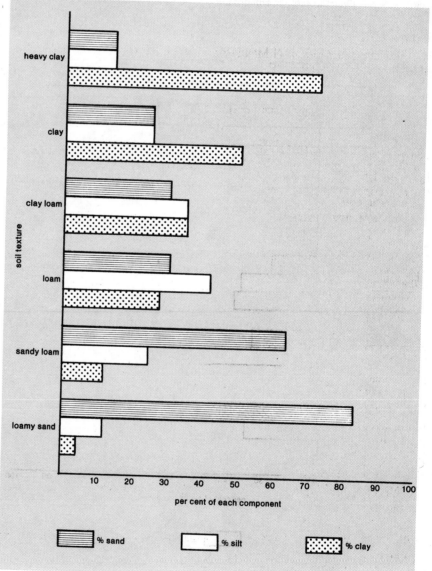

## COARSE VS FINE TEXTURE

Soils that are dominated by the sand sized fraction are referred to as being coarse or light (easy to cultivate) textured. Soils in which the texture is dominated by the clays are referred to as being fine or heavy (difficult to cultivate) textured. The more common textural names listed, in order of increasing fineness are: loamy sand, sandy loam, loam, silt loam, silt, sandy clay loam, clay loam, silty clay loam, sandy clay, silty clay, clay, and heavy clay.

The soil texture triangle is one method used to illustrate the relationships among the various soil textural groups. The diagram in Figure 1-12 shows the per cent of sand and clay in the various textures. From the diagram, a soil that contains 40 per cent sand and 20 per cent clay is called a loam. This same soil also contains 40 per cent silt (40% sand + 20% clay = 60% of the soil content, leaving 40% occupied by silt). A soil with 60 per cent sand and 15 per cent clay (25% silt) is called a sandy loam, and one with 20 per cent sand and 50 per cent clay (30% silt) is a clay. Therefore, the various textural groups are identified by names that reveal something about their relative proportions of sand, silt, and clay. Those concentrated in the upper third of the triangle contain relatively higher clay content. Those in the lower right corner contain the highest sand content. Those in the lower left corner contain the highest silt content.

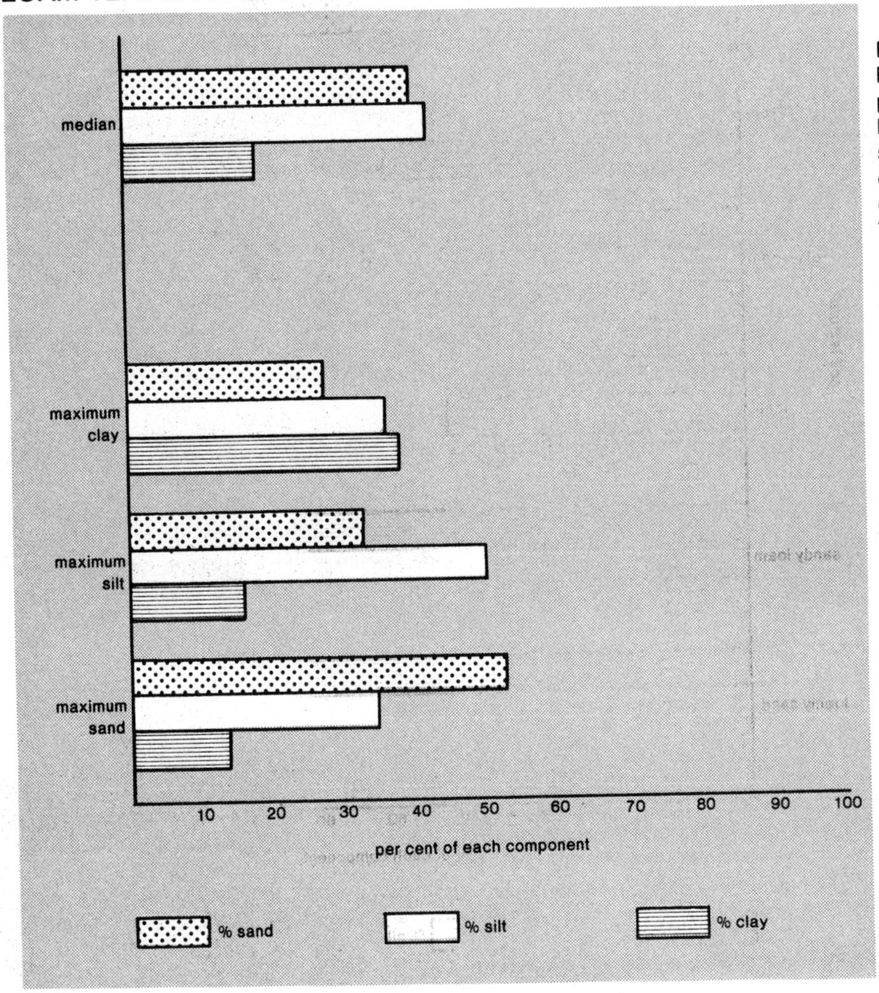

Gardens and lawns are most easily grown on soils with a loam or sandy loam texture (those concentrated in the center of the triangle). In these soils, air and water spaces are well distributed and ensure good movement of air and water. Root penetration is also good. Since most lawns and gardens are watered, vulnerability to drought should not be a major concern. In the drier regions, a slightly higher clay content is preferred if the gardens are to be grown exclusively on moisture obtained from rainfall.

Clay textured soils generally contain few of the larger pore spaces. They can be very hard to work, tend to be sticky when wet, and are quite subject to compaction. Sandy textured soils are easy to work, usually have no aeration or compaction problems, but can be quite droughty and are more prone to being deficient in nutrients. Given an adequate supply of water, sandy soils are preferred over silty and clayey soils for agricultural or horticultural uses.

## IDEAL TEXTURE DEPENDS ON USE

For most gardening and landscaping purposes, loams, silt loams, and sandy loams are considered to be the most suitable soil textures because their characteristics are intermediate to the extremes of the sandy or the clay soils. The blend of soil particles that such 'loamy' soils contain ensures the desirable characteristics, with respect to water retention, percolation, aeration, nutrient supply, and soil aggregate strength, are provided. Soils of other textural classes can be made more suitable for gardening and lawn building by the addition of soil amendments (see IMPROVING SOIL STRUCTURE).

It should be pointed out that an ideal soil texture for farming can be quite different from that desired by the home gardener. Furthermore, the ideal soil texture for farming conditions varies with regional climatic conditions. In the low rainfall regions of the southern prairies (e.g., Regina-Moose Jaw region), farming a soil with a high clay content is desirable because of its impressive ability to store soil water. However, due to the high clay content and the soils subsequent tendency to compact, these soils are hardly ideal for gardening. In the higher rainfall areas of the prairies, clay soils can also be very difficult to farm, particularly during wetter years (e.g., Red River Valley). In the southern prairies under natural rainfall, a sandy

### Figure 1-11
### EXTREMES AND MEDIAN MINERAL PARTICLE CONTENT WITHIN LOAM TEXTURAL GROUP

Figure 1-12
## TEXTURE TRIANGLE

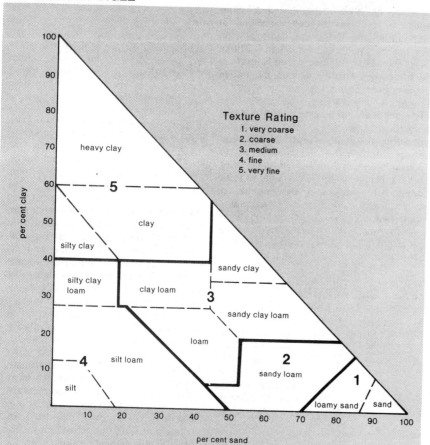

Texture Rating
1. very coarse
2. coarse
3. medium
4. fine
5. very fine

Table 1-4
## PREDICTED WATER SUPPLYING POWER OF SELECTED TEXTURAL GROUPS AT FIELD CAPACITY

| Soil Texture | Available Water of Moist Soil | |
|---|---|---|
| | cm/m | in./ft. |
| sandy loam | 8.0 | 1.0 |
| loam | 12.5 | 1.5 |
| clay loam | 16.7 | 2.0 |
| heavy clay | 20.8 | 2.5 |

garden fork can be used to test the soil structure; the larger clods should readily break down into smaller aggregates or crumbs. If the soil breaks down into a fine powder, it is lacking in structure and probably contains an excessive amount of sand-sized particles. If the soil remains in large, hard lumps, it probably contains an excessive amount of clay-sized particles.

## SOIL STRUCTURE AND TILTH

While coarse, sandy soils can be structureless, individual soil particles in most other soils are arranged into aggregates or groups of particles. The way in which the particles are grouped together is termed **soil structure**. The action of wetting and drying, as well as freezing and thawing, contribute to the development of soil structure within the soil profile. Although structural patterns can normally be detected in the subsoil (B-horizon), the structure of the surface layer (A-horizon) is the most critical for gardening purposes. In a topsoil with good structure, individual soil particles are bound together in clusters, soil crumbs, aggregates, or 'peds' of various sizes. These naturally formed aggregates are relatively water stable and remain fairly intact, even when the soil is wet. This type of soil structure has good soil drainage and aeration, and helps to ensure a good seedbed in which young seedlings can quickly become established. Although clay is a very important binding agent in helping to maintain soil aggregates, soil organic matter (humus) most strongly influences the formation of aggregates and the structure of surface soils.

The word **tilth** refers to the physical condition of the soil as it relates to ease of tillage, fitness as a seedbed, and its impedance to seedling emergence and root penetration. In soils with poor structure, individual soil particles are poorly aggregated into larger crumbs. Such soils are compact and relatively impervious to water and air. They are often very difficult to work and tend to puddle and crust quite readily. By resisting puddling (breakdown of aggregates into smaller soil particles), crusting of the surface layer is prevented upon drying. Crusting of the surface layer can seriously hinder the emergence of seedlings. Usually, crusting of the surface soil is most serious in soils with low organic matter content (e.g., soils that were formerly

soil is quite droughty and unproductive. With proper irrigation, however, these soils can be the most productive and the easiest to manage for farming or gardening purposes. In regions of higher rainfall, the lighter textured soils can also be very productive.

If water is limited, one should choose a soil with a relatively high clay content and use considerable care during cultivation to avoid compacting the soil.

If water is abundant, a gardener should then choose a soil with a higher sand content, since it is easier to manage. Depending on its texture, soil varies in its ability to retain moisture. This difference is shown in Table 1-4, where the moisture-holding capacity of several different soil textures are compared.

For gardening purposes, a soil that crumbles and easily breaks down into smaller granules is preferred. A spade or forested). Good soil structure is also critical to proper root development.

# CHEMICAL ASPECTS OF SOIL

## SOIL COLLOIDS

The most chemically active portion of soil is confined primarily to very finely divided particles called **colloids**. Soil colloids are small enough to stay suspended in water without dissolving or settling. These particles are so small, they can only be seen through a microscope. They consist of clay and humus and, because they are negatively charged, are able to retain and store many positively charged plant nutrient particles on their surface. The extent to which these particles are able to store nutrients in this manner is referred to as the **cation exchange capacity** (CEC). The size of the CEC varies in direct proportion with the amount of colloidal materials present and is an indirect measure of a soil's fertility. Furthermore, the presence of colloids is beneficial because they prevent the loss of certain nutrients (native and applied fertilizer) in water that drains through the soil.

## SOIL REACTION (pH)

The terms **acid**, **neutral** and **alkaline** refer to the relative concentrations of hydrogen ions ($H^+$) and hydroxyl ions ($OH^-$) in the soil solution. These concentrations are expressed in terms of a pH scale, which indicates the active acidity (see Figure 1-13).

The pH scale ranges from 0 to 14. In a neutral soil (pH 7.0), there are equal amounts of hydrogen and hydroxyl ions. A pH below 7.0 is considered to be **acidic** (i.e., surplus of hydrogen ions), while a pH above 7.0 is considered to be **basic** or alkaline (i.e., surplus of hydroxyl ions). Each pH unit represents a ten-fold increase or decrease in relative acidity or alkalinity. Therefore, a pH of 5.0 is ten times more acidic than a pH of 6.0.

Acid soils are sometimes referred to as being 'sour', while alkaline soils are called 'sweet' soils. The most favorable soil reaction for the growth of most plants is in the neutral range (i.e., pH of 6.5-7.5). However, a neutral pH is not ideal for growing all plants (see Table 1-5) since some plants are more **acid-loving** (see Plant Nutrition lesson, Figure 4-12 and Table 4-3). An alkaline soil condition indicates the presence of

## ANIONS, CATIONS, AND CEC

by John Harapiak

The most chemically active part of the soil consists of small particles known as colloids. Clay minerals are classified as colloidal materials, as is the bulk of the stable organic matter (humus) present in the soil.

All soil particles have a net negative charge on their surface. However, the amount of charge is much greater for colloidal material (i.e., clay and/or humus) than in a comparable weight of sand. The amount of this charge is usually referred to as the CEC (i.e., cation exchange capacity). Obviously, the size of the CEC is much greater in soils with a high clay and/or organic matter content.

Positively charged ions, such as nitrogen in the ammonium form ($NH_4^+$), calcium ($Ca^{++}$), magnesium ($Mg^{++}$), and potassium ($K^+$), are attracted to and effectively held on the surface of the negatively charged colloids, where they can be taken up by the plant roots as required. The positively charged ions are called **cations**. The negatively charged ions, such as nitrogen in the nitrate form ($NO_3^-$), sulphate ($SO_4^-$), and chloride ($Cl^-$), are repelled by the surface of the colloids and, therefore, tend to stay dissolved in the soil water that surrounds the colloids. The negatively charged ions are called **anions**. The anions move more readily in the soil than do the cations and can, therefore, be lost from the rooting zone of the crop through leaching if excessive amounts of water are applied to the soil. Plant nutrients that are cations are less subject to leaching losses than anions.

## Figure 1-13
### THE pH SCALE AND ASSOCIATED SOIL REACTION

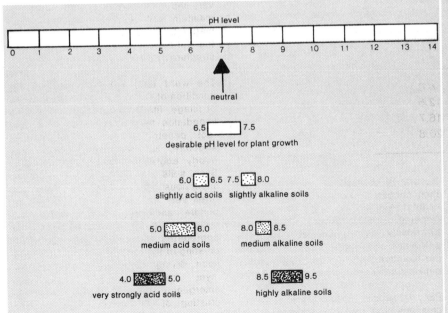

Table 1-5

## OPTIMUM SOIL ACIDITY FOR GROWTH OF SOME PLANTS

| OPTIMUM pH RANGE | PLANTS |
|---|---|
| **Very Acid** (pH 4.0 - 5.0) | Azalea, rhododendron, cranberry, and blueberry |
| **Moderately Acid** (pH 5.0 - 6.0) | Snap bean, potato, watermelon, aster, lily-of-the-valley orchid, holly, juniper, lily, phlox, and hydrangea |
| **Slightly acid** (pH 6.0 - 6.8) | Asparagus, spinach, beet, celery, cantaloupe, lettuce, onion, rose, chrysanthemum, sweet pea, and snapdragon |
| **Slightly and moderately acid** (pH 5.0 - 6.8) | Apple, pear, plum, pecan, grape, raspberry, blackberry, strawberry, cabbage, radish, squash, tomato, pepper, sweet corn, carrot, carnation, and gerbera |

excess amounts of free calcium, sodium carbonate, or bicarbonates. Similarly, an acid condition usually indicates a surplus of aluminum. Both conditions can interfere with the availability of plant nutrients from the soil (see Plant Nutrition lesson, Figure 4-11).

### FREE LIME

Although free lime is usually present in parent materials, many of the soils located in the more arid portions of the prairies contain free lime (calcium carbonate) at the surface. Soils with free lime will have a pH that exceeds 7.0. The presence of excessive amounts of free lime in the surface layer is undesirable, since it can interfere with the uptake of several plant nutrients. Iron is one micro-nutrient that may become relatively unavailable to plants in a soil with a high free lime content. Evergreen shrubs, raspberries, roses, mountain ash, currants, and cranberry are among the plants that are most susceptible to 'iron chlorosis' (i.e., yellowing of leaves between the veins).

The presence of free lime can only be corrected slowly by the application of acid forming materials such as a sphagnum peat moss and acid forming fertilizer such as ammonium sulphate (21-0-0-24). In extreme cases, more drastic procedures involving the application of elemental sulphur or aluminum sulphate may be considered. However, such procedures should not be attempted without seeking expert advice on the subject.

## SALINITY AND ELECTRICAL CONDUCTIVITY (EC)

Salts are a common and natural constituent of all soils. Some soils contain excessive amounts of soluble salts that can be harmful to plant growth. Such soils are frequently referred to as 'alkali' but should be correctly identified as 'saline'. The parent material from which our soils were formed frequently contain substantial amounts of salts. The upward movement of water can result in the salts being deposited in the surface layer. High salt content in soil is usually evidenced by a white crust on the surface of a dry soil. There is no chemical treatment that removes or counteracts salt accumulations. To reduce the salt level, the soils must be managed so as to move the salts downward, out of the rooting zone.

The presence of dissolved salts increases the ability of water to conduct an electrical current. Therefore, the electrical conductivity (EC) of a soil can be used as a measure of the level of soluble salts that are present in the soil. If the soil water extract tests medium to high, crop production may be hindered. To counteract this problem, steps should be taken to reduce the level of soil salinity and to grow some of the more salt tolerant crops (see Table 1-6).

## MICROBIAL ACTIVITY

It is frequently suggested that a productive soil is a living soil. This statement is made in recognition of the enormous contribution to soil productivity made by an invisible army of active soil microbes. Besides the role that soil microbes play in soil development through the formation of humus, these organisms continue to make an important contribution to plant growth through their influence on the fertility level of the soil. They decompose organic residues and recycle nutrients such as nitrogen (N), phosphorus (P), and sulphur (S) to growing plants.

Bacteria, fungi, actinomycetes, and algae are some of the important types of soil micro-organisms. All are present in very large numbers under favorable soil conditions. A single gram of soil may contain as many as 4 million bacteria, 1 million fungi, 20 million actinomycetes, and 30,000 algae.

In addition to mediating the breakdown of crop residues, soil micro-organisms are involved in a number of important plant nutrient reactions. Mineralization, nitrification, denitrification, nitrogen fixation, sulphur oxidation, and immobilization comprise the key reactions.

- **Mineralization** is the process of organic matter decomposition that results in the breakdown of complex organic substances into simpler compounds, accompanied by the release of carbon dioxide, water, and plant nutrients. Organic matter cycling is an important source of nitrogen, sulphur, and phosphorus. Continued productivity of a garden soil is dependent on the maintenance of a stable level of soil organic matter (humus) through the return of plant residues and the addition of supplementary organic matter.

- **Nitrification** is the conversion of immobile ammonium-nitrogen ($NH_4^+ - N$) to mobile nitrate-nitrogen ($NO_3^- - N$). Nitrate-nitrogen is the form of nitrogen taken up by most crops.

- **Denitrification** is the conversion of nitrate-nitrogen ($NO_3^- - N$) to gaseous forms of nitrogen that are lost to the air from the soil under conditions of poor aeration. This process represents a potentially serious loss of a vital plant nutrient from the soil.

- **Nitrogen fixation** results from soil microbes fixing atmospheric nitrogen to be subsequently used by plants. Some of these organisms are free-living (e.g., blue-green algae), while others exist in nodules on the roots of legume plants such as clover, alfalfa, peas, and beans. These microbes obtain their energy from the plant. In turn, the host plant obtains nitrogen from the nodules. Legume seeds may require innoculation to promote the development of nitrogen-fixing nodules.

- **Sulphur oxidation** involves oxidizing elemental sulphur and organic sulphur into plant available sulphate-sulphur.

- **Immobilization** is the process whereby soil micro-organisms convert plant available inorganic forms of nitrogen to unavailable organic forms. Soil micro-organisms require supplemental ammonium and nitrate during decomposition of organic matter, if the nitrogen content of the added plant residue is low. This nitrogen is tied up and temporarily unavailable to plants, but is released slowly later in the season and during subsequent years for use by crops.

## SOIL MANAGEMENT

A definition of the word **manage** as it relates to soil management is, "to use the soil to the best advantage". This implies using the best available knowledge, techniques, and materials to produce a crop. In order to achieve a productive garden, it is important that the gardener have a good understanding of the soil with which he is working, and know its strengths and limitations. Maintenance of soil fertility is not necessarily identical to maintenance of soil productivity. Soil productivity depends not only on the fertility of the soil, but also on the skills of the gardener in growing the most suitable crops, selecting the right fertilizer, controlling weeds and pests, and a host of other factors about which the gardener must become aware.

The nature of soil profoundly affects the growth of plants. Sunlight, air, and warmth are essential, but are factors that are beyond the control of the gardener. On the other hand, the fertility, structure, and moisture-holding capacity of the garden soil lend themselves to practical methods of modification.

Understanding how and when to work the soil to achieve the best soil tilth for crop emergence and development is very critical, as is knowing the proper use of fertilizers and soil amendments to improve the chemical and/or physical aspects of soil.

## IMPROVING SOIL STRUCTURE AND TILTH

Because of the importance of soil structure and the fragile nature of soil aggregates, extreme care must be exercised in managing the soil so that the structure is maintained or improved. For home gardens, soil quality is usually most strongly judged by its water-holding capacity and its ability to provide good aeration. Far less importance is placed on fertility, since a lack of adequate plant nutrients can be solved by proper fertilization and liming (see ADJUSTING SOIL pH). The amount of moisture that a soil can provide for crop uptake is determined by its texture, porosity, and organic matter content. A sandy soil usually has excellent porosity, but low water-holding capacity. The opposite is true for a heavy soil. Sandy soils can be improved by applying a 5-8 cm (about 2-3 in.) layer of clay or clay loam topsoil. A heavy clay soil can be improved by applying an 8-15 cm (about 3-6 in.) layer of loamy sand or sandy loam topsoil. These soil amendments should be incorporated to a depth of 12-15 cm (5-6 in.) in the original topsoil. Coarse, sandy materials can be used to improve clay soils. However, addition of insufficient sand to clay soils can compound compaction problems. In many cases, improvement of the fine clayey textured topsoils may also require proper surface and sub-surface drainage.

Annual additions of organic materials, such as chopped crop residues, peat moss, compost, or well-rotted manure, help to maintain the garden soil in good physical condition. Researchers have discovered that soils, to which organic matter is regularly added, display better soil tilth, are more friable, and compact

less readily under foot. The true benefits of the improved tilth resulting from routine application of organic matter are really expressed in terms of improved soil aeration, increased water infiltration, and an improved ease of management. These benefits can be directly attributed to the increased humus content of the soil. Other researchers have discovered that regular incorporation of organic matter into the soil appears to make the soils more productive. It is possible that this can be attributed, at least partially, to the fact that bacterial decomposition of plant residues produces gums that help to bond soil particles together, thereby providing a more desirable soil structure.

### CULTIVATION

Flower-beds and gardens usually benefit physically from rough or coarse preparation in the fall of the year. This type of condition is best achieved by turning the soil with a spade (see Vegetables lesson, CULTIVATING THE SOIL). The use of a rototiller may excessively pulverize the soil. Proper fall tillage insures that an excellent seedbed can be accomplished with minimum effort in the spring. For best results, soils should be cultivated at an intermediate moisture content; that is, neither too wet nor too dry. It is also very important to avoid recompaction of freshly cultivated soils by not walking on the soil when it is wet.

### SOIL COMPACTION

The movement of water and fresh air into the soil is dependent on soil porosity, which is markedly influenced by soil structure (see SOIL STRUCTURE AND TILTH). Soil structure is especially important to ensure the presence of larger soil pores. Improper management of some soils can contribute to decreased porosity as a result of soil compaction (see Figure 1-9). Compaction changes the size and character of the soil pores such that the larger soil pores are destroyed. Compacted soils provide a poor medium for plant growth because of poor root penetration into the soil and the reduced movement of water and air in the soil.

In building lawns, the use of heavy machinery should be avoided, especially when the soil is wet. To avoid compaction, excessive walking should also be avoided in gardens and flower-beds when they are wet, particularly in cases where the soils are fine textured (i.e., high clay content). Excessive pulverization (e.g., rototilling) during preparation of the soil prior to seeding makes the soil more vulnerable to compaction, as does working soils while they are wet. Addition of organic matter can help reduce the effects of compaction.

## ADDITION OF ORGANIC MATTER

Poor tilth or physical condition is probably one of the most common garden soil problems. In many cases, this problem occurs because the soil contains low organic matter levels or excessive amounts of clay. Lack of organic matter can be an inherent property of the soil, or it can be the result of continuous cropping of the soil for many years without replenishment with soil building organic materials.

The amount of crop residue produced in a garden is usually quite limited. Furthermore, for purposes of disease control, this material is normally removed rather than incorporated into the garden. The net result is that little organic matter is routinely added to the garden soil through the production of vegetable crops.

Addition of organic matter is actually a universal soil amendment. Peat, well-rotted manure, or compost can be used for soil improvement at the rate of 1.6 - 3.3 m³/100 m² (about 2-4 cu. yd./1000 sq. ft.) of surface area. These materials should be thoroughly incorporated into the top 12-15 cm (5-6 in.) of soil. If large amounts of sawdust, shredded straw, or green grass clippings are used, 0.5 kg of nitrogen per 100 m² (1 lb./1000 sq. ft.) should be added to assist the soil micro-organisms with the decomposition of these materials and to prevent a severe nitrogen deficiency from occuring (immobilization) as they contain relatively low amounts of nitrogen.

## ADJUSTING SOIL pH

Soil alkalinity can be corrected to some extent through the addition of acidic sphagnum peat or acid forming fertilizers such as 21-0-0-24 (ammonium sulphate). The pH can be reduced more rapidly through the addition of aluminum sulphate or finely divided elemental sulphur. However, these and other methods of pH correction should only be

attempted after accurate soil tests have been made and professional advice obtained. Generally, alkaline soils are most likely to be found in the more arid, southern portions of the prairie region.

Soil acidity is often overlooked as a possible problem contributing to poor plant growth. Approximately one-third of the soils in central and northern Alberta are slightly to moderately acid in reaction. Significant amounts of acid soils also occur in north-western Saskatchewan. The grey, forested soils are most likely to be acidic in nature.

Generally, if the soil pH is lower than 5.5, the soil should be amended by the addition of lime. Soil testing is the only accurate method for determining the amount of lime required to raise the soil pH to a more favorable level. The amount of lime to be applied depends upon the the degree of acidity, soil type, its organic matter content, and on the fineness and nature of the liming material (see SOIL TESTING). The majority of prairie soils do not require the application of additional lime. In fact, unnecessary lime application will make these soils less productive (see FREE LIME).

## CONTROLLING SOIL SALINITY

Soil test analyses can identify the amount of salt contained in the soil. Although there is no chemical treatment that can be used to remove or counteract these salts, the following management practices may be beneficial

for reducing the effects of excess soil salt:

- **Improve drainage.**
  Installing subsoil drainage allows excess salts to be drained out of the soil as they are leached downwards with the application of surplus water. If subsoil drainage cannot be installed, digging shallow ditches to remove surface runoff may help to prevent further accumulation of salts, as will the use of raised beds (see Vegetables lesson, GARDENING METHODS).

- **Grow salt tolerant plants.**
  Plants differ widely in their ability to tolerate salt concentrations in the soil. Table 1-6 lists the vegetable plants with high and low salt tolerance.

- **Adding organic matter.**
  The application of organic matter (peat or manure) is often beneficial because increasing the organic matter content helps the soil to increase its water-holding capacity. High water-holding capacity results in the dilution of the salts. Addition of organic matter also makes heavy watering more acceptable, which may help to move the salts out of the soil.

- **Avoid use of saline water.**
  In some cases, soil salinity results from the application of poor quality well or slough waters. These salts remain in the soil after the water has

Table 1-6
### RELATIVE SALT TOLERANCE OF SOME VEGETABLE CROPS

| High Salt Tolerance | Medium Salt Tolerance | Low Salt Tolerance |
|---|---|---|
| beet | tomato | radish |
| kale | broccoli | celery |
| asparagus | cabbage | bean |
| spinach | cauliflower | |
| | lettuce | |
| | corn | |
| | potato | |
| | muskmelon | |
| | carrot | |
| | onion | |
| | pea | |
| | squash | |
| | cucumber | |

*Relative salt tolerance decreases down each column (e.g., tomato is more tolerant than cucumber).

been used by the plants or lost through evaporation. Continual application of water with a moderate salt content eventually results in a serious salt build-up in the soil and renders the soil useless for gardening. If you are in doubt about the salt content of your water supply, have it analyzed by a qualified water testing lab.

## PROPER USE OF FERTILIZERS
The judicious use of fertilizers, which includes using the most suitable analyses and rates of plant nutrients, as well as the proper timing and placement, is very important. Improper use of fertilizer can result in disappointing crop growth and can contribute to environmental problems. Soil tests are one of the best ways for determining which nutrients may be deficient in the soil and the rate of fertilizer needed to correct the problem (see SOIL TESTING).

The balance of nutrients that should be applied is influenced by the nutrient status of the soil. In addition, the nutrient requirements of the crop being fertilized should also be taken into consideration to ensure that the most appropriate fertilizer is applied. For example, fertilization of lawns usually requires the application of 2-4 times as much nitrogen as phosphate. This high nitrogen requirement is necessary to encourage the lush vegetative growth associated with attractive lawns. However, the use of a lawn fertilizer program in flower-beds and gardens will result in a poor set of blossoms and excessive leafy growth. In these situations, approximately equal amounts of nitrogen and phosphate is usually more appropriate.

Plant nutrients, whether supplied by the soil or from fertilizer, must be taken up by the roots. It makes sense, therefore, to place the fertilizer nutrients in the rooting zone of the crop being fertilized. Surface applied fertilizer may encourage shallow rooted plants. Furthermore, surface applied nitrogen fertilizer is vulnerable to atmospheric losses (see FATE OF NUTRIENTS IN SOIL). In the case of lawn fertilization, especially in warm weather, the lawn should be well watered following fertilizer application to move the nutrients into the soil where the chances of volatile losses are minimized. However, excessive watering can contribute to losses in run-off water,

particularly on sloping lawns.

Because they are deeper rooted, trees grown in lawns benefit very little from lawn fertilization. To properly fertilize trees, the nutrients should be injected to a depth of 30-60 cm (12-24 in.) where the soil is dominated by the roots of the trees, rather than the roots of the lawn grasses.

## FERTILIZER AND FOOD QUALITY
In recent years, there have been many vigorous debates about the merits of using 'chemical' fertilizers and the possible negative influence of these manufactured plant nutrients on food quality. Such arguments ignore some basic facts of plant nutrition (see ORGANIC VS INORGANIC GARDENING). Plants take up the same types of nutrients whether they are supplied to the soil in the **organic** or **inorganic** form. Secondly, it is not economically feasible to supply all of the fertilizer required in the organic form.

Food quality is most adversely affected by the lack of an adequate supply of plant nutrients in the soil. Therefore, the addition of fertilizer nutrients, whether in the organic or inorganic form, can improve the quality of the produce that is harvested by providing the growing crop

with an improved and properly balanced supply of plant nutrients.

## PLANT NUTRITION

Like all living organisms, plants must obtain a balanced amount of nutrients for normal growth and development. Sixteen elements are considered to be essential nutrients for plant growth. Carbon (C), hydrogen (H), and oxygen (O) account for 90 - 95 per cent of the plant weight. These nutrients are obtained from air (carbon dioxide) and water. The soil or fertilizer must supply the remaining thirteen elements (see Table 1-7). Nitrogen and phosphorus are the elements most frequently supplemented by way of fertilizer application. However, increasing amounts of potassium and sulphur are also supplied in fertilizer.

## NITROGEN

Nitrogen promotes rich, lush growth and a healthy, dark green color. Nitrogen is primarily used in the building of plant proteins. Lawns, lettuce, spinach, and other green, leafy plants require a plentiful supply of nitrogen to maintain good growth. Excessive amounts of nitrogen can, under some conditions,

Table 1-7
## NUTRIENTS OBTAINED FROM THE SOIL

| CHEMICAL NAME | SYMBOL | PLANT REQUIREMENTS |
|---|---|---|
| **Major or Macro–nutrients** | | |
| **Nitrogen** | N | Relatively large amounts required |
| **Phosphorus** | P | Frequently deficient |
| **Potassium** | K | |
| **Calcium** | Ca | Relatively large amounts required |
| **Magnesium** | Mg | Seldom deficient |
| **Sulphur** | S | |
| **Minor or Micro–nutrients** | | |
| **Boron** | Bo | |
| **Chlorine** | Cl | Very small amounts required |
| **Copper** | Cu | Seldom deficient |
| **Iron** | Fe | |
| **Manganese** | Mn | |
| **Molybdenum** | Mo | |
| **Zinc** | Zn | |

prolong the growing period and delay crop maturity. The effect of nitrogen delaying maturity can largely be overcome by the provision of adequate supplies of phosphorus and potash. Nitrogen is the nutrient that usually most strongly limits growth on western Canadian soils.

## PHOSPHORUS

The nutrient phosphorus promotes the development of strong, healthy root systems (particularly in the case of storage roots such as beets), seed development, early maturity and a normal, healthy, dark green color. Phosphorus is relatively immobile in the soil and its levels can be significantly built up over time through regular application of phosphorus containing fertilizers. Excessive applications of phosphorus fertilizers should be avoided. Most prairie soils, however, are still deficient in phosphorus.

## POTASSIUM

The majority of prairie soils are considered to be adequately supplied with potassium. In many cases, however, potassium is included in lawn and garden fertilizers to ensure against unsuspected potassium deficiencies resulting from the unbalanced application of nitrogen and phosphorus. Potassium helps to promote strong stems and roots, and is involved in maintaining a proper water balance within the plant. It also helps plants resist disease infection. Potassium is involved in influencing most of the reactions that take place in living plant cells. Potassium is quite mobile in the soil and can be leached with excess watering. In addition, large amounts of potassium are contained in vegetative plant materials such as grass clippings. If grass clippings are routinely removed, a large amount of the potassium that is normally recycled is lost from the system. For this reason, soils in which lawn grasses are grown may require additional potassium. Sandy textured soils are more likely to be deficient in potassium than clayey soils.

## SULPHUR

Like nitrogen, sulphur helps promotes dark green growth and is essential to protein formation within the plant. A lack of adequate sulphur may result in the failure of the plants to properly set seed. Sulphur is particularly important for cole crops (cabbage, broccoli, and cauliflower). Sulphur is most likely to be limiting on sandy soils and (especially) on soils that were formerly forested.

## FATE OF NUTRIENTS IN SOIL

Once a plant nutrient is released from soil (i.e., decomposition of organic matter or weathering of soil minerals) or added as fertilizer, there are several ways in which it can be lost from the soil system including:

* **Crop Removal**
  The portions of plants that are removed from the garden or the lawn contain all of the nutrients essential to sustain plant growth. If the nutrients contained in this material are not returned to the soil, they must be replaced by soil mineralization or fertilizer if soil fertility levels are to be maintained.

* **Leaching**
  Water that percolates through the soil profile carries dissolved nutrients. In the arid soils of the southern prairies, this water seldom percolates beyond the rooting depth of the crop. However, in higher rainfall regions, or if irrigation water is applied, particularly on sandy soils, significant amounts of nutrients can be lost through water movement beyond the rooting depth of the crop. Nitrogen (in the nitrate form) and sulphur (in sulphate form) are the two plant nutrients that are most vulnerable to leaching losses.

* **Erosion**
  The organic matter contained in topsoil is a rich reserve of the nutrients required to sustain plant growth. Therefore, if this layer of soil is lost through erosion, losses of plant nutrients are very high. Eroded soils require additional amounts of organic matter and more than the normally applied amounts of fertilizers to help restore soil productivity. In addition, eroded soils are more prone to deficiency of some micro-nutrients (e.g., zinc).

* **Denitrification**
  Under conditions of excess water and/or poor drainage, both soil and fertilizer nitrogen in the nitrate form ($NO_3^-$) is subject to gaseous losses as various nitrogen oxides. When first applied to the soil, fertilizers supplying nitrogen in the ammonium form (e.g., ammonium sulphate and urea) are not subject to denitrification losses. As the soil warms, however, the nitrogen in these products is rapidly converted to nitrate, at which stage these fertilizer materials are equally vulnerable to these losses.

* **Volatilization**
  Nitrogen fertilizers containing ammonium are subject to atmospheric losses of gaseous ammonia ($NH_3$) if they are not incorporated into the soil. Urea based fertilizers are particularly vulnerable when applied to grass or to a sandy soil in warm, dry weather. Losses can be minimized by watering the fertilizer into the soil.

* **Fixation**
  Nutrients can be lost by immobilization into the soil organic matter pool, precipitation into insoluble compounds, or locked between the plates of swelling clays. For example, phosphorus is very vulnerable to being made less soluble and, therefore, less useful to the crop. In high pH soils, the phosphorus readily combines with calcium to form insoluble compounds. Similarly in soils of low pH, it reacts with iron and aluminum. Nitrogen, in the ammonium form ($NH_4^+$), and potassium are often trapped in the crystal lattice of clays as they shrink during the process of soil drying.

  Soil microbes also require the same nutrients to function as plants. During the process of decomposing raw organic matter, microbes usually require extra amounts of nitrogen, although other nutrients (such as sulphur) may also be needed. The subsequent rate of release of these organically bound nutrients is quite variable and, thus, provides an excellent on-going, but somewhat unpredictable, source of nutrients for plants.

* **Surface Run-off**
  Soil nutrients that are dissolved in surface water can be lost from the soil system if this water drains away. Fertilizer nutrients applied to sloping lawn surfaces are particularly vulnerable to run-off losses,

especially when excessive amounts of water are applied to move the fertilizer nutrients into the soil. Care should be exercised to prevent fertilizer nutrients from polluting water supplies in this manner.

### DEFICIENCY SYMPTOMS

When a plant nutrient is severely deficient in soil, characteristic symptoms appear in plants that can be used to identify the nutrient lacking. However, chances are that by the time these trouble signs appear, it is too late to do much to salvage the crop. Furthermore, by the time deficiency symptoms or 'hunger signs' appear in the crop, the damage is quite severe. To ensure satisfactory crop production, possible deficiencies can be averted by following the recommendations of a soil test. Only in this manner can a gardener ensure that the crop is not suffering from 'hidden hunger'.

## SOIL TESTING

An accurate measurement of the nutrient status of the soil can be obtained by submitting a representative soil sample to a reliable laboratory for a soil test. The soil test should indicate the status of the major plant nutrients (N, P, K, and S) as well as provide a recommendation for the amount of fertilizer nutrients to apply in order to optimize plant growth. The soil test also includes information on other soil characteristics, such as salinity and acidity.

Soil sampling and chemical analysis is the most accurate method for predicting the fertilizer needs of crops. Soil testing and fertilizer recommendation is a three-step process; sample collection, sample analysis, and fertilizer recommendation. When the soil test is correlated with crop responses, the test results can form the basis of an effective fertilizer **program**.

### HOW TO TAKE A SOIL TEST

Soil test results can only be as accurate as the sample that is tested. Proper collection of soil samples is very important.

1. Size up the areas to be sampled. Where practical, sample separately areas which show variation in: texture, color, previous crop, and past treatment (fertilizer, manure).

## SOIL TESTING LABORATORIES

Lakeside Research
P.O. Box 800
Brooks, Alberta
T0J 0J0          (403) 362-3326

Alberta Soil & Feed Analysis Ltd.
204, 324 - 7 Street South
Lethbridge, Alberta
T1J 2G2          (403) 329-9266

Saskatchewan Soil Testing Laboratory
University of Saskatchewan
Saskatoon, Saskatchewan
S7N 0W0          (306) 966-6890

Chemex Labs (Alberta) Ltd.
2021 - 41 Avenue N.E.
Calgary, Alberta
T2E 6P2          (403) 291-3077

Core Laboratories-Canada, Ltd.
1540 - 25th Avenue N.E.
Calgary, Alberta
T2E 7R2          (403) 250-5600

Jass Laboratories Ltd.
3510 - 6 Avenue North
Lethbridge, Alberta
T1H 5C3          (403) 328-1133

Monenco Analytical Laboratories Ltd.
Bay 2, 2023 - 2nd Avenue S.E.
Calgary, Alberta
T2E 6K1          (403) 273-2525

Barringer Magenta Labs
4200B - 10 Street N.E.
Calgary, Alberta
T2E 6K3          (403) 250-1901

Crossfield Laboratories Ltd.
Bay 3, 900 Mountain Avenue
Crossfield, Alberta
T0M 0S0          (403) 946-4364

Access PTI Technical Services Ltd.
Bay 1, 3521 - 78 Avenue S.E.
Calgary, Alberta
T2C 1J7          (403) 279-2487

Alpha Laboratory Services Ltd.
10504 - 169 Street
Edmonton, Alberta
T5P 3X6          (403) 489-3754

Norwest Labs
9938 - 67 Avenue
Edmonton, Alberta
T6E 0P5          (403) 438-5522

Manitoba Provincial Soil Testing Lab
University of Manitoba
Winnipeg, Manitoba
R3T 2NT          (204) 474-8155

Alberta Soil and Feed Testing Lab
6th Floor, O.S. Longman Building
6909 - 116 Street
Edmonton, Alberta
T6H 4P2          (403) 436-9150

# SAMPLE INFORMATION SHEET FOR GARDEN AND LAWN SOIL TESTS

<u>Submitter Information</u>

Submitter Name: _____

Address: _____

Town or City: _____

Postal Code: _____  Phone Number: _____

Indicate ( ) Analyses Required

☐ Standard Garden

☐ Other (specify)_____

<u>District Information</u>

County No.____, M.D. No.____, I.D. No.____, or S.A. No.___, Dist. Ag. Office at_____

| Lab. No. (For Lab. Use Only) | Sender Number | Sample Depth Cm (Inches) | Area No | Area Size Sq. Ft. | Number of Places Sampled | Date Sampled |
|---|---|---|---|---|---|---|
| _____ | _____ | ☐ 0-15(0-6) | _____ | _____ | _____ | _____ |
| _____ | _____ | ☐ 15-30(6-12) | | | | |
| _____ | _____ | ☐ 30-60(12-24) | | | | |

<u>IF AN ACCURATE RECOMMENDATION IS REQUIRED THE FOLLOWING INFORMATION SHOULD BE SUPPLIED</u>

Garden to be Grown
or Present Garden  _____

Previous Garden  _____

Indicate Condition of Garden Plants or Garden

Good ☐    Fair ☐    Poor ☐

Good ☐    Fair ☐    Poor ☐

<u>Condition of Plants in Present Garden</u>

| | | | | |
|---|---|---|---|---|
| Roots: | Well Rooted ☐ | Few Roots ☐ | | No Roots ☐ |
| Plants: | Strong ☐ | Spindly ☐ | | Stunted ☐ |
| Upper Leaves: | Dark Green ☐ | Light Green ☐ | | Yellow or Brown Spots ☐ |
| Lower Leaves: | Dark Green ☐ | Light Green ☐ | | Yellow or Brown Spots ☐ |

<u>Condition of Soil</u>

Soil Condition:    Loose ☐      Hard ☐    Easily Worked ☐      Difficult to Work ☐

Depth of Top Soil: _____ inches

<u>Organic Matter Added</u>

Type:    Peat ☐    Manure ☐    Clippings ☐    Other (Specify) _____

When and Amount: _____

<u>Fertilizer Applied</u>

Type (Analysis): _____ _____  Application Rate _____ lb/1000 ft²

Method of Application:    Broadcast ☐    Below Seed ☐    With Seed ☐

Time of Application(s) (month): _____

If this request is related to a previous soil analysis report from this laboratory state Report Number _____

OTHER INFORMATION OR SPECIAL CONCERNS SHOULD BE NOTED AND ATTACHED TO THIS SHEET:
    Example:  Factors affecting crop growth, special problems, etc.

2. Avoid taking samples from fertilizer bands, or where manure has been piled or spilled.

3. Soil is easiest to sample when it is moist and suitable for spading.

4. Take a uniform core or thin slice of soil from at least 10-12 places in a given area. Garden and flower-beds should be sampled to a 20 cm (8 in.) depth and lawns should be sampled to a 10-15 cm (4-6 in.) depth.

5. If a spade is used, dig a spade full of soil to the depth of the spade and throw to the side. Then dig a slice 2.5 cm (1 in.) thick and keep on the spade (see Figure 1-14). Use a knife to mark off a 2.5 cm (1 in.) core. Discard the edges and place the core in a clean pail. Repeat 10-12 times (see Figure 1-15).

6. Collect in a clean pail and mix all cores together thoroughly, crushing small lumps with fingers. Remove about 0.5 kg (1 lb.) of the mixture.

7. Spread the sample on a clean sheet of paper and allow to air dry.

8. Place the dried sample in a sample box or shipping container.

9. Complete the information sheet, especially noting any problems.

10. Deliver or mail the sample and information sheet to the soil testing laboratory.

## HOW TO INTERPRET SOIL TEST RESULTS

The following information will help you to better understand your soil test results and recommendations.

**Available nutrients** are a measure of the essential building blocks for all plant growth. The four that are measured on your soil report are required in the largest quantities and are called macro-nutrients. Nitrogen, phosphorus, potassium, and sulphur are supplied at proper levels in a healthy soil. Sometimes one or more of these nutrients become deficient and requires the addition of a fertilizer. See how your soil test results compare with the guidelines in Table 1-8. The guidelines are only averages. Some plants require much more of some nutrients and less of others.

Nitrogen is required for the development of healthy green leaves and for overall plant health. Phosphorus is essential for the growth of strong healthy roots and the development of flowers, fruit, and seeds. Potassium has a balancing effect on plant growth, promoting strong root and stem development; it is also needed for the development of good color and disease resistance. Sulphur is an important component of plants and is needed for the growth of healthy leaves. When these macro-nutrient levels are low, fertilizer recommendations are made to raise and balance plant nutrients to optimum levels for that growing season. If medium levels are obtained for all nutrients, no fertilizers are required. Very high test results indicate possible over fertilization or poor soil drainage which will affect plant growth by accumulating excess nutrients. Improper soil sampling and drying may also be responsible for very high results.

**Soil reaction** (pH) is a test which indicates whether a soil is acidic or alkaline. Most garden plants and lawn grasses grow best at a pH of 5.8 to 7.3. If your soil is within this range, there is usually no need for correction. An acid soil condition is indicated when the pH is less than 5.5. This can harm the growth of most plants and may require an addition of lime to raise the pH to an optimum level. A pH greater than 7.5 can also be harmful. The application of peat moss and acidic type fertilizers will help reduce this problem.

**Salts** in your soil are required for plant growth, but too much of the wrong kinds of salt can be very damaging. A salt is any mineral that dissolves in water and includes all the soil nutrients. See how your soil test results compare with the guidelines in Table 1-9.

Electrical conductivity or EC is a measure of the total dissolved salts in your soil. It is measured in mS, which indicates how well electricity travels through a water extract of the soil. If your soil tested medium to high in any one of these salts, plant growth may be

### Figure 1-14
### USING A SPADE TO COLLECT A SOIL SAMPLE

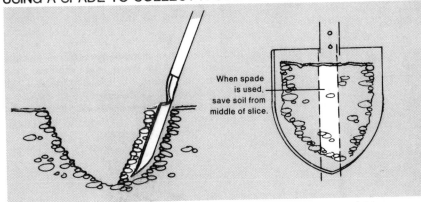

When spade is used, save soil from middle of slice.

### Figure 1-15
### OBTAIN A REPRESENTATIVE SAMPLE

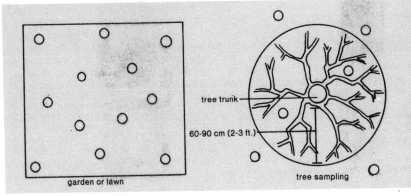

garden or lawn

tree trunk

60-90 cm (2-3 ft.)

tree sampling

## Table 1-8
## RELATIVE PROPORTIONS OF MACRO-NUTRIENTS

| MACRO-NUTRIENT | VERY LOW | MEDIUM | VERY HIGH |
|---|---|---|---|
| **Nitrogen - N** | Less than 15 lb/acre | 70-90 lb/acre | Over 100 lb/acre |
| **Phosphorus - P** | Less than 10 lb/acre | 70-80 lb/acre | Over 200 lb/acre |
| **Potassium - K** | Less than 100 lb/acre | 250-400 lb/acre | Over 800 lb/acre |

## Table 1-9
## RELATIVE CLASSIFICATION OF SOIL SALINITY

| | LOW | MEDIUM | HIGH | VERY HIGH |
|---|---|---|---|---|
| **Total Salts** (mS/cm) | 0-0.5 | 0.5-3.0 | 3.0-8.0 | over 8.0 |
| **Sodium and Sulfate** | L | M | H | H+ |

## Table 1-10
## NUTRIENT CONTENT OF THREE TYPICAL FERTILIZERS

| FERTILIZER | QUANTITY OF NUTRIENTS IN 10 kg OF PRODUCT | | |
|---|---|---|---|
| | NITROGEN | PHOSPHORUS | POTASSIUM |
| 21-0-0 | 2.1 kg of N | no $P_2O_5$ | no $K_2O$ |
| 16-20-0 | 1.6 kg of N | 2.0 kg of $P_2O_5$ | no $K_2O$ |
| 8-24-24 | 0.8 kg of N | 2.4 kg of $P_2O_5$ | 2.4 kg of $K_2O$ |

hindered. Improving soil drainage, drenching with heavy applications of water, and selecting salt tolerant plants are some options when soluble salts are present in very high amounts. Never use softened water or water from high salt wells for irrigation purposes as sodium will accumulate to toxic levels.

**Free lime** indicates the presence of excess lime in your soil. Some soils are naturally high in lime. This material usually restricts a plant's uptake of many essential nutrients. The addition of more lime will compound this problem. Therefore, **never apply lime to a soil unless a soil test shows the need for it** to raise soil pH. Ideally, garden soils should contain little or no free lime.

**Texture** is the proportion of soil particles and the sizes of these particles. The quantity of sand, silt, and clay determines the textural class. For convenience, five broad numerical categories are frequently used to classify mineral soils (see Figure 1-12).

Often, soils with textures of medium, fine, or very fine are hard and difficult to work. The addition of 5-7 cm (2-3 in.) of peat moss will improve water penetration and ease of working (tilth). Spread material over soil surface and rototill 12-15 cm (5-6 in.) deep.

**Organic matter** or humus content of the soil is probably the most important factor affecting physical condition or tilth. The material is necessary for maintaining good soil structure, aeration, and moisture holding ability. It also serves as a storehouse for plant nutrients. Annual additions of peat moss, manure, compost, or lawn clippings (without herbicide treatment) will help maintain this level.

**Fertilizer recommendations:** The Fertilizer Act requires that all fertilizer materials be labeled according to their guaranteed analysis of nitrogen, phosphorus, and potassium. The three large numbers separated by a hyphen on a container give the per cent by weight of nitrogen (N), phosphate ($P_2O_5$), and potash ($K_2O$). They are always reported in this order. Table 1-10 gives three examples of common fertilizers and the amounts of actual nutrients in 10 kg of product.

Some fertilizer materials are labeled with a fourth number. This will always represent the per cent of elemental sulphur (S) by weight in the container.

**Fertilizing:** Fertility levels in your soil are expressed in kilograms of nutrient per hectare (kg/ha). The quantity of fertilizers recommended in your soil report are expressed in kilograms of product per 100 square metres (kg/100 m²). To convert kg/100 m² to lbs./1000 sq. ft., just multiply by 2 (e.g., 5 kg/100 m² x 2 = 10 lbs./1000 sq. ft.). Since fertilizers can only be purchased in kilograms, this is more convenient for the average homeowner to calculate the right quantity of fertilizer to use. To apply the proper amount of fertilizer, first determine the total area to be fertilized. Multiply the length times the width in metres to get the area in square metres. Divide this number by 100 and multiply the result by the quantity recommended on the report. For example: A lawn soil test recommends using 2.5 kg of 21-0-0 per 100 m². The homeowner has a small yard measuring 10 m wide by 15 m long. The calculations are:

10 m x 15 m = 150 m²
150/100 = 1.50
1.50 x 2.5 kg = 3.75 kg

Therefore, 3.75 kg of 21-0-0 fertilizer should be applied to this lawn area.

Measure out the required amount of fertilizer carefully. Use a kitchen weigh scale or bathroom scale. If this is not convenient, then use a measuring cup. It takes about 5.5 cups of the average fertilizer to make one kilogram. Do not handle or transfer fertilizer on the lawn or garden area where a spill can be very difficult to clean up.

There are two basic methods for applying a fertilizer. These are the broadcast method and side-dressing method. If a fertilizer is broadcast onto the surface of a garden, it should be worked in or incorporated into the soil prior to seeding or planting. This can be done with a rototiller or by hand with a spade or rake. Try to spread the fertilizer as uniformly as possible to prevent excessive amounts in certain spots and deficiencies in others. When fertilizing a lawn, apply one-half of the total required fertilizer in one direction and the other half perpendicular or 90° to that direction. Fertilize only when grass plants are dry, preferably before a heavy rainfall or irrigation. Always water in the fertilizer immediately with 3-5 cm (1½-2 in.) of water to prevent salts from burning the leaves and roots. Avoid fertilizer deposits on the leaves of broadleaf plants or in direct contact with seeds or young seedlings. When using the side dressing method, use one-third of the total recommended nitrogen and one-half of the phosphorus and potassium in the furrow. Place the fertilizer 3 cm (1½ in.) below and 5 cm (2 in.) on each side of the seed.

## ORGANIC VS INORGANIC GARDENING

The use of organic materials such as animal manures, green manure, plant refuse, and compost has long been recognized as being important to the soil building process. However, it is virtually impossible to supply all the nutrients that are required for food production in organic form alone. However, some organic gardening advocates suggest that our soils are being destroyed and that our food is being poisoned by fertilizer salts which are mined or manufactured and placed on the soil by man.

There is no question that organic materials can help to improve the structure of the soil. On sandy soils, for example, additional organic matter helps the soil retain moisture more effectively. Organic matter also helps to improve the heavier, clay soils by improving their drainage, granulation, and aeration. The addition of organic matter can often result in increased yields. However, it is unrealistic to think that organic materials alone can supply enough nutrients for all crops that are grown. For example, muck soils are almost entirely composed of organic matter. If they are to become truly productive, however, these soils need regular additions of fertilizer. Some people feel that there is some intrinsic difference between plant nutrients derived from organic and inorganic

materials. In fact, plants do not and cannot differentiate between nutrients derived from these different sources. Furthermore, there is no difference in the nutritional value of crops that are fertilized with organic or inorganic fertilizers. In other words, there is nothing magical or superior about the plant nutrients supplied by organic materials. Nutrients derived from decaying organic matter are neither better nor worse than nutrients from other sources.

Organic materials are very useful, but their value as a source of plant nutrients should not be over-sold. For the home gardener, making compost from leaves, grass, and other organic wastes for application to small plots of ground should be encouraged. However, attempting to fertilize large acreages with compost is impractical and costly. For the farmer, producing high yielding crops every year and returning as much organic matter as possible (in the form of crop residue) to the soil is one of the most practical ways of maintaining a productive soil.

It should be pointed out that green plants can function very effectively in a completely inorganic environment. Crops grown without the benefit of soil are nutritionally equivalent to organically grown crops because plants are unable to utilize organic nutrients. Furthermore, the nutrient content of plants is mainly controlled by genetics, rather than by the medium in which it is grown. Any fertilizer applied to the soil, whether it is organic or not, is reduced to a common inorganic unit before it can be taken up by the plant.

Every gardener is encouraged to be an organic gardener for the right reasons (i.e., the recycling of plant materials and other organic wastes in the interests of building the soil is encouraged). This approach is completely supported by science. However, the dogma surrounding the use of natural fertilizers in preference to the manufactured or mined types of fertilizers is an emotional issue that cannot be scientifically defended.

## CONCLUSION

Working with soils can be very rewarding, whether in terms of being able to produce some of your own food supply, or as a source of pride as a

result of creating an attractive, well landscaped yard, or simply from improving the resale value of your property as a result of your gardening efforts.

Whether growing flowers, vegetables, shrubs, trees, or grass, the key to success is having a properly prepared soil in which to get your plants started. A poor or improperly prepared soil can result in disappointment and frustration. By developing an insight into what plants require in terms of soil quality, your chances of being successful are greatly enhanced.

Although soils are extremely complex, the basics involved in creating a productive soil are within easy grasp of all home gardeners. The key lies in gaining an understanding of how to properly manage soils, in learning how to improve soils that are less than ideal for gardening, in developing an appreciation of the vital role that organic matter plays in maintaining a favorable environment for plant growth, and in learning to understand the role of plant nutrients in maintaining balanced and healthy growth of plants.

Man is very dependent on soil to ensure his continued existence. The earth richly rewards the knowledgeable and diligent gardener, but it can frustrate and punish the uncaring. Civilizations have perished because of their failure to recognize the fragile relationship of soil and food supply. The preservation of this vital and limited resource is very much dependent on the activities of man and how he manages this important natural resource.

Soils are one of man's most valuable natural resources. They are a living part of nature which, when properly managed, fertilized, and watered, provide the foundation for the production of bountiful yields of crops.

Soils are a precious resource that does not automatically last forever. Within a small garden, however, where economics are not a major concern, no matter how poor a soil is naturally, it can be made productive by additions of water, organic matter, and generous applications of fertilizer. Given time and patience, an unproductive soil can be made highly productive as a result of proper planning. Properly managed soils produce the desired, vigorous growth of plants for food, fibre, protection, recreation, and beauty.

## SELF CHECK *QUIZ*

1. What are some of the soil features that make **degraded** or grey soils less desirable for gardening?

2. Distinguish between soil texture and soil structure.

3. Name the four main soil components and indicate their relative proportion in an ideal soil.

4. What is soil pore space and how is it modified?

5. How does the size of soil pores vary and how does this influence soil air and water supplies?

6. What is the meaning of the term 'loam'?

7. Define field capacity and wilting point.

8. What is meant by the terms 'coarse and fine textured'?

9. Differentiate between nitrogen fertilizer losses due to denitrification and volatilization.

10. Is food quality dependent on whether plant nutrients are supplied in the organic or inorganic forms?

## GLOSSARY

**A-Horizon** - top layer of soil, commonly referred to as topsoil.

**acid soil** - soil material having a pH of less than 7.0.

**aeration** - process by which air in the soil is replaced by air from the atmosphere.

**aerobic** - having molecular oxygen as a part of the environment.

**aggregate** - group of soil particles cohering in such a way that they behave mechanically as a unit.

**agricultural lime** - soil amendment consisting principally of calcium carbonate, and including magnesium carbonate and perhaps other materials. It is used to supply calcium and magnesium as essential elements for growth of plants and to neutralize soil acidity.

**alkali soil** - soil having a high degree of alkalinity (pH of 8.5 or higher), or having a high exchangeable sodium content, or both. A soil that contains enough alkali (sodium) to interfere with the growth of most crop plants.

**anaerobic** - having no molecular oxygen in the environment.

**available nutrient** - portion of any element or compound in the soil that can be readily absorbed and assimilated by growing plants.

**available water** - portion of water in a soil that can be readily absorbed by plant roots.

**azonal soil** - soil without distinct genetic horizons.

**B-Horizon** - second layer in the soil profile, commonly referred to as subsoil.

**C-Horizon** - third layer in the soil profile comprised of parent material from which the particular soil has evolved.

**cation exchange capacity** - total amount of exchangeable cations that a soil can adsorb.

**chernozemic** - type of soil developed under grassland.

**clay** - as a particle-size term: a size fraction less than 0.002 mm in equivalent diameter, or some other limit (geologists and engineers). As a rock term: a natural, earthy, fine grained material that develops plasticity with a small amount of water. As a soil term: a textural class. As a soil separate: a material usually consisting largely of clay minerals but commonly also of amorphous free oxides and primary minerals.

**clayey** - containing large amounts of clay, or having properties similar to those of clay.

**clod** - compact, coherent mass of soil produced by digging or plowing. Clods usually slake easily with repeated wetting and drying.

**coarse texture** - texture exhibited by sands, loamy sands, and sandy loams (except very fine sandy loam). A soil containing large quantities of these textural classes.

**colloid** - substance in a state of fine subdivision, whose particles are $10^{-4}$ to $10^{-7}$ cm in diameter.

**compost** - organic residues, or a mixture of organic residues and soil, that have been piled, moistened, and allowed to decompose. Mineral fertilizers are sometimes added. If it is produced mainly from plant residue, it is often called 'artificial manure' or 'synthetic manure'.

**degradation** - changing of a soil to a more highly leached and weathered state, usually accompanied by morphological changes such as the development of an eluviated, light-colored A-horizon.

**electrical conductivity** - measurement of the ability of a soil water extract to conduct an electrical current expressed in mmhos or mS.

**erosion** - wearing away of the land surface by running water, wind, ice, or other geological agents, including such processes as gravitational creep. Detachment and movement of soil or rock by water, wind, ice, or gravity.

**fertilizer** - any organic or inorganic material of natural or synthetic origin that is added to soil to supply certain elements essential to the growth of plants.

**field capacity** - percentage of water remaining in the soil 2 or 3 days after the soil has been saturated and free drainage has practically ceased. The percentage may be expressed in terms of weight or volume.

**fixation** - process or processes in a soil by which certain chemical elements essential for plant growth are converted from a soluble or exchangeable form to a much less soluble or non-exchangeable form, for example, phosphate fixation.

**friable** - consistence term pertaining to the ease of crumbling of soils.

**humus** - fraction of the soil organic matter that remains after most of the added plant and animal residues have decomposed. It is usually dark colored.

**immobilization** - conversion of an element from the inorganic to the organic form in microbial tissues so that the element is not readily available to other organisms or plants.

**impervious** - resistant to penetration by fluids or roots.

**infiltration** - downward entry of water into the soil.

**irrigation** - artificial application of water to the soil for the benefit of growing crops.

**luvisolic** - type of soil developed under forests.

**macronutrient** - chemical element necessary in large amounts, usually greater than 1 ppm in the plant, for the growth of plants and usually applied artificially in fertilizer or liming materials. 'Macro' refers to the quantity and not to the essentiality of the element to the plants.

**micronutrient** - chemical element necessary in only small amounts, usually less than 1 ppm in the plant, for the growth of plants and the health of animals. 'Micro' refers to the amount, not the essentiality of the element to the organism.

**muck soil** - organic soil consisting of highly decomposed materials. Mucky peat and peaty muck are terms used to describe increasing stages of decomposition between peat and muck.

**neutral soil** - soil in which the surface layer, to plow depth, is neither acid nor alkaline in reaction.

**nitrification** - biochemical oxidation of ammonium to nitrate.

**parent material** - unconsolidated and more or less chemically weathered mineral or organic matter from which the solum of a soil has developed by pedogenic processes.

**porosity** - volume percentage of the total bulk not occupied by solid particles.

**reproductive growth** - usually follows vegetative growth stage and results in the growth of flowers, fruits and seeds.

**saline soil** - nonalkali soil that contains enough soluble salts to interfere with the growth of most crop plants.

**sand** - as a particle term: soil particle between 0.05 and 2.0 mm in diameter. As a soil term: soil textural class.

**saturate** - to fill all the voids between soil particles with a liquid.

**silt** - as a particle term: particle between 0.05 and 0.002 mm in equivalent diameter. As a soil term: textural class.

**soil air** - soil atmosphere, the gaseous phase of the soil, is the volume not occupied by solid or liquid.

**soil organic matter** - organic fraction of the soil; includes plant and animal residues at various stages of decomposition, cells and tissue of soil organisms, and substances synthesized by the soil population.

**soil permeability** - ease with which gases and liquids penetrate or pass through a bulk mass of soil or a layer of soil.

**soil pH** - negative logarithm of the hydrogen-ion activity of a soil. The degree of acidity or alkalinity of a soil as determined by means of a suitable electrode or indicator at a specified moisture content or soil-water ratio, and expressed in terms of the pH scale.

**soil profile** - vertical section of the soil through all its horizons and extending into the parent material.

**soil reaction** - degree of acidity or alkalinity of a soil, usually expressed as a pH value.

**soil salinity** - amount of soluble salts in a soil, expressed in terms of percentage, parts per million, or other convenient ratios.

**soil structure** - combination or arrangement of primary soil particles into secondary particles, units, or peds. The peds are characterized and classified on the basis of size, shape, and degree of distinctness into classes, types, and grades.

**soil texture** - proportion of sand, silt, and clay in a soil.

**solum (plural sola)** - upper horizons of a soil in which the parent material has been modified and in which most plant roots are contained. It usually consists of A- and B-horizons.

**tilth** - physical condition of soil as related to its ease of tillage, fitness as a seedbed, and impedance to seedling emergence and root penetration.

**topsoil** - layer of soil moved in cultivation. The A-horizon. Presumably fertile soil material used to topdress roadbanks, gardens, and lawns.

**unavailable water** - portion of the soil water that clings so closely to the solid particles in the soil that it cannot be taken up by the plant.

**water-holding capacity** - amount of water a soil can hold, influenced by the size and mix of mineral particles and the amount of organic matter present.

**weathering** - physical and chemical disintegration, alteration, and decomposition of rocks and minerals at or near the earth's surface by atmospheric agents.

**wilting point** - moisture content of a soil at which plants (specifically sunflower plants) wilt and fail to recover their turgidity when placed in a dark, humid atmosphere.

**zonal soil** - any one of the great groups of soils having well-developed soil characteristics that reflect the zonal influence of climate and living organisms, mainly vegetation, as active factors of soil genesis.

1. The soils that develop under heavy forest cover tend to contain low organic matter levels and are characterized by a lack of structure that makes them susceptible to crusting. Generous application of organic materials can help improve the structure of these soils (see SOIL PROFILES - page 103).

2. Soil texture refers to the relative proportion of sand, silt, and clay sized particles within the soil. Soil structure refers to the manner in which these individual soil particles are bound together into larger aggregates (see SOIL TEXTURE - page 110 and SOIL STRUCTURE AND TILTH - page 112).

3. The four main soil components are mineral matter, organic matter, soil water, and soil air. Their relative proportion on a volume basis in an ideal soil amounts to 45%, 5%, 25% and 25% respectively (see SOIL COMPONENTS - page 104 and Figure 1-3 - page 104).

4. Pore spaces are the voids between soil particles (minerals and organic matter) that are occupied by air and water. Compaction and declining organic matter can result in a reduction of available pore space within the soil. Addition of organic matter can result in an increase in pore space (see SOIL COMPONENTS - page 104 and SOIL COMPACTION - page 115).

5. The proportion of larger sized pores is increased in light (sandy) textured soils and/or soils with a high organic matter content. Large pores help to facilitate the movement of water and air within the soil. In compact, clayey soils, the entry of moisture into the soil is hindered and the soils tend to be poorly aerated (see SOIL AIR - page 108 and SOIL WATER - page 106).

6. A loam soil is one that contains a certain proportion of sand, silt, and clay (see Figure 1-10 and 1-11). It does not refer to the color or organic matter content of the soil. This definition is not in keeping with the common usage of this term in the landscape industry (see SOIL TEXTURE - page 110, Figure 1-10 - page 110 and Figure 1-11 - page 111).

7. Field capacity is the amount of water that will be retained by the soil against the force of gravity. Wilting point is the moisture content at which the plant cannot remove significant amounts of water from the soil. The difference between these two characteristic points represents the water available to support plant growth (see SOIL WATER - page 106, Figure 1-5 - page 107 and Figure 1-7 - page 108).

8. Coarse textured soils are those that contain a high proportion of sand sized particles. These are also referred to as light textured due to the relative ease of cultivation of these soils. Fine textured soils are dominated by clay sized particles. These soils are also referred to as heavy textured due to their difficulty of cultivation (see COARSE VS FINE TEXTURE - page 111).

9. When soils contain excess water, nitrogen in the nitrate form ($NO_3^- - N$) is vulnerable to losses whereby some of the oxygen combined with the nitrate is lost due to the activity of soil micro-organisms. As a result, the nitrogen is lost to the atmosphere as a gas. This process is called denitrification. Nitrogen fertilizer in the ammonium form can be lost to the atmosphere if applied to the surface of the soil in warm, dry weather. This type of loss is called volatilization and can be overcome by working the fertilizer into the soil (see MICROBIAL ACTIVITY - page 114 and FATE OF NUTRIENTS IN SOIL - page 118).

10. Before organically combined nutrients can be taken up by a crop, they must be broken down into inorganic components of the type that are supplied by fertilizers. Therefore, the nutrients taken up by plants are the same regardless of whether they were initially supplied in the organic or inorganic form (see ORGANIC VS INORGANIC GARDENING - page 123).

## RESOURCE MATERIALS

*Alberta Acreage Course: Soils and Fertilizers*. Edmonton: Alberta Agriculture, 1977.

Course lesson 3.

A somewhat different approach (eg., degree of emphasis) to this Soils lesson.

Bentley, C.F. and J.A. Robertson. *Soils and Fertilizers for Gardens and Lawns*. Edmonton: Faculty of Agriculture and Forestry, University of Alberta, 1977.

Additional detail on some of the items covered in lesson one.

Bentley, C.F., T.W. Peters, A.M.F. Hennig & D.R. Walker. *Grey Wooded Soils and Their Management*. Edmonton: U of A Bulletin B-71-1, 1971.

Deals in more detail with the problems more specific to grey wooded soils.

Toogood, T.A. and R.R. Cairns. *Solonetzic Soils, Technology and Management*. Edmonton: U of A Bulletin B-78-1, 1978.

Deals more specifically and in greater detail with the problems of solonetzic soils.

- CLASSIFYING CLIMATE
- CLIMATIC FACTORS INFLUENCING GROWTH AND DEVELOPMENT
- CLIMATE AND HORTICULTURE
- MODIFYING CLIMATIC EFFECTS

# CLIMATE

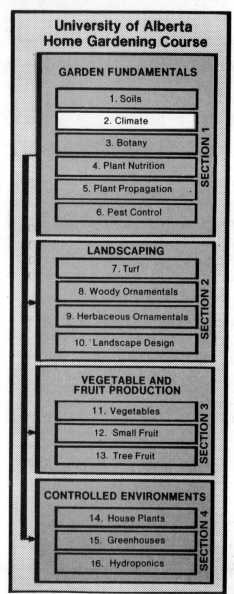

**University of Alberta
Home Gardening Course**

**GARDEN FUNDAMENTALS**

1. Soils
2. Climate
3. Botany
4. Plant Nutrition
5. Plant Propagation
6. Pest Control

SECTION 1

**LANDSCAPING**

7. Turf
8. Woody Ornamentals
9. Herbaceous Ornamentals
10. Landscape Design

SECTION 2

**VEGETABLE AND
FRUIT PRODUCTION**

11. Vegetables
12. Small Fruit
13. Tree Fruit

SECTION 3

**CONTROLLED ENVIRONMENTS**

14. House Plants
15. Greenhouses
16. Hydroponics

SECTION 4

# SELF-STUDY LESSON FEATURES

Self-study is an educational approach which allows you to study a subject where and when you want. The course is designed to allow you to study efficiently and incorporates the following features:

**OBJECTIVES** — are found at the beginning of each lesson and allow you to determine what you can expect to learn in the lesson.

**LESSON MATERIAL** — is logically organized and broken down into fundamental components by ordered headings to assist you to comprehend the subject.

**REFERENCING** — between lessons and within lessons allows you to integrate course material.

The last two digits of the page number identify the page and the digits preceding these identify the lesson number (eg., 107: Lesson 1, page 7 or 1227: Lesson 12, page 27).

Referencing:

sections within the same lesson (eg., see OSMOSIS)

sections in other lessons (eg., see Botany lesson, OSMOSIS)

figures and tables (eg., see Figure 7-3)

**FIGURES AND TABLES** — are found in abundance throughout the lessons and are designed to convey useful information in an easy to understand form.

**SIDEBARS** — are those areas in the lesson which are boxed and toned. They present information supplementary to the core content of the lesson.

**PRACTICAL PROJECTS** — are integrated within the lesson material and are included to allow you to apply principles and practices.

**SELF-CHECK QUIZ** — is provided at the end of each lesson and allows you to test your comprehension of the lesson material. Answers to the questions and references to the sections dealing with the questions are provided in the answer section. You should review any questions that you are unable to answer.

**GLOSSARY** – is provided at the end of each lesson and alphabetically lists the definitions of key concepts and terms.

**RESOURCE MATERIALS** — are provided at the end of each lesson and comprise a list of recommended learning materials for further study of the subject. Also included are author's comments on the potential application of each publication.

**INDEX** — alphabetically lists useful topics and their location within the lesson.

---

© 1986  University of Alberta Faculty of Extension

**Written by:  R. Hugh Knowles, Professor Emeritus F.C.S.L.A.**

Technical Reviewer    Dr. C. Stushnoff

**THE PRODUCTION TEAM**

Managing Editor ....................................................... Thom Shaw
Editor ................................................................. Frank Procter
Production Coordinator ....................................... Kevin Hanson
Graphic Artists ......................................................... Lisa Marsh
Carol Powers
Melanie Eastley Harbourne
Data Entry ...................................................... Joan Geisterfer

ISBN 0-88864-852-9

(Book 1, Lesson 2)

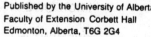

Published by the University of Alberta
Faculty of Extension Corbett Hall
Edmonton, Alberta, T6G 2G4

After completing this lesson, the student should be able to:

1. appreciate the effects of climate on the global distribution of vegetation.
2. understand how the climatic factors - light, temperature and moisture - relate to plant growth and development.
3. understand how general climate is modified by physical geography and recognize the importance of site selection in horticulture.
4. determine the limiting factors imposed on horticultural production by the climate of the prairie region.
5. consider ways and means for modifying climate for the benefit of the crop.

## TABLE OF CONTENTS

## LIST OF FIGURES AND TABLES

# INTRODUCTION

Climate, the term commonly used to summarize an area's weather, involves light, temperature and the effects of moisture. Because climate is so largely responsible for determining what plants will grow where, then vegetational distribution becomes an obvious indicator of climate. This lesson begins with a general classification of climate in which attention is directed to the nature of the landscape in each of the world's climatic regions and the productive capability of each.

Because climate plays such a significant role in determining where the main concentrations of commercial horticultural production **should be** located, this subject is also examined, but within the Canadian context. Finally, the horticultural potential of the western climate is dealt with.

The specific impacts on plant growth and development by the three chief components of climate are discussed. The details of the processes affected and the physiological reactions of the plant are not covered in this lesson on climate, but will be found more appropriately in the Botany lesson.

The lesson concludes with a section on climate modification, an important consideration for success in the protection of high value horticultural crops.

# CLASSIFYING CLIMATE

The most widely used system for classifying climate is the one developed by the Austrian geographer Wilhelm Köppen. It is based on temperature, precipitation, seasonal characteristics and the fact that the natural vegetation (a major element of landscape) is the best available expression of regional climate.

The Köppen system acknowledges five basic climates: A.    tropical rainy, B. dry, C.    humid, mild winter temperatures, D.    humid, severe winter temperatures and E.    polar. Within this broad classification, each class is further divided to describe different sub-climates, each with its typical landscape; thus, steppe and desert comprise the B category (see Table 2-1). The D category, the one with which most Canadians are familiar, is broken

## Table 2-1
## CLIMATE CATEGORIES AND THEIR DIVISIONS

| CATEGORIES | CLIMATE | LANDSCAPE |
|---|---|---|
| A. | Tropical Rainy | Tropical Rainforest<br>Monsoon Rainforest<br>Tropical Savannah |
| B. | Dry Climates | Desert<br>Steppe |
| C. | Humid, Mild Winter Temperatures | Dry Summer Sub-tropical<br>Humid Sub-tropical<br>Marine West Coast |
| D. | Humid, Severe Winter Temperatures (Continental) | Continental, Cool Summer<br>Taiga (Boreal Forest)<br>Northern Grasslands<br>Continental, Warm Summer<br>Temperate Grasslands |
| E. | Polar | Boreal Tundra |

down into humid continental, warm summer and humid continental, cool summer.

# TROPICAL RAINY CLIMATES

These climates are characterized by the absence of winter. Precipitation is seldom less than 75 cm (29.5 inches) per year and the principal landscapes are distinguished by the amount and distribution of rainfall.

## TROPICAL RAINFOREST
Because the climate of this landscape is characterized by a uniformly high temperature and heavy precipitation uniformly distributed, plant growth is luxurient and the number of plant types is large. Most plants are what might be called broad leaved evergreens since they retain their foliage the year round. The soils of the tropical rainforests are quickly exhausted when cultivated because of the high temperature and heavy continuous rainfall. Consequently, the tropical rainforest is a very fragile ecological system that should not be tampered with. The tropical rainforest is common to the jungles of Central and South America.

## MONSOON RAINFOREST
The climate of this landscape is characterized by a long season of fairly evenly distributed rainfall and a short but pronounced dry season. Because of the dry season, the trees of the monsoon rainforest are only semi-evergreen with all or most losing their leaves during the dry season. This is the classical landscape of the rainforests of India, Burma, West Africa and northern Australia.

## TROPICAL SAVANNAH
This landscape is transitional between that of the tropical rainforest and that of the dry climate. The annual rainfall is much less evenly distributed throughout the year than the precipitation of the rainforest. Temperatures are also variable and are distributed over distinct cool/dry and hot/wet seasons. The savannah landscape consists typically of tall coarse grass punctuated with clumps of trees. Trees are widely spaced and are leafless during the dry season. This is the typical landscape of the African plains and the Australian outback. Soils here are low in organic matter and poor in fertility, however, the African savannah supports the richest fauna of grazing animals in the world.

## DRY CLIMATES

The main features of dry climates are low humidity, scanty and unreliable rainfall, intense radiation and high winds.

Desert and steppe landscapes are typical of dry climates.

### DESERT

The annual rainfall for most deserts is less than 15 cm (6 inches) but when rain does fall, it often results in torrential floods. Because of the limitations imposed by rainfall, the plants of the desert are spaced out with bare soil existing between them. Contrary to what one might expect, desert soils are quite fertile and are very productive under irrigation. This, of course, is due to the fact that there is very little leaching taking place under natural conditions. Desert agriculture, however, calls for good management practices because with high evaporation, irrigation water tends to leave salt concentrations dangerously close to the surface.

### STEPPE

The steppe landscape is typical of the grasslands of southeastern Alberta and Saskatchewan. The steppe climate is semi-arid and, even though cultivation is easy, agricultural success is not always assured. Wheat seems to be the one crop that is most readily adapted to this climate.

## HUMID CLIMATES

Humid climates are characterized by seasonal variation in temperature. Indigenous vegetation goes through an annual period of dormancy but, in this instance, dormancy is a response to low temperature rather than drought.

There are three principal landscapes produced in response to this kind of climate. They are dry summer sub-tropical, humid sub-tropical and marine west coast.

### DRY SUMMER, SUB-TROPICAL

This landscape is typical of those found in coastal southern California and the Mediterranean regions of southern France and Spain, South Africa and southern Australia. Vegetation is variable. Glades of open woodland comprise the tree vegetation and both shrubs and trees are usually dwarfed with small, thick, glossy leaves to prevent excessive transpiration.

The climate responsible for this landscape type is characterized by hot dry summers and winter temperatures that are mild. Winters are generally sunny though most of the annual rainfall, 30 - 60 cm (12 - 24 inches), falls at that time.

This landscape is well suited to agriculture. With irrigation it is possible to grow an extremely wide variety of horticultural crops. Citrus, fig, date, olive, grape and the prune-plum are typical of the range of fruit crops. Vegetable growing is also a major agricultural enterprise. It owes much of its success to the fact that a high quality

## Figure 2-1
## MAJOR CLIMATIC REGIONS OF THE WORLD

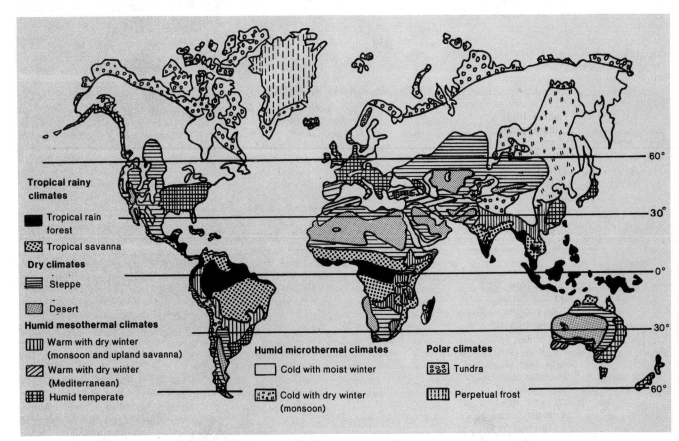

**Tropical rainy climates**
- Tropical rain forest
- Tropical savanna

**Dry climates**
- Steppe
- Desert

**Humid mesothermal climates**
- Warm with dry winter (monsoon and upland savanna)
- Warm with dry winter (Mediterranean)
- Humid temperate

**Humid microthermal climates**
- Cold with moist winter
- Cold with dry winter (monsoon)

**Polar climates**
- Tundra
- Perpetual frost

product can be produced during the winter months.

## HUMID SUB-TROPICAL

These are landscapes that are typical of those found on the eastern side of the Asian continent. The climatic determinants are high summer rainfall, high summer temperatures and mild winters. Such climates are conducive to agriculture, particularly to crops that require a long frost free period. Rice is the main cereal crop and cotton and tobacco are also commonly grown.

## MARINE WEST COAST

These landscapes are common to the west coasts of all continents at the middle latitudes. Generally, they exist as narrow strips. The important climatic factors responsible for this unique landscape are the air masses that move in from the oceans. As a result, the general climate is one of cool summers and moderate winters.

Commonly the marine climates and landscapes give way to others that are markedly different within a short distance. This is very noticeable in parts of California where the foggy/humid marine climate gives way to a very dry one.

The marine west coast climate varies with respect to precipitation from very high to moderate. In many cases, it is the fog associated with this type of climate that moderates what might otherwise be a summer with little rainfall. Fogs are the determinants of agricultural production in these landscapes. Cool season crops like apple, pear, strawberry, lettuce and peas all do well in the open, but warm season things like cucumber and tomato must be grown under glass or plastic.

## CONTINENTAL CLIMATE - HUMID, SEVERE WINTER TEMPERATURES

There are two main subdivisions of this climate; the humid cool summer type of northern latitudes and the humid warm summer type typical of regions further south. Both are distinguished by cold snowy winters and wide annual ranges in temperature. Because their controlling climatic forces originate over large land masses, the term continental climate has been applied to them. Only in North America and Eurasia are there land masses large enough for the development of such climates. Those of

Canada, north central U.S. and the Soviet Union are typical.

## TAIGA (BOREAL FOREST) - COOL SUMMER

The landscape of the most northerly continental climate is one of dense stands of conifers. The soils are podsols with a heavy cover of litter. They are generally unsatisfactory for agricultural purposes though the long days of the short summer compensate to some extent for the lower temperatures.

## NORTHERN GRASSLANDS - COOL SUMMER

These landscapes lie to the south of the taiga. Their soils are deep, fertile, highly productive and their general use for agricultural production testifies to their capability. Forages, cereals and oilseeds are the major crops.

## TEMPERATE GRASSLANDS - WARM SUMMER

The landscape of the temperate grasslands is similar to that of the northern grasslands. However, the very long growing season and the warm summer and summer precipitation tend to make this landscape of great agricultural importance. Corn and soy bean are the major crops of the temperate grasslands in North America.

## POLAR CLIMATE

The bitter cold, the fact that the sun appears above the horizon only for six months and is absent for an equal length of time, makes the polar climate agriculturally unimportant. Nevertheless, in the warmer parts of the polar region a typical living landscape does exist.

## BOREAL TUNDRA

Tundra vegetation is basically of two types. One type is a mixture of cushion-type flowering herbs, sedges, and lichens and the other type is of low distorted woody shrubs - plants that in warmer climates would have been trees. The soil of the tundra is very shallow and is, in most cases, only a few centimetres deep.

## CLIMATIC FACTORS INFLUENCING PLANT GROWTH AND DEVELOPMENT

## LIGHT

Light has many direct or indirect influences on plants. It provides the energy for the synthesis of carbohydrates (sugars) and it has a profound effect on many physiological processes such as germination, flowering, maturation and dormancy. The effect of light alone lends credence to the fact that the environment is really the foster parent of every plant and plays a role as indispensable to the plant's development as the hereditary factors which have been transmitted from its biological parents.

Normal plant growth requires the entire range of the visible spectrum of white light. The various light dependent processes – photosynthesis, phototropism and photoperiodism all involve photochemical reactions mediated by specific pigment systems that respond to various wavelengths of the visible spectrum.

The sun's energy travels across space in the form of electromagnetic waves. When absorbed by a surface, this radiation is transformed to heat energy and produces an increase in temperature. Thus, when short wave energy is absorbed at the earth's surface, the earth becomes a radiating body. The energy re-radiated, however, is entirely in the long wave (low frequency) range.

Solar energy received at the edge of the earth's atmosphere has a great frequency range but most of it never reaches the earth's surface. This is due to the ozone layer of the atmosphere which is one of nature's most effective filters. It absorbs much of the ultra-violet and cosmic frequencies entering the atmosphere, and radiation shorter than 2.9 microns seldom reaches the earth. It also absorbs and re-radiates long wave radiation from the earth.

Water vapor also acts as part of the atmosphere's filtering system. Although it is not too effective in absorbing the

## Figure 2-2
## THE ELECTROMAGNETIC SPECTRUM OF SOLAR RADIATION

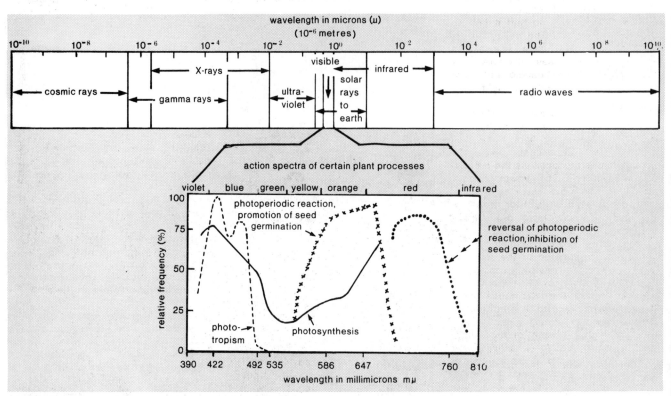

## Figure 2-3
## FILTERING OF SOLAR RADIATION

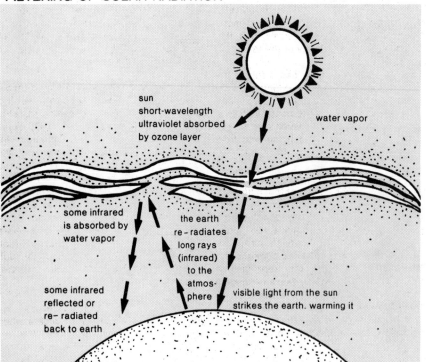

incoming short wave radiation, it is very effective in absorbing the long wave radiation from the earth and thus, helps to maintain surface temperatures much higher than what they might be otherwise.

The radiation absorbed by plants and soil takes one of several routes. Some is conducted into the soil as heat energy. A large part is used in the evaporation of water. A smaller amount is transferred by convection through the layers of air above the soil and a small, but extremely important part (the visible frequencies) is captured by the photochemical processes of the plant. Eventually, however, all is returned to the atmosphere as long wave radiation.

In the absence of light, plants will grow until their food reserves are exhausted, but their growth in darkness will be abnormal. Typical symptoms are whitish spindly stems, exceptionally long internodes and poor roots. This is known as etiolated growth. Nevertheless, horticulturists still grow some crops by withholding light from the portion of the plant they wish to have etiolated. One of the better examples of this practise is the 'blanching' of celery in order to get a product with white, rather than green, 'stems'. The grower simply withholds light from the leaf stem, the edible portion of the plant, so that it fails to produce chlorophyll. The celery bunch, however, does not show any of the structural weaknesses displayed by plants growing in total darkness because the leaves are exposed to full light.

Many growth processes involved in flower, fruit and seed production are indirectly affected by light, since their growth is dependent on the carbohydrates produced via the process of photosynthesis. The growth of roots, structures which are never exposed to light, still depend on light for growth. In this case, carbohydrates produced in the leaves that are surplus to the needs of the above ground portions of the plant, are translocated to the roots for growth. Since the greatest translocation of sugars to the root system occurs in the late summer after the needs of the top have been satisfied, it is not hard to imagine how devastating a late summer hail storm or a plague of leaf eating insects would be to a plant's root system and indirectly to the total plant. Such impacts would have noticeable dwarfing effects on the top of a tree, since anything that affects growth and development of the root system will indirectly influence growth of the top.

The 'turning' phenomenon expressed by the heads of sunflowers is also something that is mediated by light. Actually it is a growth response or more correctly an elongation phenomenon resulting when light shining on one side of a stem impacts the hormone responsible for the elongation of cells. The response is an enlargement of cells only on that side of the stem away from the light, hence, the bending or turning of the flowerhead.

Light also indirectly affects the opening of stomata in the leaves of plants, thereby determining the rate of gas exchange between leaves and the environment. In the absence of light, stomata tend to close. Plants which may show symptoms of wilting during the latter part of a sunny day will regain their turgor when darkness falls, if soil moisture is not a limiting factor.

Light can affect the anatomy of plant foliage. Some plants will develop 'sun leaves' when exposed to intense light while others of the same species,

## Figure 2-4

## SECTIONS TAKEN THROUGH A SUN LEAF AND A SHADE LEAF

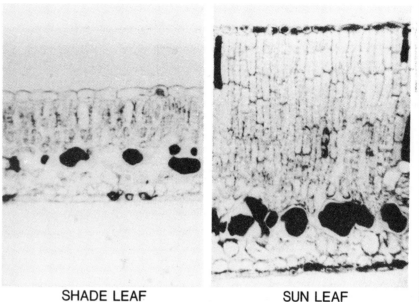

SHADE LEAF          SUN LEAF

growing in regions where light is less intense, will develop shade leaves. The difference between the two leaf types is one of thickness and area. The sun leaf is thicker and frequently smaller. This is actually a survival response. Reduction of the surface area will reduce moisture stress. Thickening of the leaf is actually due to the development of many more layers of cells, thereby increasing the photosynthetic efficiency of the foliage.

High light intensity also has a role in the autumn coloration of plants. Intense light, when accompanied by low night temperatures, favors the accumulation of sugars. The pigments responsible for red color in foliage are in turn derived from these.

The specific length of day (photoperiod) to which a plant is subjected also sets limits upon its development. For example, under short day conditions, a radish plant will continue to grow vegetatively for an indefinite period of time. Even though radishes possess the hereditary capacity for reproductive development, the short day environment imposes a barrier to the expression of this potentiality. Under long day conditions, however, if other factors are favorable, the radish will flower and set seed within the course of a few weeks.

## TEMPERATURE

The intensity and duration of radiation are the two factors upon which temperature depends. The more vertical the sun's rays, the less atmosphere they have to penetrate, thus sunlight over the middle latitudes provides a greater concentration of energy per unit area than do the oblique rays which reach the poles and regions in between.

Temperature is also affected by altitude. For every 300 m (985 feet) of elevation there is a decrease in temperature of 3.6°C. This is approximately 1000 times the rate of temperature change for comparable latitudinal differences. The reason for this is that much of the atmospheric thermal energy is received directly from the earth's surface and only indirectly from the sun. In addition, the lower tropospheric air contains more water vapor and dust and is a more efficient absorber of terrestrial radiation whereas the same radiation at high elevations has a much greater opportunity to escape.

Temperature is also affected by landform. In valley sites, on nights when radiation cooling occurs and the air closest to the ground on the sides of the slopes is colder and heavier than the air above, it will flow or drain down slope

Figure 2-5
**INVERSION LAYER PHENOMENON**

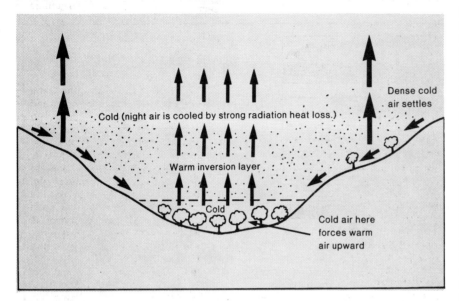

Figure 2-6
**AIR MOVEMENT IN VALLEYS INFLUENCED BY TIME OF DAY**

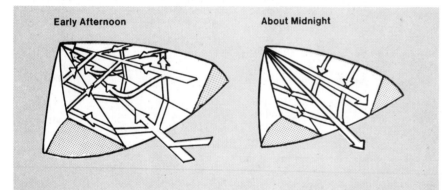

and build up in the valley bottom. Such 'temperature inversions' can have serious implications for horticultural crops, particularly in the early spring. Because of this phenomenon, valley bottoms are to be avoided while upland slopes within the influences of the upper, warmer air are preferred. (see Figure 2-5)

With annual crops, the important temperature considerations during the growing season are mean and extreme values. Perennial crops, on the other hand, are not only affected by the length of the growing season, but also by temperature values over the twelve month period.        Peaches and apricots for example, require a long growing season and warm summer temperatures. The

northern distribution of these tender fruits is limited by the hardiness of their flower buds; temperatures below -25°C will cause injury. In Alberta we find similar things occurring with the blossoms of shrubs like The Golden Bell (*Forsythia*) and the Double Flowering Plum (*Prunus*) even though the winter temperatures are not usually severe enough to cause injury to wood or to shoot buds.

Injury to plants is frequently caused by sudden drops in temperature during the growing season. There are two types of weather conditions responsible for this. The first is the rapid cooling which occurs during a radiational frost. The second is a freeze that results when a

cold air mass (cold front) with a temperature below 0°C moves into a region.

Radiation frost is common under conditions of clear skies while a freeze may occur with an overcast sky and usually involves considerable wind. Frost, because of its local nature, may occur when the official temperature is above freezing. As pointed out earlier, the earth re-radiates energy, but at night, when it is receiving no solar radiation, there is a net loss of heat. Frost occurs when the loss of heat from the earth's surface permits the temperature to drop to or below the freezing point. Radiation cooling takes place not only from the ground surface but from all objects upon it. On a cool clear night, for example, fruit trees will lose heat by radiation. However, if the soil beneath the trees is bare, then radiation from the soil may keep frost out of the tree. In situations where the surface of the soil is covered by a grass mulch, radiation from the soil is prevented and frost forms both on the mulch and in the tree above.

Because heat moves from depth to the surface of soil by conduction, the conductivity of the soil will affect whether or not frost occurs at the surface. Frost on muck soil can be a serious problem because organic soils tend to be poorer conductors of heat compared to mineral soils. More important than soil type in the occurrence of frost is the amount of moisture in the soil. By replacing air (a poor conductor) with water (a better conductor) the danger of frost can be reduced. Frost, therefore, may be prevented on muck soils by flooding.

White frost, commonly seen in the morning, is actually frozen dew. Its occurrence depends on the dew point (the temperature at which the relative humidity reaches 100%). If the ambient temperature is above 0°C then dew forms, but if the temperature is below this, a white frost occurs.

When humidity is low, frost may also occur when the temperature is below 0°C but above the dew point. This is known as a black frost because the only visible indication of it is when the vegetation is blackened due to cold injury.

When water changes to ice, the change in state is accompanied by the release

## Figure 2-7
## FACTORS AFFECTING RADIATION FROST

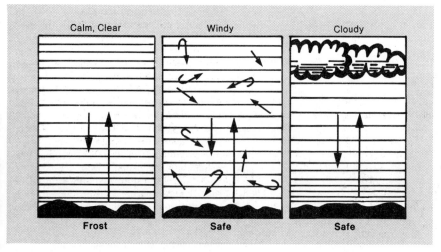

of energy, the heat of fusion. Consequently, if the temperature does not go too low, the freezing of water or the occurrence of a white frost will actually protect plants from damage. This phenomenon is exploited in the use of sprinkler irrigation as a method of frost protection.

Frost is of vital horticultural concern. It defines the season for annual crops in the middle latitudes and it is potentially destructive to perennial crops that flower in the early spring. In the latter case, damage is usually confined to temperature sensitive flower parts.

Temperature plays one other important role with respect to plants. Depending on the species, trees and shrubs will require exposure to a specific number of hours near 5°C during the dormant season if buds are to open and shoots are to grow normally when growing conditions return. The condition of inactivity that is broken in this way is known as the rest period. Many people will react to this phenomenon and when they are sure the rest period has been completed (January 1 for most plants in this region) they will cut branches from flowering trees and shrubs, put them in water and enjoy out of season bouquets, months in advance of the normal blossoming period. When a plant does not receive the required amount of low temperature (chilling) to complete its rest period, growth (if it occurs at all) will be sluggish and quite definitely abnormal. Such problems do not

normally occur above latitude 49° North but they can arise in the more southernly climates. Peaches, for example are a tender fruit that can be grown safely in favorable locations between 35° and 50° North. In orchards south of 35° North, peach buds will not receive sufficient chilling to grow and produce normally except at higher elevations.

While the rest period is of relatively short duration when compared to the total length of the dormant season, it is the continued presence of low temperature and short days that maintains the plant in a state of inactivity when the rest period has been completed. Occasionally, when

unseasonably warm periods are sustained, as sometimes happens in the Chinook belt, plants that have completed their rest period may be brought out of dormancy to their ultimate disadvantage when low temperatures return.

## MOISTURE

In a discussion on climate, the term moisture refers to precipitation (rain and snow) and atmospheric humidity. The average precipitation of a region is of less value agriculturally than effective precipitation (i.e., the water that is available to the plant and not lost to run-off or evaporation). For example, there is a marked difference in the effective precipitation of the Calgary and Edmonton areas. That at Edmonton is much higher and, consequently, a wider variety of plant material can be expected to survive there.

The value of moisture to horticultural crops is clearly demonstrated in irrigated areas of southern Alberta. The dryland landscape is predominantly grassland as far as the eye can see but as one approaches an irrigation district, immediately the featureless landscape is relieved by the living windbreaks of the irrigated farmsteads. For many years the town fathers of Brooks, Alberta, provided irrigation water to the community for the support of trees. This resulted in Brooks becoming a literal oasis in the grasslands of the south.

## Table 2-2
## MOISTURE REQUIREMENT OF PLANTS
## AT EACH STAGE OF GROWTH

| STAGE OF CROP DEVELOPMENT | STAGE | YIELD REDUCTION DUE TO STRESS (%) |
|---|---|---|
| Emergence to Establishment | 1 | 3 |
| Establishment to Rapid Growth | 2 | 25 |
| Rapid Growth to Flowering | 3 | 50 |
| Flowering to Dough Stage | 4 | 21 |
| Dough Stage to Maturity | 5 | 1 |

Some years later, the town reconsidered its benevolence and within a very short time the trees that had contributed so much to the community began to decline by the hundreds. Fortunately, the importance of moisture to the survival of woody vegetation in the town was recognized before deterioration had gone too far.

These days, with more and more horticultural production located in irrigation districts, it is becoming a commonly accepted practise to deliver moisture to the crop based on the crop's requirements at each stage of growth or development. This not only conserves moisture but reacts to the changing needs of the plant. Table 2-2 illustrates the sorts of yield reductions that can be expected in a corn crop when moisture stress occurs at any one of five stages of growth and development shown.

While adequate moisture is of vital concern to the producers of horticultural crops, excesses can also be very serious. Much of the damage arising from excess moisture results directly from root damage which can occur when water replaces oxygen in the soil for sustained periods. This is particularly devastating to tree crops.

## CLIMATE AND HORTICULTURE

The distribution of land suitable for cultivation is primarily determined by the nature of the physical environment, climate, soil and land form. No agricultural enterprise is more dependent on the climatic factors of temperature, long frost free periods and mild winters than is horticulture. In Canada, where happy combinations of these climatic factors are rare in their totality, major areas of commercial horticultural production are usually found in regions where climate has been modified by some local condition. The more important of these have been proximity to large bodies of water, amenable land form and height above sea level.

These climatic modifiers (microclimates) can be particularly important for perennial crops like tree and small fruits and nursery crops. Commercial vegetable growing too, may be concentrated in regions where the climate is amenable, however, there is

much more flexibility in selecting areas for horticultural crops of the annual persuasion. The main reason for the difference lies with the fact that plant breeders have been able to develop cultivars of annual crops that are capable of producing a quality product in climates that lack one or more of the optimum requirements for the crop in question. Very long frost free periods and mild winters are not as vital to the success of vegetable crop production as long as soil and moisture conditions are favorable.

The fruit growing regions of British Columbia have achieved their distinction largely because of climate. For example, the climate of the southern portion of the Okanagan valley is very mild, thus it is possible to grow the tender soft fruits with an acceptable degree of risk. The buds of the soft fruits, peaches and apricots, are very susceptible to low temperature injury when winter temperatures drop below -24°C. Grapes also are now being grown in the region, partly for the same reason; but also because of the nature of the growing season, that is, high daily maximum temperature and a long frost free period.

Altitude has also had a significant effect on fruit growing in British Columbia. Apples grown in the 'high' mountain valleys owe their exceptionally good color to the clear skies and abundant sunshine usually found at higher altitudes. Fruit experts frequently comment that a B.C. apple does not have the 'sprightliness' of the same product produced in Eastern Canada. This may be true but it cannot be denied that B.C. apples are more highly colored, sweeter, crisper and firmer than their eastern counterparts. These characteristics of the B.C. apple are products of a climate with clear sunny days and cool nights whereas those of the eastern apple are produced in a climate that is more humid, with less hours of sunlight and warmer nights.

The fruit growing regions of Ontario are all located within the influence of the Great Lakes and this factor plays an important role in climate modification. These large bodies of water are gigantic heat reservoirs and the temperature of

## Figure 2-8
## ORCHARD CONCENTRATIONS—MONTEREGIAN AREA

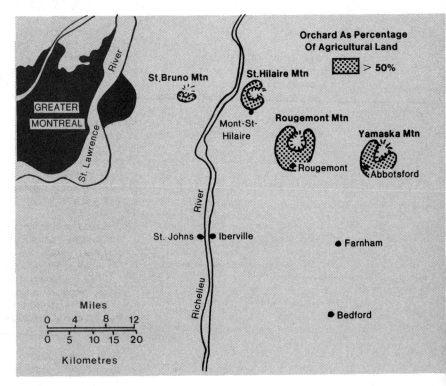

Figure 2-9
ORCHARD REGION—ANNAPOLIS VALLEY

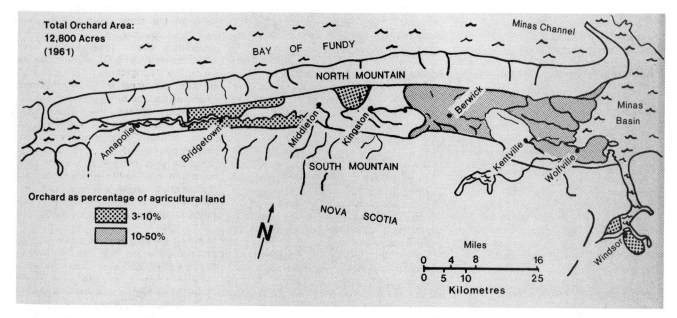

arctic air blowing across open water can be significantly raised to the benefit of nearby orchards. It has been shown, for example, that winter winds leaving the state of Wisconsin at -34°C and blowing across the open water of Lake Michigan will arrive on the eastern shore of the lake at a temperature of 0°C. Such a phenomenon cannot help but have a marked effect on the suitability of an area for the growing of perennial crops.

Water bodies may have other climate moderating effects. It is not uncommon to find that on-shore winds during the late summer will significantly prolong the growing season by delaying the date of the first killing frost. Also, if the water body is small enough to freeze over during the winter, then winds blowing across the frozen surface during the spring can effectively delay the blossoming of fruit trees until the danger of spring frost is past.

In Quebec, most of the important commercial orchard concentrations are found on land types that exhibit a considerable degree of slope. It is interesting to note (see Figure 2-8) the concentrations of orchards that are clustered about the south, east and western aspects of the ancient volcanic peaks of the Monteregian area just east of Montreal. These hilly locations offer good air drainage as well as a variety of aspects for all of the various cultivars

being grown. Hence, some of the risks associated with the growing of fruit in an uncertain climate have been partially avoided. Slope and landform in this case have a major effect on the avoidance of radiation frosts.

As far as climatic modification goes, the Annapolis Valley of Nova Scotia has been thrice blessed (see Figure 2-9). The Bay of Fundy and Minas Basin offer the climate moderating effects of large water bodies on cold continental winds from the north and north-west. The landform, known as North Mountain which runs along the northern boundary of the valley, offers further protection from north winds and provides south facing slopes that offer some protection from radiation frost. Thirdly, the valley is within the moderating influence of the Gulf Stream and winds that enter the valley from the south and south-west are warmed by this ocean current.

There are few major areas of commercial horticulture in the prairie provinces. Certainly, commercial tree fruit production as noted in all other regions is non-existent. The 'continental' characteristics of the regional climate tend to overwhelm any of the geographic modifiers so important to climate in other parts of the country.

There are some areas where vegetable growing on a commercial scale is

practiced but, because of the limits of the western and export markets, size of the operations is much more modest than what may be found elsewhere in Canada. Southern Alberta and Manitoba are the major areas of vegetable production in the region.

Small fruit production (strawberries, for example) is expanding. At the moment, the main obstacle to a viable industry is the lack of high quality, fully hardy cultivars. This fact was highlighted in 1977 when the strawberry producers of Manitoba suffered a $700,000 loss because their main high quality cultivar was not fully winter hardy.

## REGIONAL CLIMATE AND HORTICULTURE

The general climate of the prairie provinces falls into the category 'continental, cool summer'. This is an apt description, but within the region there is such a wide climatic variation insofar as horticulture is concerned that horticultural practises will vary greatly from north to south.

In the northern parts of the region, moisture is seldom a limiting factor to horticultural productivity. The length of the growing season puts some restrictions on the number of species and cultivars of woody plants that may be grown. However, with some annual

Figure 2-10
## CLIMATIC MAP OF THE PRAIRIE REGION

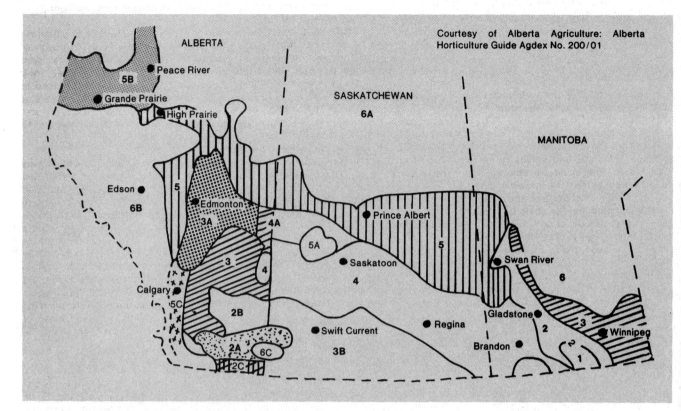

Courtesy of Alberta Agriculture: Alberta Horticulture Guide Agdex No. 200/01

Zone 1 is the most favorable fruit-growing locality due to high precipitation, a long frost-free period, and the presence of natural shelter.

Zone 2 differs from Zone 1 by having lower winter temperatures and a shorter frost-free period. Subzones 2A, 2B, and 2C are less favorable because of drought and rapid winter temperature fluctuations caused by chinook winds. Supplemental moisture and shelter are particularly beneficial in these subzones.

Zone 3 has climatic conditions similar to Zone 2 but is often characterized by less favorable soil conditions. Subzones

3A and 3B are colder and drier than Zone 3.

Zone 4 has moderate precipitation and lower winter temperatures than the preceding zones.

Zone 5 consists of northern areas with short growing seasons and cold winter temperatures. Subzones 5A, 5B, and 5C are less favorable; the latter subzone is subject to drying chinook winds.

Zone 6 is a northern area or one with a high altitude, leading to the least favorable conditions for fruit growing on the prairies.

crops, the longer day that prevails at the northernmost latitudes more than makes up for the limitations imposed by the dates of spring and fall frosts.

The minimum temperatures of the northern climate can have adverse effects on some perennial crops. It is well known that while the above ground infrastructure of a tree may be able to tolerate extremely low temperatures when the tree has been fully hardened for winter, certain parts may not. Both roots and flower buds are more

susceptible to low temperature injury than most other tissues and are frequently damaged by these temperatures.

Snow cover in the north is generally reliable and it can also make an important contribution to winter survival. Snow, when not compacted, is an effective insulating material, and in northern Alberta, it can be relied upon to protect the crowns and roots of strawberry plants which would not survive winter temperatures otherwise.

In the southern part of the region, moisture is the major limiting factor and all horticultural production must be irrigated. In this part of the region, effective precipitation is much less than that normally occurring in the north. This is because of the high evapotranspiration caused by the almost continuous wind and aggravated by the occasional hot, dry chinook. Snow cover is also limited during the winter and seldom lasts long enough to give protection from low temperature extremes. Desiccation and low temperature injury to all types of perennial vegetation is common. The temperature of the growing season in the south, however, is generally favorable and in areas where the crop can receive irrigation and some protection from wind, conditions for the production of warm season crops are excellent.

Even though there are large climatic differences between the north and south, there is one characteristic common to both that all horticulturists must respect. It is the limitation imposed on woody plants by the length of the growing season. For trees and shrubs to survive the winter, they must be able to grow and mature before the growing season ends. If they cannot, then they will be unable to cold harden their tissues for winter and will thus be subject to low temperature injury. The length of the growing season, then, imposes severe restrictions on the pallete of woody materials that can be used in the region. Many of the finer woody ornamentals that do so well in eastern Canada have no chance of survival in the prairie provinces simply because they require so much more growing season before maturation can begin. For the same reason, we cannot expect McIntosh and Delicious apples to survive here. Because of the relative shortness of the growing season, we are restricted to the use of those cultivars derived from culturally more primitive parental material, things that can more readily adapt to this climate. For the most part, the vast majority of our apple cultivars fall into this category.

Plants that are hardy in the region prepare for winter by responding to environmental cues. By mid-August, a plant that is hardy here will have completed its elongation growth for the season with the formation of a terminal bud. About this time, day length will be noticeably shorter than what it was at the height of the growing season and this does not go unnoticed by the plant. The receptor of the short day stimulus is a photoreceptive pigment in the leaves which detects the change in day length and then transfers the information to other parts of the plant, causing changes which lead to the condition known as maturity. Dr. James McKenzie of the Canada Research Station, Beaverlodge has studied some of these changes taking place in the Red Osier Dogwood. He has noticed that the control of transpiration by leaves that is so obvious

and effective during the growing season, no longer functions normally when short days arrive. He has also noticed, at about the same time, that roots tend to function less effectively as structures in the uptake of moisture. All this results in a net loss of free water from plant tissue. Later, as temperatures begin to drop and leaves begin to fall, the plant undergoes a process known as 'cold hardening' by getting rid of freezable water. To facilitate this, the cell membranes change by becoming more permeable. With this change, water is able to move more freely out of the cell and into the intercellular spaces where it can freeze solid without damaging the cells. Had it been retained and then frozen within the cell, ice crystals would have destroyed the cells and caused death of the tissues.

It must be noted that to sustain life, all water does not leave the cell. The water remaining becomes tenaciously bound to proteins and other cell constituents and, for the most part, is retained by the cell in an unfreezable condition.

When plant tissues have undergone this process of cold hardening, a plant's resistance to low temperature injury increases dramatically. Most plants that are fully cold hardened will withstand temperatures of -50°C without injury to their trunks and branches, although some plants may suffer from loss of flower buds when temperatures of -50°C are sustained for several days.

## MODIFYING CLIMATIC EFFECTS

The selection of site is the most important single aspect in establishing a horticultural enterprise. However, no site is perfect and the horticulturist will use any means that is economically feasible to ameliorate the effects of climate if such steps are going to maximize production or protect the crop.

Many practical and innovative ways have been used to modify the effect of light and temperature on production. Shade structures are commonly used to reduce transpiration of young transplants at a stage in their growth when they are soft and most susceptible to transpirational loss. Reduction of light intensity is also important to the maintenance of quality

of containerized nursery stock and the retention of color in commercial flower crops like roses. This is most important in areas of intense summer sunlight.

Mulches are commonly used to moderate the effects of temperature on growth of warm season crops. In the summer, when soil temperatures are at their highest, plastic mulches can be used to effectively maintain soil temperatures at higher and more acceptable levels and thus reduce the time from planting to maturity.

Mulches are also used in a practical way to provide winter protection with some crops. In this instance they are not used 'to keep plants warm' but rather, used to prevent those temperature fluctuations that can have such devastating effects on the root systems of plants (strawberries, for example) when they are subjected to freeze/thaw cycles. Winter mulches then, should not be applied until after the soil has frozen. When this is done, the dormant condition is maintained and the physical lifting of plants by freeze/thaw conditions is prevented.

Structures of various kinds have been used to control temperature. Cold frames, inexpensive low enclosed beds covered with a removable sash or plastic, are commonly used by homeowners to extend the growing season so that plants can be started before the growing season begins. In some cases, people will even go so far as to use these structures for the *in situ* growing of such exotics as peppers and melons. The cold frame is ideally suited for this purpose since it has all of the qualities required to accept short wave radiation. Since it can store and re-radiate heat, it is able to provide the environment required for warm season crops.

The harvest dates of some warm season crops can be predicted because the time required to reach a harvestable stage is a function of the total heat received. In such cases, the time required to reach a harvestable stage may be expressed in terms of temperature-time values called heat units. Heat units are calculated by measuring time relative to temperature above a certain minimum. If the minimum for a certain crop is 10°C, then a day with a mean temperature of 18°C would provide eight degree days of heat units.

## Figure 2-11
## TUNNELS AND HOT CAPS

A day with a mean temperature of 5°C, on the other hand, would provide zero degree days of heat units. The use of the heat unit is a very useful means for estimating the practicality of things like cold frames as growing structures.

Protective structures are also employed at field scale during the early part of the season. Cones of translucent paper or plastic called 'hot caps' are frequently used for crops that have reached the stage for transplanting but are still too tender to stand the rigors of the outdoor environment. These little tents simply act like miniature greenhouses, not only by protecting the plant from frost but also by conserving heat. They also give the young plant a good start on its way to maturity.

In recent years, there has been widespread field use of plastic tunnels to facilitate early vegetable production. Tunnels are made from sheets of clear polyethylene plastic laid down mechanically, usually over wire hoops. Soil is used to seal the sides of the tunnels at ground level. As temperatures rise, the plastic is perforated for ventilation and later slit in increasingly more places. In many instances, the plastic tunnel is thus converted to a plastic mulch, anchored where necessary by soil.

For centuries, horticulturists have made use of structures like masonary walls that will absorb radiant energy during the day and release it gradually at night. It is very common in Europe to find two-dimensional trees trained against such structures to take advantage of the heat necessary to mature the crop. Homeowners frequently will use this principle to produce vine ripened tomatoes by growing them on a trellis in front of the south facing wall of a building.

Wind has always been of serious consequence to horticultural production and when accompanied by rain, hail, or even high temperature, the impact can be devastating. The damage from wind varies with the season. At blossom time, wind can seriously affect pollination of fruit trees by either reducing the duration of receptivity of the flower stigma or by reducing bee activity or both. During the time of most rapid crop growth, wind can increase transpiration to the point of incipient wilting. In winter, winds may cause the desiccation and browning of some conifers.

Wind protection, however, can be achieved to some degree by the planting of shelterbelts. Figure 2-12 provides some indication of the amount of shelter one might expect from a solid planting of trees of modest height. Shelterbelts are planted at right angles to the direction of the prevailing wind. The density of the belt depends on the amount of shelter required. The type of shelterbelt and its location is important because the hazard of frost can be increased if it prevents the flow of cold air from the field or orchard or prevents air mixing that would bring warm air to the plantation from an inversion layer.

## CONCLUSION

It was noted earlier that environment is the foster parent of every plant and plays as indispensable a role in its development as do hereditary factors which have been transmitted to it from

## Figure 2-12
## THE EFFECT OF SHELTERBELTS ON WIND VELOCITY

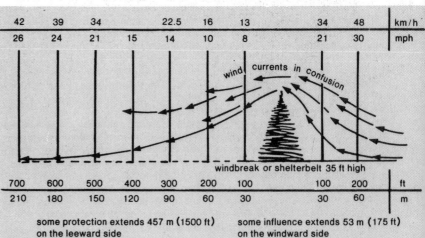

| 42 | 39 | 34 | | 22.5 | 16 | 13 | | 34 | 48 | km/h |
| 26 | 24 | 21 | 15 | 14 | 10 | 8 | | 21 | 30 | mph |

wind currents in confusion

windbreak or shelterbelt 35 ft high

| 700 | 600 | 500 | 400 | 300 | 200 | 100 | | 100 | 200 | ft |
| 210 | 180 | 150 | 120 | 90 | 60 | 30 | | 30 | 60 | m |

some protection extends 457 m (1500 ft) on the leeward side

some influence extends 53 m (175 ft) on the windward side

450 m (about 1500 ft)     50 m (about 165 ft) achievement

its biological parents. The elements of climate are powerful components of environment and it has been shown that they, perhaps more than any other set of environmental factors, will determine what crops can be economically grown in the various regions of the world.

Like all living things, plants respond quickly to environmental stimuli. In some instances, the response will be positive and lead to increased production. In others, the response will be equally positive but lead to conservation and survival. In still other cases, one set of climatic factors may favor growth but prevent development.

While the elements of climate are fundamental to growth and development of plants, it is interesting to note how subject the elements of climate are to modification by the elements of geography. In so many cases, successful production of horticultural crops is so very dependent on amelioration by the microclimate.

Finally, we must not discount the importance of man in climatic modification. Innovation coupled with a broad understanding of factors affecting plant growth can mean the difference between success and failure.

The conservation of moisture at ground level is one other important aspect of climate amelioration. Organic mulches are frequently used for this purpose. They may be used to reduce evaporation and to increase the absorptive capacity of the upper layer of soil. At the same time, these moisture conserving materials can play another very important role in protecting soil structure from the devastating effect of heavy rainfall.

## SELF CHECK *QUIZ*

1. In selecting a site for the growing of tree fruits, the orchardist must be more selective in the choice of sites than the vegetable grower. Discuss the reasons for the difference.

2. Under what conditions might it be possible to use sprinkler irrigation to protect a crop from frost injury?

3. Show how you might use innovative microclimatic modification techniques to (a) increase the frost-free period, (b) increase the number of heat units, and (c) cause developmental change.

4. Show how the defoliation of a tree in late summer would have a more stressful effect on the tree than a similar occurrence in early June.

5. What are the prospects and limitations for horticultural production in south, central and northern Alberta?

6. In spite of the fact that rolling topography can be more difficult to manage, orchardists will invariably consider upland areas on rolling terrain more valuable for tree fruit production. Explain.

7. A woody plant must achieve maturity before cold hardening can take place. Indicate two phenomena associated with the mature condition that must precede cold hardening.

# GLOSSARY

**ambient temperature** - temperature of the environment in contact with the subject (i.e., temperature of the air surrounding a plant).

**black frost** - frost that occurs when the temperature is below 0°C but above the dew point.

**cold hardiness** - condition which must be acquired by perennial plants in order to avoid injury when exposed to freezing temperatures.

**cosmic radiation** - extremely short-wave radiation, from the sun, which is below the wavelengths of the visible spectrum.

**desiccation** - type of plant tissue injury resulting from extreme moisture loss. In continental climates, it is generally associated with low temperatures and wind.

**dew point** - temperature at which the relative humidity reaches 100%.

**effective precipitation** - net amount available to plants following run-off and evaporation losses.

**electromagnetic radiation** - solar radiation consisting of electromagnetic waves including radio, light, x-ray and gamma rays.

**etiolation** - morphological expression of a leafy plant that has been grown in the absence of light.

**evapo-transpiration** - total water transferred from the earth to the atmosphere by evaporation and transpiration.

**indigenous** - native

**incipient** - initial stage

**in situ** - in its original place

**micron** - unit of length equivalent to $10^{-2}$ metres

**microclimate** - climate of a small area as opposed to that of a region of which the small area is a part.

**ozone layer** - region in the upper atmosphere where most atmospheric ozone is concentrated.

**photoperiodism** - growth or developmental response of a plant to the length of daylight.

**phototropism** - process whereby the directional growth of a plant is altered by its reaction to light.

**radiation frost** - condition which commonly occurs on a clear cold night when the earth and things upon it lose heat by radiative cooling.

**rest period** - physiological condition common to the buds of woody plants beginning at the time of terminal bud formation and ending after exposure to a discrete number of hours of critical low temperature.

**sprightliness** - term used to describe the flavor of a fresh, mature apple containing a combination of acidity, sweetness and aroma.

**sun-leaves** - leaves possessing several layers of palisade cells due to prolonged exposure to intense sunlight.

**tropospheric** - pertaining to the inner layer of the atmosphere.

**white frost** - frozen dew.

# INDEX

## RESOURCE MATERIALS

Geiger, R. *The Climate Near the Ground*. 5th German ed. Cambridge: Harvard University Press, 1971.

The definitive work on microclimate.

Griffiths, J.F. and D.M. Driscoll. *Survey of Climatology*. Ohio: C.E. Merrill Publishing Co., 1982.

One of the better all-round texts on climatology.

Janick, J., R.W. Schery, F.W. Woods, and V.W. Rutten. *Plant Science*. 2nd ed. San Francisco: W.H. Freeman and Co., 1974.

A good general university level text with good coverage of climate and its components.

Klages, K.H.W. *Ecological Crop Geography*. New York: Macmillan, 1958.

An excellent treatise, though dealing chiefly with climate and agronomic crops.

Krueger, R.R. "The geography of the orchard industry in Canada." *Readings of Canadian Geography*. Toronto: Irving, Holt, Rinehart & Winston, Ltd., 1972.

An excellent treatise on horticultural microclimate.

Westwood, M.N. *Temperate Zone Pomology*. San Francisco: W.H. Freeman and Co., 1978.

An excellent text for sections dealing with the effect of climate on woody plants, specifically tree fruits.

## SELF CHECK ANSWERS

1. a. Tree fruits are woody perennials. Therefore, both length of growing season and severity of winter climate are important.

   b. Site and climate or microclimate have an important role in winter survival of fruit trees and their flower buds.

   c. Climate and microclimate are also important with respect to pollination and fruit set and with the quality of fruit produced.

   d. The growing season must be long enough and warm enough for the fruit to mature.

   e. Vegetables are annuals for the most part. Hence, winter temperatures are of no consequence.

   f. Through plant breeding and selection, vegetable cultivars have been developed that are much more climate selective than are tree fruit cultivars, hence, climate is not an insurmountable problem for the vegetable grower.

   g. Long growing seasons, fertile soils and adequate water supply are more important than microclimate because microclimate modification, in so many cases, can be made artificially in vegetable production (see CLIMATE AND HORTICULTURE - page 208, REGIONAL CLIMATE AND HORTICULTURE - page 209).

2. Sprinkler irrigation can be used to protect crops from light frosts because water, in the act of freezing, releases enough heat to prevent tissue injury (see TEMPERATURE - page 205).

3. a. To increase frost free period — use tunnels; cold frames

   b. To increase number of heat units — black plastic mulch — south facing masonary walls

   c. To cause developmental change — mild moisture stress; reduction of day length with shade cloth or extending it with light (see MODIFYING CLIMATIC EFFECTS - page 211).

4. June defoliation - Tree will produce new leaves and still have sufficient time to grow and produce surplus metabolites for translocation to roots for growth of these structures. There will, therefore, be little if any reduction in root growth and, consequently, no effect on top growth of the tree the following year.

   Late summer defoliation - The tree will be able to replace little, if any, foliage at this time of year. Hence, there will not be a supply of metabolites for the roots. Shoot growth will be limited since growth of the top of the tree in the following year is dependent on the root system. Anything that adversely affects the root system will adversely affect the top (see LIGHT - page 203).

5. Southern Alberta - high winds and limited precipitation make tree fruit production difficult, except in sheltered, irrigated areas. Warm season vegetable crops do well under irrigation. High lime and saline soils call for special attention by growers of all horticultural crops.

   Central Alberta - tree fruits (apples, apple crabs) all perform well in this climate. Irrigation not required. Cool season vegetable crops grow well.

   Northern Alberta - day length tends to make up for cool temperatures in vegetable production, though the latter favors cool season crops, except in a few areas where the microclimate favors the growing of warm season crops. Apples, apple crabs and crab apples do well although certain cultivars do better than others (see REGIONAL CLIMATE AND HORTICULTURE - page 209).

6. Low temperature injury during the growing season can be serious with tree fruit crops, particularly at blossom time. Since cold night air tends to move downwards to valley bottoms, upland areas on the valley sides tend to be preferred orchard locations. Also, when temperature inversions occur, warm air moves up slope causing upland areas to be warmer than valley bottoms (see TEMPERATURE - page 205 and Figures 2-5 and 2-6 - page 206).

7. The two phenomena associated with woody plants that must precede cold hardening are:

   The formation of a terminal bud, which indicates the end of extension growth.

   The plant's ability to respond to the shortening daylength of the region and, as a result, undergo important physiological change (see REGIONAL CLIMATE AND HORTICULTURE - page 209).

# BOTANY

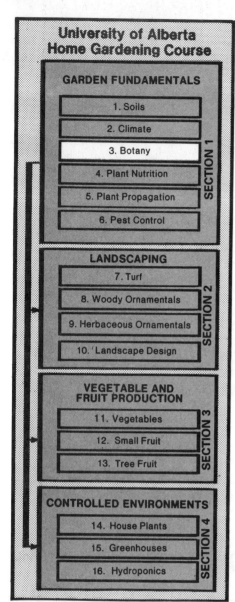

**University of Alberta Home Gardening Course**

**GARDEN FUNDAMENTALS**

1. Soils
2. Climate
3. Botany
4. Plant Nutrition
5. Plant Propagation
6. Pest Control

SECTION 1

**LANDSCAPING**

7. Turf
8. Woody Ornamentals
9. Herbaceous Ornamentals
10. Landscape Design

SECTION 2

**VEGETABLE AND FRUIT PRODUCTION**

11. Vegetables
12. Small Fruit
13. Tree Fruit

SECTION 3

**CONTROLLED ENVIRONMENTS**

14. House Plants
15. Greenhouses
16. Hydroponics

SECTION 4

# SELF-STUDY LESSON FEATURES

Self-study is an educational approach which allows you to study a subject where and when you want. The course is designed to allow you to study efficiently and incorporates the following features:

**OBJECTIVES** — are found at the beginning of each lesson and allow you to determine what you can expect to learn in the lesson.

**LESSON MATERIAL** — is logically organized and broken down into fundamental components by ordered headings to assist you to comprehend the subject.

**REFERENCING** — between lessons and within lessons allows you to integrate course material.

The last two digits of the page number identify the page and the digits preceding these identify the lesson number (eg., 107: Lesson 1, page 7 or 1227: Lesson 12, page 27).

Referencing:

sections within the same lesson (eg., see OSMOSIS)

sections in other lessons (eg., see Botany lesson, OSMOSIS)

figures and tables (eg., see Figure 7-3)

**FIGURES AND TABLES** — are found in abundance throughout the lessons and are designed to convey useful information in an easy to understand form.

**SIDEBARS** — are those areas in the lesson which are boxed and toned. They present information supplementary to the core content of the lesson.

**PRACTICAL PROJECTS** — are integrated within the lesson material and are included to allow you to apply principles and practices.

**SELF-CHECK QUIZ** — is provided at the end of each lesson and allows you to test your comprehension of the lesson material. Answers to the questions and references to the sections dealing with the questions are provided in the answer section. You should review any questions that you are unable to answer.

**GLOSSARY** — is provided at the end of each lesson and alphabetically lists the definitions of key concepts and terms.

**RESOURCE MATERIALS** — are provided at the end of each lesson and comprise a list of recommended learning materials for further study of the subject. Also included are author's comments on the potential application of each publication.

**INDEX** — alphabetically lists useful topics and their location within the lesson.

© 1986 University of Alberta Faculty of Extension

**Written by: Gail Rankin**

Special Technical Material by: Dr. E.W. Toop

Technical Reviewers:  Dr. E.W. Toop
Dr. K.E. Denford

**ISBN 0-88864-852-9**

(Book 1, Lesson 3)

THE PRODUCTION TEAM

Managing Editor .................................................... Thom Shaw
Editor ................................................................. Frank Procter
Production Coordinator ...................................... Kevin Hanson
Graphic Artists ....................................................... Lisa Marsh
Carol Powers
Melanie Eastley Harbourne
Data Entry ..................................................... Joan Geisterfer

Published by the University of Alberta
Faculty of Extension Corbett Hall
Edmonton, Alberta, T6G 2G4

## LEARNING OBJECTIVES

After completing this lesson, the student should be able to:

1. identify the system of classification used for naming plants and understand why and how plants are classified.
2. understand the structure of plants and appreciate how the structures relate to the internal functions.
3. identify the various ways water is utilized by plants.
4. understand how photosynthesis, respiration, and other plant processes operate within plants.
5. understand how light affects plant growth.

## TABLE OF CONTENTS

## LIST OF FIGURES AND TABLES

# INTRODUCTION

Botany is that branch of science which studies plants. This lesson deals with the plant itself - from the microscopic cell to the macroscopic tree. It looks inside the plant to find out what it is and how it lives, functions and grows. A basic knowledge of botany will help the home gardener appreciate the intricacies and life processes of plants. As well, it will help in diagnosing plant ailments and perhaps in understanding how and why plants react to adverse environmental factors. Some of these environmental factors include topics previously dealt with. For example, soil compaction adversely affects water uptake, thereby hampering photosynthesis which, in turn, will produce a weak, unthrifty plant. There are also many climatic factors which affect the physiological processes of plants.

Knowing the way in which plants are identified and classified can assist in the search for more information on a particular plant. Students are introduced to both the scientific classification and the descriptive classification of plants.

A good knowledge of botany is essential to understanding plant nutrition and all of the ensuing lessons. The reasons will become evident as you progress through the course. For example, the main reason why many gardeners are unsuccessful in grafting is improper alignment of the anatomical areas of both plants. If proper alignment does not occur, the graft will die. This lesson will deal with this and many other anatomical concerns.

Morphology is that branch of botany which studies the structure and function of plants. Morphology will be followed from a single cell through tissue development to plant organs - roots, stems, leaves and flowers.

Once students know what a plant is composed of, the study of plant physiology can begin. Plant physiology is the study of vital plant processes - photosynthesis, respiration, and water uptake.

As light is fundamental to photosynthesis, the lesson will include information on the effects of light on plants.

# SCIENTIFIC CLASSIFICATION

The study of plant classification is also called **systematics**. Looking closely at plants, it is found that some have many of the same characteristics. For example, garden mint, Salvia, garden sage, hemp-nettle and creeping charlie have three common characteristics - square stems, opposite leaves, and the 'mint type' flower. These characteristics allow us to broadly group or classify a large number of plants into the mint Family (*Labiatae*). Scientists through the ages have looked for a similarity in characteristics which serves as the basis for classification.

## NAMING PLANTS (Taxonomy)

That branch of science dealing with the naming of plants is called **Taxonomy**.

All creatures on earth have names and it certainly simplifies things when one wishes to talk about each other or other plants and/or animals. Scientists seem to speak a different language and hence, no one knows what they are talking about. They refer to potatoes as *Solanum tuberosum*, Canada thistle as *Cirsium arvense* plus many, many more. This binominal or double name system is the internationally accepted standard for naming plants.

## BINOMIAL SYSTEM OF NOMENCLATURE

When we talk about naming plants, one man comes to mind - Carolus Linnaeus. He was a brilliant Swedish botanist who developed a system of naming which we still use today. This is called the Binomial System of Nomenclature wherein 'Bi' means two, 'nomial' means name and 'nomenclature' means naming or a 'two name system of naming' (most of us have a minimum of two names, e.g., John Doe). Not only did Linnaeus name plants, but he was vitally interested in all life - he named insects, birds and other animals too.

During Linnaeus' time and before, there was much interest in the plants explorers were bringing home. In fact, there were so many names for plants that it was totally confusing. As Latin was widely learned in schools and universities at that time, it was natural for Linnaeus to use it to describe plants (Greek has also been used). What Linnaeus proposed

was that each plant be given two names - the first is the generic name or the Genus (plural Genera), the second is the Species (eg., potato: *Solanum* is the Genus and *tuberosum* is the Species). When a scienfitic name is written correctly, the Genus and Species will always be italicized or underlined and have an initial or a shortened name behind it (*Solanum tuberosum* L). The initial refers to the person responsible for giving the plant its scientific name. 'L' of course stands for Linnaeus. The names, especially the Species names, are usually quite descriptive. A tuber is the swollen underground part of the potato, hence *tuberosum* tells you something about this particular *Solanum* plant.

Color is often used to identify a particular Species. Therefore, some Species names include the Latin word for the color of the plant part that uniquely identifies the plant. For example, *albus* in Latin means white and could be used in a Species name to identify the plant's flower color.

(See Latin colors below)

### Colors

| Latin | English |
|-------|---------|
| *albus* | white |
| *aureus* | golden yellow |
| *griseus* | blue gray |
| *luteus* | yellow |
| *niger* | black |
| *ruber* | red |
| *violaceous* | violet |
| *virens* | green |

Don't be afraid of making mistakes when pronouncing Latin names. A mispronounced scientific name is still more descriptive than 'that green thing'.

Plants also have **common names** but these are frequently confusing. For example, in one part of Alberta, *Thermopsis rhombifolia* is known as Golden Bean whereas in another part of the province, it is called cow cockle. Cow cockle most commonly refers to *Vaccaria pyramidata* which is a completely different plant.

## Figure 3-1
### CLASSIFICATION HIERARCHY

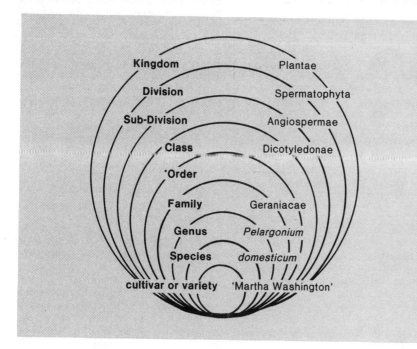

Kingdom — Plantae
Division — Spermatophyta
Sub-Division — Angiospermae
Class — Dicotyledonae
*Order
Family — Geraniacae
Genus — *Pelargonium*
Species — *domesticum*
cultivar or variety — 'Martha Washington'

*frequently deleted in modern botanical classifications.

## CLASSIFICATION HIERARCHY

Varieties are usually considered to be naturally occurring hybrids, whereas cultivars or clones are cultivated varieties, or ones in which man has been involved. Cultivars are not latinized and, when written, are placed in single quotation marks (eg., *Pelargonium* 'Martha Washington', a cultivar of geranium). There are two main Divisions in the plant Kingdom with which the home gardener is concerned. Pteridophyta - the ferns and fern allies, and Spermatophyta - the seed plants.

### PTERIDOPHYTA OR FERNS
There are approximately 11,000 species of ferns which vary in size from 10 mm plants to 25 m trees (1/2 in - 80 ft). The most important difference between ferns and seed plants is that ferns reproduce by means of spores, not seeds. Spores are very small and can only be seen individually under magnification. Spores are enclosed in a casing called a sporangium (plural sporangia). Together, many sporangia form a sorus (plural sori) which is usually located on the underside of the leaf and is visible to the naked eye. Some ferns have sori dotted in an organized pattern on the underside of the leaf while others have one long continuous sorus along the margin of the leaf (see Figure 3-2). Leaves of ferns are called fronds and are usually feathery in appearance. When fronds first appear, they are tightly coiled and are called fiddleheads (see Figure 3-3). The fiddleheads of the Ostrich fern are considered to be quite a delicacy.

### SPERMATOPHYTES OR SEED PLANTS
Seed plants are considered to be more recent plants (geologically) than the primitive ferns. Ferns, in order to reproduce, must have water so that the motile sperm may swim to fertilize the egg. Seed plants have evolved on land and have nonmotile male cells which do not need water to reproduce.

Within the Division Spermatophyta there are two Sub-Divisions - Gymnospermae and Angiospermae.

### GYMNOSPERMS
Many fossils which have been identified are related to the ferns and the Gymnosperms. 'Gymnos' (Greek origin) means naked while 'sperma' means seed. This refers to the seeds being produced in open structures (cones) instead of being enclosed in a mature ovary or fruit, as is the case with Angiosperms.

Within the Gymnosperm Sub-Division there are many Families. The most

## Figure 3-2
### SORI

Courtesy of Rudi Kroon

## Figure 3-3
### FIDDLEHEADS

Courtesy of Rudi Kroon

## Table 3-1
## THE DIFFERENCES BETWEEN MONOCOTS AND DICOTS

| DICOTS | MONOCOTS |
|---|---|
| flower parts in 4's or 5's or multiples thereof with two seed leaves or cotyledons | flower parts in 3's or multiples thereof with one seed leaf or cotyledon |
| leaves net-veined | leaves with parallel veins |
| vascular cambium present | vascular cambium absent |
| vascular bundles organized | vascular bundles scattered |
| Future references to monocots and dicots can be made to this chart. | |

commonly represented Family in Alberta is the Pinaceae Family or Pine Family. It includes such Genera as the spruce (*Picea*) and pine (*Pinus*). The house plant, Norfolk Island Pine, is in the Araucariaceae Family in this Sub-Division and, although not a true pine, it is related. Most people think of Gymnosperms as having awl-shaped leaves that remain evergreen throughout the year, but this is not the case. The Ginkgo or maidenhair tree has broad leaves that drop in the fall.

ANGIOSPERMS

Angiosperms are characterized by having their seeds enclosed in fruits. This Sub-Division is divided into two large Classes, the Monocotyledonae (monocots) and the Dicotyledonae (dicots). Table 3-1 indicates the differences between monocots and dicots. The name refers to the number of cotyledons. Hence, monocots have one (mono) cotyledon whereas dicots have two (di) cotyledons.

Future references to monocots and dicots can be made to this table.

## DESCRIPTIVE CLASSIFICATION

Plants may also be classified as to their use by man (for example, drug, food, lumber, animal feed and fuel plants). They can also be classified by where they grow (for example, terrestrial plants, epiphytic plants, aquatic plants, etc). In horticulture, there are several descriptive classifications used. Table 3-2 provides an example of descriptive classification.

## STRUCTURE AND FUNCTION

Each plant has a certain capacity for growth that is dependent on its internal structural components. That branch of science which studies plant structure is known as morphology. It is important to know not only the structural elements of plants but, also, how these elements function. Plants are primarily composed of cells, tissues and organs.

### THE CELL

The cell is the basic unit of plant structure. It varies in size, shape and function and is the smallest structure capable of growth and reproduction. It is highly complex in that it can take carbon dioxide and water and convert them into sugar. A living plant cell is composed of 85-95 per cent water with organic and inorganic salts, proteins, fats and carbohydrates making up the remainder. Included in the microscopic anatomy of the cell are the cell wall, cell membrane, cytoplasm (mitochondria and plastids), and the nucleus of the cell. These comprise the cell structure (see Figure 3-4).

## Figure 3-4
## THE CELL

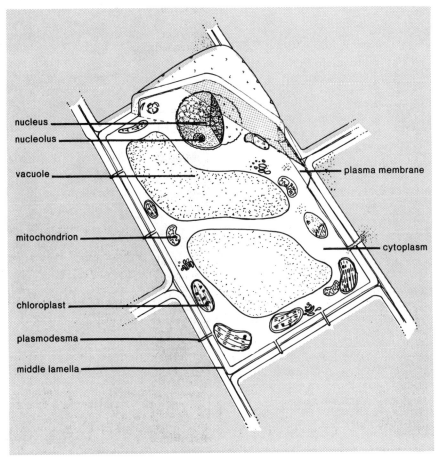

- nucleus
- nucleolus
- vacuole
- mitochondrion
- chloroplast
- plasmodesma
- middle lamella
- plasma membrane
- cytoplasm

Table 3-2
## DESCRIPTIVE CLASSIFICATION

| CLASSIFICATION | CHARACTERISTICS | EXAMPLE |
|---|---|---|
| **GROWTH HABIT** | | |
| ANNUALS | • Those plants which complete their growth in one season<br>• Go from seed to seed | marigold |
| WINTER ANNUALS | • Planted in summer or fall of one year and mature the following year. | kochia |
| BIENNIALS | • Takes two seasons to grow from seed to seed (to complete life cycle)<br>• First year accumulates food reserves in roots and shoots<br>• Second year flowers and fruits | carrots, beets, parsnips |
| PERENNIALS | • Grow three or more years--some people say they grow indefinitely<br>• Ambiguous due to natural senescence and climatic factors<br>• Some perennials are annuals on prairies<br><br>• Roots become woody in second year and are not used for food only for seed products. | delphinium<br><br><br>snapdragons, petunias, |
| **STRUCTURE AND FORM** | | |
| HERBACEOUS | • Soft succulent<br><br>• Little or no secondary (woody) tissue<br>  - HERB - A plant with no persistent woody stem above ground<br>          - Also aromatic species used for scent or flavouring<br>  - VINES - Trailing or climbing plants<br>          - Herbaceous or not woody enough to support themselves<br>          - May have tendrils (modified leaf)<br>  - WOODY - Hard stems due to development of secondary tissues<br>          - Cell walls contain cellulose and lignin<br>  - SHRUBS - Low woody plants<br>          - Usually multi-stemmed; no trunk<br>  - TREES - Single main trunk<br>          - Can grow very tall | thyme<br><br>clematis<br><br><br><br>mountain ash<br><br>honeysuckle<br><br>poplar |
| **LEAF RETENTION**<br>DECIDUOUS | • Drop leaves annually<br>• On Prairies this occurs in fall<br>• Mostly Angiosperms except Larch (Tamarack) | birch |
| EVERGREEN | • Remain green all year<br>• They do drop their needles but not simultaneously (eg., pines in the fall are notorious leaf 'droppers'). A plant growing under stress (lack of water, excess water, poor location, etc) will aid in the drop. Usually pines retain 3-4 year needles. Any stress can cause them to drop all but the current season's growth.<br>Be wary: There are leaf spot diseases as well. Make sure it is properly identified before spending money on a miracle cure.<br>• Not all evergreens are Gymnosperms | spruce, pine, juniper<br><br><br><br><br><br>cliff green, vinca, arctic phlox. |

Table 3-2: CONTINUED

| CLASSIFICATION | CHARACTERISTICS | EXAMPLE |
|---|---|---|
| **CLIMATIC ADAPTATIONS** | | |
| TROPICAL | • plants which grow in warm climates where freezing temperatures are rare. | palm, weeping fig |
| TEMPERATE | • plants which grow where there is a marked winter season of freezing temperatures<br>• these plants require a rest period and a dormant period. | apple, pear |
| BOREAL | • those plants which grow in the colder areas of the Temperate Zone. These can include the mountainous areas as well as the far north (Arctic)<br>• these plants may only have 3 weeks of temperatures above freezing. They are highly adapted to their climate. | arctic phlox |
| **WATER REQUIREMENTS** | | |
| HYDROPHYTES | • those plants which grow in water<br>• have low oxygen requirements<br>• poorly developed root system | waterweed, pond weed |
| MESOPHYTES | • those plants intermediate in water requirements<br>• have well developed root systems and are commonly found growing in soil | garden bean, elm tree |
| XEROPHYTES | • those plants growing in dry habitats<br>• have various adaptations which enable them to grow and reproduce | cacti, conifers |

## CELL WALL

The cell wall provides mechanical support for the cell. It is strong, semi-rigid yet flexible. The cell wall is composed of layers of cellulose, hemi-cellulose and/or lignin. Lignin is only produced in those plants having woody tissues. There is a cementing layer located between cells. This layer is called the middle lamella and consists of mucilaginous pectic compounds which 'glue' the cells together. If you are familiar with making jams and jellies, pectin is a familiar compound. Commercial pectin actually comes from the white, pulpy part of citrus fruits. Pectin is added to jams and jellies to make them jell. When fruit ripens, the pectic compounds break down and the middle lamella becomes 'unstuck'. One way of telling whether or not a jam or jelly will need commercial pectin is to consider when the fruit was picked. If there was still a lot of green or yellowish color present, the middle lamella would still be intact and pectic compounds would be present. Jelly made from such fruit should therefore jell on its own with no added pectin. If, on the other hand, the fruit were picked red (eg., raspberries), there would be no pectic compounds left, so a commercial pectin would need to be added.

Cell walls contain pits which are thin areas in the cell wall. Water and nutrients are able to flow between cells via these pit membranes.

## CELL MEMBRANE

Cell membrane (also referred to as the plasma membrane) is located just inside the cell wall and encloses the cytoplasm. The cell membrane is a most interesting structure as it allows some, but not all, chemical compounds in and out and is described as being differentially permeable. It regulates the flow of nutrients and water in and out (see OSMOSIS). If the cell membrane is ruptured, the cell dies. It is extremely thin and composed of proteins and fats. If 12,500 cell membranes were stacked on top of each other, they would achieve the thickness of a sheet of paper.

## CYTOPLASM

The cytoplasm is a liquid gelatinous material in which all the physiological activities of the cell occur.

## ORGANELLES

### Mitochondria

These are frequently referred to as the 'power house' units of the cell. It is in the mitochondria that energy is released from sugar by the process of respiration. The process is analagous to the release of energy (in the form of heat) when wood is burned. It is this released energy that keeps the individual cell and, therefore, the whole plant functioning. There are many mitochondria within a cell but they are very abundant in actively growing areas such as root tips and shoot tips (see MERISTEMS).

### Plastids

There are several kinds of plastids to be found in a cell and they are usually the most conspicuous of the components

Figure 3-5
CHLOROPLAST

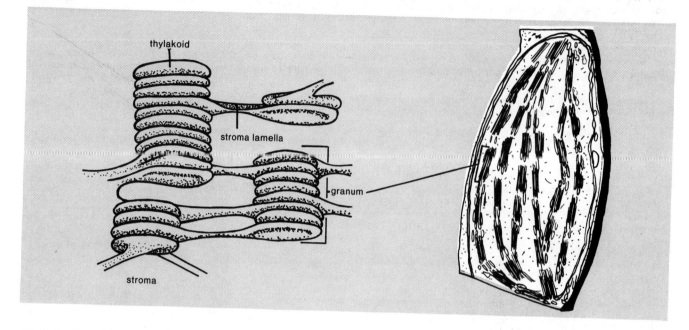

present. Two kinds of plastids are important to the home gardener. **Chromoplasts**, which contain the carotenoid pigments, are yellow, orange or red in color. **Chloroplasts** contain the green colored pigment chlorophyll. Plants, such as the Coleus which can have brightly colored foliage, do not appear to have any chloroplasts present. This is not true. The chromoplasts mask the chloroplasts. Chloroplasts are often called the 'seat of food manufacturing' for a plant.

A chloroplast is composed of a complex system of membranes embedded in a matrix called the stroma. The stroma contains many proteins (called enzymes) which act as catalysts for many life processes. The internal part of a chloroplast can be compared to many stacks of coins, interconnected by wires or strings (see Figure 3-5).

Each stack of 'coins' is called a granum and each individual 'coin' is called a thylakoid. The strings which connect the grana are called stroma lamella.

Right now you are most likely asking, "Why do I need to know all this?" The answer will be found when you begin studying photosynthesis. It will also help you answer that age old question, "Why do houseplant leaves turn yellow and drop off?"

In the thylakoid membranes of the chloroplast are found the pigments. The pigments of interest to the home gardener are the chlorophylls. Other pigments, such as the carotenoids, can also be found in chloroplasts. The function of the pigments and the chloroplast will be discussed later in the lesson under the topic of photosynthesis. It may be useful to note that a mature tree has chlorplasts providing a surface area for light absorption equal to 400 km$^2$ (about 150 square miles) and each cell may have as many as 150 chloroplasts.

### NUCLEUS
The nucleus is the control centre of the cell; it directs activities and stores hereditary information. Each living cell contains a nucleus at some point in its lifetime. Normally, there is only one per cell although there are exceptions. Within the nucleus is a darker body (sometimes more than one) called the nucleolus (plural nucleoli). The nucleolus is composed mostly of protein. It is involved in the synthesis and exportation of a form of RNA (ribonucleic acid) to other parts of the cell. RNA is a special protein involved in the synthesis of genetic material.

Also within the nucleus, in cells near growing tips (meristematic tissue), it is possible to see strands of chromatin

material. During cell division this chromatin material clumps into structures called chromosomes. Genes composed of genetic material called DNA (deoxyribonucleic acid) are located on the chromosomes.

### TISSUES

Cells function singly but are usually grouped with other similar cells. Where this occurs, the group of cells is called a tissue. Look at your hand and arm. You have skin which covers and protects your muscles and your bones. The outer part of the skin is made up of epidermal cells and collectively, the skin is called a tissue. Just under the epidermis is the dermis which also has a specific function and is called a tissue. Plants too have tissues and have specific cells associated with each tissue.

### MERISTEMATIC TISSUES
There are many regions in a plant where active growth occurs. This growth occurs in regions where actively dividing cells are present. These actively dividing cells are called meristematic tissue. There are several different types of meristematic tissue found in plants including apical meristems, vascular cambium, cork cambium and intercalary meristems.

## APICAL MERISTEM

The root system of a plant has many roots, each with a growing point. Similarly above the ground, the plant has many growing points. These growing points are made up of many cells which are actively dividing. They are called apical meristems and perform a primary plant function — growth. We take advantage of apical meristem growth when we take cuttings (see Plant Propagation lesson).

## VASCULAR CAMBIUM

Have you ever wondered how trees increase their girth? Just under bark tissue is a moist, creamy white area called the vascular cambium (usually shortened to cambium). As a child, you may have carved your initials into a poplar tree. If you did, you will be familiar with the cambium. In fact, if you were successful in getting through to the cambium, you most likely permanently damaged it and that is why your initials may still be found in the tree today. The cambium is a most amazing tissue because it is only one cell layer in thickness. Its main function is to produce new conducting tissue for the plant (see Figure 3-7). It is found as a continuous sheet in the form of a cylinder just under the bark which runs the entire length of the tree from its root system to the tips of each branch. Most perennial dicot plants have a well-developed vascular cambium.

## CORK CAMBIUM

When a tree is increasing in girth from the activity of the cambium, the bark could strangle the tree if it didn't grow at the same rate. A single layer of actively dividing cells just under the inner bark, called the cork cambium, is responsible for increasing the outer bark in trees. This outer bark becomes cracked and furrowed or noticeably 'flakes off' as the tree ages and enlarges.

## INTERCALARY MERISTEM

After a lawn has been fertilized and watered in the spring, it continues to grow mowing after mowing. Grasses, being monocots, do not possess a vascular cambium. They do, however, have special groups of cells called the intercalary meristems. A grass plant has several such meristems which permit the continual elongation of the leaf blades between mowings.

## PERMANENT TISSUES

Permanent tissues contain cells that are no longer dividing. The cells have been produced by meristems and are now mature and able to carry on specific functions such as water uptake or protection. Permanent tissues can be divided into two groups: **simple tissues** (surface tissues) consisting of only one kind of cell and **complex tissues** (storage and support tissues) consisting of two or more kinds of cells.

## SURFACE TISSUES

### Epidermis

The outer layer of cells on all young plants is called the epidermis which, as mentioned earlier, can be compared to human skin. Although there are many exceptions, the epidermis is usually only one cell layer in thickness. It is composed of living cells and functions primarily as mechanical protection for the plant; it covers and protects the underlying tissues. It may be covered with a waxy, waterproof coating called the cuticle. The thickness of the cuticle varies. On desert plants, the cuticle can be very thick and functions to prevent underlying tissues from drying out. The cuticle also repels water. Water droplets falling on a houseplant with glossy leaves will tend to bead and drop off. This is important in pesticide application. Frequently, a **surfactant** is used with the pesticide to change the surface tension of water, thereby spreading the water and pesticide over the leaf surface. Liquid dishwashing detergent mixed with water and sprinkled on a glossy plant leaf will act as a surfactant and allow water to spread evenly over the leaf surface.

Specialized epidermal cells include root hairs, guard cells, and secretory glands.

### Periderm

As a young woody plant begins to mature, the epidermis is replaced by a corky protective sheath called the periderm. The periderm includes the cork cambium and the corky tissue we call bark. Some plants produce an extensive amount of cork, namely cork oak which supplies us with the cork used for bottle stoppers.

Some areas of the periderm may rupture and form rough, pit-like areas called **lenticels**. Lenticels primarily function in gas exchange between the internal atmosphere and the external on birch bark, pin cherry, choke cherry and saskatoon bushes.

## STORAGE AND SUPPORT TISSUES

Plants are a very diverse group. Some have specialized structures capable of storing vast quantities of food and water (eg., carrots, beets and cacti), while others function more in the support of the plant. For example, support tissues in trees keep them erect and give them form. Support and storage tissues are composed of cells. There are eight different types of cells to be found in plants but not all plants have all eight types (see Table 3-3).

### Parenchyma Cells

These cells are living at maturity, thin-walled and unspecialized. They form the bulk of the tissue found in all parts of higher plants. If there are chloroplasts in parenchyma cells, we frequently call them **chlorenchyma** and their chief function is photosynthesis. Parenchyma cells main function is storage and conduction of water and nutrients. In the carrot, for example, the bulk of the tissue is composed of parenchyma cells.

### Collenchyma Cells

These too, are living at maturity but they have unevenly thickened walls which are pliable yet strong and function in mass as weak mechanical support tissue. Monocots and herbaceous dicots have this type of flexible support tissue. The 'strings' of celery are perhaps the most familiar collenchyma tissue.

### Sclerenchyma Tissue

This support tissue consists of two types of cells - stone cells (sclerids) and fibers. Both are non-living at maturity, are thick-walled, and the cell walls usually contain lignin. Fibers are elongated cells which can be short or very long (eg., in trees, fibers can be up to 60 cm or 24 inches in length). Fibers give plants strength and are associated with both phloem and xylem tissue. Fibers form interlocking sheets of tissue in roots, stems and leaves and are partially responsible for a plant's ability to stand and retain its form under exposure to external forces such as wind. Sclerenchyma fibers are used to make linen (from flax) ropes, string and canvas. Stone cells are responsible for the grittiness in pears.

Table 3-3
CELL TYPES

| CELL TYPES | CELL STRUCTURE |
|---|---|
| parenchyma | |
| collenchyma | |
| sclerenchyma sclerids | |
| fibers | |
| xylem vessel | |
| tracheid | |
| phloem sieve tube | |
| companion cell | |

## CONDUCTING TISSUE

Conducting tissues are complex tissues which are composed of several different types of cells. These cells are specially adapted for moving water and soluble food within the plant. Conducting tissues can be thought of in terms of the plant's circulatory system, with the xylem tissue being involved in moving water and the phloem tissue being involved in moving the food.

## XYLEM

Xylem is a Greek word meaning 'wood'. The inner part of the stem of a tree, for example, contains the xylem or wood. This can be confusing however, as all higher plants contain xylem including

monocots and non-woody herbaceous dicots. The xylem, is the **water conducting tissue** in plants and consists of **vessels** and **tracheids**. Both cells are non-living at maturity which accounts for the dead inner wood of a tree. Vessels form long tubes of individual cells called **vessel elements**. Tracheids are similar to vessels but are mostly confined to Gymnosperms. Most water conduction is up (parenchyma ray cells in the xylem moves water laterally as well). Fibers may also provide support for the xylem tissue.

## PHLOEM

Phloem is the **food conducting tissue** of plants and includes **sieve tubes** and **companion cells**. Sieve tube elements

are laid end to end with sieve plates at the end of each cell or element. Movement of cytoplasm through the sieve plate aids in food conduction. Sieve tube elements are living at maturity but the nucleus disappears. Control of the cell's activity is taken over by a row of cells beside each sieve tube called companion cells. These are specialized parenchyma cells. Also associated with phloem tissue are fibers, sclerids, and parenchyma ray cells. Food conduction is up, down and lateral. The xylem and phloem together form the vascular system.

## ORGANS

An organ can be defined as a structure containing a group of different tissues cooperating functionally to perform a composite task. These include roots, stems, leaves, flowers, fruits and seeds.

### ROOTS

Roots are quite often the least considered part of a plant, perhaps because they are usually underground. It is a case of 'out of sight, out of mind'. The roots function is in anchoring the plant, absorbing water and nutrients and storing food. Roots normally do not contain chloroplasts, however, epiphytic roots (eg., some orchids) and some aquatic plant roots may contain chloroplasts.

**Tap roots** consist of one or more primary roots which remain larger than the secondary roots and continue to grow in a downward direction. This type of root system is found in dicots. Sometimes, the tap root can become enlarged and function in food storage (eg., carrot and dandelion).

**Fibrous roots**, as a root system, are those found mainly in grasses and other monocots. These consist of numerous, slender roots of equal or near equal size.

**Adventitious roots** are those roots which are found on parts of the plant where they wouldn't ordinarily be expected (eg., roots forming on leaves and stems).

**Lateral roots** are creeping, underground roots which run horizontal to the soil surface. They are easily confused with rhizomes which are underground stems. The difference, while relatively unimportant to the home gardener, can

## Figure 3-6
## LONGITUDINAL SECTION OF XYLEM AND PHLOEM

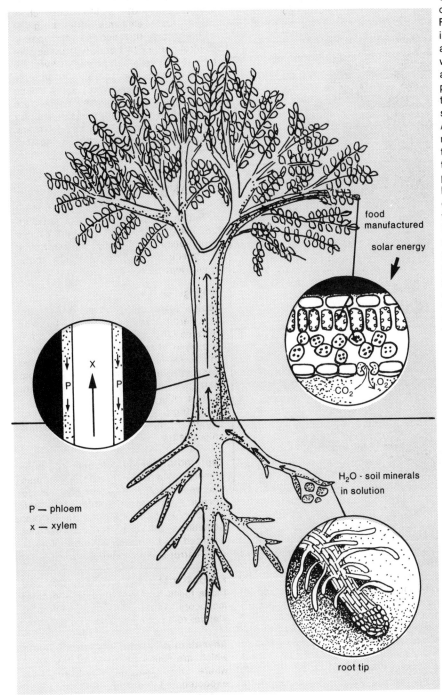

food manufactured

solar energy

$CO_2$  $O_2$

P — phloem
x — xylem

$H_2O$ - soil minerals in solution

root tip

epidermis is replaced by periderm. Roots are capable of absorbing enormous amounts of water. At the tips of most roots, epidermal cells develop outpockets called root hairs (see Figures 3-8 and 3-9). Root hairs form irregular shapes around soil particles and, thereby, come in contact with soil water. They greatly increase the water absorption area of roots. An individual plant of the cereal, rye can have more than 14 billion root hairs which, in total surface area, is roughly equivalent to an American football field. They can also release pectic-like substances that help to increase soil contact – making it hard to remove soil from root hairs. These pectic-like substances also act as lubricants which facilitate the movement of roots through soil. Because of the tremendous absorptive capability of root hairs, it is important to include as many of them as possible when transplanting a plant. For example, when a seedling is pulled out of the soil instead of being gently lifted out, most of the root hairs are pulled off. This practise can cause transplant failure. The same principle holds true for transplanting large trees. The bulk of the root hairs are at the **drip line** and beyond (see Figure 3-10). If a rootball is undersized when dug, most of the root hairs are eliminated. If too few root hairs are present on the transplant, the tree will not survive. Because of stored up food in a large plant, such as a tree, transplant failure may not occur for up to five years from the time of transplanting.

Some plants do not have root hairs (eg., many conifers and terrestrial orchids). These plants frequently have a fungus associated with the root system. These fungi, called **mycorrhizae**, aid in absorption of water and some nutrients.

The cortex is found beneath the epidermis. In some plants, it is more prominent than others (eg., in storage roots such as carrots and beets, the bulk of the tissue seen in a cross section is cortex). It is primarily a food storage tissue.

The next tissue found on the inside of the cortex is the **endodermis**. It is a single layer of cells which separates the vascular system from the cortex. It is only found in roots and appears to have a protective function. A waxy substance, **suberin**, forms on the endodermal cells and protects the vascular system from desiccation.

be significant for the weed scientist who develops specific herbicides for plants. An example of a plant that produces lateral roots is Canada thistle. Sometimes, these roots become tuberous and function as storage organs (eg., dahlia and sweet potato).

Roots are covered with an epidermis composed of a single layer of parenchyma cells. As roots mature, the

Figure 3-7
ROOTS  (cross sections)

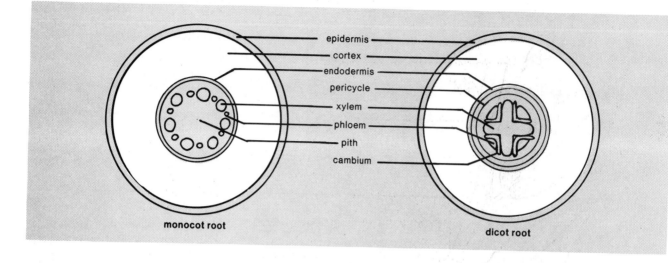

monocot root                                  dicot root

Figure 3-8
ROOT TIP (longitudinal section)

Figure 3-9
ROOT HAIRS

Figure 3-10
DRIP LINE OF A TREE

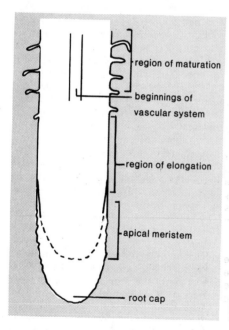

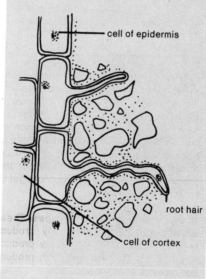

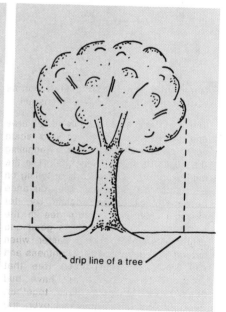

Next to the endodermis in dicots is another layer of cells called the **pericycle**. It gives rise to secondary roots.

The vascular system of monocots and dicots is very different. The xylem in dicots extends out in star-like fashion and occupies the centre of the vascular cylinder. In monocots, the xylem alternates with the phloem. The phloem in dicots lies between the xylem arms and the pericycle. In woody dicots, the vascular cambium develops between the phloem and xylem. There is no vascular cambium in monocots (see Figures 3-6 and 3-7).

**STEMS**
Stems function as storage organs, a place of attachment for leaves and the connecting link for the vascular system from the roots to the leaves. Some stems are green and are capable of photosynthesis whereas others are woody and incapable of photosynthesis. Stems are usually thought of as 'upright' but some hug the ground and grow horizontally. These have a 'prostrate' growth habit. The leaves plus the stem

## Figure 3-11
## WOODY TWIG

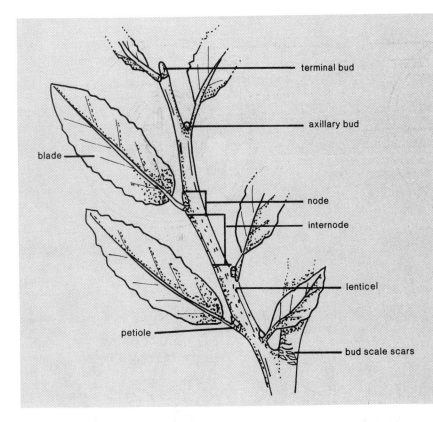

(labels: terminal bud, axillary bud, blade, node, internode, lenticel, petiole, bud scale scars)

is called a shoot. Stems start out as buds produced by the apical meristem.

The appearance of the internodal area and the distance between bud scale scars can be very useful in determining the health of a plant. Any change in the quality and the amount of light falling on a plant will influence the distance between nodes. The English ivy, for example, has short internodes in the summer when natural light is good and longer internodes in the winter when natural light decreases in brightness and day length. A transplanted tree that produces little growth will have bud scale scars that are close together. After the transplant shock is over, the tree will return to producing a normal amount of growth during the growing season. By observing the distance between bud scale scars (equivalent to one year's growth) it is possible to determine the health of a tree.

The buds of a stem are capable of dormancy. In fact, one function of stem buds on outdoor plants is to overwinter the plant. In spring, growth may originate

from the terminal bud, the lateral or axillary buds, or adventitious buds. Adventitious buds may not be visible on the stem surface as they are frequently embedded in stem tissue. They are found in the internodal stem region as well as on leaves and roots. Adventitious buds often grow as a result of an injury to the plant. We take advantage of this phenomenon and use it as a propagation tool.

Buds can also be of three types. These include leaf buds which only produce leaves, flower buds which only produce flowers, and mixed buds which produce both leaves and flowers.

Young stems of monocots and dicots are covered by the epidermis which can be covered by a cuticle. As dicots age, the epidermis may be replaced by periderm. The epidermis of stems may have areas for gas exchange. In stems and leaves, these areas are pores called stomata or stomates. These pores are flanked by two specialized epidermal cells called **guard cells**. The guard cells

plus the pore are also referred to as a stoma or stomate. In woody dicots, the periderm also has areas for gas exchange but these are different in structure and are called lenticels. Stems of monocots differ from those of dicots as shown in Figure 3-12.

### STEM MODIFICATIONS
Some stems differ from the norm. In fact, they may not even look like stems but structurally and anatomically they are. These are called specialized or modified stems and can be divided into two distinct groups - those above ground and those below ground (see Figure 3-13).

### Above Ground Modifications
**Stolons** are stems that grow horizontally along or above the ground. They characteristically have long internodes (eg., strawberry and spider plants).

**Spurs** are found on woody plants like apple or crabapple trees. Spurs are characterized by restricted longitudinal growth. They have greatly shortened internodes and usually appear on axillary branches. They can revert to normal growth.

**Crown** is that part of a plant at ground level. It may become enlarged or compressed and can develop buds which can produce a new plant (eg., *Aloe, Agave, Echeveria*).

### Below Ground Modifications
Underground stems are modified for storage and reproduction.

**Bulbs** are short, disk-shaped stems surrounded by fleshy, leaf-like structures called scales. There are two types of bulbs common to horticulture: laminate and scaly. **Laminate** or **tunicate bulbs**, such as onions and tulips, have closely wrapped concentric layers of scales which are protected from desiccation and mechanical injury by an outer layer of dry scales. **Scaly** or **imbricate bulbs**, such as the Easter lily and garlic have loosely wrapped small scales which are attached to a basal plate and slightly overlap one another like shingles on a roof. **Bulblets** are miniature bulb propagules formed in the axils of the scales. **Bulbils** are sometimes produced by lilies in the axils of leaves on aerial stems. Their importance will become

### Figure 3-12
### STEMS (cross section)

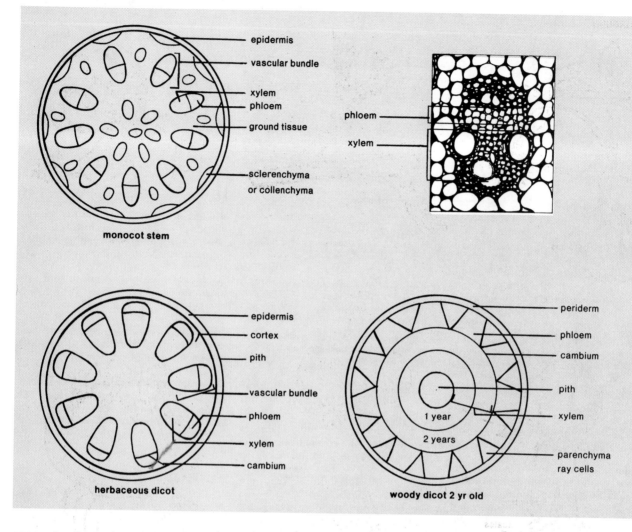

epidermis
vascular bundle
xylem
phloem
ground tissue
sclerenchyma
or collenchyma

**monocot stem**

phloem
xylem

epidermis
cortex
pith
vascular bundle
phloem
xylem
cambium

**herbaceous dicot**

periderm
phloem
cambium
pith
xylem
parenchyma
ray cells

1 year
2 years

**woody dicot 2 yr old**

apparent when plant propagation is studied.

**Corms** are often mistakenly called bulbs. Corms are short, fleshy underground stems made up of a solid mass of tissue having nodes and internodes. **Cormels** are small propagules formed by buds at the nodes. They are important in propagation (eg., crocus, gladiolus).

**Rhizomes** are horizontal underground stems having nodes, internodes, buds and adventitious roots. The most common headache plant for gardeners, quack grass, is a good example of this modification. Many of the hardy irises also have rhizomes.

**Tubers** are swollen, underground thickened stems. Tuber in Latin, means 'lump' which is quite descriptive of their appearance. Tubers have 'eyes' or buds at the nodes which are capable of growth (eg., potato).

Sometimes, all of these below-ground modified stems are classed as 'bulbs' and this can lead to confusion.

### LEAVES
Leaves perform two major functions. Firstly, leaves are the site of the food manufacturing process (photosynthesis) for the plant and secondly, leaves are the site of water vapor loss (transpiration). Since these two life processes are of utmost importance, they will be dealt with in detail at the end of

the lesson. In order to understand photosynthesis, it helps to have a basic knowledge of the structure and anatomy of leaves.

Leaves grow from special meristems. The surface area of leaves is usually large which enables the plant to capture as much light as possible. In fact, plants arrange their leaves with the upper flat surface more or less at right angles to the light's rays.

Stipules, which are leaf-like structures, may be associated with the **petioles** in the region of the axillary bud. Where they occur, they are paired at each axil of the dicot leaf and are capable of photosynthesis.

# Figure 3-13
## STEM MODIFICATIONS

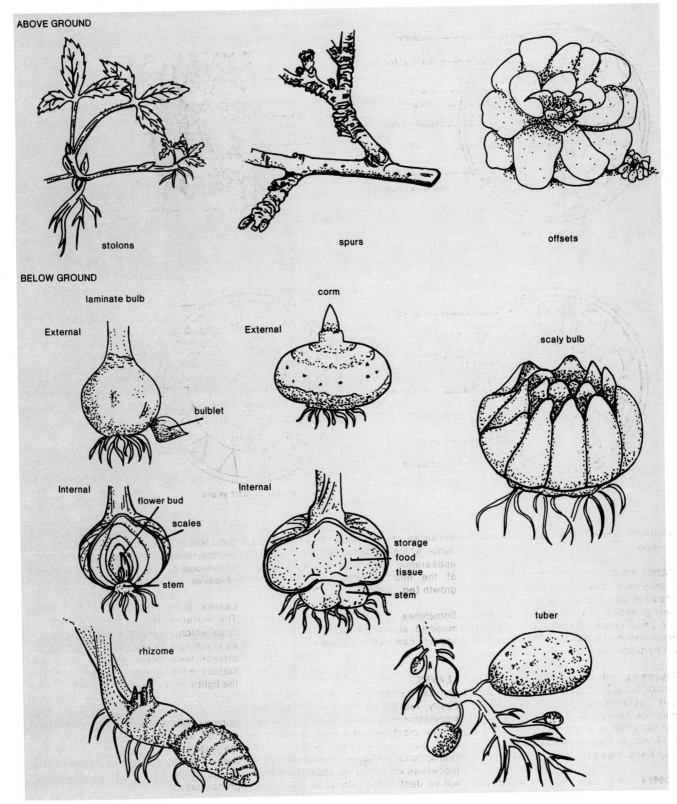

ABOVE GROUND

stolons

spurs

offsets

BELOW GROUND

laminate bulb

External

bulblet

Internal

flower bud

scales

stem

corm

External

Internal

storage
food
tissue
stem

scaly bulb

rhizome

tuber

## Figure 3-14
## MONOCOT AND DICOT LEAVES

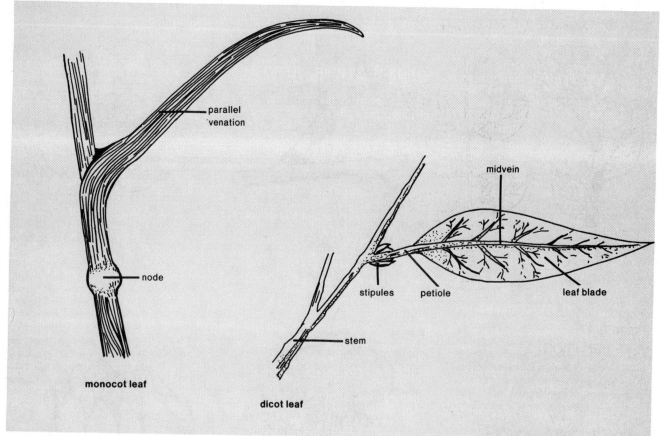

parallel venation

midvein

node

stipules

petiole

leaf blade

stem

**monocot leaf**

**dicot leaf**

## Figure 3-15
## LEAF ATTACHMENT

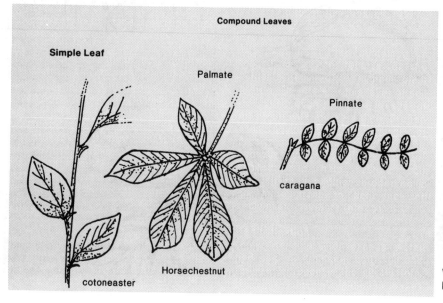

Compound Leaves

Simple Leaf

Palmate

Pinnate

caragana

Horsechestnut

cotoneaster

Leaves are attached to a stem at the nodes in one of three ways. Their attachment is either **alternate**, **opposite** or **whorled**. Alternate leaves zig zag up a stem, one at each node (eg., apple). In opposite attachment, leaves are arranged opposite one another on a stem , two at each node (eg., dogwood, lilac). Whorled attachment means three or more leaves at each node (eg., northern bedstraw).

Leaves may be simple or compound. If compound, several leaflets make up one leaf. **Pinnately compound leaves** have leaflets that are arranged in pairs. **Palmately compound leaves** have leaflets that are all attached at a point near the top of the petiole. Their appearance is similar to fingers radiating out from the palm of your hand (see Figures 3-16 and 3-17).

With net venation, it is also possible to have pinnate and palmate venation on

## Figure 3-16
## LEAF ARRANGEMENT

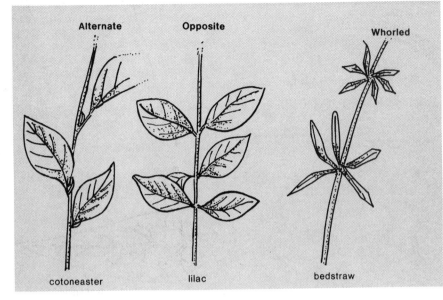

## Figure 3-17
## LEAF VENATION

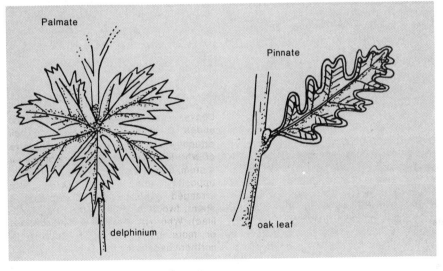

leaves (see Figures 3-16 and 3-17). The pattern of the vascular system (veins) in leaves may be either netted or parallel. Most dicot leaves show **net** venation while monocots show **parallel** venation.

In Figure 3-18, note that the leaf is covered by an upper and lower epidermis with a cuticle appearing on the upper side. In addition to the epidermis, some plants have **epidermal** **appendages**. These are just extensions of the epidermal cell. They can be classified as glandular or non-glandular. Glandular appendages or secretory hairs are common on geraniums (*Pelargoniums*), petunias, birch twigs and leaves, as well as the infamous stinging nettle (see Figure 3-19). Crushing these hairs causes secretions (fragrances or poisons) to exude from the cut surface. With stinging nettles, skin irritation occurs when the tips of the stinging hairs are broken off, thereby allowing the poison sap to leave the cell and enter the skin. Non-glandular appendages can be in the form of hairs as in the star-shaped hairs of the mustard family, or scales as in the Bromeliads. Both glandular and non-glandular appendages are visible under magnification.

### STOMATAL APPARATUS
In order for gas exchange to occur and for excess water vapor to escape, it is necessary for the plant to have pores in its epidermis. These microscopic pores are called stomata (singular - stoma). The term stoma also refers to the pore plus the two cells on either side of it called the **guard cells** (see Figure 3-20). They are specialized epidermal cells which contain chloroplasts and regulate the pore opening. In dicots, there are more stomata on the lower epidermis than the upper. There are some exceptions, however. In aquatic plants with floating leaves, all the stomata are on the upper surface (eg., water lily) whereas on desert plants (eg., olive tree) all of the stomata are on the lower surface and none on the upper surface of the leaf. The number of stomata varies. It is estimated that a mature European oak leaf would have 1400 stomata/mm$^2$ while a garden pea leaf would have approximately 300 stomata/mm$^2$.

### MESOPHYLL TISSUES
The mesophyll tissue or middle region of the leaf is characterized by an abundance of chloroplasts and large intercellular spaces. In dicots, this area usually consists of two layers. The layer of cells beneath the upper epidermis is called the **palisade layer**. It is made up of cells that are elongated and arranged perpendicular to the surface. There may be one or more layers of these cells. The second layer is called the spongy mesophyll. It consists of cells that are irregular in shape and have large spaces separating them. These spaces are high in carbon dioxide and water vapor - two of the ingredients for photosynthesis. Oxygen, which is a 'waste' product of photosynthesis, is released to the atmosphere through the stomata via these spaces. Monocots lack the palisade layer with the bulk of the inner cells being spongy mesophyll.

The vascular system of the roots and stems extends out into every leaf on a plant and terminates at the margins of

## Figure 3-18
## INTERNAL STRUCTURE OF A DICOT LEAF

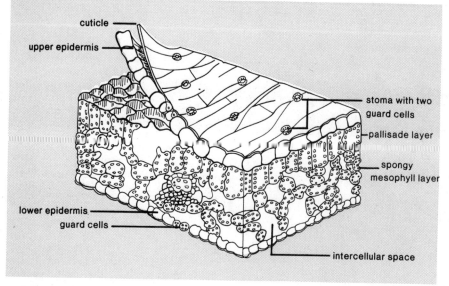

- cuticle
- upper epidermis
- stoma with two guard cells
- pallisade layer
- spongy mesophyll layer
- lower epidermis
- guard cells
- intercellular space

## Figure 3-19
## STINGING NETTLE GLANDULAR HAIR

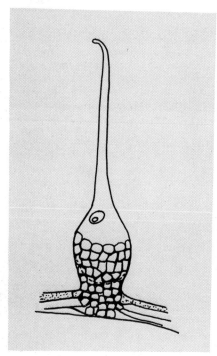

the leaf blades. Water and nutrients flow up the plant in the xylem to the leaf tissue. Photosynthesis in the leaves then produces food which is carried in the phloem to all other parts of the plant.

Any excess food is stored in stem and root tissues. The phloem and xylem comprise the vascular system. The vascular system of the mid-vein of dicots is continuous with the vein in the petiole and stem (see Figure 3-14).

PETIOLE AND LEAF DROP

The internal structure of the leaf petiole is similar to that of a young stem. In deciduous dicots, a special layer of cells, called the abscission layer, forms at the base of the petiole where it attaches to a stem. It does not extend through the vascular bundles. In autumn, the middle lamella between the cells dissolves, leaving the petiole attached to the plant by its vascular bundles. These leaves are easily blown off by the wind. Suberin is produced by the plant to seal off the scar area to disease organisms (see Figure 3-21)

SPECIALIZED LEAVES

In addition to photosynthesis and transpiration, some leaves take on other functions and appearances. These leaves result from individual and specialized plant requirements and are usually associated with a plant's ability to adapt to its environment.

### Tendrils
In garden peas, the uppermost leaflet of the compound leaf is reduced to a whip-like structure which will curl around anything it touches and, thereby act as a support for the plant. Certain other plants also develop tendrils which may consist of an entire leaf being reduced to a tendril.

### Spines
Many cacti and other desert plants have reduced their leaves to non-photosynthetic spines. In this way, excess evaporation from delicate tissues is eliminated. Stems of most of these plants are photosynthetic.

### Window Leaves
Examples of plants with window leaves include the Lithops (living stones). The leaves are thick and mostly buried in the growing medium (soil, sand or gravel). They have a very thick cuticle, several layers of epidermal cells and very few stomata. Below the epidermial layers of colorless cells are very large, tightly packed water storage cells. These cells allow the sun's rays (where air temperatures can reach 40°C+) to be deflected so as not to burn up the plant. Enough sunlight still reaches the innermost or deepest part of the leaf for photosynthesis to occur in cells which contain chloroplasts.

### Reproductive Leaves
Some plants produce little plantlets on their leaves. The Mexican Hat plant and the Mother Fern are two examples of plants with such reproductive leaves.

### Floral Bracts
The 'flower' of the poinsettia (the red, white or pink structures) are actually modified leaves called bracts. These 'flowers' serve to attract insects for pollination. The true flowers appear as a cluster of rather inconspicuous 'nobs' in the center of the rings of bracts.

### Insect-Trapping Leaves
These plants have leaves modified for trapping insects. Examples include the Venus fly trap, the Pitcher plant, sundews, bladderworts and butterworts. The last three are common to 'boggy' places on the prairies.

## Figure 3-20
## STOMA

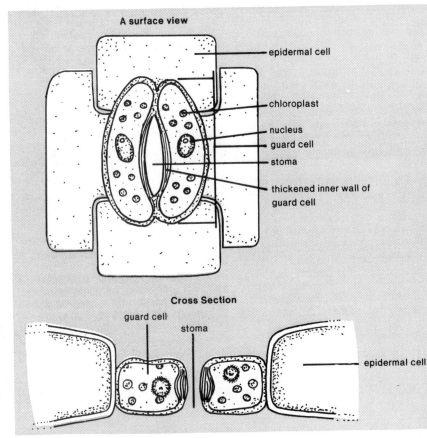

**A surface view**

- epidermal cell
- chloroplast
- nucleus
- guard cell
- stoma
- thickened inner wall of guard cell

**Cross Section**

guard cell
stoma
epidermal cell

## Figure 3-21
## ABSCISSION LAYER IN PETIOLE

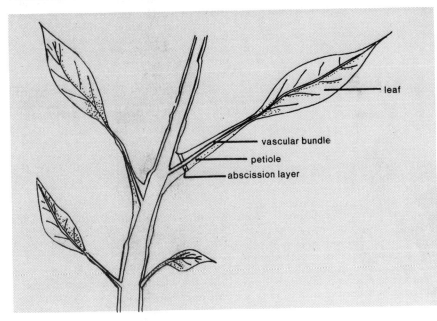

- leaf
- vascular bundle
- petiole
- abscission layer

## FLOWERS

Many researchers believe that flowers are in fact modified leaves. Flowers, nevertheless, arise from apical meristems and their prime function is that of reproduction, thereby perpetuating the species.

All plant identification is based on the flower, so it is absolutely essential to know its parts.

- **sepals** - These structures are usually green and enclose the other parts of the flower in the bud. Usually, there are several sepals which together are called the **calyx**.
- **petals** - These structures are usually brightly colored. The petals collectively make up the **corolla**. The corolla with the calyx is called the **perianth**. In some members of the lily family, the three sepals and three petals are the same color, that is, the perianth is said to be petaloid. The six individual segments are then called petals.
- **stamens** - These are made up of the **anther**, which contains the pollen, and the **filament**, a stalk-like structure on which the anther sits. The pollen grains produce male gametes or sperm.
- **pistil** - This structure consists of three parts: the **ovary** (containing one to many ovules), the style (which connects the ovary to the stigma) and the **stigma** (which is the surface on which the pollen lands). Each ovule contains a female gamete or egg.

Not all flowers consist of these four parts. If a flower does consist of all four parts, it is said to be complete. If it is missing one or more flower parts, it is considered incomplete. A flower containing both stamens and pistil is said to be perfect while a flower lacking either stamens or pistil is said to be imperfect. Staminate flowers have male parts but lack female parts, whereas pistillate flowers have female parts but lack male parts. **Receptacle** is another term frequently associated with flowers. It is the swollen end of the stem or **peduncle** on which the above flower parts are inserted.

There are two terms used to describe the sex of plants. Monoecious (meaning one house) plants have separate male and female flowers on the same individual. Corn is an example of this. The tassels at the top of the plant contain staminate flowers and the ears contain the pistillate flowers. The silks

## Figure 3-22
### PARTS OF A TYPICAL FLOWER

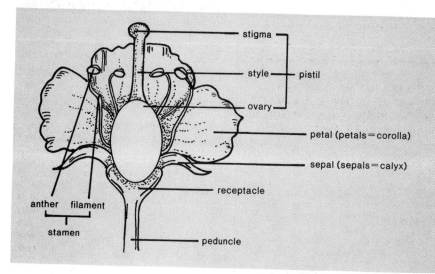

are the styles and stigmas of the many ovaries covering the tiny, immature cobs.

Dioecious (meaning two houses) plants have staminate and pistillate flowers on separate plants. Poplar, for example, is a dioecious tree. The 'fluff' from poplar contains the seeds and is produced by the female tree. Male poplar trees do not produce 'fluff'.

Flowers can often appear in a cluster on a stem. When flowers are arranged in a cluster, it is called an inflorescence (see Figure 3-23). A daisy or dandelion-type flower is often considered to be a single flower. This is an incorrect assumption. These flowers are more accurately called inflorescences because they are made up of hundreds of flowers. This becomes apparent when a dandelion head goes to seed. Hundreds of seeds are produced from a single head. The head inflorescence can be made up of two types of flowers: **ray florets** and **disk florets**. Ray florets are strap-shaped flowers like the 'petals' of a daisy. Disk florets are the yellow structures at the centre of the daisy. Not all head inflorescences contain both. In fact, the first breakdown in identifying a flower with a head is to distinguish if there are only ray florets present, only disk florets present, or if both are present.

Plants are identified by use of a 'key'. A plant key consists of a series of two contrasting statements. A choice is made as to which statement most aptly describes the plant in question. Following each statement there will either be a number or a name which will lead the user to another set of contrasting statements or a name. See the example in Table 3-4.

Example: The plant to be identified (Plant **X**) has pink ray florets and yellow disk florets.

By 'working' a key it is possible to identify a plant. When the plant name is identified, it is cross referenced with the description of the plant to see if, in fact, the identification is correct. If the description does not match, the key is reworked to find where the mistake was made. It is essential that the key chosen includes the plant to be identified.

## Figure 3-23
### INFLORESCENCES

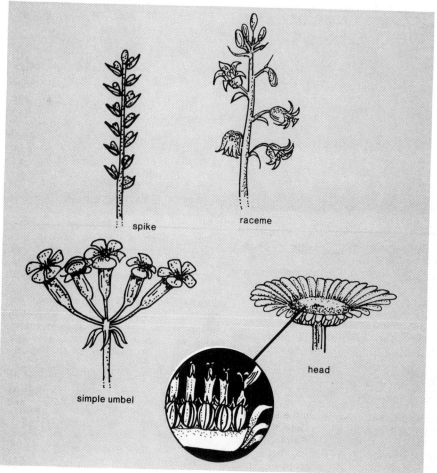

## Table 3-4
## CLASSIFICATION KEY

| KEY | EXPLANATION |
|---|---|
| 1. Flowers all rays and perfect; sap milky . . . . . . . .Dandelion Group | Plant X also has disk florets so we eliminate this statement and go on to next statement in 1. Also our plant doesn't resemble a dandelion. |
| 1. Flowers not all rays but when present either pistillate or neuter; sap watery. . . .2 | Plant X fits this description as indicated. Go to statement 2. |
| 2. Heads having ray florets . . . . . . . .3 | Plant X has both ray and disk florets. Go to statement 3. |
| 2. Heads having only disk florets . . . .5 | As this statement does not pertain to plant X, it is eliminated. |
| 3. Ray florets yellow or orange. . . . . .4 | Plant X has pink rays. Go on to next statement in 3. |
| 3. Ray florets pink, purple or blue . . . . . . . . . . . . . . . .Daisy Group | Plant X has pink rays and fits in here. The key tells us to go to that part of the key listing the Daisy Group. |

## POLLINATION

Pollination is the term used to describe pollen transfer to the stigma. If the stigma is receptive, the pollen grain grows a tube-like projection down through the style and into the ovary. Some plants have flowers that are self-pollinating wherein the pollen lands on the stigma of the same flower or on the stigma of other flowers of the same plant in order to bring about successful germination of the pollen grains. Cross pollination occurs when the pollen from one plant lands on the stigmas of flowers of another plant of the same species in order to accomplish successful germination of the pollen grains. Cross pollinated plants have a mixture of genetic material acquired from each parent plant. This can be important to anyone who collects seeds. For example, seeds taken from orange snapdragons may not produce all orange offspring because the genetic material inherited from each parent would not necessarily be identical.

Pollinating agents, such as the wind, help in transferring pollen to the stigmas. Wind pollinated flowers are not showy, in fact, they may be quite inconspicuous.

They have no nectar producing structures (nectaries). They produce an abundance of pollen and the stamens are well exposed. Also, their stigmas are feathery and usually branched. These adaptive features help plants, such as grasses, to become pollinated. Other agents are insects, such as bees, ants, moths and butterflies as well as larger animals, such as bats. Most insect pollinated flowers are brightly colored and showy. They attract the insects — in fact, some flowers (some orchid species, in particular) mimic insects in appearance. These insects try to mate with the flower which, of course, is unsuccessful for the poor insect because the insect pollinates the plant in the process. Insect pollinated plants are fragrant, have nectaries and, quite often, their pollen is sticky. The sticky pollen adheres to an insect's feet and body and is thereby transported to other flowers.

## FERTILIZATION

Fertilization occurs when the sperm from the pollen grain unites with the egg in the ovule of an ovary. Fertilization may occur within hours after pollination or, in the case of some gymnosperms, it may take one to two years. Once fertilization has occurred, an embryo develops. In some plants, fertilization may not take place. Instead, some of the ovule tissue starts to divide and produces an embryo. This production of fruit without fertilization is called **parthenocarpy**. An example of parthenocarpic fruit is the seedless tomato. There are other instances where fruit production can occur without fertilization and subsequent seed production.

## FRUITS AND SEEDS

Is a tomato a fruit or a vegetable? Although it is always classified as a vegetable, it is actually a fruit. A fruit is defined as a 'mature ovary' and normally contains seeds. Garden peas, then, are also fruits, the pod being the ovary wall and the peas being the matured, fertilized ovules or seeds.

Inside each seed is a new plant in miniature. Monocots and dicots differ considerably. In dicots, two cotyledons or seed leaves are produced from tissues surrounding the ovules at the time of fertilization. In monocots, one cotyledon is produced and is usually quite small. The main food storage tissue in such seeds is called the endosperm and is not a part of the embryo. The endosperm or cotyledons contain nutritive tissue to feed the developing embryo before the first true leaves are produced. Some dicots, like the garden bean, also have photosynthetic cotyledons but, as soon as the first true leaf appears, the cotyledons begin to deteriorate and die.

# PLANT PHYSIOLOGY

Plant physiology is that branch of botany which deals with organic plant functions. More specifically, plant physiology includes the absorption of water and nutrients from the outside world into the plant; photosynthesis, digestion, metabolism, assimilation, secretion, respiration, transpiration, growth and movement. The scope of this course doesn't allow for discussion of all of these topics. In this lesson, light and its effects on plant physiology, as well as water uptake, photosynthesis and respiration are dealt with.

## LIGHT (Solar Radiation)

The sun is a source of light for us on earth. The sun's rays reach earth in the form of solar energy or radiation. Plants are able to take that solar energy and transform it into chemical energy which is used in food manufacture (see Climate lesson, LIGHT).

Light (solar energy) is usually thought of in terms of waves and is commonly described in terms of wavelength. Light waves are not the only waves present in solar radiation (see Figure 2-2).

Visible light is broken down into all the colors of the rainbow; violet, indigo, blue, green, yellow, orange and red. Plants primarily use only the blue and red wavelengths (with some overlap into orange and indigo) and it is these wavelengths that stimulate chlorophyll production. The actual energy present in light varies with the wavelength and is conceived as particles or units of energy called photons.

### PHOTOSYNTHESIS

It is amazing to think that all life on earth is dependent on one life process but this is indeed true. This process is called photosynthesis. Photosynthesis is a difficult concept to learn. In this lesson, the highly complex biochemical process will be presented as simply as possible. Photosynthesis is the process whereby carbon dioxide and water are transformed in the presence of light and chlorophyll to produce carbohydrates and oxygen. This process is represented in the equation below.

$$6CO_2 + 12H_2O \xrightarrow[chlorophyll]{light} C_6H_{12}O_6 + 6H_2O + 6O_2$$

Photosynthesis actually occurs in two stages; the Light Phase and the Dark Phase.

### LIGHT PHASE

This stage is dependent upon light. Sunlight or solar radiation is the usual source, however, many horticultural crops are now grown under artificial light. As long as the blue and red wavelengths are provided at an adequate intensity, growth will occur. The light phase occurs in the thylakoid membranes of chloroplasts. The thylakoids are saturated with chlorophyll pigments. When a particle or photon of light falls on a leaf, it enters the leaf and is absorbed by a chlorophyll molecule in the thylakoid membrane. When this occurs, it creates an 'over full' situation and something must be released. This something is an electron which is jolted from one energy state to another. This energy level move triggers the change of solar energy to chemical energy and acts as the driving force for reactions to come.

When the photon of light is absorbed by the chlorophyll molecule, solar energy is trapped and this, in turn, breaks up water into hydrogen and oxygen. The oxygen is released as a gas and the hydrogen is accepted by another molecule to be used in the Dark Phase.

The Light Phase is frequently called **photolysis** (photo meaning light and lysis meaning loosening) or the **Hill Reaction** after the man who discovered it. It occurs independent of temperature and is depicted graphically as:

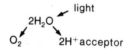

### DARK PHASE

The Dark Phase is a little more complex. In fact, 'Dark' is a misnomer. This series of reactions actually occurs independent of light (in fact, it usually occurs in light). It is readily affected by temperature and could more accurately be called the **carbon dioxide fixation phase**. This phase also occurs within the chloroplasts in the stroma region. Carbon dioxide fixation involves the addition of electrons and hydrogen atoms to the carbon dioxide molecule to form carbohydrates or sugars. In order for carbon dioxide to enter the plant, the stomata must be open.

It is now known that three types of green plants exist based on the type of reactions involved in the Dark Phase of photosynthesis. These three types of plants have different pathways by which carbon dioxide is reduced to carbohydrate. Each is favored by different environmental conditions which are reflected in the culture best suited for their optimal photosynthesis.

### $C_3$ Plants

The photosynthetic carbon reduction pathway common to the majority of horticultural crops is the **Calvin cycle**. Plants with only this pathway are frequently referred to as $C_3$ plants because the first stable product formed after the initial **carboxylation** contains three carbon atoms. These plants have a relatively inefficient photosynthesis as well as an elevated respiration rate in the presence of light (photorespiration). This high rate of respiration increases the use of photosynthate, and thereby decreases the net gain of carbon-fixation through photosynthesis.

### $C_4$ Plants

A few horticultural crops, including sweet corn and many of the noxious weeds, have a second pathway of carbon reduction called the **Hatch and Slack cycle** or $C_4$ pathway. Plants of this group have chloroplasts in the bundle sheaths (cells surrounding the vascular strands of xylem and phloem) as well as in the

## Table 3-5
## EXAMPLES OF $C_3$ AND $C_4$ PLANTS

| $C_3$ PLANTS | $C_4$ PLANTS |
|---|---|
| quack grass, lambs quarters, oats, wheat, barley, Kentucky bluegrass, beets, spinach, sunflower, soybean, beans, carrots | Russian thistle, purslane, red root pigweed, sugar cane, corn, millet, bermuda grass, barnyard grass, gramma grass |

mesophyll tissue of the leaves, more efficient photosynthesis and low to zero rates of photorespiration. As the name implies, $C_4$ plants have as their first stable product after the initial carboxylation, a compound containing four atoms of carbon.

## CAM Plants

A third type of carbon fixation, which is essentially a modification of $C_4$ metabolism, has evolved in certain plants. It is known as Crassulacean Acid Metabolism (CAM) because it was first discovered in plants of the Crassulaceae or orpine Family. Horticultural crops with this pathway are xerophytes (desert plants like the cacti and many succulents) and pineapple. These plants grow in very hot, bright, dry environments. Their stomates remain closed during the day, thus limiting water loss but also preventing carbon dioxide from entering the leaves. However, carbon dioxide enters the plant during the night when the stomates are open and is fixed into an organic acid. This acid is oxidized internally during the day and utilized to produce carbohydrate via the Calvin cycle.

The initial products of photosynthetic carbon reduction are usually converted enzymatically to make complex forms for initial storage. The two main storage forms in leaves are starch and sucrose. Other metabolic processes convert these carbohydrates into nucleic acids, proteins, lipids and other organic compounds. These compounds, in turn, are assimilated into tissues and organs which make up the plant structure.

If photosynthesis occurs faster than the food produced is used, then the leftover portion will be stored, usually in the form of starch. If photosynthesis is equal to respiration (the breakdown of food products) this is referred to as the **compensation point**. No plant can survive at the compensation point for an extended period of time. Some house plants do not survive our winters indoors because they lack sufficient light. They simply are not able to conduct enough photosynthesis to survive.

## RESPIRATION

Respiration occurs in all living organisms and the process is one in which energy is released by the breakdown of carbon-containing compounds. It is often said to be the reverse of photosynthesis. If respiration is greater than photosynthesis, storage 'foods' will be used and a food deficiency can occur. This will lead to stress causing death of cells, tissues and, ultimately, the plant.

### AEROBIC RESPIRATION

Aerobic respiration occurs in the **presence** of oxygen in the mitochondria of the cells. The end products of this type of respiration are water and carbon dioxide. Respiration is highest in meristematic tissue and lowest in dormant tissue. The rate of respiration depends on many factors. As the temperature increases, respiration increases (there is, of course, an optimum temperature for each plant). The rate of respiration also depends on the availability of oxygen and carbohydrates and is controlled by the health of cells and tissues. Whenever respiration is referred to without being specified as aerobic or anaerobic, it is usually aerobic respiration being implied.

### ANAEROBIC RESPIRATION

Anaerobic respiration occurs in the **absence** of oxygen. The end products of anaerobic respiration in plants are ethanol and carbon dioxide. This is commonly known as fermentation and is used to man's advantage in producing many foodstuffs (eg., vinegar, wine, cheese, etc.). Too high a production of ethanol can be toxic to plant tissues. For example, in waterlogged soils, aerobic respiration is stopped because all oxygen is driven out of the soil atmosphere, thereby resulting in a build-up of ethanol which subsequently kills the roots. Waterlogged soils set up anaerobic conditions under which many disease causing bacteria and fungi thrive. The result can be death to individual cells and, if the situation is not rectified, it will soon cause death to the whole plant. The death of the plant can be attributed to a lack of oxygen and/or the presence of disease organisms.

## EFFECTS OF LIGHT ON PLANTS

### ETIOLATION

In the absence of light, plants will continue to metabolize and grow until their food reserves are depleted. This growth is abnormal and the syndrome developed is called etiolation (see Climate lesson, LIGHT). It is characterized by whitish, spindly stems which are too weak to stay erect; poorly developed roots; small leaves which fail to expand; succulent tissues; and long internodes. Some of these characteristics are commonly found on houseplants in the winter months. Geraniums over-wintered in cool, dark locations demonstrate etiolation. Man has used this technique to his advantage as well (eg., white asparagus, bleached celery). Once this whitish tissue is returned to the light, chloroplasts will develop and the plant will continue normal growth. For practicality, however, it is best to prune off the etiolated growth.

### PLANT SPACING

Spacing in the vegetable garden is important for the home gardener. In order to get the maximum amount of light to each plant, it is necessary to control the density of planting. This is done through spacing, pruning and training. As well, tall plants should not be located where they will shade smaller plants. Observing where the shade occurs at certain times of the day can guide pruning, planting and spacing requirements. Initial heavy plantings help discourage weed growth. Later, when plants are large enough to sufficiently shade surrounding areas to discourage most of the weeds from growing, they can be thinned. Plants not only compete for light, but also for water and nutrients.

### PHOTOPERIODISM

Photoperiodism is a biological response by a living creature to a change in the proportions of light and dark in a 24 hour period. It has been shown to initiate mating in many animals (fish, birds, mammals and insects) and it is known to stimulate flowering in many plants.

**Short-day plants** are those which flower only when the periods of light are **less** than the critical period. They usually require 12 hours or more of uninterrupted darkness (eg., chrysanthemum, poinsettia). Early spring and fall outdoors in the prairies produce such conditions. They should really be called 'long night' plants.

**Long-day plants** flower only when the periods of light **exceed** a critical period. These chiefly flower in summer outdoors when daylength can be 16 to 18 hours and nights are short. That is why spinach, lettuce and even potatoes will produce flowers. Spinach and lettuce are normally biennials but the long, hot summer days causes this condition known as **bolting**.

**Day neutral plants** are those plants which appear to flower irrespective of daylength, provided there is sufficient light to support good growth.

There are several factors which affect photoperiodism; temperature and the age of plant are two of the most important. For example, a poinsettia will bloom in 65 days if subjected to short days at 21°C. If grown at 15.5°C under short days, it will bloom in 85 days. When plants get older, they will often flower regardless of photoperiod, although they can be forced to flower earlier at the appropriate photoperiod.

### PHOTOTROPISM

Phototropism is the effect of light on the directional growth of plants. A subtle form of movement takes place when a plant is placed on a window sill in the sunlight. After a few days, the plant will bend towards the light (see Climate lesson, LIGHT). This actually occurs as the result of a buildup of a growth hormone, auxin, on the side of the stem away from the light. As a result, cell elongation occurs at a more rapid rate on the shaded side of the stems, thus producing a 'bending' as the stems grow. Light in blue wavelengths is most effective in inducing this phenomenon.

Modern science has learned to use a derivation of auxin as a herbicide. It is called 2,4-D and it literally causes plants to grow themselves to death!

## WATER

Of all the materials used by plants, water is taken up in the largest quantities. Many plants are 90 per cent water in composition. Water participates directly or indirectly in all metabolic reactions. It is required in photosynthesis. It helps maintain plant **turgidity**. It is the medium for nutrient absorption and transport in the xylem. It is the medium for food transport in the phloem and it acts as a coolant for the plant through transpiration.

### TRANSPIRATION

Why is it important to understand transpiration? In response to this question let us ask a couple of questions. Why does your garden wilt in the summer heat even though the soil is damp? Why did your 1.2 m (4 ft) cutting of Diefenbachia die? Answers to these questions come in an understanding of transpiration. What is transpiration? It is the release of water vapor from living tissues of the plant. There are two types recognized: **cuticular**, which accounts for about 10 per cent or less, and **stomatal**, which accounts for 90 per cent plus. Since the majority is the stomatal type, it is safe to say that the bulk of transpiration occurs from leaf surfaces.

### FACTORS AFFECTING TRANSPIRATION

Some external factors affecting the rate of transpiration include the amount of radiant energy absorbed by a plant, humidity, temperature, air currents, atmospheric pressure, pollution, and soil factors (water content, soil composition).

Internal factors include the size, arrangement and position of leaves, anatomy of leaves (thickness of cuticle, double epidermis, etc.), the size of stomata and whether they are open or closed, age and maturity of a plant or tissue as well as its health, and the water retaining ability of transpiring tissue (some plants maintain stored or reserve water, eg. jade plant).

### DIFFUSION

Diffusion is the movement of molecules or ions from a region of high concentration to a region of lower concentration. This can easily be demonstrated by adding a few drops of food coloring to a container of water. The food coloring is highly concentrated and when it is added to the water (of zero color concentration) the color tends to move into all areas until it is dispersed throughout the container. Diffusion also occurs in gases.

### OSMOSIS

Osmosis is a special type of diffusion which occurs in plants. Osmosis can be defined as the movement or diffusion of water or other solvents through a differentially (or selectively) permeable membrane from a region of higher free energy to a region of lower free energy of the water or solvent molecules. Free energy refers to that energy which is available to do work. The free energy of water can be reduced by dissolving molecules in it. The differentially permeable membrane is the plasma membrane of the plant cells and it does not allow everything through. Its permeability changes with changes in metabolism and the 'environment' around the membrane.

Water moves across the plasma membrane of the root hairs into the

### Figure 3-24
### WATER UPTAKE IN ROOTS

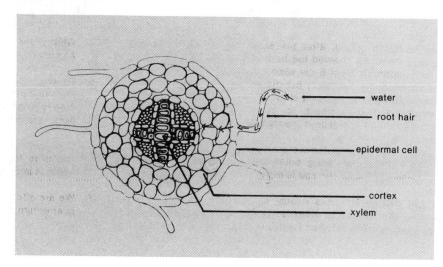

water
root hair
epidermal cell
cortex
xylem

cortex via intercellular spaces to the endodermis. It passes through the plasma membrane of the endodermis and enters the xylem. Once in the xylem, it is carried up to the leaves where photosynthesis occurs. Excess water vapor is lost through stomata so that an equilibrium is present. Too much water in plant tissues can lead to a variety of disorders.

The driving force for getting water from the roots to the leaves has led to much speculation and several theories. The cohesion-tension-transpiration theory seems to be the most accurate based on present knowledge. Water molecules cohere to each other and adhere to the walls of xylem elements, causing a tension. As water evaporates from the leaf tissues, the leaf cells become less turgid. Water is drawn in by osmosis to restore the turgid condition. The deficit created by transpiration 'pulls' water up from the roots. Quite phenomenal when one thinks of a giant redwood!

## CONCLUSION

This lesson has briefly introduced the subject of botany and the areas of taxonomy, morphology and physiology.

With knowing what a plant is composed of and how it functions, the following lesson on Plant Nutrition continues the story of how a plant lives and uses nutrients.

This lesson has followed the plant from a single cell to a collection of millions of cells where each cell has a particular function which is controlled by its genetic material. You have seen how cells, one on top of the other, form a pipeline or a circulatory system for the plant, providing it with water via the xylem tissue. Manufactured food in the form of carbohydrates produced during photosynthesis is moved throughout the plant by another pipeline system, the phloem tissue.

The knowledge of why light is required for plant growth is essential to understanding plants. One of the most common faults in growing plants lies in the poor concept of how light affects plants. If a plant is not receiving the proper amount of light for that particular plant, water uptake will be impaired. As you will learn in the lesson on House-plants, overwatering is the most frequent cause of plant death. The amount of water required by a plant is directly proportional to the amount of light it receives, assuming the temperature is adequate.

You have studied the parts of the plant, the roots, stems, leaves and flowers and have observed how each function. By studying the flower, you can now identify the male and female structures. This should enable you to determine how the plant is pollinated. The flower structure, the number of sepals, petals, stamens, pistils and their placement, aids the plant taxonomist in identifying plants.

It is hoped that by learning a bit more about the basic plant and what makes it tick, the home gardener will appreciate and, ultimately, care more about plants.

## SELF CHECK *QUIZ*

1. In the spring, after the snow melted, you noticed that mice had chewed the bark off your apple tree in a band approximately 5 cm wide all around the trunk. The tree leafed out normally but the leaves did not attain full size. By the end of June, all the leaves died and now (August) the tree appears to be dead. What is the most peripheral tissue in the tree left functional by the mice?

2. Why do your tomato plants, which are planted beside your house facing south, wilt in the hot afternoon sun even though the soil is moist?

3. Boston fern has evenly spaced rows of raised brown 'bumps' on the lower surface of some leaves. What are they? What is their function?

4. What is the main difference between Gymnosperms and Angiosperms in terms of seed development?

5. To which class (monocotyledonae or dicotyledonae) do the following plants belong? Kentucky bluegrass, creeping white clover, spider plant (*Chlorophytum*), poinsettia, tulip, daisy.

6. Speculate as to what would cause several inner, lower leaves to turn yellow and drop off your hibiscus plant, which is in a west facing window in mid-November?

7. We are often told to give a houseplant on a window sill a quarter turn every day. Why?

**aerobic respiration** - respiration occurring in the presence of oxygen.

**anaerobic respiration** - respiration occurring in the absence of oxygen.

**carbohydrate** - one of the several kinds of sugars produced by plants.

**cellulose** - carbohydrate formed from the simple sugar glucose. Major component of cell walls in plants.

**chlorophyll** - green pigment in plants essential for photosynthesis.

**chloroplasts** - plastid containing the green pigment called chlorophyll which is used in photosynthesis. Often called the 'seat of food manufacturing' for a plant.

**cotyledon** - thick leaf-like structure in seeds (often called a seed leaf) which functions in the absorption or storage of food.

**cultivar** - plant with unique characteristics considered generally superior to those of the plant from which it originated.

**deoxyribonucleic acid (DNA)** - carrier of genetic information.

**diffusion** - movement of molecules from a region of high concentration to a region of lower concentration.

**dioecious** - plants having either male or female flowers.

**epiphyte** - organism found growing non-parasitically on another organism (eg., orchids growing in trees).

**free energy** - energy which is available to do work.

**gamete** - sex cell either female (egg) or male (sperm).

**hemi-cellulose** - carbohydrate found in cell walls resembling cellulose containing sugar as well as non-sugar components.

**inflorescence** - flowers arranged in a cluster.

**internode** - section of a plant shoot between adjoining leaves or leaf sets.

**lignin** - organic substance which aids in the hardening of cell walls.

**monoecious** - plants having both male and female flowers.

**mycorrhiza** - non-parasitic fungi which grow in close association with the roots of some plants and aid in the uptake of certain nutrients.

**node** - part of the stem where leaves are attached.

**osmosis** - movement of water through a differentially (or selectively) permeable membrane from an area of higher free energy to a region of lower free energy of water molecules.

**ovule** - structure in seed plants containing the female gamete which, upon maturation, develops into the seed.

**parthenocarpy** - production of fruit without fertilization.

**petiole** - stalk or stem of a leaf.

**phloem** - food conducting tissue in plants.

**photoperiodism** - growth or developmental response of a plant to the length of day.

**photosynthesis** - process whereby plants in the presence of light are able to transform carbon dioxide and water to carbon containing energy rich, organic compounds (carbohydrates).

**phototropism** - process whereby the directional growth of a plant is altered by its reaction to light.

**protein** - group of nitrogenous compounds synthesized by plants.

**respiration** - process whereby energy is released through the breakdown of carbon-containing compounds.

**ribonucleic acid (RNA)** - cellular substance involved in protein synthesis.

**stigma** - distal portion of the pistil of a flower.

**stomata** - epidermal structure of leaves that function to permit gas exchange between plants and the atmosphere.

**surfactant** - agent which reduces surface tension and allows for a more even dispersal of a substance (eg., soap breaks the surface tension of water giving a more even spread).

**transpiration** - release of water vapor from living tissues of the plant.

**xylem** - water conducting tissue of plants.

# SELF CHECK ANSWERS

1. The xylem is the most peripheral functional tissue left by the mice (see CONDUCTING TISSUES - page 308 and Figure 3-12 - page 312).

2. The plants are transpiring at a faster rate than water is being taken up by the roots. This produces a temporary water deficit within the plant tissues. When the intensity of the sun's rays decrease, turgidity will return to normal. (see TRANSPIRATION - page 322 and OSMOSIS - page 322).

3. The 'bumps' are called sori. They contain many sporangia which, in turn, contain the spores which are the sexual propagule of ferns (see PTERIDOPHYTA OR FERNS - page 302).

4. The seeds of Angiosperms are enclosed in a fruit, whereas the seeds of Gymnosperms are naked, being produced in open structures called cones (see GYMNOSPERMS - page 302 and ANGIOSPERMS - page 303).

5. Monocotyledonae - Kentucky bluegrass, spider plant, tulip.
   Dicotyledonae - creeping white clove, poinsettia, daisy (see Table 3-1 - page 303).

6. With the intensity and duration of sunlight decreasing in mid-November, there isn't enough solar radiation penetrating the leaf layers to reach the chloroplasts. As a result, the chloroplasts die. This, in turn, causes the leaves to yellow and die. Also, inner lower leaves are usually the oldest and some leaf drop may be due to natural senescence (see PLASTIDS - page 305, LEAVES - page 312, and PLANT PHYSIOLOGY - page 319).

7. The growth hormone 'auxin' is produced on the side away from the direct light. This causes the stem to elongate on this side and the plant seems to bend towards the light. In order to have an upright plant, it is necessary to turn it each day so that stem elongation will be even (see PHOTOTROPISM - page 322).

Bailey, L.H. *Manual of Cultivated Plants*. New York: MacMillan, 1951.

A key which can be used to identify most horticultural plants. It can also be used to find out the scientific name if the common name is known.

Esau, K. *Anatomy of Seed Plants*. New York: John Wiley & Sons, Inc., 1965.

An advanced textbook on the anatomy of seed plants.

Janick, J., R.W. Schery, F.W. Woods, V.W. Ruttan. *Plant Science - An Introduction to World Crops*. San Francisco: W.H. Freeman and Company, 1981.

A textbook without any in-depth information on any one topic. It provides an adequate overview of plants and their uses.

Moss, E.H., *Flora of Alberta*. 2nd ed. edited by J.G. Parker. Toronto: University of Toronto Press, 1983.

A key to the native plants of Alberta. The classification system used in this lesson comes from this book.

Raven, P.H., R.F. Evert, H. Curtis. *Biology of Plants*. New York: Worth Publishers, Inc., 1981.

A more advanced textbook on botany - perhaps the best in print to date.

Stern, K.R. *Introductory Plant Biology*. Dubuque, Iowa: Wm. C. Brown Company Publishers, 1982.

An excellent introductory textbook on botany which is written in an interesting and easy to understand style.

*Common and Botanical Names of Weeds in Canada*. CSBN 1397, 066050547-9, revised 1980.

- PLANT METABOLISM
- PLANT NUTRIENT REQUIREMENTS
- FERTILIZERS

# PLANT NUTRITION

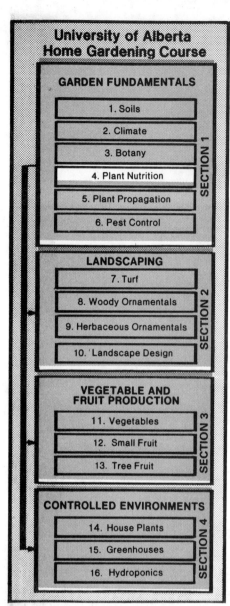

**University of Alberta Home Gardening Course**

**GARDEN FUNDAMENTALS**

1. Soils
2. Climate
3. Botany
4. Plant Nutrition
5. Plant Propagation
6. Pest Control

SECTION 1

**LANDSCAPING**

7. Turf
8. Woody Ornamentals
9. Herbaceous Ornamentals
10. Landscape Design

SECTION 2

**VEGETABLE AND FRUIT PRODUCTION**

11. Vegetables
12. Small Fruit
13. Tree Fruit

SECTION 3

**CONTROLLED ENVIRONMENTS**

14. House Plants
15. Greenhouses
16. Hydroponics

SECTION 4

# SELF-STUDY LESSON FEATURES

Self-study is an educational approach which allows you to study a subject where and when you want. The course is designed to allow you to study efficiently and incorporates the following features:

**OBJECTIVES** — are found at the beginning of each lesson and allow you to determine what you can expect to learn in the lesson.

**LESSON MATERIAL** — is logically organized and broken down into fundamental components by ordered headings to assist you to comprehend the subject.

**REFERENCING** — between lessons and within lessons allows you to integrate course material.

The last two digits of the page number identify the page and the digits preceding these identify the lesson number (eg., 107: Lesson 1, page 7 or 1227: Lesson 12, page 27).

Referencing:

sections within the same lesson (eg., see OSMOSIS)

sections in other lessons (eg., see Botany lesson, OSMOSIS)

figures and tables (eg., see Figure 7-3)

**FIGURES AND TABLES** — are found in abundance throughout the lessons and are designed to convey useful information in an easy to understand form.

**SIDEBARS** — are those areas in the lesson which are boxed and toned. They present information supplementary to the core content of the lesson.

**PRACTICAL PROJECTS** — are integrated within the lesson material and are included to allow you to apply principles and practices.

**SELF-CHECK QUIZ** — is provided at the end of each lesson and allows you to test your comprehension of the lesson material. Answers to the questions and references to the sections dealing with the questions are provided in the answer section. You should review any questions that you are unable to answer.

**GLOSSARY** — is provided at the end of each lesson and alphabetically lists the definitions of key concepts and terms.

**RESOURCE MATERIALS** — are provided at the end of each lesson and comprise a list of recommended learning materials for further study of the subject. Also included are author's comments on the potential application of each publication.

**INDEX** — alphabetically lists useful topics and their location within the lesson.

© 1986 University of Alberta Faculty of Extension

**Written by: Helge Welling and Dr. E.W. Toop**

Technical Reviewers:

Gail Rankin
Dr. Ed Redshaw
Dr. J.A. Robertson

THE PRODUCTION TEAM

Managing Editor ..................................................... Thom Shaw
Editor ................................................................. Frank Procter
Production Coordinator ...................................... Kevin Hanson
Graphic Artists....................................................... Lisa Marsh
Carol Powers
Melanie Eastley Harbourne
Data Entry ......................................................... Joan Geisterfer

**ISBN 0-88864-852-9**

(Book 1, Lesson 4)

Published by the University of Alberta
Faculty of Extension Corbett Hall
Edmonton, Alberta, T6G 2G4

QUAECUMQUE VERA

## LEARNING OBJECTIVES

After completing this lesson, the student should be able to:

1. identify and understand the function of the various processes involved in plant nutrition.
2. understand how nutrient elements are taken into the plant.
3. identify nutrient deficiency and toxicity symptoms demonstrated by plants.
4. understand the role of chemical and organic fertilizers, peat, compost, manure, etc. in supplying nutrients to plants.
5. identify the sources and functions of the various nutrient elements.

## TABLE OF CONTENTS

## LIST OF FIGURES AND TABLES

# INTRODUCTION

## DEFINITION

Many people think of plant nutrition in terms of 'plant food' yet do not equate plant food with animal or human food. Green plants require essentially the same 'food' as animals in order to grow and sustain life. However, green plants also have the capacity to synthesize food from the basic elements found in their environment. Therefore, plant nutrition refers to the supply of simple compounds and elements used by green plants to 'manufacture' their food, whereas in animal and human nutrition, plant and animal tissues are digested and 'recycled'.

Green plants utilize the products of digestion as well as animals and humans. In fact the majority of nutrients used by plants are 'recycled' and made available to them through the decay of organic matter. This aspect of recycling and both natural and intentional composting is dealt with later in this lesson.

## PLANT METABOLISM

In order to understand the physiology of plants it is important to understand the structure of plants and how the various parts function. The Botany lesson deals with the various plant organs, i.e., roots, stems, leaves, flowers, etc. It also deals with some aspects of plant metabolism, especially the unique plant process known as photosynthesis. In this lesson, we will also touch on photosynthesis but emphasize the other processes related to plant nutrition and plant metabolism.

## ABSORPTION

The uptake of water and nutrients by the roots involves both passive uptake (diffusion with a gradient or simple diffusion) and active uptake (diffusion against a gradient).

With simple diffusion, ions and molecules always move from regions of high to regions of low concentration of a given substance until an equilibrium is reached. Perhaps the simplest way to visualize this phenomenon is to imagine two rooms adjacent to one another and

separated by a screenlike wall which contains many small openings (see Figure 4-1). One room (A) is filled with bouncing balls of a size that will fit through the holes in the mesh wall. As these balls strike this wall, many will pass through into the other room (B). Once in this room, they will continue bouncing and may, in fact, bounce back into the original room. Because of the difference in concentration, there will be a **net movement** of balls from room A to room B until such time as both rooms contain an equal number of balls. With this type of diffusion, no external source of energy is needed. The ions or molecules (analogous to the bouncing

## Figure 4-1
## SIMPLE DIFFUSION

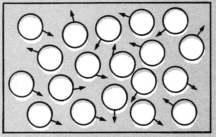

**Molecular Movement**

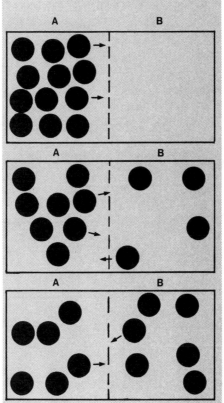

balls) by virtue of their own kinetic energy, establish a net movement from regions of their high concentration to regions of their low concentration. This phenomenon will hold for any particular type of substance, regardless of what other kinds of substances (ions and/or molecules) may be mixed with it. If the substance is water, there is net movement of molecules from a region of high concentration of water molecules to a region of lower concentration of water molecules. The process is called **osmosis**. Osmosis is a special case of diffusion limited to the diffusion of water.

With active uptake of water and nutrients by roots (diffusion against a gradient), there is a movement of ions and molecules of the given substance from a region of low concentration of that substance to a region of high concentration of the same substance. For this to occur, there must be an external source of energy. Plant roots have the ability to move certain ions and molecules against a diffusion gradient. The energy they use to do this comes from compounds made by photosynthesis and decomposed by respiration.

Water enters the plant predominantly by means of osmosis. The plasma membranes of the root hairs behave as semipermeable membranes. They allow water molecules to diffuse through them more readily than the sugar molecules that are present in the cytoplasm. Since the concentration of water within the root hair (epidermal cell) is less than that in the soil, water passes from soil into the root hair and from cell to cell until it reaches the conducting tubes (**xylem**).

Active absorption of water can also occur and may generate what is known as **root pressure**. Root pressure occurs when the soil moisture is high and the rate of transpiration or water loss from plant tissues as vapor is low. Root pressure (see Figure 4-2) is responsible for the loss of water droplets from the edges of leaves (**guttation**), the bleeding of xylem sap from cut or broken stems and the bursting of epidermal cells, usually on the underside of leaves or along succulent stems (**oedema**).

If the solute level in the soil becomes higher than that in the root cells or xylem vessels, the direction of water movement by osmosis will reverse. Unless checked, this will result in wilting

## Figure 4-2
## SYMPTOMS OF GUTTATION

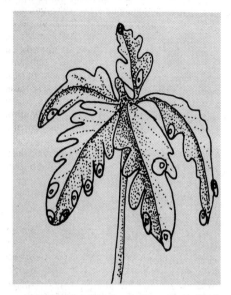

and possible death of the plant. Such reverse osmosis can be initiated by the presence of de-icing salts used on sidewalks or driveways during the previous winter, or by the presence of too much soluble fertilizer.

Mineral nutrients enter the roots as ions. These are present in the soil solution or **adsorbed** onto soil particles. Plant cell walls offer little hindrance to the movement of gaseous molecules, dissolved nutrients or ions. However, they have relatively weak attractive forces for cations (positively charged ions such as $K^+$, $Mg^{++}$, $Ca^{++}$ and others). These cations, adsorbed at a negatively charged site, can be displaced by another cation with a higher adsorptive affinity for that site. The released cation may then move inward (in leapfrog fashion) to another cation adsorptive site. Negatively charged ions (anions), some cations, gases and dissolved molecular nutrients will diffuse through the cell wall dissolved in water. The area comprised by cell walls is often termed **free space** because it does not oppose ion movement. Once ions reach the plasma membrane, they encounter an effective barrier. This may not occur until the ions reach the **endodermis** (cylinder of cells) around the roots vascular system. Ion movement across this and subsequent membranes occurs primarily by active uptake. However, some molecules may cross the plasma membrane or other

membranes by passive uptake. These molecules include gases such as oxygen, carbon dioxide, fat soluble molecules and small molecules like ammonia. The membrane may act as a molecular sieve, allowing certain sized molecules to pass through or, in the case of fat soluble molecules, the **lipid** portion of the membrane may act as a selective solvent.

Once into the cytoplasm, ions may undergo several fates. Their removal is necessary if ion absorption by the roots is to continue. Ions may be transformed by metabolic reactions within a cell into other substances. They may be adsorbed by protein molecules or transported through other cells (active and/or passive transport) until they reach the xylem. They may also accumulate in cell **vacuoles** or **organelles**.

## PHOTOSYNTHESIS

Without photosynthesis, the evolution and maintenance of life as we know it would not be possible. It is a complex series of integrated processes which

take place in the **chloroplasts** (see Figure 4-3). In its simplest definition, photosynthesis is a series of processes whereby light energy is converted to chemical energy (see Botany lesson, PHOTOSYNTHESIS). In turn, this energy is used to synthesize carbohydrates. The overall equation frequently stated to define photosynthesis is:

$$6CO_2 + 12H_2O \longrightarrow (C_6H_{12}O_6) + 6H_2O + 6O_2$$

carbon dioxide    water     carbohydrate   water   oxygen

These explanations are oversimplifications since they give no idea of the photochemical or carbon fixation steps involved. Furthermore, only some parts of photosynthesis require light (light phase); the others (dark phase) do not require it (see Botany lesson, PHOTOSYNTHESIS).

## RESPIRATION

The stored energy from photosynthesis can be released by the biological

## Figure 4-3
## CHLOROPLAST WITHIN A MESOPHYLL CELL OF A LEAF: SCHEMATIC OUTLINE OF PHOTOSYNTHESIS

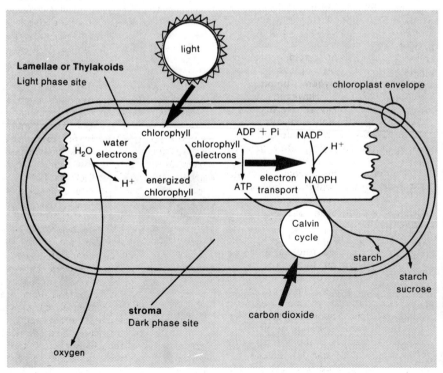

oxidation of the organic compounds resulting from that process. In fact, the maintenance of life requires the continuous use of this energy. Carbohydrates are the primary **substrates** of respiration in higher plants, with the most important ones being glucose, fructose, sucrose and starch. Other substances, to a lesser extent, may serve as respiratory substrates. These include fats (eg., endosperm of some seeds), proteins and organic acids. The most common substrate is glucose which, when oxidized in the presence of free oxygen (**aerobic respiration**), produces energy in the form of adenosine triphosphate (**ATP**).

$$C_6H_{12}O_6 + 6O_2 = 6CO_2 + 6H_2O + \text{energy}$$
Glucose Oxygen Carbon water (ATP)

This summary equation indicates that respiration, for all practical purposes, is the reverse of photosynthesis. However, like the summary equation for photosynthesis, it is an oversimplification. Many of the intermediate compounds formed during respiration may be used directly to synthesize cellular constituents.

When oxygen is lacking, respiration can still occur, but in a modified form (**anaerobic respiration**). The ultimate products of anaerobic respiration are alcohol or lactic acid. Anaerobic respiration will take place in roots deprived of oxygen because of waterlogged soils. However, vascular plants cannot usually survive for long on anaerobic respiration and usually die. Those plants with submerged roots (such as cattails, rice, etc.) generally thrive on their ability to carry out aerobic respiration with the levels of oxygen dissolved in the water or because of their specialized anatomical structure which allows for large air spaces in the submerged tissues.

The slow controlled release of energy with a minimum of heat produced is possible because of the number of biochemical steps involved, each catalyzed by one or more enzymes. About 40 per cent of the energy released during respiration of glucose is trapped in the form of the energy carrier ATP. This energy can be utilized later and even in other parts of the plant for various cellular processes.

## TRANSPIRATION

Only about one per cent of the water absorbed by plants is utilized in biochemical processes such as photosynthesis or in the maintenance of internal water pressure within the living cells (**turgor pressure**). Most of the water absorbed is lost from aerial parts of the plant through evaporation and diffusion of water vapor into the atmosphere. This process is called transpiration. Much of the water loss is through the stomates, with some loss through the cuticle and lenticels (see Botany lesson, STOMATAL APPARATUS). Under conditions of high soil moisture and high humidity, a small fraction of water may be lost by guttation (see ABSORPTION).

When the loss of water exceeds its replacement by absorption, a water deficit occurs within the plant. Water deficits reduce the turgor pressure in the cells resulting in a wilting or drooping of leaves and herbaceous stems. Such loss of turgor pressure in the guard cells surrounding each stomate will cause the aperture to decrease or close and greatly reduce the rate of transpiration. However, environmental conditions may be such that this closure is too slow to prevent major wilting. Wilting may be temporary or permanent, depending on the availability of soil moisture. Permanent wilting can cause death by desiccation if prolonged but recovery is possible if water is added to the soil soon enough.

Transpiration rates are usually higher during the day than at night because stomates are normally open during the day and closed at night. Temperatures are usually higher during the day as well. Exceptions are the many succulents with crassulacean acid metabolism (see Botany lesson, PHOTOSYNTHESIS) since their stomates are open at night rather than during the day.

Transpiration is often considered to be a very wasteful process but there are benefits to the plant associated with it. The strong cohesive forces between water molecules permit continuous columns of water to extend from the roots to the uppermost leaves of the plant. With our tallest forest species, this is a considerable distance and accounts for a much higher rise in water columns than is possible through capillary action alone. As water

molecules evaporate from the surfaces of leaf mesophyll cells, new molecules move up to replace them, creating a chain reaction down through the vascular system to the water absorbing surfaces of the roots. This mass movement of water through the plants also speeds up the movement of dissolved nutrients through the xylem to the sites of the living cells. Here, they become available in increasing concentrations for metabolism. Furthermore, the constant availability of water molecules on the surfaces of the leaf mesophyll cells permits the carbon dioxide diffusing into the leaves to be rapidly dissolved and move into the cells in solution.

## TRANSLOCATION

Translocation involves the movement of water, minerals and food from one part of a plant to another. Minerals absorbed by the roots are translocated to the stems, leaves and reproductive organs of the shoots. Once there, they may be further translocated, either up or down the vascular system, to other sites (eg., from older leaves to younger leaves). Most minerals are transported in the form of ions but nitrates, absorbed in the roots, are converted there to amino acids before translocation.

Most food is translocated as sugar, usually sucrose. The flow is from leaves (main sites for photosynthesis) to metabolically active tissues, such as areas of rapid growth (meristems) where sugar demand exceeds the synthesized supply. Insoluble carbohydrate, such as starch present in leaves, or more particularly in specialized storage organs, may be hydrolyzed to soluble sugar and translocated to meristems where the leaf supply of sugar is insufficient. Other substances are also translocated, but not in such quantities. These include amino acids, vitamins, hormones, or other growth regulators.

The xylem is the part of the vascular system through which water flows and minerals are transported from roots to the aerial portions of the plant. Some lateral movement of minerals occurs from xylem into the phloem. Minerals may also be translocated from older leaves through the phloem in either an upward or downward direction. Some sugars may also move through the xylem during certain seasons.

The phloem is the transport facility for the bulk of sugar translocation either

Figure 4-4

## TRANSLOCATION IN THE VASCULAR PLANT

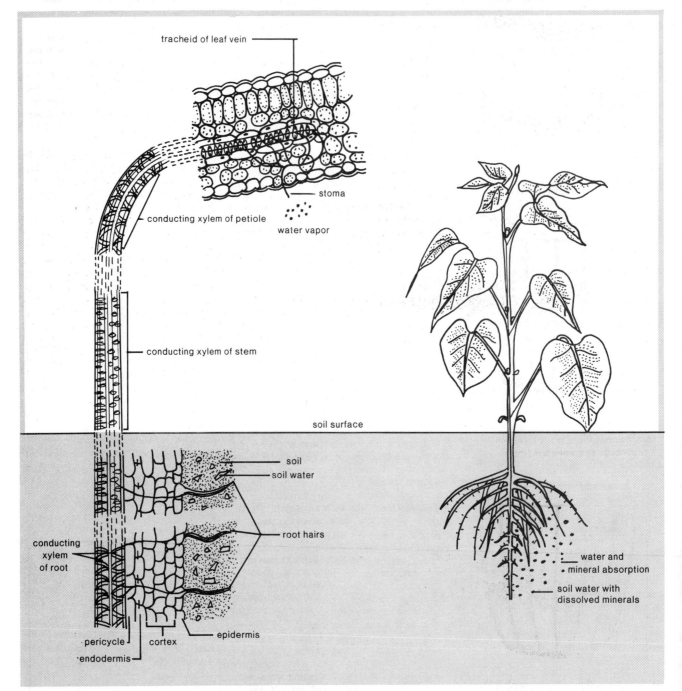

upward or downward. Sugars may also move laterally through **vascular rays**. Amino acids, organic acids, soluble proteins, auxins and vitamins are also translocated through the phloem.

Mention should be made of the importance of environmental factors on the overall nutrition of plants. Reference has been made to temperature as it affects the rate of various metabolic processes. It is a very important factor in the overall effects it can have. For example, plants growing in cold soils often show wilting or certain nutrient deficiencies (see DEFICIENCY AND TOXICITY SYMPTOMS) despite the fact that abundant (or at least adequate) amounts of water and minerals are present in the soil. Because of the low temperature, the absorptive capacity of the roots is reduced and cannot keep pace with the demand for water and mineral nutrients in the aerial portions of the plant. Similarly, low air temperatures can seriously reduce the rate of photosynthesis (both the rate of the biochemical reactions involved and the supply of carbon dioxide available within the leaves) as well as the rate of all the other processes involved in overall growth.

## Figure 4-5
### THE PRINCIPLE OF LIMITING FACTORS

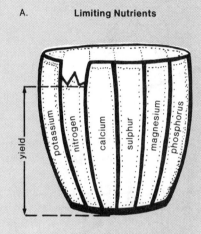

A. **Limiting Nutrients**

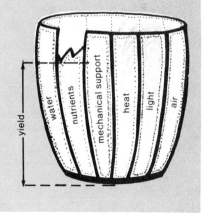

B. **An Essential Element for Plant Growth Becomes Limiting**

### PRINCIPLE OF LIMITING FACTORS

One cannot single out any particular factor as being more important than another in its effect on the overall nutrition and health of plants. Temperature has been noted above merely as an example. All factors involved must be at their optimum level for a plant to reach its full potential. When one factor is less than optimal, it then becomes the controlling or limiting entity and determines the extent to which the plant will fall short of its full potential. This concept has been identified as the principle of limiting factors (see Figure 4-5).

## PLANT NUTRIENT REQUIREMENTS

### SOURCES OF PLANT NUTRIENTS

The elements required by green plants for food synthesis include carbon, hydrogen, oxygen and many other elements. Carbon, hydrogen and oxygen are derived from carbon dioxide (absorbed mainly through the leaves) and water (absorbed mainly through the roots). The mineral elements are derived from soluble compounds (often referred to as fertilizers) which are absorbed through roots, with water serving as the carrier and transport medium.

### MAJOR AND MINOR PLANT NUTRIENT ELEMENTS

Plants get their nutrient elements from three sources - air, water and soil. Some of these elements are used in relatively large quantities and are known as major nutrient elements. Others are used in very minute quantities and are known as minor nutrient elements or, sometimes, as trace elements. Table 4-1 lists of these elements. The following sections discuss the function and source of each of these elements.

### THE FUNCTION AND SOURCE OF NUTRIENT ELEMENTS

CARBON (C)
Carbon is obtained from carbon dioxide ($CO_2$) which is taken in through the stomata of leaves and used to produce carbohydrates and oxygen through photosynthesis. Thus, carbon is part of the plant sugars which are used in respiration, energy production and are converted to cellulose and starch for cell building or food reserves. Carbohydrates may be converted to fatty substances or

used with other elements to form protein or cell components such as chlorophyll. Carbon makes up about 50 per cent of the dry weight of plant tissue.

Carbon dioxide is present in soil air in much more concentrated form than in the atmosphere. Any change in the concentration of carbon dioxide in the atmosphere or soil air influences the plant's rate of growth with minimum, optimum and maximum concentrations for plant growth varying among plants. Carbon is deposited into the soil as organic matter (recycled carbon) in forms of carbonate compounds ($CO_3^-$). These compounds provide plants with another source for carbon.

## Table 4-1
### MAJOR AND MINOR PLANT NUTRIENT ELEMENTS

| ELEMENT | SYMBOL |
|---|---|
| **Major Nutrients (macronutrients)** | |
| Carbon | C |
| Oxygen | O |
| Hydrogen | H |
| Nitrogen | N |
| Phosphorus | P |
| Potassium (Kalium) | K |
| Calcium | Ca |
| Magnesium | Mg |
| Sulphur | S |
| **Minor Nutrients (micronutrients)** | |
| Iron | Fe |
| Manganese | Mn |
| Boron | B |
| Copper | Cu |
| Zinc | Zn |
| Molybdenum | Mo |
| Cobalt | Co |
| Chlorine | Cl |
| Sodium (Natrium) | Na |
| Silicon | Si |
| Iodine | I |
| Aluminum | Al |

## OXYGEN (O)

Oxygen is one of the most important elements. Life itself (plant or animal) would not exist without oxygen. It is required in the photosynthetic process and is also required in respiration to produce energy from oxidation. Oxygen is used to build new cells and tissue and is part of hundreds of compounds found in the plant.

Gases, such as oxygen and carbon dioxide, enter the plant directly from the atmosphere through the stomata of the leaves. In the plant tissue, seemingly empty intercellular spaces exist. These spaces are typically filled with gas (air) and are part of an intercellular gas system penetrating throughout the plant tissue. This ensures that each cell will get its supply of carbon dioxide and will release the excess oxygen produced during periods of light by photosynthesis.

Oxygen is also present in soil pore space where it can enter the root system in ionic forms. Oxygen can enter the root system as $O^=$, $OH^-$, $CO_3^=$, $SO_4^=$ and $CO_2$.

The importance of oxygen to the nutritional requirements of plants cannot be overstated.

## HYDROGEN (H)

Hydrogen, along with oxygen, comprise water and as such, is absorbed into the plant (mainly through the root system). Water is essential to the life of plants and makes up 75 per cent or more of the plant's weight. Hydrogen is an important component of chlorophyll and is essential in numerous chemical reactions and processes in the plant. Hydrogen is

## Figure 4-6
## NITROGEN CYCLE

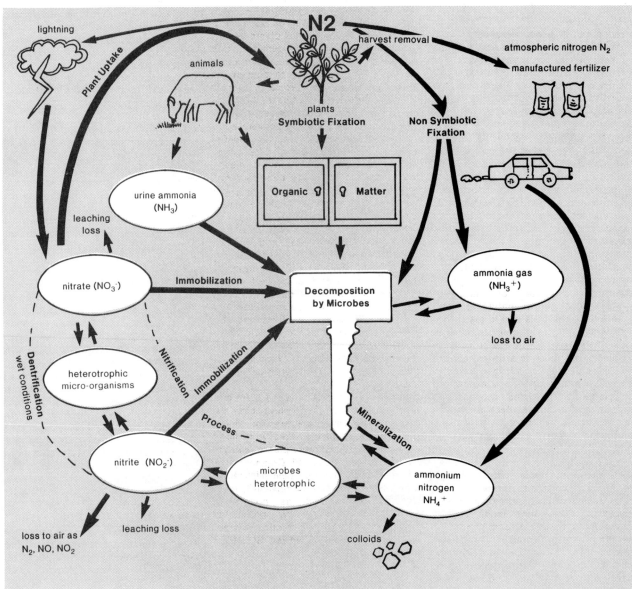

## Figure 4-7
## IMMOBILIZATION

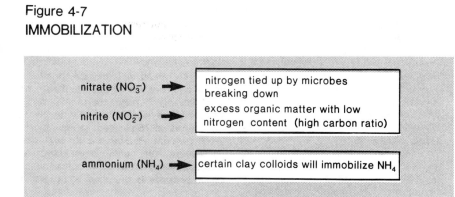

involved in acid reactions (see SOIL pH MODIFICATION) and is taken up in ionic form as $H^+$ and HOH.

### NITROGEN (N)

Nitrogen gas ($N_2$), which makes up most of the atmospheric gas, is not available to plants until it is changed to ammonium or nitrate. Plants take in nitrogen as ammonium cations ($NH_4^+$) and as nitrate anions ($NO_3^-$). Nitrogen is recycled in nature as plants and animals die and become part of the organic matter of soil. This organic matter is like a cupboard of nitrogen under lock and key (see Figure 4-6). It opens up when the key called 'decomposition' is turned on by the microbes in the soil (see ROLE OF SOME MICRO-ORGANISMS). Nitrogen then becomes available to the plants only when it has broken down completely to the ionic forms. Ammonium, the product of the first breakdown, is also available as commercial fertilizer in the form of ammonium sulphate or dissolved ammonia. Urea is a natural product excreted from animals and is also made commercially from nitrogen gas. Urea is quickly hydrolyzed in the soil to produce the ammonium form. In both cases, the soil enzyme urease changes urea to ammonium which can be absorbed by the plants or oxidized by nitrifying bacteria to form nitrate which is used by plants. Excess amounts of ammonium can cause harmful conditions for the plant.

The micro-organisms that change ammonium and nitrite to nitrate are much more sensitive than ammonium – fixing organisms. Thus, both high and low temperatures, as well as acid conditions, will stop nitrate formation. Ammonium cations ($NH_4^+$) can be held on soil colloids in an exchangeable and available form but, as long as these cations are held to colloids, they are not easily **leached**. Some specific types of clay will hold on to ammonium so tightly that it is not available to plant roots, nor can it be converted to nitrate. This, however, does not seem to be a major problem in Alberta soils. If plants take up ammonium ($NH_4^+$) during cold temperatures, the plant may have to use its stored carbohydrate to convert the ammonium to amino acids and more complex proteins. If nitrate ($NO_3^-$) is taken up during cold temperatures, it need not use stored carbohydrate but can store nitrate until warmer weather prevails before converting it to amino acids. Therefore, plants using nitrate during cold weather are more vigorous than plants using ammonium during cold weather. Some crops, such as potato and tomato, prefer nitrate nitrogen to ammonium nitrogen. Nitrogen is part of every living plant cell and a very important component in the formation of chlorophyll. Nitrogen is important in protein formation. It is part of nucleic acid and increases the cation exchange capacity in soil. It also increases leaf and stem production in plants and aids seed production of some grasses. When applied late in the season, nitrogen decreases the winter hardiness of plants. Nitrogen is easily leached out.

Nitrogen is very mobile in the plant and, if in short supply, will move from the older part of a plant into the new, rapidly growing areas. Under natural conditions, organic matter provides plants with the majority of nitrogen used. Organic matter contains about five per cent nitrogen. In agriculture (including horticulture), much nitrogen is supplied as commerical fertilizer or through the growth of legumes utilizing 'symbiotic nitrogen fixation' (see ATMOSPHERIC SOURCES OF NUTRIENTS).

### PHOSPHORUS (P)

Phosphorus originates from minerals like 'apatite' and is released through the weathering of rock containing these minerals. These minerals provide a source of phosphorus for production of commercial fertilizers. The amount of phosphorus in Alberta soils is very low; in fact, the amount of phosphorus in the average soil in North America amounts to only 0.1 per cent. Only small amounts of phosphorus are available to plants at any time. In very acid soil, phosphorus is even less available as it becomes **tied up** with aluminum and iron. In aluminum and iron compounds, phosphorus is not readily available. Phosphorus is tied up with calcium in alkaline soils to form tricalcium phosphate, which also reduces the availability of phosphorus to plants. Phosphorus is most readily available to plants at a pH between 5.8 and 6.5 and is recycled in organic matter, although only a small portion of the amount needed is obtained by recycling (see RECYCLING). Phosphorus is obtained by plants in the form of $H_2PO_4^-$ anions. The nucleus of each plant cell requires phosphorus and, without it, growth cannot take place. Phosphorus is needed in greater amounts in areas of rapid cell growth like shoots and roots. Phosphorus stimulates root development and a good supply of phosphorus will ensure a good healthy root system. Phosphorus, then, is very important for emerging seedlings. It is also quite important in flowering, pollen and seed development and the early stages of fruit formation. It helps to increase winter hardiness in plants and is very important in the breakdown of organic matter. Phosphorus is not readily mobile.

### POTASSIUM (K)

Plants take up potassium (Kalium) as $K^+$ ions which are quite mobile within the plant. In soil, potassium occurs in three forms: slowly available, readily available and unavailable for plant use. The slowly available form is associated with such clays as ilite and vermiculite. The readily available potassium is to be found in the soil solution and also adsorbed by soil colloids. The more clay there is in a soil, the greater the capacity for the soil to contain potassium.

Alberta soil contains large amounts of potassium, almost all of it in primary minerals such as feldspar and mica. Weathering makes about 1-2 per cent of this available to plants annually. Sandy and peat soils in Alberta may be short of potassium.

Potassium is used in the plant in rapidly growing tissues and is important in the formation of fruit. There is still much to learn about the role of potassium in the plant, but it is known that potassium is required for normal cell division and the synthesis and translocation of sugars. It is also needed for normal development of chlorophyll and proteins and seems to be involved in the formation of starch. Potassium aids the plant in disease resistance and winter hardiness (see Soils lesson, NUTRIENTS ESSENTIAL FOR PLANT GROWTH).

## CALCIUM (Ca)

In ionic form ($Ca^{++}$), calcium is taken up by plants from the exchangeable ions on soil colloids. It is used in the formation of the middle layer in each cell wall of the plant and is needed in large quantities for cell division and growth. Calcium affects the permeability of cell walls and make cells more selective in their absorption of nutrients. Calcium also promotes early growth and increased stiffness of plant stems.

Calcium neutralizes acids produced in the plant. One such acid is oxalic acid, which is toxic to protoplasm if allowed to build to high concentrations. Calcium renders oxalic acid harmless by forming calcium oxalate, which is insoluble. The uptake of radioactive elements by the plant is also reduced by calcium. Calcium stimulates root development and aids in the formation of nodules on legumes. Tomato blossom end rot is associated with insufficient calcium. In the soil, calcium is mainly produced from limestone (calcium carbonate). There is an important relationship between calcium, magnesium and potassium in the soil. An excess of any one or two of these ionic elements could cause exchanges with others which speed the loss by leaching, so deficiency occurs. For example, excess of calcium in comparison to magnesium results in worsened magnesium deficiency. Similarly, if a lot of potassium is present, magnesium deficiency may be more pronounced.

## MAGNESIUM (Mg)

Magnesium is taken up by the plant as $Mg^{--}$ from soil solution and soil colloids in the same way as potassium and calcium. Magnesium is a very important part of the chlorophyll molecule and, when in short supply, a condition known as **chlorosis** occurs. Magnesium helps in the formation of fats and is involved in starch movement in the plant. Spinach, cauliflower, muskmelon, Irish potato, peas, oats and corn seem to need a larger amount of magnesium than other crops.

Magnesium occurs as dolomitic limestone, which is a combination of magnesium carbonate and calcium carbonate. There is usually less available magnesium in the soil than available calcium since calcium limestone is more readily weathered than dolomitic limestone.

Magnesium makes the uptake of phosphorus take place more readily; it acts as a carrier of phosphorus in the plant. Weathering of such minerals as biotite, hornblende and chlorite also add magnesium to the soil.

## SULPHUR (S)

Soil sulphur originates from sulphide minerals in rocks, oxidized by weathering to sulphate. Sulphur makes soil acidic. Recycling of organic matter accounts for the largest amount of sulphur (see RECYCLING). Some sulphur orginates in the atmosphere in the form of sulphur dioxide ($SO_2$). It enters the soil water from rain and snow. Sulphur dioxide also comes in many fertilizers and insecticides, and is a by-product of oil recovery and refining.

Sulphur is mostly taken up by plants as $SO_4^=$ which is weakly held by soil colloids and easily leaches away. Sulphur is used in amino acids in the plant which, in turn, are used in root development and aids in the formation of nodules on legumes. It stimulates seed formation and increases plant vigor.

## IRON (Fe)

Minerals, such as pyrite, hematite, limonite and many others, contribute iron to the soil. It is taken up by the plant as $Fe^{--}$ and $Fe^{---}$, mostly through the roots. Although iron is essential for the formation of chlorophyll, it is not part of the chlorophyll molecule. Iron is needed only in small amounts by the plant and is, therefore, known as a minor nutrient. Iron is important for the activity of enzymes as well as the oxygen reducing processes. At soil pH below 5.5, iron may block translocation tissues in the plant by accumulating at the nodes. Iron becomes less available to plants as the pH of soil increases, and it is not available on highly alkaline soils. Because iron is not available to plants on highly alkaline soil, many plants growing in such soil suffer from iron deficiency. This condition is known as 'lime induced chlorosis' or 'lime induced iron deficiency'. Acid producing micro-organisms help make fixed iron available by lowering the soil pH.

## MANGANESE (Mn)

Manganese enters plants in the form of $Mn^{++}$ and, like iron, is considered a minor plant nutrient because it is only needed in small amounts. Its availability decreases as the pH increases from 5 to 7 and is affected even more by pH changes than iron, copper or zinc. The source of manganese is soil minerals and manganese is recycled in organic matter.

Manganese can easily become toxic to plants if present in more than small quantities. Soil anaerobic micro-organisms (see AERATION) tend to initiate undesirable chemical reactions such as the reduction of manganese oxide and, eventually, an excess of $Mn^{++}$ occurs under wet conditions. Aerobic micro-organisms, on the other hand, can oxidize manganese so it becomes insoluble and unavailable to plants. Manganese is important for oxygen formation in photosynthesis, for the synthesis of chlorophyll and for carbohydrate metabolism. Manganese is active in respiration and the activation of enzymes. Manganese speeds up germination of seeds, maturity of plants and affects the vitamin production and content of plants.

## BORON (B)

Boron originates in the tourmaline mineral found in igneous rock. Boron enters the plant mainly as $B_4O_7^=$ anions and, like iron and manganese, becomes less available as the pH increases from 5 to 7. Although most soils contain sufficient amounts of boron, low soil moisture can reduce boron availability. Slight excesses of boron become toxic to plants. In fact, boron based chemicals (borates) are used as weedkillers. Abnormal growth occurs in citrus fruits, apples, celery, cauliflower, beans, and corn if there is a shortage of boron.

Boron acts as a regulator in the supply of oxygen to plant roots and plant tissue. It assists in cell division and is essential for pollination and reproduction. Boron affects fibre formation, protein synthesis, carbohydrate metabolism and is closely tied to calcium performance in plants.

## COPPER (Cu)
Copper is taken up by plants as $Cu^{++}$ cations and is needed in even smaller amounts than boron. Copper becomes less available as the pH increases from 5 to 7 if leaching has occurred. Copper deficiency can occur on acid soils. Copper, like boron, becomes toxic if even a small excess of available copper is present.

Copper acts as a regulator of several biochemical processes in the plant, such as respiration and photosynthesis. It is active in enzyme systems in the plant and a deficiency of copper can result in a **dieback** of vegetable leaves and the yellowing on leaves of certain fruit trees.

## ZINC (Zn)
Zinc enters plants as $Zn^{++}$ cations and is required only in small amounts. Zinc also becomes less available as the pH increases from 5 to 7.

The availability of zinc is more important than the actual amounts present in the soil. Low temperatures and low light intensity can aggravate zinc deficiency. This deficiency can be associated with high phosphorus levels. Zinc is essential in the formation of chlorophyll and is active in enzyme systems to get some metabolic reactions going within the plant. Zinc is essential in the formation of growth hormones and influences seed production. Lack of zinc often leads to small and/or mottled leaves on trees.

## MOLYBDENUM (Mo)
Molybdenum originates in sedimentary rock and, in ionic form, is available as $MoO_4^-$ anions. Molybdenum becomes **less** available as the pH **decreases** from 7 to 5. It is unavailable in acid soil but is very available in non-acid soil.

Molybdenum is important for nitrogen fixing bacteria in legume nodules. Without molybdenum, nitrate cannot be reduced and nitrogen shortage results.

The disease 'whiptail' in cauliflowers and broccoli is caused by molybdenum deficiency. Molybdenum is important for starch formation and for amino acid and vitamin formation. Excess amounts are toxic to plants but molybdenum is required in very small quantities for normal growth of tomato seedlings (although only in amounts as low as 0.01 parts per million).

## COBALT (Co)
Cobalt originates in basic igneous rock and enters plants as $Co^{++}$ cations. Where it is needed, it is only required in very small amounts. Cobalt seems to be used by legume root nodules for effective nitrogen fixation.

## CHLORINE (Cl)
Chlorine enters the plant as a mobile anion ($Cl^-$) which activates the oxygen producing systems of photosynthesis. Chlorine anions are abundant in the soil. Since it occurs in concentrations greater than 1000 parts per million (ppm), it is sometimes considered as a major nutrient. It is, however, only needed in small amounts for plant growth. Chlorine was not proven to be an essential element for plants until 1954.

## SODIUM (Na)
Sodium (Natrium) is found in large supply in Alberta soils. It has not proven to be an essential plant nutrient, although beneficial effects on plant growth have been found (mostly in plants with a reduced potassium supply). It seems that sodium makes the amount of potassium go further. No need for sodium has been identified for horticultural crops.

## SILICON (Si)
Silicon is required for the growth of diatoms (a group of algae) where it is needed for the cell wall. Horsetail (*Equisetum*) takes up and deposits silica in cell walls, as do some grasses (including rice). Depriving these plants of silicon leads to poor growth and disease symptoms. Silicon is beneficial in sugarcane production but not essential.

## IODINE (I)
Iodine's role and effects in horticulture are not known.

## OTHER ELEMENTS
Elements such as aluminum, nickel, chromium, gallium and vanadium are not needed by plants and can be toxic if available in certain amounts.

Aluminum is part of the clay mineral and high levels of exchangeable aluminum affect the pH buffering capacity by neutralizing $OH^-$ anions, thereby freeing $H^+$ cations. Excess aluminum may tie up phosphorus, making it unavailable to plants. Aluminum ions are responsible for the blue coloring of hydrangea flowers.

# RECYCLING

The majority of nutrients used by plants are recycled. Organic matter (living or dead plant and animal residue) stores most of the nutrients required by plants. Only when active decomposition has taken place and the organic matter (no longer identifiable and called humus) has broken down to a liquid, is it available to plants in ionic form. There is a multitude of micro-organisms in the soil (one gram of soil may have from several millions to one billion). The rate of decomposition is directly related to the number of microbes present.

These micro-organisms (microbes) include bacteria, fungi, actinomycetes, algae and protozoa. Not all micro-organisms are beneficial to plants, many are harmful (causing wilts, rots, etc). Microbes absorb the nutrients released during decomposition and use them for growth and reproduction. Bacteria and fungi are the most important organic matter decomposers. Carbon and nitrogen are important for the microbes with nitrogen often being the controlling factor in organic matter decomposition. Nitrogen is needed in smaller amounts than carbon. The amount of nitrogen available, either in the soil already or in the organic matter residue, affects the rate of decomposition

## CARBON:NITROGEN RATIO
The nitrogen content in soil organic matter is given in proportion to carbon content and is called the carbon:nitrogen ratio (C:N ratio). Bacteria require one part nitrogen for each 4-5 parts carbon to effectively decompose organic matter. Sawdust and straw, which have low nitrogen content in proportion to carbon, require additional nitrogen to feed the microbes.

Immobilization of nitrogen occurs when inorganic nitrogen (such as nitrate) is tied up in organic matter. This happens when there is a large amount of organic matter with a very low nitrogen content. The microbes then utilize the available nitrogen in the soil, rendering it unavailable for plant use.

Chemically, organic matter provides 90-95 per cent of the nitrogen for use by plants, 5-60 per cent of the phosphorus, and up to 80 per cent of the sulphur.

### THE ROLE OF SOME MICRO-ORGANISMS

Mycorrhizae are fungi found on many plant roots, and aid in nutrient and water uptake. Rhizobium bacteria form nitrogen fixing nodules on legumes and on a few other non-legume plants. A group of bacteria (called **autotrophs**) benefit from oxidizing soil elements such as nitrogen, sulphur, iron, manganese and carbon monoxide. Protozoa micro-organism act as predators on bacteria. Actinomycetes

fix nitrogen and help to decompose organic matter.

Micro-organisms, while decomposing protein, release ammonium to the soil in a process called **ammonification**. All organic nitrogen released to the soil is through this process. It is the autotrophic bacteria that oxidize ammonium ($NH_4^+$) to nitrite ($NO_2^-$) and then to nitrate ($NO_3^-$) - the form desirable for plant use. This process is called **nitrification**. **Mineralization** is the change of organic nitrogen through the processes of ammonification and nitrification to the ionic forms of ammonium nitrite, and nitrate which are all forms the plant can take in (see Figure 4-8). Nitrite ($NO_2^-$) is toxic to plants. If decomposing protein is not available, the autotrophic bacteria can also utilize ammonium fertilizers, such as ammonium sulphate.

## AERATION

Aeration refers to the availability of oxygen in the pore spaces (see Soils

lesson, SOIL WATER). Aeration is dependent on fluctuations in the volumes of air and water in the pore space. Under good aerobic conditions, fluctuations always exist, whereas in poorly aerated soil, there is little or no fluctuation in the volumes of air and water.

Favorable conditions for micro-organisms include well aerated, moist soil, some calcium and the absence of strong acidic conditions. The micro-organisms function best at temperatures between 20°C and 40°C.

Micro-organisms require large amounts of nutrient elements such as nitrogen, phosphorus, sulphur and calcium. Carbon, the organic source of food for micro-organisms, is most readily used when micro-organisms compete with each other and other species for food.

Aeration is very important for the release of carbon dioxide, ammonium, nitrate, phosphorus, sulfate and water. These, along with a bit of resistant residue and very small amounts of some other elements, result in the aerobic decomposition of organic matter in well aerated soil. If soil is not well aerated, much less desirable products (such as methane, etc.) are the end products. Also in poorly aerated soil, the conversion of ammonium to nitrate is reduced when sufficient oxygen is not available (see RESPIRATION). Under wet soil conditions, anaerobic bacteria convert nitrate and nitrite to gaseous products, such as nitrogen gas ($N_2$), nitrous oxide ($N_2O$), nitric oxide (NO) and ammonia gas ($NH_3$). These gases are then lost to the air. This process is called **denitrification** (see Figure 4-9. and can lead to great losses of nitrogen. Losses are aggravated when a large amount of fresh and easily decomposed organic matter is present under warm temperatures and watery conditions in neutral or alkaline soils.

## ATMOSPHERIC SOURCES OF NUTRIENTS

Nitrogen, in the form of an inert gas which is unavailable to plants, accounts for 78 per cent of the Earth's atmosphere. Atmospheric nitrogen is made available to plants through the process of **nitrogen fixation**, which is the action of specific micro-organisms existing independently in soil and soil water. They absorb nitrogen gas ($N_2$) into their tissue when the

### Figure 4-8
## MINERALIZATION (AMMONIFICATION AND NITRIFICATION)

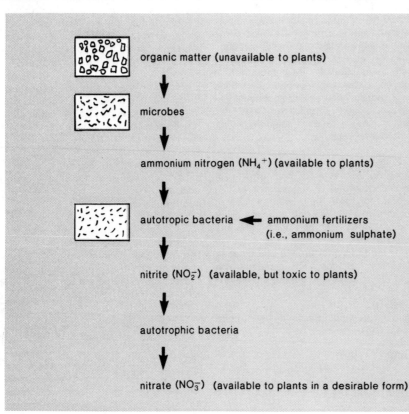

organic matter (unavailable to plants)

↓

microbes

↓

ammonium nitrogen ($NH_4^+$) (available to plants)

↓

autotropic bacteria ← ammonium fertilizers (i.e., ammonium sulphate)

↓

nitrite ($NO_2^-$) (available, but toxic to plants)

↓

autotrophic bacteria

↓

nitrate ($NO_3^-$) (available to plants in a desirable form)

## Figure 4-9
## DENITRIFICATION

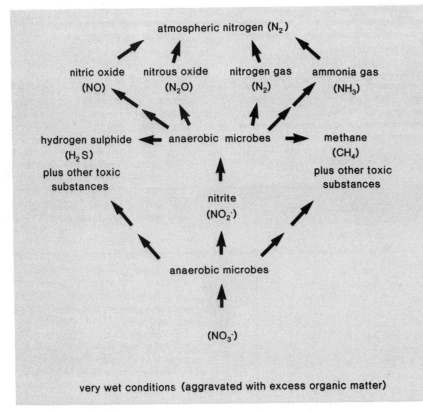

very wet conditions (aggravated with excess organic matter)

micro-organisms die. The nitrogen converted from nitrogen gas ($N_2$) is then released as the specific micro-organisms decompose. This conversion is known as **non-symbiotic nitrogen fixation.** On the other hand, certain bacteria (such as Rhizobium and actinomycetes) cause formation of nodules (abnormal root growth on some host plants - mainly legumes) and inhabit those nodules where nitrogen is fixed. This is known as **symbiotic nitrogen fixation**. The host plant provides sugars for the micro-organisms which, in turn, supply the host with usable nitrogen (neither micro-organism nor host plant alone can fix the nitrogen). Symbiotic nitrogen fixation accounts for a larger amount of fixed nitrogen than does non-symbiotic nitrogen fixation.

### INDUSTRIAL FIXATION
Large amounts of atmospheric nitrogen are fixed in commercial production of nitrogen fertilizers such as ammonium sulphate or calcium nitrate. The latter is fixed using an electrical process.

### OTHER MEANS OF FIXATION
Nitrogen also becomes fixed to nitrate ($NO_3$) and other nitrogenous compounds which are then washed down by rain. Pollution from automobiles also adds to

## Figure 4-10
## NITROGEN FIXATION

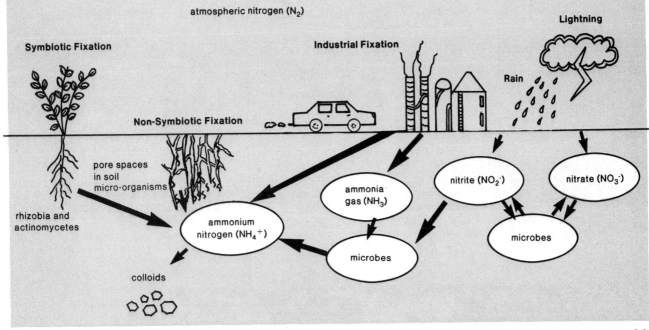

the amount of fixed nitrogen. Carbon, in the form of carbon dioxide ($CO_2$) is present in the air in a concentration of 0.03 per cent. Carbon dioxide is constantly being used by plants and constantly replenished by microbial decomposition of organic matter. Carbon makes up about 50 per cent of the dry weight of all chemical elements in plant and animal tissues. Soil contains 20-200 times as much carbon dioxide as air. The high carbon dioxide content of soil results in formation of carbonic acid, which aids in dissolving elements such as phosphorus. Oxygen is also taken in by the plant directly from the atmosphere as part of carbon dioxide (see PHOTOSYNTHESIS and RESPIRATION).

## PLANT ANALYSES AND NUTRIENT INTERACTIONS

Plants can be chemically analyzed to determine what materials are present in their tissues. Plant tissue analysis can be a useful tool for determining the nutrient status of a plant. The part of the plant that should be sampled to give reliable levels of the nutrients in question is important. For many of the mineral elements, the most reliable indicators are young expanded leaves or leaves at peak metabolic activity. One must be able to take samples of a developing plant periodically and to relate the amounts of nutrient in the samples with what should be there for the optimum

## Table 4-2
## PLANT NUTRITION FUNCTION, DEFICIENCY, EXCESS CHART

| PLANT NUTRIENT NAME SYMBOL | FUNCTION | DEFICIENCY SYMPTOMS |
|---|---|---|
| **Nitrogen** N | • reduced to $NH_2$ combined with organic acid to form amino acid and subsequently proteins, therefore part of every plant cell<br>• makes plants darker green, favoring rapid vegetative development at the expense of fibre development<br>• increases the cation capacity of the root system and enhances the uptake of other nutrients, but nitrogen also decreases calcium content in plant tissues | • leaves lose rich green color; lower leaves (eventually all leaves) become pale green; and growth is reduced. Upper leaves are small and upright; older leaves die first<br><br>Monocots (eg., corn, Draceana)<br>• middle portion of blade becomes yellowish green but the margin remains a darker green<br>Dicots (eg., bean, African Violet)<br>• leaf blade becomes uniformly yellowish green<br>• older leaves show symptoms first and may die. Leaves may remain on plant even if dead<br>• reduced yields and stunted growth |
| **Phosphorus** P | • closely tied to all life processes and a vital part of each cell. Without phosphorus, cells would not divide and grow<br>• stimulates root formation and growth<br>• speeds up maturity<br>• helps flower and seed development<br>• increases winter hardiness<br>• contributes to vigorous growth | • dark green color of upper leaves<br>• weak root system; stunted growth<br>• often purplish discoloration of leaves<br>• lower leaves turn pale green and later yellow; will die if not corrected<br>• young seedlings often show reddish-purple coloration on underside of cotyledons (this can also be brought on by low temperatures). Lack of phosphorus interferes with stomata opening, resulting in higher leaf temperature |
| **Potassium** K (Kalium) | • needed for formation of enzymes (which control carbohydrate and nitrogen metabolism)<br>• active in plant-water relationship as osmotic regulator<br>• essential for healthy fruit development<br>• encourages elongation of roots<br>• hastens maturity | • mottling of foliage<br>• pale leaf margins, increasing to brown spots along leaf edges and progressing into leaf<br>• weak stems and poor root development |

health of the plant. In addition to the nutrient elements essential for plant growth and development, there will also be non-essential materials such as silicon and aluminum. These elements have simply been absorbed by the plant by virtue of having been soluble and available to the roots in the soil.

Through research, optimal levels or ranges of essential elements (especially micronutrients) have been established in many crop plants. These published levels are really only guidelines because many interactions can occur within plants or within the soil around the roots that can alter plant requirements. Occasionally, a plant may show deficiency symptons for a particular element even though a tissue test indicates adequate levels in the plant tissue. Excessive amounts of some other element in the plant may be interfering with the proper metabolism of the element in question, and thereby create the deficiency symptoms. Therefore, the careful interpretation of tissue tests become important. The balance of nutrients in the plant tissues, as well as the availability and balance of available nutrients in the soil, is important information to have in interpreting test results.

Some of the nutrient elements become permanently fixed in plant tissue. Others may be released when deficiencies occur and become translocated to sites of high metabolic activity where the

| EXCESS SYMPTOMS | COMMENTS | REMEDY | FORM TAKEN IN BY PLANT |
|---|---|---|---|
| • rapid development of stems and large dark green leaves; some plants may develop split stems; stems and leaves are brittle<br>• carbohydrates manufactured are used up for rapid cell building leaving little for other development (such as fibre, flowers, fruits and seeds) resulting in delayed flowering and fruiting and low yield of storage organs (such as potato tubers) | • following pasteurizing of soil, or if urea is used in soil, $NO_2$ (nitrite) can build up. Nitrite is an unstable highly toxic precursor of $NO_3$ (nitrate) and is normally quickly converted to $NO_3$ (nitrate). High levels of ammonium can cause toxicity symptoms in various plants such as curving of leaves and death of cotyledons (in tomato seedlings), and development of necrotic spots on leaves. Ammonium depresses uptake of potassium and calcium and may cause deficiency of K and Ca to occur in crops such as Pea, Bean, Corn and Cucumber | • the maintenance of adequate organic matter in the soil will provide a continuing slow release of available nitrogen. Mineral fertilizers can be used to maintain adequate levels of nitrogen | $NO_3^-$ $NH_4^+$ |
| • seldom occurs<br>• browning of older leaves | | • a booster application of high phosphorus to seedlings and transplants will ensure an adequate amount of phosphorus is present for development of a good root system | $H_2PO_4^-$ $HPO_4^=$ $PO_4^=$ |
| • dwarfing<br>• shortening of internode growth<br>• eventual collapse of plant if not corrected | | • can be added as a mineral fertilizer if deficient | $K^+$ |

## Table 4-2:CONT D

| PLANT NUTRIENT NAME SYMBOL | FUNCTION | DEFICIENCY SYMPTOMS |
|---|---|---|
| **Calcium Ca** | • constituent of the middle lamella between cell walls in plants<br>  • aids the plant in absorption selection<br>  • needed for cell division<br>  • improves stiffness of stems<br>  • improves quality of fruits and seeds<br>  • needed for root development<br>  • affects pH (therefore the availability of other nutrients) | • dieback of root tips<br>  • upper leaves yellowish (sometimes with white specks) terminal growth stops often resulting in hooked appearance of tips, leaves may wrinkle and young leaves remain folded<br>  • flower buds fail to develop<br>  • fruit develops abnormalities (eg., blossom end rot in tomato) |
| **Magnesium Mg** | • vital part of chlorophyll<br> • helps to maintain green color of plants<br><br> • acts as carrier of phosphorus and regulates uptake of other nutrients<br> • closely tied to calcium and potassium use by plant<br> • involved in fat and starch development | • reduced rate of photosynthesis<br> • yellow green mottled leaves (main veins remaining green extending somewhat into branching veins)<br><br> • some plants develop red color in centre of leaf which later turns to dead spots<br> • symptoms start on lower leaves<br> • stems become weak<br> • curling of leaves upward along margins |
| **Sulphur S** | • important part of some amino acids<br> • needed for vitamin synthesis<br> • essential for nodule formation on legumes<br> • part of oil in garlic and onion | • light green color<br> • lighter green veins<br> • stunted growth<br> • upper leaves show symptoms first |
| **Iron Fe** | • essential for chlorophyll formation<br> • involved in enzyme activity and oxidation-reduction reactions | • dark veins<br> • chlorosis of young leaves, interveinal portion turning yellow and then white<br> • reduced growth<br> • symptoms most severe on young leaves<br> • twig dieback |
| **Manganese Mn** | • important for oxygen formation in photosynthesis and for carbohydrate metabolism<br>  • cofactor in enzymes<br>  • active in oxidation-reduction reactions<br>  • involved in vitamin production | • interveinal chlorosis, darker green color next to veins<br> • no sharp distinction between veins and interveinal areas (as with iron deficiency)<br> • development of specks, streaks and small dead spots |
| **Boron B** | • involved in differentiation of meristem cells<br>  • regulation of carbohydrate metabolism<br>  • involved in protoplasm formation and with movement of calcium | • cells continue to divide but growth is abnormal (Witch's Broom effect)<br> • death (necrosis) of growing plants<br> • hollow stem and brown curd of cauliflower<br> • brown heart of turnip<br> • lesions on beets, carrots and radishes<br> • black heart and pitting of celery<br> • rough skin on tomatoes |

| EXCESS SYMPTOMS | COMMENTS | REMEDY | FORM TAKEN IN BY PLANT |
|---|---|---|---|
| • interferes with availability and uptake of potassium and magnesium, and the solubility of other nutrient elements<br>• causes alkaline conditions | • an important regulator of pH | • can be added as agricultural lime (calcium carbonate) or dolomitic lime (calcium carbonate and magnesium carbonate) | $Ca^{++}$ |
| • stunted growth<br>• magnesium pectate is one of the binding agents in cell wall formation | | • magnesium sulphate can be sprayed on plant foliage from a solution of 15 g/L or 2% epsom salt or added to soil as dolomite lime or any magnesium fertilizer. 250-500 g actual Mg/acre | $Mg^{++}$ |
| | • not readily mobile in plant | • special fertilizer formulations are available for supplying sulphur, or elemental sulphur can be added (fine particles) | $SO_4^=$ |
| • loss of foliage color<br>• excess manganese may induce iron deficiency | | • cause of deficiency can be high pH making iron unavailable<br>• poor aeration<br>• unbalanced nutrient supply or root damage<br>• iron can be supplied as Iron chelate or as Iron sulphate, etc. | $Fe^{++}$<br>$Fe^{+++}$ |
| • chlorosis of young leaves<br>• stunted growth<br>• yellow cotyledons in seedling followed by death<br>• older leaves point down and curl under<br>• veins show dark purplish brown with brown interveined spotting | • toxic in small excess<br>• anaerobic condition<br>• acidic conditions<br>• after sterilization | • Brassica crops are sensitive to deficiency<br>• 5-10 g manganese sulphate/m² or spraying with 0.1% solution of manganese sulphate prevents deficiency | $Mn^{++}$ |
| • marginal necrosis of lower leaves<br>• 0.5 ppm excess can cause toxicity | | • sprays of 0.5-1 ppm Boric acid (in Borax) will help deficient plants | $B_4O_7^=$<br>$H_2BO_3^-$ |

Table 4-2:CONT'D

| PLANT NUTRIENT NAME SYMBOL | FUNCTION | DEFICIENCY SYMPTOMS |
|---|---|---|
| **BORON (cont'd)** | | • corky core of apples<br>• reduced flowering and improper pollination<br>• thickened, curled, wilted and chlorotic leaves. |
| **Copper Cu** | • regulator of enzymes and several biological processes including respiration and photosynthesis | • stunted growth<br>• dieback of twigs<br>• poor pigmentation, lack of carotine in carrots, poor color in onions<br>• poor growth |
| **Zinc Zn** | • essential for chlorophyll formation<br>• active in enzyme systems and hormones such as indoleacetic acid<br><br>• interveinal chlorosis on lower leaves **monocots** - white or yellow striping between veins and stunted growth, resetting of terminal leaves | • decrease in terminal growth and stem length<br>• reduced bud formation<br>• mottled leaves |
| **Molybdenum Mo** | • important for nitrogen fixing bacteria in legumes needed for utilization of nitrogen | • pale leaves followed by marginal scorching<br>• leaf blades fail to expand<br>• stunting and lack of vigor<br>• scorching, cupping or rolling of leaves<br>• whiptail in cauliflowers, lettuce in seedling stage<br>• outer leaves turn pale and die |
| **Chlorine Cl** | • influences cell wall permeability<br>• reduces desiccation | |
| **Sodium (Natrium) Na** | • unknown | • may improve succulence, taste and appearance of table beets<br>• may be beneficial where potassium is in low supply |
| **Fluorine F** | • stimulates germination of seeds of some species | |
| **Aluminum Al** | • not essential to plants but blue flower color of hydrangea is related to Aluminum<br>• pink flowered hydrangeas should be kept low in Aluminum. This is usually done by regulating pH levels | |
| **Cobalt Co** | • used in symbiotic nitrogen fixation of algae and legumes | |

| EXCESS SYMPTOMS | COMMENTS | REMEDY | FORM TAKEN IN BY PLANT |
|---|---|---|---|
| • reduced growth, death<br>• highly toxic at low levels | | • deficiency more likely on acid peat and organic soil<br>• spray 0.2% copper oxychloride | $Cu^+$<br>$Cu^{++}$ |
| • zinc toxicity can occur from newly galvinized pipes and tubs where water has been allowed to accumulate and then used | | • foliar spray 0.05% zinc sulphate | $Zn^+$ |
| | | • pointsettia, lettuce, primula and Brassica susceptible to deficiencies<br>• spray with 5 g Sodium molybdate in 100 L diluting 1:200 | $MoO_4^-$ |
| • burning or scorching of leaves<br>• bronzing and premature defoliation | | • gardenia, geranium, pointsetta are sensitive to excess chlorine | $Cl^-$ |
| • harms soil structure<br>• may decrease uptake of calcium and magnesium | | | $Na^+$ |
| • blackening of tips, death of leaf margins | | | $F^=$ |
| • reduces availability of phosphorus | | | $Al^{++}$<br>$Al^{+++}$ |
| | | | $Co^+$ |

demand for the element is greatest. This is reflected in the type and location of symptoms that develop when deficiencies occur (i.e., older leaves affected first versus new growth affected only). When a deficiency does occur, an application of fertilizer containing the element in question, either to the soil or in some cases to the foliage of the plant, will normally restore the plant to good health. However, by the time visible symptoms are evident, there can be a reduction in the potential yield of many crop plants. Monitoring of nutrient supply through regular soil tests, perhaps combined with tissue testing to prevent or correct deficiencies before symptoms occur, is therefore recommended for horticultural crop production. With the increasing use of soilless culture and hydroponic techniques, particularly for protected crop production, the continued monitoring of nutrient supply becomes essential. Without the buffering effects of soils and potting mixtures, imbalances in the nutrient supply can have rapid and sometimes disastrous consequences on plant growth.

## COMPETITION FOR NUTRIENTS

Competition for nutrients takes place continuously among soil micro-organisms and between various types of plants within the same locality, as well as between plants and micro-organisms. It is, therefore, essential that adequate levels are present to ensure the crop plants do not become deficient and micro-organisms have an adequate supply so that they are able to break down the soil organic matter present. Weed competition with the crop plant can seriously reduce the nutrients available to crop plants.

## DEFICIENCY AND TOXICITY SYMPTOMS

When any one nutrient becomes unavailable to a plant, the growth and development of that plant will be seriously restricted. As the supply drops below the minimum requirement, a progression of symtoms develops, often culminating in the death of the entire plant if the nutrient becomes completely lacking. For most of the essential elements the pattern of deficiency symptoms is quite distinctive allowing one to diagnose the specific nutrient required to restore the plant to good health. Therefore, a description of deficiency symptoms for many of the essential elements is given in Table 4-2.

In some instances, an overabundance of an element can be toxic to plants. Therefore, information on symptoms of toxicity and where it is likely to occur is also included.

## NITROGEN

Leaves lose their rich green color or normal greenness if nitrogen is in low supply. With monocots (corn, *Dracaena*, etc.) the middle portion of the leaf blade becomes yellowish green and the margin remains a darker green. With dicots (bean, African violet, etc.), the leaf blades become uniformly yellowish-green. Older leaves show symptoms first and, if the deficiency persists, the oldest leaves may die but remain on the plant. Growth will be stunted and yields reduced.

Excess nitrogen favors vegetative growth, resulting in rapid development of stems with large, dark green leaves. In some plants, it may cause splits to develop along the stems and both stems and leaves to become quite brittle. Such plants synthesize large amounts of sugars but these are utilized in rapid cell formation with little carbohydrate left over for the thickening of cell walls, the development of fibres or the formation of flowers, fruit, seed and storage organs. Therefore, flowering and fruiting are delayed or entirely suppressed and the yield of storage organs is likely to be low.

## PHOSPHORUS

A lack of phosphorus is indicated by a slowing down of growth with delayed maturity. The leaves of monocots often show reddish or purplish areas instead of being uniformly dark green. In dicots, the main veins of old leaves are often reddish or purple with the young leaves remaining a dark green or greyish green. The root systems of phosphorus deficient plants are weak and sparce. Browning of older leaves is a symptom of excess phosphorus. Excess or toxic amounts of phosphorus seldom occur.

## POTASSIUM

Potassium tends to balance the effects of nitrogen and phosphorus by encouraging the elongation of roots and the hastening of maturation. It is involved in the translocation and storage of carbohydrates.

The initial symptom of deficiency is the mottling of the foliage followed by yellowing of the leaf margins. Later,

these margins turn brown with the death of the cells unless the deficiency is corrected. The symptoms are evident on the oldest leaves first.

Excess potassium can cause dwarfing through the shortening of internode growth and, if excessive enough, can cause collapse of the entire plant.

## CALCIUM

Calcium is relatively immobile in plants and, therefore, the symptoms develop in the young leaves and at the growing points (meristems) before affecting older growth.

Calcium deficiency has a major effect on roots, causing the growing tips to die. This results in short stubby roots with brown tips. The upper leaves become yellowish green and terminal growth stops or terminal buds fail to develop. Inadequate calcium can cause various physiological diseases, such as bitter pit of apples, black heart of celery and blossom end rot of tomato.

The main effect of excess amounts of calcium is its interaction with other cations in the soil. It can interfere with the availability and uptake of potassium and/or magnesium. Furthermore, it regulates the acidity of the soil. The acidity of the soil, in turn, affects the availability of the various mineral elements.

## MAGNESIUM

Magnesium is part of the chlorophyll molecule as well as magnesium-pectate, one of the binding agents in the formation of cell walls. As one would expect, therefore, the outstanding deficiency symptom in practically all crops is the loss of green color in the leaf tissues between the veins. The intervascular areas change from normal green to light green and eventually to yellow, but the veins remain green. Discoloration begins at the leaf tips and gradually proceeds to the centre of the leaves, with the old leaves showing symptoms first. The reduction in chlorophyll as a result of magnesium deficiency reduces photosynthesis and, therefore, reduces the growth rate.

## SULPHUR

Sulphur deficiency leads to a yellowing of leaves but the veins become pale green to yellowish green before the tissue between the veins is affected. In general, the upper leaves show symptoms first, indicating that sulphur is not readily transferred from one part of the plant to another.

## MANGANESE AND IRON

The symptoms of deficiency are very similar for both manganese and iron. In general, the interveinal areas of young leaves become light green to yellow but the veins remain green. The young leaves show symptoms first. Dead areas develop as the symptoms advance. With manganese deficiency, these areas are relatively small and toward the middle of leaf, whereas with iron deficiency, the spots are larger and toward the tip and margin of the leaf.

## BORON

Boron and calcium have related roles in plant growth and hence their deficiency symptoms are similar. With boron deficiency, vegetative and flower buds fail to develop, leaves are misshapen and small and the tissue of storage organs (i.e. cabbage heads, turnip, carrot, etc.) breaks down.

## OTHER ESSENTIAL ELEMENTS

Deficiency symptoms for other essential elements, such as zinc, copper and molyledenum, are somewhat more variable for different crops than those previously discussed. There is, therefore, little value in attempting to describe them here. Furthermore, the problems of pollution (particularly air pollution) in many parts of the world has made the detection of nutrient deficiencies through visible symptoms less reliable. Many of the plant ailments caused by air pollutants can be misinterpreted as nutrient deficiency symptoms.

Before leaving the topic of nutrient deficiencies and toxicities, mention should be made of the overall effects of excess fertility. Since these mineral elements must be in a soluble form in order to enter the plant, their presence in the soil water dilutes the water and retards its movement into the plant roots (see OSMOSIS). As indicated earlier, the number of ions of nutrients derived from the dissociation (dissolving) of fertilizer salts can be so high that water will actually diffuse out of the roots into the soil solution, causing the plant to wilt or die. Therefore, excess amounts of potassium in the soil, for instance, could bring about total collapse of a plant because of desiccation of the roots and subsequent wilting and death of the tops

before any direct toxic effect of potassium itself could occur. It is, therefore, very important to know the total salinity or ionic content of the soil solution. This can be measured by the ability of the soil solution to conduct an electrical current. Such measurements are reported on soil tests as the **EC** or **electrical conductance**.

It is possible to reduce high electrical conductivity by leaching. Leaching is the application of water (preferably water low in solutes) in excessive amounts and its subsequent percolation downward into the subsoil or into drainage channels. This water dilutes the

concentration of solutes and removes many of the solute ions from the root zone. It is most effective when there is excellent drainage. In cases where adequate drainage is not possible, an alternative treatment is to incorporate additional soil or organic matter which is low in EC (such as peat) and will, therefore, reduce the EC level of the original soil through direct physical dilution.

The soil reaction or its acidity or alkalinity is very important in relation to plant nutrition. It determines the degree to which the various essential elements will be soluble and, therefore, available

## Figure 4-11
## COMPARATIVE SOLUBILITY OF PLANT NUTRIENTS AT VARIOUS pH LEVELS

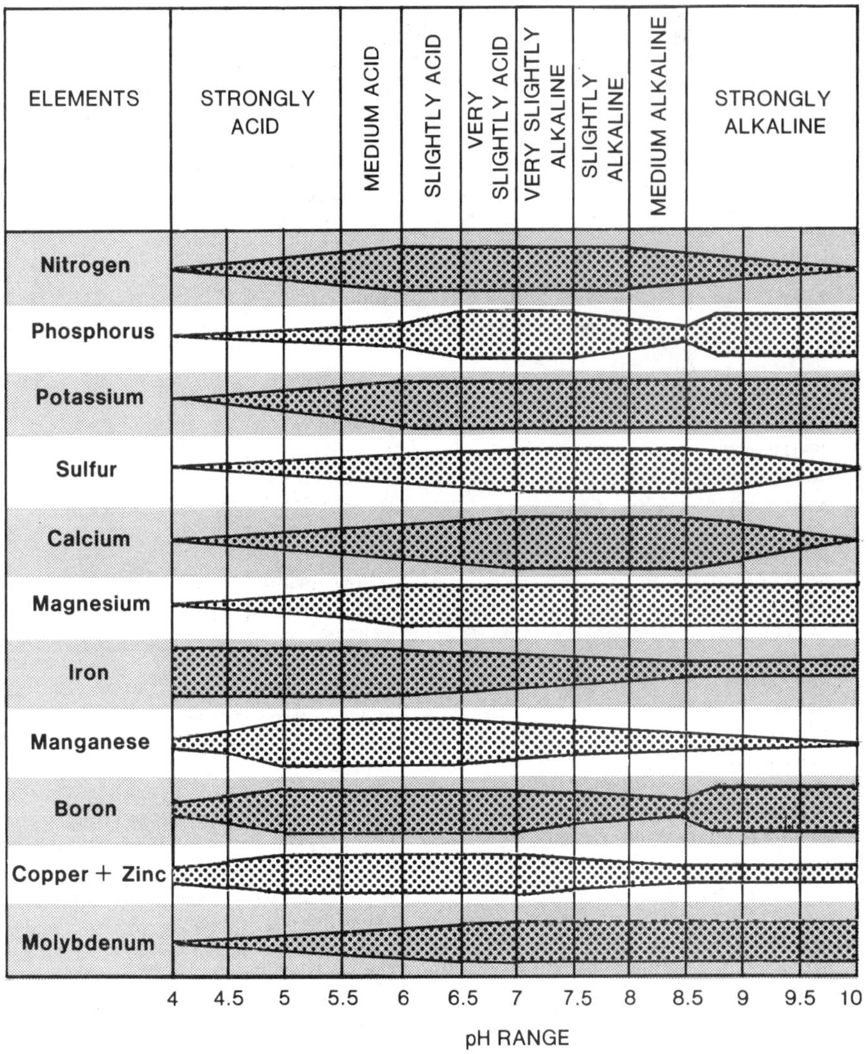

to the plant roots. It is measured as the relative concentration of hydrogen ions (H+) to hydroxyl ions (OH) and reported as a negative logarithmic function to the base 10, known as pH. The **pH scale** (see Soils lesson) is divided into 14 main divisions from 0 to 14 with the **mid-point value** of **7.0** being the reference point. At the value of 7.0, the solution is considered neutral. At values lower than 7.0, it is acidic. Because it is a logarithmic scale, every decrease of one pH unit represents a tenfold increase in H-ion concentration and a corresponding tenfold decrease in OH-ion concentration. For example, a solution of pH 5.0 is ten times more acidic than one of pH 6.0, and a solution of pH 4.0 is 100 times more acidic than one of pH 6.0.

For most plants, the optimum pH is around 6.2. At this level of acidity, all the essential elements will be soluble and available in optimum amounts, provided the compounds containing them are present. Plants with a high requirement for iron, such as azaleas or cranberries, will likely develop iron deficiency symptoms unless the pH is between 4.5 and 5.5. Plants with a high calcium requirement, such as garden peas or clover, grow best if the pH is between 6.5 and 7.5. Figure 4-11 indicates the relative solubility and availability of the mineral elements over the pH range from 4.0 to 10.0.

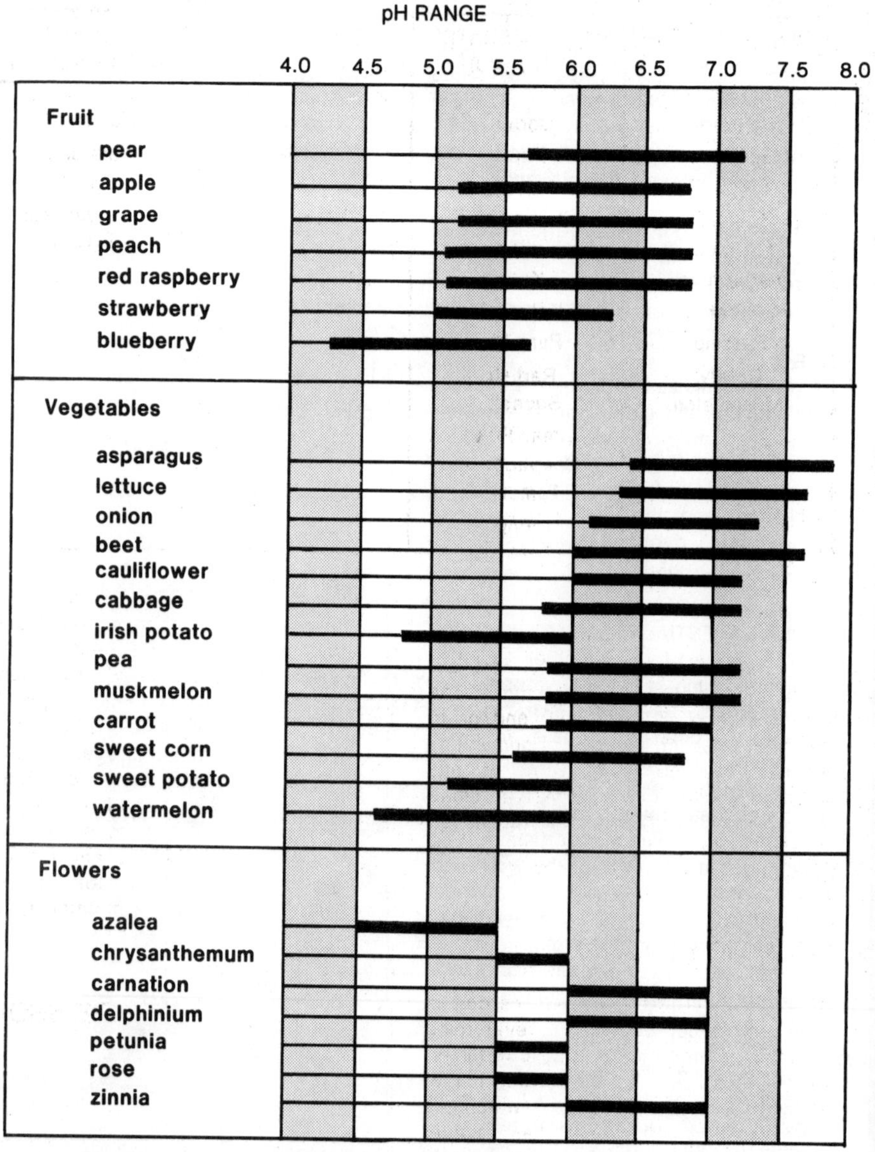

## OTHER TOXICITY SITUATIONS

In protected crop production, where the soil or potting mixture is reused for continuous year round cropping, maintenance of the soil fertility and the control of soil borne pathogens require special attention. Chemical fumigants (such as methyl bromide and chloropicrin) may be used to destroy certain harmful bacteria and fungi, as well as weeds and weed seeds. These chemicals are toxic to living plants and humans so must be handled with extreme care. They must be fully dissipated from the soil before a new crop is planted.

The most effective method of destroying soil borne pathogens involves the use of heat, particularly live steam (steam pasteurization). If the soil is heated to between 71°C and 82°C and the temperature maintained there for 30 minutes, the pathogens will be killed without harming many of the beneficial

Figure 4-12

## OPTIMUM pH RANGE FOR SEVERAL FRUITS, VEGETABLES, AND ORNAMENTALS

micro-organisms. However, because of the reduced competition among the organisms that survive, there is a differential buildup of various microbes following steaming, which takes several weeks to stabilize. For example, nitrate nitrogen levels drop during the first three weeks following steam pasteurization due to the activity of ammonifying bacteria. Ammonium levels reach a peak in about three weeks, but then decline to nil within 5–6 weeks because of the

buildup of nitrifying bacteria. Unless the ammonia initially produced is trapped in the soil as ammonium salts, such as ammonium phosphate and ammonium sulphate, it will exist as free ammonia (which is toxic to plants) and causes yellowing and dwarfing.

## Table 4-3
## PLANTS GROUPED ACCORDING TO THEIR TOLERANCE TO ACIDITY

| PLANTS SENSITIVE TO ACIDITY | WILL TOLERATE SLIGHT ACIDITY | WILL TOLERATE MODERATE ACIDITY | PREFERS STRONG ACIDITY |
|---|---|---|---|
| Cabbage | Corn | Potato | Blueberry |
| Cauliflower | Pea | Parsley | Cranberry |
| Lettuce | Carrot | Sweet Potato | Holly |
| Onion | Cucumber | Peanuts | Rhododendron |
| Spinach | Brussels sprout | | Azalea |
| Asparagus | Kale | | |
| Beet | Kohlrabi | | |
| Parsnip | Pumpkin | | |
| Celery | Radish | | |
| Muskmelon | Squash | | |
| | Lima, Pok | | |
| | Snapbeans | | |
| | Tomato | | |
| | Turnip | | |

# FERTILIZERS

The main objective of fertilizer application is to add nutrients to the growing media (usually soil) and/or to the plants, for the purpose of stimulating growth. The best utilization of any fertilizer is to apply it often in small quantities, rather than in large amounts all at once. Fertilizers are either organic or inorganic.

## ORGANIC FERTILIZERS

All organic fertilizers contain carbon in their make-up, but not everything containing carbon is an organic fertilizer. Organic fertilizers include a long list of varied organic matter, many of which are more soil conditioners than actual fertilizers in as much as they contain quite a low percentage of available nutrients.

### PEAT
Peat is used extensively in horticulture for a variety of purposes. It is classified into sapric, hemic and fibric types, which indicate the degree of decomposition, bulk density, fibre content and water-holding capacities. The fibric type has the highest fibre content, highest water-holding capacity and is not (or only slightly) decomposable. The sapric and hemic types have little or no value in

horticulture. In Alberta, most peat originates from the *Sphagnum* plant and is called 'sphagnum moss peat'. Some moss peat comes from the *Hypnum* plant and is called 'hypnum moss peat'. Among these moss peats are differences in quality. *Sphagnum* moss peat is quite acid (3.5-5) and has a high water-holding capacity, varying from 6 - 24 times its own weight at saturation. Peat originating from sedge and rushes is a less desirable peat for use in horticulture. As a soil conditioner, it

increases nutrient and water-holding capacity of the soil and improves aeration. The nitrogen content is usually about one per cent and the phosphorus content is about 0.2 per cent, which only becomes available at a very slow rate as the organic matter breaks down.

### COMPOST
Composts can be quite varied, depending on the material that is being composted. Divisions could be made between municipal sewage, industrial waste compost and that composted by the householder, gardener and farmer. Compost, like peat, is primarily a soil conditioner and, to some extent, a fertilizer. Composts from householders, gardeners and farmers are usually higher in organic matter and major nutrient element content than the sewage or waste type, whereas the latter has more ash, calcium and trace elements. One type of municipal waste compost is marketed as 'milorganite'. Compost usually has a nitrogen content of one per cent of fresh weight, 0.25 per cent phosphorus and 0.33 per cent potassium. The main benefits derived from applying compost are improvement to the soil structure and supply of micro-organisms. Nutrients from compost become available over more than one season, with about 25 per cent of the nitrogen, 100 per cent of the phosphorus and 80 per cent of the potassium being released during the first season.

### LEAF MOLD
Leafmold consists of decayed leaves, sometimes mixed with heavy clay soil. It

## Figure 4-13
## PEAT FIBRE STRUCTURE SHOWING WATER-HOLDING CAPACITY

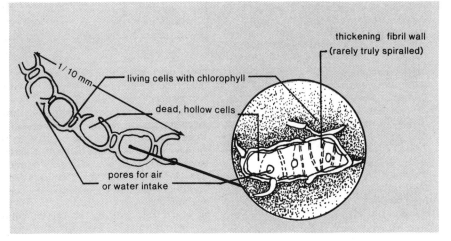

can be used as mulch or part of a potting mixture. Leafmold adds humus to the soil, but the nutritional levels are very low.

## MANURE

Animal manure was once the main source of nutrients for horticultural plants. It consists of excreta (urine and feces) from farm animals and is usually mixed with bedding (often straw). The nutritional value of manure for horticultural purposes depends on the constituents in it, not only in the proportion of bedding to excreta. Other considerations include the age and handling of the manure, as well as the kind of food that the animals producing the manure have eaten. Manure nutrients are not as readily soluble as those in inorganic fertilizers and are released over a longer period of time and in smaller quantities. For use as soil amendments, manures are best used when they have been composted or rotted with age, thus reducing odor, weed seed population and salt problems.

To obtain maximum use of most nutrients, however, fresh manure should be worked into the soil as soon as possible.

A disadvantage to fresh manure application is that the available nitrate in the micro-organisms working at breaking down the straw in the manure can be tied up. Also, because of the ammonium content, fresh manure can injure seedling roots.

Nutrients in composted or rotted manure are more readily available to plants because more of the organic matter has changed to humus. Composting increases the availability of phosphorus and destroys most weed seeds. Some of the nutrients are lost even under good composting conditions.

Sheep manure is often dried and pulverized and, as such, contains about 2.3 per cent nitrogen, one per cent phosphorus and 1.3 per cent potassium. The nutrient content of **dried** sheep manure is about equal to that of **fresh** cow manure. Fresh poultry manure contains about 2-3 times the nitrogen and 3-8 times the phosphorus of cow manure. Nitrogen is lost very rapidly from fresh manure; as much as 50 per cent may be lost within a month from fresh poultry manure. Fresh poultry manure has, on average, 1.5 per cent nitrogen, 1.2 per cent phosphorus, 0.5 per cent

potassium and has a moisture content of about 75 per cent. Dried poultry manure averages about 2.0 per cent nitrogen, 1.9 per cent phosphorus, 1.8 per cent potassium, 2.5 per cent calcium, 0.4 per cent magnesium and 5.0 per cent boron.

'Green manure' is the term used to describe growing plants turned under before maturity. This process adds organic matter to the soil as the plants have brought nutrients up from deeper layers, which are now made available near the surface for new plants as the green manure is decomposed. Green manure can conserve soluble nutrients by tying them up in the organic matter so they are not leachable. Legumes are most valued as green manure because of their nitrogen fixing capacities. The benefits derived from green manure should be weighed against the loss of a crop during that season.

## FISH FERTILIZER

Fish tankage and fishmeal are cooked and ground fish sold as fertilizer. Fishmeal contains 7-14 per cent nitrogen, 4-16 per cent phosphate and 2-3 per cent potassium.

## UREA

Urea is both a natural product from animal excreta (particularly urine) and a synthetic product made from ammonium. In the soil, urea is changed by an enzyme (urease) to ammonium carbonate, which is unstable and releases free ammonia ($NH_3$). At the soil surface, ammonia is lost to the air. Near tender roots of seedlings, root injury could result.

Urea fertilizers are made in granules or prills to overcome the water absorbing qualities of crystalline urea. Commercial urea may contain traces of biuret. Biuret is toxic to plants and can cause injury to seedlings and young plants. Modern urea production contains such small amounts of biuret that the urea produced is quite safe. Urea should be incorporated at least 8 cm (3 in) into the soil to minimize the loss of nitrogen. Synthetic urea contains 46 per cent nitrogen. Urea which has been sulphur coated, releases nitrogen more slowly. Urea-formaldehyde releases nitrogen slowly over a long period of time, similar to the way nitrogen is released from manure. Urea-formaldehyde contains 36 per cent nitrogen.

## BLOODMEAL

Bloodmeal is dried blood from slaughter houses. It contains 12-14 per cent nitrogen which is quickly made available by fungal and bacterial decomposition. It is an acid forming fertilizer which can be used at a rate of about 50 g/m² (1 lb/100 sq ft).

## BONEMEAL

Raw bonemeal contains 3-4 per cent nitrogen in a slow acting form and 20-24 per cent phosphate. The finer the grind, the more readily available bonemeal is.

Steamed bonemeal has only one per cent nitrogen but 22-30 per cent phosphate. Steamed bonemeal is usually fine ground and faster acting than raw bonemeal. It can be used at a rate of 50-150 g/m² (1-3 lb/100 sq ft).

## HOOF AND HORN

Hoof and horn comes from slaughter houses and contains 12-14 per cent nitrogen, traces of phosphorus and other elements. It acts over a long period of time and is used in the University of California (U.C.) soilless container mixtures. Hoof and horn can be applied at a rate of about 50 g/m² (1 lb/100 sq ft).

## OTHER ORGANIC FERTILIZERS

Cottonseed meal contains 6-9 per cent nitrogen, 2-3 per cent phosphate and 1-2 per cent potassium. Castor pumace contains 5-6 per cent nitrogen, 2-3 per cent phosphate, and one per cent potassium. Other humus forming products and waste utilized as organic fertilizer include hair from tanneries (2-8 per cent nitrogen), hops spent from breweries, leather waste (clippings and dust) (5 per cent nitrogen), feathers (8 per cent nitrogen), and wool waste (2-8 per cent nitrogen).

## ADVANTAGES AND DISADVANTAGES OF ORGANIC FERTILIZERS

Organic fertilizers are humus forming. Humus, from a physical aspect, improves texture, structure, color, aeration and water-holding qualities of the soil. From a chemical point of view, humus influences solubility of certain minerals. Biologically, it is an energy source for micro-organisms, providing an uninterrupted flow of nutrients. Organic fertilizers can be applied without injury to plants in amounts that would otherwise cause burning if applied as inorganic fertilizer. High amounts can be applied without injury because there are little or no soluble salts present in organic fertilizer. The nitrogen and phosphate in organic fertilizers are not water soluble, which makes them available at a slower rate, more aligned with the plant uptake and prevents loss from leaching. Disadvantages to the use of organic fertilizers lie mainly in the presence of relatively low levels of nutrients and the bulky nature of organic fertilizers. They also require more labor to apply than inorganic fertilizers. Other disadvantages lie in the variability of nutritional content and the possibility of the presence of toxic impurities, such as toxic amounts of micro-elements, particularly with industrial waste composts. Availability is a factor that can make the use of organic fertilizer either an advantage or disadvantage, depending on the user's proximity to the source.

### ORGANIC GARDENING

The concept of organic gardening is to use only naturally occurring products, staying away from products of a synthetic nature. Thus, organic gardeners will use naturally occurring organic fertilizers (such as compost, peat, manure, leafmold, etc.) as well as some inorganic substances (such as lime, rock phosphate and potash rock). The organic gardener will use urea contained in manure because it is natural, but will not use manufactured urea. The plant can only use urea (manufactured or other) when micro-organisms have reduced it to the ionic form, the ions from organic or inorganic sources being identical. The most important aspect for the gardener is to have a good understanding of all factors involved in the life processes of both soil and plants.

## HYDROPONICS

Hydroponics is a plant-feeding method in which all constituents of the normal soil-root environment are absent except water, inorganic salts and air. Modifications may include a neutral inert solid material such as gravel or volcanic scoria to aid in supporting the plant. Hydroponics avoids several problems often encountered in conventional culture such as poor soil structure, poor drainage, nonuniform texture, weeds and pathogenic soil organisms. Growing in soil is still recommended where feasible because soil has a high buffering capacity, natural fertility and well developed management programs.

For a full explanation of hydroponics and the various systems that have been developed, see Hydroponics lesson.

## INORGANIC FERTILIZERS

Inorganic fertilizers are of a mineral nature, and thus include fertilizers containing carbonates but exclude other carbon compounds.

### COMPOSITION

The percentage of the three major mineral plant nutrient elements is given on the label of the fertilizer in the order of N (Nitrogen), P (Phosphate) and K (Potassium).

This indicates the **grade** of fertilizer and should not be confused with **fertilizer ratio**. A label indicating the grade 20-20-20 contains 20 per cent each of N, P, and K in a ratio of 1:1:1. A grade like 10-30-10 has a ratio of 1:3:1 and the grade 27-14-0 has a ratio of 3:2:0. When a zero appears in one of the three places in the grade designation, this indicates that the particular nutrient is not contained in the fertilizer. The grade 27-14-0 contains both nitrogen and phosphate but potassium is missing. The nutrient content of fertilizers vary greatly. Those which supply only a single kind of nutrient are known as 'simple fertilizers'. For example, a simple fertilizer in the nitrogen group supplies only nitrogen (48-0-0). Those supplying two or more are 'multinutrient' or 'mixed fertilizers' (eg., 16-20-0). The nitrogen and the phosphate groups are the main types used on the prairies.

Included in the nitrogen supplying group, are fertilizers such as anhydrous ammonia, aqua ammonia, ammonium nitrate, ammonium sulphate, ammonium nitrate sulphate, and calcium nitrate. Among the group of mixed or multinutrient fertilizers are ammonium phosphate sulphate (16-20-0), monoammonium phosphate (11-48-0), ammonium nitrate phosphate (27-14-0) and (23-23-0), diammonium phosphate (18-46-0), magnesium ammonium phosphate (8-20-13) as well as many others. It should also be noted that many inorganic fertilizers also contain small amounts of trace elements which are not specified in the grade distinction.

### REACTION

Most inorganic fertilizers interact with the soil and soil solutions to influence the soil acidity (see Table 4-6). Some fertilizers are neutral. However, the majority are either acid forming or acid reducing (alkaline).

### RELEASE AND SOLUBILITY

Fertilizers release their nutrient content at various rates. The traditional, standard fertilizers (such as ammonium sulphate and monoammonium phosphate) are water soluble and available to the plants shortly after application (provided enough water is present in the soil for the fertilizer to go into solution). Nitrogen is quite mobile in the soil, whereas phosphates are not. Potassium is fairly mobile and quite soluble.

A group of fertilizers, known as 'slow release fertilizers', release nutrients in small amounts over an extended period of time. This group is divided into three subgroups. The first subgroup is an organic fertilizer (hoof, horn, etc.). The second subgroup is composed of fertilizer compounds with slow rates of mineralization or dissolution. The last subgroup is composed of coated fertilizers. Examples of the second subgroup are urea-formaldehyde, which is mineralized by bacteria and affected by temperatures; and magnesium ammonium phosphate, where the release is regulated by particle size (smaller particles releasing at a faster rate). The coated fertilizer subgroup includes 'Osmocote', which is a resinous coating. Its release is affected by diffusion and is controlled by the thickness of the coating (coating can account for up to 15 per cent of weight). Soil temperature also influences the rate of release. Soil pH and micro-organisms, however, do not influence the release rate. Another type of coated fertilizer is sulphur coated fertilizer (up to 20 per cent of weight). Sulphur coated urea is an example of this type. This material has different dissolution rates as temperature can influence the rate of release. Fertilizers are also sold as water soluble concentrates. These types of fertilizers instantly dissolve in water.

Most of these concentrated instant soluble fertilizers contain a dye which, when used in diluted form, can be seen to be a diluted fertilizer. Instant soluble fertilizers are usually applied with fertilizer proportioners for greenhouse operations, or simply dissolved in a small watering can for use.

## AVAILABILITY TO PLANTS

The availability of nutrients from inorganic fertilizers to plants depends on several factors, of which the pH level of the soil is primary. Nutrients must also be present near the roots in ionic form to be available to plants. Generally, a pH between 6.5 and 7.5 provides the highest availability of the three major nutrients (N, P and K) and a fairly high availability level of the other plant nutrient elements. For most horticultural plants, a pH from 6.0 - 7.0 is most desirable. Other factors affecting availability include moisture content (nutrients move mainly in the soil solution) and temperature (movement is very slow at low temperatures).

Some plant nutrients can be absorbed and made available to plants through foliar application of liquid fertilizer. This represents a very much smaller amount than that absorbed by the roots.

## PURITY OF ELEMENTS AND RELATIONSHIP TO COSTS

The label grade shows the percentage of nutrient content of N, P and K. These percentages do not add up to 100 per cent but, rather, indicate the usable nutrient content. Other materials in the fertilizer include other nutrients, such as calcium, chlorine, sulphur, oxygen and so on. These other components are known as 'carriers' and still other material may be added as 'fillers' to bring weights to a round number.

The cost of fertilizers should be compared on the basis of **price per net weight of the desired nutrient** and not on the weight of the material. Often, the cost of transporting fertilizer with a low percentage nutrient content makes that type of fertilizer too expensive in comparison to the cost of transporting a high nutrient content fertilizer. The cost of the pure nutrient can be calculated using the following formulas:

$$\frac{\text{weight in kg} \times \% \text{ nutrient}}{100} = \text{weight of pure nutrient in kg}$$

price per kg $\times$ weight of pure nutrient = price per kg of pure nutrient

EXAMPLE
formulation 34-0-0

$$\frac{25 \text{ kg} \times 34\% \text{ N}}{100} = 8.5 \text{ kg}$$

$$\frac{\$9.90}{25} = \$0.39/\text{kg} \times 8.5 \text{ kg} = \$3.36/\text{kg of pure nutrient}$$

# SOIL pH MODIFICATION

If the pH in the soil or growing medium is too low, the standard treatment is to apply or add ground limestone. The limestone may be called 'agricultural lime' or 'dolomitic lime'. Dolomitic lime has the added advantage of supplying both calcium and magnesium, as well as raising the pH. Invariably, acidic soils are low to medium in calcium content and often low in magnesium as well, so the treatment is effective. Occasionally, a soil may be deficient in calcium but have an optimum pH for the crop to be grown. In such instances, calcium can be added in the form of 'gypsum' or 'landplaster' which will supply calcium without affecting the pH. Similarly, magnesium can be added as epsom salts to supply magnesium without affecting the hydrogen-ion concentration.

If the pH is too high, an application of a salt derived from a strong acid and a weak base (alkali) will bring about a fairly rapid increase in acidity. Two compounds commonly used are iron sulphate or aluminum sulphate. If nitrogen is low and temperature and other environmental factors are ideal for rapid growth, ammonium sulphate may be used as well. For a slower but more long-term effect, pure powdered sulphur can be incorporated. Micro-organisms in the soil will slowly oxidize the sulphur to sulphate which increases the acidity level (See Tables 4-4 and 4-5 for recommended rates of application).

The choice of fertilizers for supplying plant nutrients also has a bearing on soil pH and the maintenance of that pH level. The general or residue reaction of a given fertilizer may be acid, alkaline or neutral. Such general reactions are given in Table 4-6.

# APPLICATION OF FERTILIZERS

Use of fertilizer should include considerations of the type of fertilizer to use, the right time to apply it, the method of application and whether the fertilizer is to be applied before or after planting.

As to choice of fertilizer, it is wise to have a sample of the growing media (usually soil) analysed at a soils laboratory and follow recommendations based on the analysis results (see list of soils labs in Soils lesson).

## METHOD OF APPLICATION

The kind of fertilizer to be applied greatly influences the selection of an application method. Fertilizers come in various forms. Some are in a gas form, others are liquids, powders or granules.

Gaseous fertilizers are not usually used in home gardening situations because of the need for specialized application equipment. Broadcasting, however, is a very common method, often used in combination with incorporation into the soil. Broadcasting should be done so that the fertilizer is spread uniformly on the soil surface. Various fertilizer spreaders are manufactured for this method of application. When broadcasting is done by hand, it is wise to divide the fertilizer into two equal portions. Then, spread the fertilizer by walking in one direction, south to north, for example, with one portion, and east to west with the other portion. If small amounts are involved, a filler (such as sand) can be mixed with the fertilizer to ensure more uniform distribution. Broadcast fertilizers can be incorporated into the soil using a tiller, plough, digging fork or spade.

Fertilizers can be placed with seed but there is a danger of injury to seedlings by burning. Fertilizer banding is a method where fertilizers are placed in a strip or band near the plant. If the fertilizer is placed 5 cm (2 in) to the side and 2.5 cm (1 in) below the seed or transplant (spring application), the nutrients are quickly available to the developing plant and root injury is avoided.

Fertilizer can be applied as a side dressing to rows of vegetables when

## Table 4-4
### RATE OF FERTILIZER APPLICATION

| CHEMICAL FERTILIZERS | ANALYSIS N-P-K | RATE OF APPLICATION kg/10 m² | LIQUID g/L | AVAILABILITY | GENERAL REACTION |
|---|---|---|---|---|---|
| Ammonium Nitrate | 33-0-0 | 0.25 | 1.5 | rapid | acid |
| Ammonium Sulfate | 21-0-0 | 0.5 | 3.7 | quick | acid |
| Calcium Nitrate | 15-0-0 | 0.5 | 3.7 | rapid | alkaline |
| Sodium Nitrate | 16-0-0 | 0.5 | 3.7 | rapid | alkaline |
| Urea or Nu-Green | 45-0-0 | 0.25 | 1.4 | rapid | acid to neutral |
| Urea Formaldehyde | 38-0-0 | 0.25 | Insoluble | slow | neutral |
| Treble Superphosphate | 0-45-0 | 1.0 | Insoluble | slow | neutral |
| Superphosphate | 0-20-0 | 2.45 | Insoluble | slow | neutral |
| Potassium Chloride (pink) | 0-0-50 | 0.5 | 3.7 | quick | neutral |
| Muriate of Potash (trona, white) | 0-0-60 | 0.5 | 3.7 | quick | neutral |
| Potassium Sulfate | 0-0-50 | 0.5 | 3.7 | quick | neutral |
| Mono-ammonium Phosphate | 11-48-0 | 0.5 | 3.7 | moderate | acid |
| Di-ammonium Phosphate | 21-53-0 | 0.25 | 1.5 | moderate | acid |
| Potassium Nitrate (14-0-46) | 13-0-44 | 0.5 | 3.7 | rapid | alkaline |
| Nitrophoska (mixture) | 15-30-15 | 0.5 | 3.7 | moderate | acid |

## Table 4-5
### MAXIMUM RATES OF FERTILIZERS RECOMMENDED FOR HOME GARDENING

| FERTILIZER GRADE | BROADCAST | | BANDED 5 cm to side 2.5 cm below seed (g/100 m² in row spaced 50 cm apart) | PLACED IN CIRCLE AROUND ROOT BALL | |
|---|---|---|---|---|---|
| | LAWNS (kg/100 m²) | VEGETABLES (kg/100 m²) | | 1 m TALL SHRUBS | 3 m TALL TREES |
| 21-0-0 | 3 | | | | |
| 33.5-0-0 | 2 | | | | |
| 45-0-0 | 1.5 | | | | |
| 27-14-0 | 2.5 | | 150 | | |
| 24-20-0 | 3 | | 225 | | |
| 23-23-0 | 3.3 | 3.3 | 225 | | |
| 16-20-0 | 3.5 | 3.5 | 300 | | |
| 11-48-0 | 4.5 | 3 | 525 | | |
| 13-13-13 | 4 | 4 | 450 | | |
| 10-30-10 | 4.5 | 4 | 525 | 100 g | 150 g |
| 14-14-7 | 4 | 4 | 450 | 75 g | 75 g |
| 12-5-7 | 5.5 | 5.5 | 575 | | |
| 8-12-6 | 7 | 7 | 650 | | |
| 9-11-4 | 6.8 | 6.8 | 675 | | |

Table 4-6

## FERTILIZER PLACEMENT AND REACTIONS

| NAME | GRADE | CHEMICAL FORMULA | PLACEMENT |
|---|---|---|---|
| Anhydrous Ammonia | 82-0-0 | $NH_3$ | In soil 10-15 cm |
| Aqua Ammonia | 20-0-0 | $NH_3$ In water $(NH_4OH)$ | In soil 7-10 cm |
| Ammonium Sulfate | 21-0-0 | $(NH_4)_2SO_4$ | Surface or in soil |
| Urea | 46-0-0 | $(NH_2)_2CO$ | In soil 7-10 cm |
| Ammonium Nitrate | 34-0-0 | $NH_4NO_3$ | Surface or in soil |
| Calcium Nitrate | 15.5-0-0 | $Ca(NO_3)_2$ | Surface or in soil |
| Superphosphate | 0-20-0 | $Ca(H_2PO_4)_2 + CaSO_4$ | In soil 5-15 cm |
| Phosphate Rock | 0-(11-13)-0 | $Ca_{10}F_2(PO_4)_6$ | In soil 5-15 cm |
| Monoammonium Phosphate | 11-48-0 | $NH_4H_2PO_4$ | Surface or in soil |
| | 11-51-0 | | |
| | 11-54-0 | | |
| | 11-55-0 | | |
| Diammonium Phosphate | 18-46-0 | $(NH_4)_2HPO_4$ | Surface or in soil |
| Monocalcium Phosphate (triple phosphate) | 0-45-0 | $Ca(H_2PO_4)_2$ | In soil 5-15 cm |
| Ammonium Phosphate Sulphate | 16-20-0 | $(NH_4)_2SO_4 + NH_4H_2PO_4$ | Surface or in soil |
| Ammonium Nitrate Phosphate | 23-23-0 | $NH_4NO_3 + NH_4H_2PO_4$ | Surface or in soil |
| | 27-14-0 | | |
| | 17-34-0 and more | | |
| Potassium Sulphate | 0-0-50 | $K_2SO_4$ | Surface or in soil |
| Potassium Chloride | 0-0-60 | $KCl$ | Surface or in soil |
| Potassium Nitrate | 12-0-44 | $KNO_3$ | Liquid - surface or in soil |
| Potassium Magnesium Sulphate | 0-0-22 | $K_2SO_4 + 2MgSO_4$ | |
| Magnesium Ammonium Phosphate | 8-45-0 | $MgNH_4PO_4H_2O$ | |

cultivating or can be added in liquid form through flooding, sprinkling system or watering can. Fertilizers can also be applied as a spray for foliar absorption.

Incorporation of fertilizers is done extensively in pre-plant situations such as preparations for lawns, seedbeds and flowerbeds, as well as incorporated into potting mixtures. Lettuce often receives a pre-plant broadcast of N and P which could provide enough P for the growing season. As the crop grows, more N is added in dissolved form (watering in) or as a side dressing. Side dressing is also used for crops such as peas, beans, corn, potatoes and so on. For trees and shrubs, several fertilizer application methods can be used, including broadcasting, foliar sprays and spot application (drilling holes at certain intervals and placing a concentration of fertilizer in each hole). Soil applications seem to be best for woody material as surface applications tend to stimulate herbaceous vegetation under trees. Repeated applications at four or five week intervals is an excellent way of supplying fertilizers to vegetables. Lawns benefit from application of nitrogen in the early spring with subsequent applications at six week intervals. Broadcast the fertilizer on **dry** grass and water well to fully dissolve the fertilizer. Small fruit bushes can be fertilized by digging shallow trenches around the plant near the roots and placing a band of fertilizer in the trench.

Figure 4-14

## FERTILIZER PLACEMENT

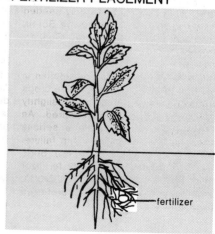

fertilizer

| COMMENT | REACTION |
|---|---|
| Can cause burns | Acid |
| Can cause burns | Acid |
| Corrosive | Acid |
| Do not store with Ammonium Nitrate | Acid |
| Avoid contact with urea. Can cause burns | Acid |
| Can cause burns | Alkaline |
| Near roots | Neutral |
| Near roots | |
| Often used preplant | Acid |
| | Acid |
| | Acid |
| | Acid |
| Can cause burns | Acid |
| Near roots | Neutral |
| Can cause burns | Acid |
| Can cause burns | Acid |
| | Neutral |
| | Neutral |
| Store dry | Alkaline |
| | Neutral |
| Slow release | Acid |

## TRACE ELEMENTS, FORMULATIONS AND APPLICATIONS

Seven essential elements are also called trace elements as they are only needed in minute quantities. They include Boron, Manganese, Zinc, Iron, Copper, Molybdenum and Chlorine.

Boron, when deficient, can be applied in very small quantities. For sensitive crops like beans, corn and other crops, slightly larger quantities may be required. An excess of boron can cause a serious toxicity problem resulting in crop failure. Boron is contained in Borax (11%), Boric acid (17%), Sodium tetraborate fertilizer borate 48 (15%) and solubor (20%). Foliar application is the preferred method of application.

Manganese, if deficient, can be applied as Manganese sulphate (26 - 28% Mn) or as chelated Manganese (12% Mn). It is best applied to the soil before planting. If needed after planting, a foliar spray can be used.

Zinc can be applied as Zinc chelate (9 - 14% Zn), Zinc sulphate (36% Zn) or Zinc carbonate (52 - 56% Zn). Soil applications before planting is best and Zinc can also be applied as foliar spray to fruit trees.

Iron deficiency is quite common on soils with high pH levels. Iron can be applied as Iron chelate in foliar spray (5 - 15% Fe) or to the soil as Ferrous sulphate (19% Fe) or Ferric sulphate (23% Fe).

Copper deficiencies are rare but when they do occur, it is often in peat soils and results in dieback of vegetable leaves. Copper can be applied as copper sulphate, copper chloride, copper ammonium phosphate or copper chelate.

Molybdenum deficiency can be corrected with ammonium molybdate, Molybdenum trioxide or sodium molybdate.

Chlorine is contained in many fertilizers and is rarely deficient.

## RATES AND FREQUENCIES

Water is necessary to utilize water soluble fertilizers. Recommendations, therefore, consider the soil types. Nitrogen and phosphorus are usually in short supply in most Alberta soils. The grey wooded soil may need an extra amount of nitrogen and sulphur which is often leached out of such soil. Some soils in the Peace River area are acid and may require the addition of lime and the use of acid reducing fertilizers. Potassium deficiency does occur in some areas and with some crops in Alberta. Fertilizer needs are best determined through soil analyses. Soils laboratories that will carry out such tests and make recommendations (see Soils lesson.)

Most crops are planted in the spring and a rush of growth usually takes place in the spring and early summer.

Consequently, this is the time when an adequate supply of nutrients is essential to produce healthy plants. If applications of nitrogen are given in late summer and early fall, it slows down the hardening off process needed for plants to survive our cold winters.

In the grey-black and grey soil zones, spring applications of nitrogen are more beneficial than fall applications. A fertilizer grade suited to supply sulphur, along with nitrogen and phosphorus, is 16-20-0-14S. Fertilizers supplying nitrogen and sulphur include 21-0-0-24S, 34-0-0-11S and 20-0-0-5S.

## COMPOSTING

Composting is a method used to decay plant and animal refuse by microbial action to form humus, a vital soil ingredient. Humus improves the chemical and physical properties of soil and supplies plants with a quantity of slowly available fertilizer elements. Compost improves soil structure, increases pore volume and increases the buffering and water-holding capacity of the soil.

The common wastes in the urban garden are grass clippings, mature and dead plants and plant parts from the fall cleanup of vegetable and flower beds, fallen leaves and dead grass from the spring raking of lawns. To this can be added vegetable peelings and other kitchen wastes. Animal wastes, except for fats, can also be used but tend to produce unpleasant odors. For the urban home gardener, it is advisable to stick to plant refuse only.

### CONSTRUCTION

Construction can be a matter of personal preference depending on the situation available for compost piles. No structure at all offers complete flexibility in the movement of the pile if needed. Unprotected compost piles must be kept moist at all times by frequent waterings. A structure can be provided by using grass sods as walls, building a bottomless wooden box of convenient dimensions with a lid or digging a pit for which a cover or lid can be provided.

The conventional system for composting is to place the organic wastes in layers approximately 15 cm thick (6 in), alternating with layers of old grass sods or soil. The material is watered down and kept moist at all times. It should be forked occasionally to avoid overheating but is generally kept covered and relatively undisturbed for one to two years, until it is thoroughly decayed.

A newer method developed at the University of California in Berkeley provide for high temperature, and rapid composing through improved aeration. While it requires considerable labor, its advantages lie in the absence of foul odors and a rapid recycling of wastes. It is this method that is well adapted to the urban scene and will be described here.

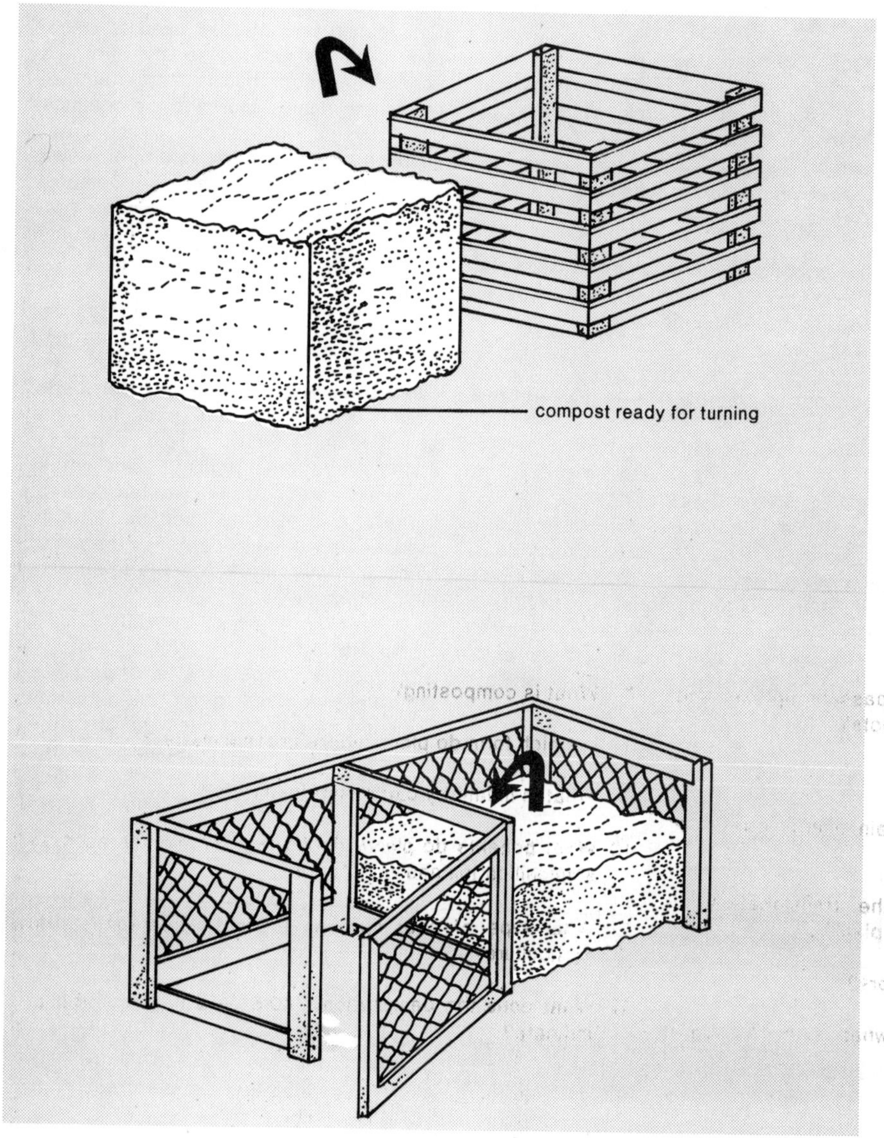

## THE FRAME

A wooden frame with either slatted or wire mesh side walls and a capacity of about one cubic metre (about one cubic yard) is adequate for the average city lot. It should have no top or bottom and will, therefore, require sturdy construction to retain its shape. It should be lightweight with the sides slightly tapered toward the top for easy removal when the pile requires turning. To turn the pile, lift off the frame, set it beside the pile and fork the compost back into the empty frame. A single bin or two bin frame can also be used with posts set into the ground. With this type of construction, a removable front panel is required (see Figure 4-14).

## PROCEDURE

Autumn is a good time to start a compost since there is an abundance of materials available at that time. Store all garden cleanup materials in the compost box until spring. Larger material should be cut up into 20-25 cm (8-10 in) lengths for better consolidation and easier future handling. Little, if any, decomposition will occur over the cold winter months. In the spring, add rakings and the first grass clippings, turning the pile to mix the old and new material. Add water if the material is dry. The pile will usually heat up in three days. Continue to add grass clippings and other materials as they become available and turn the pile at least once a week. Frequent turning and thorough mixing is essential to supply air to the interior of the pile. Water should be added as the pile is turned to provide uniform moisture throughout the pile. Enough moisture is present when the particles of compost glisten. Foul odors indicate too much moisture – the remedy is more frequent turning to speed up evaporation and improve aeration. Once the odors disappear, resume the regular routine of turning every five to seven days.

At the end of August, stop adding additional material but continue to turn the pile and keep it moist. It is finished when the pile will not heat up even though moisture and air are adequate. Finished compost is a uniformly dark color with an earthy odor. Shredding it with a mechanical shredder makes it easier to incorporate into the garden soil.

## THE COMPOSTING PROCESS

Composting is brought about by the activity of bacteria, fungi and actinomycetes. All these organisms are present in garden residues. No additives, including compost starter, fertilizer, lime or soil, are necessary to make the pile work. The first organisms involved in this process are active at ambient temperatures. These are succeeded by organisms active at successively higher temperatures. The internal temperature of a small compost pile of the type described here will reach 55-65°C or more. This range of temperature is high enough to kill flies (in all stages of development), weed seeds and plant pathogenic organisms.

## Figure 4-15
## COMPOSTING PROCEDURE

compost ready for turning

Composting organisms require a suitable carbon:nitrogen ratio for peak activity. Mixing dry garden wastes (high carbon:nitrogen ratio) with grass clippings (low carbon:nitrogen ratio) usually produces a suitable ratio. If the ratio is too high, sprinkle in nitrogen fertilizer (such as 21-0-0 or 33-0-0) on each successive layer of the pile to improve the balance.

## CONCLUSION

The nutrition of green plants is unique because it involves not only the products of digestion, typical of animal nutrition (including humans), but also the synthesis of carbohydrates from carbon dioxide and water. This synthesis of 'food' (sugars) through the trapping of solar energy (photosynthesis) makes plants self-sufficient or non-reliant on other forms of life for their continued existence. Animals, on the other hand, are ultimately dependent on plants.

## SELF CHECK *QUIZ*

1. What is the difference between passive uptake and active uptake of nutrients by plant roots?

2. What is respiration?

3. What compound constitutes the main energy carrier in living cells?

4. How does transpiration aid in the translocation of nutrients to living cells throughout a plant?

5. What is the principle of limiting factors?

6. If the pH of the soil is too low, what is the standard treatment for raising it?

7. What is composting?

8. In which form do plants utilize organic matter?

9. What is meant by carbon:nitrogen ratio?

10. What benefits do plants derive from processes such as ammonification and nitrification?

11. What type of peat has the highest value for use in horticulture?

12. What does the designation 7-40-6 on a bag of fertilizer indicate?

adsorption - concentration (gas, liquid or dissolved substance) on a surface in a condensed layer.

ammonification - reduction of ammonium due to biological decomposition of organic nitrogen compounds.

anion - ion carrying a negative charge of electricity.

autotrophs - group of bacteria capable of forming nitrite and nitrate.

carbon:nitrogen ratio - relative proportion, by weight, of organic carbon to nitrogen in soil or organic matter.

carboxylation - process whereby $CO_2$ is reduced to an organic compound in photosynthesis (carbon fixation).

cation - ion carrying a positive charge of electricity.

chlorosis - lack of chlorophyll development causing yellowing or whitening of plant tissue.

colloid - particle small enough to stay suspended in water with a high surface area per unit of mass.

denitrification - by way of anaerobic microbes, the reduction of nitrates to atmospheric nitrogen.

dieback - starting at the tips, the progressive death of shoots, branches, and roots.

fertilizer - material supplying one or more of the plant nutrient elements in a condition suitable for application to the soil.

fertilizer grade - expression of the percentage-content of the fertilizer given in the order of N-P-K.

fertilizer ratio - amount of a fertilizer in relation to another or several other fertilizers (i.e., 27-24-7 indicates a ratio of 3:2:1).

humus - well-decomposed part of organic matter.

ion - electrically charged particle.

ion exchange - replacement of an ion by another ion with the same charge.

leach - removal of materials in a solution. Usually done by washing out with water.

mineralization - change of organic nitrogen through the processes of ammonification and nitrification to forms which the plant can utilize.

nitrification - formation of nitrates from ammonia by soil microbes.

nitrogen fixation - process whereby atmospheric nitrogen is absorbed by soil micro-organisms and converted to forms available to plants.

phloem - food conducting tissue of the vascular system composed of sieve tubes with companion cells, phloem parenchyma and fibres.

pore space - space in the soil not occupied by solid particles.

symbiosis - mutually beneficial association of two or more organisms.

# SELF CHECK ANSWERS

1. Passive uptake involves only simple diffusion or the net movement of ions or molecules of a given nutrient element from a region of high concentration (soil solution around the roots) to a region of lower concentration (within the roots). Active uptake involves the net movement of such ions or molecules against the gradient. For this to occur, there must be an external source of energy supplied by the living cells of the root itself (see ABOSRPTION - page 401).

2. Respiration is the release of energy by biological oxidation of organic compounds, particularly carbohydrates (see RESPIRATION - page 402).

3. ATP - Adenosine triphosphate (see RESPIRATION - page 402).

4. The mass movement of water through the xylem during transpiration speeds up the movement of dissolved nutrients as well, thereby improving the efficiency of their translocation to living cells throughout the plant (see TRANSLOCATION - page 403).

5. When one factor (temperature, light, a particular nutrient, etc.) is less than optimal, it then becomes the controlling or limiting entity and determines the extent to which the plant will fall short of its full potential (see PRINCIPLE OF LIMITING FACTORS - page 405).

6. The application of ground limestone, either agricultural lime (calcium carbonate) or dolomitic lime (a mixture of calcium carbonate and magnesium carbonate) (see SOIL pH MODIFICIATION - page 424 and CALCIUM - page 408).

7. Composting is the production of humus from organic wastes. It involves the provision of suitable conditions to enhance the decay of plant and animal refuse by micro-organisms (see COMPOSTING - page 427 and COMPOST - page 421).

8. Organic matter must be completely decomposed so plants can take up the nutrient elements in ionic form. (see ORGANIC FERTILIZERS - page 421 and INORGANIC FERTILIZERS - page 423).

9. Bacteria require one part of nitrogen for each four to five parts of carbon to effectively decompose organic matter. The nitrogen content in soil organic matter is given in proportion to the carbon content and is called the carbon:nitrogen ratio. (see CARBON:NITROGEN RATIO - page 409).

10. Plants benefit by having micro-organisms make nitrogen available from organic sources (see THE ROLE OF SOME MICRO-ORGANISMS - page 410).

11. Peat with a high fibre content, high water-holding capacity such as sphagnum moss peat (see ORGANIC FERTILIZERS - page 421).

12. A designation such as 7-40-6 indicates the formulation and shows the percentage of the fertilizer. It is always in the order of N-P-K (Nitrogen-Phosphorus-Potassium) and in the case of 7-40-6 shows the fertilizer contains 7% nitrogen, 40% phosphorus and 6% potassium (see INORGANIC FERTILIZERS - page 423).

Baker, Kenneth F. (ed.) *The U.C. System for Producing Healthy Container Grown Plants through the use of Clean Soil, Clean Stock, and Sanitation. Manual 23.* Berkley: University of California Extension Service, 1957.

A good overall introduction to soil and problems thereof.

Bentley, C.J. and J.A. Robertson. *Soils and Fertilizers for Gardens and Lawns.* A University of Alberta bulletin, 1977.

Deals with some aspects of plant nutrition.

Donahue, R.L., R.H. Foblett, R.W. Tulluck. *Our Soils and Their Management.* Illinois: Interstate Printers and Publications, Inc., 1976.

Donahue, R.L., R.W. Milke, J.C. Schickluna. *Soils: An Introduction to Soils and Plant Growth*, 5th edition. New Jersey: Prentice-Hall Inc., 1983.

Good up-to-date introduction to soil science.

Halfacre, R.Gordon and John Barden. *Horticulture.* Toronto: McGraw-Hill Book Co., 1979.

A general textbook on horticulture. Deals with plant nutrition in Chapter 11. Related aspects, including photosynthesis, respiration and water relations, are dealt with in other chapters.

Peter, Martin Ray. *The Living Plant.* New York: Holt, Rhinehart & Winston, 1972.

Useful for understanding plant processes.

Poincelot, R.P., et. al. *Horticulture: Principles and Practical Applications.* Englewood Cliffs, New Jersey: Prentice-Hall, Inc., 1980.

A general textbook on horticulture which deals with plant nutrition in Chapters 3 and 4.

Sophee, Charles, and Jack Baird. *Soil and Soil Management.* Virginia: Reston Publishing Company, Inc., 1982.

Easy-to-read text on soils.

White, R.E. *Introduction to the Principles and Practices of Soil Sciences.* Oxford: Blackwell Scientific Publications, 1979.

Detailed scientific explanation on soil systems.

## INDEX

# PLANT PROPAGATION

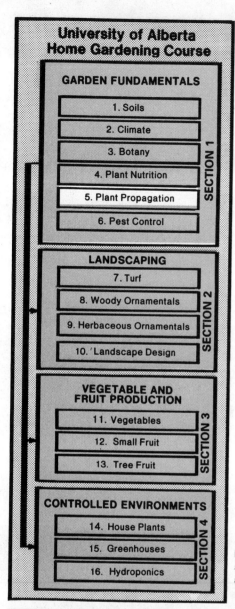

**University of Alberta Home Gardening Course**

**GARDEN FUNDAMENTALS**
1. Soils
2. Climate
3. Botany
4. Plant Nutrition
5. Plant Propagation
6. Pest Control

SECTION 1

**LANDSCAPING**
7. Turf
8. Woody Ornamentals
9. Herbaceous Ornamentals
10. Landscape Design

SECTION 2

**VEGETABLE AND FRUIT PRODUCTION**
11. Vegetables
12. Small Fruit
13. Tree Fruit

SECTION 3

**CONTROLLED ENVIRONMENTS**
14. House Plants
15. Greenhouses
16. Hydroponics

SECTION 4

# SELF-STUDY LESSON FEATURES

Self-study is an educational approach which allows you to study a subject where and when you want. The course is designed to allow you to study efficiently and incorporates the following features:

**OBJECTIVES** — are found at the beginning of each lesson and allow you to determine what you can expect to learn in the lesson.

**LESSON MATERIAL** — is logically organized and broken down into fundamental components by ordered headings to assist you to comprehend the subject.

**REFERENCING** — between lessons and within lessons allows you to integrate course material.

The last two digits of the page number identify the page and the digits preceding these identify the lesson number (eg., 107: Lesson 1, page 7 or 1227: Lesson 12, page 27).

Referencing:

    sections within the same lesson (eg., see OSMOSIS)

    sections in other lessons (eg., see Botany lesson, OSMOSIS)

    figures and tables (eg., see Figure 7-3)

**FIGURES AND TABLES** — are found in abundance throughout the lessons and are designed to convey useful information in an easy to understand form.

**SIDEBARS** — are those areas in the lesson which are boxed and toned. They present information supplementary to the core content of the lesson.

**PRACTICAL PROJECTS** — are integrated within the lesson material and are included to allow you to apply principles and practices.

**SELF-CHECK QUIZ** — is provided at the end of each lesson and allows you to test your comprehension of the lesson material. Answers to the questions and references to the sections dealing with the questions are provided in the answer section. You should review any questions that you are unable to answer.

**GLOSSARY** — is provided at the end of each lesson and alphabetically lists the definitions of key concepts and terms.

**RESOURCE MATERIALS** — are provided at the end of each lesson and comprise a list of recommended learning materials for further study of the subject. Also included are author's comments on the potential application of each publication.

**INDEX** — alphabetically lists useful topics and their location within the lesson.

© 1986 University of Alberta Faculty of Extension

**Written by: Rudi Kroon and Sharon Rempel**

Technical Reviewers:          Helge Welling
                           Dr. E.W. Toop

THE PRODUCTION TEAM

Managing Editor ................................................... Thom Shaw
Editor ............................................................. Frank Procter
Production Coordinator ..................................... Kevin Hanson
Graphic Artists ...................................................... Lisa Marsh
                                          Carol Powers
                   Melanie Eastley Harbourne
Data Entry ................................................... Joan Geisterfer

Published by the University of Alberta
Faculty of Extension Corbett Hall
Edmonton, Alberta, T6G 2G4

# LEARNING OBJECTIVES

After completing this lesson, the student should be able to:

1. identify the two basic types of plant propagation.
2. understand the principles involved in sexual and asexual reproduction.
3. identify and understand various methods of propagation.
4. select and use the appropriate propagation methods.

# TABLE OF CONTENTS

# INTRODUCTION

Plant propagation is the term loosely applied to all endeavors in the perpetuation of plants. Most home gardeners rely on specialists in the field of plant propagation to supply them with new plant material. There is no reason, however, why the home gardener should not attempt to do some of his or her own plant propagation. It could be both enjoyable and profitable. In order to be successful in such attempts, it is important to have a fairly good understanding of certain basic principles of plant growth and horticultural practices.

When looking at the general organization of the lesson, you will notice there are two major topics: sexual propagation and asexual propagation. Sexual propagation looks at reproduction through seeds. Asexual propagation deals with division, cuttings, layering, and grafting methods of reproduction. At the end of the lesson, there is a discussion of special propagation methods, including the rather new and very dynamic area of 'tissue culture'. Not included in this lesson is a 'shopping list' of specific plants and their propagation methods. However, it is hoped that after having waded through all the lesson material, you can make an intelligent decision as to the choice of methods best suited to your particular plant. Many books have comprehensive lists of methods best suited to specific plants, however, do not hesitate to try different methods.

Man has practiced plant propagation for thousands of years. When a nomadic existence was replaced by a permanent dwelling and an agricultural lifestyle, it was realized that seed for the next crop year had to be saved over the winter. By the power of observation, it was found that 'good' seed produced better crops and selected seed was saved for the next year's crop. The origin of vegetative propagation was probably accidental: a branch was hammered into the ground for a building or a fence post and roots appeared, or one tuber was planted and later yielded two tubers.

Horticulturalists still obtain new cultivars by trial and error, and accidental results are often used as a basis for further experimentation. When you work with living material, there is no such thing as the 'only' and 'absolute'.

# CHOICE OF METHODS TO BE USED

There are two basic types of plant propagation: sexual and asexual. When confronted with the choice of method to use when perpetuating a certain type of plant, you should be familiar with the growth habits of the specific plant. The amount of propagation material available and the desired number of plants are both important considerations. It should be realized that this lesson is simply not extensive enough to list all the plants with their optimum propagation method(s). There are a number of good reference books available that do list plants and the propagation method best suited to each. Some of these books are listed in the RESOURCE MATERIALS at the end of this lesson.

## CIRCUMSTANCES INFLUENCING THE CHOICE OF PROPAGATION METHODS

### EQUIPMENT AND FACILITIES

In order to propagate many types of cuttings, special equipment may be required, such as a misting tent or pressure mist system (see MISTFRAMES AND HEATING CABLES). Lack of equipment may force selection of another propagation method. Many methods require extensive skill by the propagator. Selection of these methods, however, may provide a challenge and a chance to gain new experience. As is usually the case with the home gardener, space is a limiting factor, but only a small number of plants are required. Time is not usually a critical factor for the home gardener either. Usually, the cheapest and easiest method of propagation is selected by home and commercial propagators alike. Remember that plants get bigger as they grow, so control the numbers based on available space.

The method of propagating a certain plant is strongly influenced by its form and growth habit. If there are any limitations to the methods under consideration, these should be factors in choosing a suitable method. Always try the quickest and cheapest method for commercial propagation, but for enjoyment and practice, try anything.

# SEXUAL PROPAGATION

Sexual propagation refers to propagation from seed. Seeds are viable so long as they are alive!!!! Granted, they do not lead a very exciting existence but they are alive, just waiting for the right combination of conditions to start germinating. Seeds contain a genetic code onto which all characteristics of their plant are written. This aspect of biological science is called genetics. Two aspects of genetics are important for a good understanding of plant propagation: mitosis and meiosis.

## MITOSIS

Mitosis is the process of ordinary cell division which takes place in all parts of the growing plant. One cell will split into two equal halves and will give rise to two identical cells. The chromosomes found in the original cell have divided to provide identical chromosomal content in both cells. Two identical cells taken from a plant can grow and produce two identical plants. This is exactly what happens in the practice of 'tissue culture' (see TISSUE CULTURE). This also explains why a plant with the same characteristics can be produced from a single parent plant.

## MEIOSIS

Meiosis, in contrast to mitosis (these two words are similar and can cause confusion), only takes place in those cells of the plant which are directly involved in sexual reproduction. In this process of cell division (meiosis), the chromosomes are divided in such a manner that each cell has only half the original number of chromosomes left after the division process is completed. As a consequence, these cells are not able to give rise to normal tissue which could lead to the formation of a complete and normal plant, as was the case in mitosis. In order to fully comprehend the meiotic process, it is necesary to review the typical parts of a flower that are involved in the process (see Botany lesson, FLOWERS). When one looks at a flower, the showy corolla is most noticeable and consists of a combination of colorful, modified leaves (see Figure 5-1). Other parts of the flower are often quite inconspicuous. This lesson will summarize many

## Figure 5-1

## BASIC FLOWER STRUCTURE OF AN ANGIOSPERMOUS (DICOT) PLANT

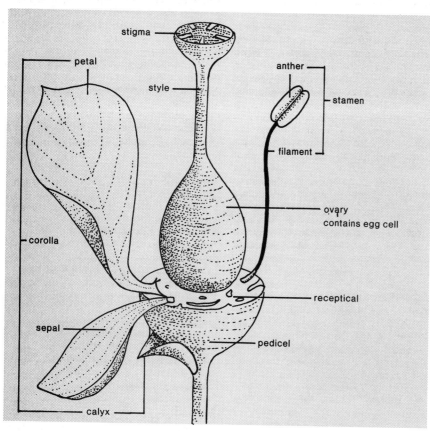

There are, however, a number of plants that have exceptional arrangements of their floral components (see Botany lesson, FLOWERS). Plants that have separate male (staminate) and female (pistillate) flowers on one plant are called **monoecious** (translated from latin to mean 'from one house'). Corn (*Zea*), pine (*Pinus*), and spruce (*Picea*) as well as a common tropical houseplant called the croton (*Codiaeum*) are examples of monoecious plants. Plants that either carry male or female flowers on one plant (but never both) are called **dioecious** (literally 'from two houses'). Some examples are cottonwood (*Populus*), willow (*Salix*), and the maiden hair tree (*Ginkgo*).

Geneticists can often predict the results of certain cross-pollinations. Plant breeders apply this knowledge to obtain certain desirable characteristics, or even new plants. In the example used earlier, flower color was discussed, but all characteristics of the plant are controlled by the genes in the chromosomes. Some of the characteristics of a plant which are controlled by the chromosomes include vigor, early-flowering and disease resistance. Certain features in the genetic coding are dominant over others and it is this trait which determines prevailing features of the plant in question. This may explain why seeds

botanical concepts to provide an appreciation for the vast differences in flower designs. These differences reflect unique adaptations that best suit the particular plant's growth and reproductive habits. With patience, you soon learn to distinguish the various parts of the flower, however well disguised they may be.

The ovary contains the ovules where one or more seeds develop after fertilization Pollination is the process whereby pollen grains, released from the anther, land on the often sticky surface of a flower's stigma. The methods by which pollen can be transferred to the stigma are numerous: insects, wind, water, birds, bats and, of course, the hand of a person. The pollen grain will be chemically stimulated by a specific substance on the stigma and will start to grow a long, tubular organ which will grow down through the style until it reaches an ovule in the ovary. Once it has penetrated the ovule, it will release

its contents into the embryo sac. Fertilization occurs when a sperm cell from the pollen tube fuses with the egg cell in the embryo sac. Each participant in the fertilization process contributes half the total number of required chromosomes, so after fertilization, the embryo has a complete set of chromosomes. The characteristics of both the mother plant and the pollen contributing plant are now stored in the chromosomes in the embryo. If the pollen came from an anther in the same flower as the ovule, or from another flower on the same plant as the ovule, then no great surprises should be expected from the seed produced. However, if the pollen produced came from a different plant of the same Species but with different colored flowers, one could expect that different colors would be produced on flowers raised from the seeds. Usually, the male (anthers) and the female parts (pistil) are found on the same flower. Such flowers are referred to as **perfect flowers.**

## Figure 5-2

## GENETIC COLOR DETERMINATION IN SNAPDRAGONS

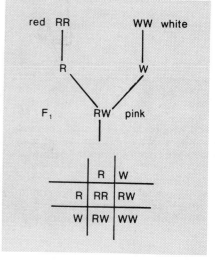

gathered from one plant can give rise to seedlings with quite different characteristics than either parent. Figure 5-2 explains how cross-pollination gives rise to hybrids because of the various dominant and non-dominant (recessive) factors. Theoretically, the outcome of cross-pollinated fertilization from parents of pure lineage can be predicted.

The number of chromosomes in each plant of any one Species is the same. However, different Genera in the same Family will have entirely different chromosomal contents. Hybridization between Species is usually easy but between Genera is extremely rare (except in Orchids and Cactus). The Gesneriadaceae (African Violet Family) is another group where intergeneric hybridization is possible. Hybridization between Families is impossible.

## F1 AND F2 HYBRIDS

When cross-pollinating a flower, the parents are referred to as the **P generation** (from the Latin word *parens*). The resulting seed generation is called the **F1 generation** (from the latin word *filius*). The result of pollination within the F1 generation is called the **F2 generation** and so on. The F1 generation usually displays more vigorous growth than successive generations. To illustrate this concept, two snapdragon plants, one with white and one with red flowers are self-pollinated. Assuming that these parents are 'pure', their seedlings will produce only white or red colored flowers. This is called a **homozygous** condition. After cross-pollination, their F1 generation results in pink flowers and the plant is markedly stronger and larger than the P generation (see Figure 5-3). If the F1 generation plants were self-pollinated, their seeds would yield flowering offspring in a ratio of 25 per cent white, 50 per cent light pink and 25 per cent red.

In the late 1950's, a seedless English type cucumber (known as President F1) was being marketed. A Danish seed company developed and sold this seed. One of the parents (P) was a cultivar known as President, but the other parent's identity was kept secret. The F1 generation was seedless and, therefore, it was impossible to produce F2 generations. The seed company was the only source of these hybrids. In cases where the parent plants (P1 and P2) are not homozygous but **heterozygous**, only the dominant factor (alleles) will be apparent in the F1 generation (see Figure 5-2). Dominant factors are always indicated by a capital letter, and non-dominant factors (recessive) would be indicated by a small letter.

## CONTROLLED POLLINATION

To experiment with hybridization, it is necessary to keep ahead of the bees. A small piece of gauze can be wrapped around a flower to prevent insect pollination. However, this will not prevent wind or self-pollination from occurring (see Botany lesson, POLLINATION). Therefore, one of the best methods is to cut the flower bud open just before it is ready to open itself and remove all the anthers with a fine pair of tweezers or scissors. Surround the pistil with a tube of material (very fine gauze works well) that will prevent stray pollen from reaching the stigma and, thereby, result in unintended pollination. Seedbeds must be isolated from one another to avoid cross-pollination with other cultivars. After one or two days, the surface of the stigma will be moist, indicating maturity. Pollen should then be applied to the stigma and (hopefully) fertilization will take place. The pistil will stay green and show swelling after a week if fertilization has been successful. Try pollinating

## Figure 5-3
## F₁ AND F₂ GENERATIONS IN SNAPDRAGONS (ANTIRRHINUM)

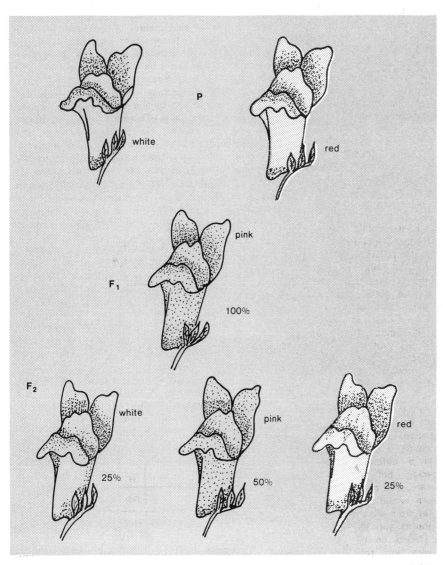

flowers at various times; pollen can stay viable for long periods of time if stored properly. The process may need to be repeated before successful pollination occurs.

After hybridization, it is necessary to keep a careful eye on the progeny. Atypical growth forms and diseased plants may occur and must be removed **(rogued)**.

Some plant types are easy to hybridize whereas others are not so easy. Information on the relative ease of hybridization can often be obtained from societies concentrating on certain Families or Genera. For example, Orchid, Cactus, Dahlia, Gladiolus and Rose societies are all very common. These organizations are excellent contacts for detailed information on breeding, showing, acquiring, or discussing plants. Your local Department of Agriculture representative may be able to supply you with the names and addresses of such societies in your area.

Lilies are a good choice for a beginning pollinator to work with. The flower buds are prominent and the various flower parts are easily distinguishable. Keep one practical detail in mind regarding the growth of the pollen tube into the ovary; there is a direct correlation between the length of the style and the length the pollen tube can grow to reach the ovary. For successful **cross-pollination** to occur, the lengths of the style and pollen tube must be matched. When hybridizing lilies, it may be noted that the length of the style of some hybrids is shorter than others. Therefore, measure the average style length from the pollen producing plant and modify the style length of the plant to be pollinated to match that of the style donor. Lily breeders do a bit of surgery to make the style the same length as that of the plant from which the pollen came. If the style has to be lengthened, a piece of style is inserted from a flower sacrificed for this purpose. Prevent flower parts from drying out by providing extra shade and high humidity around the flower. A thin, plastic tube serves the purpose of keeping pieces together.

In certain plants, it may not be possible to find anthers; sometimes double flowers have evolved to a stage where the anthers have turned into petals. Such double-flowering plants, for example, are difficult to propagate and are best reproduced from cuttings.

## COLLECTING SEED

After successful fertilization, a certain time period is required for the ovule to mature and for seeds to ripen. This period varies for each Species of plant, and is very dependent on the atmospheric conditions affecting the plant's growth. It is always best to carry out pollination work during the earlier part of the growing season to make sure the seeds have suffcent time to mature. The appearance of the fruit, pod, berry or whatever houses the seed is often a good indicator of when the seed should be collected. Seeds should be collected before natural release and dispersal occur. Collecting dry seed is easy, as the loose material around the seed is easily removed by blowing air over the seed. Seeds inside fleshy fruits can be washed out from a pulp made from the fruit. Gently mash the fruit and, after several water rinses, the seeds can usually be found on the bottom of the container. Some seeds float, so a very fine strainer may prove helpful in the washing process. Do not let the seeds remain wet for any extended period of time as the seed coat may soften and thereby shorten the storage qualities of the seed. It is not necessary to get the seeds absolutely clean. Sometimes, seed pods are stored intact over the winter and the seed separated in the spring. Sweet pea seed is a good example of this. In the fall, you may wish to do a small experiment to see if seeds stored in pods are more viable than those cleaned from the pods before storing.

Some of the large seed companies have their own plant breeding farms. These farms are often located in parts of the world where the climate is most favorable for the production of certain seeds. Seed companies strive to keep the highest quality of seed available for their customers. The larger companies are also involved with the improvement of existing cultivars and the development of new ones. Some well known international companies are Sluis and Groot of Holland, Suttons of England, Ohlsens Enkae of Denmark, Villmourin-Andreux of France, Thompson and Morgan of England, and Burpee of North America. Prominent seed companies in Canada include Stokes, Perrot, Steel Briggs and McKenzie Seed. If seeds of certain plants or their cultivars are readily available and not expensive, it is a good idea to obtain fresh seeds each season. Most seeds are viable for several years if they are stored in a cool dry place. A good storage temperature is about 3°C. The lower shelf of the refrigerator can be a good seed storage location. Be alert, however, to the location of the cooling element placed against the back wall in some refrigerators. If placed against it, the seeds will freeze, especially those from tropical plants. When normal room air is cooled, the relative humidity in a sealed container can be very high. Therefore, place the seed container without the lid closed in the refrigerator for about an hour before closing the lid tightly. Plastic or glass containers are best suited to this purpose. Be sure to label each container well. Plastic bags, since they are not vapor proof, are not recommended as seeds can still dry out in them.

Seeds are tested by seed companies and often by government departments to determine their per cent of germination. Such results are often printed on the seed package or on a separate label.

## CONDITIONS FOR SUCCESSFUL GERMINATION

Seed should generally be fresh and of good quality. It is waiting, in effect, for the right combination of circumstances to occur to start germination. These conditions for successful germination are:

• the absence of any inhibiting circumstances preventing germination. Such conditions may be present in the seed to prevent it from, for example, germinating in the fall. Such inhibitors can sometimes be removed through excessive leaching with water or by other methods.

• the presence of air (oxygen). During germination, the respiration rate increases dramatically, thereby creating a high demand for oxygen.

• a suitable temperature.

• the presence of water. The seed begins germination by absorbing water through the seed coat. Even non-viable seed may take up large amounts of water.

Once the seed coat has broken, active growth is initiated, that is, further cell division and enlargement has begun and

## Figure 5-4
## EPIGEOUS AND HYPOGEOUS GERMINATION

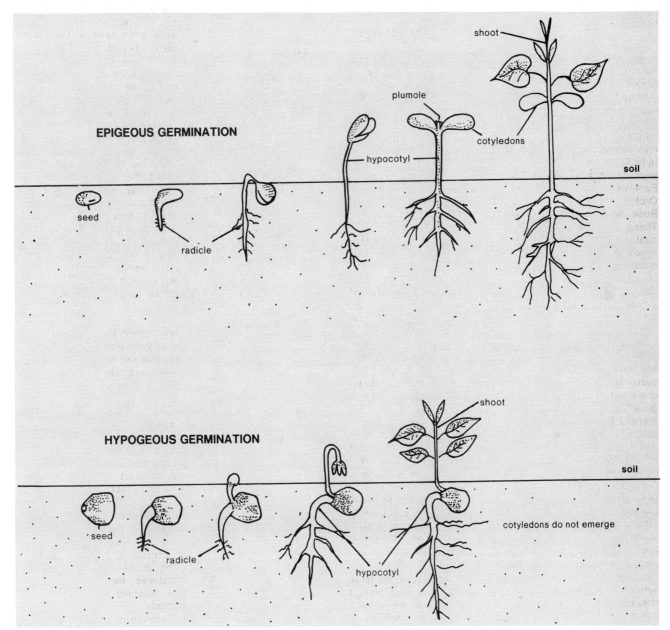

the embryo starts to develop. The onset of this process soon becomes obvious when the first sign of a root (called the **radicle**) shows. Soon the **plumule** follows which is really the young shoot or stem of the plant (see Figure 5-4). There are two different types of emergence from the seed. These two forms of germination are known as epigeous germination and hypogeous germination.

**EMERGENCE FROM THE SEED**

In **epigeous germination**, the seed leaves or cotyledons emerge, turn green (usually) and actively behave as green leaves. With **hypogeous germination**, the cotyledons remain in the seed coat under the soil surface. Food stored in either cotyledons or endosperm (if present) supplies the nutrition required by the young plant before it has leaves

and can begin photosynthesizing. Pea seeds demonstrate hypogeous germination, whereas bean **seeds** demonstrate epigeous germination.

Seed germination of monocotyledons is slightly different. Seeds stay submerged and a single green blade emerges which contains a protective cap (**coleoptile**) for the first 10 to 12 hours. The germination of corn seed illustrates this type of germination.

Each plant Species has its own specific requirements as to optimum temperature, moisture, and light requirements for germination. It is advisable to obtain specific growth requirement information before attempting to sow seeds of a plant that you are unfamilar with. On the back of purchased seed packages, specific information is detailed including depth of seeding, best time to sow, temperature and light requirements, and so on. Detailed information can also be obtained from books like those listed at the end of this lesson.

## SOME SPECIAL TREATMENTS OF SEED PRIOR TO SOWING

Certain plants require a cold, dormant period before they can be germinated. Some seeds may be difficult to germinate at first, but may easily germinate after a certain period of time has elapsed. This time period may be a month or a couple of years depending on the particular plant Species. Cotoneaster seed will take from five to six years to germinate if sown without special pre-seeding treatment. Waiting five years for a seed to germinate is not practical, especially for a nursery owner. This is an example of delayed dormancy which is especially prevalent in the Rosaceae Family.

## TREATMENT FOR SEEDS WITH A HARD SEED COAT AND OTHER BARRIERS TO GERMINATION

The seed cannot germinate until the seed coat is broken and water can enter. There are several ways to rupture the seed coat including mechanical scarification, acid scarification and warm-moist scarification. To remove other barriers to germination, such as the presence of growth inhibitors or an immature embryo, seeds are stratified (moist-chilling treatment).

### MECHANICAL SCARIFICATION

This can be done by scratching the surface of a hard seed coat with sandpaper or a fine file. Large nurseries use turning drums lined with carborundum powder to achieve scarification. The amount of scarification is dependent on the thickness and hardness of the coat which varies from Species to Species. Over-treatment will damage the seed, so caution is advised.

### ACID SCARIFICATION

Hydrochloric or sulfuric acid (in high concentrations) is used to etch part of the seed coat. The concentration of the acid and the time of treatment are interrelated, that is, the stronger the concentration, the less time required for treatment and vice versa. Hard-coated seeds should be floated on a thin layer of acid contained in a broad, shallow container (like a saucer). When acid scarification is completed, the seeds should be thoroughly rinsed outside in a sieve under a stream of cold water. Acid can cause bad burns, therefore, this method of scarification is not recommended unless experience, facilities and skill warrants its use.

### WARM-MOIST SCARIFICATION

Seeds from roses, peaches, plums, apples, pears and many other kinds of plants, require a warm, moist treatment to break the seed coat. Seed is mixed with equal amounts of coarse, wet sand and placed in a suitable box with alternating layers of moist peat. Be sure that these layers remain moist. Store in a warm place for several months away from mice - mice love to eat seeds. Seed coats become softened through the action of micro-organisms.

### STRATIFICATION

Stratification is a method of handling imbibed dormant seeds to remove internal barriers to germination. The term originated from the practice of placing the seeds in stratified layers interspersed with a moist medium such as soil, sand or peat. The usual stratification temperature is about 5°C. For this reason, the term 'moist-chilling' is used as a synonym for stratification.

### EMBRYO DORMANCY

Although some seeds look fully developed, the internal embryo development process is only partially complete. This provides a natural safeguard to prevent premature germination from occurring. This dormancy can usually be overcome by either pre-chilling (stratification) of the seed prior to seeding or by adding heat treatment, depending on the type of seed. Some seeds will require both the heat and the chilling treatments. Others may require darkness to break dormancy.

### PREPARING THE SEEDBED

When the seed is ready to be sown, the seedbed needs to be prepared.

'Seedbed' refers to any soil surface in which seed can be sown, including a simple clay pot, as well as a large nursery seedbed. The requirements of a good seedbed are:

- it should hold moisture well
- it should be able to drain excess moisture quickly and thereby remain well aerated
- it should contain sufficent nutrition for the young plants if the intention is to keep plants in there longer than the normal pricking out stage
- it should be free of harmful organisms and weed seeds
- it should have a good structure and not compact after some pressure has been applied

The type of seedbed to prepare will depend on the type of seeds to be sown. If one plans to grow tree seedlings such as oak, spruce, or pine, the seedbed should be tilled as the plants will be kept there for a relatively long period of time and will put down deep roots. Organic matter should be incorporated into the top part of the seedbed and a slow-release fertilizer (such as Osmocote) may be incorporated before planting (see Plant Nutrition lesson, RELEASE AND SOLUBILITY). Nurseries and commercial operators sterilize the soil with steam or fumigate between crops to eliminate weeds and diseases. A weed and disease free medium for growing seeds should be used regardless of the container being used.

### CHOOSING A SUITABLE CONTAINER

In the past, selecting a container meant choosing the right size of clay pot. Today, however, plastic pots are available in a wide range of sizes and shapes. There are pros and cons to both plastic and clay pots. Clay is a porous material, baked at high temperatures and will absorb a tremendous amount of water the first time it is used. Always submerge clay pots in tepid water for at least a half pots in tepid water for at least a half hour before using. Clay pots do tend to have higher soil surface evaporation rates than plastic pots and will, therefore, keep a more constant temperature when used under high light levels (germinating seeds with a piece of glass on the top of the pot, for example). There can also be a detrimental effect when a clay pot is kept in a drafty location and the soil temperature remains cooler than required by the plant. Salts from water and fertilizer tend to accumulate over a period of time in clay pots; this is due to the porosity of clay. Some plants, such as the African Violet are especially sensitive to high salt concentrations and should only be grown in plastic pots. For the purpose of seeding, a new container is best. Always wash out any container (new or old) with bleach and several rinsings of clear water before use. This method will kill or reduce the number of disease causing organisms that may be present; seedlings are very susceptible to many diseases. If many small pots are used (as opposed to one large container such as a flat) some control over disease spread can be achieved. Small pots, however, will dry out faster than large ones. Drainage holes in the bottom of the container are advisable. Broken clay pot pieces, stones, or styrofoam beads can be placed over the holes to keep the growing medium from washing out.

## SOWING MEDIUM

Moss peat is readily available at reasonable prices and is recommended for use as a component in the growing medium. It has very good moisture retaining properties and also tends to acidify a mixture. It can help to buffer the alkalinity of the soil water. Sand makes an excellent drainage material, although the quality of the sand is important. Most sand, even that labeled as a 'washed' sand, contains varying amounts of fine silt. Silt can form a hard crust on the surface of the medium and may hamper the emergence of seedlings. An Edmonton company, called 'Sil-Silica' is a source of sand which is practically dust and silt free (**7 grade**). It is a relatively inexpensive and suitable grade of sand for horticultural purposes.

An example of a sowing mixture consists of three parts loam, two parts moss peat, and two parts sand. It should be mixed well and put through a screen to remove the coarser material which can be used as a bottom layer in the container. The rest of the container should be filled with the sieved medium to about 2 cm (3/4 in.) from the top of the container. The medium around the sides of the container should be pressed down firmly and any depressions filled with additional medium.

There are numerous commercial mixes available, many using a large amount of peat and/or vermiculite. They are sold sterilized, so can be put directly into containers. There are many **soilless** medium mixes listed in horticultural publications, such as the John Innes mixture from the John Innes Institute in England, the U.C. mix designed at the University of California, and the Cornell mix from Cornell University. Local loams are unique to the area they come from, therefore, loam from Edmonton will vary greatly from British Columbian loam.

Much of the local loam contains large amounts of weed seeds and may contain residues from herbicides. Soilless mixes, therefore, are becoming more and more widely used. Pure vermiculite and perlite are often used as media for germinating seeds and are usually sterile, so subsequent sterilization is not necessary.

Weed seeds can be very troublesome in seedbeds. Some germinate quickly and play havoc with the carefully prepared surface of the seedbed, and will compete with the emerging seedlings for space, water, and nutrients. Steam sterilization usually kills weed seeds. However, for the home gardener, such sterilization is difficult. Steam sterilization can also damage the organic contents of the soil. Moss peat has been subjected to high temperatures prior to packing. Vermiculite and perlite are also heated in their manufacturing process, thus making soilless mixes popular due to reduced problems from weeds and diseases. Some people apply a fungicide to the medium before seeding to prevent diseases from developing. Like all chemicals, fungicides should be handled with extreme caution. Care should be taken not to have children or animals touch or eat treated seed. It is advisable to wash your hands before and after seeding since commercial seed is often treated with fungicides.

## SEEDING

Some seeds are large enough to be picked up with the fingers and evenly placed on the medium with sufficient space between seeds to avoid overcrowding and competition among young plants. Smaller seeds can be mixed with sand and the mixture sprinkled over the surface of the medium to obtain an even distribution. Try to keep seeds away from the very edges of the container - they dry out quickly. Once the seeds have been placed, you can cover them with a layer of sand or finely sieved medium. As a general rule, the optimal depth of planting is about two times the diameter of the seed.

## WATER AND THE GERMINATING SEEDS

The availability of sufficient moisture is one of the conditions for successful germination; excess moisture can adversely affect it. It is advisable to pre-wet the medium after you have mixed the ingredients (moss peat is very difficult to wet). There are commercial wetting agents available, however the same compounds may also cause the water to evaporate from the medium more rapidly. Hot water is better to use than cold, but all media must be allowed to cool before use. A medium is sufficently wet when it can be formed into a ball that will crumble when tapped lightly with a finger. After sowing, the container should be put into a sink or basin with about 5 cm (2 in) of water, and allowed to soak for about an hour or until you can visibly see that the seedbed has darkened with the absorption of water. Allow the container to drain. The medium should not require additional moisture until the seeds have germinated. However, if it does require addtional water, repeat the soak method. Do not sprinkle water onto the surface. Watering from the top will only encourage disease-causing organisms to grow on the wet surface.

It is not practical (or possible) to remove a nursery seedbed and soak it in the sink! Therefore, it is advisable to moisten the seedbed well before sowing, and to compact the soil surface with a flat piece of wood.

Clay pots used for seeding can be placed in about 5 cm (2 in) of moist soil or moss peat. This helps keep moisture levels constant.

Make sure that the soil temperature is high enough to encourage germination. The warm season crops will not germinate if the soil temperature is below 15°C. Cold water (below 15°C) applied to a growing media can effectively reduce the soil temperature and hamper or delay germination (eg., Petunia: 20°C). Therefore, use lukewarm water to wet the growing media. A piece of clear plastic or glass over the container may help retain both heat and moisture. Lift the cover and allow stale air to escape, but do not allow the condensed water droplets that have formed on the cover to drop onto the seedbed.

## PROBLEMS WHICH MAY BE ENCOUNTERED WITH SOWING AND GERMINATION

### POOR PRACTICES
Poor practices are those methods and techniques which cause rather than alleviate problems incurred during germination. Some of these problems include:

• seed planted too shallow — young plants dry out immediately after germination
• seed planted too deep, especially small seed — the leaves may not make it to the surface before the supply of energy in the seed is depleted
• low temperature — soil temperature should be in the optimal range for the kind of seed planted
• soil is kept too wet — seeds start to germinate but rot away due to excessive moisture
• soil is too dry and too hot — seedlings may die

### DISEASES
Diseases can often be prevented or curbed by immediate action, before an outbreak occurs. Problems can arise from the presence of disease-causing organisms, particularly fungal infections.

There are a group of fungal infections which can kill germinating seeds and young plants. In the trade, such fungal attacks are known as **damping off**. There are four organisms chiefly responsible for damping off: *Botrytis*, *Pythium*, *Rhizoctonia*, and *Phytophthora*. These fungi can exist on the surface of damp soils, especially soils with a combination of high organic content and moisture (as is the case in nurseries). The spores (reproductive organs of fungi) can be found in most fresh water, including the municipal drinking water. Spores can also be transmitted through the air so the need for cleanliness in and around the seedling nursery becomes apparent. Seed can also carry spores. Seed cleaning processes eliminate some of the spores, but others can still be present on the seed coat.

The symptoms of damping off include a girdling of the seedling stem at the soil level, which will make the plant topple over. The infection spreads very quickly from one site to another, so digging out the infected area can often stop the spread of the disease. Frequent inspection of the seedbed is necessary to stop disease at the outset.

Earlier in the lesson, it was stated that seedbeds should not be watered until seedlings have emerged. When soaking the seedbed by subirrigation methods as given above, water will rise to the surface and, if any water-carried spores are present, they will be filtered out by the soil. As long as spores stay below the soil surface, the chance of infection is reduced. Try not to touch the seedbed with your hands after seeding and watering - this will reduce the likelihood of contamination and spread. Seeds can also be disinfected by washing with a weak solution of bleach (one part bleach to nine parts water = 10% bleach solution). Fungicides (eg., Thiram 75%) can also be used as per directions on the container. Commercially prepared seed is usually treated with fungicide, and if non-treated seed is required, it must be specially ordered. Since damping off prefers moist conditions, covering the seeds with sand is recommended as sand does not retain moisture to the degree peat or loam does. It is very helpful to heat sand used in covering the seed to minimize introduction of fungal spores. The reflective properties of light colored sand helps to keep the seedbed slightly cooler in hot weather and prevents excess evaporation and unwanted cooling.

## SOIL STERILIZATION
Soils and other growing media are sterilized for a number of reasons. Pathogenic organisms (either fungal or bacterial) are usually present in unsterilized soil. Other pests may also be present in the soil, including nematodes (eelworms), insects and their larvae or eggs, weeds and/or weed seeds.

Soil sterilization can be achieved by several methods in order to destroy organisms but heat treatments are the most effective. The soil must be heated to a temperature of 82°C and maintained at this temperature for a minimum of 20 minutes. At this temperature, most weed seeds are killed. Insects are killed at temperatures of about 60-70°C. Because damping off fungi are difficult to kill, temperatures may have to exceed 82°C. However, it may not be necessary to subject the soil to such high temperatures if problems with other fungi, insects, or weed seeds have not previously existed. The lower temperature might best be used so that the soil structure and organic matter are not affected and damping off can be controlled by cultural or chemical methods. This often requires special equipment (steam for example). There are small, electrical soil sterilizers available that can handle small amounts of soil, but they are expensive. Some people have tried to 'cook' their soil, with extra water mixed in, but have found that there is more chance of infection with fungi and bacteria because of the large amount of water left in the soil after treatment.

## PRICKING OUT OR TRANSPLANTING YOUNG SEEDLINGS
Tiny seed that has been broadcast over the surface will result in plants growing very close together in the seedbed. These plants are unable to develop fully due to overcrowding. Once seedlings have reached the two-leaf stage in growth, they require removal from the seedbed and should be planted into fresh soil with more growing space. Removal and transplanting from the seedbed (**pricking out**) will remedy the situation. Those plants removed can be transplanted into flats or pots. Plants develop much stronger and more extensive root systems once they have recovered from the shock of pricking out. There is some root damage from pricking out; however, the plant responds by growing more roots which aid in the uptake of water and nutrients. Proper spacing of the young plants is critical.

Many gardeners use peat pots which can be planted directly into the ground. A **dibbler** (a flat wooden stick) or anything else that will serve the purpose of separating the young plants from the seedbed and each other can be used for pricking out. Transfer the young plants directly from the seedbed to the new container. Hold the young plant gently by its cotyledon; never grasp it by the stem. The new container should have a small hole prepared in the soil into which the plant can be gently placed. With the tip of one finger, gently compact soil around the plant. Be sure the roots make good contact with the surrounding soil, then spray the transplants with a fine mist of water to aid in moisture retention. The plant has gone through a very traumatic experience in pricking out but will usually recover soon. Do not be discouraged if a few transplants die, as good pricking out techniques are acquired by practice.

It is generally recommended that the air temperature be kept cool and the soil temperature kept warm while the plant is recovering. Keep the plant out of direct sunlight for at least three to four days after transplanting.

## HARDENING OFF PRIOR TO PLANTING OUT

Plants do not take kindly to drastic temperature changes, so do not take a plant that has been on the warm window sill in the kitchen and put it out into the garden. Young seedlings that have been raised in protected conditions will have soft tender tissues that can be easily damaged by dry winds and extreme temperatures. Plants can adapt gradually to cooler temperatures by hardening their tissues. However, the final degree of hardening is determined by the type of plant and the particular growing conditions prevailing. To acclimatize the young plants to the great outdoors, **gradual exposure is the key to survival**. Dropping temperatures gradually while slowly increasing the light intensity — use of shading material, then gradually withdrawing it for parts of the day, to final removal of it — is the process of hardening off the plant. The use of cold frames is popular for hardening off plants gradually, as are heated cold frames, greenhouses, or the use of plastic (see Climate lesson, Figure 2-11 Plants in small containers will dry out quicker outdoors; and if the plants are subjected to rainfall, excessive leaching of nutrients may occur.

## ATYPICAL SEXUAL PROPAGATION

### ORCHIDS
Both Orchids and ferns demonstrate atypical propagation. Orchids are members of the Orchidaceae Family, one of the largest plant Families with over 600 Genera and more than 1700 Species. Intergeneric hybrids are reasonably common, partly due to the fact that there is often not a great difference in chromosomal counts amongst the various Genera. For example, Cattleya, Cymbidium, Dendrobium, Paphiopedilum, and Stanhopea each have twenty chromosomes.

Without much background in genetics, it is easy to understand how accidental pollination between Genera can occur. Some such bigeneric hybrids of Orchids are Laeliocattleaya (Laelia x Cattleya), Orchiplantanthera (Planthera x Orchis) and Brassocattleya (Brassavola x Cattleya). When the parentage of hybrids is listed between brackets, the first name is the **pollen receiving** plant. Hybrids usually resemble the mother plant but also display characteristics of the pollen contributing plant.

An obvious feature of an Orchid flower is its apparent lack of style, ovary and anthers. These parts are present, however, and fertilization does occur. The stigma area is usually no more than a glossy surface area on one of the parts of the flower which could be mistaken for a petal and serves as the style. True anthers are absent but a pair of structures called **pollinia** are the special type of pollen grain carriers found only in Orchids. The flower is carried by a stem-like structure which also serves as the ovary. Often, this structure will make a 180° turn just before the flower bud opens. Such Orchids, therefore, are really upside-down flowers. This Orchid ovary initially bears little resemblance to typical plant ovaries. After pollination, the flower usually deteriorates rapidly and the ovary becomes darker green and slowly increases in size.

The seeds usually take a long time to mature. Some native Orchids, however, produce seed within a few weeks. Tropical Orchids may take up to two or more years to produce seed. For many years, Orchid seed was considered to be sterile as it was thought impossible to germinate from seeds. A French botanist, Noel Bernard, established that Orchid seed required a symbiotic relation with certain micro-organisms to initiate germination. These micro-organisms were fungi; many are Species of the Genus *Rhizoctonia* which is also responsible for damping off in other plants. Each Species of Orchid may rely on one specific fungus. Orchid seeds are some of the tiniest seeds known. The seed consists of only the embryo, surrounded by a small, transparent, protective membrane. The lack of endosperm, or other food storage tissues found in other plants, prevents the Orchid seed from germinating without the aid of such a symbiotic fungus. When the particular fungus was isolated and combined with the seed in a culture medium, germination took place. Therefore, if seeds are sown in the same pot as the original mother plant which contains the fungus, seeds will germinate.

There is an easier way to propagate Orchids thanks to the work of the American scientist, Knudson, who found that the main function of the symbiotic fungus was to provide carbohydrates and other nutrients. He determined that the nutrient requirements could be provided in a specially prepared culture material. Knudson's (or Orchid) agar is available from scientific supply houses. When working with agar and tissue culture (see TISSUE CULTURE), a supply of glassware, and other laboratory equipment is required. The medium must be kept sterile, and disinfecting the fine seeds requires special training and experience. Germination is usually rapid but fully developed young plants will take months to produce. There is often a need to prick out plants into aseptic bottles to maintain the culture by supplying additional nutrients and growth promoting materials. Commercial Orchid growers sometimes offer seedlings for sale in bottles. This described method, as well as plant division, were the only methods of Orchid propagation until the introduction of tissue culture. There are many Orchid growers worldwide. Contact one of the Orchid Societies for more information.

### FERNS
In the classification of plants (see Botany lesson, CLASSIFICATION HIERARCHY), the division of Pteridophyta — ferns — is a relatively old group of plants compared to the Spermatophyta — seed plants. The ferns differ in many respects from the seed plants, especially in their reproductive method. Many ferns have creeping rootstocks which may be growing underground (eg., Ostrich fern - *Matteuccia struthiopteris*), but there are ferns with rootstocks that creep over the soil surface and send up shoots or fronds. Such rhizomatous rootstocks can be detached from the mother plant and used as propagation material (eg.,

**Figure 5-5**
**LIFE CYCLE OF A FERN**

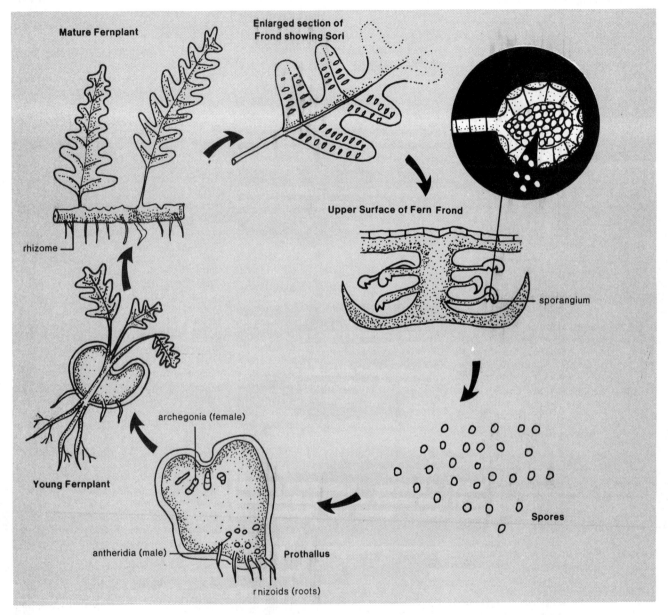

Boston fern - *Nephrolepis*, and *Davallia*). Ferns that produce thick clumps of fronds can easily be propagated by division; simply break or cut the clump into two or three pieces and repot (eg., Maidenhair fern - *Adiantum*). The Boston fern never produces spores and must be propagated this way. There are some ferns which form small bulbils or plantlets on their mature fronds (eg., Mother fern - *Asplenium viviparum* and *Asplenium bulbosum*); simply remove the bulbils and plant them in soil. Some

Hawaiian tree ferns (*Cibotium*) produce small side shoots with woody trunks. Carefully remove the shoots, plant into moist sand or fine gravel, and they will root and grow.

When studying the older fronds of many ferns, one will find many brown bumps on the underside of the fronds. These bumps are **sori** and are dense groups of spore cases (sporangia) which contain spores. Some ferns (such as the Ostrich fern) produce irregular looking, fertile

fronds. Each of the spores is a unicellular (one-celled) reproductive organ. When the spores start to grow, they will produce a small, green, leaf-like structure called the **prothallus** which is not much larger than a small pin head. The sexual organs of the fern are formed on the surface of the prothallus. The organs representing the male part are called **antheridia** and the female counterparts are called **archegonia**. In the presence of a thin film of water on the surface of the prothallus, the male sperm (from the antheridia) swim to the archegonia and fertilization can occur. A young fern plant is produced when an embryo is formed.

Sexual propagation of ferns is not difficult. Obtain a fern which will produce sori on the underside of the frond. These sori may look like small warts, however, each sorus is characteristic of the Species to which it belongs. Often the sori are along the margin of the frond, as is the case in *Adiantum* and *Pteris*. When the sori start to turn a light brown color remove the frond from the plant and store it in a paper bag, at a temperature of 21-24°C. Do not store in a plastic bag as the spores will stick to the plastic surface and will be hard to collect. When the spores are mature, they will fall from the sori. It is best to sow spores while they are fresh.

Prepare a soil mixture with a rather high water-holding capacity (one with high peat content) and fill several sterilized containers with medium. Sterilization is important to eliminate weed seeds and moss spores that could be present. Sterilize containers with a 10 per cent bleach solution, followed by several rinses with clean water. Keep the surface of the medium about 2 cm (3/4 in) below the edge of the pot. Level off the surface and compact the surface more than is usually done in typical seedbed production. Distribute the spores evenly on the surface away from the edges. Do not cover the spores, and keep the container moist and relatively warm (24°C). Cover the container with a pane of glass that has been sterilized with the bleach solution too. Cellophane or plastic wrap can also be used to seal the containers.

The light intensity required for the spores to develop is very low. Three sheets of newspaper over the top of the glass will let enough light through. The development of the prothallus is rapid; some Species will produce them in five to nine days. Prothallia manifest themselves as a solid green growth on the soil surface, so do not think that algae has invaded the pot and throw it out! Three or four days after the first prothallia are observed, spray the surface with a fine mist of distilled water (cooled down boiled water will do). Use a regular houseplant spray mist bottle for this purpose. Keep the paper on the glass until small plants are visible. Gradually remove the paper a sheet at a time, at intervals of four days. After removing the first sheet of paper, insert something under the glass to elevate it slightly to start hardening off the young plants. Remove the glass with the last sheet of newspaper. When the young ferns are 2-5 cm (1-2 in) high, small clumps can be removed and pricked out into small pots.

Cross-breeding of closely related ferns is possible, but largely experimental. Mixing of spores can be done by putting fronds from different ferns into the same bag and following the rest of the procedures. At the stage where the fertilization takes place on the prothallus, some of the sperm may end up on the 'wrong' prothallus; simply sow the spores very close together in hopes of this 'error' occurring. Do not expect startling results but do not get discouraged. Successful cross-breeding may only become apparent once the plants get larger.

## ADVANTAGES AND DISADVANTAGES OF SEXUAL PROPAGATION

Sexual propagation involves the use of seeds. A slight variation is found amongst ferns; they can be propagated sexually by means of their spores.

### ADVANTAGES OF SEXUAL PROPAGATION

• convenient when seeds are readily available

• quick and easy method to produce a large number of plants when seeds are readily available

• may be the only practical method for plants that cannot be easily propagated vegetatively

• it is a method of obtaining plants free from viral infections as most viruses are not transmitted by seed

• it is the most common method of producing new plants

### DISADVANTAGES OF SEXUAL PROPAGATION

• many cultivars of trees, shrubs, and perennials are hybrids and do not reproduce true from seed

• certain plants are slow to reach maturity if grown from seed (this last point is of great importance to commercial growers as time and space represents money)

## ASEXUAL PROPAGATION

Asexual propagation takes many forms such as division by the use of rhizomes, offsets of bulbs, tubers, tuberous roots, and pseudobulbs. Another form of asexual propagation is layering and includes air, mound (or stool), tip, or simple layering. Cuttings are a very common form and use stems, leaves, leaf tips, leaf buds, and root parts of a plant. Grafting and budding, and separation are still other forms of asexual propagation.

Before discussing the various methods of asexual propagation, there are a number of botanical details concerning the function and anatomy of plants that should be discussed. It is essential for plants to have a sufficient number of roots to take up adequate water and elements necessary for growth. Many of the asexual propagation methods are concerned with stimulating the plant to form roots, and success is subject to the plant's ability to develop roots in a short period of time. In order to be successful, a propagator must correctly determine the type of propagation, timing and material to use. Some botanical recognition of plant parts is necessary.

The two types of plants normally propagated are - angiosperms and gymnosperms (see Botany lesson). **Gymnosperms** include plants such as pine, spruce, juniper, and larix. **Angiosperms** comprise the largest group of plants worldwide. The distinction between the two groups will become apparent when discussing budding and grafting. Amongst the angiosperms are two main categories; dicots and monocots.

Figure 5-6

## ROOT TIP WITH ROOT HAIRS AND CORK LAYER

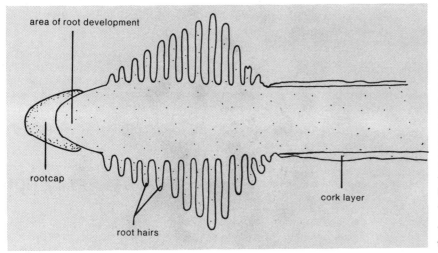

(which do not have the corky tissue) will be able to absorb water through the root hairs. It is of utmost importance that as little damage is done to the root as possible while transplanting. Water and nutrients are transported throughout the plant by means of the **xylem**. The xylem tissue in mature wood soon dies but remains functional. When propagating, it is important to know if a part of a plant that is removed for propagating is able to take up water. Plants can lose moisture through their leaves and water is used in the plant's metabolic processes. When taking a part of a plant away from the parent plant, it is beneficial to provide sufficient moisture to the exposed lower stem tissue, to keep the humidity high, and to limit the amount of direct light reaching the plant.

Vascular tissue is also used in transporting sugars produced by the plant leaves to other areas in the plant (such as the fruits or roots for storage). This tissue is called **phloem**. Both xylem and phloem tissues grow throughout the life of the plant. Because of this growth, dicot plants display increasing stem diameter when they become older and larger. The origin of this constantly expanding vascular system is a tissue called the **cambium**. The cambium is a nonspecialized tissue that can form both xylem and phloem tissues. Cambium is

## DICOTS AND MONOCOTS

Dicots or dicotyledons have leaf veins that are not parallel. The flowers have parts in multiples of four or five (see Botany lesson, DICOTS). The critical difference between monocots and dicots for propagation purposes concerns the vascular systems.

Plants take up water and nutrients through their roots and, more specifically, through their root hairs near the root tips (see Figure 5-6). Most mature roots are protected by a layer of thin corky tissue. There is, therefore, very little water uptake by mature roots. Only the extreme tip of young roots

Figure 5-7

## COMPARISON OF A YOUNG PLANT STEM WITH A MATURE PLANT STEM

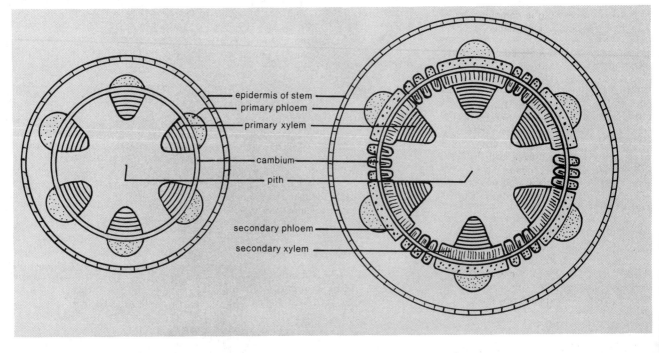

epidermis of stem
primary phloem
primary xylem
cambium
pith
secondary phloem
secondary xylem

## Figure 5-8
### COMPARISON BETWEEN YOUNG MONOCOT AND DICOT STEMS

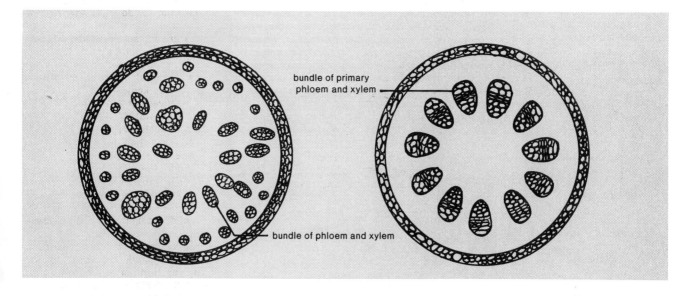

bundle of primary
phloem and xylem

bundle of phloem and xylem

located between the xylem and the phloem (see Figure 5-7). If you accidently back the car into a tree and scrape part of the tree bark, you will observe that over the years, the damaged part of the tree will heal over. This is due to the formation of wound tissue (or **callus**) that is induced by the cambium. Whenever a stem or leaf is damaged, the callus tissue will provide protection for the exposed tissue. The callus tissue formation of the cambium is important for many methods of propagation. After making cuttings, for example, callus forms on the cut and, after the inital healing is complete, roots can grow out of the callus tissue.

Monocots, or monocotyledons include corn, all cereals (wheat, barley, etc), grasses, sedges, lilies, tulips, daffodils, crocuses, amaryllis, palm trees, dieffenbachia, and others. These plants share some common characteristics although they do not visibly resemble each other at first glance. They often have strap shaped leaves with parallel veins. When the flowers are fully developed, the flower parts are in multiples of three (see Botany lesson, MONOCOTS).

Monocots have little or no secondary stem thickening. They have scattered bundles of xylem and phloem in their stems as opposed to the orderly ring arrangement inside the stems of dicots. This arrangement explains why there is no secondary thickening in monocots (see Figure 5-8).

## ASEXUAL REPRODUCTION

Many plants are able to multiply and spread by means of asexual or vegetative reproduction. Asexual reproduction makes use of plant parts that are removed from the mother plant and, when given the right conditions, will root and become independent young plants. Root formation, in many instances, need not be induced because roots have already formed while still attached to the mother plant. Asexual reproduction produces young plants which are identical to the mother plant. Some of the more common methods of asexual reproduction follow.

### RUNNERS (Stolons)
Some plants produce shoots which naturally form young plants at the end of the shoot or at the nodes. These shoots are properly called **stolons** and can be detached when there is evidence of root formation. Strawberry is a plant commercially propagated by the use of stolons. The spider plant is a house plant that produces offspring on stolons coming from the mother plant.

### SUCKERS
Suckers are shoots that arise from below ground level. To reproduce plants from suckers, they can be dug during the plant's dormant period (usually early spring). If the sucker does not have sufficient roots, some of the original root can be removed with the sucker. Raspberry is an example of a plant that can be propagated from suckers (see Figure 5-9). Be sure that only healthy plants are chosen for parent plant material.

## SEPARATION

Separation is a propagation method commonly applied to bulbs. Bulbs are really compacted plants, with the base (where the roots are attached) carrying the leaves in a circular manner. At the base of these leaves, buds form which give rise to daughter bulbs. These daughter bulbs become distinct and separable bulbs after each year of growth (eg., tulips) or may take several years to develop within the mother bulb (eg., narcissus). Tulips usually produce one large bulb, which will flower the next year, plus three or more small bulbs all loosely attached to what was the base of the mother bulb. These small bulbs, attached to the base, produce only a leaf or two the next year but can be grown in a separate bed to enlarge over a year or two until big enough to flower. Do not remove the leaves from any kind of bulb after it has finished flowering. It is from these leaves that energy is drawn for growth of the bulb and development of flowers for the next season.

Figure 5-9

## THE ORIGIN OF SUCKERS FROM A TREE ROOT

Figure 5-10

## CORM OF GLADIOLUS

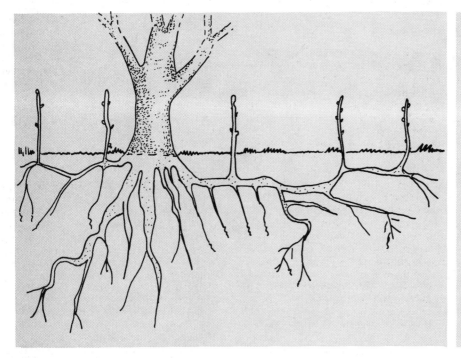

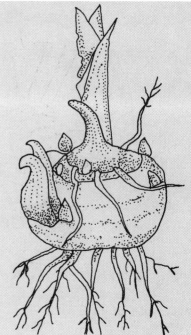

Some lilies form large numbers of bulblets around their stem, below soil level. These bulblets can be removed and planted out, and will eventually form mature flowering plants. Some lilies will produce bulbils in the leaf axes. The bulbils can be collected and grown in a shallow bulb nursery bed (see Botany lesson, BULBLETS).

### CORMS

Corms are underground swollen stems containing several buds (eg., gladiolus and crocus). The mature flowering corm exhausts its reserves the year of flowering, however, new corms will be found adhering to the remnants of the parent when they are harvested. Some small cormlets (cormels) may also form and, like the bulblets, can be sown and allowed to enlarge. The cormlets eventually flower from fully mature corms (see Figure 5-10).

### SCOOPING

If the base of a hyancith bulb is cut with a cross-shaped mark (or hollowed out) and placed upside down for several months, numerous small bulbils will form on the damaged section (see Figure

5-11). These small bulbils can also be grown in a shallow bulb nursery bed (see SEPARATION). The following information refers to Figure 5-11 and outlines the process of scooping.

1. Retain the hyacinth after it has finished flowering and allow the leaves to turn yellow naturally.
2. Take a sharp knife and make a number

of deep scores over the bottom of the bulb. Place the bulb upside down in a pot with dry sand.
3. Keep in a cool dark place for up to three months until bulbils are observable. Remove the bulbils and plant in a bulb nursery. It will take up to three years before they flower. The hyacinth is a perennial bulb and will not always successfully overwinter

Figure 5-11

## SCOOPED AND SCORED HYACINTH BULB

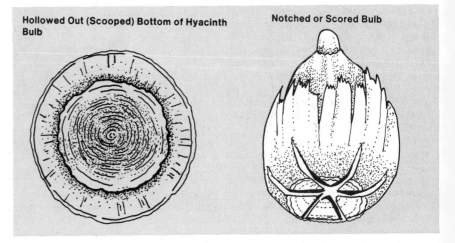

Hollowed Out (Scooped) Bottom of Hyacinth Bulb

Notched or Scored Bulb

## Figure 5-12
### DIVISION OF RHIZOMATOUS ROOTS (IRIS)

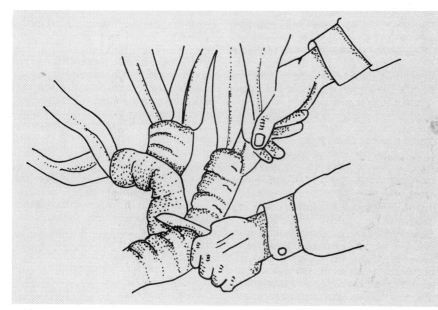

## Figure 5-13
### TUBEROUS ROOT

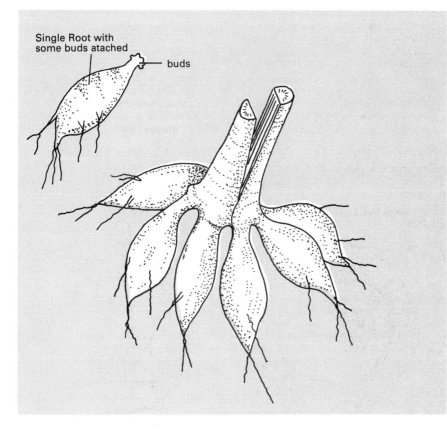

Single Root with some buds atached

buds

outdoors. The hyacinth, therefore, is not a commonly grown bulb in Alberta.

## DIVISION

Many plants produce rhizomes, tubers, tuberous roots or numerous underground shoots that remain attached to the parent plant for a period of time. To propagate such plants, simply remove one of the shoots and grow it as an individual plant (see Figure 5-12). Usually, the number of roots present is limited, but removal of the shoot usually stimulates more rooting.

### RHIZOMES
Rhizomes are stems that grow below ground. Stem tissue is able to produce buds and shoots which can grow upright through the soil surface and develop into plants. To reproduce the plants, simply cut the rhizomes off and plant in another site. Some garden examples are Rhizomatous iris and Lily of the Valley (*Convallaria majalis*)

### CROWNS
Many plants produce a large number of buds or shoots around the original parent plant. These shoots are referred to as crowns. Many herbaceous perennials, including chrysanthemums and rhubarb, can be propagated by carefully removing a shoot and some of the root, then planting in a pot. Many large perennial plants should be dug up every four to five years and the healthy, vigorous outer part of their crowns replanted to maintain healthy plants.

### OFFSETS OR OFFSHOOTS
Offsets or offshoots are similar to crowns except they do not arise from below the soil surface but from the stem above ground level. They also produce roots and will, when removed with a sharp knife, readily develop as separate plants. Many succulents display such behavior. Bromeliads, for example, produce offshoots that will replace the parent plant. The parent plant of a Bromeliad dies after it has completed the flowering process.

### TUBERS AND TUBEROUS ROOTS
Tubers display nodes and buds (eyes), whereas tuberous roots do not have eyes. Tubers can be dug up and cut into several sections, provided each section has an eye from which a shoot will be

## Figure 5-14
## TIP LAYERING OF RASPBERRY

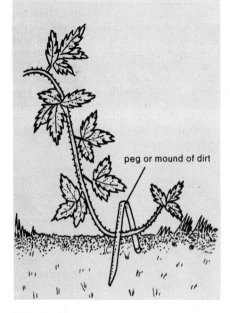

peg or mound of dirt

produced. Potatoes are tubers that are propagated by cutting and planting pieces with eyes. With tuberous roots, there must always be a small piece of stem section adhering to the upper part of the root. The new shoot develops from this part of the propagule. Dahlias are propagated this way. Tuberous begonias, when dormant, can be cut in halves or quarters, and propagated by planting the pieces. Each section must contain a bud or shoot (see Figure 5-13).

### PSEUDOBULBS
Some tropical Orchids produce swollen sections on the stem with a few leaves on the top. When removed, they can form roots and give rise to new plants. There are many Orchid Species but not all can be reproduced from pseudobulbs.

### LAYERING
Layering takes place naturally when a branch comes in contact with the soil or hangs into water, thereby promoting root formation. It is easy to imitate such a condition by bending a branch down towards the ground and tying or pegging it in that position (see Figure 5-14), with

the part touching the ground covered with soil. This method of propagation is called tip layering. Tip layering is a common way to propagate raspberries and blackberries. Other layering methods include mound (stool) and air layering.

### MOUND OR STOOL LAYERING
Apple rootstock clones are produced by taking young trees of apple that have desirable characteristics and using them as rootstock (see GRAFTING). They are partly buried in raised soil beds (**stool beds**), with shoots and branches growing out. Roots will form on the shoots and provide rootstock that can be used for grafting. The remaining stump can produce additional shoots from adventitious buds and can continue producing successive crops of rootstocks for 25 years or more.

### AIR LAYERING

Roots can be encouraged to form on stems or branches of some plants while still part of the parent plant. A stem is

## Figure 5-15
## STOOLING OF YOUNG APPLE TREE

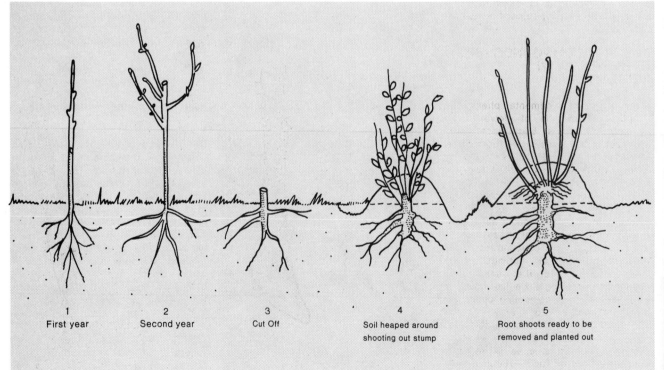

| 1 | 2 | 3 | 4 | 5 |
| --- | --- | --- | --- | --- |
| First year | Second year | Cut Off | Soil heaped around shooting out stump | Root shoots ready to be removed and planted out |

girdled just below the part where roots are desired, and the outer tissue of the stem is removed. Most of the phloem tissue will be removed when this is done, and the food supply returning to the roots will be interrupted. After the girdling, moist Sphagnum moss is wrapped around the girdled area and a layer of Cellophane or polyethylene film applied to hold the moss in place and prevent drying out. Growth regulators and metabolites will accumulate above the wound and stimulate root formation in that locality. After roots have formed, the rooted branch can be removed from the parent plant and planted. A good plant on which to practice this technique is the rubber plant (*Ficus elastica*). Older plants tend to lose their lower leaves, leaving a long stem with a few leaves on the top. Try this technique to get a short, bushy plant again.

Air layering by girdling the stem is necessary with dicot plants only. With a monocot plant, such as *Dracaena* or *Monstera*, wrapping with moist moss is sufficient to eventually produce roots. Interruption of the phloem is not possible due to the scattered distribution of the vascular tissue in monocots. When the top part of the plant is removed, water and nutrients will promote new shoot growth. Air layering is often used by commercial plant propagators of tropical house plants.

## ROOTING COMPOUNDS AND OTHER GROWTH REGULATORS

Many of the developmental phenomena in plants (formation of flower buds, development of leaf buds, roots, etc.) are influenced by chemicals (**hormones**) formed in the plant. Since their discovery in the 1930's, synthetic auxins to aid in rooting of cuttings have become useful to commercial growers. The compounds include Indole Acetic Acid (IAA), Indolbutyric acid (IBA) and Naphthalene Acetic Acid (NAA), all of which are still used in varying concentrations to promote rooting of cuttings. It is interesting to note that among the chemicals producing auxin-like activity in plant tissues is a compound called 2.4 dichlorophenoxyacetic acid, better known as 2.4-D, a chemical widely used as a herbicide. 2.4-D is an effective rooting compound if used in very low concentrations. The recommended concentration of auxins to be used for root production is variable, depending on

the type of cutting and plant material. It is advisable to observe recommendations very carefully. Most greenhouse supply companies supply rooting powder, manufactured by May and Baker (M & B) and sold under the name 'Seradix'. It is available in three concentrations: #1 for softwood cuttings (IBA 0.1%), #2 for medium softwood cuttings (IBA 0.3%), and #3 for hardwood cuttings (IBA 0.8%). A higher concentration than recommended has adverse effects, so if in doubt, use a lower concentration. 'Rootone', manufactured by Amchem, is also sold (containing IBA 0.57%). Too high a dose of Rootone can prevent cuttings from rooting.

Auxins are also used to prevent potatos from sprouting in storage, preventing flower bud loss in potted Begonias and early fruit drop in apples. Commercial growers often obtain pure auxins and make their own solution in water or ethanol (0.5 g IBA in 100 ml 95% ethanol). The use of auxins and other growth regulators (such as cytokinins, ethylene, gibberellins and many others) find more and more practical and

commercial applications, especially in the techniques of tissue culture (see TISSUE CULTURE).

Always dip freshly cut cuttings into the powder before the end dries and tap the excess powder off. It is not a good idea to dip the cutting into water before dipping it into the rooting compound as it makes a mess of the powder and far too much powder is put onto the cutting. Use a dibbler to make a hole in the propagation bed for the cutting. If the cutting is pushed into the soil, the powder may scrape off the cutting.

## CUTTINGS

Cuttings are obtained when a portion of a stem, leaf, or root is removed from the parent plant and induced under favorable conditions to form roots and, eventually, new leaves and shoots. This is the most widely adapted form of asexual propagation used commercially. There are many types of cuttings named after the part of the plant used. Some of these are root cuttings, leaf cuttings, and stem cuttings.

Figure 5-16
HEEL CUTTINGS

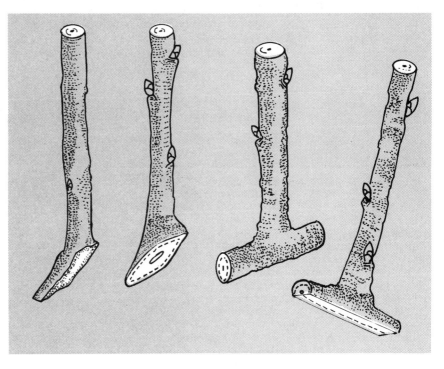

Knowledge of the vascular system of plants is important in the successful production of cuttings (see DICOTS AND MONOCOTS). Of particular importance to propagation by cuttings is the cambium because it can provide wound tissue (callus). When making cuttings, the cambium area is exposed. This callus is undifferentiated tissue and serves to prevent moisture loss from the cuttings.

### STEM CUTTINGS

Stem cuttings are made from stems of current material in varying stages of maturity: hardwood, semi-hardwood, softwood (green cuttings) and herbaceous cuttings. Stem cuttings are generally straight sections of branches from which roots are encouraged to grow. The decision as to which type of cutting should be used is dictated by the availability of material and past experience (or reference to a book on propagation methods). Some propagators have found that some plants will propagate more readily if a sliver of the older wood is included in the cutting. This sliver is called a 'heel' (see Figure 5-16). Roots will develop well using this type of cutting. Several types of cuttings may be tried to further the chances of success.

### HARDWOOD CUTTINGS

Dormant woody material (usually collected in the fall as soon as the plant, tree or shrub has dropped its leaves) is used for hardwood cuttings. The material can be stored in a cool place and later cut to the appropriate lengths in a sheltered area. The length of the cuttings is usually determined by the number of buds on a cutting. The bud immediately above the lower node is placed below soil level when the cutting is planted. A minimum of two buds is desired to 'break dormancy' when the cutting begins to grow. The optimum thickness of a hardwood cutting is about 6 to 12 mm (1/4-1/2 in) in diameter, since thin cuttings tend to dry out and thick ones may not root as well. Hardwood cuttings are often **heeled in** during the winter and planted out on site in the spring(as is the case for shelterbelt plantings). In Alberta and Arctic climates, the winter frost and cold temperatures may reduce callus tissue formation. Bundled cuttings can be stored in a cold, frost-free storage area or root cellar over the winter. The cuttings will usually have a healthy

amount of callus development on both ends by spring. The top part of the cutting will be protected from drying out by the callus and the lower part will develop roots as soon as the cuttings are planted or heeled in. Poplars (*Populus*), willows (*Salix*), alder (*Alnus*), roses (*Rosa*), and dogwood (*Cornus*) are some woody ornamentals that are produced by hardwood cuttings.

Mass production of hardwood cuttings may involve the use of a bandsaw, so bundles of cuttings are cut to a uniform length, with consideration given to the location of buds and nodes. It is advisable to keep the cuttings horizontal during storage to delay premature shooting. Hardwood cuttings from evergreen trees will only root for a limited number of Species including *Juniperus* and *Thuja*. This method is not recommended for use in dry climates due to desiccation.

### SEMI-HARDWOOD CUTTINGS

Plant material with leaves, firm stem and the start of woody tissue formation is used for semi-hardwood cuttings. The material is usually collected towards the second half of the growing season. It should be collected early in the morning when the plants are fresh and the tissues contain the maximum amount of

moisture. Keep cuttings in a cool place and away from direct sunlight; if possible collect the cuttings on a cloudy day. The length of cuttings depends on the internodal length (distance between nodes). It is best to keep two or three nodes on each cutting. The number of leaves to be retained on the cutting depends on the pattern of leaves at the node, but three or four leaves per cutting is a good target number. Certain plants with exceedingly large leaves could lose a lot of moisture through transpiration, so part of the leaves can be removed to decrease leaf surface area; simply trim the leaves by as much as one half. The leaves from the lower one or two nodes should be removed and the lower cut made on an angle just below the lowest node. Semi-hardwood cuttings should be placed into the propagation bed as soon as possible to reduce moisture loss. The medium in the bed should have good water-holding capacity. Sprinkle water over the bed after the cuttings are struck to help firm the soil around the cuttings and fill any air pockets. Place the cuttings close together to help retain humidity around them. It is advisable to keep cuttings out of direct sunlight and drafts.

Often semi-hardwood cuttings are wounded by making a longitudinal cut

### Figure 5-17
### SCOOPED LEAF BUD CUTTING

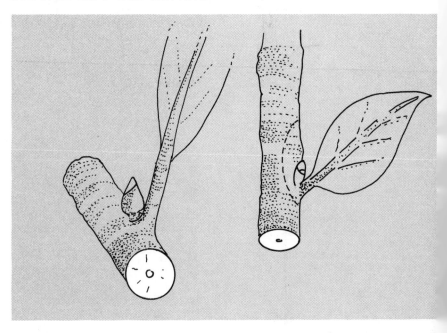

into the lower part of the stem. This will stimulate greater callus-cambium activity and will give rise to a larger number of roots. If rooting compounds are to be used, the wounding should be done before use of the compound. Cuttings will root before the end of the growing season but the buds may not break dormancy until the next season of growth. If the buds break dormancy, it is advisable to make sure the new growth has time to harden off before the cold weather arrives. Cuttings from low shrubs, which normally have little secondary thickening of the stem, should be of the semi-hardwood type to make use of the higher cambial activity of that wood. This method of propagation is used for much of our hardy outdoor material, as well as some exotic ornamentals. The indoor ornamental plants can be propagated anytime of the year in the house or greenhouse. Evergreens, like junipers (*Juniperus*) or Arborvitae (*Thuja*), propagate well by semi-hardwood cuttings taken from trees or shrubs that are vigorously growing.

A variation of semi-hardwood cuttings is the **block cutting** using cane or stem material from a plant such as the dieffenbachia. Each piece of stem should have a shoot bud and should be buried horizontally in a moist rooting medium with only the bud exposed. Young shoots and roots will appear. Keep the soil warm (23°C).

### SOFTWOOD CUTTINGS
Softwood cuttings are made from material that is actively growing and are often limited to terminal or tip cuttings. The material should be collected in the early morning or on a dark, rainy day. Cuttings should be about 10 cm (3-4 in) tall and, if cut shorter, the stem may not be strong enough and tissues may bruise too easily. Some green cuttings will root in three to four days; others take longer. Many of the commercial ornamentals, including carnations, dahlias, and many of the garden perennials are propagated this way.

Lower leaves should be removed because they can turn yellow and moldy if resting on the soil. Leaf area can be reduced to prevent excess moisture loss. Softwood cuttings can be taken when the plants are actively growing (spring and summer for outdoor material). For exotic ornamentals, year round propagation can be done, keeping in mind low light levels and shortened day length in the winter. This will slow down the growth rate and subsequent rooting rate. Artifical light can improve the situation.

Several types of plants are difficult to propagate by any method. This is due to their lack of cambial activity. The plant eventually produces roots after a long period of time and, often, the leaves fall off or the cutting dies before roots form. The invention of the mist frame has aided in the propagation of hard to root cuttings and the use of soil or bottom heat has also been helpful. The mist reduces water loss and keeps relative humidity high around the cuttings. Some plants that root well in the mist frame are clematis, apple, pear, peach, plum, maple and rose. The mist frame permits rooting under good light conditions, which has proven advantageous.

### LEAF CUTTINGS
There are a variety of ways in which the leaf of a plant can be used for propagating purposes. Only those methods which are most commonly used are discussed here.

### Figure 5-18
### REMOVING THE BUDSHIELD

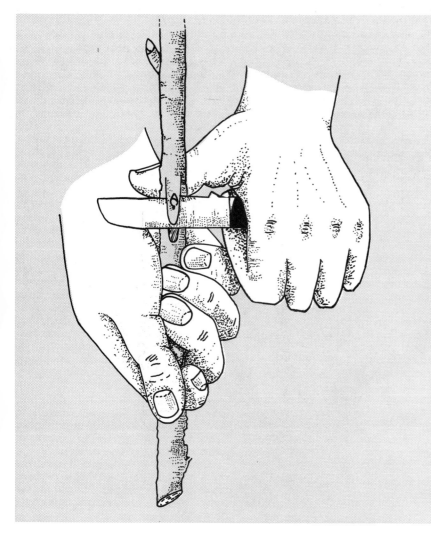

## LEAF-BUD CUTTINGS

Leaf-bud cuttings include a leaf, petiole, and short piece of the stem with an axillary bud attached. The cutting can be prepared by 'scooping' the bud from the stem (see Figure 5-18 ); rubber trees (*Ficus indica*) and hibiscus (*Hibiscus rosea*) are propagated this way. Many cuttings can be created by this method from a limited amount of plant material. An alternative is to cut short lengths of stem with a leaf and bud attached; this is called **segmenting**. The cutting is placed in the propagation bed with the stem part in the rooting medium. The leaves of the rubber plant can be rolled lengthwise and held in that position by a rubber band to help retain moisture. Moisture can also be retained by enclosing the cutting in clear plastic or cellophane. The bud on the cutting should be exposed to light to break dormancy.

## LEAF-PETIOLE CUTTINGS

African violets (*Saintpaulia ionantha*) can be propagated from leaf petiole cuttings. A healthy mature leaf, with about 2.5 cm (1 in) of petiole attached, placed in water or any growth medium will promote root development, followed by a young plant. Plants that can produce adventitious buds on their leaf petioles are able to root this way; however, many plants will produce roots on their petiole and never produce adventitious shoots. Begonia Species are examples of this. Gloxinias will produce corm-like tubers on the petiole of a leaf cutting. These 'tubers' will produce young plants the next season.

## LEAF-BLADE CUTTINGS

The leaf of a plant can be inserted into a suitable rooting mixture and will root at the same time as it produces young plantlets. Many succulent plants reproduce well this way. In fact, it is the most common way for succulent growers to build up their stock. This type of leaf cutting works well for propagating Echeveria, Crassula, Kalanchoe, Sedum and Pachyphytum. Leaves from the mother plant are broken off, allowed to dry for a few hours, then lightly pressed into a rooting mixture (a sandy mixture preferred). High light intensities speed up the rooting process. Rotting may occur if the medium is kept too wet. Commerical growers often keep the detached leaves in a cardboard box for three to four weeks before planting.

## LEAF SECTIONS

The **Begonia rex** has large colorful leaves that can be cut into 2.5 cm (1 in) squares and layed out neatly on the surface of a propagating bed filled with a peaty mixture. After producing roots, one or more young plants will grow at the edge of each leaf section. Keep a sheet of glass or plastic over the box but allow fresh air to enter at least once a day. Most of the rooting and shoot production takes place where veins are present indicating that there is cambium activity in the veins. *Gloxinia* and *Streptocarpus* (both members of the Gesneriaceae Family) are also propagated this way using larger sized leaf sections. Mother-in-law's tongue (*Sansevieria*) is propagated by cutting the long leaves into 10 cm (4 in) sections and putting them into a growing medium (somewhat on the sandy side). Roots and shoots will develop on the lower part which is in the soil. The variegated cultivar of this plant will produce only green or yellow plants, not the variegated form. The plant is a chimera (see CHIMERA AND OTHER MUTATIONS). The yellow plants will die as soon as they are removed from the leaf section as they do not contain green pigment or chloroplasts and cannot photosynthesize.

Some lilies (*Lilium*) can be propagated by removing scales from the bulbs and putting them into propagating material. Small bulbils will form on the base of these scales.

One final comment on leaf cuttings concerns propagating the Bryophyllum, a succulent plant with many young plants growing on the edges of its leaves. To propagate, simply shake the plantlets off and plant in soil.

## Figure 5-19
## CAMBIAL CONTACT

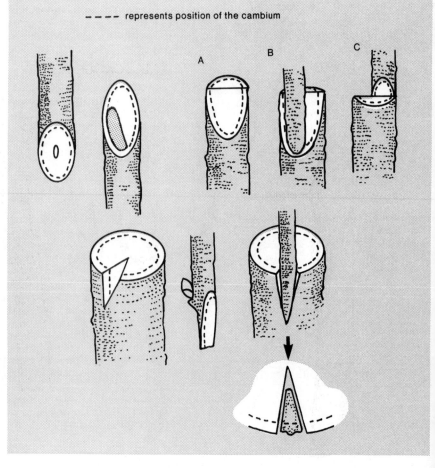

– – – – represents position of the cambium

# GRAFTING AND BUDDING

The purpose of grafting and budding is to encourage two or more parts of closely related plants to form one plant. As there is no exchange of genetic material, grafting and budding are asexual methods of propagation. Often the reasons for the grafting and budding are disease and pest resistance, growth habit modification and shape modification. Occasionally, natural grafts can be found. Root grafts often occur when plants grow close together; roots press together and form a union. Systemic diseases, caused by virus or bacteria, can spread quickly when roots touch, so adequate spacing is important, especially in nurseries. Occasionally, branches of trees will rub together and form a union. This can be of special concern to the nursery grower, due to the possible spread of systemic diseases. Strawberry clones, grown for propagation purposes, are planted in rectangular blocks with a rather wide area (50 cm or 20 in) separating the blocks. If virus is detected in a plant, the whole block must be destroyed to prevent disease spreading through the closely interwoven root system and the possible occurrence of natural root grafts.

Grafted plants consist of two parts — the **rootstock** forming the lower part, and the **scion**, the part eventually forming the top part of the grafted plant. Occasionally, an **intermediate** stock is required between the two. There are numerous methods to obtain a healthy union between the rootstock and scion. All these unions have one important requirement which is the basis for all grafts - **cambial contact**.

Grafts should always have ample cambial contact. If there is a difference in diameter between rootstock and scion, there should be at least one point where the cambium of the two parts are completely joined (see Figure 5-19). The cut surfaces where the two cambiums coincide should be flush (without air pockets between the exposed tissues). Both cut surfaces should be flat; it takes practice to get a flat cut surface with a minimum of time spent with exposed tissues. The scion should be cut first and can be kept moist by holding it in the mouth or putting it into a glass of water while the rootstock is being prepared. Knives should always be very sharp and honed after approximately every ten grafts, depending on the hardness of the material. A soft oil stone is useful for this purpose as other stones are often too hard. There are special types of grafting knives available. Grafting knives are unique in that their blades are sharpened on one side only. This allows straight cuts to be made. The blade often has a lip on the top which is used for budding. Avoid knives with sharp points as the points break off easily. Good knives are not cheap as they are made from high quality steel. When sharpening a one sided blade, sharpen only the ground side and pull the other side over the sharpening stone once or twice to remove the burr. Good straight cuts are

## Figure 5-20
## GRAFTING KNIFE

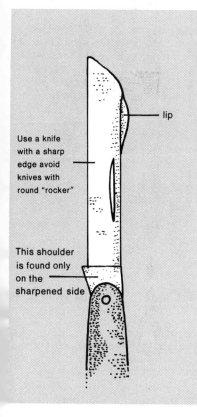

lip

Use a knife with a sharp edge avoid knives with round "rocker"

This shoulder is found only on the sharpened side

## Figure 5-21
## WHIP AND TONGUE GRAFT

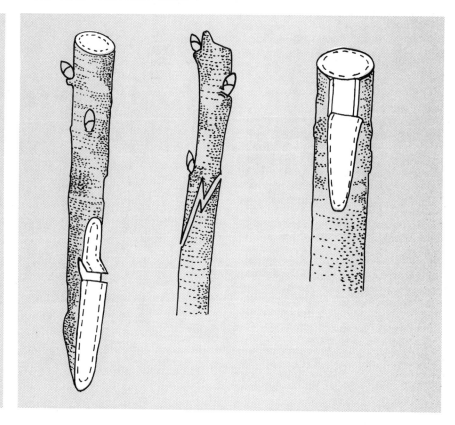

usually achieved with one quick draw. Hold the blade more or less parallel to the wood being cut. If the angle is more of a right angled cut, then the surface will usually be uneven. Keep in mind that practice makes perfect. The manner of cutting and joining is determined by the quality and nature of the plant material, as well as the skill of the grafter.

### WAXING AND REINFORCEMENT

It is important to protect the graft against drying out and from rain getting into the graft. There are several waxes available which can be used to protect the graft. Some waxes are a 'cold' type and are applied with fingers; others are 'hot' waxes applied with a brush. Waxes consist of a mixture of beeswax, resin, talcum powder and some hardening agents. The hot wax cakes are melted in a hot water bath using a small burner. The wax is applied to the plant with a brush and a good seal should be provided. Once the graft has taken, the wax will disintegrate and crumble as the stem starts to expand. Be careful not to disturb the scion when applying the wax. If grafts are kept indoors, waxing is not necessary. Grafted plants should not be

watered from above; water should be kept away from the graft. Some plants are kept under extra heat and humidity to encourage the growth of callus tissue.

### SPLICE (WHIP) GRAFT

A splice (whip) graft is a good starting graft (see Figure 5-21). Both scion and rootstock should be about the same diameter. With non-woody material the grafts slip as soon as pressure is applied. To prevent slippage, long cuts are made in both pieces. This practice increases the amount of exposed cambium and helps to hold the two pieces together.

A variation on the splice graft is the **whip and tongue graft** . After making a splice graft, both surfaces are counter-cut, providing a 'tongue'. When sliding these two surfaces together, the tongues intersect and keep the two parts firmly together (see Figure 5-21). With softer material, the tongue should be kept short to prevent buckling when pressure is applied. The whip and tongue graft is one of the most versatile grafting methods as it has a wide range of applications.

### Figure 5-22
### WEDGE OR CLEFT GRAFT

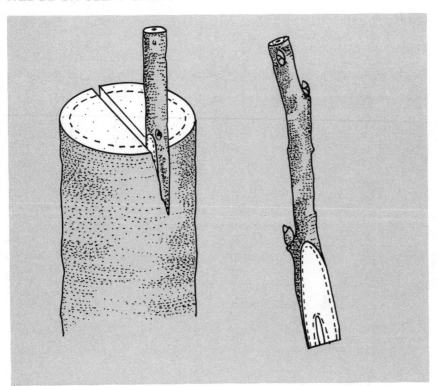

### Figure 5-23
### GRAFTING OF A CACTUS

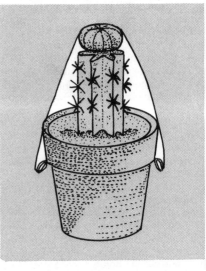

### WEDGE OR CLEFT GRAFT

This is also a simple graft but requires some skill to get a straight angle on the two cuts on the scion and a simple split made on the rootstock surface. The cleft made in the rootstock supplies steady pressure on the scion to keep the two pieces together. The cut should not be too deep (see Figure 5-22).

Wedge grafting works well on soft material like cucumber and tomatoes. There are many other grafting methods (too numerous to mention), but the main purpose is to strive for good cambial contact between the two parts. A more complicated cut will need more time to prepare and will increase the risk of tissues drying out.

One additional grafting method worth mentioning is used for cacti. These plants have their cambium in the central core of the stem, so the scion is placed right in the middle of the rootstock. Often the scion is kept in place with a rubber band or a long cactus spine through its middle section (see Figure 5-23).

Grafts need some protection and reinforcement. Cotton thread, rubber strips, or plastic strips (available from horticultural supply outlets) can be used for reinforcement, keeping in mind that should not inhibit the growth of the plant. Cotton twine has to be cut, which is

## Figure 5-24
### SPLICED APPROACH GRAFT

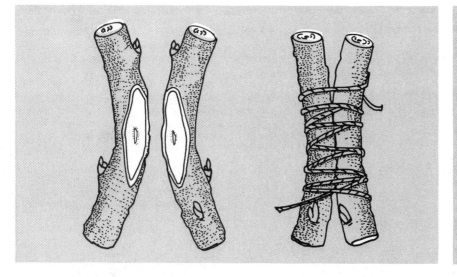

## Figure 5-25
### TONGUED APPROACH GRAFT

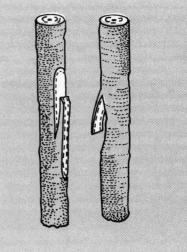

tedious job. Some topworked grafts are kept in place with nails. Plastic or rubber strips, about 1 cm (1/2 in) wide, are started on the lower part, just under the lowest extent of the scion and wrapped around the stem in an overlapping fashion, with some pressure applied. A loop is left at the end which can be pulled loose if required.

### APPROACH GRAFTING
Two plants are grown close together for approach grafting. They can either be in one pot, separate pots, or in the garden. Both plants are brought together, a small part of each stem is cut away thereby exposing the cambium, and the two plants are bound together at the cuts. When it appears that a successful union has taken place, the plant which is to become the scion is cut below the graft and the other is cut above the graft. The advantage of using this method is that if the graft does not 'take', the plants are not lost. The disadvantage is that if one plant has a stronger sap flow than the other, significant pressure can build up which will push the two surfaces apart. A tongue cut is recommended to help reduce pressures.

The two different plants can be in individual pots or a potted plant can be hung in a tree and grafting can take place. **Bottle grafts** incorporate a 'cutting' from the scion plant (with its lower part in a bottle of water), while the top part is an approach graft. The bottle is removed as soon as the union seems to be successful (see Figures 5-24 and 5-25).

### SCION GRAFTING
Scion grafting has the widest commercial application. Rootstocks can be grown in the nursery as free growing stock — lined out in rows or planted as young seedlings in pots which have been sunk into the nursery bed.

The weather and season can affect the procedure; often one waits for good weather and misses the optimum grafting period. The weather may also hamper the successful joining of the graft union (see TIMING). Rootstock in pots can be dug up and brought into a sheltered location where the grafting can be done. Such grafts are usually kept in a greenhouse until the union has firmly taken. The plants are then hardened off before planting outside and adequate growing time is provided before the onset of the cold weather.

The rootstock is cut off about 2.5 cm (1 in) higher than the location of the graft union. The scion is cut first, then the rootstock is trimmed. Do not cut or dig more material than can be grafted in one session. There will be a certain amount of transplant shock, so the sooner the grafted rootstocks are planted, the

greater their chance of survival.

When working with woody rootstock, latent buds are often removed. If the terminal bud is not present and dormancy is broken, nutrients and water will go to the grafted area. Many nurserymen do not remove latent buds until the graft has taken.

If the graft fails, a bud or shoot may rejuvenate the rootstock and allow for future grafting use. Just before the rootstock is cut to proper size, it should be wiped to remove soil, dust and moisture. The rootstock is re-cut at the grafting site at a slight angle. Some nurserymen maintain that this will provide a means of drainage for rain or dew. When the rootstocks are large, some trimming of the edges around the top is often done for the same reason.

**Topworking** is frequently done to rejuvenate older fruit trees. Such trees are severely pruned to the extent that only branches thicker than 5 cm (2 in) in diameter remain on the tree. Scions are grafted onto the remaining stumps using whip and tongue, wedge, or rind grafts. **Rind grafts** (see Figure 5-26), consist of a scion cut on one side only. The 'rootstock' bark is cut and peeled back with the lip of the grafting knife and the scion inserted. Experience comes in judging the number of scions each tree stump or branch can carry.

## Figure 5-26
## TOP WORKING RIND GRAFT

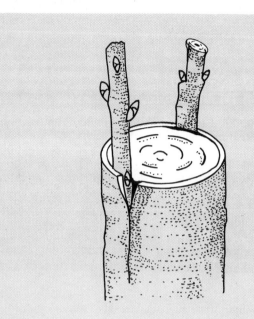

## Figure 5-27
## INARCHING AND BRIDGE GRAFTING

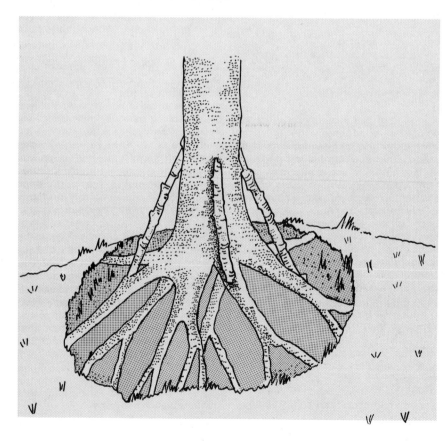

The length of the scion is subject to the distance between dormant buds; two or three dormant buds per scion is ideal. When the scion is grafted successfully, these buds will break dormancy. When this occurs, excess scion buds can be removed. The large number of buds retained is a form of insurance. Birds or the wind can damage some buds, leaving other shoots to act as replacement. When grafting, the location of the buds will determine the eventual shape of the tree. The grafter, then, can arrange even distribution of new branches and can control the shape of the tree.

### COMPATIBILITY

Close genetic relationship (Species on same Species) is usually a necessity for successful grafting, but there are a number of examples where this rule does not apply. For example, lilac (*Syringa*) can be grafted successfully on green ash (*Fraxinus*). Green ash does not sucker as do most lilacs, so grafting lilacs on green ash produces small flowering trees rather than wild thickets. In the Family of Cactaceae, there are hardly any restrictions. There are, however, many cases where an apparently successful graft will grow for several years, then develop signs of rejection of the scion. When such a graft union is investigated, much of the xylem will be unconnected and when the plant starts to increase in size and diameter at the crown, the trunk is not strong enough to support the total weight.

**Graft incompatibility** can occur for a number of reasons including:

• tissue incompatibility — either phloem or xylem tissue does not provide a good union.
• certain viral diseases prohibit good union.
• physical differences may occur (eg., the scion develops faster than the rootstock, or the rootstock grows faster than the scion).

The use of an intermediate stem piece may help overcome these problems. It can also be used to combine influences from the three graft pieces.

### INARCHING AND BRIDGE GRAFTING
Inarching and bridge grafting are often applied as a form of restoration. The scion and rootstock have been joined for years. A bridge is inserted around the

original union which may consist of several 'scions' often as thick as 3 cm (over 1 in). Usually, a large **T**-cut (see BUDDING) is made and the prepared ends of the scion inserted into it. This method may be used to allow more sap to go to the top of the tree if the original rootstock does not supply a large enough amount to the crown. It may also be used to bridge a damaged area of the trunk resulting from gnawing rodents (see Figure 5-27).

## INDEXED ROOTSTOCKS

Many countries try to use rootstocks from established clones that are known to provide successful unions with fruit trees. Previously, rootstock for many fruit trees was sown from seed obtained from fruit processing plants. Clonal rootstocks have now been established worldwide and are selected on the basis of graft union compatability as well as on inherited influences including disease resistance, dwarfing and invigorating effects, availability of intermediate stock and winter hardiness.

Two of the best known sources of these clonal rootstocks are the Malling Series (EM) from the East Malling Research Station in England and Malling-Merton (MM) - the result of cooperation between East Malling and the John Innes Institute in England. The Central Experimental Farm in Ottawa has established a hardy line of fireblight resistant apple rootstocks known as Robusta #5. The rootstocks can be obtained from tree nurseries.

## TIMING

The timing of grafting can be subject to a number of circumstances. **Hardwood grafting** requires material of which the lateral buds have not broken dormancy but the vascular tissue has become active. Scion material should be the same or slightly smaller in diameter than the rootstock. Scion material can be collected before it breaks dormancy and kept in cold storage for a limited time. It does not matter if the rootstock has broken dormancy.

Grafting of semi-hardwood material is usually carried out later in the growing season in controlled environments (i.e., growth chambers and greenhouses). Under these conditions, active growth is inconsequential. Selected scion wood should be starting to turn woody with mature lateral or terminal buds present.

The supply of grafting material is best collected during the early morning and kept moist and cool. After the graft has taken, the buds may break dormancy. Often, these buds will break dormancy the following spring, although the graft union will be complete by the fall. Grafting of clematis, for example, is always done on semi-hardwood materials.

### FRESH GROWTH (GREEN) GRAFTING

**Fresh growth (green) grafting** can be carried out under controlled conditions as soon as the material is firm enough to be cut and handled. Splice grafts and wedge and tongue grafts are the most widely adapted grafts for green wood. Use of a razor blade to make cuttings in green material is best. This method of grafting applies only to herbaceous materials. Tomatoes and potatoes can be grafted together as a home experiment.

### BUDDING

Budding is a grafting method using scions that consist of only one mature bud attached to a shield of tissue. Budding is done when the sap flow is active (bark is slipping) so that the 'shield' or outer layer tissues of the stem (containing the phloem and some cambium) can be removed easily. This 'rind', with the bud attached, is inserted under the bark of the rootstock plant. The bud is of current year's wood but it must be in 'dormancy rest'. This means T-budding can only be done successfully on the Prairies after August 1 and must be completed during the first week in August so that chances of a 'take' are good.

## Figure 5-28
## SHIELD BUD AND T-CUT

The bark is opened in the form of a **T** (see Figure 5-28). The T-cut is made with a grafting knife using the lip on the knife to loosen the rind of the T-cut. Insert the bud into the T-cut and remove excess rind above the cut. Tie the graft with cotton or budding strips; waxing may or may not be required. The top growth of the rootstock above the inserted bud is removed only after a successful union of bud and rootstock is assured. If the graft is not successful, the rootstock can still be used for future grafting. Sometimes, if the particular plant is known for difficult budding, two buds are inserted on each rootstock (eg., Walnut, *Juglans nigra*).

Patch budding is a variation of budding carried out with a double-bladed knife or special patch cutter (see Figure 5-30). Budding is an economical method as far as scion material is concerned and provides relatively better success rates than other forms of grafts.

The grafting and budding systems discussed are only a summary of the many possible graft variations. Refer to RESOURCE MATERIALS for some suggested texts on the subject. Do not be intimidated by the subject since this lesson should prepare you well enough to attempt grafting. Try grafting a backyard fruit tree with some different branches or a lilac tree with different colored flowers onto one bush. Topworking a large tree with a different cultivar could also provide interesting work.

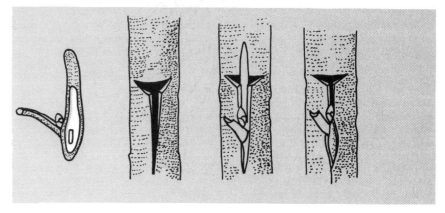

**Figure 5-29**
**PATCH BUDDING**

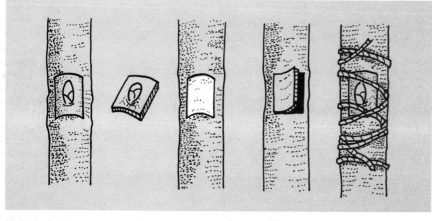

**Figure 5-30**
**DOUBLE-BLADED**
**PATCH CUTTER**

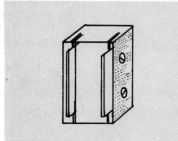

## TISSUE CULTURE

The principle of tissue culture is not new. In the early years scientists tried to grow the embryos of plants *in vitro*. Plants were grown isolated in bottles on a nutrient mixture. Knudson's Orchid Agar is the direct result of such experimentation (see ORCHIDS).

Tissue culture may have opened the door to a practical application of hydroponics. *In vitro* cultures were also used to raise virus free plants of crops which seemed to be in danger of annihilation by heavy disease infestations. It was known that the extreme growing tip of plants (meristematic area) was usually free of viruses. By isolating these areas and growing them *in vitro*, several plants could be raised which were free of

viruses. This technique was applied in the cultivation of carnations, dahlias, and tropical Orchids. Once auxins were produced synthetically (see GROWTH REGULATORS), it became less difficult to grow the young plants in isolated cultures but there were still severe limitations. Only after the discovery of kinetin (in 1957) was enough information obtained to allow complete manipulation of *in vitro* culture. France and the USA contributed much towards the basic research.

In 1960, Dutch floriculturists started to apply the technique of tissue culture to plant propagation to overcome certain problems in crops, including Cymbidium Orchids, Pointsettia and Gerbera. In 1965, there were ten commercial enterprises propagating crops by tissue culture. By 1975, the number had risen to 45 and it is estimated that, to date, there are more than 150 laboratories in Holland alone working with tissue culture. The introduction of Gerbera as a commercial cut flower crop was only possible through propagation by tissue culture. Boston fern is also propagated using tips of the rhizomes. More crops will be grown this way in the future.

Besides the commercial applications, tissue culture holds exciting possibilities for plant propagators and other scientists working in the field. One meristem tip has the potential of producing thousands of new plants.

As early as 1954, the first complete plant (a carrot) was grown from a single cambium cell removed from a mature

carrot plant. In 1960, large scale production of Orchids began. In 1967, pollen grains from tobacco were grown into a complete plant. Such plants have only half the number of chromosomes than sexually propagated plants. In 1973, the technique had developed to such an extent that it was possible to fuse the contents of two cells into one cell and produce an intergeneric hybrid, thus, tissue culture entered the field of plant breeding.

The *in vitro* technique requires the same type of laboratory equipment as described for the seeding of Orchids on Knudson's Agar. There are many amateur Orchid growers using tissue culture in their own laboratories. A thorough knowledge of the handling of the various chemicals and their concentrations is required. It is absolutely essential to produce cultures under aseptic (sterile) conditions. Once the culture is growing, it can be maintained under fluorescent lights at a temperature of 18-21°C and a relative humidity of 65 per cent.

Tissues removed from plants have to be disinfected. Tips are washed with bleach solutions or alcohol to kill micro-organisms on their surface. Any organisms missed will appear as contaminations on the culture, since bacteria and fungi also grow well in the rich, nutrient mediums.

Chemicals can also be ordered through local supply firms. Equipment, such as autoclaves (sterilizing units), can be obtained through scientific supply outlets.

Two commercial sources of tissue culture supplies are:

Flow Laboratories Inc.
1760 Meyerside Drive, Unit 3
Mississauga, Ontario L5T 1A3

Gibco Canada Inc.
2260A Industrial Street
Burlington, Ontario L7P 1A1

Research is being done at two universities in Alberta. The Alberta Tree Nursery and Horticulture Centre in Edmonton is currently involved in a program of Saskatoon (*Amalanchier alnifolia*) and blackcherry (*Prunus serotina*) propagation through tissue culture. California tissue culture laboratories are becoming successful in supplying young plants from croton, ficus, hydrangea, nerine, philodendron and more.

Due to the vast amount of work being done in the field of tissue culture, books on the subject soon become obsolete. Tissue culture has great potential for application in horticulture.

## MIST FRAMES AND HEATING CABLES

Cuttings, which have a number of leaves attached to them or consist of soft green growth, are subject to excess water loss and eventual wilting. Although it is recommended that all such tender propagation material be kept cool and moist, the chances of such material producing roots is severely restricted by desiccation. Plants with a rather inactive vascular cambium will be difficult to propagate as soon as the shoots become woody.

In the late 1950's, many nurseries started to use mist systems in their greenhouses. One of these, the 'fog system', used high pressure air jets to atomize water into small particles. The suspended fog in the greenhouse atmosphere reduces the light intensity and maintains high humidity which, in turn, reduces evaporation of moisture from the plant tissue. This application aids in the production of cuttings, not only the problem ones, but all semi-hardwood or softwood cuttings. The fog system is rather expensive to buy and maintain but can pay for itself in a short period of time. Some problems were encountered with the cooling influences of the evaporating moisture, the hardening off processes and the reduced light intensity during dark days resulting in a low photosynthetic rate.

A modified form of the fog system is the 'mist frame'. This consists of a number of nozzles spaced evenly along the base of the propagation bench, either in the greenhouse or outside. Water released from these nozzles is under pressure, but the pressure is not sufficient to atomize the water. Atomizing the water is accomplished with fine nozzles and deflectors. Mist systems do not spray constantly but are controlled by timers. The rate of release is adjustable through the use of an 'electronic leaf'. This device consists of an anode-cathode contact which will turn on the water

through a solenoid valve. As soon as the surface of the 'leaf' is wet by the spray it will automatically shut off the water. As soon as the 'leaf' is dry the solenoid is reactivated and the spray comes on again. Nozzles are available with a choice of jet sizes; adjustments are made to provide exactly the amount of water to prevent cuttings from desiccating. There are also 'weaning' devices available that gradually decrease the amount of water released and assist in hardening off the plants.

One of the manufacturers of material to build a mist frame is MacPenny's Automatic Mist Propagation Equipment (which can be obtained from major greenhouse supply companies). Such suppliers can also provide more details regarding construction.

Cuttings usually root faster if a source of heat is provided to the rooting media. Heating cables are often incorporated into mist frame bottoms to counteract the cooling effects of evaporation. Many other propagation beds (besides mist systems) are equipped with heating cables. Maintaining the rooting media temperature at an optimum for the plant will allow the surrounding air temperature to be kept cooler. The cable does not give off enough heat to affect the air temperature. The reason why warm rooted plants survive in colder air temperatures is physiological and proves to be a great cost saver for greenhouse owners.

Heating cables are available in a variety of lengths. Cables should rest on a metal screen to provide even distribution of heat through conductivity. Special thermostats are available to control and monitor the soil temperature.

## CHIMERAS AND OTHER MUTATIONS

One of the advantages of asexual propagation is that identical offspring are produced from the parent plant. Over time, however, variations can occur due to a mutation. Such changes may provide a permanent variation in the genetic make-up of the young plant. Often, such changes may not even be noticeable from the external (or morphological) appearance of the plant. However, it may turn out to affect the drought resistance of the plant, its frost hardiness, or its resistance to pests and

diseases. For this reason, it is advisable to select propagation material from plants which look representative of their Species. Plants that are slightly taller, shorter, or have different sized leaves often give rise to new cultivars.

Occasionally, these mutations give rise to larger or different colored flowers; these mutations are called **sports**. Certain groups of chrysanthemums (Princess Ann), carnations (William Sim), dahlias, and tulips (Apeldoorn) have sports that give rise to numerous new cultivars. Mutations are obtained by experiment and can be induced with the aid of chemicals, X-rays and other forms of radiation.

Another type of mutation results from the formation of adventitious buds in areas of the plant where two different types of tissue are present. Such variations are called **chimeras**. One of the variants of the mother-in-law's tongue (*Sansevieria zeylandica*) is a plant with long green leaves and yellow margins. If a section of this leaf is rooted, the resulting shoots that originate from the green part will be entirely green while those from the yellow part will be partly yellow. If an adventitious bud originates exactly from the point where the green and yellow tissues meet, a green plant with yellow margins will be obtained. Therefore, the variegated or yellow-edged plant can only be duplicated successfully from suckers. Chimeras are also encoutered in the Pelargonium cultivars with multicolored leaves. Sometimes, a branch will develop that has only green or all white leaves. In the latter case, the branch will survive only if it is connected to the mother plant since it lacks chlorophyll and cannot manufacture its own food as a cutting or individual plant.

Certain cacti produce chimeric variations which cannot sustain themselves once they have been removed from the parent plant. As a result, the yellow chimeric cacti are grafted onto a green photosynthetic rootstock which will support growth. Graft chimeras are also known to occur. They are produced when an adventitious bud develops from the cambium (callus) on a graft and this bud contains cells derived from both the scion and the rootstock. These occurrences are rare. The most famous example is that of the Adam's Laburnum. The grower tried to graft a golden-chain Laburnum (*Laburnum anagyroieles*) onto a purple broom (*Cytisus purpureus*) to provide a taller stem. The graft failed but a graft chimera grew out of the callus tissue which produced a pink flowering shrub known as Adam's Laburnum (*Laburnocytisus adami*).

## ADVANTAGES AND DISADVANTAGES OF ASEXUAL PROPAGATION

Asexual or vegetative propagation makes use of parts of a plant which when removed from the mother plant and given the right conditions, will regenerate missing parts and become independent young plants. In some instances, root formation will not have to be induced; parts of the plant can be removed which have already formed roots while still attached to the mother plant (a mature spider plant with 'babies' is a good example of this). Asexual propagation produces young plants which are identical to the mother plant.

### ADVANTAGES OF ASEXUAL PROPAGATION
• plants display the exact characteristics of their parents
• certain plants are unable to produce seeds (are sterile) due to genetic reasons or because the growing season is too short to complete the plant's lifecycle
• some plants produce non-viable seed or seed that takes a long time to germinate
• combinations of different grafted rootstocks and scions can influence the growth pattern of a mature tree (apples, pears, peaches, etc.)

### DISADVANTAGES OF ASEXUAL PROPAGATION
• some plants do not easily produce roots from cuttings
• viruses and other infections are easily transmitted
• requires more skill by the propagator than propagation from seed
• can be time consuming
• usually elaborate equipment and facilities are required

## CONCLUSION

Plant propagation comprises two divergent approaches.

1. **sexual** propagation — by which plants are raised from seed.
2. **asexual or vegetative** propagation — by which plants can be reproduced in a variety of ways other than seed.

In the sexual method, genetic information from the male (pollen producing) and the female (seed producing) plants are combined. Often, this results in the production of seedling plants which display characteristics of both parent plants. In most cases, this is hardly noticeable. Annual plants reproduced from seed show a minimum of variation.

Sexual propagation reduces the possibility of disease transfer from one generation to another whereas one of the drawbacks of asexual reproduction is the possibility of transmitting diseases from one generation to another.

Asexual propagation is practised where seed production is difficult or slow, or where certain desirable characteristics are not reproduceable from seed.

Most of the propagation methods discussed do not require a special skill or knowledge but simply an understanding of the factors which influence the behavior and nature of plants. Plant propagation is a subject which most hobby gardeners can practice, either for their enjoyment or for more practical reasons.

## SELF CHECK *QUIZ*

1. What conditions must be met before seeds will germinate?
2. What qualities must a seed sowing medium provide for successful germination to occur?
3. Why is peat moss often used in seedbeds?
4. Which methods are used to propagate annual cultivars? Why?
5. What is the main advantage of asexual reproduction?
6. What time of the year is best for taking root cuttings? Why?
7. How can transpiration from cuttings with leaves be reduced?
8. What are the advantages of budding over other forms of grafting?

**adventitious** - arising from an unusual place.

**annual** - plant which completes its life cycle and dies within one year.

**antheridia** - male sex organs of ferns. Found on the prothallus.

**archegonia** - female sex organs of ferns. Found on the prothallus.

**auxins** - growth regulating substances.

**callus** - layer of thin walled, undifferentiated cells developing on wound surfaces.

**corm** - underground swollen base of a stem which stores food.

**cross-pollination** - transfer of pollen from a stamen to the stigma of a flower of another plant.

**dioecious** - plants having either male or female flowers but not both.

**epigeous** - pattern of germination in which the cotyledons emerge from the soil.

**F-1 hybrid** - first-generation of hybrids which arise from the cross-fertilization of two distinct Species.

**frond** - name usually applied to leaves on ferns.

**heterozygous** - gene pair in which the genes are not identical.

**homozygous** - gene pair in which both genes are identical.

**hybridization** - the process of creating a new plant by combining the gametes from two separate Species.

**hypogeous** - pattern of germination in which the cotyledons do not emerge from the soil.

**monoecious** - a single plant having both male and female flowers.

**mutation** - a sudden unexpected heritable change produced by a plant.

**P generation** - Parental Species which are used in cross-fertilization to create hybrids.

**perennial** - plant which lives for more than two years.

**perfect flower** - stamens and pistil found in the same flower.

**prothallus** - small, green, leaf-life structure which develops from the spores of ferns.

**rhizome** - horizontal underground stem.

**rootstock** - stems or roots of a plant to which scions are grafted.

**runner** - stem which grows horizontally over the surface of the soil. Often develops new plants at its tips.

**scarification** - cutting or scratching of the seed coat to facilitate the entry of water and oxygen.

**scion** - bud or stem of a plant grafted to the rootstock.

**sori** - dense groups of spore cases (sporangia) which contain spores.

**sucker** - shoot arising from underground parts of a plant.

**tuber** - enlarged fleshy underground stem.

## SELF CHECK *ANSWERS*

1. The conditions for successful germination include:

   a. seed must be viable

   b. the presence of water

   c. the presence of air

   d. a suitable temperature

   e. absence of conditions inhibiting germination
   (see CONDITIONS FOR SUCCESSFUL GERMINATION - page 504)

2. Seed sowing medium should:

   a. hold moisture well

   b. be able to drain out excess moisture; be well aerated

   c. be free of harmful organisms (pests, weeds and diseases)

   d. contain sufficient nutrition

   e. have a good texture
   (see PREPARING THE SEEDBED - page 506)

3. Peat moss is often used in seedbeds because it has a good water-holding capacity and good aeration (see CHOOSING A SUITABLE CONTAINER - page 506).

4. Annual cultivars are best suited to reproduction by seed. Seed provides a quick, easy and cheap method of producing large numbers of plants that are reasonably true to type (see CIRCUMSTANCES INFLUENCING THE CHOICE OF PROPAGATION METHODS - page 501).

5. The main advantage of asexual reproduction is that plants can be produced that are exactly like the parent plant (see ADVANTAGES OF ASEXUAL PROPAGATION - page 528).

6. Fall and early spring are usually the best times to take root cuttings because the root cuttings contain the maximum amount of stored food at these times (see CUTTINGS - page 517).

7. Transpiration can be reduced by reducing the number of leaves, by reducing the leaf area and by raising the humidity around the leaves (see TIMING - page 525).

8. Budding can be done more quickly than most other forms of grafting; it requires less skill; it uses less scion wood and the rootstock can be used again if the graft does not take (see BUDDING - page 525).

Arditti, Joseph. *Orchid Biology. Reviews and Perspectives*. Ithica: Cornell University Press, 1977.

Recommended for Orchid growers; many details on tissue culture.

Browse, D. McMillan. *Plant Propagation*. New York: Royal Horticultural Society. Simon and Schuster Publ. Co., 1979.

Informative, with excellent illustrations.

Free, M. and Eliot M. Dietz. *Plant Propagation in Pictures*. Garden City, New York: Double Day Publishing, 1979.

An entertaining popular book.

Garner, R.J. *The Grafters Handbook*. London: Faber, 1979.

One of the best books ever written about this subject with clear text and good illustrations. Should be in any good library.

Hartmann, H.T. and D.E.Kester.*Plant Propagation: Principles and Practices*. 4th Ed. Englewood Cliffs, New Jersey: Prentice-Hall Inc., 1983.

Wright, R.C. M. and A. Titchmarsh. *The Complete Book of Plant Propagation*. London: Ward Lock Publishing Ltd., 1981.

Recommended literature.

## INDEX

# PEST CONTROL

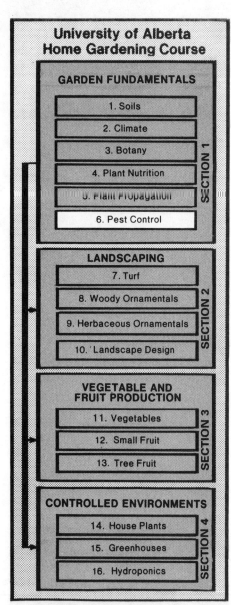

### University of Alberta Home Gardening Course

**GARDEN FUNDAMENTALS**
1. Soils
2. Climate
3. Botany
4. Plant Nutrition
5. Plant Propagation
6. Pest Control

SECTION 1

**LANDSCAPING**
7. Turf
8. Woody Ornamentals
9. Herbaceous Ornamentals
10. Landscape Design

SECTION 2

**VEGETABLE AND FRUIT PRODUCTION**
11. Vegetables
12. Small Fruit
13. Tree Fruit

SECTION 3

**CONTROLLED ENVIRONMENTS**
14. House Plants
15. Greenhouses
16. Hydroponics

SECTION 4

# SELF-STUDY LESSON FEATURES

Self-study is an educational approach which allows you to study a subject where and when you want. The course is designed to allow you to study efficiently and incorporates the following features:

**OBJECTIVES** — are found at the beginning of each lesson and allow you to determine what you can expect to learn in the lesson.

**LESSON MATERIAL** — is logically organized and broken down into fundamental components by ordered headings to assist you to comprehend the subject.

**REFERENCING** — between lessons and within lessons allows you to integrate course material.

The last two digits of the page number identify the page and the digits preceding these identify the lesson number (eg., 107: Lesson 1, page 7 or 1227: Lesson 12, page 27).

Referencing:

> sections within the same lesson (eg., see OSMOSIS)

> sections in other lessons (eg., see Botany lesson, OSMOSIS)

> figures and tables (eg., see Figure 7-3)

**FIGURES AND TABLES** — are found in abundance throughout the lessons and are designed to convey useful information in an easy to understand form.

**SIDEBARS** — are those areas in the lesson which are boxed and toned. They present information supplementary to the core content of the lesson.

**PRACTICAL PROJECTS** — are integrated within the lesson material and are included to allow you to apply principles and practices.

**SELF-CHECK QUIZ** — is provided at the end of each lesson and allows you to test your comprehension of the lesson material. Answers to the questions and references to the sections dealing with the questions are provided in the answer section. You should review any questions that you are unable to answer.

**GLOSSARY** – is provided at the end of each lesson and alphabetically lists the definitions of key concepts and terms.

**RESOURCE MATERIALS** — are provided at the end of each lesson and comprise a list of recommended learning materials for further study of the subject. Also included are author's comments on the potential application of each publication.

**INDEX** — alphabetically lists useful topics and their location within the lesson.

© 1986 University of Alberta Faculty of Extension

Compiled by: Buck Godwin

Special Technical Material and Assistance:
Mike Dolinski, I.R. Evans, D. Sippell, S. Ali, W. Yarish, D. Maurice, M.K. Price of Alberta Agriculture, Crop Protection Branch

ISBN 0-88864-852-9

(Book 1, Lesson 6)

### THE PRODUCTION TEAM

Managing Editor .................................................... Thom Shaw
Editor ................................................................ Frank Procter
Production Coordinator ...................................... Kevin Hanson
Graphic Artists ...................................................... Lisa Marsh
Carol Powers
Melanie Eastley Harbourne
Data Entry ...................................................... Joan Geisterfer

Published by the University of Alberta Faculty of Extension Corbett Hall Edmonton, Alberta, T6G 2G4

# LEARNING OBJECTIVES

After completing this lesson, the student should be able to:

1. determine what a pest is/define pest.
2. identify a pest and determine the extent of damage that has and can occur in a backyard gardening situation.
3. select and use appropriate and reasonable pest control measures.
4. identify, develop and implement preventive control measures.

# TABLE OF CONTENTS

# LIST OF FIGURES AND TABLES

# INTRODUCTION

Pests include all insects, weeds, plant diseases and vertabrates that hinder or diminish growth and production of desirable vegetable, fruit, and ornamental plants. In order to provide these desirable plants with an environment in which to reach their full potential, control of pests is a fundamental concern to gardeners. For most types of pests, control can be accomplished through a variety of means. However, no control measures can be adequately implemented without a knowledgeable determination of the problem.

This lesson stresses the importance of pest identification as a means of assisting the gardener in making reasonable decisions regarding the control of insects, weeds, plant diseases and vertebrate pests.

# INSECTS

Alberta is home for an estimated 20,000 Species of insects. The vast majority pose no problem and make a positive contribution to the interesting fauna of the region. Insect numbers are normally kept in reasonable bounds by unfavorable weather conditions and by various insect and animal predators. Still a few Species do, at times, mar the beauty of the landscape and others reduce the gardeners' supply of vegetables, fruit and flowers. In order to minimize such losses, gardeners need to understand insects. Control without understanding is neither desirable nor feasible.

This lesson attempts to provide a basis for such understanding with special attention given to Alberta's horticultural insect pests. The following information deals primarily with:

• how to recognize developmental stages and damage caused by insect feeding
• aspects of insect biology that enable insects to survive and compete so successfully with man
• insect control

With this information, gardeners will better understand and appreciate their insect neighbors and also be equipped to make informed decisions when necessary.

## INSECT CLASSIFICATION

The identification of Genera and Species of insects is often difficult and requires special training. In the broad sense, an insect is a land animal with three pairs of walking legs. This distinguishes insects from the Arachnids (spiders, ticks, mites) which have four pairs of walking legs, and from the Myriapods (millipedes and centipedes) which have more than four pairs.

The word 'insect' is derived from the Latin *insecare* meaning 'to cut into' and refers to the bodies of some insects that are almost cut in half by a constriction at the neck or waist.

A scientific classification of insects is listed in Figure 6-1. This classification lists most insects Orders that are of interest to the home gardener (see Botany lesson, Figure 3-1).

## RECOGNITION OF INSECTS AND THEIR DEVELOPMENTAL STAGES

Insects may be recognized by their body form which is distinctly segmented into head, thorax and abdomen (Figure 6-2). The head bears a pair of antennae, eyes, mouthparts; the thorax bears wings (in adult insects) and three pair of legs; the abdomen has the sex organs. Although this description is adequate for most adult insects, it does little to distinguish many insect larvae (the immature stages) from non-insects. For this, it is important to understand how insects develop.

Insect development proceeds either by a series of distinctly different growth forms (i.e., by complete development) or by gradual development, in which the young look very similar to their adult counterparts. Of these two developmental groups, insects with

## Figure 6-1
### SCIENTIFIC CLASSIFICATION OF INSECTS

KINGDOM
Animal

| PHYLUM | PHYLUM | PHYLUM |
|---|---|---|
| Arthropoda (Jointed Legs) | Molusca | Annelida |

| CLASS | CLASS | CLASS |
|---|---|---|
| Arachnida (Spiders, Ticks, Mites) | Gastropoda (Slugs) | Oliogochaeta (Earthworms) |
| Diplopoda (Millipedes) | | |
| Chilipoda (Centipedes) | | |
| Crustacea (Sow Bugs, Pill Bugs) | | |
| Insecta | | |

ORDER
Collembola (Springtails)
Odonata (Dragonflies, Damselflies)
Orthoptera (Grasshoppers, Crickets)
Dermaptera (Earwigs)
Thysanoptera (Thrips)
Hemiptera (Stink Bugs, Tarnished Plant Bugs)
Homoptera (Whiteflies, Aphids, Scale Insects)
Neuroptera (Lacewings)
Coleoptera (Flea Beetles, Colorado Potato Beetle)
Lepidoptera (Butterflies, Moths)
Diptera (Houseflies, Currant Fruit Flies, Onion Root Maggot)
Hymenoptera (Ants, Bees, Wasps, Sawflies)

complete development are the more recent and advanced in insect history. As will be seen later, they possess biological traits which make them the most numerous group of insect pests.

## COMPLETE DEVELOPMENT

Insects hatch from the egg stage into the non-reproductive, feeding and growing stage (larva). Upon completion of growth, the larva changes to a nonfeeding, resting stage (pupa) within some sort of covering (such as the last larval skin). It is during the pupal stage that the insect transforms to the adult (see Figure 6-3). The group of insects which display this type of development includes many kinds of common crop and garden insects, such as beetles, flies, moths and butterflies, as well as many others (see Figure 6-5). Most often, it is the larva of these insects that damage plants. The larval stages (see Figure 6-6) are known by various common names, such as:

  • **caterpillars** — are the larvae of the butterflies, moths (some of which are cutworms) and sawflies. These larvae have six clawed legs at the front of the body and numerous fleshy legs at the rear.
  • **maggots** — are the headless, legless larvae of flies.
  • **grubs** — are beetle larvae having jointed legs and well developed heads.

The wings of the complete development insects develop internally in the larva and can be seen in outline on the pupa. For example, the wings are outlined in a cutworm pupa. When the pupa is gently squeezed, the segmented abdomen moves, proving that the pupa is alive!

## GRADUAL DEVELOPMENT

Gradual development insects also arise from eggs but, unlike complete development insects, they go through a series of growth (nymph) stages before becoming adults (see Figure 6-3). Nymphs and adults look very similar, except that adults are larger and may have wings. There is no resting stage (pupa) in this group; the mature nymph sheds its skin for the last time when it becomes a reproductive adult. For those insects in this group which have wings as adults, the nymphs show the gradual enlargement of wing pads, which are often used to determine the growth stage (**instar**) of the nymph. The age structure of the insect pest population can be determined by comparing the

## Figure 6-2
## DISTINGUISHING FEATURES OF INSECTS

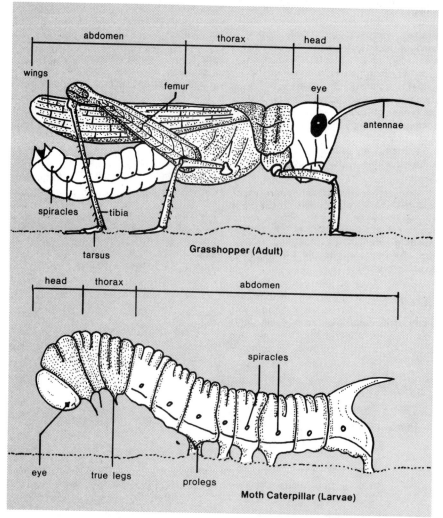

**Grasshopper (Adult)**

**Moth Caterpillar (Larvae)**

sizes of the nymphs to the adults and by noting the size of the developing wing pads.

The outside surface of all insects is a tough, waxy covering called the **cuticle**. Insects grow by periodically molting (shedding the cuticle). Since the cuticle is also the skeleton, the soft, newly-molted insect is easy prey for predators and is most vulnerable to injury by machinery. Once hardened, the waxy coating of the cuticle serves to prevent water loss. Newly-molted insects, however, are susceptible to both dehydration and (especially) insecticide sprays. Many insects die during molting.

Insects breathe through a network of internal tubes which open to the outside of the body as tiny holes called **spiracles** (see Figure 6-2). Movement of the thorax and abdomen pumps air in and out of the tubes. The tubes are lined with the same material as the cuticle and this lining is shed with the cuticle at molting. Insecticidal soaps suffocate insects by coating the insect's body with a soap film that does not permit breathing. It is also likely that very young insects suffocate when covered in water during rainstorms.

## INSECT REPRODUCTION

Population growth depends on environmental conditions, as well as three biologically pre-determined (genetic) factors. The factors include:

• the capacity of individuals to produce offspring,
• the generation time
• the proportion of females in the population.

Reproductive capacity is a characteristic of a Species. An example of a Species having a high reproductive potential is a pea aphid, which may have 20-30 generations in a single growing season, with females each producing up to 150 offspring. The honeybee is another example of an insect with a high reproductive potential; the queen honeybee is prolific and can produce as many as 100,000 eggs in a season. Low reproductive potential is demonstrated by some rangeland grasshoppers which have two-year life cycles (generation time of two years).

Cicadas (the best known is the 17-year cicada) are particularly long-lived insects; the shortest generation time known for them is four years. Although most insects fall between the extremes in generation times and egg-laying capacities, pest Species typically have one or more generations per year and produce moderate to high numbers of eggs.

The female reproductive system (see Figure 6-7) consists of paired ovaries and oviducts. The oviducts unite to form a common oviduct which opens into the external egg-laying apparatus (ovipositor). The number of eggs a female is capable of laying at any one time is determined by the number of egg tubules (ovarioles) within each ovary. Since eggs within these tubules develop sequentially, only the last mature egg in each tubule will be laid. The number of eggs laid in groups of eggs (eg., 'rafts' of mosquitos laid on the surface of still pools or 'pods' of grasshoppers) is limited in such masses by the number of ovarioles. Thus, while pods of migratory grasshoppers contain an average of about 20 eggs, those of the two-striped grasshopper average about 80 eggs; the anatomy of the two 'hopper' species is fundamentally different. Sperm are stored in a pouch (the spermatheca) where they are nourished for variable periods of time and released as needed to fertilize the eggs. Paired accessory glands release materials which, at oviposition, cover the egg mass or glue the eggs to a support.

Although most insects produce offspring from fertilized eggs, the phenomenon of

## Figure 6-3
## COMPLETE DEVELOPMENT

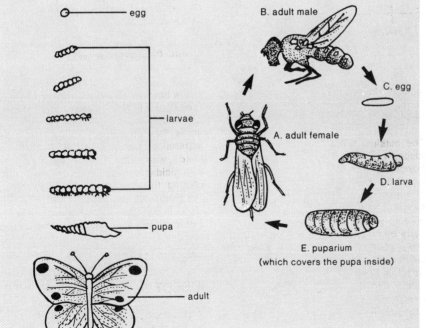

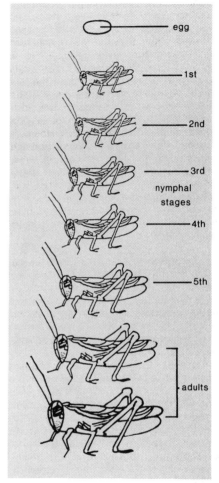

### Figure 6-4
### GRADUAL DEVELOPMENT OF THE MIGRATORY GRASSHOPPER

producing young from unfertilized eggs is not uncommon. Ants, bees and wasps can typically lay either unfertilized eggs (which develop into males) or fertilized eggs (which develop into females). Some grasshoppers and other insects can produce female offspring from unfertilized eggs. In either case, such insects can reproduce even in the absence of mates. This is of particular advantage to colonizing individuals (those that disperse to find new habitats) and is another reason why insects have inhabited the earth for over 300 million years.

Although most insects produce offspring by laying eggs, many variations exist. It

Figure 6-5

## INSECT ORDERS OF THE TWO DEVELOPMENTAL TYPES

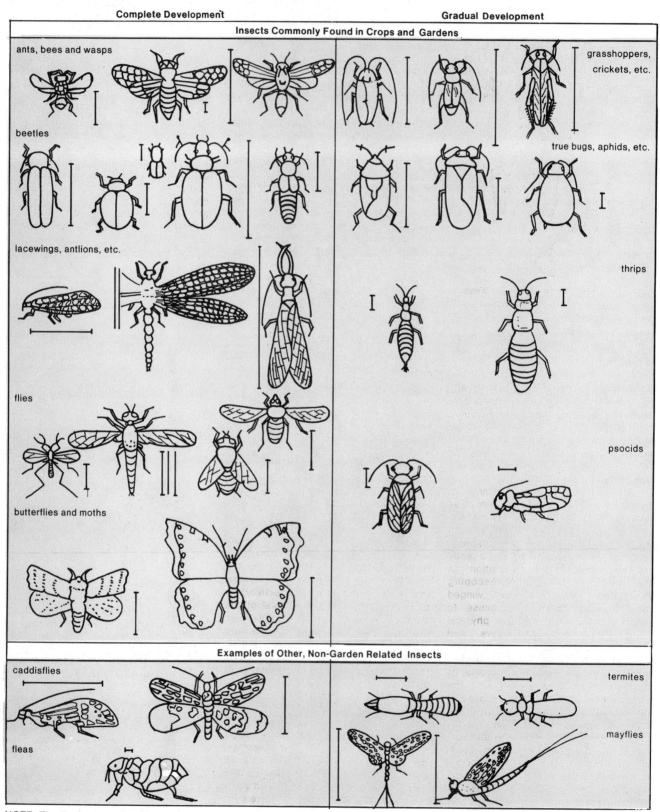

**Complete Development**     **Gradual Development**

Insects Commonly Found in Crops and Gardens

ants, bees and wasps

grasshoppers, crickets, etc.

beetles

true bugs, aphids, etc.

lacewings, antlions, etc.

thrips

flies

psocids

butterflies and moths

Examples of Other, Non-Garden Related Insects

caddisflies

termites

fleas

mayflies

NOTE: The line or lines beside each insect indicate its true size

## Figure 6-6
## COMMON TYPES OF INSECT LARVAE

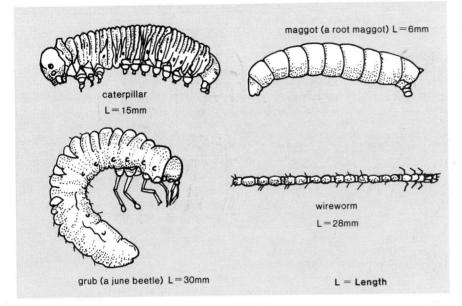

caterpillar
L=15mm

maggot (a root maggot) L=6mm

wireworm
L=28mm

grub (a june beetle) L=30mm

L = Length

is worthwhile knowing some of these lesser-known, although no less important, types of proliferation.

• Summer populations of aphids may be entirely female and, therefore, reproduce without mating. In addition, these virgin females bear living young which have been nourished in the mother's ovarioles before hatching. At birth, the nymphs are able to feed and fend for themselves.

• The production of young by immature (nymph) insects occurs in the aphids as well. At the time of birth, the summer (non-mating) aphid has within her the developing embryos of her offspring, each of which carries an already developing grandchild generation (a phenomemon called **telescoping generations**). In the summer, winged aphids are produced in response to declining host plant quality, physical contact of colony neighbors and shortening day lengths. While the first two factors are results of overcrowding in the aphid colonies, some combination of these three factors stimulates the production of winged forms. Because of the telescoping of generations, it is the grandparents (or an even earlier generation) which received the stimulus, started the production of winged aphids and, thus, initiated the colony's dispersal to a new food plant. This is yet another example of how insects adjust to changing environmental conditions. This also explains why aphid populations can quickly disappear once winged aphids start being produced by the previous generation.

• Production of many offspring from one egg can also occur. Certain parasitic wasps lay an egg within the host insect which develops into two or more larvae. In the case of one tiny wasp (which attacks the red-backed cutworm) one egg can give rise to as many as 2,000 larvae which ultimately consume the caterpillar. Such a mechanism ensures survival of the parasite whose hosts are rare.

In cases where the females retain eggs until hatching or for varying periods of larval development, the cost to the mother of nourishing the young (measured as lowered productivity) is offset by the increased survival of the offspring due to the maternal protection. Producing many offspring from one egg allows those Species having very scarce or limited food supplies, the opportunity to produce multiple (though identical) offspring.

## HOW INSECTS FEED

Insects consume their food in a variety of ways. A primitive but important method is by chewing off the external parts of a plant, grinding them up and swallowing them (solids and liquid parts together). Most gardeners will have seen the results of this type of injury to plants. Cabbage worms, grasshoppers and Colorado potato beetles are common examples of insects which cause plant injury by chewing.

### PIERCING AND SUCKING INSECTS

A second important way in which insects feed on growing plants is by piercing the epidermis (outer layers) of plants and sucking out the sap from the cells within. Only internal and liquid parts of the plant are ingested. The insects, of course, feed from the outside of the plant. Their work is accomplished by means of an extremely slender and sharp, pointed portion of the mouth parts called a **proboscis**, which is thrust into the plant and through which the sap is sucked. This results in a very different looking, but nonetheless severe injury. The hole made by the proboscis is so small that it cannot be seen. The withdrawal of the sap, however, results in either minute spotting of white, brown, or red on leaves, fruit or twigs, curling of the leaves, deforming of the fruit, or a general wilting, browning, and dying of the whole plant. Aphids, scale insects, leaf hoppers and plant bugs are common examples of piercing and sucking insects.

## Figure 6-7
## REPRODUCTIVE SYSTEM OF A FEMALE GRASSHOPPER

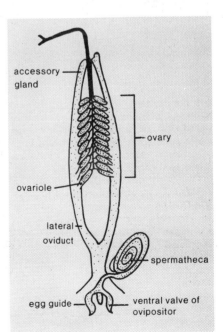

accessory gland

ovary

ovariole

lateral oviduct

spermatheca

egg guide

ventral valve of ovipositor

### INTERNAL FEEDING INSECTS

A number of insect pests feed within the plant tissue during a part or all of their destructive stages. They gain entrance to the plant either by having the egg thrust into the tissue by the sharp ovipositor of the parent insect or by eating their way in after they hatch from the eggs. In either case, the hole by which they enter is very small and (generally) invisible. The chief groups of internal feeders are indentified by their common group names: 'borers' in wood or pith, 'worms' or 'weevils' in fruits, nuts or seeds; 'leaf miners'; and 'gall insects'. Alberta gardeners will likely be most familiar with leaf miners on Birch and Lilac and gall insects on Willow, Goldenrod and Roses.

### SUBTERRANEAN INSECTS

Subterranean insects include chewers, piercers and suckers, root borers and gall insects, the attacks of which differ from those already described with reference only to the soil surface. These insects may spend their entire life cycle below ground (eg., the woolly apple aphid); but more often there is at least one life stage of the insect above ground, as in the case of wireworms, root maggots and cutworms.

## CONTROL OF INSECTS

Despite the fact that insects are capable of rapidly increasing in numbers, severe outbreaks of any of Alberta's insect pests are rare. Damage from insects affecting gardens can usually be reduced or eliminated with a combination of cultural methods, management practices or the proper use of recommended insecticides.

It is normal for the gardener to expect some insect damage; most plants can tolerate some damage. Whenever an insect infestation is severe or has been a problem before, then control is definitely in order.

### NATURAL CONTROL BY OTHER INSECTS

Many insects feed on other insects. This is a most significant factor that keeps plant-feeding insects to almost harmless numbers from year to year. Of the different kinds of insects which inhabit Alberta, nearly half of them can exist only by devouring the members of the other half. Birds and diseases may destroy large numbers of both groups,

and are important in determining how numerous any particular kind of insect will be. Nearly every Species of plant-feeding insect is preyed upon by a number of other kinds of insects. These enemies are of two main types — predators and parasites.

Predators are those insects which 'run down' and feed on their victims, much as a cat catches and eats entire mice. Relatively large insect predators, like ladybird beetles or dragonflies, devour large numbers of aphids or mosquitoes (respectively) at a single meal, whereas bugs and predatory ground beetles may eat only part of each victim they kill. Predators are effective in reducing a pest population quickly.

Parasites are insects which reduce population density by limiting reproduction of their **hosts** although they do not immediately destroy the host. A parasitized cutworm is not killed until after feeding is complete. By one means or another, their eggs or larvae are placed inside the victim host. During the first few weeks of inhabiting its body, parasitic larvae rarely kill their host. Thus, during the current year, parasites do not reduce the damage caused by the hosts in which they are living. However, such a large percentage of the host insects are killed at the end of the season, that their numbers are greatly reduced the following year. Normally, the combined activity of predators and parasites is sufficient to keep numbers of various plant-feeding pests below significant damage levels.

## PREVENTION

It is easier and more economical to prevent, rather than control, insect infestations. Plants grown on fertile soil can withstand insect attacks better than those grown on infertile soil. Prevention of insect damage can be achieved by adopting good garden management practices.

• use a system of rotation — don't plant the same crop in the same spot each season

• destroy garden residue (refuse) which can be a site for insect or disease overwintering

• make a compost or dig residue (refuse) into the soil (see Soils lesson)

• place tar paper and tin-can collars around each plant to reduce or prevent

insect damage

• eliminate weeds; some insects reproduce rapidly on weeds, then turn to the garden crop for food

• where practical, hand pick and destroy egg bands, galls or infested leaves or caterpillars

## INSECTICIDES

Control begins with identification. Home gardeners may wish to learn to distinguish between certain main groups, or classes, of insects and the disorders to which they give rise. One then selects a treatment that is known to be effective for that insect or group as a whole.

Insecticides are pesticides used to control insects. Chemicals are used by the home gardener (on a limited basis) to protect gardens against various pests.

Insecticides work (kill) differently, depending on the major group of insects one wants to remove. There are four types of insecticides:

1. **systemic** insecticides are those which, when applied to a plant, seed or soil, are taken into the plant and transported throughout the plant tissue. Insects that feed by sucking plant juices are controlled as they feed on poisoned sap.

2. **non-systemic** insecticides are those chemicals applied to the surface of a plant where the chewing and biting insects ingest the poison along with the plant tissue.

3. **natural insecticides** are produced by processing plants which have insecticidal properties (i.e., Derris powder is extracted from roots of Rotenone-bearing plants. Pyrethrum is obtained from the heads of certain plants belonging to the Chrysanthemum Genus).

4. **Biological agents** are natural viruses or bacteria that act to control insects. A bacteria (*Bacillus thuringiensis*) is available for control of the larval stage of butterflies and moths.

Because there are extensive differences in the poisonous characteristics of chemicals and people's reactions to them, each chemical must be handled carefully. Always read the label instructions carefully as pesticides can be extremely hazardous materials. Misuse of such poisonous chemicals can result in serious consequences.

For safe use of pesticides, follow these precautions:

1. identify the insect to insure that it is a pest that needs to be controlled by an insecticide rather than by some cultural control practice;
2. read the label carefully to be sure it is for control of the problem insect and that it is safe to use for the intended application;
3. always note the **wait period** between application and eating of the fruit or vegetable treated;
4. wear protective clothing — especially rubber gloves;
5. mix and handle pesticides carefully, outdoors if at all possible;
6. avoid prolonged exposure; do not inhale sprays or dusts; never smoke when applying chemicals;
7. store unused pesticides in their own container and in a safe place out of children's reach; and
8. shower with adequate amounts of soap and water, then put on clean clothes.

For both cultural and chemical control recommendations for specific insects, check the Alberta Agriculture, 'Back Yard Pest Management' (Agdex 605-3) reprinted in this lesson. This publication identifies the major insects which cause problems in our vegetable gardens, on small fruits and fruit trees, ornamental shrubs, shade trees and flowers.

# WEEDS

A weed might best be defined as a plant growing where the gardener does not want it to grow or, simply, a plant out of place. Therefore, creeping charlie in a lawn is a weed, as is dill in a petunia bed. Weeds encompass all types of undesirable plants including trees, broadleaved plants and grasses. Weeds are classified as pests as are insects, plant diseases and some animals, particularly rodents. Losses caused by the presence of weeds include:

- reduced garden yields
- additional costs associated with control measures
- poorer quality products
- reduced worker efficiency
- weeds may act as hosts for diseases and insects
- weeds may cause allergic reactions in some individuals

# LIFE CYCLE OF WEEDS

Plants are divided according to their lifespan. There are four divisions or types of plants (see Botany lesson).

- **annuals** (summer annuals)
- **winter annuals**
- **biennials**
- **perennials** (simple or creeping).

The life cycle of seed plants (annuals) begins with seed germination, continuing with the development of roots, stems, leaves, flowers and, finally, seed production. In **summer annuals**, this development cycle is completed in one growing season. Red root pigweed and lamb's quarters are examples of summer annual weeds. In **winter annuals**, the seed germinates in the fall and a mat of leaves (**rosette**) is formed near ground level. The plant grows from the fall rosette during the following spring and produces seed in late spring or summer of that year. Stinkweed and Shepherd's Purse are common winter annual weeds. Many winter annuals may also perform as summer annuals if germination begins early in the growing season. All methods of controlling annual weeds have one common and fundamental purpose — to prevent seedset. Annuals have no other way to regenerate if their top is killed. Therefore, germination of annual weeds should be **encouraged** prior to planting the crop. Fall tillage and/or early spring tillage is commonly practiced to control winter annuals. Any tillage should be shallow, with the aim of destroying all top growth.

**Biennials** complete their life cycles within two years, then die. Burdock and common mullein produce tap roots and a rosette of leaves in the first year, then flower and seed in the second year. Biennials are controlled like annuals; the optimum time to destroy them is during the rosette stage of growth in the first year.

**Perennials** live for more than two years and may live almost indefinitely. In many cases, no seed is produced the first year, but seeding occurs each successive year thereafter for the life of the plant. In many cases, only the root system is perennial and the top growth is annual. Dandelion and quack grass are examples of perennial weeds. Perennials can be divided into two types: creeping perennials and simple perennials.

Creeping perennials are characterized by their ability to develop extensive patches from aggressive root systems and to grow from considerable depth in the soil. They normally store large amounts of carbohydrates in the root system which, in turn, supports the production of numerous shoots along the full length of the expanding rootstocks. Canada thistle and toad flax are typical examples of hardy, creeping perennial weeds.

Stems, rhizomes, roots and buds are vegetative methods by which weeds reproduce. A most difficult weed to control is quackgrass, which spreads chiefly by vegetative means. Another example is smooth brome grass. Both plants spread by means of true underground stems (rhizomes). These aggressive, horizontal, underground stems are characterized by numerous joints, each with vegetative buds capable of producing upright stems.

Creeping perennials may invade new soil and spread very rapidly by vegetative means alone. A small root cutting of Canada Thistle, less than 2 cm (3/4 in) long can, in one season, produce a mature plant with underground rootstocks spreading over an area of 4.5 m (15 ft) in diameter.

Simple perennials reproduce from seeds only since they do not possess any means of vegetative reproduction. The common dandelion is an example of a tap-rooted perennial weed which regularly reproduces from wind-borne seed. Foxtail barley is an example of a well-known, fibrous-rooted, grassy weed which depends entirely on seed for spread and survival.

### ORIGIN AND SPREAD OF WEEDS

Many plants considered as weeds are not native to the area in which they are now problem plants. For example, some of the common weeds and their native lands are listed in Table 6-1.

The control of introduced weeds is often more difficult than the control of native weeds. For example, the control of Canada thistle and knapweed is made more difficult, in part, because natural control factors (including insects and diseases), which help to keep them in check in their native countries, are not present in western Canada. Both Canada thistle and knapweed (several types) were accidentally introduced into Canada as impurities in seed grain. They proved to be well adapted to the climate and soils of Canada; their natural enemies were left behind, thereby allowing them to prosper and multiply in this new land.

Although plants themselves cannot move, their seeds, fruit, runners, rhizomes and rootstocks can. Seed is the method by which weeds are usually spread in spite of the fact that, in general, seeds cannot move themselves. They must depend on other forces to move them. Man is the major force responsible for the spread of weed seeds through his transfer of seed and, to a certain extent, through carelessness. The spread of common tansy, toad flax and scentless chamomile in central and northern Alberta are examples of weed spread by man. These plants were originally brought in as flowering ornamentals. They proved to be very well adapted to both soils and climate and spread rapidly from the original garden plantings. More recently, common groundsel has arrived as an impurity in vegetable seed such as carrots. Chickweed has spread from soil in bedding plants and that accompanying the roots of balled and burlap shipments of trees and shrubs.

### SEED PRODUCTION
The seed is the primary survival mechanism for annual and biennial weeds. One characteristic common to weedy plants is their ability to produce seed in abundance as indicated in Table 6-2.

### SEED DISSEMINATION
Most common weeds tend to produce large numbers of small seeds which help to insure their spread and survival.

## Table 6-2
## SEED COUNTS OF SOME COMMON WEEDS

| WEED | NUMBER OF SEEDS PER PLANT |
|------|---------------------------|
| Canada Thistle | 680 |
| Kochia | 14,600 |
| Purslane | 72,500 |
| Lamb's Quarters | 193,000 |
| Red Root Pigweed | 196,400 |
| Shepherd's Purse | 38,500 |

## Table 6-1
## ORIGIN OF SOME COMMON WEEDS

| EUROPE | EURASIA | WESTERN CANADA |
|--------|---------|----------------|
| Canada Thistle | Stinkweed | Field Horsetail |
| Chickweed | Baby's Breath | Foxtail Barley |
| Quackgrass | Knapweed | Milkweed |
| Scentless Chamomile | Purslane | American Dragonhead |
| Shepherd's Purse | Wild Carrot | Rough Cinquefoil |
| Flixweed | Ground Ivy | Poison Ivy |
| Round-leaved Mallow | Toad Flax | Water Hemlock |
| **Oxeye Daisy** | Nodding Thistle | Yarrow |

Agents involved in seed dispersal include wind, birds and animals, run-off water, the use of weed-infested manure and mulches, and seed supplies containing weed seeds.

### SEED GERMINATION
Many seeds do not germinate immediately after ripening but will do so over a period of years. This built-in mechanism is known as **seed dormancy**. Seed dormancy may be an important factor that favors the survival of weedy plants. Table 6-3 indicates the lifespan of weed seeds which have been buried in the soil for extended periods of time and tested regularly to determine their ability to germinate.

## WEED SEEDS IN ORGANIC MATTER

Gardeners regularly attempt to improve the structure and tilth of garden soils by incorporating various kinds of organic matter such as manure, moss peat, straw, sawdust and compost. The gardener's concern is for all these products to be free of viable weed seeds. A careful watch for the presence

of weeds is necessary. For example, moss peat imported into Alberta has been identified as a source of sheep sorrel infestations. Also, unclean straw and partially decomposed manures routinely contain weed seeds. Manures, in various stages of decomposition, can still be the source of many garden weeds since an estimated 75 per cent of common weed seeds retain their ability to germinate even after passing through the digestive tract of some farm animals (see Table 6-4).

If problem weeds are known to exist in hay, straw, coarsely-ground feed grain, or screenings, then such materials should always be treated to destroy the seeds before they enter the soil. For example, manure containing weed seeds, litter and bedding should be well rotted to destroy weed seeds before use. The effectiveness of rotting depends on the size of the pile, type of manure, moisture content, temperature generated within the pile, condition of weed seeds, climate and length of storage.

## Table 6-3
## LIFESPAN OF WEED SEEDS

| UP TO 10 YEARS | 11 TO 20 YEARS | 21 TO 40 YEARS |
|----------------|----------------|----------------|
| Chickweed | Canada Thistle | Lamb's Quarters |
| Green Foxtail | Ox-Eye Daisy | Purslane |
| | Plantain | Red Root Pigweed |

## DEPTH OF ROOTS

The depth to which a root system will penetrate depends on the soil, depth of the water table and nature of the subsoil. In untilled soils, the major part of the root system of weeds (such as Canada thistle) develops within the top 30 cm (1 ft) of the soil, while in loose, well-tilled garden soils, roots could extend 2 m (6 ft) or more.

## METHODS OF WEED CONTROL

Weed control is a technology, an understanding of weed control principles is essential before the techniques can be adopted or modified. Weed control may be defined as 'killing or suppressing weeds to a degree that permits satisfactory gardening operations'.

Three fundamental methods of weed control include:

- preventive methods
- cultural control
- chemical control

### PREVENTION

The best general check against all weeds plants is to prevent their entry and, hence, blooming and seed setting. Some preventive methods of weed control are:

1. Use only clean seed. Do not knowingly plant weed-contaminated seed of any sort (i.e., grass, vegetable, or flower seed).
2. Strive to ensure that any purchase or imported topsoil, sand or manure is weed free.
3. Check for weeds in the container or root ball of nursery stock material. After setting out nursery stock, periodically check for and destroy all weed growth at the base of new plants.

### CULTURAL CONTROL

Effective weed control is achieved when weeds are mechanically destroyed at their weakest or most susceptible stage of growth. This can be done by a variety of methods including:

- **Hand Weeding** is best accomplished when the soil is soft and weeds are small enough to allow for the entire removal of the plant. Perennial weeds require extra attention.
- **Hand Digging** is often used to remove perennial weeds. The gardener must

## Table 6-4
## GERMINATION OF WEEDS SEEDS IN MANURES

| WEED | HORSES | CATTLE | SWINE | SHEEP |
|---|---|---|---|---|
| Quackgrass | + | + | - | + |
| Red-root Pigweed | + | + | + | + |
| Curled Dock | + | + | + | + |
| Lamb's Quarters | + | + | + | + |
| Ox-Eye Daisy | - | + | | + |
| Canada Thistle | + | + | + | + |
| Dog Mustard | - | - | + | + |
| Common Purslane | - | + | | |
| Broadleaved Plantain | + | + | + | + |
| Green Foxtail | + | + | + | + |
| Nightflowering Catchfly | + | + | + | + |
| Corn Spurry | - | | + | + |
| Chickweed | + | + | + | + |
| Dandelion | - | - | + | + |
| Per cent of weeds from germinating seeds | 64% | 71% | 83% | 92% |

be persistent and thorough so that every piece of the underground rootstock is removed as very small sections will surely result in regrowth.

- **Hoeing**-a sharp hoe is a valuable tool for general weed control. Hoeing cuts young weeds off just below the soil surface. They are then left to wilt and dry. Most will not regrow but succulent weeds (eg., Purslane) may have to be removed as they can re-establish from plant fragments.
- **Rototilling** can be an effective method of weed control, particularly when the weeds are small and tillage operation shallow. Deep rototilling can bring new crops of weed seeds to the surface where they will likely germinate easily.
- **Fallow**-as much as half of the garden area can be left unseeded each year. This allows for several cultivations during the unseeded portion during the growing season which serves to eliminate successive crops of annual weeds, as well as creeping, rooted perennial weeds such as Canada thistle, horsetail and quackgrass.
- **Mulches** are usually organic materials like weed-free straw or grass clippings placed on the soil to retard weed growth and conserve moisture. Plastic mulches, usually in the form of sheets of black plastic, may enhance the production of warm season

vegetables.

### CHEMICAL CONTROL

Chemical treatment will likely continue to find favor for weed control in lawns and will also continue to be of limited value in smaller flower and vegetable gardens where a wide assortment of plants grow in a relatively small area. Herbicides do have some specialized advantages. For example:

1. Carefully selected herbicides can be applied to selected row crops where cultivation is difficult.
2. Cultivation may injure root systems and foliage. Selected herbicides may eliminate the need for cultivation.
3. Herbicides may be particularly useful in the eradication of creeping, rooted perennial weeds as an alternative to laborious hand digging.

### KINDS OF HERBICIDES

Herbicides are available in a variety of forms. They may be liquid, granular, dust or pellet which allows for a variety of application methods. Selection of herbicide is based on the type of plant (weed) to be controlled. Susceptible plants are those which may be harmed if they come into contact with the wrong heribicide or an incorrect rate of application. The types of herbicides available include:

1. **Contact herbicides** kill only the plant or plant part on which it has been placed.
2. **Systemic herbicides** are absorbed and translocated throughout the entire plant by the flow of the plant sap.
3. **Soil sterilants** are non-selective herbicides applied to the soil to prevent growth of all plants.
4. **Selective herbicides** kill the target weeds and leave others undamaged.
5. **Non-selective herbicides** damage or kill all vegetation to which they are applied.
6. **Pre-plant herbicides** are applied to the soil before the desired crop is seeded.

### ADDITIONAL WEED CONTROL INFORMATION

Information on specific weeds can be found at the end of this lesson which can be used for the purpose of selecting effective methods of control. The listing is in no way complete for all the weeds that the home gardener may encounter in Alberta. However, the 15 weeds listed are representative of the types that continue to compete for nutrients and space in backyard gardens and lawns. More comprehensive listings can be obtained from some of the books listed in Resource Materials.

The 'Backyard Pest Management' (Agdex 605-3) reprinted in this lesson, provides a very good overview of weed control principles and their application to home gardening. This information is contained in the section entitled, 'Weed Control for Home Grounds', which also gives some general chemical application recommendations for specific weeds. This, and all other publications dealing with weed control techniques, emphasizes safe use of chemical products and the need to follow label directions in order to achieve effective and safe weed control.

## PLANT DISEASE

The science of plant disease or disorders is called **plant pathology**. Plant disease affects all aspects of plant growth from seedling to harvest and storage. The study of plant diseases includes:

- causes of disease
- effects of disease on crop or flower production
- recognition and development of diseases
- control of plant diseases.

This section will enable home gardeners to become more aware of plant diseases in the landscape and garden. Based upon this awareness, precautions can be taken to eliminate or reduce losses from plant diseases.

## WHAT IS A PLANT DISEASE?

Diseased plants are distinguished by changes in their shape or growth patterns which are brought about by unfavorable environmental conditions or by parasitic diseases. They are not growing normally and something is wrong. Diseases such as fireblight of apple trees and botytris blight on peonies may be easily detected at certain growth stages. Root rot in peas or sweet peas, however, may be less obvious. These are all infectious diseases caused by parasitic living organisms such as fungi and bacteria. Examples of disease caused by non-living causes are:

- lime-induced chlorosis in mountain ash, plums and roses, evidenced by abnormal yellowing of leaves (see Plant Nutrition lesson, IRON).
- herbicide damage to green ash and Manitoba maple evidenced by narrow, elongated leaves with twisted margins and prominent light-colored veins.
- winter injury to raspberry evidenced by failure of upper parts of canes to leaf out.

Thus, diseases in vegetable crops and ornamentals, as well as turf, can be caused by **biotic** (living organisms) or **abiotic** (non-living) factors.

## SYMPTOMS OF DISEASE

Plant diseases may be grouped by their symptoms and named accordingly; scab on cucumber, wilting on sunflowers, mildew on phlox, rots, and so on. However, the same symptoms may be caused by entirely different agents and, therefore, require entirely different methods of control. Wilting in plants may be caused by bacterial or fungal infection or insufficient moisture in the

soil. The identification of individual diseases is often difficult and requires considerable training and field experience before a diagnosis can be made with confidence. Examples of diseases and their symptoms follow.

### Figure 6-8
### COMMON LEAF SPOT OF ROSES

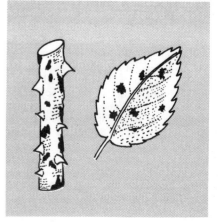

**SPOT DISEASES**

Spots on leaves and stems are often the first clue that plants are diseased. They are caused by various fungi, bacteria and environmental conditions. Generally, the size, shape and color of the spot is constant for the disease. Black spot of roses is a good example of a disease that causes distinctive spots on the leaflets of roses (see Figure 6-8).

### Figure 6-9
### SEEDLING BLIGHT ON PEAS AND BEANS

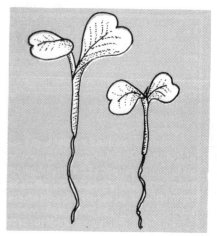

## BLIGHT

A blight typically kills young growing tissues. Seedling blights are very common throughout Alberta. The blight fungus kills the young stems and roots. The disease is very active during dry, cold soil conditions on such crops as cabbages, beans, cauliflower and turnip in early May (see Figure 6-9).

## SCORCH

During very hot weather, the sun's rays may cause a browning or bleaching and shriveling of leaves. A variety of woody ornamentals, including notably hardy types like poplars, can show scorch symptoms during sudden periods of extreme heat. Similar symptoms on trees may result from high levels of soil salts in poorly drained areas or from roadside salt run-off used on streets during winter (see Figure 6-10).

## Figure 6-10
## LEAF SCORCH

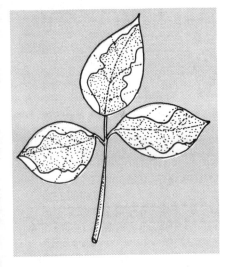

## WILT

Wilting is due to a deficiency of water in the leaves and stems. This may be due to lack of water in the soil, injury to the root system by root maggots, or to the effects of root and stem diseases. Fusarium wilt of asters, for example, is caused by a soil-borne fungus that attacks plants through their roots (see Figure 6-11).

## DAMPING-OFF

Certain fungi frequently attack seedlings, and kill the tissues of stems and roots near the soil surface.

## Figure 6-11
## FUSARIUM WILT

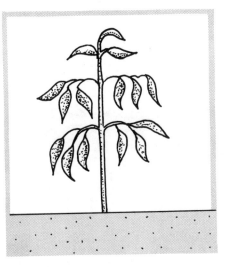

The disease is active under wet soil conditions. Fungal infection causes the plants to fall over and rot. Greenhouse seedlings are most susceptible to damping-off, particularly under conditions of overwintering and poor sanitation (see Figure 6-12).

## Figure 6-12
## DAMPING OFF OF SEEDLINGS

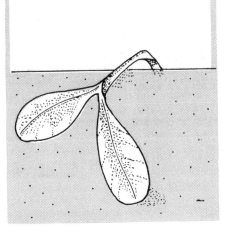

## ROTS

An organism which causes the distintegration of a large part of a plant causes rot. Commercial greenhouse growers of poinsettias often have problems with root rot diseases caused by several distinct types of fungi (see Figure 6-13).

## Figure 6-13
## ROOT ROT OF POINTSETTIAS

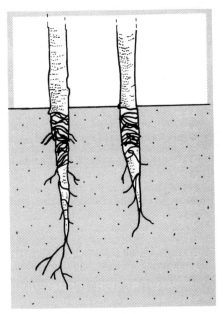

## STUNTS

Plants may be stunted from a number of causes, including living and non-living diseases. Rhizoctonia root rot and potato leaf roll virus in potatoes can be important disease problems in commercial potato production. Root knot nematode causes stunting in greenhouse tomatoes (see Figure 6-14).

## Figure 6-14
## STUNTING

## LIVING (BIOTIC) CAUSES OF DISEASE

The most important causes of infectious plant diseases are fungi, bacteria, viruses and nematodes. As a group, they are referred to as microbes or germs.

## FUNGI

Fungi are living plants that are unable to manufacture their own food. Familiar fungi are molds, mushrooms, yeasts, and fungi that produce penicillins. Depending on the fungus, they may be destructive pests or highly useful organisms.

Fungi that obtain their food from dead plants or animals are **saprophytes**. Fungi that obtain their food from living plants and animals are **parasites**. Fungi, along with other microbes, are nature's primary means of 'recycling' dead plants and animals back to their elemental components by a process called **rotting**. They are mainly responsible for the disappearance of vegetable refuse roots and lawn clippings turned into the soil or used to produce compost. Fungi that feed directly on living plants and cause diseases are called **pathogens** (disease-causing organisms). Worldwide, more than 100,000 types of fungi have been identified. One-third of these can cause plant diseases.

Fungi and other microbes are given Latin (scientific) names just like green plants so that they may be internationally identified. The fungus responsible for cottony snow mold of turf is given the Latin name *Coprinus psychromorbidus*. The fungus causing scab of potatos is called *Streptomyces scabies*. Plant parasitic fungi are usually limited in the kinds of plants they attack.

### WHAT DOES A FUNGUS LOOK LIKE?

Growing fungi are composed of very fine, hair-like white or colored threads called **hyphae**. Hyphae form the body of the fungus called **mycelium** which appears as the fluffy growth on rotting food. For a practical demonstration, place some moist bread inside an airtight plastic bag for a week and then examine the contents. Fungi reproduce by means of minute spores (seeds) of variable shape, size and color. These spores can be produced directly from the hyphae. Alternatively, spores may be formed in specialized structures called **fruiting bodies** (eg., mushrooms).

Disease develops when a fungus spore is able to infect and grow on a healthy plant. The reaction of the plant to the infecting fungus is the expression (symptom) of the disease (see Figure 6-15).

Spores are the seeds in the life cycle of

## Figure 6-15
## FUNGI

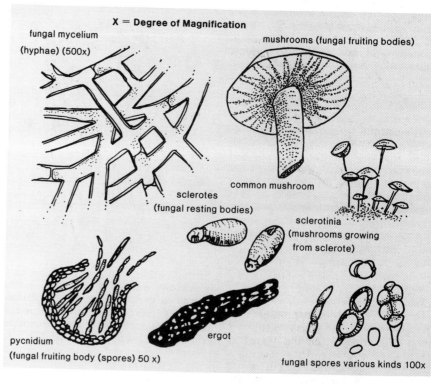

X = Degree of Magnification

fungal mycelium (hyphae) (500x)

mushrooms (fungal fruiting bodies)

common mushroom

sclerotes (fungal resting bodies)

sclerotinia (mushrooms growing from sclerote)

pycnidium (fungal fruiting body (spores) 50 x)

ergot

fungal spores various kinds 100x

the fungus. Spores have these characteristics:

- they are the reproductive structures of the fungus
- they spread fungi to new locations
- they survive over winter or other periods of adverse weather conditions.

Spores can be dispersed or spread, sometimes for great distances, by various means including air currents, running water, splashing rain and insects. Some fungi, such as *Sclerotinia* (white mold of snapbeans and cottony snow mold of turf) produce special resting bodies called **sclerotes** or **ergots** which may be much larger than spores. They are about the size of cereal grains and can survive in or on the soil for a number of years. They are composed of mycelium inside a tough, protective, blackish rind. Sclerotia will germinate during moist, favorable summer weather and produce tiny mushrooms that release infectious spores. Sclerotinia spores attack snapbeans, sunflowers, petunias and carrots in storage; ergot spores attack the developing cereal grains.

## BACTERIA

Bacteria are essential for the production of cheese, yogurt, many drugs, vitamins and other complex chemicals. They form the nodules on the roots of legumes that fix nitrogen (alfalfa, beans, peas, clovers). Some bacteria cause diseases in man, animals and plants.

Bacteria are the smallest free living organisms known to man. Some are so small that 5,000 of them laid end to end would measure only one centimetre (about 1/2 in). Bacteria are invisible to the naked eye. They are generally single-celled organisms that cannot produce their own food. A bacterial population can double in as little as 20 minutes under ideal growing conditions. (see Figure 6-16).

### HOW DO BACTERIA GET AROUND?

Unlike fungi, bacteria cannot penetrate an intact surface of a plant, so they invade plants through natural openings or wounds. They need free water to enter natural breathing pores on plant leaves and stems. Thus, bacteria can multiply quickly and are most destructive under moist, warm conditions. Bacteria

## Figure 6-16
## BACTERIA

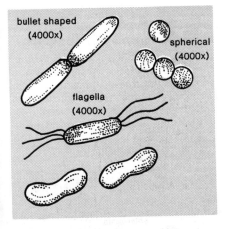

bullet shaped
(4000x)

spherical
(4000x)

flagella
(4000x)

are spread by splashing rain, plant to plant contact and insects. They are also spread on or inside seed and by wind-blown infected plant debris.

### SYMPTOMS OF BACTERIAL DISEASE
Bacterial infections cause distinctive, water-soaked spots on the leaves of many kinds of plants. They cause leaf blights, wilts, scabs and cankers, as well as soft rots of fruit, root and storage organisms. Bacterial diseases cause leaf and stem blights (fireblight) in many Species of the rose Family. Leaf and tuber diseases of potato (bacterial ring rot) also result from bacterial invasion.

### VIRUSES
Viral diseases cause such conditions as colds, influenza and smallpox in man; foot and mouth in cattle; swine fever in hogs; and mosaic stunts and yellows in crop plants. Viruses are named for the symptoms they produce (eg., tobacco mosaic virus and aster yellows).

Viruses are smaller than bacteria and can multiply, reproduce and survive only in living cells. Viruses are systemic (i.e., they are present in all parts of infected plants). Most viruses are transmitted by insects such as aphids, leafhoppers and mites which transfer the viruses from one plant to another during feeding. These insect carriers are referred to as **vectors**. They overwinter in perennial or biennial weeds and, in some cases, inside seeds (see Figure 6-17).

### VIRUS DISEASES IN ALBERTA
There are thousands of viral diseases of plants worldwide. Fortunately, only a few

## Figure 6-17
## VIRUSES

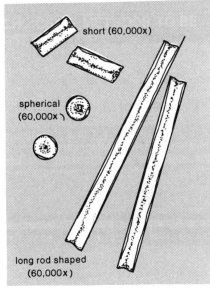

short (60,000x)

spherical
(60,000x)

long rod shaped
(60,000x)

of the horticultural crops grown in Alberta have viral diseases. Two examples are leaf roll of potato and tobacco mosaic virus in tomato.

### NEMATODES
Nematodes are small, worm-like creatures. They may exist on organic matter in the soil or as parasites of plants, fungi, insects, animals and even man. They are the cause of such disorders as trichinosis and elephantiasis. The life cycle of nematodes can be divided into six stages: egg, four larval forms and the adult, which may take from weeks or months to complete (see Figure 6-18).

Symptoms of nematode injury are often visible on plant roots or in above-ground plant parts. Below-ground symptoms of nematode injury are visible as excessive root formations, galls, or root knots, whereas above-ground symptoms include yellowing, stem swelling, stunting or reduced vigor of infected plants.

In warmer climates, nematode diseases are major barriers to crop production and cause millions of dollars in losses annually. While nematodes are common in Alberta soils, nematode diseases are serious problems in only a few crops. The stem nematode causes stunting and yield losses in alfalfa stands in southern Alberta. The sugar beet cyst nematode causes problems in beets and in plants of the cabbage Family.

### NEMATODE SURVIVAL
Mobility in nematodes is never great. Survival is achieved by the ability of the nematode to exist for years in soil as eggs or cysts which hatch when a suitable host is grown. Nematode pests are carried to new areas by man, wind, water or animals. Nematode spread may be restricted by quarantine measures. This is the case with the golden nematode of potatoes, which occurs in soils on Vancouver Island and Newfoundland. Stringent quarantine measures on the movement of potatoes, other plant parts and soil have prevented this pest from being introduced to the rest of Canada for over 30 years.

## Figure 6-18
## NEMATODES

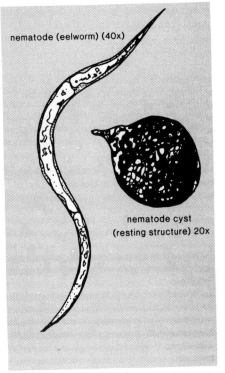

nematode (eelworm) (40x)

nematode cyst
(resting structure) 20x

## NON-LIVING (ABIOTIC) CAUSES OF DISEASE

### NUTRITIONAL FACTORS
In addition to diseases caused by parasitic organisms, there are a number of unhealthy conditions of growing plants (non-parasitic diseases) caused by improper nutrition. These conditions can

be corrected if their cause is understood. The appearance of affected plants usually provides the clue to the disorder.

To grow normally, all plants require nutrients from the soil in definitive quantities. Nutritional diseases can result from a deficiency or an excess of a particular soil nutrient. For example, too little available nitrogen may result in chlorosis (general yellowing) and stunting. In other situations, patches of alkaline soils resulting from the accumulation of certain salts can seriously interfere with plant growth. Plants vary in their ability to tolerate soil alkalinity or acidity. For example, an overabundance of lime tends to 'bind' iron; that is, to hold this micronutrient in a form that plants cannot utilize (see Plant Nutrition lesson, PLANT ANALYSES AND NUTRIENT INTERACTIONS and Table 4-2). This can sometimes be remedied by spraying affected plants (roses maples, mountain ash) with a solution of iron sulphate or chelated iron.

## ENVIRONMENTAL FACTORS

Sudden changes in a plant's environment will sometimes produce symptoms that may be confused with those of an infectious disease. Late spring frosts may cause abnormal growth in some crops. When the growing point of peas, potatoes or sunflowers is killed by frost, new growth will begin from a dormant bud or buds below the damaged area. This results in a plant with a distorted appearance or an excess number of branches. Purpling of leaf tissues may be symptomatic of chilling injury or phosphorus deficiency. Damage to plants can also be associated with exposure to toxic emissions (or their by-products) in the atmosphere. For example, ozone concentrations of more than eight parts per million (ppm) may damage leaf tissues of crops such as snap beans. The inappropriate use of herbicides, insecticides and growth regulators may also cause serious injury to plants.

Many gardeners will be familiar with herbicide damage in situations where application rates, timing with respect to plant growth, and limitations of crop and cultivar sensitivity are not followed. Much too frequently, damaged ornamental trees and ornamentals of all kinds, suffer after the inappropriate use of soil sterilants in driveways and back alleys. Some herbicides cause a slight

chlorosis after application, while general yellowing, loss of vigor and wilting or browning of leaf tips may occur in combination with moisture or temperature stress. Symptoms of herbicide injury can resemble those produced by nutritional disorders, infectious diseases, or insect damage.

Insecticides can cause foliage damage to crops, particularly if used at higher than recommended rates. Both insecticides and fungicides used as seed treatments may cause seedling damage if used improperly.

## ADDITIONAL PLANT DISEASE INFORMATION

The publication, 'Backyard Pest Management', reprinted in this lesson, details most of the plant diseases that attack Alberta gardens. For easy reference, the section on Plant Diseases is further divided into sections based on the type of plants attacked by various diseases. Therefore, if you seek information particular to diseases of small fruits, refer to the section entitled, 'Control of Small Fruit Diseases'. Note that most of the control recommendations for plant diseases stress the importance of prevention.

# VERTEBRATES

Vertebrates include a wide array of animals characterized by a segmented spinal column or, in simple terms, a backbone. Included are mammals, birds, reptiles and fish, but the gardener's problem may be as close as the neighbor's cat or a troublesome robin. Prevention of damage is the primary objective and control methods may vary from complete eradication to screen protection of plants or the use of chemical repellents.

The following information can be regarded as supplementary or further information to that already contained in the 'Backyard Pest Management' publication reprinted at the end of this lesson under the heading 'Control of Vertebrate Pests'.

## MICE

Mice are nocturnal animals, being most active at night and in situations that provide shelter. Gardeners know that

mice wreak havoc in stored seed supplies; they consume a variety of emerging seedlings in greenhouses and, sometimes, work under the snow in winter and strip the bark from shrubs like Nanking cherry.

Mice are best controlled by eliminating tall grass, garden debris and any situation which provides shelter and food for survival. Traps are effective when properly baited with tasty morsels of bacon rind, peanut butter, cheese and sunflower seeds. Traps need to be checked often and reset regularly.

Ready mixed baits containing anticoagulants are available from commercial sources. Rodent repellents that contain the bitter tasting chemical Thiram, may be applied in the autumn to the bark of valued shrubs and trees.

Chances of mouse damage will decrease if lawns are neatly mowed and long grass and vegetation are removed from adjacent areas. Mice can best be removed from homes and out buildings with traps. If mice are a continuing problem, all holes and cracks wider than 65 mm (1/4 in) should be sealed with concrete mortar, galvanized sheet metal, heavy-gauge hardware cloth or other material that will resist rodent gnawing.

## POCKET GOPHERS

Pocket gophers are thickset, grey-brown rodents, 18-24 cm long, with small ears, large cheek pouches and long, protruding front teeth. Their common name 'mole' comes from their habit of building a network of underground passages 8 cm in diameter and 10-20 cm below the soil surface. The exhausted soil is disposed of in the conspicuous but unwelcome 'hills' in lawns and gardens.

Pocket gophers eat a variety of garden crops and kill woody plants and shrubs by feeding on the roots. They also deface lawns with the mounds of soil that are deposited above ground by their burrow building. After the mound is built, the gopher plugs the burrow entrance with soil so the entrances may not be conspicuous. There are several gopher traps available including the 'Guardian', 'California', and 'Victor'. These traps must be set within the burrow. The burrow will be 2-20 cm (3/4-8 in) below ground level and can be located with a long screw driver or probe. Begin to probe 1-2 cm (1/2-1 in) from the edge of the mound. The burrow will be located upslope from the mounds and at the base of fan-shaped mounds or in the indentation of horseshoe-shaped mounds. Place the trap within the burrow as directed on the product label.

## RICHARDSON GROUND SQUIRREL

Although several types of ground squirrel inhabit the prairie provinces, the most widespread and abundant is the Richardson Ground Squirrel. This 'flicker-tail' or 'gopher' is a widespread resident of the treeless plains and parklands. They tend to live in colonies and, when unchecked, can multiply rapidly.

Ground squirrels occasionally move into lawns and gardens in mid-summer. They dig a burrow system with a 5-6 cm (2-2 1/2 in) diameter entrance. The simplest method of removing ground squirrels is to fill the burrow with water from a garden hose. The squirrels can then be dispatched when they emerge from the burrow. Alternatively, ground squirrels will often move elsewhere and bother someone else if the burrow is filled with water several times.

Ground squirrels can also be poisoned within urban areas with a prepared bait containing 0.005 per cent chlorophacinone. Six pellets or 15 mL (1/2 fl. oz.) of bait should be placed within each ground squirrel hole. After 48 hours, re-bait all holes where the soil covering has been disturbed or removed. Remove and bury any poisoned ground squirrel bodies found above ground. A third baiting might be required for complete control.

## RABBITS AND HARES

Rabbits and hares are cyclic, reaching peaks in populations approximately every ten years. During these peak population periods and, to a lesser extent in other years, rabbits will feed on the bark of fruit trees and various ornamental and shelterbelt plants.

There are a number of ready-made repellents that discourage rabbits from feeding on the bark and twigs. Most contain the bitter tasting chemical Thiram. Repellents should be applied in the fall, when the leaves have fallen, the bark is dry and temperatures are above freezing. The repellent should cover the

trunk of the tree 60-100 cm (24-40in) above the snow line. When only a few trees are involved, an alternative to chemical repellent is to use are tree guards. Tree guards are made of 0.65 cm (1/4 in) wire screening set 7-10 cm (3-4 in) into the ground and extending 60-100 cm (24-40 in) above the snow line.

## YELLOW-BELLIED SAPSUCKER

Yellow-bellied sapsuckers attack only living trees. In urban areas, where trees are planted for ornamentals and shelter, they seem to prefer birches, Colorado spruce, Scots pine and Siberian elm. The adult birds cause damage to trees by pecking horizontal rows of regularly spaced, small, oval or squarish holes through the bark and into the sapwood. Sapsuckers then use their brush-like tongue to drink the sap that oozes into the holes. They also eat the outer wood layers. As one row of holes becomes dry, another row is drilled. Rows of holes may extend for some distance up the trunk and along heavier branches. Injury is most pronounced in the spring and early summer when sap pressure is greatest.

The extent of sapsucker damage varies. Lightly attacked trees usually make a complete recovery but, where several rows of holes are present, branches may be permanently damaged and tops of trees killed. Secondary damage may result from the entry of harmful insects and disease organisms by way of these holes.

Control is difficult because the yellow-bellied sapsucker is protected under the Migratory Birds Convention Act and may not be killed or captured, nor can its eggs be destroyed.

Serious damage can be prevented, to some extent, by frightening devices (flutters) in affected trees. Wrapping damaged areas with strips of burlap and leaving it in place from April to late summer can also be effective. Sealing holes with pruning paint (spray form) will reduce sap flow and prevent entry of insects and disease.

## ROBINS

Although the first robins to appear are warmly greeted as harbingers of spring,

and their removal of earthworms and insects is generally applauded, they often wear out their welcome as the strawberry season appears and saskatoons and Nanking Cherries hang heavy on the bushes. Frightening devices (flutters) have generally proven ineffective, as have rubber hoses coiled to resemble snakes and pans of water placed among the rows. Wherever possible, the best control appears to be total exclusion of birds through the construction of a 4 cm (1 1/2 in) poultry wire mesh covering placed 10 cm (4 in) above the plants so that the birds cannot reach the fruit.

## DOMESTIC ANIMALS

This vertebrate concern is usually centered on neighborhood cats and dogs that are simply going about normal activities of 'marking territories' and necessary activities of life. To keep peace in the neighborhood, the problem is probably best solved by adequate fencing to act as a deterrent.

Several spray-ons are commercially available and repellents such as 'Scent-off' can be effective when hung on lower branches of plants, taped to steps and railings, or put in flower boxes or beds.

## CONCLUSION

Pest control may be defined as suppressing undesirable forces that limit production to a degree that permits satisfactory gardening operations. Implicit in the control of pests is a necessity for sound judgement to be excercised by the pest controller. Each pest control situation requires a knowledgeable assessment to be made regarding the present and potential extent of the problem. Such assessment provides a base upon which reasonable control measures can be implemented.

The basic principles of pest control are:

Insects

1. Insure that the insect is a pest that needs to be controlled.
2. Use preventive control measures where pest problems are common and cultural control practices where

available.
3. Ascertain the extent of the insect infestation and select a suitable control measure.

## Weeds

1. Suppress or prevent weed seed production.
2. Reduce weed seed reserves in the soil.
3. Prevent weed seed spread.
4. Suppress growth of existing weeds.

## Plant Diseases

1. Prevent disease organisms from entering the plant by using chemical or physical barriers.
2. Grow varieties that are resistant to disease organisms.
3. Use disease free stock.

Source: Weed Control For The Home Grounds (Agdex 641-1)

## SELF CHECK *QUIZ*

1. List the three fundamental methods of weed control.

2. List four factors that may reduce the effectiveness of herbicides?

3. How should pesticides be stored?

4. How do systemic insecticides differ from non-systemic?

5. What plants are susceptible to fireblight and what are the symptoms of fireblight?

6. What is the best method to protect a strawberry patch from robins?

7. What chemical is available to protect trees and shrubs from damaged caused by mice and rabbits? How does it work?

8. What is the evidence that a sapsucker has been on a birch tree?

9. Why is chemical control of dandelions easier than that of quackgrass in lawns?

# COMMON GARDEN WEEDS

### BROAD-LEAFED PLANTAIN - *PLANTAGO MAJOR*

Plantain is a perennial with a short, vertical rootstock and many slender lateral roots. The large and oval leaves lie close to the ground. The inconspicuous flowers are crowded on slender spikes, 5-30 cm (2-12 in) long. Birds are fond of the tiny, dark-brown, angled seeds.

#### Control

The thick, tenacious rootstock makes hand pulling in gardens difficult. Timely hoeing in the garden and mowing the lawn from July to September reduces seed production. Plantain can be controlled in lawns with 2,4-D amine or MCPA amine. Spot treatments in September or October also aid in its control. It is resistant to dicamba.

### COMMON GROUNDSEL - *SENECIO VULGARIS*

This annual is hollow stemmed with many branches; it has become a widespread weed of lawns, gardens and wherever the soil has been disturbed. The leaves are alternated, deeply lobed and toothed. The flowers are yellow and surrounded by slender bracts. The tiny slender seeds have a cluster of fine hairs attached to the upper end.

#### Control

Groundsel is readily controlled in gardens by hoeing, especially before the seeds are mature in the fall.

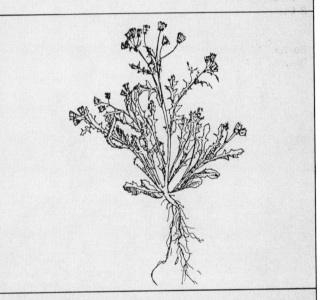

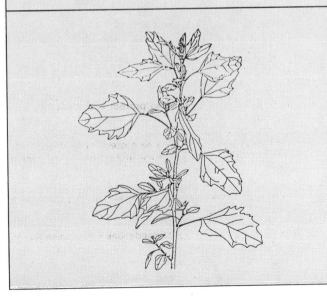

### LAMB'S QUARTERS - *CHENOPODIUM ALBUM*

Lamb's quarters is a widespread and abundant annual garden weed. Plants are identified by angular streaked stems with alternate leaves varying from spade-shaped to somewhat triangular, the lower surface is grey-green and covered with mealy particles; leaf margins coarsely toothed to nearly entire. Flowers are small, greenish and crowded in leaf axils and at the stem tips. Flowers do not have petals.

#### Control

Timely cultivation to destroy seedlings and prevent all plants from producing seed is recommended.

In lawns, chemical control can be achieved with selective herbicide mixtures applied in the spring.

Source: *Weed Control for the Home Grounds*. Alberta Agriculture, Agdex 641-1

## PURSLANE - *PORTULACA OLERACEA*

Purslane is an annual, prostrate, fleshy weed. It is troublesome in lawns, gardens and orchards. The reddish stems are often 30 cm or more in length. The yellow flowers appear in small clusters at the end of stems and in the axils of leaves. Many shiny, black seeds are produced throughout the growing season and may remain viable in the soil for several years.

### Control

Barnyard manure and mixed seed packets are common sources of infestation. As it is a vigorous competitor for space in the garden, continuous hoeing (especially in August) will help to eliminate the weed problem for the next spring. Always remove the cut off plants since the cut pieces may take root and a plant cut off while in bloom may mature its seeds before dying. Rotate your garden plots and summer fallow the unplanted portion to control this weed. In lawns, treat when young and actively growing with a selective herbicide mixture.

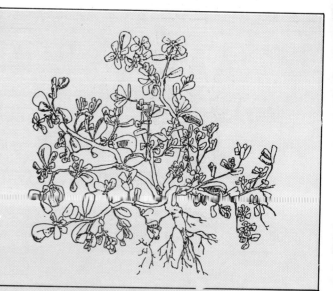

## COMMON CHICKWEED - *STELLARIA MEDIA*

This low-lying annual is commonly found in lawns and gardens. The weak, branch stems take root at the nodes. The leaves are opposite, oval, pointed at the tips and mostly smooth. The flower, like a 10-pointed star, is 6 mm (1/4 in) wide, white with five deeply lobed petals. It produces flowers and seeds throughout the growing season. It often grows where soils are compacted and in moist shady areas.

### Control

Compacted areas on the lawn should be aerated and re-seeded. Heavy trampling in one area should be avoided. Well trimmed lawn edges prevent the spread into the garden. In lawns, apply any brand of 'Chickweed and Clover Killer' in late spring. These products will contain mecoprop or mecoprop + 2,4-D + dicamba. In gardens, remove the shade where possible, till shallowly so the weed seeds are near the surface where they are encouraged to germinate and can be controlled by hoeing.

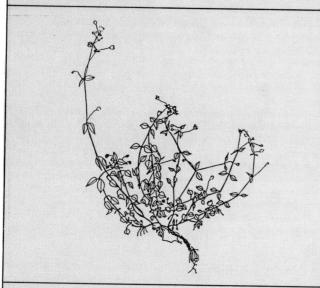

## ROUND-LEAVED MALLOW - *MALVA ROTUNDIFOLIA*

This is an introduced annual or biennial. The root is a taproot producing many branches. The lower branches spread out on the ground. The tiny white-mauve flowers are clustered in the leaf axil. The fruit is a circle of orange-like segments. The leaves are round with wavy edges. It is a nuisance in gardens and along fences.

### Control

Plants should be destroyed before the seeds can mature. If weeding in the garden has been delayed too long, the plants should be pulled, carried off and destroyed. Once established, it is difficult to control, so **good lawn** and **garden care** is essential. It can be controlled in lawns with repeated applications of selective herbicide mixtures.

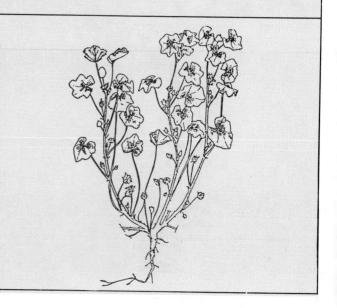

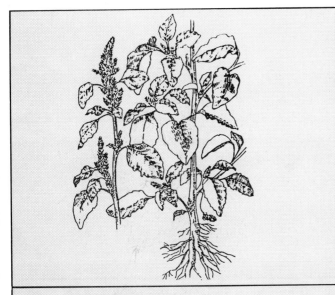

## REDROOT PIGWEED - *AMARANTHUS RETROFLEXUS*

This annual weed multiplies very rapidly from the abundant seeds produced. Seedling roots are pinkish and the stems toward the base and the roots of mature plants are reddish. The leaves are hairy below. Flowers, without petals, grow in dense spike-like clusters. The seeds are small, black and shiny. Pigweed is troublesome in gardens, in fence corners or sites where the soil has been disturbed.

**Control**

Remove all pigweed plants in the late summer and fall to save work the next spring. Seeds germinate very readily and can be encouraged to begin growth early in the spring, thus allowing control of seedlings prior to planting the garden. Weed preventers (such as EPTC and Trifluralin) applied as recommended in gardens, will kill germinating pigweed seeds. Spot treatments with selective herbicide mixtures containing dicamba will control this weed in lawns.

## ANNUAL BLUE GRASS

This is a short-lived annual grass with stems that spread on the ground and form mats. Because it is an annual, it causes unsightly dead patches in the lawn in the spring and fall. The weedy grass grows in lawns, gardens and around ornamental shrubs and trees.

**Control**

Selective removal of undesirable grasses from lawns through the use of herbicides is impossible. For immediate results in lawns, dig out isolated patches, re-seed and maintain a healthy turf. Paraquat applied to newly germinating seeds will kill annual blue grass before it becomes established. Seed or sod a lawn directly on the bare ground. Treflan, **applied as directed**, around shrubs, trees, beds and in gardens will kill the germinating seeds.

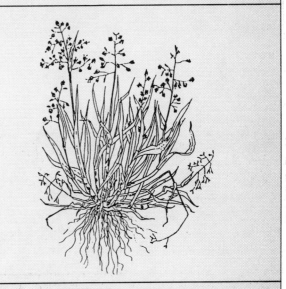

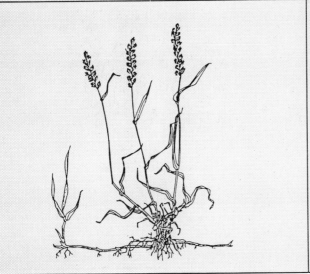

## QUACK GRASS - *AGROPYRON REPENS*

Quack grass is probably the most troublesome lawn weed in Alberta. It can be recognized by its conspicuous, creeping, underground rootstocks, which are whitish-yellow in color and by the finger-like appendages which clasp the stems at the base of the leaf blade. The wide leaved, rich green colored grass multiplies readily by seeds and a creeping rootstock. When rootstocks are broken by cutting with a shovel or rototiller, each segment is capable of reproducing a new plant.

**Control**

A relentless maintenance program is required to control quack grass.

1. A healthy, well established lawn discourages the rapid spread of quack grass.
2. Cut the lawn frequently to 3-5 cm (1 1/2-2 in).
3. For localized patches, allow to grow to 10-15 cm (4-6 in) in height, spray with glyphosate (Roundup) and after two weeks, work up and re-seed.

## DANDELION - *TARAXACUM OFFICINALE WEBER*

This perennial is probably the best known of all lawn and garden weeds. It is stalkless and has a deep tap root. Leaves form a rosette on the ground, and one or more flower heads develop on each plant. Dandelions flower from early spring throughout the growing season.

### Control

Avoid close mowing which promotes low lying leaf growth. Spray with 2,4-D or MCP amine early in the spring (early to mid-May), well before the dandelion flowers appear, and again in late summer if plants are evident in the lawn (late August to mid-September).

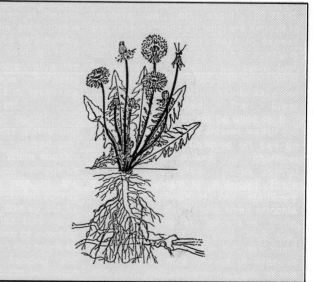

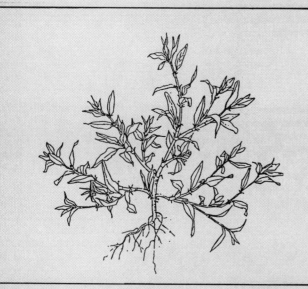

## PROSTRATE KNOTWEED - *POLYGONUM AVICULARE*

This annual weed, with prostrate wiry stems, is found spreading over the hard dry soil of foot-paths, along driveways and entrances. The small leaves are on short stems with a papery sheath at the union of the plant stem. The tiny pinkish or white flowers are formed in sheaths. The seeds are three-sided, smooth, brown and 3 mm (1/8 in) long.

### Control

Aerate compacted areas to stimulate grass growth. Hand pull old plants. Vigorous lawn growth and well trimmed edges will keep knotweed from spreading. If knotweed becomes a problem in lawns, or if chemical control on foot-paths and driveways is required - apply a selective herbicide mixture containing dicamba and 2,4-D when weeds are in seedling stage.

## SHEPHERD'S PURSE - *CAPSELLA BURSA-PASTORIA MEDIC*

This weed may behave as an annual or winter annual. Plants in almost any stage of development may be found through the summer. It has a solid, deep taproot and a rosette of leaves lying flat on the ground. The leaves are elongated and deeply lobed. Many small white flowers are produced on a flowering stem. The seedpods are heart-shaped. This common lawn and garden weed occurs throughout Alberta.

### Control

Fall hoeing will destroy rosettes and prevent early ripening the following summer. Thereafter, routine cultivation will afford effective control of this annual in gardens. In lawns, apply 2,4-D or selective herbicide mixtures containing dicamba and mecoprop when the weed is in the seedling or rosette stage, either in the fall or early spring.

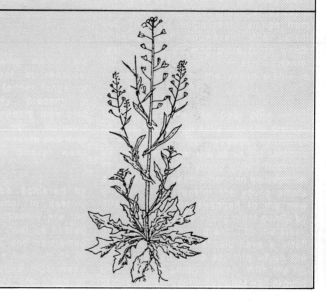

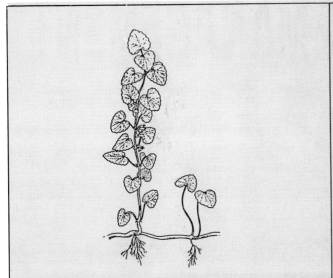

## GROUND IVY - *GLECHOMA HEDERACEA*

Also known as Creeping Charlie, this common perennial infests lawns, gardens and orchards. It is low growing and spreads by creeping stems that root at the nodes. The leaves are opposite, hairy and kidney-shaped with wavy round margins. The bluish-purple flowers are funnel-shaped and short lived. The rough, dark brown seeds are occasionally found in rock garden mixtures.

### Control

Continuous hoeing reduces garden infestation and good management controls the spread of ground ivy in the lawn. Chemical control in lawns involves spraying in late spring and again in the fall when annual growth has ceased. Selective herbicide mixtures containing 2,4-D + dicamba are effective but retreatment might be required.

## CREEPING BELLFLOWER - *CAMPANULA RAPUNCULOIDES*

This perennial, when grown as a border plant in gardens reaches 40-60 cm (6-24 in) in height. If neglected, it spreads by means of creeping underground rootstocks to the lawn and assumes a lower growth habit. The flowers are bluish-purple and bellshaped. The lower leaves are long-stemmed and heart-shaped while the upper leaves may be stemless. This invasive plant is prevalent in rock gardens.

### Control

When hand pulled, the plant breaks off at a heavy feeder root a few centimetres below ground level and the rootstock sends up another plant. Continuous cultivation helps reduce its growth in gardens. If the problem is severe in lawns, digging out the clumps and re-seeding will speed up control.

It can be controlled in lawns with selective herbicide mixtures containing dicamba + 2,4-D + mecoprop. Repeated treatments may be necessary.

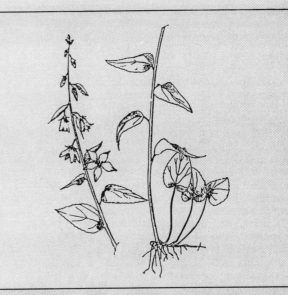

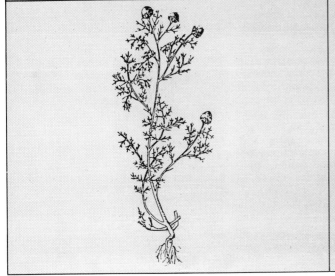

## PINEAPPLEWEED - *MATRICARIA MATRICIOIDES PORTER*

This annual persists on roadsides, along foot-paths, along edges of lawns and in gardens. It is low growing with many branches of finely divided leaves. The flower heads are yellowish-green, cone-shaped and on the ends of the branches. The plant emits an odor of pineapple when crushed.

### Control

Keep edges between lawn and driveways or sidewalk well trimmed. Compacted areas should be aerated. It is best controlled in gardens by hoeing. For control in lawns, repeated treatments with selective herbicide mixtures containing 2,4-D and MCPA are needed to effectively control pineappleweed.

# BACK YARD PEST MANAGEMENT

**BACK YARD PEST MANAGEMENT** COVERS MOST OF THE PEST-RELATED PROBLEMS THAT THE ALBERTA GARDENER IS LIKELY TO ENCOUNTER AND OFFERS PRACTICAL, COST-EFFECTIVE SOLUTIONS. KEEP THIS PUBLICATION IN A HANDY PLACE. THE INFORMATION IT CONTAINS WON'T GO OUT OF DATE.

## INTRODUCTION

This publication has been developed to provide the homeowner with basic information on control of insects, diseases, weeds and vertebrate pests around the home. The publication covers most pests common to Alberta and will help you to identify and solve pest problems using both chemical and non-chemical approaches. In many cases, pests do not build up to significant levels and controls are not necessary; in other cases, simply removing insects by hand will reduce the problem. As another alternative, application of a pesticide may be required at some time during the season. Consider the magnitude of your problem and select your solution accordingly.

## ALTERNATIVES TO PESTICIDES

Certain naturally occurring insecticides, such as pyrethrum and rotenone (derris dust), are readily available and relatively safe to use. Even so, many pest problems around homes do not require control with pesticides and can be solved using cultural or biological approaches. Some alternatives to control with pesticides in various situations follow:

## TREES AND SHRUBS:

Most trees and shrubs, especially deciduous types, can withstand substantial defoliation. Insect pests can be picked off trees, or leaves harboring pests can be removed and the insects killed. Such pests as caterpillars, leaf rollers, woolly bears and galls can be dealt with in this fashion at low infestation levels.

Pruning diseased branches can eliminate or delay spread of disease. Scrap-

ing off the egg bands of such insects as the forest tent caterpillar from twigs and branches of trees and shrubs can reduce infestation.

Spraying trees and shrubs with a strong stream of water can dislodge and kill pests such as spider mites, pear slugs and tent caterpillars. Repeated applications of soap flakes (30 mL (2 Tbsp) per litre of water) or Safer's Insecticidal Soap in spray solution will provide good control of many insects.

Another alternative is to use a **biological insecticide** containing a bacteria called **Bacillus thuringiensis** sold under the names Dipel, Thuricide, or Biological Insecticide.

With vertebrate pests, trapping, drowning, or exclusion techniques can be used to prevent or solve problem situations.

## LAWNS:

Whenever possible, dig out weeds by hand. Keep your lawn well watered and fertilized — a healthy lawn is a strong deterrent to weed establishment and growth.

## VEGETABLE GARDENS:

Insects like Colorado potato beetle can be picked off plants while cutworms can be prevented from attacking plants by sinking tin cans with both ends removed down into the soil around plants. Tar paper can be placed tightly around the base of cole crops and onions to prevent egg laying at the base of these maggot-susceptible crops. Each year, rotate crops from one part of the garden to another to prevent the build-up of soil-borne organisms which in many cases are specific to only a few crops. Use soap as discussed earlier to

dislodge and suffocate insects. Keep plants well spaced and foliage off the ground to reduce damage by slugs. In addition, place boards between rows to provide artificial hiding places for slugs, then destroy the slugs which take shelter under the boards during the day. Biological and natural insecticides can be used to control many of the insects found in the garden. Check the label carefully to determine which insects can be controlled with these products.

Many gardening books and journals on the market provide information on cultural control of pests and are a good source of additional information.

## PROPER USE OF PESTICIDES

The following safety tips should be followed by homeowners:

1. Identify the problem and use a pesticide which lists both the pest and the plant it is infesting on its label. Use only those pesticides marked "Domestic" around the home.

2. Carefully read and follow label directions for use. Pay particular attention

to mixing directions and wait period to consumption for applications to vegetables, berries, and fruits.

3. Mix pesticides outdoors, standing upwind. Do not spray on a windy day. Avoid inhaling the pesticide at all times. Always use safety equipment listed on the label. Never smoke, eat, or drink when handling pesticides.

4. Use different sprayers for insecticides and herbicides or wash the sprayer thoroughly after using herbicides since traces of herbicide can kill sensitive plants.

5. Keep your skin covered. Remove clothing after spraying and wash them in hot soapy water separate from other clothing. Wash your hands and face thoroughly after using pesticides. Do not allow children or pets to play on or in the treated area for 24 hours.

6. When spraying do not allow drift onto your neighbours' ornamentals or vegetables. To protect pollinators, do not spray trees and shrubs when they are in bloom.

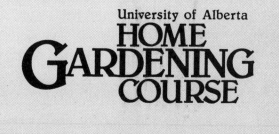

For further information contact your local garden supply centre:

University of Alberta
HOME GARDENING COURSE

Alberta Agriculture is the original publisher of this document - Backyard Pest Management. It is being reprinted in the University of Alberta Home Gardening Course through Alberta Agriculture's cooperation and approval. Any changes or additions to the original publication made for the University of Alberta Home Gardening Course are printed in italics. Therefore, text material that is printed in italics is not information supplied by Alberta Agriculture but is information prepared by the authors of the University of Alberta Home Gardening Course.

Alberta
AGRICULTURE

# INSECTS

## CONTROL OF INSECTS ON VEGETABLES

| PEST | CROP | INJURIOUS STAGES AND DAMAGE | SUMMARY OF LIFE HISTORY | CONTROL* |
|---|---|---|---|---|
| Cruciferous root maggots | Cabbage, radish, turnip, other crucifers. | Roots are grooved or tunnelled by small, white, legless maggots. Injury allows entry of root rot organisms. Damaged plants appear stressed and outer leaves may yellow. If severely damaged, plants may wilt and die. | Root maggots overwinter as brown puparia in the soil. Greyish flies resembling houseflies emerge in early to mid June and females lay white eggs on the soil at the base of plant stems. Newly hatched maggots chew seedling rootlets or bore into larger roots. After about one month, mature maggots pupate and give rise to a second generation of flies in early to mid August. Resulting maggots cause further damage to late-harvested root crops like rutabaga. | **Cultural** - Remove all cruciferous weeds (e.g. stinkweed, shepherd's-purse) from the garden. Aluminum or tar paper 15 cm diameter discs give some protection to nonroot crops when placed around stems at soil level. **Chemical** - Apply one of the following: a) diazinon granular in-furrow at seeding or with transplants. For seeded crops, repeat 2 weeks after thinning as a row-top application **or** b) diazinon EC as a drench at seedling emergence or with transplants. Repeat at 7-10 day intervals until end of June and again from late July to mid August for root crops or c) chlorpyrifos granular as a pre-plant, broadcast treatment. Use diazinon EC if further treatments are required. |
| Onion maggot | Onion, chive | Bulbs are tunnelled at their base by white, legless maggots similar to cruciferous root maggots. Rot organisms may compound damage. Attacked plants appear stressed and may wilt. One maggot may move along a row of seedlings, destroying several. | Adult flies are greyish. The life cycle is very similar to the cruciferous root maggot. Infestations tend to be heaviest in irrigated areas. | **Cultural** - Destroy infested plants and remove crop refuse in the fall. Use older plants, which flies prefer, as a trap crop. **Chemical** - Apply one of the following: a) diazinon or ethion granular in-furrow at planting **or** b) diazinon EC as a foliar spray if adults are numerous in late spring or c) chlorpyrifos granular as a pre-plant soil-broadcast treatment. |
| Cruciferous flea beetles | Cabbage, radish, turnip, other crucifers | Several species of flea beetle are injurious. Adults are very small, black or black and yellow beetles which jump actively like fleas. They eat pinhead-sized holes in the leaves, sometimes destroying much of the leaf surface of young plants. Small seedlings and transplants may be killed if attack is prolonged. Larvae are small white 'worms' which feed on host plant rootlets or roots but, unless numerous, cause little damage. | Adults overwinter in protected areas under plant debris or in the top 2-5 cm of soil. They become active in early spring and females lay eggs in the soil near food plants. Larvae feed for 3-4 weeks before pupating. New fall adults continue feeding until freeze-up. There is only one generation a year of most species. | **Cultural** - Control cruciferous weeds such as stinkweed, shepherd's-purse and wild mustard. Clean up garden refuse. Keep young plants well watered so they can outgrow damage. **Chemical** - Apply either carbaryl, diazinon, malathion, methoxychlor or rotenone as a foliar treatment. Repeat as necessary. |
| Potato flea beetle, tuber flea beetle | Potato, tomato, eggplant | Both tuber flea beetle and potato flea beetle are now present in Alberta. They resemble crucifer flea beetles and cause similar leaf damage. Damage by young Colorado potato beetle larvae may resemble or mask the shot-holes produced by flea beetles. Tuber flea beetle larvae in particular feed on potato tubers, producing surface tracks and shallow tunnels which fill with corky material. | Life history is similar to that of cruciferous flea beetles. There is probably only one generation a year under Alberta conditions. Netted gem (Russet Burbank) is very susceptible to damage. | **Cultural** - Clean up garden refuse and do not leave piles of potato culls. Plant resistant potato varieties (e.g. Pontiac). **Chemical** - When damage or beetles are first observed on the leaves (late June), treat plants with carbaryl, diazinon or methoxychlor. Repeat at 7-10 day intervals as necessary to control adult beetles before they can lay eggs. |
| Colorado potato beetle | Potato, tomato, eggplant | Both adults and larvae eat the leaves of host plants. Adults are rounded, hard-shelled beetles, 12 mm long, with alternating black and yellow stripes running lengthwise on the wing covers. Larvae are soft, hump-backed and brick-red, with two rows of black spots on each side. | Winter is passed in the adult stage several centimetres below the soil surface. Beetles emerge about the same time as the potato sprouts leaf out. Females lay clusters of orange eggs on leaf undersides over an extended period. In 7-10 days, larvae hatch and feed voraciously, completing development in about 2-4 weeks. They pupate in the soil and new adults emerge about a week later. There may be one or more generations a year, depending on location. Heavy snow fall will increase winter survival of beetles. | **Cultural** - Clean up potato culls. Hand-pick adults if few in number. **Chemical** - Apply either carbaryl, diazinon, methoxychlor, rotenone or endosulfan as a foliar treatment when beetles are first observed. Repeat as necessary to control both adults and larvae. |
| Cutworms | All garden plants | Several species of cutworm damage plants. They are soil-dwelling, fleshy and catepillar-like, up to 25 cm long when fully grown, characteristically curl up when disturbed. Most feed at night, destroying seedlings and transplants by cutting them off at or just below ground level. A few species climb plants and eat foliage or fruit. | Adults are the well-known 'miller moths' which are attracted to lights in mid summer. Common species, such as the red-backed cutworm, overwinter as eggs in soil. These hatch in early spring and cutworms feed on nearby weeds or crops until late June, pupating in the soil. Adult moths emerge in July or August. There is one generation a year. | **Cultural** - Keep weeds under control and cultivate soil in the fall. Use physical barriers such as milk cartons around individual plants. Hand-pick cutworms from soil around newly damaged plants. **Chemical** - Apply either: a) diazinon granular in-furrow or around transplants or b) chlorpyrifos as a broadcast pre-plant soil treatment. For climbing cutworms, spray or dust plants with carbaryl. |

| PEST | CROP | INJURIOUS STAGES AND DAMAGE | SUMMARY OF LIFE HISTORY | CONTROL* |
|------|------|------------------------------|--------------------------|----------|
| Imported cabbageworm, diamondback moth | Cabbage, radish, turnip, other crucifers | These caterpillars chew ragged holes in the foliage. Imported cabbageworms may also bore into heads and contaminate edible portions with their droppings. The cabbageworm grows into a velvety green, 20 mm long caterpillar with a faint gold line down the back. Diamondback larvae are pale-green, much smaller (10 mm), and wriggle quickly when disturbed. | Some imported cabbageworms overwinter as chrysalids (butterfly pupae) above ground. The familiar white cabbage butterfly emerges in spring and is joined by waves of migrants from the south. Eggs are laid singly on leaf undersides. There may be two or more generations a season. Diamondbacks have a similar life history but don't overwinter in Alberta. The adult is a small brownish moth which usually goes unnoticed. | **Cultural** -Hand-pick low numbers of larvae. **Biological** - Apply Bacillus thuringiensis as a foliar spray. **Chemical** - Apply diazinon, malathion, carbaryl, methoxychlor or rotenone as necessary. |
| Slugs | Most garden crops | Slugs are greyish-brown, soft-bodied, slimy creatures up to 30 mm long, which leave glistening trails. They feed mostly at night by rasping holes in plant foliage. Small backyard gardens provide favorable humid conditions and debris under which slugs can hide. | Slugs overwinter under boards or debris, or in soil as clear, spherical eggs or sometimes as adults. Eggs hatch in late spring and young slugs are usually observed in mid summer. There is only one generation a year. | **Cultural** -Dispose of all debris under which slugs can hide and lay eggs. Maintain a border of bare soil around garden. Use traps such as boards laid on the soil, or saucers of beer. Keep the garden dry and plants well spaced. **Chemical** - Apply slug baits or sprays containing metaldehyde or methiocarb around garden. Protect baits from pets. Start control early in the season. |
| Wireworms | Potato tubers, seeds, root crops | Larvae are injurious. They are shiny, yellowish-brown, somewhat cylindrical and distinctly segmented. They cause wilting and poor germination by boring into seeds and underground parts. Potatoes particularly are tunnelled and may later rot. | Adults are the so-called black or brown 'click' beetles. Females deposit eggs in the soil in spring, usually in grassy or weedy areas. On hatching, larvae feed on plant parts below soil level. Three to seven years are required by most destructive species to complete their life cycle. | **Cultural** -Avoid planting root crops and large seeds in land recently in grass or with heavy weed cover. **Chemical** - If damage is expected, apply a broadcast application of diazinon granular just prior to planting or seeding. |
| Aphids | Crucifers, dill, potato, other garden plants | Aphids are small, soft-bodied insects often found in colonies. Adults may be winged or wingless; nymphs are wingless. Most species are pale green but some are yellow, brown, black or pink. Both adults and nymphs injure plants by sucking sap, causing leaf distortion and reduced growth. Some transmit diseases, such as potato leaf roll. | Most species overwinter as eggs on the stems of a perennial plant. The eggs hatch in the spring and after one or two generations, winged migrants fly to summer hosts, an annual. Adults produce living young continuously and without mating. Population growth is usually rapid, therefore. Sexual forms produced in the fall mate and lay the overwintering eggs. | **Cultural** -Hose down plants frequently with forceful sprays of water to keep populations down. Use aluminum foil mulch. **Chemical** - Apply either diazinon EC, malathion EC, rotenone dust or insecticidal soap as necessary. |
| European corn borer, corn earworm | Sweet corn, tomato | The corn earworm feeds on the developing silk and corn kernels and occasionally bores into tomatoes. It is a large (3.8 -5 cm) green, brown or pink worm-like caterpillar. The European corn borer is smaller (about 2.5 cm at maturity) and light brown to pink. Just after hatching, it feeds briefly on leaves then bores into the stalk or ears to feed on the cob and kernels. | Corn earworm infestations result from an invasion of adult moths from the U.S. in early summer. They are not very common and usually confined to southern Alberta. Eggs are laid singly on the silk. The European corn borer recently re-established itself in southern Alberta and has the potential to spread north. Larvae overwinter near the soil in infested stalks and pupate in the spring. Adult moths are brown with yellow markings. Females lay eggs in masses on leaf undersides in July. There is one generation a year of both of these corn pests. | **Cultural** -Destroy infested ears. Remove all crop refuse in the fall. **Chemical** - For European corn borer, dust or spray with carbaryl when egg masses or feeding damage on leaves is first noticed. Repeat in 7 days. Corn earworm infestations are difficult to predict. Dust developing silks with carbaryl if eggs are observed. |
| Thrips | Onion, cabbage, pea, bean and other crops | Onion thrips attack several garden plants. They are pale yellow, greenish or brown and injure plants by rasping at leaf tissues and consuming plant juices. This produces white or silvery blotches on the leaves, and eventually browning and leaf death. Similar damage is caused by several other thrips species to peas, beans and cabbage. On cabbage, damage may produce scarring and corky tissue on leaf undersides. Flowers of many vegetables may be heavily infested. | Adult thrips overwinter in crop refuse, greenhouses, weeds, and grass. Eggs are laid in leaf tissue in the spring and hatch in about a week. Nymphs feed for a week or more and drop to the ground to pupate. There are three or more generations a year. Hot, dry weather favors a rapid population increase in dispersal flights over long distances. | **Cultural** -Keep garden free of weeds and refuse. **Chemical** - Apply diazinon or malathion, EC or dust, to foliage. Dust onion bulbs with malathion prior to storage or setting out. |
| Grasshoppers | All garden crops | Adults and nymphs of several species chew all green plant material. Adults of most species are winged; nymphs are wingless. | Most economic species overwinter as eggs in pods in the soil. They hatch in early spring and young hoppers feed for 2-4 weeks before the final moult to the adult stage. Adult females begin egg-laying in late July. Serious outbreaks may occur after 2-3 years of hot, dry weather and good snow cover, particularly in low rainfall areas of southern and eastern Alberta. | **Cultural** -Cultivate garden and weedy areas in the fall to discourage egg laying. **Chemical** - Apply carbaryl, dimethoate, or malathion as a spray to control young hoppers before they become egg-laying adults. Wire netting may be the only protection against very severe infestations. |

| PEST | CROP | INJURIOUS STAGES AND DAMAGE | SUMMARY OF LIFE HISTORY | CONTROL* |
|---|---|---|---|---|
| Aster leafhopper | Carrot, lettuce, celery, potato | These leafhoppers are small, pale yellow insects which jump or fly actively. They suck sap but unless numerous cause minimal damage. Some, however, carry and transmit aster yellows mycoplasma, which causes stunted, distorted and yellowed plants. | The darker-colored western strain overwinters as eggs or is blown in from the west. The more common pale strain originates in the United States and adults arrive on southeasterly winds from mid June onwards. Cereals are the preferred host but many vegetables and weeds are also eaten. Eggs are inserted into leaf tissue. There may be two or more generations a year. Primarily a pest in central and southern Alberta. | **Cultural** -Immediately rogue out all plants showing aster yellows symptoms. Control weeds. Use certified seed potatoes. **Chemical** - Apply a spray of either malathion or carbaryl as necessary.<br>* Chemicals are in active ingredients rather than trade names, with rare exceptions (Dutox®). Check label for rates. |

## EQUIVALENT NAMES FOR COMMON DOMESTIC PESTICIDES

| Active Ingredient | Product Name* | Active Ingredient | Product Name* |
|---|---|---|---|
| acephate | Orthene | gamma BHC | Lindane |
| carbaryl | Sevin | malathion | Malathion |
| chlorpyrifos | Dursban | metaldehyde | Slug Bait |
| diazinon | Diazinon, Maggot Granules | methiocarb | Mesurol (Slug bait) |
| dicofol | Kelthane | methoxychlor | Methoxychlor |
| dimethoate | Cygon, Lagon | oxydemeton-methyl + trichlorfon | Dutox |
| endosulfan | Endosulfan | propoxur | Baygon |
| ethion | Onion Maggot Granules | rotenone | Rotenone, Derris Dust |

* This is a partial list of products available. Many product names do not refer to the principal ingredient. Check the guaranteed (active) ingredients listed on the label.

# CONTROL OF INSECTS ON CONIFEROUS ORNAMENTALS

| PEST | CROP | INJURIOUS STAGES AND DAMAGE | SUMMARY OF LIFE HISTORY | CONTROL* |
|---|---|---|---|---|
| Spruce spider mite | Spruce, juniper, cedar | Damage is caused by adults and nymphs sucking the plant sap, causing the foliage to lose color and eventually dry up and drop. They also spin fine silken webbing which traps dust particles, dandelion seeds and shed needles, giving the plant a dirty appearance. Discoloration typically is more evident initially in the inner portions of the plant and spreads outwards as the summer progresses. Severe infestations will lower the aesthetic value of the plant and may eventually cause its death. | This mite overwinters as tiny red eggs at the base of needles or under loose bud scales. Hatching occurs about mid May and new adults are found by early June. New generations are produced every 2-3 weeks during the summer, so populations can build up rapidly if unchecked. Wet weather is detrimental to them. | **Cultural** -Hose down trees and shrubs with a forceful spray of water once a week. **Chemical** - If infestations persist at damaging levels, apply a foliar spray of dicofol, diazinon or malathion. Repeat in 7-10 days. |
| Spruce gall aphids | Spruce, pine, larch, fir, hemlock | Several species of aphids cause the growth of variously shaped galls on new growth of spruce. The galls are initially green but later turn purple or brown before opening and releasing mature aphids. Pine, larch, fir or hemlock act as secondary hosts. On these and for later generations on spruce, the presence of aphids is indicated by white cottony specks on needles. The white fluff covers and protects the eggs and nymphs. Galls cause tip kill and the open-feeding stages may distort and yellow needles and give them a dirty appearance. | The life cycle is complex and varies with the species. On spruce, eggs are laid in the fall at the base of needles and it is the nymphs hatching from these that overwinter. Further development occurs in early spring and adult females lay eggs near the buds. These hatch to produce nymphs which feed on the newly emerging needles. They become enclosed by gall tissue and feed within. When the galls dry in mid summer the nymphs molt to females. Generations continue to cycle as the non-gall forming, 'white fluff' stage. | **Cultural** -Pick off new galls as they are formed. Hose off the 'white fluff' generation with a forceful spray of water. **Chemical** - To prevent gall formation, spruce must be sprayed with carbaryl or malathion just as the buds begin to open. Control of the 'white fluff' generations on host plants can be controlled with the same materials. Apply twice at 7-10 day intervals. |
| Yellowheaded spruce sawfly | Spruce | Green striped larvae with yellow or orange heads consume needles, particularly on open-growing trees. Heavily infested trees appear ragged, especially near the top, and take on a yellowish-brown color. Successive heavy defoliation may kill the tree. | Adult wasp-like sawflies emerge from the soil from late May to mid June and females lay eggs at the base of developing spruce needles. Larvae hatch in about a week and feed on the new needles until mid July. They drop to the ground to spin a cocoon in the soil, where they remain until spring. There is only one generation a year. | **Cultural** -Hand-pick larvae where practical or; **Chemical** - apply a foliar spray of malathion when larvae are still small. |
| White pine weevil | Spruce, occasionally pines | White, legless larvae with brown heads feed under the bark of new leaders eventually girdling the stem. The leader wilts and dies. Usually 2 years of growth are affected. Open-growing trees less than 10 m high with a leader that is 13 mm or more thick are most likely to be attacked. Attacks result in crooked or forked trees. | Dark brown, adult weevils overwinter in soil under infested trees. In the spring they feed on the soft inner tissues of the new leader and deposit eggs in the feeding punctures in late May. Resin beads indicate their activity. Larvae hatch in 2 weeks and travel downward as they feed. In late July, when full grown, they bore into the wood to form wood chip cocoons in which to pupate. Adults emerge from early August to late September, feed for a short period, and then overwinter in the soil. | **Cultural** -Prune out all infested leaders and burn. **Chemical** - Protect susceptible trees from adult egg-laying by spraying the leader with methoxychlor in late April or early May. Repeat in 10-14 days. |

| PEST | CROP | INJURIOUS STAGES AND DAMAGE | SUMMARY OF LIFE HISTORY | CONTROL* |
|------|------|------------------------------|--------------------------|----------|
| Spruce budworm | Spruce, balsam fir | Yellowish to purplish-brown caterpillars with small white spots, light underside and black head begin mining the buds in early to late May, feeding on the developing needles. As the buds elongate they feed openly, webbing the partially eaten needles together to form a shelter. In severe, consecutive infestations, all the new foliage and some of the older needles are consumed, so that the tree top and later the whole tree may die. Other budworms may cause similar injury but are generally not as damaging. | Spruce budworms overwinter as young larvae in bark crevices. They emerge in early May and complete feeding by mid to late June. Pupation occurs on the tree. Small, brownish-grey moths emerge in late June to early July and females lay clusters of green eggs on the undersides of needles. Eggs hatch in about 10 days. There is one generation a year. | **Cultural** -Hand-pick larvae where practical early in the season. **Biological** - Apply a foliar spray of Bacillus thuringiensis. **Chemical** - Apply a foliar spray of malathion or dimethoate when larvae first appear, and repeat as necessary. |
| Sawflies | Spruce, larch, cedar, pine | Several species of sawfly larvae defoliate conifers. Most are naked, greenish larvae, often with black heads. The larvae have 6 pairs of legs on the abdomen in addition to the 3 pairs on the thorax. They are generally gregarious. | Most species overwinter in coccoons in the soil. Adults emerge in the spring or early summer and females insert eggs in host foliage. Larvae when full grown descend to the ground to pupate. There is one generation a year. | **Cultural** -Hand-pick larvae where practical. **Chemical** - Apply a foliar spray of carbaryl, malathion or diazinon when larvae are first observed. |
| Aphids | Most conifers | Several open-feeding species of aphid are sap-suckers on the branches or needles of conifers. They reduce plant vigor and also excrete sticky honeydew on which an unsightly black mold grows. | Most species attacking conifers overwinter as shiny black eggs on stems and needles. These hatch in spring and large brown or black aphids form colonies, often tended by ants. There are several generations a year. | **Biological** - Avoid spraying if large numbers of parasites, or predators such as lady beetles, are present. **Cultural** - Hose off aphids weekly. **Chemical** - If necessary, apply a foliar spray of malathion, dimethoate or diazinon. |
| Pine needle scale | Spruce, pines, and occasionally Douglas-fir | Tiny, white elongated scales suck sap from the needles, causing yellowish spots and premature needle drop. Tree vigor is reduced if heavy populations are present. | This insect overwinters on the needles as eggs, beneath the scale covering. These hatch in early June and walk or are blown to other needles, where they insert their mouth parts and become stationary. As they develop they become flattened and secrete a white scale covering. The female lays eggs beneath the cover in mid August. There is one generation a year. | **Biological** - Predators and parasites generally exert some control. **Chemical** - If necessary, apply a foliar spray of malathion, dimethoate, diazinon or carbaryl in mid June or soon after new needles appear. Reapply in early August to kill surviving females. |
| Northern pitch twig moth | Lodgepole pine | Pale-reddish caterpillars bore into new and old growth of pine stems at nodes or whorls of branches, causing a brown pitch nodule to form on the outside. Small branches are weakened and break easily. They may be common in nurseries, shelterbelts and forested areas. | Two years are required to complete the life cycle. Larvae overwinter in the pitch nodules on the tree. Pupation occurs in spring, and moths emerge in early summer. Eggs are laid on the new shoots and upon hatching the larvae construct a small pitch blister under which they winter. Next spring they resume feeding and construct a second pitch nodule adjacent to the original one. In May or early June, larvae move to the stem and form large hollow nodules at a crotch where they again feed and spend the second winter. | **Cultural** - There are no chemical controls. Remove resin nodules by hand as they form. Avoid bringing in trees from infested forested areas, or remove all nodules before transplanting; examine periodically thereafter.<br><br>* Chemicals are in active ingredients rather than trade names, with rare exceptions (Dutox®). Check label for rates. |

## CONTROL OF INSECTS ON DECIDUOUS ORNAMENTALS *AND FRUIT TREES*

| PEST | PLANTS ATTACKED | INJURIOUS STAGES AND DAMAGE | SUMMARY OF LIFE HISTORY | CONTROL* |
|------|-----------------|------------------------------|--------------------------|----------|
| Aphids | Most trees and shrubs | Small, soft-bodied, variously colored insects usually found in colonies. They suck sap from leaves, stems or roots causing loss of vigor, wilting, distortion or spots. They also excrete sticky honeydew on which black sooty mold grows. Some, such as woolly elm aphid, curl the leaves and are protected both by the leaf and a waxy coating.<br><br>*Aphids may be winged or wingless and are usually green, brown or black. They feed on fruit of all fruit trees. Aphids concentrations can generally be found on terminal buds, flower buds, and young, undeveloped fruit. Trees show loss of vigor and wilting. Aphids are also vectors which spread disease.* | Aphids overwinter as eggs on a perennial winter host. They hatch in spring and produce 1 or 2 generations before winged forms are produced which fly to summer hosts. Several generations of living young are produced in rapid succession. Overcrowding encourages migration to other plants. In the fall, sexual forms are produced which mate and lay the overwintering eggs. | **Cultural** - Prune off heavily infested branches and destroy. Hose aphids off with water. **Chemical** -If lady beetles and other natural enemies are not present, apply a spray of either dimethoate, diazinon, malathion or insecticidal soap as required. For woolly elm aphid, use trichlorfon + oxydemeton-methyl (Dutox®).<br><br>*Apply chemicals as a spray when leaves appear in spring and later as necessary.* |

| PEST | PLANTS ATTACKED | INJURIOUS STAGES AND DAMAGE | SUMMARY OF LIFE HISTORY | CONTROL* |
|---|---|---|---|---|
| Spider mites | *Elder, mountain ash. other ornamental trees and fruit trees and shrubs* | Damage is caused by both the tiny, sap-sucking adults and nymphs feeding on leaf undersides. Leaves show speckles and as damage becomes more severe, lose color and dry out. Fine webbing may be visible. | Adults are believed to overwinter in protected habitats. Some may be carried in on infested nursery stock and greenhouse plants. Females lay clear, spherical eggs on leaf undersides. Nymphs may complete development in as little as a week, depending on temperature. There are several generations a year. | **Cultural** - Hose plants down frequently with water. **Chemical** - Apply a spray of either dicofol, dimethoate, malathion or Dutox® at 7-14 day intervals as necessary. |
| Gall insects and mites | Poplar, elm, other trees and shrubs | Gall mites are almost invisible to the naked eye, whereas insects such as gall aphids and gall midges are quite visible when galls are opened. The galls usually take the form of bumps, finger-like extensions or felty growths on leaf surfaces and sometimes on petioles or stems. They rarely cause any serious damage. Common examples are poplar leaf-petiole gall aphid, boxelder leaf gall midge, oak petiole gall wasp, elm finger gall mite, and rose leaf and stem gall wasps. | The life histories are very complicated and for some species not well known. Most mites overwinter under bud scales, bark and other protected places and move onto new growth in the spring. Aphids often have an alternate summer host. Galls are formed by the plant in response to feeding by the pest. Development proceeds within the gall. Adults may emerge in spring or fall, depending on species. | **Cultural** - Prune out galls as these form where practical. **Chemical** - Chemical control is difficult and careful timing critical so it is generally not recommended. For damaging populations of gall mites on valuable trees, use a dormant oil just prior to bud-break and follow with foliar sprays of dicofol, carbaryl or Dutox® as the new leaves expand. Repeat foliar spray after 7-14 days. |
| *Erophyid mite* | *Leaves of plum and cherry plum* | *Cause galls to form at right angles on the leaves.* | | *Spray must not be applied within two days of harvest.* |
| Poplar bud-gall mite | Poplar | Cauliflower-like galls are formed from new leaf clusters in the spring by the feeding of tiny mites. Galls grow actively for 3-4 years, resulting in stunted and crooked branches, particularly lower ones. A serious pest in southern Alberta on hybrid poplars. | Mites spend the winter inside an active gall and in the spring either feed on the gall's new growth or migrate to uninfested buds where they form new galls. A new generation is produced every 2-3 weeks. Mites may be blown to other trees where they start a new infestation. | **Cultural** - Prune out and burn all galls on dormant trees in the fall and new ones as they form. Native trees and some hybrids such as Dunlop or Griffin are more resistant to attack. **Chemical** - There is presently no practical or registered chemical control. |
| Ash flower-gall mite | Ash | Tiny mites attack the staminate flowers of ash, causing them to develop abnormally and form galls up to 12 mm in diameter. The dried-out clusters of galls remain on the tree through the winter. | Adult female mites overwinter on the trees and migrate to developing flower buds in the spring to lay eggs. Several generations are produced in the summer. Attacks are sporadic. | **Cultural** - Control measures are generally not necessary. They can be controlled with a dormant oil spray prior to bud break and/or dicofol applied after buds swell but before new growth emerges. |
| Willow red gall sawfly | Willow | Pale larvae feeding in the leaf produce green, yellow or red oval galls the size of cherry pits on the leaf surface, each containing a single larva. Low populations will not harm the tree or shrub. | Larvae overwinter in the galls on fallen leaves. Small black, adult sawflies emerge in spring and mid summer, and females lay eggs in the leaf. Feeding by larvae causes the galls. There are two generations a year. | **Cultural** - Prune off galls as they form and collect and burn leaves in the fall. **Chemical** - Some control of the early generation has been reported with carbaryl and diazinon sprays on newly developing leaves. Usually no control is necessary. |
| Birch leafminers | Birch | White, grub-like, flattened larvae of three species of sawfly feed within the leaf tissue from early June onwards, producing pale green spots which expand into brown, blister-like blotches. | Larvae overwinter in earthen cells in the soil or in the leaf. Small, black, wasp-like adults emerge in mid May and lay eggs in the upper leaf surface. Eggs of the common species hatch in early June. Larvae feed within the leaf and emerge in early July, dropping to the ground to pupate. There are one or two generations a year, depending on species. | **Chemical** - Apply one of the following treatments: (1) a foliar spray of acephate, carbaryl, dimethoate, diazinon or malathion in early June and again in mid July, (2) a band of undiluted dimethoate around the lower tree trunk when the new leaves are fully open (2.5 cm width band for every 2.5 cm of tree diameter for medium sized trees), (3) a soil drench of undiluted dimethoate in late May at a rate of 50 mL per 2.5 cm diameter trunk, applied within the drip line in 4 or more shallow holes (approximately 2 cm in diameter). Fill with soil and water well. Properly applied, the soil drench has provided the best control of these sawfly species. |
| Lilac leafminer | Lilac | Small, flattened, yellowish caterpillars mine initially within the leaf causing yellow or brown blotches. They then exit, roll up the leaf from the tip, and continue to feed, skeletonizing the upper leaf surface. Damage is unsightly but not fatal. | Pupae overwinter in the soil. Tiny, greyish moths emerge in late spring and females lay eggs on the undersides of leaves. They hatch in early July and larvae burrow into the leaf, feeding for a few days before emerging to continue feeding in the rolled leaves until mid July. They drop to the ground to pupate. In early August a second generation of moths appears and the life cycle is repeated. | **Cultural** - If few in number, pick off infested leaves and destroy them. **Chemical** - Apply either (1) dimethoate to main stems as a paint-on band treatment in mid to late June, and again if necessary 1st August, or (2) a foliar spray of dimethoate, acephate, malathion or diazinon in early July and early August. |

| PEST | PLANTS ATTACKED | INJURIOUS STAGES AND DAMAGE | SUMMARY OF LIFE HISTORY | CONTROL* |
|---|---|---|---|---|
| Caterpillars | Many trees and shrubs | A variety of caterpillars attack trees and shrubs, chewing holes or various portions of the leaves. Unless defoliation is severe, overall tree health will not be affected. Common caterpillars are linden loopers, cankerworms, woolly bears, and larvae of the pepper and salt moth, tiger swallowtail, and rusty tussock moth. Leaf-rolling caterpillars are sometimes common on fruit trees and poplars. | Life history varies depending upon the species of caterpillar. Most overwinter as pupae in the ground, and the moths or butterflies emerge in the spring and lay eggs on the leaves. Caterpillars grow and feed for 2-4 weeks (longer for a few). Some species overwinter as larvae or eggs. The great majority have only one generation a year. | **Cultural** - Handpick caterpillars and destroy where possible. **Biological** - If necessary, apply a foliar spray of Bacillus thuringiensis. **Chemical** - Alternatively, apply a foliar spray of malathion, diazinon, methoxychlor, carbaryl or Dutox. |
| Sawflies | Willow, birch, poplar, rose and others | Larvae resemble caterpillars but have at least 6 pairs of legs on the abdomen in addition to the 3 pairs on the thorax. Most species are green with brown or black heads and often have black or black and yellow spots or stripes on the body. When touched the tail end is raised up in the air. They often feed gregariously, either skeletonizing leaves or feeding in from the edges. | Most overwinter as larvae in cocoons in the soil, completing development in the spring. Adult sawflies emerge in May to June and lay eggs in the leaf which hatch about 3 weeks later. The larvae feed for 3 weeks or more before dropping to the ground to spin their cocoons. There is one generation a year. | **Cultural** - Handpick larvae where possible. **Chemical** - Apply a spray of malathion, carbaryl or diazinon as necessary. |
| Forest tent caterpillar | *Poplar, apple, other fruit trees and shrubs* | Large, blue and brown caterpillars marked with a row of keyhole-shaped white spots along the back chew holes in new foliage or completely defoliate trees and shrubs. They tend to be gregarious, particularly when resting at night. Periodically, they occur in outbreak numbers, infesting large areas. Several years of heavy defoliation will result in die-back, reduced growth and death of trees under stress. | Overwinter as eggs in brown bands around twigs of broad-leaved trees and shrubs. The caterpillars hatch about the time the trembling aspen leaves unfold in mid May. They complete their growth in 5 to 8 weeks and spin yellowish cocoons on leaves and buildings, where they pupate. The brown adult moths emerge about 10 days later in early July and disperse either locally or over long distances before females lay the overwintering egg bands. | **Cultural** - Remove egg bands and destroy them before the larvae hatch in the spring. Hand pick colonies of larvae or, **Biological** - apply a foliar spray of Bacillus thuringiensis or, **Chemical** - apply a foliar spray of malathion, carbaryl, methoxychlor or diazinon when larvae are still small. |
| Large aspen tortrix | Poplar, birch, willow, alder | The principal host, aspen poplar, is attacked by dark green caterpillars with black heads which chew into developing buds in early spring, making holes in the new leaves. Later they tie several leaves together with silken threads, forming a tent in which they continue to feed. This is a serious pest during outbreaks which may last 2-3 years. | Young larvae overwinter at the base of trees in silken cells in cracks and crevices. They emerge in early May and enter buds. Older larvae consume leaves in their tents until early to mid June, when they pupate within the tent. Nondescript grey moths emerge two weeks later and lay clusters of eggs on the upper surface of trembling aspen leaves. Tiny larvae web leaves together and skeletonize the leaf surface before congregating at the base of the tree in early August to overwinter. | **Cultural** - Prune out webbed leaf clusters. **Chemical** - Apply a foliar spray of carbaryl, Dutox®, or oxydemetonmethyl when larvae or damage is first observed. |
| Ash plant bug | Ash | Small, greenish-yellow plant bugs with black or red markings suck sap from leaves, flowers, buds and seeds. They leave white specks and black dots of excrement. When infestations are severe, leaves appear scorched. This pest is increasing in Alberta. | It is believed this pest overwinters as eggs on the tree. Nymphs and adults are numerous in July and August. There are two or more generations a year. | **Chemical** - Apply a foliar spray of malathion, diazinon, carbaryl, or Dutox® as necessary. |
| Poplar and willow, leaf and flea beetles | Poplar, willow | Both adults and larvae of a number of species feed on foliage, chewing holes or skeletonizing the leaf. Adult leaf beetles are small, black, brown or black and yellow insects, which often drop to the ground when disturbed. Flea beetles are very small, shiny-black beetles which hop. Larvae of both are elongate black or black and yellow in color. They are usually found in clusters on leaf undersides. | Adult flea and leaf beetles overwinter on the ground under dead vegetation or litter. Eggs are laid on the leaves from late May onwards. Larvae complete development on the leaf and pupate there. Most species have more than one generation a year so all stages may be found on the host by late summer. Infestations tend to be sporadic. | **Chemical** - Apply a foliar spray of carbaryl, malathion or diazinon as necessary. |
| Pear slug | Fruit trees, cotoneaster, mountain ash, hawthorn | Small, dark, slimy, slug-like larvae feed on the upper leaf tissue leaving greenish spots. Leaves may later appear scorched if damage is severe. Since most damage occurs late in the season, plant growth is not seriously affected. | Pear slugs overwinter in earthen cocoons just below the soil surface. Small, black, adult sawflies emerge in spring and females lay eggs singly on the underside of leaves in late June. Larvae feed for two or three weeks, turning bright orange when mature. A second, much more numerous generation appears in mid August and feeds into September before dropping to the ground to overwinter. | **Cultural** - Hose off larvae with water. **Chemical** - Apply a foliar treatment of insecticidal soap, malathion, carbaryl or rotenone when larvae or damage is first observed. |

| PEST | PLANTS ATTACKED | DESCRIPTION OF DAMAGE | SUMMARY OF LIFE HISTORY | CONTROL* |
|------|-----------------|-----------------------|-------------------------|----------|
| Wood borers | Poplar, willow, birch, ash, elm, etc. | White, legless larvae of several species of beetles and moths bore into the sapwood of the tree. External symptoms include holes in the bark through which the insect expels sawdust-like excrement. Small branches may wilt. There may be death of branches or whole trees. Diseases often gain a foothold. Common borers include long-horned and metallic wood borers in poplar, carpenterworms in ash and poplar, bronze birch borer in birch, and poplar-and-willow borer in poplar and willow. | Life cycle varies with species of insect involved; most take 2 years or more to complete. Eggs are generally laid in the bark. Larvae bore into the tree and eventually pupate in their tunnels. Adults emerge in the spring to mate and lay eggs. Most common species are beetles in the adult stage except carpenterworms which develop into large grey moths. | Satisfactory controls are not yet developed. **Cultural** - For carpenterworms, wrap trunks with burlap from May to August to prevent adult moth emergence and egg-laying. For poplar borers, remove heavily infested 'brood trees.' Use flexible wire in new holes to kill larvae. Provide plants with good growing conditions. For shoot-borers, prune out and destroy infested shoots. **Chemical** - For bronze birch borer and poplar-and-willow borer, spray with lindane in spring or early summer to kill borer larvae. |
| Boxelder bug | Boxelder (Manitoba maple) | Both nymphs and adults are sap suckers which feed on the seeds, foliage and tender twigs of female (seed-bearing) boxelder trees. Occasionally other maples and ash are attacked. Nymphs are bright red when young. Adults are medium-sized, winged, grey-brown to black insects with a few conspicuous red lines on the body and red eyes. They occur primarily in south and southeastern Alberta. Damage to trees is generally minor. | Adult boxelder bugs emerge from winter hibernation in spring and females lay red eggs primarily in bark crevices. Nymphs, and later adults feed on developing foliage. In the fall, they become gregarious and congregate in sunny areas, from where they migrate to dry, sheltered places to hibernate. While migrating they frequently enter houses and become a nuisance. | **Cultural** - If possible remove female boxelder trees. **Chemical** - Apply a spray of diazinon, carbaryl or Dutox® to boxelder trees. On buildings, seal entry joints well and use diazinon or methoxychlor if necessary.<br><br>* Chemicals are in active ingredients rather than trade names, with rare exceptions (Dutox®). Check label for rates. |
| *Plum Curculio* | Plum, apple and pear | *Adult beetles damage fruit by feeding and egg-laying which is characterized by a small crescent shaped scar. Grubs are small, curved and greyish-white. They burrow into and feed on fruit causing a gummy substance to exude from fruit.* | | *Spray with methoxychlor when fruit is just beginning to form and repeat in ten days.* |

## CONTROL OF INSECTS ON SMALL FRUITS

| | | | | |
|------|-----------------|-----------------------|-------------------------|----------|
| Raspberry Crown Borer | Raspberry | Thick bodied, white larvae damage plants by tunneling extensively in bases of canes, crowns and roots. Mature larvae may be up to 25 mm long. | Eggs are deposited on foliage in late summer. Larvae burrow into bases of canes where they winter. Development continues during the second summer. Larvae pupate in the bases of canes; the yellow and black adults emerge in mid summer. | **Chemical** - Diazinon applied as drench to crown area in October or in spring when new shoots are about 10 cm high. |
| Caterpillars | All fruit species | Caterpillars are the larvae of moths and butterflies. May be up to 5 cm long, and any color. Chewing insects that feed mainly on leaf tissue. Damage may consist of removal of all or part of leaf blade, leaf skeletonization, or leaf mining. | Depending on species, eggs may be laid on or near host plants any time during the season. Hatching may occur immediately, or eggs may overwinter. There may be one or several generations per year. May overwinter in any stage. | **Chemical** - Ensure good coverage if using rotenone dust, or spray malathion to run-off. |
| Imported currantworm | Currant, gooseberry | The larvae are leaf feeders and when feeding in groups can completely defoliate a bush in early spring. When mature, they are green and almost 2 cm long. Disturbed larvae raise front and rear ends of body. | Eggs are laid on the underside of leaves in May and June. Larvae feed for 2 - 3 weeks, then pupate in leaf litter. The yellow and black adult sawflies deposit their eggs in mid summer. Larvae or pupae from this second generation overwinter. Adults emerge in May and June. | **Chemical** - Ensure good coverage if using rotenone dust, or spray diazinon or malathion to run-off. |
| Currant Fruit Flies | Currant, gooseberry, saskatoon | The legless white larvae cause "wormy fruit." Larvae develop within fruit which turn red and drop prematurely. | Small yellowish flies with dark bands on their wings emerge from puparia in the soil. Eggs are deposited singly into developing berries, where larvae develop. Mature larvae return to soil to pupate and overwinter. One generation annually. | **Chemical** - Two applications of malathion or methoxychlor, the first at petal fall and the second one week later. |
| Aphids | Most fruits | All stages (except winter eggs) damage crop plants by sucking sap. Several species transmit viruses. Symptoms of feeding include yellowing, stunting and leaf distortion. Some species excrete sticky honeydew. | Most aphids overwinter as eggs on stems of perennials. These produce aphids that give birth to live young. Winged adults are produced whenever population densities are high and in fall when winged adults start new colonies on other hosts. Both males and females develop in late fall, mate, and winter eggs are laid. | **Cultural** - Hose down plants with a forceful spray of water directed at the aphid colonies. **Chemical** - Ensure good coverage if using rotenone dust, or spray malathion to run-off. |

| PEST | | DESCRIPTION OF DAMAGE | SUMMARY OF LIFE HISTORY | CONTROL* |
|------|------|------|------|------|
| Spider mites | All fruits | Both nymphs and adults suck plant juices, usually from the undersides of leaves, resulting in a yellow stippling of upper leaf surfaces. Heavy infestations produce webbing on leaves and stems and may cause leaves to dry up completely. In strawberries, mites attack young leaves in crowns, resulting in crinkled, stunted and browned leaves; no fruit will form. | Females winter on soil in protected areas. In spring, eggs are laid on plants. Under hot, dry conditions, a new generation may occur every two weeks. | **Cultural** - Hose down plants with a forceful spray of water directed at the infested parts. **Chemical** - In strawberries, use dimethoate, diazinon, malathion, and dicofol. In raspberries use malathion and dicofol. |
| Slugs | Strawberries, blueberries | Immature and mature slugs, feeding primarily at night, rasp holes into foliage and gouge grooves into ripe and unripe fruit. May leave slime trails. | Clear, spherical eggs are laid in moist places such as under boards, in plant debris, etc. where they overwinter. Slugs appear in late June and multiply rapidly under moist conditions. Young resemble adults. | **Cultural** - Sanitation (debris removal) is most important. Place boards on the ground under which slugs gather and can be destroyed. **Chemical** -Slug baits containing metaldehyde or methiocarb can be applied in noncrop areas. Use fresh material only. Start treatment in July. |
| Leafrollers | Strawberry and various other species | Larvae feed on fruit, buds and leaves. Typical symptoms of infestation include a leaf or leaves rolled together and fastened with silk. The greenish-white larvae live in these leaf tubes. | Overwinters in egg stage sometimes in egg masses attached to twigs, branches and occasionally trunks. Larvae hatch at bud break and feed within rolled or folded leaf tubes and feed on leaf tissue. | **Chemical** - Malathion applied as foliar spray. Spray to run-off. |
| Strawberry root weevils | Strawberry, raspberry, blueberry | Plants damaged primarily by the white legless larvae feeding on roots and crowns. Plants appear stunted and the leaves may be bunched. Adult feeding results in "notched" leaf margins. | The small brown beetle overwinters in the soil, emerges in late May and deposits its eggs near host plants. Some of the larvae develop into adults; others overwinter as pupae or larvae. | **Chemical** - Apply one of the following when leaf notching is first seen: malathion, diazinon, methoxychlor. |
| Sawflies | Various fruits of rose family | Caterpillar or sluglike larvae are foliage feeders. In severe cases entire bushes may be stripped. | Larvae or pupae usually overwinter in underground cocoons. Wasplike adults emerge in spring, place their eggs into or on leaves. One to three generations annually, depending on species. | **Chemical** - Diazinon or rotenone dust applied as foliar treatment. |
| Raspberry sawflies | Raspberry and other care fruits | Mature larvae are 10 mm long, light green in color with all segments but the head covered with spiny, whitish bristle. They feed on the underside of leaves causing elongated holes between the veins. Adult sawflies are black with yellow and reddish margins. | Adults emerge from the soil in early spring and lay eggs within the leaf tissue during the blossom period. Larvae then hatch and feed for 2-3 weeks in the summer, then drop to the ground to pupate overwinter. | Damage is often not severe enough to require control measures.<br><br>Chemical - Malathion, Diazinon as a foliar treatment prior to blossoming. |
| Raspberry Fruitworm | Raspberry | The tiny brown beetles feed on emerging foliage, damaging unfolding leaves, buds, and blossom clusters. Heavy feeding may reduce the crop. Wormlike larvae penetrate flower buds and developing fruit; wormy fruit cannot be marketed. | The tiny brown beetles emerge from soil in April and May. Eggs are deposited on flower clusters or developing fruit. Mature yellow larvae drop to the ground, pupate and become adults, the overwintering stage. | **Chemical** - Two applications of diazinon a) when flower buds appear, and b) just before flowering.<br>* Chemicals are in active ingredients rather than trade names, with rare exceptions (Dutox®). Check label for rates. |
| Uglynest Caterpillar | Chokecherry | The green larvae spin dense silken webs which tie together several leaves to form the "colony." These caterpillars are leaf feeders. | This species overwinters as eggs deposited in loose bands around bases of young trees. Larvae develop in May and June; adults emerge in June and July. | **Cultural** - Sanitation: prune out all nests in mid May. Follow up with a foliar application of malathion. |
| Cylamen Mites | Strawberry | Adults are tiny, clear to pale yellow or brown in color. Both immature and adult stages can cause injury by attacking young, unfolding leaves causing stunting, distortion and browning of leaves. Flowers shrivel and no fruit is produced. | Cylamen mites overwinter in the crown of old plants and become active in the spring, moving along the runners to new plants. They dislike light and take to the shady areas in the folds of unopened leaves. A new generation is produced every two to three weeks. | Chemical - Dicofol or Malathion as a foliar treatment when growth begins in spring and later as necessary. Do not use within 7 days of harvest. |
| Tarnished Plant Bug | Strawberry | Adults and nymphs are 6 mm long the former a mottled brownish-bronze color and the latter yellowish-green. Both damage the plant by piercing and sucking its sap. Fruit may also be malformed. | Adults overwinter in debris and emerge in spring. Females insert eggs in plant tissue. | Chemical - Dimethuate, methoxychlor spray just before first blossom opens. |

# CONTROL OF INSECTS ON FLOWERS

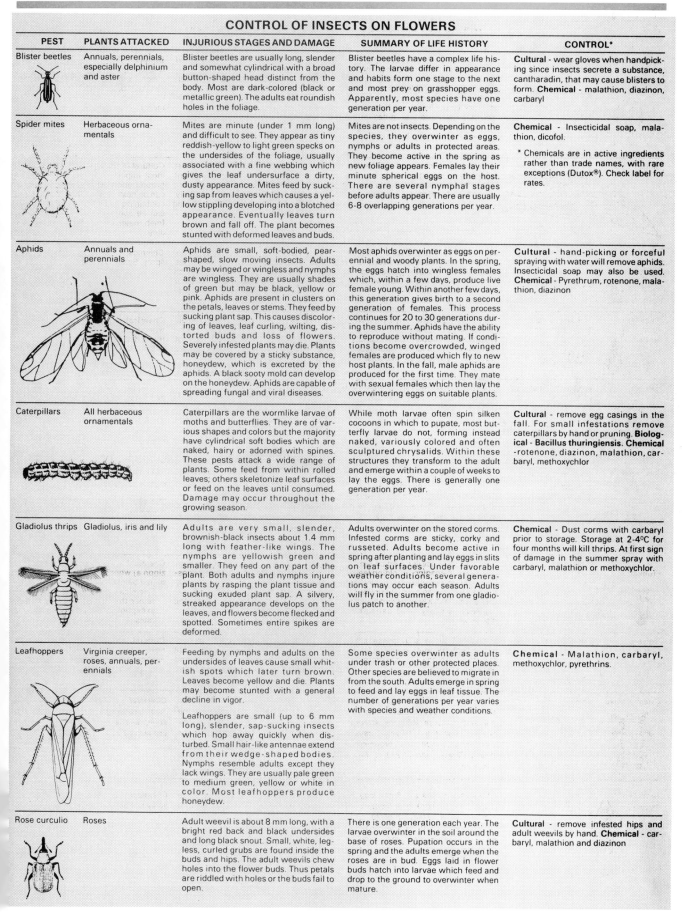

| PEST | PLANTS ATTACKED | INJURIOUS STAGES AND DAMAGE | SUMMARY OF LIFE HISTORY | CONTROL* |
|---|---|---|---|---|
| Blister beetles | Annuals, perennials, especially delphinium and aster | Blister beetles are usually long, slender and somewhat cylindrical with a broad button-shaped head distinct from the body. Most are dark-colored (black or metallic green). The adults eat roundish holes in the foliage. | Blister beetles have a complex life history. The larvae differ in appearance and habits form one stage to the next and most prey on grasshopper eggs. Apparently, most species have one generation per year. | **Cultural** - wear gloves when handpicking since insects secrete a substance, cantharadin, that may cause blisters to form. **Chemical** - malathion, diazinon, carbaryl |
| Spider mites | Herbaceous ornamentals | Mites are minute (under 1 mm long) and difficult to see. They appear as tiny reddish-yellow to light green specks on the undersides of the foliage, usually associated with a fine webbing which gives the leaf undersurface a dirty, dusty appearance. Mites feed by sucking sap from leaves which causes a yellow stippling developing into a blotched appearance. Eventually leaves turn brown and fall off. The plant becomes stunted with deformed leaves and buds. | Mites are not insects. Depending on the species, they overwinter as eggs, nymphs or adults in protected areas. They become active in the spring as new foliage appears. Females lay their minute spherical eggs on the host. There are several nymphal stages before adults appear. There are usually 6-8 overlapping generations per year. | **Chemical** - Insecticidal soap, malathion, dicofol.<br><br>\* Chemicals are in active ingredients rather than trade names, with rare exceptions (Dutox®). Check label for rates. |
| Aphids | Annuals and perennials | Aphids are small, soft-bodied, pear-shaped, slow moving insects. Adults may be winged or wingless and nymphs are wingless. They are usually shades of green but may be black, yellow or pink. Aphids are present in clusters on the petals, leaves or stems. They feed by sucking plant sap. This causes discoloring of leaves, leaf curling, wilting, distorted buds and loss of flowers. Severely infested plants may die. Plants may be covered by a sticky substance, honeydew, which is excreted by the aphids. A black sooty mold can develop on the honeydew. Aphids are capable of spreading fungal and viral diseases. | Most aphids overwinter as eggs on perennial and woody plants. In the spring, the eggs hatch into wingless females which, within a few days, produce live female young. Within another few days, this generation gives birth to a second generation of females. This process continues for 20 to 30 generations during the summer. Aphids have the ability to reproduce without mating. If conditions become overcrowded, winged females are produced which fly to new host plants. In the fall, male aphids are produced for the first time. They mate with sexual females which then lay the overwintering eggs on suitable plants. | **Cultural** - hand-picking or forceful spraying with water will remove aphids. Insecticidal soap may also be used. **Chemical** - Pyrethrum, rotenone, malathion, diazinon |
| Caterpillars | All herbaceous ornamentals | Caterpillars are the wormlike larvae of moths and butterflies. They are of various shapes and colors but the majority have cylindrical soft bodies which are naked, hairy or adorned with spines. These pests attack a wide range of plants. Some feed from within rolled leaves; others skeletonize leaf surfaces or feed on the leaves until consumed. Damage may occur throughout the growing season. | While moth larvae often spin silken cocoons in which to pupate, most butterfly larvae do not, forming instead naked, variously colored and often sculptured chrysalids. Within these structures they transform to the adult and emerge within a couple of weeks to lay the eggs. There is generally one generation per year. | **Cultural** - remove egg casings in the fall. For small infestations remove caterpillars by hand or pruning. **Biological** - Bacillus thuringiensis. **Chemical** -rotenone, diazinon, malathion, carbaryl, methoxychlor |
| Gladiolus thrips | Gladiolus, iris and lily | Adults are very small, slender, brownish-black insects about 1.4 mm long with feather-like wings. The nymphs are yellowish green and smaller. They feed on any part of the plant. Both adults and nymphs injure plants by rasping the plant tissue and sucking exuded plant sap. A silvery, streaked appearance develops on the leaves, and flowers become flecked and spotted. Sometimes entire spikes are deformed. | Adults overwinter on the stored corms. Infested corms are sticky, corky and russeted. Adults become active in spring after planting and lay eggs in slits on leaf surfaces. Under favorable weather conditions, several generations may occur each season. Adults will fly in the summer from one gladiolus patch to another. | **Chemical** - Dust corms with carbaryl prior to storage. Storage at 2-4°C for four months will kill thrips. At first sign of damage in the summer spray with carbaryl, malathion or methoxychlor. |
| Leafhoppers | Virginia creeper, roses, annuals, perennials | Feeding by nymphs and adults on the undersides of leaves cause small whitish spots which later turn brown. Leaves become yellow and die. Plants may become stunted with a general decline in vigor.<br><br>Leafhoppers are small (up to 6 mm long), slender, sap-sucking insects which hop away quickly when disturbed. Small hair-like antennae extend from their wedge-shaped bodies. Nymphs resemble adults except they lack wings. They are usually pale green to medium green, yellow or white in color. Most leafhoppers produce honeydew. | Some species overwinter as adults under trash or other protected places. Other species are believed to migrate in from the south. Adults emerge in spring to feed and lay eggs in leaf tissue. The number of generations per year varies with species and weather conditions. | **Chemical** - Malathion, carbaryl, methoxychlor, pyrethrins. |
| Rose curculio | Roses | Adult weevil is about 8 mm long, with a bright red back and black undersides and long black snout. Small, white, legless, curled grubs are found inside the buds and hips. The adult weevils chew holes into the flower buds. Thus petals are riddled with holes or the buds fail to open. | There is one generation each year. The larvae overwinter in the soil around the base of roses. Pupation occurs in the spring and the adults emerge when the roses are in bud. Eggs laid in flower buds hatch into larvae which feed and drop to the ground to overwinter when mature. | **Cultural** - remove infested hips and adult weevils by hand. **Chemical** - carbaryl, malathion and diazinon |

| PEST | PLANTS ATTACKED | INJURIOUS STAGES AND DAMAGE | SUMMARY OF LIFE HISTORY | CONTROL* |
|---|---|---|---|---|
| Rose gall wasps | Roses | Several species of wasp-like insects lay their eggs in stems of roses causing large swellings or galls. Galls may resemble hairy moss on the stem or large wart-like swellings covered with spines. | Insects overwinter in the galls. Adults emerge in the spring. One generation occurs per year. | **Cultural** - prune out and destroy infested stems. **Chemical** - dimethoate as soil drench in the spring. |
| Whiteflies | Annuals and perennials, especially coleus, fuchsia, hollyhock and impatiens | Adult whiteflies are small (1-2 mm), delicate insects covered with a white powdery wax. They resemble tiny moths and swarm when plants are disturbed. Nymphs appear as soft, flat, oval spots on the undersides of leaves. All stages are sap-suckers causing leaves to yellow and die. Severely infested plants wilt. Leaves become coated with sticky honeydew on which a black sooty fungus grows. | There are continuous generations in the greenhouse. Whiteflies overwinter only in greenhouses. Small white "crawlers" move around on leaves after eggs hatch. Nymphs are fully developed in 2 weeks and the complete life cycle takes about 4 weeks. In the summer whiteflies can infest plants outdoors. | **Chemical** - Insecticidal soap, malathion, methoxychlor, resmethrin. |

## CONTROL OF INSECTS ON TURFGRASS

| PEST | INJURIOUS STAGES AND DAMAGE | SUMMARY OF LIFE HISTORY | CONTROL* |
|---|---|---|---|
| Ants | Ants live in nests in the soil and may form large mounds. As mounds are pushed up, plant roots are cut. The mounds smother the turf and are unsightly. Passages are dug through the soil and cause irregular drying. | Ants live in colonies that may have hundreds or thousands of individuals. The eggs, larvae and pupae are tended by adults in the nest. The adults have hard, shiny, black or brown bodies and may have wings. The head and thorax are separated from the abdomen by a thin waist. Size varies from 1 - 14 mm long, depending on the species. Ants can be helpful, as they eat decaying organic matter and harmful insects. Some species eat plant seeds. | **Chemical** - Carbaryl - do not water for two days after treatment; repeat in 2-3 weeks if necessary. Chlorpyrifos and diazinon - water lawn thoroughly after treatment. |
| Glassy cutworm | The immature (larval) stage is a cutworm. The body is smooth, round, thick and segmented, and a dull greenish-grey, brown or blackish with a dark head. There are three sets of legs near the front and five sets of "false legs." Mature larvae are 3.5 - 5.0 cm long. When disturbed the larvae curl into a "C" shape. At night the larvae feed around the mouth of the tunnels they live in during the day. They eat the stems, leaves and crowns of any type of grass. | The adults, gray-brown moths, are active at night. The wings span 2.5 - 3.7 cm and are marked with light and dark spots and bands. The forewings are darker than the hind pair. Adults are often attracted by street lamps at night. A few days after eggs are laid on grass blades the larvae hatch and start feeding. The full-grown cutworm tunnels into the soil to spend the winter as either a larva or pupa. | **Chemical** - Diazinon |
| Sod Webworm | The caterpillars are up to 2 cm long, a dirty white or tan color, and may have rows of darker spots on their backs. They have a few long hairs on the back, a brown plate on the thorax, and a dark brown head. There are three pairs of legs near the front and five pairs of "false legs." Webworms live in silk-lined burrows in the soil or thatch. They chew off grass close to the crown and pull the blades into their tunnels to feed. Larvae feed at night and as they grow eat all parts of the plant. Damage begins as irregular brown patches in the turf, which grow larger and can cover entire lawns. Damage is most severe during the late part of the summer. Webworms may go unnoticed unless one sees either birds digging into the turf seeking the worms, or the greenish frass at the tunnel entrance. All grasses are attacked, especially bentgrasses, bluegrasses and newly seeded lawns. | The adults are 6 - 12 mm long, tan colored, and may have a white stripe on the edge of the forewing. The moths hide in the grass during the day and fly a zigzag path during warm evenings in late May and June. Eggs are laid throughout the lawn, hatching on the leaves in 6 - 10 days. The young larvae mine the leaf surface as they work their way to the soil to build tunnels. Webworms cease feeding in late September and overwinter in the soil or thatch. They pupate in spring and emerge as moths. | Apply insecticides about 2 weeks after moths appear. Carbaryl - do not water after treatment. Chlorpyrifos -do not water for 12 - 24 hours after treatment. Diazinon - water well after treatment. |
| Earthworms | Earthworms can grow to 20 cm long. Their burrowing and hard casts make a lawn lumpy and difficult to mow. They are particularly troublesome on lawn bowling greens and golf greens. Earthworms burrow through the soil feeding on organic matter and will feed on dead leaves and stems at the soil surface. They decompose thatch, mix organic material through the soil, and aerate the soil with their tunneling. | Earthworms need a moist environment. Soils with high worm populations often have high organic matter levels. Saline soils, sandy soils and soils with a pH of 4.5 or lower usually have few worms. Earthworms are usually found in the top 30 - 45 cm of the soil. They come to the surface at night and after heavy rains. They will move deeper if the soil becomes dry or cool. | **Chemical** - Carbaryl<br><br>* Chemicals are in active ingredients rather than trade names, with rare exceptions (Dutox®). Check label for rates. |

# WEED CONTROL FOR HOME GROUNDS

## Introduction

Well-kept grounds, whether simple or elaborate, provide an attractive surrounding for a home. Controlling unwanted plants (i.e. weeds) to maintain an attractive appearance demands more time and energy than any other gardening chore. This publication provides a guide to the recommended cultural and chemical means for controlling weeds in your lawn, garden and ornamental plantings.

Effective weed control requires proper identification of the weed problem followed by good cultural or chemical treatment at the correct time. Sound management, including the use of good growing practices, and cultural weed control methods in conjunction with herbicides, is essential for good weed control.

Chemical weed control used according to recommendations is not always 100 per cent effective. The action of chemicals depends upon several factors, such as age of the weed, the temperature at which the chemicals are applied, the fertility of the soil and the amount of available moisture. If it rains or irrigation water is applied within 6 hours after herbicide application, the activity of the herbicide may be reduced and reapplication of the chemical will be necessary.

Once the particular weed problem is controlled, do not expect it to be permanently eliminated as seeds remaining in the soil will likely germinate. Topsoil, unrotted manure, or soil around nursery stock that is brought into the home grounds may contain weed seeds, stolons (creeping stems that root at the nodes), rhizomes (underground, root-like stems), and roots. Weed seeds can also be introduced by air, (e.g. dandelion seed) or in run-off water, or by birds, animals and humans.

## Safe Use of Herbicides

1. READ AND FOLLOW EXACTLY THE HERBICIDE LABEL INSTRUCTIONS.
2. Never smoke, eat or drink while applying herbicides.
3. Avoid inhaling sprays or dusts. Wear protective clothing and a respirator when directed to do so on the label. Always wash your hands and face thoroughly after handling herbicides.
4. Buy herbicides for home use in small quantities. Herbicide should be labelled "DOMESTIC."
5. Store herbicides where there is no chance of contact with human food or livestock feeds. KEEP HERBICIDES OUT OF REACH OF CHILDREN.
6. Keep chemicals in their original containers - never in unmarked containers or bottles used for food or drink. Use a special container for measuring herbicides. Do not use kitchen utensils. Generally, do not allow any liquid herbicide to freeze.
7. Empty containers should be broken or punctured and buried at least 50 cm deep.
8. Mark herbicide application equipment "Herbicide Only." Do not use sprayer for any other purpose. Do not apply herbicides on a windy day.
9. If dusts or sprays are spilled on skin or clothing, wash skin immediately with soapy water. Remove contaminated clothing and clean before reusing.

## Weed Control In Lawns

A sound management program to promote vigorous growth of grass will help control weeds. The program should include fertilizing, watering and cutting at the proper height. Herbicides may, nevertheless, be required to keep the lawn free of weeds.

Care should be taken in the application of herbicides to prevent drift; flowering plants and many trees and shrubs are susceptible to herbicides. Precautions that can be taken include use of low pressure or no pressure applicators, application on calm days, the covering up of susceptible plants with newspapers or plastic, and spraying when temperatures are 16° to 25°C. After mowing, allow the grass to grow for about three to five days before spraying and do not mow for a day after spraying.

## New Lawns

Before establishing a lawn by either seeding or sodding, perennial weed problems such as Canada thistle, perennial sow thistle and quack grass must be brought under control. Weed seed germination should be promoted and the young weed seedlings destroyed with shallow cultivation to reduce weed problems later. Precautions should be taken to prevent reinfestation from contaminated lawn seed and weeds in sod or topsoil. Canada No. 1 seed may contain a certain percentage of weed seeds, but premium quality contains fewer. When buying premium quality seed, you can specify that it be free of a particular weed.

The following steps can be taken to control perennial weeds before establishing a lawn:
a) Ensure that the top soil brought into your yard is free of perennial grass rhizomes or root pieces of perennial plants.
b) Perennial weeds in the area to be seeded or sodded can be controlled by treatment with glyphosate (Roundup) or amitrole (Cytrol, Amitrol T). Rotovate about two weeks after treatment then seed or place your sod.

New lawns can be sprayed with selective herbicides after the second cutting unless otherwise stated. Selective herbicides are those that will kill certain weeds without damaging the lawn (or crop). In contrast, nonselective herbicides such as Amitrol T destroy all vegetation including lawn (or crop) and weeds.

## Established Lawns

Selective herbicides are able to control most broadleaved weeds in established lawns. However, because of the wide range of susceptibility of the many different weeds found growing in lawns, the correct selective herbicide or mixture of herbicide must be chosen.

These herbicides are commercially available in different formulations, therefore, you should check the instructions carefully to determine the proper application rate.

## Weed Control in Gardens

The two general methods of controlling weeds in the vegetable garden are cultural control, such as hoeing and mulching, and chemical methods.

Cultural control of weeds is more practical for the home gardener. Gardeners may not be prepared to cope with problems involved with applying chemicals in the home garden. For example, home gardeners usually grow several kinds of vegetables and these may require different chemicals. Also, some herbicides may leave residues which can injure different vegetables grown in that area the next year. Applying the correct rate of herbicide on a small scale without proper equipment is also difficult.

Gardeners who feel that the use of herbicides is not appropriate or practical for their home garden should rely on cultural methods of weed control such as mulching and hoeing or cultivation.

## Mulches

Mulches are any materials applied to the soil surface for protection or improvement of the area covered. Mulches with organic material such as weed-free straw, 7 to 10 cm thick, will retard weed development, conserve moisture and help to maintain a uniform soil temperature. After the crop is removed, the mulch layer can be incorporated into the soil to enhance its organic matter content.

Plastic mulches, either black or white, increase the soil temperature and also conserve moisture. Black plastic mulches, with openings for the crop, will prevent weed growth except where the opening occurs. Clear plastic, however, permits weed growth since light can penetrate through the plastic. Plastic mulches are best suited for warm season vegetables.

## Hoeing or Mechanical Cultivation

Hoeing or cultivation should be carried out when weeds are small and the soil surface is dry. After hoeing, most annual weeds can be left on the surface, however, succulent weeds such as purslane must be removed. Purslane will re-establish itself if plant fragments are left on the soil surface. Cultivation should be shallow so that the root systems of garden annuals are not damaged and to keep the number of new weed seeds brought to the soil surface at a minimum.

## Chemical Control

Chemical control of weeds, while not practical for the small home garden, can be useful for large gardens (1/5 hectare or more) with some herbicides. Two her-

bicides which can be used on a wide variety of vegetable crops are Treflan (trifluralin) and Eptam (EPTC). Both herbicides must be incorporated thoroughly into the top 7 to 10 cm. of soil. For uniform treatment the crops that are tolerant to one herbicide could be located in one area. Treflan and Eptam control green foxtail, chickweed, lamb's-quarters, pigweed, purslane and some other weeds.

Vegetable crops tolerant to Treflan are beans, (dry and smap), cabbage (direct seeded or transplants), carrots, rutabagas, sunflowers, cauliflower (direct seeded or transplants), peas, and transplants of tomato, pepper, broccoli, brussels sprouts and annual flowers.

Vegetable crops tolerant to Eptam are beans (not lima beans and aduzki beans), rutabagas and potatoes. Eradicane (EPTC + saftener) can be used for sweet corn. Eptam is available in 4 and 20 L containers and 22.7 kg bags of 10% granules. Eradicane 8E is available only in 22.7 L containers. Trifluralin is available in 10 L and larger containers, in 25 kg bags of 5% granules and it is also available in small containers for home use, e.g. Co-op Weed Preventer (1.47% granules).

For information on application rates and soil incorporation, please consult the appropriate herbicide label. Quack grass and perennial thistles can be controlled according to recommendations for lawn renovation. The affected area may have to be left out of production for at least part of the year.

## Ornamental Shrubs, Trees and Flowers

Herbicides can be used to control annual weeds, reducing the amount of hand weeding required. Hoe-No-More and No-Hoe contain 4% chloramben and control barnyard grass, green and yellow foxtail, chickweed, lamb's-quarters, pigweed, purslane, ragweed and annual smartweed species. A 500 gram (17.6 oz) package can be used in perennial flowers, shrubs and trees, transplanted annual flowers and certain vegetables. Refer to the label for rates for specific situations. Apply to bare soil or after tilling or hoeing. Do not disturb treated soil. Avoid application to foliage of desirable plants and do not apply when foliage is wet.

Rainfall after application will improve control. If no rain falls within three to four days after application, water the area to activate the herbicide. If water is not available, shallow cultivation may be necessary. Weeds are controlled as they begin to grow. Control can be expected for six to eight weeks depending on weather conditions.

Weed Preventers containing 1.47% trifluralin will control barnyard grass, green and yellow foxtail, chickweed, knotweed, pigweed, lamb's-quarters and annual smartweed species. Apply product before weeds emerge; weeds already growing will not be controlled.

Soil to be treated should be loose and free of clods. Apply by shaking container over the area. Incorporate into the top 2 cm (0.8 in) of soil by hand raking. Water lightly. For best results, apply in the spring. For annual flowers, apply only after they become established (about two weeks after transplanting). Use only around ornamentals, shrubs and other established plants not used for food.

Co-op Weedrite, Weedrite, or compounds containing 5% paraquat (or paraquat and diquat) will control top growth of all weeds. This product can be used around ornamental shrubs and trees, however, the spray must not contact green bark or foliage. Further treatment will be required for regrowth of perennial weeds. It does not provide any residual effect since this chemical is inactivated by the clay particles of the soil.

## General Vegetation Control

### Driveways, Patios, Fencelines

Cultural control methods may be tedious but prove safest for vegetation control in areas such as driveways, walks, under fences, backlanes and parking areas, tennis courts and bricked-in patios. However, herbicides are available which are specifically designed for complete vegetation control in these areas.

Herbicides such as Gramoxone or Weedrite kill annual weeds and top growth of perennial weeds. These are contact herbicides, i.e. they destroy or burn off the treated foliage, but these chemicals are not translocated into the root system of plants. Roundup (glyphosate) and Amitrol-T (amitrole) can be used to eradicate most perennial weeds, although repeated applications may be required for some species. These chemicals are safe to use on slopes or around trees and shrubs, provided sprays are kept off foliage and green bark. Roundup and Amitrol-T are systemic herbicides which move throughout the plant, including the root system, when sprayed on the foliage.

Soil sterilants are total vegetation control products which act in the soil, kill existing vegetation and prevent any plant growth for one or more years. THE USE OF SOIL STERILANTS IN THE HOME GROUNDS POSES GREAT DANGER TO DESIRABLE PLANTS.

- Soil sterilants should be used only where the objective is to have bare ground, and should not have wide use around the home.

- In using soil sterilants, use strictly according to directions.
- Roots of trees and shrubs extend laterally approximately twice their height. Accordingly, leave a "safety zone" between the area you treat and nearby trees or shrubs to prevent root uptake of the soil sterilant.
- Do not apply soil sterilant chemicals on sloped areas where runoff water will carry the treated soil into areas where desirable plants are growing or may later be planted.

### Killing Unwanted Trees

In urban areas, trees designated for removal cannot be safely sprayed and furthermore the standing dead tree would be unsightly. Therefore, unwanted trees should be manually removed with chain saws, etc. Deciduous trees will normally resprout vigorously from the base, and may also sucker profusely (e.g. poplar) after the main stem has been removed. After the tree has been felled, another cut to reduce the stump height to a minimum would be useful to minimize interference with mowing or other operations.

To kill the remaining stump, drill holes about 1 cm in diameter in the stump, fill these holes with 2,4-D and close with a plug of clay. Some formulations of 2,4-D may be more effective than others and repeat treatments may be necessary. The herbicide will move into the root system and kill suckers as they develop.

CAUTION: If desirable trees, particularly those of the same species are located in close proximity to the cut tree, damage may occur to these trees where root intertwining has taken place.

Once the stump is killed, it can be left to the elements and natural decay-causing organisms will gradually break it down. Some commercial products containing saltpetre (potassium nitrate) are available in home garden centres, nurseries, etc. to aid in burning the stump; however, most urban communities have by-laws prohibiting open fires. Hence the options for stump removal appear to be limited to natural decay or removal by mechanical means.

| WEEDS | RECOMMENDED HERBICIDE |
|---|---|
| Dandelions, Canada thistle, sow thistle, plantain, mustards, lamb's-quarters | Use 2,4-D amine or MCPA amine. Treat for dandelions preferably in early fall (late August to mid September) or in early spring before flowering. Spring treatments (early to mid May) should be made before bedding plants have been set out. |
| Chickweed, creeping Charlie (ground ivy), knotweed, clover, black medick, plus 2,4-D susceptible weeds | Apply any brand of "Chickweed and Clover Killer." These products will contain mecoprop or mecoprop + 2,4-D + dicamba. |
| Creeping bellflower | Use a product that contains a mixture of mecoprop + 2,4-D + dicamba. Treat regrowth as required. |
| Quack grass, foxtail barley (Note: crab grass and quack grass are not the same. Crab grass does not occur in Alberta). | No selective herbicide is available for an overall application that will remove unwanted perennial grasses from a blue grass lawn. Severely infested lawns may require complete renovation. Blades of unwanted grasses can be wiped with a sponge using a weak solution (2%) of Amitrol-T, Cytrol or Roundup. CAUTION: use rubber gloves for this procedure. Spot treatment with these herbicides, followed by reseeding is another possible alternative. |

# PLANT DISEASES

## INTRODUCTION

Any plant in an unhealthy condition caused by unfavorable environmental conditions as well as parasitic microorganisms is said to be diseased. Parasitic microorganism are very tiny plants or animals that live on, or in and obtain their food from other living plants or animals. Several types of microorganisms cause plant disease, such as fungi, bacteria, and viruses.

Fungi are usually invisible to the naked eye but some types produce large structures which can be easily seen. Mushrooms are one example. Fungi proliferate by spores which are really very small seeds. Single spores are invisible to the naked eye and can be spread great distances by wind, water, insects, man, tools and vehicles. Fungi can survive for years in soil, plant debris and dormant plants.

Bacteria are microorganisms, usually single-celled, and multiply with astonishing rapidity. Bacteria enter plants through wounds or natural plant openings since they cannot actively penetrate the plant cuticle. Insects are often important in spreading bacteria.

Viruses are extremely small microorganisms that cannot multiply outside living plants. They are spread by insect vectors, usually aphids or leafhoppers, or mechanically, that is, by the spread of plant sap from an infected plant containing the virus to a healthy plant as can occur during cultivation and pruning.

Thousands of different microorganisms are potentially infectious to trees and plants. Some of the major diseases encountered in home gardens are described below but, unfortunately, such descriptions are not foolproof. Many site and environmental stress factors such as drought, cold temperatures and salinity may cause symptoms that are very similar to those caused by disease organisms.

Herbicides can cause symptoms that may be confused with disease symptoms. Injury from herbicides is difficult to diagnose accurately on the basis of symptoms and usually requires an investigation into the pattern of damage and a history of the types and rates of the chemicals applied.

Insect damage, too, can be mistaken for disease. Since such damage is often noticed only after the insect has left, it is sometimes more important to become familiar with the type of damage an insect causes than with being able to identify the insect. (See the section on insect pests.)

Do not be surprised if the disease symptoms expressed by your plant do not fit any of the disease descriptions given or, on the contrary, if they seem to describe half a dozen diseases. Accurate diagnosis of a disease usually requires a trained plant pathologist and some special equipment. Luckily, accurate diagnosis of a disease is not always necessary in order to control it.

For practical purposes, it is very often possible to talk of diseases and control measures in terms of the general symptoms that are produced (see Figure 1). Although a particular symptom can be caused by a variety of environmental and biological factors, the treatment of these factors involves many of the same cultural practices and controls.

### CONTROL

Control methods seek to achieve either eradication or prevention. Eradication consists of procedures that stop the development of a disease by destroying the disease microorganism, whereas prevention is designed to protect your plant from infection.

Most controls for plants are preventative and non-specific cultural methods such as pruning, sanitation, watering and fertilizing. Very few diseases can or need to be controlled by chemical pesticides. Pruning can control a number of diseases and prevent others from infecting your plants. The healthier your plant, the more resistant it will be to infection by microorganisms. If your plant does not seem healthy, review your watering, fertilizing and other gardening practices. Experiment with your cultural practices. Too much of a good thing is sometimes as bad as too little. Every plant has to be treated somewhat differently since no two growing sites are exactly the same. Watch your plants and see how they respond to your care and to changes in weather conditions. Eventually you will come to know exactly what your plants require to be healthy and vigorous.

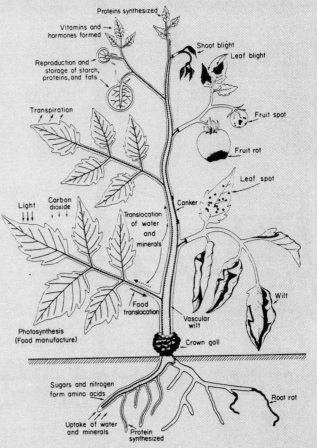

**Figure 1**. Basic functions in a plant and interference with these functions by some common plant diseases.

## CONTROL OF VEGETABLE DISEASES

Growing vegetables successfully requires that you have some knowledge of a plant's growth requirements. Information on home vegetable growing can be found in numerous books and several government publications including the "Alberta Horticultural Guide." Specific information on growing practices is also often presented on seed packets.

Practices that improve the vigor of your plants will help your plants resist infection by disease microorganisms. Obtaining good quality seed is essential in preventing the introduction of a new disease into your garden. Good sanitation including disposing of or composting plant debris reduces the buildup of disease microorganisms in your garden. Rotating your vegetable growing area will also help to reduce the buildup of specific diseases in your garden.

Disease incidence varies considerably from one area to another and from one garden to the next. Different soil types, site location and cultural practices all contribute to produce a unique situation. Consequently, it is often useful to determine for yourself whether or not specific control practices are indeed necessary. One way in which this can be done is to apply a particular control procedure (such as application of a pesticide) or a change in cultural practice (watering, fertilizing or cultivating) to half of your planting only. During and after the season, compare your plants' responses to the different treatments. Trying different varieties is another good way of determining how best to control diseases and maximize your production. Practising the preventive methods outlined below should mean that you will have few serious disease problems in your garden.

### PREVENTION

a. Plant resistant varieties if available. Information on resistant varieties is sometimes available in seed catalogues, on seed packets and at horticultural supply centres.

b Apply a seed-protectant fungicide, purchase seed pre-treated with fungicide, or buy seed that is certified disease-free or has been hot-water or chemically treated.

c. Follow good cultural practices, e.g. plant in warm, fairly moist soil, properly prepare the seed bed, correctly fertilize, avoid cultivation when the soil is wet, water during dry periods, do not overfertilize, and maintain good soil drainage.

d. Rotate your vegetables yearly. Although there is no standard rotation, a good starting place is a four-year rotation. This involves dividing your garden (if possible) into four distinct plots. In one plot, plant all of your cole crops (cabbage, cauliflower, broccoli, etc.), in another plant your vine crops (squash, cucumber, etc.), in another miscellaneous vegetables including onions, beets, carrots, radishes and so on, and finally in your fourth plot, plant your potatoes and tomatoes. Remember, this is only a suggestion and your crop rotation will depend very much on how large your garden is and which vegetables you decide to grow. You may also need to adapt your rotation if you have problems with specific diseases. If possible, changing the location of your garden is a good way to control many soil diseases.

e. Maintain good sanitation. This includes good weed control, including volunteers (i.e. vegetables that have seeded themselves), turning under or cleaning up crop debris, removing and destroying diseased plants.

f. Some diseases are favored by dense foliage and a moist environment. To avoid problems, avoid heavy seeding rates and dense foliage. Water early in the day so that plants do not remain wet overnight, and avoid long periods of overhead watering, particularly during flowering.

g. Apply an appropriate fungicide.

Check the label for information on which plants the pesticide can be used on and note how many days before harvest the last spray can be made. For details on the timing of application and the application rates carefully read the product label. Some fungicides are applied prior to planting (drenches), some are applied directly to your vegetables, and others are applied to the plant residues.

h. Proper harvesting practices are essential if storage problems are to be avoided. Although harvesting practices will vary somewhat for different vegetables, some common methods of avoiding problems are: dig late in the fall when the soil is cooler; avoid harvesting in wet weather; avoid bruising or skinning the vegetables.

i. Prior to storing, dry vegetables in a cool dark place. If possible, before storing onions, keep them at temperatures of 32 - 35°C for one to two weeks under continuous air movement.

j. Sanitation and proper environmental conditions determine the life of your stored vegetables. Storage areas should be cleaned thoroughly with a disinfectant prior to introducing your harvest. Most vegetables will store best at a temperature of 0 - 4°C and a relative humidity of less than 70%. Avoid warm, humid storages. Storages should be well ventilated. Potatoes and carrots must be stored at a high humidity. Onions should be stored at low humidity.

k. At least six weeks prior to planting add enough lime to your soil to obtain a pH of approximately 7.0. Note: this practice could result in an increase in potato scab

l. Control insects which may cause extensive defoliation or transmit viruses and diseases. Defoliation can expose fruits to sunscald.

m. Remember to use a different sprayer to apply insecticides or fungicides to your garden than you used to apply herbicides because of possible residual contamination. Pesticides, and especially herbicides, applied at the wrong rate or time, can cause substantial damage to your garden plants. Avoid planting in an area where a residual herbicide has been used.

| DISEASE | PLANTS ATTACKED | DESCRIPTION OF DAMAGE | SUMMARY OF LIFE HISTORY | CONTROL* |
|---|---|---|---|---|
| Viruses | Most vegetables | The most common and sometimes the only symptom produced is reduced growth of the plant, resulting in various degrees of dwarfing or stunting of the plant. Viruses can cause a variety of symptoms ranging from ringspots and mosaics to tumors and distortion of stems and leaves. (See Viruses under "Small Fruits" for a more detailed description of virus symptoms.) | Viruses are spread by contact of diseased with healthy plants as might happen, for instance, directly by vegetative propagation, or indirectly by means of gardening tools, your hands, or by the feeding habits of insects or other pests. Once a plant is infected, there are no chemicals that will eliminate the virus. It is therefore important to obtain seed that is certified virus-free. | **Prevention:** a, b, e, l |
| Rot | Most vegetables | Rot consists of softening, discoloration, and often disintegration of plant tissue. | These symptoms are produced by many of the same organisms that are responsible for causing leaf spots and blights. Some environmental factors such as excessive sunlight or wide fluctuations in soil moisture can also result in fruit rot. | See leaf spots and blight. |
| Wilts | All vegetables | Wilt is a loss of rigidity or a drooping of plant parts generally caused by insufficient water in the plant. Certain disease organisms cause this condition by interrupting the regular flow of water. Fungal wilts are characterized by discolored brown areas on infected stems and twigs. Bacterial wilt can usually be identified by the presence of a sticky substance in the stem tissues. | Wilts can be caused by bacteria, fungi, viruses or environmental factors. Wilt organisms may overwinter in plant debris, in the seed, in vegetative propagative material or in insects. They enter plants through wounds and are spread by working infected soil, by direct contact of plants, or by insects. | **Prevention:** a, b, c, d, e |
| Herbicide injury. | Most vegetables | Many plants, especially tomatoes, are susceptible to 2,4-D injury. The first symptom is a downward curvature of the leaves and the tips of the growing points. Even minute amounts of 2,4-D drift can cause noticeable distortion of growth. In more severe cases, stems become thick, stiff and brittle and show a whitening of the external surface accompanied by a severe curvature and twisting of the leaves. New leaves do not expand fully and are elongated with abnormally pointed tips. Picloram and dicamba are residual herbicides that cause a "fiddlehead" type symptom on tomatoes and potatoes. | Herbicide sprays often drift from their intended area of use and into gardens. Residual herbicides may remain in your soils for several years and cause damage to your garden plants. | **Prevention:** m |
| Common scab | Potatoes | Symptoms of the disease are distinct, irregular, rough, corky spots on the tuber. | This disease is caused by a bacteria-like organism. It is most damaging in alkaline or freshly manured soils. Uniform watering during tuber initiation results in less disease. | **Prevention:** a, c, d |
| Potato greening and glycoalkaloids | Potato | The skin and flesh of tubers turn green when exposed to light over a period of time. Glycoalkaloids are naturally occurring chemicals in potatoes that normally occur in low concentration. Glycoalkaloids increase in tubers that are exposed to light resulting in bitter tasting potatoes. | High glycoalkaloid levels may be harmful to humans. Peeling removes most of the glycoalkaloids unless the potatoes have been stored for some time thus allowing the glycoalkaloids to spread toward the centre of the tuber. | **Prevention:** i |
| Neck Rot | Onion | The tissue about the neck of the onion may become sunken and have a dried-out appearance. A gray mold with many black kernel-like bodies may appear about the neck of the onion or cover most of the surface. Inner scales are soft, appear as if they have been cooked and have a light-brownish color. Between the scales, the mycelium of the fungus may be observed as a gray mass. When soft rot bacteria follow neck rot, the entire onion is reduced to a soft, wet, foul-smelling mass. | Neck rot is principally a storage disease and seldom attacks onion bulbs while they are in the ground. The fungus that causes neck rot overwinters in trash, soil and buildings that have been used to store diseased onions. | **Prevention:** a, c, d, h, i, j |
| Blossom End Rot | Tomatoes and peppers | A slight water-soaked area forms at or near the bottom of the fruit (blossom end) and later enlarges and darkens. Eventually the cankers become dry, sunken, flat, leathery and finally dark brown to black in tomatoes or light colored and papery in peppers. | An irregular water supply produces a water deficit in the fruit resulting in blossom end rot. Blossom end rot is also associated with an unbalanced nutrient supply, particularly, deficient calcium or excess nitrogen in relation to phosphorus, potassium and other major nutrients. | **Prevention:** c |
| Sunscald | Tomato, pepper | A light-colored area develops on the side of the fruit exposed to the sun. These areas become slightly sunken or wrinkled and creamy white on older fruit. Spots appear light brown on young fruit. Scaled tissues dry out rapidly in hot weather and become thin and papery. | This disease is caused by high temperatures at the fruit surface as a result of exposure of the fruit to direct sunlight. | **Prevention:** l |

| DISEASE | PLANTS ATTACKED | DESCRIPTION OF DAMAGE | SUMMARY OF LIFE HISTORY | CONTROL* |
|---|---|---|---|---|
| Blackleg | Crucifers (broccoli, brussel sprouts, cabbage, cauliflower, rutabaga) | Symptoms appear 2-3 weeks before transplanting. Well-defined, ashen-grey spots occur on the leaves, and similar spots surrounded by a purplish border occur on stems. If large areas of stem tissue are killed, the affected plants will die. | This fungus disease is carried on the seed and persists on plant refuse for one or two years. The disease usually starts in the field from infested soil or seed. Sprinkler irrigation and rain may spread this microorganism. | **Prevention:** b, c, d, e |
| Tipburn | Lettuce | The first symptoms are small, brown spots about 0.6 cm from the edge of the leaf. The tissue around these spots often dies and turns brown. Tipburn may also occur internally. Such dead areas within the head offer excellent places for rot-producing organisms to become established, especially certain bacteria that cause a watery tissue breakdown commonly known as "slime rot." | This disease is caused by environmental factors and appears to be most prevalent when bright, warm days follow periods of damp, foggy weather. Several factors or conditions have been reported to increase the incidence and severity of the disease: 1) rapidly growing, succulent plants tend to be more susceptible than plants that have developed more slowly, 2) high humidity, as well as high temperatures, 3) fluctuating or inadequate soil moisture may increase the amount of tipburn, and 4) the disease may be related to calcium and/or boron deficiencies. | **Prevention:** a, c |
| White rot | Onion, Welsh onion, garlic, leek, shallot | The leaves of an infected plant decay at the base, turn yellow, wilt and fall over, the older ones being the first to collapse. The roots of such plants usually are badly rotted so that the plant can be pulled up easily. Numerous black kernel-like bodies about 0.5 cm in diameter are formed throughout the infected parts and on the surface of the onion. | The white rot fungus persists in the soil for many years. It is spread by running water or carried in soil clinging to transported seedlings or tools. The disease is most severe in cool, fairly moist soil. | **Prevention:** a, d, e |
| Storage problems | All stored vegetables | Various fungi, bacteria and environmental factors can cause problems with stored vegetables. Symptoms range from rotting vegetable tissue to an abundance of fluffy white, brown, grey or pink fungus growth. | Storage vegetables are often infected in the field and the disease progresses in storage. Relatively warm and humid storages promote the development of storage diseases. Malformation of stored vegetables, however, is usually the result of suboptimal growing conditions. | **Prevention:** e, f, h, i, j |
| Clubroot | Crucifers (broccoli, brussel sprouts, cabbage, cauliflower, rutabagas) | Affected plants show almost normal vigor at first, but then gradually or suddenly pronounced stunting sets in, which may be followed by death of the plant. The most obvious symptom appears on the roots and sometimes the underground part of the stem. The symptom consists of knobby club-shaped swellings on the roots and rootlets. These malformations may be individual or coalesce and cover the entire root system. | This fungus overwinters in the soil and can remain there indefinitely. Once a field becomes infested, it becomes unsuitable for growing cruciferous plants unless costly methods and materials are used to sterilize the soil. | **Prevention:** a, k |
| Leaf spots and blights | All vegetables | Leaf spots cover a limited area of the leaf or stem whereas blight is characterized by general and rapid killing of leaves, flowers, and stems. A powdery white growth is sometimes associated with leaf spots. | Bacteria and fungi are responsible for causing these symptoms. Leaf spots are rarely severe enough in Alberta to warrant control measures. However, some blights and leaf spots can cause extensive damage, especially if moist weather conditions prevail. These diseases overwinter in crop debris. | **Prevention:** e, f, g **Preventive Fungicide:** maneb, zineb |
| Asparagus rust | Asparagus, onion, shallot and chives | The first symptom is the browning or reddening of the smaller twigs or needles. The discolored area spreads rapidly until the entire plant appears as if it had ripened prematurely. The red color is caused by the stems and the needles being covered with small pustules, which emit a dusty cloud when touched. | Fungus spores are blown by wind or washed by rains. The fungus requires droplets of water for germination. Heavy dews are especially effective. Plants growing in relatively dry soil are injured much more than those planted in wet soil. If the young shoots are cut, the disease does not have an opportunity to develop. | **Prevention:** a, e, f, g **Preventive fungicides:** zineb |
| Damping-off/ seedling blight | All vegetables | Seedlings either fail to emerge or become stunted and collapse before the first leaves unfold. Some plants survive but carry a scar known as "wirestem" near the soil line. | Various fungi, capable of thriving in a wide range of conditions, can cause damping-off. In general, conditions that are sub-optimal for plant growth favor at least one of the damping-off fungi. | **Prevention:** b, c, d, e, f |
| Powdery mildew | Most vegetables | See Powdery Mildew under "Small Fruits" | See Powdery Mildew under "Small Fruits" | See Powdery Mildew under "Small Fruits" |
| Botrytis Grey Mold | Beans | See Botrytis Grey Mold under "Small Fruits" | see Botrytis Grey Mold under "Small Fruits" | See Botrytis Grey Mold under "Small Fruits" |

* Chemicals are in active ingredients rather than trade names, with rare exceptions (Dutox®). Check label for rates.

# CONTROL OF ORNAMENTAL AND FRUIT TREE DISEASES

Diseases can be reduced by preventing environmental stress. Proper tree maintenance prevents the development of many diseases and can be accomplished by following these three steps:

1. Match the Tree or Shrub to the Site

The decision as to choice of plant material depends on what requirements must be met. For example, plants might need to be salt and drought tolerant, be easily maintained, be colorful or a combination of these other factors. Determine your selection guidelines.

After establishing guidelines, determine what plants are available that fit your needs. The **Alberta Horticultural Guide** is available free from the Communications Division of Alberta Agriculture and is an excellent source of information on tree characteristics and cultural practices.

2. Maintain Tree Health

Newly planted trees should be kept uniformly moist throughout their first growing season. Once your trees are established, water them during periods of low rainfall. Evergreen trees and shrubs should also be watered prior to freeze-up to help prevent winter drought injury. Watering should also be done if warm weather occurs during the winter causing the soil to become dry.

When you are watering, always use enough water to soak the soil properly; do not water a small amount each day because this encourages shallow rooting, which makes the tree susceptible to future droughts and frost damage.

Tree should be lightly fertilized every spring. Inadequate fertilization can result in yellowing foliage, small leaves and winter injury. Most good lawn fertilizers with a high nitrogen content

(10-8-6, 10-6-4 or 16-20-0) are acceptable for trees. Late application of fertilizers should be avoided since this will promote succulent growth that will not mature soon enough and may be damaged by freezing.

Pruning of shade trees is important in keeping them symmetrical and in a healthy condition. Flowering trees need pruning more often to let light and air into them to encourage the production of healthy growth and bloom. Your local nursery, garden supply centre, and library have many useful hints or publications on this subject.

3. Avoid Changes in the Growing Site

A delicate balance exists between the root system of a plant and its soil environment. Site change almost always result in root damage. This will weaken the tree and make it more susceptible to attack by insects and disease organisms. Your tree gradually will lose vigor and may show off-color, small leaves, poor growth, early leaf drop and dieback of twigs and branches. This condition is usually progressive over several years. To prevent the decline of your plant, prune away dead wood. This will reduce the crown size and will promote new growth. And don't forget, water and fertilize.

PREVENTION—Ornamentals

a. Avoid selecting susceptible varieties or species when planning a new planting. Information on disease resistance can be found in the Alberta Horticultural Guide and other publications. Most garden centres will also have this type of information.

b. At pruning time, and this will vary for different trees and shrubs, several practices should be followed to help prevent your tree from being infected by a disease. It is important that sprouts from the base of a tree, and water shoots on the trunk and larger limbs be removed since they can easily be infected. Tree wounds or cuts over 5 cm should be treated with pruning paints. Pruning paints are not recommended or necessary for evergreen trees. When pruning, properly and repeatedly disinfect shears with a solution such as lysol (1 part to 500 parts of water), household bleach (1 tablespoon to 1 pint of water), or mercuric chloride (1:1000). Always work on healthy looking trees and branches first.

c. Maintain the vigor of susceptible trees by proper fertilization and regular watering. Avoid excessive use of high nitrogen fertilizers which promote soft susceptible growth. Control wood boring and other insects which appear to be stressing your trees. Water after leaf drop but before the ground freezes; water again when the trees are breaking dormancy. Thin out stands to promote good air circulation. Provide good soil drainage and avoid planting in poor sites.

d. Apply an appropriate fungicide. See label instruction for details on the rate and timing of application. Spraying of isolated trees may be safely omitted if thorough eradication is practised.

e. Do not carry firewood on your holiday. Elm wood with bark can spread the disease. Report diseased elms to your agricultural office or city parks department.

f. *Protect the southwest side of the trunk.*

g. *Reduce watering late in summer and in wet years, plant a cover crop to help deplete moisture and hasten cold hardening.*

ERADICATION — Ornamentals

A. In late fall, winter or early spring, remove and burn all cankered limbs. Where possible, make these cuts at least 30-45 cm back along healthy wood. Remove dying trees and known sources of infection on your property by destroying badly infected trees and pruning unhealthy or infected branches of other trees. Encourage your neighbors to do likewise.

B. During the growing season, cut off and destroy any infected twigs several inches below the infection, but avoid excessive pruning at this time. Proper disinfection of tools is necessary when pruning.

C. Destroy alternate hosts in the vicinity of valuable evergreen plantings.

D. Infected bark on large roots and the trunk should be cut out. Do not cover with soil until the fall. This will allow a healthy callus to form.

E. Collect and destroy all fallen leaves.

| DISEASE | PLANTS ATTACKED | DESCRIPTION OF DAMAGE | SUMMARY OF LIFE HISTORY | CONTROL |
|---|---|---|---|---|
| Apple-cedar Rust/ Juniper Rust | Primary hosts: cedar or juniper Secondary hosts: apple, crabapple, saskatoon, cotoneaster, quince, pear, hawthorn, mountain ash, and other rosaceous plants. | On the primary host: symptoms consist of reddish-brown galls from 3-50 mm in diameter on the branches. Older galls have circular depressions with small protuberances which enlarge to form gelatinous, yellow-orange 'sporehorns' following rainy periods in the spring. These should be pruned out to prevent infection of the secondary host. On secondary host: small, pale yellow spots appear on the upper surface of leaves in the spring. These gradually enlarge and turn orange. Numerous spots may occur on a single leaf and young fruits may become similarly infected. These spots which may occur on both leaves and fruits may be covered with numerous spiny projections. | Apple-cedar rust is a fungal disease that requires two different host species in order to complete its life cycle. Both primary and secondary hosts must be growing in close proximity for the disease to develop. Spores are released from the horns on the primary host and are carried by wind to apple leaves. Infected secondary hosts then produce spores that are carried back to the primary hosts to complete the life cycle. | **Eradication:** A, B, C **Prevention:** a |
| Apple Scab | Apple, applecrab, crabapple | *Infection results in pale, chlorotic, water-soaked spots which become dark green, velvety spots on leaves and fruit. Leaves may curl and drop prematurely. Scab of fruit may cause skin to rupture causing a whitish ring to form around the scab. As scab spot enlarges the centres become brown and corky.* | *Fungus overwinters on fallen leaves and in spring when conditions are moist produces spores which are transported by air currents to young foliage and fruit. Unopened blossoms are susceptible also and infection may lead to blossom abortion or severe infection of fruit.* | **Eradication:** e **Prevention:** d |
| Black Knot | Plums, cherries and chokecherries | Small, light brown swellings of the current or previous season's growth are the first symptoms observed. The knots may only reach a size of 1-2 cm in diameter. In the spring, knots turn olive green and have a velvety textured surface. By autumn, they turn black and harden and may be 10-15 cm long completely encircling the limb. The knots continue to expand during successive seasons and may eventually kill the branch. | Black knot is a fungus that produces spores which are wind-blown or rain-splashed from knots to healthy branches in the spring. | **Eradication:** A, B **Prevention:** b |
| Browning of evergreens | Evergreens | Some needle shed is natural. Excessive defoliation may result from frost injury (sudden droop of growing tips), herbicide injury (curl, twist or distortion of new stems; whole branches with needles that are light yellow or white; green tips following severe crown discoloration), drought (trees gradually turn brown from top down and outside in), cold or winter injury (sudden deep red-discoloration of branches), dog damage (browning of outer, lower branches) and iron deficiency (gradual yellowing of foliage during several years). | Browning of evergreen needles is caused by a variety of environmental and site factors. The color change is usually definite and sometimes quite spectacular. Often the change occurs long after injury, so that recovery may not be possible. | **Prevention:** c |

| DISEASE | PLANTS ATTACKED | DESCRIPTION OF DAMAGE | SUMMARY OF LIFE HISTORY | CONTROL* |
|---|---|---|---|---|
| Canker disease | Most trees and shrubs | Canker disease symptoms usually consist of death to tree tissues which crack open and expose the wood underneath. In some cankers, the healthy tissues next to the canker may increase in thickness and appear higher than the normal surface of the stem. | Cankers can be caused by fungal or bacterial infections and/or by environmental stresses such as frost, fire and hail. A wound is the key event in canker formation. The most common wound site is a branch stub although mechanical injuries are also common sites for cankers on shade trees. Given a wound and a host in susceptible condition, canker fungi or bacteria can invade healthy bark and produce a canker. The spores produced by the invading fungus are blown to other trees. | Eradication: A, B Prevention: b, c |
| Leaf scorch, yellowing and dieback | Deciduous trees and shrubs | Symptoms of scorch include yellowing and/or darkening of tissues between the main leaf veins or along the leaf margins. Rapidly wilted leaves may retain a pale green color. As the condition progresses, entire leaves may dry up, turn brown and become brittle. Damage is usually more pronounced on the upper, windward or southern side of trees. Plants may lose many leaves prematurely during late summer and exhibit some twig dieback. | Leaf scorch is caused by adverse environmental conditions such as soil compaction, transplant shock, nutrient deficiency, drought, salt toxicity, weed killer injury, etc. | Prevention: b, c |
| Cytospora canker | | On deciduous trees, sunken elongated cankers form on the trunk or branches. The bark on the canker face is often cracked and discolored with a callus ridge at the margin. Small black pimples appear on the dead bark on the canker face. Small branches and twigs are rapidly girdled while larger branches and the main stem may take several years to become girdled. On conifers, the lowest branches are killed and then branch death progresses up the tree. Dying branches first exhibit yellow-green then purple foliage and later drop their needles. A large amount of resin flows from infected branches and coat the entire surface of the bark around the cankers and drips onto lower branches. | The Cytospora fungus overwinters on the bark and in the cankers. During wet weather in the spring, spores are formed and are washed to other branches by rain splash. These spores can also be transported by insects, pruning tools, and clothing. If the spores land on a wound they can cause an infection. A canker will eventually develop as the fungus invades healthy bark. | Eradication: A, B Prevention: b, c |
| Dutch elm disease | American elms are highly susceptible. Chinese and Siberian elms are highly resistant. At present, Dutch elm disease is not known to occur in Alberta. | The earliest symptoms on trees are yellowing and/or wilting of the leaves on a single branch usually in the upper crown. Yellow or wilted leaves quickly turn brown and die. This symptom is known as a "flag." The symptoms rapidly spread, usually one branch at a time, to progressively larger branches and eventually the entire tree. | Dutch elm disease is caused by a fungus which overwinters in infected and recently killed trees, in stumps and in recently cut brush and logs. It is carried from infected wood to healthy trees by elm bark beetles. The disease may also invade trees through root grafts from adjacent infected trees. | Eradication: A, B Prevention: a, b, e |
| Dwarf mistletoe | Evergreens | Infected branches increase in thickness. Large numbers of smaller branches called witches' brooms are formed on the infected branches. Broomed branches usually have dense foliage, outlive the noninfected branches around them and continue to enlarge. Infections on small trees may result in rapid mortality. Large trees decrease in growth and progressively decline as witches' brooms develop. | Dwarf mistletoe is a plant that feeds on other plants. The aerial shoots of dwarf mistletoe plants bear male and female flowers on separate plants. During mid to late spring, male flowers produce pollen that is usually carried to female plants by insects. When mature, the fruits are oval berries. Each berry contains a single seed in mid summer; the mature seeds are dispersed by "explosive discharge." Water pressure builds up inside the berries during maturation and this pressure propels the discharge seed at high velocity (approximately 27 m/sec) to a maximum horizontal distance of about 16 m. Many of the seeds land on needles and branches and trunks of adjacent trees while others land on the soil. | Eradication: A, B Prevention: b, c |
| Fireblight | Apple, crab-apple, mountain ash, cotoneaster, hawthorn, Saskatoon berry, pear | Infected blossoms suddenly become blighted and turn brown. Later, twigs may appear as if scorched by fire. Leaves on infected branches often remain on the trees all summer and well into the winter. The disease also produces cankers. These cankers are discolored, slightly sunken and tend to crack at their edges. | Fireblight is a destructive bacterial disease. During the spring and early summer in moist, warm weather, cankers that were not removed may exude a slimy bacterial ooze. This ooze, consisting of millions of bacterial cells is easily spread to blossoms by flies, ants and beetles. Honey bees and wild bees spread the organism from blossom to blossom after the first few blooms have become infected. The disease may also be spread by rain, wind and pruning shears. Fireblight epidemics can develop during early summer warm periods (over 18°C) when there are alternating intervals of rain and sunshine. | Eradication: A, B Prevention: a, b, c |
| Leaf spots, blotches, shot-holes | *Most deciduous, ornamental and fruit trees.* | Symptoms range from well defined dead areas on the leaf to superficial growth of white to grey-white fungus material on leaves and shoots. Despite what appears to be extensive damage, most leaf diseases are not very damaging to shade trees. When leaves are dropped each fall or winter, the effect of an infection usually ends. In some cases premature defoliation lowers food reserves. | Various species of fungi can cause leaf spots. The fungi that attack different tree species usually have similar life cycles. Most remain dormant in the dead leaves on the ground during the winter. Some fungi survive in the buds or on dead twigs and branches. In the spring during wet weather, the fungi become active and discharge spores that are carried by wind and rainsplash and land on the young expanding leaves. The spores quickly penetrate the leaves and produce disease symptoms. During summer more spores are produced in these infected areas and can cause new leaf infections during wet weather. Thus, during wet growing seasons a considerable buildup of infections can occur. | Eradication: E Prevention: a, b, c |

| DISEASE | PLANTS ATTACKED | DESCRIPTION OF DAMAGE | SUMMARY OF LIFE HISTORY | CONTROL |
|---|---|---|---|---|
| Shoot blight of lilac | Lilac | Symptoms seen in spring are black spots on stems and leaves of young shoots. These increase in size forming large blotches. Immature leaves may turn black and die along with entire shoots which frequently curl over and wither. Flower clusters turn brown and flowers fail to develop when infected by the bacterium. | Both a bacterium and a fungus can cause shoot blight. The bacterium overwinters in stems and branches. Disease spread occurs most rapidly during rainy periods when bacteria are splashed from infected to healthy tissue. The fungus persists in the soil. | **Eradication:** A, B  **Prevention:** a, b, c |
| Shoestring root rot | Shoestring root rot affects a wide range of shrubs and trees that are commonly used for ornamentals. | The first observable symptoms of shoestring root rot can range from a slow gradual dieback, to the sudden death of a tree. Examination of infected roots reveals the presence of mats of the fungus between the bark and the wood. In the late summer or early fall, honey colored mushrooms may appear around the base of infected trees. They only persist for a few weeks but the black shrivelled remains of the mushrooms can often be found for many months. | Shoestring root rot is a fungal disease that overwinters in both living and dead trees. During the spring the fungus resumes growth through the soil and infects healthy roots. After the infected tree is killed, the fungus lives for many years in the soil. | **Eradication:** D  **Prevention:** c |
| Silverleaf | *Deciduous, ornamental and fruit trees and shrubs.* | The most characteristic symptoms are a silvery or leaden sheen to the foliage in marked contrast to the deep green of healthy leaves. When silvered branches die, fruiting bodies may appear on the bark. As the disease progresses, the metallic color intensifies and rusty-looking streaks may develop along the leaf midribs. Dry or alkaline soils may produce a form of leaf silvering that can be mistaken for silverleaf. | Silverleaf is a fungus that produces spores during wet periods in the growing season. The spores are wind borne to healthy trees where the fungus can successfully infect the tree through wounds. Fruiting bodies (mushrooms) on dead branches, old stumps or heaps of prunings are the sources of new infection. | **Eradication:** A, B  **Prevention:** b, c |
| Slime Flux | Poplars, American elms, and Siberian elms are the most common hosts of this disease in Alberta. | Typical symptoms are wilting, branch dieback and an external or internal slime flux. Affected wood generally is dark, water-soaked and has a foul odor. | Slime flux is caused by a bacterium. Infection usually originates in a crotch of the tree where water accumulates and does not run away. Insect and mechanical or pruning injuries provide wounds where bacteria can enter the tree. | **Eradication:** A, B  **Prevention:** b, c |
| Western gall rust | Hard pines | This disease stimulates the stem cells to divide rapidly causing pronounced swellings. Infections generally remain localized and do not progress from branches into the main stem. Galls may persist for many years without killing branches; however, a noticeable reduction of host growth often occurs. Masses of orange spores are released when the bark layer over the galls is ruptured. | This fungal disease can cause serious damage to pines. Two or three years after infection, the galls or blisters rupture, allowing powdery, yellowish-orange spores to be spread by the wind. | **Eradication:** A, B  **Prevention:** a, b |
| Winter Injury Sunscald | Apple, pear and other ornamental trees and shrubs | *Occurs on the southwest side of the bark resulting in serious damage or killing of the bark. This may also predispose the wound to entry of disease organisms. Bark appears darkened and rough, often blistered and peeling.* | *Late afternoon sun reflects off snow onto bark causing tissues to thaw. Sudden drop in temperature at sundown causes freezing and rupturing of tissue.* | *Prevention:* a, f, g |
| Frost cracking | ornamental trees and shrubs | *Cracking occurs along trunks and major limbs* | *A sudden decrease in temperature as in an early fall prior to trees being fully cold hardened results in water present freezing and expanding causing cracking.* | *Prevention:* g |
| Tip dieback | ornamental trees and shrubs | *Dead terminal growth is blackened in color* | *Water sprouts, suckers and late season growth brought on by overwatering or overfertilizing results in succulent growth that does not harden off adequately.* | *Prevention:* b, g |

## CONTROL OF SMALL FRUIT DISEASES

Diseases can seriously damage small fruits in Alberta and growers should be aware of the threat they pose. Preventive disease control programs, including sanitation, the use of resistant varieties and proper cultural practices, should reduce or eliminate the need for chemical control. If fungicides must be used, carefully follow the manufacturer's recommendations for rates and timing of application.

Information on varieties and general growing practices for small fruits is available in the "Alberta Horticultural Guide." The most destructive diseases of small fruits are caused by viruses. It is imperative that virus-free plants be obtained. If plants in your garden are suspected of having a virus that appears to be significantly affecting production, get rid of them. Most other fungal and bacterial diseases can be controlled quite effectively with good preventive cultural practices.

PREVENTION — Small Fruits

a. Plant resistant varieties or use planting stock that is certified disease and virus free. Select only winter-hardy varieties. Select healthy looking plants with well-developed root systems.

b. Create optimal growing conditions by providing adequate water and fertilizer especially during the blossoming and early fruiting periods and by controlling harmful insects which may cause extensive defoliation, or transmit viruses or other diseases. Avoid unnecessary injury to plants during cultivation. Provide good soil drainage. Avoid over-fertilization and prune plantings to allow for good air circulation.

c. Plant in an area that has been used for growing small fruits for the past 3-4 years.

d. Apply a protective fungicide. See label instruction for details on rates of application. Check label for information as to which plants the pesticide can be used on, and note how many days before harvest the last spray can be made.

e. Avoid excessive water applications during the fall hardening-off period. Avoid fertilizing, cultivating or pruning in late summer as this stimulates succulent growth. Provide winter cover by bending raspberry canes and covering the tips with soil.

f. Usually not serious, control measures are seldom necessary.

g. Plant in a protected or sheltered area.

h. Use herbicides judiciously and with

ERADICATION — Small Fruits

A. Prune and discard old raspberry canes or infected branches after harvest. Pruning should be done approximately 10 cm below infected areas. Remove and destroy badly infected plants. Properly and repeatedly disinfect shears with a solution such as lysol (1 part to 500 parts of water), household bleach (1 tablespoon/pint of water), or mercuric chloride (1:1000). Always work on healthy looking trees and branches first.

B. Remove and destroy leaves and plant debris after harvest.

C. Pick and pack only sound fruit. Discard damaged fruits or store separately.

D. Do not plant within the immediate vicinity of an adequate host!

| DISEASE | PLANTS ATTACKED | DESCRIPTION OF DAMAGE | SUMMARY OF LIFE HISTORY | CONTROL |
|---|---|---|---|---|
| Botrytis Grey Mold | Strawberries, raspberries, saskatoons, and chokecherries | Blossoms, blossom stalks, and green and ripe fruit may be attacked. Infection usually starts in young blossoms which are very susceptible. Several blossoms in a cluster may turn brown, dry up and eventually the entire blossom stalk dies. Some blossom infections spread only as far as the calyx or hull where the fungus remains dormant until the fruit ripens, at which time a fruit rot will occur. Ripe fruit is very prone to infection and the fungus spreads rapidly between berries that are in direct contact in a cluster. Grey mold may not appear on ripe fruit until 1-2 days after picking. | Grey mold is a fungal disease that is favored by shade and dense foliage where air circulation is poor and sustained periods of high humidity are likely to occur. Under humid conditions, an abundance of light grey spores are produced on infected plant parts. These are easily dislodged and spread by wind currents. The fungus overwinters on various types of plant debris in the soil. | **Eradication:** C **Prevention:** a, b |
| Powdery Mildrew | Strawberries, raspberries, currants, and gooseberries *grape and saskatoon* | Infected leaves turn purple and curl upwards exposing undersides which are coated with a dusty, greyish-white fungal growth. Severely affected leaves may wither and die. | Powdery mildew is a fungal disease that often appears shortly before fruiting. Warm, dry weather accentuates the symptoms of powdery mildew. The fungus spreads by air-borne spores. It overwinters on diseased leaf debris. | **Eradication:** B **Prevention:** a, b, g, h, i, k **Preventive fungicide:** Sulphur, zineb |
| Black leaf and witches' broom | Saskatoon | Diseased plants have extensive branch development in a small area producing a witches' broom appearance. The undersides of leaves are covered with a dense black fungus growth. | This disease is caused by a fungus that overwinters on twigs and branches of Saskatoon bushes. The fungus also survives on dead leaves on the bush and on the ground, from which it infects new growth in the spring. The disease can grow into new growth, but does grow back down into older wood. | **Eradication:** A, B |
| Mummy berry and brown rot | Saskatoon, blueberries, chokecherry | Infected twigs and flower clusters suddenly darken and wilt. Infected tissues generally exhibit a felty brown mass of fungal growth (spores) during humid periods. Infected berries turn tan to salmon in color and are small and wrinkled. | This fungus disease infects both twigs and flowers. Dead infected berries (mummies) usually cling to the trees after the foliage and other berries have fallen. These overwinter and may produce spores the following spring under favorable conditions. Wind and rain splashing are the major means by which the spores are spread to healthy tissues. | **Eradication:** A, B, C |
| Verticillium wilt | Raspberries, strawberries | Symptoms include leaves which turn yellow, wither and fall. Lower leaves generally show these symptoms first. The wilt progresses up the canes and they usually darken in color and die. Wilt symptoms may appear suddenly with the onset of warm, dry weather. | The fungus disease is particularly damaging to black raspberries. The fungus may survive in the soil for several years. It attacks through the roots. Poor soil drainage and cool, wet weather favor the disease. | **Prevention:** b, c |
| Spur blight | Raspberries | Weakened plants often have a reduced yield and may winterkill. Purplish to chocolate brown spots and bands appear on young canes directly below the points where the leaves are attached. The diseased areas often enlarge and girdle stems, and may spread to buds, petioles and leaves. Leaves may fall prematurely especially on lower portions of the plant. Infected bark may dry out and crack by late summer. | This fungal disease is a common and damaging disease of red raspberries. The fungus survives from season to season on infected plant parts. Spores are produced during wet periods and spread by wind or rain. Infection occurs through healthy or wounded tissue. | **Eradication:** A **Prevention:** a, b, d **Preventive fungicide:** Sulphide sulphur |
| Crown and cane galls | Raspberries and many other woody and herbaceous plants | Plants develop galls or knots the size of peas to golf balls on the roots and crown. The galls are white at first, turn brown and warty with age, and finally decay. Cane galls appear as small, warty out-growths on the sides of raspberry canes. Plants infected with cane or crown gall may or may not exhibit any reduction in vigor or fruit set. | This is a bacterial disease which survives for extended periods in the soil. The bacteria invade plants only through breaks in the bark and wounds made by insects, pruning and cultivating. | **Eradication:** A **Prevention:** a, b, c |
| Cane blight | Raspberries | Symptoms include dark brown to purplish cankers which form at wounds (from pruning, insects, etc.) on new canes usually towards the end of the season. As the cankers enlarge and extend down the cane, lateral shoots may suddenly wilt and die. Infection, wilting and death of side branches on second-year canes may occur if wounds are present. Infected canes are brittle and snap off easily. Infected fruiting canes generally die between blossoming and fruit set. | The fungus overwinters on diseased canes. Spores are wind-blown, rain-splashed or carried by insects. | **Eradication:** A **Prevention:** a, b |
| Anthracnose | Raspberries, strawberries, and blueberries | In Alberta, anthracnose often affects black raspberries. All above-ground plant parts may be attacked. Small, circular, slightly raised, purple spots appear on young canes in mid summer. The spots may enlarge and turn a grey color in the centers with purple margins. Some leaves may show 'shot-hole' symptoms if the spots fall out. Infected green fruits fail to mature and dry up, white ripe fruits turn brown and soft. | Several different fungi can cause anthracnose. The fungi overwinter on diseased canes. Spores are produced in the spring and spread by rain or wind. | **Eradication:** A, B **Prevention:** b, d **Preventive fungicide:** Captan |
| Leaf spots | Strawberries | Symptoms vary somewhat depending on which fungus is responsible. In general, they consist of spots of damaged or destroyed areas of the leaves. These spots can enlarge and cause leaves to have a scorched appearance. Fruits and fruit stems may also be affected. | Leaf spots are caused by several different fungi. These fungi produce spores in the spring which are carried by wind and rain to healthy foliage. Leaf spot diseases are often brought into a field when new plants are set out. Overwintering occurs on live and dead leaf tissue. Moist warm weather favors the development of leaf spots. | **Eradication:** A **Prevention:** a, b |
| Black root rot | Strawberries | Plants with black root rot generally have much smaller root systems than normal. Main roots show patches or zones that are darker than the rest of the root. Small feeder roots may show a similar patchiness or be entirely lacking. Tips or major sections of main roots may be killed, and in cross section they show a black color throughout. Foliar growth is often stunted and reduced and fewer runner plants are produced. Leaves often show marginal burning and fruits are usually small and leathery with prominent seeds. Plants with severe black root rot may die outright or winter kill. | Black root rot can be caused by a number of fungi, environmental conditions, herbicide or fertilizer burn or a combination of these. The fungi that can cause this disease can all be found in soil. They will infect and damage plants only if growing conditions are suboptimal. | **Prevention:** a, b, c |

| DISEASE | PLANTS ATTACKED | DESCRIPTION OF DAMAGE | SUMMARY OF LIFE HISTORY | CONTROL* |
|---|---|---|---|---|
| Virus | All small fruit | *Mottle:* Tissues between the veins on younger leaves characteristically show an irregular yellowing. Some vein clearing also occurs. Leaves are sometimes puckered or curled and plants may be stunted. Severe strains may markedly distort leaves and flowers. <br> *Yellows (Yellow Edge):* The main symptom is yellowing of leaf margins. Leaves may be stunted, and curl and cup upward. Petioles are short, giving plants a compact habit. Autumn reddening usually appears earlier. <br> *Veinbanding:* Narrow yellow bands develop along the main and secondary veins. Vein clearing, leaf twisting, shortening of petioles, rugosity and faint yellowing also may be seen. <br> *Crinkle:* Crinkle is characterized by the appearance of numerous small, yellowish spots scattered irregularly over the leaf. On young leaves, the spots are small but they gradually enlarge as the leaves expand. With severe crinkle the yellow tissues turn reddish-brown. Vein clearing, leaf crinkling, petiole stunting and a pale green color are often seen. | There are many different viruses that infect small fruits. Although different viruses produce different symptoms, the control of all viruses is basically the same. Once a plant is infected by a virus, the virus cannot be eliminated. Viruses can be introduced with the plant stock or by insects such as aphids and leafhoppers, which transmit viruses. | **Prevention:** a, b <br> **Eradication:** A |
| Drought | All small fruits | Plants appear wilted and unhealthy. Fruit set and yield are poor. | Lack of water. This can be accentuated during hot, windy weather when plant transpiration is very high. Drought can be especially damaging during the blossoming and fruiting periods. | **Prevention:** b |
| Poor drainage | All small fruits | Roots fail to develop and plants become weak. Root rot diseases may follow. | Root rot results when soils are very wet for prolonged periods of time. | **Prevention:** b |
| Sunscald | All small fruits | Exposed surfaces become discolored at first then later turn to greyish-white patches. | This problem often develops on ripening fruit during hot sunny weather. | **Prevention:** b |
| Winter injury | All small fruits | This can be a severe problem in certain Chinook areas. Fruiting canes usually produce blossoms but berries fail to develop or may dry up before ripening. Canes may die after leafing out. Tip dieback frequently occurs. <br> *Tip dieback of raspberries is especially prevalent in chinook zones where they have a tendency to break bud dormancy early during a warm spell.* | Winter injury resulting from root injury occurs most commonly during winters of little snowfall or in soils bare of vegetation. Damage usually occurs when temperatures fluctuate excessively or rapidly. | **Prevention:** a, e |
| *White Pine Blister Rust* | *Currant, gooseberries, white pines* | *Very little damage occurs to the currant gooseberry, but they act as an alternate host of the disease which can be devastating to White Pine. Infected White Pine develop small cankers surrounded by a narrow band of yellow-orange bark. This takes on a blister like appearance and oozes an orange-yellow substance. On currants, the symptoms appear as slightly raised yellow-orange spots.* | *The pathogen, which is a fungus, overwinters on White Pine and produces spores in the spring which are transferred to the currant or gooseberry where the life cycle is completed and a different type of spore is again transferred to the White Pine.* | **Eradication:** D |
| *Red Steele* | *Strawberry* | *This disease results in wilting or death of the plant. The steele or core of the strawberry root becomes reddish-brown and plants appear wilted and stunted. Roots appear greyish with a rattail likeness.* | *Red Steele is a fungus disease that is prevalent in cold, wet soils and may remain in soils more than 10 years.* | **Prevention:** a |
| Inadequate pollination | All small fruits | In the absence of insects, berries tend to be small and are frequently malformed. Stamens of primary flowers may not form well during the cool weather of early spring, thereby creating a shortage of pollen. In such cases, large numbers of pollinating insects are needed to insure a good fruit set. The careless application of insecticides during blooming could seriously reduce populations of pollinating insects. | Maximum yields and fruit size are achieved when abundant pollinating insects are present. On cool windy days pollinating insects do not fly. On some days pollinating insects are only active in protected areas such as shelterbelts. | **Prevention:** g |
| Frost | All small fruits | Damage to flower pistils prevents pollination and produces misshapen berries. | At temperatures of -3°C severe injury to open flowers, buds, and developing berries will occur. | **Prevention:** a |
| Fireblight | Raspberries, saskatoons | See Fireblight under "Ornamentals." | See Fireblight under "Ornamentals." | See Fireblight |
| Juniper rust | Saskatoon | See Apple-Cedar Rust/Juniper Rust under "Ornamentals." | See Apple-Cedar Rust/Juniper Rust under "Ornamentals." | See Apple-Cedar Rust |
| Black Knot | Chokecherries | See Black Knot under "Ornamentals." | See Black Knot under "Ornamentals." | See Black Knot |
| *2,4-D Damage* | *All small fruits* | *Damage appears as twisted and curling foliage and growing point which eventually turns brown and dries up. Plants will be stunted and may even be killed.* | *Occurs when 2,4-D is being used near small fruit plant or a slight breeze causes chemical drift.* | **Prevention:** h |

**Chemicals are in active ingredients rather than trade names, with rare exceptions (Dutox®). Check label for rates.**

## CONTROL OF DISEASES ON GARDEN FLOWERS

| PEST | PLANTS ATTACKED | INJURIOUS STAGES AND DAMAGE | SUMMARY OF LIFE HISTORY | CONTROL* |
|---|---|---|---|---|
| Black spot | Roses | Round black spots with fringed margins develop on the leaves, stems and leaf stalks. Spots enlarge, slowly developing a yellow zone around the spots. Entire leaves will yellow and fall prematurely. Severely infested plants may lose most of their leaves. | Disease is caused by a fungus which overwinters on stems and infected leaf debris. Fungus becomes active during warm wet weather in the late spring and summer. Within two weeks of a spot appearing, spores are produced and the infection is carried by water to other leaves. | Cultural -Plant disease-free roses in a sunny area with good ventilation and soil drainage. Destroy all fallen leaves from infected plants. Stems should be pruned back severely, within 5-8 cm of the graft union. Chemical - Spray applications are more effective than dusts. Use benomyl, captan, sulphur, chlorothalonil, diclone, mancozeb, folpet. |
| Botrytis | Peony | Young stalks suddenly wilt and fall over. Buds turn black and dry up. Opening flowers may be destroyed. Leaf spots may develop when infected petals fall on foliage. In wet weather the diseased parts become covered with a brown felty coat of spores. | The fungus overwinters at the base of infected stalks or infected leaf debris. Other plants become infected from spores that are spread by wind or rain. | Cultural - sanitation is the most important step in control. Destroy diseased plant parts immediately. Remove tops just below ground level in the fall. Avoid dense plantings and overhead watering. Chemical - zineb and sulphur, benomyl at 7-10 day intervals during shoot growth. |
| Powdery mildew | Annuals, perennials and roses | Disease starts on young leaves as raised, blister-like areas that are soon covered with a grayish-white powder or talcum-like mold. The fungus growth develops on the surfaces of leaves, stems, buds and flowers. The fungus feeds only on the plant's surface and slowly injures the plant. Symptoms of injury are: stunting, distortion of leaves and buds, yellowing of leaves, premature leaf fall and a general decline in plant growth. | Fungi overwinter on diseased plant debris, stems and dormant buds. Spores are dispersed by wind and rain. Mildew is favored by humid conditions with widely fluctuating temperatures. It is most common in crowded plantings where air circulation is poor. | Grow mildew-tolerant or resistant cultivars wherever possible. Avoid planting in shady locations. Space plants out to avoid overcrowding and allow air circulation. Chemical - Apply protective fungicides at first sign of infection. Use dinocap, benomyl, sulphur, folpet, or tribasic copper sulphate.<br>* Chemicals are in active ingredients rather than trade names, with rare exceptions (Dutox®). Check label for rates. |

## CONTROL OF TURFGRASS DISEASES

| PEST | DESCRIPTION OF DAMAGE | SUMMARY OF LIFE HISTORY | CONTROL* |
|---|---|---|---|
| Fairy Ring | Fairy rings are circles or arches of dark green grass in the turf. Areas of dead brown grass may develop inside the band of green grass. Tan-colored mushrooms often appear during the summer and/or autumn. The soil beneath the fairy ring is infested with white "threads" of fungus. Fairy rings enlarge as they grow out from the outer edge. A ring may take 2-3 years to become visible. | This fungus is found on all kinds of turf, including highly maintained greens-type turf and pastures. Generally, fairy ring is more common in dry, under-fertilized lawns and on sandy soils. | Cultural: The dark green rings can be masked with fertilizer applications. The dead turf can be brought back by aerating the ring and watering heavily and frequently. To eradicate the ring, the infested and surrounding soil must be completely dug out and removed. Chemical: Formaldehyde. To use this fumigant, the turf should be stripped and the infected soil cultivated. A formaldehyde solution is watered on and the treated area is sealed off with a tarp for 10-14 days. |
| Powdery Mildew | Grass blades become coated with a grey or white powder. Leaves may turn yellow, orange, or brown. Occurs all through the growing season but is not usually severe until autumn. | Most common in shaded areas of lawns (e.g., under trees and on north sides of buildings). New seedlings of some Kentucky blue grass cultivars in sunny locations may be damaged. Excessive or deficient nitrogen favors the disease. | Cultural: Use the more shade-tolerant Creeping Red Fescue, instead of Kentucky blue grass in shaded areas. Raise the height of cut in shaded areas and avoid excessive nitrogen. Cultivars that show little powdery mildew are 'Dormie,' 'Nugget' and 'Sydsport.' Chemical: Thiophanate methyl, apply every 10-14 days. This disease is rarely severe enough to require chemical control. |
| Snow Moulds (pink snow mould, gray snow mould, snow scald, cottony snow mould) | There are four types of snow mould diseases in Alberta. The disease-causing fungi grow at low temperatures -during cold, wet autumn and spring weather and under the snow in winter. As snow melts, patches of grey, white or pink fuzzy mould appear on the grass. The grass blades may turn yellow or brown; circular to irregular patches of turf may die and eventually form large areas of dead grass. | Turf is most at risk when snow falls on unfrozen, wet ground. Heavy snow accumulation that lasts late into spring allows the disease a long time to develop. Excessive nitrogen fertilizer forces the turf to grow late into autumn and so the turf does not 'harden-off' for winter and is more susceptible to snow mould. | Cultural: Reduce fertilizing and irrigation in late summer to allow the turf to harden off. Rake up fallen leaves. Break up piles of snow to speed their melting in spring. Pick up grass clippings and/or dethatch the turf to keep the thatch layer less than 2 cm thick. When the turf has dried in spring, use a stiff broom to break up the patches of mould. Chemical: Chlorothalonil, Benomyl. The fungicides must be applied in late autumn, just before the first snow falls. Snow moulds are often severe on bowling and golf greens. However, they rarely require chemical control on home lawns. |
| Slime moulds | Patches develop in the lawn where leaf blades are coated with clusters of tiny 'beads' that are sticky and lilac-grey. The appearance is similar to patches of spilled oil. Little damage is done to the grass. | Prolonged periods of wet weather. | Cultural: Patches can be removed by sweeping or mowing when the turf dries. Chemical: None required.<br>* Chemicals are in active ingredients rather than trade names, with rare exceptions (Dutox®). Check label for rates. |

# CONTROL OF VERTEBRATE PESTS

## Ground Squirrels

Ground squirrels will occasionally move into lawns and gardens in mid summer. They will dig a burrow system with an entrance 5-6 cm in diameter. The simplest method of removing ground squirrels is to fill the burrow with water from a garden hose. The squirrels can then be dispatched when they emerge from the burrow; alternatively, squirrels will move elsewhere and bother someone else if the burrow is filled with water several times.

Ground squirrels can also be poisoned within urban areas with a prepared bait containing 0.005% chlorophacinone. Six pellets or 15 mL of bait should be placed within each ground squirrel hole. After 48 hours, re-bait all holes where the bait has been disturbed or removed. Remove and bury any squirrel bodies above ground. A third baiting might be required for complete control.

## Pocket Gophers

Pocket gophers, also called "moles," eat garden crops and kill woody plants and shrubs by feeding on the roots. They also deface lawns with the mounds of soil that are deposited above ground by their burrow building. After the mound is built, the gopher plugs the burrow entrance with several cm of soil, so the entrances may not be conspicuous. There are several gopher traps available including the Guardian, California, and Victor. These traps must be set within the burrow. The burrow will be 2-20 cm below ground level and can be located with a long screw driver or probe. Begin to probe 1-2 cm from the edge of the mound. The burrow will be located upslope from the mounds and at the base of fan-shaped mounds or in the indentation of horseshoe-shaped mounds. Place the trap within the burrow as directed by the label.

## Mice and Rabbits

Mice and rabbits will occasionally girdle trees and shrubs during the winter. There are a number of ready-made repellants that discourage rabbits and mice from feeding on trees. Most contain thiram which has a bitter taste. All repellents should be applied in late fall when the leaves have fallen and the bark is dry. The temperature should be above freezing and the repellent should cover the trunk of the tree 0.6-1 m above the snow line. Tree guards can be used where only a few trees are involved. The guard should be made of 0.65 cm (¼ inch) wire screening set 7-10 cm (3 to 4 inches) into the ground and should reach a height of 0.6-1 m above the snow line.

Chances of mouse damage will decrease if lawns are neatly mowed and long grass and vegetation are removed from adjacent areas. Mice can best be removed from homes and out buildings with traps. If mice are a continuing problem, all holes and cracks wider than 0.65 cm (¼ inch) should be sealed with concrete mortar, galvanized sheet metal, heavy-gauge hardware cloth or other material that will resist rodent gnawing.

## Bats

Bats are beneficial insect-eating animals, but they can be a nuisance if they take up residence in attics or unoccupied buildings. The discovery of one or two bats in a house is a frequent problem. A bat usually will find a way out by detecting fresh air movement. The simplest solution is to open all windows and doors leading outside. If the bat is still present at nightfall, the lights should be turned off to help it find open doors or windows.

The only long-term solution for ridding bats from an attic is to seal up all cracks and openings larger than 0.65 cm (¼ inch). Care must be taken to ensure that bats are not sealed within the house. The best time to start is in the fall after young bats have learned to fly and before the advent of cold weather.

Bats can sometimes be removed from an attic by repellents. Naphthalene crystals can be placed in traps or loose-meshed bags and suspended from the rafters. About 2.3 kg (5 lb) for every 60 cu. m (2000 cu. ft.) will treat an average attic. Lights can also be an effective repellent. Large attics may require four or more 100-watt bulbs, but a 150-watt spot light is more effective. Drafts can repel bats where it is possible to open doors or windows and create strong breezes with an electric fan.

abiotic - non-living.

biotic - living.

cuticle - tough, waxy covering found on the outside surface of insects.

host - Species from which a parasite obtains nourishment.

hyphae - single tubular filament of a fungi.

instar - stage in the life of an insect between two successive molts.

larva - immature, wingless, wormlike creature hatched from an egg which goes through minor changes to form a pupa.

molting - shedding and replacement of an outer covering on insects.

mycellium - mass of interwoven hyphae forming the body of fungi.

nymph - juvenile insect resembling an adult which becomes an adult without an intervening pupa stage.

ovipositor - external egg-laying apparatus of insects.

parasite - lives in or on host from which it obtains nourishment.

pathogens - disease-causing organisms.

plant pathology - science of plant diseases or disorders.

predator - Species which kills and devours other Species.

proboscis - extremely slender and sharp, pointed portion of the insects' mouth parts.

pupa - intermediate form from larva to maturity.

saprophyte - insect which obtains its food from dead plants or animals.

sclerotes (ergots) - dense, compacted hyphae remaining dormant during harsh conditions but germinates upon favorable ones.

spiracles - tiny breathing opening on the body surface of insects.

telescoping generations - new-born insect already carrying the next generation of insects.

vector - transporter of viruses from one plant to another.

# SELF CHECK ANSWERS

1. Preventive methods, cultural control and chemical control (see METHODS OF WEED CONTROL - page 609).

2. a. age of the weed being treated
   b. temperature at which chemicals are applied
   c. fertility of the soil
   d. amount of available moisture

   (See WEED CONTROL FOR HOME GROUNDS in 'Backyard Pest Management').

3. Chemicals should always be stored in their own containers out of children's reach and in a place where there is no chance of contact with human or animal food (see SAFE USE OF HERBICIDES in Backyard Pest Management).

4. Systemic insecticides are taken into the plant. Non-systemic insecticides sit on the surface of the plant (see INSECTICIDES - page 606).

5. apple, crabapple, mountain ash, cotoneaster, hawthorn saskatoon berry (see CONTROL OF ORNAMENTAL AND FRUIT TREE DISEASES in Backyard Pest Management).

6. Prevent robins from reaching the strawberries by covering the crop with a wire mesh (see ROBINS - page 615).

7. Thiram is a bitter tasting chemical used to deter mice and rabbits from chewing bark and twigs. The repellent containing thiram should be applied to the bark in late fall when the leaves have fallen and the bark is dry (see Mice and Rabbits in 'Backyard Pest Management' and MICE - page 614 and RABBITS AND HARES - page 615).

8. A tree that is speckled with horizontal rows of regularly spaced small, oval or squarish holes through the bark on trunk or large branches demonstrates yellow-bellied sapsucker damage (see YELLOW-BELLIED SAPSUCKER - page 615).

9. Dandelion, being a broadleaved weed, is susceptible to different types of chemical weed killers than is quack grass. Any chemical that could eradicate quack grass would kill the lawn grass as well (see ESTABLISHED LAWNS and CHEMICAL CONTROL in 'Backyard Pest Management').

Alberta Agriculture, Alberta Environmental Centre. *Weeds of Alberta*. Alberta: Alberta Agriculture and Alberta Environmental Centre, 1983. Agdex 640-4.

Wide general appeal because of excellent color illustrations on Alberta weeds.

Alberta Agriculture. *Crop Protection '86*. Alberta: Alberta Agriculture 1986.

Alberta Agriculture. *Major Diseases of Turf Grasses in Western Canada*. Alberta: Alberta Agriculture, undated. Agdex 273-636-3.

Excellent publication for prairie conditions. Well illustrated with color photographs.

Alberta Agriculture. *Tree and Shrub Diseases and Their Control*. Alberta: Alberta Agriculture, 1978. Agdex 275-635-4.

Brief and helpful account of infectious and noninfectious diseases of ornamental plants.

MacNab, A.A., A.F. Sherf, and J.K. Springer. *Identifying Diseases of Vegetables*. Pennsylvania: The Pennsylvania State University, 1983.

A well-illustrated color reference guide.

Ministry of Agriculture and Food. *Ontario Weeds*. Toronto: Ministry of Agriculture and Food, undated. Publication #505.

An inexpensive publication with excellent references and line drawings.

Philip, Hugh G. *Insect Pests of Alberta*. Alberta: Alberta Agriculture, undated. Agdex 612-1.

The best work currently available on problem insects in Alberta.

## INDEX

# TURF

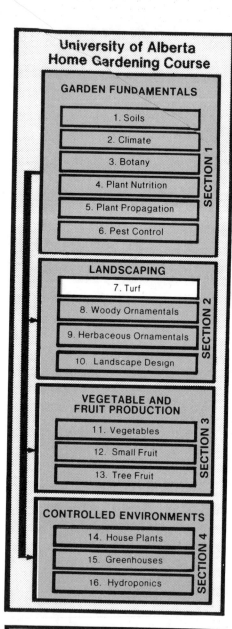

**University of Alberta Home Gardening Course**

**GARDEN FUNDAMENTALS** — SECTION 1
1. Soils
2. Climate
3. Botany
4. Plant Nutrition
5. Plant Propagation
6. Pest Control

**LANDSCAPING** — SECTION 2
7. Turf
8. Woody Ornamentals
9. Herbaceous Ornamentals
10. Landscape Design

**VEGETABLE AND FRUIT PRODUCTION** — SECTION 3
11. Vegetables
12. Small Fruit
13. Tree Fruit

**CONTROLLED ENVIRONMENTS** — SECTION 4
14. House Plants
15. Greenhouses
16. Hydroponics

# SELF-STUDY LESSON FEATURES

Self-study is an educational approach which allows you to study a subject where and when you want. The course is designed to allow students to study the course material efficiently and incorporates the following features.

**OBJECTIVES** — are found at the beginning of each lesson and allow you to determine what you can expect to learn in the lesson.

**LESSON MATERIAL** — is logically organized and broken down into fundamental components by ordered headings to assist you to comprehend the subject.

**REFERENCING** — between lessons and within lessons allows you to integrate course material.

The last two digits of the page number identify the page and the digits preceding these identify the lesson number (eg., 107: Lesson 1, page 7 or 1227: Lesson 12, page 27).

Referencing:

sections within the same lesson (eg., see OSMOSIS)

sections in other lessons (eg., see Botany lesson, OSMOSIS)

figures and tables (eg., see Figure 7-3)

**FIGURES AND TABLES** — are found in abundance throughout the lessons and are designed to convey useful information in an easy to understand form.

**SIDEBARS** — are those areas in the lesson which are boxed and toned. They present information supplementary to the core content of the lesson.

**PRACTICAL PROJECTS** — are integrated within the lesson material and are included to allow you to apply principles and practices.

**SELF-CHECK QUIZ** — is provided at the end of each lesson and allows you to test your comprehension of the lesson material. Answers to the questions and references to the sections dealing with the questions are provided in the answer section. You should review any questions that you are unable to answer.

**GLOSSARY** — is provided at the end of each lesson and alphabetically lists the definitions of key concepts and terms.

**RESOURCE MATERIALS** — are provided at the end of each lesson and comprise a list of recommended learning materials for further study of the subject. Also included are author's comments on the potential application of each publication.

**INDEX** — alphabetically lists useful topics and their location within the lesson.

---

1986  University of Alberta Faculty of Extension

Written by:  Lorraine Taylor

Technical Reviewers:            R. Hugh Knowles
                                Roger Vick

**ISBN 0-88864-852-9**

(Book 2, Lesson 7)

THE PRODUCTION TEAM

Managing Editor .................................................... Thom Shaw
Editor ....................................................................... Frank Procter
Production Coordinator ........................................ Kevin Hanson
Graphic Artists ...................................................... Lisa Marsh
                                                                          Carol Powers
                                                     Melanie Eastley Harbourne
Data Entry ............................................................ Joan Geisterfer

Published by the University of Alberta
Faculty of Extension Corbett Hall
Edmonton, Alberta, T6G 2G4

After studying this lesson, the student should be able to:

1. determine whether to use seed or sod for constructing a new lawn.
2. select and use the most suitable grass variety for particular lawn sites.
3. understand the steps involved in building a lawn.
4. understand the importance of proper lawn maintenance.
5. select and apply the correct lawn fertilizer at the appropriate time.
6. recognize when a lawn needs watering and determine how much water should be applied.
7. understand and implement basic cultural control methods for lawn weeds.
8. select and use the appropriate herbicides to control weeds in lawns.
9. identify the five most common lawn insect pests in Alberta.
10. understand how to avoid common lawn diseases through proper maintenance.
11. list the steps involved in non-routine maintenance practices (eg., aeration, dethatching, spot repairs, topdressing, renovation).

## TABLE OF CONTENTS

## INTRODUCTION

This lesson details a variety of aspects regarding lawn construction, maintenance and renovation. Specifically, this lesson provides information on:

- selection of seed or sod for lawn building

- steps involved in preparing the site for seed and sod

- the importance of establishing a regular maintenance program including mowing, fertilizing and watering

- cultural and chemical pest control specific to lawns

- special lawn maintenance practices including aeration, dethatching and renovation

Wherever necessary, procedural information is presented in listed form to allow for reference. Charts are also incorporated to provide the student with comparison information.

## WHY HAVE A LAWN?

Lawns can be both decorative and functional. They are an integral part of the entire landscape. They provide a unifying base for the house and its surroundings. As well as enhancing the appearance of a landscape, lawns serve several functional purposes. They provide a clean, soft surface for play areas and reduce dust and mud. On steeply sloped banks, grass holds the soil and prevents erosion. Grass helps reduce the glare of summer sun and cools the surrounding air.

## LAWN CONSTRUCTION

Lawn construction incorporates all the aspects of building a new lawn. It includes the steps for preparing the soil and the procedures for laying sod and planting seed. With proper maintenance, lawns can be practically trouble free for many years. Grassy weeds, compaction and uneven surfaces are problems that are often difficult to correct in established lawns but easily prevented with proper construction.

The decision to use seed or sod may be based on several considerations including the type of grass desired or required, the time available to establish the lawn and cost.

### LAWN GRASSES

Several types of grasses can be used for lawns. In Alberta and throughout

Figure 7-1
LAWN GRASSES

Crested Wheatgrass

Red Fescue

Kentucky Bluegrass

Table 7-1

## TURF GRASS CHARACTERISTICS

| NAME | GROWTH HABIT | TEXTURE | MOISTURE REQUIREMENTS | NUTRIENT REQUIREMENTS per growing month | CULTIVARS |
|---|---|---|---|---|---|
| **Kentucky Bluegrass** *Poa patensis* | sod forming rhizomatous | fine-coarse, blade width 2-4 mm | medium drought resistance | 0.2 - 0.6 kg N / 100 m² 0.4-1.3 lb N / 1000 ft² | 32 licensed in Canada, some recommended in Alberta: Dormie Banff, Nugget, Eclipse, Mystic, Touchdown |
| **Creeping Red Fescue** *Festuca rubra var. rubra* | sod forming (slower than KBG) rhizomatous, slow vertical growth | fine blade width 0.5-1.5 mm stiff | good drought resistance | 0.1 - 0.2 kg N / 100 m² 0.2-0.5 lb N / 1000 ft² | Boreal, Pennlawn |
| **Chewings Fescue** *Festuca rubra var. commutata* | bunch-type high density | fine blade width 1-2 mm stiff | good drought resistance | 0.1 - 0.2 kg N / 100 m² 0.2-0.5 lb N / 1000 ft² | Agram' |
| **Crested Wheatgrass** *Agropyron cristatum A. dersertorum* | bunch-type upright | coarse blade width 2-5 mm | excellent drought resistance | 0.1 - 0.3 kg N / 100 m² 0.2-0.7 lb N / 1000 ft² | Fairway, Nordan, sod forming types being developed |

Canada, Kentucky bluegrass is most commonly used. Where a low maintenance lawn is desired and where there is too little water or light for Kentucky bluegrass, other lawn grasses can be sown. Table 7-1 describes the grasses most frequently used in Alberta.

### CULTIVARS

The word 'cultivar' is derived from condensing the words 'cultivated' and 'variety'. As with other horticultural plants, plant breeders have developed many grass cultivars. In fact, there are over thirty Kentucky bluegrass cultivars licensed for use in Canada. Each cultivar has special characteristics. Specific cultivars may be chosen for a lawn seed mix because of certain characteristics, such as resistance to a disease common in the area or shade tolerance in a heavily treed lawn. Table 7-2 lists the characteristics of several Kentucky bluegrass cultivars that grow well in Alberta.

### OTHER TURF GRASSES

Many other grasses are used in lawn seed mixes but are not suitable for entire lawns. Creeping bentgrass (*Agrostis palustris*) is the closely mown

grass used on golf and lawn bowling greens. It is an extremely high maintenance grass, requiring daily mowing during much of the growing season. For practical purposes then, creeping bentgrass is not a suitable grass for home lawns.

Table 7-2

## KENTUCKY BLUEGRASS CULTIVAR CHARACTERISTICS

| | |
|---|---|
| **Banff** | dwarf plant, high tolerance to short mowing, broad leaf, dark green, stays green late in autumn. |
| **Dormie** | upright growth, deep green, highly resistant to *Typhula* and *Fusarium* snow molds and powdery mildew, fairly broad leaf, early dormancy, early spring green-up. |
| **Eclipse** | very low growing, dark green, medium texture, good shade tolerance |
| **Mystic** | light to medium green, powdery mildew resistant, narrow leaf, good autumn color; little thatch |
| **Nugget** | very dense, dark green, good tolerance to low mowing, narrow leaf |
| **Touchdown** | moderately low growing, medium green, good density |

## Table 7-1 CONT'D

| SOIL PREFERENCE | LIGHT REQUIREMENTS | WEAR TOLERANCE |
|---|---|---|
| moist, fertile, well drained pH 6.0-7.0 | full sun – light shade | medium-good good recuperative ability |
| pH 5.5-6.5, will tolerate down to 4.5; grows in dry, sandy soil, must be well drained | prefers full sun; better than other grasses in shade | medium slow recuperative ability |
| 5.5-6.5, will tolerate pH as low as 4.5 | good growth in shade | medium-poor recuperative ability |
| fertile, will tolerate moderately alkaline grows on all soils, best on sandy loam - clay | prefers full sun; moderate shade tolerance | |

## Figure 7-2
## RHIZOME TYPE VS BUNCH TYPE GRASS

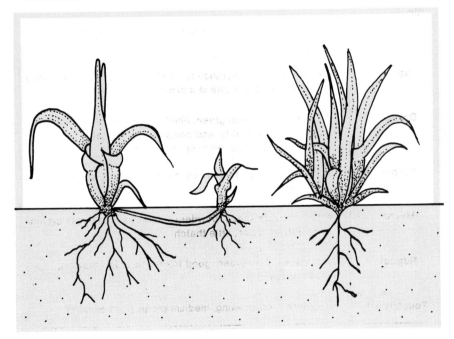

Because perennial ryegrass *(Lolium perenne)* germinates and establishes quickly, it is often used in seed mixes. However, it is not fully hardy in Alberta. It gradually dies out so cannot be used alone.

Although not a grass, white Dutch clover *(Trifolium repens)* was often used in lawn mixes. The broad leaves and white flowers of clover do not blend well in a lawn. In recreational lawns, clover is a nuisance because it stains clothing. Redtop *(Argostis abla)* was another common constituent of lawns. Both white Dutch clover and redtop became less commonly used as Kentucky bluegrass and fesque cultivars were improved.

All of the grasses mentioned so far are classified as 'cool season' grasses. Gardening magazines from the United States often discuss the desirable features of some 'warm season' grasses including slow growth, tolerance to low mowing and drought tolerance. However, grasses like Zoysiagrass, Bermudagrass and St. Augustine grass grow best at 26-35°C and will not survive in Canada.

## SOIL PREPARATION

Soil preparation is one of the most important steps in building a lawn to ensure trouble-free maintenance. Problems with soil texture, drainage and slope are easily corrected at this stage. The steps for preparing a lawn are the same for seeded and sodded lawns.

### SOIL TESTING
Ideally, soil preparation begins with a soil test. Figure 7-3 shows a soil test kit and core sampler which can be used to collect soil samples. The laboratory report, based on the soil sample submitted, determines whether the soil texture needs improvement or whether the soil pH needs adjustment. The report also identifies the salt content of the soil. Excess salts are difficult to reduce but a start can be made before the lawn is planted (see Soils lesson).

### WEED CONTROL
It is important to have most weeds under control **before** the lawn is planted. Annual weeds (such as stinkweed, shepherd's purse,

Figure 7-3

## SOIL TEST KIT AND CORE SAMPLE

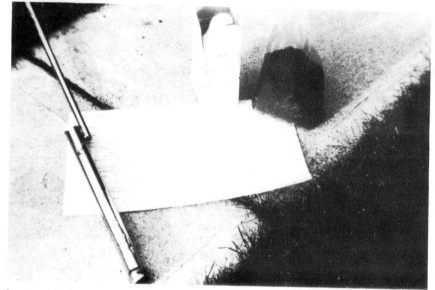

**Courtesy of Alberta Agriculture**

### SOIL AMENDMENTS

Soil amendments may be needed to improve the soil and make it more suitable for grass growth. Amendments are used to adjust:

* **soil pH**
* **soil texture**
* **nutrient levels**

### SOIL pH AMENDMENTS

Most grasses grow best in soil that ranges in pH from 5.5 to 7.0 (see Table 7-1). Occasionally, soils are too acidic and lime must be added to raise the pH. Lime (eg., dolomitic lime) can be spread over the soil and mixed into the top l5 cm (6 in) of soil. A soil test is necessary to determine how much lime, if lime is required, can safely be incorporated. Sulphur is sometimes used to lower soil pH (if the soil is too alkaline). Again, a soil test should be taken to determine the amount to use. Like lime, sulphur can be spread over the soil surface and tilled in (incorporated).

chickweed, and purslane) are of least concern. If they do grow in a newly seeded lawn, they die soon after mowing begins Perennial weeds are more troublesome if they become established. Of these, grassy weeds are most difficult to remove because they cannot be 'selectively' controlled with a herbicide (see CHEMICAL CONTROL OF LAWN WEEDS). Many weeds can be killed by cultivating the soil two or more times (see Figure 7-4). The weeds can be allowed to grow to a height of about 15 cm (6 in) then turned under with a shovel or rototiller. The bare soil can even be watered to encourage weed growth. When the soil is tilled, more weed seeds come to the surface. They will germinate and can be killed. It is important to kill the weed plants before they set seed.

Herbicides can also be used to control weeds prior to planting (see Pest Control lesson, BACKYARD PEST MANAGEMENT). Both perennial and annual broadleaf weeds can be controlled with selective herbicides (see CHEMICAL CONTROL OF LAWN WEEDS). If there are grassy weeds like quackgrass, non-selective herbicides are required. Do not plant immediately after using a herbicide. If some weeds are missed they will regrow and require a second treatment. Some herbicides require a wait period to avoid seed or root damage. The wait period can be up

to four weeks for some herbicides. Check the herbicide label for wait periods between application and seeding or sodding. While clearing the lawn site of weeds, it should also be cleared of stones, roots and any other debris.

### SOIL TEXTURE AMENDMENTS

'Sandy loam' is the best soil texture for lawns (see Soils lesson). Very sandy soils tend to dry out quickly and, therefore, require frequent irrigation. Organic

Figure 7-4

## ROTOTILL SOIL AMENDMENTS

materials like peat, compost and manure can be incorporated with sandy soils to improve their moisture-holding ability. Soils composed of a lot of clay often become hard and cracked when dry, and waterlogged when wet. The same organic materials (peat, compost and manure) help to loosen the soil and prevent it from becoming compacted. The choice of organic material usually depends on its availability and cost. Packaged peat moss is likely the most convenient to use. Depending on the source, it may be quite acidic and could benefit soils with a pH above 7.0. If animal manures are used, they must be well rotted and free of weeds. Some manure, particularly from feed lots, has high salt levels. If a lot of manure is to be added, it may be best to have it tested first.

Coarse sand improves soil drainage to reduce waterlogging. It is important to use coarse or washed sand when amending any lawn or garden soil. Fine sand combines with the clay and makes the soil even harder. Any of the soil amendment materials can be added to a lawn area to make up about 10 to 15 per cent of the soil mix. A 2.5 cm (1 in) layer of organic material can be spread over the soil surface and mixed into the top 12.5 cm (5 in.).

### SOIL NUTRIENT AMENDMENT

Fertilizers are often used to amend soil nutrient levels prior to planting. Generally both nitrogen and phosphorus are required. Phosphorus is especially important for new lawns because it promotes root growth (see Plant Nutrition lesson, PHOSPHORUS). A soil test will reveal the type and amount of fertilizer to use (see Table 7-3 for general fertilizer recommendations).

All of the soil amendments can be added and cultivated into the soil together, before packing and levelling. Alternatively, fertilizer can be spread on the final prepared surface and raked in. Neither seed nor sod should be in direct contact with fertilizer as the seeds and roots can be burned when the fertilizer dissolves.

### DRAINAGE

Excess water limits the supply of oxygen to grass roots. None of the common lawn grasses grow well in poorly drained soils because winterkill is also common to plants in waterlogged

Table 7-3

### LAWN FERTILIZER RATES FOR SOME COMMON LAWN FERTILIZERS

| FERTILIZER | ANALYSIS | APPLICATION RATE | |
| --- | --- | --- | --- |
| | | kg / 100 m$^2$ | lb / 1000 ft$^2$ |
| Ammonium Phosphate | 11-48-0 | 4.5 | 9 |
| Ammonium Phosphate Sulphate | 16-20-0 | 3.0 | 6 |
| Ammonium Nitrate | 34-0-0 | 1.5 | 3 |
| Ammonium Nitrate Phosphate | 27-14-0 | 2.0 | 4 |
| Ammonium Sulphate | 21-0-0 | 2.5 | 5 |
| Complete | 6-10-4 | 8.0 | 16 |
| Complete | 10-32-10 | 5.0 | 10 |

soils. Minor drainage problems can be solved by incorporating coarse sand or by slightly sloping the lawn to allow water runoff. This topic will be dealt with in greater detail in subsequent lessons.

### GRADING

A lawn should have a slope of at least three per cent. Slopes greater than 30 per cent are too steep to mow safely. A slight slope is needed to drain water away during heavy rainfall, when the water comes too quickly to soak in. The grade should run away from buildings and may be sloped toward trees or shrub beds. Terraces may be used to divide up a steep slope (see Figure 7-5). To calculate per cent of slope, determine the drop in elevation over a certain distance. For example, if the elevation drops one metre from the house to the front road (a distance of 50 m), there is a two per cent slope (1 ÷ 50 = 0.02 or 2%).

Figure 7-5
### TERRACED LAWN

Courtesy of Alberta Agriculture

Make the desired grade in the subsoil. Topsoil should only be added after a suitable subsoil grade has been established. Otherwise, expensive topsoil will be used to fill low spots and will produce uneven topsoil depths throughout the lawn. The lawn does not need to be absolutely level, but do consider water drainage and ease of mowing when shaping mounds into the site. Because settling sometimes occurs on new lawns, it is advisable to delay final grading until one or two heavy rains have fallen on the area.

Grading must be done with special care around trees already established in the future lawn area. The addition or removal of as little as 2.5-5.0 cm (1-2 in) of soil around the roots of trees may cause their eventual death. If soil is removed, many of the fine feeder roots that gather water and nutrients may be destroyed. With shallow rooted trees, some of the large supporting roots might be damaged. When soil is spread over top of tree roots, water and air movement can be impaired.

### THE FINAL SURFACE
Topsoil is to added when the subsoil grading is complete (see Figure 7-6). Fertilizer can be mixed in as the topsoil is spread. Other soil amendments may also be added at this time. Ideally, add at least 15 cm (6 in) of topsoil. If an

irrigation system is to be installed (either professionally or by yourself), it is usually done before the final packing and levelling. For a fee, some companies will design systems for do-it-yourself installation.

The final planting surface should be firm to provide good root or seed contact with the soil, allowing quick establishment. It should also be free of humps and depressions as uneven spots make future mowing difficult. The soil is most easily packed with a water-filled roller (see Figure 7-7), which is usually available from rental shops. As the soil is packed (rolled), uneven spots become apparent. To cut down high spots and fill depressions, a long heavy object (like a ladder) should then be dragged across the area (see Figure 7-8). This will pull (shear) soil from the high spots and drop it into low spots. The ladder should be dragged at an angle other than 90° to the direction of pull. Otherwise, the final surface may be wavy. Repeat rolling, levelling several times, and working from a different direction each time. The soil is packed firmly enough when footprints just show on the surface.

When the final packing and levelling is complete, the site is ready to receive sod. If the area is to be seeded, the surface should be lightly raked. Raking

### Figure 7-6
## TOPSOIL ADDED TO LAWN SITE

Courtesy of Alberta Agriculture

### Figure 7-7
## SOIL ROLLER

allows for good contact between seed and soil.

## LAWNS FROM SOD

Table 7-4 compares the advantages and disadvantages of starting lawns from sod and seed. Cost is most often the major drawback of using sod. Sometimes, to offset the cost, both sod and seed are used to estalish lawns. Sod may be used for the front yard or a children's play area while the rest of the lawn may be started from seed (see Figure 7-9).

### BUYING SOD
Cost is an important consideration when buying sod but, like any other large purchase, price should not be the only deciding factor. If you have a choice of companies from which to purchase sod, telephone or visit the suppliers. Ask questions about the grasses, sod thickness, freedom from weeds and services offered. Do any local sod suppliers use Kentucky bluegrass cultivars that are suited to your lawn; ones that are particularly wear tolerant, for example? Sod re-roots best when it is cut thinly. The sod pieces should be no more than 1.5-2.5 cm (about 1/2-1 in) thick. The sod should be free of weeds, particularly grassy weeds. Sod production is a competitive business and companies that sell sod offer a variety of services to assist in sod use. Is information on installing the sod

Table 7-4
SOD VS SEED

| FACTORS | SOD | SEED |
|---|---|---|
| **Planting Season** | whole growing season, approximately late April - late October | early June best; May - early Sept. with special care for watering |
| **Establishment Rate** | very fast, can be used within 3 weeks; establishment almost guaranteed | about 3 months before useable; can be lost to excess water or dryness; could be patchy |
| **Grass Mix** | usually limited to Kentucky Bluegrass/Fescue (approximately 80/20%) | unlimited choice (although prepared mixes may be limited), can blend selected cultivars, specialty grasses for specific conditions |
| **Weeds** | little problem, if sod is clean | can be serious; need excellent control prior to seeding |
| **Use on Slopes** | excellent and immediate cover; roots quickly to hold soil | very susceptible to erosion by heavy rain or improper watering |
| **Soil Preparation** | follow steps given in SOIL PREPARATION | same as for sod plus final light raking |
| **Cost** | $.80 - $1.25/sq yd (approx.) avg lawn = 4000 sq ft $355 to $555 per lawn | $6.50/lb, 5 lb/1000 ft², $130.00/4000 sq ft |

Figure 7-8
LEVEL THE LAWN AREA

Courtesy of Alberta Agriculture

given? What arrangements are made for returning the pallets? What is the cost of delivered sod compared with sod picked up at the source? Note that one pallet of rolled sod — 75 sq yd — weighs approximately 1300 kg or 2900 lb. Sod is sold in either rolls (see Figure 7-10) or slabs. If you have a preference, inquire about which way it is sold. Some sod companies encourage customers to inspect their sod in the field. If making a large purchase, it may be well worth your time to do so.

## SOIL PREPARATION

The previous section described the steps for preparing the soil prior to laying sod. Here is a quick review:

1. Start with a soil test to determine if soil texture, soil pH, or nutrient levels need to be amended.

2. Use cultivation and/or herbicides to control weeds. Annual weeds rarely invade sod because the grass is already established, but quackgrass can be a troublesome pest.

3. Remove all stones and other debris (lumber, nails and bits of concrete are often left behind at newly constructed home sites).

4. Be sure that the subsoil is well drained.

5. Grade the soil to have at least a three per cent slope, which falls away from the house.

6. Add topsoil if necessary. Soil amendments (such as organic matter, sand and/or fertilizer) can be incorporated into the uppermost 15 cm (6 in) of topsoil.

7. Pack and level the soil surface to make a firm seedbed free of small hills or depressions.

8. The level of the lawn should be even with adjacent sidewalks. When making the final grade for sod, the soil surface should be slightly lower than the sidewalk to allow for the thickness of the sod.

## LAYING THE SOD

Sod companies often give verbal or written instructions about laying their sod. Be sure to follow their advice. These are the important steps:

Figure 7-9
SODDED PLAY AREA

Courtesy of Alberta Agriculture

1. Just prior to laying the sod, thoroughly moisten the soil.

2. Lay the first row of sod in a straight line, using a sidewalk, driveway, or tightly stretched string as a guide (see Figure 7-11).

3. Lay each successive row against the sod pieces already laid. In brick-like fashion, alternate the location of sod ends (see Figure 7-12).

4. To lay each successive row, work from the sod pieces already laid.

5. Butt each piece of sod tightly against adjoining pieces. The edges should not overlap each other, nor should there be gaps between the sections.

6. Some sod companies recommend brushing or raking a soil/peat mixture into the joints between the sod pieces to help them knit together faster.

7. Sod is easily cut with a sharp knife to fit irregularly shaped areas (see Figure 7-13). Weeds can also be cut out and removed from the sod pieces.

8. Once laid, the sod can be lightly rolled to press the grass roots into the soil (see Figure 7-14). If using a water-filled roller, empty it.

9. It is **most important** to water the sod immediately after it is laid. If the lawn is large, or if it is a hot, dry day, watering should begin even before the entire lawn is finished.

10. Sod is a very perishable product. Be prepared to lay it as soon as it is delivered. If sod must be stored, put it in a shady spot, out of the wind. Use a covering of moist burlap to prevent the sod from drying.

Figure 7-10
SOD IN ROLLS

Courtesy of Alberta Agriculture

### MAINTAINING A NEWLY SODDED LAWN

Until the sod roots into the soil, the grass must be kept constantly moist. Depending on the weather, the new lawn may need daily watering for a week or more. The grass should be kept almost 'spongy' wet. For the next two or three weeks, the area should be watered often enough to keep the soil moist.

## Figure 7-11
## LAYING SOD

## Figure 7-12
## LAY IN BRICK-LIKE FASHION

Once the grass roots have grown into the soil, the sod pieces cannot be lifted and the lawn will require less watering. The lawn can be mowed when the grass blades are about 7 cm (about 3 in) long. Do not mow when the soil is wet. If fertilizer was mixed into the soil before the sod was laid, the lawn should not need fertilizing for another six weeks. The sod supplier may recommend which fertilizer to use and the best time to apply it. Because root development is still important, phosphorus fertilizers (like 16-20-0 and 11-48-0) can be used (see Plant Nutrition lesson, Tables 4-4, 4-5, and 4-6).

## Figure 7-14
## LIGHTLY ROLL SOD AFTER LAYING

## Figure 7-13
## CUT SODS TO FIT AREA

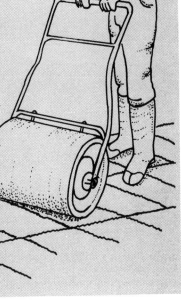

## LAWNS FROM SEED

Lawns are less expensive to grow from seed than from sod (see Table 7-4), but seeded lawns take longer to establish. While sodded lawns rarely fail, seeded lawns can be ruined by heavy rain, high winds, poor weed control, overwatering, or unexpected human, animal, or mechanical traffic.

### SOIL PREPARATION
Preparing the soil surface for seeding is similar to that for sodding. The following reviews the steps required to prepare the soil surface for seeding:

1. Begin with a soil test to determine if soil pH, texture, salt levels, or nutrient levels need to be adjusted.

2. Use cultivation and/or herbicides to control weeds. This is a particularly important step for seeded lawns as the young grass seedlings can be choked out by weeds.

3. Clear the lawn area of stones and debris.

4. Ensure that the soil is properly drained.

5. Grade (slope) the lawn away from buildings.

6. Soil amendments such as organic matter and sand can be incorporated into the soil. Add topsoil if needed.

7. The final grading of the topsoil should make it about level with the sidewalk.

8. Pack and level the soil surface, making a firm seedbed.

9. Lightly rake the soil just prior to seeding (see Figure 7-15).

### THE SEED MIX
Most lawns in Alberta are grown from a seed mixture of Kentucky bluegrass and creeping red fescue or Chewings fescue. Low maintenance lawns and unirrigated lawns in southern Alberta are often seeded to crested wheatgrass. Some acreage and farm owners with large lawns grow a Kentucky bluegrass lawn near the house and seed the remaining area to crested wheatgrass.

Figure 7-15
### RAKE THE LAWN SEEDBED

Courtesy of Alberta Agriculture

A general seed mix recommendation is 80 per cent Kentucky bluegrass, composed of two or more cultivars, plus 20 per cent fescue by weight. The proportions can be adjusted, depending on site conditions. Because fescue germinates more quickly than the bluegrass, such a mixture is useful in preventing erosion and slowing weed growth during establishment. As well, the fescue grows better in shade than does the bluegrass. It fills in the shady spots beneath trees and around buildings. A combination of bluegrass cultivars is recommended to get the benefit of their varied characteristics.

Figure 7-16
### DIFFERENT RATES OF SPRING GREENING - 'NUGGET'(L) 'SYDSPORT'(R)

Courtesy of Alberta Agriculture

For instance, one cultivar might be selected for its early spring green-up (see Figure 7-16) and another selected for its ability to stay green well into autumn. A mix of grasses and cultivars guards against the loss of an entire lawn to disease. This could happen if a single grass (susceptible to the disease) was planted. Table 7-5 lists several seed mixes and the rates at which they should be sown.

## WHEN TO SEED A LAWN
In Alberta, June is usually the best time for seeding because:

- there is an adequate level of soil moisture

- the soil is warm enough for rapid seed germination

- June rainfall will supplement irrigation

- weed growth is not at its peak

- temperatures are not high enough to impair seedling growth.

Lawns **can** be seeded almost any time from mid-May until early September. Seeding should not begin until the soil has warmed to 15°C. No seeding should be done within six weeks before dormancy, to allow the plants time to establish and prepare for winter. Lawn seeding is often unsuccessful in July because of low soil moisture and rainfall combined with high temperatures.

## SEEDING THE LAWN
When the soil is carefully prepared and the steps listed below are followed, a high quality lawn can be grown. After about one full growing season, a seeded lawn can be as dense and attractive as a sodded lawn. These are the steps to seed a lawn:

1. Begin with a thoroughly moistened lawn site.

2. Divide the total amount of required seed in half. Spread half over the entire area working in one direction. Then spread the other half — working from a different direction. This serves to spread the seed evenly. Seed can be applied by hand or with a mechanical seeder. Large grassed areas, such as sod farms and parks, are usually seeded with tractor pulled 'Brillion' seeders. Many county offices have Brillion seeders available for loan. The seeder forms furrows, drops the seed into the furrow and presses the seed into the soil.

3. Lightly rake the seeded area to cover the seed. Rake across the slope or the water may run down the raked furrows and wash the seed out.

4. Lightly roll the area to press the seed into the soil. Good seed/soil contact is needed for seed germination.

5. Gently water the area. Once the

seed has been moistened and begins germinating it must be kept moist, otherwise the seedling will die. Depending on the weather, the lawn area may need watering several times a day. Sprinklers that apply water in a fine spray are best. Until the grass has sprouted, the lawn must be watered very carefully. If the sprinkler is left on too long, puddles may form and wash the seed away. After the grass sprouts, it may need less frequent watering, but the soil must be kept constantly moist.

6. Mulches of burlap, chopped straw, or peat moss are sometimes used to help keep the seed moist and to protect it from washing away on steeply sloped areas. Such mulches are not usually necessary on flatter areas unless seeding during hot, dry, windy weather. Burlap mulch must be removed before the grass seedlings begin to grow into the cloth, otherwise the seedlings can be pulled out as the burlap is lifted.

## MAINTAINING A NEWLY SEEDED LAWN
As the seedlings grow and develop roots, less frequent watering is required. However, the soil should be kept moist until the grass plants are well established.

The lawn can be mowed when the grass blades are about 7 cm (about 3 in) long. Until a dense stand of grass covers the soil, the lawn requires careful mowing to avoid tearing, especially when turning corners with the mower. Be sure the soil is dry before mowing or it may become compacted.

Mowing removes most annual weeds. Even if the annual weeds are numerous, they rarely require chemical control. Grass seedlings are very sensitive to the common lawn herbicides. If herbicides must be used, do not apply any until the lawn has been mowed twice (at least).

About six weeks after seeding, the lawn can be fertilized. A phosphorus containing fertilizer like 16-20-0 or 11-48-0 can be used. However, do not fertilize after mid-August (see AUTUMN CARE).

## Table 7-5
## LAWN SEED MIXES AND PLANTING RATES

| SEED MIX | SITE CONDITIONS | kg/100 m² (lb/1000 sq ft) |
|---|---|---|
| 80% Kentucky Bluegrass 20% Creeping Red Fescue or Chewing Fescue | suitable for high quality, well maintained lawn; some irrigation usually required; full sun | 2.5 (5) |
| 50-25% Kentucky Bluegrass 50-75% Creeping Red Rescue or Chewings Fescue | semi-shady lawn; use higher rate of fescue with more shade | 2.5–3.0 (5-6) |
| 100% Crested Wheatgrass | low rainfall areas with no irrigation, a bunch-type grass and therefore considered a lower quality lawn | 3.0 6 |

## MULCHED SEED

A second method of seeding lawns uses mulched seed. This is referred to as hydroseeding. The seed is mixed with water and a mulch (like straw or paper fibre). This mixture is sprayed over the lawn area (see Figure 7-17). This is a useful method for seeding large sites, steep slopes, or other areas that are difficult to seed by conventional means. The mulch helps hold the seed on slopes and retains moisture for germination. Large tanks and sprayers are required which makes this an expensive procedure and rarely practical for home lawns.

# LAWN MAINTENANCE

## INTRODUCTION

**Mowing, watering,** and **fertilizing** are the **three fundamentals of lawn care.** Few lawn problems are likely to occur if lawn care is performed regularly and properly on a well constructed lawn. There is a minimum level of maintenance required to keep lawns healthy (see Figure 7-18). That level varies with the type of grass used. If more than just the minimum amount of maintenance is carried out, the quality of the lawn can often be improved. Maintenance of a healthy lawn involves performing the appropriate operation at the appropriate time.

## MOWING THE LAWN

### MOWING HEIGHT

Kentucky bluegrass grows best when it is kept at 4-5 cm (about 1 1/2-2 in). Some cultivars ('Baron' and 'Fylking' for example) grow well when mowed lower. Crested wheatgrass grows best when cut to 4-6 cm (about 1 1/2 - 2 in). Creeping red fescue should be mown at 2.5-5.0 cm (about 1-2 in) and Chewings fescue at 3.7-5.0 cm (about 1 1/2 - 2 in). When cut within these ranges, the grasses grow vigorously. The grasses are able to compete with weeds and reduce the spread of weeds in the lawn. Healthy grass is able to resist many disease attacks and, if damaged, quickly recovers. Mowing grass shorter than the optimum height (see Figure

### Figure 7-17
### MULCHED SEED

7-19) or letting it grow very long can weaken the grass plants, reduce the root growth and allow unwanted plants to grow.

The frequency of mowing depends on the weather, amount of water the grass has received (rainfall or irrigation) and amount of fertilizer applied. At each

### Figure 7-18
### DIFFERENT LEVELS OF LAWN MAINTENANCE

Courtesy of Alberta Agriculture

## Figure 7-19

### SHALLOW ROOT SYSTEM WHEN KENTUCKY BLUEGRASS MOWN TOO SHORT

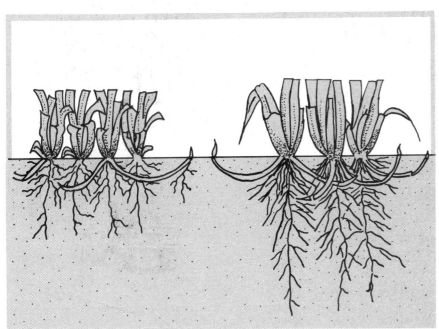

mowing, no more than one-third of the blade should be removed. As the plants grow taller, they become coarse at the base (see Figure 7-20). As a result, the lawn looks sparse and coarse if tall plants are cut back to 5 cm (2 in). If the lawn does become overgrown, as often happens after a long, rainy spell, raise the cutting height. Gradually lower the cutting height on the mower with each successive mowing until it is returned to

the usual height. The mowing height may also be raised during hot, dry, summer weather. If the plants are left to grow about 0.5 cm (about 1/4 in) longer than normal, the roots are slightly more shaded and suffer less heat stress.

### LAWN MOWERS

Lawn mowers are of two main types: reel and rotary mower. The **reel type**

mower cuts with a shearing action. It gives the finest cut but requires level ground. Motorized models are used on golf and bowling greens; push models are used on home lawns. Reel type mowers can cut very low.

The **rotary mower** blade spins horizontally and lops the tops off grass blades. Rotary mowers are the most commonly used type for home lawns. There are walk-behind gas and electric models as well as riding mowers available. **Mulching mowers** have rotary blades which cut the grass, chop it into small pieces, and blow it back into the lawn to decompose. Alberta's growing season may not be hot or humid enough to decompose all clippings in one year (see GRASS CLIPPINGS). **Air cushion** rotary mowers ride on a layer of air rather than wheels. They are easy to manoeuver on level and sloped lawns, but clippings cannot be picked up when using this type of mower. **Flail mowers** and **sickle mowers** are used in rough areas, such as ditches. They give a poor quality cut.

Regardless of the type used, keep lawn mower blades sharp. Ragged leaf tips (caused by dull mower blades) turn brown or grey and make the lawn look unattractive (see Figure 7-21). The poorly cut tips heal slowly and are more susceptible to entry of disease organisms than are cleanly cut plants. Lawns cut with a dull mower use more water than those cut with sharp mower blades.

### LAWN MOWER SAFETY
Every year many people are injured while using lawn mowers. Some safety pointers should be kept in mind:

1. Before each mowing, clear the lawn of anything that will interfere with the mower; stones, twigs, and toys, for example. Rotary mowers can hurl such items at great speed. As well, hard objects will damage mower blades.

2. Wear sturdy footwear while mowing the lawn.

3. Before making any adjustments to the lawn mower, turn it off and wait until the blade(s) stop turning.

4. Never allow passengers on riding mowers.

## Figure 7-20

### GRASS BECOMES COARSE IF LEFT TO GROW LONG

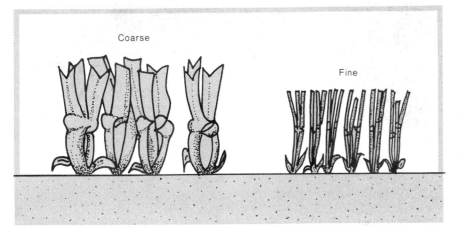

Coarse

Fine

Figure 7-21

## RAGGED GRASS BLADES WHEN CUT WITH DULL MOWER

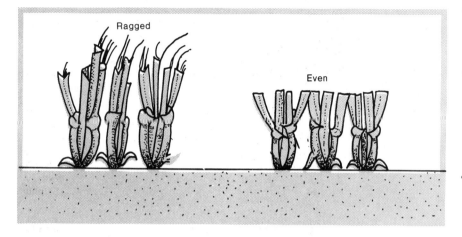

### GRASS CLIPPINGS

Thatch is the layer of organic matter (including grass clippings) that accumulates at the soil surface. When the weather is hot and humid, thatch breaks down (decomposes) and supplies the lawn with nutrients and organic matter. The grass blades have a high nitrogen content which is, through decomposition, returned to the soil. As much as 1 kg of nitrogen/100 m²/season (2 lb/1000 sq ft/season) may be returned to the soil if clippings are left. However, Alberta's season is usually too short for complete decomposition so the thatch only accumulates. If thatch is allowed to accumulate in lawns, it interferes with water and fertilizer movement to the grass roots. Eventually then, thatch must be removed from most Alberta lawns.

Many people prefer to pick up the clippings at each mowing. Clippings can be collected in a bag attached to the lawn mower or raked up by hand. Even with such regular collection, spring dethatching is occasionally required (see LAWN DETHATCHING).

If the grass is long or wet when cut, the clippings often come out of the mower in clumps (see Figure 7-22). Always remove these clumps or they will smother and kill patches of lawn. Hand or mechanical lawn edgers can be used to give a final, tidy appearance to the lawn (see Figure 7-23).

## FERTILIZING THE LAWN

### LAWN FERTILIZERS

Why fertilizers are needed and how they should be applied is discussed in previous lessons (see Plant Nutrition lesson, FERTILIZERS). The important points are reviewed here:

• The four nutrients used in largest

Figure 7-22

## PICK UP GRASS CLIPPINGS

amounts by grass are nitrogen, phosphorus, potassium and sulphur.

• Nitrogen is needed for lush green leaf growth. It leaches out of the soil readily and so requires frequent application.

• Phosphorus is needed for root growth. It is especially important on newly seeded and sodded lawns. Phosphorus is quite immobile in the soil. The phosphorus that is not used up by plants right away remains to be used later.

• Potassium is needed to give plants a sturdy structure and disease resistance (see Figure 7-24). Most Alberta soils are high in potassium so many fertilizers do not contain it in their formulations (eg., 16-20-0, 11-48-0, 34-0-0).

• Sulphur is used to make proteins in plants so if it is in short supply, plants will not grow properly.

• Grass plants require many other elements for growth. These minor elements are only needed in trace amounts and are usually in adequate supply in Alberta soils.

• All fertilizers are identified by three

Courtesy of Alberta Agriculture

## Figure 7-23
## NEATLY EDGED LAWN

Courtesy of Alberta Agriculture

numbers (see Figure 7-25). They indicate the per cent of nutrients contained in the fertilizer. The first number indicates the per cent nitrogen, the second number identifies the per cent phosphate (which supplies phosphorus), and the third number indicates the per cent available potash (which supplies potassium). For example, a 25 kg bag of 20-10-5 contains 20% nitrogen (or 5 kg), 10% phosphate (or 2.5 kg), and 5% potash (or 1.25 kg). The various elements that combine to make the compounds supplying the NPK, make up the remaining 65 per cent.

The two main types of fertilizers are **organic** and **chemical** (or commercial). Most of the organic fertilizers need to be incorporated into the soil (animal manures, for example) and are, therefore, unsuitable for use on lawns. Many of the commercial fertilizers commonly used for agriculture are suitable for lawns. However, some special lawn fertilizers are available:

**Herbicide/fertilizer combinations** are used to weed and feed lawns at the same time. They save time by combining both operations and provide a convenient way to apply herbicides. However, you must avoid spreading them into adjacent flower beds, gardens, and near tree roots as the herbicides contained will kill broadleaved plants. On a small home lawn, this may be impossible. If there are only a few weeds in the lawn, spot applications of herbicides are likely to be less expensive than treating the entire lawn with a herbicide/fertilizer combination (see Figure 7-26).

**Slow release fertilizers** release nutrients gradually over several weeks, whereas most fertilizers dissolve and release their nutrients within a few days. Slow release fertilizers give slow, even growth rather than sudden flushes. Fewer fertilizer applications are needed. The same growth can be achieved with typical commercial fertilizers by applying them in small amounts each week. The slow release products are convenient, but more expensive. A common example is SCU (Sulphur Coated Urea).

**Winterizer fertilizers** are meant to be used at the end of the growing season. Their purpose is to give resistance to winter diseases and to speed spring greening. Lawns that are properly maintained and regularly fertilized throughout the growing season usually have good disease resistance. If the winterizer is applied before the grass is dormant in autumn, it might encourage late season growth that is readily winterkilled. If lawns green up too early in spring, the tender new growth may be damaged by late spring

## Figure 7-24
## POTASSIUM IS IMPORTANT FOR DISEASE RESISTANCE

Courtesy of Alberta Agriculture

Figure 7-25
LAWN FERTILIZER

storms. These fertilzers may force early leaf growth when root growth is actually needed. Some examples of fertilizers sold as 'winterizers' are 13-16-0, 12-3-5 and 4-8-16.

- Fertilizer prices should be calculated on a per unit nutrient basis, rather than by comparing bag prices (see Plant Nutrition lesson, PURITY OF ELEMENTS AND RELATIONSHIP TO COST). Generally, the more concentrated fertilizers are less expensive per unit of nutrient. The more concentrated fertilizers are used in smaller amounts and must be applied carefully to avoid burning the grass.

### SOIL TESTING

General rates for lawn fertilizers are given in Table 7-3. The only way to know the exact needs of a lawn is to have a soil test (see Soils lesson). For home lawns, soil testing every 4-5 years is normally sufficient to see that the nutrient levels are adequate. With experience, you will know by the lawn's appearance when nutrients, particularly nitrogen, are needed. On an established lawn, a soil test will determine phosphorus and potassium levels. The nitrogen level is also tested but this figure is less useful because nitrogen changes so quickly in the soil. Regular testing helps monitor changes in soil pH and salt levels and may show that maintenance practices should change. For example, repeated use of acidic fertilizers (like 21-0-0 which is high in sulphur) may gradually lower the pH. It is helpful to have the same soil test laboratory do the analysis each time so that reports are consistent and comparisons can be made from year to year.

Figure 7-26
COMBINATION FERTILIZER - HERBICIDE

### WHEN TO FERTILIZE THE LAWN

Table 7-1 lists the nutrient requirements of lawn grasses. A general recommendation for a typical Kentucky bluegrass lawn is 1.5 kg actual nitrogen/100 m²/season (3 lb/1000 sq ft/season). This amount can be spread on the lawn with as few or as many applications as desired. Good results can be expected from three applications of 0.5 kg nitrogen/100 m² (1 lb/1000 sq ft) each time. The first application should be made in mid-May, the second in early July, and the third in mid-August. Some people use fewer applications to save time. Remember though, increased rates of fertilizer application also increase the likelihood of burning the grass. Some references recommend using no more than 0.5 kg nitrogen/100 m² (1 lb /1000 sq ft) at each application. Another disadvantage of making only one or two applications is that nitrogen, which is not taken up by the grass immediately, may leach out and be lost. Some people prefer to use more than three applications. Frequent fertilization allows the grass to grow evenly, with fewer flushes of lush growth. The number of applications is limited only by the amount of time available.

Mid-May is the recommended time for the first application of fertilizer. Many people fertilize their lawns earlier than this (as much as a month earlier), but there are several problems associated with very early application including:

- **late spring storms** - Very often the weather warms up and the grass begins to grow in early April. Early fertilizing will force even more tender new growth. Late spring storms are common and can easily damage the new growth.

- **root damage repair** - Some of the grass plant roots and crowns have likely been damaged during the winter. As the soil begins to warm in spring, the plants are able to repair that damage. If, however, the lawn is fertilized immediately in the spring, the nitrogen forces the plant to promote leaf growth at the expense of root development.

- **soil compaction** - After a long winter, gardeners are usually eager to get out and work on the lawn. If fertilization, as well as raking and aerating, begins too soon, the soil will still be wet and easily compacted.

### HOW TO APPLY FERTILIZER

Fertilizer can be applied by hand although the method requires practise to give even coverage. Dribble or drop type spreaders are fairly accurate and drop fertilizer in a narrow band (see Figure 7-27). They must be used with care; missed rows and overlaps are obvious when the grass greens up. Rotary spreaders throw fertilizer in a wide arc. A lawn can be fertilized quickly with either the hand–held or push rotary spreaders.

To achieve good results when fertilizing a lawn, there are several important steps to remember:

- Divide the total amount of fertilizer to be applied in half; apply each half over the entire lawn, in two directions (lawn seed is spread the same way). Uneven application

### Figure 7-27
### ROTARY SPREADER - DRIBBLE SPREADER

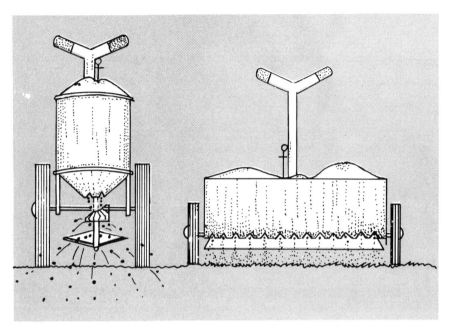

shows up later as dark green or pale strips (see Figure 7-28).

- Spread fertilizer on a dry lawn; wet grass (even with dew) can be burned when the fertilizer dissolves on the leaves.

### Figure 7-28
### POORLY APPLIED FERTILIZER

Courtesy of Alberta Agriculture

- Water the lawn heavily immediately after fertilizing to dissolve the fertilizer. This makes it available to the plant by washing it off the grass leaves and down to the roots.

- If the lawn cannot be watered, try to apply fertilizer just prior to a heavy rainfall. There is less chance of the lawn being damaged if a small amount of fertilizer is used — about 0.4 kg N/100 m² (about 3/4 lb N/1000 sq ft).

- Move the spreader off the lawn when filling it. Accidentally spilled fertilizer is difficult to pick off grass. The consequence may be a very lush patch or a burned spot.

- Close the spreader whenever you stop or turn, otherwise the fertilizer continues to spill out.

## WATERING THE LAWN

### HOW MUCH WATER TO USE
Kentucky bluegrass needs about 4 cm (1 1/2 in) of water/week for best growth. The frequency of watering depends on the amount of rainfall received. If the grass receives less than

Figure 7-29
EFFECT OF FERTILIZER ON LAWNS

Soil moisture levels and grass appearance indicate when to water the lawn. The following indicators can be used to determine when the lawn needs water:

- Use a soil probe or small trowel to check the soil moisture. When the soil is dry 5 cm (2 in) below the grass, it is time to water.

- Grass short of water begins to wilt.

- The grass blades do not spring back when the lawn is walked across and footprints are obvious.

- Kentucky bluegrass turns a slate blue color.

- The edges of older grass blades begin to curl inwards.

the optimum amount of water, it grows less vigorously and weedy plants may gain a foothold in the lawn. If unwatered during hot, dry spells, the grass will stop growing and turn brown (become dormant). After a heavy rainfall or thorough watering, the grass usually greens up and begins growing again. But, while in the dormant state, weeds can easily invade the lawn (see Figure 7-30).

The method of irrigating affects rooting depth and, consequently, the drought tolerance of the lawn. At least 5 cm (2 in) of water should be applied at each irrigation. The soil should be wetted to about 15 cm (6 in) deep. If lawns are frequently and lightly watered, the grass roots remain near the soil surface. Shallow rooted lawns suffer in very dry weather because the plants have no deep roots to seek out more water (see

Figure 7-30
UNDERWATERED LAWN

Courtesy of Alberta Agriculture

Figure 7-31
DEEP ROOTS ON HEAVILY WATERED LAWNS VS SHALLOW ROOTS ON LIGHTLY WATERED LAWNS

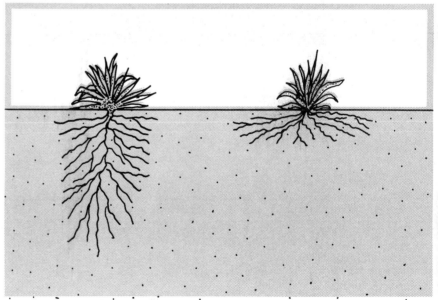

Figure 7-31). Underground watering systems may cause shallow rooting because they are often programmed to turn on automatically, without consideration for what the grass needs. It is easy to measure the amount of water applied (see Figure 7-32). Set out several containers (tin cans, for example) on the lawn under the sprinkler. Record the time it takes to apply 5 cm (2 in) of water. The time required varies with the type of sprinkler and the time of day. In urban areas, water pressure usually drops during dry summer evenings when water use is heavy. If water infiltration is slow and puddles form before the necessary amount of water is applied, move or turn off the sprinkler and continue irrigating once the water has soaked in.

## LAWN SPRINKLERS

The choice of sprinkler may be determined by the lawn shape (see Figure 7-33). The best type of sprinkler is one that covers the lawn area with little overlap onto sidewalks, roads, driveways, or other such areas. Sprinklers that cover a large area, irrigate the lawn quickly but are easily affected by wind.

## WHEN TO WATER

Signs of wilting (eg., footprints in the lawn, slate gray color, curled leaves) and dry soil 5 cm (2 in) deep indicate a need for watering. Early morning is the best time of the day for watering. If watering during midday heat, some of the water will be lost to evaporation. If plants are watered in late evening, they may stay wet through the night. Damp, cool grass provides an ideal environment for disease growth. Early morning and evening are usually the calmest times during the day (least wind) and sprinkler patterns are least affected. The least amount of water is lost to evaporation when the lawn is watered on a calm, cloudy day.

## SPRING CARE OF LAWNS

Spring lawn care activities include a clean-up raking and fertilizing (see Figure 7-34). A vigorous raking removes dead grass leaves and clippings and improves the appearance of the lawn. This is also the best time for aerating and dethatching (if necessary). With all of these tasks, it is important to wait

### Figure 7-32
### MEASURE AMOUNT OF WATER APPLIED

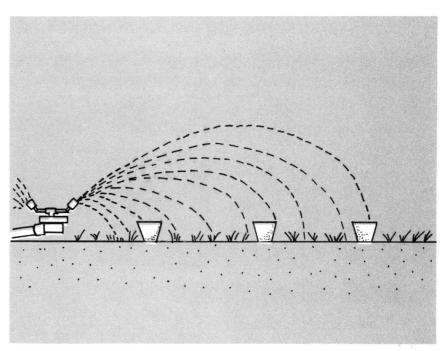

until the soil is dry. Lawns still soggy with melted snow are easily damaged.

If salt was used to melt sidewalk ice, the salt laden snow should be shovelled off the grass before the snow begins to

melt. Salts can damage grass plants and can make the soil unsuitable for growth. If puddles form as the snow melts, they should be drained off (if possible).

### Figure 7-33
### LAWN SPRINKLER

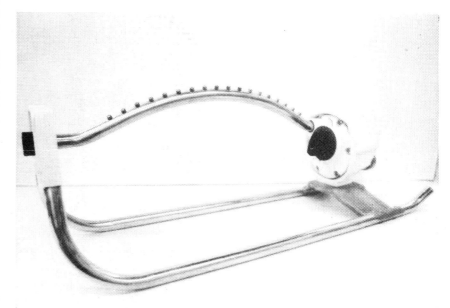

Figure 7-34

RAKE IN SPRING TO REMOVE DEAD GRASS

## AUTUMN CARE

As temperatures drop, lawn growth gradually slows and the plants harden off for winter. Mowing should continue until all growth has stopped. Do not alter the mowing height. Grass that is left to grow long for winter may be more susceptible to snow mold damage. Very low mowing just prior to winter dormancy exposes the plant crowns, which can be damaged by desiccation and low temperature (see Figure 7-35).

Both fertilizer and water cause grass plants to continue growing when they should be going dormant. August 15 is a generally suggested cut-off date for fertilizer application. Reduce watering in early autumn. However, lawns should not be dry at the onset of winter.

Rake tree leaves off the lawn before the first permanent snowfall (see Figure 7-36). If left on the lawn, leaves may become wet and form a compact layer which provides an ideal site for the growth of snow mold diseases.

Figure 7-35

GRASS MOWN TOO LOW IN AUTUMN

Courtesy of Alberta Agriculture

## SKATING RINKS ON LAWNS

When built properly, backyard skating rinks do not kill lawns. Proper construction involves the following:

1. Begin with a 2.5 cm (1 in) base of lightly packed snow. This acts as a barrier between the grass and the ice.

2. Apply several light sprinklings of water on top of the snow and allow the water to freeze before flooding the rink. This ice layer prevents water from soaking through the

Figure 7-36

RAKE UP LEAVES IN AUTUMN

Courtesy of Alberta Agriculture

snow and reaching the grass. A sheet of plastic laid over the packed snow will also keep the water from soaking through to the grass.

3. Once the base is formed, the rink can be flooded. A water-snow slush works well to fill in holes and cracks.

4. Most winterkill on lawns occurs in spring, when snow and ice repeatedly freeze and thaw. Once the skating rink begins to melt, take measures to speed melting and draining of the water. Snow banks and boards around the edges of the rink should be removed so the water can run off. Punching holes in the ice and spreading out dark materials (like charcoal) may speed the melting.

# LAWN PROBLEMS

## INTRODUCTION

This section discusses problems that lawn owners may encounter. The five main types include: weeds, diseases, insects, vertebrate pests, and physiological disorders. In comparison with lawns in milder and more humid climates, Alberta lawns are relatively trouble free. Insect and disease control measures are not, as they are in many other places, routinely part of lawn maintenance. Most importantly, if lawns are built properly and well maintained, lawn disorders due to pests may never become a problem.

If a problem does develop in the lawn, there are three important steps to follow:

1. **Identify the problem** — Identification can be made using past experience, reference books, horticulturists at garden shops or local horticultural societies, or district agriculturists. Plant samples can be sent to diagnostic laboratories for identification and control recommendations. Submit these samples through the Alberta Agriculture district offices.

2. **Find the primary cause of the problem** — Most lawn pests do not appear unless the lawn is under stress and is not growing well. If the primary cause is not found and corrected, control of the pest is likely to be only temporary. For example, chemical moss killers can be used to control moss in lawns. However, if the soil is too acidic for vigorous grass growth, the moss will reappear until the acidity is corrected.

3. **Repair damage quickly** — As pest populations increase, they become harder to combat, so should be dealt with as soon as they are discovered. A lawn damaged by pests or environmental stress is weakened and susceptible to invasion by other pests until the damage is repaired.

## LAWN WEEDS

### CULTURAL CONTROL
'Cultural control' refers to the control of pests through the use of proper maintenance practices rather than the use of pesticide chemicals. Cultural methods can be used to **prevent** establishment of the pest in the lawn (see Pest Control lesson, CULTURAL CONTROL). Weeds do not easily become established in a lawn where the grass is growing well and forms a dense turf. Begin with the correct types of grasses for the lawn site. Watering and fertilizing schedules that suit the types of grasses used are important. Deficiencies or excesses of water or fertilizer give weeds a competitive edge. The following three lawn weeds are best controlled culturally.

### ANNUAL BLUEGRASS (*Poa annua*)
Annual bluegrass makes an attractive, dense and low growing turf. It is sometimes used for golf greens. Generally, however, annual bluegrass is considered a weed in home lawns. Being an annual plant, it dies each winter. It has poor tolerance to drought and turns brown in hot weather. Its light green color and its ability to set seed often, make it conspicuous in Kentucky bluegrass lawn mixes. Annual bluegrass is very susceptible to snow mold diseases. Because it produces a lot of seed, annual bluegrass can take over a

lawn in as little as three years.

To prevent the growth of annual bluegrass by cultural means, follow the procedure outlined:

1. Mow at 4-5 cm (1 1/2-2 in). Annual bluegrass grows best at 2.5 cm (1 in) or lower. Do not lower the mowing height to try to cut off the seed heads. This puts the Kentucky bluegrass under stress and favors the annual bluegrass.

2. Water heavily and infrequently. Light, frequent irrigation promotes germination and growth of annual bluegrass.

3. Follow fertilizer recommendations for the lawn grass being used. Annual bluegrass thrives when soil nitrogen is high. It also competes well with other grasses when soil phosphorus is high. Unlike nitrogen, phosphorus is relatively immobile in the soil. Repeated use of fertilizers containing phosphorus can cause phosphorus build up.

4. Repair any damaged spots in the lawn, either with seed or sod (see SPOT REPAIRS IN LAWNS). Annual bluegrass often becomes established in bare patches and spreads from there.

If there are small patches of annual bluegrass in a lawn, they can be dug out. If the plants have had a chance to set seed, new plants will likely grow for some time. Non-selective herbicides can also be used to kill annual bluegrass but such herbicides also kill desirable grasses.

### CREEPING BENTGRASS (*Agrostis palustris*)
Like annual bluegrass, creeping bentgrass is a difficult weed to control with herbicides because it, too, is a grass. Any herbicide that kills weed grasses also kills desirable grasses. Creeping bentgrass is primarily used for closely mown golf and lawn bowling greens (see OTHER TURF GRASSES). It is not suitable as a lawn grass because of its very high maintenance requirements. If it invades Kentucky bluegrass lawns, bentgrass spreads vigorously and makes lawns look patchy. Bentgrass is not compatible

with bluegrass because it is slower to green in spring, turns brown earlier in autumn, is very susceptible to snow mold damage and has poorer wear tolerance. When mown higher than about 2 cm (3/4 in), bentgrass develops a lot of thatch. Creeping bentgrass seems to be a particular problem in southern Alberta lawns. The most effective cultural method to control bentgrass growth is watering deeply and infrequently. Frequent irrigation provides the moist environment needed for bentgrass seed germination. Bentgrass is spread throughout the lawn when stem pieces are cut up by the lawn mower. Under moist conditions these pieces can take root and grow. The bentgrass root system is much more shallow than bluegrass and so requires frequent irrigation for good growth.

If bentgrass becomes established in patches, a vertical mower can be used to cut out the plant stems (see DETHATCHING). The clippings and stems must be picked up to prevent further spreading. Where lawns have become badly infested with bentgrass, a non-selective herbicide can be used to kill the weedy areas. If the thatch is thick, it should be removed by raking, by a vertical mower, or with a sod cutter. The bare patches can then be reseeded or sodded with the desired grasses.

## MOSSES

Lawn mosses are the most notable example of weeds that only appear when the lawn is growing poorly. The conditions that interfere with good grass growth and consequently favour moss growth are:

- low or unbalanced soil fertility
- compacted or wet soils
- heavy shade
- acidic soil
- a thick thatch layer

Because moss is not deeply rooted, it can be raked out of the lawn. Just before mowing, vigorously rake the mossy patches. Large areas left bare after removing moss should be seeded. Chemical 'moss killers' are available to control moss but, unless the conditions favoring moss growth are corrected, the weed will return.

## CULTURAL CONTROL PRACTICES

Cultural control practices that favor growth of desirable grasses in lawns include:

1. Fertilize the lawn regularly.

2. Keep traffic off wet lawns to avoid compacting the soil. Aerate compacted lawns.

3. Avoid overwatering — measure the amount applied.

4. Prune large trees to allow some light through their canopy and, thereby, reduce shade.

5. In very shady areas, plant shade tolerant grasses (fescue) or other plants that grow well in shade.

6. Soils too acidic for good grass growth can be amended with lime, based on the recommendation from a soil test.

7. Reduce thatch build up by avoiding excess application of nitrogen and by picking up clippings at each mowing. A thatch layer can be picked up by vigorous raking or with power raking equipment.

## CHEMICAL CONTROL OF LAWN WEEDS

Careful lawn maintenance is required for effective weed control. Sometimes, chemical control is necessary as well (see Pest Control lesson, LIFE CYCLE OF WEEDS and KINDS OF HERBICIDES). Several terms are important to remember:

- **Annual weeds** grow from seed; they flower, produce seed, and die in one season.

- **Perennial weeds** grow for several years; they spread by seed and by vegetative means, and most have some type of storage root that allows them to survive the winter.

- **Grassy weeds** and desirable grasses are so similar to one another that herbicides which kill the grassy weeds also kill the desirable grasses.

- **Broadleaved weeds** have wide leaves and their physical make up differs enough from lawn grass that they can be killed without affecting the grass.

- **Selective herbicides** for lawns kill only broadleaved weeds and do not harm the grass.

- **Non-selective** herbicides kill both the lawn and weeds — they are used for spot applications or complete renovation.

- **Contact** herbicides kill the part of the plant contacted, so complete spray coverage is important.

- **Translocated** herbicides move through the plant, often into the roots.

Table 7-6 lists the common lawn weeds and the chemical names of the herbicides used to control them. They are available under several trade names. Crabgrass (*Digitaria*) is a serious lawn weed in many places, but it **does not** grow in Alberta and is, therefore, not listed in Table 7-6.

## APPLYING LAWN HERBICIDES

The timing of herbicide application is important for good results. Translocated herbicides are best applied when the weeds are growing quickly. If treatment is made when the lawn is growing well, the bare spots left by dead weeds will fill in rapidly. Late May and June are good times of the year to apply translocated herbicides. September, after a hard frost, is also a good time to control perennial weeds. The almost dormant plants will not have time to repair the herbicide damaged roots before winter, so winterkill is common. The herbicide label often makes recommendations for time of application.

There are many pesticide chemicals available for home garden use and many ways to apply them. If used according to the directions on the product label, pesticides can be used safely (see Pest Control lesson, WEED CONTROL FOR HOME GROUNDS in BACKYARD PEST MANAGEMENT).

The safe use of chemicals is very important. A review of pesticide chemical safety is included here:

- identify the pest and select the right product to control it

## Table 7-6
### HERBICIDES FOR LAWN WEED CONTROL

| WEED | PLANT TYPE | LIFE CYCLE | HERBICIDES | |
| --- | --- | --- | --- | --- |
| | | | SELECTIVE | NON-SELECTIVE |
| **Broadleaved Plantain** *Plantago major* | broadleaved | perennial | 2,4-D mecoprop, MCPA * | |
| **Canada Thistle** *Cirsium arvense* | broadleaved | perennial | 2,4-D * dicamba * mecoprop* MCPA * | glyphosate (c) |
| **Chickweed** *Stellaria media* | broadleaved | annual | ioxinyl, mecoprop | |
| **Dandelion** *Taraxacum officinale* | broadleaved | perennial | 2,4-D, ioxinyl | |
| **Ground Ivy (Creeping Charlie)** *Glechoma hederacea* | broadleaved | perennial | mecoprop | |
| **Prostrate Knotweed** *Polygonum aviculare* | broadleaved | sometimes perennial | dicamba mecoprop (young plants) | |
| **Purslane** *Portulaca oleracea* | broadleaved | annual | 2,4-D, ioxynil | |
| Quackgrass *Agropyron repens* | grassy | perennial | | glyphosate (c) gramoxone (c) amitrol (c) |
| **Wild White Clover** *Trifolium repens* | broadleaved | perennial | dicamba mecoprop | |
| **Bluegrass** *Poa annua* | grassy | annual | | |
| **Creeping Bentgrass** *Agrostis stolonifera* | grassy | perennial | 2,4-D * | |

(c)Registered for agricultural or commercial use, not for homeowner use.

* Suppress weed growth only

- mix only enough of the pesticide as is needed
- mix in a well ventilated area
- no smoking while mixing or applying pesticides
- use the application rates recommended on the label
- always wear proper protective clothing eg., cover arms, legs and heads)
- never spray when windy
- store in original container and out of reach of children

Herbicides can be applied to lawns in several ways. Motorized **sprayers** may be used for large farm and acreage lawns. Tank and backpack sprayers (pressurized with air) can be used for smaller areas. Small hand sprayers and watering cans may be used for spot treatment of weeds (see Figure 7-37). **Weed bars** release herbicide as they are dragged over the lawn. These should not be used on very hot days because excess herbicide may be released. Check the label for the maximum temperature. Herbicide **canes** are used to treat individual weeds. The herbicide is released as the cane is pressed down on the weed. Weedy grasses can be treated **individually** with a small paint brush or sponge tipped tweezers. With this treatment, non-selective herbicides can be used without damaging the lawn. Any bare spots left by killed weeds should be re-grassed. Otherwise, weeds can re-establish in the lawn.

Figure 7-37

## HOSE END SPRAYER FOR PESTICIDE APPLICATION

Courtesy of Alberta Agriculture

## LAWN INSECTS AND RELATED PESTS

Unlike other lawn pests, insect infestations are not usually related to lawn conditions and few cultural control methods are successful. Fortunately, there are few types of lawn insects in Alberta and infestations are uncommon. Most home gardeners in Alberta never have to treat their lawns for insects.

It is important to identify the pest before selecting a treatment. If insect damage is discovered but the pest cannot be found, the insects can be brought to the surface by flooding the soil. Remove the top and bottom of a large tin can and set it on the damaged area of the lawn. Flood the can with a soapy water solution or a weak solution of insecticide. This causes the pests to come to the surface so an identification can be made and a method of treatment selected. Refer to Figures 7-38 to 7-41 and the Pest Control lesson, CONTROL OF INSECTS ON TURFGRASS in BACKYARD PEST MANAGEMENT. It must be stressed that lawns should not be treated for insects as a 'just in case' measure. Insecticides should be used only when damage warrants it.

Figure 7-38

## ANT

Figure 7-39
## GLASSY CUTWORM

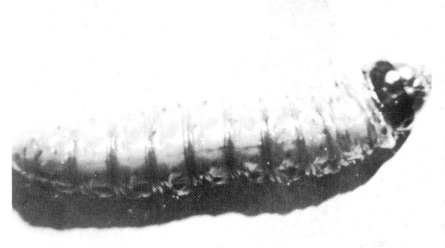

Courtesy of Alberta Agriculture

## LAWN DISEASES

In warmer, more humid areas of Canada, chemical prevention of lawn diseases is a necessary part of regular lawn maintenance. In Alberta, lawn bowling greens and golf greens need annual treatment for snow mold but, otherwise, diseases are rarely a serious problem. Most lawn diseases can be prevented or controlled by using the maintenance practices discussed previously (see LAWN MAINTENANCE). These are the important points for maintaining a disease-free lawn:

- Use a balanced fertilizer program. Excess nitrogen causes lush grass growth that is susceptible to disease attack. A deficiency in nitrogen weakens the grass, making it unable to resist disease.

- Fertilize at the right time of year. Fertilizing late in the season forces grass growth when it should be becoming dormant.

- Occasionally check soil pH. Most grasses grow best in the pH range 5.5-7.0. Lawns growing on soils outside that range are unthrifty and are unable to resist disease attack.

- Use the grasses adapted to the specific growing conditions.

Figure 7-40
DEWWORMS

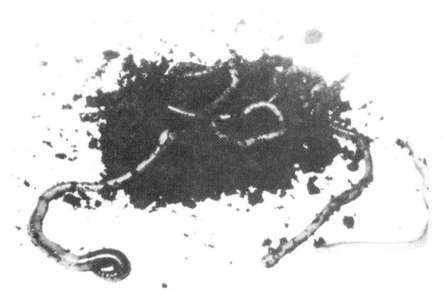

Courtesy of Alberta Agriculture

Creeping red fescue, for example, grows more vigorously than Kentucky bluegrass in shade and is, consequently, more disease resistant in shaded sites.

• Select specific cultivars for

Figure 7-41
SOD WEBWORM

Courtesy of Alberta Agriculture

resistance to a disease that might be common in your area (see Table 7-1). Detailed information on disease resistant cultivars can be obtained from various sources, including some of the publications listed in RESOURCE MATERIALS.

## DESCRIPTION AND CONTROL RECOMMENDATIONS FOR SOME LAWN DISEASES

Table 7-7 and the following identifies the more common lawn diseases and outlines various prevention methods.

FAIRY RING

Fairy ring is likely the most common lawn problem in Alberta. This fungus disease is found throughout the world on all types of grassed areas. Fairy rings are identified by dark green or brown circles and arches in the lawn (see Figure 7-42). During rainy weather, small tan colored mushrooms often appear in the ring. Digging into the fairy ring reveals a white, fibrous growth (mycelium) throughout the soil. As the root-like mycelium spreads, the fairy ring enlarges from the outer edge, anywhere from a few to 60 cm (25 in) in diameter per season. The mycelium can become so dense that water is unable to penetrate it. Consequently, the grass above the mycelium dies.

Fairy ring mushrooms should not be confused with random clumps of mushrooms that also appear during rainy spells or in newly laid sod that is kept constantly moist. These mushrooms are harmless. If you consider them unattractive, pick and discard the mushrooms.

It has not yet been determined exactly how fairy ring spreads. The mushrooms are the reproductive stage, producing seed-like spores. However, it is not known if new fairy rings ever grow from the spores. The growth of fairy rings is usually halted when they reach sidewalks and cultivated soil, such as flower beds and gardens. Growth also stops when rings grow into one another.

Although fairy rings are a common problem, no simple means of control has been found. Some fungicides will kill the mushrooms, but there are none that will kill the fungus in the soil. Fairy rings can grow in any kind of lawn but are more frequently found on dry, under-fertilized lawns. Control, then, begins with proper lawn maintenance. Four methods of control or eradication are recommended:

1. **Mask** the symptoms by heavily watering and fertilizing the entire lawn. This keeps the lawn dark green and the dark green fairy rings

Figure 7-42
FAIRY RING FUNGUS IN SOIL

Courtesy of Alberta Agriculture

Figure 7-43
FAIRY RING REPAIR

B. REFILL FAIRY RINGS WITH CLEAN SOIL

C RESEED OR SOD TO PREVENT WEED INVASION

Courtesy of Alberta Agriculture

are not obvious. This does not kill the fungus.

2. **Spike and soak** the fairy ring to penetrate the mat of mycelium and allow water to reach the grass roots. Use a garden fork or root feeder to aerate the entire ring, and a 20 cm (8 in) band beyond the inner and outer edges. Water repeatedly to keep the grass soaked. This allows the grass to regrow which only masks the symptoms. Occasionally, heavy watering seems to kill the fungus.

3. Fairy rings can be removed by **digging** them out (see Figure 7-43A, B, C). Begin digging at least 40 cm (16 in) beyond the outer edge of the ring and remove all of the soil up to 40 cm (16 in) beyond the inner edge of the ring. The depth of the fungal growth depends on the soil type. The mycelium grows deepest in sandy soils. It is most important that **all** the fungus is removed or the ring will re-establish. Be careful to keep the infested soil from falling onto the lawn. Fill in the hole with topsoil and cover with seed or sod.

4. A **biological** control method has been tested a few times and may be especially useful where there are numerous rings. Remove the grass

over the fairy rings, either by stripping it off (sod harvesters can be rented) or rototilling it into the soil. Rototill the stripped area in several directions to completely mix the soil. Ideally, this is done in autumn and the cultivated soil is left over winter. Once thoroughly mixed, the soil is prepared as for a new lawn and can be seeded or sodded. The same antagonism that causes two rings to die when they meet causes the fungus to die when several rings are mixed together.

## POWDERY MILDEW

Powdery mildew is a fungal disease which generally occurs in shaded areas of lawns, such as under trees or on the north side of buildings and fences. White or grey powder-like spores cover the grass blades. The leaves may eventually turn yellow and die. Although powdery mildew affects grasses all season, it is often most severe in autumn.

Powdery mildew is rarely serious enough to warrant chemical control. Avoid excesses or deficiencies of nitrogen, as both increase mildew damage. Grass will grow more vigorously in shaded areas if the mowing height is raised slightly. Less water is needed here because the soil dries out more slowly. Use shade tolerant grasses in areas prone to mildew growth. Three Kentucky bluegrass cultivars that have some resistance to powdery mildew are 'Dormie', 'Nugget', and 'Sydsport'.

## SNOW MOLDS

The four types of snow molds that grow on Alberta lawns are so called because they are active at low temperatures. These diseases grow under the snow and sometimes during cold, wet weather in early spring and late autumn. The first sign of snow mold is usually grey, white, or pinkish moldy patches of mycelium that appear on the lawn as snow melts in spring (see Figure 7-44). This is often the only evidence of snow mold on home lawns. The mold can be swept off and no chemical treatment is required. Where snow mold is severe, the lawn may be killed and annual applications of fungicide are needed in autumn.

The severity of snow mold damage depends on the weather and the

## Figure 7-44
## SNOW MOLD

Courtesy of Alberta Agriculture

condition of the grass plants. Damage is favored by wet autumn weather, early snowfall on unfrozen soil and deep snow that lasts late into the spring. The following precautions can help to prevent snow mold damage:

## Figure 7-45
## SPREAD SNOW TO SPEED MELTING

Courtesy of Alberta Agriculture

- avoid excess nitrogen fertilization

- cease fertilizing in early autumn

- rake up tree leaves before the first permanent snowfall

- spread out snow drifts to speed melting in spring (see Figure 7-45)

- use a broom or rake to break up patches of mold in spring, this allows the grass plants to dry and fungus to stop growing

- if patches larger than 15 cm (6 in) of lawn are killed by snow mold, repair them quickly to avoid weed invasion of the bare spots

## OTHER LAWN DISEASES

Several other lawn diseases are only infrequently found on Alberta lawns. Identification and control recommendations are best obtained from reference books, horticulturists, or a diagnostic laboratory. **Melting-out** (*Drechslera spp.*) appears during long spells of cool, humid, cloudy weather. Damage begins at the base of grass blades. The blade turns red-brown and later changes to a straw color. Control measures include using resistant cultivars ('Merion', 'Sydsport', 'Touchdown'), avoiding close mowing, and heavy nitrogen applications (especially during wet weather). **Red thread** (*Corticium fuciforme*) appears as irregularly shaped patches of bleached looking grass. As leaves die, coral to red 'threads' of jelly-like fungus grow during cool, wet weather. To control this disease: be sure nitrogen is not deficient; prevent prolonged leaf wetness by watering infrequently; provide good soil drainage and encourage air movement; and control thatch development. **Slime molds** make greasy looking white, grey, or purple patches on lawns. The fungus grows during cool, wet weather. It does not harm the grass but is unsightly. The patches can be removed by vigorous raking or sweeping or with a strong spray of water. Slime molds disappear during dry weather.

## VERTEBRATE PESTS

Mice, ground squirrels, and pocket gophers can damage lawns by making

Table 7-7
## FUNGICIDES FOR LAWN DISEASES

| DISEASE | FUNGICIDE | APPLICATION |
|---|---|---|
| **Fairy Ring** (*Marasmium oreades*, most commonly) | none registered | only control measures available are: <br> 1. mask with fertilize <br> 2. spike and soak <br> 3. dig out <br> 4. biological |
| **Powdery Mildew** (*Erysiphe graminis*) | thiophanate methyl | every 10-14 days rarely required |
| **Fusarium Patch** (*Fusarium nivale*) <br><br> **Gray Snow Mould** (*Typhula spp.*) <br><br> **Snow Scald** (*Myriosclerotinia borealis*) <br><br> **Copririus Snow Mould** (*Caprinus psychromorbidus*) | benomyl <br> thiophanate methyl <br> others registered <br> commercial use only | must be applied just prior to permanent snowfall; identification of snow mould type needed before selecting fungicide; rarely required |

tunnels and mounds. They are most common on farm and acreage lawns. Refer to the Pest Control lesson for details regarding identification, damage and control of these vertebrate pests. Some control measures are reviewed here:

- Remove their natural cover (eg., keep lawn short; cut tall grass and weeds in ditches and at edges of fields adjacent to lawns; remove rock and wood piles and old buildings on lawns).

- Remove food sources (eg., avoid dumping vegetables and grain near lawns, prevent rodents from entering grain storage bins).

- Make the lawn unsuitable for mouse tunneling (see Figure 7-46). Pack the first 10-15 cm (4-6 in) of snow around walls, fences, trees, and other areas where mouse damage has occurred. The packed snow acts as a barrier. If snow mold has been a problem, this method of control is not recommended.

Figure 7-46
## MOUSE DAMAGE

Courtesy of Alberta Agriculture

- Encourage predators (dogs, for example).

- Trapping and poisoning may be effective but they can be harmful to pets and other non-target animals. As well, the control may only be temporary as new animals move into the area.

- Further advice on controlling rodents is available from government and university extension personnel.

## LAWN AERATION

### THE PROBLEM OF COMPACTION
Grass grows poorly and becomes thin on lawns that become hard or compacted. Weeds may invade, water is slow to soak in, and puddles form after rainfall or irrigation. Compaction occurs in areas that receive a lot of traffic (where a pathway cuts across the lawn, for example). Soils become compacted quickly if they are repeatedly walked on when they are wet. Lawns built with clay rich soils are especially prone to compaction.

### AERATION
Compaction can be reduced by removing cores of soil, thereby allowing better movement of air, water, and fertilizer to the grass roots. Both manual and mechanical aerators can be used to remove the soil cores (see Figure 7-47). The manual aerator is only practical for small areas. Mechanical aerators remove soil cores approximately 7 cm (about 3 in) long and 2 cm (3/4 in) wide (see Figure 7-48). Because aeration is not a routine maintenance practice, most people rent aerators. They are available from many rental companies.

### WHEN TO AERATE
Unless a lawn becomes compacted, aeration may not be required for several years. When necessary, spring is the best time to aerate the lawn. By aerating in spring, the disturbed grass plants have all season to recover. Aeration can be done at the same time as spring raking and fertilizing. The soil should be moist, not wet, so the aerating tines can penetrate the soil. In most cases it is best to remove the soil

## Figure 7-47
## HAND AERATOR

cores that are left on the lawn surface. This can be done by raking or with a grass catching attachment on a lawn mower. In large turf areas, the cores are

## Figure 7-48
## AERATION CORES

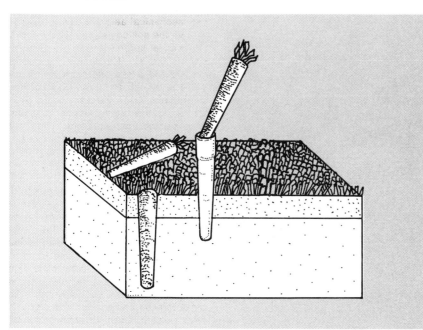

often left on the grass because it is not practical to pick them up. If left on the lawn, the soil plugs can be broken up and spread out with a mower, rake, or metal mats. This soil brought to the surface can help speed thatch decomposition. When fertilization follows aeration, the fertilizer reaches the grass roots quickly. If the compaction problem has developed over many years, the lawn may need to be aerated several times to remedy the problem.

## LAWN DETHATCHING

### THE PROBLEM OF THATCH
The thatch layer builds up as grass leaves are continuously dying and being replaced with new ones (see Figure 7-49). As well, grass clippings accumulate with each mowing. Even if clippings are picked up after mowing, some are left on the lawn. A thin layer of thatch is helpful to insulate grass roots from heat and cold. However, if the layer becomes too thick, water, air, and fertilizer penetration is slow. A thick thatch layer makes the lawn feel spongy. Grass roots grow in the thatch. During hot spells, the thatch dries out

## Figure 7-49
## THATCH LAYER

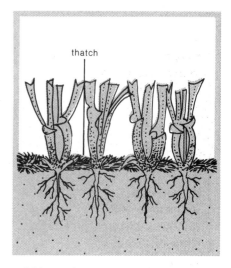

quickly and any roots growing in it suffer. During wet weather, the thatch holds water. This moist environment is an ideal site for disease organism growth.

### DETHATCHING
Much of the thatch can be removed by raking the lawn. If there is a lot of thatch, several rakings may be required (see Figure 7-50). Because hand raking is slow, hard work, many people choose to use a motorized dethatcher. Some lawn mowers have 'power rake' attachments which can be used. However, the mower must have a powerful motor for good results. Like aerators, dethatchers can be rented. Dethatchers may be called 'vertical mowers' (see Figure 7-51). These machines have a series of blades attached vertically to a horizontal axle. As the machine runs, the blades spin around and pull up the thatch. The operating depth should be adjusted so that the blades just reach the top of the soil level. The thatch is brought to the lawn surface and must be removed, either raked, lawn vaccuumed or picked up with a grass catcher on a lawn mower.

### WHEN TO REMOVE THATCH
A general rule of thumb is to remove thatch when the layer is more than 2 cm (3/4 in) thick. Use a sharp knife to cut a small section from the lawn. From this, the depth of the thatch layer can be easily measured. Dethatching is not a routine maintenance practice. The frequency of dethatching depends on

## Figure 7-50
## RAKE UP THATCH

Courtesy of Alberta Agriculture

how often clippings are picked up, the weather, how much nitrogen is used on the lawn and how frequently the lawn is mowed. The type of grass and cultivar also affects the rate of thatch accumulation. 'Fylking' and 'Merion' (Kentucky bluegrass cultivars), for example, are considered more prone to thatching than other cultivars. If the thatch has accumulated over many years, one pass of the dethatcher does not usually lift out all the debris and the operation needs to be repeated, in a different direction.

Both aerating and dethatching are best done in spring. The vigorously growing grass plants quickly repair any damage and fill in bare spots before weeds can invade the lawn. If done in midsummer, plants may be slow to recover because of the heat. If done too late in autumn, the plants may not have enough time to repair themselves and to prepare for winter. For best results, the soil and thatch should be dry at the time of dethatching. When dethatching is needed, a logical sequence in spring is to:

1. mow the lawn to remove dead grass blades

2. dethatch

3. pick up thatch

4. repeat steps 2 and 3 if thatch layer is still deeper than 2 cm (3/4 in)

5. fertilize (it will penetrate quickly with thatch removed)

6. water well

## Figure 7-51
## VERTICAL MOWERS OR DETHATCHERS

## SPOT REPAIRS IN LAWNS

It has been stressed several times in this lesson that damaged parts of lawns should be repaired quickly, before weeds can establish. If salts, such as fertilizer, deicing salts and animal urine, cause dead, 'burned' grass, the grass leaves alone may be killed but the plants usually recover. Repeatedly flood the damaged site. Water dissolves the harmful salts and washes them below the 'plants' roots. Animal urine and manure contain nitrogen and, in small amounts, cause patches of lush green growth (see Figure 7-52). If the entire lawn is kept well supplied with nitrogen, such patches are less likely to be noticed.

## Figure 7-52
## LAWN "OVERFERTILIZED" BY DOG

Courtesy of Alberta Agriculture

If the grass has been killed, it must be removed and replaced with seed or sod. Small patches can be raked vigorously to remove the dead plants and expose bare soil. If a large area is to be repaired, it may be simpler to rent a sod cutter and remove the dead grass in strips. When using seed, use the same mixture as in the surrounding grass so the patched area will eventually blend in. Add fresh soil to the repair site (if needed) to raise it to the level of the surrounding grass. Spread a light covering of seed over the raked soil (see Figure 7-53). The seed can then be covered with a fine layer of soil or peat moss and tamped down with a foot, the back of a rake, or with a roller (in large areas). Until the seed has germinated and plants begin to grow, keep the repaired area constantly moist. As with a newly seeded lawn, this grass can be mowed when it is about 7 cm (about 3 in) tall. Mow carefully until the new seeding is established.

## Figure 7-53
## SPOT RESEEDING

The fastest way to regrass bare spots in lawns is to use sod. Clear the area of dead grass. Some soil may have to be removed so the sod patches lie level with the lawn (see Figure 7-54). The edges of the lawn adjacent to the repair area may need trimming so the sod can be laid snuggly beside them. Lay the sod in the area to be patched and tamp the grass down with feet or a roller (see Figure 7-55). Be sure there is good contact between the grass roots and the soil. Keep the area well watered until the sod has taken.

### STORING GRASS SEED
Grass seed may be stored for a few years. It is helpful to keep leftover seed from a seeded lawn. If repairs are necessary, you will have a seed mix that matches your lawn. Store seed in a

## Figure 7-54
## REMOVE SOIL SO SODS LAY EVEN WITH EXISTING LAWN

dry, cool location (just above freezing is ideal). There will be a slight drop in germination rate after the first two years in storage. After that, there is a big decrease in germination. If seed has been stored a long time, its viability can be tested before use. Sprinkle a small amount of seed on a paper towel and keep it moist for at least 15 days. By looking at the number of seeds that germinate, you will have an idea of the per cent germination.

## Figure 7-55
## SOD USED TO PATCH DAMAGED LAWN

Courtesy of Alberta Agriculture

## TOPDRESSING

Topdressing a lawn involves spreading a fine layer of soil mix over the grass and working it in. Topdressing is used on home lawns for several reasons. Most commonly, it is used to level uneven areas. For example, if new lawn areas are not given time to settle before planting, some low spots may develop. On farms and acreages, it is not unusual for escaped livestock to walk across newly seeded or wet lawns leaving a pock-marked surface. Topdressing is frequently used on high maintenance turf (such as golf greens) for several reasons; thatch control, modifying the soil, winter protection from desiccation, and reseeding sparse grass stands. Topdressing is not a routine maintenance practice and many gardeners will never use it. Only a fine layer of soil mix can be spread on at each application and so many applications are needed before results are seen. These are the steps for topdressing:

1. Use a topdressing mix of soil, organic matter and sand that is similar to the soil beneath the grass. If any of these are used alone, layers develop and water movement is affected.

2. The topdressing mix may need to be screened to remove debris and dried before it can be spread evenly.

3. Mow the lawn just prior to topdressing. The grass should be dry.

4. Use a shovel to sprinkle a 3-6 cm (1/8-1/4 in) thick layer of topdressing over the uneven areas of the lawn. A thicker layer may kill the grass.

5. Work the topdressing into the lawn with a rake, broom, metal door mat, or pushboard (see Figure 7-56).

6. Topdress at a time when the grass is growing well, so it quickly grows through the added soil.

## RENOVATING A LAWN

Sometimes it is necessary to renovate a lawn, most often because the lawn has been poorly maintained for many years

### Figure 7-56
### WORK TOPDRESSING IN WITH BACK OF RAKE

or because it was improperly constructed. Determining whether partial or complete renovation is needed depends on the condition of the lawn. Partial renovation is successful when the lawn problems include weeds, compaction, thatch, or poor soil conditions (low nutrients and incorrect pH). Complete renovation is usually required if the problems include unsuitable grass, poor drainage, incorrect grade, poor soil (high salts, high clay content), or lumpy surface.

### PARTIAL RENOVATION
These are the steps that might be taken in a partial renovation program. Complete descriptions for each activity have been discussed earlier in the lesson.

1. Begin with a soil test to determine what fertilizers are needed and if pH needs to be adjusted.

2. Identify weeds to select and identify the appropriate herbicide. Several applications may be required throughout the season.

3. Regrass any bare spots left after the weeds have died.

4. Dethatch (may require more than one pass over the lawn to pull out all the thatch).

5. Aerate.

6. Fertilize according to soil test recommendations.

7. Establish and begin a program of regular maintenance (i.e., mowing, watering, fertilizing) (see LAWN MAINTENANCE).

### COMPLETE RENOVATION
If you have determined the lawn cannot be salvaged, it can be taken out and replaced.

1. Begin with a soil test to determine what fertilizers and soil amendments are necessary. The test results may reveal some of the reasons for the poor grass growth.

2. Remove the existing grass. It can be stripped off with a sod cutter or rototilled into the soil. The latter method has the advantage of adding organic matter to the soil. However, repeated rototilling will be necessary to break up the sod and incorporate it into the soil. It is often helpful to kill the grass with a non-selective herbicide prior to rototilling. This is a necessary step if the lawn had many perennial and grassy weeds.

3. Special care must be taken when working around trees growing in the lawn area so as not to damage roots.

4. Once the old grass has been removed, drainage and grade can be corrected.

5. Incorporate organic matter, sand and fertilizer as needed to improve the soil. Topsoil may need to be added.

6. Prepare the soil for seed or sod.

7. Lay sod or spread seed and keep moist.

8. Establish a regular maintenance program.

## WHERE LAWNS WILL NOT GROW

There are some places where lawns cannot grow (where the soil is unsuitable, where there is too little sun, or where slopes are so steep it would be hazardous to mow, for example). In these areas, other landscape plants may be more appropriate. Plants such as annual flowers and ground covers are often used. Other alternatives are ground cover mulches like bark chips and pine cones. Some homeowners use decorative paving blocks to fill in these troublesome areas.

## CONCLUSION

Lawns are an important part of the home landscape. A well-landscaped yard contributes significantly to the value of the property. This lesson has outlined the steps involved in building and maintaining a high quality lawn. Lawn grasses, like most horticultural plants, have been greatly improved over the years. We have come a long way from the days of sod cut with shovels from pastures. The types of grasses and the improved cultivars best suited to Alberta were discussed.

Because the lawns are **permanent**, it is important to pay particular attention to the construction of the lawn as problems are difficult to correct later. Once established, properly constructed lawns require relatively little care. This lesson has presented the necessary information for building and growing an easily maintained lawn.

As you study subsequent lessons, the basic gardening principles outlined in this lesson apply to most types of plants. Instructions like water deeply, improve the soil with organic matter, and select plant types recommended for Alberta are repeated throughout the Home Gardening Course. Experienced, successful gardeners recognize the importance of proper maintenance practices applied to their lawns and do not judiciously apply fertilizers and pesticide chemicals. This not only saves time and money, but also represents wise stewardship of our resources. All these basic principles, as well as maintenance procedures specific to the lawn have been thoroughly described in the lesson.

The weather is a popular topic with gardeners. Although our short season and cold winters seem to severely limit the kinds of plants we can grow, remember that it also limits the number of pests with which we must contend. Although the careful use of chemical pesticides to control pests has been discussed, special emphasis has been placed on prevention and control through cultural means.

## SELF CHECK *QUIZ*

1. If 21-0-0 is selling at $7.95/25 kg bag and 34-0-0 is selling at $10.55/25 kg bag, which fertilizer would you choose? Other than price, what else should you consider?

2. List reasons for using several grasses and cultivars in a seed mix.

3. A lawn is to be seeded with a 20 per cent Fescue / 80 per cent Kentucky Bluegrass mix. The lawn area is 20 m X 15 m. How much seed is needed?

4. Why is spring the best time to aerate and dethatch lawns?

5. How can you prevent or delay having to aerate?

6. What three types of soil amendments are used when constructing a lawn?

Agriculture Canada. *Home Lawns*. Ottawa, Ontario: Minister of Supply and Services Canada, 1980. Publication 1685. Agdex 273/20-1.

Details on preparing the lawn site, seed mixes, seeding, and sodding. Also describes lawn maintenance and pest control. Well illustrated.

Agriculture Canada. *Turfgrass Problems in the Prairie Provinces*. Ottawa, Ontario: Minister of Supply and Services Canada, 1984. Publication 1767. Agdex 273/636-4.

Good description of lawn diseases in the Prairie Provinces.

Alberta Agriculture. *Garden Fax: Fairy Ring Control in Lawns*. Alberta: Alberta Agriculture, 1986. Agdex 273/636-2.

Description of the symptoms, disease cycle, and three control recommendations for fairy ring.

Alberta Agriculture. *Garden Fax: Laying Sod*. Alberta: Alberta Agriculture, 1983. Agdex 273/22-1.

Outlines soil preparations, buying and laying sod, and maintenance of a new lawn.

Alberta Agriculture. *Major Diseases of Turf Grasses in Western Canada*. Alberta: Alberta Agriculture, 1985. Agdex 273/633-3.

Describes over 20 diseases. Includes predisposing factors and cultural and chemical control. Well illustrated with color photographs.

Andrews, Brian. *Gardening with Brian Andrews*. Edmonton: reprinted from the Edmonton Journal, 1967.

A good review of lawn construction and care. Source of local information.

Beard, James B. *How to Have a Beautiful Lawn*. College Station, Texas: Beard Books, 1979.

A detailed reference with answers to most questions. Information on warm season grasses and suggested schedules for lawn maintenance irrelevant in Alberta, but still a useful reference.

Beard, James B. *Turfgrass: Science and Culture*. Englewood Cliffs, New Jersey: Prentice-Hall Inc., 1973.

An excellent scientific reference for turfgrass culture. Too much detail for backyard gardening.

Fushtey, S.G. and M.K. Sears. *Turfgrass Diseases and Insect Pests*. Ontario Ministry of Agriculture and Food (Agdex 273/600).

Good color photographs and descriptions to help identify pests.

Hawthorn, R. *Dawson's Practical Lawncraft*. London: Crosby, Lockwood, Staples, 1977.

A good reference with practical applications and considerations.

Pycraft, David. *Lawns, Ground Cover and Weed Control*. London: Mitchell Beazley Publishers Ltd., 1980.

Excellent detailed descriptions of lawn building and maintenance tasks. Filled with helpful drawings. Must make allowances for differences in English weather.

# SELF CHECK *ANSWERS*

1. 21-0-0 is more acidic because it contains sulphur - long term use could be detrimental to soils with a low pH. 34-0-0 is more concentrated and, therefore, burn potential is higher so must be applied with great care. If the lawn needs phosphorus or potassium, neither of these fertilizers are suitable (see SOIL AMENDMENTS - page 704 and Table 7-3 - page 705).

2. Rapid germination to prevent soil erosion and excessive weed growth. Variation in grasses to suit variation in the site (eg., shady spots, dry areas). Benefits of different characteristics (eg., color, texture). Disease resistance - a monostand could be completely killed by a disease (see THE SEED MIX - page 710).

3. 20 X 15 m = 300 m² / seeding rate = 2.5 kg/100 m² therefore = 7.5 kg of seed for total area (see Table 7-5 - page 711).

4. Lawns then have all season to recover. Mid-summer adds heat stress to recovery. Plants growing vigorously to compete with weeds that will try to establish in the exposed soil. Soil will be moist from snow melt. Can be done at same time as spring fertilization and raking for good spring clean-up (see WHEN TO AERATE - page 728 and WHEN TO REMOVE THATCH - page 729).

5. Amend clay soils with sand and organic matter before building. Put sidewalks in obvious traffic paths. Restrict traffic to sidewalks; use hedges and flower beds to guide traffic. Keep all traffic off the lawn when it is wet (see LAWN AERATION - page 728).

6. Lime and sulphur to adjust soil pH - only need occasionally and must only be used upon recommendation from a soil test. Organic matter and sand to improve soil texture. Fertilizer (see SOIL AMENDMENTS - page 703).

# GLOSSARY

**cultural control** - prevention or control of pests using non-chemical means.

**disease resistance** - ability of a plant to prevent the development of a disease on or in it. Resistance varies from complete immunity to slightly less than susceptible.

**dormancy** - plant state where growth stops. Growth usually resumes when growing conditions are more suitable.

**grade** - slope of the lawn.

**mulch** - layer of organic or inorganic material laid on the ground to slow soil moisture evaporation, prevent erosion, and control weeds.

**mycelium** - thread-like vegetative stage of a fungus.

**organic matter** - substances derived from living things.

**pesticide chemicals** - materials (e.g., herbicides, insecticides, and fungicides) applied to prevent or control pests.

**sod** - commercially grown grass. Harvested with a small amount of soil and planted to establish a lawn.

**soil amendment** - material incorporated into the soil to make it more suitable for plant growth.

**spore** - seed-like reproductive structure of a fungi.

**thatch** - layer of dead and living organic matter found between the grass leaves and the soil surface.

# INDEX

# WOODY ORNAMENTALS

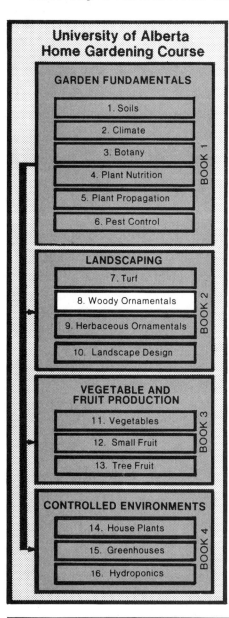

**University of Alberta Home Gardening Course**

### GARDEN FUNDAMENTALS

- 1. Soils
- 2. Climate
- 3. Botany
- 4. Plant Nutrition
- 5. Plant Propagation
- 6. Pest Control

BOOK 1

### LANDSCAPING

- 7. Turf
- 8. Woody Ornamentals
- 9. Herbaceous Ornamentals
- 10. Landscape Design

BOOK 2

### VEGETABLE AND FRUIT PRODUCTION

- 11. Vegetables
- 12. Small Fruit
- 13. Tree Fruit

BOOK 3

### CONTROLLED ENVIRONMENTS

- 14. House Plants
- 15. Greenhouses
- 16. Hydroponics

BOOK 4

# SELF-STUDY LESSON FEATURES

Self-study is an educational approach which allows you to study a subject where and when you want. The course is designed to allow students to study the course material efficiently and incorporates the following features.

**OBJECTIVES** — are found at the beginning of each lesson and allow you to determine what you can expect to learn in the lesson.

**LESSON MATERIAL** — is logically organized and broken down into fundamental components by ordered headings to assist you to comprehend the subject.

**REFERENCING** — between lessons and within lessons allows you to integrate course material.

The last two digits of the page number identify the page and the digits preceding these identify the lesson number (eg., 107: Lesson 1, page 7 or 1227: Lesson 12, page 27).

Referencing:

> sections within the same lesson (eg., see OSMOSIS)

> sections in other lessons (eg., see Botany lesson, OSMOSIS)

> figures and tables (eg., see Figure 7-3)

**FIGURES AND TABLES** — are found in abundance throughout the lessons and are designed to convey useful information in an easy to understand form.

**SIDEBARS** — are those areas in the lesson which are boxed and toned. They present information supplementary to the core content of the lesson.

**PRACTICAL PROJECTS** — are integrated within the lesson material and are included to allow you to apply principles and practices.

**SELF-CHECK QUIZ** — is provided at the end of each lesson and allows you to test your comprehension of the lesson material. Answers to the questions and references to the sections dealing with the questions are provided in the answer section. You should review any questions that you are unable to answer.

**GLOSSARY** – is provided at the end of each lesson and alphabetically lists the definitions of key concepts and terms.

**RESOURCE MATERIALS** — are provided at the end of each lesson and comprise a list of recommended learning materials for further study of the subject. Also included are author's comments on the potential application of each publication.

**INDEX** — alphabetically lists useful topics and their location within the lesson.

---

© 1986 University of Alberta Faculty of Extension

**Written by: R. Hugh Knowles, Professor Emeritus, F.C.S.L.A.**

Technical Reviewers:      Brendan Casement
Duncan Himmelman

**ISBN 0-88864-852-9**

(Book 2, Lesson 8)

THE PRODUCTION TEAM

Managing Editor ................................................... Thom Shaw
Editor ................................................................ Frank Procter
Production Coordinator ..................................... Kevin Hanson
Graphic Artists ...................................................... Lisa Marsh
Carol Powers
Melanie Eastley Harbourne
Data Entry ...................................................... Joan Geisterfer

Published by the University of Alberta
Faculty of Extension, Corbett Hall
Edmonton, Alberta, T6G 2G4

After completing this lesson, the student should be able to:

1. identify the influences that limit growth of woody plants.
2. identify the control systems that operate within woody plants and regulate their growth.
3. identify and determine which factors are important in the selection of woody ornamentals.
4. identify and perform the proper method of planting to avoid possible future problems.
5. appreciate the need for proper maintenance, training and pruning to control woody ornamental growth.
6. identify woody plant disorders and determine the appropriate corrective action.

## TABLE OF CONTENTS

## LIST OF FIGURES AND TABLES

# INTRODUCTION

This lesson is concerned with that group of woody plants commonly referred to as ornamentals. Since they are woody, they can be expected to respond to the stresses and stimuli affecting all woody plants even though their culture can be markedly different from that of tree fruits and forest crops. The difference, of course, lies with the fact that woody ornamentals are not required to produce a commercial crop of food or fibre. Hence, woody ornamentals are not generally subject to the same intense management pressures affecting tree fruits and forest crops.

In spite of these differences, a brief exposure to the patterns and processes that control growth of the woody plant is presented to help convey a better understanding of why and when certain things are done to promote growth of woody ornamentals. The balance of the lesson is devoted specifically to woody ornamentals and deals with their shortcomings, their use, their origins, and their management.

# GROWTH PATTERNS

Physical growth of the above ground portions of the woody plant is expressed in two ways: by elongation of the shoots of the current year and by increase in stem diameter. Elongation growth can be seen and measured from the time of bud break at the start of the growing season until the formation of a terminal bud. The latter generally develops sometime during the period from late July to mid-August and this indicates the end of elongation growth. Increase in stem diameter as growth is not so apparent and usually continues beyond the time elongation growth has ceased for the year. Foresters, who are very much interested in the production of wood, will evaluate this latter type of growth by use of the increment borer. The increment borer is a tool that removes a horizontal core of wood from the tree trunk to allow for examination of the width of the annual growth rings. Such examination provides an accurate determination of the history of the tree through analysis of the annual amount of diameter growth.

Elongation growth of the woody plant is controlled by the **endogenous** growth regulators auxin, cytokinin and gibberellin and is fueled by nutrients and moisture from the soil (see Plant Propagation lesson, ROOTING COMPOUNDS AND OTHER GROWTH REGULATORS). In the spring, when the sap is rising in the plant, cytokinins produced in the roots are attracted to the buds, the sites of annual activity. Cytokinins are responsible for cell division, so if the ambient temperature is high enough when transfer from the roots takes place, growth proceeds (see Figure 8-1).

The growth regulator - **auxin** - which is produced by the buds, creates a physiological sink to which nutrients and cytokinins are attracted. All this stimulates growth from the bud; that is, the production of a leafy shoot. The young leaves of the shoot are, in turn, the source of a growth substance - **gibberellin** - which is responsible for elongation of shoots. When optimum supplies of this substance are available, then a leafy shoot is produced with its leaves spaced wide apart. If it were not for this substance, the plant would produce a leafy shoot in which the leaves would be much closer together.

The growth pattern of the new shoot continues as long as young leaves are present. As shoot and leaves age, however, the amount of cytokinin available to the shoot diminishes and leaves which formerly produced gibberellin now tend to produce another growth regulating substance known as **abscisic acid**. This substance acts as a growth inhibitor to slow, and eventually stop, elongation growth. The visible manifestation of this is where the youngest leaves at the ends of shoots fail to develop as leaves. Rather, the process aborts and the structures develop, not as leaves, but as bud scales with the ultimate formation of the terminal bud.

When the terminal bud is formed, the shoot goes into a period of inactivity known as **summer dormancy**. The control point is the terminal bud and, if the terminal bud is removed or unseasonably wet weather occurs

## Figure 8-1
## GROWTH REGULATORS IN WOODY PLANTS

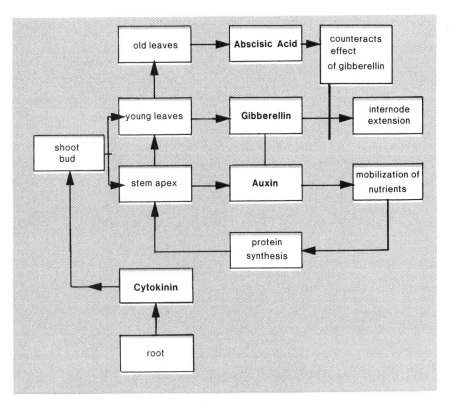

shortly after it is formed, the plant is still capable of producing new growth from the most distal lateral buds. However, should the period between the formation of the terminal bud and its removal be delayed for a few days, little, if any, response will be obtained from the most distal lateral buds. In other words, as time elapses, summer dormancy deepens and no external stimulus is capable of causing growth. When this stage is reached, buds on the tree or shrub are in a period of profound rest. This cannot be overcome until the buds receive a certain length of exposure to low temperature (about 5°C) in order to release the bud from dormancy (see Climate lesson, TEMPERATURE). This phenomenon can be examined by carrying out a simple experiment. Starting about the first of November, take branchlets from a tree or shrub and place their bases in a jar of water. Check the effect of this treatment in seven days time. Repeat the experiment at weekly intervals. When the branches in one of the time treatments breaks bud and shows normal growth, it can be concluded that by the time that particular treatment was begun, the normal rest period was over for that particular tree or shrub.

Tangential growth (i.e., growth in diameter of stems) continues long after extension growth has ceased. This is a logical sequence because when extension growth is over, the leaves and shoots of the plant are now able to produce and translocate food materials to sites where they will be used to increase diameter growth of stems and enlargement of roots.

While growth of top and roots can be examined independently, it is important to note that the two are interdependent (see Botany lesson, ORGANS). If the growth of the top is large and vigorous, the root growth will be the same. However, if something should impact the top of a tree or shrub during the latter part of the growing season, it will also have an effect on the root system. Thus, hail damage to leaves and stems or defoliation by insects in August, will reduce production of food material normally translocated to the root system. Reduced growth of the root system is the direct result of such top damage. The ultimate effect, something that will not be seen until the following growing season, will be reduced growth of the

top of the plant as a result of subnormal growth of the root system during the previous year. This explains why pruning practiced late in the season has a dwarfing effect on trees, whereas pruning prior to the start of the season, has no such effect.

In the discussion of elongation growth, it was mentioned that when terminal buds are formed on most woody plants, the buds enter a period of **summer dormancy**, a change that becomes deeper and more profound as time goes on (see Figure 8-2). The period of inactivity following summer dormancy is referred to as **dormancy rest**. The length of **dormancy rest** varies among Genera but is quite consistent within a Species or cultivar. In the north temperate zone, **dormancy rest** is usually completed before the winter season is over. When this period has been completed (even though the plant is now in a condition to commence growth), it will remain dormant as long as favorable conditions for growth are absent. The retention of dormancy totally imposed and controlled by the environment, is known as **dormancy quiescence** and is responsible for maintaining a plant's state of inactivity until growing conditions return in the spring.

While dormancy rest and dormancy quiescence are important to the survival of the woody plant, these are not the only factors responsible. The phenomenon of **winter hardiness** is also vital. The development of winter hardiness by a plant is an event that is synchronized with the onset of dormancy rest (see Climate lesson, TEMPERATURE).

What changes occur in the indigenous woody plant when the hours of daylight begin to decline? As the days shorten, the indigenous plant and, for that matter, all others that normally survive in the region, receive the message that the seasons are about to change. The message is received by a photoreceptive pigment in the leaves and transmitted to other parts of the plant (see Climate lesson, LIGHT). The plant responds by making certain biochemical changes that are used in preparing the plant for winter.

The changes triggered by the shortening daylength are collectively responsible for the development of **maturity** in the plant. Maturity is a prerequisite for winter hardiness. If maturity is not achieved, a plant cannot initiate fundamental changes in preparation for winter. One could not expect a woody plant from California, for example, to achieve maturity in any Alberta climate. In such plants, something tends to block the way so that photoreceptive pigment in the leaves is unable to receive or convey the short day message to the rest of the plant.

This phenomenon is demonstrated in an experiment conducted on plants from three geographical sources. The plant material selected was the ubiquitous red osier dogwood (*Cornus sericea*), one clone from Minnesota, a second from North Dakota and a third from Seattle,

## Figure 8-2
## THE DORMANCY PHENOMENON OF WOODY PLANTS

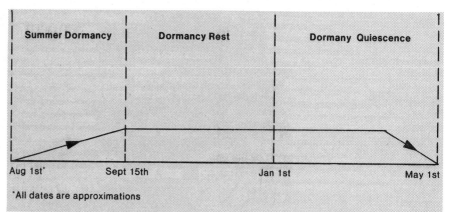

| Summer Dormancy | Dormancy Rest | Dormany Quiescence |

Aug 1st*      Sept 15th      Jan 1st      May 1st

*All dates are approximations

Washington. The three clones were brought to St. Paul, grown for a year in the nursery and in September/October, twigs from each were taken at weekly intervals and subjected to low temperature. This was to determine if and when maturity had occurred within plants from each of the three sources. In Figure 8-3, two of the three curves representing plants from two sources reached a point where a significant change in response to low temperature resulted prior to the occurrence of killing temperatures. Plants from Seattle, however, failed to achieve maturity early enough and were damaged when killing temperatures occurred.

## Figure 8-3
## WOODY PLANT RESPONSE TO CLIMATIC VARIATIONS

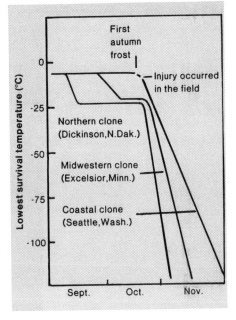

What changes take place in a woody plant following the achievement of maturity? From the curves in Figure 8-3, it is obvious that some substantial change was taking place in the two strains that were able to make stem tissues more resistant to low temperature injury. An examination of Figure 8-4 helps to explain what happens in mature tissue when it is exposed to the steadily lowering temperatures of autumn. Since it is well known that water releases measurable amounts of heat when it freezes, the curve in Figure 8-4 demonstrates that

## Figure 8-4
## WOODY PLANT RESPONSE TO STEADILY DECREASING TEMPERATURE

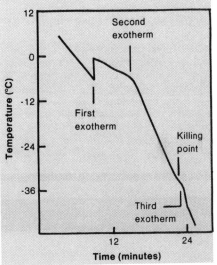

water in the tissues does not freeze at 0°C. In fact, no obvious measurable change occurs until the temperature reaches -5°C. The ability of water to remain liquid well below its normal freezing point is known as **super-cooling** and water still present in mature tissue is said to be super-cooled. When freezing eventually occurs, heat is released. It is this increase in temperature that shows up as a 'blip' on the curve. Fortunately for the plant, the ice is not forming within the cell. When mature tissue is subjected to slow, steadily decreasing temperature, the cell membranes become more permeable and free water moves out of the cells and into the spaces between them. Here it can freeze solid without injuring cells or tissues.

Notice that a second 'blip' occurs as the temperature is further reduced. The second 'blip' is much smaller than the first but indicates the same thing, that more water is freezing. Again, it is freezing outside the cells in the intercellular spaces. This water also comes from within the cells but, this time, it is water more closely associated with cell constituents. At this stage, the cell contents change quite drastically. Thus, any water remaining becomes so much a part of the molecular structure of cell components, that it is almost impossible to remove from the cell. Certainly, the water remaining is

unfreezable within the cell and only exposure to exceedingly low temperatures will have any effect upon it. As the temperature drops further, note from the curve that a third and hardly noticeable 'blip' occurs. This signifies that a critical low temperature has been reached, one that is capable of extracting even the most tenaciously bound water from the cell constituents. At this stage, death of the mature plant occurs.

Further reference to the influence of climatic variations and the effect of these variations on woody plants is contained in this lesson. Read the LIMITS TO WOODY PLANT SURVIVAL reprinted from *Woody Ornamentals for the Prairie Provinces*. The Climate lesson also provides useful information that can be applied to growth of woody ornamentals.

# ORIGINS OF TREES AND SHRUBS FOR THE PRAIRIE PROVINCES

The woody ornamentals that have proven themselves satisfactory in the prairie region have been derived from a number of sources. In some cases, the 'ordinary' indigenous plant has been brought into cultivation and, when found satisfactory, propagated by seed or other means. Such things as red osier dogwood (*Cornus sericea*), paper birch (*Betula papyrifera*), white spruce (*Picea glauca*), silver buffalo berry (*Shepherdia argentea*), lodge-pole pine (*Pinus contorta latifolia*) and golden flowering currant (*Ribes odoratum*) can be found growing on the Prairies (see Figure 8-5). All have been found satisfactory under cultivation. In other cases, some sharp-eyed plants-person has noted a peculiarity in an indigenous plant and vegetatively propagated the special plant to perpetuate its unique character. There are quite a number of these native selections that are now obtainable from local sources. Some of the better known are the three junipers — Wapiti, Dunvegan Blue and Prince of Wales (*Juniperus horizontalis* cultivars) as well as the Garry Pink (*Viburnum trilobum* 'Garry Pink') and the Isanti dogwood (*Cornus sericea* 'Isanti') .

Some of our woody plants have originated as chance seedlings. The

## Figure 8-5
## PAPER BIRCH│SUB-ALPINE FIR

## Figure 8-6
## SCHUBERT CHOKECHERRY

of the region would be complete without some reference to the contribution made by the plant hunters. Most successful introductions from other parts of the globe have come from expeditions to places like northwest China, Manchuria, Siberia and North Korea. Horticulturists are constantly reminded of this when they are confronted by such Species names as *sibirica, mandschurica* and *koraiensis.* Northwest Europe has also been a reasonably productive source of hardy materials. The Scots pine (*Pinus sylvestris*), the European white birch (*Betula alba*) and Norway spruce (*Picea Abies*) all originated in this part of the globe (see Figure 8-8). The fact that northern Asia and northwest Europe have been such good sources of woody plants for western Canada should not surprise anyone since these places have climates and growing seasons quite similar to our own.

## Figure 8-8
## NORWAY SPRUCE

Schubert chokecherry (*Prunus virginiana melanocarpa* 'Schubert'), a small, red-leaved tree, was found as a single plant among a number of chokecherry seedlings produced from a bulk seedlot (see Figure 8-6).

Plant breeders have also contributed greatly to the pallette of materials available. The Muckle plum (*Prunus X nigrella* 'Muckle'), one of our more attractive, small-flowering trees has arisen as the result of a single cross between the native plum of Manitoba (*Prunus nigra*) and the Russian almond (*Prunus tenella*). Quite recently, the highly regarded Tower poplar (*Populus X* 'Tower') has been introduced (see Figure 8-7). It is a hybrid between the Swedish columnar aspen (*Populus tremula erecta*) and the White poplar (*Populus alba*).

No discourse on the woody ornamentals

## Figure 8-7
## THE TOWER POPLAR

# SELECTING WOODY ORNAMENTALS

In choosing woody ornamentals, there are many things to be considered. While most people have some idea of what they want in terms of ultimate plant size, shape, or color, these are only a few of the things upon which choices should be made.

**Hardiness** is, unquestionably, an important consideration. If a plant is known to be not hardy, then it should be rejected. On the other hand, there are plants of borderline hardiness which should not be rejected out of hand if their performance has not been evaluated in several microclimates. This approach of the dedicated horticulturalist can frequently prove worthwhile. If it were not for those who have experimented and discovered the appropriate environmental niches for plants, such great ornamentals as the Oregon grape (*Berberis aquifolium*), Korean golden bell (*Forsythia ovata*) or the hardier rhododendrons (*Rhododendron sp*) might never have been found adaptable to some regional conditions.

Another important consideration is **compatibility**, not simply the compatability of plants with other plants, but the compatability of the plant with the life style of the user. With reference to compatability between plants, one plant should not interfere with the growth of another. Plants should not make work for the gardener. Even the devoted enthusiast is unable to enjoy the most enchanting ornamental if its bad habits create excessive problems.

Some other very important incompatabilities exist between plant Genera. The rusts, an important group of plant diseases, are dependent on having two generically different hosts within reasonable proximity. For example, the disease, cedar apple rust (caused by *Gymnosporangium spp.*) is dependent on having either juniper or cedar growing within spore flying distance of such things as hawthorn, mountain ash or crabapple (see Figure 8-9). Another rather distressing disease of this type is the spruce needle rust (*Chrysomyxa ledicola*) that occurs in the wild between spruce and the small, common, understory plant called Labrador tea (*Ledum groenlandicum*). Spruce, when

## Figure 8-9

### CEDAR APPLE RUST SYMPTOMS ON JUNIPER AND MOUNTAIN ASH

infected, loses its needles and deteriorates rapidly.

Not all such incompatabilities are vigor or disease oriented. There are still others relating to insect pests. The grower who plants domesticated roses near areas where the wild rose is growing runs the risk of having the plantation invaded by the rose curculio (*Rhynchitis bicolor*). The woolly elm aphid (*Eriosoma americanum*) provides a similar case. It spends part of its life history associated with the American elm (*Ulmus americana*) and the balance in association with the native saskatoon (*Amelanchier alnifolia*).

There are several ways in which plants can impact a person's life-style. Some say there is no free lunch when it comes to assessing the virtues of trees. All appear to have one problem or another. For instance, there are those that drop things. Willows (*Salix*), for example, tend to drop branchlets all year round. The Ussurian pear (*Pyrus ussuriensis*) drops its crabapple-sized fruit in August and the green ash (*Fraxinus pennsylvanica subintegerrima*) hangs onto its fruit over the winter but deposits them on the ground early the following year. However, the tree in this class that is likely the least compatible with people

and their lifestyles is the Manchurian elm (*Ulmus pumila*). In May, it produces a super-abundance of fruit which it drops over a three week period. The fruit, which is the color, shape and size of a flake breakfast cereal, scatters over a wide area. Those that strike the bare soil, germinate with impunity. But the production of fruit is not the only problem associated with the Manchurian elm. In addition, it has what might be called deciduous branchlets that drop to the ground with the slightest breeze. Finally, the foliage is retained by the tree for a very long period and usually dropped long after the pleasant weather of autumn has gone (see Figure 8-10)

There are other woody plants that have the annoying habit of producing new shoots from the root system, sometimes at the base of the plant and sometimes at some distance from the trunk or crown. The poplar (*Populus*) frequently produces many surface roots which are easily injured. In response to injury, the poplar produces an adventitious shoot or sucker. The common lilac (*Syringa vulgaris*), the sumac (*Rhus glabra*) and the sea buckthorn (*Hippophae rhamnoides*) are also suckering plants but confine their suckering to the base of the plant.

Figure 8-10
MANCHURIAN ELM

**Fruit Clusters**

**Covers The Lawns Of Adjoining Properties**

Some woody plant cultivars are perpetuated by being grafted on a compatible roofstock. The double-flowering plum (*Prunus triloba multiplex*) is one such cultivar. When these plants are set in the ground with the swollen graft-union above the soil, suckering invariably occurs. If nothing is done about it, the suckers will eventually thrive at the expense of the cultivar. Home gardeners should be made aware of this problem as it happens far too frequently but can be easily prevented. All that is required is deeper planting. When the graft-union is placed 5 cm (2 in) below the soil surface, few problems will be encountered with suckers. It also makes sense to learn to recognize the difference between the growth characteristics of the cultivar and those of the rootstock so that suckers from the rootstock can be pruned out if they show up.

Many woody plants have the unfortunate characteristic of being attractive to specific insect pests. The May Day tree (*Prunus padus commutata*) is an example of this as it attracts the tent caterpillar.

Leaf miners are also a problem with some plants. The birches (*Betula*) and some of the lilacs (*Syringa*) have been particularly hard hit by such pests. In fact, a few people have actually lost interest in these plants because of the difficulties and costs of control. Aphids are bothersome on a great many plants. The aphid is a small sucking insect that confines its feeding activities to new growth. When infestations are heavy (and they usually are), the plants frequently show some abnormalities. Aphids have one other claim to unpopularity; that is, their ability to produce and exude 'honey-dew', a sticky substance that literally drips from trees to destroy the finish of anything that happens to lie beneath their canopy. The Manitoba maple (*Acer Negundo*) is very prone to aphid infestation.

Some plants are subject to plant diseases. This may lead to their rejection by some people. Fireblight, a bacterial disease caused by the organism *Erwinia amylovora* that attacks apple, crab-apple, mountain ash, cotoneaster and pear is likely the most common and destructive plant disease in the region. Within recent times, horticulturists have become aware of the effects of the parasitic shoe-string fungus (*Armillaria mellea*) on some of our better woody ornamentals. This, no doubt, is because it attacks one of our more attractive ornamental trees, the Amur cherry (*Prunus Maackii*), shortening its effective life span to less than twenty years.

The foregoing is only part of the plant selection problem. The other part involves selection on the basis of ornamental characteristics. Because **scale** is so very important in the appreciation of landscapes, ultimate **size** of the plants used is an important characteristic. There is an unfortunate tendency among home gardeners to select plants that grow to a size that is so far out of scale with their surroundings, that they feel they must chop them down to size, rather than remove them. This practice leads to some grotesque looking landscapes and worse looking plants. On the typical urban lot, shrubs that normally grow more than 1 m (4 ft) tall should be selected very carefully and used with discretion. The most satisfactory shrubby material for small properties are the plants that naturally stay within the range of 30 - 75 cm (1 - 2 1/2 ft). Such plants can then be grouped to achieve the density and mass required, without having to resort to oversized material.

A second important characteristic of ornamental plants is **texture**. Texture is determined largely by the size and coarseness of leaves. The range is quite broad and plants can be grouped so that textural contrasts (coarse versus fine) can be developed or that gradations (from coarse to medium to fine) may be achieved (see Figure 8-11).

Another consideration that must be addressed in plant selection is derived from the fact that woody ornamentals are used to provide **interest** on a year round basis. Plants with colorful bark, interesting branching habits and attractive fruit have a great deal to offer throughout the winter as well (see Figure 8-12).

During the growing season, two additional ornamental characteristics are considered important. These are **leaf color** and **flowering habit**. The predominant leaf color in the landscape is green and its various shades. However, some leaf color variety exists and it ranges from variegated white and green, yellow and green, to golden, purple or reddish purple through to silver

## Figure 8-11
## PLANT TEXTURES

(see Figure 8-13). Flowering shrubs and trees are important sources of summer color. Admittedly, the color source is brief so the contribution from each plant lasts but a couple of weeks. However, by getting to know the material, a skilled gardener can choose, distribute and often achieve interest from flowering woody plants over an extended period of several weeks (see Figure 8-14).

Finally, the characteristic of **form** is

something to be considered when selecting plants. Form is important in combining plants to achieve effective contrasts or harmonious combinations. As with the characteristics discussed earlier, the extremes can be combined to provide contrast but, for the more harmonious combinations, intermediates can be used to bridge the gap between the extremes.

The ornamentals with the most distinctive form characteristics are the conifers. Among the conifers, there is the columnar form of the arborvitae, the pyramidal form of the spruce, the globular forms of mugo pine (*Pinus mugo*) and the globe cedar (*Thuja occidentalis cultivars*) and, finally, the horizontal form of some junipers. Deciduous woody plants also display form which can serve as a basis for classification. However, because their density and color of foliage is, in most instances, not as strong and distinctive as that of the conifer, form tends to become slightly less important as an ornamental characteristic (see Figure 8-15)

Refer to the 'Plant Selector Key' reprinted in this lesson from *Woody Ornamentals for the Prairie Provinces*. Although not comprehensive, it will provide you with useful information on the types of trees and shrubs suitable for growth in this region. The Plant Selector Key lists those plant types with specific characteristics that you can match to your requirements.

## Figure 8-12
## COLORFUL BARK OF DOGWOOD

# THE USE OF WOODY ORNAMENTALS

### SELECTING THE APPROPRIATE PLANT ENVIRONMENT

In using woody plants wisely, **site**, **aspect** and **microclimate** are important considerations. Plants have preferred environments and, unless these are provided, a plant's full potential may never be realized. Pine trees, for example, prefer open sunny locations on lighter soils. It is not uncommon to see the effect of shade on the mugo pine when it is located on the north side of a house or beneath the canopy of a tree. In such locations, it quickly loses its

Figure 8-13
## LEAF COLOR OF WOODY ORNAMENTALS

Silverleaved Dogwood

Russian Olive

Figure 8-14
## FLOWERING OF WOODY ORNAMENTALS

Skinners American Lilacs

Double Flowering Plum

is retained during this very critical spring period, they are never damaged.

The golden bell (*Forsythia ovata*), a plant that is not widely grown in the region, is capable of providing a spectacular show of blossoms if adequate snow cover is provided over the dormant season. However, when snow cover is not deep or heavy enough to cover the plant completely, those flower buds that are exposed to the elements are frequently damaged (see Figure 8-16).

Aspect plays a very important role in determining whether or not a plant that is capable of providing bright, fall color will achieve its maximum potential. The Amur maple (*Acer ginnala*) and some Species of the burning bush (*Evonymus*) never display their best autumn color unless they are exposed to full sunlight.

Shade may also have an adverse effect on flower bud initiation of the flowering crabapples (*Malus sp*). When a major portion of a tree is in constant shade, it is not uncommon to find that part of the tree remains vegetative while the portion in full sunlight blossoms heavily.

In some instances, reflected light and heat from buildings can have an adverse effect on the survival of plants. The arborvitae or white cedar (*Thuja occidentalis*) seldom does well in such exposures and dessication injury frequently shows up after exposure to the warming rays of early, spring sunshine.

## PLANTING DESIGN

Landscapes are of two types; the **natural**, which is composed of the land, its topography and the plants upon it, and the **urbanized**, in which the works of man predominate. Plants in the natural landscape tend to be used more freely although layouts are subject to both environmental and practical aesthetic considerations. In the natural landscape, the design practitioner will be concerned with **three levels of vegetation**:

1. that above eye level (the trees and tall shrubs),
2. the shrub layer that exists below eye level, and
3. the vegetation providing cover on the ground.

tight compactness and becomes loose, open and uncontrollable. Similar things happen to some of the broadleaved evergreens when planted in the 'wrong place'. Two of these, the Oregon grape (*Berberis aquifolium*) and cliff green (*Paxistima myrsinites*), native plants from the foothills and mountain valleys,

never achieve their potential if located where snow cover is lost early in the spring. When the foliage of these plants is exposed to strong, spring sunlight before the start of new growth, they seldom survive intact although they may be restored later. When such plants are grown in locations where the snow cover

Figure 8-15
## FORM OF CONIFERS

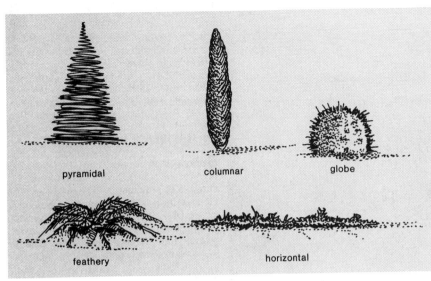

pyramidal          columnar          globe

feathery          horizontal

Figure 8-16
## GOLDEN BELL

naturalness of the site and still recognize the importance of the existing natural amenities. The objective here is to break up the existing area into a series of **interconnecting spaces of variable size**. A series of oval shapes have been used to show all open space. This includes the open space defined by the two waterbodies. In Figure 8-17C, the spaces are now defined by massed vegetation. The result is a landscape with connecting open spaces that relate to site amenities. The visual impacts of offsite things are either softened or eliminated (visually) by the vegetation masses.

In all landscape situations, it is important to choose a predominant tree type. If the predominant tree type chosen is not indigenous to the region, it makes visual sense for it to possess some of the characteristics of the natural vegetation.

With spaces defined and the major trees located on plan, then placement of large shrub masses can be determined. On natural sites such as this, there may be special areas that call for special vegetation. For example, areas close to the waterbodies or stream may have a high water table and call for the use of trees like willow (*Salix*) and other water tolerant plants. Another concern that must be addressed is what to do about the proportion of deciduous to coniferous material. On a site of this magnitude, conifers must be concentrated at important visual locations and used in significant numbers. It is also important not to mix the two. The reason for this is that faster growing deciduous materials, when interspersed with conifers, can destroy the form of the conifers.

In the highly urbanized landscape, where the works of man dominate, the three levels of vegetation may be used. However, their use, patterns and alignments will conform to the urbanized nature of the site. Uniformity in shape and size of trees and shrubs frequently becomes very important. Tree alignments tend to conform to pre-conceived geometry. Surface vegetation, where function decrees, may give way entirely to hard surfacing.

Figure 8-18 shows a small space or courtyard within the confines of two wings of a building. Because of the rectilinear nature of the space, it follows that the use of plant materials must

In large areas like parks, all three levels of vegetation can be utilized fully. In places like golf courses, the use of the shrub layer may be minimized in order to promote the game of golf. In athletic fields, only the ground vegetation may be retained.

Figure 8-17A illustrates a site in a completely rural area. The site is

bounded on the north by a county road, on the south by a wooded hillside and on the east and west by developed farmland. Note that the site has natural amenities - a couple of small waterbodies and a small stream flowing from east to west.

Figure 8-17B illustrates an approach that might be taken to enhance the

Figure 8-17
DESIGN APPROACH FOR A RURAL LANDSCAPE

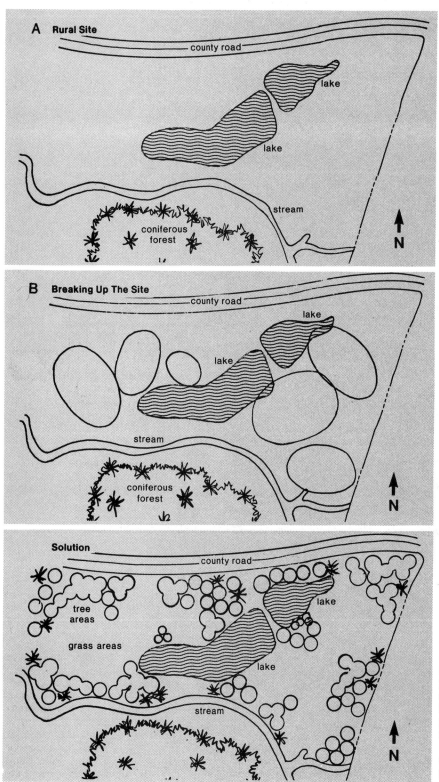

conform to the nature of the space, otherwise a chaotic and totally illogical design will result. In this plan, as with the previous one, all three levels of vegetation are used in a logical way. That is, trees are not placed in front of windows, shrubs are employed in places where they seem more appropriate and, finally, there is a strong cohesion between all parts, derived from the use of ground covers to tie things together.

## PLANTING TREES AND SHRUBS

There are two very important things to be considered when planting trees and shrubs. The first consideration is the **soil** in which they are going to be planted. The second consideration is the **size of the plant pit** in which each is going to be placed. In most cases, soil dug from the plant pit is satisfactory for backfilling around the roots. This is particularly true for bare-root plants. With container stock, care should be taken to see that the backfill material is not finer in texture than that of the root-ball soil. Otherwise, water will tend to flow around the root-ball, rather than entering it. In soils that have good structure, the plant pit need only be dug large enough to hold the root-ball. The recommended practice is to **plant high,** that is, 5 cm (2 in) less than the depth of the soil in a 20 L (about 4 gal) container and 2.5 cm (1 in) less than the depth of soil in a 4 L (about 1 gal) container (see Figure 8-19). The reason for this is to counter the settling of the plant where its root-ball ends up below the level of the surrounding soil. It should be noted, however, that **high planting is not recommended for sandy soils** that have the tendency to hold less moisture.

The diameter of each pit should be twice that of the container or root-ball so that backfill soil can be worked in easily around the root-ball. To minimize 'glazing' of the sides when pits are dug with a power auger, digging should be done when soil moisture levels are well below field capacity. No matter how the pit is dug, it is always advisable to scarify the sides and bottom to meld the backfill soil with the field soil and so provide easier access to the field soil by developing roots.

Containerized woody plants frequently have major roots circling around the

Figure 8-18
URBANIZED LANDSCAPE DESIGN

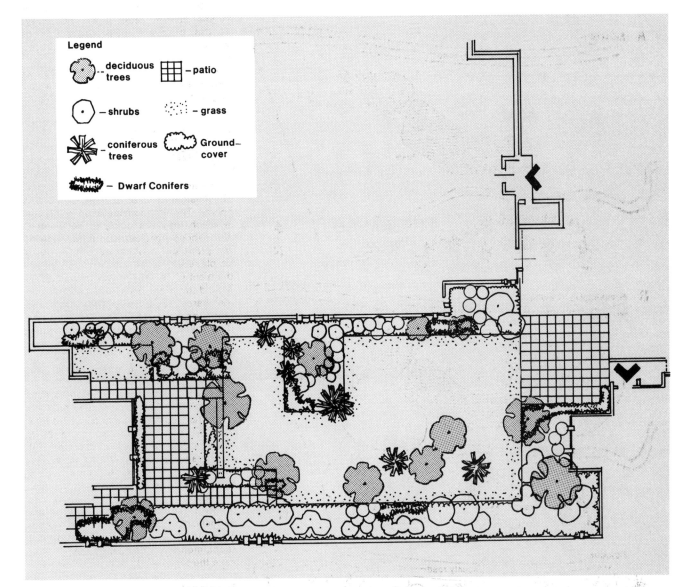

Legend

![deciduous trees] — deciduous trees
![patio] — patio
![shrubs] — shrubs
![grass] — grass
![coniferous trees] — coniferous trees
![Ground-cover] — Ground-cover
![Dwarf Conifers] — Dwarf Conifers

root-ball. Some horticulturists will go so far as to cut the root-ball vertically on two opposite sides for at least half the distance to the trunk in order to decrease the chance that hidden, encircling roots will girdle the root system later. With container stock, it is a standard practice to free the roots at the periphery of the root-ball by combing them gently upwards. If these roots are then straightened out in the backfill soil, root establishment will be much quicker. When planting bare-root stock, any weak, damaged or twisted roots should be cut back into healthy wood.

Just prior to setting the plant, mound 2.5 cm (1 in) of the loosened soil in the bottom of the pit, firm it and set the plant on top. With bare-root plants, the largest root should be placed on the **downwind** side to stabilize the tree.

When the plant has been placed and its pit backfilled, the base of the plant, in all but the sandiest soils, should be 2.5 - 5 cm (1 - 2 in) above the finished ground level. If this practice is followed, a basin can be made around the plant, with the lowest part of the basin near the periphery. This will prevent collar rot that frequently occurs when the lowest part of the basin is at the trunk (see Figure 8-20).

Should a tree be staked? This is a question for which there is no generally accepted answer. Staking or guying is sometimes practical on windy sites or where the tree is weak and cannot support itself. If a tree has good structure and an adequate root-ball,

## Figure 8-19
## PLANTING A ROOT-BALL

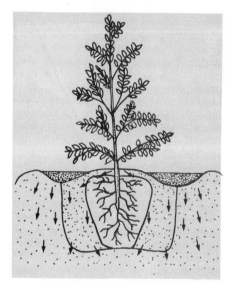

there is seldom any need to support it. On the other hand, if the tree is bare root material, support will be necessary until it is established. Shrubs are never supported and it is seldom necessary to support spruce or pine when the root-balls are adequate.

With deciduous plants at planting time, pruning will benefit bare-root materials, particularly those plants that have begun to leaf out. Such pruning will make it easier for the reduced root system to support the top. Container stock does

## Figure 8-20
## PLANTING HIGH

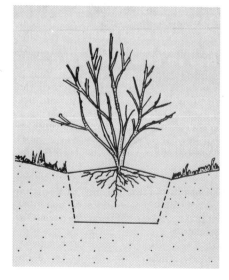

not require pruning because the root system, if handled properly at planting time, will continue to support the existing top.

Some **corrective** pruning at planting time is advisable for the following reasons:

*   To encourage well branched plants — cut back major branches lightly; that is, make cuts only in wood of the previous season.

*   To open up the plant and reduce its density — prune interior wood only, directing attention to weak growth, crossed branches and any wood showing injury.

# MAINTENANCE PRACTICES

If trees and shrubs are going to achieve their full potential, a certain amount of maintenance will be required. There are three practices that are particularly important. These are training, pruning and feeding.

## TRAINING YOUNG DECIDUOUS TREES

## Figure 8-21
## EXCURRENT AND DECURRENT GROWTH HABITS

Training is a technique involving shortening and removing branches from trees in their formative years. The objective of training is to develop a well distributed, permanent branching system. In the practice of tree training, there are two types of trees to deal with. There are those like the basswood or linden (*Tilia*) that have lateral branches on current growth of the leader (weak apical dominance). The growth habit of such trees is **excurrent** and characterized by a strong central leader and conical shape (see Figure 8-21). There are others with no lateral shoots on current growth (strong apical dominance) like the American elm (*Ulmus americana*) which has quite an irregular growth habit and forms vigorous laterals in the second year. Such trees have a **decurrent** growth habit, which requires considerable attention during the training period in order to develop a central trunk and a strong branch structure. The tendency is for scaffold branches to make up the main framework of decurrent trees. In contrast, most excurrent trees with weak apical dominance have strong central trunks with many laterals that are much smaller in diameter.

During the training period, most trees are trained (cut back) to central leaders so

**Little Leaf Linden Showing the Excurrent Habit of Growth**

**American Elm Showing the Decurrent Habit of Growth**

## Figure 8-22
## TREE TRAINING PRACTICES

they have one main trunk. The practice is to cut the laterals on the lower half of the developing leader to stubs 10 - 15 cm (4 - 6 in) long. These stubs will tend to slow extension growth of the leader. However, they must be kept within bounds so that the leader is not slowed unnecessarily. Therefore, all laterals up to the height of the lowest permanent branch are cut back, but not removed. Those above the lowest permanent branch are thinned so they are about 15 cm (6 in) apart vertically, and spaced radially around the trunk. None should be allowed to compete strongly with (or outgrow) the leader (see Figure 8-22)

For small trees, where a strong central trunk is not required, the modified central leader system is a practical one to follow. This system is commonly used in fruit orchards. Figure 8-23 illustrates development of such a tree. First, the leader is **headed back** to encourage growth of laterals. The laterals themselves are then headed back to encourage further branching, with the tree on the right being the ultimate objective.

## PRUNING

Pruning is one of the more important practices for every home gardener to master. Good pruning inevitably means good plants. Its purpose is to direct growth and maintain the natural size and appearance of a plant by ˙removing unnecessary growth.

Pruning can be done most easily during the dormant season, when there are no leaves to contend with. That is not to say that pruning should never be done during the growing season because there will be occasions when it is necessary. However, when done in the spring while the plants are still dormant, there are fewer questions as to what should or should not be removed.

### PRUNING SHRUBS
The natural form of a plant is one of its most important attributes. Pruning should enhance, rather than destroy, the natural form (see Figure 8-24). If a shrub is too large for a particular site or situation, there is only one way to deal with it — dig it up and use it in a more appropriate spot.

In striving to maintain the natural form of a shrub, there will be occasions when removal or shortening of a branch may be all that is required. In removing a branch, the most desirable practice is to simply cut the offending stems from the plant right at the base. In shortening a branch, it is important to determine the consequences of the cut to be made. First, such cuts should be made in relation to either a bud or to another stem (see Figure 8-25). If a cut is made within 6 mm (1/4 in) above a bud, then further extension growth from the branch or stem will come from that bud. If the bud is located on the outside of the stem, then new growth will be directed outward. On the other hand, if the bud is on the inside of the stem or branch, then new growth will be directed towards the inside of the plant and may cause problems later. The point of making the cut 6 mm (1/4 in) above a bud is important. When this point is ignored and a longer stub is left above the bud, problems arise with respect to healing of tissues (see Figure 8-26). It appears that the bud to which the pruning cut is made has some positive influence on the healing of the cut surface. When the cut is made 12 mm (1/2 in) or more above the bud, this influence is then lost; the cut remains open and the plant becomes subject to invasion by harmful organisms.

## Figure 8-23
## DEVELOPMENT OF THE MODIFIED CENTRAL LEADER TREE

Figure 8-24

## PRUNING TO RETAIN A NATURAL FORM

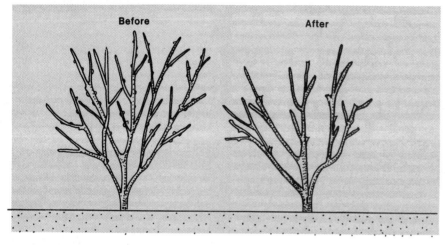

Figure 8-25

## HEADING BACK TO A BUD

While pruning to maintain the natural form of a plant is an important reason for annual pruning, there are other important reasons for pruning. One reason is the removal of weak and undesirable wood. Branches have a tendency to interfere with one another and, if this is permitted, one or both are damaged by the friction generated. In such cases, it is customary to remove the least desirable of the two branches, or to prune each in such a way as to remove the point of contact.

After a shrub has been in place and neglected for a few years, the tendency for it to accumulate an overabundance of wood becomes quite evident. In such cases, the thinning out or removal of interior wood is a logical approach to maintaining the health and vigour of the plant. In these situations, attention is directed more to complete removal of stems than to anything else. Since this practice may call for the removal of a lot of wood, it falls to the person using the pruning equipment to decide whether or not all stems slated for removal should be taken at one time. It is important to recognize that when very large amounts of wood are taken from a tree or shrub and the root system is undisturbed, the plant will respond by producing a large amount of vegetative growth. If the shrub is a flowering type, the effect of all this pruning can be disastrous. In such cases, it makes sense to rejuvenate the plant over a period of three or more years, rather than to remove all the wood at once.

## PRUNING TREES

All of the pruning practices referred to in respect to shrubs apply equally to pruning trees. However, trees require additional pruning considerations that must be emphasized. The most important involves **heading back.** When heading back, there is an unfortunate tendency among the uninitiated to make cuts into older wood. The product of this is something that looks more like a scarecrow or hat rack, rather than a tree (see Figure 8-27). Heading back cuts on trees should never be made into wood older than three years.

In addition to heading back, cuts to laterals are also important in tree pruning. The diameter of the portion of

Figure 8-26

## DIEBACK AFTER IMPROPER PRUNING

## Figure 8-27
## THE EFFECTS OF IMPROPER PRUNING

the branch removed should be close to that of the lateral that is being retained (see Figure 8-28).

When removing a major branch from a tree, it is very important to ensure that the basal collar of the branch to be removed is retained by the plant. The reason for this is that the collar contains cells that are very important in isolating

exposed plant tissues from invasion by wood-rotting and pathogenic organisms (see Figure 8-29).

In the past, it was customary to cover the surfaces of pruning wounds with an asphalt emulsion to counter dessication and promote healing. In recent years, however, the usefulness of this practice has been questioned. It is now suggested that such coatings may promote, rather than counter, infection.

confined to new growth at the time of shoot elongation. A new shoot at this stage is about the size and shape of a human finger and removal of a piece of the shoot will reduce growth proportionally. The increase in density that accompanies pinching is dependent on it being done prior to visible needle formation. When pinching is done just after the shoots have begun to elongate, the plant will respond by producing buds on the decapitated shoot. Since growth has been shortened, the new growing points (buds) will be closer to the body of the plant. Hence, when pinching is practiced on an annual basis, the density of the plant will be greatly increased as time goes on.

### PRUNING FLOWERING TREES AND SHRUBS

While all trees and shrubs blossom and produce fruit and seed, only those that have large and distinctive blossoms are considered (by horticulturists) as flowering plants. This group can be divided into two types: those that produce blossoms on wood of the **current** season and those that produce their blossoms on wood of the **previous** season. Because of these distinctions, each of the two types must be handled in a different way.

Those that produce their flower buds on wood of the current season must be pruned (when pruning is necessary) before new growth occurs. In other

## Figure 8-28
## CUTTING BACK TO A LATERAL

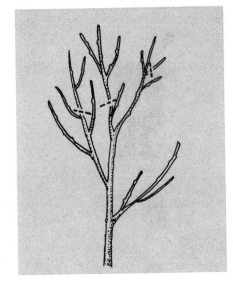

### PRUNING CONIFERS

Conifers are pruned only when necessary. In some cases (arborvitae, for example), pruning actually becomes **shearing** — a practice which, when performed just at the time of new growth, will promote an increase in the density of the plant. The upright, pyramidal-shaped junipers also respond favorably to spring shearing. However, it is not desirable to shear those conifer forms whose branches grow along the ground. Much of the value of these conifers lies in their natural form, which shearing would destroy. Nevertheless, it is occasionally necessary to prune this type of juniper. Pruning to a lateral is the accepted practice, with special attention given to hiding the site of the pruning cut.

Dwarf pines are frequently pinched to increase their density and control their size (see Figure 8-30). Pinching is

## Figure 8-29
## PRUNING TO A BASAL COLLAR

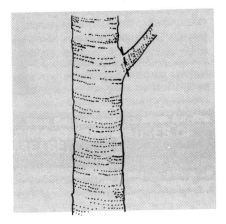

Figure 8-30
## PINCHING TO CONTROL ANNUAL GROWTH

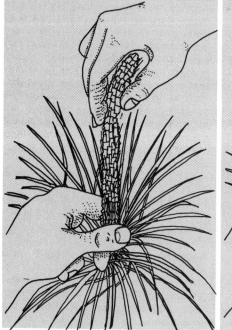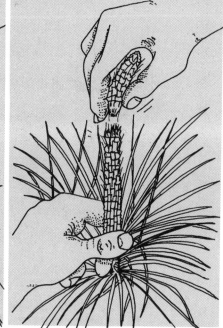

words, if pruning is done **before** growth takes place and before flower buds form, then pruning will not seriously reduce the flowering surface of the plant. On the other hand, if the second group of flowering plants (those that blossom on wood of the previous season) were to be pruned just prior to blossoming, much of the flowering surface would be reduced. In some cases, flower buds cannot be distinguished from shoot buds. Hence, even an expert may inadvertently reduce the flowering surface by pruning at the wrong time. Plants that produce blossoms on wood of the previous season, then, should be pruned (when pruning is necessary) **after, not before,** blossoming has taken place.

The two types of flowering plant can be easily distinguished. Those that blossom on wood of the previous season are the **spring flowering plants** and include lilacs (*Syringa sp.*), apples and crabapples (*Malus sp.*), plums, cherries, apricots and flowering almonds (*Prunus sp.*). Those that blossom on wood of the current season are **summer flowering plants** such as the pink or red flowered Spirea (*Spiraea bumalda*) and the large 'white flowered' plant known as the snow hills hydrangea (*Hydrangea arborescens grandiflora*) (see Figure 8-31).

## TREE SURGERY

Mechanical injury to trees is not uncommon so when bark-destroying injuries occur, some response must be taken to promote healing. When the injury is irregular, it should be trimmed to a vertical spindle form by cutting into healthy bark and cambium. The spindle form will heal more effectively than a circular form because the two sides of the wound are closer together than the ends (see Figure 8-32). Wound covering callus generated from cork cambium on the two sides will, in time, cover the wound and come together along the central axis of the spindle-shaped wound.

Cabling and bracing trees is sometimes necessary when trees age and develop structural weaknesses (see Figure 8-33). However, such practices are only advocated for use on trees where it is warranted by the value of the tree and its life expectancy. **Cabling** involves the attachment of a flexible steel cable between branches to limit excessive limb motion and reduce stress on crotch or branches. **Bracing** uses bolts or threaded rods to rigidly secure weak or split crotches, to unite split trunks or branches, or to hold rubbing limbs together or apart.

## FEEDING

Generally, the nutrition of woody ornamentals is not considered very important. This is partly due to the fertility of soils in the region and partly

Figure 8-31
## SNOW HILLS HYDRANGEA

## Figure 8-32
## WOUND TREATMENT AND HEALING

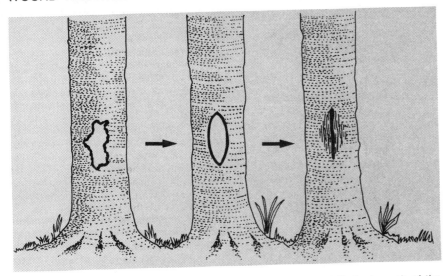

because the plants in question are not food producing. If they were, productivity would then become part of the equation and nutrition would be an important consideration.

Unlike herbaceous plants, trees and shrubs do not respond immediately to nitrogen when it is applied to the soil. Soil applications in early spring may not be utilized by the plant until much later in

## Figure 8-33
## CABLING

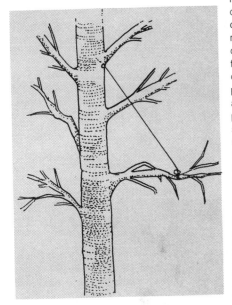

the growing season. In fact, much of the nitrogen taken up by woody ornamentals may actually be stored by the plant for use the following year. Because of this, when nutritional deficiencies are detected early in the growing season, nutrients should be applied as a foliar spray of soluble, non-burning fertilizer to the leaves. Such applications have almost immediate effects.

## CHEMICAL CONTROL OF PLANTS

Suckers from roots are a nuisance in the landscape. Those that arise at the base of trees lend themselves to treatment by chemicals, provided the chemicals are not injurious to turfgrass. Those that occur within the lawn at some distance from the source are generally controllable by mowing. The chemical plant growth regulator, naphthalene acetic acid (NAA), has been found to provide adequate control of basal suckers. However, treatment must be repeated each year. This same growth regulator can also be used in the control of fruit set where fruit is either not required or desirable.

The growth of roots in sewers is a perennial problem in cities. Willows and poplars enter older sewer lines through the lower quadrants of joints and grow longitudinally along the bottom of the pipe. The availability of moisture, aeration and nutrients are so favorable for root growth, that roots inevitably clog

the sewer. Mechanical treatments can be used. However, they are effective only back to the point where the root system enters the sewer, so the treatment must be repeated every one to three years. In recent years, chemical treatments have proven more economical. The most satisfactory materials have been mixtures of vapam and dichlorobenyl. Vapam kills the roots, while dichlorobenyl inhibits regrowth. Used in the sewer as an air-aqueous foam, it fills the sewer to give an effective kill. Precautions must be taken, however, to prevent chemical back flow through plumbing fixtures and sewer vents.

## DIAGNOSING PLANT PROBLEMS

Landscape plantings get off to a good start during their first year if the stock is satisfactory and the project well managed. With time, however, certain changes in the plant materials may become evident and create cause for concern. In some cases, the changes may be a result of normal growth behavior, whereas in other cases, the changes may be symptoms of something serious.

If a plant is treated for the wrong malady, problems may actually be compounded or, at best, corrective treatment may have no effect at all. Accurate diagnosis is very important and generally depends on the following:

- observation of subtle differences from the normal in plant appearance,
- knowledge of plants, soils, climate, pests and diseases, and
- accurate information regarding the recent history of the affected plant, the site, the climate, and prevailing cultural practices.

Some 'abnormalities' are simply manifestations of the normal condition. Each spring, for example, professional horticulturists are bombarded with questions concerning strange 'growths' that appear on spruce trees 'for the first time'. The growths are small, purple, egg-shaped structures that later give off a flour-like powder. These structures are nothing more than male cones providing pollen for the fertilization of the female cones which are borne near the top of the tree. Similar concerns are expressed in autumn, when some of the older needles of pine and branchlets of arborvitae turn brown and later shed. These too, are normal conditions, even though the amount of shedding may seem excessive some years.

Occasionally in the spring, people are concerned about what seems like abnormal foliage color on some deciduous plants. This phenomenon is quite common; the color variation is something that normally occurs, every spring.

As it gets older, the trunk of the Manitoba maple takes on somewhat voluptuous contours that have been associated, mistakenly, with disease or insect infestation (see Figure 8-34). These swellings are actually due to concentrations of trace buds beneath the bark that become active and grow as water sprouts if stressful conditions occur.

## Figure 8-34
## SWELLINGS ON THE TRUNK OF MANITOBA MAPLE

# THE DIAGNOSTIC APPROACH

Because of their diversity, the characteristics and requirements of landscape plants are not that well understood by most people. However, there is no reason why people should not become familiar with the plants commonly grown in the region, their problems and their response to environment and cultural practices.

The more perplexing plant problems can be classified according to the following criteria: symptoms, kind of plant affected, or plant parts involved. There are, however, others (like mechanical injury) that are more obvious and can be solved without having to take the more complex, analytical approach.

## PLANT INJURY

### MECHANICAL INJURY
Mechanical injury is usually the easiest to diagnose. However, it may require close scrutiny to spot the site of the injury.

### CHEMICAL INJURY
Symptoms of chemical injury show up readily on leaves and new shoots. The **epinasty** (see Figure 8-35) shown by plants affected by one of the phenoxy herbicides is quite common, although it can sometimes be confused with symptoms expressed by virus infected plants.

Symptoms of soil borne chemical injury are generally seen as dead areas on the margins and tips of leaves. Air-borne chemicals, on the other hand, may promote interveinal chlorosis or sizeable 'water-soaked' or dead areas on the leaf blades.

### THERMAL INJURY
On the Prairies, thermal injury to plants is generally of the low temperature variety. The most common is **tip-kill**, a symptom of an injured plant's failure to fully mature its tissues. The loss of flower buds but survival of shoot buds is also a common symptom of thermal injury. This, however, is nothing more than an expression of the relative lack of hardiness of flower buds compared to shoot buds.

One of the most perplexing symptoms of thermal injury is the one expressed by trees with root systems that are incapable of withstanding extremely low temperatures. The symptoms of this type of injury are initial bud-break, quickly followed by the death of the tree. Such behavior is diagnosed as follows. The buds of the tree have sufficient materials and moisture in the bark and wood to cause initial bud-break but, because the roots are damaged, the tree is unable to transport moisture to the sites of growth. The tree, therefore, dies before any further expansion of leaves can take place.

## NON-INFECTIOUS DISORDERS
One of the more common non-infectious disorders is lime-induced chlorosis. Lime induced chlorosis is quite common in Alberta, though more so in some areas than others. The symptom, failure of the interveinal portion of young leaves to produce chlorophyll, is fostered by high

## Figure 8-35
## THE EFFECT OF THE HERBICIDE 2,4-D ON SPRUCE

lime soils. An excess of lime causes a change in soil pH, which reduces the availability of iron to the plant. These symptoms are usually more pronounced in the early spring, when the soil is cold and wet (see Figure 8-36).

## Figure 8-36
## LIME INDUCED CHLOROSIS ON ROSE

Slow growth, incipient wilting and death of tissues on the southwest part of a smooth-barked tree are all symptoms of 'sun scald' injury. Sun scald damage occurs in winter when the late afternoon sunlight raises the temperature of the

bark in the southwest portions of the trunk or branch, causing ice in the bark to melt and move back into the cells. When the sun drops below the horizon, the temperature drops quickly. Ice crystals form within cells, rupturing them and causing death of tissues in that part of the tree.

### INFECTIOUS DISEASES

Fungal, bacterial, viral and mycoplasmic diseases are common to woody plants. Symptoms vary from damage concentrated in a small area of a plant to complete destruction.

The bacterial disease, fireblight (caused by the organism *Erwinia amylovora*), has a number of symptoms, since the disease may be expressed as a potential killer in one of its forms and as a milder malady in another. As a killer disease, the symptoms of fireblight are stem swellings, highly colored dead leaves and cracks in swollen stems that ooze an infectious bacteria. The symptoms of the other form of fireblight are confined to fruiting portions of the tree. Typically, these are dead leaves and mummified fruit which are frequently no larger than a pea.

Fruiting bodies (spores) or spore bearing structures, are symptomatic of most fungal diseases. Virus and mycoplasmic diseases are not as easily verified. However, the mycoplasmic disease, silver leaf (*Stereum purpurea*), has a single identifiable symptom in the appearance of the silvered leaf.

Virologists, no doubt, have a pallette of symptoms on which they too, can rely.

## CONCLUSION

The woody plant is a composite of interrelated systems. Because of this, it is apparent that influences to one part of a plant indirectly affects other parts. The severity of these indirect effects is largely determined by the time of the initial influence. Because of this basic complexity, some knowledge of the systems involved make the management of the woody plant a more rational process.

This lesson has emphasized the need for sound management of woody ornamentals based on a knowledge of plant growth patterns and the expected response of the plant to treatment.

Woody ornamentals are important elements in the landscape. However, they must be chosen carefully and used wisely to avoid the array of problems to which most are subject. Fortunately, selection and use of woody plants is made easier because some woody plants have fewer 'warts' than others.

## SELF CHECK *QUIZ*

1. With woody plants, growth is of two types: extension and tangential. Discuss the relationship of one to the other in the total annual growth of a woody plant.

2. What general inference, relative to the importing of nursery stock, can be made from the results of the three dogwood clones experiment?

3. What is the importance of a physiological sink to growth and/or development in woody plants?

4. What is the first important physical change to take place in mature plant tissues as cold hardening proceeds? What phenomenon occurs as a result of this change?

5. In order to minimize problems that could occur later, list four things upon which woody plant selection might be based.

6. What are the three levels of vegetation that can be used in designing a landscape?

7. What are the reasons for (a) pruning to a lateral, and (b) heading back?

## THE LIMITS TO WOODY PLANT SURVIVAL By R.H. Knowles
*From Woody Ornamentals for the Prairie Provinces*

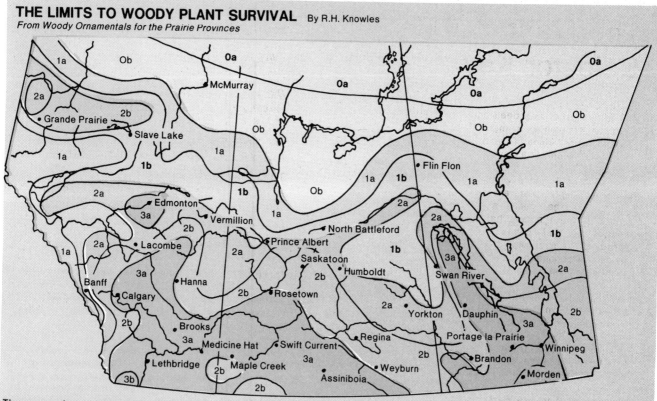

The map shown here indicates, in a relative way, the range of growing conditions to which woody plants will be exposed in the Prairie Provinces. The zones delineated are not governed simply by winter isotherms, but rather by a number of factors which may be identified within each zone. These operate collectively to impose the limits to winter survival.

If there is one factor that affects the survival of woody plants in this part of Canada more than any other, it would have to be the length of the growing season. When this period is not long enough for a plant to complete its annual growth and mature its tissues, the plant will then be incapable of acclimating those tissues to the low temperatures of winter.

The length of growing season strongly limits the variety of plants that can be grown in any zone, but is found most limiting in Zones 1 and 2. Zone 3 is favored by a longer growing period and a wider variety of plants can be successfully grown as a result. However low rainfall and greater exposure to the elements place some additional limitations on the growing of woody plants in this zone and those not capable of tolerating these do not survive. On the other hand, there will be

areas, in Zone 3, with favorable microclimates, that will sustain a larger than average variety of plants because of the protection factor.

In some zones, particularly the southern portion of Zones 2 and 3, soil conditions have an important limiting role. In these areas the lime content is frequently high enough to cause iron salts to be insoluble and thus unavailable to the plant. When plants are exposed to such conditions, chlorophyll, the green coloring matter of leaves, is suppressed and the plants are subject to stress, loss of vigor, and if the condition is not corrected, eventually death.

The effects of winter conditions on woody plants may be manifested in several ways. When the growing season is obviously too short to permit full maturation, the amount of winter injury will vary from tip-killing (loss of a few inches of the previous year's growth) to complete killing of the plant. Plants that tip-kill are obviously growing just beyond their region of adaptation. Sometimes, however, certain factors will make it possible to grow plants successfully beyond their region of adaptation by contributing the means whereby the plant gains the necessary time to mature, e.g. large cities often generate enough heat to ward off the

danger of fall frosts and may thereby effectively extend the growing season within their area of influence. However, for that group of plants that kill out completely after a normal winter we can be sure that no alteration of climate, cultural practice, or technology is going to make it possible for such plants to mature their tissue in the time available to them.

There is also one other facet to the winter survival of woody plants, one directly connected with the tolerance of already matured plants to low temperature. Plants that have achieved annual maturity will not generally be injured by temperatures within the range of 0 to -25°C however with some, injury to such things as flower buds and roots may be noted when temperatures exceed -40°C. With such plants snow cover is very important during periods of low temperature. Those plant parts that are beneath the snow line will generally survive with roots and flower buds intact.

In the Prairie Region, the southern parts of Zone 2b and 3a, particularly in Alberta and Saskatchewan, are within the influence of the Chinook winds. The Chinook seldom blows without completely eliminating the protective snow cover.

# The Plant Selector Key

The following key has been designed to help in the selection of plants. It makes no attempt to be specific, nevertheless, it can be helpful to the person looking for a plant for a particular situation.

The listing of a genus within a particular category does not imply that all species and varieties belonging to that genus show the characteristics referred. Rather it means that one or more species or varieties of that genus will have the desired character. The user should employ the Selector Key only as a directional guide to the part of the text that describes a plant or plants that may suit their need.

It will be noted that the genus *Berberis* appears in various places in the Plant Selector Key. This may alarm some people since it is well known that certain members of the genus have been black-listed by Agriculture Canada. These species are the alternate hosts for the disease 'stem rust of wheat', *Buccenia graminis*.

It is not illegal to use *Berberis aquifolium*, *Berberis circumserrata* and *Berberis koreana* for landscape purposes.

## Trees

### Conifers
#### High-headed at maturity
*Larix, Pinus, Pseudotsuga*

#### With branches to the ground at maturity
*Abies, Juniperus, Larix, Picea, Taxus, Thuja*
50 feet
*Picea, Larix*
30 feet
*Abies, Taxus*
20 feet
*Juniperous, Thuja*

### Broad-leaved deciduous
#### High-headed at maturity
*Acer, Betula, Celtis, Fraxinus, Juglans, Populus, Prunus, Quercus, Ulmus.*

With good fall color
*Acer, Betula, Celtis, Fraxinus, Populus, Quercus.*

#### Low-headed
*Acer, Aesculus, Alnus, Amelanchier, Betula, Cornus, Crataegus, Elaeagnus, Malus, Ostrya, Populus, Prunus, Pyrus, Salix, Shepherdia, Sorbus, Syringa, Tilia.*

With conspicuous flowers
*Aesculus, Amelanchier, Cornus, Crataegus, Malus, Prunus, Pyrus, Sorbus, Syringa, Tilia.*

With good fall color
*Acer, Aesculus, Amelanchier, Betula, Sorbus.*

Sometimes multi-stemmed
*Alnus, Amelanchier, Betula, Malus, Prunus, Salix, Sorbus, Syringa.*

With good bark color
*Betula, Prunus, Salix.*

## Shrubs

### Conifers
#### Low spreading
*Abies, Juniperus, Picea, Taxus.*

Low globe shape
*Juniperus, Pinus, Thuja.*

Columnar
*Juniperus, Thuja.*

Pyramidal
*Juniperus, Thuja.*

With foliage other than green
*Juniperus.*

### Broad-leaved
#### Shrubs up to 2 feet
*Amorpha, Chaenomeles, Cornus, Cotoneaster, Daphne, Euonymus, Genista, Lonicera, Berberis Paxistima, Potentilla, Prunus, Rosa, Spiraea, Viburnum.*

With conspicuous flowers
*Amorpha, Chaenomeles, Daphne, Genista, Berberis , Potentilla, Rosa, Spiraea.*

With attractive fruit
*Cotoneaster, Euonymus, Berberis , Rosa.*

With good fall color
*Cotoneaster, Euonymus.*

### Shrubs 2 to 4 feet
Amorpha, Berberis, Caragana, Clematis, Cornus, Daphne, Euonymus, Hydrangea, Lonicera, Mahonia, Ostryopsis, Physocarpus, Potentilla, Prunus, Rhamnus, Rhus, Rosa, Sambucus, Shepherdia, Spiraea, Viburnum.

#### With conspicuous flowers
Amorpha, Caragana, Clematis, Cornus, Daphne, Hydrangea, Lonicera, Mahonia, Physocarpus, Potentilla, Prunus, Rosa, Spirea, Viburnum.

#### With attractive fruit
Berberis, Cornus, Daphne, Euonymus, Lonicera, Mahonia, Physocarpus, Rosa, Shepherdia, Viburnum.

#### With good fall color
Berberis, Cornus, Euonymus, Ostryopsis, Physocarpus, Rhus, Viburnum.

#### With foliage color other than green
Berberis, Cornus.

### Shrubs between 4 and 6 feet
Amorpha, Berberis, Caragana, Cornus, Corylus, Elaeagnus, Euonymus, Forsythia, Hydrangea, Holodiscus, Lonicera, Oplopanax, Philadelphus, Physocarpus, Prinsepia, Prunus, Rhamnus, Rhus, Ribes, Rosa, Salix, Sambucus, Shepherdia, Sibiraea, Spiraea, Syringa, Viburnum.

#### With conspicuous flowers
Amorpha, Berberis, Caragana, Cornus, Forsythia, Hydrangea, Holodiscus, Lonicera, Philadelphus, Physocarpus, Prunus, Ribes, Rosa, Sibiraea, Spiraea, Syringa, Viburnum.

#### With attractive fruit
Berberis, Cornus, Elaeagnus, Euonymus, Lonicera, Oplopanax, Physocarpus, Rhus, Rosa, Shepherdia, Viburnum.

#### With good fall color
Berberis, Cornus, Euonymus, Rhus, Viburnum.

#### With leaves other than green
Berberis, Cornus, Elaeagnus, Rosa.

### Shrubs over 6 feet
Acanthopanax, Acer, Amelanchier, Caragana, Cornus, Cotoneaster, Euonymus, Halimodendron, Hippophae, Lonicera, Lycium, Philadelphus, Physocarpus, Prunus, Rhamnus, Ribes, Rhus, Rosa, Salix, Sambucus, Shepherdia, Sorbaria, Sorbus, Syringa, Tamarix, Viburnum.

#### With conspicuous flowers
Amelanchier, Caragana, Lonicera, Philadelphus, Physocarpus, Prunus, Ribes, Rosa, Sambucus, Sorbaria, Sorbus, Syringa, Tamarix, Viburnum.

#### With attractive fruit
Acanthopanax, Hippophae, Lonicera, Physocarpus, Rhus, Rosa, Shepherdia, Sorbus, Viburnum.

#### With good fall color
Acer, Amelanchier, Cornus, Cotoneaster, Euonymus, Sorbus, Syringa, Viburnum.

#### With leaves other than green
Physocarpus, Prunus, Salix, Shepherdia.

## Plants for special purposes

### Trimmed Hedges
Acer Negundo, Caragana arborescens, Caragana pygmaea, Cotoneaster lucida, Malus niedswetskiana Leslie, Potentilla fruticosa, Prinsepia, Prunus virginiana, Ribes alpinum, Spiraea bumalda Anthony Waterer.

### Untrimmed Hedges
Cornus alba sibirica. Lonicera Maximowiczii sacha-linensis, Rosa X Therese Bugnet, Rosa Betty Bland, Syringa Meyeri, Syringa Prestoniae.

### Groundcovers
Arctostaphylos, Cornus, Cotoneaster, Daphne, Euonymus, Genista, Juniperus, Mahonia, Pachysandra, Paxistima, Polygonum, Potentilla, Salix.

### For High Lime Soils
Caragana, Eleagnus, Halimodendron, Hippophae, Juniperus, Picea, Potentilla, Rosa spinosissima, Rhamnus, Rhus, Shepherdia, Syringa, Tamarix.

## Plants with bad habits*

Aesculus—fruit drop
Eleagnus—winter injury
Fraxinus—fruit on femaie trees
Populus—fluff from female trees
Rhus glabra—suckering habit
Rhus typhina—suckering habit
Ulmus pumila—fruit drop, deciduous twigs and late leaf drop.

*Other than insect and disease problems.

Carpenter, P.L., T.D. Walker and F. Lanphear. *Plants in the Landscape*. San Francisco: W.H. Freeman and Co., 1975.

A well illustrated, broad treatise dealing with the horticultural side of landscape architecture. A good book for the landscape contractor.

Davidson, H. and R. Mecklenburg. *Nursery Management*. Englewood Cliffs, New Jersey: Prentice-Hall Inc., 1981.

The definitive work on nursery management.

Harris, R.W. *Arboriculture*. Englewood Cliffs, New Jersey: Prentice-Hall Inc., 1983.

A most comprehensive and up-to-date book on the care and management of trees and shrubs.

Janick, J. *Horticultural Science*. San Francisco: W.H. Freeman and Co., 1972.

An excellent basic text dealing with the whole field of horticulture and the science behind it.

Knowles, R.H. *Woody Ornamentals for the Prairie Provinces*. Edmonton: University of Alberta Bulletin 58, 1975.

An illustrated compendium of woody plants hardy in the region.

Luckwill, L. *Growth Regulators in Crop Production*. London: Edward Arnold, 1981.

A very fine book on the use of growth regulators by one of the foremost authorities in the field.

Luckwill, L. and C.V. Cutting, eds. *Physiology of Tree Crops*. London: Academic Press, 1970.*

A number of excellent papers on a wide variety of topics given at the 2nd Long Ashton symposium.

Shigo, A.L. "Tree Decay in Our Urban Forests" *Plant Disease*, 66(9): 763-768, 1982.

An interesting paper dealing with current thinking on the subject of pruning practises as they relate to wound healing.

Tucker, Stuart C. *Pruning in Alberta*. Alberta: Agdex 270/24-1, 1984.

Weiser, C.J. "Cold Resistance and Acclimation in Woody Plants" Hort Science, 5(5): 403-410, 1970.

An excellent review paper.

## SELF CHECK ANSWERS

1. Extension growth begins at the end of dormancy quiescence. Because growing points (buds) are the prime physiological sinks at this time, extension growth takes precedence over all other forms of growth. The formation of a terminal bud in mid-summer indicates the end of extension growth. When the terminal bud has been laid down, nutrients from the soil and metabolites produced by the plants can be translocated to other growth sites. Some of these materials will be used for tangential growth of stems and the growth of roots. Prior to this time both had lower priority than extension growth of stems (see GROWTH PATTERNS, page 801).

2. The experiment results point out the fact that when nursery stock comes from regions where the length of growing season is quite different from that of our own, the risk of winter damage to such imports is very real (see GROWTH PATTERNS, page 801).

3. Physiological sinks are important to growth and development in woody plants because they provide a means for a plant to priorize its growth and developmental requirements (see GROWTH PATTERNS, page 801).

4. The first important physical change to take place in mature plant tissues as cold hardening proceeds is an increase in permeability of cell membranes. The phenomenon that occurs as a result of this change is the movement of free water out of the cells and into intercellular spaces (see GROWTH PATTERNS, page 801).

5. Four things upon which woody plant selection might be based are:

   a. hardiness

   b. compatibility

   c. susceptibility to insect pests

   d. susceptibility to diseases (see SELECTING WOODY ORNAMENTALS, page 805)

6. The three levels of vegetation are:

   a. that above eye level

   b. the shrub layer that exists below eye level,

   c. the vegetation providing cover on the ground (see PLANTING DESIGN, page 808).

7. a. Pruning to a lateral is done primarily to direct growth, that is, in the direction of the lateral.

   b. Heading back is done for two reasons: first, to shorten a stem or branch and, second, to encourage branching from lateral buds (see PRUNING TREES, page 814).

**abscisic acid** - naturally occurring plant growth regulator with growth inhibiting properties.

**adventitious shoot** - shoot that has arisen from a secondary site of activity rather than a primary site (like a bud).

**collar rot** - condition of deterioration occurring at the base of a tree trunk when the surface of the soil at the base of the tree is lower than the soil farther from the trunk. Rot is fostered by excess moisture coming in contact with the tree trunk.

**cytokinin** - naturally occurring plant growth regulator that plays a major role in cell division.

**distal end** - end farthest from the source (i.e., the tip of a plant shoot).

**dormancy quiescence** - inactive plant state that prevails following the completion of dormancy rest until growing conditions return.

**dormancy rest** - profoundly inactive state displayed by a plant during late fall and early winter. The condition is overcome following exposure to a discrete number of hours of critical low temperature. During dormancy rest, no external growth stimulus can cause active growth.

**desiccation injury** - type of injury commonly seen on broadleaved evergreens and conifers due to the effect of low temperatures, drying winds and bright sunshine.

**endogenous growth regulator** - growth regulator that is produced naturally by the plant.

**epinasty** - twisting of an actively growing shoot, generally in response to some external stimulus.

**gibberellin** - naturally occurring growth regulator that promotes stem elongation.

**graft-union** - point of union occurring when a shoot of one plant is grafted to the stem or root of another.

**growth regulator** - chemical substance that affects growth and development of plants.

**heading back** - type of pruning cut that is confined to stems of plants where the distal portion of the stem is removed or headed back to a lateral bud.

**incipient wilting** - first symptoms of wilting.

**increment borer** - instrument used for taking a horizontal core of tissue from a tree trunk to measure tangential growth.

**interveinal chlorosis** - condition confined to leaves of plants, the symptom of which is failure of leaves to produce chlorophyll in the area between veins.

**lateral bud** - bud located on the side of a shoot rather than at the terminal end.

**leader** - leading shoot at the top of a spruce tree; in young deciduous trees, the leader is the main stem.

**lime-induced chlorosis** - failure of leaves of broadleaved plants to produce chlorophyll when the amount of free-lime in the soil is sufficient to decrease soil acidity to the point where the availability of iron is interfered with.

**maturity** - annual state reached by woody plants that must be achieved before tissues can be cold hardened for winter.

**mycoplasmic disease** - disease caused by a strange group of organisms that differ from bacteria, fungi and viruses even though they may have characteristics common with each.

**phenoxy herbicide** - herbicide with auxin-like properties capable of killing most broadleaved plants.

**photoreceptive pigment** - pigment such as phytochrome which is known to initiate developmental changes in plants when significant alteration in the length of day takes place.

**physiological sink** - site of activity in a plant to which a significant portion of available plant nutrients and certain growth regulators are attracted.

**profound rest** - dormancy rest.

**scaffold branches** - main structural lateral branches of a tree, generally distributed around the tree so that no two interfere with one another, either vertically or horizontally.

**site aspect** - main direction to which a site is oriented to light.

**strong apical dominance** - form expressed by the leading shoot of a tree whereby all currently produced buds below the tip remain dormant until the following year.

**summer dormancy** - dormant condition which occurs in buds following the end of extension growth. As time goes on, the dormant conditions deepen until the condition of dormancy rest has been fully achieved.

**super-cooling** - process whereby the temperature of water in plant tissue can go several degrees below the freezing point without changing state.

**suckering** - characteristic of some plants to produce new growth from adventitious buds.

**tangential growth** - increase in diameter of a stem.

**terminal bud** - bud formed at the end of a shoot that normally heralds the end of extension growth for the season.

**texture** - fineness or coarseness of a plant, usually due to foliage and twigs.

**variegated** - of two distinct colors in combination.

**vegetative propagation** - reproduction of a plant from vegetative parts of the parent.

**weak apical dominance** - form expressed by the leading shoot of a tree wherein the buds of the current year grow and produce short lateral shoots.

# HERBACEOUS ORNAMENTALS

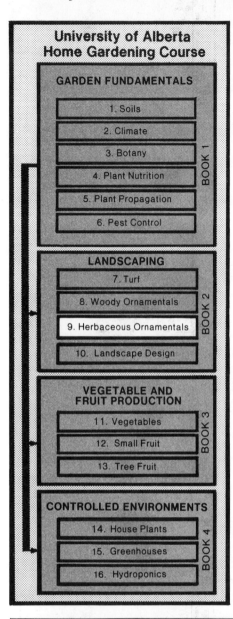

**University of Alberta Home Gardening Course**

**GARDEN FUNDAMENTALS**
- 1. Soils
- 2. Climate
- 3. Botany
- 4. Plant Nutrition
- 5. Plant Propagation
- 6. Pest Control

BOOK 1

**LANDSCAPING**
- 7. Turf
- 8. Woody Ornamentals
- 9. Herbaceous Ornamentals
- 10. Landscape Design

BOOK 2

**VEGETABLE AND FRUIT PRODUCTION**
- 11. Vegetables
- 12. Small Fruit
- 13. Tree Fruit

BOOK 3

**CONTROLLED ENVIRONMENTS**
- 14. House Plants
- 15. Greenhouses
- 16. Hydroponics

BOOK 4

# SELF-STUDY LESSON FEATURES

Self-study is an educational approach which allows you to study a subject where and when you want. The course is designed to allow students to study the course material efficiently and incorporates the following features.

**OBJECTIVES** — are found at the beginning of each lesson and allow you to determine what you can expect to learn in the lesson.

**LESSON MATERIAL** — is logically organized and broken down into fundamental components by ordered headings to assist you to comprehend the subject.

**REFERENCING** — between lessons and within lessons allows you to integrate course material.

The last two digits of the page number identify the page and the digits preceding these identify the lesson number (eg., 107: Lesson 1, page 7 or 1227: Lesson 12, page 27).

Referencing:

> sections within the same lesson (eg., see OSMOSIS)

> sections in other lessons (eg., see Botany lesson, OSMOSIS)

> figures and tables (eg., see Figure 7-3)

**FIGURES AND TABLES** — are found in abundance throughout the lessons and are designed to convey useful information in an easy to understand form.

**SIDEBARS** — are those areas in the lesson which are boxed and toned. They present information supplementary to the core content of the lesson.

**PRACTICAL PROJECTS** — are integrated within the lesson material and are included to allow you to apply principles and practices.

**SELF-CHECK QUIZ** — is provided at the end of each lesson and allows you to test your comprehension of the lesson material. Answers to the questions and references to the sections dealing with the questions are provided in the answer section. You should review any questions that you are unable to answer.

**GLOSSARY** — is provided at the end of each lesson and alphabetically lists the definitions of key concepts and terms.

**RESOURCE MATERIALS** — are provided at the end of each lesson and comprise a list of recommended learning materials for further study of the subject. Also included are author's comments on the potential application of each publication.

**INDEX** — alphabetically lists useful topics and their location within the lesson.

## THE PRODUCTION TEAM

Managing Editor ................................................... Thom Shaw
Editor ............................................................. Frank Procter
Production Coordinator ..................................... Kevin Hanson
Graphic Artists ...................................................... Lisa Marsh
Carol Powers
Melanie Eastley Harbourne
Data Entry ..................................................... Joan Geisterfer

Published by the University of Alberta
Faculty of Extension Corbett Hall
Edmonton, Alberta, T6G 2G4

After completing this lesson, the student should be able to:

1. define 'herbaceous ornamental' and identify the plants included in the category.
2. identify the criteria for selecting plant material.
3. define the term 'bedding plant'.
4. develop a plan for using herbaceous ornamentals most effectively.
5. identify and implement a plan for preparing and maintaining flower beds and borders.
6. select the propagation method best suited to various plants and identify the criteria for selection.

## TABLE OF CONTENTS

## LIST OF FIGURES AND TABLES

# INTRODUCTION

Herbaceous ornamentals refers to all those non-woody plants that can be used attractively in the landscape. Some of the plants included in this category develop fairly woody stems by the end of each growing season, but are either killed back or cut back to ground level each winter.

Herbaceous plants may be annual, biennial or perennial in their growth habit (see Botany lesson, Table 3-2). **Annuals** are those which grow from seed, produce flowers and seeds during the growing season, then die, regardless of whether or not the environmental conditions continue to be favorable for growth. The life of these plants can be extended by preventing seed set, either by removing faded flowers or selecting clones or hybrids that are genetically sterile.

**Biennials**, by definition, are those plants which take two years to complete their life cycle. During the first growing season, they produce only vegetative growth, usually a rosette of leaves and (often) a storage organ, such as a fleshy taproot. If they are hardy enough to survive the winter, they produce flowers and seeds during the second year, then die. A few popular biennial flowers, such as hollyhock and sweet William, often survive as perennials for a few years. There are also selections available that flower from seed during the first season and can be used as bedding plants.

**Perennials** are those herbaceous plants that, once established, continue to produce new top growth and flowers each season. This growth can come from a hardy perennial crown and root system, an underground bulb, or other storage organ. Those that produce bulbs, such as tulips, daffodils and lilies, are often dealt with as a separate group of herbaceous perennials. Included in this grouping are both hardy and tender bulbs. Tender bulbs are those that require lifting and special storage to bring them through the winter.

Many of the plants grown as annuals or bedding plants are true annuals. Others are perennials or modified biennials that flower from seed the first year, but are too tender to survive our winters. In all cases, these plants survive only one season and new plants must be started each year. For this reason, the term 'bedding plants' is a more appropriate reference for this category of herbaceous ornamentals than is 'annual flowers'.

# USES IN THE LANDSCAPE

Herbaceous ornamentals, because of their limited season as functional landscape plants, are usually of secondary importance to landscape planners. Woody plants (both evergreen and deciduous) are much more useful in defining space relationships and tying the structural elements on a given site to the natural setting (see Woody Ornamentals lesson, PLANTING DESIGN). Herbaceous ornamentals serve more as 'cosmetics' that, when used carefully, can enhance the landscape features and add color and interest during the growing season.

**Bedding plants** are particularly useful for mass plantings of solid, brilliant colors in both beds and borders (see Figure 9-1). Their use should be mainly confined to the outdoor living area of the yard, where their beauty can be enjoyed from the patio, deck or family room picture window. Masses of solid color are usually more effective than mixed colors. This is not to say that masses of different colors cannot be used together.

Color planning, however, is influenced by light and shadow, climate and humidity. Therefore, color theories (which apply where lighting is controlled) must be modified. Nonetheless, it is possible to use both complementary and analagous colors for harmonious results.

Suggested combinations, according to the Birren system for outdoor color use are included as a sidebar in this lesson.

Hardy perennials are useful for large border plantings (see Figure 9-2). If these borders are 2-3 m (about 6-10 ft) in depth and 15 m or more (50+ ft) in length, a variety of heights covering a wide range of hardy perennials can be used (from very low ground covers to plants 2 m or 6 ft high). With proper planning, such a border can be aesthetic as well as interesting from early spring to late fall each year. Annual flower plantings tend to remain quite static throughout the summer season. Perennial plantings, on the other hand, constantly change as different kinds progressively come into bloom, then fade away as the season advances.

Mixed borders can be an attractive garden feature and may be more practical than a purely herbaceous perennial border for the average city lot. Such a border may be a combination of

## Figure 9-1
## MASS PLANTING OF HERBACEOUS ORNAMENTALS

The Birren system for outdoor color uses six basic colors which are listed here in a descending order of the amount of light reflected from each (a value scale):

White 80%
Yellow 55%
Green 35%
Red 25%
Blue 20%
Black 0%

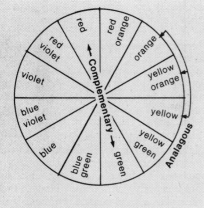

Masses of high value color are not too effective in full sunlight - they tend to produce glare. For those borders located in strong sunlight, lower values should predominate. In shady borders, colors of high value can be used more freely. In deep shade, colors which possess a high degree of luminosity (orange and scarlet) are more satisfactory than yellow or white in spite of the fact that both yellow and white have higher color values.

Flower colors are seldom pure. Usually they are tints, shades or tones of the pure color or hue.

Tints are derived from yellow, green, red, or blue by the addition of white.

Shades of these colors are obtained by the addition of black.

Tones result from the addition of grey.

In each case (tint, shade or tone), as a measure of white, black or grey is added to a pure color, that color decreases in strength, or purity. This decrease is said to be a decrease in **chroma**.

In spite of the fact that light, climate and humidity play an important part in the way colors can be arranged in the landscape, it is still possible to use either complementary or analagous colors (those which adjoin one another in the color circle) for harmonious results.

## SUGGESTED COMBINATIONS

### BLUE

1. With scarlet and buff.
2. With white and yellow.
3. With orange and scarlet.
4. With various chromas of blue.
5. With yellow or orange of the same chroma (but use sparingly).

### VIOLET, PURPLE and MAGENTA
(These colors lie between red and blue).

1. Those hues nearer blue - group together or use with tints and shades of blue.
2. Those hues nearer red - group together or use with tints or shades of red.
3. Violet or purple should be used with plenty of yellow or yellow-green foliage.
4. Violet and purple can be contrasted with whites and yellows of equal chroma.

### RED and SCARLET

1. With dense green backgrounds.
2. For sharp contrast, with white or clear blue.
3. With analagous hues, red-violet and red-orange.

### PINK (Tint of Red)

1. Will gain more strength if interspersed with white.
2. Goes well with other colors of the same chroma.

### ORANGE

1. With darker colors - red, browns and bronzes.
2. With turquoise blue (complement).
3. With purple flowers and bright green foliage (split complement).
4. With creamy white or yellow.

### YELLOW

1. With blue of equal chroma.
2. With white (but use sparingly).
3. Small amounts will liven up cold, heavy compositions.

### WHITE

1. Frequently turns out to be a tint of one color or another. If so, use with other chromas of same color, or as a contrast with that color's complement.
2. If interspersed among low value colors, it softens them.
3. If interspersed among high value colors, it strengthens them.

### GREENS

There are a great many foliage greens varying from deep, dull green through light grey-green, blue and yellow-green to the darkest of the evergreens. Foliage color must be secondary to flower colors and be carefully chosen to intensify the effect of anything placed in front of it. Thus, yellow-green or blue-green foliage can spoil the effect of a carefully arranged harmony that will not be at its best if yellow or blue is included.

### GREY and SILVERY FOLIAGE

They can be used to lighten heavy or monotonous masses of dark green and, at the same time, heighten the effect of distance. They can also bring conflictiing colors into pleasing relationships. Ineffective when dotted among bright colors, but effective in similar surroundings if used in mass. Most effective with light-tinted flowers.

## Figure 9-2
## PERENNIAL BORDER

## Figure 9-3
## ANNUALS AS SHRUBS AND HEDGES

woody shrubs and perennials, perennials and annuals, or a mixture of shrubs, perennials and annuals. If early spring flowering bulbs are included in a perennial planting, it is advisable to replace them with bedding plants as the bulb foliage dies back after flowering.

Although woody plants are preferable to herbaceous ones for foundation plantings, one may not wish to spend the money required for shrubs, especially for summer homes or cottages that are closed-up for the winter. Tall, massive perennials, such as bleeding heart or peony, and annuals such as castor bean and kochia, can serve well as seasonal shrubs. Some can even be used to provide summer hedges (see Figure 9-3). Some herbaceous ornamentals are very useful as accent plants in a foundation planting of woody material. Small groupings of bedding begonias or tuberous begonias, for instance, with evergreen shrubs as a backdrop, can be very striking and require a minimum of bedding plants.

Planters and hanging baskets of various kinds and sizes are very useful containers for bedding plants. Usually, a combination of upright plants and trailing or cascading types work well in most types of containers. It is not recommended to use perennials or woody plants in planters unless the

containers are large and well insulated against severe winter temperatures.

Annual vines, such as scarlet runner bean, canary creeper and morning glory, can be useful to cover bare or uninteresting walls, old stumps, gazebos, or trellises. Annual vines can also be useful for covering rough or unsightly areas of ground (or compost piles, etc.). Hardy perennial and woody vines **(lianas)** however, may be more effective cover plants. Some examples are clematis, Virginia creeper and the Dropmore scarlet honeysuckle.

## CULTURE

### SELECTION AND PLANNING

The Alberta Horticultural Guide should be used to select those bedding plants and perennials that perform well in a specific location and are hardy in Alberta. Those sections pertinent to this lesson are reprinted (as a sidebar) through permission of Alberta Agriculture.

Three factors must be considered when planning for perennials: **color, height** and **season of bloom**. The object is to have a flower garden which is interesting and colorful from spring to fall. In order

to achieve this, it is best to prepare detailed plans. On a sheet of graph paper, an outline drawing of the property can be made (to scale) showing the position of permanent structures and the garden beds and borders to be developed. It may be desirable to make larger diagrams of the major planting areas, particularly a perennial border if one is to be included. The border can be outlined to scale on the graph paper and sheets of tracing paper or onion skin used as overlays to develop appropriate height zones and color zones. Figure 9-4 demonstrates a method for determining the placement of herbaceous ornamentals within a border. The plan identifies the areas to be developed through considerations of the height and color of plants.

Combine the height-color distribution plan with one which considers the seasonal distribution of flowers (see Figure 9-5). Figure 9-5A identifies the placement of perennials that bloom in fall. The placement of summer flowering perennials is identified in Figure 9-5B and the placement of spring flowering perennials is identified in Figure 9-5C. The method for designing a seasonal distribution plan for a perennial border is detailed below.

To make sure of an attractive combination of flowers blooming in a perennial border through spring, summer and fall, sketch the locations of plants on sheets of tracing paper laid over an outline of the bed. If you use the height - color distribution plan as the outline (Figure 9-4), your final plan will include height-color distribution as well. On the first sheet of tracing paper, select tall **fall**-blooming varieties; draw these in as clumps (light green) spaced along the back. Then add complementary fall plants (also indicated in light green), placing medium-sized ones in the center and short ones towards the front (see Figure 9-5A).

On a second sheet of tracing paper laid over the first, plan your **summer** blooms. Since most plants that flower in summer are medium-sized, select these first as your main display; draw these in as clumps, concentrating them in the center of the bed and locating the plants (indicated in medium green) in some of the open areas not already occupied by fall flowers. Then place in front and back, a few tall and short summer-blooming varieties whose colors will complement the flowers you have chosen for the center.

On a third sheet of tracing paper laid over the other two, plan your **spring**-blooming plants (dark green) in the remaining spaces (see Figure 9-5C). As most spring perennials are short, they naturally look best in the front of the bed. Some medium-sized and tall

spring-flowering plants should be interspersed in the center and back. Now you can trace the outlines of your fall and summer displays through to the top sheet. If your seasonal distribution plan was created in conjunction with the height-color distribution plan, you are ready to select and determine perennial border plants that reflect height-color-season of bloom considerations.

Any gaps on the finalized plan can be filled with bulbs or annuals in desired quantities. Although height must be taken into consideration to prevent taller plants from hiding shorter ones, there should not be a rigid demarcation of height. A gentle blending of the planned height zones will help to prevent monotony. Once this has been achieved, specific plants can be chosen (using reference books and catalogues) for each designated height-color area and seasonal distribution area. For convenience at planting time, include a legend in the margin of the plan that details the mature spread of the plant and the time and length of its blooming period.

Considerable planning is required for perennnial flower beds and borders. The majority of perennials have a definite (limited) season of bloom. If this is not taken into consideration, succession of bloom will not be achieved and the

garden will not be alive with bloom throughout the season.

To achieve a **continuous display of blooms**, it is necessary to make the border more than one row deep. The border should be at least 1.5 m (5 ft) deep or wide. From the standpoint of maintenance, a border wider than 3 m (10 ft) is cumbersome. The length of a border can be determined by the space available. For most residential lots, the border length is not likely to exceed 20 m (65 ft).

The **shape** of the perennial border may be a strict and formal rectangle or, possibly, an L shaped combination of two rectangles. A natural, gently curved edge makes the planting appear less formal and adds interest by providing a variation in the width of the border. It also allows for a variation in the number of height zones along its length. A scalloped or patterned edge not only detracts from the beauty of the flowers but can make lawn edge maintenance more difficult. It is easier to use a lawn mower along a straight or gently curved edge than along sharply cornered edges. A row of flat bricks laid at the interface of the lawn and border can further reduce the requirement for trimming.

In order to produce a sense of **balance** in the border, it is best to limit the height of the tallest plants to approximately one half the width of the border. Edging

## Figure 9-4
## PLANNING A PERENNIAL BORDER FOR COLOR-HEIGHT DISTRIBUTION OF FLOWERS

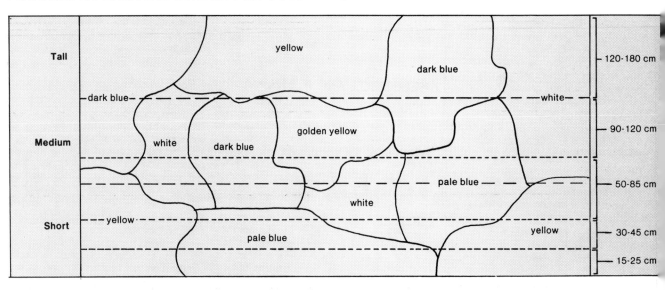

Figure 9-5
PLANNING A PERENNIAL BORDER FOR SEASONAL DISTRIBUTION OF FLOWERS

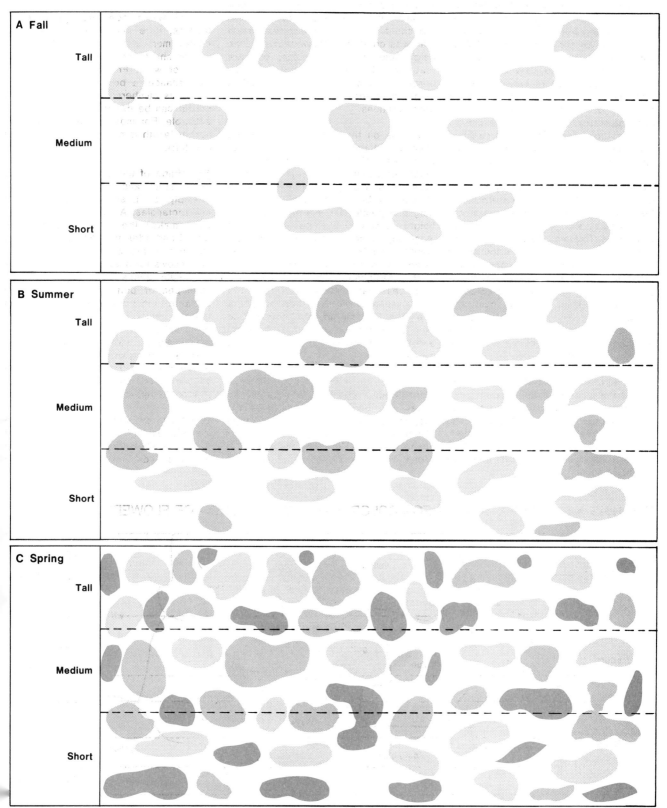

A Fall
Tall
Medium
Short

B Summer
Tall
Medium
Short

C Spring
Tall
Medium
Short

plants are the shortest in a well planned border and should provide a good ground cover that remains attractive throughout the season. Bedding plants may be used as edging material to achieve an attractive continuity to the front of the border, particularly if early spring flowering bulbs are used (i.e., those which require replacement once their flowers and foliage fade).

To create **unity**, color groups should be repeated at regular intervals throughout the border. It is best to plant in groups that imitate the shape of the border (rectangles for a strictly rectangular border, soft curved areas for a naturalistic or informal border). More than one type of plant is used in any one color zone to provide blooms in succession. This means that color zones will overlap height zones. Furthermore, not only should these color zones repeat throughout the border, but the actual kinds of plants should repeat as well, although to a lesser extent.

To assist in the selection of hardy perennials, it is necessary to use reference material that describes their height, spread, color and season of bloom. It is best to select six to ten basic perennials that bloom successively throughout the season and can be used in the various height and color zones of your plan (see Table 9-1). Others that may be less dependable (or of more limited season of bloom) can then be chosen to round out the planting. A well planned border of relatively few, well-chosen, dependable kinds, appropriately repeated throughout the length of the border, are more attractive than a hodge-podge of many kinds of different plants. Furthermore, plants provide the best effect when planted in groups of three or more. Exceptions are large, massive plants, such as the peony and common bleeding heart, which are best maintained as individual plants within the border.

Bedding plants are very versatile and can be used in mass plantings of solid color in beds or borders of various dimensions (see USES IN THE LANDSCAPE). They are also well adapted to growing in planters and hanging baskets. The benefit of using bedding plants is that a different combination of plants and color schemes can be used each year. Depending on the color of the house, garage, fence or

other permanent features of the yard, choice of color schemes for the garden may be somewhat restricted. In any event, bedding plants should be chosen with care and considerable thought given to the color of the blooms and the mature height of the plants.

## LOCATION EXPOSURE

The majority of both annuals and perennials perform best in full sun. If possible, place flower beds where sunlight is received for at least six hours a day. A west exposure is ideal for many plants but some, such as begonias and patience plants, can wilt and scorch in the heat of the late afternoon sun. Air should freely circulate around the plants to reduce disease problems. A solid colored background, such as a wall, fence, shrub or hedge planting, is desirable for concentrating attention on the flowers and, perhaps, to provide wind protection. However, the background must not compete with or limit the availability of light, nutrients or moisture to the plant. If woody plants are used as background material, they should be situated 60-100 cm (24-39 in) from all herbaceous plants (particularly perennials). Bedding plants can be planted a little closer than perennials and successfully compete for water and nutrients because the surface roots of the woody plants will be disturbed and, likely, destroyed in preparing the area for planting the bedding plants each spring. To prevent the penetration of shrub or tree roots into a flower border, a barrier sheet of thin, rigid plastic or galvanized iron can be sunk (60-100 cm (24-39 in) into the soil between the woody and herbaceous material.

Not all herbaceous ornamentals are suited to all garden locations. In general, bedding plants are limited only by availability of moisture and light. Suitability to specific locations, such as partial shade and hot sandy soil, are noted in the section of the Alberta Horticultural Guide reprinted in this lesson.

In areas where the frost free period is short, it is desirable to select annuals and bedding plants that can tolerate light frost. Table 9-2 indicates the tolerance to frost of some common bedding plants. In some instances, plants can be conditioned to withstand

considerable frost by being exposed to low temperatures for several days prior to freezing. Furthermore, plants can often be protected from frost damage by watering them just prior to freezing temperatures and allowing the plants to be covered by a thin coating of ice (see Climate lesson, TEMPERATURE).

## PREPARATON FOR PLANTING

The preparation of a bed for annuals need not be as extensive as for perennials since the bed can be worked annually. However, the better the bed is prepared with deep tillage to produce a well drained, well structured soil, the better the plants will do. Deep spading in the fall, to allow frost action to improve the soil structure, is a recommended practice. Light cultivation in the spring (prior to planting) completes the settling and leveling of the site. All weeds, especially perennial weeds, should be eliminated by either chemical or cultural means before planting annuals or perennials (see Pest Control Lesson, METHODS OF WEED CONTROL and BACKYARD PEST MANAGEMENT).

After weeds have been controlled, soil can be readied for planting. Initial cultivation need penetrate only about 8-10 cm (3-4 in) to loosen the soil. Following this, soil amendments can be added to the surface and incorporated as the soil is further worked. Amendments to incorporate are: a fertilizer high in phosphorus (rates based on the results of soil tests) and about 5 cm (2 in) of peat moss to increase moisture retention. To provide a satisfactory rooting zone, an annual flower bed should be prepared to a minimum depth of 15 cm (6 in) and a perennial flower bed to a minimum of 25-30 cm (10-12 in). A depth of 45 cm (18 in) may be preferable, particularly if the subsoil is hard and drainage is poor.

To do a thorough job of preparing a perennial border, one should remove a narrow strip of topsoil (15 cm or 6 in deep) at one end of the border, then spade up the subsoil area to another 15-30 cm (6-12 in) depth while incorporating peat, fertilizer and, if drainage is poor, perhaps some coarse sand. Once this is accomplished, the adjoining strip of topsoil can be placed on the newly tilled strip of subsoil and the process continued until the entire

Table 9-1

## A SELECTION OF 20 EASY TO GROW, READILY OBTAINABLE, HERBACEOUS PERENNIAL FLOWERS

| SCIENTIFIC NAME | COMMON NAME(S) | HEIGH CM | COLOR | TIME OF FLOWERING | COMMENTS |
|---|---|---|---|---|---|
| *Dianthus deltoides* | Maiden Pink | 25 | red | June | 1. Very hardy<br>2. Good for front of dry sunny border |
| *Allium schoenoprasum* | Chives | 30 | mauve / pink | **June** | 1. Grows anywhere<br>2. Useful for kitchen as well as front of ornamental border |
| *Dicentra eximia (formosa)* | Fernleaf Bleeding Heart | 35 | pink | July onwards | 1. For front of border or rock garden<br>2. Long flowering season |
| *Achillea millefolium* | Common Yarrow | 30-60 | pink | July onwards | 1. A common native of Alberta<br>2. Improved dark pink or red cultivars available |
| *Bergenia crassifolia* | Giant Rockfoil | 45 | pink | May | 1. Tough plant and good ground cover<br>2. Large glossy leaves with red-purple tints in fall |
| *Campanula glomerata* | Clustered Bellflower | 45 | blue | July | 1. Excellent ground cover<br>2. Profusion of dark purple-blue flowers clustered into heads |
| *Chrysanthemum coccineum* | Painted Daisy or Pyrethrum | 45-60 | pink or red | June | 1. Best in well drained sunny location<br>2. Large daisy flower heads with bright yellow centers |
| *Doronicum caucasicum* | Leopard's Bane | 45 | yellow | late May | 1. Valuable for cheerful early flowers<br>2. Easily grown with tidy low foilage |
| *Anthemis tinctoria* | Golden Marguerite | 60 | yellow | July-August | 1. A vigorous spreading plant for a dry place or poor soil<br>2. Valuable for ferny foliage and long flowering season |
| *Chrysanthemum leucanthemum* | Ox-Eye Daisy | 60-100 | white | late June onwards | 1. Tough, commonly grown but invasive daisy<br>2. Useful for its long flowering season |
| *Gaillardia aristata* | Blanket Flower | 60-100 | yellow: yellow / red | June onwards | 1. Native plant with attractive daisy flowers<br>2. Some greatly improved cultivars are available |
| *Iris sibirica* | Siberian Iris | 60-120 | blue | late June | 1. Flowers held well above grassy foliage<br>2. Sword shaped leaves and seed heads make an attractive contrast with other plants |
| *Lychnis chalcedonica* | Maltese Cross | 60-90 | red | July | 1. Stiffly erect plant with dense scarlet flowers<br>2. Popular plant - will grow anywhere |
| *Phalaris arundinaceae* | Ribbon Grass | 60-100 | --- | --- | 1. Grown for its green and creamy white striped leaves<br>2. Typical grass flowers are not showy |
| *Trollius hybridus (T. chinensis or europaeus)* | Globe Flower | 60-100 | yellow | June-July | 1. Excellent garden plant<br>2. Bright shiny globe shaped "buttercup" flowers |
| *Filipendula ulmaria* | Meadow Sweet | 90-130 | white | late July | 1. Large but very attractive plant<br>2. Does well in semi-shade |

Table 9-1 CONT'D

| SCIENTIFIC NAME | COMMON NAME(S) | HEIGHT CM | COLOR | TIME OF FLOWERING | COMMENTS |
|---|---|---|---|---|---|
| *Hemerocallis Hybrids* | Day Lily | 90 | yellow: orange: dark red | July onwards | 1. Excellent hardy plant<br>2. Iris-type leaves |
| *Lythrum* | Loosestrife | 90-180 | pink: red/purple | August | 1. Cultivars available specifically developed for the prairies<br>2. Cultivars include: Morden Pink, Morden Gleam, Morden Rose and Dropmore Purple |
| *Aconitum napellus* | Monks Hood | 120-180 | dark blue | July | 1. A good plant for the back of a border<br>2. Similar to delphinium |
| *Rudbeckia laciniata* | Golden Glow or Cone-Flower | 180 | yellow | July-August | 1. Cultivar 'Golden Glow' most often grown<br>2. Useful at back of a large border |

border is completed. Such deep tillage requires a great deal of effort and time but should ensure a vigorous, long-lived perennial flower bed. Leaving such a deeply disturbed area to settle over winter before planting is a good idea.

## TIME OF PLANTING

Annuals are planted outdoors when the soil has dried sufficiently after the spring thaw to allow cultivation. Temperatures should be high enough to support growth (usually late May to early June). Annuals may be planted directly outdoors as seeds or as transplants (bedding plants). Transplants can be purchased or started from seed by the homeowner in a greenhouse or other warm, well-lighted area. Seeding dates for transplant production in the average home are given in the Alberta Horticultural Guide reprinted in this lesson. Planting the seed too early is the most common mistake made in the production of herbaceous ornamentals. Unless a greenhouse type of environment can be provided (bright light during the day and cool temperatures at night), the seedling growth cannot be controlled and plants become tall and spindly very quickly. Even with judicious pruning and pinching back (see PINCHING AND DISBUDDING), the plants can be ready for hardening off and transplanting to the garden before it is safe to do so. With the use of a greenhouse, one can sow seed earlier and control the growth so that shoots remain short but stocky.

Few annuals are seeded directly in the Alberta garden because the growing season is so short. Exceptions are those which do not transplant well and those that develop to flower in 60 days or less (eg., bachelor button, California poppy, cosmos, godetia, larkspur and Shirley poppy).

Many perennials can be started from seed as well. This is an inexpensive way to propagate large numbers of plants, but is only possible for species and mixed hybrid strains which come **true from seed**. Direct seeding outdoors is recommended. As these are hardy perennials, there is really no need to get a jump on the season. The best time for seeding perennials outdoors depends on the individual plant's germination requirements and rate of growth. Seed of some kinds require chilling before they germinate. Such seed can be planted in the fall rather than the spring or given a chilling treatment prior to planting (see Plant Propagation lesson, COLLECTING SEED and TREATMENTS FOR SEED WITH A HARD SEED COAT AND OTHER BARRIERS TO GERMINATION). Seedlings require thinning or transplanting (pricking out) when they are large enough to handle by the first set of leaves. When the young plants have become well developed, they can be transplanted to their permanent location in the garden. Some kinds, when

Table 9-2
FROST TOLERANCE OF SOME ANNUALS OR BEDDING PLANTS

| WITHSTAND FROST | WITHSTAND LIGHT FROST | NO FROST |
|---|---|---|
| Sweet Alyssum | Phlox | Zinnia |
| Pansy | Stock | Nasturtium |
| Sweet Pea | Lobelia | Salpiglossis |
| California Poppy | Globe Amaranth | Marigold |
| Cornflower | Wallflower | Salvia |
| Snapdragon | Cosmos | Dahlia |
| | Calendula | Begonia |
| | African Daisy | |
| | Verbena | |

seeded in the spring, produce a small flower stalk by early fall of the same year.

Established perennials are usually planted or transplanted in the spring or late summer to early fall. When to plant depends on the growth habit of the perennial and climatic factors. As a general rule, late flowering and less hardy perennials are planted in the spring, whereas early spring flowering perennials are planted in late summer. Cool weather aids root establishment and minimizes watering. In Alberta, planting is usually done in the spring with the following exceptions: iris (plant right after flowering), peony (plant in late summer) and Oriental poppy (plant in August when plant is dormant or inactive).

To reduce wilting and excessive loss of moisture, planting should be done on a cool, overcast day or in the cool of the evening. Holes should be dug that are large enough to accept the roots without crowding. Plants should be set no deeper than 2 cm (about 3/4 in) lower than their original depth before transplanting. The former planting level will be obvious by the soil mark on the stem. Sufficient space should be left between plants to allow for their maximum potential or mature spread. Following planting, firm the soil around the roots to eliminate air pockets and water each plant well. If fertilizer was not incorporated at the time of soil preparation, a fertilizer solution can be used to water-in new transplants. A 'starter solution' is often used (10-52-10 or 10-52-17) at the dilution rate recommended on the package.

For bulbs or similar storage organ plants, the depth of planting varies with the size of the bulb and the kind of plant.

Figure 9-6 gives the recommended planting depths for fall planted hardy 'bulbs'.

## MAINTENANCE

### CULTIVATION
When the soil is dry enough to work and growth has begun, perennial and annual beds should be lightly cultivated to a depth of about 3-5 cm (1-2 in). This will eliminate germinating weed seeds and break up any crusting of the soil surface, thus improving aeration and moisture penetration. Cultivation of this sort should continue on a regular basis throughout the growing season.

### FERTILIZATION
Specific requirements can only be

## Figure 9-6
## PLANTING DEPTHS FOR "BULBS" PLANTED IN THE FALL

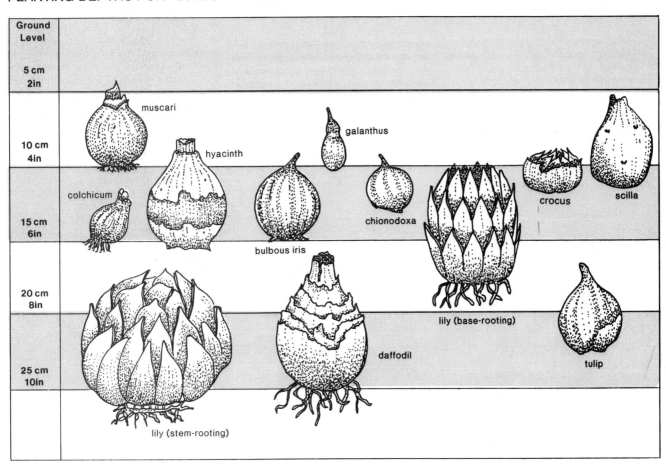

determined if the soil is tested for nutrient content (see Soils Lesson). In general, however, Alberta garden soils tend to be low in phosphorus but contain adequate potassium and calcium. Therefore, higher phosphorus fertilizers, such as 11-48-0 and 10-30-10, are usually good choices for incorporation into both the subsoil (for deep tillage of a proposed perennial border) and the topsoil (for all flower beds). Yearly applications of a complete fertilizer in the ratio of 1:2:1 or 1:3:1 (see Plant Nutrition lesson, INORGANIC FERTILIZERS) should maintain good fertility. The rate of application depends upon the per cent analysis of the fertilizer used and the residual levels in the soil. Periodic soil tests are recommended as a means of monitoring the fertility levels over a span of several years.

Unless the nitrogen level of the soil is extremely low, it is unwise to use those fertilizers recommended for lawns. High nitrogen levels favor vegetative growth and delay maturity, two undesirable aspects for a flower garden (see Plant

Nutrition Lesson, DEFICIENCY AND TOXICITY SYMPTOMS). As a further caution, some lawn fertilizers contain herbicides (weed and feed types) and should never be used on garden areas reserved for flowers or vegetables (see Turf lesson, LAWN FERTILIZERS).

## WATERING
When irrigating the garden, always apply enough water to penetrate to a depth of 15 cm (6 in) — even deeper for deep rooted plants. In order to encourage deep rooting, periodic heavy irrigation is preferable to frequent light waterings. If sufficient water to wet only the top few centimetres of soil is all that is ever applied, the soil below this level will dry out and restrict root growth to the moist surface layer. This makes the plants dependent upon frequent applications of water which, if not forthcoming, cause rapid and severe wilting and even death of the plants.

Applying moisture in the early part of the day allows any wet foliage to dry before temperatures drop at sundown. This can

aid in disease control, especially of mildew and leaf spotting diseases. Because of a shallow and limited root system, annuals require more frequent watering than perennials. Mulches may be used to reduce evaporation, conserve moisture and, therefore, reduce the need for watering, especially for perennials (see Climate lesson, MODIFYING CLIMATIC EFFECTS).

## STAKING
Many of the larger and taller plants require additional support to prevent them from falling over in wind or heavy rain. Staking is a method of providing this additional support. Staking is most frequently required by perennials, but tall, slender annuals may also need to be staked. The stakes used should be inconspicuous and placed while the plants are young. Green colored bamboo or heavy gauge wire rods are usually used. Long twisties or strong, thin twine tied to the stake and loosely looped around individual stems or small groups of stems keep plants upright without appearing strangled or bundled together. Metal rings or hoops, supported on metal wire legs, placed over the crowns of massive plants (such as peonies and bleeding hearts) provide a sturdy, unnoticeable support to plants growing up through them (see Figure 9-7). Narrower 'tomato' hoops can be used for staking tall, slender plants like delphiniums.

## PINCHING AND DISBUDDING
Pinching, the removal of the top 3-5 cm (about 1 1/2 - 2 in) of growth, is done to encourage side branching and to develop more compact plants with more flowers. Pinching is practiced on both annuals and perennials when they are about 5-10 cm (2-4 in) tall. Many annuals self-branch readily and do not require pinching. Some other plants, depending on the nature of their growth pattern, do not lend themselves to pinching.

Disbudding is the practice of removing side flower buds to encourage the development of large terminal blooms. In disbudding, buds are removed as soon as they are large enough to **roll out**. Disbudding is commonly done to plants with 'head' inflorescences (see Botany lesson, FLOWERS) such as chrysanthemums and dahlias, as well as tuberous begonias and roses.

## Figure 9-7
## STAKING

Tomato Hoop          Peony Hoop

## FADED FLOWER REMOVAL

The removal of faded flowers and developing seed pods not only keeps the garden tidy but encourages the development of more flowers. Once seed begins to set, flower production usually ceases. Many of the annual flower cultivars today, however, are extremely **floriferous** and continue to flower despite not having their faded flowers removed (which can be a tedious and almost impossible task). This occurs as a result of these plants being sexually sterile and unable to set seed.

## PRUNING

Pruning, in the sense of thinning out shoots or removing side branches, is unlikely to be a requirement for any herbaceous plant. However, pruning to limit the spread of certain perennials is often necessary and may be done by removing stray shoots or by spading around the plant to eliminate the outer fringes of growth. Some removal of weak spindly shoots within a plant crown may also be beneficial, as it reduces competition and encourages even stronger growth from the remaining shoots.

## TRANSPLANTING

Some sort of rotation should be established to renew sections of perennial borders every 3-5 years to keep borders healthy and prevent the establishment of disease. Periodic rotation also serves to control perennial weed growth. Transplanting of established plants may also be necessary if any one of the following conditions exists:

1. A certain plant or group of plants does not flower well or look attractive in relation to the other plants around it in its present location.

2. The plant is too large or has become crowded.

3. The center of the plant is dying or has naturally declined because of the competition from vigorous peripheral growth (a natural development with plants such as rhizomous irises).

# PROPAGATION

## ANNUALS

For the most part, annuals are propagated from seed and can be grown from seed by the homeowner. Some kinds germinate easily and can be self-perpetuating once they have been introduced (eg., California poppy and nasturtium). Many cultivars are hybrids which either do not produce seed or do not come true from self-seed. For these, new seed must be purchased each year.

A limiting factor in starting annuals from seed indoors is light (see Plant Nutrition lesson, PRINCIPLE OF LIMITING FACTORS). If plant growth is thin and leggy, natural light is insufficient and should be supplemented with artificial light (see TIME OF PLANTING). Many people buy annuals as bedding plants which have been produced from seed by greenhouse operators. A few common annuals or bedding plants are propagated from cuttings, the prime example being the large-flowered bedding geraniums.

## PERENNIALS

Perennials are usually propagated vegetatively rather than from seed because more time is required to produce a flowering plant from seed. Furthermore, like many of the annuals, certain perennials will not come true from seed. Propagation of perennials usually takes one of three forms: division, cuttings and layering.

### DIVISION

Division is the separation of a large plant into smaller portions. Some perennials thrive on division and should be divided every few years (eg., summer phlox, iris, campanula, geum, lychnis, columbine, delphinium). Other types should be left undisturbed for up to ten years or more, unless one wishes to obtain more plants (eg., peony, gypsophila, bleeding heart, gas plant, adonis). For the majority of perennials, the best time to divide is in the spring, when new growth is starting (see TIME OF PLANTING for exceptions).

## Figure 9-8
## DIVISION OF HERBACEOUS PERENNIAL CROWN

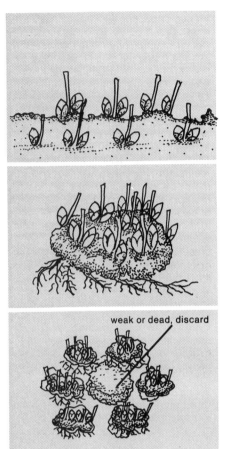

weak or dead, discard

To lift a plant for division, dig around its outer edges. Dissect the clump into pieces of desired size with at least 3-5 buds present. If the center portion has died or is lacking in vigor, discard it (see Figure 9-8).

For bulbous plants, such as tulips, daffodils and lilies, the bulbs can be dug after flowering and the tops have died down. The bulbs can then be separated from one another and individually replanted. How frequently this needs to be done to keep the plants vigorous and the flower size at its best depends on the kind of plant.

### CUTTINGS (CUTTAGE)

Stem cuttings can be taken from parent

plants in the spring or early summer when the new shoot growth is about 15 cm (6 in) high. Terminal **slips** 7-10 cm (3-4 in) long are removed at or just below a node. The bottom leaves are then removed and the cuttings **stuck** into a suitable rooting medium in flats or pots. To enhance the rooting process, the base of each cutting may be dipped into a rooting hormone (available from garden supply outlets) prior to being stuck. To induce rapid rooting, the medium must be kept moist and the surrounding area maintained at a high relative humidity. Plants such as lythrum, summer phlox, chrysanthemum, delphinium and sedum can be readily propagated from stem cuttings.

Root cuttings are a useful method of propagating plants with heavy roots such as anchusa, bleeding heart, echinops, gaillardia or gypsophila. Plants are lifted in the fall and straight root segments about 0.5 cm (about 1/4 in) in diameter are removed and cut into sections 3-5 cm (about 1-2 in) long. The sections are then planted horizontally (or at a slight angle) 1.5 to 2.5 cm (1/2-1 in) deep in flats of rooting medium. The flats can be stored in a building maintained at 5-10°C or outside if protected from severe winter temperatures. Buds will initiate and give rise to shoots in the spring. When the top growth is 8-10 cm (3-4 in) tall, the plants can be transplanted to the garden.

### LAYERING (LAYERAGE)

A few rapidly spreading ground cover plants, such as arctic phlox, pinks (Dianthus) and creeping thyme, layer naturally. That is to say, the stems spread along the surface of the ground and naturally become rooted. Such rooted stems can be severed easily from the parent plant and transplanted as small separate plants. Many other plants can be induced to successfully root through layerage by bending over the stems and pinning them to the soil (see Plant Propagation lesson, DIVISION). If the stem is wounded or partially cut at the point of contact with the soil, this aids the rooting process. Mounding up earth around the base of the plants (mound layering) when the shoots are still quite young often induces adventitious roots to form on the covered basal portion of these shoots.

Once this occurs, the soil can be gently pulled away and the shoots cut off as rooted cuttings ready for transplanting.

## WINTER PREPARATION AND PROTECTION

With respect to annual flowers, no winter protection is required since the plants are merely allowed to freeze out. However, it is wise to remove the plants after they are severely frost damaged and spade over the beds to allow the winter weather to break the soil clods into a crumb-like structure. If there was any disease or insect problem present during the growing season, removal of the plant debris in the fall will minimize the possibility of the problem re-occurring or becoming worse the next growing season.

Since perennials are intended to survive the winter and revive with new top growth in the spring, they do warrant concern on how best to promote their survival over winter. Perennials may be damaged or killed during the winter for any one or more of the following three reasons:

1. Alternate freezing and thawing of the ground causing heaving and the subsequent breaking of roots. This problem is especially prevalent in the Chinook belt of Alberta, where frequent and rapid temperature fluctuations can occur several times throughout the winter.

2. Water collecting over the crown of the plant and limiting its supply of oxygen. Maintaining a slight slope to the surface of the flower bed or border and good drainage minimizes this possibility. Even if drainage is normally adequate, rapid thawing of snow cover can cause this problem, especially when the ground underneath remains frozen. If this water remains standing for several days or if it freezes as a solid layer of ice, the plant may suffocate. If the plant is not killed outright, it may have been weakened sufficiently for pathogens to attack and bring about decay.

3. Desiccation or loss of moisture caused by drying winds and low soil moisture.

To minimize the possibility of winter damage, it is important to ensure that the soil is moist to an adequate depth before freeze-up. Furthermore, a winter mulch maintains an evenly frozen ground condition throughout the winter and, thereby, prevents heaving. Snow is the best mulch. However, as snow cannot be effectively trapped or retained, evergreen boughs or peat moss may be used as mulch. It is best to delay applying winter mulch until the ground has become thoroughly frozen.

The placement or orientation of a border may also determine the survival of perennials. South facing plantings, especially if the land slopes to the south, are more subject to alternate freezing and thawing conditions and to the drying warmth of the late winter sun than any other exposure. North facing slopes, especially those protected from the wind, are ideal for ensuring winter survival of perennials.

Whether borders should be cleaned in the spring or fall is a matter of preference. The removal of dead tops is easier in the fall since they have not yet been flattened by snow. Also, there is no new growth to interfere with this task. Fall removal also ensures that no residue is left to harbour disease organisms, insects or rodents over winter. On the other hand, if stalks are left through the winter, they may trap snow. This can be especially useful on windy sites or areas of low snowfall. Snow traps can also be provided through judicious placement of snow fences or burlap screens.

## TENDER BULBOUS ORNAMENTALS

Plants that produce a bulb or similar underground storage organ are perennial in growth habit. Those that are hardy in our climate can be used and handled in much the same as any other hardy herbaceous perennial. However, those that are tender must be treated as bedding plants if they are to be used as garden plants. Because such plants produce storage organs, it is possible to save these structures, store them over winter and replant them in the spring (see Figure 9-9). For this reason, they can be considered as special crops. The special aspects of handling a few popular plants classed as tender bulbous ornamentals are given below:

## DAHLIA

There are 12-14 classes of dahlias, ranging in flower form from singles through anemone flowered, colarette, cactus, decorative, ball and pompon to miniatures (see Figure 9-10). Propagation is by division of the tuberous roots (see Figure 9-11), rooting cuttings taken from the new shoot growth in the spring, or planting seed. The dwarf bedding type of dahlia, such as the Unwin Hybrids, is invariably started from seed indoors or in a

greenhouse. These dwarfs also develop storable tuberous roots but flower best and remain more uniform in growth habit if started from seed each year.

Dahlias are very frost sensitive and should be planted outdoors only after all danger of spring frost is past. Use of hot caps may permit earlier planting. Tuberous roots can be planted a week earlier than green plants.

Tall, large-flowered dahlia cultivars require poles or stakes for support. It is important to place the stake at the time of planting to avoid damaging the tuberous roots. A short stake may be used and replaced later with a support stake of the required height. Dahlias require large amounts of water and, if they do not receive sufficient water, their growth and subsequent flowering stops.

After the plants are blackened by the first killing frost of early autumn, the stalks should be cut back to within 10 cm (4 in) of the ground surface and the roots lifted. Most references suggest cleaning the roots of soil and storing them in a dark, moist, cool place(3-6°C). Thin or stringy roots should be wrapped in moist sphagnum moss or coated with paraffin to prevent shrivelling. However, roots have been found to store better if left undisturbed in the clump of soil adhering to them at the time of digging. The soil is allowed to dry out completely during storage in a dark, cool place and, unless the roots show evidence of shrinking, no additional moisture needs to be added. Dahlia roots should not be saved from any plant that showed evidence of virus infection during its growing season.

In the spring, the roots are removed from

## Figure 9-9
## PLANTING DEPTHS FOR "BULBS" PLANTED IN THE SPRING

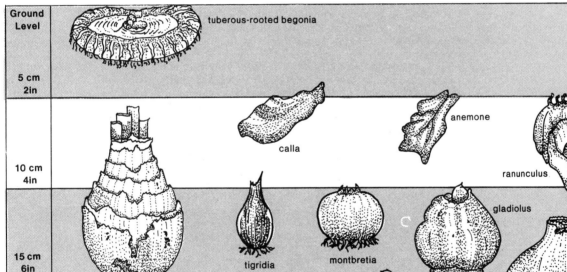

Figure 9-10
FLOWER FORMS OF DAHLIAS

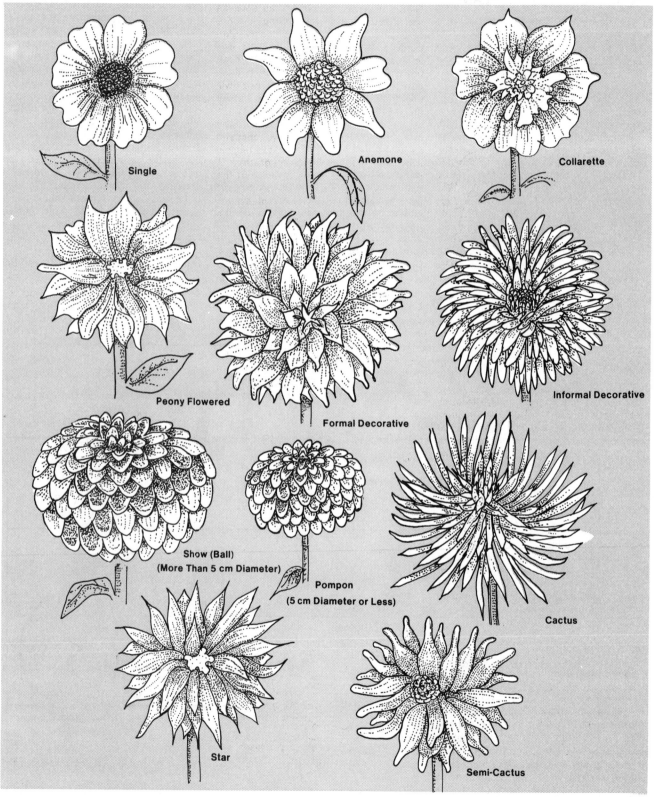

## Figure 9-11
## DIVISION OF A DAHLIA PLANT

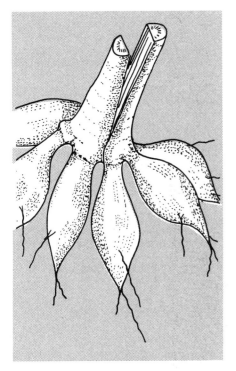

storage, cleaned of soil (if necessary) and divided with one strong eye to each root (see Plant Propagation lesson, DIVISION). Because dahlia roots do not possess the genetic capability of initiating adventitious buds, it is essential that each tuberous root contain a small portion of stem where the buds are located.

### GLADIOLUS

The gladiolus (glad) is not a particularly useful flower for enhancing the garden landscape but it does make an excellent cut flower and is popular in flower shows, where the competition among glad fanciers can be very keen.

The glad produces a corm (rather than a bulb) which can be dug and stored over winter. Glads propagate naturally through the formation of baby corms or cormels around the edge of the main corm during the summer season (see Figure 9-12). These cormels may be harvested in the fall, stored slightly moist over winter and planted out in nursery rows in the spring. By fall, corms of varying size will have developed from these cormels and many will be of flowering size (2.5 to 3.5 cm (1 - 1 1/2 in) in diameter or larger).

Glad corms can be planted as soon as the soil is worked in the spring. In order to assure a succession of blooms, glad corms can be planted at 7-10 day intervals until the first of July. Although there are several buds present on each corm, only one (occasionally two) will develop into a shoot. Each shoot produces a central flower spike and a succession of grass-like leaves arranged in overlapping fashion in two opposite rows. As the plant develops, the original corm shrivels and disintegrates. A replacement corm forms above it at the base of the new shoot. For each corm planted, therefore, only one replacement corm is produced, keeping the population of corms rather static. Only when two shoots emerge from a corm are two replacement corms formed. However, to increase the number of corms, very large corms (well above the minimum diameter for flowering size) can be cut into two or three segments. Each segment must have a strong eye or bud. The segments should be dusted with fungicide before planting to prevent disease. In this way, two or three replacement corms will be assured for each original corm sacrificed. During the growing season, it is especially

## Figure 9-12
## GLADIOLUS CORM PLUS CORMELS

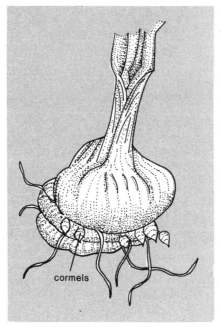

cormels

important that moisture does not become limiting during the critical period, when the new corm is forming and developing its own root system.

Glads should be left in the garden until they are severely damaged by hard frosts (usually early to mid-October). They should be dug, the soil removed and the plants bundled in sheaves of convenient size for hanging to dry and cure. Some references suggest cutting the tops back to within a few centimetres of the corms and allowing the corms to dry a few hours in the sun before storing to cure. In either case, the corms should be cured by storing for two to three weeks at 27-35°C. When the curing is complete, the corms will be firm and the shrivelled remains of old corms, the stem and the husks can easily be removed. Some references suggest leaving a few inner husks around the corm but this makes the detection of any corm rotting diseases difficult to detect. Corms should be sorted and those that show evidence of disease should be discarded. Dusting with a fungicide or fungicide-insecticide powder is recommended prior to storage in shallow trays or boxes at 5-10°C.

Other tender bulbous plants that can be handled in much the same way as the gladiolus are acidanthera, anemone (*Anemone coronaria*), Ismene-lily (*Hymenocallis narcissiflora*), Mexican tiger flower (*Tigridia pavonia*) and montbretia or tritonia (*Crocosmia x crocosmiiflora*).

### TUBEROUS BEGONIA
Tuberous begonias (see Figures 9-13 and 9-15) can be propagated from seed, soft terminal stem cuttings or division. Propagation from seed is the most difficult method. If started in February in a greenhouse, plants of flowering size can be produced by summer. The seed is very fine and, therefore, requires a very fine seeding medium. The seed must be barely covered and kept at a high humidity until germination occurs and the young seedlings have established roots. The surface of the sowing medium must be kept uniformly moist and the temperature held at 20-22°C for uniform germination.

Large tuberous roots with several buds or eyes can be cut into segments each with one or more eyes (see Figure 9-14).

## Figure 9-13
### TUBEROUS BEGONIA FLOWER

dry until the tops wither, then cleaned of all soil and fine fibrous roots. The tops should be removed as close to the tuberous root as possible without damaging the root surface where new buds will arise. The corm-like tuberous roots can be washed, dried, then stored in dry peat moss, vermiculite, or sand at cool temperatures. Some references suggest storing at 7-15°C, whereas others recommend 2-5°C. At the lower range, growth is inhibited until the roots are removed from storage. When stored at the higher range, buds swell and begin growth by February or March. Once growth starts, the roots should be removed from storage, planted in pots and placed in warm temperatures with sufficient light. Tuberous roots, whether purchased or stored from the previous season, should be started in pots by mid-March in order to obtain plants in bud ready to flower by late May or early June.

## Figure 9-14
### DIVISION OF A TUBEROUS BEGONIA

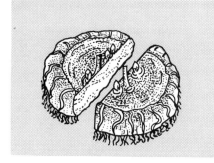

The cut surfaces should be dusted with a fungicide to protect against disease and the wounds allowed to dry and begin healing before planting.

Terminal cuttings can be taken from well developed shoots leaving 2-4 leaves on the parent plant below the cut. A peat or peat-lite mix makes a good medium for rooting. The humidity should be kept high to minimize wilting.

Tuberous begonias flower best in partial shade and should receive no direct sunlight after mid-morning. Like dahlias, they are extremely frost sensitive. Once blackened by frost in the late summer or early fall, they should be dug, allowed to

## Figure 9-15
### THE FLOWER FORMS OF DOUBLE-FLOWERING TUBEROUS BEGONIAS

**Carnation (Flowered)**

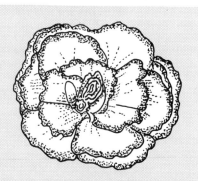
**Picotee (Flowered)**

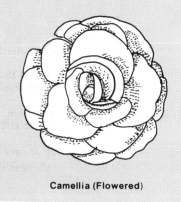
**Camellia (Flowered)**

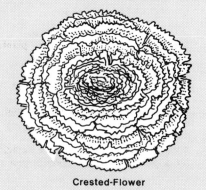
**Crested-Flower**

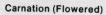

Other bulbous tender plants that can be handled in much the same way as the tuberous begonia include: caladium, giant summer hyacinth (*Galtonia candicans*), tuberose (*Polianthes tuberosa*), ranunculus (*Ranunculus asiaticus*) and yellow calla (*Zantedeschia elliottiana*).

## CONCLUSION

Herbaceous ornamentals, because they do not produce perennial woody top growth, have a limited seasonal function as landscape material. On the other hand, woody plants, both deciduous and evergreen, are much more useful in defining space relationships and tying the structural elements on a given site to the natural setting. They contribute to the landscape design and add interest year round. Nevertheless, herbaceous ornamentals, if carefully used, can enhance the landscape features and add color and interest during the growing season. A judicious combination of bedding plants and herbaceous perennials can add color to the home ground from early spring to late fall, even in the relatively short growing season of Alberta. With a careful choice of plant Species and cultivars, a gradual increase in flowers can be achieved. For example, flowers of early spring bulbs can be later joined by mid-season perennials and mass plantings of annuals. The beauty can climax by mid-summer and gradually taper off as the annuals decline and eventually disappear with the first killing frost. Fall flowering perennials continue to add color until the onset of winter.

## SELF CHECK *QUIZ*

1. Are the terms 'bedding plants' and 'annuals' synonymous?

2. How are bedding plants used in the landscape?

3. How does one achieve balance and unity in a perennial border?

4. If woody plants are used as a background or wind break for a perennial flower border, how close to the woody plants can the herbaceous perennials be planted?

5. What is the general rule for determining when a perennial flower should be transplanted?

6. What are three reasons for transplanting established perennial flowers?

7. What are four ways in which perennials may be propagated?

# PERENNIAL FLOWERS

## SPRING FLOWERING BULBS

### Outdoor Culture

Although tulip, narcissi (daffodils) and scilla (squills or bluebells) are the spring bulb crops most commonly seen in Alberta gardens, several other less familiar kinds have proven hardy in the province.

### Preparation for planting

1. Any garden soil that is well drained and does not cake or harden is good for bulbs.
2. Work soil to a depth of 30-45 cm and incorporate fertilizer such as 4-10-8 at the rate of 1.5 kg/10 m² of ground.
3. Most any location in the garden is suitable for bulbs. Planting near building foundations will result in earlier growth and flowering. Premature development in exposed areas could result in damage from severe night frosts or late winter cold snaps.
4. Select large sized bulbs of standard varieties for greater vigor and performance.

### Planting

1. Set bulbs in the ground in early September or as soon as they are available in the fall.
2. Bulbs should be planted at least three weeks before the ground freezes if possible.
3. Plant tulip 20 cm deep (from soil surface to base of bulb), narcissus 25 cm deep, and scilla 10-12 cm deep.
4. After the ground has frozen apply a 6-8 cm mulch of peat or clean straw to prevent heaving of the soil and premature growth. Remove this mulch in stages in the early spring.

### Care after flowering

1. When flowers fade remove the flower heads but not the stems or leaves.
2. Allow foliage to mature and die down undisturbed. Annual flowers may be planted amongst the bulbs to hide the maturing tops.
3. Tulips and narcissi can be left for 2 to 3 years before lifting and replanting. When lifting is necessary, do so when the tops have died and store the bulbs in a cool dry place until time to replant in the fall.

### Species

The following species have performed well in Alberta and are considered worthy of trial.

### Tulips

Most tulip cultivars will perform well the first season after planting but gradually deteriorate in subsequent years. Cultivars like Single Early, Double Early, Mendel, Triumphs, Darwin Hybrids, Lily Flowered, Darwins, Single Lates, Double Lates and species can be tried.

### Grape Hyacinth

*Muscari Alpina
Muscari armeniacum
Muscari azureum
Muscari botryoides (Common Grape Hyacinth)

### Squill

Scilla bifolia
Scilla sibirica (Siberian squill)

### Ground Lily or Trillium

*Trillium grandiflorum (large white trillium)
*Trillium nivale (dwarf white trillium)
*Not readily available.

### Glory of the Snow

Chionodoxa luciliae
Chionodoxa sardensis

### Others:

Bulbocodium vernum
Colchicum autumnale
Convallaria majalis
Crocus spp.
Fritillaria spp.
Narcissus spp.
Puschkinia libanotica

## CHRYSANTHEMUM

### Cultural Notes

1. Prefer full sunlight but will tolerate some shade.
2. Good drainage essential; will not tolerate "wet feet".
3. Grow in good garden soil into which well rotted barnyard manure has been deeply worked.
4. Rooted cuttings or divisions should be spaced 45-60 cm apart.
5. Firm soil around roots and water well until established.
6. Heavy, but infrequent, waterings are best.
7. Chrysanthemums may be treated as annuals. Roots may be stored over winter and new plants propagated by herbaceous cuttings after March 1.
9. Chrysanthemums may require irrigation in early spring before growth starts.

## GERANIUM

### Propagation and Storage

1. Cuttings should be taken before early fall (end of August or first week in September).
2. Cuttings should be 10-15 cm long, of firm but not hard shoots.
3. Make bottom cut immediately below a node, remove leaves from lower half of cutting.
4. Allow cuttings to dry on bench for minimum of 6 hours (preferably overnight).
5. Using a shallow pot, flat or wooden box with good drainage and a minimum depth of 8 cm, fill with perlite or sand, moisten and firm.
6. Place cuttings into medium to depth of 6-8 cm.
7. Place container near window (avoid direct sunlight for first week).
8. Keep perlite or sand moist but not wet.
9. After cuttings have rooted (6-10 weeks) put into 8 cm clay pots using mixture of garden loam (7 parts), peat (3 parts) and sand (2 parts).
10. Place in sunny window (south or east side). After cuttings are established keep soil on dry side. Do not encourage much growth.
11. Pinch out growing tips to keep plant compact and bushy. (Do not pinch after March 15).
12. A second crop of cuttings can be taken from established plants as late as February. Treat as above.
13. Apply some fertilizer first week in May.
14. Plant out in planter or garden at end of May.
15. Cultivars grown from seed, e.g. Carefree and New Era series, are available but require early seeding.
NOTE: Old plants may be dug and placed in pots or boxes and stored in a cool dark spot over winter. Prune them back, water and place in a sunny window in late February to encourage growth. Plant outside the end of May.

## IRIS

### Cultural Notes

1. Plant or transplant in early August.
2. Grow well in most soils of good tilth and good drainage.
3. Best in full sunlight.
4. Propagated by division of rhizomes.
5. Each division for planting should have roots and at least one growing point.
6. When planting be certain the roots are well spread apart and the top of the rhizome level with the surrounding soil. Pack well and water.
7. For good color displays plant in groups of three or more spaced 45 cm apart.

### Species

Bearded iris — *Iris germanica* — Height 30-60 cm.

Siberian iris — *Iris sibirica* — Height 60-100 cm.

Dwarf iris — *Iris pumila* — Height 20-30 cm.

Other Species — Blueflag iris — *Iris versicolor*, Goldbeard iris — *Iris flavissima*, Grass iris — *Iris graminea*, Pilgrim iris — *Iris ruthenica*, Seashore iris — *Iris spuria*, Virginia iris — *Iris virginica*, Yellow flag iris — *Iris pseudacorus*.

*I. pseudacorus*, *I. virginica* and *I. versicolor* are tall-growing species with yellow, purple and blue flowers respectively. All three species are good for wet locations.

## LILY (Hardy garden types)

### Cultural Notes

1. Must have deeply worked, well drained soil
2. Heavy soils can be improved with well-rotted organic matter, peat, sand or inert materials such as perlite or vermiculite.
3. Fall is the best time for planting or transplanting. Mulches of peat moss in the late fall to a depth of 10-12 cm will aid in the establishment of bulbs after planting.
4. Application of nitrogenous fertilizer after shoots have emerged promotes strong early growth. Application of a complete fertilizer when flower buds are showing improves flower quality and bulb vigor.
5. The removal of faded blossoms (pods included) will aid bulb production. Leaves and stems should be left intact.
6. In the fall, mature stems with bulblets attached are removed. This is done by placing the feet firmly on either side of the stem so that a quick twist and a pull will separte it from the large parent bulb.

### Species

**Early flowering** (June and July). Planting depth — top of bulb to soil surface.

    10 cm — *canadense, cernuum, concolor, dauricum, pumilum*

    15 cm — *amabile, amabile var. luteum, callosum, martagon var. album, martagon var. dalmaticum, hansonii\*, tsingtauense\**

    20 cm — *davidii regale*

**Late flowering** (August)

    20-25 cm — *auratum var. platypnyllum, speciosum, tigrinum*

    25-30 cm — *henryi*

    hybrids — various available

    \*tolerate partial shade

## PEONY

### Cultural Notes

1. Grow best in a deeply worked rich clay loam soil. Do not use manure.
2. Prefer full sunlight.

3. Plant or transplant in September.
4. Each crown or division should have at least five buds.
5. Plant so that buds are 5 cm below the surface and firm the soil around the crown.
6. Apply garden fertilizer in the spring for added vigor and better blooms.
7. Support against wind or heavy rain.
8. Remove tops just above crowns in September and burn (Botrytis blight control).

# OTHER PERENNIALS

**Key to colors:**

| | | |
|---|---|---|
| Pk — pink | Y — yellow | W — white |
| R — red | B — blue | V — violet |
| O — orange | P — purple | sh — shades |

(‡Indicates plants suitable for shade)

### OVER ONE METRE

| Common Name | Botanical Name | Color |
|---|---|---|
| New England aster | *Aster novaengliae* | P Pk |
| ‡Common bleeding heart | *Dicentra spectabills* | Pk |
| Solitary clematis | *Clematis integrifolium* | B |
| ‡Columbine meadowrue | *Thalictrum aquilegifolium* | P to W |
| Daylily | *Hemerocallis* | P Y O R Pk |
| False dragonhead | *Dracocephalum virginianum* | P |
| Gasplant dittany | *Dictamnus albus* | P W |
| Garden heliotrope | *Valeriana officinalis* | V |
| Rough heliopsis | *Heliopsis scabra* | Y |
| ‡Ledebour globeflower | *Trollius ledebourii* | Y |
| Small globe thistle | *Echinops ritro* | B |
| Greatleaf golden ray | *Ligularia speciosa* | Y |
| Mongrel larkspur | *Delphinium hybridum* | B W |
| Lythrum (cultivars) | *Lythrum virgatum* | Pk R |
| ‡Monkshood | *Aconitum napellus* | B |
| ‡Shell-leaf penstemon | *Penstemon grandiflorus* | P |
| Oriental poppy | *Papaver orientale var.* | R Y W O |
| Common sneezeweed | *Helenium autumnale* | Y O |
| Washington lupine | *Lupinus polyphyllus* | P R Y sh |

### OVER 60 cm

| Common Name | Botanical Name | Color |
|---|---|---|
| New York aster | *Aster novibelgi* | B R W |
| Rhone aster | *Aster acris* | Pk |
| Baby's breath | *Gypsophila paniculata* | W |
| Danesblood bellflower | *Campanula glomerata* | P |
| Peachleaf bellflower | *Campanula persicifolia* | B W |
| Black-eyed Susan | *Rudbeckia hirta* | Y |
| Mountain bluet | *Centaurea montana* | B |
| Bouncing Bet | *Saponaria officinalis* | Pk |
| ‡Italian bugloss | *Anchusa azurea* | B |
| Tall buttercup | *Ranunculus acris* | Y |
| Clammy campion | *Lychnis viscaria* | R |
| Maltesecross campion | *Lychnis chalcedonica* | R |
| ‡Longspur columbine | *Aquilegia longissima* | B R Y sh |
| Coral bells | *Heuchera sanguinea* | Pk |
| Bigflower coreopsis | *Coreopsis grandiflora* | Y |
| Gloriosa daisy | *Rudbeckia (hybrids)* | Y |
| Shasta daisy | *Chrysanthemum maximum* | W |
| Ruyschianum dragonhead | *Dracocephalum ruyschianum* | P |
| Perennial flax | *Linum perenne* | B |
| Oregon fleabane | *Erigeron speciosus* | P |
| Common perennial gaillardia | *Gaillardia aristata* | R Y |
| Tall gayfeather | *Liatris scariosa* | Pk |
| Caucasus geranium | *Geranium ibericum* | B |
| Siberian larkspur | *Delphinium grandiflorum chinense* | P B W |
| Caucasian leopardsbane | *Doronicum caucasicum* | Y |
| Lupin minarette | *'Lupinus polyphyllus 'Minarette'* | sh |
| ‡European meadowsweet | *Filipendula ulmaria* | W |
| Penstemon | *Penstemon barbatus* | R |
| Decussata phlox | *Phlox decussata var.* | R B W |
| ‡Blue plantainlily | *Hosta caerulea* | P |
| Greekvalerian polemonium | *Polemonium caeruleum* | B |
| Florists pyrethrum | *Chrysanthemum coccineum* | R Y W sh |
| Meadow sage | *Salvia pratensis* | B R W |
| Caucasian scabious | *Scabiosa caucasica* | B Pk W |
| Seaholly eryngo | *Eryngium alpinum* | B |
| Golden spurge | *Eurphorbia epithymoides* | Y |
| ‡Spotted St. John's-wort | *Hypericum punctatum* | Y |
| ‡Wildbergamot beebalm | *Monarda fistulosa* | P |
| Sneezewort yarrow | *Achillea ptarmica* | W |

### OVER 30 cm

| Common Name | Botanical Name | Color |
|---|---|---|
| †Wood anemone | *Anemone sylvestris* | W |
| Bergenia | *Bergenia cordifolia* | P |
| Bergenia | *Bergenia crassifolia* | P |
| †Pacific bleeding heart | *Dicentra formosa* | Pk |
| Golden camomile | *Anthemis tinctoria 'Kelway'* | Y |
| Arkwright campion | *Lychnis arkwrightii* | O to Pk |
| Dwarf campion | *Lychnis haageana* | R |
| Evergreen candytuft | *Iberis sempervirens* | W |
| †Bethlehem lungwort | *Pulmonaria saccharata* | R to W |
| Sweet William phlox | *Phlox divaricata* | P B |
| Pinks | *Dianthus var.* | Pk to R |
| Iceland poppy | *Papaver nudicaule* | R Y W O |
| Spike speedwell | *Veronica spicata* | B |
| Pink spike speedwell | *Veronica spicata rosea* | Pk |
| Woolly speedwell | *Veronica incana* | P |

## PERENNIALS SUITABLE FOR ROCK GARDENS

### 15 - 30 cm

| | | |
|---|---|---|
| Golden tuft alyssum | *Alyssum saxatile* | Y |
| Silver mound artemisia | *Artemisia 'Silver Mound'* | |
| Alpine aster | *Aster alpina* | B |
| Multicolor bugleweed | *Ajuga reptans multicolor* | P |
| †Alpine columbine | *Aquilegia alpina* | B Y |
| Blue sheep's fescue | *Festuca ovina glauca* | |
| Golden flax | *Linum flavum* | Y |
| Fleece flower | *Polygonum cuspidatum 'Spectabile'* | |
| †Alpine forget-me-not | *Myosotis alpestris* | B Y |
| Hascomb gentian | *Gentiana hascombensis* | B |
| Lady slipper | *Cypripedium calceolus pubescens* | Y |
| †Lily of the valley | *Convallaria majalis* | W |
| European pasqueflower | *Pulsatilia sp.* | P |
| †Sawsepal penstemon | *Penstemon glaber* | B |
| Periwinkle | *Vinca minor* | B W |
| Auricula primrose | *Primula auricula* | P R Y sh |
| Polyantha primrose | *Primula polyantha* | R O W |
| Dwarf ribbon grass | *Phalaris arundinacea picta 'Alta Dwarf'* | |
| Golden spurge | *Euphorbia epithymoides* | Y |
| Japanese spurge | *Pachysandra terminalis* | |
| Stonecrop | *Sedum spp.* | R Y P |
| Saxifrage tunicflower | *Tunica saxifraga* | Pk |

### UNDER 15 cm

| | | |
|---|---|---|
| Carpathian bellflower | *Campanula carpatica* | B to W |
| Bird's-foot trefoil | *Lotus corniculatus fl. pl.* | Y |
| †Bloodroot | *Sanguinaria canadensis* | W |
| Draba | *Draba aizoides* | Y |
| Common edelweiss | *Leontopodium alpinum* | W |
| Creeping gypsophila | *Gypsophila repens* | W |
| Hens and chicks | *Sempervivum tectorum* | |
| Houseleek | *Sempervivum sp.* | R Pk |
| Arctic phlox | *Phlox borealis* | P |
| Moss phlox | *Phlox subulata* | R to W |
| Maiden pink | *Dianthus deltoides* | Pk |
| Alpine rockcress | *Arabis alpina* | Pk W |
| Cortusa primrose | *Primula cortusoides* | P R W sh |
| Larchleaf sandwort | *Arenaria laricifolia* | W |
| Saxifrage | *Saxifraga decipiens var.* | R |
| †Common shooting star | *Dodecatheon media* | P W |
| Moss silene | *Silene acaulis* | Pk |
| Snow-in-summer | *Cerastium tomentosum* | W |
| Rock soapwort | *Saponaria ocymoides* | Pk |
| Blue king speedwell | *Veronica repens* | B |
| Comb speedwell | *Veronica pectinata* | Pk |
| Hungarian speedwell | *Veronica latifolia* | B Pk |
| Stonecress | *Aethionema pulchellum* | Pk |
| Stonecrop | *Sedum spp.* | R Y P |
| Yellow strawberry | *Duchesnea indica* | Y |
| Thyme | *Thymus spp.* | |
| †Horned violet | *Viola cornuta* | B R Y W |

# ANNUAL AND BIENNIAL FLOWERS

## Cultural Notes

1. To obtain early flowering of annual flowers, seed should be planted indoors.
2. If a greenhouse or bright sun room is not available, a shelf or cabinet can be built in the basement with ample light provided by fluorescent lighting fixtures.
3. Seeding dates given below are for transplant production and should be used merely as a guide. The most common mistake is sowing the seed too early.
4. For seed sown indoors use pots or flats and a lightweight porous soil mixture.
5. When seedlings are large enough to handle, transplant to 6-8 cm apart.
6. Place outside to harden off about May 15 but protect from night frosts.
7. Plan your garden arrangement.
8. Prepare land thoroughly, adding organic matter with well-rotted manure, peat moss, or compost.
9. Do not work soil that is wet.
10. Transplant to the garden the last week of May or first week of June.
11. Plant into moist soil, leaving adequate room for development.
12. Practise shallow cultivation to avoid damage to feeder roots.
13. Thorough soakings every 7-10 days are more beneficial than frequent light waterings.
14. Remove faded flowers to keep plants blooming.

## Key to Colors:

| | | |
|---|---|---|
| **B — Blue** | **Pk — Pink** | **W — White** |
| **O — Orange** | **R — Red** | **Y — Yellow** |
| **P — Purple** | **V — Violet** | |

\* Indicates plants suitable for partial shade.

\*\* Indicates plants adapted to hot sandy soil and full sunshine.

+ Indicates plants which could be seeded directly outdoors after May 15.

† Indicates plants which also have cultivars grown as biennials.

## COMMON ANNUALS

| Common Name | Generic Name | Color | Average Seeding Day-Month |
|---|---|---|---|
| **Tall - 45 cm. or over** | | | |
| +\*\*Bachelor's button | *Centaurea* | B P Pk W R | 10 - 3 |
| Castor bean | *Ricinus* | | 20 - 3 |
| +Chrysanthemum | *Chrysanthemum* | R Y W | 15 - 4 |
| \*Cockscomb | *Celosia* | R Y | 20 - 4 |
| +Cosmos | *Cosmos* | R W Pk O | 15 - 4 |
| Dahlia | *Dahlia* | Y to R | 10 - 4 |
| Dusty miller | *Cineraria* | Grey Foliage | 15 - 3 |
| †Foxglove | *Digitalis* | R W Pk V | 20 - 3 |
| Garden or China aster | *Callistephus* | B R W P Pk | 21 - 3 |
| +Gloriosa daisy | *Rudbeckia* | Y | 15 - 4 |
| +Gourds | *Curcurbita* | Decorative vine fruit | 15 - 4 |
| †Hollyhock | *Althaea* | R Y W Pk | 20 - 3 |
| Larkspur | *Delphinium* | B R W Pk V | 20 - 3 |
| Marigold | *Tagetes* | R to Y | 10 - 4 |
| Mealy cup sage | *Salvia* | B W | 1 - 3 |
| Money plant or honesty | *Lunaria* | Silver membranous fruit | 20 - 4 |
| Morning glory | *Ipomoea* | B R W Pk | 20 - 4 |
| \*Nicotiana | *Nicotiana* | R Pk V P W Y | 15 - 4 |
| \*Painted tongue | *Salpiglossis* | Y to R to B | 15 - 3 |
| +Poppy | *Papaver* | Pk R W O | 15 - 4 |
| Salvia (scarlet sage) | *Salvia* | R Y P | 1 - 3 |
| Scarlet runner bean | *Phaseolus* | R | 20 - 4 |
| Snapdragon | *Antirrhinum* | P R Y W Pk O | 15 - 3 |

| Common Name | Generic Name | Color | Average Seeding Day-Month | Common Name | Generic Name | Color | Average Seeding Day-Month |
|---|---|---|---|---|---|---|---|
| *Spiderflower | Cleome | Pk to W | 1 - 4 | Statice | Limonium | B R Y W V Pk | 1 - 4 |
| Statice | Limonium | B R Y W Pk V | 1 - 4 | Sweet scabious | Scabiosa | B R W | 1 - 4 |
| Straw flower | Helichrysum | R Y W Pk | 15 - 4 | **Sweetsultan | Centaurea | B R Y W | 10 - 4 |
| Stocks | Matthiola | B R Y W Pk P | 30 - 3 | | | | |
| Stocks (evening scented) | Matthiola | V | 20 - 3 | **Medium — 25 - 45 kcm** | | | |
| +Sunflower | Helianthus | Y | 15 - 4 | +Baby's breath | Gypsophilia | Pk W | 15 - 3 |
| +Sweet pea | Lathyrus | B R W | 1 - 4 | +Bartonia | Mentzelia | Y | 1 - 4 |
| +**Zinnia | Zinnia | R Y O P V Pk | 15 - 4 | Basil 'Black Opal' | Ocimum | Colored foliage | 15 - 4 |
| | | | | +Butterfly flower | Schizanthus | P R W Y | 15 - 3 |
| **Medium — 25 - 45 cm** | | | | *Chinese forget-me-not | Cynoglossum | B | 25 - 3 |
| Balsam | Impatiens | R W Pk | 20 - 4 | Didiscus or blue lace flower | Trachymene | B | 20 - 3 |
| Begonia (fibrous rooted) | Begonia | R P W | 1 - 3 | Fairy bouquet | Linaria | B Y W R | 1 - 4 |
| Carnation | Dianthus | R W Pk Y O | 20 - 3 | +Flax | Linum | R B | 1 - 4 |
| Dusty miller | Centaurea | Grey foliage | 15 - 3 | +**Golden African daisy | Dimorphotheca | R W Y O | 20 - 4 |
| Geranium | Pelargonium | R W Pk | 1 - 3 | Heliotrope | Heliotropium | B | 1 - 3 |
| +Annual gaillardia | Gaillardia | R Y O | 20 - 3 | Snow on mountain | Euphorbia | W | 15 - 3 |
| +*Nasturtium | Tropaeolum | R Y O | 15 - 4 | Swan River daisy | Brachycome | B W V | 20 - 4 |
| +Painted daisy | Chrysanthemum | Y | 1 - 4 | | | | |
| **Petunia (single) | Petunia | B R W P Pk V Y | 1 - 3 | | | | |
| **Petunia (double) | Petunia | B W Pk R P | 1 - 3 | | | | |
| *Annual phlox | Phlox | R Y W Pk P | 15 - 4 | **Dwarf — Less than 25 cm** | | | |
| +**Pot marigold | Calendula | Y O | 20 - 4 | +Butterfly flower | Schizanthus | Pk to V | 15 - 3 |
| Salvia | Salvia | R Y P | 1 - 4 | +Calliopsis | Coreopsis | Y to R | 1 - 5 |
| +*Satin flower | Godetia | P R W | 20 - 4 | +Catchfly | Silene | Pk | 20 - 4 |
| Snapdragon | Antirrhinum | P R Y W Pk | 15 - 3 | Cup flower | Nierembergia | B | 25 - 3 |
| Stocks (dwarf) | Matthiola | W R Y V B P | 30 - 3 | Gazania | Gazania | Y R O | 20 - 4 |
| *Verbena | Verbena | B R W Pk | 1 - 3 | Gilea | Gilea | R Pk Y W | 15 - 4 |
| | | | | Heliotrope | Heliotropium | B | 1 - 3 |
| **Dwarf — Less than 25 cm** | | | | *Annual phlox | Phlox | B R Y W Pk | 15 - 3 |
| **Ageratum | Ageratum | B Pk W | 15 - 4 | +Viscaria | Lychnis | R B | 1 - 4 |
| +Bachelor's button | Centaurea | B P Pk W R | 10 - 4 | | | | |
| +**California poppy | Eschscholtzia | O Y W R | 10 - 4 | | | | |
| +*Candytuft | Iberis | P R W Pk | 1 - 4 | | | | |
| Ice plant | Mesembryanthemum | R B P | 15 - 3 | | | | |
| Patience plant | Impatiens | P O Pk R W | 20 - 3 | | | | |
| *Lobelia | Lobelia | B W V R | 20 - 3 | | | | |
| +French marigold | Tagetes | R to Y | 10 - 4 | | | | |
| *+Nasturtium | Tropaeolum | R Y O | 15 - 4 | | | | |
| +Nemesia | Nemesia | R Y Pk W | 25 - 3 | | | | |
| +Ornamental kale | Brassica | Colored foliage | 20 - 4 | | | | |
| *Pansy | Viola | P B Y W | 15 - 3 | | | | |
| +**Portulaca | Portulaca | R Y W O Pk | 20 - 4 | | | | |
| Salvia | Salvia | R Y P | 1 - 4 | | | | |
| Snapdragon | Antirrhinum | R Y W Pk | 15 - 3 | | | | |
| +*Sweet alyssum | Lobularia | P W Pk V | 10 - 4 | | | | |
| Sweet pea | Lathyrus | P Pk B R W V | 15 - 4 | | | | |
| †Sweet William | Dianthus | R W | 1 - 4 | | | | |
| Verbena | Verbena | R Pk W P | 15 - 3 | | | | |
| *Viola | Viola | B Y W | 1 - 3 | | | | |
| +Zinnia | Zinnia | R O Pk Y | 15 - 4 | | | | |

**Everlasting Flowers**

| Common Name | Generic Name | Color | Average Seeding Day-Month |
|---|---|---|---|
| Eryngo | Eryngium | B | 20 - 4 |
| **Globe amaranth | Gomphrena | R-P O W Pk | 15 - 4 |
| Globe thistle | Echinops | B | 15 - 4 |
| Immortelle | Xeranthemum | Pk P | 15 - 4 |
| Money plant or honesty | Lunaria | Silver membranous fruit | |
| Statice or sea lavender | Limonium | Y Pk B V R W | 15 - 4 |
| Strawflower | Helichrysum | Y R W Pk | 15 - 4 |
| *Sunray or acroclimium | Helipterum | Pk W | 15 - 4 |

# UNCOMMON ANNUALS

**Tall — 45 cm or over**

| Common Name | Generic Name | Color | Average Seeding Day-Month |
|---|---|---|---|
| African daisy | Arctotis | W | 20 - 4 |
| +Canterbury bells | Campanula | B W Pk | 20 - 3 |
| +*Calliopsis | Coreopsis | Y to R | 20 - 4 |
| +*Clarkia | Clarkia | R W Pk O | 10 - 4 |
| **Globe amaranth | Gomphrena | R-P O W Pk | 15 - 4 |
| Globe thistle | Echinops | B | 15 - 4 |
| +Love-in-a-mist | Nigella | B W | 15 - 3 |
| Madagascar periwinkle | Vinca | Pk W | |
| +Mallow | Lavatera | R W | 20 - 4 |

analagous colors - colors which lie near each other on the color wheel (i.e., yellow-orange and yellow).

complementary colors - combination of two colors directly opposite each other on the color wheel (i.e., yellow and violet).

corm (cormels) - swollen base of a stem axis enclosed by dry, scale-like leaves.

disbudding - removal of lateral flower buds.

foundation plantings - plantings at the base of a structure which tie the structure to the landscape.

peat-lite mix - general term referring to any soilless growing medium containing peat and vermiculite and/or perlite.

pinching - pruning the soft succulent tip of a shoot to stimulate lateral growth.

roll out - term with respect to disbudding. One rolls out a bud when it is small and easily removed.

rossette - circular cluster of leaves or other plant organs.

slips - terminal herbaceous cutting.

true from seed - genetically homogeneous.

tuberous (tuber) - special kind of swollen modified stem structure that functions as an underground storage organ.

# SELF CHECK ANSWERS

1. Not in the strict definitions of the terms. Bedding plants include all those herbaceous ornamentals that we must replant each spring. Many of those are started from seed and many are true annuals. However, bedding plants also include such kinds as petunias (which are really tender perennials that will produce flowers the first year from seed) and tuberous begonias (tender perennials with a corm-like tuberous root that must be lifted for the winter in Alberta and replanted the next spring) (see INTRODUCTION - page 901).

2. Bedding plants are particularly effective as mass plantings of solid colors in both beds and borders. They are also prime candidates for planters and hanging baskets or as accent plants in foundation plantings. Vine or creeper types can be used on gazebos or trellises or to cover unsightly rough areas of ground, etc., where perennial vines will not survive or are not desired. Some bedding plants, such as castor bean and kochia, can serve as seasonal shrubs or summer hedges (see USES IN THE LANDSCAPE - page 901).

3. A sense of balance is achieved mainly by limiting the height of the tallest plants to approximately one half the width of the border. Unity is established and balance enhanced by repetition across the length of the border. Color groups should be repeated at regular intervals across the length of the border and actual kinds should repeat as well, but to a lesser extent (see SELECTION AND PLANNING - page 903).

4. About 60-100 cm (24-39 in) (see LOCATION EXPOSURE - page 906).

5. In general, early spring flowering perennials are planted in late summer to early fall, whereas most others, particularly late flowering or less hardy species, are planted or transplanted in the spring (see TIME OF PLANTING - page 908).

6. a. The plant is too large and is crowding neighboring plants.
   b. The center of the plant is weak or dying with only the periferal growth being healthy and vigorous.
   c. The plant does not look attractive in relation to the plants around it (see TRANSPLANTING - page 911).

7. a. from seed
   b. by division of crowns or separation of bulbs
   c. from cuttings of various kinds, including root cuttings
   d. by layering (see PERENNIALS - page 911).

Agriculture Canada. *Coral-bells for Canadian Gardens*. Publication 1755/E, 1983.

A short five page leaflet on ornamental species and cultivars of Heuchera.

Agriculture Canada. *Herbaceous Perennials for the Prairie Provinces*. Publication 1769/E.

A bulletin covering the cultural aspects and descriptive information on herbaceous perennials recommended for the prairies.

Alberta Agriculture. *Classification of Roses*. Agdex 283, October 1972.

A one page fact sheet taken from "The 1968 Prairie Garden".

Alberta Agriculture. *Flowering Bulbs for Canadian Gardens*. Agdex 280/20, AC 996, Revised 1984.

A 42 page bulletin on the classification of bulbs, their use in the landscape and the cultural practices for both hardy and tender kinds.

Alberta Agriculture. *Ground Covers and Climbing Plants*. Agdex 274/20-1, AC 1698, 1980.

A 39 page bulletin covering both woody and herbaceous vines and ground covers.

Alberta Agriculture. *Growing Gladiolus*. Agdex 281/20-1, AC 1229, Revised 1984.

A 20 page bulletin on the culture of gladiolus including insect and disease control.

Alberta Agriculture. *Horticultural Guide*. Agdex 200/01, 1986.

A must for Alberta home gardeners.

Alberta Agriculture. *Lythrums for Home Gardens*. Agdex 282/30, AC 1285, Revised 1983.

A fold-over leaflet on the pertinent aspects of growing Lythrums or Loosestrife as a home garden perennial flower.

Alberta Agriculture. *Nursery Propagation of Woody and Herbaceous Perennials for the Prairie Provinces*. Agdex 275/16-1, AC 1733, 1982.

A 51 page bulletin covering seed propagation and vegetative propagation of both woody and herbaceous perennials.

Alberta Agriculture. *The Rock Garden*. Agdex 271/17, AC 1243, Revised 1971.

A short bulletin on the construction of a rock garden and selected listings of rock garden plants.

Alberta Agriculture. *Rose Growing in Alberta*. Agdex FS283/20-1, Revised 1980.

A fact sheet format covering the culture of roses in Alberta.

Alberta Agriculture. *Roses Recommended for Alberta*. Agdex FS283/32-1, Revised 1980.

A single leaflet fact sheet listing roses recommended for Alberta. Includes shrub roses as well as hybrid teas, floribundas, grandifloras and hybrid perpetuals.

Buckley, A.R. *Canadian Garden Perennials*. Saanichton, BC: Hancock House Publishsers Ltd., 1977.

A soft cover manual dealing with perennials recommended for the various regions across Canada.

Crockett, J.U. *Annuals*. New York: Time Life Books, 1971.

A well illustrated book on how to grow annuals for outdoor beauty and for cut flower use. Includes an illustrated dictionary or encyclopedia of annuals available to Canadian and American home gardeners.

Crockett, J.U. *Bulbs*. New York: Time Life Books, 1971.

A well illustrated book on ornamentals that produce an underground storage organ (bulb, corm, tuber, etc.). The format is very similar to that of the Time-Life book on annuals.

Drew, John K. *Pictorial Guide to Hardy Perennials*. Kalamazoo, MI: Merchants Publishing Company, 1984.

A magazine-sized soft cover booklet with good color pictures of hardy perennials.

Fell, D. *New Ideas in Flower Gardening*. Barryington, Illinois: Countryside Books, 1976.

A magazine-sized soft cover booklet on the culture and use of bedding plants and herbaceous perennials. Many suggestions for using specific kinds of flowers effectively.

Ford, Gillian. *Herbaceous Perennials Suitable for Central Alberta*. Devon: Friends of the U of A Devonian Botanic Garden: Publication No. 6, May 1976.

The what, why, where, and how of growing herbaceous perennials with a descriptive listing of the author's selection of some of the more satisfactory herbaceous perennials for central Alberta.

Grayson, Rockwell and Esther. *The Complete Book of Bulbs*. New York: J.B. Lippincott Co., 1977.

An excellent general reference on bulbs for the home garden.

Hay, R. and P.M. Synge. *The Color Dictionary of Flowers and Plants for Home and Garden*. New York: Crown Publishers, Inc., 1969.

Over 2000 small, but excellent, color photographs of both woody and herbaceous plants for the home and garden with short descriptions and pertinent cultural information for each plant illustrated.

Kramer, Jack. *1000 Beautiful Garden Plants and How to Grow Them*. New York: William Morrow and Company, Inc., 1976.

The planning of a home garden, including vegetables, but predominantly a plant dictionary of trees, shrubs, annuals, perennials, bulbs and vines.

Millarville Horticultural Club. *Gardening Under the Arch*. Calgary: Friesen Printers, 1983.

Advice by amateurs on how to be successful gardeners in the "chinook belt" of Alberta.

Potter, C.H. *Perennials in the Garden.* New York: Criterian Books, 1959.

A somewhat outdated book but a good general guide to raising perennials.

Shewchuk, G.W. *Growing Roses in the Prairie Provinces.* Edmonton: G.W. Shewchuk Publisher, 1981.

An excellent book for all Alberta rosarians. A comprehensive book on growing roses in the prairie climate.

Still, Steven. *Herbaceous Ornamental Plants.* Champaign, IL: Stipes Publishing Company, 1982.

A dictionary of herbaceous ornamentals with line drawings to illustrate the form of each entry. An excellent reference book.

## INDEX

# LANDSCAPING

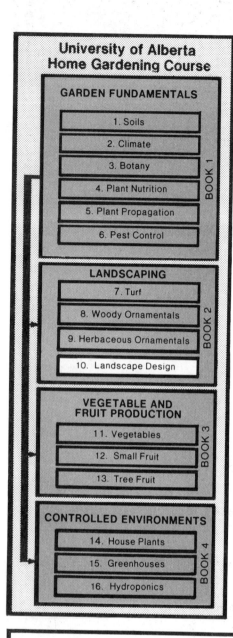

**University of Alberta Home Gardening Course**

**GARDEN FUNDAMENTALS**
- 1. Soils
- 2. Climate
- 3. Botany
- 4. Plant Nutrition
- 5. Plant Propagation
- 6. Pest Control

BOOK 1

**LANDSCAPING**
- 7. Turf
- 8. Woody Ornamentals
- 9. Herbaceous Ornamentals
- 10. Landscape Design

BOOK 2

**VEGETABLE AND FRUIT PRODUCTION**
- 11. Vegetables
- 12. Small Fruit
- 13. Tree Fruit

BOOK 3

**CONTROLLED ENVIRONMENTS**
- 14. House Plants
- 15. Greenhouses
- 16. Hydroponics

BOOK 4

# SELF-STUDY LESSON FEATURES

Self-study is an educational approach which allows you to study a subject where and when you want. The course is designed to allow students to study the course material efficiently and incorporates the following features.

**OBJECTIVES** — are found at the beginning of each lesson and allow you to determine what you can expect to learn in the lesson.

**LESSON MATERIAL** — is logically organized and broken down into fundamental components by ordered headings to assist you to comprehend the subject.

**REFERENCING** — between lessons and within lessons allows you to integrate course material.

The last two digits of the page number identify the page and the digits preceding these identify the lesson number (eg., 107: Lesson 1, page 7 or 1227: Lesson 12, page 27).

Referencing:

    sections within the same lesson (eg., see OSMOSIS)

    sections in other lessons (eg., see Botany lesson, OSMOSIS)

    figures and tables (eg., see Figure 7-3)

**FIGURES AND TABLES** — are found in abundance throughout the lessons and are designed to convey useful information in an easy to understand form.

**SIDEBARS** — are those areas in the lesson which are boxed and toned. They present information supplementary to the core content of the lesson.

**PRACTICAL PROJECTS** — are integrated within the lesson material and are included to allow you to apply principles and practices.

**SELF-CHECK QUIZ** — is provided at the end of each lesson and allows you to test your comprehension of the lesson material. Answers to the questions and references to the sections dealing with the questions are provided in the answer section. You should review any questions that you are unable to answer.

**GLOSSARY** — is provided at the end of each lesson and alphabetically lists the definitions of key concepts and terms.

**RESOURCE MATERIALS** — are provided at the end of each lesson and comprise a list of recommended learning materials for further study of the subject. Also included are author's comments on the potential application of each publication.

**INDEX** — alphabetically lists useful topics and their location within the lesson.

1986 University of Alberta Faculty of Extension

**Written by: R. Hugh Knowles, Professor Emeritus, F.C.S.L.A.**

ISBN 0-88864-852-9

(Book 2, Lesson 10)

THE PRODUCTION TEAM

| | |
|---|---|
| Managing Editor | Thom Shaw |
| Editor | Frank Procter |
| Production Coordinator | Kevin Hanson |
| Graphic Artists | Lisa Marsh |
| | Carol Powers |
| | Melanie Eastley Harbourne |
| Data Entry | Joan Geisterfer |

Published by the University of Alberta
Faculty of Extension Corbett Hall
Edmonton, Alberta, T6G 2G4

# LEARNING OBJECTIVES

After completing this lesson, the student should be able to:

1. recognize the importance of beginning all landscape planning and design with a statement of objectives.
2. identify and incorporate good functional relationships between the parts in order to establish if the plan is to work and conflicts are to be avoided.
3. recognize the importance of the visual aspects of landscape design and determine the degree to which such aspects promote unity.
4. identify the three ways in which unity can be expressed.
5. appreciate that good functional and aesthetic design solutions are not always compatible with the environment.
6. define foundation planting in terms of its purpose in the overall design of the landscape.

# TABLE OF CONTENTS

# LIST OF FIGURES AND TABLES

# INTRODUCTION

Landscape horticulture, within the context of this lesson, addresses the subject only as it applies to residential landscape design. The approach taken is one that is directed toward meeting the needs and desires of the users, one that recognizes the realities and limitations of the site and one that is guided in its entirety by adherence to aesthetic principles.

The acceptance of solutions to design problems is based primarily on how well the designer has met the set of original objectives. Therefore, one must recognize the fact that the final solution is not necessarily the best or only one. In most instances, the development of alternatives does not mean going back to 'square one'. Rather, the modification of a part or parts of the scheme may well generate changes that result in a well conceived plan. It is common practice for even the experienced designer to develop and explore a number of alternatives before arriving at a workable solution.

One of the objectives of this lesson is to have the student think of landscape in terms of the three elements: **trees**, **shrubs** and **groundcover** (see Woody Ornamentals lesson, PLANTING DESIGN). Each is of equal importance in its contribution. Trees, because of their size, can dominate things very readily and this must be recognized. Shrubs must be selected very carefully because most of the materials readily available from nurseries can often achieve a stature far greater than what the urban property can accommodate. If most shrubs for use on the urban property did not exceed 60 cm (2 ft.), garden design would be much easier. Later in this lesson, a planning concept for an urban property is shown (Figure 10-8). In it, trees and 'specimen' shrubs read as individuals, but the smaller shrubs are massed. Groundcover is also massed on the plan. The apparent role of groundcover is to provide continuity between the larger elements and to contribute some interest of its own, chiefly in foreground areas.

Case studies are used in this lesson. The first demonstrates the process used to develop a final working plan. Through the use of case studies, particular design problems are identified and dealt with. Some of these you will encounter when you start planning and designing your own garden.

It should be pointed out here that 'garden' is the term used in this lesson to describe an outdoor space designed for human use and enjoyment and it is often comprised of a number of parts. Because 'garden' denotes the **designed** outdoor space, it is not synonymous with the undesigned 'yard'.

## WHAT IS DESIGN?

In the design of anything, be it an ark or an automobile, a residential landscape or a transit terminal, work must be preceded by a **statement of objectives** which defines the functions to be served. Such a statement constitutes what is commonly referred to as a **design program**.

The statements used in the design program are of two types. There are those that are precise and measurable such as, 'the plan must provide parking space for six vehicles', and there are those that must be stated in a more abstract manner. For example, a statement that says 'some screening will be required on the north and west sides of the property', could be an appropriate abstract design statement. Such a statement encourages examination of more than one design solution. Alternately, if the statement says 'screening will be provided on the north and west sides of the property by a wooden fence', then the designer's freedom to examine and test alternative types of screening has been eliminated.

If program statements are well conceived and the program is in itself complete, then the approach to design can be uncomplicated, logical and fun. In design, some people are naturally more innovative than others. However, innovation is something that can be acquired with experience.

## THE FUNCTIONAL SIDE OF DESIGN

An early step in the design process is **transformation of the words of the program to a simplified graphic statement** which shows, in abstract form, only the parts and the relationships between them. Figure 10-1 shows this sort of abstraction as it applies to the problem of house design. Note that there is a difference in magnitude (strength or importance) in the relationships between the parts. Thus, strong relationships exist between entry and kitchen as well as kitchen and deck. Less strong relationships exist between both entry and living room and living room and deck. Graphic abstraction such as this leads to the next planning stage, that of **assigning approximate sizes and preferred locations to the various parts**. In landscape design, this stage is known as land-use planning, the outcome

Figure 10-1

## GRAPHIC STATEMENT OF RELATIONSHIPS

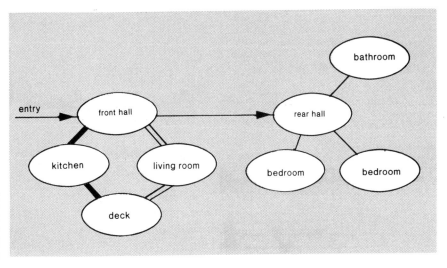

of which is the **land-use plan**. Figure 10-2 shows a simple floor plan (the equivalent of the landscape land-use plan) derived from the abstraction shown in Figure 10-1. Both the relative sizes of the parts and the relationships between them are expressed at this stage.

Since the land-use plan establishes the appropriate relationships between the parts, design beyond this point involves decisions on precise size and shape, on the choice of materials, on the environments in each part of the plan and, finally, on the total product.

## THE AESTHETIC SIDE OF DESIGN

Because the final solution must also be visually pleasing as well as functionally appropriate, the designer must have some familiarity with design principles. Primarily, **composition** is important. What is composition? Simply put, composition is the product of **unity**. If unity or 'oneness' is not apparent in the plan being created, then composition does not exist.

Composition can be fostered in one of three ways:

1. by repeating certain elements in different parts of the plan (**repetition**),

2. by utilizing a high degree of similarity between the elements (**harmony**), or,

3. by using **contrast** and developing a dominant theme. In this case, unity is achieved by the dominance established.

While unity is necessary to assure that a design is visually acceptable, there can still be a range of solutions within the limitations of composition. For example, a design that relies heavily on repetition can be uncomplicated. To some, such repetition is unimaginative and, when carried to the extreme, is boring or monotonous. Yet, such design may still fall within the limits of composition.

In those designs where unity is achieved by the development of harmony, interest lies somewhere between those developed with a high degree of repetition and those in which variety (contrast) is emphasized. With respect to variety, such compositions are always interesting because of contrast, a form of relationship that is dynamic and exciting.

Depending on the means used to achieve unity, composition can be of three types. Each type has its place, hence, no single type of composition is appropriate to all situations. Within composition, the range of aesthetic values wherein unity is readily maintained, is summarized in Figure 10-3. If this range is exceeded in either direction, then composition, if it continues to exist at all, does so by expressing exceptional 'dullness' on the one hand (B) or extreme 'busyness' on the other (A). With the amount of repetition and variety shown in (C) however, there should be no difficulty in achieving composition at this point. Within the upper and lower limits of the range, it should be possible to develop compositions that vary from the dynamic to the conservative.

Of the three types of composition, the one that derives its unity almost entirely

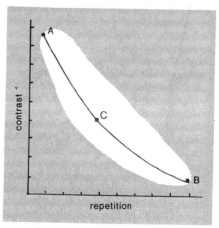

## Figure 10-3
## EFFECT OF CONTRAST AND REPETITION ON COMPOSITION

through repetition is the type best suited to the design of great formal landscapes. Many of the world's grand urban designs relied heavily on repetition to achieve their unity. Compositions that depend on harmony are more apt to be found in the sylvan settings of the 18th Century English garden, an art form that received its inspiration from the French school of landscape painting. As previously stated, the third type of composition, the one that achieves a basic degree of contrast (with dominance), is the most dynamic and exciting of the three and is typical of much contemporary design. Examples can be found in everything from mainstream modern architecture to residential gardens.

In the design of the contemporary residential garden, many (including this author) advocate an approach that first calls for the creation of a basic development plan in which unity and interest are incorporated. This can only be achieved by paying particular attention to the arrangement of the parts. Once the requirements of this stage are met, then other decisions can be made concerning the materials (architectural and plant) that should be used to articulate the plan and complete the job. At this second stage, unity is still of primary concern. Hence, most professionals work within a modest pallette of materials with enough variety to provide interest, but not so varied that unity is sacrificed to diversity.

## Figure 10-2
## FLOOR PLAN DERIVED FROM GRAPHIC STATEMENT

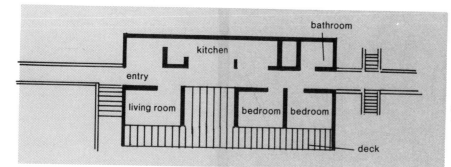

While the choice and distribution of plants is important from the standpoint of visual design, such decisions are not based solely on aesthetic principles. Each material, each plant, each group of plants must be looked at on the basis of what they can do to make the plan work. If a major element does not fulfill some important function relating to the plan, then it should not be selected, regardless of its individual appeal.

Case Study #1

The first case study highlights the **process** of designing a garden on a residential property.

Mr. and Mrs. A live in a house situated on a large, pie-shaped lot. They have three children in their family, a pre-schooler and two teenagers. The living room of the house faces the back yard and, at ground level, there is good visual and physical connection between indoors and out. Figure 10-4 shows part of the main floor plan of the house and the back yard.

The A's wish to develop a garden that can be visually enjoyed year round. They frequently entertain and often extend these activities to the out-of-doors, as weather permits. In addition, they want a special play space for the pre-schooler and her friends and, finally, they wish to have a paddle tennis court for use by the adults and teenagers.

Figure 10-5 illustrates, in a very abstract way, the sorts of relationship that must be addressed within the existing limitations of site plan and floor plan. It identifies the need for a strong relationship between kitchen and outdoor living. It emphasizes both the desirability of having the outdoor living area (patio) connected to the kitchen and extended from the indoor living area, as well as the importance of integrating both living areas with the garden. Figure 10-5 also identifies two more fundamental considerations. First is the desirability of separating the children's sand box and play area from the main adult parts of the site while assuring that it is located close to the part of the

house where it is conveniently possible to maintain supervision. It also illustrates the necessity for visually separating the paddle tennis court from the rest of the garden. The court is within an enclosed wire cage; hence, its visual separation is an absolute necessity.

Having established, in abstract form, the relationship between elements that must be considered, the A's can now develop a land-use plan (see Figure 10-6). Note that the approximate sizes of the various parts are displayed on the land-use plan without detailing their form. This is accomplished through refinement of the land-use plan to produce the basic development plan (see Figure 10-7).

Figure 10-7A shows one such refinement of the land-use plan. Compare this plan with the next refinement in Figure 10-7B, the basic development plan. The allocation of space is very similar in both. However, in the basic development plan (plan B), the parts are more fully integrated. Note that the eastern edge of the outdoor living area in Figure 10-7A is

## Figure 10-4
## SITE PLAN

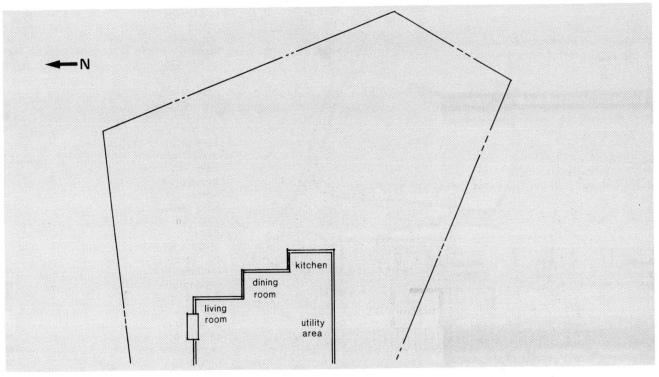

N

kitchen

dining room

living room

utility area

## Figure 10-5
## DESIGN RELATIONSHIPS

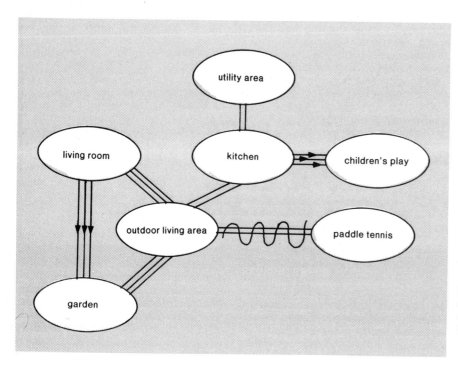

a straight line parallel to the house. This implies that the outdoor living area is simply part of the house. This is changed in Figure 10-7B. The eastern edge of the outdoor living area now parallels the house for only part of its distance, then changes direction and invades the garden. This relatively small change produces a major impact since the group living area is no longer simply a part of the house, but is now related to both house and garden (the way it should be).

Things can be 'fleshed out' when a satisfactory basic development plan has been achieved. By this time, the designer has recognized the strengths and weaknesses of the site and has some thoughts on how design problems can be handled. Since the property in this case backs onto a service lane, there is no question that some form of enclosure is required. As no one purposely develops a garden with a service lane as background, a substantial, solid fence along both the northern and eastern property lines is

## Figure 10-6
## LAND-USE PLAN

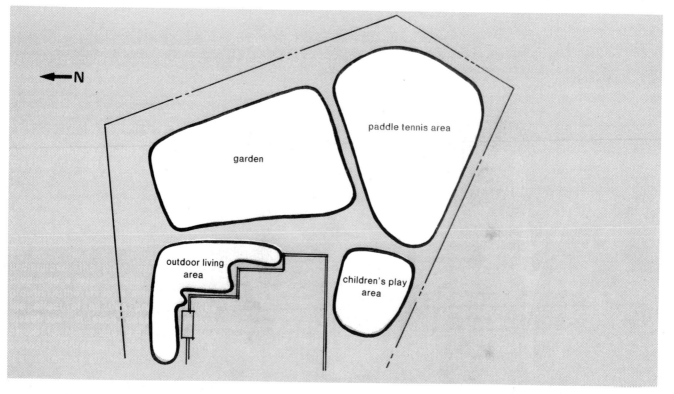

Figure 10-7A
REFINEMENT OF LAND-USE PLAN

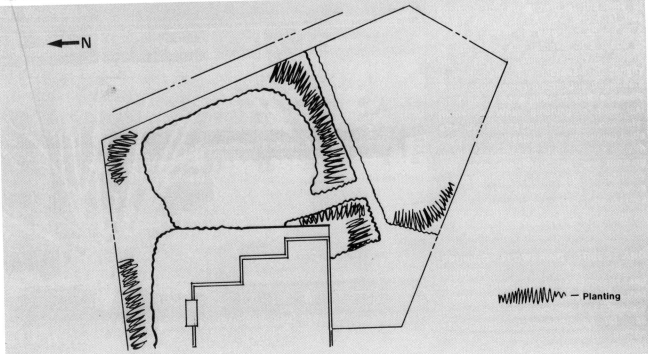

Planting

Figure 10-7B
BASIC DEVELOPMENT PLAN

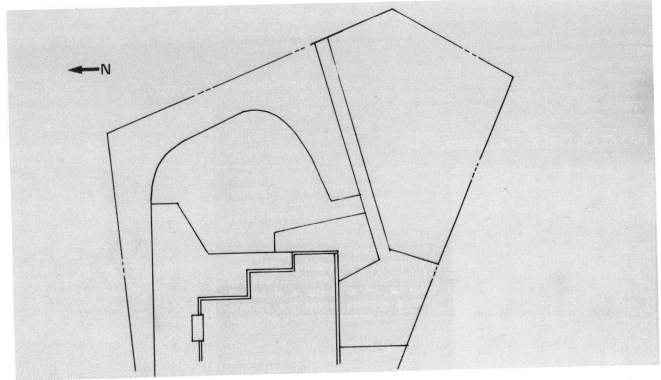

called for. However, land-use changes occur at a point on the eastern property line where the route to the garbage drop meets the lane. Because of the very marked difference in land use that occurs south of this point, it falls to the designer to justify the southern extension of the solid fence (if that is to be the decision). Since this is also the area assigned to paddle tennis, is there any justification for using the same type of fence? Although the need for a fence may well exist here to discourage trespass by animals and children, this can be achieved by use of a simple, low maintenance type of fence (such as chain link). However, there may be some justification for reverting to the original screen fence type adjacent to the children's play area. Such a consideration may be more for the benefit of the next-door neighbor than for the children. Children's play areas can be cluttered with toys and other things so, for the sake of harmony with neighbors, the children's play area is screened from the adjoining property.

Having integrated the functional elements within the basic development plan, attention can now shift to selection and placement of plant materials. Figure 10-8 shows the planting concept developed for the A's property.

Note that the trees used on, or adjacent to, the outdoor living area are all high headed. This is a 'people space', hence, the trees chosen must be compatible with the activities of people. The inclusion of a high headed conifer just south of the fence on the northern property line is of special significance. Its primary function throughout the year is to screen the group living area from a nearby window in the house next door.

At the southern end of the garden area, there is no fence to help screen the paddle tennis court. Hence, screening falls totally to plant material. The primary elements chosen to do the job are a cluster of three well-placed spruce trees and a low headed deciduous tree. These are supported by masses of shrubbery.

The combination of elements used reflects a necessity to achieve a practical screen without getting out of scale. Scale is also an important consideration in the two planting areas adjacent to the pre-schooler's area. Here the plants have been chosen and used to soften things rather than screen them. Single trees and masses of low shrubbery accomplish this without losing sight of scale.

A somewhat less than conventional solution to the landscape plan is expressed on the eastern boundary of the site. The fence line is located 1 m (about 3 ft) inside the eastern property line. Trees are planted outside the fence rather than inside. The planting of trees outside the fence may well be questioned, but there are perfectly logical reasons for doing this. The fence itself presents a long horizontal line at eye level, something that would be less dominant if it were broken up. This can be achieved by the use of a few well placed trees which are capable of

**Figure 10-8
CONCEPT**

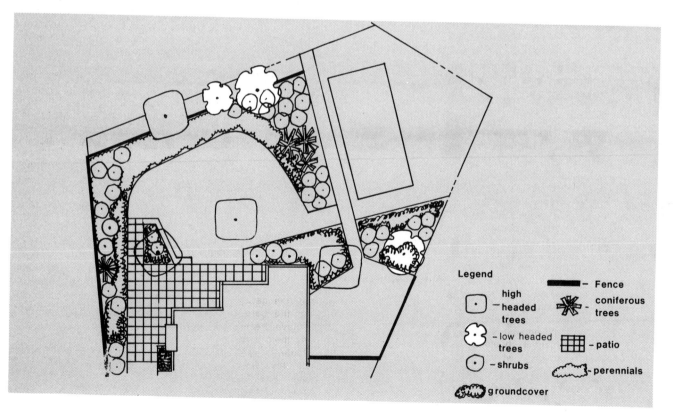

Legend

☐ – high headed trees

✿ – low headed trees

◉ – shrubs

▨ groundcover

▬ – Fence

✳ – coniferous trees

▦ – patio

〰 – perennials

raising their canopies above the top of the fence. Also, because the family living room faces east, it was decided that something of high interest should be planted on the garden side of the enclosure. What better spot for a perennial border — a feature capable of providing exceptional interest throughout the entire growing season (see Herbaceous Ornamentals lesson, SELECTION AND PLANNING). Because most herbaceous perennials are unable to compete with woody plants, the planting area is reserved exclusively for the perennials and the woody plants are relegated to space on the far side of the fence.

This case study shows that good landscape design depends on how well the solution meets the needs and requirements of the users, and on how well the parts fit together. Like other forms of art, landscape design must conform to the universal principles of artistic expression.

Case Study #2

The second case study emphasizes the need to recognize site limitations that affect landscape design and to solve these problems creatively.

The most common stereotype of the small urban garden is a patch of lawn at the back of the house surrounded by perimeter beds of shrubs or flowers with the entire space enclosed by a single fence type. There may or may not be a vegetable plot but, if present, it will not likely be screened from the house and garden.

One of the objectives of this lesson is to counter this design stereotype and foster a desire for innovative problem solving. There is seldom justification for a single fence type around the whole yard. Yet, how often do you see enclosure change in response to a change in land-use. As a result, a trip down a service lane in any new middle class neighbourhood is not unlike a trip by the livestock pens at a packing plant. If a barrier is required for privacy, screening, or shelter, then it should be high enough and solid enough to satisfy those requirements, but it should never extend beyond the area where it is needed.

The property shown in Figure 10-9 is a corner lot with a bus route on the west side, which justifies the need for solid fencing on that side of the property. In terms of the need for enclosure within the garden itself, it becomes obvious that separating the vegetable plot from the garden space must be achieved in some way. A similar need can be identified at one point on the eastern boundary of the garden, where the garden space would otherwise be completely exposed to the house next door. If these two needs for screening were to be solved by repeating the fence used on the west side of the property, the effect would be overpowering. In design, too much repetition fosters monotony (see THE AESTHETIC SIDE OF DESIGN). This is the main reason for selecting a different screen material, since screening is still required. The plan shows that the vegetable plot is screened from the garden by a hedge, while the house next door is visually eliminated by a low headed tree and a few shrubs.

Another point worth talking about is the plan's deviation from property lines. Property lines are not so important that all edges within the garden must parallel them. The plan in Figure 10-9 demonstrates this. In fact, this deviation in alignment introduces a degree of contrast that contributes a certain amount of interest to the scheme.

With respect to the question of unity, note that the parts hang together as they did in the first case study. This is accomplished by careful repetition of edge alignments in various parts of the garden, although the parts are separated in space.

There are a number of points that could be raised related to planting and environments in this garden. Since the garden faces south, the location of the tree next to the patio can be justified, provided it is a type that provides some overhead canopy and, at the same time, does not attract pests or drop things onto the patio beneath it.

Because of their locations, the garage and the hedge separating the garden from the vegetable plot have heavily shaded environments on their north sides. In fact, only shade tolerant material can grow within the areas affected. For this reason, turf grass has been eliminated and other materials substituted in both areas. North of the hedge, a bed of shade tolerant groundcover solves the problem. North of the garage, brick paving is used to eliminate the problem of having to grow something in that spot. In addition, it provides a necessary and practical space for barbecuing.

One of the things called for in this garden is space for perennial flowers. The bed along the west property line is highly desirable for this purpose as there is a suitable background in the form of the screen fence. To minimize the competition between tree and shrub roots with the perennials, trees and shrubs (with one exception) are located on city property outside the fence. These materials are tall enough to create an impact within the garden without occupying useable space. A further attempt is made to minimize root competition by raising the soil in the perennial bed by 15 cm (6 in) to help get the roots of the perennials above those of the nearest woody plants.

Finally, to prevent the garden space from 'leaking out' through the vegetable plot, a single small tree is planted in a strategic spot in a location that is relative to the patio and the path to the vegetable plot. Since this is a small tree, it provides the screening necessary without occupying too much space in the vegetable garden.

In the design of gardens, the consequences of all decisions must be carefully weighed. Designers must constantly be aware of the implications brought about by design conditions and elements. What are going to be the consequences of any changes? How can adverse impacts be minimized? Since designers must frequently compromise otherwise good solutions, they must be prepared to look for innovative ways of solving the problems created.

Case Study #3

Case Study #3 illustrates the importance of edge and enclosure to garden design. In this example, a major problem is avoided by a simple, but well conceived, strategy.

Figure 10-10 presents a solution to the problem of developing a garden in a shallow but wide space at the rear of a house. In this situation, it would have

## Figure 10-9
## GARDEN DESIGN - CASE STUDY TWO

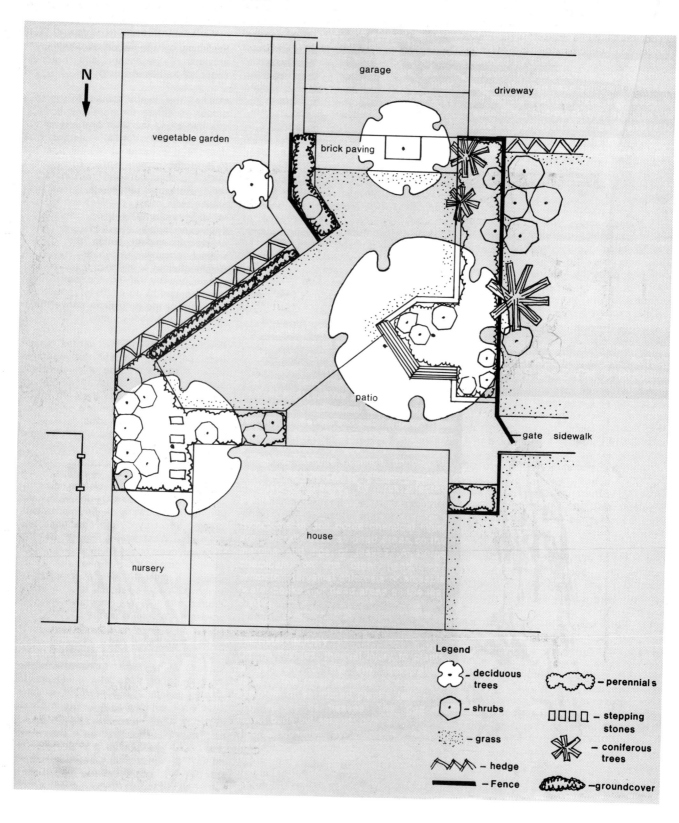

N

vegetable garden

garage

driveway

brick paving

patio

gate   sidewalk

house

nursery

**Legend**

- deciduous trees
- shrubs
- grass
- hedge
- Fence
- perennials
- stepping stones
- coniferous trees
- groundcover

been very easy to become locked into the stereotype referred to earlier. The family room is located in the north east part of the house and relates to a wooden deck some 45 cm (18 in) above the lawn area. Fortunately, the designer of the deck had the good sense to orient its northern edge to the northwest and, thus, relate the user to much more of the space than would otherwise have been available. Imagine how things would have looked had the northern edge of the deck paralleled the north face of the house. The relationship of the deck with the whole western part of the garden would have been lost. Instead, the deck edge is turned to the northwest and the alignment of the edge between lawn and

## Figure 10-10
## GARDEN DESIGN - CASE STUDY THREE

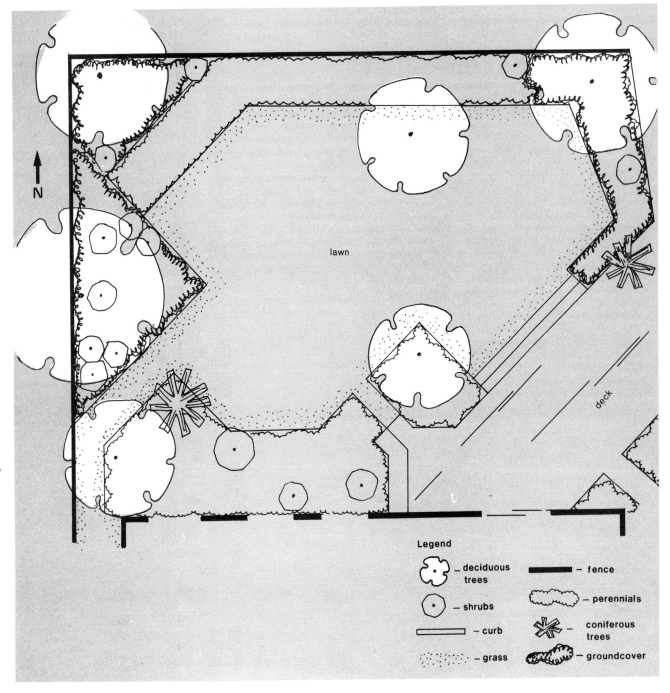

Legend

- deciduous trees
- shrubs
- curb
- grass
- fence
- perennials
- coniferous trees
- groundcover

planting area adjusted so that, in part at least, it relates to the alignment of the deck edge. The plan then takes on a coherence and a degree of unity that otherwise would not have been achieved.

In this plan, land-use is **monotypical**. There is, therefore, justification for using one type of enclosure throughout. It should be noted, however, that enclosure here consists of far more than a fence. The trees and shrubs provide a counterpoint that makes the combination of trees and fence far more acceptable than either fence or trees alone.

Case Study #4

When lots are very large it is easy to develop spaces that are larger than what the owner actually has time (or the inclination) to care for. Because of this, it is important to examine the land-uses carefully in the beginning, so that the proposed sizes for the various parts fit the functions they are to serve and the efforts required to maintain them.

Figure 10-11 is the plan developed for a garden at the rear of a house on a large pie-shaped lot. The rear property line abuts a service lane. Both the depth of the back yard and the width of the property at its rear extremity assure space of generous proportions. However, the lane that runs along the edge of the property for more than 30 m (100 ft) is a major visual detraction.

Figure 10-11
GARDEN DESIGN - CASE STUDY FOUR

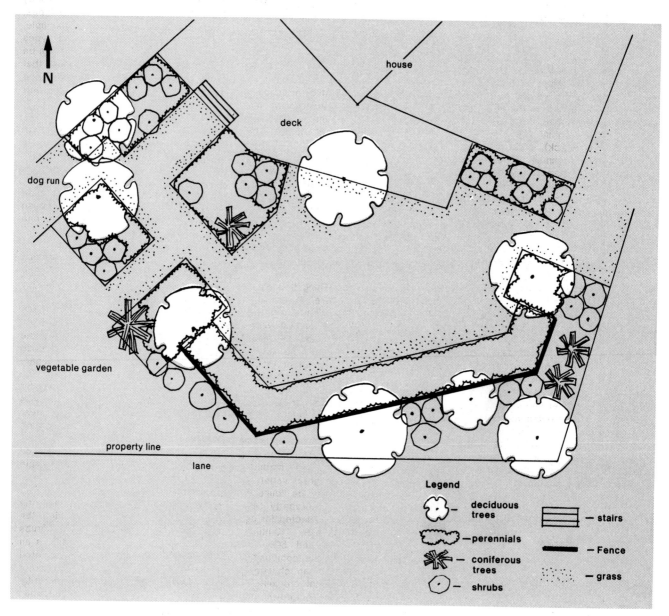

The four objectives of this landscape problem are:

1. to develop an interesting garden space of manageable size that becomes an extension of the house and deck,

2. to set aside a separate space for a large vegetable garden that is visually separate from the house and its outdoor living area,

3. to provide an unobtrusive, fenced-in run for the family dog, and

4. to develop an innovative solution to the problem created by the service lane.

The problem of the lane is dealt with first. To reduce the impact of the service lane, an edge to the garden is chosen that deviates strongly from the alignment of the rear property line. If the garden is examined from within (i.e., from a viewpoint on the deck), it can be seen that neither the alignment of edge nor enclosure (the screen fence) bear any relationship to the lane. Edge and enclosure, however, do bear more than a subtle relationship to house and deck. This affinity is most obvious from within the garden.

The other three objectives are also satisfied by this solution. The hidden dog-run and the visually separate vegetable garden are easily accommodated within this concept and no apparent awkwardness is required to do the job.

While large lots frequently appear to have too much space, they do provide more of an opportunity to do things than properties at the other end of the scale. Nevertheless, this freedom should not be accepted by the designer as an excuse to waste or 'throw away' parts of the property. With this freedom goes a responsibility to devise innovative ideas for use of the extra space.

## LANDSCAPE PROBLEMS AND PRACTICAL SOLUTIONS

Many of the problems that people encounter in gardens are of their own making. Invariably, such problems arise from failure to recognize the consequences of a choice or action.

### SUN AND SHADE

Shade from trees is sometimes difficult to deal with. In certain places and at certain times of the day, shade is highly valued. Yet, what are the consequences of that shade on other parts of the garden at other times of the day? The whole question of natural light in the garden is a subject that must be addressed early in the design stages so that appropriate materials can be used in places where light levels may otherwise become a limiting factor.

The large-leaved golden ray (*Ligularia*) is an interesting case. If it is grown in a location where it gets afternoon sun, its leaves hang like damp dishrags from 2 p.m. until the sun drops below the horizon. On the other hand, many of our more popular perennials (plants like Peony, Iris and Lily) never reach their full potential unless planted in full sun.

Turfgrass is also something that should be commented on here. If shade is intense, as is the case on the north side of buildings, then shade tolerant weeds, weedy grasses and moss can easily take over. There is really no way of coping with this situation other than to eliminate grass as the surfacing material and to substitute a broad-leaved, shade-loving groundcover or to pave over the area.

While turf grass has its limitations in the shadiest parts of the garden, the use of turfgrass mixtures has made it possible to handle the great variety of light conditions that may be found on various parts of the property. For example, if the mixture selected for use is one containing 50% Kentucky bluegrass (sun loving) and 50% fine fescue (shade loving), the composition of the established turf can change in response to environmental pressure. In shady areas, fescue outgrows the

bluegrass and becomes dominant, while the opposite occurs in the sunnier areas that favor the Kentucky bluegrass.

### PLANTING DESIGN

Another problem in landscape design arises out of woody plant distribution in the garden. In all gardens, the owners must first try to achieve interest over a long season by selecting an array of plants that display their best effects at different times of the year. This is never easy, however, primarily because of space limitations in the small garden. It may be necessary to restrict woody plant selection to perhaps three types, which are then repeated. For example, suppose that one of the three types selected is the Nanking cherry. It can be distributed throughout the garden so that when its season (early spring) arrives, it provides interest in more than one part of the garden.

Again, because of spatial limitations, the designer of the small garden would do well to look for plants that have more than one 'best' season. For example, some plants produce a good display of bloom and their foliage shows good autumn coloration. The highbush cranberry (*Viburnum trilobum*) is one such plant.

One of the imaginative design strategies frequently employed by landscape architects involves choosing a flowering tree and a flowering shrub that bloom at the same time with the same color. Such combinations provide the repetition necessary to give unity and, at the same time, give the degree of contrast (size and form in this case) necessary to provide interest For example, the Nanking cherry can be used with the Pincherry (*Prunus pennsylvanica*) or with Ussurian pear (*Pyrus ussuriensis*) to create this effect. The double-flowering plum (*Prunus triloba multiplex*) is a good companion plant with the rosybloom crabapple (*Malus niedzwetzkyana* 'Hopa').

There are two approaches that might be taken to the problem of planting the small garden. One uses trees, shrubs and groundcovers. The other utilizes an infrastructure of only a few well selected and well placed trees and shrubs. Major interest in the latter case is provided by a good selection of herbaceous perennials and bulbs, supported by annual flowers to give a good succession of bloom. A garden of the first type has groups of shrubs linked by groundcover and trees located at strategic locations to give some variety to the skyline. This type of garden lends itself to north facing properties where shade is the major limiting factor to the growing of perennial and annual flowers.

## NON-PLANT PROBLEMS

There are non-plant problems caused by climate, soils and combinations of the two that are unique to the Prairie Provinces. Consequently, one can not pick up a book written for southern Ontario, the lower mainland of British Columbia or sunny California and expect to find totally practical solutions. One such problem is that often referred to as the 'sinking sidewalk' or the 'plunging patio', wherein a perfectly good and expensive bit of paving loses its equilibrium a year or two after construction. This type of failure is caused by frost action on soils with significant shrink/swell properties. In all the black soil zones in the prairie provinces, soils tend to be noticeably heavy. This gives them the ability to swell when wet and shrink when dry. Because of the strength of the shrink/swell forces, it is absolutely necessary to completely remove the topsoil from beneath any proposed hard surfacing in the garden. In some cases, it simply means a 22.5 cm (9 in)

excavation to a solid base of subsoil clay, replacing the soil removed with a 15 cm (6 in) layer of crushed rock and 7.5 cm (3 in) of concrete. If the excavation exceeds these depth requirements, then compacted subsoil clay can be used to reduce the depth of the excavation. The subsoil clay in Edmonton, for example, is so resistant to the penetration of moisture that it provides a very suitable base on which to place the granular material for sidewalks and patios.

Brick or uni-stone pavements have become very common in gardens and because stability is of great importance, the base for these surfaces should be prepared as carefully as those for concrete. Once the topsoil has been removed, well compacted sand makes a satisfactory material on which to set the surfacing material.

Frost action in the region can have equally devastating effects on retaining walls, which are frequently used in gardens. Most of these structures do not require massive foundations. Nevertheless, they must have foundations that respect the action of frost.

For most garden retaining walls, a suitable foundation consists of a modest 30 cm (12 in) horizontal beam of reinforced concrete poured with its upper surface at, or just above, ground level. Such structures are known as grade beams and are not free floating,

but are supported by concrete piles drilled to frost line (1.7 m or about 6 ft at Edmonton). The piles are placed at intervals beneath the grade beam. The distance between piles depends on the load being supported by the beam. There is an added precaution against frost action that is recommended with this type of construction, that being to build a form that gives the grade beam a V bottom (see Figure 10-12). This configuration tends to dissipate the upward acting, frost-motivated forces. Since these forces push against a sloping bottom, there is a tendency for the uplifted soil to slip against the surface of the beam, rather than to act upon it squarely.

Because of heavy soils and frost action, the stability of fences and screens is frequently a problem. The common practice is to build them completely of wood and replace them when they start to deteriorate. The trouble with this philosophy is that wooden fences tend to either sag or lose their horizontal alignment within five years of construction. While this is disturbing, most homeowners are inclined to live with the sagging structure for a few more years before considering a replacement. It makes far more sense to put in a structure that retains its stability indefinitely. Experience favors steel posts to frost line and set into concrete. There are modifications of this technique which may be somewhat less expensive. The point to be made, however, is that whatever vertical support structure is chosen, its base must be set to just below the frost line to avoid heaving.

## FOUNDATION PLANTING

Foundation planting is used at the front and, sometimes, the sides of the house. It is the planting in the public part of the property, the part people see when walking or driving down the street. Because of its location, the main function of foundation planting is to provide a setting for the house; that is, to help the house become a part of the neighborhood.

Foundation planting comprises two parts. The first is the **base planting**, which consists of the shrubbery and groundcover adjacent to the house. The second part involves only tree planting. Trees are frequently used as elements of 'enframement' but are always used to

### Figure 10-12
## GRADE BEAM FOUNDATION FOR RETAINING WALL

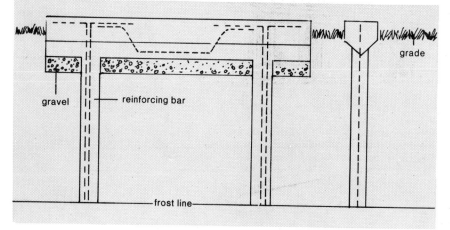

complete the picture.

## THE BASE PLANTING

Shrubs used in the base planting must be in scale with the building. If the house is large, then the use of larger plants and larger plant masses is justified. If the house is small, the plants and plant masses must conform. A designer also makes further concessions to the structure by emphasizing important parts with base planting material. The main entrance is always of special importance. This is the point to which guests are directed, hence, it must say 'you have arrived'. Corners are other important spots but here, the concern is of a different nature. The function of corner plantings is to tie the house to the ground.

The major elements of a good base planting should be linked with groundcover plants or inert groundcover material (eg., bark chip). When living groundcovers are used, they must be planted close enough to provide complete cover in a single growing season. When this is done, they are able to compete with weeds and, at the same time, provide a maintenance-free carpet.

The use of color is the final thing to be addressed on the subject of base planting. How much color should be used and where? Because the house is the dominant element and the base planting is used to complement it, color must be incorporated carefully. It is not uncommon to see homeowners use a single color to complement the green foliage of the more important elements of the base planting. Scarlet geraniums are commonly used for this purpose since, with a small amount of scarlet, a large amount of green gains in intensity. This is often referred to as the structural use of color.

## THE TREE PLANTING

While the base planting serves a useful purpose, such planting alone can only go so far toward making the house a part of the neighborhood. Trees are actually more important in meeting this objective. However, the effect is greatly increased when both the tree planting and the base planting are used in a complementary fashion.

Trees and their locations must be carefully selected since trees can often be out of scale with their surroundings.

For example, the huge American elm would hardly be an appropriate tree to complement a small bungalow. With regard to tree location, there is nothing that applies to all situations. In most cases, however, trees are used to enframe buildings and to screen other things. Thus, the choice and location of trees on the property is usually determined by the functions they are to serve.

Two foundation planting examples are presented to demonstrate the technique.

Example #1

The house shown in Figure 10-13 is a conventional two story with the usual set back from the street. A sidewalk leads directly to the front door. Because the house is of simple, straightforward design, the base planting is also simple and straightforward. Emphasis is placed near the main entrance and the corners. The major shrubs are linked together with groundcover.

One of the more important considerations in this example is the scale of plant material used. Plants achieving a stature of more than 75 cm

## Figure 10-13A
## FOUNDATION PLANTING - EXAMPLE ONE

Figure 10-13B

Figure 10-13C

(30 in) are obviously too large. Selecting shrubs for base planting is not always easy. Certain plants of a particular stature are often unavailable. However, the same required effect can sometimes be achieved by massing several smaller plants together. In many instances, this solution is actually the preferred arrangement.

Figure 10-13B shows that the base planting makes a significant contribution but, on further examination, it seems of little consequence without the trees. This fact is very apparent in new residential neighborhoods during the early years of development.

The placement of trees in this example, plays an important role in enframing the house. The solution (Figure 10-13C) shows that it is not necessary to choose identical locations on either side of the property for the trees. In fact, it is not necessary that trees be the same Species or even the same size. A small tree placed forward on the property, as in Figure 10-13C, can be as important as a larger tree placed further back from the street.

In Example #2 (see Figure 10-14), the house is an unconventional box-like structure with a degree of busyness expressed in the facade. A person looking at this house for the first time would have great difficulty in deciding whether the vertical panels dominate the horizontal or whether it is the other way around. It is one of the functions of foundation planting to resolve such contradictions.

In this example, the base planting (see Figure 10-14B) is a good deal more intricate than in the previous one (see Figure 10-13B). The edges of the planting beds quite obviously reflect the squareness of the building and a good deal of attention has been paid to the use of groundcover. In this plan, groundcovers are a major (but not dominant) element. The shrubs in the base planting are located in strategic positions and are all in scale with the house. There does not appear to be any real problem with their placement, provided the groundcover is used to link them.

The base planting in Figure 10-14B is

nevertheless most ineffective without the tree planting (see Figure 10-14C). When these are added, the importance of the tree component becomes obvious. As mentioned earlier, the vertical and horizontal panels in the house facade conflict with one another. How can this conflict be resolved by foundation planting? Obviously the choice of a tall, vertical, high-headed tree can go a long way toward resolving such conflict. Because of the form of the trees and their placement, the vertical elements of the house are now able to dominate the horizontal and resolve the conflict.

## CONCLUSION

This lesson shows that good gardens don't just grow. It should be obvious, at this stage, that gardens require a good deal of planning and design. Both planning and design of the garden are straightforward logical processes. They begin with a statement of objectives and a site plan.

The planning process is a broad brush technique that establishes relationships

Figure 10-14A
FOUNDATION PLANTING - EXAMPLE TWO

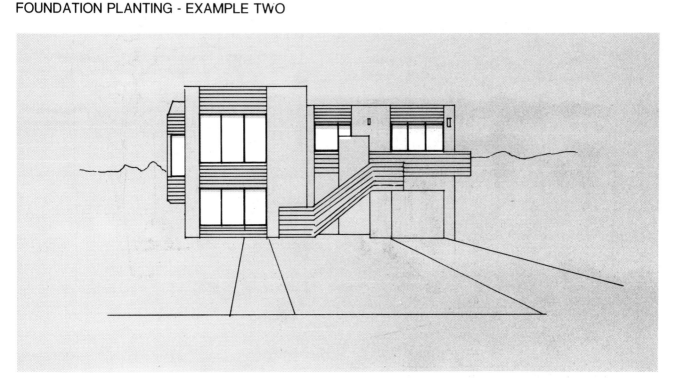

Figure 10-14 B

Figure 10-14 C

between the parts and selects appropriate parts of the site for the various components. The end point of planning is the land-use plan. From this point forward, the process is referred to as landscape design.

In design, adequate size and shape become the first concerns, although integration of the parts into some well unified configuration proceeds at about the same time.

When the designer is satisfied with the appearance of the basic development plan, then landscape horticulture begins. Appropriate plants must be chosen for the various parts of the site, their requirements must be met, and their contribution to the landscape must be assessed so that they might add to the unity and interest already established in the basic development plan.

Planting the front of the house is less demanding than planting the garden because space is not being dealt with to the same degree. In foundation planting, a setting is being created and, while aesthetic considerations are similar to those used in garden design, the functional requirements are much simpler.

## RESOURCE MATERIALS

Eckbo, Garrett. *Landscape for Living*. New York: F.W. Dodge Corp., 1950.

A well documented, easy to read, little book on the subject of planning and design of the residential landscape.

Graves, Maitland. *The Art and Color of Design*. New York: McGraw Hill, 1951.

An exceptionally good, readable, very well illustrated text dealing exclusively with the universal principles of fine arts.

Hoag, Donald C. *Trees and Shrubs for the Northern Plains*. Fargo, North Dakota: North Dakota Institute for Regional Studies, 1965.

A good text on the subject of landscape horticulture in the prairie region.

Knowles, R.H. *Woody Ornamentals for the Prairie Provinces*. Edmonton: University of Alberta Bulletin 58, 1975.

A good reference when looking for descriptions of hardy trees, shrubs and groundcovers.

Pierceall, G.M. *Residential Landscapes*. Reston, Virginia: Reston Publishing Co. Inc., 1984.

The complete guide to residential landscape design. Deals with plans for all housing types from the single family home to multi-family housing.

Vay Dyke, Scott. *From Line to Design*. West Lafayette, Indiana: PDA Publishers Corp., 1982.

A good text for those interested in the planning and design processes.

Wang, Thomas C. *Plan and Section Drawing*. Toronto: Van Nostrand Reinhold, 1979.

A good landscape graphics handbook.

## SELF CHECK *QUIZ*

1. Describe the difference between a land-use plan and a basic development plan?

2. Why is it necessary to use dominant elements in compositions involving contrast?

3. Harmonic repetition is a form of relationship involving both harmony and repetition. Think about it and then describe how a composition employing circular elements only, would differ from another composition employing circular elements only, if the first involved harmonic repetition and the second, just pure repetition.

4. Describe compositions A, B, and C, shown in Figure 10-3, in terms of their content of contrast and repetition.

5. Looking at edge in Figure 10-9 and 10-10, identify two sets of alignments in each (by letter A and B) that have a critical role in establishing unity within each plan. What form of relationship has been expressed by these sets of alignments to assure unity?

6. Why are dwarf conifers so well suited to base planting situations?

## SELF CHECK *ANSWERS*

1. A land-use plan establishes the appropriate locations for and relationships between the parts of a landscape plan based on the objectives to be met and the nature of the site.

   A basic development plan is derived from the land-use plan. It displays the relationships and locations established in the land-use plan but carries them forward to the point where the refinements of shape and size of the ground plane components have been determined (see Case Study #1 - page 1003, Figure 10-6 - page 1004 and Figure 10-7B - page 1005).

2. Dominant elements are used in compositions involving contrast to create unity, which would otherwise be sacrificed to diversity (see THE AESTHETIC SIDE OF DESIGN - page 1002).

3. In a composition that uses harmonic repetition, the elements consist of circles of varying size. In a composition that uses repetition, the elements consist of circles of the same size (see THE AESTHETIC SIDE OF DESIGN - page 1002).

4. In A, the composition contains chiefly elements of contrast with little repetition. It could be either very dynamic or downright busy. In B, the composition contains much repetition and very little contrast. This composition will be very dull and un-interesting. In C, there is both a moderate amount of contrast and repetition. The composition is likely quite interesting and strongly unified (see THE AESTHETIC SIDE OF DESIGN - page 1002).

5. Repetition is the form of relationship expressed by these sets of alignments (see THE AESTHETIC SIDE OF DESIGN - page 1002).

6. Small scale, form and density are important in base planting situations. Dwarf conifers have all three characteristics (see THE BASE PLANTING - page 1010).

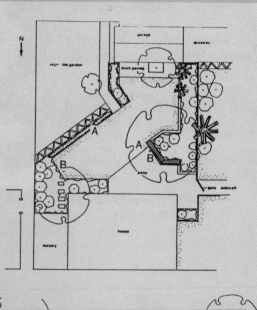

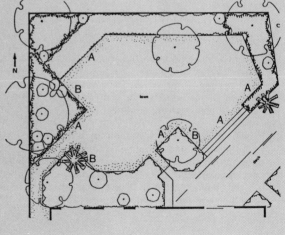

**aesthetic principles** - principles involved with artistic expression (eg., composition; unity; dominance).

**aesthetic values** - good and bad, depending on how a design relates to aesthetic principles.

**alignment** - line or direction expressed by a fence, pathway, or road.

**backyard** - unimproved portion of the property behind the house.

**basic development plan** - plan developed as a result of refinement of the land-use plan. This plan shows ground form only — no plant materials.

**canopy** - branch structure of a tree.

**composition** - organization of the parts of a plan to achieve a unified whole.

**complementary** - situation that prevails when two things are associated and the one gains from the other and vice versa.

**contrast** - form of relationship between elements in which maximum differences exist.

**edge** - line of demarcation separating two kinds of material (eg., turf and pavement; turf and woody or herbaceous plants).

**enclosure** - structure (architectural or plant) used to delineate a space.

**floor plan** - plan of a building that deals with room and corridor arrangement.

**foundation planting** - planting used on the public or street side of the house. It consists not only of the materials used against the foundation but also the trees used on this part of the property.

**garden** - designed outdoor space for use and enjoyment.

**grade beam** - horizontal beam at grade level supported by piles which go down to the frost line.

**granular material** - sand, gravel, or crushed rock used to provide a suitable base for poured hard surface areas and flexible paving, such as uni-stone.

**groundcover** - low woody or herbaceous ornamental plants seldom more than 15 cm (6 in) high that are capable of covering the soil quickly and economically so that they might compete with weeds.

**harmony** - form of relationship between elements in which strong similarities exist.

**high headed tree** - tree that carries its branches above 2 m (over 6 ft).

**infrastructure** - basic elements of a plan.

**land-use plan** - plan derived from the analysis of site in relation to functions to be provided.

**monotypic** - single type.

- part of the garden used chiefly for entertaining; the counterpart of the living room.

**pile** - columnar structure of reinforced concrete used in the support of a grade beam.

**repetition** - form of relationship between elements in which there is no difference expressed.

**shrink/swell properties** - property of something expressed by its ability to shrink when dry and swell when fully imbibed with water.

**site plan** - plan showing the raw site prior to planning and design.

**subsoil clay** - B-horizon of a soil. The material found below the topsoil.

**uni-stone paving** - type of paving material consisting of interlocking pieces.

**unity** - state of being one in which all the parts express strong relationships with one another.

# VEGETABLES

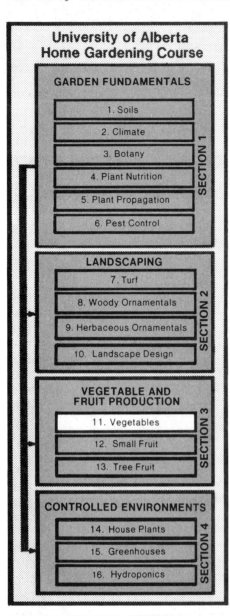

**University of Alberta Home Gardening Course**

GARDEN FUNDAMENTALS — SECTION 1
1. Soils
2. Climate
3. Botany
4. Plant Nutrition
5. Plant Propagation
6. Pest Control

LANDSCAPING — SECTION 2
7. Turf
8. Woody Ornamentals
9. Herbaceous Ornamentals
10. Landscape Design

VEGETABLE AND FRUIT PRODUCTION — SECTION 3
11. Vegetables
12. Small Fruit
13. Tree Fruit

CONTROLLED ENVIRONMENTS — SECTION 4
14. House Plants
15. Greenhouses
16. Hydroponics

# SELF-STUDY LESSON FEATURES

Self-study is an educational approach which allows you to study a subject where and when you want. The course is designed to allow students to study the course material efficiently and incorporates the following features.

**OBJECTIVES** — are found at the beginning of each lesson and allow you to determine what you can expect to learn in the lesson.

**LESSON MATERIAL** — is logically organized and broken down into fundamental components by ordered headings to assist you to comprehend the subject.

**REFERENCING** — between lessons and within lessons allows you to integrate course material.

The last two digits of the page number identify the page and the digits preceding these identify the lesson number (eg., 107: Lesson 1, page 7 or 1227: Lesson 12, page 27).

Referencing:

> sections within the same lesson (eg., see OSMOSIS)

> sections in other lessons (eg., see Botany lesson, OSMOSIS)

> figures and tables (eg., see Figure 7-3)

**FIGURES AND TABLES** — are found in abundance throughout the lessons and are designed to convey useful information in an easy to understand form.

**SIDEBARS** — are those areas in the lesson which are boxed and toned. They present information supplementary to the core content of the lesson.

**PRACTICAL PROJECTS** — are integrated within the lesson material and are included to allow you to apply principles and practices.

**SELF-CHECK QUIZ** — is provided at the end of each lesson and allows you to test your comprehension of the lesson material. Answers to the questions and references to the sections dealing with the questions are provided in the answer section. You should review any questions that you are unable to answer.

**GLOSSARY** — is provided at the end of each lesson and alphabetically lists the definitions of key concepts and terms.

**RESOURCE MATERIALS** — are provided at the end of each lesson and comprise a list of recommended learning materials for further study of the subject. Also included are author's comments on the potential application of each publication.

**INDEX** — alphabetically lists useful topics and their location within the lesson.

---

1986 University of Alberta Faculty of Extension

**Written by: Leonard Eckberg**

Technical Reviewers:
Phil Dixon
Dr. W.T. Andrew

**ISBN 0-88864-852-9**

(Book 3, Lesson 11)

THE PRODUCTION TEAM

Managing Editor .................................................. Thom Shaw
Editor .............................................................. Frank Procter
Production Coordinator ....................................... Kevin Hanson
Graphic Artists .......................................................... Lisa Marsh
Carol Powers
Melanie Eastley Harbourne
Data Entry ...................................................... Joan Geisterfer

Published by the University of Alberta
Faculty of Extension Corbett Hall
Edmonton, Alberta, T6G 2G4

After completing this lesson, the student should be able to:

1. determine the most satisfactory garden size.

2. choose the best types of vegetables and cultivars to satisfy his family's needs.

3. objectively choose a garden site.

4. plan the layout of a vegetable garden plan.

5. calculate the proper amounts of fertilizer to apply to a garden soil and the best time and methods of application.

6. understand how to condition and cultivate a soil.

7. determine the best time and methods for sowing vegetable seeds.

8. manage and set out vegetable transplants.

9. choose and incorporate one or a combination of several gardening methods.

10. extend the growing season by using various cultural techniques.

# TABLE OF CONTENTS

## LIST OF FIGURES AND TABLES

# INTRODUCTION

A vegetable is a plant that is cultivated for its edible part or parts. This can be its roots, stems, leaves, petioles, flowers, fruit or seed. For centuries, man has gathered plants and learned how to use and cultivate them to feed himself and his family. Today, gardeners have an impressive variety of nutritious vegetables to choose from. This lesson deals with those vegetables that are suitable for growing in our northern climate and the techniques required to grow them successfully.

## WHY GROW VEGETABLES

There are probably as many reasons for growing a vegetable garden as there are people doing it. Since local food stores usually fulfill most of the fresh vegetable needs year round, there must be some benefit for people to produce their own vegetables. The rewards must outweigh the disadvantages for people to work so hard year after year.

Fresh vegetables play an important role in maintaining man's physical health as they provide an important source of many vitamins and minerals. Gardening can also be therapeutic, both physically and emotionally. It provides plenty of fresh air and exercise while being a wholesome form of recreation and relaxation. A vegetable plot can provide function and utility to a garden landscape and give the owner more pride in his home (see Figure 11-1). The whole family can participate in this activity, thereby enhancing community spirit. Some households use gardening to help teach their children responsibility by having them look after their own private plot. The advantages of vegetable gardening seem limitless.

Successful vegetable gardening is not difficult and does not require a 'green thumb'. 'Green thumb' is simply a term used to describe the sum of a person's experience and understanding of the local climate and of plant requirements.

## ORIGINS OF VEGETABLES

Sometimes it helps to understand the background of the vegetables that are grown. Most of the common types have been cultivated since before recorded history. For example, Moses referred to cucumbers, garlic, leeks, melons and onions in writings dated about 1400 BC. The tribes of India and Persia were among the first vegetable growers. The native Indians of tropical America raised vegetables for centuries before any white men appeared. In most cases, the ancestral prototype has disappeared or is not recognizable. Some exceptions are the wild Jerusalem artichoke of Canada, the kidney bean of South America, the wild parsnip, carrot and cabbage of Europe, and the wild onion of Asia.

The original habitat of the wild plants from which modern vegetables have sprung is listed in Table 11-1.

# PLANNING THE VEGETABLE GARDEN

## BASIC CONSIDERATIONS

Many people have become very discouraged by their poor quality crops or their tremendous surplus of crops like lettuce or zucchini. Both problems tend

Figure 11-1
## VEGETABLE GARDENS

Courtesy of Lynn Dennis

Table 11-1

## ORIGINS OF VEGETABLES

| NORTH AMERICA | JAMAICA | CENTRAL AND SOUTH AMERICA | EUROPE | ASIA | EURASIA | AFRICA | NEW ZEALAND |
|---|---|---|---|---|---|---|---|
| summer squash | gherkin (pickler) cucumber | bush bean pole bean kidney bean scarlet runner bean | beet celeriac celery swiss chard kale | broad bean Chinese cabbage cress cucumber | asparagus carrot cauliflower water cress dandelion | watermelon okra | New Zealand spinach |
| Jerusalem artichoke | | flint corn eggplant potato sweet potato pumpkin tomato | Brussels sprouts kohlrabi cabbage leek parsley | endive lettuce muskmelon onion pea radish | horseradish | | |
| | | winter squash pepper | parsnip rutabaga salsify turnip | rhubarb spinach | | | |

to be due to poor planning and management. It is essential for the gardener to have a clear idea of what the garden will look like before starting to prepare the vegetable plot for planting. The first things that should be considered are:

- space available or needed,

- time that can realistically be devoted to gardening,

- ultimate purpose of having a garden, and

- total volume of each vegetable required (based on likes and dislikes of the family).

### SPACE AVAILABLE
A farmer or acreage owner obviously has much more space to work with than a city dweller, but both have viable gardening spaces. Even apartment dwellers with a balcony or sunny roof top can use containers to make a suitable garden (see CONTAINER GARDENING).

The thing to keep in mind is that the entire space available need not be planted immediately. A beginner should always start out small to avoid major disappointments. Think about what could be managed and cut this area roughly in half. This prevents backbreaking frustration in trying to keep up with maintenance requirements. With experience, the vegetable garden can be expanded with confidence.

### TIME REQUIREMENTS
There is no disputing the fact that gardening does take time. Every garden needs soil preparation, planting, weeding, mulching, watering, pest control and harvesting during the growing season. The time required to perform some of these tasks can be reduced with various labor saving techniques. However, it's still better to keep a garden on the small side as an oversized garden can soon become overgrown and overrun with weeds. With experience and development of proper management techniques, more efficient use of gardening time can be realized.

### PURPOSE OF A GARDEN
There are three common types of vegetable gardens. A **salad garden**, for example, is a relatively small plot with easy access to the kitchen. The cook can step out and gather an assortment of fresh greens, radishes, onions, baby carrots, beets or tomatoes. These crops can all be closely spaced (see Table 11-13) and a succession of plantings (see SUCCESSION PLANTING) can ensure an adequate supply of salad fixings all summer long.

A **soup (summer) garden** is a little larger than a salad garden. It is intended to supply the family's fresh vegetable needs throughout the growing season without leaving any surplus for storage or processing. Successive small plantings provide several harvests that can be eaten immediately without spoilage or waste. Any vegetable that grows successfully in our northern climate can be grown in this type of garden. Only short season crops can be harvested more than once per season. Many of the crops grown in either salad gardens or soup gardens can be raised in containers.

The **surplus garden** is the largest of the three types of home vegetable gardens. It usually supplies all the fresh vegetable needs of the family during the growing season with excess being stored, frozen or canned for consumption throughout the winter. Such a garden can decrease dependence on outside sources, particularly when prices are highest during the winter. To make processing easier, a large quantity of plants are sown so that a sizable volume of mature vegetables are available at the same time (see VOLUME OF PRODUCE DESIRED).

## LIKES AND DISLIKES

It is a waste of time, money and gardening space to plant a large quantity of vegetables that the family does not like. When trying a new vegetable, plant it sparingly. If it grows successfully and the family likes it, then increase its production next year. Discuss preferences with the family and base planting decisions on how much of each vegetable was consumed in previous years.

## WHAT VEGETABLES AND CULTIVARS TO GROW

Decisions regarding which vegetables and which cultivars of these vegetables to grow should be given careful consideration. To help make a garden more productive and rewarding, investigate the characteristics of particular vegetables before purchasing seed or transplants. The following sections outline the characteristics of vegetables that are important considerations in the selection process.

## SIZE AND GROWTH HABIT

The size of a garden plot directly affects the choice of vegetable and/or cultivar. A small container garden or salad garden cannot accommodate a large, sprawling vine crop like cucumbers or pumpkins. Fortunately, plant breeders have developed dwarf and non-vining forms. If space is at a premium, pay attention to those cultivars that are labelled 'dwarf', 'compact', or 'balcony' types. Such space limitations do not usually apply to a surplus garden.

## DISEASE RESISTANCE OR TOLERANCE

Plant breeders are always developing new disease resistant and disease tolerant cultivars. **Disease resistance** means that a plant is not susceptible to

attack from particular diseases. **Disease tolerance** implies that a plant is capable of withstanding a certain level of infection before its productivity is severely reduced. Check with local information services to determine which cultivars are resistant or tolerant to the diseases in the vicinity. Organic gardeners, in particular, try to select disease resistant and tolerant cultivars in order to reduce the need for pesticide treatment.

## TIME TO MATURITY

When faced with a short growing season, northern gardeners must be concerned with the length of time it takes a plant to grow from a seed or transplant to where the crop is ready for harvesting. This 'time to maturity' is

usually quoted in days on seed packets or in catalogues. Special gardening techniques (like succession planting and interplanting) require careful consideration of this time. Short season vegetables are faster to mature and will be in and out of the garden in a relatively short period of time. Long season crops, however, may not be able to produce before the end of a season. Some are offered as early-, mid-, or late-season cultivars. This sometimes makes it possible to grow a long season crop in an area with a short growing season. Sweet corn is a good example of this.

## COOL SEASON AND WARM SEASON

All vegetables are classified into two major groups: **cool season** and **warm**

Table 11-2

## COOL SEASON AND WARM SEASON CROPS

| WARM SEASON VEGETABLES | COOL SEASON VEGETABLES |
|---|---|
| Bean (snap and dry) | Asparagus |
| Squash | Broad Bean |
| Corn | Beet |
| Pumpkin | Broccoli |
| Tomato | Brussels Sprout |
| Muskmelon | Cabbage |
| Watermelon | Carrot |
| Pepper | Cauliflower |
| Eggplant | Celery |
| | Chinese Cabbage |
| | Garlic |
| | Leek |
| | Lettuce |
| | Onion |
| | Parsley |
| | Parsnip |
| | Pea |
| | Potato |
| | Radish |
| | Rutabaga |
| | Spinach |
| | Swiss Chard |
| | Turnip |

season. This classification is based upon their temperature requirements for seed germination and growth above ground. All cool season crops are grown for their vegetative parts. They tend to be cool hardy or frost tolerant. Warm season crops are vegetables grown primarily for their fruits. They require a long growing season and generally need to be transplanted in order to extend the season long enough to produce. The only two exceptions are peas and broad beans, which are actually cool season crops. Warm season crops also benefit from the use of hot caps, plastic mulches and tunnels (see PLANT PROTECTORS).

## INTENDED USE

Several vegetables have been bred for specific uses such as canning, freezing, storage, or for fresh use. Cultivars of crops bred for processing, such as beans, peas, and tomatoes tend not to be as succulent, sweet or tender as the cultivars bred for fresh use. The cultivars for processing have been specifically developed for their firm textures and lasting flavors when preserved.

## NUTRITIONAL VALUE

All vegetables contain varying amounts of vitamins and minerals. Generally, most contain notable amounts of vitamins A, B1 (Thiamine), B2 (Riboflavin), B3 (Niacin) and C, as well as calcium, iron and potassium. The 'TOP TEN' vegetables, in order of vitamin and mineral content, are:

- broccoli
- spinach
- Brussels sprouts
- lima beans
- peas
- asparagus
- artichokes
- cauliflower
- sweet potatoes
- carrots

Nutrient content may be important to people who wish to select and grow vegetables to maximize possible health benefits from the garden.

## OTHER CONSIDERATIONS

There are many other factors to consider when choosing vegetables. One is the permanence of a garden. A renter, for example, may not want to plant a perennial crop like asparagus or rhubarb as both take several years before a crop can be harvested.

Some people may be concerned with seed quality. Qualities like viability, weed content, dockage and trueness to type are important when buying large quantities of seed. Always use fresh Canada No. 1 seed (see TESTING FOR VIABILITY).

Some seed is pre-treated for disease control. These seeds may be coated with a fungicide to help combat damping off while germinating in cool, damp soils. The coating is a chalky substance that is either bright pink, purple or dull green in color. Others are treated with hot water to kill the organisms causing anthracnose, black leg and black rot. Hot water treated seeds are completely safe to handle with bare hands and are preferred by organic gardeners.

To find out which vegetable cultivars are suitable often requires some research. Watch out for those cultivars that are specifically designed for commercial growers. Prices are generally higher for seed that is pelleted or precision sized for use in mechanical seeders. Newly introduced cultivars are not always the best for all geographical areas unless otherwise stated. For example, 'All America Selections' have been thoroughly tested in 50 trial sites in Canada and the United States, but trial and error will still prove which vegetable cultivars grow best in specific garden sites.

Seed catalogues can often provide one of the best sources of information. Many seed suppliers are advertised in magazines and newspapers and their catalogues can often be obtained free of charge (see RESOURCE MATERIALS). Other sources of information are the Alberta Horticultural Guide, extension horticulturists, district agriculturists, garden centers and the backs of seed packets. Neighbors can often provide useful information as there are so many different cultivars of vegetables to choose from. One nationally known seed company lists 45 different cultivars of sweet corn, 12 cultivars of peas and 54 cultivars of tomatoes. Only a select few of these are suitable in a prairie garden.

## SELECTING THE SITE

Very few gardeners are blessed with the ideal garden site. To grow well, all vegetables need optimum levels of light, heat, water, soil and protection. All gardens have varying degrees of these factors but various techniques can be used to compensate for the flaws. The closer a garden site comes to meeting the 'ideal site', the better is its potential for producing healthy crops that mature quickly. Many people have little or no choice as to location of their garden but if a choice does exist, the following sections can provide useful information to assist in site selection.

## LIGHT

The availability of light is a very important consideration in selecting a garden site. Most plants require a minimum of six hours of direct sunlight, with eight to ten hours per day preferred. Many crops only do well in the north because the daylength is so long and the light intensity less strong. When plants do not receive enough light, they become weak, spindly and slow to mature. They are also more susceptible to attack by diseases and insects. Therefore, always try to plant a garden in a sunny location away from trees, fences and buildings (see Figure 11-2). When prolonged shade is unavoidable, plant only shade tolerant vegetables like

**Figure 11-2
PREVENT SHADING**

Courtesy of Alberta Agriculture

bunching onions, peas, carrots, and leafy vegetables like lettuce, spinach and chinese cabbage (see SHADE GARDENING). When planning the garden, place tall vegetables like corn, asparagus, sunflowers, staked tomatoes, peas and pole beans on the north side. This prevents shorter crops from being shaded when taller plants near maturity (see Figure 11-3).

## HEAT

The availability of adequate warmth is another priority in site selection. All plants have a minimum base temperature for growth. Below this temperature, plants do not grow, rather, they remain in suspended animation. Some examples of base temperatures for various vegetable plants are: spinach (2.2°C), peas (5.5°C), corn and beans (10°C) and tomatoes and pumpkins (13°C). Plants growing very near their base temperatures tend to be more susceptible to diseases and insects. In northern areas, the lack of adequate heat can be the most limiting factor in plant growth.

Several things can be done to increase temperatures in the soil and around plants. The velocity of wind, which has a cooling effect, can be reduced with some form of protection. Shading should also be minimized. Depending on the size of the vegetable bed, raised beds can increase soil temperature in the spring. Hotcaps, plastic mulches and tunnels can also be used to promote warming in the spring. Even cold frames or hot beds can be used to a limited degree. If the area has a very short growing season, plant on a south facing slope or, when all else fails, grow only fast-growing, frost-tolerant crops.

## SLOPE

The topography of a garden site and surrounding area greatly affects the growth rate of vegetables. When a plot is located on a south facing slope, it receives more direct sunlight. As a result, the soil warms up faster in spring and stays warm longer into fall. All warm season crops grow better when planted on a south facing slope. The opposite is true for north facing slopes which favor the growing of cool season crops.

The degree of slope must not be too great. A two per cent slope is ideal (see Turf lesson, GRADE). Grades steeper than this can result in severe erosion problems. To prevent erosion, the garden may be terraced or rows of vegetables planted along contours rather than up and down the slope. Both methods help to trap running water during heavy rainfall.

Avoid planting gardens at the bottom of hills. Cold air, being heavier than warm air, sinks down and settles in these areas. As a result, the growing season is shortened by late-spring and early-fall frosts. Even physical barriers (like shelterbelts or buildings) have been known to trap cold air on a slope and cause frost problems. Water also tends to collect at the bottom of hills or in depressions. Excess water and dissolved salts brought down from higher elevations can make gardening difficult.

## WATER

All plants need water to survive. Not only is the quality and quantity of water important for plant growth, but so is the timing of water application. Plants occasionally suffer from water stress when a gardener relies on nature to provide sufficient quantities of rain when needed. Severe deficiencies can quickly kill an entire garden while slight deficiencies can register on only the most sensitive crops and retard the growth of others. Supplemental watering is essential if gardeners expect to maximize production. Therefore, a garden should be planted where there is access to an adequate supply of good quality water. Well water that is 'softened' or high in sodium should never be used to water plants. Sodium accumulates in the soil with each application until toxic levels are reached (see WATERING).

## SOIL

Vegetables are capable of growing in almost any kind of soil. However, poor soils produce poor quality crops that are slow to mature and are susceptible to insects and diseases. An ideal garden soil is deep, well-drained, friable and fertile. Loam, sandy loam, or sandy clay loam soils are usually the best types for gardens (see Soils lesson, SOIL TEXTURE).

The quality of the soil in a newly selected garden site can be determined by inspecting the soil in a hole dug 30 cm (12 in) deep. The soil should be of a suitable texture and organic matter content (see Soils lesson, SOIL TEXTURE). Keep in mind that soil can be improved over a period of time with the addition of organic matter, fertilizer and other amendments (see HOW TO IMPROVE SOIL QUALITY). Sometimes it

### Figure 11-3
### CONSIDER HEIGHT TO PREVENT SHADING

Courtesy of Alberta Agriculture

is necessary to completely replace the native soil with fresh topsoil from another area. Another alternative is to collect what topsoil is available in raised beds. Some reasons for this may be that the topsoil is too thin, too high in clay content, too high in salts, or too low in nutrients and organic matter. Choosing a site with the best possible soil available minimizes the amount of time, money and effort required to improve it.

## SHELTER

Protection from strong winds is the final consideration. Reducing wind velocities will help reduce soil drying, excess evapotranspiration, excess cooling and mechanical damage. Choosing a garden site with adequate shelter already in place will minimize the need to erect or plant a new one (see Figure 11-4). Windbreaks can be fences, hedges, trees, or walls (see Climate lesson, MODIFYING CLIMATIC EFFECTS). A barrier that is one metre (about 4 ft) in height will provide protection for up to 50 m (about 165 ft). Located on the north and west sides of a garden plot, a

shelterbelt will generally trap snow to improve soil moisture in the spring. As mentioned before, be sure to allow for the passage of cold air falling down a slope. Adequate wind protection will give comfort to garden plants and gardeners. The length of the growing season may also be improved.

## GARDEN LAYOUT PROCEDURE

After determining the requirements of a vegetable garden and selecting a suitable site, a gardener can begin planning the actual garden layout on paper. Begin by measuring the dimensions of the proposed area. Determine a suitable scale to use in order to fit and draw the representation of the plot on one sheet of paper. Using graph paper often makes this easier as one square can represent a certain unit of area. Draw the outline of the garden and indicate the garden's orientation (mark north). Use the information in the following sections to complete the garden layout plan. To further assist in

this task, an example of a garden layout plan is included (see Figure 11-5) as well as the step-by-step procedure at the end of this section (see PLANNING THE LAYOUT OF A GARDEN).

## VOLUME OF PRODUCE DESIRED

Most gardeners know which vegetables they want but are unsure of how much to plant in order to satisfy their family's needs. Although trial and error can provide the best solution to this problem, a simple reference is needed to keep from drastically overplanting or underplanting a crop. Table 11-3 can be used to estimate the number of plants required to feed each person per growing season. Balance the estimate listed with the particular likes and dislikes of family members. If the vegetable is intended for storage, as well as for fresh use, add the two columns together.

It is seldom necessary to plant all seeds in a package. It is cheaper to discard seeds than to waste time, money and space on unwanted vegetables. Some vegetable seeds can be stored and used later to replant if the crop fails or to supply seed for next year's crop (see PROPER STORAGE OF SEED).

## GROWTH HABIT

All vegetables require a certain amount of garden space in order to grow healthy and produce a satisfactory crop. Overcrowding causes stress from competition for light, water, and nutrients. Excess stress leads to slower growth rates and weak plants which are more susceptible to insect and disease attacks. Always allow the recommended spaces between and within rows.

Plant each vegetable in an area that can accommodate its special growing habits. Vine crops (like cucumbers and pumpkins, for example) are best planted on the outside edge of the garden. This allows them to spread out and fill in unused areas. Tall crops (like corn and staked or trellised vegetables) should be located on the north side of the plot to prevent unnecessary shading of shorter ones.

## Figure 11-4
## WELL PROTECTED GARDEN

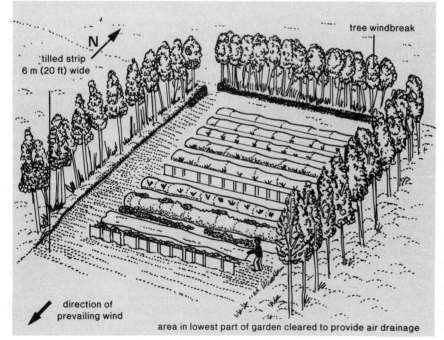

N
tilled strip 6 m (20 ft) wide
tree windbreak
direction of prevailing wind
area in lowest part of garden cleared to provide air drainage

## Figure 11-5
## GARDEN LAYOUT PLAN

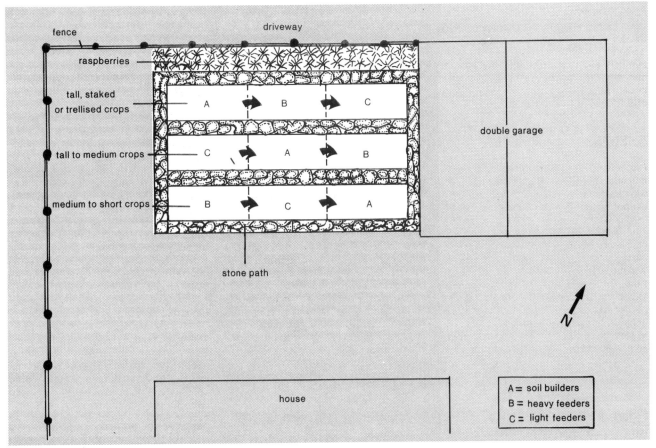

## ORIENTATION

Many gardening books give conflicting advice on which direction to orient the rows or beds of a garden. Some suggest rows should run north to south while others recommend east to west. The most important consideration regarding orientation is the slope of the land. Rows should always run across a slope (along contours) to minimize erosion problems regardless of the direction the rows take.

If mainly tall or medium height crops are grown, it is probably best to have the rows running east to west in order to maximize exposure to light. If shade loving crops are preferred, then a north to south direction is better. For an all purpose garden in the north on relatively flat land, most gardeners recommend an east to west orientation of garden rows or beds.

## SEASON LENGTH

It is usually an advantage to plant crops with similar growing seasons together, particularly if the gardener plans on using succession planting (see GARDENING METHODS). Harvesting short season crops opens up a block for further plantings. Placing long season crops together keeps them out of the way until they are ready to harvest. A spot set aside for perennials prevents them from being disturbed when cultivating the soil. Corn should always be planted in blocks rather than single rows to provide better pollination. Keep sweet corn well away from popping corn as cross pollination adversely affects eating quality.

## GARDENING SYSTEM

There are four basic gardening systems. These are 'single row', 'temporary wide row', 'permanent wide row' and 'container gardens'. Each system has advantages and drawbacks. Succession planting, interplanting and companion planting can be incorporated into any of these systems. Each of these methods are discussed later in this lesson (see GARDENING METHODS). The gardening system employed ultimately affects the amount of gardening space required.

## CROP ROTATION

Rotation is a very important part of responsible garden management. Planting different crops in a particular spot each year helps to prevent the depletion of soil nutrients and the build-up of soilborne insects and

## Table 11-3
## VOLUME OF VEGETABLES TO PLANT

| VEGETABLES | NUMBER OF PLANTS PER PERSON | | VEGETABLE | NUMBER OF PLANTS PER PERSON | |
|---|---|---|---|---|---|
| | FRESH | STORAGE | | FRESH | STORAGE |
| Asparagus | 5 | 10-20 | Kohlrabi | 3-5 | 5-10 |
| Bean, snap bush | 5-10 | 30-40 | Lettuce, head | 5-10 | 2-3 |
| snap pole | 5 | 15-20 | leaf | 5-10 | 0 |
| lima | 0 | 50 | | | |
| broad | 0 | 50 | Mustard greens | 5 | 0 |
| Beet | 10 | 20-30 | | | |
| Broccoli | 3-5 | 10-15 | Onion, bunching | 30-50 | 0 |
| Brussels sprout | 2-3 | 5-10 | storage | 5-10 | 30-40 |
| Cabbage, early | 2-3 | 0 | Parsnip | 0 | 25-30 |
| late | 0 | 5-10 | Pea | 10-15 | 40-50 |
| Chinese | 3-5 | 3-5 | Pepper, sweet | 2-3 | 0 |
| | | | Potato, early | 4-6 | 0 |
| Carrot | 30-50 | 75-100 | late | 2-3 | 15-20 |
| Cauliflower | 2-3 | 5-10 | Pumpkin | 1 | 1 |
| Celeriac | 2-3 | 10-15 | | | |
| Celery | 2-3 | 5-10 | Radish, spring | 30-50 | 0 |
| Chard, Swiss | 5-10 | 0 | winter | 0 | 15-20 |
| Cucumber, pickler | 0 | 5-10 | Rhubarb | 2-3 | 2-3 |
| slicer | 2-3 | 0 | Rutabaga | 0 | 15-20 |
| Eggplant | 2-3 | 0 | Spinach | 10-20 | 0 |
| Endive | 3-4 | 0 | Squash, summer | 1-2 | 0 |
| | | | winter | 0 | 4-6 |
| Garlic | 3-5 | 5-10 | | | |
| | | | Tomato, slicing | 2-3 | 2-3 |
| Horseradish | 0 | 1-2 | cherry | 2-3 | 0 |
| | | | Turnip | 5-10 | 15-20 |
| Kale | 2-3 | 5-10 | | | |

Crop rotation keeps a check on soilborne diseases. Many fungi, bacteria and viruses build up in population during the growing season when feeding on a specific plant host. When crops are not rotated, the population of pathogens can increase exponentially, making control virtually impossible for several years. Some examples of such diseases are bean blight, black rot, cabbage black leg, clubroot, cucumber anthracnose, fusarium wilt, pea root rot and potato scab. When the host plant is unavailable, the disease population decreases.

Rotating crops also helps to reduce insect problems. Most insects have a very narrow range of host plants and overwinter in the soil near their food source. Moving the host each year makes it a little more difficult for newly emerging insects to find their food source. Be careful not to plant another closely related vegetable in this spot as it, too, will likely be a suitable host.

The easiest method of getting a crop rotation system going is to divide the vegetable plot into three or four sections. Parallel sections running east to west make it easier to keep tall crops on the north side when moving them to a new location each year. A garden divided into growing beds already has clearly defined units to work with. Each year an entire section is moved with very little juggling of a crop's position within each unit. Creating the satisfactory units of vegetables is the most difficult planning process when keeping heavy feeders and related vegetables apart.

If succession planting is practiced, crops are rotated within the same year. Soil depletion is prevented by alternating root crops such as beets, carrots and radishes with leafy crops like lettuce, spinach and Swiss chard. Shallow rooted crops, like green onions, can be alternated with deep rooted ones, like parsnips, to vary the soil levels from which the nutrients are drawn. Do not plant vegetables closely related to each other in the newly vacated spot as insects or diseases may become a problem.

## PLANNING THE LAYOUT OF A GARDEN

Now assemble all the necessary information and decide on which vegetables, how much of each and where each is to be grown in the plot based on growth habits. Orient the rows

diseases. Unfortunately, very few gardeners practice crop rotation because they feel their garden is too small to do this adequately. Their decreasing yields and increasing pest problems are an unnecessary result.

Each vegetable crop varies in its nutrient requirements. For the purpose of crop rotation, vegetables can be grouped into three categories, based on what they remove from the soil and give back to it.

The three groups include **heavy feeders**, **light feeders** and **soil builders**. A satisfactory rotation of these involves planting a heavy feeder one year, a light feeder the next year and a soil builder during the third year. Every effort should be made not to plant heavy feeders in the same spot two or more years in succession. Table 11-4 lists common vegetables with similar nutrient needs.

Table 11-4
## VEGETABLES WITH SIMILAR NUTRIENT REQUIREMENTS

| HEAVY FEEDERS | LIGHT FEEDERS | SOIL BUILDERS |
|---|---|---|
| Asparagus | Carrot | Alfalfa |
| Beets | Garlic | Beans, broad |
| Broccoli | Leek | Beans, lima |
| Brussels Sprout | Mustard | Beans, snap |
| Cabbage | Onion | Clover |
| Cauliflower | Parsnip | Green Manure Pea |
| Celery | Pepper | |
| Corn | Radish | |
| Cucumber | Rutabaga | |
| Eggplant | Shallot | |
| Endive | Swiss Chard | |
| Kale | Turnip | |
| Kohlrabi | | |
| Lettuce | | |
| Potato | | |
| Pumpkin | | |
| Parsley | | |
| Rhubarb | | |
| Spinach | | |
| Squash, winter | | |
| Squash, summer | | |
| Tomato | | |

or beds to accommodate for slope or prevent shading. Place crops with similar growing seasons together. Determine which gardening system will be used. Allow for rotation of crops annually. Mark off spaces that will be occupied and jot down the dates each crop will be planted. Succession crops can be put in parenthesis with expected planting dates. All of these steps will help determine the quantity of seeds or transplants to buy. The drawing (see GARDEN LAYOUT PROCEDURE) will also serve as a seasonal reminder and for future planning. Good documentation of a garden's performance prevents having to rely on memory when making decisions in subsequent years.

## THE GARDEN SOIL

The composition and quality of soil in a vegetable garden is very important. Vegetables must produce an edible crop from a seed in a relatively short period of time. Therefore, there must be a steady supply of nutrients for plants to achieve maximum growth rates. Yields, appearance, and even the taste of vegetables are all directly affected by nutrient availability and balance.

The soil must also provide structural support to hold up both short and tall plants. At the same time, it must be loose enough to allow water and air to penetrate. Root crops like carrot, potato and turnip must also be allowed to expand unimpeded during the growing season. To create and maintain a soil that satisfies all these criteria requires sound management practices.

## HOW TO IMPROVE SOIL QUALITY

The ideal garden soil is seldom found just waiting to be planted. To correct inadequacies, a gardener needs to know what is in his soil. Periodic laboratory tests should be carried out to monitor all of its qualities and to maintain nutrients at optimum levels. It is, therefore, recommended that a garden soil test be done every three to four years with soil samples taken during the fall (see Soils lesson, SOIL TESTS). Fall is the best time to take samples as nutrient levels are stabilized and give more accurate readings. Microbial activity during a growing season sometimes distorts true nutrient content readings. It also allows ample time for corrective action to be taken before planting the following spring.

A soil changes annually as new materials are used and/or added. Plants, insects, earthworms and micro-organisms remove and release nutrients. Structural changes in the soil are obvious while chemical alterations are less noticeable. Nutrients soon become depleted if not continually replenished. All soils need improvement every year in an ongoing management program. A soil test serves as a guideline for determining how much material to add in order to achieve and maintain ideal soil conditions.

### FERTILIZERS AND FERTILIZING
There are a great many types and kinds of fertilizers available on the market today. No one fertilizer can solve all of a gardener's nutritional needs. This section deals with both natural and chemical fertilizers and how to use them.

Organic fertilizers, like animal manures and compost, solve some nutritional deficiencies while improving soil structure. Generally, however, they are very weak fertilizers and not very well balanced. For example, even generous applications of manure may supply adequate amounts of nitrogen but not much phosphorus or potassium. Continued exclusive use of manure may lead to nutrient deficiencies unless other fertilizers are added (see Plant Nutrition lesson, ORGANIC FERTILIZERS).

The timing of any fertilizer application depends upon the nature of the material itself. Soil texture, soil pH and the type of vegetable being planted also affects timing. For example, most natural

Table 11-5

## NATURAL FERTILIZERS

| ORGANIC MATERIAL | % OF NUTRIENT BY WEIGHT | | | |
| --- | --- | --- | --- | --- |
| | NITROGEN | PHOSPHORUS | POTASSIUM | |
| Activated Sludge (Melorganite) | 5.0 | 3.0 | 0 | medium |
| Alfalfa Hay | 2.5 | 0.5 | 2.1 | |
| Animal Tankage | 8.0 | 20.0 | 0 | medium |
| Blood Meal | 15.0 | 1.3 | 0.7 | |
| Blood (dried)* | 12-15 | 3.0 | 0 | medium-rapid |
| Bone Meal | 2-4.0 | 11-21.0 | 0.2 | slow |
| Brewer's Grains (wet) | 0.9 | 0.5 | 0.1 | |
| Cattle Manure (wet)* | 0.3-0.57 | 0.15-0.2 | 0.4-0.53 | medium |
| Coffee Grounds (dried) | 2.0 | 0.4 | 0.7 | |
| Cornstalks | 0.8 | 0.4 | 0.9 | slow |
| Fish Emulsion* | 5.0 | 2.0 | 2.0 | medium-rapid |
| Fish Meal | 10.0 | 4.0 | 0 | slow |
| Fish Scrap | 7.8 | 13.0 | 3.8 | slow |
| Guano (bird droppings) | 12.0 | 8.0 | 3.0 | medium |
| Hoof and Horn Meal | 12.5 | 1.8 | 0 | slow |
| Horse Manure (wet)* | 0.4-0.66 | 0.2-0.23 | 0.4-0.68 | medium |
| Leaf and Grass Compost* | 0.6-1.0 | 0.2-0.25 | 0.33-0.4 | medium |
| Mushroom Compost* | 0.4-0.7 | 57-62 | 0.5-1.5 | slow |
| Phosphate Rock | 0 | 30-32 | 0 | very slow |
| Pig Manure (wet)* | 0.56-0.6 | 0.32-0.4 | 0.1-0.52 | medium |
| Pine or Spruce Needles | 0.5 | 0.1 | 0 | slow |
| Poultry Manure (wet)*. | 0.97-2.0 | 0.77-1.9 | 0.41-1.9 | medium-rapid |
| Rabbit Manure (wet) | 2.4 | 0.6 | 0.1 | medium |
| Sawdust | 4.0 | 2.0 | 4.0 | very slow |
| Seaweed | 1.7 | 0.8 | 5.0 | slow-medium |
| Sheep Manure (wet)* | 0.6-0.9 | 0.3-0.34 | 0.2-1.0 | medium |
| Wood Ashes* | 0 | 1.5 | 7.0 | rapid |

(wet)  Material is moist or damp, not dried

* Most commonly used by organic gardeners

fertilizers require that soil micro-organisms break them down to a soluble form before a plant can take them up. This takes a fair amount of time and gives the appearance of being a slow release type fertilizer. Therefore, by the time a deficiency is detected, treatment with an organic fertilizer likely means that its nutrients will not be available in time to correct the condition. If applied too early, in anticipation of a deficiency, nutrients are lost or reduced by leaching. Chemical fertilizers, because of their quick release of nutrients, are better able to correct plant nutrient deficiencies.

Tables 11-5 and 11-6 list some of the

Table 11-6
COMMON CHEMICAL FERTILIZERS

| FERTILIZER | | NITROGEN | PHOS-PHORUS | POTASSIUM | RELATIVE AVAILA-BILITY | GENERAL REACTION |
|---|---|---|---|---|---|---|
| | | % OF NUTRIENT BY WEIGHT | | | | |
| Ammonium Sulphate | * | 21 | 0 | 0 | quick | acid |
| Ammonium Nitrate | * | 33 | 0 | 0 | rapid | acid |
| Calcium Nitrate | | 15 | 0 | 0 | rapid | alkaline |
| Sodium Nitrate | | 16 | 0 | 0 | rapid | alkaline |
| Urea | | 45 | 0 | 0 | rapid | acid |
| Ammonium Phosphate Sulphate | * | 16 | 20 | 0 | moderate | acid |
| Mono-ammonium Phosphate | * | 11 | 48 | 0 | moderate | acid |
| | | 11 | 51 | 0 | | |
| | | 11 | 55 | 0 | | |
| Di-ammonium Phosphate | | 21 | 53 | 0 | moderate | acid |
| Superphosphate | | 0 | 18 | 0 | slow | neutral |
| | | 0 | 25 | 0 | | |
| | | 0 | 20 | 0 | | |
| Treble Superphosphate | | 0 | 45 | 0 | slow | neutral |
| Potassium Phosphate | | 0 | 22 | 28 | moderate | neutral |
| Potassium Chloride | | 0 | 0 | 50 | quick | neutral |
| Muriate of Potash | * | 0 | 0 | 60 | quick | neutral |
| Potassium Sulphate | | 0 | 0 | 50 | quick | neutral |
| Potassium Nitrate | | 13 | 0 | 44 | rapid | alkaline |
| | | 14 | 0 | 46 | | |
| Common Mixtures or Blends | | 8 | 24 | 24 | | |
| | | 8 | 38 | 15 | | |
| | | 13 | 16 | 10 | | |
| | * | 10 | 52 | 10 | | |
| | | 15 | 30 | 15 | varies | varies |
| | * | 20 | 20 | 20 | | |
| | | 20 | 10 | 5 | | |
| | | 4 | 12 | 4 | | |
| | | 5 | 10 | 5 | | |
| | | 25 | 5 | 20 | | |

* Most readily available fertilizers on the market

more common natural and chemical fertilizers and their relative availabilities in a soil after application. Soils rich in organic matter minimize some of the problems associated with nutrient availability. Organic matter promotes good soil pH for solubility, cuts down on leaching, and supplies the necessary micro-organisms for breakdown of organic materials.

After a gardener has brought all nutrients up to optimum levels (based on the recommendations of a soil test), the vegetable garden should be fertilized annually to replace those nutrients lost during a growing season. This is called maintenance fertilizing. In an ideal maintenance fertilizing program, the gardener maintains optimum levels of nutrients by determining nutrient loss to plants. Then, through the addition of the proper amount of fertilizer, the gardener replenishes the lost nutrients in one calculated application. Maintenance fertilizing maintains soil fertility levels and keeps a garden producing at maximum capacity. When all the plants are removed, an average vegetable garden plot loses approximately:

 0.5-1.5 kg nitrogen / 100 m²
 (1-3 lb / 1000 sq ft)
 0.25-0.75 kg phosphorus / 100 m²
 (1/2-1 1/2 lb / 1000 sq ft)
and 1.0-2.0 kg potassium / 100 m²
 (2-4 lb / 1000 sq ft)

Many gardeners simply fertilize each spring with 16-20-0 or 20-10-5 (or other similar fertilizer) at an approximate rate of 2-3 kg / 100 m² (4-6 lb / 1000 sq ft). Although such annual applications serve to supply a boost to the nutrient level of the vegetable garden, long-term use of this method may still lead to nutrient deficiencies. Some crops feed more heavily on specific nutrients than others. Table 11-7 indicates the actual nutrient losses more accurately. It lists some of the more common vegetables with similar nutritional needs.

Plants are not the only cause of nutrient loss. Nitrogen levels can be decreased by a process called ammonification. This occurs when $NH_4$ is converted to ammonia gas and is lost to the atmosphere (see Plant Nutrition lesson, RECYCLING). Leaching also causes a loss of nutrients. Highly soluble nutrients (like $NO_3$ and $K_2O$) are washed down

## Table 11-7
## NUTRIENT REQUIREMENTS OF COMMON VEGETABLES

| | Nitrogen (N) | | | Phosphorus (P) | | | Potassium (K) | | |
|---|---|---|---|---|---|---|---|---|---|
| | H | M | L | H | M | L | H | M | L |
| Asparagus | ● | | | | ● | | ● | | |
| Beans | | | ● | | | ● | | | ● |
| Beets | | ● | | | ● | | | ● | |
| Broccoli | | ● | | ● | | | ● | | |
| Brussels Sprouts | | ● | | ● | | | ● | | |
| Cabbage | | ● | | ● | | | ● | | |
| Carrots | | ● | | | ● | | | ● | |
| Cauliflower | | ● | | | ● | | ● | | |
| Celery | ● | | | | ● | | ● | | |
| Corn | | ● | | | ● | | | ● | |
| Cucumbers | | ● | | ● | | | | ● | |
| Eggplant | | ● | | ● | | | ● | | |
| Horseradish | | ● | | | ● | | | ● | |
| Kale | | ● | | ● | | | ● | | |
| Lettuce | | ● | | | ● | | | ● | |
| Onions | | ● | | | ● | | | ● | |
| Parsnips | | ● | | | ● | | | ● | |
| Peas | | | ● | | | ● | | | ● |
| Peppers | | ● | | ● | | | ● | | |
| Potatoes | | ● | | ● | | | ● | | |
| Pumpkins | | ● | | ● | | | ● | | |
| Radishes | | | ● | | ● | | | ● | |
| Rutabaga | | ● | | | ● | | | ● | |
| Squashes | | ● | | ● | | | ● | | |
| Swiss Chard | | ● | | | ● | | | ● | |
| Tomatoes | | ● | | ● | | | ● | | |
| Turnips | | ● | | | ● | | | ● | |

| Nutrient Use | Nitrogen (N) | Phosphorus (P) | Potassium (K) |
|---|---|---|---|
| High (H) | 1.5 kg +/100 m² | 0.4 kg +/100 m² | 2.0 kg +/ 100 m² |
| Medium (M) | 0.5-1.5 kg/100 m² | 0.2-0.4 kg/100 m² | 1.0-20 kg/100 m² |
| Low (L) | less than 0.5 kg/100 m² | less than 0.2 kg/100 m² | less than 1.0 kg/100 m² |

and away from plant's roots through heavy rainfall or irrigation. Quantities lost depend upon soil texture, drainage, organic matter content and volume of water applied. Gardeners must guess at these amounts in order to maintain optimum nutrient levels. Experience and periodic soil tests will confirm the amount of loss from these sources.

Only after calculating how much of each nutrient the garden requires, can the amount of actual fertilizer to apply be determined. Whether to use natural or chemical fertilizers is a matter of personal preference and costs. The total amount of any type of fertilizer is determined by the percentage of nutrient in the material (see Plant Nutrition lesson, PURITY OF ELEMENTS AND RELATIONSHIP TO COSTS). A small amount of a concentrated fertilizer will do the same job as a large amount of a weak one. The following example shows how the calculations are done.

Example

Mr McDonald, a retired farmer, now lives in the city and wishes to plant celery, corn and tomatoes in a small garden plot 4 m (13 ft) wide and 6 m (20 ft) long. This means he has 4 m X 6 m = 24 m² (13 ft X 20 ft = 260 sq ft) to fertilize. He estimates from Table 11-7 and from previous experience of natural losses, that he needs about 1.5 kg of nitrogen and 0.5 kg of phosphorus per 100 m² (3 lbs N / 1000 sq ft and 1 lb P / 1000 sq ft). Additional potassium is seldom required in Prairie soils, but its level should be checked periodically with a soil test. Very sandy areas and peaty or high organic areas are exceptions in that soils in these areas are often deficient in potassium. Mr. McDonald's soil, a silt loam with an excellent supply of organic matter, does not require additional potassium at this time.

The proper way to calculate the amount of fertilizer to apply is to divide the number of kilograms (number of pounds) of nutrient required in 100 m² (1000 sq ft) by the percentage of nutrient in the fertilizer (expressed as a decimal).

Since Mr. McDonald's soil is slightly basic (high pH), he wants to use mono-ammonium phosphate (11-55-0) and ammonium sulphate (21-0-0) which are both acidic in nature (see Table 11-6). He starts by calculating how much phosphorus to apply (Both metric and imperial units are given):

$$\frac{0.5 \text{ kg of phosphorus required}}{55\% / 100} = \frac{0.5}{0.55} = 0.9 \text{ kg of } 11\text{-}55\text{-}0 \text{ per } 100 \text{ m}^2$$

OR

$$\frac{1.0 \text{ lb of phosphorus required}}{55\% / 100} = \frac{1.0}{0.55} = 1.8 \text{ lbs of } 11\text{-}55\text{-}0 \text{ per } 1000 \text{ sq ft}$$

Since the fertilizer 11-55-0 also supplies some nitrogen, Mr. McDonald needs to know how much actual nitrogen is in the 0.9 kg (1.8 lbs) he will be applying. He does this by multiplying (instead of dividing) the weight of nitrogen required by the percentage of nitrogen in the 11-55-0.

$$0.9 \text{ kg of } 11\text{-}55\text{-}0 \times \frac{11\%}{100} = 0.9 \times 0.11 = 0.1 \text{ kg of nitrogen } / 100 \text{m}^2$$

OR

$$1.8 \text{ lb of } 11\text{-}55\text{-}0 \times \frac{11\%}{100} = 1.8 \times 0.11 = 0.2 \text{ lb of nitrogen } / 1000 \text{ sq ft}$$

Mr. McDonald wants to apply a total of 1.5 kg of nitrogen per 100 m² (3 lb N / 1000 sq ft). Therefore, he must subtract the amount of nitrogen being applied in the 11-55-0.

1.5 kg - 0.1 kg = 1.4 kg of nitrogen still needed.
(3.0 lb - 0.2 lb = 2.8 lb of nitrogen still needed.)

Now he can calculate how much 21-0-0 to apply.

$$\frac{1.4 \text{ kg of nitrogen required}}{21\% / 100} = \frac{1.4}{0.21} = 6.7 \text{ kg of } 21\text{-}0\text{-}0 \text{ per } 100 \text{ m}^2$$

OR

$$\frac{2.8 \text{ lb of nitrogen required}}{21\% / 100} = \frac{2.8}{0.21} = 13.3 \text{ lb of } 21\text{-}0\text{-}0 \text{ per } 1000 \text{ sq ft}$$

But Mr. McDonald's garden is not 100 m² (1000 sq ft) so less fertilizer is required to bring nutrients back up to optimum levels. To calculate the right amounts of fertilizer, he divides the weight by 100 m² (1000 sq ft) and multiplies by his true area of 24 m² (260 sq ft)

$$\frac{0.9 \text{ kg of } 11\text{-}55\text{-}0}{100 \text{ m}^2} \times 24 \text{ m}^2 = 0.009 \times 24 = 0.22 \text{ kg of } 11\text{-}55\text{-}0$$

and

$$\frac{6.7 \text{ kg of } 21\text{-}0\text{-}0}{100 \text{ m}^2} \times 24 \text{ m}^2 = 0.067 \times 24 = 1.61 \text{ kg of } 21\text{-}0\text{-}0$$

OR

$$\frac{(1.8 \text{ lb of } 11\text{-}55\text{-}0 \times 260 \text{ sq ft} = 0.5 \text{ lb})}{1000 \text{ sq ft}}$$

and

$$\frac{(13.3 \text{ lb of } 21\text{-}0\text{-}0 \times 260 \text{ sq ft} = 3.4 \text{ lb})}{1000 \text{ sq ft}}$$

All fertilizers should be applied as accurately as possible. There is no sense in calculating accurate weights on paper if the gardener is just going to throw fertilizers on his garden indiscriminately. Use a weight scale, a bathroom scale, or a measuring cup to measure the fertilizer. It takes approximately five cups of fertilizer to equal one kilogram (about 2.5 cups / lb). Using this information, Mr. McDonald will apply:

5 cups X 0.22 kg = 1.1 cups of 11-55-0

and

5 cups X 1.61 kg = 8 cups of 21-0-0

on his garden before rototilling and planting this spring.

Mr. McDonald thought he might like to apply organic fertilizer instead. He saw horse manure on sale at one of the garden centers. Its analysis is 0.6 per cent N - 0.2 per cent P - 0.6 per cent K. To compare this fertilizer with chemical fertilizer, he calculated the following:

$$\frac{1.5 \text{ kg of nitrogen required}}{0.6\% / 100} = \frac{1.5}{0.006} = 250 \text{ kg of manure per } 100 \text{ m}^2$$

$$\frac{250 \text{ kg of manure}}{100 \text{ m}^2} \times 24 \text{ m}^2 = 60 \text{ kg of manure for his garden}$$

This manure will also supply the needed phosphorus of 0.5 kg (250 kg X 0.2/100 = 250 X 0.002 = 0.5 kg of phosphorus). Instead of applying 0.22 kg (1.1 cups) + 1.61 kg (8 cups) = 1.83 kg (9.1 cups) of fertilizer salts, Mr. McDonald would have to apply 60 kg (132 lb) of horse manure. Costs for this quantity of manure (even on sale) are many times greater than the chemical equivalent and is much more difficult to apply and incorporate.

## SOIL CONDITIONERS AND CONDITIONING

Organic matter is the fundamental part of a good, healthy soil (see Soils lesson, ORGANIC MATTER). It is continuously being broken down to release its nutrients. In addition to this, organic matter maintains soil porosity for air and water penetration while minimizing nutrient and water losses. It also provides an ideal environment for beneficial micro-organisms. Every gardener should replace lost organic matter annually by applying animal manure, compost, or peat moss, or by rotating vegetables with a green manure crop.

### ANIMAL MANURE

Animal manures are still considered to be the foundation of good vegetable gardening. Most are fairly good soil conditioners that also add some nutrients. Nutrient levels contained in animal manures depend upon the type of animals, what they were fed and how the manure was handled. Improper handling can reduce nutrient levels by leaching and ammonification. Manure is available in three forms. These are **fresh** (green), **rotted** (composted) and **dried**.

Fresh manure, which is usually the least expensive form of manure, should never be used on a vegetable garden. It contains high levels of ammonia which, when released, are toxic to plants and burn sensitive, young roots. Any weed seeds present are still likely to be viable and can infest an otherwise clean garden. There is also the possibility of fresh manure introducing other pests or pathogens into the soil. Manure that comes from a feed lot often contains high levels of salts and antibiotics so it, too, should not be used in the garden (neither should mushroom manure, as it also has a high salt content).

Composted or well-rotted manure is generally safe to apply to a vegetable garden, except where soil salts are high or in areas where potatoes or rutabagas will be planted. Salts tend to accumulate with unnecessary applications. Potatoes are particularly sensitive to the scab organism which manure encourages. Such soils will benefit more from an application of peat moss.

Manure is composted in the same manner as plant refuse. When the composting process is completed, the manure is free of all insects, weed seeds and diseases. It is virtually odor free, with a mild, earth smell and a soft, crumbly texture. The percentage of nutrients (by weight) in well-composted manure is actually higher than that of fresh manure, as a compost heap condenses in size with the breakdown of fibrous materials.

The recommended, general purpose application rate for composted animal manures is a 2-5 cm (1-2 in) layer worked in 15 cm (6 in) deep. This averages out to approximately 5.5 kg of manure/m² (10 lbs/sq yd). The nutrient levels of poultry manure are about twice that of most other animal manures, so about one half the general purpose rate should be used. Incorporate any manure thoroughly with a rototiller or shovel to ensure there are no clods or concentrated layers within the soil. Fall is the best time to apply a manure in order to allow it time to decompose before spring. Fertilizers may be added during incorporation.

### COMPOST

Compost from various plant refuse has very similar properties to composted manures (see Plant Nutrition lesson, COMPOSTING). Both may be incorporated into a soil during the spring or fall (fall is preferred). Application rates are the same as for composted manures of animals. They may also be used as a mulch on top of the soil to keep temperatures more moderate, reduce moisture loss, and suppress weed growth. The mulch can then be plowed under after a growing season instead of being removed.

### PEAT MOSS

Horticultural peat moss may be somewhat more expensive to buy than

manure, but the advantages of using peat moss are greater (see Soils lesson). Over the long term, costs actually become less because less material is needed. Organic matter levels are maintained as peat moss is slow to break down, unlike manures and compost. There is also little danger of applying too much peat moss in a garden. Thorough incorporation ensures an adequate amount of mineral soil is available to provide the necessary support and nutrients for plant growth. Start by applying a 5-8 cm (2-3 in) layer of peat moss and incorporate it 15-20 cm (6-8 in) deep. Add 3-5 cm (1-2 in) annually, until the desired texture is reached. The value of peat moss is in its organic matter building ability and, because it contains virtually no nutrients, its application does not confuse the determination of fertilizer rates. Maintain nutrient levels with annual applications of natural or chemical fertilizers as previously described. Since peat moss is usually acidic, there is the added benefit of reducing soil pH of alkaline soils (Prairie soils are typically alkaline).

Unfortunately, peat moss does not make a very good mulching material. It tends to dry out and form a crust, making it very difficult for water to penetrate and rewet. Other organic substances or plastics make better mulches (see GROWING SEASON EXTENDERS).

Peat-like materials (from sloughs containing sedges and rushes) are not always recommended for garden use. Although they look and smell good, they tend to be high in accumulated salts. Overuse of such materials can lead to excessively high electrical conductivities and poor plant growth. Horticultural peat moss comes from black spruce and tamarack bogs or muskegs where the sphagnum moss plant grows. This material is more coarse and lighter brown in color. It also does not break down like the sedges and rushes peat.

### MINERAL SOURCE CONDITIONERS

There are several mineral-based soil conditioners available, not all of which are recommended for the vegetable garden. The most common are sand, perlite and vermiculite. Sand is probably the most tempting material to use when trying to loosen a heavy clay soil. However, many gardeners have found that when sand is mixed with clay, the result is a 'concrete'. Vast quantities of very coarse, washed or sharp sand have been used with limited success but costs and labor requirements make the use of this type of sand very impractical.

Perlite and vermiculite are two common materials used in greenhouse and houseplant growing media. They do an excellent job of maintaining soil porosity, particularly for soilless mixes (see Plant Propagation lesson, SOWING MEDIUM). When used in an outdoor garden soil, however, both materials lose their desirable properties with seasonal freezing and thawing. The pulverized product cannot maintain its porosity and tends to bind nutrients, making them unavailable to plants.

## GREEN MANURE
A gardener can build up a rich soil, high in organic matter, without applying peat moss or animal wastes. This can be done by rotating vegetable crops with a green manure crop. Green manure is a legume (like clover or alfalfa) or non-legume (grass or grain) that is cultivated for part of a season, then plowed under while it is still green. The crop protects fallow land from wind and water erosion while preventing weeds from infesting and becoming a nuisance. All nutrients used for the crop's growth are returned to the soil when the crop is plowed in. Soil fertility actually increases as nutrients from great depths are brought to the surface and made available to shallow rooted vegetables.

Green manure incorporation is a very practical technique for use on larger gardens on which it would be very time-consuming and expensive to add manure or peat moss. One half or one third of a garden plot can be set aside for growing the green manure crop. The location of this crop is rotated annually. Alfalfa and various other clovers are best suited to this purpose. Both fix atmospheric nitrogen and bring up nutrients from as deep as 10 m (over 30 ft). During the growing season, these plants make good forage and honey crops. Some even have leaves, flowers, or seeds that can be used for teas or as pot herbs.

If a soil is too acidic, wet, or infertile, or if the creation of organic matter is the prime objective, then a non-legume is a better choice of green manure crop.

Brome, buckwheat, oats, rye, wheat and barley are all excellent soil improvers. They produce considerably more succulent top growth than legumes in a shorter period of time.

Regardless of the green manure crop grown, periodic mowing or scything is needed to prevent blossoming, as any seeds produced will become weeds during the succeeding year. Otherwise, minimal maintenance is required. Some possible exceptions are emergency weeding and watering. Legumes should probably be inoculated to increase the population of *Rhizobia*. This is the bacteria responsible for fixing nitrogen. Plow under all green manure crops in late summer or early fall, just before buds appear. The garden will then be ready for spring planting. Extra nitrogen may be applied to counteract that tied up in micro-organisms and to speed up decomposition.

## CHEMICAL IMPROVEMENTS
There are two chemical conditions, other than fertility, which have been known to adversely affect a garden soil: soil salinity and soil pH. With both of these, a soil test is required to assess the severity and determine corrective measures.

### SALINITY
Soils can have a very high salt content that is harmful to plants. This is indicated by a high EC or electrical conductivity number on a soil test report. High salt levels may occur naturally or result from overfertilization. These soils are commonly called 'alkali' but are more correctly referred to as 'saline'. A saline soil contains large quantities of magnesium or sodium sulphates. Evidence of the presence of this condition is a white crust on the soil surface and very poor plant growth.

Unfortunately, soil salinity is a very difficult condition to correct. Water, moving by capillary action, brings salts to the surface. Improving downward flow of water minimizes this salt accumulation. To help dilute some of the excess salts, gardeners can increase organic matter and watering when conditions are not too severe. Never use soft water for this purpose. The high sodium and magnesium contents of soft water only serves to aggravate the problem (see WATERING).

When salinity is too great, the soil must be completely replaced with fresh topsoil from a non-saline site. It is recommended that raised beds then be used to improve drainage and prevent the problem from recurring (see RAISED BED GARDENING).

In those areas that only have high sodium levels, the use of gypsum or calcium sulphate is sometimes recommended. The theory is that the calcium ion will displace the sodium ion, thereby allowing the sodium to be leached away. This practice is not always successful and should only be attempted on the recommendation of a soils specialist.

### SOIL pH
The pH of a soil refers to its acidity or alkalinity. The ideal soil pH for most vegetables is between 6.0 and 6.5, which is slightly acidic. Most soils in the Prairies are somewhat alkaline (pH greater than 7.0). For this reason, acidic type fertilizers are preferred to help lower pH over an extended period of time. Table 11-6 indicates which chemical fertilizers are acidic by nature. Soil pH is very resistant to change because of its powerful buffering ability (inherent in most soils). Do not use sulphur, aluminum sulphate, or ferrous sulphate unless recommended by a professional.

Occasionally, acidic soils are found with a soil pH below 6.0. These areas probably had or still have coniferous trees growing on them. When soil pH is low enough, the application of agricultural limestone is recommended. Gardeners in Europe and eastern North America must use limestone annually, but, because Prairie soils are built on limestone parent material, lime only needs to be used if it is recommended by a soil test.

## CULTIVATING THE SOIL

Cultivation is a difficult task, but is necessary for maintaining good soil tilth. It involves spading, hoeing, turning, rototilling and raking. All of these operations serve to improve soil structure, drainage, and soil atmosphere. Cultivation removes woody plant residues, diseased debris and rocks. It also provides a uniform, flat seedbed.

Most gardeners cultivate in two stages: once in the fall and once again in the spring. During the fall, most of the plant debris is removed. Organic matter and slow release fertilizers are then added before the soil is turned over and broken up. This stage may be left until spring but this makes the task of spring planting much larger and harder. Fall cultivation exposes insects to birds and cold temperatures. It opens the ground to frost action and helps break up hard clods. Snow catch is maximized to improve spring moisture content. Increased exposure to the sun also means that planting may begin earlier in the spring with less work. Fast acting fertilizers should still be added in the spring and any undecomposed debris removed. More organic matter can also be incorporated. The soil is smoothed with a rake to a fine (but firm) seedbed which is then ready for planting.

## DIGGING AND DOUBLE DIGGING

Digging, or any other form of cultivation, requires that the soil be at the proper moisture content. If a soil is too wet when cultivated, extremely hard clods of earth develop when it dries. If too dry, a soil pulverizes to a dust. Always check the soil first. Grab a handful of soil from a depth of 5-10 cm (2-4 in) and squeeze it hard. No water should ooze out when pressure is applied and the soil should hold its molded shape when released. Only then is it safe to cultivate.

A common technique for cultivating a soil by hand is to dig a series of trenches. This is called the 'trenching and turning' method. It is preferred when creating a new garden where sod presently exists but it can also be used in many existing gardens. Surface plant material (like sod) is usually stripped off and clinging soil removed. Plant material can then be composted before being returned to the soil.

Dig a trench 30 cm (12 in) wide and 20 cm (8 in) deep along one side of the plot. Use a wheelbarrow to transport this soil to the opposite side. If deep-rooted vegetables are to be grown, dig the trench 30 cm (12 in) deep. Be careful not to dig too deep as this brings up very poor subsoil which is low in organic matter and nutrients. A gardener may have to add several centimetres of new topsoil in order to obtain the proper depth of good quality soil (15-30 cm or 6-12 in). Fertilizers and extra organic

matter may also be applied to the surface for incorporation with the digging process.

When the first trench is finished and the soil removed, dig a parallel trench of equal width and depth next to it. Use the soil from this trench to fill the first (see Figure 11-6). Hard clods and plant residues should be broken up and mixed in. Continue digging trenches while keeping edges straight and parallel. When finished, the final trench is filled with the soil from the first. If cultivation is done in the fall, leave the soil rough and lumpy.

## Figure 11-6
## TRENCHING AND TURNING METHOD

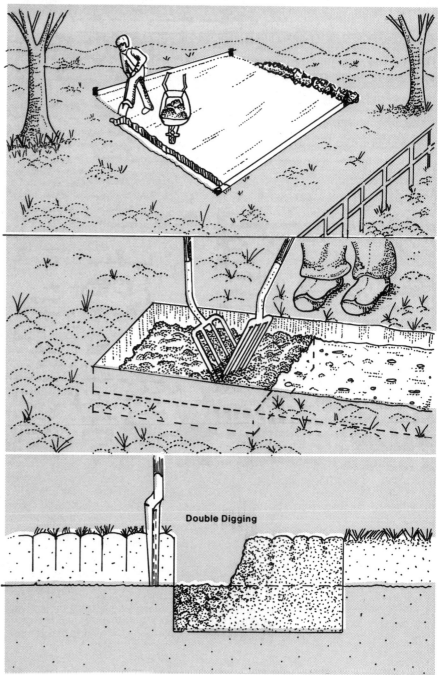

Double Digging

Double digging uses a two step process. A trench is dug as in the trenching and turning method but before refilling the previous trench, the subsoil is loosened an additional 10 to 15 cm (4-6 in) deep. This is done by stabbing and rocking a heavy garden fork back and forth. If the subsoil is exceptionally hard, organic matter may be incorporated into this layer or drainage tiles put in place. Always try to keep the topsoil and subsoil layers separate.

If a soil is particularly poor in a double dug bed, it can be improved during cultivation. Alternating layers of soil with peat moss, manure or compost, each 7-8 cm (about 3 in) thick, works well in improving the texture of a heavy clay or sandy soil. One drawback to double digging is that it is a very difficult and tedious task when all the work is done by hand. The use of a rototiller make incorporating soil amendments much easier.

## ROTOTILLING

Because hand digging is slow, difficult work, gardeners with very large plots obviously prefer using a rotary tiller to a shovel for garden cultivation. Normally, rototilling is done in the spring to prepare a very fine seedbed. It gives maximum incorporation or mixing of soil amendments and fertilizers. There is, however, some controversy about its use.

## Table 11-8
### FROST DATA FOR SOME LOCATIONS IN ALBERTA

| LOCATION | ALTITUDE | NO. OF YEARS RECORDED | AVG. FROST -FREE PERIOD | AVG. DATE OF LAST SPRING FROST | AVG. DATE OF FIRST FALL FROST |
|---|---|---|---|---|---|
| Athabasca | 1700 | 23 | 70 | June 15 | Aug 25 |
| Bow Island | 2612 | 10 | 125 | May 18 | Sept 20 |
| Brooks | 2487 | 28 | 114 | May 23 | Sept 16 |
| Calgary (airport) | 3540 | 30 | 106 | May 28 | Sept 12 |
| Cold Lake | 1784 | 18 | 112 | May 26 | Sept 16 |
| Coronation | 2618 | 30 | 111 | May 25 | Sept 13 |
| Drumheller | 2255 | 25 | 108 | May 25 | Sept 12 |
| Edson | 3033 | 30 | 67 | June 18 | Aug 25 |
| Fairview | 2160 | 30 | 111 | May 21 | Sept 10 |
| Edmonton (Fort Saskatchewan) | 2050 | 13 | 115 | May 19 | Sept 14 |
| Fort Vermilion | 915 | 30 | 91 | June 6 | Sept 6 |
| Grande Prairie | 2190 | 29 | 113 | May 19 | Sept 10 |
| High Prairie | 1965 | 30 | 91 | June 2 | Sept 1 |
| Lac la Biche | 1835 | 12 | 97 | June 1 | Sept 7 |
| Lethbridge (airport) | 3018 | 30 | 118 | May 21 | Sept 16 |
| Medicine Hat | 2365 | 30 | 125 | May 17 | Sept 20 |
| Peace River (airport) | 1866 | 17 | 88 | June 3 | Aug 31 |
| Red Deer | 2820 | 22 | 105 | May 28 | Sept 11 |
| Rimbey | 3020 | 10 | 107 | June 1 | Sept 16 |
| Rocky Mountain House | 3330 | 26 | 95 | May 31 | Sept 5 |
| Stettler | 2700 | 30 | 114 | May 22 | Sept 14 |
| Strathmore | 3160 | 21 | 109 | May 23 | Sept 10 |
| Taber | 2650 | 24 | 127 | May 15 | Sept 21 |
| Vegreville | 2082 | 29 | 99 | May 30 | Sept 7 |
| Vermilion | 2037 | 26 | 90 | June 5 | Sept 4 |

Courtesy of Alberta Agriculture: Alberta Vegetable Production Guide    Agdex 250/13-1

Figure 11-7
## AVERAGE FROST FREE DAYS

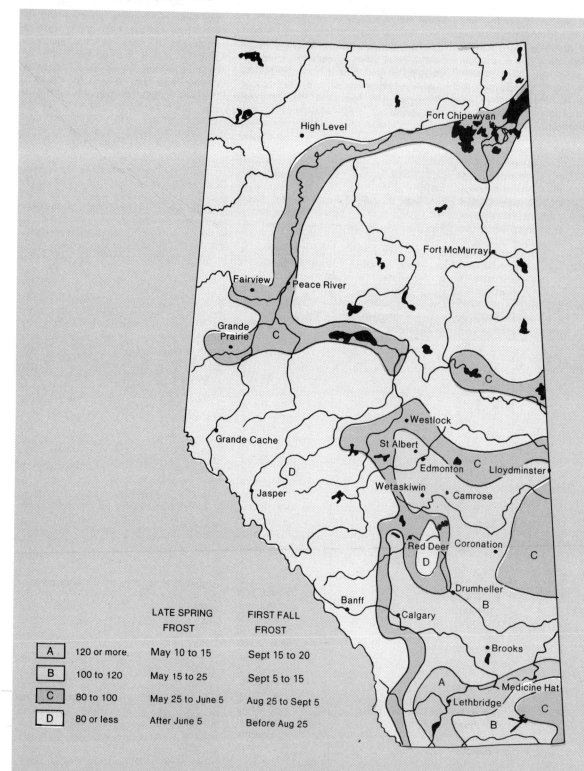

| | | LATE SPRING FROST | FIRST FALL FROST |
|---|---|---|---|
| A | 120 or more | May 10 to 15 | Sept 15 to 20 |
| B | 100 to 120 | May 15 to 25 | Sept 5 to 15 |
| C | 80 to 100 | May 25 to June 5 | Aug 25 to Sept 5 |
| D | 80 or less | After June 5 | Before Aug 25 |

Courtesy of Alberta Agriculture: Alberta Vegetable Production Guide Agdex 250/13-1

Some horticulturists claim that overuse of a rototiller can destroy soil structure. It tends to pulverize the desirable, small, dirt lumps, which leads to compaction and erosion. This is usually overcome by the incorporation of additional organic matter and cultivating at the proper moisture content.

Another problem is that it tends to cultivate only the top 10 cm (4 in) of soil. Good soil management requires that at least 15-20 cm (6-8 in) be cultivated. Proper adjustment of the tiller and using it at a slower pace generally means that greater depth can be achieved. A rototiller is like any other tool. If it is not used properly, it cannot do the job. It is an indispensable tool for many gardeners.

### FALL CLEAN UP

One of the more important tasks after a growing season is the removal of all diseased and woody plant materials. This is essential to minimize reinfection of many plant diseases, as well as to control insect populations . Pull up all cabbage, cauliflower and broccoli stalks to help remove overwintering root maggots. Also pull up corn stalks, tomato vines and bean plants as these are too woody and do not decompose fast enough. Bury all plant materials in a compost heap or dispose of them by trashing or burning. Remove all plastic mulches and plant protectors. The soil can then be turned over to speed the decomposition of remaining plant residues.

## SOWING SEEDS

In order to take maximum advantage of the growing season, a gardener must practice careful planning and patience. Also, a gardener must have a basic knowledge of soil quality, local climatic conditions and the time it takes a vegetable to reach maturity. Knowing when the last spring frost occurs or when soil temperatures are sufficiently warm enough determines the best planting dates for each crop. Plants that are tolerant to cool temperatures can be planted outside much earlier than those that are not so tolerant. A gardener must determine which crops are to be directly seeded outdoors, which are to be transplanted, and which technique to use to ensure maximum yields.

## WHEN TO PLANT

Many gardening books and seed catalogues contain basic climatic maps which indicate broad zones of similar growing seasons. This information is generally misleading. The dates for the last spring frost and first fall frost can vary dramatically from several days to weeks in a particular garden within each zone. Many gardeners often add a 2-3 week grace period to improve the odds (see Figure 11-7 and Table 11-8).

### DETERMINING LAST SPRING FROST DATE

The date of the last spring frost is the most important date in vegetable gardening. The best method of determining this date is to keep personal weather data in a record book or gardening file each year. The microclimate of a vegetable garden may be quite different from its surroundings. Predictions of frost from the local weather stations are only accurate for that particular location.

Microclimate is affected by a countless number of weather modifiers (see Climate lesson, MODIFYING CLIMATIC FACTORS). Large bodies of water, for example, tend to moderate temperature shifts and keep temperatures lower in the spring and higher in the fall. Higher elevations generally have cooler temperatures year round. The bottoms of small valleys are also cooler due to cold air drainage. Windbreaks, buildings and southern exposures, however, act as buffers. Even raised beds have a similar, beneficial effect. A gardener has to become familiar with his particular area in order to take maximum advantage of the growing season.

Gardeners new to an area should first contact local weather stations and any agricultural or horticultural information offices. The people in these offices are usually able to give approximate dates for the last spring and first fall frosts. Neighbors may prove to be an invaluable source of such information. Thereafter, keep accurate records of these dates, based on practical experience. Using averages will help determine the frost free period and, ultimately, determine the types of vegetables and their cultivars which can be grown successfully.

### MINIMIZING RISKS

In order to minimize the risk of a crop failure, the seeding dates for each vegetable must be calculated as accurately as possible. Mark, on a current or perpetual calendar, the dates of the last spring and first fall frosts. On one side of the calendar, place a '0' beside the week each date appears. Then number the weeks backward from 0 to 10 and forward from 0 to 5. These numbers will be useful for determining when to start transplants and when to plant outdoors (see Table 11-9).

In areas with a short growing season, transplants may be used. This is essential for some warm and long season crops to bear fruit. Transplant material can be grown at home or purchased from local nurseries or greenhouses. There are also many cultural techniques that may be employed to lengthen the growing season (see GARDENING METHODS). Many provide frost protection, faster warming of soil temperatures and more rapid growth. Experimentation with different cultural and propagation techniques will determine which is most successful in a particular microclimate.

Table 11-9 can be used as a guideline for planning the seeding date of each vegetable. All figures are expressed in weeks with respect to the last spring frost. Use the calendar with its numbered weeks in conjunction with this table. Record each vegetable's planting date, whether it be for direct seeding outdoors or transplants. From this table, it is obvious that not all the vegetables in a garden should be planted on the same day.

In the first column (Indoor Seeding Dates), each number refers to the number of weeks to sow seeds prior to the date of the last spring frost. The numbers in brackets indicate the absolute earliest that these crops should be started.

The second column gives the preferred age of transplants. Growing longer than these times produces overgrown and poor quality transplants for setting outdoors. Those crops with a * beside them indicate those crops that are very sesitive to transplant damage. Use only individual containers for sowing and growing these crops. When setting out, minimize root disturbance. For very

Table 11-9

## WHEN TO PLANT SEEDS

| VEGETABLE | INDOOR SEEDING DATES (BEFORE LAST SPRING FROST) | PREFERRED AGE OF TRANSPLANTS | OUTDOOR SETTING DATE | | OUTDOOR DIRECT SEEDING DATES | AVERAGE WEEKS TO MATURITY FROM SOWING DATE |
|---|---|---|---|---|---|---|
| | | | BEFORE LAST FROST TO | AFTER LAST FROST | | |
| Asparagus | 10(18) | 12-14 | 3-4 | 4 | 3-4 | — |
| Beans, lima | 3 | 3-4* | — | 1-2 | 1-2 | 8.5-10.5 |
| Beans, broad | — | — | — | — | 5-7 | 12-13 |
| Beans, pole | 3 | 3-4* | — | 1-2 | 0 | 10 |
| Beans, snap | 3 | 3-4* | — | 1-2 | 0 | 5.5-8 |
| Beets | 8 | 4* | 4 | — | 3-4 | 7-8 |
| Broccoli | 6(12) | 6-8 | 4 | 2-3 | 3-4 | 8-10 |
| Brussels Sprouts | 6(12) | 6-8 | 4 | 2-3 | 4-6 | 12-16 |
| Cabbage, green  late | 4(6) | 6-8 | 0 | 2-3 | 0 | 10-16 |
| Cabbage, green  early | 6(11) | 6-8 | 5 | 2-3 | 3-4 | 8.5-10 |
| Cabbage, red | 6(8) | 6-8 | 0 | 2-3 | 0 | 10 |
| Cabbage, savoy | 4(6) | 6-8 | — | 2-3 | +3-4 | 11-17 |
| Cabbage, chinese | — | none | — | — | +3-4 | 8.5-12 |
| Carrots | 9(10) | 5-6* | 4 | — | 5-7 | 8.5-13.5 |
| Cauliflower | 6(12) | 6-8 | 4 | 2 | 0 | 8-16 |
| Celeriac | 7 | 6-8 | — | 1 | — | 16-17 |
| Celery | 5(7) | 6-8 | — | 1-2 | 1-2 | 13-20 |
| Corn, sweet | 2 | 4* | 0 | 2-3 | 2-3 | 8.5-14 |
| Cucumbers, pickling | 4(5) | 2-3* | 1t | 2 | +1 | 7-9 |
| Cucumbers, slicing | 4(5) | 2-3* | 1t | 2 | +1 | 7-9 |
| Eggplant | 10 | 8-10 | 0t | 2-3 | 0 | 8-12 |
| Endive | 4(8) | 4-5 | 4 | 2 | 2-4 | 11-14 |
| Garlic, cloves | 8(10) | 4-6 | 2-4 | 1 | 4-6 | 13-16 |
| Kale | 6(11) | 6-8 | 5 | 2 | 4-6 | 7-9 |
| Kohlrabi | 6(11) | 6-8 | 5 | 2 | 4-6 | 9-10 |
| Leeks | 10 | 4-6 | 5 | 2 | 1-2 | 12-21 |
| Lettuce, head | 6(12) | 4-6 | 6 | 3 | 3-4 | 10-14 |
| Lettuce, leaf | 5(8) | 3-5 | 2-3 | 3 | 5-7 | 6-7 |
| Mustard | 10 | 4-6 | 5 | 2 | 2-4 | 5-7 |
| Okra | 3 | 6-8* | 0 | 3-4 | 0 | 7-9 |
| Onions, bunching | 10 | 4-6 | 4-5 | 2 | 4-6 | 8-17 |
| Onions, cooking  sets | — | — | 0 | — | 0 | 14 |
| Onions, cooking  seed | 10 | 4-6 | 5-7 | 2 | 5-7 | 13-25 |
| Parsley | 9 | 4-6 | 5-7 | 4-6 | 5-7 | 10-11 |
| Parsnips | 8(10) | 4-6* | 4 | 3-4 | 2-4 | 11-17 |
| Peas | 8 | 4* | 4 | 2-3 | 5-7 | 8-11 |
| Peppers | 10 | 6-8* | 0t | 2-3 | 1 | 9-10 |
| Potato  eyes | 3-4 | 4-6 | 0 | 2-3 | 3-4 | 12-16 |
| seeds | 6-8 | 6-10 | 0 | 2-3 | | 13 |
| tubers | — | — | — | — | 2-4 | 10-16 |

Table 11-9 CONT'D

| VEGETABLE | INDOOR SEEDING DATES (BEFORE LAST SPRING FROST) | PREFERRED AGE OF TRANSPLANTS | OUTDOOR SETTING DATE | | OUTDOOR DIRECT SEEDING DATES | AVERAGE WEEKS TO MATURITY FROM SOWING DATE |
|---|---|---|---|---|---|---|
| | | | BEFORE LAST FROST TO | AFTER LAST FROST | | |
| **Pumpkin** | 4-5 | 4* | 1t | 1-2 | +1-2 | 13-16 |
| Radish **early** | — | none | — | — | 4-6 | 3-4 |
| **storage** | — | none | — | — | 3-4 | 6-9 |
| **Rutabaga** | 7(8) | 3-4 | 4 | — | +4 | 12-13 |
| **Spinach** | 7(12) | 4-6* | 3-6 | — | 5-7 | 6-7 |
| **Squash summer** | 1 | 4* | 0t | 3-4 | 0 | 7-10 |
| **winter** | 1 | 4* | 0t | 3-4 | +1-2 | 11-17 |
| **Swiss Chard** | 7(8) | 4* | 3-4 | — | 2-4 | 7-9 |
| **Tomato cherry** | 6-8 | 6-10 | 0t | 3-4 | 0 | 8-9 |
| **determinant** | 6-8 | 6-10 | 0t | 3-4 | 0 | 8-10 |
| **indeterminant** | 6-8 | 6-10 | 0t | 3-4 | 0 | 8-11 |
| **Turnips** | 7(8) | 3-4* | 4 | — | 4-6 | 5-8 |

sensitive crops, consider using direct seeding outdoors instead.

Many vegetable crops may be transplanted from several weeks before the last frost date to several weeks beyond this date. Consider the desired age of the transplant and the proposed date for setting outdoors when calculating the time to sow seeds. Crops like cucumbers and pumpkins have a 't' beside the number of weeks before last frost. This means that the crops require adequate frost protection. If protection is impractical, then set plants out a couple of weeks after the last frost date.

Most outdoor direct seeding dates are prior to the last spring frost. Those with a '+' sign are sown only after the last frost. This is because the seeds or seedlings cannot tolerate cold soils or freezing night temperatures. A '0' means the crop is planted on the frost date itself.

The final column gives the approximate time that it takes a seed to produce a harvestable crop. This time varies greatly, depending upon the vegetable cultivar, cultural practices and weather during the growing season. Similar information is given on seed packets and in seed catalogues. Use this information and compare it to the frost free period of

the garden. This determines if direct seeding is possible or whether transplants have to be used.

This table is only a guideline for the gardener to use in calculating his own particular planting dates. Many tables, with exact planting dates like the one in the Alberta Horticultural Guide, are not applicable to every garden. A planting schedule must be individually prepared for each garden and its particular microclimate. Practical experience, and the use of Table 11-9, can minimize risks and maximize yields. Keep an accurate record of each vegetable's success or failure. You can then modify subsequent planting dates.

## SEEDS

Most vegetable crops can be propagated from seed. For most crops, this is the easiest and best method. Seed can be purchased from local grocery stores, hardware outlets, garden centers, nurseries, or through the mail. Many mail-order seed companies offer a wider selection of cultivars of each vegetable than do stores. Seed packages are usually stamped with an expiry date. Do not purchase outdated seed.

**TESTING FOR VIABILITY**

Viability is the quality or ability of a seed to germinate and produce a healthy seedling or plant under favorable growing conditions. If every seed in a package were to germinate and grow, a 100 per cent viability would exist. However, even with fresh seed, a certain percentage does not succeed. Most seed direct from the grower has a tested germination rate of 80-95 per cent. This means that 80-95 seeds out of 100 can germinate under proper conditions. Losses are mainly due to insufficient maturity, insect or disease damage, or physical damage to the embryo.

The viability of seeds decreases with time. All vegetable seeds should be tested for viability if they have been stored for a year or more. To do this, place 10-50 seeds on a moistened blotter of paper towels or cotton cloth. Cover with another blotter or with a glass plate, plastic sheet, or wide-mouthed jar. This covering helps to maintain a constant, high humidity. Lift the cover daily to provide aeration and ensure adequate moisture. Allow an additional week beyond the average number of days for germination (usually listed on the seed packet) before counting the number of seeds that show emergence of a radicle or root. Carefully count all the seeds that have germinated and divide this number by the total number of seeds tested. Multiply the resulting fraction by 100 to arrive at per cent germination for these seeds. eg.,

$$\frac{16 \text{ seeds germinated}}{20 \text{ seeds tested}} \times 100 = \begin{array}{c} 80 \\ \text{per cent} \\ \text{viability} \end{array}$$

If the resulting per cent germination is below 60, consider buying new seed. If it is between 60 and 80 per cent, plant additional seeds to ensure the desired number of plants. Carrot and celery seed are usually lower in viability, so extra seed must always be sown to ensure an adequate stand.

### PROPER STORAGE

Theoretically, in an ideal environment, a seed can survive almost indefinitely. For practical purposes, however, most vegetable seeds last at least two years. With good garden management and planting only what is needed, there are usually many vegetable seeds left over after planting. Record the date of purchase on each seed packet that contains leftover seeds and save money on next year's garden by storing excess seeds.

The most important quality of proper seed storage is moisture content. It must be low enough to reduce the respiration rate and enzyme activity of the embryo. If humidity is too high, partial germination may occur. Storage rots and molds are often able to kill the seed.

To prepare seeds for storage, thoroughly dry all seeds (even fresh ones). Place seeds in a warm, dry location with good air circulation. While drying, the temperature should not exceed 37°C. If drying outside, bring the seeds inside at night and before damp weather to prevent them from getting wet.

Another condition of good storage is temperature, as temperature directly relates to moisture content. Ideally, most seeds should be stored in an area of low humidity with storage temperatures kept between 4 and 10°C.

Most seeds store best in sealed containers (see Figure 11-8). Two exceptions are peas and beans, which need to breathe. For these, use a paper bag or jar with holes punched in the lid. All others can be stored in metal tins or

### Figure 11-8
### STORING SEEDS

Courtesy of Alberta Agriculture

glass jars with tight fitting lids. Reduce humidity in the container by placing a couple of spoonfuls of powdered milk, corn starch or silica gel (wrapped) in tissue in with the seeds. Store the sealed containers in an unheated garage, attic, refrigerator or any other cool, dark place. When stored in this manner, vegetable seeds should remain viable for as long as listed in Table 11-10.

## DIRECT SEEDING OUTDOORS

Most vegetables are started by sowing seeds directly into the garden. Their success generally depends upon the growing season and the length of time it takes for the vegetable to mature. Direct seeding avoids the initial shock of exposing transplants to the more severe climate outside and requires somewhat less work in preparation and planning.

Begin with a well prepared seedbed (see Figure 11-9). Use good quality seed and sow at the proper depth. Plant additional seeds to allow for losses and thin out excess seedlings to maintain the proper plant spacings (see Table 11-13). Practice early cultivation and watch for insect and disease attacks.

Not all seed needs to be sown at the same time (see MINIMIZING RISKS and Table 11-9). Successive sowings allow for dispersed harvests (see SUCCESSION PLANTING). This can prevent the feast and famine cycle that is so common in many gardens. Allow enough time for plants to reach maturity before the first fall frost. Sow only when soil temperatures are high enough for seed germination. Warm season crops are particularly sensitive to cold soils. Beans, for example, will rot before germinating in cool, damp soils.

Choose a calm, sunny day for direct seeding a garden. Before beginning, mark off the areas for each vegetable from the garden layout plan (see GARDEN LAYOUT PROCEDURE). Measure carefully and follow the plan closely. Do not feel that all seed must be used or that the entire garden plot must be planted. A gardener can always transplant seedlings later when thinning. Leave areas for this and subsequent sowings.

### Table 11-10
### LONGEVITY OF VEGETABLE SEEDS IN STORAGE

| 1-2 YEARS | 2-3 YEARS | 3-4 YEARS | 4-5 YEARS | 5-6 YEARS |
|-----------|-----------|-----------|-----------|-----------|
| corn | leek | asparagus | all members of | cucumber |
| onion | pepper | bean | the cabbage | endive |
| parsley | | carrot | family | muskmelon |
| parsnip | | celery | squash | watermelon |
| | | lettuce | pumpkin | |
| | | pea | swiss chard | |
| | | spinach | | |
| | | tomatoe | | |

# Figure 11-9
## WELL PREPARED SEEDBED

There are several problems associated with direct seeding. Losses can result from bird and rodent feeding, insect and disease damage, wind and water erosion, or bad weather. Cold spring soils lead to very slow germination. Individual plant care is usually less than adequate but losses can be offset with a variety of cultural measures.

## SOWING TECHNIQUES
There are two basic ways to plant seeds by hand. Seeds may be **broadcast** (scattered) randomly over the soil surface when sowing entire beds or blocks. For more control in conventional rows and intensive plant spacing patterns, seeds are usually **sown individually**. There are many mechanical devices available on the market to assist in this method of planting. Wide row plantings can be made using either method.

### BROADCAST
Broadcasting involves scattering or flinging seed outward over a prepared seedbed. Scattered seeds separate before falling onto the soil. Extra fine seeds can be broadcast more evenly if the seeds are mixed with sand. After broadcasting, cover the seed with a thin layer of fine soil, sand or peat moss. Water the area gently with a fine spray, taking care not to flood the soil surface and wash seed away.

Broadcasting is a good method for sowing cover crops like herbs and greens or other small-seeded crops for which spacing is not important in the early stages. It can also be used for crops like carrot, onion, radish and turnip as it guarantees a good stand of plants. The need for thinning is inevitable. Broadcasting can lead to a rather messy operation for transplanting seedlings to another area. If sown too thickly, a dense and tangled bed will result. Damping off can also be a major problem with broadcast seeding. Otherwise, it is an excellent technique for getting a quick and even planting.

### ROWS
Conventional row gardens are still the most popular method of planting vegetables. Garden space efficiency in row gardens is low when compared to other methods. Depending upon the desired depth, rows or furrows can either be dug with a hoe handle or corner of the blade. A general rule is to sow seeds at a depth that is 2-3 times the seed's width. Sowing too deep results in poor germination. Sowing too shallow causes malformed seedlings.

Use minimum between-row spacings or wider to accommodate traffic and machinery. Take care not to seed between rows of small seeded crops. Use the seed packet as a shaker to place seeds or an old salt shaker may just do the trick. Alternatives are to drop pinches of fine seed from between the thumb and forefinger or to sow with a mechanical seeder. Mixing extra fine seed with sand or sugar can also help to control seeding rates. Cover the seed with fine textured soil or compost to prevent moisture loss from the ground. Gently firm the covering material to provide good seed-to-soil contact and still allow for seedling emergence.

It is much easier to get uniform spacings with larger seeds. Always plant closer than recommended and thin later. Cover the seeds adequately with soil, firm the covering soil and water carefully.

### HILLS
Crops like bean, corn, cucumber, melon, pumpkin and squash are often planted in hills. This provides seeds with a somewhat warmer germinating area. More direct exposure to sunlight and cold air drainage also results in faster warming of soil temperatures in the spring. Unfortunately, drier conditions during hot summer days is also a result of using hills.

To build hills, soil is taken from the pathways and piled. When soil quality is poor, or heavy feeding crops are grown, dig a hole or trench and refill it with soil that has been amended with fertilizers and organic matter. This procedure tends to make a much deeper soil and provides a reserve of nutrients, strategically placed for an early boost in growth. For vine crops, plant 4-6 seeds per hill, spaced evenly along the top and sides. Bury the seeds at the correct depth and thin later to three seedlings per hill.

### RAISED BEDS
There are a number of individual seeding patterns that can be used in raised beds. When planted in blocks, vegetables are spaced according to the intensive spacings listed in Table 11-13. It requires a rich, fertile soil that is well prepared. The closer overall spacing does not usually stunt growth and average yields are dramatically increased. Raised bed planting requires a greater degree of precision and a knowledge of minimum space requirements. Large individually seeded crops may be sown this way, while small seeded crops can be sown in small pinches at the appropriate spacings.

The clusters of resulting seedlings are carefully thinned later to single plants to minimize root damage to the remaining plants.

When raised beds are seeded in rows, the crops are spaced closely together with a different crop in each row. This gives a diversified crop mix and takes advantage of interplanting and companion planting techniques. Neighboring rows take advantage of each other's spaces. For example, snap beans require a minimum space of 15 cm (6 in.) and carrots require 8 cm (about 3 in.). When these crops are beside one another, the rows are spaced $(15 + 8)/2 = 11.5$ cm (about 4½ in.) apart.

Some consideration must be given to plant height when planting a raised bed in rows. When the bed is running north to south, the tallest crop can be put in the center row, with successively shorter crops to the outside. If the bed is running east to west, the tallest crops should still be on the north side to prevent shading of shorter, sun-loving crops. Generally, up to six rows can be planted in each standard sized bed, depending on the crops grown and spacing required.

### WIDE ROWS
Wide rows are useful for small and large seeded crops alike. The technique of wide row planting is also called **band planting**. Seeds are planted in several, very close, parallel rows to form a single 45 cm (18 in) wide band of a single crop. A similar effect is achieved when seed is evenly broadcast in a wide strip. Bands are spaced the usual 60-75 cm (24-30 in) apart to form the pathways.

The major advantage of using wide rows is the greater yields per garden area achieved. It makes more efficient use of space by having fewer pathways and more plants. Individual plants may produce less, but the overall garden yield is higher. Weeding requirements are reduced as weeds are more successfully crowded out. The dense, leafy canopy (depending on the the type of crop) shades the ground and the soil remains cooler. This provides another advantage for cool season crops. Fertilizers are also more easily applied and are used more efficiently by the crops, instead of by weeds in unseeded areas.

There are, however, some disadvantages. The technique encourages excessive dampness and poor air circulation, which fosters disease growth and spread. Peas and beans are very susceptible to this problem. Fortunately, disease spread can be stopped by removing every second pea or bean plant. Maturity of the crop is also delayed due to the competition for light, water and nutrients.

### FLUID DRILLING
Fluid drilling is an excellent technique for getting uniform spacings of small seeded crops like carrot, lettuce, onion, and radish. In fluid drilling, seeds are suspended in a jelly-like fluid and sown by squeezing the mixture through a small hole in a plastic bag. The greatest advantage of fluid drilling is that it minimizes the need for tedious thinning of small seeded crops.

The fluid or gel is easily made from cornstarch or gelatin. To make the fluid carrier, mix 30-45 mL (2-3 tbsp) of cornstarch in 600 mL (about 1 pint) of cold water. Heat the solution and bring it to a full boil while constantly stirring. Continue to stir (to prevent lumps) while the solution cools in a pan of water. The consistency to strive for is similar to that of thick shampoo. A solution with the consistency of toothpaste is too thick. If the fluid is too thin, the seeds will settle to the bottom and squirt out too fast. Some practice is needed to get it just right.

When the proper thickness is achieved, pour about 120 mL (about 1/2 cup) of cooled gel into a sandwich-sized plastic bag. Add the seed and mix together thoroughly. Tie the bag closed and cut the tip off one corner with scissors. The hole should be slightly larger than the diameter of the seed. To sow the seed, gently squeeze the bag and squirt the gel and seeds onto the soil. Seeds should come out evenly and uniformly. Cover the seeds and gel with the appropriate thickness of covering material (soil, compost, or peat moss). Water immediately. If the gel is allowed to dry out before being diluted, the cornstarch forms a very hard ribbon and prevents germination.

The other alternative is to use gelatin (flavored or unflavored gelatin crystals). Prepare the gelatin as usual but, before it sets, stir in additional water to obtain the desired consistency. Mix in the seeds and apply in the same manner as described previously. The main advantages to using gelatin over cornstarch is that gelatin is easier to make and it does not form a hard ribbon when dry. Experimentation will determine the amounts of water, seed and gel to use.

Fluid drilling can be used to sow single rows, wide bands or entire blocks. It reduces seed losses from thinning and from blowing winds. To get faster growing plants (1-2 weeks earlier), pre-germinated seed may be used with minimum damage (see PRE-GERMINATING SEED).

### FALL SEEDING
Fall seeding is a gamble which may produce extra early crops. Fall seeded garlic and onion have been known to mature 2-3 weeks earlier than those seeded in the spring. Fall seeded leaf lettuce and spinach may produce a harvestable crop in late June; carrots may be ready for harvest in early July and parsnips may be ready in August.

Light soils, finely prepared with lots of organic matter, are needed for fall seeding. Heavy clay soils that form a crust could prevent seedling emergence. Fall seeded crops should be planted in an area that is out of the way of spring cultivation. Seeds are sown when soil temperatures are still above freezing (about 5°C). Such soil temperatures normally occur during late October to early November. If planted too early, water is taken up by the seed, causing the seed to die when it freezes.

The seeds should be sown at their usual depth and covered with a sand and peat moss (or compost) mixture. Irrigate in early spring at the first indication of water stress. The gamble with fall seeding is that heavy frosts will not occur in late spring to damage or kill the seedlings. Crops that have proven successful with fall seeding are leaf lettuce and spinach. Carrots, garlic, leeks, onions (seed) and parsnips can also be fall seeded but are usually less successful.

### PRE-GERMINATING SEED
All seeds germinate better at temperatures higher than those preferred by the resulting plants themselves. This creates a bit of a

problem of how to germinate seeds in a warm environment and grow them in a cooler one, particularly if the crop is to be direct seeded outside. The solution is to pre-germinate the seed before sowing. The technique works very well for both indoor transplants and outdoor direct seeding.

Seed is pre-germinated by the same method as used in testing viability (see TESTING FOR VIABILITY). The only difference is that the viable seed, instead of being discarded, is planted when the radicle or root appears. The seeds are sown at the normal depth with the root pointing downwards. Be very careful not to damage the seed when handling it and water immediately to keep the soil damp.

Culturing and picking out germinated seed is more easily done with larger seeded crops. The most popular pre-germinated vegetable seeds are bean, corn, cucumber, eggplant, melon, pea, pepper, squash and tomato. When small seeded crops are pre-germinated, the sorting process is eliminated. To minimize damage to the tender, immature seedlings, the seeds should be sown by fluid drilling.

Growth rates are significantly improved when pre-germinated vegetable seeds are sown. Plants may reach maturity 1-2 weeks earlier. When seeds are not subjected to cool, damp soils in the spring, losses are reduced. By pre-germinating seeds, the gardener plants only viable seeds and avoids wasteful thinning of healthy seedlings.

### THINNING SEEDLINGS
Weak and overcrowded seedlings (whether indoors or outdoors) need to be thinned in order to allow for proper development. Thinning requires a certain amount of care to minimize damage to the remaining seedlings. Carefully pull out or cut off (with scissors or knife) all unwanted seedlings, leaving the strongest and healthiest to continue growing. Choose a calm, cloudy day or wait until late in the afternoon to thin the outside garden. To make the task easier, soils should be loose and moist. Remove all excess plants to obtain the desired between – plant spacing (see Table 11-13). Thinning should commence soon after the first true leaves appear.

It is sometimes necessary to transplant overcrowded seedlings into gaps in the garden (see Plant Propagation lesson, PRICKING OUT OR TRANSPLANTING YOUNG SEEDLINGS). Doing this on a cloudy day, or late in the afternoon, reduces stress and allows the plant to become better re-established and settled in. Use a trowel or popsicle stick to dig deep enough to get out most of the roots, keeping as much soil intact around the root ball as possible. Hold the seedling gently by its leaves — not by the stem. Use a dibbler or sharp stick to make the new planting hole. Transplant carefully and water-in with a mild starter solution (see STARTER SOLUTIONS) immediately. Wilting is likely to occur for several days due to the trauma of the move. Daily waterings should minimize transplant losses and setbacks. Some shading should be provided to transplants located in areas where the sun is particularly harsh.

# VEGETABLE TRANSPLANTS

Transplants make it possible to shorten the length of time it takes to produce an edible vegetable crop outdoors. Transplanting increases the variety and range of crops that can be grown in an area with a short growing season. Transplants may be purchased from local nurseries or garden centers. Examine each transplant carefully before taking it home (see BUYING TRANSPLANTS).

### HOME GROWN TRANSPLANTS
With only a moderate investment, a gardener can produce his own healthy transplants at home. Almost any vegetable can be grown successfully from transplants, although some crops are more suited to transplanting than others. Beans, corn and peas, for example, should only be direct seeded as they are very sensitive to transplant shock. Table 11-9 provides information on when to sow seeds for transplanting.

Determine when to sow each vegetable in relation to the last spring frost (see DETERMINING LAST SPRING FROST DATE). Timing is very important to produce properly aged transplants. Starting the seed too early results in weak and overgrown transplants that are less likely to produce well in the garden. It is better to start them late and set them out later in the spring. Create a custom tailored planting schedule and

modify it annually as experience dictates.

### BUYING TRANSPLANTS
Not all gardeners are able to (or want to) start their own transplants. Limitations on time and space make it necessary for these gardeners to rely on professional growers to supply them with transplant materials. The quality of the transplants depends upon the grower's expertise and management levels. Always select seedlings carefully. Ask questions about fertilizers and pest control measures that have been used. Inquire about the varieties that are available and select only those cultivars that are known to grow well in your area. Whenever possible, buy only locally grown plants to minimize the risk of transplant failure or poor production.

### QUALITIES TO LOOK FOR
Do not be tempted into buying the largest transplants with the idea of getting extra early yields. These are usually the more expensive ones but are not always the strongest. Plants always experience some degree of transplant shock and plants with flowers, or even some fruits, could actually be set back further in early production than other, smaller plants. Also, tall, top-heavy plants tend to grow abnormally after being moved.

The best transplants are short, sturdy seedlings with healthy green leaves. They should not show any sign of insect feeding or plant disease. Cole crops should be checked for clubroot by gently scraping away the soil surface around the root. Clubroot either shows up as very soft, yellow tissue or as extremely woody tissue.

Purchased transplants in individual containers are preferred. These can be separate pots or flats with distinct cavities or cells. Plants in crowded, open flats tend to have very tangled root systems that suffer a great deal of damage when separated. This is especially true for sensitive crops like cucumber and squash.

Check for adequate rooting depth. If many roots protrude out of the drainage holes, this indicates that the plant is pot bound, which could lead to serious developmental problems in the future. Inquire about whether the transplants have been properly hardened off as hardened off plants respond better to transplanting.

## HARDENING OFF

Home grown or purchased transplants both need to be **hardened off** (conditioned to the more severe climate of the outdoor garden). Young plants growing indoors or in a greenhouse are tender and succulent. The hardening off process prepares the plant for the inevitable change. It reduces the time it takes the plant to become accustomed to outdoor conditions and resume growing.

Start hardening off the transplants prior to setting them out by dropping the air temperature (for cool season crops only) or withholding water, or both. The best way to accomplish this is to move them outside on a calm (about 16°C) day and leave them in a shady spot for about one hour before bringing them back inside. On the next day, leave them in the shade outside for two hours. On the following day, allow them one hour of full sun and two hours of shade. By the end of the week, they can be left outside all day. If there is no danger of frost, they can be left outside all night as well. Keep them slightly moist so they do not dry out and wilt. A cold frame makes the process of hardening off much easier (see COLD FRAMES).

## COLD TREATMENT

Cold treatment is somewhat different than hardening off. Cold treatment causes some vegetables to blossom and set fruit earlier than normally possible. It is a premature hardening off process used on vegetables like tomatoes and peppers and more closely duplicates the typical spring temperatures of their native habitat. Tomatoes are grown at 10-13°C for three weeks following the appearance of their first true leaves. After three weeks, the temperatures are maintained at 16-18°C day and night before setting out. Similarly, when the third set of true leaves appear on peppers, they are subjected to 12-13°C night temperatures for four weeks. After this, the plants are kept at 21°C day and night. The procedure does not increase overall yields, but does encourage the development of the important first fruits.

## PLANTING OUT

As soon as plants are completely hardened off and the weather permits, transplants should be planted out. This usually occurs close to, or soon after, the proposed setting out date as calculated from Table 11-9 and the planting calendar (see MINIMIZING RISKS). Planting out is best conducted on a cloudy day. If the day is sunny and warm, delay transplanting to later in the afternoon.

### PROPER TECHNIQUE

Follow the proposed garden plan developed in GARDEN LAYOUT PROCEDURE. At the proper spacings, dig a hole with a trowel for each transplant. Once the holes are dug, planting can begin. Start from the center and, when planting into beds, work outwards to prevent reaching overtop of seedlings. Potted seedlings slip easily out of containers when the container is turned upside down and gently tapped. Support the plant and the soil surface with the fingers and palm of the other hand. There should be no need to handle the stem or foliage.

Peat pots can be planted without removal, although they tend to impede root growth when their decomposition is slow. Be sure to bury the entire pot. If the rim of the pot is exposed above the soil surface, it acts like a wick and dries out the peat pot (see Figure 11-10).

Roots are then unable to penetrate and the plant may die. If necessary, the top rim of the pot can be torn or cut off down to the soil line and discarded.

Always try to minimize root damage. If the plant is pot bound, very carefully try to straighten out the roots with a pencil. Never let the roots become dry or exposed to sunlight for too long a period. Place the plant into its hole as soon as it is removed from the container. Most vegetables should be buried at the same depth as they were in their potting medium. Cole crops can be transplanted 1-2 cm (about 3/8-3/4 in) deeper for additional support. Tomatoes may be transplanted several centimetres deeper to encourage more roots to form on their stalks. Some of the lower leaves may even have to be removed to promote root development further along the stalk.

When the transplant is properly located at the desired depth, support it vertically and fill in the hole with good quality soil. Gently firm the soil with the hands; just enough to provide good support for the plant. Leave a shallow depression around the base. This hollow keeps water from draining away from the stem. Water thoroughly to help settle roots and further firm the soil. A starter solution can be applied at this time. Provide protection for warm season crops with hot caps, cloches or row covers (see PLANT PROTECTORS).

## Figure 11-10
## POOR TRANSPLANTING TECHNIQUE

Courtesy of Alberta Agriculture

## STARTER SOLUTIONS

Starter solutions are dilute fertilizers designed to stimulate growth of new transplants by increasing the availability of nutrients near their roots. Many nutrients are not easily obtained by new transplants, particularly in cool soils. For warm season crops, a high phosphorus type fertilizer (like 10-52-10 or 15-30-15) can be used. For cole crops and other cool season crops, a fertilizer like 20-20-20 (at slightly lower concentrations) can be used. The solution is poured into the hole before planting, or around the plant after planting. Either method is equally effective for supplying the required nutrients.

Large batches of starter solution can be mixed in a bucket. The quantity required depends upon the number of plants and the volume of solution to be applied to each plant. The standard recommendation is to mix 45-60 mL (3-4 tbsp) of fertilizer per 4.5 L (1 gal) of water. Apply about 120 mL (about 1/2 cup) of solution to each plant. Many gardeners prefer using a larger volume of solution in a weaker concentration. These gardeners mix 15-30 mL (1-2 tbsp) of fertilizer in 4.5 L (1 gal) of water with about 230 mL (about 1 cup) applied to each plant. This reduces the need for extra hand watering and makes it easier to completely dissolve the fertilizer.

cultivated ground must be devoted to pathways. Traffic on the pathways causes compaction of soil, poor drainage and poor soil aeration. Cultivation practices, especially on very large gardens, do not counteract these major disadvantages. It can be as much as thirty times less space efficient when compared with other intensive planting techniques.

Some advantages to the conventional row garden are that planting plans are easier to make and follow. Cultivation by machine is also straightforward. There is easy access to the garden and even the pathways of large plots can be cultivated (where hand weeding and mulching are impractical). Recommendations for between-row and within-row spacings are readily available from most reference sources. Crops best suited to row gardening are asparagus, corn and potato.

## TEMPORARY WIDE ROW GARDENING

Temporary wide rows are long, wide rows of mounded soil which provide a seedbed for vegetable gardening. Temporary wide rows are the traditional growing beds of Oriental gardening (called Chinese mounds) (see Figure 11-11). They are also used in French intensive gardening. They provide for greater efficiency of land use as more vegetables can be grown in the same amount of space. Overall yields can be as much as four times greater than that from conventional rows. Other advantages over row gardening include better maintenance of soil structure, less compaction, and a reduced need for weeding. Cultivation of temporary wide rows can also be done by machinery.

Dimensions of the mounded wide rows vary according to the amount of garden space available. The rows can be of any length but are usually 120 cm (about 4 ft) wide at the base and 90 cm (about 3 ft) wide at the top surface with gently sloping sides. These dimensions provide easy access to plants in the center. Valuable topsoil from the pathways is piled into rows to a depth of 30-40 cm (12-16 in). This provides an adequate depth of high quality soil in which plants can grow. The top surface should be at least 15 cm (6 in) above the surrounding ground level for water and cold air drainage. Mulches, stones, bricks, or planks can be laid alongside the mounded wide rows to enhance pathways.

Temporary wide rows are easily prepared and planted year after year without ever being walked on. This keeps soils light and friable. Since the beds are open to the air and more exposed to sunlight, the soil becomes

# GARDENING METHODS

## ROW GARDENING

Planting vegetables in long, straight rows is by far the most popular gardening method in use today. The vegetable plot used in row gardening is usually rectangular, level with the surrounding land, and contains a series of narrow, parallel rows of vegetables. When the plot is level with its surroundings, there is little, if any, allowance for surface drainage of water or cold air. As a result, soils take much longer to warm and dry in the spring. Such a system is primarily used for larger gardens that are cultivated, planted and harvested by machine. However, this gardening method requires a very high investment in land and equipment. Also, it is a rather inefficient use of arable land as large portions of

## Figure 11-11
## CHINESE MOUNDS

warmer and drier much earlier in the spring. Mounded rows are best oriented in an east to west direction for maximum exposure. After harvesting, all or part of the garden is cultivated, with the possible exception of pathways. If the pathways are cultivated, their locations should be marked so they always remain in the same place. This avoids the problem of compaction. Cultivation can easily be done with mechanical tillers on mounded wide row gardens.

## PERMANENT WIDE ROW OR RAISED BED GARDENING

Raised beds make it possible to raise the soil surface as much as 60-100 cm (about 2-3 ft) above ground level (see Figure 11-12). Soil can be amended to meet specific plant requirements. Topsoil can be mixed with various organic materials to arrive at a soil that possesses all the optimum growth qualities needed. In one or two seasons of work, a raised bed gardener can achieve even higher yields than those achieved with temporary wide row gardening.

The sides of a raised bed can be fabricated of any suitable container construction material. Common materials for such purposes include planks, beams, railroad ties, bricks, cement blocks, or rocks. If wood is used, it should be pressure-treated with copper naphthanate to prevent rotting. Creosote should not be used as it damages plant tissues in close proximity to wood treated with it. The choice of materials for construction of raised beds depends upon costs, availability and the desired aesthetics.

In areas with high saline soils, or where drainage is poor, a thick layer of sand or fine gravel should be put in the bottom of the raised bed. Drainage tiles can also be used to prevent soils from becoming waterlogged or contaminated with natural salts.

In early spring, the soil tends to remain wetter than in mounds as the walls prevent air circulation. Drying, however, is still much faster than on flat land. The growing season is much longer as there is some frost protection from warmer soils and cold air drainage. Gophers and moles also tend to leave raised beds alone. The better drainage, faster drying and higher spring soil temperatures

provided by raised beds can often cause problems. For example, if sandy soils are used in a raised bed, the effects of a drought can actually be worsened. Side walls of the beds may heave with frost and wooden frames eventually need to be replaced. The permanent walls also provide a hiding place for slugs and snails.

Raised beds require a geat deal more initial work and are much more expensive to develop than are flat gardens. When constructed, however, they are easier and less expensive to maintain. Sowing, weeding, mulching and cultivating are still required, but these tasks need only be done in a relatively small area. The soil surface is closer to the gardener's working level, so there is less need for stooping and straining. The raised bed makes it possible for the handicapped and elderly to enjoy gardening as well. One can sit on the bed edges to cultivate, sow, or harvest in comfort.

Pathways around raised beds are permanent. Paving them with gravel or any other ground covering material makes access to the garden much easier, even in the wettest of weather. Pathways should be made wide enough to accommodate a wheelbarrow. This usually requires a minimum of 50 cm (about 20 in) between beds and 60 cm (about 24 in) between the corners of adjacent beds. When access to a raised bed is from one side only, the bed should be a maximum of 1 m (about 3 ft) wide. For raised beds with access from

more than one side, a width of up to 1.5 m (about 5 ft) is suitable.

## SQUARE FOOT GARDENING

Square foot gardening is a relatively new gardening method which is very similar to raised bed gardening. In square foot gardening, vegetable plots can be raised or level with the surroundings. The square plots are encircled by permanent, all-weather pathways. The efficient use of space is slightly less than that of either temporary wide row or raised bed gardening, but convenience and aesthetics may be greater. Crops are always planted intensively in blocks, so production is correspondingly high. The dimensions of square foot garden beds are usually 1.2-1.5 m (4-5 ft) square. Soil in such plots can only be cultivated by hand. There are now two excellent books on this subject written by Mel Bartholomew (see RESOURCE MATERIALS).

## VERTICAL GARDENING

Vertical gardening is not a method unto itself but a space saving enhancement of any gardening method. It takes advantage of the fact that some plants can grow just as well (or better) when supported vertically than when laying on the ground. By growing vertically, fruits are kept cleaner and relatively free of pests, diseases and rodents associated with growing next to the soil. It also provides much easier access to picking.

Figure 11-12
RAISED BED

Plants that are natural clingers, climbers, or twiners are ideally suited to vertical gardening. Some examples are pole beans, peas, and all the vine crops including cantaloupe (muskmelon), cucumber, pumpkin, squash and watermelon (so long as they are not bush type cultivars). The larger fruits require individual slings to prevent them from pulling the vine down or breaking away and falling off. The slings for each fruit are tied onto the supports and not onto the vines.

Supports must be of sufficient size and strength to carry the weight of a mature plant and its fruit. Supports can be made from wire or wood fences, wooden arches or lean-to's, teepee-shaped tripods, or quadripods. Climbing or twining plants are encouraged to cling to and climb guy wires or strings suspended from these supports. Tomatoes do not normally climb, but can be staked or caged.

## SHADE GARDENING

Partial or complete shade is often unavoidable in a garden plot. Fortunately, these shady spots can still grow an adequate supply of vegetables if the right crops are selected. Vegetables that are cultivated for their leaves and roots generally do best in such areas. Some actually grow better in shade than if grown in the open sun. Gardeners often erect shade screens or other devices to grow shade loving crops. This makes it possible to grow these crops through the hottest part of the summer. Vegetables grown in shade are often more succulent and less bitter than vegetables grown in full sunlight.

Where shade is unavoidable, some vegetables (except salad greens) do not reach full size as compared to growth in full sun. Maturity may also be delayed. This can be offset by using transplants or light reflecting walls. Plant out in shady areas before the leaves on trees begin to open. Provide extra space between plants, as vegetables tend to spread out or sprawl when competing for light. Some crops worth trying in a partially shaded garden plot are: beet, broccoli, cabbage, carrot, Chinese cabbage, endive, kale, leaf lettuce, mustard greens, bunching onion, pea, radish, spinach, Swiss chard, turnip and herbs like chive, mint and parsley.

## CONTAINER GARDENING

Growing vegetables in containers may be the only gardening option available to those people who have very limited garden space (i.e., apartment dwellers, condominium owners, inner-city residents or people in mobile-home parks). Besides plant pots, containers may be anything from window boxes and hanging baskets to variously shaped vessels placed on doorsteps, patios, balconies and rooftops. Container gardening requires a suitable container of growing medium, an adequate supply of light, water, fertilizers, and some appropriate vegetable seeds or transplants. Fortunately, plant breeders have developed many new cultivars specifically for such growing purposes.

These are labelled on seed packages and in seed catalogues as bush, dwarf, midget, or balcony types.

### CONTAINERS

Prospective container gardeners can purchase a wide selection of new and decorative containers or recycle materials from around the home (see Plant Propagation lesson, CHOOSING A SUITABLE CONTAINER). The container needs to be large enough to accommodate a mature plant and durable enough to last through the season. People have used old buckets, garbage cans, dishpans, waste baskets, ice cream pails, styrofoam coolers and even leaky aquariums. Wood can also be used to fabricate a container. Only cedar

## Table 11-11
## CONTAINER GARDENING GUIDE

| VEGETABLE | CONTAINER SIZE PER PLANT |
|---|---|
| Beans, bush | 20 cm wide / 20-25.5 cm deep (3 plants per container) |
| Beans, pole | 30 cm wide / 20 cm deep (staked) |
| Beets* | 15-30 cm deep |
| Broccoli<br>Brussels Sprouts<br>Cauliflower | 30 cm wide / 30 cm deep |
| Cabbage | 20-25.5 cm wide / 30 cm deep |
| Carrots* | 25.5-30 cm deep |
| Corn* | 53 cm wide / 20 cm deep (3 plants per container) |
| Cucumbers* | 20 cm wide / 30 cm deep (bush or staked) |
| Eggplant* | 30 cm wide / 30 cm deep |
| Endive | 15 cm wide / 15 cm deep |
| Kale | 20 cm wide / 20 cm deep |
| Lettuce* | 20 cm wide / 15-20 cm deep (2 looseleaf or 1 head) |
| Mustard | 20 cm wide / 15-20 cm deep |
| Onions and Garlic | 15 cm deep |
| Peas* | 30 cm deep (staked) |
| Pepper* | 30 cm wide / 30 cm deep |
| Potato | (not recommended for containers) |
| Radish | 10-15 cm deep |
| Spinach | 15 cm wide / 10-15 cm deep |
| Squash, summer and winter* | 61 cm wide / 61 cm deep (bush) |
| Swiss Chard | 20 cm wide / 20 cm deep |
| Turnips | 15 cm wide / 15-30 cm deep |
| Tomato, dwarf* | 30 cm wide / 61 cm deep (staked) |
| Tomato, standard | 15 cm wide / 25.5-30 cm deep |

or wood that has been treated with copper naphthanate should be used. Copper naphthanate is a wood preservative and is sold as Cuprinol, Cupricide, Cop-R-Nap and Pentox. Allow newly treated wood to weather about a week before using for container gardening purposes.

Adequate drainage is an absolute must for successful gardening in containers. Without drainage, the soil becomes soggy and root rot sets in. Holes should be at least 6 mm (1/4 in) in diameter along the lower edge of a container near (not in) the bottom. Place about 13 mm (1/2 in) of drainage material like gravel, pebbles, crushed brick, or broken clay pots in the bottom of the container. If there are no drainage holes in the container, double or triple the depth of the drainage material layer.

The size of the container should correspond to the type of vegetable being grown. Table 11-11 can be used to select containers based on the minimum size requirements per individual plant. The table is only a guide for determining minimum widths and depths of containers for various vegetable plants. Containers that are too small cause plants to become pot bound and unproductive. Vegetables that are listed without width dimensions are given the same spacings as for intensive gardening. Those crops that have a * beside them in Table 11-11, have cultivars available that are specifically bred for their smaller growth habit and are more suitable for container gardening.

### GROWING MEDIA

The growing medium or soil is one of the most important factors in determining the success of a container garden. It must be of the proper texture to support all of the plant's needs throughout the growing season. Mineral soil may or may not be included in a growing media recipe (see Plant Propagation lesson, SOWING MEDIUM). Soilless mixes have the advantage of being much lighter in weight. Such mixes weigh approximately one-half that of an equal volume of mineral soil. Any sizeable volume of soil used in containers can easily overload balconies and rooftops.

There are countless recipes for growing media for use in container gardens and there appears to be no best one for all purposes. The constituents are usually determined by accessibility and cost. Pasteurization or sterilization of the media is not necessary but has been known to reduce disease, insect and weed problems. A recipe for growing media that has had excellent results is one that combines seven parts of rich garden soil to one part each of peat moss, vermiculite and perlite. A more common potting soil is called **SOD**. It is made by combining equal parts (by volume) of **S**oil, **O**rganic matter (peat moss or compost) and **D**rainage material (sand, perlite, or vermiculite).

There are many kinds of commercial soilless mixes on the market; the most common being Cornell Mix. It is made by combining equal parts of peat moss and perlite or vermiculite. All fertilizers and trace elements must be added to this peat-lite mixture continuously and in the right proportions. With proper management and fertilizing, all growing media can be reused year after year.

### CONTAINER CULTURE

Vegetables can be planted in containers as either seeds or transplants in the same way as described for outdoor gardening. However, it requires a certain amount of skill and know-how on the part of the gardener to grow vegetables successfully in containers. The microclimate of a rooftop or balcony is quite different from that at ground level. As a result, the growing season in such locations can be much longer and temperatures much higher.

Plants in containers require adequate amounts of light. There should be at least six hours of direct sunlight available for fruiting vegetables and slightly less for leafy ones. Light-colored (reflecting) walls can be used to supplement light levels. Dark colored containers get very hot in direct sunlight. As a result, the plant's root system can literally be baked inside a dark colored pot. Provide shade for such containers or cover them with light colored paint or aluminum foil. Containers on wheels or on dollies can easily be moved which allows the gardener to control the amounts of light plants receive (see Figure 11-13).

Always try to shelter plants from drying winds. Balconies and rooftops usually offer little protection. Boards, painted white or covered with aluminum foil, can serve as windbreaks while supplementing light levels.

Soil in containers dries out rapidly. Therefore, plants require watering much more often than those growing in a standard garden (as much as once or twice a day in hot weather). When the top 2.5-5 cm (1-2 in) of soil becomes powdery dry, apply water to the soil surface until it starts to run out of the drainage holes. To reduce chlorine levels in tapwater used for watering plants, tapwater should be allowed to sit for 12-24 hours before application. Organic mulches help to reduce moisture loss and maintain cooler soil temperatures.

### Figure 11-13
### MOVEABLE CONTAINER GARDEN

Courtesy of Alberta Agriculture

Due to the limited volume of soil and the repeated waterings, nutrients can quickly become depleted from a container. Frequent feedings are required to maintain optimum nutrient levels. Many gardeners feed their container vegetable plants a dilute solution of a complete fertilizer with every third watering or once a week. The application of slow release fertilizers, like Mag Amp or Osmocote, reduce the need for such frequent feedings.

## YIELD IMPROVING TECHNIQUES

Any gardener can turn even the smallest garden into a heavy producer of vegetables by making more efficient use of space. Techniques like band planting, succession planting, interplanting and companion planting are used to maximize production. All are relatively easy to use but do require a little planning and forethought.

## BAND PLANTING

Band planting is the same as wide row planting (see SOWING TECHNIQUES). It is a useful technique for all small seeded and some large seeded crops. Crops are grown in 45 cm (18 in) wide strips (see Figure 11-14). Yields are significantly higher than for the same area planted to single rows. Cultivation, weeding and fertilizing are easier and more efficient in band planting. This technique is primarily used for crops like snap bean, beet, carrot, lettuce, onion, pea and radish. An added bonus with onions is that they mature much earlier, although their bulb size may be smaller.

## SUCCESSION PLANTING

There are three main forms of succession planting used to produce a continuous supply of vegetables. All of them ensure that every bit of garden space is utilized to capacity. The most common form is called 'true succession planting' (see Figure 11-15). It involves planting a new crop into the spot vacated by another so that no part of the garden remains fallow for the rest of the growing season. Short season crops that were planted first thing in the spring are followed by another short season crop. Be sure to rotate crops properly

### Figure 11-14
### PREPARATION FOR BAND PLANTING

Courtesy of Alberta Agriculture

### Figure 11-15
### SUCCESSION PLANTING

Courtesy of Alberta Agriculture

(see CROP ROTATION). Peas, for instance, are soil builders that add some nitrogen to the soil. Lettuce or spinach, which are fairly heavy feeders on nitrogen, are good successor crops to peas.

Another form of succession planting is called 'successive planting or relay planting'. In successive planting, the same vegetable cultivar is planted and replanted every 7-10 days over the course of several weeks. This guarantees a much longer harvest than when everything matures together. This is especially useful when only small quantities of particular vegetables are desired over a long period of time. Some examples of crops suited to successive planting are bean, lettuce, green onion, pea, carrot and radish. The technique can be easily combined with true succession planting by replanting in vacated spots.

The final form of succession planting is a variation of successive planting. This procedure involves planting early-, mid- and late-season cultivars of the same vegetable on the same day. The results are the same in that harvests are spread out over a longer period of time. Many long season crops have cultivars with varying lengths of time to maturity. Crops like cabbage, corn, tomato and potato are the most common. The approximate time it takes to reach maturity is usually indicated on the seed packet or in seed catalogues. Inaccuracies may be a result of where the seed was packaged as 'days to maturity' varies with geographic location. Be aware of this time requirement as the frost-free period of the garden may not provide a long enough growing season for some late cultivars.

## INTERPLANTING

Interplanting is also called **intercropping**. It involves growing plants in the same space at the same time to make more efficient use of the garden area. Crops grown together must be compatible. Generally, fast growing crops are put next to slow growing ones; small plants are grown between taller ones; and shade tolerant plants are raised in the shadow of taller, sun-loving plants. This takes advantage of different growth habits, rooting depths, nutrient needs and light requirements. Small, compact crops, such as beet, lettuce, onion and radish, can grow amongst almost any larger, upright plants. Pole beans benefit from growing near corn (and vice versa) as one supports the other nutritionally and physically. Carrots and onions are commonly mixed together in a band. One is deep-rooted while the other is shallow-rooted.

## COMPANION PLANTING

Companion planting is actually interplanting with specific plant-to-plant relationships in mind. It is thought that certain roots, flowers, leaves and fruits contain beneficial materials that repel insects, weeds or rodents. Such plants not only protect themselves, but often protect the surrounding growth as well. Some herbs are alleged to improve the flavor of certain other crops when grown nearby. Companion planting also involves the practice of preventing antagonistic crops from being planted next to each other. Certain secretions that may assist one plant may be harmful to another.

The technique of companion planting is religiously practiced by many organic gardeners who swear by its benefits. Unfortunately, there is little scientific proof to support these claims. There are many books written on this subject; two very informative ones are by Louise Riotte (see RESOURCE MATERIALS).

## GROWING SEASON EXTENDERS

Vegetable gardening does not necessarily have to begin after the last spring frost and end with the first fall frost. Many devices and techniques are available to extend the growing season. Starting seeds indoors is one method (already discussed). Using cold frames, hot beds and plant protectors is another. With these devices, a gardener can start planting earlier in the spring and continue growing longer into the fall.

### COLD FRAMES

Cold frames are simply enclosures with a glass or plastic covering or lid. They are very good devices to use in the spring to modify temperatures. Through radiation, they are able to keep the soil and air temperatures inside several degrees warmer than the outside temperatures. As a result, they are also useful for providing frost protection to plants at night. Ventilation is provided during the day by holding the lid open progressively wider as the season grows warmer. This prevents overheating and promotes air circulation. Cold frames require routine monitoring to maintain the proper growing environment for the plants contained within. A thermometer suspended inside the cold frame can be used to determine when the lid should be opened and closed. With good soil and proper management of the environment, plants can be set out several weeks before normally permitted. Transplants are much more successfully hardened off when left outside in a cold frame.

Cold frames can be made from recycled lumber and old window sashes, or they can be purchased commercially as assemble-yourself kits or as ready-made (see Figure 11-16).

The most popular dimensions of a cold frame are 1 m x 2 m (3 ft x 6 ft). If it is too small, it becomes difficult to ventilate properly. If larger than 2 m x 3 m (6 ft x 10 ft), it becomes difficult to handle. Glass is the best glazing material for use in cold frame lids. Cross braces should be avoided as they stop the downward flow of water, causing a build-up that can freeze and break the glass. Overlapping the panes (like shingles) prevents this from occurring. A double thickness of glass lasts longer and provides better insulation. Sashes with a polyethylene sheet covering produce a similar effect. Plastic covers discolor and transmit progressively less light. They also become brittle and must be replaced every 2-3 years. For those who prefer durability, fibreglass, acrylics or plexiglass can be used, but these materials cost much more than either polyethylene sheeting or glass.

## Figure 11-16
## COLD FRAME

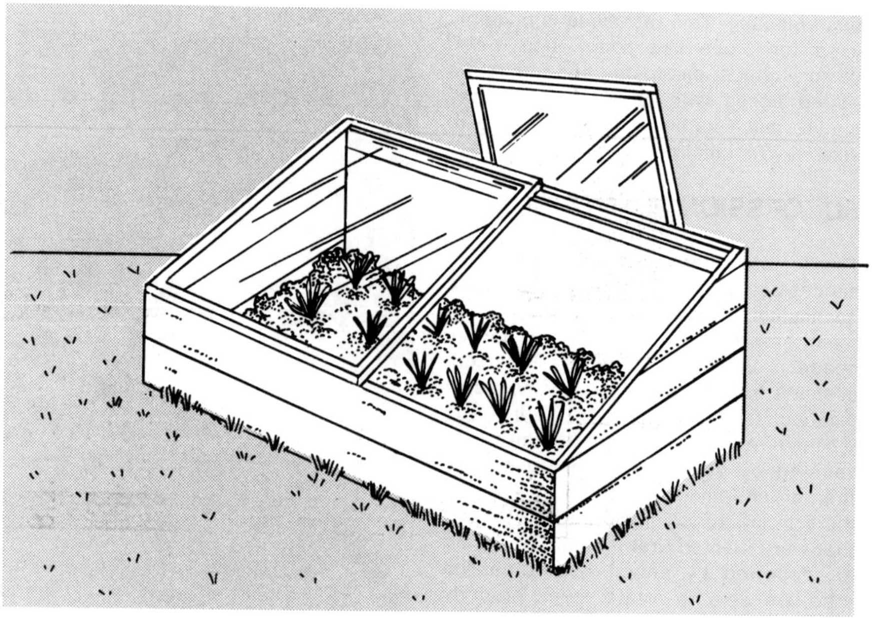

Wooden cold frames should be painted or treated with a copper naphthanate to prevent rotting. The sides are usually insulated and all the seams caulked. They are best located where they can receive maximum daylight exposure. The lid should slant at a 30-45° angle and should face directly south. Protection from strong winds is very important. Cold frames are usually located against the south side of a house or shed for convenient access and maximum protection.

Permanent structures are further insulated by piling soil against all exposed walls. During the summer, permanent cold frames can be completely opened and used as nursery areas. Temporary cold frame structures can be placed directly in the garden and removed when the fear of frost is over. With this procedure, plants get a much earlier start in their final growing position (without having to be transplanted).

## HOT BEDS

Hot beds provide their greatest benefits to gardeners in the more severe northern climes. Their construction is similar to that of cold frames but their walls generally penetrate 30 cm (1 ft) below the soil surface and their interior is heated. Heat can be supplied by electric heating cables, incandescent light bulbs or other such devices. Thermostatic controls are generally used to regulate and maintain uniform temperatures.

The typical dimensions of a practical hot bed are 1 m x 2 m (3 ft x 6 ft). First, a 5 cm (2 in) layer of vermiculite is placed on the bottom of the bed and covered with 25 cm (10 in) of soil (see Figure 11-17). Heating cables, which are available in various lengths and wattages, are laid on this surface in loops that are 12-18 cm (5-7 in) apart. A disadvantage to using heating cables is that they tend to dry out the soil very quickly and moisture levels must be

checked daily. Cover the loops with 2-3 cm (1 in) of soil before applying a meshed screen material. This screen prevents roots from penetrating too deeply. The screen is then covered with a final layer of topsoil 12-20 cm (5-8 in) deep.

About 200 watts of power are required to heat a typical hot bed. Incandescent light bulbs can be used in conjunction with heating cables or used alone for this purpose. Eight, 25-watt light bulbs mounted at equal spacings and wired to a thermostat adequately supply the required heat for a hot bed of typical size. The bulbs should be kept at least 50 cm (20 in.) above the soil surface to prevent burning the vegetable's leaves.

Interior carwarmers are very popular and effective for heating hot beds. Many have their own thermostat or can be wired to one quite easily. The car warmer fan circulates the air and keeps temperatures fairly uniform within the hot bed.

## Figure 11-17
## SIDE VIEW OF CABLE HEATED HOT BED

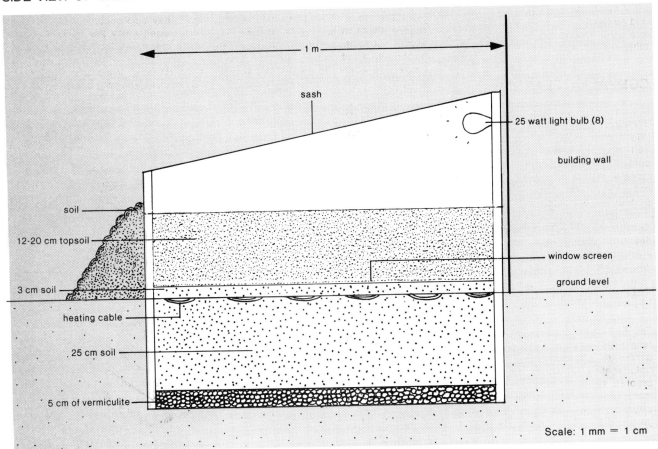

1 m

sash

25 watt light bulb (8)

building wall

soil

12-20 cm topsoil

window screen

ground level

3 cm soil

heating cable

25 cm soil

5 cm of vermiculite

Scale: 1 mm = 1 cm

## PLANT PROTECTORS

Many different kinds of plant protectors have been developed to provide frost protection and to improve plant growth. They range from waxed paper hot caps (hot tents) and glass bell jars for individual plants, to plastic row covers for large groups of plants. All were originally referred to as 'cloches' which is a French word for 'bell' - the original plant protector.

### HOT CAPS

Hot caps (hot tents) generally describe any individual plant protector. The primary function is to provide some frost protection and thereby enable a crop to get a good start. They are removed when plants outgrow them or when all danger of frost has passed. Hot caps have the advantage of being easy to handle and set up, which is a particular advantage when a frost seems imminent. They are easily removed the next day, if desired.

Most hot caps are not terribly useful as long-term, daytime plant protectors. Their small size does not allow them to adequately trap enough solar radiation to provide heat during very cold spells, but then, neither does anything else short of hot beds. They also tend to overheat during the day as they do not allow for ventilation. Glass type hot caps may even cause plants to burn on sunny days by magnifying the sun's rays.

Hot caps should be used sensibly on primarily warm season crops. Commercial waxed paper hot caps are the most common type used. They provide about 2-3°C of frost protection. Newspaper hats work equally well, but must be removed daily to allow sunlight to reach the plants. Most waxed paper hot caps on the market incorporate a wire for structural reinforcement. The V-15 size is used for small transplants, while the T-20 size is used for tomatoes. Larger sizes permit more room for growth (see Figure 11-18).

Plants should be well watered before covering with a hot cap. The flaps around the base are covered with soil to prevent the hot cap from blowing away. A small cut on the side facing away from prevailing winds allows for ventilation. As the plant grows, the cut is torn open progressively wider for greater air circulation. By mid-June, hot caps can be removed completely and destroyed.

### Figure 11-18
### HOTCAPS
**A.**

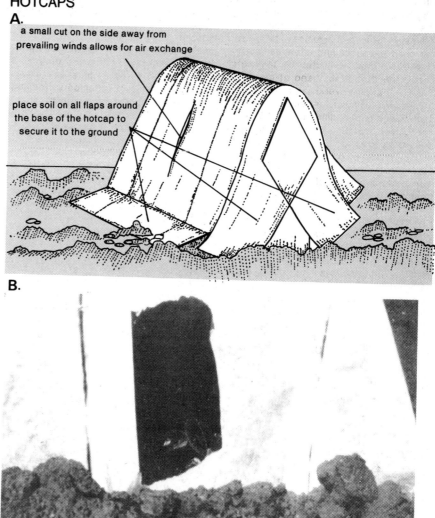

a small cut on the side away from prevailing winds allows for air exchange

place soil on all flaps around the base of the hotcap to secure it to the ground

**B.**

**C.**

Large, translucent plastic jugs (like the kind that vinegar comes in) make good and reusable substitutes for paper hot caps. The cap of the jug is discarded and the bottom completely cut away. The bottomless jug can then be placed over the top of each transplant and pushed 1-2 cm (3/8-3/4 in) deep into the soil for anchorage. These hot caps allow enough sunlight to penetrate without causing overheating.

Special glass or plastic bubbles are also available commercially. Some are tent-shaped and capable of covering several plants. These are usually made of glass panes fastened over wire A-frames. The glass allows for very good transmission of light and ample frost protection.

Courtesy of Alberta Agriculture

The inclusion of water provides for heat storage. A new type of cloche, marketed as 'Wall-O-Water' has several clear plastic cavities that are filled with ordinary water. Columns of water surround the plant and allow sunlight to penetrate. Heat, collected by the water during the day, is released at night and gives the plant several degrees of frost protection. Similar effects can be achieved by encircling a plant with an automobile tire filled with water. The tire is then covered with glass or plastic. On exceptionally cold nights, this, or any other type of cloche, can be covered with newspapers or blankets for added frost protection.

PLASTIC MULCHES
Plastic mulches (inorganic mulches) can be considered as plant protectors because they, too, can be used to modify temperatures and encourage early plant growth. A clear plastic sheet placed over the soil surface can raise soil temperatures by as much as 7°C. This additional soil warmth offers some frost protection, as heat is released during the night. Use 2 mil thick polyethylene sheeting that is 1.22 m (4 ft) wide and any desired length. This plastic sheeting is available in rolls at many graden centers and hardware stores. Apply the sheeting to a well-prepared, moist soil surface, one week prior to seeding or setting out transplants. This allows the soil time to warm up first. Anchor all the outside edges of the plastic with soil. Make a

small, X-shaped cut in the center of the sheet, through which seeds or plants can be inserted into the soil (see Figure 11-19).

Another advantage to plastic mulches is that they also retain soil moisture. This can be a valuable attribute in northern latitudes where low soil temperatures and moisture often limit plant growth. Black plastic is less effective for raising soil temperatures, but controls weeds much better because no light passes through the plastic. For this reason, black plastic is preferred by most gardeners, particularly when clear plastic tunnels are used in addition to the mulch. Both clear and black plastic are useful for warming garden soils in the spring.

TUNNELS OR ROW COVERS
Tunnels or row covers are excellent devices for protecting entire rows of vegetables. They look like long, miniature, quonset-style greenhouses and provide an ideal environment for fast plant growth during the spring by increasing air and soil temperatures as well as humidity. Growth rates of any warm or cool season vegetable rival those of plants started in cold frames. The device is primarily used on all warm season crops, but is not recommended for tomatoes. Tomato plants grown under row cover produce excessive amounts of vine growth which dramatically delays fruit setting. Vine crops, like cucumbers, respond best to row covering.

Tunnels are almost always used in conjunction with plastic mulches. Black plastic mulches are preferred since weed growth can be overwhelming in the greenhouse environment. Lay the mulch a week before planting. Plant the seeds or transplants on a calm day and erect tunnels immediately after planting.

There are no set standards for the construction and installation of row covers. All experienced gardeners have developed their own methods. However, the following steps can be used as a guideline for those wishing to use row covers for the first time:

1. Pound wooden stakes into the ground at each end of the row, at least 1 m (3 ft) beyond the last plant in the row.

2. Bend 1.2-1.4 m (4-5 ft) lengths of #8 or #9 galvanized wire into arches that are able to span the mulch. Exposed mulch will normally be about 1 m (3 ft) wide.

3. Push the ends of the wire arches into the soil 15 cm (6 in) deep, one end on either side of the row. Space the wire arches 1 m (about 3 ft) apart.

4. Use double wire arches at each end of the row to provide additional support.

5. Lay a (2 mil) clear polyethylene sheet 1.8 m (6 ft) wide over the wire arches.

6. Tie one end of the plastic sheet to one of the wooden stakes. Strech the plastic sheet firmly over the arches. Tie the other end of the sheet to the other wooden stake.

7. Cover all the outside edges of the plastic with soil.

8. Ventilate the tunnel by making 12-15 cm (5-6 in) slits spaced 3-5 cm (1-2 in) apart along the length and on both sides of the tunnel. Another alternative to ventilating the tunnel is to poke circular holes through the plastic with a very hot tin can 5-7 cm (2-3 in) in diameter at 30 cm (1 ft) intervals (see Figure 11-20).

## Figure 11-19
## INORGANIC MULCH

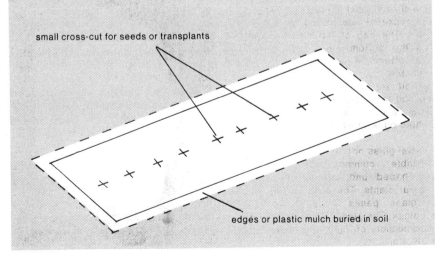

small cross-cut for seeds or transplants

edges or plastic mulch buried in soil

**Figure 11-20**

## PLASTIC MULCH AND TUNNEL

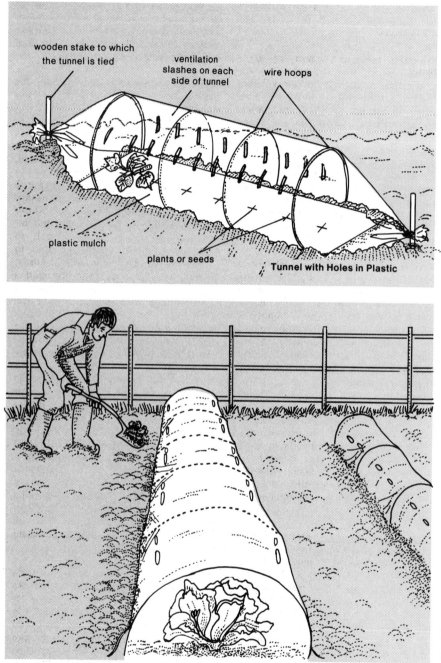

wooden stake to which the tunnel is tied

ventilation slashes on each side of tunnel

wire hoops

plastic mulch

plants or seeds

**Tunnel with Holes in Plastic**

some seed catalogues. The increase in vegetable production attributed to their use makes them well worth trying. The plastic only lasts one season as sunlight makes it brittle and subject to tearing. Heavier gauge plastics have been tried but are harder to handle and they sag between the wire hoops. Removal, storage and reapplication are impractical.

Some gardeners have used corrugated fibreglass tunnels successfully. Sheets, that are 1.2 m (4 ft) wide and 2.4 m (8 ft) long, are bent lengthwise into arches and held in place with stakes. The ends of the tunnel are left open during the day and covered up at night. Tunnels offer only at 1-2°C of frost protection. When severe frosts are predicted, the tunnel can be covered with blankets. Corrugated fibreglass is reusable and easier to erect and dismantle than polyethylene sheeting.

## CULTURE

Good gardening practices take time. Proper culture produces healthy crops that are, to a certain degree, able to withstand unfavorable conditions. Each crop requires special care to meet its particular requirements. Watering, fertilizing, mulching, weeding and control of insects and diseases are needed in varying degrees. Some crops also require pruning, staking, or other special practices to produce the desired crop. A certain amount of perseverance is needed to keep up with these demands. Knowing what needs to be done and how to do it makes cultural tasks easier.

## WATERING

Water is probably the most misunderstood of all plants' needs. It must be supplied in the right amounts and at the right time to allow plants to achieve their optimum growth potential. Water must be available to the feeder roots and not just the leaves or top few centimetres of soil.

Irrigation cannot be applied on a typical schedule. Light applications of water can actually do more harm than good as roots will remain close to the soil surface, instead of penetrating to deeper levels. At the lower depths, moisture and nutrients remain in fairly stable supply. Watering, therefore, should be done less

A tunnel is removed when plants begin to flower or when leaves begin to push up against the plastic wall. This usually occurs by the end of June or after 4-6 weeks. Removal of the tunnel from flowering plants may be delayed by pulling up the side of the tunnel most protected from the wind and pinning the

plastic sheet to the top of the wire hoops with clothes pins. This allows bees to enter and pollinate the flowers. The tunnel can be easily closed for the evening.

Mulch and tunnel kits are now available at some garden centers and through frequently but in greater volumes to get moisture deep enough to feed the main root masses. This serves to stimulate deep root growth.

Mulches help to reduce water loss from surface evaporation. Very often, a gardener notices a dry soil surface and assumes the entire soil profile is also dry. This may not necessarily be true. Always check the soil to the approximate depth of the root zone before watering the garden. Use a spade to dig a hole 30-45 cm (12-18 in) deep in a vacant spot in the garden. Grab a handful of soil from various levels and squeeze it. When soil is holding as much water as it can, it is said to be at field capacity. If at field capacity, particles of soil stick together (regardless of the soil's texture) and can be formed into a durable, pliable ball. The more crumbly the soil is, the less water it contains and the further it is from field capacity. When the soil is at 50 per cent field capacity, it is time to water. At this point, the soil is probably unable to be formed into a ball. This depends upon the soil's clay content. If soil is known to be high in clay content, try to roll it out in a ribbon. If this cannot be done successfully, the garden should be irrigated. A simpler check can be made with a hollow metal rod or a specially designed probe. Insert the probe deep into the soil. If it penetrates easily, chances are there is still sufficient water available. If the probe is difficult to insert or it comes out perfectly clean, the soil is well below field capacity and should be watered.

Plant behaviour is also a good indicator of when to water. The most obvious symptom of insufficient available moisture is wilting, but this can be misleading. Some plants respond to excessive heat by wilting, even when there is sufficient moisture available. Vine crops, eggplants, lettuce, peppers, sweet corn, and tomatoes wilt almost every day in the heat of the summer sun and recover late in the afternoon, when temperatures are cooler. If they begin wilting early in the day or do not recover, apply water immediately. Wilted plants that still do not recover may be suffering from root damage or some other vascular disease (see Pest Control lesson, PLANT DISEASE).

Overwatering can also cause wilting. This is due to a lack of oxygen in the soil. Carbon dioxide accumulates in soil pores and is unable to escape. Plants soon use up all of the available oxygen and suffer from 'physiological drought'. Soils prone to this problem can be corrected by adding organic matter or other drainage material to amend the soil structure.

During the course of a growing season, a plant's water requirements change dramatically. Generally, larger volumes of water are consumed during the early growth, flowering, and fruit set stages. Moisture stress during any of these periods results in a poorer crop. Blossom end rot of tomatoes, splitting of cabbages and blossom drop in peppers are prime examples of water related problems. Sweet corn is the heaviest drinker and most inefficient user of water and requires vast quantities, particularly during silking, tasseling and ear development.

Except for emergency applications, watering should always be done in the afternoon or (preferably) early in the morning. Allow several hours before sunset to give the leaves a chance to dry before dark. If the plants are still wet at night, disease-causing fungi tend to grow. Powdery mildew and cucumber scab are two very common diseases attributed to this.

The quantity of water to apply varies with each garden and with each season. During some years, a garden may need to be watered every few days; during other years, it may not need to be watered at all. The volume and frequency of watering must be determined on the basis of need and not on the basis of habit or schedule.

Knowing when to stop watering requires physically checking the soil. An inexperienced gardener may need to do this several times, until experience allows him to determine how much water needs to be applied to bring the root zone up to field capacity. Watering by hand may be sufficient in the spring but can be very impractical later in the summer. It can take several hours for some sprinklers (even at full volume) to apply only a small amount of water over the entire garden.

Gardening methods and irrigation equipment both have an effect on watering volume. Raised beds, particularly those without retaining walls, require more frequent watering than do level plots of land. Intensively planted beds require more water than conventional rows due to the increased competition for moisture. With these gardening systems, however, it is easier to direct water only where it is needed. This avoids wastage of water between rows or other unplanted areas. The total volume of water that needs to be applied may actually be less in such gardening systems. Mulches are useful for diminishing water losses (see MULCHING).

There are many types of irrigation equipment available, each type having its own advantages and inefficiencies.

Some sprayers or sprinklers disperse water unevenly and into areas where water is not needed. As much as 50 per cent of the water sprayed into the air and onto leaves can be lost to evaporation. Other types are able to concentrate water in well-defined areas. Soaker hoses and trickle irrigation systems are of this type. Choose the type of equipment that best suits the gardening requirements and make allowances for any faults. Try to minimize any contact with the wet foliage of vegetable plants as this tends to cause or spread disease. Firmly anchored metal or wooden stakes, placed in strategic locations (corners, for example) in the garden, make it easier to move a garden hose from place to place. Using stakes greatly reduces the amount of physical damage to plants that can occur if the hose is dragged over the garden. Placing a bucket or sauce pan in the garden to catch a sample of the water being applied helps in determining the amount (depth) of water applied. Timing the application can provide useful information for subsequent applications.

Quality and temperature of the water is also important in any type of garden irrigation. Warm water is much better for plants than cold water as warm water is more readily absorbed and helps to speed up growth. Cold water can actually slow or stop growth temporarily. Use clean water that is low in salts. **Never irrigate a vegetable garden with softened water or water that is high in sodium or magnesium salts.** These elements accumulate in the soil and eventually make it unsuitable for plant growth.

Household 'grey' water from washing or bathing may be used for about half the irrigation needs. Water that is filtered should not contain any borax, fabric softeners, bleaches or detergents. Soap, if not too concentrated, is acceptable. Dilute this water if necessary. Dugout or river water should have an irrigation water quality test carried out before using it on the garden. Samples of water can be taken to a local agriculturalist who will send it to the appropriate lab for testing (Irrigation and Water Check).

## MIDSEASON FERTILIZING

Soil that is properly prepared and fertilized before planting seldom requires supplemental feeding. When a deficiency is detected in the garden, however, apply only fast-acting fertilizers. Fertilizers can be applied in liquid form to the soil, sprayed on the leaves, or side-dressed in dry form alongside established crops. For solution feeding, enriched water is poured onto the soil to soak in around the plant's roots. The recommended mixing rate is 15 mL (1 tbsp) of fertilizer per 4.5 L (1 gal) of water. Apply 230 mL (about 1 cup) of solution to each plant. Additional water after application leaches nutrients down to feeder roots. Another alternative is to apply the proper amount of water-soluble fertilizer to the soil surface and water in well with about 2.5 cm (1 in.) of water.

Foliar feeding is particularly useful during very wet or very dry spells. This is when nutrient uptake through the soil is difficult for most plants. The fertilizer solution is sprayed directly onto the leaves until they start to drip. Leaves will absorb the nutrients almost immediately, so results are very rapid (but short lived). A common type of fertilizer to use for foliar feeding is 20-20-20, mixed at the same proportions as described above.

Side-dressing involves applying a dry fertilizer into furrows alongside an existing crop. This procedure is particularly beneficial for crops lacking phosphorus. Results are relatively slow, as roots must first find this nutrient supply to take it up. Furrows are 5-7 cm (2-3 in) deep and about 10 cm (4 in) away from the plants. Fertilizer is placed in the bottom of the furrow and buried.

The timing of any fertilizer application is very important, especially with nitrogen.

Plants that are flowering or beginning to bear fruit, slow down in nitrogen uptake and leaf production. Applying too much nitrogen at this stage can cause the plants to abort fruiting and resume leaf production. This delays harvesting of fruit bearing crops and makes their tissues succulent and more prone to frost damage.

## MULCHING

Mulching is a valuable tool for water conservation and weed control. It also provides physical protection for growing crops. Vine crops and other fruits close to the ground are kept cleaner and drier, which reduces disease. Soil compaction and root damage are also reduced. Organic mulches form an insulating blanket that reduce temperature shifts in the soil. They keep cool season plants cooler in summer. Organic mulches also help to extend the growing season of some root crops by protecting their edible parts from frost damage. Inorganic mulches raise soil temperatures in early spring and make it possible to plant warm season crops earlier.

For organic mulches to be effective, they must be applied in sufficiently thick layers. Loose materials, like straw or leaves, should be applied 20-25 cm (8-10 in) thick. This thickness later compresses to about 10 cm (4 in). Finer materals, like sawdust or compost, can be applied at 5-8 cm (2-3 in) to get satisfactory weed control. Lawn clippings can be applied at the same rate. Organic mulches are applied only after plants are taller than the mulch layer is thick. Covering vegetable seeds with mulches makes it difficult for the seedlings to emerge. With heat-loving crops, mulching too soon before the soil has warmed can retard their development. Mid-June is the usual time for application of organic mulches on Prairie gardens.

Symptoms of transplant shock can be reduced when cool season crops are mulched immediately after being set out. Minimize contact between the mulch and the stalks of new plants. A rotting mulch can cause disease problems in tender shoots. To prevent this, leave an unmulched circle around tha base of each plant.

Organic mulches need to be replenished

throughout the summer to replace the material that has decomposed. When weeds begin popping through, pile on more material to maintain a thick barrier. Newspapers can be used under a mulching material that is in short supply. Newspaper that is printed with black ink only is safe to use for this purpose (some colored dyes have been known to be toxic). Newspaper can even be used alone if anchored with small amounts of soil. It usually decomposes in one season, or faster when Incorporated into the soil

Organic mulches should not be used in areas that are very wet or have a very short growing season as they tend to increase disease and slug problems. In such areas, confine their use to pathways and drier areas, or forego their use entirely.

The beauty of most organic mulches is that they need not be removed at the end of the growing season. Fall incorporation of such mulches adds to soil organic matter and nutrient reserves. All plastic mulches must be removed and disposed of after harvesting the crop.

## WEEDING

Weeding is a necessary evil in every garden. It's simply a matter of removing each weed one by one, and requires perseverance and recognition (which is not always easy). Certain preventive and control measures must be used to ensure that weeds do not take over the garden.

Mulching is one of the best weed control methods. A thick layer of organic material or a single sheet of black plastic will suffice. Weeds can then be quickly spotted and easily uprooted. The use of some organic materials can actually increase weed populations. To avoid this, use only clean straw (instead of hay) and well-composted manure (instead of fresh) to minimize the introduction of new seeds.

Gardens that are not mulched must be cultivated with a trowel, rake, hoe, or tiller to keep weeds under control and to loosen the soil. Begin weeding three days after seeds are sown. The early start guarantees that the vegetable seedlings are given a fighting chance, as weeds are much better competitors for water, light and nutrients than are vegetable seedlings. Be very careful not to damage tender vegetable seedlings when weeding by hand or machine.

It is essential that all weeds be killed before they flower and go to seed since seed production is enormous for most weeds. If left too long, the task of weed control can be several times greater. The best time to weed a garden is during mid-day, when the sun is hottest and the soil surface is driest. Uprooted weeds then die quickly, instead of re-rooting. The shallow cultivation associated with hand weeding actually reduces water losses from surface evaporation and minimizes raising new viable seeds.

Pathways may be cultivated with tillers to incorporate weedy plant refuse and undo soil compaction. Be careful not to cultivate the root systems of vegetable plants. For weeding next to plants, use a scuffle hoe, Dutch hoe or stirrup hoe. These will get rid of the weeds without digging into the soil. The blade is pushed

across the soil surface to chop weeds off at ground level, thereby diminishing their chances for survival.

Chemical herbicides are not generally recommended for use in the vegetable garden. Any domestic product that kills weeds will also kill vegetables. Chemicals should only be used as a last resort and with extreme care. Spot treatments with a carefully directed spray or with a paint brush, will minimize the amount of chemical that drifts onto neighbouring, non-target plants. Herbicides that are advertised for control of weeds in pathways and around the perimeter of a garden are unreliable and tend to persist for more than one year in areas with a short growing season. Continual cultivation and perseverance will eventually reduce or eliminate even the hardiest perennial weed.

## ENVIRONMENTAL PROTECTION

The climate of the Prairies is extremely severe and unpredictable. Many gardeners have become very disillusioned after their entire garden has been devastated by frosts, winds, hail, droughts or floods. Very little can be done to avoid most of these catastrophes. However, winds and frosts are environmental conditions that man can have some effect on.

Winds are best controlled by windbreaks and shelterbelts (see SHELTER). Properly located and constructed windbreaks are able to provide protection from wind damage and can improve the overall microclimate of the garden. They can even lengthen the growing season. Gardeners and vegetable plants alike appreciate the benefits of windbreaks.

## Table 11-12
## FOUR NATURAL STORAGE CONDITIONS

| STORAGE TYPE | PRODUCE | BULK (5) DENSITY (kg/m³) | TEMPERATURE °C | RELATIVE HUMIDITY (%) | STORAGE PERIODS (MONTHS) |
|---|---|---|---|---|---|
| **Cold and Humid** | Beets | 650 | | | 4-6 |
| | Cabbage (3) | 500 | | | 2-6 |
| | Carrots | 550 | 0-1 | 90-95 | 4-6 |
| | Parsnip | 500 | | | 2-5 |
| | Radish | 600 | | | 0.5-3 |
| | Rutabaga | 650 | | | 4-6 |
| **Cool and Humid** (1) | Potatoes - seed | | 4-5 | | |
| | - table | 670 | 5-6 | 90-95 | 5-10 |
| | - process | | 7-9 | | |
| **Cool and Less Humid** (4) | Squash | 500 | 7-10 | 70-75 | 4-6 |
| | Pumpkin | | | | 2-4 |
| **Cold and Dry** | Onions (cured) (2) | 600-700 | 0-3 | 70-75 | 4-8 |

1. Potatoes are normally cured 2-3 weeks at 10-15°C and high RH, then cooled slowly to storage temperature. Storage conditions highly dependent on variety and use.

2. Onions are either field cured, or cured in storage at 32-36°C with high air flow prior to long term storage.

3. Cabbage storage quality and time is highly variety dependent.

4. Squash and pumpkin should be well ripened; cure at 30°C then reduce temperature.

5. Bulk density varies 5-10%, use as a guide for estimating storage size requirements. (kg/m³ X 0.0625 = lb/ft³ or kg/m³ ÷ 16 = lb/ft³).

Note: Most produce, particularly cabbage and potato, react to light; store in dark conditions.
The above values are for commercial storage. Home storage would likely result in a shorter storage period because conditions are usually less than ideal.
Courtesy of Alberta Agriculture

Table 11-13
VEGETABLE PLANTING GUIDE

| VEGETABLE | RECOMMENDED CULTIVARS | SEEDING DEPTH (cm) | DISTANCE BETWEEN ROWS (cm) | WITHIN ROW DISTANCE BETWEEN PLANTS (cm) |
|---|---|---|---|---|
| Asparagus | California Selections<br>Viking KB3<br>Mary Washington<br>Viking 2K | 2.5-4.0 | 90-120 | 30-60 |
| Beans - Green | Blue Lake, Bush<br>  Selections<br>Dwarf Stringless<br>Gator Green<br>  Improved<br>Green Crop<br>Provider | 4-5 | 60-90 | 8-10 |
| Beans - Wax or Yellow | Gold Crop<br>Honey Gold<br>Sun Gold<br>Topnotch Golden<br>  Wax | 4-5 | 60-90 | 8-10 |
| Beans - Pole | Blue Lake, Pole<br>Kentucky Wonder<br>Scarlet Runner | 4-5 | 75-90 | 15-20 |
| Beans - Broad or Faba | Broad Windsor<br>Exhibition Long<br>  Pod<br>Green Windsor | 4-5 | 60-90 | 10-15 |
| Beans - Lima | Baby Potato Bush<br>Burpee's Improved<br>  Bush<br>Fordhook Bush | 4-5 | 60-90 | 10-15 |
| Beans - Novelty | French Horticultural<br>  Bush<br>Royal Burgundy<br>Royalty | 4-5 | 60-90 | 8-10 |
| Beets | Detroit Dark Red<br>Early Wonder<br>Formanova<br>Ruby Queen<br>Vermilion | 1-2.5 | 30-60 | 5-10 |

| BAND, BLOCK OR INTENSIVE PLANT SPACING (cm) | AVERAGE MATURE HEIGHT OF PLANTS (cm) | WEIGHT OF SEED TO DIRECT SEED 5 m ROW (g) | TIMING OF SUCCESSIVE SOWINGS | WHEN TO HARVEST |
|---|---|---|---|---|
| 45 | 150 | 4.6-5 | None | Cut 1.0 cm below soil when spears are 20-25 cm tall and less than 2.5 cm in diameter. |
| 15 | 30-45 | 40-70 | Sow every 1-2 weeks until 8 weeks before First Fall Frost (FFF) | Once per week as pods become plump but before they become lumpy from seed development. Cut off plants at end of season (leaving roots) to supply nitrogen to soil. |
| 15 | 30-45 | 40-70 | same as for green beans | Same as green beans. |
| 20 | 200+ | 30-40 | Requires only one planting at start of season | Same as green beans |
| 20 | 60-75 | 35-50 | Same as pole beans | Use like a snap bean when immature or wait until inside turns cottony. |
| 20 | 60-75 | 35-50 | Same as pole beans | When pods start to shrivel. |
| 15 | 30-45 | 40-70 | Same as green beans | Same as green and yellow beans. |
| 8-14 | 30 | 2.5-4.5 | Sow every 2-3 weeks until 8 weeks before FFF | When 5 cm across. |

Table 11-13: CONT'D

| VEGETABLE | RECOMMENDED CULTIVARS | SEEDING DEPTH (cm) | DISTANCE BETWEEN ROWS (cm) | WITHIN ROW DISTANCE BETWEEN PLANTS (cm) |
|---|---|---|---|---|
| Beets - Novelty | Albino White<br>Burpee's Golden | 1-2.5 | 30-60 | 5-10 |
| Broccoli | Cleopatra<br>Green Comet<br>Green Hornet<br>Goliath<br>Premium Crop | 0.5-1.5 | 45-90 | 30-45 |
| Broccoli - Novelty | King Robert Purple | 0.5-1.5 | 45-90 | 30-45 |
| Brussels Sprouts | Half Dwarf<br>Jade Cross<br>Prince Marvel | 0.5-1.5 | 60-90 | 45-60 |
| Cabbage - Early | Copenhagen<br>Market Early<br>Early Marvel<br>Emerald Acre<br>Golden Acre<br>Golden Cross<br>Tucana | 0.5-1.5 | 60-90 | 35-50 |
| Cabbage - Mid-Season | Blue Heaven<br>Bonanza<br>Jet Pak<br>Prime Pak<br>Princess<br>Stonehead | 0.5-1.5 | 60-90 | 35-50 |
| Cabbage - Late | April Green<br>Danish Ballhead<br>Houston Evergreen<br>Storage Green<br>Ultra Green | 0.5-1.5 | 60-90 | 35-50 |
| Cabbage - Red | Red Head<br>Red Meteor<br>Ruby Ball | 0.5-1.5 | 60-90 | 35-50 |
| Cabbage - Savoy | Ace, Savoy<br>Canada Savoy<br>Chieftain Savoy<br>Solarite | 0.5-1.5 | 60-90 | 35-50 |

| BAND, BLOCK OR INTENSIVE PLANT SPACING (cm) | AVERAGE MATURE HEIGHT OF PLANTS (cm) | WEIGHT OF SEED TO DIRECT SEED 5 m ROW (g) | TIMING OF SUCCESSIVE SOWINGS | WHEN TO HARVEST |
|---|---|---|---|---|
| 8-14 | 30 | 2.5-4.5 | Same as beets | Same as beets |
| 38-45 | 75 | 0.6-1.2 | Sow 2-3 weeks after first sowing ensuring 11-12 weeks before FFF | Cut central head just before flowers open. Cut side florets every 7-10 days. |
| 38-45 | 75 | 0.6-1.2 | As above | As above |
| 45 | 75 | 0.6-1.2 | Only one planting possible | Cut bi-weekly when sprouts are 2.5 cm across. |
| 35-45 | 60-75 | 0.6-1.2 | Sow again 3-4 weeks after first planting ensuring 10 weeks before FFF | Cut when heads are very firm but before cracked. |
| 35-45 | 60-75 | 0.6-1.2 | Same as early cabbage | Same as early cabbage. |
| 35-45 | 60-75 | 0.6-1.2 | Only one sowing possible | Same as early cabbage. |
| 35-45 | 60-75 | 0.6-1.2 | Only one sowing possible | Same as early cabbage. |
| 35-45 | 60-75 | 0.6-1.2 | Only one sowing possible | Same as early cabbage. |

Table 11-13: CONT'D

| VEGETABLE | RECOMMENDED CULTIVARS | SEEDING DEPTH (cm) | DISTANCE BETWEEN ROWS (cm) | WITHIN ROW DISTANCE BETWEEN PLANTS (cm) |
|---|---|---|---|---|
| **Cabbage - Chinese** | Jade Pagoda<br>Summertime<br>Wintertime | 0.5-1.5 | 60-90 | 35-50 |
| **Carrots - Standard** | Amsterdam, Coreless<br>Canuck<br>Chantendy Types<br>Dess-Dan<br>Gold Pak 28<br>Imperator Types<br>Nantes Strong Top<br>Orange Sherbet<br>Spartan Types<br>Touchon Coreless | 0.5-1.0 | 30-60 | 2.5-5 |
| **Carrots - Baby** | Baby - Finger Nantes<br>Baby Orange<br>Baby Sweet Hybrid<br>Frantes<br>Nangro<br>Parisienne<br>Vita Sweet | 0.5-1.0 | 30-60 | 2.5 |
| **Cauliflower** | Andes<br>Igloo<br>Self Blanche<br>Snowball Types<br>White Fox<br>White Rock<br>White Soils | 0.5-1.5 | 60-90 | 30-45 |
| **Cauliflower - Novelty** | Burgundy Queen<br>Early Purple Head | 0.5-1.5 | 60-90 | 30-45 |
| **Celery** | Improved Utah 52-70<br>Self Blanching<br>Tendercrisp | 0.3-0.5 | 60-90 | 15-20 |
| **Celeriac** | Prague | 0.3-0.5 | 60-90 | 10-20 |

| BAND, BLOCK OR INTENSIVE PLANT SPACING (cm) | AVERAGE MATURE HEIGHT OF PLANTS (cm) | WEIGHT OF SEED TO DIRECT SEED 5 m ROW (g) | TIMING OF SUCCESSIVE SOWINGS | WHEN TO HARVEST |
|---|---|---|---|---|
| 35-45 | 60-70 | 0.6-1.2 | Use transplants first in spring then sow 12 weeks before FFF | Cut when heads are large and firm. |
| 5-10 | 30 | 0.6-2.5 | Sow every 2-3 weeks until 8-10 weeks before FFF | After 6 weeks, pull out roots to thin stand and use as desired. |
| 6 | 20-25 | 1.2-2.5 | Sow every 2-3 weeks until 7-8 weeks before FFF | After 4-5 weeks, pull out roots to thin stand then use as desired. |
| 45 | 75 | 0.6-1.2 | Sow every 2-3 weeks but ensure 9-10 weeks before FFF | Cut when head has reached maximum size and firmness just before buds open. |
| 45 | 75 | 0.6-1.2 | Same as cauliflower | Same as cauliflower |
| 15-28 | 45 | 0.3-1.2 | Only one planting possible | After 8 weeks, cut as desired. |
| 20-25 | 45 | 0.3-1.2 | Same as celery | Same as celery. |

Table 11-13: CONT'D

| VEGETABLE | RECOMMENDED CULTIVARS | SEEDING DEPTH (cm) | DISTANCE BETWEEN ROWS (cm) | WITHIN ROW DISTANCE BETWEEN PLANTS (cm) |
|---|---|---|---|---|
| **Cucumber - Pickling** | Early Pik<br>Mincu<br>Morden Early<br>Tempo Pioneer | 2-5 | 120-180 | 20-30 |
| **Cucumber - Slicing** | Slicemaster<br>Sweet Slice<br>Sweet Success | 2-5 | 120-180 | 20-30 |
| **Cucumber - Novelty** | Lemon<br>Patio Pik<br>Pot Luck<br>White Wonder | 2-5 | 120-180 | 20-30 |
| **Eggplant - Cylindrical** | Ichiban<br>Moneymaker | 1.5-2 | 60-90 | 45-90 |
| **Eggplant - Oblong** | Black Beauty<br>Black Bell<br>Dusky | 1.5-2 | 60-90 | 45-90 |
| **Kale** | Dwarf Green Curled<br>Tall Scotch Curled | 0.5-1.5 | 60-90 | 45-60 |
| **Kohlrabi** | Early Purple<br>Vienna<br>Early White<br>Vienna<br>Grand Duke | 0.5-1.5 | 45-60 | 20 |
| **Leek** | Large American<br>Flag<br>Titan<br>Unique | 1.5-2 | 40-60 | 15-25 |

| BAND, BLOCK OR INTENSIVE PLANT SPACING (cm) | AVERAGE MATURE HEIGHT OF PLANTS (cm) | WEIGHT OF SEED TO DIRECT SEED 5 m ROW (g) | TIMING OF SUCCESSIVE SOWINGS | WHEN TO HARVEST |
|---|---|---|---|---|
| 30-45 | 20-30 | 2.3-2.5 | Sow every 2-3 weeks until 7-8 weeks before FFF | Pick fruits from vines when desired size of cucumber is achieved. Check every 2-3 days. |
| 30-45 | 20-30 | 2.3-2.5 | Sow every 2-3 weeks until 8-9 weeks before FFF | Pick fruits when cucumbers have reached desired size but before they turn yellow. |
| 30-45 | 20-30 | 2.3-2.5 | Sow every 2-3 weeks until 7-8 weeks before FFF | Same as pickling cucumber. |
| 60 | 60 | 0.3-0.6 | None | Cut when fruit is 15 cm long and the skin is shiny. |
| 60 | 60 | 0.3-0.6 | None | Cut when fruit is dark, shiny color and suitably large. |
| 38-45 | 60 | 0.6-1.2 | None | After 8 weeks, cut outside leaves as needed until hard frost. |
| 20-25 | 45 | 0.6-1.2 | Sow every 2 weeks until 4 weeks before FFF | Cut from root and remove leaves when greater than 5 cm across. |
| 15 | 45 | 1.2-1.5 | None | Pull when 3-5 cm across until hard frosts. |

Table 11-13: CONT'D

| VEGETABLE | RECOMMENDED CULTIVARS | SEEDING DEPTH (cm) | DISTANCE BETWEEN ROWS (cm) | WITHIN ROW DISTANCE BETWEEN PLANTS (cm) |
|---|---|---|---|---|
| Lettuce - Crisphead or Iceberg | Great Lakes Selections Ithaca Mesa 659 New York Pennlake | 0.5-1.0 | 30-60 | 20-35 |
| Lettuce - Butterhead | Buttercrunch Butter King White Boston | 0.5-1.0 | 30-60 | 20-35 |
| Lettuce - Cos or Romaine | Cosmo Parris Island Valmaine | 0.5-1.0 | 30-60 | 20-30 |
| Lettuce - Leaf | Grand Rapids Royal Oak Salad Bowl Waldman's Dark Green | 0.5-1.0 | 30-60 | 20-35 |
| Lettuce - Novelty | Red Sails Ruby Tom Thumb | 0.5-1.0 | 30-60 | 20-35 |
| Muskmelon or Cantaloupe | Alaska Burpee Hybrid Delicious 51 Maine Rock | 1.5-2.5 | 150-180 | 30-60 |
| Mustard | Green Wave Florida Broadleaf | 0.5-1.5 | 30-60 | 20-35 |
| Onions - Yellow or Cooking | Canada Maple Early Yellow Globe Eskimo Improved Autumn Spice Norstar Stokes Exporter II | 1-2 | 30-60 | 5-10 |

| BAND, BLOCK OR INTENSIVE PLANT SPACING (cm) | AVERAGE MATURE HEIGHT OF PLANTS (cm) | WEIGHT OF SEED TO DIRECT SEED 5 m ROW (g) | TIMING OF SUCCESSIVE SOWINGS | WHEN TO HARVEST |
|---|---|---|---|---|
| 30 | 30 | 0.6-2.5 | Only one sowing possible | Cut when head is firm. Use thinned-out seedlings. |
| 25 | 25-30 | 0.6-1.8 | Sow every 2-3 weeks until 10 weeks before FFF | Use thinned-out seedlings. Cut when firm head forms. |
| 15-20 | 30-35 | 0.6-2.5 | Sow every 2-3 weeks until 11 weeks before FFF | Use thinned-out seedlings. Cut when suitable size. |
| 20-25 | 25-30 | 0.6-1.8 | Sow every 2-3 weeks until 7 weeks before FFF | Same as for cos lettuce. |
| 25 | 25-30 | 0.6-1.8 | Same as leaf lettuce | Same as leaf lettuce. |
| 38-45 | 20-30 | 2.0-2.5 | None | Pick fruits when most of green color between netting disappears. |
| 25 | 30-35 | 0.6-1.8 | Sow every 2-3 weeks until 7 weeks before FFF | Use thinned seedlings and cut when suitable. |
| 15 | 45 | 1.2-5.0 | None | Pull when needed or after tops fall over. |

Table 11-13: CONT'D

| VEGETABLE | RECOMMENDED CULTIVARS | SEEDING DEPTH (cm) | DISTANCE BETWEEN ROWS (cm) | WITHIN ROW DISTANCE BETWEEN PLANTS (cm) |
|---|---|---|---|---|
| **Onions - Spanish** | Fiesta<br>Gringo<br>Sweet Spanish<br>  Utah Strain | 1-2 | 30-60 | 5-10 |
| **Onions - Red** | Carmen<br>Red Wethersfield<br>Southport Red<br>  Globe | 1-2 | 30-60 | 5-10 |
| **Onions - White** | Ringmaster<br>Southport White<br>  Globe<br>White Sweet<br>  Spanish | 1-2 | 30-60 | 5-10 |
| **Onions - Bunching** | Beltsville Bunching<br>Evergreen<br>Bunching<br>White Lisbon | 1-2 | 15-30 | 5 |
| **Onions - Perennial** | Egyptian<br>Multiplier<br>Shallot | 1-2 | 30-60 | 5-10 |
| **Onions - Pickling** | Silver Queen<br>White Barletta<br>White Pearl | 1-2 | 15-30 | 5 |
| **Parsnip** | All American<br>Half Long<br>Harris Model<br>Improved Hollow<br>  Crown | 0.5-1.5 | 45-60 | 5-10 |
| **Peas - Early** | Dane<br>Jade<br>Laxton's Progress<br>Little Marvel<br>Pep<br>Spring | 2.5-5 | 15-60 | 7-8 |

| BAND, BLOCK OR INTENSIVE PLANT SPACING (cm) | AVERAGE MATURE HEIGHT OF PLANTS (cm) | WEIGHT OF SEED TO DIRECT SEED 5 m ROW (g) | TIMING OF SUCCESSIVE SOWINGS | WHEN TO HARVEST |
|---|---|---|---|---|
| 15 | 45 | 1.2-5.0 | None | Pull when tops fall over. |
| 12-15 | 45 | 1.2-5.0 | None | Pull when tops fall over. |
| 12-15 | 45 | 1.2-5.0 | None | Same as red onions. |
| 6-8 | 30 | 2.4-5.0 | | Pull as required after 6 weeks. |
| | 45 | 1.2-5.0 | None | Sow every 3-4 weeks until 9 weeks before FFF |
| 7-8 | 30 | 2.4-5.0 | None | Pull when bulb size is sufficient. |
| 15 | 35-40 | 1.2-2.5 | None | Pull after frosts but before freeze-up or leave till thaw next spring. |
| 8-10 | 45-150 | 40-75 | Sow every 2-3 weeks until 9-10 weeks before FFF | Remove pods every few days as pods begin to plump up but before they become lumpy and wrinkled. |

Table 11-13: CONT'D

| VEGETABLE | RECOMMENDED CULTIVARS | SEEDING DEPTH (cm) | DISTANCE BETWEEN ROWS (cm) | WITHIN ROW DISTANCE BETWEEN PLANTS (cm) |
|---|---|---|---|---|
| Peas - Mid-Season | Lincoln or Homesteader Novella | 2.5-5 | 15-60 | 7-8 |
| Peas - Late | Bounty Green Arrow Puget | 2.5-5 | 15-60 | 7-8 |
| Peas - Edible Podded | Sugar Ann Sugar Snap | 2.5-5 | 15-60 | 7-8 |
| Peppers - Sweet (Green) | Ace Bell Boy Early California Wonder Lady Bell | 0.5-1.0 | 45-75 | 30-45 |
| Peppers - Sweet (Yellow) | Castle Golden Bell Gypsy | 0.5-1.0 | 45-75 | 30-45 |
| Peppers - Hot | Cayenne (Red) Hungarian Wax (Yellow) Large Red Cherry (Green) | 0.5-1.0 | 45-75 | 30-45 |
| Potatoes - Early | Carlton Irish Cobbler Norland (Red) Yukon Gold (Yellow) | Tubers 7-15 cm below soil | 50-75 | 25-45 |
| Potatoes - Mid-Season | Norchip Norgold Russet Pontiac (Red) Superior Viking | Tubers 7-15 cm below soil surface | 50-75 | 25-45 |
| Potatoes - Late | Explorer (Seeds) Kennebec Russet Burbank or Netted Gem | 0.5-1.0 | | |

| BAND, BLOCK OR INTENSIVE PLANT SPACING (cm) | AVERAGE MATURE HEIGHT OF PLANTS (cm) | WEIGHT OF SEED TO DIRECT SEED 5 m ROW (g) | TIMING OF SUCCESSIVE SOWINGS | WHEN TO HARVEST |
|---|---|---|---|---|
| 8-10 | 45-150 | 40-75 | Allow 10 weeks before FFF | Same as early peas. |
| 8-10 | 45-150 | 40-75 | Allow 10-11 weeks before FFF | Same as early peas. |
| 8-10 | 45-150 | 40-75 | Allow 9-10 weeks before FFF | Remove pods before they fill out. |
| 35-40 | 60 | 0.3-0.6 | None | Pick fruits when large enough to eat until just before FFF. |
| 35-40 | 60 | 0.3-0.6 | None | Same as green peppers. |
| 35 | 50-60 | 0.3-0.6 | None | Pick fruits late in season when most mature for greatest flavor. |
| 23-40 | 60 | Varies | None | Dig up hilled potatoes after vines have died. |
| 23-40 | 60 | Varies | None | Same as early potatoes. |
| 23-40 | 60 | 0.3-0.6 | Start as transplants only | As late as possible. |

Table 11-13: CONT'D

| VEGETABLE | RECOMMENDED CULTIVARS | SEEDING DEPTH (cm) | DISTANCE BETWEEN ROWS (cm) | WITHIN ROW DISTANCE BETWEEN PLANTS (cm) |
|---|---|---|---|---|
| **Pumpkin - Vine** | Connecticut Field<br>Jack O'Lantern<br>Small Sugar<br>Spookie | 2.5-3 | 240-480 | 60-90 |
| **Pumpkin - Bush** | Spirit | 2.5-3 | 240-300 | 45 |
| **Radish - Summer** | Champion<br>Cherry Belle<br>Comet<br>Early Scarlet Globe<br>French Breakfast<br>White Icicle | 0.5-1.5 | 20-30 | 2.5-5 |
| **Radish - Winter** | Black Spinach<br>Chinese Rose<br>Chinese White | 0.5-1.5 | 30 | 10 |
| **Rhubarb** | Early Sunrise<br>German Wine<br>MacDonald | Crowns<br>5-8 cm<br>deep | 120 | 90 |
| **Rutabaga or Swede Turnip** | Altasweet<br>Laurentian | 1-2 | 45-60 | 10-15 |
| **Spinach** | America<br>Cold Resistant<br>  Savoy<br>King of Denmark<br>Long Standing<br>  Bloomsdale | 2-3 | 30-45 | 5-10 |
| **Spinach - Perennial** | New Zealand Spinach | 2-3 | 90 | 30 |
| **Squash - Summer (Green Zucchini)** | Ambassador<br>Diplomat<br>President<br>Zucchini Select<br>Goldbar | 2.5-5 | 90-120 | 45-90 |
| **(Yellow Crookneck) (or straightneck)** | Gold Neck<br>Gold Rush<br>Goldzini<br>Straightneck | 2.5-5 | 90-120 | 45-90 |

| BAND, BLOCK OR INTENSIVE PLANT SPACING (cm) | AVERAGE MATURE HEIGHT OF PLANTS (cm) | WEIGHT OF SEED TO DIRECT SEED 5 m ROW (g) | TIMING OF SUCCESSIVE SOWINGS | WHEN TO HARVEST |
|---|---|---|---|---|
| 90 | 75 | 0.6-2.5 | None | Cut stem of fruit when vine leaves have died and when pumpkins have turned orange color. |
| 60 | 75 | 0.6-2.5 | None | |
| 5-7 | 20 | 2.5-5.0 | Sow each week (except during hot part of summer) until 4 weeks before FFF | Pull when radish is over 2.5 cm across. |
| 10 | 30 | 2.5-4.0 | Sow every 2-3 weeks until 8 weeks before FFF | Pull just before freeze-up. |
| 90 | 120-150 | Varies | None | Pull stalks (not cut) when 60-90 cm long for 8-10 weeks only. |
| 20-25 | 40 | 0.6-2.5 | None | Pull when about 10 cm across before freezing. |
| 10-15 | 30 | 1.2-2.5 | Sow every 2 weeks (except hottest part of season) until 7 weeks before FFF | Cut outer leaves as required after 6 weeks. |
| 30 | 45 | 1.2-2.5 | None | Same as spinach. |
| 60 | 75 | 2.3-2.5 | None | Pick when at least 2.5 cm in diameter or when a suitable size before reaching overmaturity. |
| 60 | 75 | 2.3-2.5 | None | Same as summer squash. |

Table 11-13: CONT'D

| VEGETABLE | RECOMMENDED CULTIVARS | SEEDING DEPTH (cm) | DISTANCE BETWEEN ROWS (cm) | WITHIN ROW DISTANCE BETWEEN PLANTS (cm) |
|---|---|---|---|---|
| (Patty Pan or Scallop) | Early White Scallop<br>Scallopini<br>St. Pat | 2.5-5 | 90-120 | 45-90 |
| (Vegetable Marrow) | Vegetable Marrow (Bush) | | | |
| Squash - Winter | Golden Nugget (Bush) | 2.5-5 | 180 | 45-90 |
| (Acorn or Pepper) | Jersey Golden Acorn (Bush)<br>Table King (Bush)<br>Table Queen | | | |
| (Buttercup) | Buttercup (Bush)<br>Kindred (Vining)<br>Sweet Mama | | | |
| Butternut | Early Butternut (Bush)<br>Eastern Butternut<br>Waltham Butternut | | | |
| (Delicious) | Golden Delicious<br>Green Delicious | | | |
| (Hubbard) | Baby Hubbard<br>Kitchenette<br>Blue Hubbard<br>Golden Hubbard<br>Hubbard Improved Green<br>Warted Hubbard | | | |
| (Others) | Banana Squash<br>Vegetable Spaghetti | | | |
| Sweet Corn - Early | Altagold<br>Butter Vee<br>Earlivee<br>Northern Vee<br>Northlite<br>Polar Vee<br>Seneca 60<br>Spring White<br>Sunny Vee | 3-6 | 55-90 | 30 |

| BAND, BLOCK OR INTENSIVE PLANT SPACING (cm) | AVERAGE MATURE HEIGHT OF PLANTS (cm) | WEIGHT OF SEED TO DIRECT SEED 5 m ROW (g) | TIMING OF SUCCESSIVE SOWINGS | WHEN TO HARVEST |
|---|---|---|---|---|
| 60 | 75 | 2.3-2.5 | None | Pick when suitable size before over maturity. |
| 75-90 | 75 | 1.5-2.5 | None | Pick when fruit slips off vine easily or when skin is tough enough to resist pressure from a thumb nail. |
| 45 | 120 | 10-20 | Sow every 3 weeks until 9-10 weeks before FFF | Break off cobs when silk is brown and the juice inside the kernels is milky. If watery, corn is too young. If pasty, then corn is over mature. |

Table 11-13: CONT'D

| VEGETABLE | RECOMMENDED CULTIVARS | SEEDING DEPTH (cm) | DISTANCE BETWEEN ROWS (cm) | WITHIN ROW DISTANCE BETWEEN PLANTS (cm) |
|---|---|---|---|---|
| **Sweet Corn - Mid-Season** | Early Bird<br>Early Gem<br>Jazz<br>Northern Super Sweet<br>Seneca Star<br>Spirit<br>Sunny Vee | 3-6 | 55-90 | 30 |
| **Sweet Corn - Late** | Butter and Sugar<br>Calypso<br>Flavorvee<br>Golden Beauty<br>Reliance<br>Sugar Loaf<br>Sunburst Improved | 3-6 | 55-90 | 30 |
| **Swiss Chard - White** | Fordhook Giant<br>Lucullus<br>White King | 1-2.5 | 30-60 | 10-20 |
| **Swiss Chard - Red** | Burpee's Rhubarb<br>Ruby Red | | | |
| **Tomatoes - Bush** | Brookpact<br>Cold Set<br>Earlibright<br>Earlirouge<br>Improved Starfire<br>Quinte<br>Rocket<br>Subarctic Maxi | 1-1.5 | 60-90 | 45-60 |
| **Tomatoes - Staking** | Early Girl<br>Stokes Early Hybrid<br>Ultragirl | 1-1.5 | 45-60 | 45-60 |

| BAND, BLOCK OR INTENSIVE PLANT SPACING (cm) | AVERAGE MATURE HEIGHT OF PLANTS (cm) | WEIGHT OF SEED TO DIRECT SEED 5 m ROW (g) | TIMING OF SUCCESSIVE SOWINGS | WHEN TO HARVEST |
|---|---|---|---|---|
| 45 | 150 | 10-20 | Sow every 3 weeks allowing 10-11 weeks before FFF | Same as for early corn. |
| 45 | 180-200 | 10-20 | None | Same as early corn. |
| 20 | 30 | 2.5-4.5 | Sow every 2-3 weeks until 9 weeks before FFF | Cut outer leaves as required after 8 weeks. |
|  |  |  | Same as white chard. | Same as white chard. |
| 45-60 | 60-90 | 0.3-0.6 | None | Pick when fruits are ripe. Green ripe condition is determined when gell-like substance surrounds seeds. |
| 45-60 | 180-200 | 0.3-0.6 | None | Same as bush tomatoes. |

Table 11-13: CONT'D

| VEGETABLE | RECOMMENDED CULTIVARS | SEEDING DEPTH (cm) | DISTANCE BETWEEN ROWS (cm) | WITHIN ROW DISTANCE BETWEEN PLANTS (cm) |
|---|---|---|---|---|
| **Tomatoes - Cherry** | Stokes Alaska<br>Subarctic Delight<br>Subarctic Plenty | 1-1.5 | 45-60 | 30-45 |
| **Tomatoes - Paste** | Nova<br>Veeroma | 1-1.5 | 45-60 | 45-60 |
| **Turnip** | Purple Top White<br>Globe<br>Tokyo Cross | 0.5-1.5 | 30-40 | 10-15 |
| **Watermelon** | Early Canada<br>Supersweet<br>Stokes Sugar<br>Hybrid (large)<br>Sugar Baby<br>Yellow Baby<br>(yellow flesh) | 2.5-3 | 180-240 | 60-90 |

The arrival of the first fall frost signals the close of another growing season for many vegetables. Covering sensitive plants with newspapers or blankets can provide some protection against light frosts. This may allow those plants the few extra days they need to reach maturity. Applying a light sprinkling of water before sunrise has also proven successful against frost damage. Plants that are coated with ice often show little or no sign of injury if allowed to thaw slowly. When a hard frost occurs, the gardener should leave the vegetables alone until warmer temperatures permit a slow thaw. The worst thing to do would be to harvest the frozen vegetables and thaw them out quickly inside. Frozen water in plant cells will rupture the cell walls and cause a water soaked appearance of the affected tissues. Produce damaged in this manner is not suitable for processing or storage.

## STORAGE OF VEGETABLES

Almost any vegetable crop can be stored indoors (in some form) over the winter. Methods of storage include: pickling, canning, freezing, drying, natural storage, and the preparation of jams or jellies. In every case, the maturation or spoilage of the vegetables is either greatly slowed or stopped completely. Each method has its own advantages and disadvantages.

Most of these techniques require some degree of processing which alters the natural flavor and texture of the vegetable. Natural storage is often the most appealing as it involves storing fresh, raw, whole vegetables in natural conditions. Quality is rarely improved by storage. At best, the vegetable quality is only maintained.

The storage area and containers should be as clean as possible. Harvest the vegetables during the coolest part of the day which is usually in the morning. This makes it so that field heat does not need to be extracted from the vegetables. Store only top quality produce. Damaged or overmature vegetables should be used immediately and not stored. Check produce regularly and remove any that show signs of decay. Keep any ethylene producing stored fruits (like apples and pears) in a separate location. Ethylene gas stimulates respiration and maturation of vegetables. Keep all vegetables in the dark (especially potatoes) or greening will occur. Table 11-12 indicates four natural storage environments and those vegetables best suited to each.

## CONCLUSION

Vegetable gardening can be a highly profitable and enjoyable pasttime. Careful consideration of all the gardening inputs and use of proper management techniques can maximize a gardener's benefits and minimize his disappointments. Both experienced and beginning gardeners learn through trial-and-error as to what works best and what does not in their particular garden site. Experimentation and research into new cultivars of vegetables and gardening methods often leads to greater yields, less work and more satisfaction. Maintaining accurate records on weather data and actual production levels of each vegetable crop will greatly aid the gardener in this endeavor.

| BAND, BLOCK OR INTENSIVE PLANT SPACING (cm) | AVERAGE MATURE HEIGHT OF PLANTS (cm) | WEIGHT OF SEED TO DIRECT SEED 5 m ROW (g) | TIMING OF SUCCESSIVE SOWINGS | WHEN TO HARVEST |
|---|---|---|---|---|
| 45 | 45 | 0.3-0.6 | None | Same as bush tomatoes. |
| 60 | 180 | 0.3-0.6 | None | Same as bush tomatoes. |
| 15 | 30 | 0.6-1.2 | Sow every 3-4 weeks until 8 weeks before FFF | Pull when over 2.5 cm across. |
| 60-75 | 60 | 0.6-2.5 | None | Pick fruits when they have a hollow thump sound and when skin turns yellow on bottom. |

## SELF CHECK *QUIZ*

willow and poplar shelterbelt

house, family of 5

lettuce
watermelon · 'allsweet' 104 days
zucchini
asparagus
radish
peas
cabbage
rhubarb
broccoli
rhubarb
tomato
potato
high nitrogen fertilizer
corn · 'silver queen' 94 days

thistles

sowing on a hot sunny day
seed source: Ontario
seeding date: May 24  1979 1980 1981 1982 1983 1984 1985 1986

1. Study the garden layout plan and list at least 10 problems that would be encountered if this plan was actually used this year in the Prairies.

2. What are the 5 main factors in an ideal garden site that all vegetables require in order to grow well?

3. Mr. McDonald decided not to use 11-55-0 on his garden as he found 16-20-0 on sale. Recalculate the amounts of fertilizer he should apply to his 24 m² plot assuming he still requires 1.5 kg of nitrogen and 0.5 kg of phosphorus per 100 m². The fertilizer 21-0-0 will be used to apply the remaining quantity of nitrogen required.

4. Why is it necessary to cultivate a garden soil every year?

5. What are some of the problems that can occur with direct seeding of vegetables?

6. List some of the qualities to look for when selecting vegetable transplants.

7. Which gardening methods make the most efficient use of gardening space?

8. What are the three forms of succession planting?

9. What devices can be used to extend the growing season in a vegetable garden?

10. Why is mulching an important cultural practice?

# SELF CHECK *ANSWERS*

1. Shelterbelt is too close and shades the garden. It will also compete with the vegetables for water and nutrients.

   There is no turn around space at the end of the rows which could cause a problem if a rototiller is used midseason to cultivate the pathways.

   There is far too much zucchini and lettuce planted to feed the family.

   All rows have the same space between them and this does not allow for spreading crops like watermelon or other vine crops.

   Perennial crops like asparagus and rhubarb should have been planted off to one side to prevent damage during spring cultivation.

   Corn is planted on the south side instead of the north to prevent shading of shorter sun loving plants.

   Corn is planted in a single row instead of a block which will lead to poor pollination of the cobs.

   All crops are planted on the same day. Many crops should be seeded earlier than May 24 while others should be later.

   Corn and watermelon cultivars are not recommended for the Prairies as they require too long a growing time to mature.

   High nitrogen fertilizers are used exclusively, which will promote lush leaf growth at the expense of flowers and fruit.

   Perennial weeds (like thistles) should be controlled to prevent spreading and competition for light, water and nutrients.

   Planting is done on a hot sunny day. For transplants, a cool cloudy day is best.

   No crop rotation is indicated to prevent the buildup of diseases and insects.

   Related crops are planted beside each other. Separation of crops like tomato and potato helps to slow the spread of common pests.

   No provision for succession planting has been made. Short season crops like radish and lettuce would be better planted in several shorter rows every few weeks for a longer harvest period.

   Note: There are probably many more faults with this garden plan but this list touches on most of the more important points discussed in the lesson. (See WHAT VEGETABLES AND CULTIVARS TO GROW, SELECTING THE SITE, and GARDEN LAYOUT PROCEDURE — pages 1103 to 1109).

2. All vegetables require optimum levels of light, heat, water, soil and shelter (see SELECTING THE SITE — page 1104).

3. Begin by calculating the amount of phosphorus to apply.

$$\frac{0.5 \text{ kg of phosphorus}}{20\%/100} = \frac{0.5}{0.20} = 2.5 \text{ kg of 16-20-0 / 100 m}^2$$

$$2.5 \text{ kg of 16-20-0} \times \frac{16\%}{100} = 2.5 \times 0.16 = 0.4 \text{ kg of nitrogen}$$

1.5 kg of nitrogen required - 0.4 kg applied = 1.1 kg still required

$$\frac{1.1 \text{ kg of nitrogen}}{21\%/100} = \frac{1.1}{0.21} = 5.24 \text{ kg of 21-0-0 per 100 m}^2$$

$$\frac{2.5 \text{ kg of 16-20-0} \times 24 \text{ m}^2}{100 \text{ m}^2} = 0.025 \times 24 = 0.6 \text{ kg of 16-20-0}$$

$$\frac{5.24 \text{ kg of 21-0-0} \times 24 \text{ m}^2}{100 \text{ m}^2} = 0.0524 \times 24 = 1.26 \text{ kg of 21-0-0}$$

   Therefore, Mr. McDonald will now have to apply 0.6 kg (1.3 lbs) of 16-20-0 and 1.26 kg (2.8 lbs) of 21-0-0 to his garden (see FERTILIZERS AND FERTILIZING — page 1109).

4. Cultivation is required to improve soil structure, drainage and soil atmosphere and to facilitate the removal of plant residue, diseased debris and rocks while providing a uniform, flat seedbed (see CULTIVATING THE SOIL — page 1115).

5. With direct seeding of vegetables, losses can occur from bird and rodent feeding, insect and disease damage, wind and water erosion, and adverse weather conditions. Thinning of seedlings is often required to obtain the proper plant spacing (see DIRECT SEEDING OUTDOORS — page 1122).

6. The main qualities to look for when buying transplants are:

   * short, stocky plants that are not top heavy.

   * healthy, green leaves

   * no evidence of insects or disease

   * no fruits, flowers or flower buds

   * plants in individual pots, cavities or cells

   * adequate rooting depth with no evidence of being pot bound

   * properly hardened off (see VEGETABLE TRANSPLANTS — page 1125).

7.  The gardening methods that make it possible to grow the most vegetables in the least amount of space are:

    - temporary wide row gardening
      or Chinese Mound gardening
      or French intensive gardening
    - raised bed gardening
    - square foot gardening
    - vertical gardening
    - container gardening

      Note: all these gardening methods make use of intensive plant spacing (see GARDENING METHODS — page 1127)

8.  True succession planting involves replanting a vegetable crop into the space vacated by another crop.

    Successive or relay planting involves sowing the same crop every one or two weeks to extend the length of time that the crop will be ready for harvest.

    A variation of successive planting involves sowing early-, mid- and late-season crops at the same time to obtain an extended harvest period (see SUCCESSION PLANTING — page 1131).

9.  The devices that are used to extend the growing season are:

    - raised beds
    - cold frames
    - hot beds
    - hot caps or hot tents
    - mulches (organic or plastic)
    - tunnels or row covers
    - newspaper or blankets (for frost protection)
    - water (surrounding plants or sprayed on plants) (see GROWING SEASON EXTENDERS — page 1132).

10. Mulching is important in a vegetable garden. It is a valuable tool for water conservation and weed control while providing physical protection for growing crops. Fruits close to the ground are kept cleaner and more free of disease and insects. Soil compaction and root damage are reduced. Soil temperatures are kept more moderate when organic mulches are applied. Soil temperatures are dramatically increased when plastic mulches are used. Root crops are protected from frosts in the fall. Organic mulches can be incorporated to help increase soil organic matter and improve soil tilth (see MULCHING — page 1138).

## GLOSSARY

alkali - soil that contains sufficient sodium salt levels so as to interfere with normal plant growth.

bolting - premature flowering of a plant, usually at the expense of normal vegetative development.

cole crops — vegetables in the cabbage family or belonging to the genus *Brassica* (i.e., broccoli, Brussels sprouts, cabbage, cauliflower, Chinese cabbage, kale, kohlrabi, radishes, rutabaga and turnips).

damping-off - disease of seeds and seedlings caused by a fungus or group of fungi under conditions of cool, damp soils.

determinate - growth habit of a plant depicted by flowers and fruit formed at the ends of branches and main stems. Usually results in a bush-like form of the plant.

friable - easily crumbled.

germination - sprouting of a seed to form a seedling.

green manure - crop that is specifically grown for the purpose of being plowed under while still green. Process undertaken to improve soil organic matter and nutrient levels.

grey water - household waste water from washing or bathing that can be used to irrigate a garden. It should not contain detergents, borax, bleaches or other chemicals.

hardening-off - process by which plants are gradually acclimatized from an indoor to an outdoor environment.

indeterminate - growth habit of a plant that forms flowers and fruits from lateral buds along the stems. Usually results in elongated plant growth.

inoculation - process of adding the proper type of *Rhizobium* bacteria to legume seeds to help increase nitrogen fixation.

mulch - layer of organic or inorganic material laid on the ground to slow moisture evaporation, prevent erosion and control weeds.

pesticide - substance, usually synthetic, that kills or inhibits a selected type of living thing (e.g., insecticides, herbicides, fungicides, nematicides, ovicides, rodenticides and biocides).

radicle - part of an embryo inside a seed that is first to emerge from the seed coat and develops into the root.

seedling - young plant that usually only continues its cotyledons or first true leaves.

set - small bulb usually of onions or shallots.

side-dressing - method of applying fertilizer to soil surface under plants or in trenches beside plants.

**subsoil** - layer of mineral soil beneath topsoil generally containing much less organic matter and nutrients. Unsuitable to support plant growth by itself.

**tendril** - slender shoot that coils and twines itself around anything it touches in order to help support the plant.

**tilth** - condition of soil under cultivation.

**transplant** - plant that is capable of being moved from one location to another. Can also denote the action of transferring a plant from one growing medium to another.

**true leaf** - leaf that develops after the development of the cotyledon leaves or seedling leaves.

## RESOURCE MATERIALS

Alberta Agriculture. *Alberta Horticultural Guide*. Revised 1986. Agdex 200/01.

Alberta Agriculture. *Common Soil and Fertilizer Questions and Answers*. 1983. Agdex 520-1.

Alberta Agriculture. *Cucumber Diseases*. AC 1684, 1979. Agdex 256/635-1.

Alberta Agriculture. *Diseases of Potatoes and Their Control*. Revised 1981. Agdex FS 258/635-3.

Alberta Agriculture. *Growing Garden Potatoes*. AC 1559, Revised 1980. Agdex 258/20-1.

Alberta Agriculture. *Growing Garden Tomatoes*. AC 1558, Revised 1980. Agdex 257/20-1.

Alberta Agriculture. *Growing Savory Herbs*. AC 1158, Revised 1980. Agdex 263/20-1.

Alberta Agriculture. *Growing Vegetables in the Prairie Garden*. AC 1033, 1980. Agdex 250/20-1.

Alberta Agriculture. *High Salt Content in Garden Soil*. 1980. Agdex FS 518-6.

Alberta Agriculture. *Home Storage Room for Fruits and Vegetables: Construction and Operation*. AC 1478, Revised 1978. Agdex 250/60.

Alberta Agriculture. *Home Vegetable Gardening in Alberta*. 1983. Agdex 250/20-3.

Alberta Agriculture. *Mice and Their Control*. Revised 1983. Agdex FS 683.

Alberta Agriculture. *Non-Parasitic Disorders of Potatoes*. 1979. Agdex FS 258/07-2.

Alberta Agriculture. *Northern Gardening*. AC 1575, 1976. Agdex 200/14-1.

Alberta Agriculture. *Perennial Weed Control*. 1983. Agdex FS 641-11.

Alberta Agriculture. *Pesticides for the Home and Garden*. AC 1543, (annual) Agdex 606-1.

Alberta Agriculture. *Rhubarb Culture*. AC 1664, 1978. Agdex 254/20-2.

Alberta Agriculture. *Tomato Diseases*. AC 1479, Revised 1980. Agdex 256/635.

Alberta Agriculture. *Trickle Irrigation for Home Gardens and Shelterbelts*. 1977. Agdex FS 568-1.

Alberta Agriculture. *Vertebrate Pest Control*. 1977. Agdex FS 680.

Alberta Agriculture. *Wood Preservatives for Home and Horticultural Use*. 1982. Agdex FS 200/23-1.

Andrews, Brian R. *Brian Andrews on Gardening*. Edmonton: Reprinted from the files of The Edmonton Jounal, 1968.

Good softcover text on all aspects of gardening with only a few illustrations.

Bartholomew, Mel. *Square Foot Gardening*. Emmaus, Pennsylvania: Rodale Press, 1981.

Paperback, describes intensive method of gardening using an area similar to raised beds.

Bartholomew, Mel. *Cash from Square Foot Gardening*. Pownal, Vermont: Storey Communications Inc, 1985. Vermont, 1985.

Softcover, continues with advice on management and marketing of vegetables from this type of garden.

Bennett, Jennifer. *The Harrowsmith Northern Gardener*. Camden East, Ontario: Camden House Publishing Ltd. 1982. Also available through Harrowsmith Books. #286B

Hardcover, one of the most complete books on organic growing of vegetables and herbs north of the 40th parallel.

Biggs, Tony. *Vegetables*. The Simon and Schuster Step-By-Step Encyclopaedia of Practical Gardening. New York: Simon and Schuster. 1980.

Softcover, many helpful line drawings.

Anna Carr. *Rodale's Color Handbook of Garden Insects*. Emmaus, Pa.: Rodale Press, 1979

Softcover, contains over 300 color photographs of insects throughout Canada and the United States giving descriptions, lifecycle, host plants, feeding habits and natural controls.

Crockett, James. *Crockett's Victory Garden*. Toronto: Little, Brown and Co., 1977.

Softcover, great pictures; planting dates and other data not relevant in Prairie cimate.

Crockett, James Underwood. *Vegetables and Fruits*. New York: Time-Life Books, 1972

Many volumes of hardcover books on individual subjects of horticulture including vegetables.

Cullen, Mark. *Weeds, Pests, and Diseases:* Cullen Canadian Garden Guide, Toronto: Summerhill Press Ltd., 1975.

Softcover, excellent reference for all forms of container gardening.

Faust, Joan Lee. *The New York Times Book of Vegetable Gardening.* New York: Quadrangle - The New York Times Book Co., 1975

Softcover, excellent coverage of the subject with pictures and diagrams.

Gardella, Maureen Nehnberg, editor. "Grow Your Own", *Successful Gardening Encyclopedia.* Westport, Connecticut: H.S. Stuttman Inc., 1977.

A 5 volume set of hardcover books with excellent pictures and diagrams for specific culture of individual vegetables.

Harp, H.F. *The Prairie Gardener.* Edmonton: Hurtig Publishers, 1970.

A good source for local information.

Millarville Horticultural Club. *Gardening Under the Arch.* Calgary: c/o Mrs. Theresa Patterson, Site 30, Box 1, R.R. 8, Calgary, Alberta. 1982.

Softcover, written by members of the club, contains practical hints.

Mother Earth News Editors. *The Abundant Vegetable Garden: A Handbook for Success.* Mother Earth News Inc. Hendersonville, N. Carolina, 1985.

Ogden, Samuel, *Step-by-Step to Organic Vegetable Gardening.* Emmaus, Pa.: Rodale Press, Inc., 1971.

Ortho Books. *All About Vegetables.* San Francisco, Cal.: Chevron Chemical Co., Consumer Products Division, 1980.

Softcover, one of many good books in the "All About" series containing plenty of pictures and diagrams.

Reader's Digest editors. *Illustrated Guide to Gardening in Canada.* Montreal, Quebec: The Reader's Digest Association (Canada) Ltd., 1979.

Hardcover, very complete coverage of all horticultural subjects with many line drawings and tables.

Riotte, Louise. *Carrots Love Tomatoes. Secrets of Companion Planting for Successful Gardening.* Charlotte, Vermont: Garden Way Publishing, 1975.

Softcover, excellent manual for using plant interrelationships for deterring insects and weeds.

Riotte, Louise. *Roses Love Garlic. Secrets of Companion Planting with Flowers.* Charlotte, Vermont: Garden Way Publishing, 1983.

Softcover, a continuation with little duplication but designed more for flower gardening.

Rodale editors. *The Organic Gardener's Complete Guide to Vegetables and Fruits.* Emmaus, Pa: Rodale Press, 1982. #437B

Hardcover, exhaustive compendium of facts and crop-by-crop description of vegetables and fruits.

Seymour, John. *The Self-Sufficient Gardener.* Garden City, New York: Dolphin Books, Doubleday & Company, 1978.

Softcover, excellent guide for raised bed gardening.

Sunset Book editors. *How to Grow Vegetables and Berries.* Menlo Park, California: Lane Publishing Co., 1982.

Softcover, filled with good diagrams and pictures.

Sunset Books editors. *Introduction to Basic Gardening.* Menlo Park, California: Lane Publishing Co., 1981.

Softcover, with good diagrams and instructions for the beginner.

Sunset Books editors. *Container Gardening.* Menlo Park, California: Lane Publishing Co., 1984.

Softcover, plenty of pictures and instructions on all forms of container gardening indoors and outdoors.

Taylor, Norman. *Taylor's Encyclopedia of Gardening.* Boston: Houghton Mifflin Co., 1961.

Hardcover, large and comprehensive text of all aspects of gardenign

Wilson, Lois. *Chatelaine's Garden Book: The Complete All Canada Guide to Garden Success.* MacLean Hunter Ltd., Toronto, 1986.

Wright, Michael (ed.) *The Complete Book of Gardening.* available through Harrowsmith Books. #177A Warner Books, New York, 1983

Paperback, good coverage of all aspects of gardening

Young, Isabelle and Charles. *Better Ways to Successful Gardening in Western Canada.* Calgary, Alta.: The Calgary Albertan, 1978.

Softcover, deals with all aspects of gardening in the Prairies.

*Canadian Magazines and Newsletters.*

*Alberta Horticulturist*, c/o Muriel Conner, Secretary, Alberta Horticultural Association, Box 223, Lacombe, Alberta T0C 1S0.

Published quarterly.

*Canadian Garden News*, 36 Head Street, Dundas, Ontario L9H 3H3.

Published 10 times yearly.

*The Edmonton Horticultural Society Bulletin*, Edmonton Horticultural Society, Membership Director, 11507-141 Street, Edmonton, Alberta T5M 1T7.

Published monthly.

*The Prairie Garden*, P.O. Box 517, Winnipeg, Manitoba R3C 2J3.

Western Canada's only gardening annual written by and for western gardeners and homeowners; published by The Prairie Garden Committee of the Winnipeg Horticultural Society.

Published annually.

*Seed Catalogues*

Alberta Nurseries and Seeds Ltd., Box 20, Bowden, Alberta TOM OKO. Specialty - Flowers, vegetables, nursery stock and supplies.

Ashby's Seeds, Cameron, Ontario KOM 1GO. Specialty - Vegetables and herbs.

Dasha Barinka, 46232 Strathcona Road, Chilliwack, B.C. V2P 3T2. Specialty - Unusual vegetables and herbs.

Bishop Seeds, Box 338, Belleville, Ontario K8N 5A5. Specialty - Vegetables, flower and lawn seed as well as small quantities of farm and green manure seed.

C.A. Cruickshank Ltd., 1015 Mount Pleasant Road, Toronto, Ontario M4P 2M1. Specialty - Vegetables, flowers, flowering bulbs and supplies.

William Dam Seeds, Box 8400, Dundas, Ontario L9H 6M1. Specialty - Untreated vegetable and flower seeds plus small quantities of green manure seed.

Dills Pumpkin Farm, Windsor, Nova Scotia BON 2TO. Specialty - Giant pumpkin seed only.

Dominion Seed House, 115 Guelph Street, Georgetown, Ontario L7G 4A2. Specialty - Vegetable and flower seeds and gardening supplies.

Early's Farm and Garden Centre, Box 3024, Saskatoon, Saskatchewan S7K 3S9. Specialty - Vegetable seed and supplies for northern climates.

Garden Import Inc., Box 760, Thornhill, Ontario L3T 4A5. Specialty - Vegetable and flower seeds from Britain.

Gardener's Supply Co. Ltd., 949 Wilson Avenue, Downsview, Ontario M3K 1G2. Specialty - Gardening tools and growing devices for vegetables.

Halifax Seed Co. Ltd., Box 8026, Station A, Halifax, Nova Scotia B3K 5L8. Specialty - Vegetables, flowers and herbs plus garden supplies.

Island Seed Co. Ltd., P.O. Box 4278, Station A, Victoria, B.C. V8X 3X8. Specialty - Tomatoes.

Lindenberg Seeds Ltd., 803 Princess Avenue, Brandon, Manitoba R7A 0P5. Specialty - Vegetables, flowers and herbs that are Prairie hardy.

McFayden Seed Co. Ltd., Box 1800, 30-9th Street, Brandon, Manitoba R7A 6N4. Specialty - Vegetables, flowers and nursery stock.

Northern Star Plants and Herbs, Box 2262, Station A, London, Ontario N6A 4E3. Specialty - Herbs, spices and other unusual seeds.

Ontario Seed Co. Ltd., Box 144, Waterloo, Ontario N2J 3Z9. Specialty - Vegetable and flower seeds.

George W. Park Seed Co., Box 31, Greenwood, South Carolina 29647. Specialty - Vegetable and flower seeds.

W.H. Perron and Co. Ltd., 515 Labelle Blvd., Chomedy, Laval, Quebec H7V 2T3 Specialty - Vegetables, flowers, nursery stock and supplies. French Catalogue only.

Rawlinson Garden Seed, 269 College Road, Truro, Nova Scotia B2N 2P6 Specialty - Vegetable, flower and herb seeds.

Richters, Otto Richter and Sons Ltd., Box 26, Goodwood, Ontario LOC 1AO. Specialty - Herbs only.

Robertson-Pike Seeds, 10320-80 Avenue, Edmonton, Alberta T6E 1T9. Specialty - same as McFaydens.

Sanctuary Seeds, 2388 West 4th Avenue, Vancouver, B.C. V6K 1P1. Specialty - Untreated, nonhybrid vegetables and herbs.

Seed Center Ltd., Box 3867, Station D, Edmonton, Alberta T5L 4K1. Specialty - Vegetables, flowers, nursery stock and supplies for northern gardeners. Price - free.

Semences Laval Inc., 3505 Boulevard St. Martin Ouest, Laval, Quebec H7T 1A2. Specialty - Vegetables, flowers and garden supplies.

Siberia Seeds, Box 3000, Olds, Alberta TOM 1PO. Specialty - cold-resistant tomatoes only.

Stokes Seeds Ltd., Box 10, 39 James Street, St. Catherines, Ontario L2R 6R6. OR: 4066 Stokes Building, St. Catherines, Ontario L2R 6R6 Specialty - Vegetables and flower seeds, large selection.

T and T Seeds Ltd., Box 1710, Winnipeg, Manitoba R3C 3P6. Specialty - Vegetables, flowers and supplies for northern gardens.

Thompson and Morgan, Inc., Box 1308, Jackson, New Jersey 08527. Specialty - Vegetable and flower seeds, wide choice.

Tregunno Seeds Ltd., 126 Catharine Street N., Hamilton, Ontario L8R 1J4. Specialty - Vegetable and flower seeds plus garden supplies.

Vessey's Seeds Ltd., York, P.E.I. COA 1PO. Specialty - Vegetable and flower seeds.

A.J. Woodward and Sons, 635 Fort Street, Victoria, B.C., Specialty - Vegetable and flower seeds from England.

# SMALL FRUIT PRODUCTION

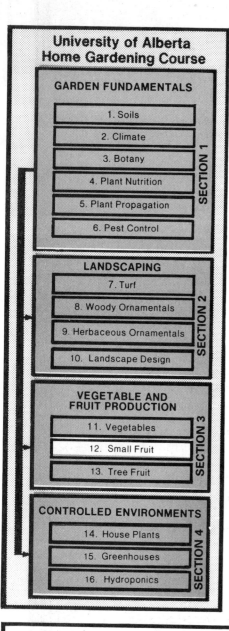

**University of Alberta Home Gardening Course**

**GARDEN FUNDAMENTALS**
- 1. Soils
- 2. Climate
- 3. Botany
- 4. Plant Nutrition
- 5. Plant Propagation
- 6. Pest Control

SECTION 1

**LANDSCAPING**
- 7. Turf
- 8. Woody Ornamentals
- 9. Herbaceous Ornamentals
- 10. Landscape Design

SECTION 2

**VEGETABLE AND FRUIT PRODUCTION**
- 11. Vegetables
- 12. Small Fruit
- 13. Tree Fruit

SECTION 3

**CONTROLLED ENVIRONMENTS**
- 14. House Plants
- 15. Greenhouses
- 16. Hydroponics

SECTION 4

# SELF-STUDY LESSON FEATURES

Self-study is an educational approach which allows you to study a subject where and when you want. The course is designed to allow students to study the course material efficiently and incorporates the following features.

**OBJECTIVES** — are found at the beginning of each lesson and allow you to determine what you can expect to learn in the lesson.

**LESSON MATERIAL** — is logically organized and broken down into fundamental components by ordered headings to assist you to comprehend the subject.

**REFERENCING** — between lessons and within lessons allows you to integrate course material.

The last two digits of the page number identify the page and the digits preceding these identify the lesson number (eg., 107: Lesson 1, page 7 or 1227: Lesson 12, page 27).

Referencing:

    sections within the same lesson (eg., see OSMOSIS)

    sections in other lessons (eg., see Botany lesson, OSMOSIS)

    figures and tables (eg., see Figure 7-3)

**FIGURES AND TABLES** — are found in abundance throughout the lessons and are designed to convey useful information in an easy to understand form.

**SIDEBARS** — are those areas in the lesson which are boxed and toned. They present information supplementary to the core content of the lesson.

**PRACTICAL PROJECTS** — are integrated within the lesson material and are included to allow you to apply principles and practices.

**SELF-CHECK QUIZ** — is provided at the end of each lesson and allows you to test your comprehension of the lesson material. Answers to the questions and references to the sections dealing with the questions are provided in the answer section. You should review any questions that you are unable to answer.

**GLOSSARY** – is provided at the end of each lesson and alphabetically lists the definitions of key concepts and terms.

**RESOURCE MATERIALS** — are provided at the end of each lesson and comprise a list of recommended learning materials for further study of the subject. Also included are author's comments on the potential application of each publication.

**INDEX** — alphabetically lists useful topics and their location within the lesson.

1986 University of Alberta Faculty of Extension

**Written by: Jan C. Hardstaff**

Technical Reviewers

Betty Vladicka
Al Schernus

THE PRODUCTION TEAM

| | |
|---|---|
| Managing Editor | Thom Shaw |
| Editor | Lois Hameister |
| | Frank Procter |
| Production Coordinator | Kevin Hanson |
| Graphic Artist | Melanie Eastley Harbourne |
| Data Entry | Lois Hameister |

Published by the University of Alberta Faculty of Extension Corbett Hall Edmonton, Alberta, T6G 2G4

ISBN 0-88864-852-9

(Book 3, Lesson 12)

After completing this lesson, the student should be able to:

1. select a suitable site for the small fruit plantation, avoiding certain factors that may be limiting.

2. properly prepare the soil to ensure successful establishment and optimum growing conditions of small fruits.

3. plan the layout of the small fruit plantation.

4. choose suitable cultivars of various small fruits.

5. identify each kind of small fruit and have an understanding of its growth, flowering and fruiting habits.

6. be able to successfully culture strawberries, raspberries, saskatoons, black and red currants, gooseberries or grapes.

7. be able to take preventive measures to avoid physiological, insect, disease or pest problems.

## TABLE OF CONTENTS

# INTRODUCTION

Every home gardener, whether rural or urban, should set aside some space for growing a variety of small fruits. A wide range of small fruits can be successfully produced on the prairies including: strawberries, raspberries, saskatoons, currants, gooseberries, grapes, highbush cranberries, blueberries and huckleberries. The resulting fruit yields much pleasure and satisfaction to the home gardener and those who share the rewards of his labor.

This lesson provides both the experienced and amateur gardener with a comprehensive, practical study of small fruit culture. It begins with an overview that deals with the suitability of small fruits to the home garden and the criteria which must be met to successfully produce quality small fruits.

The next section looks at the importance of selecting an optimum site for the small fruit plantation within the space available. Various characteristics of the site, including slope and air drainage, exposure to the sun and wind, soil conditions, moisture supply, soil drainage and climate influence the overall environment. This section provides guidelines for choosing an appropriate site and points out things to avoid that may limit the growing of certain types of fruit. The previous lessons on Soils, Climate and Plant Nutrition are applicable to site selection.

Soil preparation is of vital importance to the successful establishment of a small fruit plantation. It is really the preparation of a somewhat permanent home for the plants and should, therefore, be done properly to provide optimum growing conditions. Controlling the weeds, adding organic matter and ensuring adequate fertility levels contribute to good response and quick establishment of the small fruit plants.

Careful consideration with respect to management and spacing requirements helps to make culture of the small fruit plants easier and increases the chances of successfully producing a high yielding, quality plantation. The section on establishing the small fruit plantation provides information on how to plan the layout of the plantation.

Next, guidelines in choosing cultivars of the various small fruits are discussed.

Because the cultivar chosen depends on your horticultural climatic zone (see Climate lesson, Figure 2-10), it is difficult to give specific recommendations. Instead, a table lists the more commonly grown cultivars. The RESOURCE MATERIALS at the end of the lesson provide a list of sources where information can be obtained on which cultivars are best suited in certain zones.

The final sections cover the culture of the various small fruits commonly grown on the prairies. These sections give the homeowner practical cultural guidelines. Each section begins with a brief discussion of the unique botanical characteristics of each of the small fruits. This is followed by information on plant establishment and management practices that ensure maximum longevity and productivity of the plantation. The problems and prevention section at the end of the lesson is provided to help the gardener avoid situations which increase disease and pest problems, and enables early detection of these problems. The information in the Pest Control lesson is also valuable in diagnosing and controlling diseases and pests.

# AN OVERVIEW OF SMALL FRUIT GROWING ON THE PRAIRIES

## SMALL FRUITS IN THE HOME GARDEN

### ADVANTAGES

Small fruits grown in the home garden are of a higher quality than those obtained in the supermarket. The home gardener does not have to sacrifice quality for high yields and maximum profits. Fruit can always be picked fresh, and if suitable cultivars of each fruit are chosen so as to stagger the harvest, fruit will be available throughout the season. By preserving the fruit through canning or freezing, or the making of jams, jellies and juice, availability is extended well into the winter months.

Certain kinds of small fruits are valuable as ornamentals. Properly trained grapes, along a well protected south wall, have a very elegant look and provide an interesting contrast against brick, stone or siding. Strawberries, particularly the runnerless types which are low yielding, can be used as ground cover material. Various bush fruits, when strategically located in the garden, can be used to screen the garden from the rest of the yard, as well as provide a barrier to deter those who might like to partake of the delights of one's garden.

The small fruit plantation, although more expensive to establish than the vegetable garden, provides long-term enjoyment. If properly cared for, it can supply fruit for many years. In comparison to a fruit tree plantation, small fruits have the advantage of providing a quicker return on one's investment.

### DISADVANTAGES

Although the advantages of growing small fruits outweigh the disadvantages, these disadvantages are worth mentioning. The short growing season on the Prairies seriously limits the extent of small fruit production. Spring and fall frosts pose a very real threat to certain small fruit crops and, indeed, almost any cultivated plant on the Prairies. Because of the short growing season, unless cultivars are carefully chosen, much of the fruit may ripen at the same time. If the fruit is not harvested when it is at its optimum stage of ripeness, there is a reduction of quality and a large amount of wastage. Because small fruits do not store well, they must be preserved if there is a substantial yield. This takes time and effort. Most of the disadvantages of growing small fruits can be overcome by careful site selection, planting hardy cultivars that ripen at different times, and limiting the size of the planting to meet the needs and requirements of the gardener and his family.

## SUMMARY FOR SUCCESS

The following criteria must be met for the home gardener to successfully produce quality small fruits:

- The selected site must provide optimum growing conditions for the plants, taking into account microclimatic and soil conditions.

- Adequate soil preparation helps the plants establish themselves by reducing competition with weeds and increasing the organic matter content, a condition favorable to most small fruits. Ensuring adequate fertility by having the soil tested and supplementing any nutrients that are lacking helps improve the health and yield potential of the small fruits.

- Proper planning with respect to the spacing and placement of various small fruits in relation to one another and other existing plants is important. A well thought out planting plan avoids competition among plants, reduces the spread of disease among various susceptible small fruits by not planting them close together, and makes management of the plantation easier by grouping plants with similar requirements.

- Choose cultivars that are hardy, offer disease resistance, have acceptable quality and are true-to-type. Purchase disease-free stock from reputable nurseries.

- Consistent management is essential in the maintenance of a healthy and productive small fruit plantation. This involves training young plants, cultivating to control weeds, mulching to maintain organic matter levels, providing winter protection as necessary, following an irrigation schedule, pruning the plants to maintain fruit bearing wood, renovating the plantation as required, and controlling insects, diseases and other pests in the plantation.

## SITE SELECTION

Choosing an appropriate site is important in the establishment of a successful small fruit planting. This section outlines the basic requirements of most small fruits so that optimum growing conditions and productivity can be achieved. Specific requirements of some small fruits that differ significantly from the rest are also mentioned.

Consider the following factors when selecting a site:

- slope and air drainage
- exposure to the sun and wind
- soil conditions
- moisture supply and soil drainage

## SLOPE AND AIR DRAINAGE

All small fruits benefit from being planted on a gentle slope with a gradient of about five per cent. This allows surface runoff of water, particularly in the spring when frost in the soil may impede drainage. Avoid steep slopes as these are prone to soil erosion. Plant along the contour of the slope to help prevent erosion.

The site chosen should be higher than surrounding areas to permit good air drainage through and away from the planting. This is important for two reasons. First, cold air drains from high to low elevations (see Climate lesson, Figure 2-5). Consequently, depressed spots can become frost pockets. Early blooming plants, such as the June-bearing strawberry, currants and gooseberries, are especially vulnerable to early spring frosts. Fruits that mature late in the season may suffer damage from early fall frosts. Planting in higher spots will help extend the growing season.

Good air drainage also improves air circulation and reduces the incidence of diseases that thrive in warm, moist spots. Fungal diseases, such as powdery mildew, are especially prevalent under warm, moist conditions.

## EXPOSURE TO THE SUN AND WIND

In general, it is best to plant most small fruits on a north- to east-facing slope. This exposure takes slightly longer to warm up in the spring and will, therefore, delay the opening of buds, preventing their exposure to early spring frost. This is especially important for early-blooming crops, such as the strawberry, currant and gooseberry, as the blossoms are very susceptible to frost and, if damaged, may result in the loss of a season's crop. Currants, gooseberries and blueberries like semi-shade and moist conditions. They thrive with a northern exposure that tends to stay cool and moist.

Planting with a southern exposure to the early spring sun promotes the premature breaking of buds, thereby increasing the risk of early spring frost damage. Southern exposures are also more prone to soil heaving in the winter. This can damage strawberries. Raspberries,

planted on the south side of buildings where reflected heat may be trapped in the winter, may prematurely break their dormancy during warm spells. Subsequent cold spells result in the opening buds then being damaged by freezing. During the growing season, the soil tends to dry out quickly when it is exposed to the south. This is especially detrimental to strawberries, which have a shallow root system. Irrigation requirements of all small fruit crops may increase with a southern exposure.

The grape is the only small fruit that benefits from a southern exposure. This plant requires a very warm location during the growing season and prefers the south side of an east-west wall, where it receives the most exposure to the sun. It must be emphasized that the grape needs a great deal of winter protection because of the southern exposure (see GRAPE CULTURE - WINTER PROTECTION).

Exposure to drying winds may result in a condition of physiological drought where moisture is drawn out of the tissue, causing the buds and bark to dry out. Provide protection from wind exposure for all small fruits. In rural locations, this should be in the form of a shelterbelt on the north and west sides to protect the plants from the prevailing winds. More information on establishing a shelterbelt can be obtained from local district agriculturists or from publications on shelterbelts (see RESOURCE MATERIALS). In urban locations, plants can be protected from the wind by planting them on the lee side of fences, hedges or buildings.

## SOIL CONDITIONS

Soil conditions vary widely across the prairies (see Soils lesson). Small fruits can be adapted to a number of soil types. Most small fruits prefer a light loam soil with good drainage. Currants and gooseberries like a bit heavier loam with a higher moisture-holding capacity. Avoid coarse, gravelly soils as these have low fertility and water-holding capacity. Also avoid soils with a high clay content because they have poorer drainage, are more difficult to manage and may become compacted. These heavier soils are also colder which can delay blooming and the production of fruit.

All small fruits require a high organic matter content in the soil. High levels of organic matter improve the soil's tilth, drainage, aeration, water-holding capacity and nutrient availability. There are a number of practices that can increase the amount of organic matter in the soil (see SOIL PREPARATION).

The pH requirement of most small fruits is slightly acidic to neutral (pH range of 6.0 to 6.5). Extremely acidic soils may require liming with dolomitic limestone to increase pH and the availability of calcium and magnesium which become tied up under conditions of high acidity. However, most Prairie soils have adequate amounts of lime in the soil, so this is not a problem. On the other hand, extremely alkaline soils may be detrimental to plants and even cause lime-induced chlorosis. This results when iron, necessary for the making of chlorophyll used in photosynthesis, becomes chemically tied up with other elements under conditons of high soil pH. Raspberries have exhibited iron deficiency symptoms related to these conditions.

Blueberries and huckleberries prefer acidic soils in the pH range 4.0 to 5.5. This makes their culture limited to places that are naturally acidic, such as where peat bogs have developed or the land was previously cleared of coniferous vegetation whose shedding needles acidified the soil. Adding soil acidifier, such as aluminum sulphate, may temporarily solve the problem, but where soils have a high lime content, as in the Prairies, this acidifying effect will quickly be neutralized.

## MOISTURE SUPPLY AND SOIL DRAINAGE

All small fruits grown on the Prairies require moist, but well-drained conditions. Soil drainage is therefore important, which is why lighter textured soils and higher levels of organic matter are beneficial. Hard pans, which are compacted layers beneath the soil surface, should be avoided. Surface drainage is also important. Water should not be allowed to stand, which is another reason a slight slope is preferred and depressed areas avoided. Standing water eventually results in root damage due to poor aeration and prevents the uptake of nutrients and moisture. The exception is the true cranberry, which is not hardy on the Prairies. These plants

are usually grown in bogs that can be flooded during harvest so that the cranberries can be skimmed off the surface of the water.

A reliable supply of water must be available for the irrigation of small fruits during the growing season. Moisture is especially required in the spring during periods of vegetative growth and also during the period of fruit development. The strawberry, because of its shallow root system, requires more frequent irrigation than other fruits. Currants and gooseberries are moisture loving plants and benefit from irrigation. It is important to water these plants deeply to ensure deep rooting. If plants, such as raspberries and saskatoons, develop deep root systems, they require irrigation only during especially dry periods.

## SOIL PREPARATION

Once the site is selected, the soil must be adequately prepared before establishing any small fruit crops. This should begin the year prior to planting. The main objectives in soil preparation are to:

- control weeds
- increase the amount of organic matter in the soil
- ensure adequate levels of fertility

## WEED CONTROL

Small fruits do not thrive under weed infested conditions. This results in intense competition for moisture, nutrients and light. The year prior to planting, take measures to reduce the weed populations to manageable levels (see Pest Control lesson, METHODS OF WEED CONTROL).

Summerfallowing can be used to discourage the growth of weeds and grasses. The site is left uncropped the year prior to planting and is periodically cultivated to control weeds while they are still small and have not yet set seed. During this period, cultivation can be reduced, but not substituted with the use of a herbicide. The top growth of perennial weeds such as Canada thistle, sow thistle and quack grass can be controlled with paraquat (or a

combination of paraquat and diquat) although further treatment will be required for regrowth of the perennial weeds. However, cultivation together with a few treatments of herbicide will seriously knock them back.

An alternative to summerfallowing is to grow a row crop, such as potatoes, the year prior to planting, that will be hoed or cultivated to control weeds. Whichever method is used, cultivate the site deeply the fall previous to planting. The following spring, a light cultivation will eliminate early germinating annual weeds and prepare the site for planting.

## INCREASING ORGANIC MATTER

Small fruits benefit in many ways from increased levels of organic matter in the soil (see Soils lesson, ORGANIC MATTER). Soils with high levels of organic matter have improved tilth and drainage capacity, and increased aeration, water-holding capacity and nutrient availability.

There are numerous sources of organic matter. Well-rotted cattle manure that is free of weeds is probably the best. However, it must be stressed that the manure be well-rotted, or the new plants may be burned by the high levels of ammonia gas that are given off from fresh manure. Well-rotted manure can be applied to a depth of 7.5-10 cm (3-4 in) in the fall or early spring prior to planting and should be cultivated in to a depth of 20 cm (8 in). Strawberries especially benefit from well-rotted manure added to the soil. Poultry manure can also be used, but with caution. It is twice as strong as cattle manure and should be applied to a depth of 4-5 cm (1.5-2 in.). Again, thoroughly work it into the topsoil.

If manure is not available, other sources of organic matter can be used: leaves, grass clippings, compost, peat moss, sawdust or straw. However, these materials have a much lower content of nitrogen than manure and if nitrogen fertilizer is not added, will reduce the levels of nitrogen available in the soil as they decompose. For example, every 100 m² (1000 sq.ft.) of straw applied 7.5-10 cm (3-4 in.) in the fall, should be accompanied with a 2.5 kg (5.5 lb) of nitrogen fertilizer such as 21-0-0 in the fall, and a second application of 2.5 kg (5.5 lb) nitrogen fertilizer in the spring.

## SOIL FERTILITY

Soil type, climate, management practices, previous crops grown and the amount of organic matter added to the soil all influence soil fertility. Have a soil test conducted to determine the soil's texture, fertility, organic matter content and pH. Soil sample boxes, instructions and soil probes are available from your local district agriculturist or soil testing laboratory.

From the results of the soil test, determine your fertilizer requirements. Usually, if you indicate the crop being grown, a recommendation will be made for you by the soil testing laboratory. On the Prairies, levels of the nutrients should be maintained as follows: 35 kg/acre of nitrogen, 27 kg/acre of phosphorus, and 136 kg/acre of potassium. Soils will generally not require lime or potassium as these occur naturally in most Prairie soils. Prairie soils may be low in phosphorus so incorporating a high phosphorus fertilizer, such as 0-20-0 or 11-48-0, into the subsoil is beneficial. Most small fruits grow within a pH range of 5 to 8. If your soil is significantly above or below this range, the soil testing laboratory should be able to recommend how to amend it.

# ESTABLISHING THE SMALL FRUIT PLANTATION

## PLANNING THE LAYOUT

The layout of a small fruit plantation should be planned in such a way that:

- possible disease and insect problems are reduced

- plants of the same type are grouped in blocks and not interplanted, thus making management practices easier

- adequate spacing is provided to reduce competition among plants and leave room for management practices

## PREVIOUS CROPS AND ALTERNATE HOSTS

Two factors influence the presence or absence of disease and insect problems. The first of these is the previous crop(s) that was grown where the small fruit planting is to be established. Rural gardeners should avoid planting small fruit crops where a grain crop was grown the previous year. During the harvest, grain seeds remain on the soil, resulting in the establishment of volunteer grain the following season. Strawberries and raspberries should not follow one another, nor should they be planted where potatoes, tomatoes, eggplant or peppers were grown in the previous four to five years. Every four to five years, rotate strawberries to a location that has not grown strawberries for four to five years. This prevents the buildup of disease in the soil, such as black root rot of strawberries. It also reduces populations of a destructive insect pest, the strawberry root weevil.

The second factor that influences disease and insect problems is alternate host availability. Disease and insect problems can be avoided by planting small fruits away from alternate hosts that are susceptible to the same insect or disease problems. Because currants and gooseberries belong to the same genus (*Ribes*), they are affected by the same pests and diseases and, therefore, should not be planted next to one another. Saskatoons should not be planted near native saskatoons which may pass on disease and insect pests. They should also not be planted near juniper which is an alternate host for the fungal disease saskatoon-juniper rust (see Pest Control lesson, BACKYARD PEST MANAGEMENT - CONTROL OF SMALL FRUIT DISEASES).

## MANAGEMENT CONSIDERATIONS

Plant small fruits in blocks such that the strawberries are planted in one spot (keep the June-bearing and everbearing varieties separate), raspberries are planted in another, saskatoons in another, and so on. Cultivars of the same kind of fruit may differ in the time it takes to ripen and therefore the date of harvest. Quality may also vary. For these reasons and for easier management, if different cultivars are to

be grown, group them together within the block. Arrange the blocks of small fruits in such a manner that mutual disease and insect susceptibility is avoided. The placement and spacing should also accommodate cultural practices such as cultivation between rows, spraying, irrigation, fertilization and harvesting.

Avoid interplanting small fruits with vegetables. Although some space may be conserved, this greatly hampers the management practices of both crops. Vegetables have different requirements for water, nutrients and cultivation than do small fruits and competition will develop between the vegetables and small fruits. Spraying small fruits to control disease or insect pests may contaminate vegetables grown between the rows. The ability to cross cultivate between the rows with a power cultivator or tractor-drawn cultivator is a convenience that would have to be dispensed with if small fruits were interplanted with vegetables. For similar reasons, small fruit should not be interplanted with fruit trees. The exception might be strawberries when the fruit trees are small and not yet productive. In this case, the land can provide some fruit for the gardener while awaiting the return from his fruit tree orchard. Since strawberries are not a permanent crop, they can be removed when the fruit trees begin to bear.

## SPACING REQUIREMENTS

Adequate space is essential to reduce competition among plants and allow for the cultural practices of the small fruits. Table 12-1 lists the spacing requirements for the small fruits commonly grown on the Prairies. These spacings vary according to the planting system and cultural practices used. For example, a hedgerow planting of saskatoons requires greater row spacing and less distance between plants than the spaced planting system where the distance between plants is equal in all four directions. The available cultivating equipment also influences the row spacing. Plants grown under irrigation can be more closely spaced than those that are not irrigated.

It is important to measure carefully the size of the plot that is to be used for growing small fruits. Based on the spacing requirements of the various

Table 12-1
## SPACING GUIDELINES FOR SMALL FRUITS

| SMALL FRUIT | SYSTEM[1] | INITIAL PLANT SPACING IN ROW[2] (cm) | EVENTUAL PLANT SPACING IN ROW (cm) | ROW SPACING CENTER TO CENTER[3] (cm) | EVENTUAL ROW WIDTH[4] (cm) |
|---|---|---|---|---|---|
| June-Bearing Strawberry | Matted Row | 45-60 | — | 120-150 | 60-75 |
| | Spaced Row | 45-60 | 12 | 120-150 | 60-75 |
| Ever-Bearing Strawberry[5] | Single Row Hill | 30 | — | 90-100 | — |
| | Double Row Hill | 30 | — | 120-150 | 60 |
| Raspberry | Hedge Row | 70-100 | 15 | 300-400 | 45 |
| | Hill[6] | 180 | — | 180 | — |
| Saskatoon | Hedge Row | 180 | 50 | 450-500 | 200 |
| | Spaced Planting | 250 | — | 250 | — |
| Currants | Hedge Row | 150 | 50 | 200-300 | — |
| Gooseberry | Hedge Row | 150 | 50 | 200-300 | — |
| Grape[7] | Trellis | 200 | — | — | — |
| High Bush Cranberry | Spaced Planting | 300 | — | 300 | — |
| Low Bush Cranberry | Hedge Row | 60 | — | 100 | — |
| Bush Cherry | Hedge Row | 150 | — | 300 | — |
| | Spaced Planting | 200 | — | 200 | — |

[1]Systems of planting various small fruits are discussed in each of the cultural sections.
[2]Initial plant spacing varies with soil fertility, moisture and training systems.
[3]Below are found the spaces to which certain plants are thinned in the row.
[4]Row spacing and width varies according to the width of cultivation equipment used.
[5]Ever-bearing (and day-neutral) strawberries produce fewer runners than June-bearing and thus can be more closely spaced.
[6]Plant two canes per hill. Note that hill system and spaced planting system are synonymous with plants being equidistant in all four directions.
[7]Plant grapes 30 cm (12 in) from a south-facing wall.

small fruits in Table 12-1, determine how many plants can be accommodated in each block set aside for their culture. Besides physical limitations, the overall size of the planting should be influenced by the gardener's needs and preferences and the amount of time that can realistically be spent looking after the planting.

## CULTIVAR SELECTION

### CHARACTERISTICS OF GOOD CULTIVARS

Cultivars of the various small fruits grown must be hardy in the climatic zone in which they are to be grown (see Climate lesson, REGIONAL CLIMATE AND HORTICULTURE). They should also be disease free and (preferably) disease and insect resistant. It is no use planting

inexpensive plant material or plants donated from a well-meaning neighbor if they are diseased. Many small fruits are susceptible to viral diseases which can be easily transmitted to newly propagated plants.

Select cultivars so as to stagger the harvest season. If room permits, plant early, mid-season and late-season cultivars to extend the availability of fresh fruit and allow the harvesting to be staggered at different times during the growing season. For the home gardener, quality of fruit should be of greater importance than yield. Finally, it is important that the plants be true-to-type, so that genetically identical plants of the same cultivar have similar growth habits and ripen at the same time.

Purchase plants from a reliable local nursery. Hardiness can almost be ensured if the plants are propagated and raised locally. If ordering plants from a nursery that is not on the Prairies, make

sure the cultivar is hardy for the Prairies. Plants should be vigorous, well-rooted and (preferably) only a year old, as these plants suffer less transplanting shock than older plants. Table 12-2 is a general guideline that lists cultivars recommended for the Prairies.

## STRAWBERRY CULTURE

### BOTANICAL CHARACTERISTICS

Botanically, the strawberry plant consists of a rosette of leaves which arises from a crown (Figure 12-1). Buds develop in the axils of the leaves and differentiate to become flower buds or runners. Runners are the means by which the plants propagate themselves. Runner plants develop from the second node of the runner; they root and become

Table 12-2
## SMALL FRUITS RECOMMENDED FOR THE PRAIRIES

| SMALL FRUIT | TYPE | RECOMMENDED CULTIVARS | | |
| --- | --- | --- | --- | --- |
| | | ALBERTA HORTICULTURAL GUIDE | RECOMMENDED ON PRAIRIES | WORTHY FOR TRIAL |
| **Strawberry** | June-bearing | Protem, Redcoat, Veestar, Senga Sengana, Vibrant | Porter's Pride, Kent, Bounty | |
| | Ever-bearing | Jubilee, Ogallala | | Fort Laramie, Quinalt |
| **Raspberry** | Red | Boyne, Chief, Killarney | | Lathom, Trent, Madawaska, Festival, Fraser |
| | Yellow | Honeyqueen | | |
| **Saskatoon** | Purple/Black | Northline, Smoky, Pembina, Thiesen, Moonlake, Honeywood and seedlings of selected strains | | |
| | White | Altaglow | | |
| **Currant** | Red | Perfection, Prince Albert, Red Cross, Red Lake | Viking A, Stephens | |
| | White | Large White, White Grape, White Imperial | | |
| | Black | Boskoop, Consort, Magnus, Willoughby[1] | | |
| | Albol[2] | Black Giant and other Golden-, Black- and Red-fruited cultivars | | |
| **Gooseberry** | | Pembina Pride, Pixwell[3], Welcome | | |
| **Grape[4]** | Native | Beta, Riding Mountain, Fredonia and selections | White Smith | |
| **Mongolian Cherry[5]** | | Selected seedlings | | |
| **Nanking Cherry[5]** | | Selected seedlings | | |
| **Sandcherry[5]** | | Brooks Sandcherry, Mando, Manmoor and selected seedlings | | |

[1]Resistant to powdery mildew
[2]Also known as Colorado, California Golden, Clove, Cross, Buffalo, Missouri and Golden Flowering Currant.
[3]Fewer thorns
[4]Some European grapes (e.g., Concord) have been grown in very sheltered locations or in greenhouses where they have winter protection.
[5]Ensure two bush cherries are present for cross-pollination.

daughter plants. The crown consists of a vascular cylinder of branched strands that arise from the base of the leaves and spiral part way around the crown, producing primary and secondary roots at the base of the strands. The advantage of this vascular cylinder is that if the roots are damaged or removed on one side of the plant, the leaves connected to these roots can still obtain moisture and nutrients from other leaves and roots that are tied into the vascular cylinder. However, this also means that loss of roots on one side of the plant adversely affects the whole plant. Because of the vascular cylinder around the crown of the plant, proper placement of the plant during planting is important (see Figure 12-2).

Buds of the June-bearing strawberry that give rise to fruit or runners, are initiated under conditions of short day length and cool temperatures, usually experienced the previous fall. In the spring, these buds then flower and give rise to fruit. Ever-bearing strawberries initiate flower buds throughout the summer under conditions of long days and warm temperatures. Because of this continuous production of flowers and subsequent fruits, runner production of ever-bearing strawberries is poor.

The day-neutral strawberry is a fall-bearing type of strawberry that is not

## Figure 12-1
## ANATOMY OF A STRAWBERRY PLANT

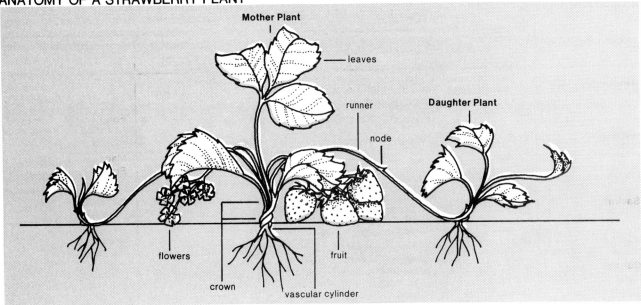

unlike the common ever-bearing strawberry. However, it is notable for its large fruit, greater productivity and superior quality. It is a recent discovery that is being tested at the University of Saskatoon and is not yet available. Preliminary results indicate the cultivars Hecker and Fern are the best and earlier than most ever-bearing cultivars. They are fairly hardy and will respond well to winter protection in the form of straw mulching.

One advantage of this and the ever-bearing strawberry is that a crop of fruit can be produced the first year the plants are set. A second is that there is no danger of damage to the blossoms by spring frost which can significantly reduce yields with June-bearing types.

The strawberry flower is usually perfect and self-pollinating, although the Chilean strawberry has imperfect flowers that require cross-pollination. The flower

buds are borne in the axils of leaves on the crown (see Figure 12-3). The fruit of the strawberry is an accessory fruit that results when several ovaries belonging to a single flower ripen and enlarge while remaining adhered to the receptacle, which becomes the core of the fruit. The seed produced on the surface of the fruit is called an 'achene'. If the flower is incompletely fertilized, a physiological disorder called 'catfacing' results (see Figure 12-4). This is because there is

## Figure 12-2
## PROPER PLANTING DEPTH FOR STRAWBERRY

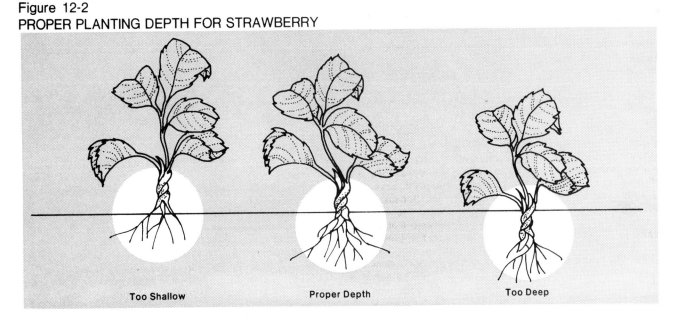

Figure 12-3
## FLOWERING AND FRUITING HABITS OF STRAWBERRY

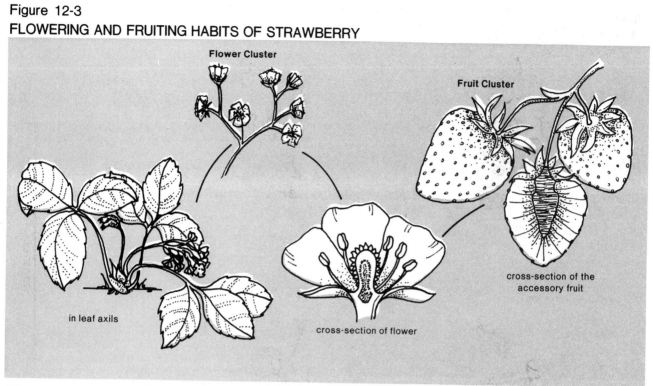

Flower Cluster

Fruit Cluster

cross-section of the
accessory fruit

in leaf axils

cross-section of flower

Figure 12-4
## CATFACING OF STRAWBERRY

Courtesy of Al Schernus (Olds College)

not a uniform developing of seeds on the surface of the fruit and it is the developing seeds which produce a hormone that causes the berry to swell.

## PLANTING

### WHEN TO PLANT
Set plants out early in the spring, usually in mid-May, or as soon as the soil can be worked to provide a level and pulverized planting bed. By planting early, June-bearing strawberries have good runner production and a number of daughter plants established by the end of the first season. In the case of ever-bearing strawberries, some fruit may be obtained during the first season if they are planted early. Planting later in the spring or early summer is only successful if plenty of water is applied, and even then, runner production and plant vigor may be poor. Fall planting is not recommended.

### PLANTING STOCK
Obtain plants from the nursery close to planting time. They should arrive in a dormant state already trimmed for planting. If the plants cannot be planted immediately, they can either be stored in polyethylene bags in a refrigerator at 1-4°C or they can be temporarily heeled-in in a sloping trench that is out of direct sunlight, with soil pressed firmly around the roots, and care taken so that the crown is not covered with soil. Figure 12-24 shows a similar way in which saskatoons can be heeled in while awaiting planting. If plants are home-grown or obtained from a neighbor, they should be vigorous runner plants. These should be dug carefully, runner ends and old leaves removed, and the roots trimmed to 12 cm (about 5 in) prior to planting. Remember that planting home-grown plants increases the risk of introducing disease to the planting.

### PLANTING SYSTEMS
The three most common planting systems are:

• matted row system
• spaced row system
• hill system.

Figure 12-5
STRAWBERRY PLANTING SYSTEMS

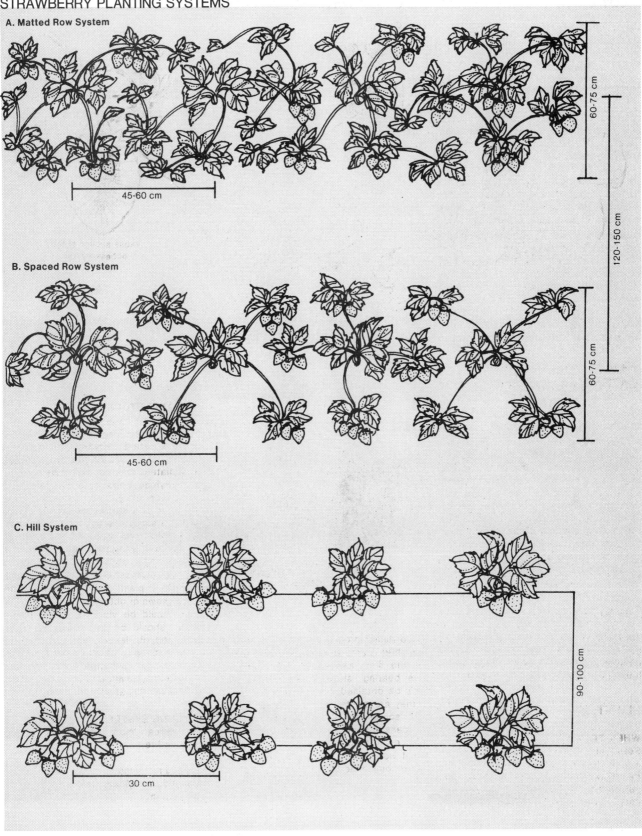

A. Matted Row System

60-75 cm

45-60 cm

120-150 cm

B. Spaced Row System

60-75 cm

45-60 cm

C. Hill System

90-100 cm

30 cm

## MATTED ROW SYSTEM

The matted row system is perhaps the easiest and most practical method for the gardener (see Figure 12-5A). It is best suited to June-bearing strawberries which have good runner production. Spacing requirements are listed in Table 12-1. Mother plants are planted 45-60 cm (18-24 in) apart in rows 1.2-1.5 m (4-5 ft) apart, and encouraged to produce all the runners and daughter plants they can in the first season. Cultivars of ever-bearing and day-neutral strawberries, which produce few runners and daughter plants, may be planted closer. Weed control and the de-blossoming of plants is recommended, as weeds can compete with the new daughter plants, and flowers produced by the mother plants can divert energy away from the production of runners. In the event of excessive runner production, a certain amount of thinning and runner placement may be necessary to reduce competition between plants. Once the matted row has developed to a width of 60-75 cm (24-30 in), cultivate between the rows to maintain this width.

## SPACED ROW SYSTEM

The spaced row system can be used for June-bearing strawberries (see Figure 12-5B). Although this system produces fewer plants, the resulting berries are usually larger and easier to pick. Mother plants are spaced in the same manner as for the matted row system. However, runners produced are placed such that the resulting daughter plants are no closer than 12 cm (about 5 in) apart and are evenly spaced about the mother plant. All other runners are removed. The row is maintained at a width of 60-75 cm (24-30 in) by cultivating between the rows.

## HILL SYSTEM

This system works well for cultivars of ever-bearing or day-neutral strawberries with low runner production (see Figure 12-5C). Planting beds are hilled up to 20-25 cm (8-10 in) high and allowed to settle prior to planting. Plants can be planted in single or double rows and spaced 30 cm (12 in) apart. If double rows are used, stagger the plants. Row spacing from center to center varies from 90-100 cm (36-40 in). Remove all runners so that only the mother plants are maintained. Plastic mulch can be placed over the plants and the plant

drawn through openings in the plastic (see Figure 12-6). The mulch prevents the rooting of any daughter plants.

## SETTING THE PLANTS

Once the beds are prepared and the plot marked out to ensure accurate spacing, begin setting the plants. It is important that the plants be kept moist and not allowed to dry out. This can be done by placing them in containers between layers of moist moss and covering with moist burlap. If the roots are dry, they can be placed in water long enough to wet them and then excess water drained off. Plants should not be submerged in water for more than a few minutes as this can result in root damage.

The depth of planting is very important. Set plants so that the midpoint of the crown is at the same level as the soil surface (see Figure 12-2). If set too deeply, runner production can be delayed, and the crown may rot. If set too shallowly, the crown and top of the roots may dry out.

Hand planting is easily accomplished by

## Figure 12-6
## MULCHING AND OTHER METHODS TO PROTECT PLANTS

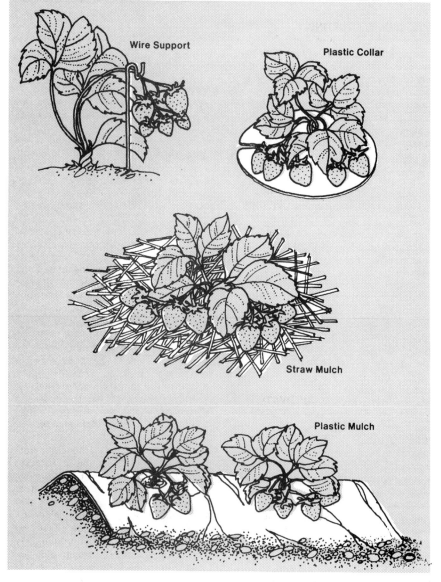

inserting a spade to a depth of about 20 cm (8 in) into the ground and prying open a cavity. Place the plant at the correct depth, with the roots well distributed and fanned out in the hole. Then, withdraw the spade and firm the soil around the plant. Plants should be watered-in after planting to firm the soil around them, reduce transplanting shock and help the plant to become established quickly. A soluble starter fertilizer with a good amount of phosphorus (such as 10-52-10) can also be applied at the correct rate (see STRAWBERRY CULTURE - FERTILIZING).

## MANAGEMENT PRACTICES

### CARE OF THE PLANTING
Management practices in the first season after planting largely determine the success of the crop in terms of quality and yield. Watering during the period of runner development and rooting is important for the plants to become well established the first season. Shallow cultivation, as required to control weeds and prevent crusting of the soil surface, reduces competition and allows for easier rooting of daughter plants. It must be stressed that cultivation be kept shallow so that the root system is not damaged and the soil quickly dried out. With June-bearing strawberries, blossom removal from mother plants throughout the first season after planting promotes earlier and increased runner production. Blossoms developed by ever-bearing strawberries after July may be left to produce berries. Runners should be spaced or thinned to prevent competition among plants for water, nutrients and light. Allow approximately four plants to develop per 0.09 m² (1 sq ft).

### WEED CONTROL AND CULTIVATION
Practice weed control and cultivation the year prior to planting (see SOIL PREPARATION - WEED CONTROL). At this time, eliminate serious weed problems with cultivation and, if necessary, combine this with use of the herbicide paraquat. Other preventative measures against future weed infestations include using a mulch that does not contain weed or grain seeds (see STRAWBERRY CULTURE - MULCHING) and eliminating external sources of weeds in vacant lots, ditches, or the periphery of the planting by keeping these areas mown short or sprayed with an effective herbicide.

For the small planting, use a hand hoe several times during the season to keep the weeds in check. Hoeing should be kept shallow and not too close to the plants to prevent damage to the crown or root system. A small, powered hand cultivator can also be used between the rows on small plots which can reduce the amount of time it takes to weed the plot. Only shallow cultivation is recommended to prevent damaging the root system. Larger plantings may warrant the use of a garden tractor or larger implement. Consider the size of the cultivator before establishing the planting, so that there is sufficient room between the rows to cultivate. The use of herbicides is recommended only for commercial use in large plantings of strawberries.

### IRRIGATION
Strawberries require a continuous moisture supply if fruit size and yields are maximized. Approximately 90 per cent of the root system is found in the top 15 cm (6 in) of the soil. To supply adequate moisture to this root zone, 2.5-3.8 cm (1-1.5 in) of water needs to be added weekly. What is not provided by natural rainfall must be supplemented by irrigation. Sprinkler irrigation or the use of a soaker hose are common methods of adding water.

It is very important that the strawberry plants never be subjected to drought conditions and allowed to wilt. Irrigation is necessary following planting, during runner development and rooting, during fruit production, and at the time of renovation. Frost damage to the blossoms in the early spring can be reduced by irrigating. As the water freezes on the surface of the plants, it gives off heat and reduces the decline in temperature of the tissues, thus preventing or reducing frost damage.

Although strawberries benefit from supplemental irrigation, avoid overwatering. During fruit production, excess moisture results in soft fruit of poor quality. These conditions also predispose plants to greater incidence of disease, particularly those caused by fungi. Nutrients, especially nitrogen, may be leached or flushed through the soil profile to the subsoil under very wet conditions. It is, therefore, a good practice to measure and keep track of the amount of water that is applied to ensure that it is adequate, but not excessive. This can be done by placing rain gauges in several places throughout the planting. These can simply be shallow containers that are marked to indicate their depth. Time how long it takes to add 2.5 cm (1 in) of water. Instruments which measure available soil moisture can also be inserted permanently into the soil, but these are costly.

Cut back watering gradually in the late summer and early fall to permit the plants to prepare themselves for winter by entering a dormant state. After the first few fall frosts, but prior to freeze-up, water the planting heavily to avoid drying out during the winter. Resume irrigation as required the following season.

### FERTILIZING
A soil test is recommended the fall prior to planting to determine the nutrient levels present in the soil (see SOIL PREPARATION). If the soil test indicates any nutrient deficiencies in the soil, correct these by adding the appropriate fertilizer at the recommended rates and working it into the top 20 cm (8 in) of the soil. No further applications of fertilizer should be required the first growing season. The kind and amount of fertilizer will vary considerably according to the soil type, climate, management practice and previous crop, and whether or not manures, composts and mulches are used. Generally, a starter fertilizer (such as 0-20-0 or 11-48-0) that is high in phosphorus should be broadcast over the soil and incorporated prior to planting together with a soluble starter solution (such as 10-52-10) at planting time. After the harvesting of berries, fertilizer containing nitrogen may be added to increase foliage production and leaf size. Nitrogen fertilizer should not be applied to June-bearing strawberries in the early spring as increased vegetative growth may result at the expense of a good yield of berries. Fertilizer should also be added during the renovation of the planting (see RENOVATION).

### MULCHING AND WINTER PROTECTION
There are a number of advantages to mulching strawberry plantings:

- it helps to conserve water by reducing losses to evaporation

- it keeps the fruit cleaner (see Figure 12-6)

- as it decomposes, it maintains a high level of organic matter (nitrogen fertilizer may need to be added to prevent this process from depleting nitrogen available to the plants)

- it can help to suppress weeds

- it can help prevent soil erosion during heavy rains

- it can help prevent heaving due to alternate freezing and thawing

- it can provide winter protection by preventing desiccation and excessive freezing of plants

There are several kinds of mulch that can be used. However, a good mulch should be easily obtained, inexpensive, not so light that it blows away, not prone to packing down, and free from weed seeds, harmful disease organisms and insects. Clean wheat straw is the best, but oat or rye straw are also suitable. Sawdust or woodchips can be used, but require nitrogen fertilizer to break them down. Woodchips may also be rather expensive. Leaves are not recommended as they tend to pack too tightly around plants and smother them. Peat moss is not a good mulch for this application as it sticks to the fruit. Polyethylene can be used as a summer mulch to help control weeds, but may make the plants more susceptible to frosts. This is because the plastic prevents the soil from radiating heat at night and warming the air around the plants. Plastic mulch can be applied after the mother plants have set daughter plants. Stretch the plastic over a row or bed of strawberries on a calm day. Pull the plastic tight and tie it to a stake at either end of the row, then keep soil along the edges of the plastic to keep it from blowing away. If the hill system is being used, the plastic should be put down after the newly planted plants have become established, and these should be pulled through slits in the plastic (see Figure 12-6). The plastic will then prevent the rooting of daughter plants.

For winter protection, apply an organic mulch such as straw after a few light frosts, when the plants have stopped growing and are dormant. If the

## Figure 12-7
## STRAW MULCHING OF STRAWBERRY

### A. APPLY MULCH IN FALL

### B. IN SPRING RAKE MULCH BETWEEN THE ROWS

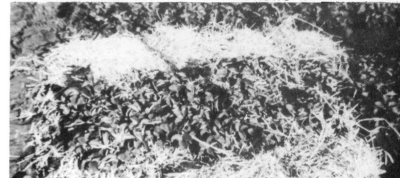

Courtesy of Al Schernus (Olds College)

temperature drops to -7°C and stays, it is time to cover the plants.

Mulch should be applied to cover the strawberries to a depth of 10 cm (4 in) (see Figure 12-7A). When the danger of severe frost is past in the spring and prior to any yellowing of the leaves, remove the mulch from the surface of the plants (see Figure 12-7B). If it is removed too late, blossoming and maturation of the fruit crop is delayed. Some mulch can be worked in around the plants to conserve moisture and discourage weeds. The excess mulch is then raked into the space between the rows. This also helps in weed control and can later be cultivated in to add organic matter to the soil.

## HARVESTING

For maximum quality, pick strawberries on the day they ripen. The berries should have a good red color, but be firm in texture (see Figure 12-8). Overripe berries are easily damaged and spoil readily. At peak harvest, pick berries at least every other day and sometimes every day. The frequency of harvesting depends on the cultivar. The best time of day to pick is early in the morning, when the air temperature and the field heat of the berries are low. Quickly place the berries in a cool place to keep them fresh. Do not wash the berries as this causes them to spoil faster.

## Figure 12-8

## RIPE BERRIES READY FOR HARVEST

Courtesy of Al Schernus (Olds College)

Handle the berries as little as possible to reduce bruising. Separate the large quality berries from the small or misshapen ones during harvesting. When picking, grasp the stem just above the berry and remove it with a slight twist and a pull. This leaves a 1.3 cm (1/2 in) stem on the berry. Place berries in shallow boxes or trays to avoid crushing.

Once picked, the berries deteriorate quickly unless they are cooled to remove the field heat and reduce respiration. Rapid cooling to 0°C reduces the rate of deterioration. Home gardeners should immediately place the berries in a refrigerator.

Pick-your-own operations have increased in popularity as a marketing strategy for commercial small-fruit growers on the Prairies. This method of harvesting allows customers to obtain fresh, high-quality fruit at a more reasonable price than would otherwise be paid at the supermarket. This also reduces the amount of labor, grading, packing and storing that would otherwise need to be provided by the grower, thereby reducing the cost of production.

## RENOVATION

Renovation is usually followed soon after the harvest of June-bearing strawberries to achieve two objectives. The first is to remove old leaves and debris, and expose weeds that need to be removed. This process of sanitation helps in controlling disease. The second objective is to rejuvenate the planting. By fertilizing and watering the planting, new vegetative growth is encouraged which 'sizes up' the plants by increasing the size and numbers of leaves on them.

Plantings are mown at a high enough setting that the growing point of the crown is not damaged, but most of the leaves are removed. The leaves and other debris are then raked aside, composted, burned or otherwise removed. Cultivate between the rows to narrow the row to the desired width and control weeds. Carefully remove weeds that are exposed between the plants by hand cultivation or hand pulling. If the planting is relatively large, herbicides may be used to control weeds (see STRAWBERRY CULTURE - WEED CONTROL). A soil test should indicate the type and amount of fertilizer to be added. Apply fertilizer when harvest is complete, broadcasting it evenly over the plants. Do this prior to mowing. If the plants are mown, the fertilizing must be immediately followed by irrigation to wash the fertilizer off the surface of the leaves and prevent fertilizer burn. Continue irrigation to promote the rapid development of new foliage during the period from mid-July to the end of August. Remove all runners unless they are needed to fill in the gaps. If plants

## PICK-YOUR-OWN OPERATIONS
Vol. 1 No. 1 *The Fruit Grower.* Christina Grant (ed.)

Ten years from now, Susie and Dwayne Frostad may well have ten carefully nurtured acres of strawberries under cultivation on their farm near Beaverlodge. But for now, like many other northwestern fruit growers, they are starting small.

Last summer, Susie and Dwayne managed to set in the ground a half acre of strawberries in rows three feet apart, each plant two feet apart. This past spring, the couple increased the commercial bed to one acre in size, maintaining the previous year's system.

Despite the small size of most of her 1984 berries, Susie encountered ready acceptance at both the local Farmers' Market and in pick-your-own situations. "People seemed to be happy with them anyway; they were glad to get fresh, local fruit." About 100 pounds were snapped up by eager consumers, and the tremendous local demand - and hence potential for growers - became apparent.

Discussing demand for local fruit, the Frostads foresee almost limitless possibilities. "There is a big demand for strawberries. Stores have them for such a limited time." Also, Susie notes, the freshness and quality of local produce does not go unnoticed by the public.

## Figure 12-9
## RENOVATION OF STRAWBERRY PLANTING

Courtesy of Al Schernus (Olds College)

are to be kept for several years, a few runners can be trained to produce daughter plants in the alley along one side of the row (see Figure 12-9). At the end of the season, the row width can be narrowed by removing some of the older plants next to the alley on the other side of the row. This results in one-third to one-half of the bearing row being replaced by younger plants. However, if there is evidence of viral disease, this may not be a practical way of renewing the planting as the mother plants will pass on the disease to the newly established daughter plants. Usually after three harvests, it is less work, yield begins to decline, and it may be desirable to move the bed to another site and start again with fresh plants from the nursery. If the new planting is established in the spring of the old planting's third harvest, it is possible to have strawberries every year.

Renovation is not generally practiced on the Prairies unless the planting becomes overwhelmed with weeds, or the presence of debris increases the incidence of disease such as gray-mold fungus (see Pest Control lesson, BACKYARD PEST MANAGEMENT — CONTROL OF SMALL FRUIT DISEASES). The duration of a strawberry planting may extend from two to four fruiting seasons, depending on the vigor and health of the planting.

# NOVELTY GROWING SYSTEMS

### STRAWBERRY BARRELS

Growing strawberries in a barrel is a unique way to maximize limited space. It may be the only answer for those balcony gardeners who could not otherwise enjoy fresh, home-grown strawberries. Ever-bearing cultivars are commonly used. Figure 12-10 illustrates how to make a strawberry barrel.

Remove one end of the barrel (which is to be the top). Treat the inside of the barrel with a wood preservative. Drill the bottom of the barrel to create a number of drainage holes approximately 5 cm (2 in) apart. Also, drill holes at 30 cm (12 in) intervals along the sides of the barrel. The diameter of the holes should be 5-7.5 cm (2-3 in). If the barrel is to remain in one place permanently, the bottom of the barrel may be removed. However, it is a good idea to leave this in place and put the barrel on casters so that it can be easily moved. To facilitate watering, a central core of perforated tile 10-15 cm (4-6 in) in diameter and extending the full height of the barrel should be placed vertically in the center prior to filling.

Fill the bottom 5 cm (2 in) and the central core with coarse sand or gravel. Then fill the barrel to the level of the first holes with growing medium. Potting soil or a 2:1 mixture of garden soil and peat moss can be used. Water the first layer and allow it to settle before planting. Insert plants into each hole, fitting the

## Figure 12-10
## STRAWBERRY BARREL

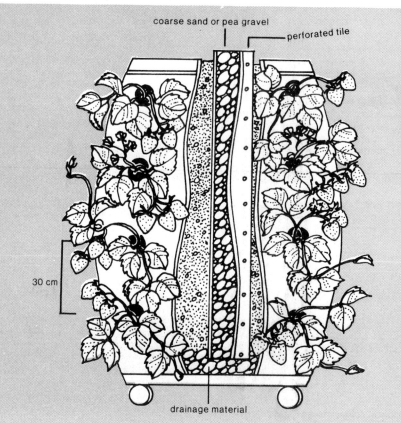

coarse sand or pea gravel

perforated tile

30 cm

drainage material

crown so that it is perpendicular to the surface of the barrel. Be careful not to plant too deep or too shallow (see PLANTING - SETTING THE PLANTS). Spread the roots carefully and cover with soil to the level of the second set of holes. Repeat this process, watering down each layer of soil, until the barrel is filled. When this is accomplished, place an inverted flower pot or can over the central core to prevent debris from entering. The top of the barrel can then be planted as well.

Water the barrel every five to seven days, or when it is dry, by adding water to the central core. This permits a more even distribution of water throughout the barrel. Fertilizer will also need to be added as potting soil is usually void of any nutrients, and even garden soil will have the nutrients leached out after numerous waterings. After planting, add a starter solution that is high in phosphorus (such as 10-52-10) to promote root development. After the harvest of berries, add a solution of tomato-type, soluble fertilizer.

Remove runners as they form, since there is no place for them to root. To overwinter the barrels, wheel them into a garage or cooler that maintains a temperature just above freezing throughout the winter. If there is any chance that temperatures may fall below freezing, wrap the barrel with insulation to protect the plants.

## Figure 12-11
## STRAWBERRY PYRAMID

Courtesy of Alberta Agriculture

### STRAWBERRY PYRAMID

Strawberries may also be planted in a tiered fashion with circular, square or rectangular tiers (see Figure 12-11). Such a system can be used to increase the planting area where space is limited. For a circular shaped pyramid, the bottom tier may be 1.8 m (6 ft) in diameter, with successive layers being 30 cm (12 in.) smaller in diameter and 15-20 cm (6-8 in.) in height. A column filled with sand or gravel may be placed in the center of the planting to facilitate watering or a small cone shaped sprinkler placed on the top of the planting. Lawn-edging strips or wooden boards may be used to create the benches, which are then filled with soil. Plants are then set in alternating rows in each layer.

Such planting systems require more frequent watering than a normal garden. The plants are also more subject to frost damage and winter kill because the temperature of the soil in the tiers fluctuates. Therefore, winter protection must be provided. One method is to water-in the plants well just prior to freeze up and cover with a heavy blanket of straw. Piling snow on the planting also helps to insulate it from winter damage.

### FORCING STRAWBERRIES

For those strawberry lovers who would like to extend their growing season and availability, there is a way in which the plants can be forced by covering them with a plastic tunnel. For an early crop of June-bearing strawberries, cover the plants with double layers of plastic over a U-shaped aluminum frame about March 1. Use a propane heater to prevent the night temperature from falling below 0°C (32°F) and to maintain the daytime temperature at about 15 to 20°C (60 to 70°F). Berries can then be produced starting around the first or second week of April. During the day some solar heat can also be utilized to maintain the temperature inside the structure. If waste heat is available in a fashion that can be economically channeled to the structure, it could reduce the cost of heating with propane.

Plastic tunnels over ever-bearing strawberries can also be used to force a late fall crop of strawberries into October. Place the plastic tunnel over the plants at the end of August. One drawback with this practice is that it prevents the strawberries from entering dormancy in preparation for winter and more winterkill may be observed.

## RASPBERRY CULTURE

### BOTANICAL CHARACTERISTICS

The underground portion of the raspberry plant is perennial. The red raspberry propagates itself by producing suckering canes, which are biennial and arise from adventitious buds on the roots (see Figure 12-12). These canes are rather prickly, and have a semi-erect growth habit. During their first year, they produce only vegetative growth and increase in size and height. The following year, flowers are produced in small clusters on short shoots which arise from the axils of the leaves on two-year old canes. Once the canes have borne a crop of fruit they die. Pruning to remove these spent canes is therefore important (see RASPBERRY - PRUNING).

The flowers of the raspberry are self-pollinating and arise from mixed flower buds (see Figure 12-13). The fruit that results when the flowers are fertilized is called an aggregate fruit and consists of a collection of 'druplets'. Each druplet contains a seed surrounded

## Figure 12-12
### GROWTH HABIT OF RASPBERRY

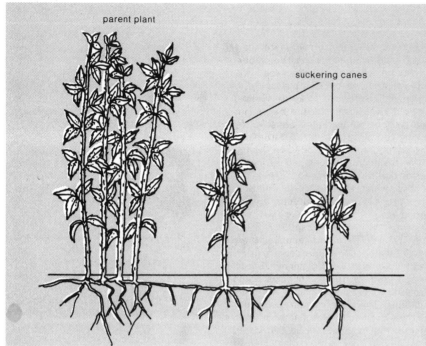

parent plant

suckering canes

with flesh. Unlike the strawberry, the receptacle or core remains on the plant when the fruit is picked. It is important that a high percentage of druplet set be achieved. Crumbly berry is a disease caused by the tomato ringspot virus, which may result in low druplet set and serious reductions in yield.

## PLANTING

### WHEN TO PLANT
Raspberry plants have a tendency to break their buds rather early. To reduce transplanting shock, plant raspberries while still dormant early in the spring, as soon as the ground can be worked. Prepare the soil well, prior to planting, by adding organic matter and controlling weeds (see SOIL PREPARATION).

### PLANTING STOCK
Obtain dormant plants from a reliable nursery close to planting time. Use planting stock that is free of common viral diseases. The plants should be strong, vigorous suckers that have

## Figure 12-13
### FLOWERING AND FRUITING HABIT OF RASPBERRY

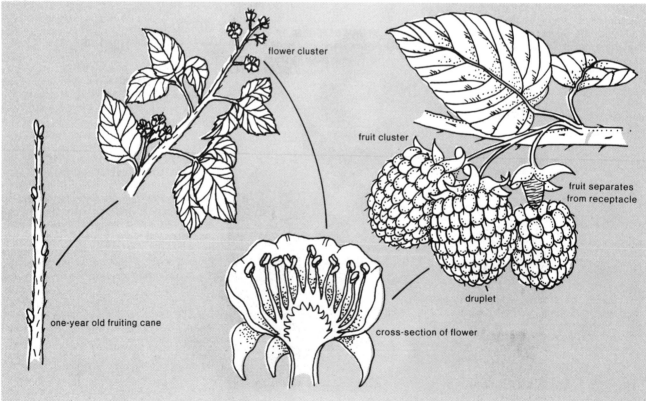

flower cluster

fruit cluster

fruit separates
from receptacle

one-year old fruiting cane

druplet

cross-section of flower

completed one season of growth and are dormant. They should also have a well developed root system. If home-grown plants are to be used, obtain them from a healthy plantation that has no symptoms of viral disease.

Plants can be purchased bare-root or in pots. If bare-root plants have dried out during shipping, allow their roots to soak in water for several hours. Avoid drying out the plants if possible. Potted plants, although more expensive, have the advantage of an established root system which gets the plants off to a better start. If planting is delayed, temporarily heel-in the plants in a sloping trench (see Figure 12-24).

### PLANTING SYSTEMS
Raspberry plants are commonly planted in one of two systems: the **hedgerow** system, or the **hill or spaced row** system. Plant spacings for both systems are given in Table 12-1.

### HEDGEROW SYSTEM
In the hedgerow system, plants are planted from 70-100 cm (26-38 ft) apart in rows 3-4 m (10-13 ft) apart (see Figure 12-14). Suckers that are produced between the original plants are thinned to a 15 cm (6 in) spacing and allowed to develop. The width of the row is maintained at 45 cm (18 in) by means of cultivation. Plants are then allowed to form a hedgerow which may or may not

be modified by some type of training system (see RASPBERRY CULTURE - TRAINING AND SUPPORT SYSTEMS).

### HILL SYSTEM
The other type of planting system is the hill system in which one or two raspberry canes are planted in hills placed 1.8 m (about 6 ft) apart. These plants are then allowed to produce suckers, which are thinned and trained at the beginning of the second growing season (see RASPBERRY CULTURE - TRAINING AND SUPPORT SYSTEMS).

### SETTING THE PLANTS
Once the soil has been prepared and the plot marked out to ensure accurate row spacing, set the raspberry plants. Cross-marking the distances between plants is not necessary with the hedgerow system, but should be done for the spaced row or hill system. Set the plants slightly deeper than they previously grew in the nursery. If planting by hand, set the plants in a similar manner as that described for strawberries, by prying open the soil, inserting the plant, then withdrawing the shovel and firming the soil around the plant. It is important to keep the plants from drying out during planting by wrapping them in moist burlap. It is also important that the soil be firmly tamped and the plants watered in well soon after planting to prevent them from drying out. A starter solution of soluble fertilizer

### Figure 12-15
### PRUNE RASPBERRIES AT PLANTING

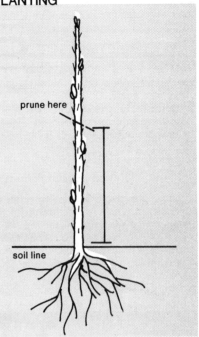

(such as 10-52-10) with a high content of phosphorus can also be added at this time. Once planted, cut the canes back to a height of 15-30 cm (6-12 in) (see Figure 12-15). This promotes early root establishment and the production of vigorous new canes which will arise from lateral buds on the stem and adventitious buds on the roots. If plants are set late in the spring or early summer, do not prune them back as this causes a loss of food reserves and results in a poor stand.

## MANAGEMENT PRACTICES

### WEED CONTROL AND CULTIVATION
Weed control and cultivation begins the year prior to planting (see SOIL PREPARATION). Eliminate perennial weeds, such as quack grass or Canada thistle, during this period, either by continued cultivation or with the treatment of herbicides (see SOIL PREPARATION - WEED CONTROL). Weed control is especially important in the first season after planting, when competition with weeds may significantly reduce the vigor of the plants and even prevent their establishment.

### Figure 12-14
### HEDGEROW SYSTEM

Courtesy of Alberta Agriculture

Chemical weed control is limited to commercial plantings only. Once the plants have been set, cultivate between the rows to keep the weed population down. In small plantations, hand hoeing may be sufficient to kill weeds between the rows. Loosen weeds between the plants with a fork and remove them. Using a hoe this close to the plants may risk root damage. In larger plantations, a tractor drawn cultivator is most practical for weeding between the rows. Consider the width of the cultivator when deciding on the spacing between the rows. Maintain row width at 45 cm (18 in) with hand cultivation.

During the first season, cultivate the space between the rows in both directions, and keep it shallow so that only weeds and suckers between the rows are eliminated and the roots are left undamaged. Since the upper 25 cm (10 in) of soil can contain up to 70 per cent of the root system, cultivation should not exceed a depth of 5 cm (2 in). If roots are damaged by cultivation, the places of injury may become infected with crown gall (see Pest Control lesson, BACKYARD PEST MANAGEMENT — CONTROL OF SMALL FRUIT DISEASES).

When the plants are mature, cultivate in one direction only to minimize injury to the canes. Continue cultivation from the early spring throughout the growing season at regular intervals. During the harvest, cease cultivation, as this may knock berries off the plants and dirty those remaining on the bushes. Following harvest, allow weeds to grow between the rows to use up moisture that might otherwise keep the canes growing vigorously and prevent the plants from entering dormancy before the arrival of cold weather. However, do not allow weeds to go to seed. If a year is particularly wet, seed a cover crop of rye or oats between the rows to help deplete excess moisture. This will cause growth to slow down and allow the plants to harden-off so that they can better withstand the severe cold of winter. After a few fall frosts, the planting can be cultivated to eliminate any weeds, or the cover crop plowed under while it is still green.

If snow cover is poor in the winter, heaving due to alternative freezing and thawing may damage the plants. To reduce this, especially in the case of a new planting, plow a couple of furrows up to the row on both sides of the plants. If a cover crop has been planted, it can be left on during the winter to help catch snow and reduce soil erosion. Plow this under the following spring and add a nitrogen fertilizer to aid in decomposing the added organic matter (see RASPBERRY CULTURE - FERTILIZING).

## IRRIGATION

For high yields and good cane production, irrigation is essential. Small garden plots may be irrigated with a sprinkler or soaker hose. Larger rural plantations may be irrigated with sprinkler systems or by running water into furrows on either side of the row.

Raspberries require approximately 2.5-3.8 cm (1-1½ in) of water per week from the time of blooming until the end of harvest. Water that is not provided naturally by rain should be supplemented with irrigation. Never allow the raspberry plants to wilt. To avoid this situation, begin irrigation when the amount of available soil moisture reaches 50 per cent (see Soils lesson, SOIL WATER). By adding the amount of water mentioned above, the available soil moisture can be brought back to 100 per cent.

Avoid excessive irrigation. Too much water added during fruit development may result in soft fruit, which does not handle or store well. This may also cause leaching of nutrients (especially nitrogen) below the root zone. If proper drainage is not provided, poor aeration may hinder normal root growth and development.

## FERTILIZING

It is strongly recommended that a soil test be conducted in the fall prior to planting to determine the nutrient levels of the soil and to determine what must be added to bring these levels to their optimum. Adequate soil preparation to increase the amount of organic matter in the soil will benefit the planting by increasing the soil's ability to hold moisture and nutrients (see SOIL PREPARATION).

Raspberries require large amounts of nitrogen, phosphorus and potassium to promote vigorous cane production early in the growing season. High yielding, thicker and taller canes result when nutrient levels are optimum. However, a significant amount of vegetative material, and consequently nutrients and organic matter, is removed during pruning each year (see RASPBERRY CULTURE - PRUNING). This material is not left in the soil because it would increase the incidence of disease and would take a long time to break down.

In the early spring, apply a complete fertilizer containing nitrogen, phosphorus, potassium and trace elements in their proper balance. This promotes vigorous cane production. Do not apply excess amounts of fertilizer, especially nitrogen. Excess nitrogen results in very succulent cane production and softer fruit. Fertilizer is usually banded on either side of the row, as application directly to the base of the plants may result in injury.

## MULCHING

Mulch is sometimes used on small plantings of raspberries to conserve soil moisture, control weeds and prevent erosion. By applying a 10-15 cm (4-6 in) layer of straw mulch, for example, weed seedlings are shaded and unable to become well established. This shading also reduces water loss due to evaporation from the soil surface, resulting in a more uniform soil moisture. Mulch is not usually applied during the first year of planting. In the fall or spring, after the first season's growth and a good rain, mulch may be worked in among the plants. The soil should be wet prior to application as, initially, the dry

## Figure 12-16
## PROPER METHOD OF THINNING CANES

prune close to ground without leaving stubs

## Figure 12-17
## THINNING RASPBERRY CANES

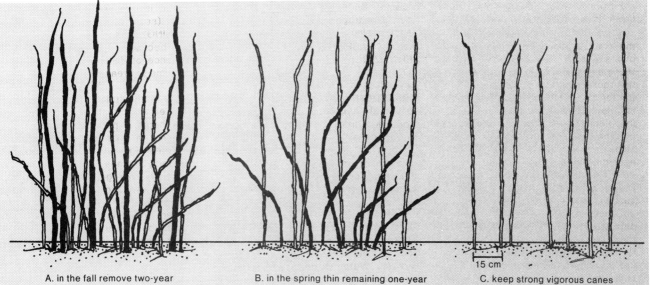

A. in the fall remove two-year
old canes that have borne fruit

B. in the spring thin remaining one-year
old canes

C. keep strong vigorous canes
(10-12 / m of row)

15 cm

mulch will impede the penetration of moisture. It is, therefore, a good idea to wet down the mulch to prevent this. Once wet, the mulch helps to maintain a moist environment.

Mulch may not be practical for larger plantations because of the cost of the material and its application. Damage from mice may also increase if there is a mulch layer for them to nest in. If the year is particularly wet and the mulch prevents the soil from drying out late in the season, maturity of the canes and the onset of the hardening-off process in preparation for winter may be delayed.

## PRUNING
Raspberries should be pruned at planting time to encourage strong lateral branching (see RASPBERRY CULTURE - SETTING THE PLANTS). Red raspberries produce new canes from leader buds found at the base of one-year old canes and from adventitious buds formed on underground stems. These canes have a biennial habit of growth. Their vegetative growth is completed the first year and they produce fruit the following year. After the canes bear fruit, they die. A system of training is necessary to control the natural propagation of the red raspberry canes and prevent them from becoming a dense thicket. Annual pruning and some type of support system is recommended to maintain an

optimum number of strong, vigorous canes which can be easily managed and harvested.

Allow the plants to sucker freely to fill the row during the first year, but cultivate to maintain the row width at 45 cm (18 in). The following spring after planting, thin out the young canes by cutting them out at ground level with 'secateurs' (see Figure 12-16). Remove weak, spindly looking canes first. Thin the remaining strong canes so that they are at least 15 cm (6 in) apart, with an average of 10 to 12 canes per lineal metre of row (see Figure 12-17B and 12-17C). These canes will produce fruit in their second growing season.

After the fruit has been harvested in late summer, remove and burn the fruit-bearing canes (see Figure 12-17A). This practice of sanitation helps to prevent the spread of diseases, such as spur blight (see Pest Control lesson, BACKYARD PEST MANAGEMENT — CONTROL OF SMALL FRUIT DISEASE). However, in those areas where there is minimal snow cover in the winter, the old canes may be left to help trap snow, which is a good insulating material for the plants. The old canes are then removed in the spring. At this time, the new canes produced the previous year should be thinned to a stand of healthy strong canes as mentioned above.

## Figure 12-18
## PRUNE RASPBERRIES IN SPRING TO REMOVE WINTER TIP KILLING

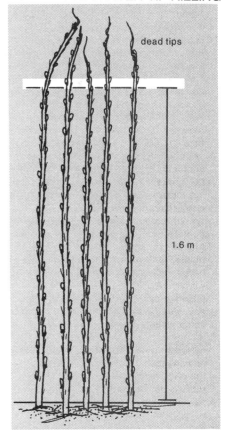

dead tips

1.6 m

Winter tip killing is common with red raspberries. This can be reduced by providing winter protection (see RASPBERRY CULTURE - WINTER PROTECTION). Canes that are injured should be headed back early in the spring, when the extent of damage has been assessed. Canes can be headed back to a height of 1.6 m (about 5 ft) (see Figure 12-18). This only slightly reduces the yield and may delay the harvest by a few days. Severe spring pruning significantly reduces yields and delays harvest even longer. Studies have shown that buds 10-15 (counting down from the tip) are the best yielding and should, therefore, be left if possible.

## TRAINING AND SUPPORT SYSTEMS

Support systems make harvesting and management easier and keep the fruit clean by maintaining the canes in an upright position. Plants left unchecked results in overcrowding, poor light distribution to the whole plant, weak canes that may bend over, and berries that are often difficult to get at. Fungal diseases are more prevalent because air circulation is reduced.

## MODIFICATIONS OF THE HEDGEROW SYSTEM

In this system, place fence posts at intervals down the center of the row with 45 cm (18 in) cross arms nailed to the fence post at a height of 90 cm (3 ft). Run wires down either side of the row at this height and encourage the canes to grow up between the wire support (see Figure 12-19A). With the two-sided trellis, bend half of the fruiting canes to one side of the row and half to the other. Hold the canes in place with clips or ties to the support wire. This gives the row a V-shaped appearance. New suckers tend to be produced down the center of the row. In the one-sided trellis system, bend canes to one side of the row and secure with clips or ties (see Figure 12-19B). A wire on a swinging arm can also be used to secure the canes. Hold the two wires together with clips every 3-4.5 m (about 10-15 ft). New suckers tend to be produced on the opposite side of the row to the fruiting canes. The following year, bend these new canes to the other side.

## MODIFICATIONS OF THE HILL SYSTEM

The hill system is well suited to the small garden plot where space permits the

### Figure 12-19
### TRAINING AND SUPPORT SYSTEMS FOR RASPBERRIES

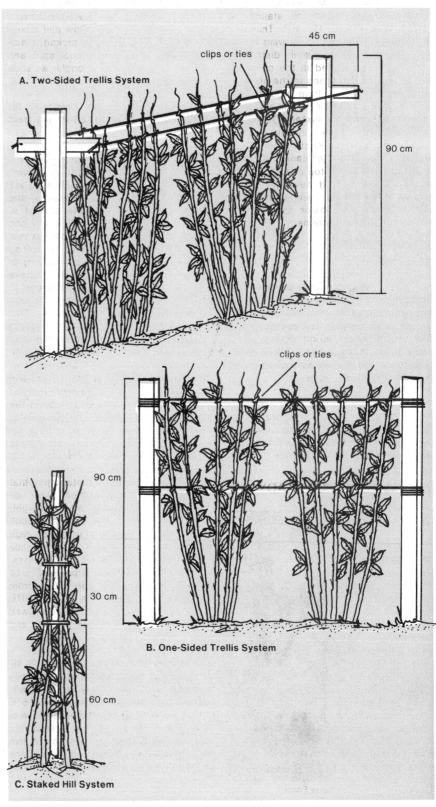

A. Two-Sided Trellis System

clips or ties

45 cm

90 cm

clips or ties

90 cm

30 cm

60 cm

B. One-Sided Trellis System

C. Staked Hill System

growing of only a few raspberry plants. With this system, raspberries are trained to grow in clumps. One way to support these canes is called the staked hill system (see Figure 12-19C). Thin new canes early in the spring, leaving five to eight vigorous ones well distributed around a stake placed in the center of the clump. Tie the canes to the stake at about 60 cm (24 in) from ground level. Another modification of the hill system is called the teepee-hill system. Select 5-8 canes spaced in such a manner that the base of the hill is at least 35 cm (14 in) across. Then tie the canes together tightly, one tie at the top and another 20 cm (8 in) lower. Fruit develops on the outside of the circular cane arrangement and is, therefore, easier to pick with either of these hill systems.

## HARVESTING

Pick raspberries when they are ripe (see Figure 12-20). Firm, well-colored berries that easily separate from the receptacle are ready for harvest. Raspberries ripen over a 2-3 week period during which berries should be picked every other day. To extend the season, plant early, mid-season and late varieties.

The best time of day to pick is early in the morning when the temperature is cool and the field heat of the berries is low. Picking in the heat of the day results in softer, drier berries. Handle

### Figure 12-20
### RIPE RASPBERRIES READY FOR HARVEST

Courtesy of Birchland Berry Farm

berries as little as possible, and place them in shallow trays to avoid crushing the berries on the bottom. If large quantities are to be harvested, construct picking trays to hold shallow pint boxes (see Figure 12-21). Once picked, place the berries in a shady, cool spot and transfer to a refrigerated cooler as soon as possible.

The optimum storage condition for raspberries is 0°C and 85-90 per cent relative humidity. Under these conditions, quality berries can be maintained for two to three days. This can be extended somewhat by placing dry ice in the storage room. The dry ice gives off carbon dioxide, reducing the rate of respiration and the spread of fungal growth. If these special conditions are not available, place the berries in a refrigerator immediately after harvesting and preserve the surplus by freezing or canning. Berries which have over-ripened in the field and dropped to the ground should not be included with those picked from the canes. This increases the incidence of soft rotting due to fungi. For rural gardeners who have larger raspberry plantations with commercial potential, a pick-your-own operation, in which customers come and harvest the berries themselves, may be the best and easiest way to market the berries (see PICK-YOUR-OWN OPERATION).

## WINTER PROTECTION

There are two types of winter injury that commonly affect raspberries grown on the Prairies. The first is winter drought, which is especially prevalent in chinook zones and other areas prone to high winds during the winter. These winds tend to draw moisture out of the canes, leaving the plants dessicated. To prevent this, shelter the plants from prevailing winter winds (see SITE SELECTION). Also, water-in plants well in the fall after growth has stopped and prior to ground freezing.

The second type of winter injury is tip killing. Raspberry buds have a tendency to break their dormancy in the early spring if temperatures remain above 5°C for three or four days. This occurrence of false spring, followed by a return to freezing temperatures, kills the active buds. It is usually the top portion of the canes that are affected, since they break dormancy first. Consequently,

### Figure 12-21
### PICKING TRAY FOR RASPBERRIES AND OTHER SMALL FRUITS

many of the raspberry canes will have dead tops when real spring does arrive.

To avoid the problem of winter injury, take these precautions:

- Grow only hardy varieties recommended for your horticultural climate zone.

- To prevent early breaking of dormant buds, avoid establishing plants on a site with a southern exposure.

- Shelter plants from prevailing winds to prevent desiccation.

- Ensure that plants are allowed to harden-off late in the growing season. If excess soil moisture is present to prevent this, sow a deep rooted cover crop after harvest to help draw this moisture off. It is also important to choose a site with adequate drainage.

- In places where snow cover is poor, leave old canes and the cover crop, if present, through the winter to catch snow. Remove the old canes the following spring.

- Water-in plants well in late fall after growth has stopped and prior to the ground freezing.

- In areas where snow-cover is not maintained, bend the canes over while they are still relatively flexible and cover them with soil to a depth

## Figure 12-22
## PREVENTING WINTER TIP KILLING

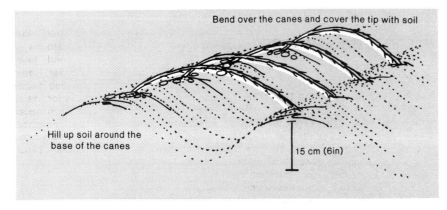

Bend over the canes and cover the tip with soil

Hill up soil around the base of the canes

15 cm (6in)

of 10-15 cm (4-6 in) at their highest point. Remove soil the following spring, before the buds swell. They are able to withstand -15°C temperatures without injury. A fork can be inserted and used to pry the plants out of the soil, which should then be leveled around the plants. Uncovering the plants too late, when succulent shoots have sprouted from the buds, may make the plants more susceptible to frost injury.

In areas with a greater amount of snow cover, it may only be necessary to cover the growing tips with soil (see Figure 12-22). With two people working together, one bends the canes over, while the other shovels soil onto the tips to hold the plants in place. Remove the soil in the spring, as mentioned previously.

### DURATION AND RENOVATION OF THE PLANTING

Raspberry plantings can remain productive for 8-10 years if properly managed. Regular irrigation, fertilization and weed control extends the life of the plantation. Controlling insect and disease problems as they arise helps to maintain the health of the plants.

Once the root system becomes crowded within the row, sucker production decreases. At this time, renew the plantation or replant. If the plantation appears to be free of disease, particularly viral diseases, suckers can be allowed to form between the rows and these transplanted to a new site. It is recommended, however, that certified,

disease-free plants be purchased from a nursery to ensure that a healthy new stand is established. Locate the new planting in a place that has not grown raspberries for at least four or five years to ensure that the soil is not infected (see SOIL PREPARATION). This new location should be some distance from the old, especially if the old planting was diseased.

## SASKATOON CULTURE

### BOTANICAL CHARACTERISTICS

The saskatoon is a native shrub that grows to a height of 4-5 m (13-16 ft). It is most successfully propagated by seed, although this results in variations among seedlings. Seeds must go through a process called 'after-ripening' in order to germinate (see SASKATOON CULTURE - GROWING PLANTS FROM SEED). There has been limited success in vegetative propagation by means of suckers, root cuttings and softwood cuttings. Although these asexual means of propagation result in plants that are identical to the parent plant, it is not as easy as growing seedlings from seed. The shrub itself has quite a long juvenile phase. It usually takes six or more years before the plants produce any fruit and eight or more years before they are fully productive. Once mature, however, the stand should remain productive for up to 15 years.

The white flowers of the saskatoon are borne on short racemes and are

generally self-pollinating, with the exception of the white-fruited cultivar Altaglow which is self-sterile and requires cross-pollination. The fruit is usually a purplish-blue to black, although there are red- and white-fruited cultivars as well. Botanically, it is a 'pome fruit' (see Figure 12-23).

## PLANTING

### GROWING PLANTS FROM SEED
Saskatoons are most commonly propagated from seed. The seed is collected as soon as the fruit is ripe, separated from the fruit and dried. Scratching the seed scars the seed coat and allows moisture to enter the seed. The imbibing of moisture takes place during a process called stratification, which subjects the seed to cold, moist conditions that bring about after-ripening of the seed and the breaking of dormancy (See Plant Propagation

## Figure 12-23
## SASKATOON FRUIT

Courtesy of Birchland Berry Farm

lesson, TREATMENT FOR SEEDS WITH A HARD SEED COAT AND OTHER BARRIERS TO GERMINATION). Seed is layered in damp peat moss and stored at 2-7°C for a period of about 90 days. When the seed begins to germinate, it should be planted.

### TRANSPLANTING SEEDLINGS
From seed, it takes approximately two years to produce seedlings of suitable size for planting. Although purchasing seedlings from nurseries is considerably more expensive than purchasing seed, it is much more expedient. Young saskatoon plants are ready to transplant when they have developed good root systems and the top growth has reached 15-30 cm (6-12 in) in height.

Plant early in the spring, as soon as the ground can be worked. Soil should be well prepared prior to planting to ensure good weed control and high organic matter content (see SOIL PREPARATION). Because young saskatoons compete poorly with weeds, avoid a weedy situation as it may frustrate efforts to establish a saskatoon plantation.

Plant spacing is listed in Table 12-1. The spacing varies, depending on whether one is establishing a hedgerow or spaced row system (see Figure 12-14). Mark or stake the plot prior to planting to ensure adequate and even spacing.

When planting the young plants, keep the roots moist and intact. Place the plants in a bucket of water to avoid drying out. Set plants slightly deeper than they were in the nursery. Hand planting is the same as that described for strawberries and raspberries. Firm the soil around the plants. Water-in plants at the time of planting and add a starter solution of fertilizer (such as 10-52-10) that is high in phosphorus. If watering is to be done by hand, form a circular depression around the plant to retain the water.

Limited success can be achieved by vegetatively propagating saskatoons by means of suckers taken from established bushes. Although this may result in establishing the plantation more quickly, there is no guarantee that the suckers are disease-free, and there is, therefore, the risk of introducing diseases, particularly viral diseases, into the new plantation.

If planting is delayed, the plants can be temporarily heeled-in in a sloping trench (see Figure 12-24). Keep them moist and plant as soon as possible.

## MANAGEMENT PRACTICES

### WEED CONTROL AND CULTIVATION
Because young saskatoon plants compete poorly with weeds, maintain a clean planting. Cultivate at regular intervals on either side of the row to maintain a 50 cm (20 in) row width. Keep cultivation shallow to maintain a favorable condition for root development. When the plants are small, cross cultivation with a rototiller may be possible to control weeds. Later, control weeds within the row by hand hoeing. Eventually, allow suckers to grow and fill in the row if a hedgerow system is being established. If a spaced row system is used, continue cross cultivation for the life of the planting, and do not allow suckers to become established between the plants. Because saskatoons have such a long juvenile period before fruit production begins, it may be practical to interplant the plantation with strawberries or some type of vegetable row crop between the rows until maturity

is reached. Maintain shallow cultivation of 1 m (3 ft) strips down either side of the row of saskatoons, however, to allow for good root development.

There are currently no herbicides registered for use on saskatoons. A number of herbicides are currently being tested and one has, so far, been proposed. It should not be long before one or more will be registered for use on larger size plantations. However, cultivation still must be practiced regularly to control weeds. Herbicides, when they become available, should complement cultivation.

### IRRIGATION
Irrigation must be available for saskatoons. Although the saskatoon plant is fairly drought tolerant, the fruit is small, drier and ripens unevenly in the clusters in dry years. This poses problems in harvesting. Provide good drainage in a very wet season, as saskatoons won't tolerate wet feet.

When the orchard is young, especially the first season after planting, plants need continual spot irrigation. Once the plants are established, irrigation may only be necessary during dry spells. When the plants are mature and

### Figure 12-24
### HEELING-IN OF SASKATOONS OR OTHER SMALL FRUITS PRIOR TO PLANTING

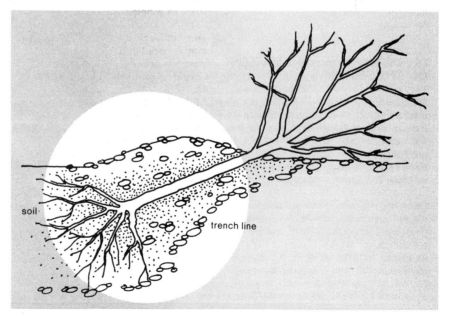

producing fruit, irrigation from the time of fruit set until harvest promotes maximum fruit size, quality and even ripening. Under dry conditions, uneven ripening can extend harvest over a period of a few weeks, while in wet years, the harvest period is significantly shorter.

Discontinue irrigation after August 1 to permit the plants to harden off. In a very wet year, if there is no other crop growing between the rows to take up the excess moisture, a deep-rooted cover crop, such as annual rye or oats, may be seeded after harvest and grown to promote hardening-off of the plants. This crop may be plowed under in the fall or early spring. Late fall watering, prior to freeze up, ensures an adequate moisture supply throughout the winter and early spring and reduces winter injury due to desiccation. Desiccation is generally rare with saskatoons as they are very winter-hardy, native plants.

### FERTILIZING
Determine fertilizer requirements from the results of a soil test the previous fall (see SOIL PREPARATION). It is generally a good idea to water-in plants at planting time with a starter solution containing phosphorus to promote root development. For the first few years during the juvenile period, apply fertilizers with relatively high amounts of nitrogen to promote the development of strong, vigorous, bushy plants. When the plants have reached maturity (in six to eight years), apply nitrogen in proper balance with phosphorus and potassium to maximize fruit production.

### MULCHING
Mulching between the plants may assist in suppressing the establishment of weeds within the row. The mulching layer should be 7.5-10 cm (3-4 in) thick to keep weeds from pushing through. One grower tried sawdust over a generous application of well-rotted manure. Clean straw can also be used. Remember that some types of organic matter, such as sawdust and straw, require nitrogen for decomposition. This should be supplemented with either an application of well rotted manure or nitrogen fertilizer. Plantings should always be irrigated after mulch is applied in the spring, as it takes a lot of moisture to wet dry mulch and this may otherwise prevent the penetration of moisture. Straw mulch should be removed in the

fall as it may attract mice, which can do considerable damage to the plants.

### PRUNING
When they are juvenile, saskatoon bushes are trained to develop and maintain a desirable form and to promote vigorous vegetative growth. Maintain row width by cultivating on either side to remove stray suckers. Prune to shape the bushes in the early spring when the plants are dormant. This reduces desiccation and winter injury where the cuts are made. Do not allow height to exceed 1.8 m (6 ft). Select several main stems that are well spread, so that the center is not too dense. Remove weak stems and dead, diseased or damaged wood. When removing diseased wood, disinfect pruning tools in a disinfectant solution of 50 mL Lysol per 1 L water (4 tbsp Lysol per qt water) to prevent the spread of infections. Remove all cuttings from the site and burn them to maintain sanitation.

When the plants have matured and fruit production has begun, pruning should not only maintain shape, but promote productivity as well. Fruit is produced on short lateral branches arising from wood that is one or more years old and is usually borne in clusters containing 7-13 berries. Flower bud initiation begins the previous season. These buds are subjected to a cold treatment during the

winter to break their dormancy, and produce flower clusters the following growing season. Young wood produces the highest quality berries which are large, juicy and sweet, while older stems with more branches produce greater yields. These stems may produce for 15-25 years. However, productivity may decline when stems reach 4-5 years of age, at which time they should be removed to allow younger, more vigorous ones to replace them. Pruning reduces the total yield in the following season. It should, therefore, be conducted with great moderation and on a consistent basis, so that severe pruning is not necessary.

There are two types of pruning cuts. The first is called a **heading back cut**. This involves the removal of the terminal portion of a branch or stem and should be made just above an outward-facing lateral branch or bud (see Figure 12-25A). This type of cut encourages lateral branching below the cut. Although it has not been proven, this would likely result in a greater amount of young fruiting wood. The second type of pruning cut is the **thinning cut** (see Figure 12-25B). The purpose of this cut is to remove dead, diseased, damaged or crowded branches and open up the center of the bush to allow better light distribution and air circulation. These cuts are made flush to the branch from which the portion being removed has

### Figure 12-25
### CONTRAST OF HEADING BACK AND THINNING CUTS

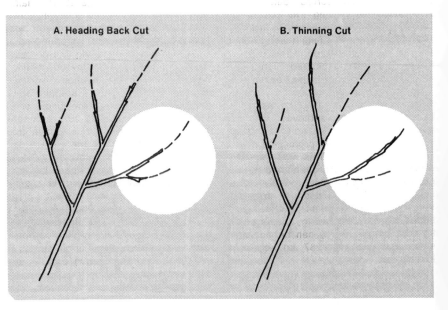

A. Heading Back Cut   B. Thinning Cut

originated. Again, conduct all pruning in the early spring when the plants are dormant, and disinfect pruning tools if disease is apparent.

It should be mentioned that the effects of pruning saskatoons have not yet been tested in scientific trials. The above information can only be provided as general guidelines until more conclusive information becomes available.

## HARVESTING

Under ideal moisture conditions or irrigation, clusters of saskatoon fruit ripen fairly evenly over a short period of time. In drier years without supplemental irrigation, it may take a few weeks for the crop to ripen, which hampers harvesting procedures.

Fruit is ready for picking when it is ripe and blue-black in color. When picking and handling the fruit, avoid damaging the berries. Shallow trays reduce the possibilty of crushing berries at the bottom of the container with the weight of those on top (see Figure 12-21). Overripe, shrivelled or damaged fruit decrease the quality and shelf life of the berries.

Harvest in the early morning when it is cool. Keep berries in the shade after picking and transfer to cool storage as soon as possible. Clean the fruit by immersing it in cold water and allowing debris to float to the top. Afterward, cull berries can be sorted out. Before packaging and placing the fruit in the cooler, it should be surface dried to reduce the spread of fungi (such as gray botrytis mold) in storage. If fruit is being frozen, it can be packaged slightly wet to minimize drying out in the freezer.

A maximum yield of 1097 kg/ac (2417 lb/ac) has been achieved with an average yield of 777 kg/ac (1713 lb/ac) in the first six years of production of one saskatoon orchard. This was possible without irrigation, fertilization and regular pruning. It works out roughly to a maximum of 2.3 kg/bush (5 lb/bush). With proper management practices, it is believed yield from healthy plants of 4.5 kg/bush (10 lb/bush) can be achieved with yields up to 2287 kg/ac (5040 lb/ac).

# CURRANT AND GOOSEBERRY CULTURE

## BOTANICAL CHARACTERISTICS

Currant plants have fairly upright stems which are not prickly. It is important to distinguish the black currant from the red and white currant, particularly when considering their pruning requirements (see TRAINING AND PRUNING - BLACK CURRANTS). Black currants produce fruit on young new wood of the previous season's growth. Red and white currants, on the other hand, produce fruit on short spurs found on two- and three-year old wood. Currants are usually propagated by hardwood cuttings, although if only a few plants are to be produced, trench layering can be used(see Plant Progatation lesson, LAYERING).

The flowers are borne in elongate clusters and are rather inconspicuous (see Figure 12-26). In almost all cases, the currant is self-pollinating. However, some black currants are self-sterile because their floral structure is such that the stigma of the pistil extends past the anthers, making it difficult for insects to transfer pollen to the stigma. These rare exceptions would require cross-pollination. Botanically, the fruit is a true berry.

The gooseberry belongs to the same genus (*Ribes*) as the currants. The woody stems are erect and covered with spines. Gooseberries are propagated in quantity by mound layering, but can also be propagated by hardwood cuttings (see Plant Propagation lesson, CUTTINGS). The flowers are similar to the currant, but are borne singly or in pairs (see Figure 12-26) and are self-pollinating. The fruit is also a true berry. It is larger than the currant and can be red, green, yellow or white in color with longitudinal stripes. The fruit of the European gooseberry is slightly hairy while that of the American gooseberry is smooth. The fruit is borne on spurs of two- and three-year old branches. Some fruit may also be borne along the sides of one-year old shoots. It is pruned in the same manner as red and white currants.

## PLANTING

### WHEN TO PLANT
Currants lose their leaves early in the fall and resume their growth early the following spring. While the plants are still dormant in early spring is probably the best time to plant. However, currants can be planted successfully in the fall. In this case, plant in early September or after the plants have lost their leaves. This should enable the establishment of some root growth prior to the onset of winter. Water plants heavily before the ground freezes to help reduce winter injury and to provide an ample supply of water for the plants the following spring. Hilling up soil around fall set plants provides additional winter protection. Rake level again in the spring.

Gooseberries may not respond as well as currants to fall planting. They generally lose their leaves later in the fall and, therefore, may not be ready for fall planting in time to allow for some root development. Early spring planting is more successful.

### PLANTING STOCK
Obtain healthy, vigorous, one-year old plants with a well established root system from a reliable nursery. Two-year old plants are more expensive and suffer greater transplanting shock.

Plants may also be propagated from a neighbor's bush by means of cuttings or layers, however, it will take at least a year to obtain sizable plants ready for planting (see Plant Propagation, ASEXUAL PROPAGATION). Take hardwood cuttings in the fall from dormant, vigorous shoots of the current season's growth. Make sure the parent plant is healthy so that no disease is passed on. Figure 12-27 demonstrates how to propagate currants and gooseberries from cuttings. Store the cuttings over the winter in a box containing moist sand. Keep them in a cool place. In the spring, plant cuttings in a sheltered moist location 15 cm (6 in) apart and deep enough so that one or two buds are exposed in the case of black currants and three or four for red or white currants and gooseberries.

Figure 12-26
FLOWERING AND FRUITING HABIT OF CURRANT AND GOOSEBERRY

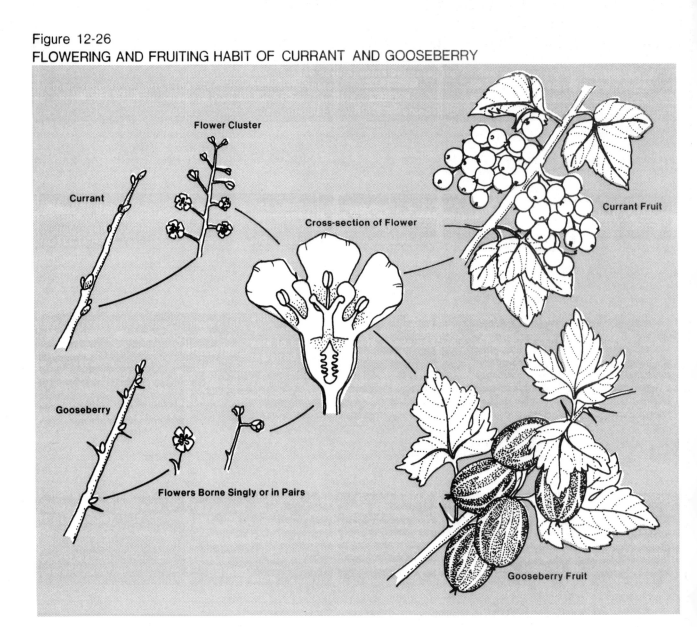

Flower Cluster

Currant

Cross-section of Flower

Currant Fruit

Gooseberry

Flowers Borne Singly or in Pairs

Gooseberry Fruit

Currants and gooseberries can also be propagated by trench layering. A few lower branches are bent over, partially covered with soil, and held in place with the tips of the branches exposed. Scarring the branches slightly with a sharp knife in the spot where it will be in contact with the soil may enhance rooting. Rooting usually takes a year, after which the newly rooted plants may be removed. They may need an additional year in a nursery to develop good root systems before they are ready to plant.

## SETTING THE PLANTS

Currants and gooseberries are commonly planted in hedgerows. Spacing requirements are given in Table 12-1. Keep plants moist during planting. If this should be delayed for an extended period of time, heel-in the plants in the same manner as described for other small fruits prior to planting. Prune off any damaged roots with a sharp knife or pair of secateurs. Set the plants slightly deeper than they were previously grown in the nursery. This can be most easily done with two people working together,

as previously described for other small fruits. Prune the plants back to a height of 15 cm (6 in) subsequent to planting, to encourage the development of lateral buds. Water-in the plants immediately after planting. A starter fertilizer solution high in phosphorus may also be applied at this time.

## Figure 12-27
## PROPAGATING CURRANTS AND GOOSEBERRIES BY HARDWOOD CUTTINGS

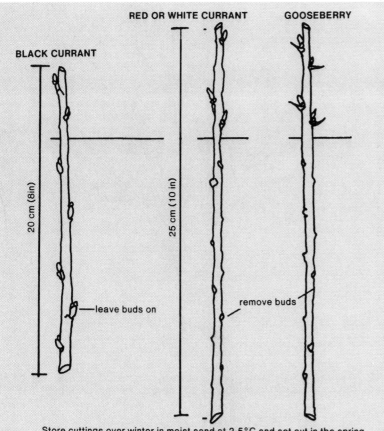

BLACK CURRANT
RED OR WHITE CURRANT
GOOSEBERRY

20 cm (8in)
25 cm (10 in)

—leave buds on
remove buds

Store cuttings over winter in moist sand at 2-5°C and set out in the spring.

# MANAGEMENT PRACTICES

## WEED CONTROL AND CULTIVATION
Begin weed control during soil preparation (see SOIL PREPARATION) and continue throughout the life of the planting. Both currants and gooseberries are moisture-loving plants. To maintain ideal growing conditions:

- Eliminate weeds which compete for moisture, nutrients and light.

- Keep cultivation shallow to prevent excessive drying of the soil.

- Prevent exposure of feeder roots close to the surface.

There are no herbicides registered for use on currants and gooseberries.

## MULCHING
Although clean cultivation helps control weeds throughout the growing season, weeds can also be suppressed with a layer of mulch applied in early spring. This also considerably reduces the amount of moisture lost from the soil due to surface evaporation. As well, mulch keeps the soil temperatures cool, which both currants and gooseberries like. Mulch thickness should be 10-15 cm (4-6 in) for currants and 5-7.5 cm (2-3 in) for gooseberries. Clean straw or some other suitable material can be used. After harvesting, incorporate the mulch into the soil and cultivate the planting through to the fall to control weeds.

## IRRIGATION
As mentioned, currants and gooseberries thrive under moist conditions. Provide irrigation to maintain soil moisture especially when the plants are becoming established. Irrigation during the period between fruit set and ripening increases yield. Cut back irrigation after harvesting to encourage the onset of dormancy. Grow a green manure crop such as peas, oats or rye the season before planting and turn under while it is still green to add organic matter and nitrogen.

## FERTILIZING
A soil test the fall prior to planting and periodically throughout the life of the planting assesses the fertility status of the soil and indicates what nutrients soil requires to provide optimum growing conditions for the plants. Both currants and gooseberries are heavy feeders. In subsequent years, this can be maintained in the planting by adding manure in the fall and working it in the following spring or by fertilizing with a suitable nitrogen fertilizer early each spring. Adding phosphorus at planting time encourages root development. Because phosphorus is also used by mature plants for fruit development, add it in balance with nitrogen.

## TRAINING AND PRUNING
The training and pruning of black currants differs from that required for red and white currants and gooseberries. The reason for this difference arises from the age of fruiting wood. As discussed earlier in this lesson, black currants bear fruit on one-year old wood of the previous season's growth. Therefore, the main objective is to promote a good supply of vigorous young wood. With red and white currants and gooseberries, fruit is borne on older wood, generally on short spurs produced laterally from two- or three-year old wood. The objective of pruning these fruits is to remove wood that is older than three years and replace it with younger growth in a continuous thinning and renewal process. Prune in the early spring, while plants are still dormant.

### BLACK CURRANTS
After planting, prune black currant plants back to 15 cm (6 in) leaving several buds close to the soil level. These buds develop into shoots the season after transplanting. The following year, these shoots bear fruit. In the spring of the first year after planting, select 6-8 fruiting canes and head back the rest, leaving

## Figure 12-28
## PRUNING CURRANTS AND GOOSEBERRIES

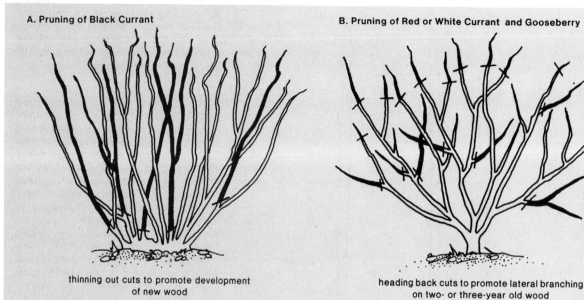

**A. Pruning of Black Currant**

thinning out cuts to promote development
of new wood

**B. Pruning of Red or White Currant and Gooseberry**

heading back cuts to promote lateral branching
on two- or three-year old wood

only one or two buds. This promotes the production of young shoots from the base of these canes.

The tips of remaining canes should not be headed back. Each succeeding spring select six canes of the previous season's growth and leave 2-4, two- or three-year old canes, provided this older wood is well-equipped with vigorous, young lateral shoots. Remove the undesirable canes with a thinning cut (see Figure 12-25B). Figure 12-28A demonstrates how to prune a mature black currant bush.

### RED OR WHITE CURRANTS AND GOOSEBERRIES
Plants can be trained to produce shoots from a short single stem, or from stools similar to that described for black currants. The advantage of training them as stools is that winter injury or disease that affects one branch does not necessarily involve the entire bush. This latter training system is perhaps more practical for the Prairies. At planting, choose 3-4 main stems that are well distributed and head them back to leave two buds per stem, reducing the height of the plant to about 15 cm (6 in). The spring of the second year after planting, select six of the strongest shoots of the previous season's growth and remove weaker canes. Head back (see Figure

12-25A) these shoots one-third their length to promote lateral branching. The spring of the third year following planting, leave the six shoots selected the previous year, which are now two-year old shoots, and select three, one-year old shoots from the previous season's growth. Terminal growth of all main branches should be headed back to promote lateral branching, or the further development of existing laterals and fruiting spurs on two-year old wood. In subsequent prunings, maintain a total of nine shoots, with three, one-year old shoots; three, two-year old shoots; and three, three-year old shoots. Remove wood that is older than three years, unless the plant is especially vigorous, in which case a few four-year old stems containing good amounts of two- and three-year old lateral branches may be allowed to remain. Figure 12-28B illustrates how to prune mature red or white currants and gooseberries.

## WINTER PROTECTION

Currants and American gooseberries are hardy plants which rarely suffer from winter injury. In particularly wet years, when the hardening of bushes in preparation for winter is delayed, there may be some injury. This situation can be alleviated somewhat by planting a cover crop after harvest to draw excess water from the soil.

The large-fruited European gooseberry varieties are less hardy. To protect these plants from winter injury, hill soil up around the base of the plants and cover with a heavy mulch of straw. Rake this cover away from the plants early in the spring prior to the breaking of buds.

Ensure protection from cold winter winds for both currants and gooseberies (see SITE SELECTION).

## HARVESTING

Although currants remain in good condition on the bushes up to a month after ripening, quality and yield are higher if they are picked as soon as they are ripe. Black currants are slightly more durable than red currants due to their thicker skins. This protects them from tearing and being crushed during harvesting and handling. Remove whole clusters or pick the berries individually. Pick red and white currants by removing the whole cluster. If they are picked as individual berries, the more delicate skin may tear at the base of the fruit, resulting in much of the juice being lost. Pick gooseberries as individual berries. For jelly-making, they should be slightly green, but for preserving they should be ripe or slightly pinkish in color. Protect yourself and the berries from the thorns!

## GRAPE CULTURE

The grape is currently a fruit of minor importance on the Prairies, chiefly because of its tenderness and need for winter protection. Nevertheless, there are a few hardy, early-maturing cultivars that can be grown in sheltered, sunny locations (see Table 12-2). The hardiest grapes are cultivars developed from the native Canadian grape, the American grape or hybrids of the two. However, there has been some success in growing more tender European grapes on hardy rootstocks under well-protected conditions.

## BOTANICAL CHARACTERISTICS

The grape is a woody vine which climbs by the aid of tendrils which are produced opposite the alternately arranged leaves. It is propagated by cuttings or by grafting scions onto rootstocks using the whip or tongue method of grafting. The flowers are small and greenish and are borne in clusters opposite the leaves (see Figure 12-29). The flowers are of three types:

1. staminate, in which only male stamens are present and female pistil is absent;

2. perfect and self-fertile, in which both stamens and pistil are present; and

3. perfect and self-sterile, in which stamens and pistil are present, but the stamens are malformed and do not produce viable pollen.

The staminate and perfect, but self-sterile flowers require cross-pollination. Some European hybrid varieties and a few cultivars of American grapes require cross-pollination. However, the majority of American grapes and the native Canadian grape are self-pollinating. The fruit is a pulpy

Figure 12-29
### FLOWERING AND FRUITING HABIT OF GRAPE

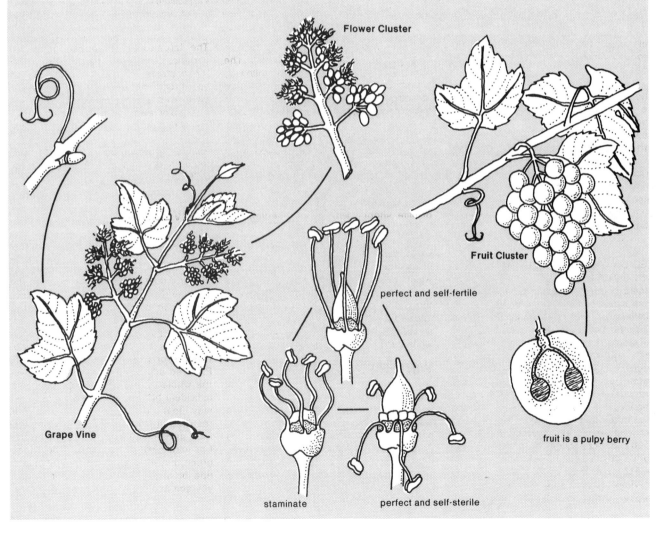

Flower Cluster

Fruit Cluster

perfect and self-fertile

Grape Vine

fruit is a pulpy berry

staminate

perfect and self-sterile

berry and ranges in color from red through purple, violet, blue, green, to nearly white.

## PLANTING

In addition to the use of hardy cultivars, the selection of a suitable site is a critical factor determining the success or failure of grape culture on the Prairies. As mentioned earlier in the section SITE SELECTION, young plants should be planted where they can be trained in an east-west fan system with a good southern exposure. There should be enough space provided in the planting bed so that the vines can be laid flat to the ground and covered with soil (see WINTER PROTECTION).

Obtain well-rooted, one-year old plants from a reliable nursery. The best time for planting grapes is in the spring, when the ground can be easily worked. Prevent the plants from drying out. If planting must be delayed, soak the plants for several minutes in water and heel-in to a well-drained, shady area and keep moist. Set plants in their permanent location while they remain dormant, as they suffer greater transplanting shock once growth of the buds starts.

## Figure 12-30
## PRUNING GRAPE AT PLANTING

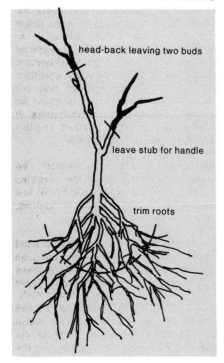

head-back leaving two buds

leave stub for handle

trim roots

Prepare plants prior to planting by trimming off extra-long or damaged roots (see Figure 12-30). Prune the top portion, removing all but the most vigorous cane and cut this back so that only two buds remain. This forces lower shoots to develop and helps to prevent the vines from drying out before growth starts. A small stub can be left from one of the removed canes, for use in tying the vine to the wire or trellis system used for training the plant. Next, dig a hole large enough to accommodate the root system. Do not put fresh manure or fertilizer in the hole as this will burn the root system. Instead, work well rotted manure or fertilizer evenly into the soil prior to planting. Set plants in the hole with their roots well distributed and at about the same level as they were grown previously in the nursery. Work good topsoil around the roots and firmly tamp in the plants to ensure good soil-root contact. Then water the plants thoroughly and give them some starter solution containing phosphorous. It is a good idea to make a slight depression around the base of the plants to facilitate watering during the first growing season.

## WEED CONTROL AND CULTIVATION

Do not allow weeds or invading lawn grass to compete with plants for water and nutrients, as this will seriously set the plants back. Begin shallow cultivation in the spring and continue until mid-summer. Avoid damaging the roots. Later in the summer, weeds reduce available moisture. This helps the plants harden-off for winter. However, if the plants are growing poorly, weeds may restrict growth even more. If this is the case, continue cultivation throughout the growing season. Herbicides are not recommended for home grape plantings. However, a mulch of clean straw or other suitable material to a depth of 5-10 cm (2-4 in) can help to suppress weeds and reduce the cultivation needed. This also helps conserve soil moisture and add organic matter to the soil.

## IRRIGATION

Do not allow new plants to dry out. Make moisture available to the plants throughout the active growing season. If soil conditions are dry, plants will be stunted and maturity delayed. Towards the end of the summer, cut back watering to encourage wood to harden-off. Once the vines are dormant, a late fall watering helps protect the roots from winter damage.

## FERTILIZING

Grapes are not heavy feeders. This may be partly due to the heavy annual pruning of the plants which keeps their size in check. The general rule in fertilizing grapes is to do so sparingly. If the soil has been prepared the fall prior to planting by adding well-rotted manure, the need for additional nutrients is reduced. Most garden soils that have been fertilized regularly in the past usually have adequate supplies of nutrients for grapes, at least for the first few years of their establishment. In later years, some fertilizing may be necessary. Working in well-rotted manure after a few years will benefit the plants as this allows for the continuous release of small amounts of nutrients. Avoid root injury with commercial fertilizers; use reduced rates or relatively low analysis fertilizer.

## WINTER PROTECTION

On the prairies, where winter temperatures fall below -30°C, remove vines from the trellis after pruning in the fall and lay them flat on the ground. Then heap soil around the primary trunk and cover the vines with at least 15 cm (6 in) of soil. In addition, mulch the vines with straw and ensure a good snow cover over the winter to help insulate them from severe cold temperatures. Water-in the plants well in the late fall prior to the ground freezing to protect the plants from winter injury. Remove soil the following spring when the danger of severe cold is past and prior to the breaking of buds.

## TRAINING AND PRUNING

Annual pruning is required to encourage the production of new wood which bears the fruit. As described earlier, the first pruning is given at planting time. Do all subsequent prunings in the fall to reduce the amount of growth that needs to be covered for the winter.

There are a number of systems used for pruning grapes. The best-known is the

Kniffen system. It is widely used where grapes do not need winter protection, but is not of practical use for the Prairies. The system that is commonly used on the Prairies, where temperatures fall below -30°C, is the fan system. In training the grape to the fan system, keep the primary trunk below the first wire to permit the vines to be laid down in the fall and covered with soil. During the growing season, train the vines to a trellis of three wires running between strongly braced posts at either end of the row. The bottom wire should be 45 cm (18 in) from the ground and subsequent wires 45 cm (18 in) apart.

### FAN SYSTEM

During the first season after planting, growth should be directed into the two shoots which develop from the two buds left at planting. In the fall, prune each cane back, leaving only two upward pointing buds which have developed on the current season's growth. The following season, allow these buds to produce vertical shoots and tie these to the wire trellis. These four canes will be the main arms for the first several years. In the fall after the second season's growth, prune the canes to a length of

about 60 cm (2 ft), leaving 4-5 buds on each cane. In the third year, the plants may begin to produce fruit. However, flower clusters should be removed, so that fruit does not develop at the expense of vegetation that is necessary to build a strong framework. Until the plants become mature, usually at about six years of age, maintain the canes 60-100 cm (about 2-3 ft) in length and remove fruit, or at least thin it to one-third the annual crop. Each fall, prune the canes back, leaving 4-5 buds on the current season's growth. Remove all lateral shoots from the arms, except the lowest one on the arm just above the primary trunk. These shoots are pruned to leave only one node and are called renewal spurs. After the sixth year, the full crop of fruit can be allowed to develop. When the main arms become brittle after several years, remove them and allow the renewal spurs to produce shoots that are trained to replace the old arms of the framework. Figure 12-31 shows a grape trained to the fan system.

### HARVESTING

Harvest grapes at their proper maturity. Unlike most other fruits, the grape does

not continue to ripen after picking. Often grapes reach their full size and have good color several days before they have reached maturity. The best indicator of maturity is the sugar content of the fruit. As grapes ripen, the sugar content increases and they become less acidic and more sweet. For wine-making or table use, pick grapes when both color and flavor have reached their peak. Pick the grapes earlier for jellies and jams, as the pectin content is greatest before maturity is reached. On the Prairies, warm soils and a good exposure to the maximum amount of sunlight are necessary to have any hope of reaching maturity within the short growing season. With this crop, however, there can be no guarantee that fruit will be produced every year. Regardless, the hardy grape vines make an attractive ornamental addition to yard or garden.

## OTHER SMALL FRUITS

### BLUEBERRY, HUCKLEBERRY AND TRUE CRANBERRY

The blueberry, true cranberry and the huckleberry all share a unique requirement for acidic soil. This has made their cultivation on the Prairies somewhat difficult. The pH levels for successful berry production must range between 4.0 and 4.5. Acidification of most soils in the Prairies is not practical as there is a very high lime content present which neutralizes any acidifiers (such as aluminum sulphate) that are applied to the soil. If one is intent on growing blueberries or huckleberries, it is advisable to find isolated regions which have naturally acidic soil.

The true cranberry cannot be successfully grown on the Prairies because it is not sufficiently hardy and requires extremely moist conditions, such as found in a bog.

The blueberry can be propagated most successfully by mound layering, although softwood and hardwood cuttings have been used as well (see Plant Propagation lesson, ASEXUAL PROPAGATION). The plants also spread by underground rhizomes which produce suckers. The flowers and fruits of the lowbush blueberry are borne on the

## Figure 12-31
## FAN SYSTEM

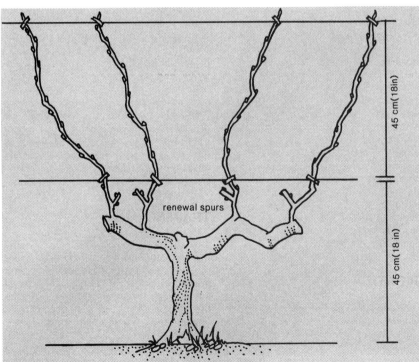

renewal spurs

45 cm(18in)

45 cm (18 in)

previous year's growth. The flowers are self-pollinating, but it has been found that cross-pollination increases fruit set and size. Flower buds are borne laterally or terminally on one-year old wood. The highbush blueberry is composed of a number of tall canes which increase in height with added terminal growth each year. The older canes are relatively unproductive and eventually die to be replaced by younger canes from the crown. The highbush blueberry is not very hardy on the Prairies, although some are being grown for trial in the Peace River Region near Fairview.

## HIGHBUSH CRANBERRY

The highbush cranberry plant is not a true cranberry. It is native to North America and grows best under moist soil conditions that are neutral or slightly acidic. This plant is also shade-tolerant. It is used widely as an ornamental, but its berries make good jelly. It is not used for jams because of the prominent seeds within the fruit. The highbush cranberry plant grows from 2.5-3.0 m (7.5-9 ft) tall and can be propagated by seed. Its flowers are white and borne in large, broad and flattened clusters and are self-pollinating (see Figure 12-32). The fruit is red and drupe-like with a prominent pit.

## BUSH CHERRIES

The Nanking cherry, Mongolian cherry, sandcherry, chokecherry, pin cherry and Chinese bush cherry are all valuable as ornamentals and quite widely used in landscapes. The Nanking and Mongolian cherries are excellent for use in jelly and wine making. They are also used as pollinators for early blooming *Prunus* fruit trees, such as the apricot and some cultivars of plums. The sandcherry is good for eating out of hand or used for jams and canning. It is also useful as a pollinator for late-blooming *Prunus* fruit trees. The chokecherry can be used to make jelly, syrup and wine. The pin cherry and Chinese bush cherry also make excellent jelly.

These plants are propagated by seed, suckers and, in some cases, by trench layering. The Nanking can also be propagated by softwood cuttings. The flowers are borne either singly or in clusters and require cross-pollination with another member of the *Prunus* genus. The fruit that results is a drupe or stone fruit, in that it contains a prominent pit (see Figure 12-33).

Figure 12-33
NANKING CHERRY

Courtesy of Alberta Agriculture

## PROBLEMS AND PREVENTION

### PREVENTATIVE MEASURES

By following good management practices, small fruit plants can be maintained in a healthy, vigorous state. Take the following preventative measures to reduce the incidence of physiological, insect, disease or pest problems:

AVOID ENVIRONMENTAL STRESS
• Grow only hardy cultivars.

• Select a site that is protected from frosts and has adequate soil drainage (see SITE SELECTION).

Figure 12-32
HIGHBUSH CRANBERRY

Courtesy of Birchland Berry Farm

## PRACTICE GOOD MANAGEMENT

- Do not crowd plants so that adequate air circulation is maintained and competition is reduced.

- Never allow plants, especially newly planted ones, to dry out. Always give the plants a deep soaking, as shallow watering encourages shallow root systems which are more susceptible to drought conditions.

- Discontinue irrigation after harvest to permit the plants to harden off.

- Water early in the day to permit the foliage to dry before the cool evenings. This will help reduce fungal disease problems.

- Practice consistent weed control to prevent competition of weeds with the plants.

- Use of fertilizers and their rates should be based on a soil test that determines what nutrients are deficient.

- Use herbicides only on large plantings where cultivation has failed. Apply only those registered for use on a particular crop. Use caution to avoid spray drift which may cause serious injury to desirable plants.

- Do not apply pesticides when the plants are in full bloom as this may injure the blossoms and harm beneficial pollinating insects.

- Prune annually to remove dead, diseased, damaged or crowding branches. This reduces the entry or spread of disease. When necessary, disinfect tools after each cut with a solution of 50 mL Lysol per 1 L water (4 tbsp per 1 qt water).

- Provide winter protection to help plants survive the severe cold temperatures experienced on the Prairies.

## MAINTAIN SANITATION

- Remove all pruned material from the site and haul away or burn.

- Remove mulch and leaves from among the plants and cultivate into the soil at the end of the season for decomposition and to prevent overwintering diseases, insects and mice from taking refuge in it.

## PROVIDE PROTECTION

- Locate plants where they are sheltered from the cold harsh winter winds. In rural locations, if no natural windbreak exists, establish a shelterbelt.

- Provide winter protection to help plants survive the severe cold temperatures experienced on the Prairies.

# DETERMINING WHAT THE PROBLEM IS

Even with the best of management practices and preventative measures, the plants may suffer from problems arising from one or more of the following:

- physiological disorders
- insect pests
- diseases
- animals and birds.

## PHYSIOLOGICAL DISORDERS

### ADVERSE ENVIRONMENTAL CONDITIONS

- Lack of light due to excessive shading causes growth to be spindly, the leaves small and pale, and the fruit quality poor.

- Poor drainage decreases aeration (the amount of oxygen the roots receive) and may cause rotting of the roots. This, in turn, causes the foliage to wilt, yellow and drop off.

- Dry soil conditions for extended periods cause wilting and, eventually, the tissues die and dry up.

- Saline soils (soils with salt accumulations) produce symptoms of water stress as the roots are unable to take up moisture. Run-off from roads or driveways may be high in salt which was applied in the winter.

- High pH causes iron (Fe) to become unavailable in the soil solution resulting in iron deficiency symptoms (see NUTRIENT IMBALANCE)

- Low pH may prevent the uptake of calcium (Ca) or magnesium (Mg) resulting in deficiency symptoms of these two nutrients.

- Overfertilizing, especially with nitrogen, shows scorching and browning symptoms on the leaves and may result in the over-production of vegetative growth and the inhibition of flower bud initiation and, thus, fruit development.

- Underfertilizing results in a number of nutrient deficiency symptoms (see NUTRIENT DEFICIENCY).

- Mechanical damage may result from careless or too deep cultivation, injuring roots and branches of the plants.

### WINTER INJURY

- Frost cracking of branches results from a sudden decrease in temperature in the fall or the onset of an early winter. This may be contributed to by late season watering or fertilizing which encourages active growth and delays the onset of cold hardening. These practices should not be continued past late July or early August.

- Winter tip killing or dieback usually affects the succulent terminal growth and fruiting spurs. Younger wood is more susceptible than older wood. The symptoms of this injury will be evident the following spring. The growing tips will be dead and may turn black.

- Winter desiccation may be prevalent in regions that experience high winter winds or warm periods throughout the winter due to chinook conditions. The wind or warm temperatures cause moisture to be lost from the tissues. Warm temperatures also cause premature opening of the buds. Continuous winds or subsequent cold temperatures will freeze the tissue or cause it to dry out.

### NUTRIENT IMBALANCE

- Nitrogen - leaves are chlorotic, with a light green color, and small lower leaves on older wood turn yellow, and may dry up and fall off. Growth of the terminal shoots will be weak, and fruit development will be poor. Bark will have a reddish color. Nitrogen deficiency may be brought on by competition with grass, weeds or other trees and shrubs; large amounts of organic matter, such as straw, being worked into the soil requiring nitrogen to break it down; and leaching of available nitrogen from the soil solution by heavy rains. Excess nitrogen will result in large dark green leaves and excessive lush growth. Leaf fall and the onset of winter hardening may also be delayed. Trees may also be more susceptible to fireblight.

- Phosphorus - deficiency in fruit trees is uncommon but, if present, may show sypmtoms of small, dark green leaves with a bronze tinge and purple or brown spots.

- Potassium - this nutrient is rarely deficient in prairie soils. If this nutrient is limited, deficiency is evidenced by interveinal purpling of older leaves, browning of the tips and scorching of the leaf margins. Leaves may also curl up and inwards. Shoot development is weak and may experience dieback in the winter. Fruit ripens unevenly.

- Magnesium - interveinal chlorosis of older leaves, with neurotic or dead spots developing later. Leaves fall off prematurely. Fruit also matures and drops early. Flower bud initiation is limited for the following year.

- Manganese - high soil pH can cause manganese to be tied up in the soil. Symptoms include bright yellow interveinal chlorosis on the tips of young leaves with veins remaining a dark green. Eventually, the entire leaf will become yellow and prematurely drop. Excess manganese may occur where soil pH is low and causes stunting of growth and mottling of bark with necrotic spots.

- Iron - high soil pH results in iron being made unavailable in the soil solution. Interveinal chlorosis of young leaves starting near the growing tip may occur. Small veins also turn yellow. Shoots may suffer dieback.

- Zinc - if limited will result in stunting of the terminal. Leaves are small and seem crowded on the branches because of the reduced amount of extension growth. Leaves become chlorotic and may drop off early, starting with the older leaves first. Fruit production will be poor.

- Calcium - fruit disorders are the result of a shortage of calcium. Calcium is necessary for sound cell wall structure and, if absent, may result in breakdown of the fruit.

- Boron - deficiencies show up as fruit disorders. Internal breakdown of the fruit and premature drop may result. This nutrient is more limiting where it is dry and pH is high.

- Copper, sulfur, molybdenum, chloride, and sodium - these micronutrients are usually adequate in prairie soils.

## INSECT PESTS

Insects have the ability to reproduce themselves very quickly. Some insects, such as the aphid, may produce several generations of offspring during the growing season. If insect pests are not controlled early, their population may increase to the point of becoming unmanageable later on. There are three basic categories of insects pests:

- **Chewing** insects which eat the foliage, fruit and bark (caterpillars, imported currantworm, currant fruit fly, slugs, leafroller, strawberry root weevil, sawfly, raspberry fruitworm, uglynest caterpillar)

- **Sucking** insects which remove nutrients from leaves, branches or fruit (aphid, spider mite, cyclamen mite, tarnished plant bug)

- **Burrowing** insects which may infest the bark or fruit (raspberry crown borer).

CONTROL OF INSECTS ON SMALL FRUITS in the Pest Control lesson describes the pest, which host it attacks and the damage that is caused and gives a brief description of its life cycle and recommended control measures.

## DISEASES

The incidence of disease is very much influenced by the weather. When conditions are moist, diseases caused by fungi and bacteria flourish. Fortunately, the dry climate of the Prairies discourages these diseases from becoming serious problems. There are, however, certain plants that are quite susceptible to infection even on the Prairies. Most diseases can be prevented by pruning with disinfected tools to maintain an open habit of growth allowing good air circulation. Make clean cuts to encourage rapid healing and discourage the entry of pathogens. Remove dead, diseased or damaged wood and burn or dispose of it to maintain sanitary conditions and prevent the spread of disease. Good management practices promote healthy, vigorous plants that are more resistant to disease infestations. CONTROL OF SMALL FRUIT DISEASES in the Pest Control lesson lists some of the more common diseases. The name of the pathogen, the type of disease, the host it infests, the damage that results, a brief description of its life cycle, and control recommendations are given.

## DAMAGE FROM ANIMALS AND BIRDS

Mice and rabbits can cause serious damage to small fruit plants by feeding on the tender bark of the stems. If these stems are girdled, they may die. Rodent repellents (containing thiram) work well on rabbits, but not mice. Mice can be lured into half open cans laying on their side that contain poisoned grain. Removing mulch from around the base of the plants will discourage mice from nesting there, but must be weighed against the advantage of retaining the mulch for winter protection. Fencing in the small fruit plantation with a wire mesh fence will discourage animals from entering.

Birds can also be troublesome pests. If the planting is a small one, plants can be covered with cheese cloth or some other type of netting (such as old shear drapery), when the fruit becomes ripe. Birds especially like June-bearing strawberries which is the only fruit around that early in the season. Later on, there may be other fruits and seeds that will distract the birds from the small fruit plantation. Hanging several noisemakers throughout the plantation helps frighten birds away.

# CONCLUSION

This lesson applies much of the material covered in *Book One - Gardening Fundamentals* to the culture of small fruits. Selecting the appropriate site for the establishment of the plantation requires an understanding of how both climate and soils influence growing conditions. The Soils and Plant Nutrition lessons are both applicable to the preparation of the soil prior to planting and the maintenance of adequate nutrient levels and organic matter content throughout the plantation's duration. The Botany lesson gives an understanding of the physiology of each small fruit which is often important in performing such cultural practices as pruning. Under the cultural descriptions of each small fruit, the methods in which these plants are propagated were indicated and descriptions and diagrams of these are found in the Plant Propagation lesson. Finally, the Pest Control lesson is a valuable tool in determining the cause of any problems that may arise and also gives suggested preventative and control measures to take.

This lesson also provides a fairly complete description of the culture of the commonly grown small fruits. Each section covers such topics as planting, planting systems, management practices (including: weed control, fertilizing and irrigation, mulching and winter protection), training and pruning systems and harvesting. This should enable both the rural and urban home gardener to successfully grow a wide variety of delicious small fruits.

## SELF CHECK *QUIZ*

1. Organic matter is an important amendment to the soil.

   a. List four kinds of organic matter.

   b. List ways in which organic matter improves the soil.

2. When selecting cultivars of small fruits, what characteristics are important?

3. Compare the growing, flowering and fruiting habit of the June-bearing and ever-bearing strawberry.

4. a. What are the criteria for a good mulch? List two kinds of mulch.

   b. List six advantages of using mulch.

5. What novelty system can be used to grow strawberries on a balcony?

6. Describe one way in which raspberries can be trained to keep the fruit clean and provide new canes with plenty of room to grow?

7. How long does it take for a saskatoon bush to bear fruit?

8. Why are black currants pruned differently than red or white currants and gooseberries?

9. List four main cultural considerations that help to prevent physiological, insect and disease or pest problems in small fruits.

Alberta Agriculture. *Alberta Horticultural Guide*. Revised 1986. Agdex 200/01.

Alberta Agriculture. *Bush Fruits in Alberta*. Revised, 1979. Agrifax (FS) 230/20-1.

Alberta Agriculture. *Lowbush Blueberry Production*. AC 1477, Revised 1979. Agdex 235/20.

Alberta Agriculture. *Raspberries in Alberta*. Revised 1979. Agrifax (FS) 230/20-1.

Alberta Agriculture. *The Saskatoon*. AC 1246, Revised 1979. Agdex 235/20.

Alberta Agriculture. *Strawberries in Alberta*. Revised 1979. Agrifax (FS) 230/20.

*American Fruit Grower*. Published by Meister Publishing Co. Address inquiries and orders to: Meister Publishing Co., 37841 Gullid Ave, Willoughby, OH 44094.

Bilderback, Diane E. and Dorothy Hinshaw Patent. *Backyard Fruits and Berries*. Emmaus, P.A.: Rodale Press, 1984.

Comprehensive advice on establishing and managing small fruits and fruit tree.

Billit, Arthur. *The ABC's of Fruit Growing*. Toronto: Hamlyn, 1979.

Childers, N.F. *Modern Fruit Science*. Newbrunswick, N.J.: Horticultural Publications, Rutgers University, 1975.

Hill, Lewis. *Fruits and Berries for the Home Garden*. New York: Alfred A Knoff, 1077.

*Kinnikinnick*. Published monthly by Friends of the Garden, University of Alberta. Address inquiries to: University of Alberta Devonian Botanic Garden, University of Alberta, Edmonton, Alberta T6G 2G1.

Readers Digest. *Illustrated Guide to Gardening in Canada*. Montreal: The Reader's Digest Association (Canada) Ltd., 1979.

Shoemaker, J.S. *Small-Fruit Culture*. Toronto: Blakistons Co., 1975.

Detailed cultural information for home gardener and commercial grower.

*The Fruit Grower*. Published quarterly by the Fruit Growers Society of Alberta. Address inquiries and orders to: The Fruit Growers Society of Alberta, Box 861, Beaverlodge, Alberta T0H 0C0.

*The Prairie Garden*. Published annually by The Prairie Garden Committee of the Winnipeg Horticultural Society. Address inquiries and orders to: The Prairie Garden, P.O. Box 517, Winnipeg, Manitoba R3C 2J3.

Westwood, M.N. *Temperate Zone Pomology*. San Francisco: W.H. Freeman & Co., 1978.

University level text on culture and physiology.

## GLOSSARY

**accessory fruit** - a fruit formed from an enlarged receptacle attached to the ovary.

**achene** - dry, fruit-type seed on the surface of strawberry fruit.

**aggregate fruit** - a fruit formed by closely clustered carpels called druplets that easily separate from the receptacle.

**berry (true)** - fleshy fruit derived from swollen ovary. Also used to describe strawberries, raspberries and other small fruits, some of which are not true berries.

**bramble** - cane with spines.

**cane** - woody, pithy stems of bush fruits.

**catfacing** - puckering of the strawberry fruit due to incomplete fertilization that often originates with frost damage to the blossoms.

**cultivar** - a group of closely related plants propagated and cultivated from a plant with common origin and similar characteristics. Often used in place of the term variety, although these are usually selections of the species.

**de-blossoming** - the removal of blossoms during the early establishment of the plant to divert energy and nutrients away from blooming and fruit development toward vegetative growth.

**field heat** - the heat given off by living, respiring fruit after harvest that should be removed by cooling to prevent deterioration.

**forcing** - causing plants to produce flowers and develop fruit by artificial means at times of the year when the plant would not normally be productive.

**fruit** - the edible product of a plant which is closely associated with the flower in its development: a ripened ovary.

**fruiting habit** - the location and manner in which fruit is borne on woody plants.

**gradient** % - $\dfrac{\text{distance of rise} \times 100}{\text{distance of run}}$

**hardiness** - the characteristic of a plant that determines its ability to resist cold temperature injury.

**mixed structures** - buds that contain both vegetative and flower structures.

**mulching** - placing one of a number of materials on the soil surface.

**physiological** - problems which arise from adverse environmental conditions, winter injury, mechanical injury, chemical injury or nutrient deficiency.

**renewal spurs** - grape canes near the trunk cut back to two buds to provide new fruiting wood that will eventually be encouraged to replace framework.

**renovation** - rejuvenation of plants or the moving and reestablishment of plants to a new site.

**ripeness** - state of maturity prior to breakdown.

**tender** - not reliably hardy.

**true-to-type** - identical to the parent plant type that the plant was vegetatively propagated from.

1. a. well-rotted manure
   leaves
   grass clippings
   · straw

   b. improved tilth
   better drainage
   increased aeration
   greater water holding capacity
   more nutrient availability
   (See SOIL PREPARATION-INCREASING ORGANIC MATTER, page 1203)

2. - cultivars should be hardy on the Prairies
   - disease free (preferably disease and insect resistant as well)
   - vigorous young plants with good root systems
   - cultivars with a variety of harvesting periods (early-season, mid-season and late-season) to stagger the harvest period and provide fresh fruit for a longer season.
   - quality, high yielding fruit production
   - plants that are true-to-type
   (See CULTIVAR SELECTION-CHARACTERISTICS OF GOOD CULTIVARS, page 1205)

3. **June-bearing**:
   Growing - Numerous runners produced from mother plants and spreads more quickly. Matted- or spaced-row system suitable.

   Flowering - Flower buds initiated under conditions of short day length and cool temperatures. Blooms in spring.

   Fruiting - Fruits borne in the spring from late May to early July with greatest production in June.

   **Ever-bearing**:
   Growing - Little runner production, spreads slowly. Hill system more suitable.

   Flowering - Flower bud initiation is not dependent on day length or temperature. Flowering is continuous throughout summer.

   Fruiting - Fruits are usually a bit smaller and borne throughout growing season.

   (See STRAWBERRY CULTURE-BOTANICAL CHARACTERISTICS, page 1205)

4. a. A good mulch should be:

   - easily obtained (many things can be recycled from your own garden as mulch)
   - inexpensive
   - not so light that it blows away
   - not prone to packing
   - free from weed seeds and harmful disease organisms and insects

   b. Using mulch helps to:

   - conserve moisture by reducing loss to evaporation
   - keep fruit cleaner
   - add organic matter to the soil (if the mulch is organic)
   - suppress weeds
   - prevent soil compaction and erosion during heavy rains
   - reduce temperature fluctuation in winter and thus protect plants from alternate freezing and thawing of soil
   (See STRAWBERRY CULTIVARS-MULCHING AND WINTER PROTECTION, page 1211)

5. The strawberry barrel (see STRAWBERRY CULTURE-NOVELTY GROWING SYSTEMS-STRAWBERRY BARREL, page 1214, and Figure 12-10).

6. Two-sided Trellis Hedgerow System - In this system, posts are set in at either end of the row. Crossbars are nailed to the post and wire supports run down either side of the hedgerow. Half of the fruiting canes are bent to one side of the row and tied or clipped to the wires and half to the other side of the row. New canes arise from the center of the V-shaped row where there is plenty of light and room to grow. At the end of the season, the fruiting canes tied to the wires are removed and the new canes are tied to either side of the row after thinning the following spring. Other training systems include the one-sided trellis and the staked hill system. (See RASPBERRY CULTURE - TRAINING AND SUPPORT SYSTEMS, page 1220.)

7. Saskatoon bushes may start to bear a crop when they are six years old, but it may be 8 to 10 years before they are fully productive. Once bearing begins, the plant remains productive until it is 20 to 25 years old. (See SASKATOON CULTURE-BOTANICAL CHARACTERISTICS, page 1222.)

8. Black currants produce fruit on young, one-year old wood of the previous season's growth. To promote a good supply of vigorous young wood, older wood is removed in a continuous thinning and renewal process. The primary pruning cut is the thinning cut (see Figure 12-25).

   Red or white currants and gooseberries produce fruit on short spurs found on two and three-year old wood. Shoots are headed back to produce lateral branching on older wood. A total of about nine shoots are maintained with 3 one-year old shoots, 3 two-year old shoots and 3 three-year old shoots. Wood older than three years is thinned out (see Figure 12-25).

   (See CURRANT AND GOOSEBERRY CULTURE-BOTANICAL CHARACTERISTICS, page 1225, and Figure 12-28.).

9. a Avoid environmental stress by growing hardy cultivars and selecting a suitable site.

b. Practice good management including: irrigation, weed control, fertilization, pruning and providing winter protection if necessary.

c. Carry out sanitary measures, removing all pruned material, old mulch, and leaves (especially if disease is present).

d. Protect plants with a windbreak or by planting in a sheltered location (see PROBLEMS AND PREVENTION-PREVENTIVE MEASURES, page 1232).

## INDEX

# TREE FRUIT PRODUCTION

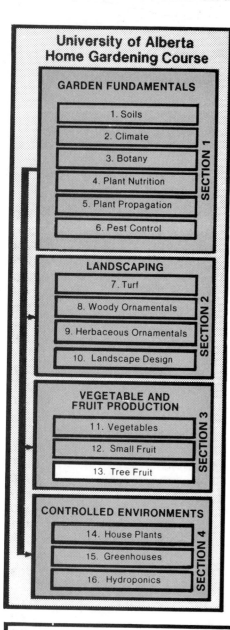

**University of Alberta Home Gardening Course**

GARDEN FUNDAMENTALS — SECTION 1
1. Soils
2. Climate
3. Botany
4. Plant Nutrition
5. Plant Propagation
6. Pest Control

LANDSCAPING — SECTION 2
7. Turf
8. Woody Ornamentals
9. Herbaceous Ornamentals
10. Landscape Design

VEGETABLE AND FRUIT PRODUCTION — SECTION 3
11. Vegetables
12. Small Fruit
13. Tree Fruit

CONTROLLED ENVIRONMENTS — SECTION 4
14. House Plants
15. Greenhouses
16. Hydroponics

# SELF-STUDY LESSON FEATURES

Self-study is an educational approach which allows you to study a subject where and when you want. The course is designed to allow students to study the course material efficiently and incorporates the following features.

**OBJECTIVES** — are found at the beginning of each lesson and allow you to determine what you can expect to learn in the lesson.

**LESSON MATERIAL** — is logically organized and broken down into fundamental components by ordered headings to assist you to comprehend the subject.

**REFERENCING** — between lessons and within lessons allows you to integrate course material. ·

The last two digits of the page number identify the page and the digits preceding these identify the lesson number (eg., 107: Lesson 1, page 7 or 1227: Lesson 12, page 27).

Referencing:

    sections within the same lesson (eg., see OSMOSIS)

    sections in other lessons (eg., see Botany lesson, OSMOSIS)

    figures and tables (eg., see Figure 7-3)

**FIGURES AND TABLES** — are found in abundance throughout the lessons and are designed to convey useful information in an easy to understand form.

**SIDEBARS** — are those areas in the lesson which are boxed and toned. They present information supplementary to the core content of the lesson.

**PRACTICAL PROJECTS** — are integrated within the lesson material and are included to allow you to apply principles and practices.

**SELF-CHECK QUIZ** — is provided at the end of each lesson and allows you to test your comprehension of the lesson material. Answers to the questions and references to the sections dealing with the questions are provided in the answer section. You should review any questions that you are unable to answer.

**GLOSSARY** — is provided at the end of each lesson and alphabetically lists the definitions of key concepts and terms.

**RESOURCE MATERIALS** — are provided at the end of each lesson and comprise a list of recommended learning materials for further study of the subject. Also included are author's comments on the potential application of each publication.

**INDEX** — alphabetically lists useful topics and their location within the lesson.

1986 University of Alberta Faculty of Extension

**Written by: Jan C. Hardstaff**

Technical Reviewers:
    Grant Gillund
    Betty Vladicka

ISBN 0-88864-852-9

(Book 3, Lesson 13)

THE PRODUCTION TEAM

Managing Editor ................................................. Thom Shaw
Editor ............................................................ Lois Hameister
    Frank Procter
Production Coordinator ...................................... Kevin Hanson
Graphic Artist ........................... Melanie Eastley Harbourne

Data Entry ..................................................... Lois Hameister

Published by the University of Alberta
Faculty of Extension Corbett Hall
Edmonton, Alberta, T6G 2G4

# LEARNING OBJECTIVES

After completing this lesson, the student should be able to:

1. understand fruit tree physiology.

2. propagate fruit trees.

3. plan an orchard containing a variety of fruits to fit the gardener's needs.

4. select, plant and establish the trees.

5. train the tree to the modified central leader system.

6. maintain form and vigor with annual pruning.

7. manage and maintain healthy fruit trees.

8. prevent problems from arising or becoming too serious.

# TABLE OF CONTENTS

## LIST OF FIGURES AND TABLES

# INTRODUCTION

Home production of fine fruit can be challenging and rewarding. Whether the home gardener be urban or rural, amateur or experienced, it is important to learn the cultural and management practices that produce and maintain quality fruit.

This lesson focuses on tree fruit production on the Prairies. Commercial tree fruit production on the Prairies is not presently viewed as a profitable venture. For this reason, this lesson adapts much of the cultural and management information available for commercial growers so that it will be practical for the home gardener. For those who have never attempted growing a fruit tree, or those who have and want to know more about how to care for existing fruit trees, this lesson should provide valuable information on:

- selecting hardy cultivars

- planting fruit trees

- training fruit trees to become vigorous bearing trees

- pruning to maintain the tree or rejuvenate old neglected trees

- performing basic propagation and grafting techniques

- maintaining healthy fruit trees

# OVERVIEW

## COMMERCIAL FRUIT PRODUCTION

There are three major fruit growing regions in Canada:

- the Okanagan and Fraser Valleys of British Columbia

- the Niagara Peninsula of southern Ontario

- the Annapolis Valley of Nova Scotia.

Major geographical factors which determine the suitability of a region for successful commercial tree fruit production include climate, site and soil.

Prairie conditions may adequately meet site and soil requirements, but unfortunately become limiting with respect to climate. The number of growing degree days on the Prairies is considerably less than in the more suitable regions. The result is that fruit trees take longer to become bearing trees. Consequently, the return on investment from a prairie orchard would be longer term than in one of the more suitable regions. In addition, many of the desirable commercial fruit trees are just not hardy on the Prairies and, with the improved transportation systems, quality fruit produced commercially in the milder climates is readily available.

## ADAPTING TREE FRUITS TO THE HOME

Because of the year-round availability of fruit from other commercially suitable areas, the amount of fruit grown by the home gardener has declined sharply. However, there is still a great deal of interest in the production of fruit on the home grounds on a modified scale. Growing fruit trees can be a rewarding hobby, but to obtain an abundance of quality fruit takes time and care on a regular basis.

The home orchard is easier to adapt to a rural or suburban situation. The trees can be given greater spacing and more uniform treatments of fertilizer and pest control measures in an area set aside solely for their production. This by no means should discourage the urban dweller from including fruit trees in the landscape of his yard. Fruit trees can contribute ornamental value year round with fragrant blossoms in spring, lush green beauty in summer, attractive color in fall and elegant form in winter (see Figure 13-1). Fruit trees provide some shade, although fruit drop is undesirable close to patios or walks. Dwarf trees would be ideal for the urban home owner where space is limiting. However, they are generally not recommended on the Prairies because they have not been proven consistently hardy. There are a few people who have grown semi-dwarf apple trees with some success. Perhaps in the future more research and testing will provide the homeowner with a reliable and convenient dwarf fruit tree (see USE OF DWARF FRUIT TREES ON THE PRAIRIES).

## CRITERIA FOR SUCCESS

Follow these criteria for successful fruit production:

- Select a site that offers optimum growing conditions, shelter and accessibility.

- Choose hardy cultivars recommended for the area.

## Figure 13-1
## APPLE TREE IN BLOSSOM

Courtesy of Alberta Agriculture

- Plan carefully with respect to spacing, pollination requirements and the effect of existing plant material.

- Plant and train the trees carefully.

- Follow a management program that includes: regular pruning, spraying, fertilizing and watering to maintain healthy vigorous trees.

# ENVIRONMENTAL CONSIDERATIONS

## CLIMATE

The semi-arid climate of the Prairies is characterized by limited precipitation, extremes of temperature, a short growing season and drying winds. Fruit trees require a cumulative precipitation of at least 50 cm (20 in) to produce a crop of fruit; this exceeds the 40 cm (16 in) or less that the Prairie climate offers. This makes supplemental irrigation a necessity for maximum production. Sufficient water not only increases yields, but increases the fruit tree's ability to withstand the severe seasonal temperatures. Adequate soil water and sap moisture in the tissues of the tree, particularly during blossoming, fruiting and just prior to the onset of winter, enable the trees to withstand the drying heat of summer and the intense cold of winter.

Injury to the trees resulting from temperature extremes can occur in several ways. Late spring frosts seriously reduce yields by damaging or killing blossoms or young fruit. During the growing season, hot temperatures under conditions of little rainfall cause trees to dry out and seriously reduce their vigor and yield of fruit. Early fall frosts, before the trees are able to harden-off for the winter, result in frost cracking on the trunk and die-back of the growing tips and buds. During the winter, mild temperatures and drying winds in chinook zones desiccate or dry out the bark and bud tissue (see PROBLEMS AND PREVENTION).

The Prairies are divided into zones according to the amount of precipitation received, the length of the frost-free period, and temperature extremes and fluctuations (see Climate lesson, Figure 2-10). Although the Prairie climate is far from optimum for the growing of fruit trees, injury and loss can be prevented. Select a protected site, choose the hardiest recommended cultivars and carry out whatever management practices, such as irrigation and wind protection, necessary to modify the severity of the climate.

## SITE SELECTION

The selection of site has a tremendous influence on the performance of fruit trees, whether they be in a small rural orchard or a city yard. Consider the following factors:

- slope and air drainage
- direction of exposure
- shelterbelt protection
- soil and water drainage
- water source and the effects of bodies of water

### SLOPE AND AIR DRAINAGE

Fruit trees do best when planted where there is a gentle slope of approximately five per cent permitting adequate air drainage away from the orchard. Avoid low lying hollows because cold air drains into these spots and creates frost pockets (see Climate lesson, Figure 2-5). A site that is higher than surrounding land gives good air drainage through and away from the orchard, thereby reducing the risk of frost damage. As well, increased air circulation minimizes the spread of fungal disease.

### DIRECTION OF EXPOSURE

When choosing a site, consider its orientation to the sun as well as to prevailing winds. Select a site on a north- to northeast-facing slope which is protected from the prevailing winds. Where this is not possible, establish the fruit trees in a sheltered location, protected from southern exposure by a building, fence or existing plant material. Ensure enough space is allowed to avoid shading later in the growing season.

A southern exposure should be avoided for two reasons. First, trees on a south-facing slope, or in a yard with a southern exposure, tend to prematurely bud in the spring. This increases the risk of damage to the buds by early spring frost. With a more northerly exposure, the temperature remains cooler longer, delaying budding until true spring arrives and the danger of frost is past. The second reason for avoiding southern exposure is the increase of winter injury from sunscald. This is especially prevalent when the orientation is to the southwest. Northern exposures protect the bark of the tree from the late afternoon sun that causes sunscald (see PROBLEMS AND PREVENTION).

### SHELTERBELT PROTECTION

Protect trees from prevailing winds. On the Prairies where the wind is so prevalent, particularly in chinook zones, fruit trees need shelter. Avoid exposed hill tops and west- to northwest-facing slopes because of high velocity winds. In the winter, these drying winds cause desiccation of bark and buds. During the growing season, high wind discourages pollinating insects, increases moisture loss from the soil and trees, causes soil erosion, interferes with spraying and increases fruit drop. Where wind is severe, trees are deformed.

Urban gardeners can provide wind protection by making use of existing buildings, board fences or hedges that provide shelter on their leeward side. In the rural situation, a shelterbelt is essential to reduce the force of the wind. The shelterbelt illustrated in Figure 13-2 includes, from the windward side, a row of shrubs, one or two rows of deciduous trees and to the leeward side, a row of evergreens. Recommended shelterbelt material varies according to region but caragana, poplar and spruce are most common. Avoid fireblight susceptible material such as mountain ash and cotoneaster. A well established shelterbelt provides protection on the leeward side to a distance of twenty times its average height.

Plant fruit trees a distance of 25 m (82 ft) on the leeward side of the shelterbelt for two reasons. First, snowdrifts in the lee of the shelterbelt may result in limb breakage if the fruit trees are planted too close. Allowing the recommended space minimizes this problem by trapping the snow between the shelterbelt and the fruit trees. If space is limited, plant a row of caragana 10 m (32 ft) inside the windbreak to trap the snow. Secondly, shelterbelts trap cold air, especially at the bottom of slopes. For this reason, leave gaps open in these

## Figure 13-2
## SHELTERBELT

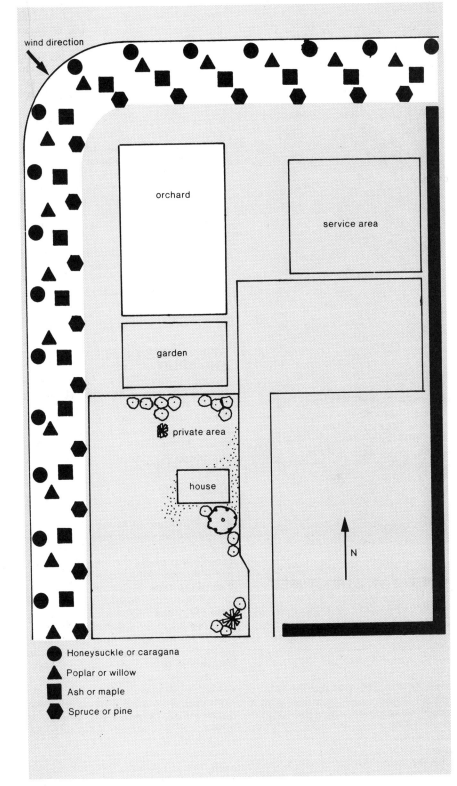

wind direction

orchard

service area

garden

private area

house

N

● Honeysuckle or caragana

▲ Poplar or willow

■ Ash or maple

⬡ Spruce or pine

spots to allow air drainage away from the orchard. See RESOURCE MATERIALS for more information on shelterbelt planning.

### SOIL AND WATER DRAINAGE

The ideal soil for fruit trees is a deep, well-drained silt loam or clay loam with good fertility. If you are unsure of your soil condition, soil sampling instructions can be found in the Soils lesson. Have a soil testing lab conduct a soil analysis. The results of the tests tell you the nutrient level, pH and salt content of your soil. If your soil shows extremes of pH or a high salt content, fruit trees will not do well. If you specify that you plan to grow or are presently growing fruit trees, the laboratory will usually provide a fertilizer recommendation to correct any deficiencies.

A deep topsoil gets young trees off to a good start, but the subsoil is of even greater importance (see Figure 13-3). Ideally, a soil depth of 2 m (6½ ft) provides for adequate rooting, although trees will grow in shallower soils. Avoid compact soils and hard pans near the surface as they impede root penetration and prevent good water drainage. The subsoil must be well drained and the water table at least 1 m (about 3 ft) below the soil surface as fruit trees don't thrive with "wet feet". A gentle slope helps drain off water accumulating on the surface in late winter and early spring when water drainage is poor.

### WATER SOURCE AND THE EFFECTS OF BODIES OF WATER

Quality water should be easily accessible for use in supplemental irrigation. Tap water can be used by urban home owners. For rural gardeners, a reliable well can provide water for irrigation, but should be tested for high concentrations of salt, sodium and other minerals that may accumulate in the soil and harm the fruit trees. A river, stream, lake or dugout would be a better source of quality water provided it can be economically pumped to the trees.

Planting fruit trees near a body of water is beneficial because of its moderating effects on temperature. Premature spring budding can be delayed until the danger of frost is past because the cool air over the frozen water keeps air temperatures around the trees cool. After thawing, the open body of water absorbs heat during

## Figure 13-3
## DEPTH OF SUBSOIL FOR ROOTING

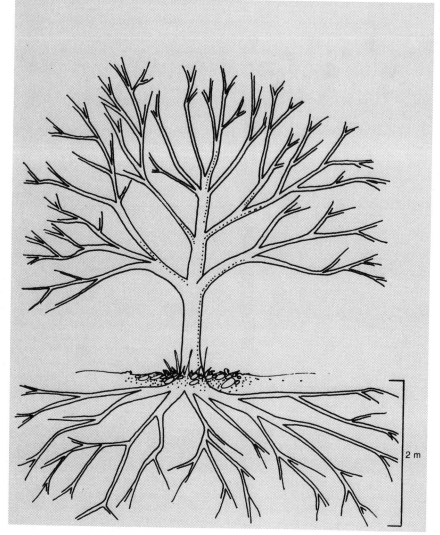

2 m

the day and gives it off at night, preventing temperatures from dropping drastically overnight. This can protect the fruit trees from late spring frosts that might damage blossoms or young developing fruit. It also helps to extend the season by protecting maturing fruit from early fall frosts.

## FRUIT TREE ANATOMY

This section on anatomy is a basis for studying other sections in the lesson where much of the terminology will apply.

## VEGETATIVE STRUCTURES

Figures 13-4 and 13-5 illustrate the various components of a fruit tree's anatomy. Fruit trees are planted as one-year old maiden whips or two-year old branched trees. A whip is an unbranched stem that is usually 1-2 m (3-6½ ft) in length. The young fruit tree consists of the upper stem and a root system joined together by a bud or graft union. This union (see Figure 13-15) is characterized by a slight swelling on the stem.

Once the tree is planted, the **lateral buds** give rise to branches and the **terminal bud** produces the central leader. The **lateral branches** that are chosen to remain during the training period to form the eventual framework of the tree are called **primary scaffold branches**. These will ideally have wide crotch angles in relation to the main trunk. The **head height** of the tree is the distance from the ground to the lowermost scaffold. The **drip line** of the tree is the area beneath the outermost branches. **Secondary branches** and spurs are produced from lateral buds. **Spurs** are short, woody fruit-bearing branches. Undesirable drooping secondary branches are called **hangers**. When a tree is under stress, **trace buds**, located just beneath the bark that generally do not develop, give rise to vigorous shoots called **water sprouts** that grow vertically from the main branches or **trunk** of the tree. **Suckers** often sprout from the base of the tree. If they point above the union, they are called **crown suckers**. Suckers developing from the rootstock are called **root suckers**.

## STRUCTURE OF FLOWERS AND FRUIT

The flower and fruiting habits of the various tree fruits are quite distinct. They fall into two basic categories, the pomes and the stone or drupe fruits. Figure 13-6 shows the differences between these two groups.

### POME FRUITS

APPLE
The buds of an **apple** tree differentiate to become vegetative buds (giving rise only to leaves and shoots) or mixed buds (giving rise to an influorescence of five blossoms with a rosette of leaves at the base) (see Figure 13-6A). Mixed flower buds are formed terminally on two-year and older spurs. This influorescence is **determinate**, that is, the blossoms open from the center outward. The flowers of an apple are **epigynous**, that is, the ovary is inferior and the floral parts arise above it. Each flower has 5 petals and sepals, 15 or more stamens and 2-5 pistils. The fruit is referred to as a **pome** and is derived from the fusion of the ovary with the receptacle. The ovary is composed of five carpels that may contain two seeds each.

Figure 13-4
ANATOMY OF A FRUIT TREE

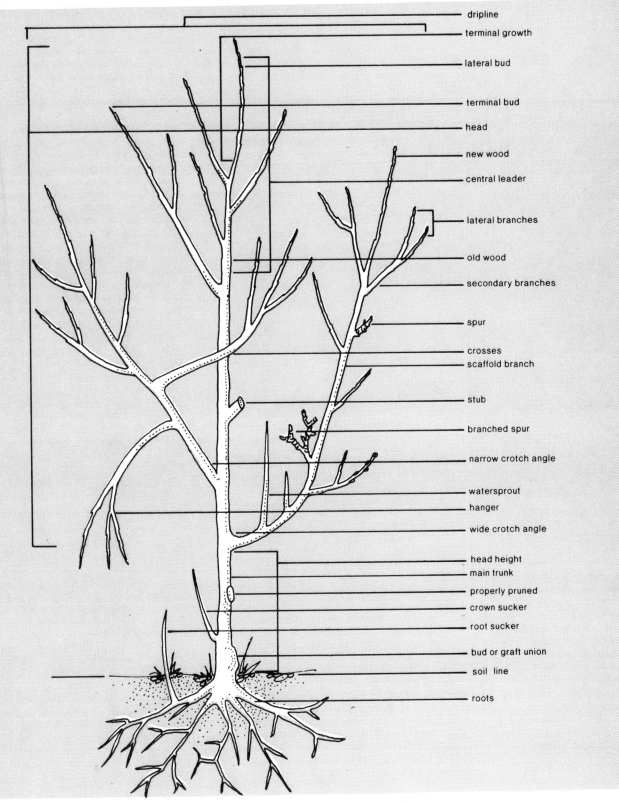

dripline
terminal growth
lateral bud
terminal bud
head
new wood
central leader
lateral branches
old wood
secondary branches
spur
crosses
scaffold branch
stub
branched spur
narrow crotch angle
watersprout
hanger
wide crotch angle
head height
main trunk
properly pruned
crown sucker
root sucker
bud or graft union
soil line
roots

## Figure 13-5
## PARTS OF THE BRANCH

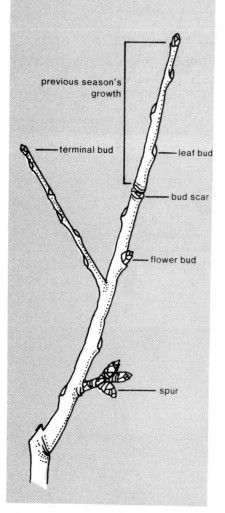

- previous season's growth
- terminal bud
- leaf bud
- bud scar
- flower bud
- spur

### PEAR

The **pear** also produces both mixed or vegetative buds. The mixed buds of the pear are formed on two-year and older spurs as well (see Figure 13-6A). The influorescence has from 6-8 blossoms which flower **indeterminately**, that is, the lateral flowers on the outside of the influorescence open first and the central flower last. Like the apple, the flower is epigynous with 5 petals and sepals, 20 stamens and 2-5 pistils. The fruit is a pome and is similar to the apple except for its teardrop shape and coarser texture (because of the presence of stone or grit cells).

### STONE FRUITS

#### PLUMS, APRICOTS AND CHERRIES

The buds of **plum**, **apricot** or **cherry** fruit trees are either vegetative or unmixed flower buds (see Figure 13-6B). Plum and cherry flower buds develop laterally on two-year and older spurs giving rise to a few flowered influorescence. Apricot flower buds develop laterally on one-year old and older wood and each gives rise to a solitary flower. These flowers are in both cases **perigynous**, that is, the flower parts arise from beneath the ovary. The flowers have five petals and sepals, one pistil and numerous stamen. The fruit is referred to as a **drupe** or **stone fruit** containing one seed formed between two ovules. The flesh of the fruit is derived entirely from the ovary.

## PHYSIOLOGY OF FRUIT

### JUVENILE STAGE TO MATURITY

Following a successful grafting or budding operation (see PROPAGATION OF FRUIT TREES), the buds produce an abundance of vegetative growth the following spring, resulting in whips that are longer than 1 m (over 3 ft). However, no flowers or fruit are produced. After the first season's spurt of growth, start training the maiden whip (see TRAINING AND PRUNING). The following year, the tree again exhibits vigorous vegetative growth, but no flowers or fruit. The tree is in a juvenile stage and does not yet have reproductive tissue that is capable of producing flower buds. The length of the juvenile phase varies with the kind of tree (see Table 13-4) and whether or not the tree is a dwarf.

Some cultivars come into bearing sooner than others and those exhibiting dwarfing characteristics also tend to reach maturity earlier than most trees. The juvenile phase is characterized by the production and utilization of large quantities of carbohydrates for cell elongation and differentiation as the shoots, leaves and roots develop at a rapid rate. The transition from this juvenile vegetative phase to the adult reproductive phase takes place when a certain size is reached, the rate of growth is slowed and carbohydrates begin to accumulate in the tissues (see Figure 13-7). The fruit tree reaches maturity when there is a greater amount of carbohydrates (starches and sugars) relative to nitrogen-containing compounds (proteins). This is also referred to as the C:N ratio. The naturally occurring hormone 'florigen' then begins to stimulate differentiating cells to form the reproductive tissue of flower buds. Once mature, fruit trees remain productive for many years. Table 13-4 indicates the various ages to which fruit trees are able to produce fruit.

A number of practices can bring on the production of flower buds if maturity is delayed. Bark ringing or girdling encourages branches that are not bearing fruit to initiate flower buds for the following year (see Figure 13-8). Do this early in the growing season, between full bloom and petal fall. Weak trees should not be ringed. This ringing or girdling of the bark around the trunk or at the base of limbs breaks the vascular system that is translocating nitrogen (necessary for vegetative growth), upward from the roots. This break also prevents the translocation of carbohydrates from the leaves where they are manufactured downward. This forces accumulation of carbohydrates by trapping them above the wound, resulting in hormone initiation of flower bud development. The width of the strip of bark removed varies according to the diameter of the trunk or branch (see Table 13-1). Notching or scoring, by making two or more cuts to the sapwood below a bud, causes flower bud initiation above it due to carbohydrate accumulation above the wound.

### THE MATURE FRUIT TREE

Figure 13-9 indicates when the physiological processes of vegetative growth (flowering and fruit development) occur during the course of a year. The diagram shows how these processes are interrelated.

#### VEGETATIVE GROWTH

In late April and early May, environmental factors, particularly the increase in temperature and longer days, indicate to the lateral and terminal buds that spring has truly arrived. The tissues thaw and the **buds begin to swell**, absorbing the moisture immediately around them. The roots begin to draw soil moisture and nutrients upward into the tree. The bud scales, which encased the bud during the winter, supply the initial nitrogen that

## Figure 13-6
## FLOWERING AND FRUITING HABITS OF TREE FRUITS

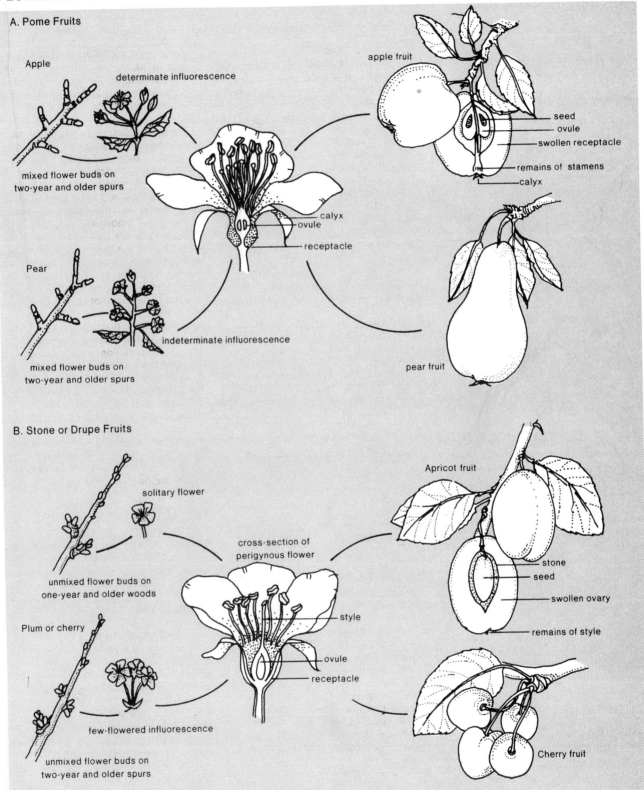

A. Pome Fruits

Apple

determinate influorescence

apple fruit

seed
ovule
swollen receptacle
remains of stamens
calyx

mixed flower buds on
two-year and older spurs

calyx
ovule
receptacle

Pear

indeterminate influorescence

mixed flower buds on
two-year and older spurs

pear fruit

B. Stone or Drupe Fruits

solitary flower

cross-section of
perigynous flower

Apricot fruit

unmixed flower buds on
one-year and older woods

stone
seed
swollen ovary
remains of style

Plum or cherry

style

ovule

receptacle

few-flowered influorescence

unmixed flower buds on
two-year and older spurs

Cherry fruit

## Figure 13-7
## TRANSITION FROM JUVENILE STAGE TO MATURITY

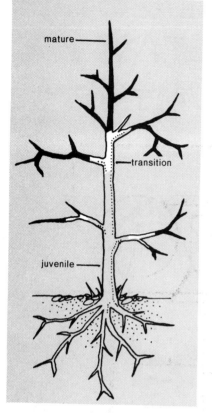

is needed in making protein for the developing shoots. In mid-May, when the temperatures are beginning to remain above freezing, the buds begin to expand. By the third week in May, many of the leaves have opened and begin photosynthesizing. **Shoot extension** then takes place until early summer. Extension of terminal and lateral buds ceases when **the formation of the terminal bud** at the end of the shoot begins. This process is completed by late July or early August, at which point the terminal bud enters a state called **summer dormancy**. If severe pruning, over-watering or over-fertilizing occurs during this period, it may result in the tree stimulating the terminal buds to begin growing.

Under normal circumstances in late summer, nutrients are diverted away from the terminal buds and utilized in the **radial growth** of the tree. The cambium layer (see Botany lesson, Figure 3-12), which has been active but not extremely productive in the early part of the growing season, now begins to divide

and contribute to the growth of the sapwood and bark. Besides the radial growth in the upper part of the tree, the **roots are also stimulated** to put forth new rootlets and enlarge the root system.

By late summer, the days begin to shorten, the nights become cooler and the initiation of **cold temperature acclimation** begins. With the coming of the first frosts and the drop of temperature to 0° to -5°C, the metabolic processes of the plant are slowed and the tissue begins to dehydrate. As the night temperatures drop, cold hardening takes place and any water left in the cells of the tissue becomes bound to substances within the cells. Water between the cells then freezes and the tree is **cold hardened** and prepared for winter.

At this point, the buds are in a physiologically controlled state (that is chemically induced) called **dormancy rest**. This dormancy rest can only be broken with a cold treatment of certain temperature and duration. Once this requirement has been met, the tree is in

a state of **spring dormancy quiescence** which can be broken when environmental conditions are conducive to plant growth. If warm temperatures come too early and the plants respond, subsequent cold temperatures can cause injury to the trees. This is why it is a good idea to locate trees with a northern exposure so that they are not fooled by a false spring.

### FLOWERING AND POLLINATION
**Flower bud initiation** occurs in the spring immediately following the extension growth of the shoots. At this point, the carbohydrates that were being manufactured and utilized at a rapid rate for cell division and elongation now begin to accumulate in the tissues. Generally, factors that increase carbohydrate accumulation in the tree (e.g., ample light, pinching the growing point prior to terminal bud formation, ringing or notching) increase the number of flower buds initiated. On the other hand, factors that decrease the amount of carbohydrate accumulation (e.g., early summer pruning, defoliation, excessive nitrogen or water, and high temperatures

## Table 13-1
## GUIDELINES FOR BARK RINGING

| BRANCH DIAMETER | | RING WIDTH | |
|---|---|---|---|
| (cm) | (in) | (cm) | (in) |
| 0.6-2.5 | 0.25-1.0 | 0.3 | 0.125 |
| 2.6-5.0 | 1.1-2.0 | 0.6 | 0.25 |
| 5.1-7.5 | 2.1-3.0 | 0.9 | 0.375 |
| 7.6 + | 3.1 + | 1.2 | 0.5 |

## Figure 13-8
## BARK RINGING

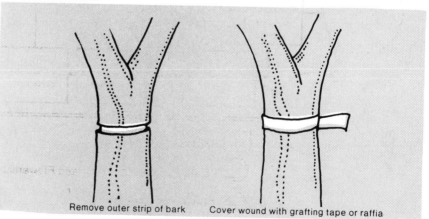

Remove outer strip of bark          Cover wound with grafting tape or raffia

Figure 13-9
FRUIT TREE PHYSIOLOGY

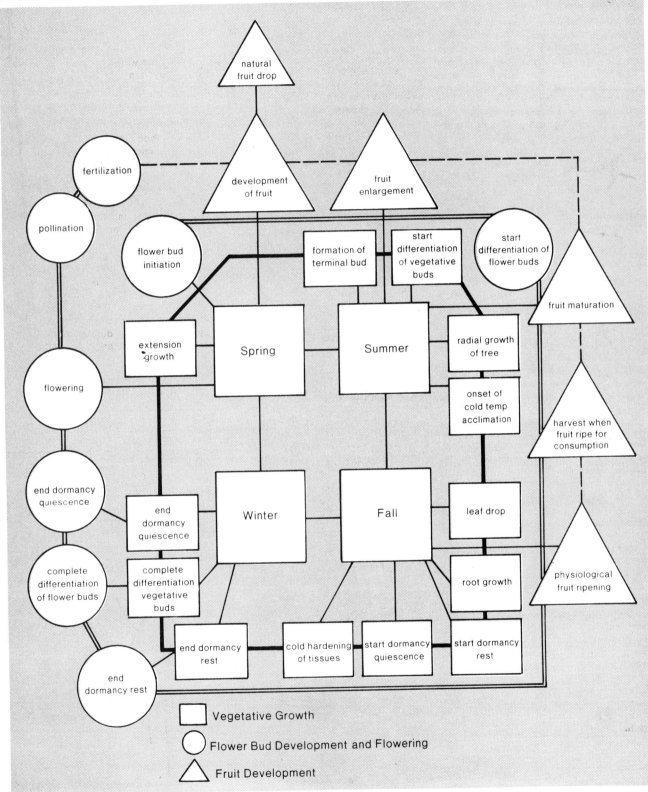

that increase respiration) reduce the number of flower buds initiated.

Once flower buds are initiated, the process of **differentiation** begins. This is quite similar to that of vegetative buds in that they need a certain period of cold temperature treatment to complete differentiation and break the dormancy of the buds. The following spring when environmental conditions are right, the buds open and **blossom**. Apples and pears blossom from mixed buds at the same time the leaves are expanding from their buds, usually in mid- to late-May. Plums and apricots blossom from unmixed buds from early to mid-May (see Table 13-2).

**Pollination** is the transfer of pollen from the anther (male reproductive structure) to the stigma of the pistil (female reproductive structure) (see Botany lesson, FLOWERS). Because tree fruit pollen is heavy and sticky, it is not easily carried by the wind. Insects, primarily honeybees or wild bees, are responsible for carrying the pollen from flower to flower (see Figure 13-10). These insects work best when the temperatures are warm, winds are calm, and weather is dry. Temperatures below 10°C, winds above 35 km/hr (20 mph) and rainy weather, inhibit bee activity. If these conditions persist during the bloom period, there will be a low percentage of fruit set. Pollination is best immediately after the flowers have opened, but can still occur within two or three days of initial bloom.

If conditions are favorable and pollination takes place, the pollen grain germinates and sends a pollen tube down into the ovary where it fertilizes an egg in the ovule (see Botany lesson, FLOWERS). This **fertilization** process results in seed formation. The majority of fruit trees on the Prairies require pollination, fertilization and seed formation to stimulate fruit set. If these requirements are not met, the trees may bloom profusely, but bear no fruit.

The flowers of pome and stone fruits are perfect, that is, they contain both anthers and pistil. However, even though both male and female parts are present on the same flower, many of these fruits are **self-sterile**, that is, they cannot be fertilized by their own pollen. A few cultivars of fruit trees are **self-fertile**, that is, the ovaries of the flowers can be fertilized by their own pollen. It is wise to

consider apples, apple-crabs, crabapples, pears, plums, apricots, cherry-plums and bush cherries as self-sterile.

In order to pollinate a self-sterile fruit tree, a pollinator must be provided that:

- is a different cultivar, preferably within the same species

- is compatible with the cultivar to be pollinated

- has a bloom period that overlaps with that of the cultivar to be pollinated

- comes into bearing at the same time

- does not have an alternate bearing habit (an alternate bearing or biennial bearing fruit tree is one that bears a heavy crop of fruit one year and almost nothing the following season)

In the urban situation, suitable pollinators are often found in neighboring yards. If

## Figure 13-10
## INSECTS ARE AGENTS OF POLLINATION

Courtesy of Alberta Agriculture

these are within 500 m (about 1600 ft) and are different cultivars, they should do the job. For the rural gardener, pollinating cultivars need to be provided as any fruit tree on a neighboring farm or acreage is not likely to be close enough for the insects to cross-pollinate. It is also a good practice, particularly if a small orchard with several trees is being grown, to place a hive of honeybees on the edge of the orchard. One colony of bees can service over two acres of fully grown trees.

Although the most permanent and effective way to ensure cross-pollination is to plant at least two compatible cultivars, this may not always be practical for the home gardener, especially where space is a limiting factor. In this case, collect a bouquet of branches of a desirable cultivar that is compatible and hang them in the tree you wish to pollinate just after the blooms have opened. If the bouquet is not in bloom, force the blooms indoors by placing them in a bucket of warm water. Another solution is to topwork the fruit tree with a suitable cross-pollinating cultivar whose blossoms open about the same time as the cultivar to be pollinated (see TOPWORKING). This is a practice which grafts scions of a desirable pollinating cultivar to an existing tree.

### POLLINATION REQUIREMENTS
For **apples and pears**, a sufficient overlap of bloom allows for cross-pollination. Within this group, the period of bloom is not as important as it is for the *Prunus* species. Cultivars of apples, apple-crabs and crabapples of the genus *Malus* will cross-pollinate within this group, even though they represent different species and, in the case of apple-crabs, interspecific hybrids. Apple pollen may also pollinate pear trees of the genus *Pyrus* and vice versa. However, a greater percentage of higher quality fruit results when the pollinating cultivar is closely related.

The **Prunus** species includes all of the stone fruits that can be grown on the prairies. The irregularity of bloom period among *Prunus* species makes the selection of a pollinator, whose bloom period overlaps, an important consideration. As a general rule, early-flowering *Prunus* species can be effectively pollinated by the Nanking cherry. For the late-flowering *Prunus* species, the sandcherry is a successful

Table 13-2

## BLOOMING PERIOD AND SUITABLE POLLINATORS FOR VARIOUS *PRUNUS* TYPES AND CULTIVARS[1]

| *PRUNUS* FRUIT TYPE | BLOOM PERIOD[2] | CULTIVAR | |
|---|---|---|---|
| Apricot | Early-Bloom | Brookcot<br>Scout<br>M604<br>Manchurian Apricot | - Nanking Cherry<br>- Other Early-Blooming *Prunus* Fruits |
| Plum | Early-Bloom | Acme<br>Bounty<br>Brookgold<br>Dandy<br>Fofonoff<br>Prairie | - Nanking Cherry<br>- Other Early-Blooming *Prunus* Fruits |
| | Mid-Bloom | Elite<br>Perfection<br>Norther[3] | - Nanking Cherry + Sandcherry<br>- Other Early-Blooming *Prunus* Fruits<br>- Other Mid-Blooming *Prunus* Fruits |
| | Late-Bloom | Brook Red | - Sandcherry<br>- Other Mid-Blooming *Prunus* Fruits<br>- Other Late-Blooming *Prunus* Fruits |
| Plum Hybrids | Mid-Bloom<br>Late-Bloom | Grenville[4]<br>Pembina[4] | - Assiniboine, Bounty, Cheney, Kaga |
| Cherry Plums | Mid- to Late-Bloom | Alace<br>Opata<br>Dura<br>Manor<br>Sapa | - Sandcherry<br>- Other Cherry Plums<br>- Manchurian Plum (Ptitsin Series) |

[1] Adapted from "Pollination and Production of Tree, Bush and Small Fruits", Alberta Horticultural Research Centre Pamphlet 85-11, Brooks, Alberta, March, 1985.

[2] In Brooks, Alberta: Early-blooming would be from April 25 to May 4    Mid-blooming would be from April 29 to May 6
       Late-blooming would be from May 4 to May 9
Blooming periods for regions in north-central Alberta would be approximately two weeks later.

[3] Norther Plum is not a good pollinator, therefore, when growing Norther, plant a third cultivar so that the pollinating tree can in turn be pollinated by the third cultivar.

[4] Self-sterile hybrids - incompatible with cultivars of similar parentage.

pollinator. Table 13-2 should help in the selection of suitable pollinators for *Prunus* species.

## FRUIT DEVELOPMENT

Successful fertilization of flowers results in the formation of embryos which mature to become seeds. These seeds produce a hormone which stimulates **fruit set**, or the development of fruit following pollination and fertilization. Apples and pears require a number of seeds to develop in order to achieve good size and shape. If part of the ovary is not fertilized (resulting in no seeds), the fruit will be misshapen because it is not stimulated to grow uniformly.

Following fruit set, there are **two natural fruit drops** that are nature's way of thinning the tree. The first drop occurs two or three weeks after petal fall. At this point, the fruit is merely a small swollen receptacle or ovary. Flowers that were not completely fertilized (or self-pollinated) produce weak fruit that is aborted at this time. The second drop occurs in June when damaged, malformed or incompletely fertilized fruit from 1-2 cm ($3_8$-$3_4$ in) in diameter is lost. This thinning is natural and allows remaining healthy fruit to obtain maximum water, nutrients and hormones. If a tree or branch is weak, more fruit drop results. Also, if the tree exhibits an extremely heavy blooming period, a greater number of fruits drop because of the increased competition among the young fruits. It is a good practice to thin the blossoms on fruit trees, particularly those that bloom profusely (see THINNING THE FRUIT CROP and Table 13-9). This increases both size and quality of the remaining fruit and decreases the chance of a reduced crop the following year due to alternate bearing.

As the cells divide and enlarge in the developing fruit, a hormone is produced that helps to stick or hold the fruit on. The fruit also begins to accumulate carbohydrates, which are translocated from other parts of the tree as well as produced in the outer layer of the fruit.

Apples and pears are **pome fruits** which have an embedded core (ovary) within the edible, fleshy, enlarged receptacle or base of the flower. The calyx, or remainder of the petals and sepals, remains attached to the distil end of the apple or pear fruit (see Figure 13-6A).

Figure 13-11:
PROPAGATION OF FRUIT TREES

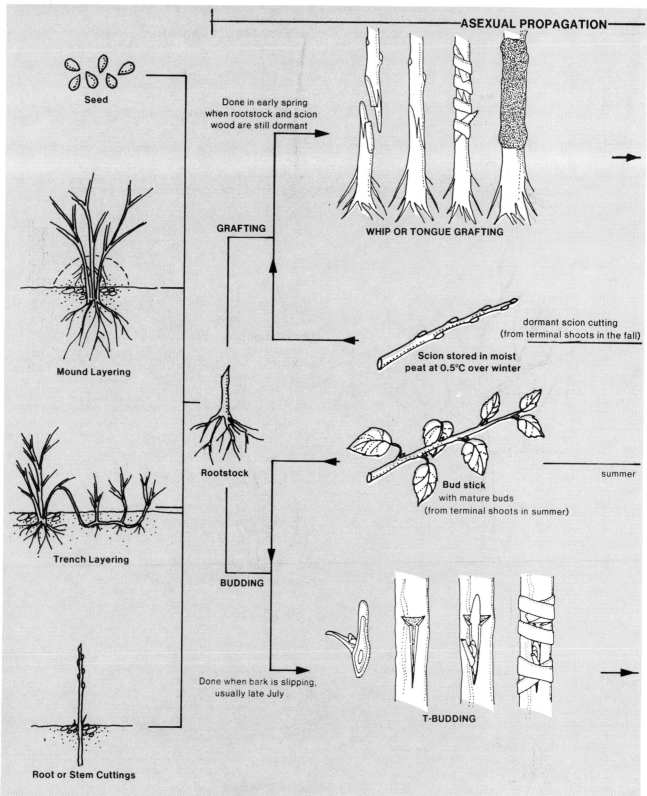

ASEXUAL PROPAGATION

Seed

Done in early spring
when rootstock and scion
wood are still dormant

GRAFTING

WHIP OR TONGUE GRAFTING

Mound Layering

dormant scion cutting
(from terminal shoots in the fall)

Scion stored in moist
peat at 0.5°C over winter

Trench Layering

Rootstock

Bud stick
with mature buds
(from terminal shoots in summer)

summer

BUDDING

Done when bark is slipping,
usually late July

T-BUDDING

Root or Stem Cuttings

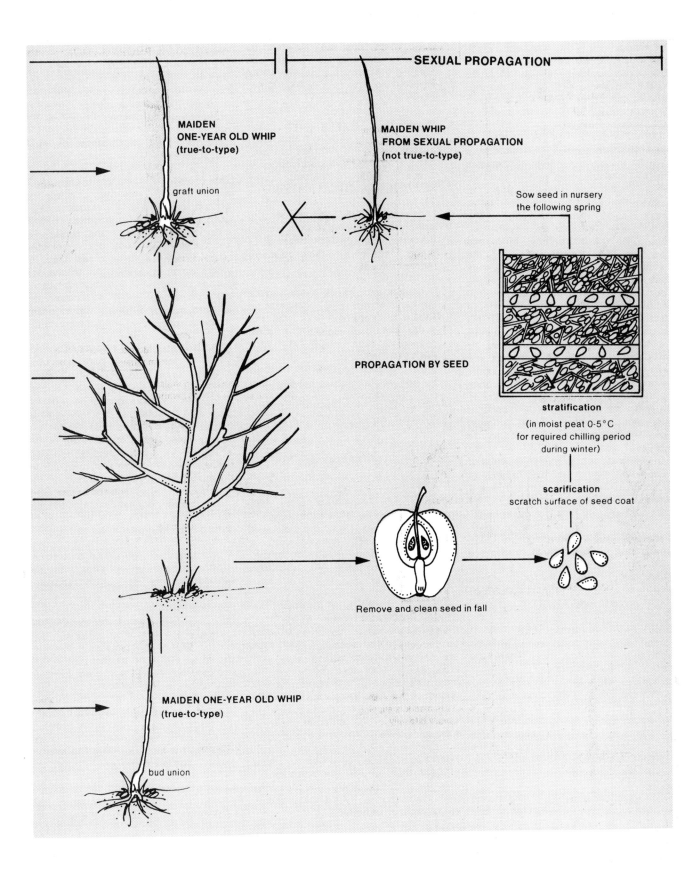

**Stone or drupe fruits** of the *Prunus* species are of quite a different origin. The edible flesh of the fruit is a result of the enlargement of the ovary wall. As the fruit enlarges, the receptacle is shed. The ovary wall, consisting of three layers; the skin, the flesh, and the part next to the stone, forms the fruit (see Figure 13-6B).

### CLIMATE AND FRUIT DEVELOPMENT

When the fruit reaches a certain size, a layer of thin-walled cells forms between the fruit and the main part of the tree which cuts off the supply of carbohydrates to the fruit. This takes place some time in July. The carbohydrates are then used by the tree for radial growth of the trunk and branches, root development, and the formation of bud scales around the buds (see VEGETATIVE GROWTH). Changes then begin to take place within the fruit as the carbohydrates that were stored as starch are converted to sugars. This is usually complete by early August, although it varies with the cultivars. At this stage, the mature fruit has the firmness, texture, color and aroma favorable for consumption. It is then ready to be harvested. Following harvest, the fruit is at a low point of respiration. Sometime during storage, however, the respiration rate begins to increase dramatically (called the **climateric stage**). At this point, the fruit is ripe. Following this, a rapid breakdown in the fruit takes place. If the fruit is a 'keeper', this climateric stage will be delayed (e.g., the Haralson apple keeps up to 25 weeks in cold storage). Generally, apples keep longer than pears. Plums, apricots and cherries are quite poor keepers. Proper storage conditions can prolong the length of time that fruit will keep (see HARVESTING FRUIT and STORING FRUIT).

### BARRENNESS IN FRUIT TREES

Periodically, there are seasons when no fruit sets on a fruit tree. There are several reasons for this:

- Winter killing of the buds may take place if there has been a period of warm weather during the winter after dormancy rest has ended. This stimulates early development of the buds. If freezing temperatures follow, the buds are killed.

- Frost during the blossoming period can injure the sensitive style and stigma of the pistil and, in some cases, destroy the pollen. (Winter killing of the buds and damage by late frosts can be avoided by choosing late-flowering cultivars, and planting the trees in a location with a north-facing or east-facing exposure.)

- Conditions that inhibit the accumulation of carbohydrates in the tissues, or an alternate bearing habit, reduces the percentage of flower buds initiated (see FLOWERING AND POLLINATION).

- Lack of pollination due to self-sterility, conditions that prevent the activity of pollinating insects, or the absence of a suitable pollinator reduce fruit set.

- Diseases and insect pests reduce the vigor of the tree in general and should be kept in check with the occasional and judicious use of pesticides (see PROBLEMS AND PREVENTION).

- Young juvenile trees do not bear fruit until they reach a certain age (see Table 13-4).

## PROPAGATION OF FRUIT TREES

Figure 13-11 demonstrates that fruit trees can be propagated either sexually by seed or asexually by budding or grafting a desired cultivar onto a rootstock (see Plant Propagation lesson, SEXUAL PROPAGATION AND ASEXUAL PROPAGATION).

### SEXUAL PROPAGATION BY SEED

Fruit trees are not usually propagated by seed because the seedlings that result are not true-to-type; that is, they vary considerably from the tree where the seed was obtained. The reason for this is that many fruit trees are self-sterile and, therefore, require cross-pollination from pollen of a different cultivar. Although the female parent of the seed is known, the male parent often cannot be traced because pollen from a number of trees may fertilize the blossoms of one tree. Consequently, the resulting tree seedling is a hybrid that exhibits characteristics of both parents.

### COMPONENTS OF ASEXUAL PROPAGATION

Asexual propagation ensures that the desirable characteristics of a cultivar are retained and the resulting new fruit tree is true-to-type. It is really like a clone of the parent. Generally, the home gardener purchases a young maiden tree propagated in the nursery. However, the following instructions explain how this is done and the significance of each component.

The **rootstock** is the plant onto which another more desirable cultivar is grafted or budded. Rootstock that is used in vegetative propagation is most commonly produced in the nursery by seed. Usually the rootstock is selected for its hardiness, disease resistance or vigor, which it passes on to the top portion of the tree. Dwarfing rootstocks are sometimes used to dwarf the ultimate size of a tree. However, many dwarfing rootstocks are not very hardy on the Prairies (see USE OF DWARF FRUIT TREES ON THE PRAIRIES).

A **scion** is a hardwood cutting taken from a desired cultivar's terminal shoots of current season's growth in order to graft onto a rootstock. A scion diameter the size of a pencil is best. Scions are usually taken during the dormant period of the stock tree. The best time is after the leaves have fallen, but they can be taken before the buds swell in the spring. Once the scion wood is gathered, it must be kept dormant until it is set into the rootstock. This can be done by storing it in moist peat moss at 1-2°C.

A **budstick** (although similar to a scion) is a softwood cutting taken from the terminal shoots of current season's growth when the buds are mature, but not dormant. If the leaf at the base of the buds separates cleanly (without tearing) when it is pulled off, the bud is mature. Again, the budstick's diameter should be the same as that of a pencil. Remove the leaves to prevent moisture loss. Leave a short piece of the petiole for a handle to hang onto when the bud is being removed and budded onto the rootstock. Keep the budsticks moist. If they are not to be used immediately, wrap them in moist toweling and keep in plastic bags in a cool place.

Aside from hardiness, which is usually passed on by the rootstock, an **interstem** grafted between the rootstock and the desired cultivar can contribute other desirable characteristics. There are two methods of doing this. The first is to graft on the interstem and, once it has taken in a year or so, graft the desirable cultivar onto the interstem piece (see Figure 13-12A). Usually whip or tongue grafts are used (see METHODS OF ASEXUAL PROPAGATION and Plant Propagation lesson, GRAFTING AND BUDDING). The tree is then trained to its ultimate form. This is the common practice used to dwarf fruit trees on the Prairies, with the short dwarfing interstem piece being grafted between a hardy rootstock and a desirable cultivar. The reason dwarf rootstock is not used directly is that it is not generally hardy here (see USE OF DWARF FRUIT TREES ON THE PRAIRIES).

The second way in which interstems are used is to graft them onto a hardy rootstock, grow and train them until a framework is established, then topwork this established framework (see Figure 13-12B and GRAFTING TECHNIQUES).

## Figure 13-12
## USING INTERSTEMS

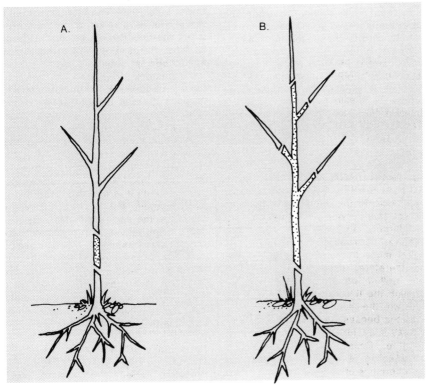

### Table 13-3:
### STANDARD GRAFTING WAX RECIPE

| INGREDIENTS | QUANTITIES |
|---|---|
| Resin | 500 g (1 lb) |
| Linseed Oil | 90 mL (3 fl. oz.) |
| Parawax | 2.5 kg (5 lb) |

Certain cultivars of apples have narrow crotches. This results in a weak framework. However, an interstem framework, with strong, wide angle crotches, will produce a tree with better form and strength (see Figure 13-24).

### METHODS OF ASEXUAL PROPAGATION

The most common methods of propagating young fruit trees are:

- whip or tongue grafting
- T-budding
- side grafting
- patch (chip) grafting

The following discussion and Figure 13-11 outline the techniques of asexual propagation. The section later in this lesson on PRINCIPLES OF GRAFTING will apply to these procedures.

### WHIP OR TONGUE GRAFTING

This method of propagation (see Figure 13-11) can be done during the winter months, usually in January or February, when there is more time available. Scions are usually taken the previous fall, but can also be taken in the spring before the breaking of dormancy. It is important that the diameter of the scion and rootstock be of similar size. Using a sharp knife, make a slanting cut on the lower end of the scion by drawing the knife forward in one smooth motion. The exposed wood should be about 5 cm (2 in) long. The tongue is made by inserting the knife one-third the length of the cut from the end of the scion to a depth of 1-2 cm (⅜-¾ in). Follow the same procedure on the rootstock, just above the root-stem junction. Then insert the scion and rootstock, one into the other, ensuring that the cambium of the scion and rootstock are in contact on at least one side for union to take place. Next, wrap the completed graft with adhesive splicing tape and coat with grafting wax (see Table 13-3). Cover and dip in dry sand to prevent the newly grafted plants from sticking together. Store the plants in a moist, dark place at 1-2°C until they can be planted in the spring.

### T-BUDDING

This method of propagation (see Figure 13-11) is generally carried out on rootstock growing in the field, when the bark on the rootstock is still slipping. This is approximately a week-long period in late July or early August. Budding has become increasingly popular with nurserymen because of the lower susceptibility to crown gall than with root grafting, the greater number of takes, and the smoother trunk that results. It is also a faster operation than root grafting. The major drawback to T-budding, however, is the rather limited time period during which it can be performed.

Make a **T**-cut on the rootstock 10-12.5 cm (4-5 in) above the ground by drawing the tip of the blade vertically through the bark, making a longitudinal cut 3-4 cm (1¼-1⅝ in) long. Next, make a horizontal cut near the top of the first cut by pressing the knife into the bark and rocking it back and forth. The bark should easily open for the insertion of the bud. Perform budding on the north side of the stem so that it will be protected from the drying effect of the sun.

Mature buds are obtained from budsticks. Keep budsticks moist. Use plump, hard, well-developed buds from the middle of the budstick. To remove these buds, insert the knife 1-1.5 cm (⅜-⅝ in) below the bud and draw it beneath the bud, removing some sapwood so that the cambium is exposed to a point 1 cm (⅜ in) above the bud.

Pry open the **T**-cut on the bark of the rootstick by holding the bud shield by its 'handle'. Insert it in an upright position beneath the flaps of bark so that only the bud is protruding through the vertical opening. Trim the top of the shield flush with the horizontal cut on the rootstock. Then use a raffia (or a rubber band) to wrap and tie the stock and bud. This material stretches as the tree grows and eventually falls off once the union has taken.

## PATCH OR CHIP BUDDING

The advantage of patch or chip budding is that it can be performed over a longer period of time than T-budding, as long as the buds are mature. The difficulty is to match the size and shape of the patch and bud with the piece removed from the rootstock. For this reason, a double bladed patch cutter is a useful tool (see Plant Propagation Lesson, Figures 5-29 and 5-30).

## SIDE GRAFTING

If a bud has dried out or winter-killed, a scion can be side grafted onto the rootstock. Make two slanting cuts on the lower end of the scion to form a wedge and trim the scion so that two buds are present. Next, make a single angular cut into the side of the rootstock below the unsuccessful T-bud. Insert the scion into the rootstock so that the cambium is in contact on at least one side. Coat the graft with grafting wax (see Figure 13-25A).

# ESTABLISHING THE FRUIT TREES

The section on ENVIRONMENTAL CONSIDERATIONS discussed how climate and site characteristics influence fruit trees. This section assumes that these factors have been considered and an optimum site chosen for the trees.

When establishing fruit trees, a number of considerations, in addition to site selection, should be considered, including:

- soil preparation
- the planting plan
- selecting cultivars
- purchasing the fruit trees
- planting the trees

## SOIL PREPARATION

Prepare the soil before planting. Ensure that weeds are controlled where the fruit trees are to be established. By summerfallowing the site the previous season, periodic cultivation will significantly reduce weeds. This may be practised in combination with the use of the herbicides paraquat, diquat, or a combination of paraquat and diquat, which eliminates annual weeds and kills back the top growth on perennial weeds.

Alternatives to summerfallowing are to plant a green manure crop, such as oats or rye, which competes somewhat with weeds and, if plowed down while still green, also adds organic matter and some nutrients back into the soil. A row crop, such as potatoes, that is hoed or cultivated to control weeds, also knocks back the weed population and provides one with a harvest as well.

Conduct a soil test to determine nutrient levels and fertilizer requirements to bring them to optimum levels for fruit trees. If it is stated that fruit trees are to be grown, a recommendation will usually be given to bring the soil fertility levels to an appropriate range for fruit trees.

Deep plowing in the fall prior to planting exposes the soil to frost action during

## Table 13-4
## PLANTING PLAN INFORMATION

| FRUIT TREE | JUVENILE PHASE (yr) | PRODUCTIVE LIFESPAN (yr) | ft (m) | HARVEST PERIOD | NO. TREES NEEDED FOR FAMILY OF 5 |
|---|---|---|---|---|---|
| Apple | 5-7 | 20-25 | 18-25 (5.5-7.6) | Aug-Oct | 2-3 |
| Crabapple | 4-5 | 25-30 | 18-25 (5.5-7.6) | Aug-Oct | 2 |
| Dwarf Apple | 2-3 | - | 8-12 (2.4-3.6) | Aug-Sept | 4-10 |
| Pear | 5-7 | 20 | 16-20 (4.9-6.1) | Sept-Oct | 2-3 |
| Plum | 4-5 | 15-25 | 16-20 (4.9-6.1) | Aug-Sept | 4 |
| Cherry Plum | 3-4 | - | 12-20 (4.9-6.1) | Aug-Sept | 3 |
| Apricot | 3-4 | 15-20 | 16-20 (4.9-6.1) | Aug | 3-4 |

the winter which breaks down large clods in the soil. Harrowing or raking in the spring will smooth out the rough surface. Some urban sites have only a thin layer of topsoil over the subsoil. If this is the case, bring in enough topsoil to work in around the roots of the newly planted trees. They quickly establish themselves in good friable topsoil. Often after a house is built, gyprock pieces may be buried in the fill close to the foundation when the yard is graded. The result may be an unfavorable pH condition for the trees. The soil test results indicate if this problem is present and recommends any amendments necessary to correct pH.

## PLANTING PLAN

### DETERMINING PLANTING SIZE

The extent of the planting size, including the number and kinds of trees selected, varies considerably depending on the existing space, personal taste, and time available to give to the planting. The rural gardener may have more space and, with the proper equipment available for cultivation and spraying, could manage a larger number of trees. The urban gardener may have less space for an extensive orchard. Therefore, he may wish to select a few fruit tree specimens to blend in as part of the landscape of the yard, utilizing their ornamental potential as well as taking advantage of their yield of fresh fruit. In some cases, there may be enough space to set aside for a vegetable garden, a cultivar of small fruits and a number of fruit trees. Fruit trees should be grouped together, as they are easier to establish and maintain in a place set aside solely for their production.

Consider the needs and preferences of the family when determining the kind of fruit trees to grow and the number of trees required Next, consider the pollination requirements of each tree (see FLOWERING AND POLLINATION section and Table 13-2). Remember that all fruit trees should be considered self-sterile. Thus, each tree requires a pollinator, although this pollinator may serve to pollinate more than one tree. Remember also that apples, apple-crabs and crabapples pollinate one another and, in some cases, may even be cross-compatible with cultivars of pears.

## DWARF FRUIT TREES
by Jan Hardstaff

There are three methods that can be used for dwarfing fruit trees:

- grafting a desired top cultivar onto a dwarf rootstock

- using a dwarf interstem between a cold hardy, non-dwarf rootstock and the desired top cultivar

- practicing pruning techniques that stunt the growth of the tree

The use of dwarf rootstock is a common method of dwarfing fruit trees. Although dwarf rootstock exists for most fruit trees, dwarfing rootstocks for apples offer the best selection. Malling 9 ($M_9$) is the name of a popular dwarf apple rootstock that can be used in milder Canadian climates and results in tree sizes of 2.4-3.0 m (8-10 ft). It is not hardy on the Prairies. Malling 26 ($M_{26}$) is somewhat hardier and sturdier and grows from 2.4-3.6 m (8-12 ft) tall. Although its framework is not hardy, the rootstock has shown some promise for use on the Prairies.

Alberta Fruit Trees, a nursery in the Edmonton area, has grafted a number of cultivars onto the $M_{26}$ rootstock and observed their response over the past five to six years. None of the trees have been lost, although some have shown more dieback due to winter injury than others. Even a McIntosh-$M_{26}$ combination, which would not normally be considered hardy, has survived.

Ottawa 3 is a cold hardy dwarf apple rootstock that limits the tree height to 2.4-3.0 m (8-10 ft). These trees also show early bearing characteristics, with significant fruit being produced after the third season.

The use of a dwarfing interstem such as Malling 27 ($M_{27}$) between the roots and a desired top cultivar has produced trees even smaller than the $M_9$ rootstock. Although $M_{27}$ rootstock is not hardy and would result in a high susceptibility to winter kill, when a $M_{27}$ interstem is grafted between a hardy rootstock and the desired top, it does not inhibit the tree's ability to survive cold winters. Because not one but two grafts are required, these dwarf interstem trees are expensive to propagate. They may, however, be a solution to the problem of adapting dwarf fruit trees to the Prairies.

It must be stressed that dwarf fruit trees are generally not recommended for the Prairies. Although they may survive for a number of years in a sheltered location, they can easily be wiped out under extremely severe winter conditions. For information on where to obtain Dwarf Fruit Trees or dwarfing material write to: Alberta Fruit Trees Farm, c/o Joe Broder, Box 87, Site 4, R.R. #2, Stony Plain, Alberta T0E 2G0.

Figure 13-13
PLANTING PLAN FOR RURAL ORCHARDS

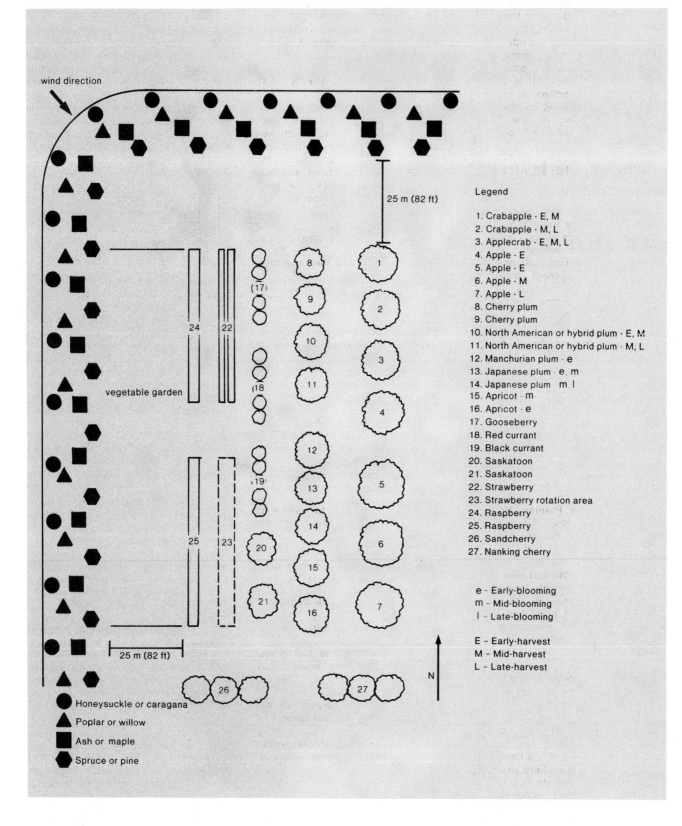

Legend

1. Crabapple - E, M
2. Crabapple - M, L
3. Applecrab - E, M, L
4. Apple - E
5. Apple - E
6. Apple - M
7. Apple - L
8. Cherry plum
9. Cherry plum
10. North American or hybrid plum - E, M
11. North American or hybrid plum - M, L
12. Manchurian plum - e
13. Japanese plum - e, m
14. Japanese plum - m, l
15. Apricot - m
16. Apricot - e
17. Gooseberry
18. Red currant
19. Black currant
20. Saskatoon
21. Saskatoon
22. Strawberry
23. Strawberry rotation area
24. Raspberry
25. Raspberry
26. Sandcherry
27. Nanking cherry

e - Early-blooming
m - Mid-blooming
l - Late-blooming

E - Early-harvest
M - Mid-harvest
L - Late-harvest

wind direction

25 m (82 ft)

vegetable garden

N

25 m (82 ft)

Honeysuckle or caragana
Poplar or willow
Ash or maple
Spruce or pine

Nanking cherries and sandcherries pollinate many of the *Prunus* species, such as plums, cherry plums and apricots while yielding fruit of their own. If pollinating cultivars are close by (in neighboring yards), they provide pollen for the fruit trees and eliminate the necessity of providing pollinators. Topworking (see GRAFTING) is another way to ensure cross-pollination between cultivars that are growing on the same tree, and cuts down on the space required to enjoy different kinds of fruits.

## DETERMINING THE PLANTING PLAN

If space permits, the rural home gardener may set the trees in a square grid system, with trees at each corner of the square to make cultivation easier. This plan has to be modified somewhat when a mixed fruit orchard (containing both pome and stone fruits) is planted, as stone fruits require less space in the row. For this reason, plant the pome fruits (apples and pears) in one group, and the stone fruits (plum, apricot and cherry-plums) in another group.

Figure 13-13 is an example of a rural orchard. It shows how the orchard should be situated with respect to the shelterbelt, small fruit plantation and vegetable garden. Do not plant the fruit trees too close to one another or to other ornamental trees and shrubs. This results in serious competition for water, nutrients and sunlight. Table 13-4 gives suggested spacings for the various fruit trees grown on the Prairies. Properly spaced trees may look rather barren initially but, as they mature, they will provide better yields of higher quality fruit as a result of the more optimum growing conditions. Note that semi-dwarf apples require considerably less space than standard apples. If semi-dwarf apples are being tried, plant them in the row with stone fruits. Remember that these trees are not predictably hardy on the Prairies.

The urban home gardener should decide what kinds of cultivars of trees to grow to provide pollinators and fruit over an extended period. The trees should be worked into the overall landscape so that they can provide ornamental value along with a harvest of fruit. Planting the trees where pesticide residues might contaminate vegetables, small fruits or outdoor living spaces

should be avoided. Messy fruit drop can also be undesirable in certain areas. Finally, planting fruit trees too close to buildings, where the tree's head and root may eventually become crowded up against the building should also be avoided.

## USE OF DWARF FRUIT TREES ON THE PRAIRIES

Dwarf apple trees, although not proven consistently hardy, have been grown with special care in certain sheltered locations in milder climatic zones on the Prairies. These trees are more semi-dwarf than true dwarf and reach between 3.6-4.2 m (12-14 ft) in height. They have a number of advantages in that they:

- are easier to prune, spray, thin and pick
- require less space than a standard tree
- usually come into bearing at an early age
- yield more manageable quantities of fruit

## SELECTING CULTIVARS

### CONSIDERATIONS

After deciding on the kinds of fruit trees to be grown and how many of each, the next step is to determine which cultivars are the most suitable. The ideal fruit tree cultivar would offer the following characteristics:

- sufficient hardiness to survive the severe Prairie climate, with little winter injury

- disease resistance and vigorous growth

- good form and structural strength

- fruit production at an early age

- good annual crop of fruit without over-production that would require thinning

- quality fruit with respect to size, appearance, texture and flavor

- variety of uses such as dessert eating, cooking, canning, jellies and jams

- long storage life

Of course, a cultivar with all of these desirable traits is extremely rare.

In selecting cultivars for the Prairies, the most important criteria to consider is **hardiness**, for without it even the tree with quality fruit is useless. Select fruit trees which are recommended for the zone in which you live (see Climate lesson, Figures 2-10). Information on what fruit trees are well adapted to growing conditions in certain zones is included in Tables 13-6, 13-7 and 13-8.

**Disease resistance**, particularly to fireblight, is another desirable trait. Table 13-5 indicates some *Malus* Species which are very susceptible, resistant or very resistant to fireblight. Most other apple cultivars and pears fall into the susceptible category.

As mentioned earlier, selection of a **suitable pollinator** is important for cross-pollination as fruit trees are generally self-sterile. Without adequate pollination, fruit set will be very low (see FLOWERING AND POLLINATION and Table 13-2 for guidelines in selecting pollinators).

The **quality of fruit** is difficult to define, as it varies considerably with people's tastes. Consider whether the fruit will be used for eating fresh, pies, sauces, jams or jellies. The time of ripeness and storage life of the fruit is also important. Choose cultivars that ripen at different times so that the harvest period can be staggered and fresh fruit will be available over a longer period of time.

### CULTIVAR DESCRIPTIONS

CRABAPPLES, APPLECRABS AND APPLES
These are the most commonly grown fruits on the Prairies. Crabapples are less than 3.5 cm (about 1½ in) in diameter and quite tart in flavor, making them more popular for canning and jellies than fresh eating. Applecrabs are from 3.5-5 cm (about 1½-2 in) in diameter and more apple than crab in flavor. These fruits are sometimes classified as crabapples because of their size. They are usually quite pleasant for fresh eating and are sometimes used for canning. Apples are more than 5 cm (2 in) in diameter and have a sweeter taste,

## Table 13-5
## FIREBLIGHT RESISTANCE RATINGS

| | |
|---|---|
| Very Susceptible: | Battleford, Hyslop, Royalty Crab[1], Transcendant, Yellow Transparent |
| Susceptible: | Most other apple and pear cultivars |
| Resistant: | Breakey, Columbia, dolgo, Haralson, Heyer 12, Rescue, Goodland |
| Very Resistant: | Trail, Ussurian Pear[1] |

1. Ornamental Tree

generally making them good for eating fresh (except when the texture is soft). Apples are often used for cooking and canning as well. Table 13-6 lists the cultivars, their fruiting season, usage and storage qualities and lists the zones in which they are hardy. There is also a brief description of each cultivar. Many of these recommendations are included in the *Alberta Horticultural Guide* (Alberta Agriculture, Agdex 200/01), and *Tree Fruits for the Prairie Provinces*

## Table 13-6
## CRABAPPLES, APPLECRABS AND APPLES FOR THE PRAIRIES

| FRUIT TYPE | CULTIVAR | FRUITING SEASON[2] | ORNAMENTAL | COOKING/CANNING | JAMS/JELLIES | STORAGE (weeks) | ZONES[3] | | | | | | | | | |
|---|---|---|---|---|---|---|---|---|---|---|---|---|---|---|---|---|
| | | | | | | | 2A | 2B | 2C | 3 | 3A | 4 | 5' | 5B | 5C | 6B |
| Crabapple | Dolgo | E | ✓ | | | ✓ | 0 | S | S | S | S | S | S | S | F | S | T |
| | Amur Red[1] | M | ✓ | | | ✓ | 4 | | | Recommended on Prairies | | | | | | | |
| | Osman | M | | ✓ | ✓ | | 4 | T | F | T | S | S | T | S | S | T | - |
| | Trailman[5] | M | | ✓ | ✓ | | 6 | T | F | T | S | S | T | S | T | T | - |
| | Columbia | L | | ✓ | | | 4 | S | S | S | S | S | S | S | S | S | T |
| Applecrab | Dawn[1] | E | | ✓ | ✓ | | - | | | Recommended for Trial | | | | | | | |
| | Rescue[4] | E | | ✓ | ✓ | | 3 | S | S | S | S | S | S | S | S | S | S |
| | Renown[1] | M | | | ✓ | | - | | | Recommended on Prairies | | | | | | | |
| | Rosybrook | M | | | ✓ | | 10 | S | S | S | S | S | S | S | S | - | T |
| | Shafer | M | | | ✓ | | - | | | Recommended for Trial | | | | | | | |
| | Trail | M | | ✓ | ✓ | | 6 | | | Recommended for Trial | | | | | | | |
| | Kerr | L | | ✓ | ✓ | ✓ | 27 | S | S | S | S | S | T | S | S | T | - |
| Apples | Heyer 12[4] | E | | ✓ | | | 4 | S | S | S | S | S | S | S | S | F | F |
| | Norland[4] | E | | ✓ | ✓ | | 8 | S | S | S | S | S | S | F | F | - | - |
| | Rosthern18[4] | E | | ✓ | | | 6 | S | S | S | S | S | S | S | T | T | T |
| | Westland[4] | E | | ✓ | | | 9 | S | S | S | S | S | S | F | F | T | T |
| | Battleford | M | | ✓ | | | 4 | S | F | S | S | S | T | T | T | T | T |
| | Carrol[1] | M | | ✓ | ✓ | | - | | | Recommended for Trial | | | | | | | |
| | Edith Smith[1] | M | | ✓ | | | - | | | Recommended on Prairies | | | | | | | |
| | Harcourt | M | | ✓ | ✓ | | 2 | F | F | F | S | S | T | T | T | T | T |
| | McLean | M | | ✓ | ✓ | | 6 | F | S | F | S | S | T | T | T | T | T |
| | Parkland[4] | M | | ✓ | ✓ | | 8 | S | S | S | S | S | - | - | - | - | - |
| | Patterson | M | | ✓ | ✓ | | 6 | F | S | T | S | S | T | T | T | - | T |
| | Sunnybrook | M | | ✓ | ✓ | | 4 | S | S | S | S | S | T | T | T | T | - |
| | Breakey[1] | L | | ✓ | | | 10 | | | Recommended for Trial | | | | | | | |
| | Collett | L | | ✓ | ✓ | | 10 | F | F | F | S | S | T | T | T | - | - |
| | Goodland | L | | ✓ | ✓ | | 20 | F | F | F | S | S | T | T | T | - | - |
| | Haralson | L | | ✓ | ✓ | | 25 | F | F | F | S | S | T | T | T | - | - |
| | Luke | L | | ✓ | | | 10 | T | T | T | F | S | - | - | - | - | - |

[1]Not a recommended cultivar in *Alberta Horticultural Guide* (Agdex 200/01).
[2]Fruiting season early (mid-late August), mid-season (early to mid-Sept), late (mid-Sept to late Sept).
[3]S=Satisfactory, F=Fair, T=Trial, -=Behavior not known (refers to hardiness of cultivar in each zone).
[4]Fruit must be picked before full maturity for storage or use.
[5]Trailman has size of applecrab but taste of crabapple.

(Agriculture Canada Publication No. 1672). In the *Friends of the Garden* newsletter 'Kinnikinnick' Volume 3, #10 published by the University of Alberta's Devonian Botanical Garden, information on crabapples (which in this case includes applecrabs) and apple cultivars is compiled into a selection key, which may also be a useful tool in making cultivar selections.

## Crabapple Cultivars

Dolgo - This early season fruit is about 3 cm (1½ in) in diameter, a bright purple-red, and excellent for making jelly, but is not a keeper. The tree is very hardy and quite an attractive ornamental, as the blossoms and fruit are quite showy. It shows a moderate resistance to fireblight. Popular seller among nurseries.

Amur Red - This mid-season crab is about 3.5 cm (1½ in) in diameter, deep red in color with red flesh, excellent for jelly, imparting a good ruby-red color. Also used as an ornamental. The tree is very hardy.

Osman - This mid-season fruit is about 3.5 cm (1½ in) in diameter, a dark, dull brown-red, good for jellies and canning, and keeps for a few weeks. The tree is quite hardy in the northern zones.

Trailman - This mid-season crab is about 4.5 cm (1¾ in) in diameter, has a greenish ground color with red blush, is tart in flavor, good for eating out of hand and canning, and keeps a little over a month. Tree comes into bearing early, is resistant to fireblight, and is quite hardy. Trailman is classified here as a crab because of its flavor, even though in size it could be called an applecrab, and is in some references.

Columbia - This late-season fruit is about 3 cm (1½ in) in diameter, and a deep red over light ground color. Its thick skin makes it only fair for canning, and it only keeps for a few weeks. The tree is very hardy throughout the Prairies and resistant to fireblight.

## Applecrab Cultivars

Rescue - This early-season fruit is about 3.5 cm (1½ in) in diameter, with solid dull red over a yellow ground color, good for canning and fresh. Goes mealy during storage which lasts only a few weeks. Very hardy throughout the Prairies.

Dawn - This early-season fruit is about 4.5 cm (1¾ in) in diameter, a light crimson color with yellowish flesh, good for eating and cooking. The tree produces heavy yields and may be subject to severe crotch injury. This cultivar is offered by many nurseries.

Renown - This mid-season fruit is 3.5 cm (1½ in) in diameter, yellow splashed with red in color, a poor canner, but a nice fresh eating apple. The tree is recommended throughout the Prairies.

Rosybrook - This mid-season fruit is 4.5 cm (1¾ in) in diameter, and is a pale green ground color mostly covered with red. The firm, sweet flesh makes it good for eatiing fresh, and it has good keeping quality up to 10 weeks. The tree is hardy throughout most of the Prairies.

Shafer - This mid-season fruit is about 4.5 cm (1¾ in) in diameter, yellow blushed with red, and excellent for eating out of hand. It is recommended for trial by the research station in Morden, Manitoba.

Trail - This mid-season fruit is 4 cm (1½ in) in diameter, orange-red in color, and good for eating and cooking, but not canning. The tree has fair vigor and because it is sometimes late in ripening should be grown where the growing season is longer.

Kerr - This late-season fruit is 3.5 cm (1½ in) in diameter, a dark, purple-red, good for jelly and eating fresh, an excellent canner, and stores up to 27 weeks. It is hardy in most of the Prairies, but recommended only for trial along the foothills.

## Apple Cultivars

Heyer #12 - This early apple is 5-6 cm (2-2½ in) in diameter, straw-colored, and good for pies and sauces. It is too tart for eating out of hand, and breaks down quickly during storage, so it should be picked before full maturity for storage and use. The tree is fireblight resistant and extremely hardy, making it a useful standard against which the hardiness of other fruits is compared. It is offered by a number of nurseries on the Prairies.

Norland - This early apple is 6-7 cm (about 2½ in) in diameter, red in color, good for eating fresh or cooking, and stores for about two months if picked

before full maturity. The tree is somewhat dwarf, and very hardy except in the chinook zones and northern zones where it is only fair with respect to hardiness.

Rosthern 18 - This early apple is 4 cm (1½ in) in diameter, is scarlet over a yellow ground in color, good for cooking and canning, and will store for a couple of months if picked prior to maturity. The tree does not have a high yield of fruit. It is hardy in most of the Prairies, with only moderate hardiness along the foothills and in the northern zones.

Westland - This fruit is 7-8 cm (about 3 in) in diameter, has a pale yellow-green ground color striped with red, is suitable for cooking and stores for nine weeks if it is picked prior to maturity. This is quite a hardy apple across the Prairies and suggested as a replacement for Heyer #12 (one of the parents of this seedling). However, it is less hardy in the northern zones and along the foothills in the chinook areas.

Battleford - This mid-season apple is 7 cm (about 3 in) in diameter, mottled and streaked red over a pale green ground color, fair for eating fresh and cooking, and stores for about a month. The tree is somewhat susceptible to fireblight, fairly hardy but not dependably productive.

Carrol - This mid-season apple is 6-7.5 cm (2½ to 3 in) in size, with a greenish-white ground color washed with stripes of red, excellent for eating fresh and good for cooking. The tree is not extremely hardy, but is recommended for trial on the Prairies.

Edith Smith - This mid-season apple is 7 cm (about 3 in) in diameter, green with a red cheek, too tough and pulpy for eating, but good for cooking and a fair keeper. It is fairly hardy on the Prairies.

Harcourt - This mid-season apple is 5 cm (2 in) in diameter, blushed bright red, has a good taste for eating fresh, but is not a good keeper. This tree is hardy across the Prairies but only moderately hardy in the chinook zones and the northern zones.

McLean - This mid-season fruit is about 6 cm (2½ in) in diameter, has yellow ground color blushed with light red, is excellent for eating, good for cooking, but does not keep more than about a month without losing its flavor. The tree yields very heavily and is fairly hardy.

Parkland - This mid-season fruit is 6-7 cm (about 2½ in) in diameter, has mildly acidic flesh that is creamy-white tinged with green, is good eaten fresh or cooked, and keeps up to two months. The tree has an alternate or biennial bearing habit, which may be corrected somewhat by thinning. It is fairly hardy but less so in the northern zones.

Patterson - This mid-season fruit is 6 cm (2½ in) in diameter, greenish-yellow blushed with red in some seasons, is good for cooking and dessert when fresh, and keeps six weeks. This tree yields heavily and is fairly hardy across the Prairies, but less so in the northern zones.

Sunnybrook - This mid-season apple is 6.5 cm (2½ in) in diameter, is yellow with red cheeks, has a sweet flavor, is good for cooking and eating fresh and excellent for pies but is only a fair keeper. Productive and hardy.

Breakey - This late-season fruit is 5-6.5 cm (2-2½ in) in diameter, striped bright red over a yellow-green ground color, excellent for eating fresh and good for cooking. Stores into November. Tree is not especially hardy or productive, but is recommended for trial in milder climatic zones.

Collett - This late-season apple is 6-7.5 cm (2½-3 in) in size, light red over a light green ground color, a good cooking and eating fresh apple, and keeps up to 10 weeks. The tree is subject to fireblight and only moderately hardy on the prairies doing best in the milder zones.

Goodland - This late-season apple is between 6-8 cm (2½-3 in) in diameter, has a creamy green ground color washed with red, is a good eating fresh and cooking apple, and stores into February. It is moderately resistant to fireblight, and only moderately hardy, doing best in the milder zones.

Haralson - This late-season fruit is 6 cm (2½ in) in diameter, brownish-red, good for cooking and for eating fresh, although the flesh is a bit tough, and an excellent keeper into March. It is a heavy producer which may require thinning. Because it ripens so late, in October, it does best where the growing season is longer.

Luke - This late-season apple is the largest grown on the prairies at 9 cm (3½ in) in diameter. Its color is mottled dark red over green, it is used primarily for cooking, and is a good keeper. However, because it is so late, it may only do well where the growing season is longer.

## PEARS

Pear trees make attractive ornamentals and their fruit can be used for cooking and canning. However, most do not have fresh eating quality, with the exception of Ure. Pears do best in the milder Prairie zones 2A to 4 (see Climate lesson, Figure 2-10), but experience severe winter dieback in the northern zones and along the foothills. They may also be difficult to establish in these areas. Table 13-7 lists some of the hardier pears suitable for certain parts of the Prairies. There is also a brief description of each cultivar.

### Pear Cultivars

Golden Spice - The fruit ripens in mid- to late September, is about 5 cm (2 in) in diameter, greenish yellow in color blushed with a dull red, is good for canning and fair for eating fresh. It is recommended for trial only in milder Prairie climates.

Tioma - The fruit ripens in mid-September, is about 7 cm (about 3 in) in diameter, yellow in color with a bronze cheek, and has a very astringent taste making it unsuitable for canning and fair for jam. The skin of the fruit is very susceptible to scab.

Ure - This pear is ripe in mid-September, is about 5 cm (2 in) in diameter, greenish yellow in color, is used for canning and is one of the few pears grown on the prairies that has good fresh eating quality. It was released in the late seventies by the Research Station in Morden, Manitoba.

David - This fruit ripens in late September, is about 5 cm (2 in) in diameter, green with a bronze cheek in color, and suitable for cooking, but not for eating fresh or canning because of its very coarse, gritty texture. May do best

## Table 13-7
## PEARS FOR THE PRAIRIES

| CULTIVAR | FRUITING SEASON[2] | ORNAMENTAL | COOKING | DESSERT EATING | ZONES[3] | | | | | | | | | |
|---|---|---|---|---|---|---|---|---|---|---|---|---|---|---|
| | | | | | 2A | 2B | 2C | 3 | 3A | 4 | 5 | 5B | 5C | 6B |
| Golden Spice | M | ✓ | ✓ | ✓ | Recommended for Trial —————————————————— Not Hardy | | | | | | | | | |
| Tioma[1] | M | ✓ | ✓ | ✓ | | | | | | | | | | |
| Ure[1] | M | ✓ | ✓ | ✓ | | | | | | | | | | |
| David | L | ✓ | ✓ | | | | | | | | | | | |
| John[1] | L | ✓ | ✓ | | | | | | | | | | | |
| Phillip[1] | L | ✓ | ✓ | ✓ | | | | | | | | | | |

[1]Recommended cultivar in *Alberta Horticultural Guide* (Agdex 200/01).
[2]Fruiting season: M=mid-Sept, L=late Sept
[3]Pears show some hardiness in zones 2A to 4, but are not consistently hardy in 5 to 6B.

where there is a longer growing season.

John - This fruit which ripens in late September is about 7.5 cm (3 in) in diameter, and greenish yellow, with fair quality for cooking. It is also quite aromatic. Because it is late, it may require a longer growing season.

Phillip - This pear is ripe in late September, thus requiring a longer growing season. It is greenish yellow in color, about 7.5 cm (3 in) in diameter, fair for canning and good for jam.

## PRUNUS SPECIES FRUITS

There are basically six types of Prunus fruits that can be grown on the Prairies including:

- native (Prunus nigra, Prunus americana and hybrids)
- Japanese plums (Prunus salicina and hybrids)
- cherry plum hybrids (Japanese plums X sandcherry (Prunus besseyi))
- apricots (Prunus armenica)
- sandcherries (Prunus besseyi)
- bush cherries including Nanking cherries (Prunus tomentosa) and Mongolian cherries (Prunus fruticosa)

To successfully grow plums or apricots on the Prairies, a site that offers protection from early spring frosts is essential. These fruit trees tend to blossom first thing in the spring, with apricots being earliest. Although the trees themselves may grow in some of the zones with shorter growing seasons, they often do not produce fruit in these regions because the blossoms are damaged by spring frosts. In areas with

## Table 13-8
## PRUNUS SPECIES OF FRUIT FOR THE PRAIRIES

| FRUIT TYPE | | CULTIVAR | FRUITING SEASON[3] | ORNAMENTAL | COOKING/CANNING | DESSERT EATING | JAMS/JELLIES | ZONES[4] | | | | | | | | | |
|---|---|---|---|---|---|---|---|---|---|---|---|---|---|---|---|---|---|
| | | | | | | | | 2A | 2B | 2C | 3 | 3A | 4 | 5 | 5B | 5C | 6B |
| Native plums | E | Bounty | L | | | ✓ | ✓ | S | S | S | S | S | - | F | U | - | T |
| (Prunus nigra, & hybrids) | E | Dandy | L | | | | ✓ | F | S | S | S | S | - | T | F | T | - |
| Prunus americana | M | Grenville²⁵ | L | | | ✓ | | ———————— Recommended for Trial ———————— | | | | | | | | | |
| | M | Norther | E | | | ✓ | | F | S | S | S | S | - | T | S | T | T |
| | L | Pembina⁵ | L | | ✓ | ✓ | | F | S | S | S | S | - | - | U | U | - |
| | E | Prairie² | L | | | | ✓ | ———————— Recommended for Trial ———————— | | | | | | | | | |
| Japanese plum | E | Brookgold | M | | | ✓ | | S | S | S | S | F | T | T | F | T | - |
| (Prunus salicina) | L | Brookred | L | | | ✓ | ✓ | S | S | S | S | F | T | T | F | T | - |
| | E | Ptitsin5,9,10 | E | | | ✓ | | S | S | S | S | S | - | F | - | - | - |
| | E | Ptitsin12 | E | | | ✓ | | S | S | S | S | S | - | F | | | |
| Cherry plum | | (green fleshed) | | | | | | | | | | | | | | | |
| (sandcherry X | | Alace | E | | | ✓ | | S | S | S | S | S | S | S | T | T | - |
| plum hybrids) | | Opata | L | | ✓ | ✓ | ✓ | S | S | S | S | S | S | S | T | T | - |
| | | (red fleshed) | | | | | | | | | | | | | | | |
| | | Manor | E | | ✓ | | ✓ | S | S | S | S | S | S | S | T | T | - |
| | | Dura | L | | ✓ | | ✓ | S | S | S | S | S | S | S | T | T | - |
| | | Sapa² | L | | ✓ | | ✓ | ———————— Recommended on Prairies ———————— | | | | | | | | | |
| Sandcherry | L | Brooks | M | | | | | | | | | | | | | | |
| (Prunus besseyi) | L | Mando | - | | | | ✓ | | | | | | | | | | |
| Cherries | L | Manmoor | E | | ✓ | | ✓ | | | | | | | | | | |
| | E | Nanking | E | ✓ | ✓ | ✓ | ✓ | | | | | | | | | | |
| | E | Mongolian | E | ✓ | ✓ | ✓ | ✓ | | | | | | | | | | |
| Apricot | E | Brookcot | E | | ✓ | ✓ | ✓ | | | | | | | | | | |
| (Prunus armenica) | E | M604 | E | | ✓ | ✓ | | | | | | | | | | | |
| | E | Manchurian | E | ✓ | | ✓ | ✓ | | | | | | | | | | |
| | E | Scout | E | | ✓ | ✓ | ✓ | | | | | | | | | | |

[1] Season of Bloom: E = April 25-May 4; M = April 29-May 6; L = May 4-9; - = unavailable.

All early-blooming cultivars of Prunus species will do best in zones and locations that are not subject to early spring frosts.

[2] Not a recommended cultivar in Alberta Horticultural Guide (Agdex 200/01).

[3] Fruiting Season: E = early Aug; M = mid-Aug; L = late Aug; - = unavailable.

[4] S = satisfactory, F = fair, T = trial, U = unsatisfactory, - = unavailable.

[5] North American plum X Japanese plum cross.

a higher risk of early spring frost, cultivars that are late-flowering are more suitable. In zones where the growing season is less than 110 days or elevation exceeds 1065 m (3450 ft), as in regions north of zone 3A (see Climate lesson, Figure 2-10) or along the foothills, it is not recommended to grow these early-flowering fruits. Table 13-8 lists some of the cultivars of *Prunus* species that are suggested for use on the Prairies. A brief description of each cultivar is also included.

## North American Plums

These are selections and crosses of native plums of Canadian and American origin and also include Native X Japanese plum hybrids (•)

Bounty - This early-blooming fruit ripens in late August, is about 3.5 cm (1½ in) in diameter, dark red with blue bloom and orange yellow flesh, fair for eating and canning, good for jam and very hardy.

Dandy - This early-blooming plum ripens in late August, is about 2.5 cm (1 in) in diameter, has yellow skin blushed with red and yellow flesh, is suitable for canning, excellent for jam, and very hardy.

Prairie - This early-blooming fruit is ripe in late August, 4.5 cm (1¾ in) in diameter, dark red in color, rather freestone and hardy.

Grenville* - This mid-blooming plum ripens in late August, is fairly large at 5 cm (2 in) in diameter, has dark scarlet skin, golden flesh and is excellent for eating. The tree is very hardy, a heavy yielder, and has a tendency to yield biennially, requiring some thinning.

Norther - This mid-blooming plum is ripe in early August, with fruit that is 3.5 cm (1½ in) in diameter, bright red with yellow flesh, good for eating, hardy and productive.

Pembina* - This late-blooming plum is ripe in early September with 4-5 cm (1½-2 in) diameter fruit that is red with a bluish bloom and bright yellow flesh, excellent for eating, good for canning and fair for jam. Very hardy and productive as late-blooming habit helps in avoiding frost damage to the blossoms. This plum is a good seller among Prairie and Alberta nurseries.

## Japanese Plums

These are selections that originated from China in Manchuria and not in Japan as the name suggests.

Brookgold - This is an early-blooming plum that is ripe in mid-August, with fruit between 2.5-3 cm (about 1 in) in diameter, golden in color with a red splash on one cheek, freestone, tender skin, excellent for eating and hardy. This plum is becoming popular with prairie nurseries.

Ptitsin 5, 9, and 10 - These plums are early-blooming with fruit ripe in early August. It is 2.5-3.5 cm (1-1½ in) in diameter, greenish yellow in color with light green flesh, is good for eating fresh and for making jam, and hardy.

Ptitsin 12 - This early blooming plum is ripe in late August, red in color with flesh to straw colored skin, good for eating, and hardy. It is considered to be the better Ptitsin by some.

Brookred - This late-blooming plum ripens in late August, producing 4-5 cm (1½-2 in) diameter fruit that is a dull, dark red in color, excellent for jam and good for eating fresh. The tree is hardy and a moderate producer. This plum is popular with prairie nurseries.

## Cherry-Plum Hybrids

These are the result of crossing the Japanese plum with the sandcherry (*Prunus besseyi*). The fruit is larger, sweeter, and better flavored than the true sandcherry, but somewhat less hardy.

Alace - This fruit ripens in early July, is about 2.5 cm (1 in) in diameter, has deep purple color with green flesh, is good to eat, and is hardy throughout the Prairies, except in the northern zones.

Opata - Ripens late August, is 2.5-3 cm (about 1 in) in diameter, has purple-red skin with bluish bloom and yellowish-green flesh, is good for eating, fair for canning and jam (used mostly as filler with other plums), very productive and quite hardy. Popular with nurseries on the prairies.

Manor - Fruit ripens in early August, is about 2.5-3 cm (about 1 in) in diameter, dark purple-red with dark red flesh, good for canning, pies and jam, and fairly hardy.

Dura - Fruit ripens late, August into September, and lasts on the tree into the fall. It is 3.5 cm (1½ in) in diameter, dull green blotches with purple and has red flesh, is excellent for canning and good for pies and jam.

Sapa - Ripens in early September and keeps well on the tree until heavy frost. It is 2.5 cm (1 in) in diameter, purple with bluish bloom and dark purple flesh, almost freestone, excellent for canning and jam.

## Apricots

These are hardy selections of Siberian and Manchurian apricots. The apricots bloom even earlier than the plums and, therefore, may not produce fruit if blossoms are killed by a spring frost.

Brookcot - The fruit ripens in early August, is 3-4 cm (1¼-1½ in) in diameter, bright yellow-orange in color with a yellow cheek, the stone is slightly clinging, and it has good canning, eating and jam qualities.

M604 - Ripens in early August with fruit 4-5 cm (1½-2 in) in diameter, the color golden yellow becoming reddish, good for eating and canning.

Scout - This fruit ripens in early August, is about 4 cm (1½ in) in diameter, bronze gold blushed with red, good for canning and jam and fair for eating.

Manchurian Apricot - Is a good pollinator for the apricot cultivars.

## Sandcherries

Hardy bush cherries, that are useful pollinators for late blooming *Prunus* species. The fruit's quality is poor for eating, but can be used for cooking or jam.

Brooks - The fruit is ripe in mid-August, about 2 cm (¾ in) in diameter, with a dark purple color and yellow-green flesh. It is good for jam and quite hardy throughout the prairies.

Mando - No information available. This is a recommendation by the ARHC in Brooks.

Manmoor - The fruit is ripe in early August, about 2 cm (¾ in) in diameter, purple black with green flesh, excellent for canning.

## Cherries
Sweet cherries such as Bing, grown in milder climates such as British Columbia, are not hardy here. Some sour cherries of the Morello-type may be grown for trial in milder zones. The Mongolian and Nanking bush cherries are reasonably hardy and productive. More than one kind of bush cherry should be planted for cross pollination and good yields.

Nanking Cherry - Early blooming, with fruit ripe in late July to mid-August, about 1.2 cm (½ in) in diameter, white to currant red in color with creamy to pink flesh. It is good for jelly, eating, canning and pies. Because it is such an early bloomer, it is a useful pollinator for other early blooming *Prunus* species. However, it is susceptible to damage by early spring frost.

Mongolian Cherry - Early blooming, its fruit is ripe in late July, is about 1.2 cm (½ in) in size, light to dark red, excellent for jelly, but can be used for canning and fresh eating. It can also be a useful pollinator for early blooming *Prunus* species.

## PURCHASING FRUIT TREES

### WHERE TO PURCHASE
Once cultivars have been selected, it is time to purchase the trees. If possible, deal with an established Prairie nursery. Cost per tree may be slightly higher for Prairie grown stock than stock grown in milder climates, simply because it takes longer to raise them under the harsher climatic conditions. However, fruit raised locally ensures their hardiness in this climate. This also results in lower shipping charges, and less transportation time in delivering the trees, thus reducing the risk of the trees drying out in transit. Choose nursery stock that is vigorous, healthy, hardy for your zone, true-to-type, and well-packed.

Do not purchase trees from garden centers without getting acceptable answers to these questions:

- Where was the stock grown?

- Is it hardy on the Prairies and for which zones?

- When was it shipped?

- How long was it in transit?

- What kind of guarantees are provided that the tree is healthy and true-to-type?

Trees grown in milder climates must be Prairie hardy. Exercise caution in buying plants that are on sale or unusually cheap. These trees may be dried out, diseased, damaged, poorly grown or wrongly named. Also, avoid seedling trees as they are not usually true-to-type and they vary widely from the mother plant. Look instead for desirable cultivars that have been grafted or budded onto hardy rootstocks.

## SIZE OF TREES
Select one-year old maiden whips that are free of root gall (warty growths on the upper roots). These should also have a vigorous stem and well developed root system. These whips are less expensive and unpruned. The latter permits the buyer to carefully train the tree to a desirable shape. Two-year old trees are usually pruned and the lower branches removed before leaving the

nursery. This may result in a tree with less desirable form than could otherwise be obtained with careful training over a long period of time. Look for wide crotch angles and scaffold branches that are well spaced on the main stem. Whether the tree is one- or two-years old, it should have a smooth, strong graft union, and a strong, well-branched root system.

If trees are being ordered from a nursery, place the order in the fall previous to planting. One-year old whips are usually purchased bare-root and should be packaged in moist peat moss. Two-year old trees can be purchased bare-root, balled and burlapped, or container grown. Be careful that the trees are not 'containerized', meaning they were dug when mature and then potted up. These trees must then suffer a second transplanting shock at the time of planting and are less likely to survive than stock that is truly container grown from day one. The advantage of container grown stock is that it can be planted almost any time during the growing season.

## PLANTING THE TREES

### TIME TO PLANT
On the Prairies, the best time to plant fruit trees is in the early spring. At this time the tree is still dormant, the soil is

## Figure 13-14
## HEELING-IN

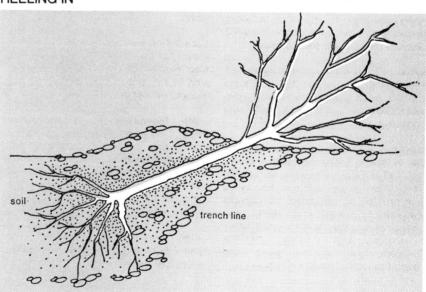

soil

trench line

moist and temperatures are cool. Later planting, when days are hot with drying winds and when the soil has lost much of its available moisture, may result in more severe transplanting shock. In milder climates, early fall planting is recommended. Theoretically, this is best as trees planted in early September may still put forth some roots before the onset of winter. However, with the extreme cold temperatures, drying winter winds and early fall frosts, winterkilling in fall plantings on the Prairies is very likely. If fall planting is necessary, plant trees in early September, thoroughly water in mid-October and hill up with 30 cm (12 in) of soil prior to freeze-up. In the following spring, remove and level the soil around the tree base.

## HEELING-IN

Nursery stock that cannot be planted for a time should be temporarily heeled-in (see Figure 13-14). Dig a trench 45 cm (18 in) deep with one side sloping about 30°. While the trench is being prepared, cover the trees with wet burlap to prevent them from drying out. Lay the trees closely in the trench and water generously. Cover the roots with fine soil. Firmly tamp the soil around the roots. Hill up soil around the trunk and apply more water. It is very important that the roots be kept moist while they are heeled-in. Water regularly until planting and protect the trees from mice and rabbits.

## PLANTING

When spring arrives, it is time to plant the fruit trees. Dig a hole large enough to accommodate the root system without crowding or folding the roots. For a one-year old tree, a hole that is 60-75 cm (24-30 in) in diameter and 45 cm (18 in) deep is adequate (see Figure 13-15). For larger trees, there should be at least a 15 cm (6 in) space on all sides of the bare roots or small root-ball. If the subsoil beneath the hole is hard, loosen it up with a spade another 30 cm (12 in) deeper. If transplanting or moving larger fruit trees with a root system 1 m (39 in) or more in diameter, allow a 30 cm (12 in) space around the root-ball. When digging the hole, retain the topsoil and remove or spread any poor subsoil. Then mix the topsoil remaining, and any extra being added, with about one-fourth (by volume) of peat moss or some other form of organic matter. This increases the moisture-holding capacity of the soil.

Avoid using manure unless it is extremely well rotted, as fresh manure will burn the roots because of the ammonium gas given off. Fertilizers that contain a high amount of phosphorus, such as 0-20-0 or 11-48-0, can also be incorporated into the soil prior to top planting to encourage root development. Starter fertilizer (such as 10-52-10) can also be applied as a liquid solution after planting when the tree is watered-in. Other types of fertilizer, particularly those with high nitrogen, should not be added during the first year.

Keep trees moist while they are waiting to be planted. Soak bare-root stock in a bucket of water for two to three hours prior to planting, then cover the roots with moist burlap until they can be set in the ground. Water the root-balls of balled and burlapped or container grown trees the day prior to planting so they are moist when the trees are planted, but not so wet that the soil falls away from the roots. This helps in removing the root-ball intact from container-grown stock in plastic pots.

Pound a stake into the north side of the hole to support the tree against strong northerly winds. Then add about 15 cm (6 in) of the topsoil mixture to the bottom of the hole. Plant the trees at a slight

## Figure 13-15
## PLANTING THE FRUIT TREE

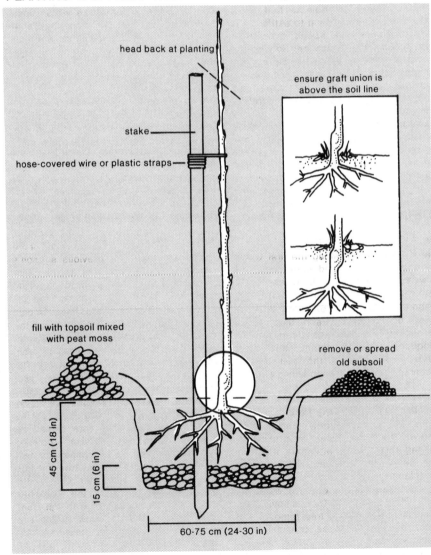

head back at planting

stake

hose-covered wire or plastic straps

ensure graft union is above the soil line

fill with topsoil mixed with peat moss

remove or spread old subsoil

45 cm (18 in)

15 cm (6 in)

60-75 cm (24-30 in)

angle into the prevailing wind. It is desirable to have a strong promising bud or lowest branch point southwest so when it develops it will provide shade to the main trunk and protection from sunscald during the winter. If the trees are bare-root, shape the soil into a cone-shaped mound around which the roots can be spread. Point the strongest roots in the direction of prevailing winds and prune any large damaged roots. Set the tree 2-5 cm (1-2 in) deeper than it stood in the nursery (the soil stain ring is visible on the stem). It is important that the graft-union remain above the soil level (see Figure 13-15). If this union is covered, the top cultivar may root, thereby losing the effect of the rootstock. Now, work the remaining topsoil around the roots or root-ball, firming it occasionally to prevent air pockets. When the hole is half filled, water the soil and allow it to settle. If the tree is balled and burlapped, remove the rope holding the burlap and loosen the burlap at this point. The burlap will eventually rot away. Plants that come in heavy pressed paper containers should have the containers cut and carefully removed prior to planting. It usually takes a long time for them to rot away with the cool soil temperatures and lack of moisture. Finally, replace the rest of the topsoil and tamp the tree in firmly, leaving a slight depression for water retention. Tie the tree to the stake using hose covered wire or plastic straps.

### WATERING-IN THE TREES

Water three times during the first week, twice during the second week, and once a week between the third and sixth weeks after planting. For the rest of the season, water the tree once a week during dry periods. Each time, water thoroughly to encourage deep rooting. Adequate watering during this early stage in the life of the fruit tree is essential to reduce transplanting shock.

### PRUNING AT PLANTING TIME

There is a controversy among fruit growers over the issue of pruning at planting time. Some advocate that this practice will result in greater transplanting shock and setback in the time it takes for the tree to establish itself. Others contend that removing the terminal portion of the tree removes the apical dominance these terminal buds possess over lateral buds and/or branches beneath them. Consequently,

more hormones and nutrients are available to encourage the production of side shoots from the lower part of the tree. Many fruit trees that are planted and not properly trained early in their development become overgrown and out of reach. On the Prairies, it is desirable to train fruit trees into a low-headed form, with scaffold branches that are well spaced and evenly distributed around the trunk. The result is a strong framework that is able to bear a good load of fruit and resist damage from heavy snowfall and strong winds. Such trees are also more accessible to the home owner. For these reasons, some degree of heading back should be practiced at planting. The general rule is to remove as little as possible to obtain the desired response.

The **one-year old maiden whip** should have from 15 cm (6 in) to one-third of its length removed, depending on the vigor of the whip. The more vigorous the whip, the less that needs to be removed to promote strong lateral branching. Some trees show good response when only the top two or three buds are removed (see Figure 13-15). Make the cut just above a strong, plump, well-developed bud that will become the new leader. (For information on how to make this heading-back cut, see TRAINING, PRUNING AND GRAFTING and Figures 13-19A and 13-22A.)

**Two-year old branched trees** should have their leaders pruned back about 15 cm (6 in) at planting time, but not more than one-third of the previous season's growth. Then select four to six side branches that are at least 15 cm (6 in) apart for *Prunus* fruit trees and 30 cm (12 in) for apples or pears. These should be well distributed in a whorl around the trunk, so they each point in a different direction. If there are not many suitable scaffolds to choose from, select the best ones and wait until subsequent years to choose the rest. It is desirable for the lowest branch to be approximately 60 cm (24 in) from the base of the tree. The tree should be planted with this branch pointing southwest. This will eventually help shade that side of the trunk from the late afternoon winter sun that can cause sunscald. The rest of the branches should be removed flush with the trunk (see Figure 13-17 for how to make a thinning cut). If the side branches are very long and succulent, they can be headed back to one-third of the previous

season's growth. If they are strong, sturdy, wide-angled branches, heading back of the side branches may not be necessary.

### LABELLING THE TREES AND KEEPING RECORDS

Labelling helps identify the different cultivars for replacement or future expansion purposes. Remove wire labels as they will eventually girdle the stem. Instead, use small labels neatly painted to wooden stakes near the trees or make a map of the orchard layout. By keeping records of the tree's hardiness to the Prairie winters, disease resistance or susceptibility, age of bearing, amount of fruit harvested annually, and growth habit, the overall performance of various kinds of trees in the planting can be assessed and compared.

## TRAINING, PRUNING AND GRAFTING

The importance of properly training and pruning fruit trees cannot be stressed enough. Begin training and pruning at the time of planting and continue annually throughout the life of the tree. This section covers the principles and techniques of training and pruning. When combined with practical application and practice, one should be able to train the fruit tree in the home garden to a desirable, well-structured shape that can be maintained throughout the tree's lifetime. The information on grafting (in the latter part of this section) will be useful if you wish to topwork scions of a desirable cultivar onto an existing tree to meet pollination requirements, or to build a hardier, sturdier tree by grafting onto a stembuilder. Grafting can also be used to repair damaged trees.

### TRAINING AND PRUNING

Although training and pruning are dealt with together in this section, it is important to distinguish between them. Training begins at the time of planting and is intended to influence the young tree to assume a certain desirable shape that ultimately determines the tree's size, shape and productivity. Pruning, on the other hand, is an annual management practice that is performed to maintain the shape and promote good fruit production of the tree. Annual pruning to keep shoot development and fruit production in a balance, results in a superior tree with higher quality fruit. A fruit tree that has been planted and left to assume its natural form eventually produces fruit, but soon becomes unmanageable and oversized without regular pruning.

## PRUNING PRINCIPLES

Even though evidence shows that pruning fruit trees improves the shape, increases fruitfulness and, in some cases, reduces or repairs injury, it remains a mystery to many home gardeners how this could possibly be so. Many people like the results of pruning, but cannot bear to carry out the procedure itself. Granted, it does seem severe, but nature also prunes trees. Broken or diseased branches, and those that are not receiving enough light, eventually fall off naturally. Pruning, however, can accomplish what nature does, but in a more orderly fashion. It can even prevent certain problems from arising.

When pruning, keep the following guidelines in mind:

## Figure 13-16
### USING SPREADERS

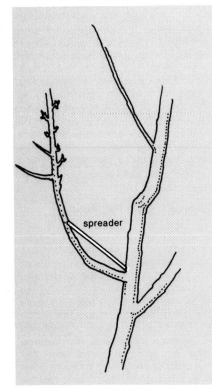

spreader

## Figure 13-17
### PRUNING CUTS

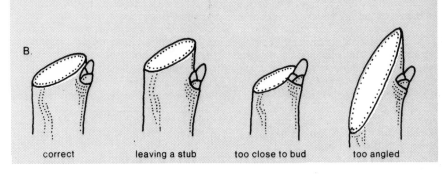

A.

prune to outward pointing buds

correct          incorrect

B.

correct          leaving a stub          too close to bud          too angled

- Encourage and maintain an attractive, low-headed form with strong scaffold branches arising from the lower portion of the trunk. This makes further pruning, spraying, thinning and harvesting much easier. The lowest scaffold should be on the southwest side, about 60 cm (24 in) from the ground, so that it will shade the trunk and prevent sunscald.

- Keep annual pruning light and, as much as possible, enhance the natural growth habit of the tree. Infrequent, heavy pruning is not only a more difficult task, but may be detrimental. It tends to dwarf the tree, causes it to come into bearing later, results in smaller crops of fruit, and stimulates succulent growth of watersprouts and suckers which are more susceptible to disease.

- Remove narrow crotch angles or use spreaders to widen them (see Figure 13-16). If allowed to develop, they will weaken the structure of the tree, and make the crotch susceptible to disease, winter injury and breakage.

- Prevent trees from becoming windswept by training them to grow into the prevailing wind.

- Make pruning cuts to an outward-pointing bud that is preferably on the lower side of the branch (Figure 13-17A). In this way, pruning is somewhat directional, as one can prune to buds that will grow in a desired direction resulting in low, spreading growth.

- Make cuts just above the bud (see Figure 13-17B). If they are too close to the bud, it may be damaged or dry up and die. Cutting too far from the bud leaves a stub that rots and predisposes the branch to disease. Sharp, clean tools give cleaner cuts that heal rapidly and prevent disease spread (such as internal rot and fireblight). If removing wood diseased by fireblight, disinfect tools after each cut (see PROBLEMS AND PREVENTION).

- To prevent leaving stubs, it is important to hold pruning tools properly, with the flat part of the shears flush with the trunk or branch where the cut is being made (see Figure 13-18A).

- Keep the tree open with periodic thinning to allow sunlight in and let air circulate to all the branches. The total yield may be reduced, but the resulting fruit will be larger and of superior quality. A crowded head promotes small, poor quality fruit and rubbing branches result in injury and provide entry for disease organisms.

- Remove diseased, dead or broken branches, as well as those that are rubbing or crowding other branches. Also remove watersprouts, suckers and old spent spurs, as they direct nutrients away from good fruiting wood.

- Maintain a proper balance between the amount of vegetative growth and the amount of fruit produced. This results in quality fruit and regular cropping.

## Figure 13-18
## REMOVING BRANCHES AND LARGE LIMBS

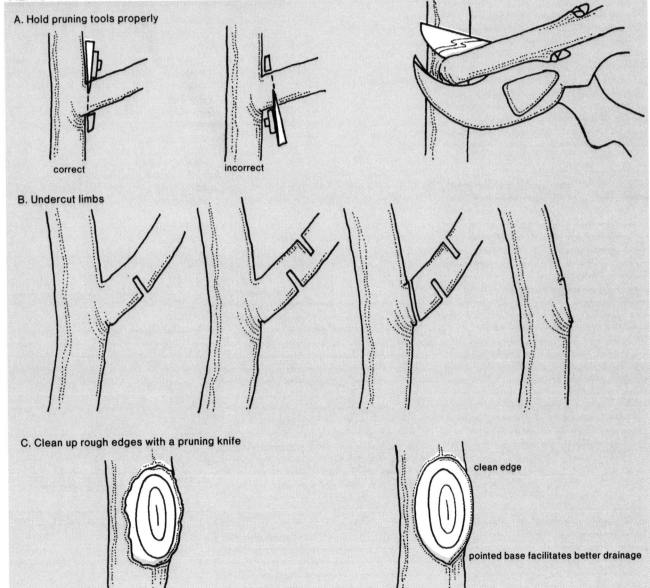

A. Hold pruning tools properly

correct    incorrect

B. Undercut limbs

C. Clean up rough edges with a pruning knife

clean edge

pointed base facilitates better drainage

- Older fruit-bearing wood can gradually be replaced by removing old limbs which began to yield less fruit or have spent fruiting spurs. New, healthy limbs can be allowed to replace them and, thus, the tree can be renewed regularly. Remember that the tree only produces good yields of quality fruit on wood that is three to five years old, so it is important that this be a gradual and continuous process (see RENEWAL PRUNING for pruning of old neglected fruit trees).

- When removing large limbs they must first be undercut (see Figure 13-18B). This prevents the limbs from tearing down the side of the trunk when they are being sawed through.

- Wounds larger than 5 cm (2 in) in diameter can be dressed with pruning paint after paring the edges with a sharp knife (see Figure 13-18C). However, the use of pruning paint is questionnable as it tends to delay callousing. In addition, trapped moisture encourages the development of rot.

- Remove all pruned wood from the site and either burn it or haul it away to a sanitary landfill to reduce the spread of any diseases that might be present.

## WHEN TO PRUNE

The best time to prune fruit trees is in the early spring while the buds are still dormant, usually in March or early April. Pruning in the fall or early winter exposes the wound to severe freezing and often increases winter injury to the tree. The wound then takes longer to heal, thereby increasing the risk of disease. It is also better to prune in the early spring in the event severe winter injury has occurred. With the absence of leaves, it is easier to locate and remove dead, diseased and broken branches. At this time, the injured branches can be pruned back to healthy tissue. Healthy tissue should have smooth bark and plump buds. Indenting with a knife should reveal living green tissue beneath the bark. Tissue infected with disease (for example, fireblight) is discolored, with the bark rough and often blistered and peeling off (see PROBLEMS AND PREVENTION).

Summer pruning is not recommended as it adversely affects the fruit tree in a number of ways, depending on when it is carried out. Heading-back to a bud or a lateral after flowering promotes vigorous growth, but inhibits flower bud initiation because less carbohydrates accumulate in the tissues. If trees are pruned in mid-summer, before the buds are resting but after extension growth has taken place, it encourages growth near the cut. This growth deprives the roots of nutrients and results in a dwarfing effect on the entire tree. Late summer pruning has the same effect on the root system as well, although to a lesser degree. Also, pruning at this time reduces the leaf surface area and may interfere with the process of cold temperature acclimation that occurs in the cold hardening process (see PHYSIOLOGY OF THE MATURE FRUIT TREE).

## TYPES OF PRUNING CUTS

There are really only two types of pruning cuts. The first is called a **heading-back cut** (Figure 13-19A). It involves the removal of the terminal portion of a twig or branch to a point between the terminal and a lateral branch or bud below it. Heading-back cuts are the principal cuts made during the training period of most fruit trees (with the exception of pears). Their purpose is to influence the eventual shape of the tree. The buds below the cut are stimulated to branch out and, eventually, these are kept or removed.

The second type of pruning cut is a **thinning or removal cut** (Figure 13-19B) which involves the removal of an entire lateral twig or branch by cutting it flush to place of origin. This type of cut is also used in training to remove unwanted laterals after scaffolds are selected and to remove any vertical or crossing branches. This pruning cut is the primary

## Figure 13-19
## TYPES OF PRUNING CUTS

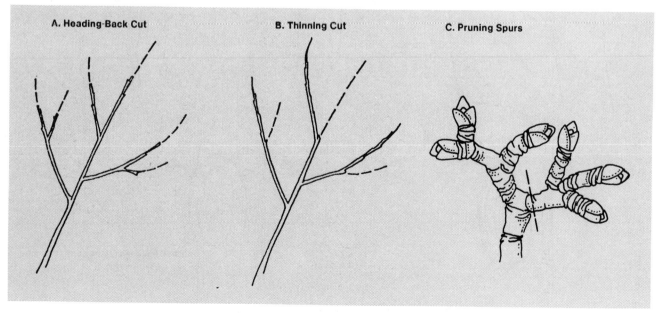

A. Heading-Back Cut    B. Thinning Cut    C. Pruning Spurs

one made on mature, bearing trees to keep the head of the tree open so as to permit optimum growing conditions. This promotes the development of fruiting wood. Thinning cuts also facilitate the removal of old unproductive wood and spurs (see Figure 13-19C).

## PRUNING TOOLS

It is much easier to prune with tools that are light, sharp and properly set. Clean cuts heal quickly. Basic pruning tools include hand secateurs, long-handled loppers, a paring knife and a choice of saws (see Figure 13-20). If the tree is a tall one, an extendable handle with a saw or lopper head mounted on the end may be required. If diseased wood is being removed, particularly if it is infected with fireblight, disinfect the tool after each cut with a solution of 50 mL of lysol/L (4 tbsp/qt) or 100 mL of bleach/L (8 tbsp/qt) of water to prevent spreading of the disease to healthy tissue (see PROBLEMS AND PREVENTION).

## TRAINING TO THE MODIFIED CENTRAL LEADER SYSTEM

On the Prairies, apples, pears, plums and apricots are usually pruned to the modified central leader system. Figure

Figure 13-20
PRUNING TOOLS

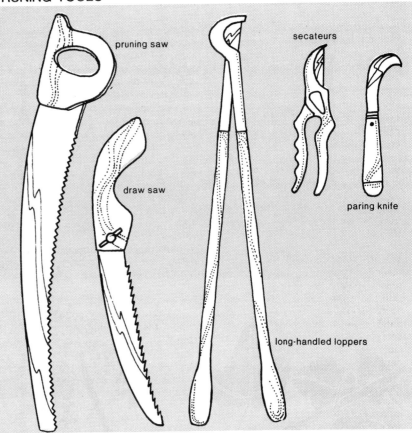

Figure 13-21
TRAINING SYSTEMS

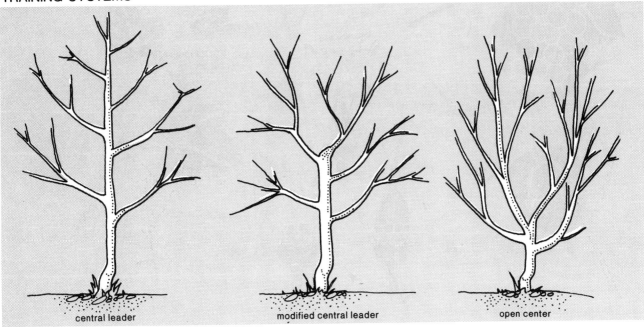

**Figure 13-22**
**TRAINING FRUIT TREES TO MODIFIED CENTRAL LEADER SYSTEM**

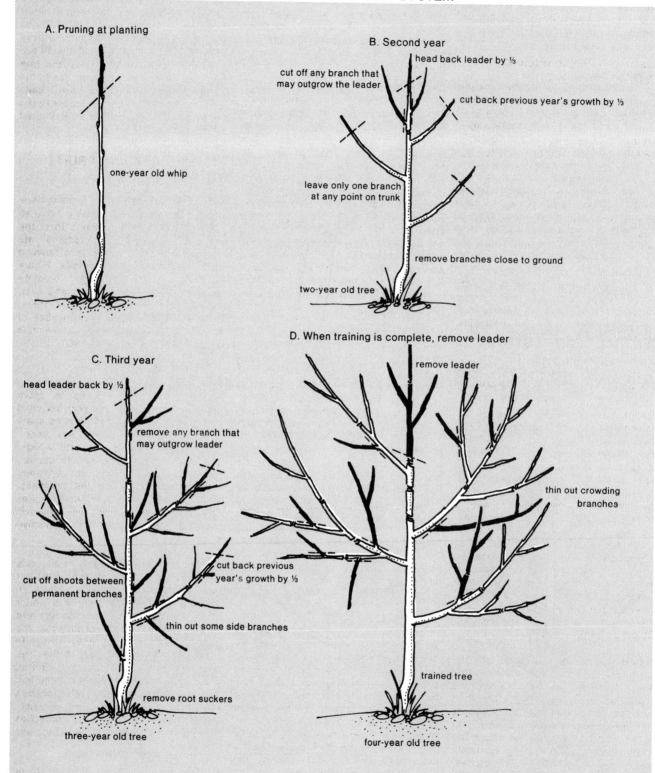

A. Pruning at planting

one-year old whip

B. Second year

head back leader by ⅓

cut off any branch that may outgrow the leader

cut back previous year's growth by ⅓

leave only one branch at any point on trunk

remove branches close to ground

two-year old tree

C. Third year

head leader back by ⅓

remove any branch that may outgrow leader

cut off shoots between permanent branches

cut back previous year's growth by ⅓

thin out some side branches

remove root suckers

three-year old tree

D. When training is complete, remove leader

remove leader

thin out crowding branches

trained tree

four-year old tree

13-21 shows this and other training systems, including central leader and open center systems. Sandcherries and cherry-plum hybrids should be trained as low bush-type trees and should not be allowed to grow to a standard tree form.

## OBJECTIVES OF THE MODIFIED CENTRAL LEADER SYSTEM

This modified central leader system promotes a low-headed tree that has four to six main scaffold branches with strong wide-angled crotches. Remember that for *Prunus* fruit trees, spacing between scaffolds should be 15 cm (6 in) and for apples 30 cm (12 in). None of these scaffold branches should be opposite, or directly below or above another, but should be whorled around the trunk of the tree. After a number of years, when a desired framework has been developed, the central leader is then headed-back to the uppermost lateral scaffold branch to prevent the tree from increasing further in height. The following describes the training procedure of a one-year old maiden whip the first four years of the fruit tree's life after planting (see Figure 13-22).

## FIRST YEAR (AT PLANTING)

Training actually begins at the time of planting with the removal of the terminal portion of the leader (see Figure 13-22A). Pears are the exception, as heading back stiffens the laterals so the leader is kept dormant (see PRUNING BEARING FRUIT TREES). This removes the apical dominance that the terminal bud exerts over the lateral buds along the stem. With this inhibition removed, these lateral buds become more active. The resulting growth of lateral branches, particularly from one-year old maiden whips during the first season after planting, permits the home gardener to select those with the widest angles and best over-all distribution for future scaffolds. As discussed previously, two-year old trees are treated somewhat differently at the time of planting (see PRUNING AT PLANTING TIME).

Delayed heading is a common practice with newly planted apple whips. In this case, only the top few buds are removed at planting time. The laterals are then produced from buds along the remaining stem. Because the shoots arising from the top part of the stem are competing for the leader position, they generally have narrow, potentially weak crotches. The shoots further down on the stem have more desirable, wide-angled crotches. When these shoots are 15-20 cm (6-8 in) long, early in the growing season, head back the top a second time. This also eliminates the upper laterals with the narrow crotches, leaving the lower wide-angled crotches from which to select the scaffold branches the next spring.

## SECOND YEAR

Early the following spring, after the first season's growth, resume training (see Figure 13-22B). Select the most vigorous, upright-growing shoot as the new leader, then head it back to one-third the previous season's growth. Remove other branches that are crowding or competing with the leader. Choose two or three scaffold branches with strong, wide crotches and proper spacing on the trunk. If these selected scaffolds are very long and succulent, head them back to one-third the previous season's growth as well. Remove all undesirable lateral branches with thinning cuts flush with the main stem.

## THIRD YEAR

The following spring, after the second season's growth, select one or two additional scaffolds (see Figure 13-22C). Thin secondary branches on the existing scaffolds. Head back all remaining secondary branches and scaffolds (both new and existing) to one-third the previous season's growth. If the leader is becoming windswept, replace it by the most upright shoot that is growing into the wind. If the tree is well sheltered from the wind, this probably won't be necessary. Install spreaders to correct any tendencies to develop weak crotches. Wedge a short piece of wood, 30 cm (12 in) in length, between the trunk and scaffold to promote a 60° angle (see Figure 13-16).

## FOURTH YEAR

In early spring, after the third growing season, cut back only the leader by one-third. Remove new secondary branches along the trunk and thin along scaffold branches. Remove branches that are growing vertically, crossing other branches, or growing into the head of the tree. Keep pruning to a minimum. With dwarf or semi-dwarf trees, cut back the leaders by one-half every year to promote growth of lateral scaffolds and keep the head of the tree low.

## WHEN TRAINING IS COMPLETE

Keep pruning light, limited to thinning and corrective directional pruning to encourage the horizontal, spreading form of the scaffolds. Do not remove short branches and spurs from the scaffolds beyond a moderate thinning. Heavy pruning delays maturation of the tissue and the bearing of fruit. Once the tree has reached bearing age, and the framework of the tree has been established, head-back the leader to the uppermost scaffold branch as illustrated in Figure 13-22D.

## PRUNING BEARING FRUIT TREES

During the training period, heading-back is the principal type of pruning cut (see Figure 13-19A). Its purpose is to shape the tree. Once the tree comes into bearing, it should receive less heading back and more thinning (see Figure 13-19B). Thinning cuts promote development of fruiting wood and keep that wood productive. In older trees, there are generally a large number of spurs which are thinned to maintain productivity (see Figure 13-19C).

### APPLES

Apples are borne terminally on spurs which have formed on two-year old wood (see Figure 13-6A). These fruiting spurs remain productive for several years, providing they receive adequate sunlight and good air circulation. Sometimes, fruit will be produced on one-year old wood or even laterally along the branches. Young, fruit-bearing spurs and branches should not be removed as they will eventually replace old, non-productive wood.

A properly trained apple tree only requires light pruning. Remove 5-10 per cent of the bearing surface annually. Thinning out entire branches is better than heading back, as this removes small, underdeveloped branches that are crowded and not receiving adequate light. By keeping the top of the tree open, light is allowed into the interior, ensuring well-developed and colored fruit throughout the tree. This also permits easier access for uniform spraying. Occasionally, heading back branches will check growth that is long and succulent.

If branches are growing parallel to, or

overhanging, one another, remove the least desirable to prevent crowding and shading. When pruning, keep scaffolds and branches in a horizontal plane as much as possible, and prevent branches from growing vertically, crowding the head, or hanging down and interfering with management practices beneath the tree. Check the height of the tree by cutting back the leader to the well-developed lateral.

## PEARS

Pears are borne in the same manner as apples (see Figure 13-6A), but generally require the least pruning of all the tree fruits as they produce few laterals. Because of this, non-bearing pear trees should not be headed back during the training period, but rather thinned to the desired number of laterals. Although the pear tends to produce upright branches with narrow crotches, the crotches widen out when the tree comes into bearing. Heading back makes the lateral branches stiff and causes them to retain this undesirable shape. Less branching also permits more scaffolds to be left on the trees.

## PLUMS

Plums are borne laterally on two- to eight-year old spurs and on short shoots (see Figure 13-6B). Some fruit may also develop at the base of one-year old wood. The fruiting spurs of the Japanese plums are short, about 7.5 cm (3 in) long. This type of plum bears rather heavily and may require heavier pruning to maintain size and quality. Remove approximately 10 per cent of the bearing wood annually. On young bearing trees, remove 25-50 cm (10-20 in) of the previous season's growth annually, and on older trees, 25-30 cm (10-12 in).

## APRICOTS

The apricot requires heavier pruning than the apple. The reason for this is that the fruit is borne laterally on one-year old branches and short-lived spurs (see Figure 13-6B). The fruiting spurs of apricots are productive for only two or three seasons. Therefore, heavier pruning is necessary to renew the fruiting wood and spurs. Some heading back is necessary to keep the tree from becoming too leggy. Thinning is also necessary to maintain adequate light distribution throughout the tree.

## SANDCHERRY AND CHERRY-PLUM HYBRIDS

These trees should be severely pruned every 3-4 years to maintain a bush-type form. This is because the fruit is borne on young wood which must be periodically renewed. After three years of bearing, cut the wood back close to the ground to promote the development of new, vigorous laterals.

## RENEWAL PRUNING

Often home gardeners who have let their fruit tree get out of hand, or have purchased a new home and inherited an unmanageable tree, wonder how they can correct the situation and bring the tree back into condition. Before attempting to revive old trees, determine whether the tree is really worth saving. If trees are very old (more than 25 years), have poor quality fruit and are diseased or damaged, remove the trees and start over with young healthy ones.

If the tree is not past its maximum bearing years (see Table 13-4) and appears to be in sound condition, with the fruit of good quality, try some renewal pruning. Renewal pruning should be done gradually over a period of years. The maximum amount of wood that can be removed at one time is between 25-30 per cent of the bearing wood. If the tree is too heavily pruned at one time, it may cause extreme shock to the tree (even killing it) or stimulate the abundant production of succulent water sprouts and suckers that are subject to winter injury and disease.

If more than one tree exists (as in an old rural orchard), first remove all worthless trees. This would include trees that have grown haphazardly from seed as they are not likely to produce fruit of any quality. Also, remove trees that have developed from the rootstock suckers. Properly space the remaining trees to allow for sufficient light, water, nutrients and room to grow.

Now start pruning the remaining good trees. The first year, prune to remove broken limbs, dead or diseased wood, sucker growth and any branches that are crossing and rubbing on others (see Figure 13-4). This kind of pruning can be done at any time during the year, although it is best performed while the trees are dormant in early spring. Keep pruning light the first year, and do no

heavy pruning of healthy limbs until the following year. Remember to first undercut when removing these large limbs (see Figure 13-18B). Make all cuts flush, leaving no stubs. Cuts larger than 5 cm (2 in) can be painted with wound dressing.

Do the second pruning the following spring when the tree is still dormant. Lightly thin the head of the tree and remove some of the bearing wood (see Figure 13-19B). This encourages fruiting on younger wood. At this time, remove some of the older branches and head back younger ones slightly to encourage their growth.

The third year, do more thinning and remove large unproductive limbs. Lower the head height by heading back the leader to a desirable lateral (see Figure 13-19A). In subsequent years, continue to carry out pruning, but keep it moderate.

## UNIQUE TRAINING SYSTEMS

Although the modified central leader system is the preferred method of training fruit trees on the Prairies, there are several other unique training systems that can be used. Most are adapted systems for fruit trees grown in a limited space or for ornamental purposes.

### ESPALIER SYSTEM

Some apple and pears can be trained to the espalier system (Figure 13-23A). Cut back the maiden tree to a bud 5 cm (2 In) above the bottom support wire, which is 45-60 cm (18-24 in) off the ground. Select and tie two lower scaffolds to the training wire and choose a leader. Remove other branches. The following spring, head the leader again to a bud 5 cm (2 in) above the next training wire and repeat the process. In this way, 6-8 scaffolds are selected and trained horizontally along wires that are spaced 30 cm (12 in) apart. Remove the leader once the scaffolds are chosen and train the tree in only two directions in the same plane. In early June, pinch back side shoots that develop off these scaffolds to 2-3 leaves. This system can be useful for the homeowner with limited space. The trees look attractive when trained along the side of a building or fence, but may be trained along wires in the garden as well. The drawback of this system is that as the tree ages, the new

Figure 13-23
UNIQUE TRAINING SYTEMS

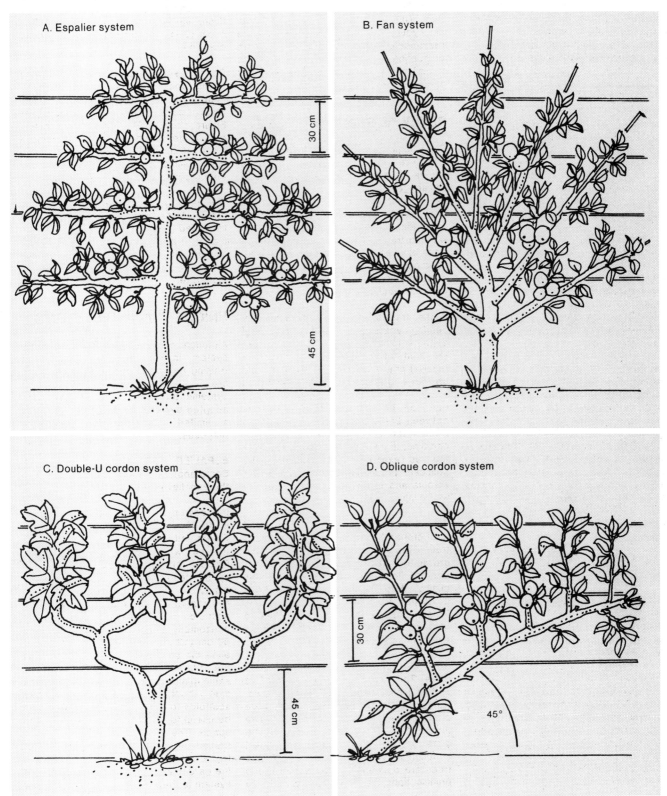

A. Espalier system

B. Fan system

C. Double-U cordon system

D. Oblique cordon system

growth tends to be concentrated along the uppermost scaffolds, causing excessive shading of the lower branches. This results in reduced vigor and poorer fruit production.

### PALMETTE OR FAN-SHAPED SYSTEM

The palmette (fan-shaped) system also trains the tree in two directions in the same plane. However, the scaffolds are trained to branch out from the main trunk and grow upward and outward in the shape of a fan. The lowermost scaffold is started about 20 cm (8 in) below the first wire (Figure 13-23B). This system has the advantage over the espalier system in that the new growth is distributed evenly throughout the whole tree.

### CORDON TRAINING

Cordon training was developed in Siberia so that apples could be grown low to the ground, thereby reducing winter injury. Head back the young plants severely to about 20-30 cm (8-12 in). Select two laterals and train them along a single horizontal wire parallel to the ground and from 30-60 cm (12-24 in) above the ground. Remove all other branches and the new leader. When they reach 45 cm (18 in) in length, bend the last 15 cm (6 in) to an upright position and allow it to grow vertically. A double-U can be formed by repeating this process on each of the now vertical branches of the cordon (see Figure 13-23C). The oblique cordon is the simplest (see Figure 13-23D). Trees are planted at 45° angles and secured to a cane at the same angle. The tree is then allowed to grow, but the terminal point is bent at an increasing angle. Vertical side growth is pinched back.

## GRAFTING

Grafting procedures accomplish one of five functions:

- **Propagation** of young fruit trees (see METHODS OF ASEXUAL PROPAGATION).

- **Frameworking** is used to work a new cultivar onto an existing tree. The objective is to retain as much of the original framework of primary and secondary scaffolds. The balance between root system and top structure is disturbed as little as possible, allowing the tree to quickly

heal and return to bearing and full production soon afterward.

- **Topworking** is used to work a desired cultivar onto an existing tree (see Figure 13-24). However, the purpose of topworking is not only to work on the desired cultivar, but also to replace as much of the limb structure as possible. This procedure can be used to some extent in renewing old trees. It is also useful in providing certain cultivars with the necessary pollinating cultivar to ensure cross-pollination and it can be a solution to growing a number of cultivars on a single tree, particularly where space is limited.

- **Stembuilders** have a number of purposes. The stembuilder may have desirable, strong, wide-angled crotches or may have a dwarfing effect on the topworked cultivar. Hardiness is another characteristic that some stembuilders pass on to

### Figure 13-24
### TOPWORKING
### USING BARK GRAFT

Courtesy of Alberta Agriculture

the desirable cultivar. Finally, a stembuilder may act as a bridge between a scion and rootstock that otherwise would not be compatible with each other, but are both compatible with the stembuilder.

- The last function of grafting is to **repair** trees that have been damaged by deer, mice or other rodents, or careless cultivation practices (see REPAIRING DAMAGE).

### PRINCIPLES OF GRAFTING

- Compatibility between the scion being grafted on and the stock receiving it is essential. Incompatible unions may result in the death of the scion, weak unions that may break under the weight of a load of fruit, uneven growth of scion and stock, or an extreme dwarfing effect on the scion.

- The best time of year to graft varies with the type of graft being performed. Side grafts, cleft grafts, bark grafts, and whip or tongue grafts are best performed when the tree is still dormant, just before buds swell in the spring (see GRAFTING TECHNIQUES). For budding, inarching or bridge grafting, the bark must be slipping or easily separated from the wood. Therefore, these procedures are done in the summer, usually in late July or early August.

- Dormant scions should be collected in the fall and stored until spring. Place them in moist peat moss, sealed in a polyethylene bag and stored in the refrigerator where temperatures are above freezing. One-year old wood, taken from the middle portion of shoots where the buds are well-developed, is preferable. The diameter of the scions should be about the same as that of a pencil.

- The cambiums of the stock and scion must have close, smooth contact and be held firmly until a successful union forms. At least one side of the scion's cambium must be in contact with the cambium of the stock.

- All grafts must be coated with grafting wax (see Table 13-3) to prevent loss of moisture and discourage entry of disease.

## Figure 13-25
## GRAFTING TECHNIQUES

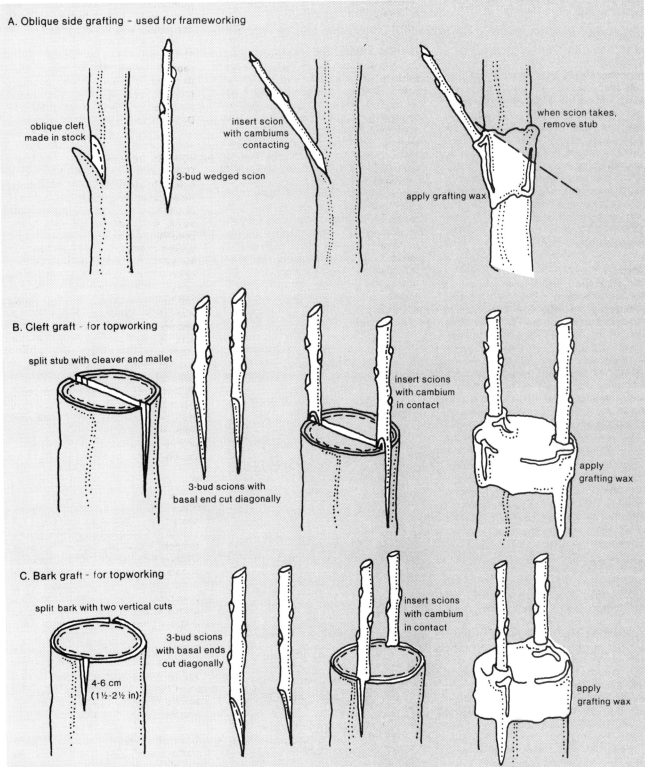

A. Oblique side grafting – used for frameworking

oblique cleft made in stock

3-bud wedged scion

insert scion with cambiums contacting

when scion takes, remove stub

apply grafting wax

B. Cleft graft – for topworking

split stub with cleaver and mallet

3-bud scions with basal end cut diagonally

insert scions with cambium in contact

apply grafting wax

C. Bark graft – for topworking

split bark with two vertical cuts

4-6 cm (1½-2½ in)

3-bud scions with basal ends cut diagonally

insert scions with cambium in contact

apply grafting wax

## GRAFTING TECHNIQUES

Now that the various functions of grafting have been discussed, the actual techniques can be explained (see Figure 13-25).

### FRAMEWORKING

#### Side Graft

The oblique side graft is a type of cleft graft that should be carried out in the spring just as the buds are beginning to swell. It is ideal for large limbs with thick bark (see Figure 13-25A). First, strip the limbs of all lateral spurs, shoots and branches where the new scions are to be grafted in. Make a shallow oblique cleft in the framework limb and insert a 3-bud scion, ensuring that the cambium of the scion and limb are in contact. Coat the graft with grafting wax.

### TOPWORKING

#### Cleft Graft

The cleft graft is commonly used to topwork a desired cultivar onto another (see Figure 13-25B). The best time to perform this type of graft is in the early spring, just after the buds begin to swell or have started to open. Select a branch of (preferably) one-year old wood and remove the top of the branch, leaving a fairly long stub, about 15 cm (6 in) long. Use a grafting tool or heavy knife to make the cleft in the stub. It may be necessary to use a mallet to insert the knife. Then hold open the cleft with the prong of the grafting tool and insert two dormant scions with at least two healthy buds on either side of the cleft. Make sure that the cambium layers are in contact. Then bind the graft and coat with grafting wax. When the two scions have taken, select the most vigorous and remove the other.

#### Bark Graft

Bark grafting is used to graft limbs that are larger than those usually cleft grafted (see Figure 13-25C). Select the branch to be topworked and remove the top. Slit the bark on either side of the stub with two lengthwise cuts and separate the bark from the sapwood with a pruning knife. Insert two, 3-bud scions so that the lowest bud is level with the surface of the stub. Then nail scions into place and wrap the graft and coat with grafting wax. This type of graft is better to use than the cleft graft where blackheart is widespread.

### Whip and Tongue Grafts

Whip and tongue grafts are also commonly used in grafting scions onto young trees (see PROPAGATION OF FRUIT TREES and Figure 13-11).

### STEMBUILDING USING INTERSTEMS

A stembuilder cultivar is budded onto a desirable rootstock and, once it takes, trained to a single trunk with well-spaced, wide-angled branches that serve as the scaffold for the top cultivar (see Figure 13-12B). When the branches reach 1 cm (⅜ in) in diameter, they are budded, in August, with the desired cultivar on the top side of the branch 20-30 cm (8-12 in) from the leader. The following spring after the buds have taken, cut back the former branch to about 5 cm (2 in) above the union and tie the growing shoot arising from the new bud to the stub for support. Prune the stub back to the established new shoot the following spring.

Anaros is a hardy, vigorous stembuilding cultivar that promotes high yields of fruit. *Malus baccata* 'Nertchinsk' is a hardy stembuilder with good, strong, wide-angled crotches, and a tendency to dwarf the topworked cultivar (see Figure 13-26). Cultivars such as Breakey, Goodland, Collet, Carroll and Garland are compatible and can be used for topworking onto Nertchinsk.

### REPAIRING DAMAGE

#### Bridge Grafting

Bridge grafting is one way to repair damage to the bark (see Figure 13-27A). Pare away the rough edges of the damaged bark. Use dormant wood of the previous season's growth for scions. These should be long enough to bridge the wound vertically on the trunk of the tree. Hold the scions in position to mark the bark. Score the bark above and below the wound and insert the scions between each pair of slits. Tack down the bark on either side of the scion to ensure a good contact of cambium layers. Cover the grafted ends of the scion and the injured area of the trunk with grafting wax.

#### Inarching

Inarching is used to repair girdled trees, trees with damaged root systems or trees whose base has been damaged by a grass fire (see Figure 13-27B). Plant small seedling trees of the desired rootstock 15 cm (6 in) apart around the base of the injured tree early in the spring. As soon as the bark is slipping, or easily separated from the sapwood, the inarching operation can be performed. Trim the wounded bark with a paring knife and top the young seedlings at the level where they will join the healthy bark just above the wound. Make

## Figure 13-26
## THE STEMBUILDER 'NERTCHINSK'

Courtesy of Alberta Agriculture

## Figure 13-27
## GRAFTING TO REPAIR DAMAGE

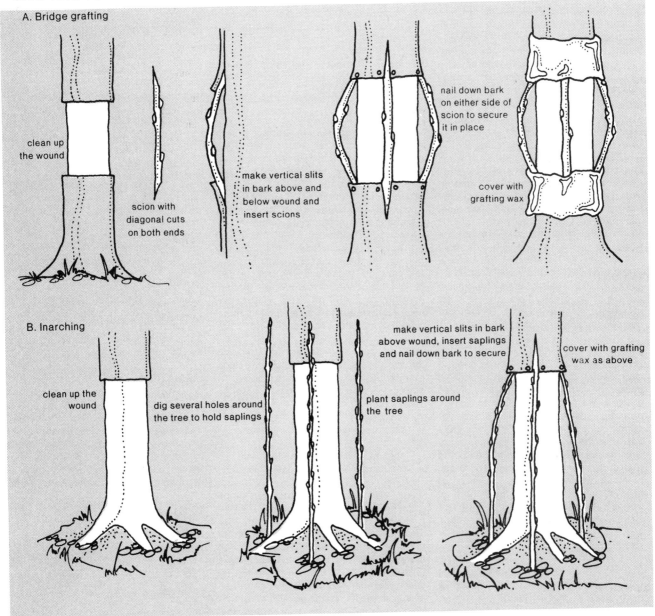

**A. Bridge grafting**

clean up the wound

scion with diagonal cuts on both ends

make vertical slits in bark above and below wound and insert scions

nail down bark on either side of scion to secure it in place

cover with grafting wax

**B. Inarching**

clean up the wound

dig several holes around the tree to hold saplings

plant saplings around the tree

make vertical slits in bark above wound, insert saplings and nail down bark to secure

cover with grafting wax as above

the cut on the diagonal on the side of the stem next to the trunk. Score the bark on either side of the seedling where the seedling stems will be inserted. Lift the bark flap and insert the end of the seedling. Then tack down the bark on either side to ensure good contact of the cambium layers. Coat the wound and grafts with grafting wax.

# MANAGEMENT OF FRUIT TREES

There is a physical law that basically states that, unless energy is applied, things go from a state of order to one of disorder. This is true of our cars if we do not keep them properly tuned and our

homes if we do not fix and replace things as they wear out. In a like manner, if we plant fruit trees and do not provide a continual system of management to nurture them and provide optimum conditions for fruit production, the trees become unmanageable and yield only poor quality fruit.

This section discusses some of the management practices that should be followed to produce beautiful trees and quality fruit in the home garden. If these management practices are followed from year to year, it should only require a small amount of time and effort. However, if maintenance is ignored for a period, a great deal of time and energy must be spent to rectify the situation.

## SOIL MANAGEMENT

### CULTIVATION
The purpose of cultivation is to control weeds, incorporate organic matter, improve water penetration and increase the amount of air in the soil. The most important of these is to control weeds which would otherwise compete with the trees for moisture and nutrients (see ESTABLISHING THE FRUIT TREES - SOIL PREPARATION). Keep cultivation to a minimum, as stirring up the soil too much causes it to break down and lose its structure. This may result in greater compaction and erosion of the soil.

Only shallow cultivation, 5-8 cm (2-3 in), is necessary. If cultivation is too deep, it may cause damage to the roots and cause the soil to dry out rapidly. Trees grown in a small rural orchard should be properly spaced at planting time to permit cultivation equipment to pass between the rows. Use this machinery with caution to prevent damage to the trunks by passing too closely. Urban home gardeners can use a hoe or shovel. Cultivate beneath the canopy of young trees at least until the trees come into bearing. This eliminates competition with weeds and allows for better establishment of the root system.

Cultivate throughout the growing season until September. If it has been a particularly wet year, however, discontinue cultivation in the latter part of the summer. This permits weeds to grow and take up excess water, causing the growth of the trees to slow down. This allows them to begin to harden off for the winter.

### COVER CROPS, SOD AND MULCHES
Cover crops planted beneath the canopy of the trees early in the summer will:

- absorb water and nutrients later in the season, helping the trees to harden off before winter

- prevent wind and water erosion of the soil

- provide some protection to the roots during the winter by catching the snow

- return nutrients and add organic matter to the soil, if plowed under late in the season.

In rural orchards, fall rye, barley or oats can be used as cover crops. In the urban garden, planting sod beneath the trees, once they have become mature, will have a similar effect. When grass is grown beneath the trees, it must be kept short to discourage rodents. Planting vegetables or small fruits beneath the trees is possible as well, however, prevent contaminating the edible portions of these plants when the trees are sprayed. When a cover crop or sod is grown beneath the trees, greater amounts of fertilizer and water are necessary as these will be used up more quickly than if the soil is cultivated.

Mulches can also be applied beneath the fruit trees. Common mulches include straw, leaves mixed with compost, sawdust or some other organic material. The advantage of mulches are that they:

- suppress weed growth

- conserve moisture in the soil by reducing evaporation loss

- provide a cushion for fruit that drops off before it is harvested.

The disadvantage is that mulches attract mice and other rodents. Remove mulch material prior to winter to discourage these pests. Also, the decomposition of mulch material may result in a decrease in soil nutrients (such as nitrogen) that are used up by the microorganisms. Nitrogen fertilizer may need to be applied to compensate for this loss.

### FERTILIZATION
Conduct a soil test to determine the soil's fertility. Information on how to take a soil sample and where to have the analysis done is contained in the Soils lesson (see Soils lesson, SOIL TESTING). Trees that have a pale green color, look unhealthy, produce small fruit, or have borne a heavy crop of fruit for several years with no fertilizer added, may require a feeding. Some symptoms

of nutrient deficiency are discussed in the PROBLEMS AND PREVENTION section.

For fertilization to be effective:

- Choose the proper fertilizer.

- Apply the right amount.

- Apply the fertilizer at the right time in the growing season.

- Spread the fertilizer in the right place.

These factors are influenced by moisture content, cover crop or previous crop grown, and the soil type. Because soils differ from location to location, it is very difficult to give a fertilizer recommendation. If the soil test is specified for fruit trees, often the soil testing laboratory will recommend an appropriate fertilizer. Spread fertilizer evenly beneath the canopy from the edge of the drip line (see Figure 13-28) to about 30 cm (12 in) from the trunk. Apply fertilizer early in the spring as soon as soil can be worked.

### IRRIGATION
A mature fruit tree requires approximately 500 kg (1100 lb) of water to produce 1 kg (2.2 lb) of dry matter. A mature peach tree produces about 20 kg (45 lb) of dry matter each season, including the production of shoots, roots, leaves and fruit. The amount of water required by the tree during the season to

## Figure 13-28
## SPREAD FERTILIZER
## BENEATH CANOPY

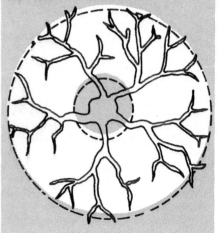

mature the crop properly is, therefore, 10,000 kg (22,000 lb). That is a lot of water!

When the tree is newly planted, it needs an almost continuous supply of moisture because the root system is small (see PLANTING THE TREES). When the trees are small, establish a basin that is about 8 cm (3 in) deep and about the same diameter as the drip line of the tree or shrub. By filling this weekly, enough water is supplied to establish a deep root system. Large trees require 8-10 cm (3-4 in) of water per week. As the tree grows, the basin is no longer able to provide adequate moisture to the active feeder roots. These roots are primarily responsible for the uptake of water and nutrients and are located roughly beneath the edge of the canopy or below the drip line. By using a sprinkler adjusted to water the area beneath the canopy, and placing a couple of cans marked to the 8-10 cm (3-4 in) level, you can determine when sufficient moisture has been added to the soil. Time how long it takes for the water to reach the level marked in the can to obtain an idea as to how long the sprinkler needs to be left on.

Another method of watering the root zone of the tree is to use a watering lance. This apparatus is a long perforated metal spike attached to a hose. By inserting the water lance in several places beneath the canopy of the tree, and watering for the length of time and at the pressure that the manufacturer suggests to saturate the soil, ample water is supplied to the trees. The grass beneath should also be surface watered to prevent competition between the grass and the tree. The canopy prevents moisture from reaching the grass beneath it.

Watering the lawn does not always sufficiently water the trees in the lawn as trees require three to four times the amount of moisture. Also, watering the foliage is not necessary and can actually be detrimental as it increases the incidence of disease, particularly those caused by fungus and bacteria. There is one exception to this rule, however. If there is a risk of spring frosts after the trees have blossomed or leafed out, spraying the canopy of the tree with water serves to help protect it from frost damage. As the water freezes on the surface, a small amount of heat is released, thereby preventing the temperature of the leaf surface from falling below freezing.

In rural orchards, the furrow method of irrigation is commonly used. Grading may be necessary so that water can be carried in furrows from one end of the planting to the other. Space furrows about 2 m (6 feet) from the tree row and 1.5-2 m (4-6 ft) apart between rows. Apply water to a depth of 10-15 cm (4-6 in) in the furrows, for about six hours.

It is important to cut back watering gradually during mid-summer, unless conditions are extremely dry. By late summer, stop watering. This permits the trees to properly harden off in preparation for the onset of dormancy rest. Excess water in late summer delays this and results in greater winter injury to the tree. In extremely wet years, allow weeds or some type of cover crop to grow beneath the trees late in the summer to deplete the excess water supply and help to harden off the trees. Once the trees have hardened off and are dormant, usually about mid-October, water them well. This prevents drying out during the winter and provides a moisture reserve for the trees the following spring. To ensure adequate moisture for the spring flush of growth, begin watering in the spring as soon as the ground has thawed.

# TREE AND FRUIT MANAGEMENT

## PRUNING
This management practice is very important in establishing and maintaining productive fruit trees with good form. Training and pruning techniques are discussed in detail in the previous section on TRAINING, PRUNING AND GRAFTING.

## THINNING THE FRUIT CROP
There are a number of reasons for thinning. Some of the reasons are to:

- improve size, color and quality of fruit

- encourage annual cropping by easing the stress on the tree that would result from over-production

- increase tree vigor

- reduce breakage by easing the weight on the branches

- reduce winter injury.

As was discussed in the section on the PHYSIOLOGY OF THE MATURE FRUIT TREE, some natural thinning takes place during the two fruit drops that occur early in the development of the fruit. This eliminates incompletely fertilized, self-pollinated, malformed or damaged fruit. However, there still may be an overabundance of healthy fruit on the tree. This is often the case with certain cultivars that have a tendency to overbear, such as the Dolgo crabapple, Haralson and Breakey apples, Dandy and Norther Plums, Sapa and Dura cherry-plums, and Scout apricot.

Thinning is a form of pruning. It should be done after the second natural dropping of fruit in June. Remove the fruit with the thumb and first or second finger by exerting a sideways pressure on the stem of the unwanted fruit. Use caution so that desirable fruit is maintained and the fruiting spur is not broken off. The amount of thinning required varies. Some sources suggest leaving one fruit per 20-30 leaves or leaving one fruit per fruiting spur. Table 13-9 gives general recommendations as to spacing of individual fruits along the branch.

## CONTROLLING INSECTS, DISEASES AND OTHER PESTS
Periodically, insects, diseases and animals may attack fruit trees. Fortunately, with the dry weather and cold temperatures experienced in the winter on the Prairies, many of the major pests that cause damage to fruit trees in major fruit growing regions are less prevalent here. Generally, if trees are healthy and proper management is being practiced, the trees are better able to withstand attacks from insects and diseases. Good sanitation practices, including disposal of fallen fruit and leaves, and burning pruned and diseased wood, reduce the incidence of disease. Protecting the trunks of the trees from rodents prevents damage. The PROBLEMS AND PREVENTION section at the end of this lesson discusses some of the more common physiological, insect, disease and pest problems/disorders that may affect fruit trees on the Prairies. It also discusses ways to prevent or control these problems.

Table 13-9

## RECOMMENDED FRUIT SPACING

| FRUIT TREE | SPACING ON BRANCH BETWEEN FRUIT cm (in) |
|---|---|
| Apple | 12-20 (5-8) |
| Crabapple | 2-5 (1-2) |
| Plum | 5-8 (2-3) |
| Apricot | 5-8 (2-3) |
| Cherry-Plum | 2-5 (1-2) |
| Pear | 12-20 (5-8) |

Source: Leslie, W.R. *The Prairie Home Orchard*,
Canada Department of Agriculture Publication 901, April, 1954, p. 36.

### HARVESTING FRUIT

Handle fruit with great care during harvesting. Fruit is perishable, and if bruised or otherwise damaged, it does not keep. Pick fruit with a twisting upward motion so as not to damage the fruiting spur which continues to produce fruit. Leave the stem on the fruit to improve its keeping quality.

Harvest fruit at the proper stage of ripeness. When the stem of the fruit is easily separated from the spur, it is probably ripe. Certainly, when the fruit begins to drop off the tree without the aid of the wind, it should be harvested. Crabapples remain on the tree well past ripeness and should be sampled periodically to determine ripeness.

Plums, apricots and cherry-plums should be picked when they are 'hard ripe'. Evidence that the fruit is ripe is indicated by the presence of a waxy bloom on the skin, a slight softness of the flesh, and (sometimes) an aroma. If plums are over-ripe when picked, the soft, juicy flesh is easily bruised. For canning purposes, plums may be harvested prior to ripeness and quickly harvested by placing a sheet of burlap beneath the canopy and shaking the tree. Pick pears when they have reached a desirable size and are firm. This is usually done prior to ripeness. After harvest, they are kept at room temperature and allowed to ripen.

Place the fruit in shallow baskets or containers that are lined with cloth or paper. Place the containers in the shade when they are full and remove them to cold storage as soon as possible.

### STORING FRUIT

Fruit is a living thing that continues to carry on respiration even after it is picked. More information on how fruit ripens, reaches maturity and subsequently deteriorates can be found in the section on PHYSIOLOGY OF THE MATURE FRUIT TREE. Store fruit in an environment that reduces respiration and slows down the deterioration of the fruit. This keeps it in a high quality eating state for the maximum amount of time. Different cultivars of fruit vary in their keeping quality. Some apple cultivars keep for several months until early spring. Others keep only a few weeks. Pears, if picked prior to ripeness and kept in cold storage, may keep for a few months. Japanese plums are poor keepers, storing for only a few days. North American and cherry-plums may keep for a month or more. Apricots keep only a couple of weeks.

Ideal storage conditons are cool temperatures, -1.1 to 0°C, and high humidity, about 80 per cent. However, most home gardeners do not have these conditions in which to store their fruit. Fruit can be stored in a refrigerator at about 4°C, with a pan of water to keep humidity high. Agriculture Canada Publication 1478, *Home Storage Room for Fruits and Vegetables*, gives some useful information on the construction and operation of a cold storage area for home gardeners with surpluses of fruits and vegetables.

Another way to store excess fruits is to preserve them. There is a great selection of fruits that make marvelous jams and jellies, sauces, or canned fruit. Agriculture Canada Publication 1560, *Canning Canadian Fruits and Vegetables*, is an excellent reference for canning fruits.

## PROBLEMS AND PREVENTION

### PREVENTIVE MEASURES

Keeping trees in a healthy, vigorous state is part of fruit tree management. The incidence of insect, disease, pest and physiological problems is much less if the following preventive measures are taken.

### AVOID ENVIRONMENTAL STRESS

As discussed early in this lesson, site selection is important:

- Frost damage in the spring or early fall can sometimes be avoided if the trees are not planted in low-lying areas. Damage due to spring frost is lessened if the trees are planted with a north-facing orientation, which delays the onset of flowering and leafing out.

- Locations with poor drainage result in root damage because of the poor aeration. Likewise, situations of high salinity or extremes of pH pose a threat to the health of the fruit tree.

- Finally, the trees should be sufficiently hardy to the climatic conditions in the zone they are growing in. If trees that are only marginally hardy are grown in a zone requiring extreme hardiness, the tree suffers severe winter injury.

If trees are subjected to any of these environmental stresses, they stand a greater chance of being attacked by insects or infected with diseases. This is the reason that site selection and choice of cultivar are very important.

### PRACTICE GOOD MANAGEMENT

Good management practices maintain the environment of the trees in an optimum condition. To achieve optimum conditions:

- Provide an adequate water supply, especially for newly planted trees and when conditions are dry. Water deeply with a good soaking as shallow watering results in shallow root systems that weaken the tree during periods of drought, extreme cold, or high wind. Holding back on water late in the summer and then watering-in well late in the fall prior to freeze-up allows the trees to harden off and prevents trees from suffering winter drought injury. This is very important in areas which experience winter chinooks or drying winds throughout the winter.

• Maintain fertility to prevent nutrient deficiency. Use the proper amounts of fertilizer as overfertilizing may damage the tree. Apply fertilizer at the appropriate time in late fall or early spring. Fertilizing too late in the season stimulates growth and delays the hardening off of the tree.

• Use chemicals at the right concentrations and as directed by the manufacturer. Spraying when the trees are in bloom may injure blossoms and, if insecticides are used, may harm beneficial pollinating insects. Use herbicides with caution around fruit trees. If herbicides meant to control weeds in the lawn are not applied at the appropriate rates, they may cause injury to the trees. In rural orchards, where herbicides may be used on other crops, make sure that the spray does not drift toward the fruit trees.

• Finally, prune annually to remove dead, diseased, damaged or crowding branches. This includes the removal of succulent water sprouts and suckers that can provide an entry to pathogens. When pruning, pare large wounds and apply wound dressing. Disinfect tools to prevent spreading of disease, particularly fireblight.

## MAINTAIN SANITATION
• Remove all pruned wood from the site and haul away or burn.

• Pick up fruit that has dropped and rake up leaves beneath the trees. Bury these in a compost pile or destroy as bugs and disease may overwinter in this litter.

• Mulch, if applied, should be cultivated into the soil at the end of the season for decomposition and to prevent overwintering diseases, insects and mice which might take refuge in it.

• Keep grass beneath the trees mown short to discourage mice, rabbits and other rodents from feeding on the trees, especially in the winter.

## PROVIDE PROTECTION
• Protect trees as much as possible from the harsh elements of the Prairies. Plant in locations that are sheltered from wind and frost. In rural situations, establish a windbreak if there is no natural shelter available to protect the trees from the wind.

• Prevent rodent damage by wrapping the trunks of the trees with plastic guards or wire mesh. Deer and other large animals that may feed on the bark of the upper portions of the tree can be discouraged by fencing in the orchard planting.

• Finally, protect trees from one another. Mixing up trees in the planting or isolating different trees in different locations in the landscape prevents disease or insect problems from spreading from one infected tree to another susceptible one.

## DETERMINING WHAT THE PROBLEM IS

Even with the best management, fruit trees can become 'sick'. Problems may arise from one or a combination of the following:

• physiological disorders

• insect pests

• diseases

• damage from animals

### PHYSIOLOGICAL DISORDERS

ADVERSE ENVIRONMENTAL CONDITIONS
• Excessive shading from buildings or large shade trees can result in less than adequate amounts of light. Growth will be spindly, leaves small and pale, and fruit of poor quality.

• Too much water damages roots and can cause rotting. Trees appear wilted, foliage yellows and drops off.

• Too little water results in wilting and eventually causes the tissues to dry up.

• Shallow soil profile results in poor root development that is unable to provide adequate water, nutrients and anchorage. This may also result if the soil is compacted.

• Salinity in soils produces symptoms of water stress as trees are unable to take up moisture. This may also be caused by road salt contaminating the soil during run-off in spring.

• High pH results in certain nutrients, such as iron (Fe), becoming unavailable in the soil solution. This may cause poor growth, certain nutrient deficiency symptoms and fruit drop.

• Low pH may prevent the uptake of calcium (Ca) or magnesium (Mg).

• Overfertilizing, especially with nitrogen, shows scorching and browning symptoms on the leaves. It may also result in too much vegetative growth and the inhibition of flower bud initiation and development.

• Underfertilizing results in a number of nutrient deficiency symptoms (see NUTRIENT IMBALANCES). Similar symptoms may arise if there is intensive competition between the tree and other plants such as grass, weeds, trees and shrubs that are planted too closely.

• Mechanical damage may result from careless cultivation and mowing too closely to the trees.

• Hail may also damage trees and fruit. In apples, russetting of fruit may occur wherein brown corky cells form to repair damage to the cuticle of the fruit and prevent further moisture loss.

• Pesticide or spray injury may occur if not applied at the proper time. Do not spray during the open blossom stage.

WINTER INJURY
• Sunscald damage is caused when the sun is low on a mid-winter

## Figure 13-29
## FROST CRACKING

Courtesy of Alberta Agriculture

afternoon, thus warming the southwest side of the trunk. As the bark absorbs the heat, the tissue may begin to thaw. When the sun sets and the temperature falls rapidly, cells in the thawed tissue freeze and rupture, killing the bark. The bark may become seriously damaged or may die in the area affected, predisposing the wound to entry by disease organisms. The bark becomes darkened and often has a roughened appearance from blistering and peeling away.

Heavy or late application of nitrogen fertilizers and planting the trees with a southwest exposure increases the incidence of sunscald. Damage can be prevented by encouraging the tree to form the lowest scaffold on the southwest side, painting the trunk with white latex, or wrapping the tree with a plastic guard. The latter method also protects trees from rodents.

- Frost cracking along the trunk and major limbs results from a sudden decrease in temperature in the fall and onset of an early winter (see Figure 13-29). If this takes place before the trees have been fully cold hardened by the process of cold temperature acclimation, the water in the tissues freezes. As it freezes,

the water expands to form ice and forces the trunk to crack.

Heavy watering late in the summer increases the chance of frost cracking. Cut back watering in late July and stop watering in early August to encourage hardening.

- Winter tip killing or dieback usually affects succulent terminal growth and fruiting spurs, especially in the case of pears. Watersprouts, suckers, and late season growth, brought on by overwatering or overfertilizing, are most susceptible to this type of winter injury. Young trees may experience dieback injury for the first few years but become more resistant as they mature. The symptoms of this injury are dead terminal growth from the previous season, which may turn a blackened color. This should not be confused with fireblight.

- Frost injury to blossoms in the spring may cause russetting of apple fruit. The greater the extent of frost damage, the larger the area of russetting on the fruit.

### NUTRIENT IMBALANCES
- **Nitrogen** - If nitrogen is deficient, leaves are chlorotic (having a light

green color) and small lower leaves on older wood turns yellow, and may dry up and fall off. Growth of the terminal shoots is weak, and fruit development is poor. Bark has a reddish color. Nitrogen deficiency may be brought on by competition of the trees with grass, weeds or other trees and shrubs; large amounts of organic matter such as straw being worked into the soil requiring nitrogen to break it down; and leaching of available nitrogen from the soil solution by heavy rains. Excess nitrogen results in large dark green leaves and excessive lush growth. Leaf fall and the onset of winter hardening may also be delayed. Trees may also be more susceptible to fireblight.

- **Phosphorus** - Deficiency in fruit trees is uncommon but, if present, may show symptoms of small dark green leaves with a bronze tinge and purple or brown spots.

- **Potassium** - This nutrient is rarely deficient in Prairie soils. If this nutrient is limited, deficiency is evidenced by interveinal purpling of older leaves, browning of the tips and scorching of the leaf margins. Leaves may also curl up and inward. Shoot development is weak and may experience dieback in the winter. Fruit ripens unevenly.

- **Magnesium** - Interveinal chlorosis of older leaves occurs, with necrotic or dead spots developing later. Leaves fall off prematurely. Fruit also matures and drops early. Flower bud initiation is limited for the following year.

- **Manganese** - High soil pH can cause manganese to be tied up in the soil. Symptoms include bright yellow interveinal chlorosis on the tips of young leaves with veins remaining a dark green. Eventually the entire leaf becomes yellow and prematurely drops. Excess manganese may occur where soil pH is low. It causes stunting of growth and mottling of bark with necrotic spots.

- **Iron** - High soil pH results in iron being made unavailable in the soil solution. Interveinal chlorosis of young leaves starting near the growing tip may occur. Small veins also turn yellow. Shoots may suffer dieback.

- **Zinc** - If limited, results in stunting of the terminal. Leaves are small and seem crowded on the branches because of the reduced amount of extension growth. Leaves become chlorotic and may drop off early, starting with the older leaves first. Fruit production is poor.

- **Calcium** - Fruit disorders are the result of a shortage of calcium. Calcium is necessary for sound cell wall structure and, if absent, may result in breakdown of the fruit.

- **Boron** - Deficiencies show up as fruit disorders. Internal breakdown of the fruit and premature drop may result. This nutrient is more limiting where it is dry and pH is high.

- **Copper, sulfur, molybdenum, chloride, and sodium** - These micronutrients are usually adequate in Prairie soils.

## INSECT PESTS

Insects have the ability to reproduce themselves very quickly. Some insects, such as the aphid, may produce several generations of offspring during the growing season. If insect pests are not controlled early, their population may increase to the point of being unmanageable later on. There are three basic categories of insect pests.

- chewing insects that eat the foliage foliage

- sucking insects that remove nutrients from leaves, branches or fruit

- burrowing insects that may infest the bark or fruit.

Information on the control of insects on deciduous ornamental and fruit trees is contained in the Pest Control lesson (see Pest Control lesson, BACKYARD PEST MANAGEMENT). A description of the pest, the host it attacks, the damage that is caused, a brief description of its life cycle, and recommended control measures are included.

## DISEASES

The incidence of disease is very much influenced by the weather. When conditions are moist, diseases caused by fungus and bacteria flourish. Fortunately, the dry climate of the Prairies discourages most diseases from becoming serious problems. Fireblight is the most severe and causes damage to apples, pears, and numerous other ornamental trees and shrubs. Most diseases can be prevented by pruning with disinfected tools, and dressing large wounds to prevent the entry of pathogens. Keeping the trees healthy and vigorous with good management practices reduces the susceptibility of the trees to disease. If disease develops, prompt eradication of the infected parts prevents spreading of the disease. Sanitation of leaf and fruit litter and any wood removed during pruning prevents the overwintering of disease organisms on infected material. The Pest Control lesson discusses the control of ornamental and fruit tree diseases (see Pest Control lesson, BACKYARD PEST MANAGEMENT). Listed are some of the more common diseases which occur on the Prairies. The name of the pathogen, the type of disease, the host it infects, the damage that results, and control recommendations are also given.

## DAMAGE FROM ANIMALS

### MICE AND RABBITS

Mice, rabbits and other animals can cause serious damage to fruit trees. Both feed on the tender bark of the trunk and, in the case of rabbits, lower limbs as well. Mice may girdle the tree at ground level and kill the tree. Rabbits may eat away large patches of bark on one side of the tree.

Repellents are available that contain bitter tasting thiram that discourages rabbits and porcupines. This should be applied in late fall on the bark after the leaves have fallen. The bark should be dry and the temperature above freezing. Cover the trunk to a height of 1 m (39 in) from the snowline. Plastic tree guards (see Figure 13-30), or wire mesh guards can be wrapped around the tree or set in the ground around the trunk and should cover the trunk to a height of 1 m (39 in). Keeping the grass and other ground coverings mowed short discourages these pests, especially mice. Any mulch

that was placed beneath the trees during the growing season should not be placed right up to the trunks. It should be removed or mixed into the soil in the fall to discourage mice from nesting in it. Partially opened cans containing poisoned grain attract and help to get rid of mice.

### DEER

Deer can also seriously injure fruit trees. The only thing that can keep deer out is a very tall fence, approximately 2.4 m (8 ft) high. However, deer may be discouraged by a smaller fence that is inside a well established windbreak and by planting trees fairly close to buildings. A large, barking dog also deters deer.

## Figure 13-30
## PLASTIC TREE GUARD

Courtesy of Alberta Agriculture

## CONCLUSION

This lesson has provided a comprehensive study of tree fruit production and applied much of the material covered in *Book One - Gardening Fundamentals*. The home gardener, with a good understanding of this lesson, should be able to apply it to the abundant production of quality tree fruits.

It is hoped that the knowledge obtained can be put to practical use in growing, training and enjoying the harvest of a good selection of tree fruits. Get growing!

## SELF CHECK *QUIZ*

1. What are the three commercial orchard regions in Canada?

2. a. Give two reasons for not establishing fruit trees with a southern exposure.

   b. How can trees be protected if a southern exposure is unavoidable?

3. How far should fruit trees be planted from the lee side of a shelterbelt in a rural home orchard?

4. How can you determine which part of a branch is the previous season's growth?

5. Distinguish between the physiology of apple and plum flowers and fruit.

6. Why will apples not grow in tropical climates?

7. Why is it sometimes necessary to buy two cultivars of a type of fruit tree if there are no existing trees of the same type in the neighborhood?

8. It is early June and your tree is dropping small undeveloped fruit. What is wrong?

9. Your tree produced an abundance of fruit last year, yet this year there is almost no fruit at all. Last summer, to encourage healthy growth of the tree, you gave your tree a high nitrogen fertilizer and an abundance of water. Why didn't your fruit tree respond to your efforts?

10. What are two common methods of asexual propagation to obtain cultivars that are true-to-type?

11. What is the most important consideration when selecting a fruit tree cultivar.

12. Why is a newly planted tree sometimes headed-back at planting time?

13. When is the best time to prune?

14. Distinguish between a heading-back cut and a thinning cut.

15. What are two objectives of the modified central leader system?

16. Which tree should not be headed-back during the training period?

17. What are the five functions of grafting?

18. What is the most damaging disease of apples and pears?

## RESOURCE MATERIALS

Alberta Agriculture. *Alberta Horticultural Guide*. 1986. Agdex 200/01.

Alberta Agriculture. *Fruit Tree Propagation*. AC 1269, 1968. Agdex 210/16.

Alberta Agriculture. *Tree Fruits for the Prairie Provinces*. AC 1672, Revised 1982. Agdex 210/20-1.

Alberta Agriculture. *Pruning and Training Fruit Trees*. AC 1513, 1973. Agdex 210/24-1. AC (1513).

Alberta Agriculture. *Shelterbelts in Alberta*. Revised 1982. (FS) Agrifax 277/20-2.

Bilderback, Diane E. and Dorothy Hinshaw Patent. *Backyard Fruits and Berries*. Emmaus, P.A.: Rodale Press, 1984.

   Comprehensive advice on establishing and managing small fruits and fruit trees.

Childers, N.F. *Modern Fruit Science*. Newbrunswick, N.J.: Horticultural Publications, Rutger University, 1975.

Cole, T.J. *Woody Plant Source List*. Ottawa: Ottawa Research Station, 1972.

Hill, Lewis. *Fruits and Berries for the Home Garden*. New York: Alfred A. Knoff, 1977.

   A well-written reference for home gardeners.

Readers Digest. *Illustrated Guide to Gardening in Canada*. Montreal: The Reader's Digest Association (Canada) Ltd., 1979.

Comprehensive reference tool for the home gardener including excellent illustrations.

Shoemaker, J.S. and B.J.G. Teskey. *Tree Fruit Production*. New York: John Wiley and Sons Inc., 1978.

   Detailed cultural information for home gardeners and commercial growers.

Westwood, M.N. *Temperate Zone Pomology*. San Francisco: W.H. Freeman, 1978.

   University-level text on culture and physiology.

Research Stations:
   Ottawa:
   Agriculture Canada Research Branch
   Ottawa Research Station, Bldg. 50
   Ottawa, Ontario K1A 0C6

Brooks:
Alberta Horticultural Research Centre
Bag Service 200
Brooks, Alberta T0J 0J0

Beaverlodge:
Beaverlodge Research Station
P.O. Box 29
Beaverlodge, Alberta T0H 0C0

Melfort:
Melfort Research Station
P.O Box 1240
Melfort, Saskatchewan S0E 1A0

Morden:
Morden Research Station
Morden, Manitoba R0G 1J0

Universities and Colleges:

Plant Science Department
460 Agriculture-Forestry Centre
University of Alberta
Edmonton, Alberta

Plant Sciences Department
University of Saskatoon
Saskatoon, Saskatchewan S7N 0W0

Horticultural Department
Olds College
Box 2000
Olds, Alberta T0M 1P0.

Periodicals: see Small Fruit Production lesson.

Societies:

Fruit Growers Society of Alberta
Box 861
Beaverlodge, Alberta T0H 0C0

# GLOSSARY

**alternate bearing** · the production of a heavy crop of fruit one year and little or no fruit the following season.

**bark ringing** - the removal of a thin strip of bark from around the trunk or at the base of main limbs to stimulate increased flower formation on vigorously growing juvenile trees which are tardy in bearing.

**barrenness** - the lack of a crop of fruit.

**bloom period** - the period following the opening of blossoms during which the flower can be pollinated and successfully fertilized (usually two or three days after initial bloom).

**budding** - a special type of grafting in which a single bud is used as the scion. There are several methods of budding. T-budding is the most common and easiest.

**budstick** - a cutting taken from the terminal shoots of the current season's growth when the buds are mature, but not dormant (usually in late July or early August). They are kept moist until they can be used as a source of buds for budding onto desirable rootstock.

**bud union** - the place along the lower stem where the bud was originally budded onto the rootstock (usually visible as a slight swelling on the stem).

**cold temperature acclimation** - the physiological changes that begin to occur with the onset of the first fall frosts resulting in the slowing of metabolic processes and the gradual dehydration of tissues.

**compatible** - different cultivars or varieties that will set fruit when cross-pollinated or make a successful graft union when integrated.

**C:N ratio** - carbon:nitrogen ratio - the balance of carbohydrates (starches and sugars) to nitrogen-containing compounds (proteins) within the tree's tissues.

**differentiation** - changes in cells and tissues with respect to their structure, composition and function during growth.

**dormance quiescence** - the state that a plant is in after its chilling requirement is met, but climatic conditions are still unfavorable to permit the breaking of bud dormancy.

**drupe** - a stone fruit which contains a seed encased in a hard shell inside fleshy tissue (e.g., plum).

**dwarf interstem** - the portion of one kind of dwarf tree that is grafted onto a rootstock and later topworked with a desirable variety.

**dwarf rootstock** - a rootstock that will pass dwarfing characteristics on to the desirable variety that is grafted onto it.

**flower bud initiation** - the initiation of buds to differentiate as flower buds usually as the result of carbohydrate accumulation in the tissues and the production of the flowering hormone florigen.

**frameworking** - a type of grafting used to work a new variety onto an existing tree while retaining as much of the

original framework of primary and secondary scaffolds as possible.

**fruit** - the ripened ovary that has developed as a result of the pollination and fertilization of the flower.

**fruit set** - the development of fruit following pollination and fertilization.

**graft** - the act of inserting the bud or scion of one variety or cultivar into the stem or trunk of another, where it continues to grow and eventually becomes a permanent part of the tree (e.g., whip or tongue, cleft, bark, side grafts).

**graft union** - the place where a successful graft has taken place.

**hardening-off** subjecting the trees to adverse conditions such as lack of moisture or nutrients in order to hasten the maturation of tissues and the proper acclimating of tissues to cold temperature.

**heading-back cut** - removal of the terminal growth, usually to a lateral bud or branch to encourage the extension growth of lateral buds below the cut. This is the principal cut made during the training period of most trees with the exception of pears.

**interstem** - the portion of some fruit trees that is grafted between the rootstock and desirable variety in order to impart some desirable characteristic to the tree (such as dwarfing, wide crotch angles or hardiness).

**maiden trees** - young one- or two-year old trees that are ready for planting and have not yet begun to be trained.

**mixed buds** - those buds containing both vegetative and floral parts.

**physiology** - the functions and vital processes of a plant or living organism.

**pome fruit** - fruit that results from a swollen receptacle that is fused to the ovary and contains a core (e.g., apples or pears).

**rootstock** - the root component of fruit tree propagation that may contribute hardiness or dwarfing characteristics to the desired top portion that is grafted on to it.

**scion** - the twig or shoot portion that is grafted onto another plant.

**take** - a successful graft union.

**thinning out** - the removal of lateral or secondary branches flush with the main stem below it.

**topworking** - changing the variety of the tree by budding or grafting on scions of the new variety to the existing branches.

**whip** - a one-year old unbranched tree.

# SELF CHECK *ANSWERS*

1. - the Okanagan and Fraser Valleys of British Columbia
   - the Niagara Peninsula of southern Ontario
   - the Annapolis Valley of Nova Scotia (see COMMERCIAL FRUIT PRODUCTION - page 1301)

2. a. Trees with a southern exposure tend to bud prematurely in the spring. Blossoms of early-flowering fruits such as apricots and some plums are especially susceptible. With a north to northeast exposure, budding can be delayed, thereby reducing the risk of frost damage. A southern exposure increases damage from unscald to the southwest side of the tree. This is caused by the late afternoon sun warming the tissues, followed by a sudden drop in air temperature at sunset. Water then freezes in the tissues, expands and ruptures the cells, killing part of the bark (see DIRECTION OF EXPOSURE - page 1302, PROBLEMS AND PREVENTION - page 1342).

   b. Train the lowermost branch approximately 60 cm (24 in.) off the ground with a southwest exposure. As the tree matures, this branch will help shade the trunk, filtering light through it to reduce the sun's intensity. Wrap a tree guard around the trunk to reflect the sunlight and protect the tree from rodent damage as well. Painting the base with a white latex paint also causes light to deflect (see PLANTING THE TREES - page 1325).

3. 25 m (82 ft) (see SHELTERRBELT PROTECTION - page 1302 and Figure 13-2 - page 1303).

4. The previous season's growth will have developed from a terminal bud at the ends of branches. This point of origin is later marked by the evidence of a bud scar (see VEGETATIVE STRUCTURES - page 1304 and Figure 13-5 - page 1306).

5. APPLE:
   - Flowers – arise from mixed buds, five flowers per influorescence, epigynous flower.
   - Fruit – pome, derived from fusion of ovary with receptacle, contains up to 10 seeds.

   PLUM:
   - Flowers – arise from unmixed flower buds, about two or three flowers per influorescence, perigynous flower.
   - Fruit – stone or drupe, derived from a swollen ovary, contains a pit with seeds (see STRUCTURE OF FLOWERS AND FRUIT - pages 1304-1306 and Figure 13-6 - page 1307).

6. They need a cold temperature treatment during which dormancy of vegetative and flower buds is broken and differentiation of buds is completed. Without a period of near freezing temperatures, the trees deteriorate significantly, become unproductive and may even die (see THE MATURE FRUIT TREE - VEGETATIVE GROWTH - page 1306).

7. Most fruit trees require cross-pollination because they are self-sterile. Although some cultivars exist that are self-fertile, most trees will produce a greater quantity of quality fruit if cross-pollinated with a compatible cultivar (see FLOWERING AND POLLINATION - page 1308).

8. Nothing is wrong. This is one of the two fruit drops which is nature's way of thinning incompletely fertilized, damaged, malformed or self-pollinated fruit (see FRUIT DEVELOPMENT - page 1311).

9. Your tree has assumed an alternate bearing habit. By adding high nitrogen fertilizer and water, you encouraged vegetative growth and utilization of carbohydrates in the tissues rather than accumulation. This results in a low C:N ratio which inhibited flower bud initiation and thus flower and fruit development the following year (see BARRENNESS IN FRUIT TREES - page 1314).

10. - Whip or tongue grafting
    - T-budding (also patch (chip) budding) (see PROPAGATION OF FRUIT TREES - pages 1314-1316 and Figure 13-11 - pages 1312-13).

11. Hardiness in the zone in which it is to be grown (see SELECTING CULTIVARS - page 1319)

12. To remove the apical dominance exerted by the terminal bud and promote the development of lateral buds into branches from which future scaffolds are to be chosen. If the tree is quite vigorous, only three or four buds may need to be removed (see PRUNING AT PLANTING TIME - page 1327 and Figure 13-22A - page 1332).

13. Early spring during March and early April. Fall pruning results in more desiccation of the bark around the wound and it takes longer to heal. Also, in the spring, you can prune out anything that exhibits symptoms of winterkill as well as diseased or broken branches (see WHEN TO PRUNE - page 1330).

14. Heading-back cut – the removal of the terminal portion of a twig or branch to a point between the terminal and a lateral bud or branch below it. Principal cut during training.
Thinning cut – the removal of an entire lateral twig or branch flush with its place of origin. Principal cut in pruning bearing trees to remove dead, damaged, diseased and unproductive older wood or spurs (see TYPES OF PRUNING CUTS - page 1330).

15. - To promote a low-head, easier-to-manage form
- To encourage the development of four to six main scaffolds with strong, wide-angled crotches (see OBJECTIVES OF THE MODIFIED CENTRAL LEADER SYSTEM-page 1333).

16. The pear. Heading-back encourages the development of upright branches with narrow crotches (see PRUNING BEARING FRUIT TREES - page 1333).

17.  propagation of young fruit trees
frameworking
topworking
stembuilding
repairing damage to the tree's base (see GRAFTING - page 1336)

18. Fireblight is the most damaging disease of apples and pears (see PROBLEMS AND PREVENTION - DISEASES - page 1345).

## INDEX

*LESSON FOURTEEN*
- GROWTH PROCESSES AND ENVIRONMENTAL FACTORS
- GROWING CONTAINERS AND TRANSPLANTING PROCEDURES
- WATER AND WATERING
- SANITATION
- SPECIAL PLANTS AND PLANT TYPES

# HOUSEPLANTS

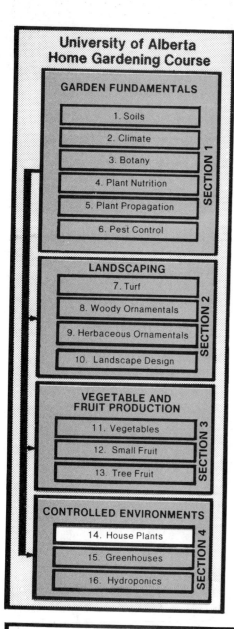

**University of Alberta Home Gardening Course**

**GARDEN FUNDAMENTALS**
- 1. Soils
- 2. Climate
- 3. Botany
- 4. Plant Nutrition
- 5. Plant Propagation
- 6. Pest Control

SECTION 1

**LANDSCAPING**
- 7. Turf
- 8. Woody Ornamentals
- 9. Herbaceous Ornamentals
- 10. Landscape Design

SECTION 2

**VEGETABLE AND FRUIT PRODUCTION**
- 11. Vegetables
- 12. Small Fruit
- 13. Tree Fruit

SECTION 3

**CONTROLLED ENVIRONMENTS**
- 14. House Plants
- 15. Greenhouses
- 16. Hydroponics

SECTION 4

# SELF-STUDY LESSON FEATURES

Self-study is an educational approach which allows you to study a subject where and when you want. The course is designed to allow students to study the course material efficiently and incorporates the following features.

**OBJECTIVES** — are found at the beginning of each lesson and allow you to determine what you can expect to learn in the lesson.

**LESSON MATERIAL** — is logically organized and broken down into fundamental components by ordered headings to assist you to comprehend the subject.

**REFERENCING** — between lessons and within lessons allows you to integrate course material.

The last two digits of the page number identify the page and the digits preceding these identify the lesson number (eg., 107: Lesson 1, page 7 or 1227: Lesson 12, page 27).

Referencing:

> sections within the same lesson (eg., see OSMOSIS)

> sections in other lessons (eg., see Botany lesson, OSMOSIS)

> figures and tables (eg., see Figure 7-3)

**FIGURES AND TABLES** — are found in abundance throughout the lessons and are designed to convey useful information in an easy to understand form.

**SIDEBARS** — are those areas in the lesson which are boxed and toned. They present information supplementary to the core content of the lesson.

**PRACTICAL PROJECTS** — are integrated within the lesson material and are included to allow you to apply principles and practices.

**SELF-CHECK QUIZ** — is provided at the end of each lesson and allows you to test your comprehension of the lesson material. Answers to the questions and references to the sections dealing with the questions are provided in the answer section. You should review any questions that you are unable to answer.

**GLOSSARY** — is provided at the end of each lesson and alphabetically lists the definitions of key concepts and terms.

**RESOURCE MATERIALS** — are provided at the end of each lesson and comprise a list of recommended learning materials for further study of the subject. Also included are author's comments on the potential application of each publication.

**INDEX** — alphabetically lists useful topics and their location within the lesson.

1986 University of Alberta Faculty of Extension

**Written by: Helge Welling**

Technical Reviewers:
Gordon Heaps
Professor Ed Maginnes

**ISBN 0-88864-852-9**
(Book 4, Lesson 14)

THE PRODUCTION TEAM

| | |
|---|---|
| Managing Editor | Thom Shaw |
| Editor | Frank Procter |
| Production Coordinator | Kevin Hanson |
| Graphic Artists | Melanie Eastley Harbourne |
| Data Entry | Lois Hameister |
| | Patricia McDonald |

Published by the University of Alberta
Faculty of Extension, Corbett Hall
Edmonton, Alberta, T6G 2G4

# LEARNING OBJECTIVES

After completing this lesson, the student should be able to:

1. recognize the influence of light, temperature, humidity, atmosphere, growing media, and water on plant growth.

2. determine the relationship between temperature and light.

3. identify the factors that influence frequency and quantity of water and fertilizer application.

4. identify the plant families that are most suitable for use as houseplants.

5. appreciate that the extent to which indoor conditions correspond to plant's native environment serves as a basis for plant selection.

6. identify plant preferences and peculiarities.

7. identify the need for transplanting and to successfully repot a houseplant.

# TABLE OF CONTENTS

# INTRODUCTION

Houseplants are plants that share and help to create the environment in our homes. The plants that are most successful as houseplants are those whose native environments are most closely matched to our indoor conditions. Climates vary worldwide so it is important to recognize the native climatic conditions of plants intended for use as houseplants. It is also important to know that the indoor conditions are not the same in all homes; they vary from house to house, and even within the house. It is, therefore, desirable to observe what kind of environmental condition exists or needs to exist in order to successfully grow houseplants. Successful growth of houseplants is dependent on matching the indoor environment to the native environment of the plant(s) or to modify indoor conditions to match plant requirements.

*Book One - Gardening Fundamentals* provides the basic information for this lesson and relates directly to important aspects of selecting and growing houseplants. This lesson identifies significant environmental factors and details their influence on the welfare of houseplants. The motivation for growing houseplants varies with each individual and influences our choice of houseplants.

- Houseplants fill a need in people to be in touch with the summer part of nature, especially so for those who live in harsh, cold climates.

- A living plant fills a psychological need in people, in as much as it is a living being and responds to the care a person gives it.

- Plants help to purify the atmosphere; they give us oxygen and they act as screens. Also, they absorb noise and some of them give us fragrance, color, or edible parts.

- Houseplants are sometimes grown for their therapeutic value (i.e., the enjoyment of raising plants from seeds or cuttings to mature plants) or grown purely for decorative value.

- Some houseplants are grown for food or garnishings for food.

# GROWTH PROCESSES AND ENVIRONMENTAL FACTORS

Plant growth is determined by the extent to which their physiological needs are met. Success with an increasing variety of houseplants is related to the degree one is able to understand the environmental needs of the plant and appreciate the growing processes of plants.

It is possible to obtain a great deal of control over our indoor climate to bring about optimum conditions for a chosen houseplant. The factors that must be controlled include **temperature**, **light** and **atmosphere** (including humidity). Other factors in the welfare of houseplants include the **growing media**, **container**, **watering** and **fertilizing practices**, as well as **sanitation** (including pest control).

## TEMPERATURE

Temperature affects a plant's physiological processes and, thus, a plant's potential for growth. Generally, cooler temperatures slow down growth processes and warmer temperatures speed up the processes. Temperatures often vary with location; soil temperature, air temperature and leaf temperature may all be different.

### SOIL TEMPERATURE

In addition to its effect on germination of seeds and rooting of cuttings, soil temperature influences the uptake of nutrients. Absorption takes place at a slower rate under cold conditions and speeds up under warmer conditions. The growth of micro-organisms is slow when soil temperatures are low, so decomposition of organic matter takes longer. Conversely, at warm temperatures, organic matter breaks down at a faster rate because of increased growth and activity of micro-organisms. High soil temperature dries out soil.

The temperature of the water used for watering affects the soil temperature. Cold water chills the soil and wilted plants take relatively longer to recover. Lukewarm water speeds up recovery from wilting by speeding uptake.

### AIR TEMPERATURE

Air temperature affects leaf temperatures and growth processes, inlcuding photosynthesis, transpiration and respiration. Respiration goes on day and night and high temperatures increase the rate of respiration. An excessive rate of respiration can result in the food supply (sugars produced by photosynthesis) being depleted. Low temperatures slow down respiration to the point of almost stopping it (as in dormancy). Since plants do not have a blood system (like animals) to keep them warm, the effect of air temperature on plants is immediate - taking a houseplant out in minus degree temperatures results in a frozen plant, even if it is only a few seconds from the door to a heated car. Insulating it with protective wrapping to delay the influx of cold temperature can keep it safe for those few seconds. (One or more layers of paper closest to the plant and a layer of plastic film outside the paper provides the necessary insulation.)

Optimum air temperature varies from kind to kind as does safe minimum and maximum air temperatures. Chilling an African violet (saintpaulia) can cause death within 24 hours. Air temperature can affect leaf and flower color and, on many plants, is responsible for initiation or development of flowers.

### LEAF TEMPERATURE

Leaf temperatures are usually close to air temperatures but certain mineral imbalances may cause a difference in leaf temperature. Leaf temperature has a significant impact on stomata opening and closing, thus affecting photosynthesis, respiration and transpiration processes. Normally, when leaf temperatures rise, the amount of water vapor that transpires increases – if transpiration exceeds absorption, the leaf wilts. This may happen in situations like the following. The houseplant is in such a location that the soil temperature is low. If the sun suddenly shines on the leaves, leaf temperature increases rapidly and wilting occurs. The wilted condition lasts until the plant is out of direct sunshine or soil temperatures have increased so absorption can again keep up with transpiration. In conditions where leaf temperature is low, the stomata are closed and, with high soil

Figure 14-1
## OEDEMA

temperature, active absorption with great root pressure takes place. Water pressure in leaf and stem cells can be so great that the cells burst and plant sap oozes out - a condition known as oedema (see Figure 14-1). This is not to be confused with guttation or cuticular transpiration (see Plant Nutrition lesson, PLANT METABOLISM).

## LIGHT

Light is the basis for all life and the ultimate source of energy. Light controls many developmental and regulatory processes in plants and animals (see Climate lesson, LIGHT). Light quality refers to intensity and duration. Light quality also refers to the spectral aspects of light and the source of light (natural or artificial).

### LIGHT INTENSITY

Insufficient light intensity causes legginess, etiolation and a different cell structure in the leaf. When light is inadequate, plants which normally have brightly colored leaves lose their brilliance (eg., coleus) and leaf damage can occur due to the breakdown of chlorophyll (see Figure 14-2). Lack of light is an aggravating factor in the condition known as oedema.

Excess light intensity causes bleaching and browning of plant leaves. Excess light is often received by African violets (saintpaulia) and many other plants. African violets usually do very well in a south window during the months of November, December and January (see Figure 14-3). However, the natural light intensity is so great in mid-February that African violet leaves turn pale and, if kept in excess light, their leaves will turn brown and the plant will die.

Light and temperature requirements are linked in numerous plants. With lower temperature, activity is slower and the plant can do with less light. Conversely, a plant can cope with higher temperatures when more light is available. Cactus, for example, would not do well at all if kept at the same high temperatures that prevail in summer with the very low light intensity that prevails in winter. Cactus should, therefore, either be kept much cooler during the winter months or given extra light.

### SEASONAL VARIATIONS IN LIGHT INTENSITY

In Alberta, the intensity and duration of light varies dramatically between summer and winter. The intensity of light is suddenly and very sharply reduced in

Figure 14-2
## INFLUENCE OF LIGHT ON PLANTS

plant on the right side has not received adequate light

Figure 14-3
## AFRICAN VIOLET

September to October. This, of course, is aggravated by cloudy days, or modified by the sunny days of Indian summer. Nevertheless, the drop in light intensity is responsible for a considerable amount of yellowing and dropping of leaves in houseplants in September and October. Another aspect of the seasonal intensity changes is the angle of the sun and its effect on houseplants. In the winter, the sun is very low in the horizon and low intensity light comes in almost horizontally through the window and across the room (see Figure 14-4). The intensity in the spring and fall is greater and the angle of the sun a little higher, consequently the direct light does not come all the way across the room, but definitely provides good light for plants in the vicinity of the windows on the east, south and west. Once summer arrives, the sun is almost directly overhead, so only those plants that are closest to the south windows receive direct sun. The light intensity, however, is very great at this time. Roof overhangs can further influence this situation and cause south windows to receive less light than east and west windows during the summer months. If light comes mainly from one direction, it is wise to turn plants 1/4 turn daily for uniform development of the plant.

## LIGHT MEASUREMENT

Plants do not 'see' light the same way as the eye does, but absorb light mainly in the blue and the red part of the spectrum. Units of light measure (such as lumen, lux and footcandles) are measurements based on the sensitivity of the human eye to light (see Greenhouse Gardening lesson, NATURAL LIGHT). Most horticultural literature still uses lux and footcandles when describing light needed by plants.

Camera light meters or photometers can be used to obtain footcandle (fc) readings of light. Two methods are described below:

**Method 1**: Set film speed dial at ASA 100, aim the meter at dull white or grey paper in the proposed plant location and orient the paper toward the maximum source of light. Get close enough so the meter sees only the paper. Determine the proper exposure. Do not block the light or create a shadow on the paper. The shutter speed indicated opposite F4 (reading it as a whole number) is the number of footcandles received at that location (eg., 1/250 sec. = 250 fc).

**Method 2**: Set the ASA at 200 and the shutter speed at 1/125 second. Focus on dull white or grey paper and adjust the F stop until a correct exposure is indicated. A correct exposure at F2 then means that the area receives 32 fc of light.

F4 = 64 fc
F5.6 = 125 fc
F8 = 250 fc
F11 = 500 fc
F16 = 1000 fc
F22 = 2000 fc

No light meter is as accurate as the plant itself in determining its needs, but we must be aware of the way light intensities vary with locations, time of day and seasons. Light at window height will be much more intense than light just below the windowsill or just off to the side of the window. As the day progresses, any trees or buildings outside the window may block the light from the sun, so intensity is greatly reduced (see Figure 14-5).

## LIGHT INTENSITY PREFERENCES OF PLANTS

Plants grow in varied locations in nature and, thus, by observing the conditions prevailing in nature where the plants do well, we can select plants for indoor locations with similar conditions or we can modify the indoor conditions to match plant requirements.

Figure 14-4
## SEASONAL ANGLE OF THE SUN

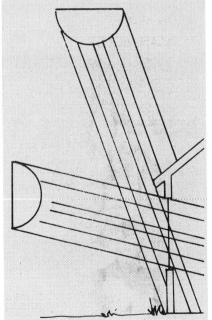

Figure 14-5
## SHADE PROVIDED BY THE TREE

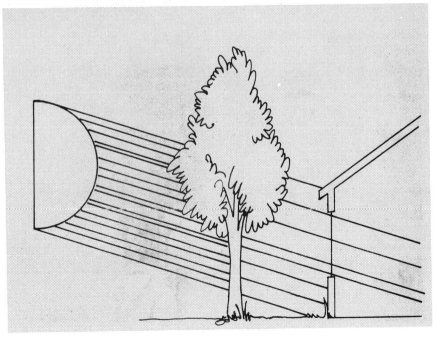

Many plants grow under **bright** light conditions and prefer the full intensity of the sun to best develop flowers, brilliance of foliage, etc. Such plants need supplementary light during the winter to bring the intensity up to a 150 fc level or higher for a 12-hour duration. Some plants grow under much less intense light and, if supplied with a medium intensity of 100 fc during a 8-12 hour day, will come through the low light winter period fine. A group of plants which can tolerate **low** light can, in fact, be damaged if exposed to bright light conditions. Light below 25 fc is insufficient for houseplants.

Some plants requiring **bright light** conditions include (see Figure 14-6):

## Figure 14-6
## BRIGHT LIGHT PLANTS

Schefflera (umbrella tree)

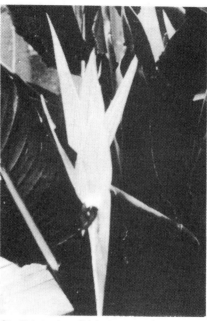

Strelitzia reginae (bird of paradise)

Beleperone (shrimp plant)

Cacti

Beleperone (shrimp plant)
Citrus sp. (orange, lemon, grapefruit, etc.)
Euphorbia sp. (crown of thorns, fat lady, poinsettia, etc.)
Hippeastrum sp. (amaryllis)
Hoya (waxplants)
Strelitzia reginae (bird of paradise)
Aloe (healing plant)
Cacti (most desert cacti)
Kalanchoe (panda plant, airplant, etc.)
Ananas (pineapple)
Impatiens (patience plant)
Coleus
Bamboo
Gynura (velvet plant, purple passion plant)
Hibiscus (hibiscus, rose of Sharon)
Nerium oleander (oleander, rosebay)
Punica (pomegranate)
Schefflera (umbrella tree)

Some plants in the **medium light** group include (see Figure 14-7):

Diefenbachia (dumb cane)
Pandanus (screw pine)
Peperomia
Philodendron
Saintpaulia (African violet)
Scindapsus (devil's ivy)
Clivia (Kaffir lily)
Cordyline (Hawaiian ti plants)
Aechmea (living vase plant)
Aphelandra (zebra plant)
Begonia
Ficus (India rubbertree, weeping fig, mistletoe fig, etc.)
Maranta (prayer plant)
Pilea (aluminum plant, etc.)
Chlorophytum (bracketplant, spiderplant)

Some plants in the **low light group** include (see Figure 14-8):

Aglaonema (Chinese evergreen)
Aspidistra (parlor palm, cast iron plant)
Chamaedorea (neanthe bella, forked blue palm)
Cyrtomium (holly fern)
Pteris ensiformis (Victoria fern)
Spathiphyllum (sailplant, white flag)
Sansevieria (swordplant, mother-in-law's sharp tongue, snakeplant)
Zingiber (common ginger)
Asplenium (bird's nest fern)
Draceana (dragonplant, cornplant, caneplant)
Syngonium (trileaf nephytus, arrowplant)
Arthurium

Figure 14-7
**MEDIUM LIGHT PLANTS**

Pandanus (screw pine)

Philodendron

Diefenbachia

Begonia

Figure 14-8
**LOW LIGHT PLANTS**

Syngonium (trileaf mephytus, arrowplant)

Asplenium (bird's nest fern)

Cyrtomium (holly fern)

## ARTIFICIAL LIGHT

### USES OF ARTIFICIAL LIGHT

The reasons for using artificial light with houseplants vary. One reason may be entirely for the decorative effect that can be brought about by highlighting some plants. Another reason may be to use artificial light as an alternative to natural light.

Artificial light makes it possible to grow plants that otherwise could not be grown. Artificial light is needed whenever the duration and intensity of natural light is inadequate for the plant to photosynthesize enough energy to maintain good health or, in some cases, even to stay alive (in winter, for example).

The purpose of using artificial light sources for plant growth is to duplicate the growth brought about by sunlight, but not necessarily to duplicate the intensity or all the spectrum of sunlight.

### FACTORS IN CHOOSING ARTIFICIAL LIGHT

When selecting lamps, you should know whether the light is intended to extend the daylength (for photoperiodic reasons), to supplement both duration and intensity of natural light, or if it is to replace natural light entirely.

For the purpose of extending the daylength only, low intensity light is needed and can be supplied by ordinary incandescent bulbs. To entirely replace natural light, lamps with the wavelengths and intensity most effective in obtaining the growth response brought about in plants by sunlight must be selected. Other factors to consider in selecting lamps are energy conversion efficiency, rated life, uniformity of light, light

### Figure 14-9
### ARTIFICIAL LIGHTING

distribution, economic operation and maintenance.

Some lamps are more efficient than others in converting electric energy into light (radiant energy). Table 14-1 shows light (radiant energy) measured as milliwatt (mW) of radiant energy obtained per watt (W) of electricity used for various types of lamps.

High intensity discharge lamps (eg., high pressure sodium) and several tubes of very high output fluorescent lamps (215 watt, 1500 mA type) can provide sufficient light for bright light preference plants if artificial light is the only source (see Figure 14-9). Medium and low light preference plant needs can be met by a lamp that produces lesser output.

### REFLECTED LIGHT

Light reflected by a mirror or white surface is very valuable and the use of reflective surfaces is an advantage when utilizing light for plant growth. Reflective surfaces and lamps can and do cause glare in some situations. Wedged louvers can be used to eliminate glare. The purpose for which artificial light is used dictates which lamps and reflective surfaces to choose. A relaxing living room setting definitely needs much softer light than a plant growth setup in the basement.

### TYPES OF LAMPS

Incandescent lamps produce light high in the red part of the spectrum and, therefore, also a lot of heat (see Greenhouse Gardening lesson, ARTIFICIAL LIGHT). These lamps should, therefore, be kept at least 50 cm (20 in) away from plants to avoid heat injury.

Incandescent lamps with reflectors that direct light down toward the plant are sufficient for extra light during winter for such plants as African violets. A few plants in close proximity to a table lamp will reward you for such attention with blooms.

Fluorescent lamps provide light mostly in the blue part of the spectrum and are much cooler than incandescent lamps. They can be placed as close as 15 cm (6 in) from plants without causing heat injury. The intensity of fluorescent light

### Table 14-1
### RADIANT ENERGY

| Light Source | Radiant Energy in mW |
|---|---|
| incandescent 100 watt bulb | 58-100 |
| incandescent 150 watt bulb | 69-500 |
| one type fluorescent tube 40 watts | 130 |
| another type fluorescent tube 40 watts | 178 |
| 400 watt high pressure sodium | 273 |

decreases with age and after about 5000 hours, it is advisable to replace the tubes. Replacement is recommended when both ends of the tube blacken or at least every two years.

High Intensity Discharge lamps (H.I.D.), like incandescent lamps, should be kept at least 50 cm (20 in) away from plants (see Greenhouse Gardening lesson, ARTIFICIAL LIGHT). High pressure mercury light appears white and metal halide light appears yellow (and makes skin appear greyish).

## CONSIDERATIONS IN INSTALLATION OF ARTIFICIAL LIGHTS

If replacing daylight entirely, artificial light should include blue, red and far red parts of the spectrum. This is often achieved by installing two types of lamps beamed at the same surface. The overall intensity should be sufficient to satisfy the plant requirements, so lamps with high energy efficiency and uniform distribution are sought. High intensity discharge lamps are well suited to this purpose.

For decorative illumination, light should be directed onto the plants (usually downward), not splashed in all directions. Downbeam or narrowbeam spotlights are often used to fulfill this objective. A 200 W bulb with a reflector can also be used. The light should emerge as a clearly defined beam.

Incandescent bulbs in a row often create 'hot spots' of bright light with valleys of low light between. This is not the case with fluorescent lamps, although the highest intensity is produced in the middle of the tube. H.I.D. lamps generally require half the wattage and electrical connections of fluorescent lamps.

Generally, the cost in artificial light lies in the initial installation (wire, luminaires, lamps, switches, timers, etc.) and in maintenance (replacement of lamps, starters, ballasts) and consumption. With respect to installation; ease of mounting and removal, size of luminaires, life expectancy of bulbs, and height adjustment are considerations in the planning and selection of lighting types.

Fluorescent lamps can be used in tiered layers as a shelf system with lamps and reflectors mounted under the shelves that hold plants. Standard fluorescent fixtures are also suitable for light

## Figure 14-10
## SHELVED LIGHT GARDENS

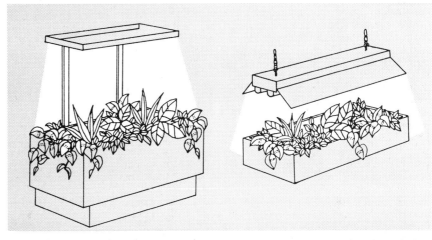

gardens placed in closets, cupboards or bookshelves or used as room dividers (see Figure 14-10). By using mirrors, aluminum foil or other reflective surfaces, the light can be maximized. Waterproof plastic trays can be used to hold the plants and timers used to turn lights on and off. If plant containers are placed on castered platforms, plants can readily be moved under artificial light for increased exposure and growth, then moved back to decorate another area.

## DISTANCE AND INTENSITY

The amount of light produced by a light source is proportionate to its distance from the surface it illuminates. Light from a lamp decreases very quickly as the distance increases. It would be easy to reason that if 400 fc is obtained at a distance of 50 cm (20 in) from a lamp, 200 fc would be obtained 100 cm (40 in) from the lamp. This is not the case; in fact, the intensity at the 100 cm (40 in) distance is 100 fc. The inverse square law governs the relationship of distance and intensity of light. As the distance is doubled, the intensity is only one-quarter (25%) of its former intensity (see Greenhouse Gardening lesson, ARTIFICIAL LIGHT).

# ATMOSPHERE

## RELATIVE HUMIDITY

One of the major factors in raising houseplants concerns humidity. The most familiar measure of humidity in the air is relative humidity (RH). It is expressed as a percentage of the amount of water the air is holding in vapor form compared to what it would hold if the air was fully saturated. Fully saturated air has an RH of 100 per cent. If the air contains only half the amount of moisture it is capable of holding, it has an RH of 50 per cent. The amount of moisture the air can hold, however, varies with the air temperature. Warm air can hold more moisture than cold air; therefore, more water must be evaporated in a high temperature to maintain a certain relative humidity than must be evaporated at a low temperature for the maintenance of the same percentage RH (Table 14-2). If the air in an inflated balloon at 20°C and 50 per cent RH is warmed to 30°C, the RH of the air inside the balloon drops to 28 per cent RH. The RH can be measured with hygrometers or calculated from the difference between a dry bulb thermometer reading and a wet bulb thermometer reading (see Figure 14-11).

At certain temperatures (Dew point temperature), condensation takes place. This happens when air is cooled to the point where it can no longer hold the water vapor it contains. Condensation forming on plants at night allows certain disease organisms to thrive, so wet foliage at night is an invitation to disaster. Relative humidity does not measure the actual moisture (water vapor) in the air. Actual moisture is measured in grams per cubic metre $(g/m^3)$. It is more practical to use percentage RH with various temperatures and moisture holding capacities.

## WAYS TO CONTROL RH

Relative humidity can be adjusted up or down by lowering or raising the temperature. Excess moisture can also be taken out of the air by moisture absorbing materials (eg., paper towels in an excessively moist terrarium) or by chemicals (eg., silicate gel). Additional humidity is often needed in the house during winter months. The cold outside air is unable to hold much moisture, so

## Table 14-2
## PER CENT RELATIVE HUMIDITY AT VARIOUS TEMPERATURES

| Wet Bulb Temp. °C \ Dry Bulb Temp. °C | 10 | 11 | 12 | 13 | 14 | 15 | 16 | 17 | 18 | 19 | 20 | 21 | 22 | 23 | 24 | 25 | 26 | 27 | 28 | 29 | 30 |
|---|---|---|---|---|---|---|---|---|---|---|---|---|---|---|---|---|---|---|---|---|---|
| 10 | 100 | 88 | 77 | 69 | 61 | 53 | 48 | 42 | - | | | | | | | | | | | | |
| 11 | | 100 | 88 | 78 | 69 | 61 | 54 | 48 | 44 | 38 | - | | | | | | | | | | |
| 12 | | | 100 | 88 | 78 | 69 | 61 | 54 | 49 | 44 | 39 | 35 | - | | | | | | | | |
| 13 | | | | 100 | 88 | 78 | 69 | 62 | 55 | 50 | 45 | 40 | 36 | - | | | | | | | |
| 14 | | | | | 100 | 88 | 79 | 70 | 62 | 56 | 51 | 45 | 41 | 37 | 33 | 28 | 25 | 21 | 18 | | |
| 15 | | | | | | 100 | 88 | 79 | 70 | 63 | 57 | 51 | 46 | 41 | 37 | 33 | 30 | 26 | 23 | 20 | 17 |
| 16 | | | | | | | 100 | 88 | 79 | 71 | 63 | 57 | 52 | 46 | 42 | 38 | 34 | 31 | 27 | 24 | 21 |
| 17 | | | | | | | | 100 | 89 | 79 | 71 | 63 | 58 | 52 | 47 | 43 | 39 | 35 | 32 | 28 | 25 |
| 18 | | | | | | | | | 100 | 89 | 80 | 72 | 64 | 58 | 52 | 48 | 44 | 40 | 36 | 32 | 29 |
| 19 | | | | | | | | | | 100 | 89 | 80 | 72 | 65 | 58 | 54 | 49 | 45 | 41 | 37 | 34 |
| 20 | | | | | | | | | | | 100 | 89 | 81 | 72 | 65 | 60 | 55 | 50 | 45 | 42 | 38 |
| 21 | | | | | | | | | | | | 100 | 90 | 81 | 72 | 67 | 61 | 56 | 51 | 47 | 43 |
| 22 | | | | | | | | | | | | | 100 | 90 | 81 | 74 | 68 | 63 | 57 | 53 | 49 |
| 23 | | | | | | | | | | | | | | 100 | 90 | 82 | 76 | 70 | 65 | 59 | 54 |
| 24 | | | | | | | | | | | | | | | 100 | 91 | 84 | 78 | 71 | 66 | 61 |
| 25 | | | | | | | | | | | | | | | | 100 | 92 | 85 | 79 | 73 | 67 |
| 26 | | | | | | | | | | | | | | | | | 100 | 93 | 86 | 80 | 74 |
| 27 | | | | | | | | | | | | | | | | | | 100 | 93 | 86 | 80 |
| 28 | | | | | | | | | | | | | | | | | | | 100 | 93 | 86 |
| 29 | | | | | | | | | | | | | | | | | | | | 100 | 93 |
| 30 | | | | | | | | | | | | | | | | | | | | | 100 |
| 31 | | | | | | | | | | | | | | | | | | | | | |
| 32 | | | | | | | | | | | | | | | | | | | | | |
| 33 | | | | | | | | | | | | | | | | | | | | | |
| 34 | | | | | | | | | | | | | | | | | | | | | |
| 35 | | | | | | | | | | | | | | | | | | | | | |

# Figure 14-11
## DRY AND WET BULB THERMOMETERS

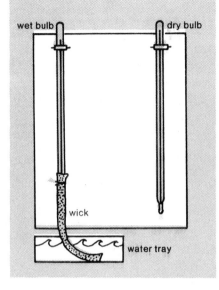

wet bulb

dry bulb

wick

water tray

when it becomes heated inside, the percentage RH is very low.

Grouping plants together can increase the local humidity by taking advantage of the evaporation of moisture from soil in the containers. Containers filled with water and placed near plants can also increase local humidity, especially if there is a large surface. The surface can be increased by adding pebbles to the water surface, and as each pebble has a large surface area, the total surface area is increased considerably. Using humidifiers which move water over a circulating disc is an efficient way of increasing the water vapor and percentage RH in the air. Manually misting a plant with a spray only increases the percentage RH for the approximate duration the mist is applied.

### PLANT PREFERENCES FOR RELATIVE HUMIDTY
Plants vary in their need for humidity. Although plants like cacti and other succulents thrive in 10 per cent RH or less, they do well in higher humidity. At the other end of the scale are plants like Spanish moss and Venus fly trap that prefer 85-95 per cent RH, but can grow successfully at 65 per cent RH and higher. A great many houseplants thrive with 50-60 per cent RH. A number of plants can tolerate the dry conditions usually found in our overheated homes. Among these are: Brassaia (umbrella tree), Cephalocereus (old man cactus), Sansevieria (mother-in-law's tongue), Philodendrons, Diefenbachia, Haworthia, Cereus, Pandanus (Screwpine), Peperomia, Scindapsus (Pothos, Devil's Ivy), Vriesea, Amonum (Cardamon), Ficus (India rubber tree, weeping fig), Opuntia (cactus), Pilea (aluminum plant), Spathiphyllum (white flag or sailplant), Saintpaulia (African violet), Aglaonema (Chinese evergreen), Chamaedorea (dwarf palm), and many more.

A large number of plants prefer bright, airy, well ventilated conditions. Plants with such a preference include: Bougainvillea, Euphorbia (crown of thorns), Zingiber (ginger), Codiaeum (croton), Coleus, Gynura (velvet plant), Hibiscus, Gardenia, several Begonia, several Figs, Citrus, Oleander, Iresine (bloodleaf), Coffee, and many others.

Among the houseplants that prefer high humidity are: Ixora (jungle geranium), Stephanotis (madagascar vine), Thrinax (key palm), Ananas (pineapple), Musa (banana), Cattleya (orchid), Dendrobium (orchid), Acalypha (red hot cattail), Cissus discolor (rexbegonia vine) Clerodendron, Ctenanthe (indian feather), Ficus (creeping fig), Fittonia (nerve plant), Maranta (prayer plant), Monstera, Pilea (silver tree), Aeschynanthus (lipstick plant), Episcia (flame violet), several Begonia including Begonia rex and Ironcross, Caladium (paperleaf), Sinningia (gloxinia), Platycerium (staghorn fern), Cordyline (tiplants) and many others.

Plants grow in climates with vast differences in humidity. Plants requiring humid conditions tend to become brittle and shrivel up when placed in the dry atmosphere of a house. Often the leaf edges are the first to show symptoms. Many plants grown outside during the summer dry up and lose their leaves when brought into the house because of the lower light and humidity inside. Plants like Kalanchoe, which are accustomed to dry atmospheres, tend to develop roots in the air when placed in humid conditions.

### POLLUTION
Pollutants play an important role in the atmosphere. The composition of the

| Dry Bulb Temp. °C | | | | | | | | | | | | | | |
|---|---|---|---|---|---|---|---|---|---|---|---|---|---|---|
| 31 | 32 | 33 | 34 | 35 | 36 | 37 | 38 | 39 | 40 | 41 | 42 | 43 | 44 | 45 |
| 14 | 12 | 10 | - | - | - | - | - | - | - | - | - | - | - | - |
| 19 | 16 | 14 | 12 | 10 | - | - | - | - | - | - | - | - | - | - |
| 22 | 20 | 17 | 15 | 13 | 11 | 9 | - | - | - | - | - | - | - | - |
| 26 | 23 | 21 | 19 | 17 | 14 | 13 | 11 | 9 | - | - | - | - | - | - |
| 31 | 27 | 25 | 22 | 20 | 18 | 16 | 14 | 12 | 10 | 9 | - | - | - | - |
| 34 | 31 | 29 | 26 | 23 | 21 | 19 | 17 | 15 | 14 | 12 | 10 | 9 | - | - |
| 40 | 36 | 33 | 30 | 28 | 25 | 23 | 20 | 18 | 16 | 15 | 13 | 11 | 10 | - |
| 45 | 41 | 38 | 34 | 32 | 29 | 26 | 24 | 21 | 19 | 17 | 16 | 14 | 13 | 12 |
| 50 | 46 | 42 | 39 | 36 | 33 | 30 | 27 | 25 | 22 | 21 | 18 | 17 | 15 | 14 |
| 56 | 51 | 47 | 44 | 40 | 37 | 33 | 31 | 28 | 26 | 23 | 22 | 20 | 18 | 17 |
| 62 | 57 | 52 | 49 | 44 | 41 | 38 | 35 | 32 | 29 | 26 | 25 | 23 | | |
| 68 | 62 | 58 | 54 | 49 | 45 | 42 | 38 | 36 | 32 | 30 | 28 | 26 | | |
| 74 | 68 | 63 | 59 | 54 | 50 | 46 | 42 | 39 | 36 | 33 | 32 | 29 | | |
| 80 | 74 | 68 | 63 | 59 | 54 | 50 | 47 | 43 | 40 | 37 | 35 | 32 | | |
| 87 | 80 | 74 | 69 | 64 | 59 | 55 | 51 | 47 | 44 | 41 | 38 | 35 | | |
| 93 | 87 | 81 | 75 | 70 | 65 | 60 | 56 | 52 | 48 | 46 | 42 | 39 | | |
| 100 | 93 | 87 | 81 | 76 | 70 | 65 | 60 | 57 | 53 | 49 | 46 | 43 | | |
| | 100 | 93 | 87 | 82 | 76 | 71 | 66 | 61 | 57 | 53 | 50 | 47 | | |
| | | 100 | 94 | 88 | 82 | 76 | 71 | 67 | 62 | 57 | 54 | 50 | | |
| | | | 100 | 94 | 88 | 82 | 77 | 72 | 67 | 62 | 58 | 54 | | |
| | | | | 100 | 94 | 88 | 83 | 77 | 72 | 67 | 63 | 58 | | |

Adapted from Taylor Instruments (1933)

atmosphere consists mainly of nitrogen and oxygen, but small quantities of carbon dioxide ($CO_2$), water vapor, smoke and other pollutants are also present. The processes of respiration, transpiration and photosynthesis, in which the atmosphere play an important role, are discussed in both the Botany and Plant Nutrition lessons.

Generally, the air in Alberta is relatively free of pollution, although in certain situations, pollution from oil wells and industry occurs. Some of the pollutants may actually be of fertilizing value, such as some nitrogenous gases. Smoke is generally detrimental to plant life as it contains sulphur dioxide ($SO_2$) and other components (smut or soot and oily vapors) which close the stomata and gradually choke the plant by blocking respiration. Plants are also sensitive to leaks of natural gas from sources such as unlit pilot valves or poorly adjusted furnaces. They are sensitive to ethylene gas as well as fumes from dry cleaning.

### VENTILATION
Fresh air brings with it carbon dioxide, which is essential for plant growth. Carbon dioxide, if not replenished, will soon be used up where plants are housed in an enclosed atmosphere. Mammals (including people) produce carbon dioxide — a happy situation for plants. Nevertheless, where plants are not doing well, ventilation may assist plants by removing excess heat, supplying $CO_2$, or removing pollutants. Moving air also discourages fungus and brings $CO_2$ close to the stomata on the plants.

## GROWING MEDIA

### FUNCTION
The function of the growing media for houseplants is to provide support (anchoring) for the plant and, at the same time, to serve as a reservoir of nutrients. The growing media must be able to hold air and water and allow roots to penetrate it (see Soils lesson, COMPOSITION OF SOIL). It must be sufficiently dense to hold the plants in place. The container and growing media together must be heavier than the total expected weight of the plant above the growing media, so the plant will remain upright even under dry conditions. The volume of growing media

must be fairly constant - not shrinking or expanding too much, whether dry or wet. It must be able to retain moisture so watering does not have to be too frequent. It must be porous enough to allow excess water to drain away and permit air to enter the pore spaces. It should have a crumb structure that allows root and water penetration and it should not cake or bake. The growing media must also be free of weed seed and undesirable pathogens.

The chemical properties should be such that an adequate amount of essential plant nutrients (in a form readily available to the plant) is present and the pH is suitable for the plant. It should not contain chemical properties in forms or amounts harmful to plants.

### SOIL CONDITIONERS
The soil conditioners (see Soils lesson, SOIL MANAGEMENT) used with house- plants include vermiculite, perlite, turface, sand, and peat.

### VERMICULITE
Vermiculite chemically is hydrated magnesium aluminum iron silicate. Natural vermiculite is a mica that has been expanded under high temperature (900°C) for horticultural purposes. It is able to hold water many times its own weight. When vermiculite is saturated with water, it holds little or no air. Vermiculite has a high cation exchange capacity which makes it suitable as a component in soilless potting mixtures. Used in soilless potting mixtures, vermiculite allows for easier rewetting, and it improves porosity of the media. Used alone, it is an excellent media for germination of seed. Vermiculite contains magnesium and potassium ions and, therefore, supply some nutrient to the growing media mixture. The pH of vermiculite is near neutral and is available in fine, regular and coarse grades.

### PERLITE
Perlite is a silica rock expanded by heat at about 1000°C. It is popcorn-like as it consists of several closed airfilled cells. As a result, water is only held on the outside surfaces of perlite. Therefore, perlite will hold as much air as water. When dry, perlite is very dusty and caution should be used when opening bags or pouring out contents. It is recommended to wet perlite before pouring to avoid inhaling harmful silicate

particles. Perlite is a very light, nearly inert material and contains some fluoride. It can be used alone as a media for rooting cuttings. Perlite is used in soilless potting mixtures to improve aeration. It has almost no cation exchange capacity and a pH of about 7.

### TURFACE (LIGHT ROCK)
Turface is baked (calcined) clay. It is primarily added to soilless potting mixtures to add weight. It has a pH of about 7 and does have a cation exchange capacity. Alone, turface is used as a media for rooting cuttings. Turface holds air and water at the same time and increases the buffering capabilities of soilless potting mixtures.

### SAND
Sand comes in various particle sizes with coarse (sharp) sand being the most desirable for use in potting mixtures. Fine particle sand, when combined with organic matter and certain proportions of silt or clay, ends up with all the characteristics of good concrete and should be avoided.

### HOUSEPLANT GROWING MEDIA
Traditionally, potting mixtures have included loam, manure, leafmold and sand. As traditions have changed and leafmold and manure have been more difficult to obtain or other problems involved in their use have made them less desirable, peat moss has replaced leafmold and manure. This does not mean that leafmold and manure should not be used but, rather, that they are used less today.

It is often more convenient to purchase ready mixed potting media but many people have the option of preparing their own houseplant growing media. When field soil is part of the mixture. it is desirable to begin with loamy soil. If the soil is high in clay, silt or sand, the proportions of other ingredients can be amended accordingly. It is also desirable to have results of a soil test on hand before preparing the mixture (see Soil Lesson, SOIL TESTING).

Preparation begins with measuring out the various components such as loam, peat and sand, along with any dry fertilizers that need to be added to bring the media up to the desired level. All the components are mixed together well, shifting them from a measured cone-shaped pile to another cone-forming pile, and then to a new pile so that the mixture is shifted a minimum of three times.

Proportions of **S**oil, **O**rganic matter, and **D**rainage material, (S.O.D.), vary, depending on the plant's preference for a particular growing media. Plants need very good aeration (eg., citrus) and should, therefore, have a higher proportion of coarse (sharp) sand in the growing media mixture. The proportion 1:1:1 S.O.D. is fine for such plants. Peat is frequently used as the organic and sand as the drainage in many growing media recipes. Some plants (eg., African violets) prefer a high humus content and should have more organic matter (i.e., peat) in the mixture (i.e., five parts loam, four parts peat and three parts sand). Charcoal is sometimes used in potting mixtures to absorb gases and foul odors from anaerobic aeration caused by overwatering, as well as to absorb excess fertilizer salts.

Before using the growing media, water should be added so a moist media is obtained. The consistency should be such that when a handful of the media is squeezed, it forms a ball that sticks together; but falls apart into a crumb structure when poked.

When mixing small quantities, it may be easier to measure components into a large plastic bag, add water and mix well by shifting the contents back and forth in the bag (about half filled).

The advantages of using soilless growing media mixtures are many. They are relatively light and much cleaner to work with than the traditional soil mixes, roots can penetrate easily and are able to fully utilize the media. Under good management, better aeration can be obtained and waterstress due to inadequate watering can be reduced. Insect and disease spread through the use of field soil is eliminated and the uniform soilless media provides for better plant growth.

There are many reasons for excluding soil from the potting mixtures. Good quality topsoil is often difficult to obtain and some soil-borne pathogens are difficult to eliminate. Inadequate aeration due to tight soil structure leads to root loss and any herbicide residues contained in the soil may cause plant loss. Consistency is difficult to maintain as soils vary considerably from one location to another.

Disadvantages of some soilless mixtures include the danger of overwatering. In the traditional soil potting mixture, soil solids account for 50 per cent of the volume, and the remainder is comprised of 25 per cent liquid and 25 per cent air in the pore space. In soilless mixes, where fine particle peat moss is used, the solids can, in some cases, be as little as 12.5 per cent of the volume, with 75 per cent water and only 12.5 per cent air comprising the remainder. Coarse particle peat moss should be used to reduce the excess water-holding capacity of these mixes. Soil-based plotting mixtures support plant growth over longer periods of time than do soilless potting mixtures. With the latter, it is necessary to repot more frequently.

The recipes for soil and soilless potting mixtures in this lesson are only to be taken as examples of mixtures being used. Since peat and soil vary in acidity and amounts of nutrient elements present, best results are obtained by following recommendations from soil test analyses.

EXAMPLES OF SOILLESS MIX RECIPES
A  35 L sphagnum peat moss
   35 L medium or coarse vermiculite
   400 g dolomite lime (may need adjustment according to pH of sphagnum peat moss)
   125 g superphosphate
   300 g calcium nitrate

B  35 L sphagnum peat moss
   35 L perlite
   400 g dolomite lime
   125 g superphosphate
   350 g calcium nitrate
   30 g potassium sulphate

C  35 L sphagnum peat moss
   35 L vermiculite
   35 L perlite
   600 g ground limestone
   675 g magnesium ammonium phosphate
   42 g potassium sulphate

Combine the ingredients thoroughly (mix at least five times) and use warm water to moisten. Start supplementary liquid fertilizing after six weeks in good light conditions.

VARIOUS SOIL POTTING MIX RECIPES
A  1 L loam
   1 L sphagnum peat moss
   1 L sand
   0-45 mL dolomite lime (according to acidity of loam and peat)
   15 mL magnesium ammonium phosphate

B  1 L loam
   1 L sphagnum peat moss
   3 L sand
   30-90 mL dolomite lime (according to pH of peat and loam)
   30-45 mL magnesium ammonium phosphate
   7 mL potassium sulphate

C  35 L loam
   15 L sphagnum peat moss
   15 L sand
   1 L dried sheep manure

## PLANT PREFERENCES FOR GROWING MEDIA

Although plants grow outdoors in so many types of soils and climatic conditions and do best when their natural requirements are met, houseplants can be categorized in terms of their growing media needs. A very large group prefers a loamy soil and includes: Aglaonema (Chinese evergreen), Aspidistra (cast iron plant), Chamaedorea (dwarf palm), Spathiphyllum (sailplant), Sansevieria (snake plant), Diefenbachia, Peperomia, Kalanchoe, Citrus, Amaryllis, Bamboo and others. Soils can be adjusted in terms of their water-holding capacities by varying the proportions of sand, peat and loam in the media. This may be necessary to suit those plants that prefer very good drainage or for those that prefer soil with less drainage.

Another very large group prefers a high humus content in the media. Some of the plants in this category are: Saintpaulia (African violet), Asplenium (birds nest fern), Aphelandra (zebra plant), Begonia, Pilea (aluminum plant), Calathea, Zygocactus (Christmas cacti), Gloxinia, Episcia (flame violet), Columnea (goldfish plants), Aeschynanthus (lipstick plant) and many more. One suggestion is to start with a proportion of 3(S), 2(O) and 1(D), then add more peat or more sand to suit the needs of the various plants.

A smaller group of plants are those plants that live in the air and cling to trees for support. They are called epiphytes (epi=upon, phyte=plant). They live on other plants but are not parasites, as they obtain nutrients from decaying leaves and from moisture in the air. Epiphytes need a media which allows a large amount of moist air to the roots. Osmunda fiber, firbark, and redwood chips are examples of growing media used for epiphytes. The largest single cause of failure with epiphytes is lack of moist air (usually because of overwatering). Some epiphytes are: Aechmea (vaseplant), Vrisea (flaming sword), Phalaenopsis (orchid), Cattleya (orchid), Tillandsia (spanish moss), Vanda (orchid), Platycerium (staghorn fern), Ripsalis (mistletoe cactus), Dendrobium (orchid), Epidendron (orchid), Polypodium (resurrection fern), Nepentes (pitcher plant) and many others.

Some plants are water plants which obtain some of their food from nutrients in the water. This category of plants include: Salvinia (floating cryptogram), Nymphea (water lily), Eichornia (water hyacinth), Azolla (water fern), and others.

## FERTILIZING HOUSEPLANTS

The growing media of newly transplanted plants should fulfil their nutrient requirements for at least six weeks, after which time a regular fertilizer program can be started. In the winter, without the use of artificial light, light is often found in such low intensity that it becomes a limiting factor. It is, therefore, of no use and can actually be harmful to add fertilizer, as the plants cannot grow further without additional light first. Adding fertilizer in such a situation only creates a buildup of fertilizer salts to such a point, often, where the salt solution in the media is higher than that in the plant. Water then begins to flow out of the plant instead of into it. This condition will kill the plant within hours. Similarly, if water is present in minimal quantities, it is of no value to add fertilizer (fertilizer salts would burn root tips). Providing sufficient light and moisture is available, fertilizers can be added and will give plants a boost, but only to the point where some of the elements may become excessive.

Of the three major mineral elements, nitrogen (N), phosphorus (P), and potassium (K), cuttings and transplants prefer a high ratio of phosphorus in the presence of high light intensity. This ratio could be 1(N)-5(P)-1(K). For vegetative growth in good light, nitrogen should be in a higher proportion, 4:1:1. For bud set, the ratio should be 1:1:1 and for maturation and blooming, 1:0:2. In lower light intensities, the ratio

## Table 14-3
## GROWING CONTAINERS

| Container Material | Advantage | Disadvantage |
| --- | --- | --- |
| Asbestos cement | durable, lightweight, strong | asbestos hazardous, rubs off, moisture seeps through to carpet unless elevated to create airspace between container and carpet |
| Ceramics and stoneware | retain moisture, cool | fragile, heavy |
| Clay | retain moisture, cool, porous | fragile, heavy |
| Fibreglass | durable, lightweight, strong | subject to hairline cracks which are difficult to detect (fill up with water before using and watch for them). Builds up heat in sun. |
| Glass | can be decorative | builds up heat in sun |
| Metals | strong | rusts (some kinds), builds up heat in sun |
| Paper (compressed) | lightweight, retains moisture | shortlived |
| Peat | allows root penetration, lightweight | shortlived |
| Plastics | durable, lightweight | becomes brittle with age and in UV light from sun |
| Polythene film | lightweight | breaks down in UV light from sun |
| Wood | resilient, strong | leaks, rots |

Some containers use liners such as wooden containers with plastic liners. Liners of certain metals such as zinc or copper should be avoided as these metals go into solution and in accumulated amounts can be toxic to plants.

for vegetative growth should be 2:1:1 and, for maturation and blooming, the ratio should be 1:0:3. (These values are based on 0.38 g of nitrate nitrogen/L or 0.06 oz/gal every two weeks.) The easiest way to uniformly add fertilizer to houseplants is by using high concentrate liquid fertilizers with every twentieth watering in good light. Other methods are to use fertilizer sticks or tablets, but these are much slower in their distribution in the media and it is difficult to tell if tablets are totally dissolved. Fertilizer in low concentrations can be applied more frequently but are a more expensive way to add fertilizer. Many low concentration fertilizers contain only one per cent or less of one of the three major elements and none of the other two, so most of the purchase of such fertilizer is filler material. There are, however, many excellent fertilizer formulations available that can be selected and used to meet particular plant requirements. A general purpose, high concentrate fertilizer that can be used is 20-20-20 (ratio 1:1:1).

## GROWING CONTAINERS AND TRANSPLANTING PROCEDURES

### GROWING CONTAINERS

Basically, any enclosure that holds growing media so a plant can thrive in it qualifies as a growing container. Growing containers vary from permanently built masonry containers to temporary structures, such as egg cartons. Sizes range from that of a thimble to containers that hold cubic metres of growing media. Some are provided with drainage holes; others are not.

A wide variety of materials are used for growing containers. Some materials are lightweight but fragile, some are heavy as well as fragile (see Table 14-3).

When choosing a container, know exactly what will be grown in it and match its function with the purpose intended. Is it to be used for a tomato plant started from seed; one that will be transplanted when it gets a little larger? If so, a temporary container, such as a peat pot, may be best suited to the

Figure 14-12
PLANT POT TYPES AND SIZES

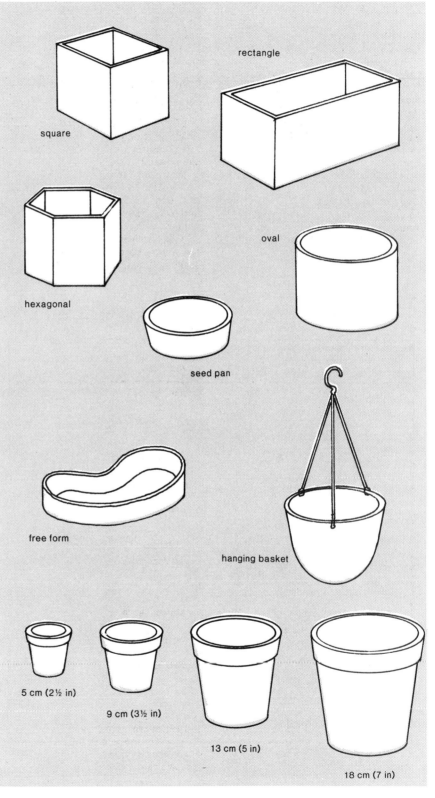

square

rectangle

hexagonal

oval

seed pan

free form

hanging basket

5 cm (2½ in)

9 cm (3½ in)

13 cm (5 in)

18 cm (7 in)

purpose. The roots of the plant can penetrate into the walls of the pot (if these are kept moist) and the plant (with pot and all) can be transplanted into a larger container or out into the garden. If the purpose is to grow a specimen palm in the living room, a decorative container may be suitable; one without drainholes into which another container with drainholes and containing growing media and the plant can be placed. Such (inside) containers must be of sufficient size to provide space for root formation and the outer container should be attractive and leakproof.

Drainage is a must if houseplants are to thrive. Often, containers without drainage holes are used as shells into which a container with drainage holes (and holds the growing media and plant) is placed. If a plant is planted directly into a container without drainage holes, then drainage inside the container must be provided. The drainage material can consist of broken crockery, gravel, polystyrene beads, or any inert material which receives excess water (acts as a reservoir) and has little or no capillary action.

Containers with drainage holes can be placed on large saucers or inside decorative containers. In either case, care should be taken not to have the container with the drainholes sitting in a pool of water. The water should be removed to allow drainage.

Most plants are sold in plastic containers. The quality of these containers varies greatly; some are very resilient and sturdy, while others are flimsy and fragile. Clay pots can still be obtained, but are rarely used in commercial pot plant production. Therefore, they are rarely sold with houseplants. With larger plants comes the choice of which type of container to use.

Some containers have plastic liners. Liners made of certain metals, such as zinc or copper, should be avoided as these metals oxidize and can, over time, become toxic to plants.

In choosing the container in which the plant grows, it is an advantage when the containers are wider at the top and the sides slope gently toward a more narrow bottom as this facilitates the removal of the plant at transplanting time (see Figure 14-12).

A container should relate to the size of the plant grown in it. A small plant in a large container cannot utilize the moisture available; soon the soil is waterlogged and the plant dies because of lack of oxygen to the roots, a situation aggravated in low intensity light. A small plant in a large container looks insignificant. Conversely, a large plant in a small container looks uncomfortable and unstable (see Figure 14-13). It is unstable because it is top heavy. A large plant in a small container uses up the available moisture quickly and also uses up the available nutrients faster and, therefore, requires very frequent watering and fertilizing.

### Figure 14-13
### PLANT TO POT COMPATIBILITY

pot too small for plant  proper balance of pot and plant  pot too large for plant

Shallow containers lose moisture much more rapidly than deep containers. However, shallow containers are better suited to creeping plants because of the proportionally larger surface area, which allows both greater evaporation and more rooting surface for creeping plants.

For tall plants and when symmetry is important, square or octagonal shaped containers are useful and well suited. Plants with a horizontal shape are complemented by oblong shaped containers. Examples of odd type containers used for plants include: cake tins, milk cartons, plastic bags, urns, kegs, barrels cut in half, washtubs, draintile, coconut halves, bottles, aquariums, tin cans and egg cups. The shape of containers is unlimited; numerous kinds of geometrical or free-flowing forms can be found and used.

### SELF-WATERING CONTAINERS
Self-watering containers have built-in water reservoirs. One type incorporate a wick put through a drainhole with one end in the growing media and the other extended into the reservoir below. This provides a means for transporting the water from the reservoir into the growing media. In other containers, numerous holes are provided which allow the roots to act as wicks that absorb water from the reservoir (see Figure 14-14). The water level can be observed through a transparent window in the water reservoir and a corner of the upper container provides an access through which water can be added. Less frequent watering is an obvious advantage of self-watering containers. A disadvantage is that fertilizer salts are often moved up to the surface with the water and, when the water evaporates, the salts leave a white toxic crust which must be removed. Closed terrariums and bottle gardens are, in a sense, self-watering as they do not need water once they have reached equilibrium (see TERRARIUMS, BOTTLE GARDENS AND DISH GARDENS).

### TRANSPLANTING PROCEDURES

In time, organic matter in the growing media breaks down and the nutrient content is gradually used up by the plant. Also, some of the nutrients are lost by being washed out with the surplus water during watering. In such cases, the plant needs to be repotted. If the growing media is completely enmeshed with roots that circle the bottom of the container, it is definitely time to transplant that plant into a roomier container. As plants grow and roots fill the growing media, they exert pressure on their container which, in some cases, is strong enough to break the container. With small containers, it is possible to examine the root system by turning the container and the plant upside down and rapping the rim of the container on a wooden edge (such as the edge of a workbench). This usually loosens the growing media and plant from the container. Transplanting procedures begin with selecting a new container.

### Figure 14-14
### SELF WATERING CONTAINERS

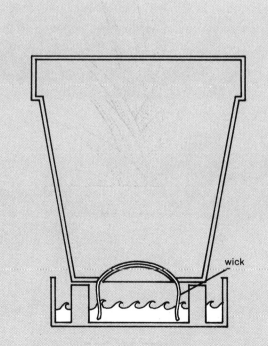

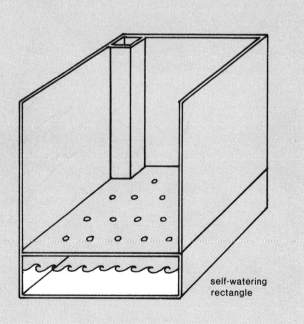

Figure 14-15
TRANSPLANTING PROCEDURE

1. a plant that needs to be repotted

2. place drainage material into the bottom of the container

3. cover drainage material with sphagnum moss

4. prepare and moisten growing media

5. adequately moistened growing media can be formed into a ball

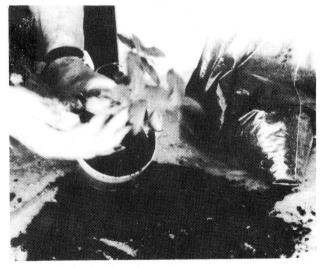

6. transplant and add growing media

If a clay pot is used for transplanting into, it must be soaked until all the air has escaped from its pores, then left to dry so it is no longer shiny wet before it is ready for use. Plastic, rubber, compressed fiber or fibreglass containers are ready to use as they are. Usually the container chosen is a size or two larger than the container the plant is presently in. There are times, however, when 'downpotting' is necessary. This is when a plant has lost much of its root system and lacks vigor. In such cases it is appropriate to put the plant into a smaller sized container.

Prepare a suitable location for transplanting and have the new container, drainage material, growing media, water and, of course, the plant for repotting on hand (see Figure 14-15).

Begin transplanting by placing drainage material (broken pottery, gravel, or polystyrene beads) into the bottom of the new container. A very thin layer of live sphagnum moss or inert fiber (like glass wool) can then be placed over the drainage material. This layer allows water to drain through but prevents the growing mixture from plugging the drainage material. The growing media on hand should be moist enough to be formed into a ball when squeezed and able to crumble when poked. If it is too dry, add water and mix well. If it is too wet, mix more dry media in until the right moisture level is obtained. The next step involves removing the plant to be transplanted from its old container

breaking off to the edges of the old growing media all the way around the top (see Figure 14-16).

Then, gently loosen the encircling root system below and, in the process, remove the old drainage material and shake loose some of the old growing media. This enables the root to grow into the new growing media without being hindered by circling, and to have space between the old rootball and the walls of the new container. Once the plant is prepared for transplanting, it can be placed into the new container to determine the amount and placement of the growing media. The final surface should allow sufficient space below the top of the rim to allow for water to be placed there during watering. This usually means that the growing media comes to within two or three millimetres (about one-eighth in) above the bottom edge of the container rim (see Figure 14-17).

### Figure 14-17
### LEVEL OF GROWING MEDIA

By placing the plant so that its base fits in this position, it is then possible to judge how much media should be placed under its rootball. Remove the plant and add the required amount of growing media to the bottom of the container. Then, replace the plant onto the growing media. Add more growing media along the sides of the rootball and firm it down with either a planting stick or with fingers to ensure that no air pockets exist and that the roots are in firm contact with the growing media (take care not to pack too hard). When the final level is reached, the new container

### Figure 14-16
### BREAKING OFF THE EDGES

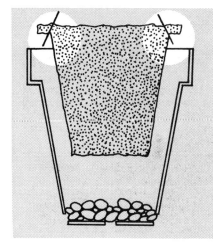

should be watered. The best way for this initial watering is to immerse the container in lukewarm water, to within one or two centimetres (about ½ in) from the rim. This is, of course, only done in cases where the container has drainage holes that allow water to penetrate from below. After the container has absorbed water (usually within 10-15 min), the container should be removed from the water and excess water allowed to drain away. If no drainage holes exist in the container, it must be watered from above.

## WATER AND WATERING

In examining water for houseplants, water quality, the frequency of water application, and the different water needs of plants are important.

### QUALITY OF WATER

Water softeners are often installed to reduce the hardness of water. During this process, sodium (Na) is added to the water. For this reason, softened water is not suitable for use on houseplants. Where water naturally contains sodium or other undesirable elements, the solution is to water more frequently to promote leaching. The excess (leached) water is discarded before it is taken up by the plant. Slough water is usually suitable for use but, in some situations, excess decaying organic matter from anaerobic decomposition may be present. An alternative to poor quality water is to use rain water that has been collected for this purpose. If rain water is collected from roof surfaces, discard the first rainfall in spring as it usually contains a lot of pollution from the roof surface. **Generally, if water is suitable to use as drinking water, then it is also suitable for plant use.**

### QUANTITY AND FREQUENCY OF WATER APPLICATION

The type of plant, temperature of air, humidity, amount of ventilation and light, growing media, plant size, container size and rate of plant growth must be considered before the frequency of watering can be determined. Sufficient water should be given a plant so that the entire root system receives it. If only a small amount of water is added to the container, just the top few centimetres are moistened. If this is done daily, only that part stays moist, while the majority of the roots receive no water. The plant lacks vigor as a result. When plants are watered sufficiently, some excess moisture will emerge through the drainage holes within 2-3 minutes of watering. Sometimes, if a plant has been allowed to dry out, the growing media pulls away from the sides of the container. If this happens and the plant is potbound, it should be repotted. If it is not potbound, or if transplanting cannot be carried out, it should be watered from the bottom. Bottom watering is recommended for most plants every few months to allow the root system to become completely saturated. It involves immersing the container in water (to within a few centimetres of the rim) until moisture can be observed on the surface of the growing media. Excess water should then be allowed to drain away and not be allowed to sit and create a stagnant, anaerobic condition (unless it is a bog plant). It should be noted that bottom watering creates an upward movement of the accumulated dissolved salts in the growing media and that sufficient watering from above in the periods between bottom watering should be done to wash out these salts.

## PLANT PREFERENCES FOR WATER

A large group of plants prefer extremes in root moisture. These include plants that naturally live in areas where flooding, followed by long periods of drought, is part of their seasonal cycle. These plants prefer to be completely soaked then left unwatered to near wilting point before being soaked again. A few of the houseplants in this category include: Sansevieria (snake plant), Schefflera (umbrella plant), Diefenbachia, Haworthia, Pandanus (screw pine), Peperomia, Scindapsus (pothos or devil's ivy), Cactus, Euphorbia (pointsettia), some Begonia, Cattleya (orchid), Dendrobium (orchid), Crassula, Citrus, and others.

A large number of plants dislike the extremes in moisture conditions and desire an evenly moist growing media. Plants in this category include: most Ferns, Paphiopedilum (slipper orchid), many Begonia, Platycerium (staghorn

fern), Sinningia (Gloxinia), Saintpaulia (African violet), Pilea, Philodendron, Aeschynantus (lipstick plant), Zebrina (wandering Jew), Maranta (prayer plant), Aglaonema (Chinese evergreen), Chamaedorea (dwarf palm), Spathiphyllum (sailplant), Aechmea (vaseplant), Aphelandra (zebra plant), Araucaria (Norfolk Island pine) and many others.

These plants should be thoroughly watered each time and not allowed to dry to near wilting. Some plants like plenty of moisture, in fact wet, but may dislike sitting in water. Among these are: Asplenium (birds nest fern), Cordyline (ti plants), Cyperus (umbrella plant), Phoenix (date palm), Zantedeszia (calla), Musa (banana), Anthurium (flamingo plants) and some others.

Lukewarm water is recommended for watering houseplants as it facilitates the uptake of water. Cold water, on the other hand, chills the growing media and slows down the root's uptake. When warm air temperatures prevail (such as a hot spell in summer), plants dry out faster. If the humidity is high (such as during a long rainy season), plants takes longer to dry out. If a fan is running for ventilation and cooling in summer, or when the furnace is constantly on during very cold weather, plants dry out faster. More light may mean higher leaf temperature but may not influence the temperature of the growing media (more evaporation, no increased uptake). A small volume container dries out faster than a large volume container. A clay pot is porous and, therefore, dries out faster than a plastic pot. A strong, vigorous plant with large leaf surfaces uses more water than a plant with a smaller leaf surface or a plant with a poor root system struggling to stay alive.

It is important for plants to get soil air. If plants are overwatered, all air spaces are filled with water and roots die from lack of oxygen. Place the water carefully so as to avoid washing growing media away from the root system. Also, avoid getting water into the crown of the plants as this provides an entryway for pathogens which can cause plant death. African violets are particularly sensitive to this. Bromeliads are the exception to this as they actually prefer to have water sitting in their vase shaped structure.

Make sure the surface of the growing media is level as water goes down

vertically. If sufficient space does not exist for water between the rim of the container and the growing media surface, plants should be transplanted so as to allow the entire growing media mass to be saturated with one watering. Double potting is sometimes done to achieve uniformly moist soil conditions. In double potting, a porous pot (such as clay) is used for the inner pot and holds the growing media and the plant. This pot is placed into a larger container of plastic or fibreglass. The space around the inner pot is filled with live sphagnum moss, vermiculite or bark chips, which should be kept moist but not wet. Excess water in the inner pot drains into the outer pot. However, surplus salts are not removed so be careful not to overfertilize such containers.

Water can be used as a growth regulator. Plants can adapt to relatively large amounts of water and grow vigorously and succulently. If prolonged intervals between watering becomes the practice, plants tend to become more woody and hardened, and growth takes place at a slower rate. This method may be adopted when houseplants are nearing their optimum decorative size in the house and it may be difficult to transplant to larger containers. Care must be taken, in such cases, to see that plants do not become too dry. Fertilizing must also be kept to a minimum to avoid salt damage.

## SANITATION

Observation and attention to detail leads to early detection of insects and disease organisms. Attention includes cleanliness, use of clean tools, and clean work area when transplanting. It also includes removing dead leaves and flowers from the plants. A good time to clean up a plant is during transplanting, at which time the whole plant can be inspected closely - roots, stem, and leaves. Keep plant pores open by washing dust and grime away with lukewarm water. Common insects on houseplants include aphids, spidermites, scales, mealybugs, thrips, white flies and springtails (see Pest Control lesson, BACKYARD PEST MANAGEMENT). Early detection of any insect problem makes control far easier than if the insects are observed at a late stage of infestation.

Aphids are very common pests on

houseplants. They can arrive from new plants already infested with aphids or they may fly in as winged adult aphids. Aphids can also be carried in on the clothing of anyone who has brushed by an infested plant. Control of aphids can involve the use of insecticidal soap or other chemicals. Use a good sprayer to apply the insecticide and be sure all parts of the plant are covered. Insecticidal soap should be applied to the 'run off' level. When using any insecticide, be sure to follow directions on the product label. The use of poisonous insecticides also means removing the plants from the living quarters for application of the insecticide. Biological control measures can also be employed. Placing an infested plant outdoors during summer may result in the aphids being accompanied by one or several of its many natural enemies, which can then be reared indoors for further natural control. There are also commercial firms in Canada that can provide insects for biological control of plant pests.

Two-spotted spider mites are notorious pests on houseplants. They are so tiny that they can barely be seen, although the damage they cause to houseplants is readily observed. The peppered and mottled appearance of the leaves, which eventually yellow and fall off, and the unmistak webbing, indicate a heavy infestation of spider mites. Before a heavy infestation occurs, tiny eggs can be seen on the undersides of infested plants. The eggs are globular and somewhat transparent. Effective biological control can be achieved by introducing a predatory spider mite which, instead of feeding on the plants, feeds off the plant-eating mite. Spider mites can be controlled with insecticidal soap which is a safe, yet effective choice if used according to directions. Miticides, such as Kelthane or Vendex, are effective but must be handled with great care and according to directions.

Scale insects, mealy bugs and thrips are among the most difficult insect pests to control on houseplants. Scale insects appear as a blisterlike scale; mealy bugs appears as a cottony white blot; and thrips are oblong spindle-shaped insects which often go unnoticed until they have done extensive damage to the leaf surfaces. All have natural enemies which can keep the infestation down to low levels. Insecticidal soap is the safest of the chemical controls. Other

insecticides (eg., Diazanon, Malathion, etc.) may also be used (see Pest Control lesson, BACKYARD PEST MANAGEMENT). Pay strict attention to directions.

White fly is a greenhouse pest which does not usually last long in the dry atmosphere of a house. If it does persist, it can be kept down with the use of a natural enemy, a parasitic wasp called Encarsia formosa. The wasp is available from commercial firms that offer insects for biological control. Insecticidal soap can also be used (as can other chemicals) but these must be used frequently (every 2-3 days) in order to achieve control. The adult white fly is capable of laying eggs when it is only two days old. The eggs hatch into a nymph stage in 5-10 days. The nymph stage lasts from as early as the fifth day after egglaying to as long as the fortieth day after egglaying. They then develop into the pupa stage, which lasts 5-7 days (usually 32-40 days after egglaying). Finally, they emerge as adults that again begin to lay eggs. Thus, the lifecycle of the white fly can be as long as 82 days. Both nymph and adult stages feed on plants.

Springtails (Collembola) are quite often found on wet soil containing plenty of organic matter. They are noticed when watering as they move about. Springtails are more a visual nuisance than anything else, and are often (not always)

associated with overwatered plants. Springtails will be less of a problem if plants are kept on the 'dry' side. Some granular forms of insecticide do control springtail, but make sure you use them safely.

Plant diseases are not usually as prevalent as insect problems on houseplants. Mildew, a fungal disease, is occasionally found on houseplants such as African violet and Begonias. One form of control for mildew is to dust the plant with elemental sulphur. Strict sanitation, such as picking off dead flowers and foliage, is very important. Mildew appears like a light sprinkling of flour on the leaves or flowers of the plant. Another fungal disease, Botrytis, is often found on the flower buds of plants such as Gloxinia. Affected buds appear tan or watery brownish and, often, buds fail to open. Control can be achieved by observing strict sanitation, good cultural practices and the careful use of a recommended fungicide (see Pest Control lesson, BACKYARD PEST MANAGEMENT). Other houseplant diseases include fungal or bacterial leaf spot, wilt, rot, and nematode infestation.

## PHYSIOLOGICAL DISORDERS

Some houseplant problems are not due to pathological organisms but are due to poor cultural practices or environmental conditions and may be:

Figure 14-18
WATER DAMAGED CITRUS PLANT

• Temperature related (i.e., too low or too high a temperature)

• Atmosphere related (i.e., air contaminated with volatile 2,4-D, SO$_2$, ethylene, dry cleaning, natural gas, soot, smoke, phenols, or salt burns aggravated by too low humidity)

• Water related (i.e., excess or insufficient quantity, unsuitable water, or poor drainage) (see Figure 14-18)

• Light related (i.e., excess light causes whitish leaves on African violet and sailplant — deficient light causes leaf drop, bud drop, or yellowing)

• Soil related (i.e., excessive fertilizer, deficient fertilizer, wrong pH, poor aeration)

Water soaked stems and limp leaves on such plants as African violets are sometimes caused by an accumulation of fertilizer salts on top of the growing media and rim of the pot. The salt is recognized as a whitish crust on the surface of growing media and as a brownish, scaly deposit on the rim of the container. The solution is to remove the salt layer, increase humidity to cut down on excess evaporation from the growing media, and **water from above to leach salts down.**

## Figure 14-19
## LOW HUMIDITY DAMAGE

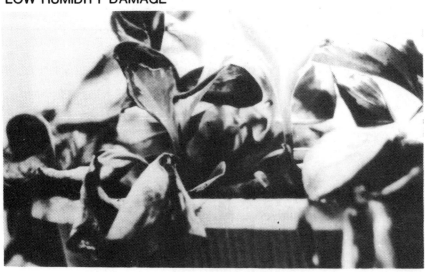

• Dry brown margins and tips of leaves can be caused by too low humidity. The solution is to increase humidity (see Figure 14-19).

• Foliage that once showed intense color appears dull, usually caused by lower light values or maturation of plant. The solution is to increase the light intensity and cut the plant back to allow the new growth to grow strong in the improved light.

• Corky brownish tan deposits may be sap dried up after cells have broken (oedema). Oedema is a problem often encountered during fall, winter and spring and is caused by the plant taking up more water from the roots than it can dispose of (see Figure 14-1). Hence, the cells are filled until the cells burst open. Factors aggravating this situation include: low light intensity, high soil temperatures combined with low leaf temperatures, overwatering, and high relative humidity (rare in Alberta).

• Flower bud drop can be caused by low humidity, fluctuations in temperature, temporary shortage of water, and fungal disease.

• Leaves full of holes can be caused by slugs in container coming out at night and eating plant leaves, by leafcutter bees, weevils, and bacterial or fungal disease.

• Brown spots or brown areas on leaves can have several causes including:

a. high sodium content in soil,

b. hot sun shining on water droplets and scorching the leaf (see Figure 14-20,

c. potash deficiency, which begins with yellowing at leaf edge and tips, later moving inwards with oldest affected area turning brown,

d. water bringing nutrient salt up from the growing media into the plant. As water is lost to the air from the edges and tips of leaves, salts are left to accumulate, building up toxic amounts and killing cells, resulting in brown tissue, and

e. chemical damage from pesticide applications.

• Black foliage can be caused by:

a. dry cleaning fumes from freshly dry cleaned clothes and ammonia cleaning remedies used in enclosed spaces,

b. overheating, such as in a closed car on a hot sunny day,

c. dry heat from touching heating elements, radiators, etc., and

d. fluoride toxicity (black tips and edges).

• Toxic effect of fluoride can be reduced by:

a. using activated charcoal in growing media (may absorb some fluoride),

b. fluoride is tied up at high pH levels. Superphosphate fertilizers increase fluoride levels, as does the use of perlite in the growing media, therefore avoid excessive use of these materials,

c. brown tips and drooping leaves can be due to excess fertilizers. The cure is to leach the soil or replant,

d. mechanical injury can occur when wiping dust off leaves (see Figure 14-21). Grit becomes imbedded in the cloth or tissue used to wipe the plant. If the cloth is used over and over without washing out, the resulting grinding action is like fine sand paper and can cause damage,

## Figure 14-20
## LEAF SCORCH

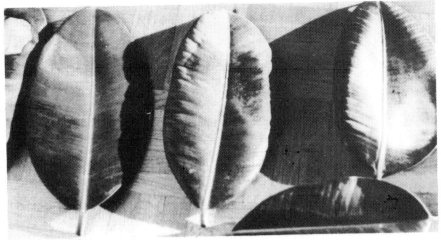

## Figure 14-21
## MECHANICAL INJURY

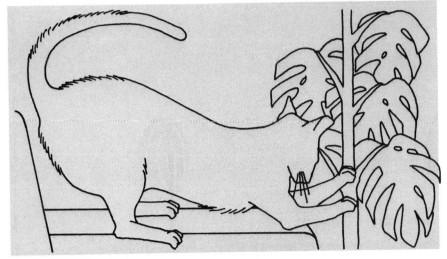

e. frequent close contact with foliage by people moving by a plant can result in mechanical damage (injured leaves, broken stems, etc.), and

f. cats and dogs occasionally injure houseplants by chewing foliage or scratching stems and trunks to sharpen claws.

## PLANT PECULIARITIES AND PROBLEMS

Individual people have their idiosyncracies, and individual species or cultivars of houseplants have their peculiarities, some of which are listed below and in the Plant Preference Tables (see Tables 14-4, 14-5, and 14-6).

**Aloe vera (healing plant)** - now known as Aloe barbadensis. When its sap is applied to human wounds, it promotes growth of new cells and thus speeds up the healing process.

**Anthurium sp. (flamingo flower)** - all parts contain some poisonous substance. The flower lasts and lasts on this plant.

**Aphelandra squarrosa (zebra plant)** - provide even moisture and good light and avoid draft to retain leaves in good health.

**Araucaria heterophylla (Norfolk Island pine)** - it is normal for the foliage to drop slightly when in too low light. This plant prefers intermediate temperature and is sensitive to drafts. It's an ideal live Christmas tree.

**Asparagus densifolia sprengeri (asparagus fern)** - is sensitive to insecticides (will show injury). Over and under watering can cause loss of foliage. A nice light green plant that prefers intermediate temperature and responds well to fertilizer in the good light of summer.

**Aspidistra elatior** - prefers warm temperatures and is called parlor palm or cast iron plant because it can put up with all kinds of abuse.

**Begonia** - if overwatered is susceptible to rot.

Table 14-4
## PLANTS TOLERATING LOW HUMIDITY (DRY CONDITIONS)

| Botanical Name | Common Name | Temp. Preferred | Light Preferred | Soil Moisture Preferred |
|---|---|---|---|---|
| Astrophytum | star cactus | W | B | Soak, Dry, Soak |
| Brassaia, Scefflera | umbrella tree | W | B | Soak, Dry, Soak |
| Cephalocercus | old man cactus | W | B | Soak, Dry, Soak |
| Cereus | – | W | B | Soak, Dry, Soak |
| Euphorbia lactea cristata | elkhorn | W | B | Soak, Dry, Soak |
| Euphorbia trigana | – | W | B | Soak, Dry, Soak |
| Opuntia | – | W | B | Soak, Dry, Soak |
| Sansevieria | mother-in-law's tongue | W | M-B | Soak, Dry, Soak |
| Coccoloba | seagrape | W | M-B | Moist |
| Graptophyllum | carricature plant | W | B | Moist |
| Philodendron eichleri | king of tree philodendrons | W | M-B | Moist |
| Philodendron oxycardium | – | W | M-B | Moist |
| Philodendron Selloum | – | I-W | M-B | Moist |
| Cissus erosa | – | W | M | Soak, Dry, Soak |
| Diefenbachia | dumbcane | W | M | Soak, Dry, Soak |
| Hawortia | – | W | M | Soak, Dry, Soak |
| Leuchtenbergia principis | prism cactus | I-W | M | Soak, Dry, Soak |
| Pandanus utilis | screw pine | W | M | Soak, Dry, Soak |
| Peperomia | watermelon, peperomia | W | M | Soak, Dry, Soak |
| Tetra plasandra meiandra | ohe | W | M | Soak, Dry, Soak |
| Cryptanthus | starplant, zebra plant | W | M | Soak, Dry, Soak |
| Scindapsus | devil's ivy, golden pothos | W | M | Soak, Dry, Soak |
| Vriesia | flaming sword | W | M | Soak, Dry, Soak |
| Anomum | cardamon | W | M | Moist |
| Costus, igneus, speciosus | spiral ginger | W | M | Moist |
| Costus malortieanus | stepladder plant | W | M | Moist |
| Ficus elastica | India rubber tree | I-W | M | Moist |
| Ficus lyrata | fiddleleaf fig | I-W | M | Moist |
| Ficus diversifolia | mistletoe fig | I-W | M | Moist |
| Ficus nitida | weeping fig | I-W | M | Moist |
| Monstera leuconeura | Prayer plant | W | M | Moist |
| Monstera delicosa | Monster plant, Mexican breadfruit | W | M | Moist |
| Monstera oblique | Laceleaf | W | M | Moist |
| Philodendron pertusum | Splitleaf Philodendron | W | M | Moist |
| Philodendron florida | – | W | M | Moist |
| Philodendron hastatum | – | W | M | Moist |
| Philodendron rubrum | – | W | M | Moist |
| Pilea cadieri | Aluminum plant | W | M | Moist |
| Pilea Silvertree | – | W | M | Moist |
| Pilea involucrata | Pan American friendship plant | W | M | Moist |
| Plectranthus | Swedish Ivy | W | M | Moist |
| Spathiphyllum | White flag, Peace lily, Sailplant | W | L-M | Moist to Wet |
| Syngonium | Trileaf nephytis, Arrowplant | W | L-M | Moist |
| Aphelandra | Zebra plant | W | M | Moist |
| Cibotium chamissoi | Tree fern | W | M | Moist |
| Cibotium menziessii | Man fern | W | M | Moist |
| Geonanthus undatus | Seersucker plant | W | M | Moist |
| Neoregela | Fingernail plant, Crimson cup | W | M | Moist |
| Nidularium | – | W | M | Moist |
| Piper nigra | Black pepper | W | M | Moist |
| Polypodium aureum | Fern | W | M | Moist |
| Saintpaulia | African violet | W | M | Moist |
| Aechmea | Grecian Vase, Christmas jewels | W | M | Moist |
| Caryota | Fishtail palm | W | M | Wet |

Table 14-4 *CONTINUED*

| Botanical Name | Common Name | Temp. Preferred | Light Preferred | Soil Moisture Preferred |
|---|---|---|---|---|
| *Chrysalidocarpus* | Butterfly palm | W | M | Wet |
| *Draceana massangeana* | Cornplant | W | M | – |
| *Draceana goldiana* | – | W | M | – |
| *Draceana godsefiana* | – | W | M | – |
| *Draceana warnecki* | – | W | M | – |
| *Phoenix* | Datepalm | W | M | Wet |
| *Aglaonema* | Chinese evergreen | W | L | Moist |
| *Chamaedorea* | Dwarf palms | W | L | Moist |
| *Polystichum aristatum* | Fern | W | L | Moist |
| *Pteris ensiformis* | Victoria fern | W | L | Moist |
| *Davallia* | Carrot fern | W | L | Moist |

**W** = warm    **I** = intermediate    **M** = medium    **B** = bright    **L** = low

Table 14-5
## PLANTS PREFERRING WELL VENTILATED CONDITIONS

| Botanical Name | Common Name | Temp. Preferred | Light Preferred | Soil Moisture Preferred |
|---|---|---|---|---|
| *Bougainvillea* | – | W | B | Soak, Dry, Soak |
| *Echinocactus* | Golden barrel | W | B | Soak, Dry, Soak |
| *Echinopsis* | Cactus | W | B | Soak, Dry, Soak |
| *Erythea armata* | Mexican blue palm | W | B | Soak, Dry, Soak |
| *Euphorbia* | Poinsettia | W | B | Soak, Dry, Soak |
| *Euphorbia* | Crown of thorns | W | B | Soak, Dry, Soak |
| *Euphorbia* | Fat lady | W | B | Soak, Dry, Soak |
| *Melocactus* | Turk's cap | W | B | Soak, Dry, Soak |
| *Polyscias* | Panax, aralia | W | B | Soak, Dry, Soak |
| *Portulaca grandiflora* | Rose-moss | W | B | Soak, Dry, Soak |
| *Setcreasea purpurea* | Purple heart | W | B | Soak, Dry, Soak |
| *Stapelia* | Starfish flower | I-W | B | Moist |
| *Vinca major* | – | W | B | Soak, Dry, Soak |
| *Zingeber officinale* | Common ginger | W | B | Soak, Dry, Soak |
| *Billbergia* | Queen's tears, rainbow plant | W | B | Moist |
| *Areca catechu* | Betelnut Palm | W | B | Moist |
| *Calliandra* | Red powderpuff | W | B | Moist |
| *Canna* | Indian shot | W | B | Moist |
| *Capsicum* | Christmas pepper | W | B | Moist |
| *Cestrum* | Night jessamine | W | B | Moist |
| *Cleome* | Spider flower | W | B | Moist |
| *Codiaeum* | Croton | W | | Moist |
| *Coleus* | Coleus | W | | Moist |
| *Gynura* | Velvet plant, purple passion vine | W | B | Moist |
| *Hibiscus* | Rosetree of China, Rose mallow | W | B | Moist |
| *Hippeastrum* | Amaryllis | W | B | Moist |
| *Hymenocallis* | Spider lily | W | B | Moist |
| *Ipomea* | Blue dawn flower | W | B | Moist |
| *Ixora* | Flame of the woods, jungle geranium | W | B | Moist |
| *Nicodemia* | Indoor oak | W | B | Moist |
| *Passiflora* | Passion flower | W | B | Moist |
| *Pentas* | Egyptian star cluster | W | B | Moist |
| *Persea* | Avocado | I-W | B | Moist |

Table 14-5 *CONTINUED*

| Botanical Name | Common Name | Temp. Preferred | Light Preferred | Soil Moisture Preferred |
|---|---|---|---|---|
| *Ricinus* | Castor bean plant | W | B | Moist |
| *Salvia* | - | W | B | Moist |
| *Solandra* | Chalice wine | W | B | Moist |
| *Gardenia* | - | W | M | Moist |
| *Siderasis fuscata* | - | W | M | Soak, Dry, Soak |
| *Begonia Dancing Girl* | - | W | M | Soak, Dry, Soak |
| *Begonia lepotrica* | Wooly bear begonia | W | M | Soak, Dry, Soak |
| *Zygocactus* | Crab cactus | W | M | Soak, Dry, Soak |
| *Brachychillum* | (a ginger) | W | M | Soak, Dry, Soak |
| *Coffea arabica* | Coffee | W | M | Moist |
| *Dizygotheca* | False aralia | W | M | Moist |
| *Ficus carica* | Common fig | W | M | Moist |
| *Ficus pumila* | Creeping fig | W | M | Moist |
| *Jacobinia* | King's crown | W | M | Moist |
| *Mimosa pudica* | Sensitive plant | W | M | Moist |
| *Rhoeo spathaceae* | Moses in cradle | W | M | Moist |
| *Sparmannia* | Zimmerlinde, African hemp | I-W | M | Moist |
| *Zamia* | Jamaica sagetree | W | M | Moist |
| *Zebrina* | Wandering Jew | W | M | Moist |
| *Begonia Joe Hayden* | Black Begonia | W | M | Moist |
| *Begonia masoniana* | Ironcross Begonia | W | M | Moist |
| *Begonia mazae viridis* | Stichleaf Begonia | W | M | Moist |
| *Pilea microphylla* | Artillery plant | W | M | Moist |
| *Rhipsalis* | Mistletoe cactus (epiphyte) | W | M | Moist |
| *Schlumbergia* | Easter cactus | W | M | Moist |
| *Platycerium* | Staghorn fern (epiphyte) | W | M | Moist |
| *Vanda* | Orchid (epiphyte) | W | M | Moist |
| *Hedychium* | Ginger lily | W | M | Wet |
| *Livinstona* | Chinese fan palm | W | M-B | Wet |
| *Musa* | Banana | I-W | M | Wet |
| *Zantedeschia* | Calla lily | I-W | M | Soak, Dry, Soak |
| *Cattleya rex* | Orchid (epiphyte) | I-W | M | Soak, Dry, Soak |
| *Dendrobium* | Ghost orchid (epiphyte) | W | M | Soak, Dry, Soak |
| *Dendrophylax* | Orchid (epiphyte) | W | M | Soak, Dry, Soak |
| *Diacattleya* | Orchid (epiphyte) | W | M | Soak, Dry, Soak |
| *Epidendron* | Orchid (epiphyte) | W | M | Soak, Dry, Soak |
| *Oncidium* | Orchid (epiphyte) | I-W | M | Soak, Dry, Soak |
| *Rhynchostylis* | Orchid (epiphyte) | W | M | Soak, Dry, Soak |
| *Coelogyni* | Orchid (epiphyte) | I-W | M | Soak, Dry, Soak |

**W** = warm   **I** = intermediate   **M** = medium   **B** = bright   **L** = low

**Caladium hortulanum (paper leaf)** - very pretty with large delicate leaves. Requires a short rest each year (dormancy).

**Caryota mitis (fishtail palm)** - tipburn can occur in low light and low humidity. It likes warm temperatures and medium to bright light.

**Chlorophylum comosum (spider plant)** - is sensitive to fluoride which can cause black leaftips. It prefers intermediate temperatures and is an excellent beginner's plant because of its vigor. It soon fills its container and wants to be transplanted.

**Citrus** (lemon, orange, grapefruit, etc.) - sudden temperature changes as well as low humidity cause flower buds to drop. Flower very sweetly fragrant.

**Codiaeum variegatum pictum (croton)** - is susceptible to spidermite. It has pretty colored foliage in bright light, but this fades to a dull color in poor light.

**Coffee arabica** - it is normal for the foliage on mature plants to hang downwards.

**Coleus blumei** - another beginner's joy. Its brilliant foliage is a pleasure to look at if in bright light. It fades to a duller color in poor light. This plant is very easy to start from cuttings.

**Crassula argentea (jade plant)** - sometimes wrongly called rubberplant. It is sensitive to overwatering and will drop its leaves. It prefers intermediate temperatures.

**Ctenante oppenheimia (Indian feather)** - is sensitive to fluoride (avoid perlite in growing media).

## Table 14-6

| Botanical Name | Common Name | Temp. Preferred | Light Preferred | Soil Moisture Preferred |
|---|---|---|---|---|
| Acalypha | Red hot cats tail | W | M | Moist |
| Calanthe | Orchid (terrestial) | W | M | Moist |
| Cissus | Rex begonia vine | W | M | Moist |
| Cordyline terminalis | Tiplant | W | M | Moist to Wet |
| Costus sanguineus | Spiral flag | W | M | Moist |
| Ctenanthe | Indian feather | W | M | Moist |
| Eucharis | Amazon lily | W | M | Moist |
| Fittonia | Nerveplant, mosaicplant | W | M | Moist |
| Maranta bicolor (and more) | Prayerplant | W | M | Moist |
| Pilea depressa, repens, etc. | Black magic | W | M | Moist |
| Sanchezia nobilis | – | W | M | Moist |
| Strobilanthes | – | W | M | Moist |
| Achimenes | Cupid's bower | W | M | Moist |
| Aeschynanthus | Lipstick plant | W | M | Moist |
| Begonia fuchioides | Fuchialeaved begonia | W | M | Moist |
| Begonia rex hybrid | Rex begonia | W | M | Moist |
| Caladium | Paperwhite, fancyleaf caladium | W | M | Moist |
| Cibotium barometz | Treefern | W | M | Moist |
| Cibotium regale | Treefern | W | M | Moist |
| Columnea | Goldfishplant | W | M | Moist |
| Crossandra | Strawflower | W | M | Moist |
| Episcia | Flame violet | W | M | Moist |
| Gesneria cuenifolia | Dwarf gesneriad | W | M | Moist |
| Nautilocalyx | – | W | M | Moist |
| Sinningia speciosa | Gloxinia | W | M | Moist |
| Smithiantha | Templebells | W | M | Moist |
| Tillandsia lindesii | – | W | M | Moist |
| Aerangis | Orchid (epiphyte) | W | M | Moist |
| Aerides | Orchid (epiphyte) | W | M | Moist |
| Angraecum | Orchid (epiphyte) | W | M | Moist |
| Ascocenda | Orchid (epiphyte) | W | M | Moist |
| Brassia | Orchid (epiphyte) | W | M | Moist |
| Vanda | Orchid (epiphyte) | W | M | Wet |
| Cocus | Coconut palm | W | M | Wet |
| Nepenthes | Pitcher plant (epiphyte) | W | M | Moist |
| Begonia smaragdina | Begonia | W | M | Moist |
| Begonia imperialis | Begonia | W | L | Moist |
| Begonia rex | Begonia King Edward IV | W | L | Moist |
| Papiopedilum | Orchid (epiphyte) | W | L | Moist |
| Phalaenopsis | Orchid (epiphyte) | W | L | Moist |

**W** = warm   **I** = intermediate   **M** = medium   **B** = bright   **L** = low

**Diefenbachia sp. (dumbcane)** - all parts are poisonous. If overwatered, it will rot. It needs good uniform light (from all around) and good care to retain all leaves.

**Dizygotheca elegentissima (false aralia)** - is sensitive to temperature fluctuations, light and moisture changes. When light level is low, foliage drop usually occurs, but this can be avoided if water is reduced when light levels drop.

**Draceana massangeana, Draceana marginata, Draceana godsefiana, Draceana goldiana, etc. (dragon plants)** - these are excellent house plants that tolerate low light, dry atmosphere and wet conditions.

**Ficus benjamina (weeping fig)** - massive leaf drop occurs if watering is neglected and plant dries out too much.

**Ficus nitida (weeping fig)** is sturdier than benjamina, and is an excellent house plant.

**Ficus elastica (India rubbertree)** - a longtime favorite houseplant tends to drop leaves when subjected to sudden temperature changes or watered with highly chlorinated water (let water sit for several hours before watering with it).

**Gardenia jasminoides (gardenia)** - flower buds drop in temperatures over 20°C and under 15°C or when placed in draft or in low humidity.

**Hedera helix (ivy)** - this plant prefers intermediate temperatures and is susceptible to spidermites and scale insects.

**Hyacinthus orientalis (hyacinth)** - the bulb is poisonous.

**Hydrangea macrophylla (hydrangea)** - blue color flowers due to aluminum uptake (low pH and therefore acid). The flower color is pink in higher pH (alkaline) conditions. Excessive iron can give bloom a brownish color.

**Lantana camara** - green berries are poisonous.

**Maranta leuconeura (prayer plant)** - foliage folds up in the dark. Sensitive to fluoride; tipburn also caused by low humidity. It dislikes wet conditions and stems rot easily then. These plants are easy to grow and attractive houseplants.

**Nephrolepsis sp. (fern)** - prefers medium light and no direct bright sun. It is sensitive to insecticides and prefers a humid atmosphere.

**Nerium oelander (oleander, rose boy)** - all parts are very poisonous.

**Peperomia sp.** - excellent houseplants but leaf stems rot at base overwatered. Likes to be quite dry before being watered.

**Persea gratissima (avocado)** - leaves can dry up due to low humidity and overwatering. This is aggravated in low light conditions. Avocado, when grown outdoors, grows into a large tree.

**Philodendron eichleri (king of the tree philodendrons)** - prefers medium to bright light and intermediate to warm temperature.

**Philodendron micans** - needs high humidity and warm temperature.

**Philodendron oxycardyum** - a vine-like P. micans tolerates a drier atmosphere and cooler temperature than micans.

**Philodendron selloum** - is a selfheading philodendron tolerating a somewhat dry atmosphere.

**Philodendron pertusom (split leaf philodendron)** - does not develop split leaves if light intensity is too low.

**Polyscias fruticosa (aralia)** - will drop leaves if exposed to gas fumes. It is sensitive to temperature changes, and susceptible to aphids and spider mites.

**Ricinus communis (castor bean)** - an exotic looking plant with poisonous seeds.

**Saintpaulia ionantha (African violet)** - stops flowering in low light. In too bright light, leaves turn first pale, then whitish, and then brown. It grows well under artificial light. Over fertilizing can result in hard crisp leaves and small, tight flower buds failing to open. It needs warm temperatures.

**Sansevieria sp. (mother-in-law's sharp tongue, snakeplant, swordplant, etc.)** - can grow in very low light but do better

in good light. The greatest cause of failure is due to overwatering, which results in it rotting away.

**Scindapsus aureus (devil's ivy, golden pothos, etc.)** - this vine-like plant is an excellent houseplant. It can tolerate quite low light, however, in too low light it loses its variegation.

**Spathiphyllum sp. (peacelily, white flag, sailplant)** - will tolerate quite low light intensities, but needs medium light to bloom.

**Sedum morgianum (burrotail)** - poisonous to some degree.

**Yucca elephantipes (elephant's foot)** - base of stem naturally swollen. In poor light, the foliage is limp.

## PRUNING AND STAKING

Houseplants belong to herbaceous and woody plants so the principles of training and pruning these types of plants are as outlined in the Woody Ornamentals and Herbaceous Ornamentals lessons. House-plants, however, also include tropical plants and are in the special situation of growing indoors. Therefore, the limitations that the residence places on the development of plants that could grow to a height of up to 100 m (over 300 ft) outdoors, and spread to include the total size of the room they share in the residence, must be considered. Plants in containers are restricted in their root development and pruning, fertilizing and watering practices can, in combination with control over the other factors (light, temperature, atmosphere), allow a plant to develop at a faster or slower rate.

Plants that grow into trees (eg., Ficus elastica or India rubbertree) should be allowed to grow to a height of 150 cm (about 5 ft), then the top should be cut off to force branching. Sometimes only one branch forms. This should be allowed to grow some distance then cut back almost to where it originated (see Figure 14-22). This type of pruning forces more branching and, eventually, the formation of a small crown. The plant must receive good light when this is done and it is advantageous to rotate it daily to obtain light on all sides of plant. Care should also be taken when pruning plants with milky sap, such as the India rubbertree. Cover the immediate surrounding areas. The sap leaves awful stains on carpet. Shrubs like Hibiscus

can be pruned in November or December and allowed to grow out during the summer. Very often, better flowers are achieved through pruning done in conjunction with good light levels.

Plants with weak stems or vines often benefit from staking. It is important to tie plants loosely enough so that growth is not restricted. This should be checked at regular intervals (perhaps monthly).

Vines can be trained to grow into any shape desired by the use of wire. Wire mesh can also be used to hold sphagnum moss (sprayed with water to keep moist) between two layers of mesh into which plants can root. The moss walls can be shaped into any design desired.

Herbaceous plants, such as Coleus, Iresine (bloodleaf), and Pilea cadieri (aluminum plant), if grown from a cutting, can be made into a bushier (branching) plant by pinching off the main stem. Allow the plant to grow 6-8 sets of leaves before pinching the stem. The topmost 2-3 sets of leaves can be rooted to start a new plant.

## HOUSEPLANT CARE CALENDAR

### January - February

Remove white crust from container if present, topdress with new soil. On African violets, watch for leaf burn due to increasing light. Avoid leaf damage from water by using lukewarm water. Rotate plants for even light distribution.

### March

Trim spindly growth; turn plants for even light; and start cuttings from plants as desired. Break dormancy of Gloxinia, Caladium, Tuberous Begonia, Achimenes and Sprekelia. Germinate seeds of Exacum, Kalanchoe, Browallia, Crossandra, Saintpaulia, Naegelia, and Sinningia if desired. Divide African violets or take cuttings for new ones. Begin fertilizer program.

### April - May

The increase in heat and light may mean more water. Time to transplant potbound plants, transplant seedlings and rooted cuttings.

## Figure 14-22
## PRUNING HOUSEPLANTS

Split-Leaf Philodendron

Diefenbachia

Ficus (rubbertree)

Hydrangea needs plenty of water. After flowers fade, cut back to two or three nodes. Grow in full sun to May, then use light shade. Topdress large container plants.

### June - August
Vacation care provisions when needed; keep up fertilizer program; wash plants off two or three times with lukewarm water during this period. Soak plants from the bottom once or twice during this period, remove white salt deposits, and topdress. Soak cacti every 2-3 weeks and prune plants to shape. Sow seed of Christmas pepper and Jerusalem cherry in June. Start pineapple, ivy, calla cyclamen and pointsettia.

### September - October
Select best plants for winter; discard the rest. Start amaryllis and avocado if desired. Increase humidity and watch for signs of insects. Wash plants off (shower gently with lukewarm water). Give short days to pointsettia, chrysanthemum and kalanchoe. Lower night temperature to 15°C for Christmas cactus for a period of three weeks.

### November - December
Stop fertilizer program. Protect plants from drafts and chills and cut back on water as required. Also increase the humidity. Use artificial light to supplement daylight. Wash plants off. Turn plants for even growth.

## VACATION CARE

Polythene film helps to conserve moisture during vacation periods. Small plants can be placed in tightly sealed bags. Restrict the folliage as little as possible and water a day before bagging as extremely wet soil encourages rot. Large containers can be wrapped with plastic film tied around the base of the plants. If practical, plants may be moved to a cool location, such as a basement (if light is available).

One method of caring for plants while on vacation is to place pots on porous bricks in tubs of water. The water level must be kept below the bottom of the pots. The porous brick absorbs water and prevents the plants from drying out for some time, provided that the plant is well watered when placed on the brick. Generally, water consumption is slowed down if temperature and light are reduced - plants still need good light but must be out of direct sunlight in order to reduce moisture loss. Automatic watering can be set up with wicks and reservoirs or wet mats, however, a reliable and knowledgeable houseplant sitter is possibly the best solution.

## PLANT IDENTIFICATION

Plant identification is made a lot easier with the use of small plastic pot labels placed in the containers (see Figure 14-23). Information on these labels may include genus, species and, perhaps, common name and a code to its care or date plant was obtained. It may also include the family it belongs to or the part of the world to which it is native. Labels come in various colors, so that they can stick out or blend in as you choose (see Figure 14-23). Identification is most helpful when you want to know more about the particular plant.

## Figure 14-23
## IDENTIFYING HOUSEPLANTS

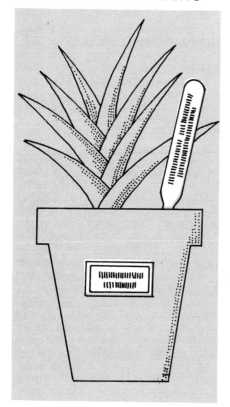

The arrangement of plant parts and its particular habits serve to distinguish one plant from another. For instance, is it a creeper or a tree? Does it have one or multiple stems? Is it woody or herbaceous? Are the leaves opposite, alternate or whorled? Does it have special patterns? Are leaves simple or compound? What shape? Does it flower? What color are its flowers? The more observant you are as to such details, the better you will be able to distinguish one plant from another to search out further information regarding the plant.

Some plant families constitute more of our houseplants than others. The following will list only a few of these families. Books such as *Exotica 3* and *Exotica 4* (see RESOURCE MATERIALS) describe thousands of plants with both pictures and text.

*Araceae* (**Aroid Family**) - this Family produces some of our best and best known houseplants. They are mostly tropical herbs with varied leaf forms. They are best identified by their often showy influorescence, which consists of a 'spathe' and 'spadix'. Houseplants in this Family include: Aglaonema (Chinese evergreen), Anthurium (flamingo plant), Alocasia, Colocasia (taro root), Caladium (paper white), Diefenbachia (dumb cane), Monstera (monster plant, Mexican breadfruit, shingle plant), Philodendron (many vines, climbers and self heading kinds), Photos, Scindapsus (devil's ivy), Nephytis, Spathiphyllum (white flag, peace lily, sailplant), Syngonium (arrowplant), Zanthedezia (calla) and many others.

*Begonicaceae* (**Begonia Family**) - almost the entire Family are houseplants, mostly tropical herbs. Begonia can be divided into the fibrous rooted Begonia (such as wax begonia, angelwing begonia, and cane begonia), Rhizamatous Begonia, Rex Begonia and tuberous rooted Begonia. Some of the prominent houseplants in this Family are Begonia 'D'Arbagas' (Queen of basket Begonia), Begonia 'Dancing Girl', Begonia lepotricha (woolly bear), Begonia semperflorens (including Callalily Begonia), Begonia 'Joe Hayden' (black Begonia), Begonia masoniana (iron cross Begonia), Begonia mazae (stitch leaf Begonia), Begonia bartonea (winter Jewel), Begonia fuchioides (Fuchia leaved Begonia), Begonia geogoensis (Fireking) and the many Begonia rex hybrids.

*Bromeliaceae* (**Pineapple Family**) - The plants in this Family are often epiphytic (grow in the air, supported on other plants). Some have stiff or fleshy leaves that form rosettes or funnels which hold water. The flowers are often colorful. Houseplants in this Family include: Aechmea (living vase), Guzmania, Neoregelia, Tillandsia, Vrisea (flaming sword), Bromelia (volcano plant), Billbergia (Queen's tears), Crypthanthos, Ananas (pineapple) and many others.

*Cactaceae* (**Cactus Family**) - Cacti are almost all American succulents. Most are tropical, some are treelike, some creeping, some epiphytic and almost all are spiny with showy flowers. Among the houseplants in this Family are: Epiphyllum (orchid cactus), Zygocactus (Christmas cactus), Schlumbergia (Easter cactus), Echinocereus (rainbow cactus), Opuntia (prickly pear), Mammilaria (pincushion cactus), Rebutia (crown cactus), Rhipsalis (mistletoe cactus), Cephalocereus (old man cactus), Melocactus (Turk's cap cactus), Astrophytum (star cactus), and many others.

*Gesneriaceae* (**African violet Family**) - Mostly moist tropical herbs and creepers, including Siningia (Gloxinia), Saintpaulia (African Violets), Aeschynanthus (lipstick plant), Nemathanthus, Aechimenes (Cupid's Bower), Columnea (goldfish plant), Episcia (flameviolet), Hypocyrta (lantern plant), Smithiantha (temple bells), Reichsteineria (Brazilian Edelweiss), Kohleria and Streptocarpus (cape primrose).

Other Families with many houseplants include: *Acanthaceae* (Acanthus Family), *Aioazaceae* (Figmarigold Family), *Amaranthaceae* (Amaranth Family), *Amaryllidaecae*, (Amaryllis Family), *Apocynaceae* (dogbane Family), *Araliaceae* (Aralia Family), *Asclepidaceae* (Milkweed Family), *Commalinaceae* (wandering Jew Family), *Compositae* (Aster Family), *Crassulaceae* (Stonecrop Family), *Cycadaceae* (Sagepalm Family), *Cyperaceae* (Sedge Family), *Euphorbiaceae* (spurge Family), *Iridaceae* (Iris family), *Malvaceae* (Mallow Family), *Maranthaceae* (Arrowroot Family), *Moraceae* (Mulberry Family), *Orchidaceae* (Orchid Family), *Palmae* (Palm Family), *Polypodiaceae*, (Common Fern Family), *Rubiaceae* (Madder Family), *Rutaceae* (Citrus

Family), *Solanaceae* (Nightshade Family), *Urticaceae* (Nettle Family), and *Zingiberaceae* (Ginger Family).

The importance of plant families is such that many societies have formed whose membership is comprised of people interested in one particular family. Examples of this are Orchid Societies, African Violet Societies, Gesneriad Societies, Cactus Societies and so on.

# SPECIAL PLANTS AND PLANT TYPES

## CACTI AND SUCCULENTS

Cacti and succulents comprise many of our houseplants. They generally require bright light and warm temperatures, and cooler temperatures when light is low (at which time they can be kept dry in near dormant conditions). These plants enjoy the added moisture that arrives with spring and better light, at which time they should be watered well and allowed to resume growth, then allowed to dry completely before being soaked again. The breaking of dormancy should be done gently with water added very sparingly. The plant can be given gradually increasing amounts of water as growth resumes and full growth takes place. They must have good drainage so that aeration can take place between waterings.

In addition to the many succulents in the Cactus family, a few other plants are also succulent and include: Aeonium (pinwheel), Crassula (jade plant), Haworthia (pearly dots), Kalanchoe (panda plant), Sedum (stonecrop) and many plants belonging to the Spurge family (*Euphorbiaceae*).

## WATER PLANTS

Water plants are often used as houseplants to enhance indoor pools. Among the plants classed as water plants are Nymphea (water lily, lotus), Eichornia (water hyacinth), Azolla (fern), Salvinia (floating fern), Marsilea (water clover), Iris (Japanese iris), Cyperus (umbrella plant and papyrus), Colocasia (taro root) and others. Iris kaempheri (Japanese Iris) and Nymphea (water lily) need full sunshine (bright light). They

can be planted in a growing media of two parts clay, one part peat moss, and one part sand. Do not fertilize. Water lilies are best planted in a reed type basket, so the new shoots come just above the media. Submerge in water to at least 20 cm (8 in) below the surface. Cyperus (umbrella plant) and Colocasia (Taro root) need only medium light and can be planted in the growing media used for water lily. Submerge roots in water, but leave the top of the plant above water. Water hyacinth, Salvinia and Azolla float on the water and need medium to bright light.

## FLOWERING PLANTS

Flowering plants generally need better light than foliage plants. They are very attractive but require more care in the way of picking up faded, dead flowers. Flowering houseplants include Saintpaulia (African violet), and its many relatives (including Gloxinia), Begonia (everblooming Begonia), Pasiflora (passion flower). Beleperone (shrimp plant), Hibiscus, Clivia (kafir lily), Amaryllis, Anthurium (flamingo plant), Zygo-cactus (Christmas cactus), Epiphyllum (orchid cactus), Jacobinia (king's crown), Orchids (the Family has over 25000 Genera), Haemanthus (blood flower), Exacum (Persian violet), Allophytum (Mexican foxglove), Cestrum (jessamine), and Ervatamia (butterfly gardenia) and Spathiphyllum (white flag).

## FOLIAGE PLANTS

Foliage plants are plants grown for their attractive foliage, and are, possibly, the houseplants that require the least maintenance. They include such plants as Diefenbachia (dumb cane), Araucaria (Norfolk Island pine), Aglaonema (Chinese evergreen), various Ferns, Aphelandra (zebra plant), Dracaena, Philodendrons, Ficus, Maranta, Bamboo, Palms, Hedera (ivy) and Scindapsus (Devil's ivy), among many others.

## BONSAI

Bonsai is the Japanese art of growing miniature trees. Plants are kept small by pruning and by keeping them in a small container which restricts their growth. Growing bonsai indoors requires the use of tropical plants. The trees are carefully pruned and trained to grow in shapes

desired by the grower. Bonsai must be watered about once a day. Their soil should never be allowed to dry out but, rather, kept moist without (overwatering) More water is required in hot, dry weather; less in dull, cool weather. Liquid fertilizer is sparingly used to feed the plant. A bonsai is never finished. Instead, it continues to grow and assume new shapes according to the plan of nature and training by its owner. The shapes desired may be such as to give the plant the appearance of an old tree with a heavy tapering trunk and drooping branches, or a crown sculptured by wind and age. Bonsai can be started from cuttings or seedlings. They are planted deep in the container and roots are snipped off as they come through drainage holes. They are transplanted within one to three years and the top is pruned. The growing media is a mixture containing granules the size of rice grains. Finer particles are removed and the remainder is mixed with coarse sand and humus. Copper wire is sometimes placed through drainage holes to hold the tree in a certain shape. For more delicate shoots, pipe cleaners are used to maintain the shape. The wire is removed within six months of placing. More information can be obtained from books that deal specifically with the subject.

## TERRARIUMS, BOTTLE GARDENS AND DISH GARDENS

Miniature landscapes can be created within any transparent enclosure such as glass, plastic or fibreglass (see Figure 14-24). These are living landscapes within the enclosures of the bottle or terrarium. Dish gardens are not enclosed but open to the atmosphere of the room.

To create a bottle garden or terrarium, begin with a dry, clean container. The tools needed for assembling the bottle garden or terrarium include: a pair of long tweezers, a pointed stick, a tamper, and a spoon tied to a long stick. There are then two ways to proceed. One method is to use live, green sphagnum moss and place the green side against the floor of container. Then add charcoal (small amount) and dry growing media. The other method is to first place a layer of pebbles for drainage. Cover the pebbles with a layer of moss or other fiber to prevent the growing media from clogging pebbles; then cover the moss

Figure 14-24
TERRARIUMS, BOTTLE GARDENS AND DISH GARDENS

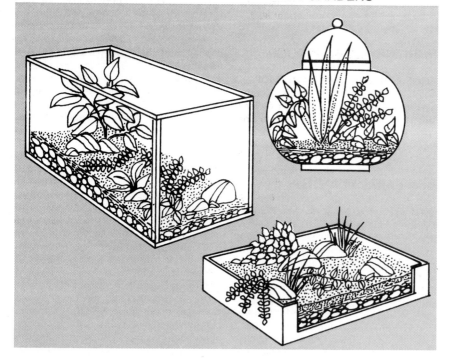

gardens are: Rebutia, Echeveria, Sedum, Haworthia, Faucaria, Lithops, Stapelia, Apteria, Portolacaria and many others.

## GIFT PLANTS

Gift plants are often plants that prefer cool temperatures. Most are grown to flowering in the cool greenhouse and sold as gifts at their peak of their attraction for special holidays. Gift plants are generally discarded after they flower in the home, although some can be kept (with great effort). A few gift plants prefer intermediate to warm temperatures and are easy to keep.

**Azalea** is a plant that prefers cool temperatures and acid, wet growing media, such as peat. It also needs bright light. If these conditions can be met, it can be grown in a home. During summer, it can be plunged in the garden (dug into the soil and left in its container) in the cool shade, then brought back indoors in September, where it needs lots of light and night temperature not exceeding 15°C. Azaleas need 4-6 weeks below 15°C for initiation of flower buds and 4-6 weeks at 5°C for development of flower buds.

**Easter lily** bulbs, which have been forced into bloom should, after blooming, have their faded flowers removed and their foliage kept alive. Easter lilies can be planted outdoors after the danger of frost has passed. Recovery often takes place and they will bloom in late summer.

**Hydrangea** are shrubs that prefer cool to intermediate temperatures with plenty of moisture (not sitting in water). After flowering, cut back to two nodes (usually one-third of their original height) and transplant into new growing media. Place them outdoors in light shade during summer, then move them to a sunny location in August. Liquid fertilizer, such as 20-20-20 (instant soluble), can be applied every two weeks during the summer with iron sulphate applied every alternate two weeks. For blue flowers, water every two weeks with aluminum sulphate (4 mL/L or 0.15 fl oz/qt). Place in a cool (8-10°C), dark place in September and let the leaves drop off. Keep moist, but only just moist. Gradually move them to warmer temperatures and increase light and water for flowering, which should take place around about February under good

with dry growing media. The growing media for the first method can be made from one part peat or leafmold mixed with ten parts of coarse sand. The growing media for the second method can be made from two parts peat to one part soil to one part coarse sand.

Vary the depth of the growing media in different places to give the effect of a pretty landscape. It should not be so deep that it detracts from the beauty of the landscape. Usually, the landscape is made to slope to the back and taller plants placed to one side toward the back, with shorter ones placed in front. Growing media is placed by spooning it in. Plants are placed by using long tweezers, a pointed stick and a tamper. As the plantscaping progresses, small pieces of rock or cork bark can be used for special effect. Pebbles can be used to create a dry stream effect and a small piece of mirror can create the effect of a lake. When everything is in place, add water very gently with an eye dropper, spoon or atomizer. It is best to err on the dry side as water can always be added as necessary. Do not place an enclosed terrarium or bottle garden in direct sun as the heat inside will build up and cook the plants.

A terrarium can be used to provide plants with high humidity and, with additional light supplied, they can serve as a 'plant hospital'; a place for ailing plants to recover.

A bottle garden is a special type of terrarium. Plants put in here must be small enough to go through the bottle's neck. Cuttings without roots can be used as they will root in the bottle. If they are already rooted, roots should be washed free of soil and carefully planted.

Suitable plants for terrariums and bottle gardens include: Allophyton (Mexican foxglove), Pilea depressa, Pilea involucrata, Pilea 'silvertree', Fittonia (nerve or mosaik plant), Sinningia pusilla (miniature plants), Rechsteineria, Begonia boweri (eyelash Begonia), Pteris ensiformis 'victoria', and more.

Dish gardens often take the form of a desert landscape and incorporate succulent plants or small cacti in a shallow, large-surface dish. These plants must be watered well enough to keep them from shrivelling, yet not watered so much as to rot the plants at their base. A sandy loam is preferable as a rooting media. Some suitable plants for dish light conditions. They need temperatures above 18°C for six weeks to initiate flower buds and between 2-9°C with leaves off for six weeks for buds to develop to flowers.

**Pointsettia** are large shrubs. They are usually grown from cuttings and sold as small plants (forced into flower for Christmas). Keep the plants moist, not wet, and keep them out of drafts. Allow plants to dry off after flowering. They can be kept moist and allowed to grow on, or dried off and placed in a dry place (such as a basement) until May. In May, cut the plant back to 15 cm (6 in) and supply light, warmth and water. They can be grown outdoors after the danger of frost has passed. Pinch off new tips until mid-August, or start new cuttings in July/August. When night temperatures go below 15°C in the fall, they should be moved indoors. Provide bright light indoors for 8-11 hours daily and provide complete darkness for 13-16 hours nightly from October 1 to mid-November/December, at which time the bracts should be colored. They need 40 short days to initiate flowering.

**Chrysanthemums** prefer intermediate temperatures and good light. After flowering, they should be cut back to about 10 cm (4 in) and divided into several smaller clumps of plants. These should be planted into containers suitable for their new size. New shoots can be pinched back when they become 10 cm (4 in) long and rooted if new plants are desired. Chrysanthemums can be grown in the garden during the summer in full sun, then moved indoors before frost. (There are also hardy varieties of Chrysanthemum which can be left outside year round.) Provide very bright light for 10-11 hours daily and complete darkness for the remainder of the day until the flower buds show color. It is not a recommended houseplant year round because of its requirement for very bright light and temperature of 15-18°C.

**Cyclamen** prefer temperatures of 10-12°C and moist, not wet, conditions. After flowering, they need a dormant period. They can be brought outdoors to a cool location in July and transferred into a cool greenhouse or cool window in September.

**Cineraria** and **Calceolaria** are usually grown from seed and are not useful after their flowers fade. **Jerusalem cherry** is

usually discarded after its fruit drops.

**Gerbera** can be grown as a houseplant if it receives intermediate to bright light.

## FORCING BULBS INDOORS

### TULIPS, HYACINTH AND DAFFODIL
Bulbs are planted indoors in October. Choose large disease-free bulbs. Cover all but the top 2 cm (3/4 in.) of the bulb when planting in a porous growing media (such as two parts sandy loam to one part peat). Provide good drainage at the bottom of the pots. After planting, soak in water and drain off the excess, then place in a 5-10°C temperature (refrigerator) and leave there for 10-12 weeks. Prevent the growing media from drying out by enclosing the container in a plastic bag. Tulips are ready to be brought out when their shoots are 5-10 cm (2-4 in) tall. Hyacinths can be brought out when their shoots are 2 cm (3/4 in.) tall. Place in an area of low temperature and low light. Gradually move them toward an area of normal light and temperature to avoid bud blasting. Water to keep moist. If plants do not receive sufficient cold treatment, the root and shoot ratio is affected and the bulb fails to flower.

## TROPICAL PLANTS

Tropical plants are best suited to our heated homes. They vary greatly in their need for light and humidity, as well as their water requirements.

Some tropical plants that tolerate low light and dry atmosphere are: Aglaonema (Chinese evergreen), Chamaedorea (dwarf palm), Spathiphyllum (sailplant, white flag), Sansevieria (mother in law's tongue) and Zingiber (ginger).

Some tropical plants that tolerate dry atmosphere and medium light are: Diefenbachia (dumb cane), Pandanus (screw pine), Peperomia (numerous, including watermelon Peperomia), Philodendron, Saintpaulia (African violets), and Scindapsus (Devil's ivy).

Some tropical plants that prefer bright light and well ventilated conditions are: Allamanda Alternanthera (Joseph's coat, parrot leaf), Areca (palm), Canna,

Codiaeum (croton), Coleus, Gynura (velvet plant), Hibiscus, Pentas (Egyptian star cluster) and Nicodemia (indoor oak).

Some tropical plants that prefer high humidity are: Stephanotis, Ananas (pineapple), Musa (banana), Dipladenia, Rechsteineria (Brazilian Edelweiss), Tillandsia (Spanish moss), Cattleya (orchid), Dendrobium (orchid), Acalypha (chenille plant), Clerodendron (glorybower), Ctenanthe (Indian feather), Eucharis (Amazon lily), Fittonia (nerve or mosaik plant), Maranta (prayer plant), Aeschynanthus (lipstick plant), Columne (goldfish plant), Medinilla (love plant), Sinningia (gloxinia), Smithiantha (temple bells), Polypodium (resurrection fern), Cocos (coconut palm), Cordyline (ti plant), Colocasia (taro root) and Adiantum (maidenhair fern).

## INTERMEDIATE TEMPERATURE PLANTS

Intermediate temperature plants prefer a lowered temperature at night. Many are excellent houseplants. A few of these are: Agave (century plant), Aloe (healing plant), Araucaria (Norfolk Island pine), Aspidistra (cast iron plant), Chlorophytum (spider plant), Crassula (jade plant), Cyrtomium (holly fern), Hedera (ivy), Kalanchoe (panda plant), Nerium (oleander), Portulacaria, Punica (pommegranate), Saxifraga (strawberry geranium) and Tradescantia (wandering Jew).

## CONCLUSION

Certain locations in the house can be problem areas for houseplant growing. These include areas near heat outlets, such as radiators or forced air duct outlets. Plants placed near these may suffer from excessive heat and loss of moisture. Another problem area for plants is near outside doors, where a cold blast of winter can freeze or chill tender foliage. Drafts from poorly insulated window areas can do the same. In choosing the location for decorative plants, think in terms of providing conditions that the plant prefers. What are the factors?

• Temperature — How is heat provided?

- Light — Plants first and foremost need light, especially when placed indoors. Is the light sufficient in summer and in winter? If not, what artificial light can be provided (quality and intensity are important)?

- Atmosphere — What needs do the plants have for humidity and ventilation? Is there any pollution? Should the conditions be modified to meet the plant requirements or should plants be selected to meet the conditions provided?

- Growing requirements — What growing media can be provided? Is it suited for the plants intended? What of fertilizers? What is the quality of the water?

- Growing containers — Are they providing drainage? Are they the right size for the plants? Proportions of plant and container are important.

Plants can be 2½-3 times the height of containers.

When choosing the container, bear in mind that it should be simple in design so as not to compete with the plant for attention. It should be of a material, design and color that harmonizes with the surroundings (furniture and background) as well as with the other plants. The effectiveness of the plant is influenced by its height, location and how it is arranged. When selecting decorative plants, design factors must be kept in mind so that the plants can provide the decorative effect sought. What gives us the pleasing results? A plant grown to perfection is healthy and vigorous. It shows lustre and has a strong framework that supports the foliage well. It is also free of symptoms of cultural neglect. Skill is involved in growing such a plant and skill is needed to display such plants effectively. A knowledge of the design elements involved is useful and include: focal point, balance, unity, dominance, harmony, contrast, repetition, texture, line, scale, proportion, shape, color, light and density. These elements are the same as those used in any design and can be studied separately.

When considering plants, time must also be considered. We must not only look at the plant as it is now, but also consider what it will be like next week, month, or year. We then need to ask questions such as: What size do they grow to? Do they bloom? Are the flowers a nuisance? Are they fragrant? Pleasantly or unpleasantly so? Do they need special care to get them to flower? What color foliage? Does the foliage color change? Is it susceptible to insects? Once we can answer such questions, we can proceed with selection of plants to raise and care for in our indoor environments.

## SELF CHECK *QUIZ*

1. Is the environment for houseplants identical in all homes in Alberta?

2. In what way is the environment for houseplants different in the winter from that in the summer?

3. Do plants differ in their need for light?

4. What is the difference in the quality of light from an incandescent light source and that from a fluorescent light source?

5. Is reflected light of any value for plants?

6. Why is it important that growing media be able to drain water away?

7. How often should a Diefenbachia be watered?

8. Should all plants be watered in the same manner?

9. Is a Cyclamen plant well suited as a houseplant?

artificial light - light provided by means other than the sun (eg., fluorescent tubes, incandescent lamps).

bonsai - Jananese art of growing miniature trees.

light intensity - amount of actual energy received from the sun (natural light).

light quality - refers to the wavelength of light and its usefulness for specific plant functions.

natural light - often referred to as white light; is a form of electromagnetic radiation plants receive from the sun.

perlite - heat-treated silicate rock used as a growing media.

photoperiod (duration) - the number of daylight hours best suited to the growth and maturation of an organism.

radiant energy - any form of energy travelling in waves, especially electromagnetic radiation as heat, light, X-rays, gamma rays, etc.

relative humidity - the amount of moisture in the air as compared with the maximum amount that the air could contain at the same temperature, expressed as a percentage.

self-watering container - a container with a built-in water reservoir.

turface (light rock) - baked clay added to soilless potting mixtures to add weight.

vermiculite - heat treated mica used as a growing media.

## RESOURCE MATERIALS

Associated Landscape Contractors of America. *Alca Guide to Interior Landscaping, Interior Landscape Div.* Virginia: Alca, 1982.

Austin, Richard L. *Designing the Interior Landscape.* New York: Van Nostrand Reinhold Company, 1985.

Blashfield, Jean F. *Apartment Greenery.* Toronto: Little, Brown and Co., 1975.

Blashfield, Jean F. *Apartment Greenery.* Boston: G.K. Hall and Company, 1976. (Large Print)

Crockett, James Underwood. *Flowering Houseplants.* New York: Time-Life Books, 1971.

Crockett, James Underwood. *Foliage Houseplants.* New York: Time-Life Books, 1972.

Drysdale, Art C. *Gardening Off the Ground.* Canada: J.M. Dent and Sons, 1975.

Elbert, Virginia F. and George A. *The Miracle Houseplants.* (The Gesneriad Family), New York: Crown Publ. Inc., 1977.

Everett, T.H. *101 More Houseplants.* Greenwich, Connecticut: Fawcett Publ. Inc., 1976.

Fitch, Charles Marden. *The Complete Book of Houseplants Under Lights.* New York: Hawthorn Books, Inc., 1975.

Futura, Tok. *Interior Landscaping.* Reston, Virginia: Reston Publ. Co. Inc., 1983.

Gaines, Richard L. *Interior Plantscaping.* New York: Architectural Record Books, 1949.

Graf, Alfred Byrd. *Exotica 3 Pictorial Cyclopedia of Exotic Plants* Vol 1. New Jersey: Roehrs Co., 1970.

Graf, Alfred Byrd. *Exotica 3 Pictorial Cyclopedia of Exotic Plants* Vol 2. New Jersey: Roehrs Co., 1973.

Graf, Alfred Byrd. *Exotic Plant Manual* 5th edit. New Jersey: Roehrs Co., 1978.

Graf, Alfred Byrd. *Exotic House Plants.* New Jersey: Roehrs Co., 1976.

Hunter, Margaret K. and Edgar H. *The Indoor Garden Design, Construction and Furnishing.* Toronto: John Wiley and Sons, 1978.

Kayetta, Ken and Steven Schmidt. *Successful Terrariums.* Boston: Houghton Miller Co., 1975.

Kranz, Frederic H. and Jacqueline L. *Gardening Indoor Under Light.* New York: The Viking Press, 1971.

McDonald, Elvin. *Little Plants for Small Spaces.* New York: Popular Library, 1974.

McDonald, Elvin. *Miniature Gardens.* New York: Grosset and Dunlap Inc., 1976.

Murphy, Wendy B. *Gardening Under Lights.* Alexandria, Virginia: Time-Life Books, 1978.

Nehring, Arno and Irene. *Propagating Houseplants.* New York: Hearthside Press Inc., 1976.

Northen, Rebecca Tyson. *Orchids as Houseplants.* New York: Dover Publ. Inc., 1976.

Northen, Rebecca Tyson. *Home Orchid Growing.* Toronto: Van Nostrand Reinhold Ltd., 1970.

Ortho Books. *Houseplants Indoors/Outdoors.* San Francisco: Ortho Book Div. Chevron Chem. Co., Canadian Edition, 1974.

Ortho Books. *The Facts of Light About Indoor Gardening.* San Francisco: Ortho Book Div. Chevron Chem. Co., Canadian Edition, 1975.

Tarrant, David. *Highrise Horticulture – A Guide to Gardening in Small Spaces.* Surrey, B.C.: Nunaga Publ. Co. Ltd., 1975.

SOURCES OF PREDATORY INSECTS

Applied Bio-Nomics Ltd., P.O. Box 2637, Sidney, B.C. V8L 4C1

Better Yield Insects, 13310 Riverside Drive, East, Tecumseh, Ontario N8N 1B2

# SELF CHECK *ANSWERS*

1. No, it varies. Some homes provide an environment with low light; others with high light intensity. Some homes provide medium range humidity; others very low humidity; etc. (see INTRODUCTION, page 1401).

2. The light intensity of natural light greatly decreases in the winter (see SEASONAL VARIATIONS IN LIGHT INTENSITY, page 1402).

3. Yes, some plants require bright light conditions; others prefer medium light intensities and yet others thrive under lower light intensities. (see LIGHT INTENSITY PREFERENCES OF PLANTS, page 1403).

4. The light from an incandescent light source radiates more of the red color and less blue colors of the spectrum, whereas the fluorescent light radiates more of the blue and less of the red colors (see TYPES OF LAMPS, page 1406).

5. Yes, reflected light is as good as nonreflected light (see REFLECTED LIGHT, page 1406).

6. It is important for growing media to drain water so air can enter the pore space to provide carbon dioxide and oxygen to the roots and prevent the buildup of anaerobic conditions (see GROWING MEDIA, page 1410).

7. A Diefenbachia should be allowed to dry to near the wilting point before being thoroughly soaked, then allowed to dry again (see Table 14-4, PLANTS TOLERATING LOW HUMIDITY (dry conditions), page 1422).

8. No, some plants dislike the extreme dry or extreme wet conditions; others prefer wet conditions (see PLANT PREFERENCES FOR WATER, page 1418).

9. No, Cyclamen require temperatures much lower than found in most homes (see GIFT PLANTS, pages 1430-31).

## INDEX

- GREENHOUSE DESIGN
- STRUCTURAL DESIGN ELEMENTS
- THE GREENHOUSE COVER
- ENVIRONMENTAL DESIGN ELEMENTS
- GREENHOUSE MANAGEMENT
- GREENHOUSE PLANTS
- PROBLEMS AND PREVENTION

# GREENHOUSE GARDENING

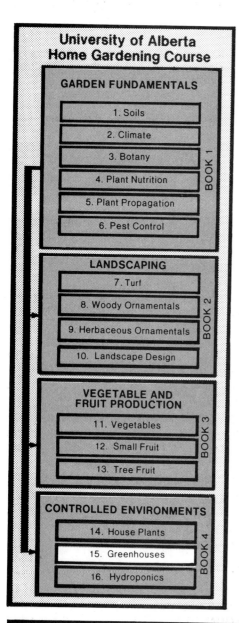

**University of Alberta Home Gardening Course**

**GARDEN FUNDAMENTALS**
- 1. Soils
- 2. Climate
- 3. Botany
- 4. Plant Nutrition
- 5. Plant Propagation
- 6. Pest Control

BOOK 1

**LANDSCAPING**
- 7. Turf
- 8. Woody Ornamentals
- 9. Herbaceous Ornamentals
- 10. Landscape Design

BOOK 2

**VEGETABLE AND FRUIT PRODUCTION**
- 11. Vegetables
- 12. Small Fruit
- 13. Tree Fruit

BOOK 3

**CONTROLLED ENVIRONMENTS**
- 14. House Plants
- 15. Greenhouses
- 16. Hydroponics

BOOK 4

# SELF-STUDY LESSON FEATURES

Self-study is an educational approach which allows you to study a subject where and when you want. The course is designed to allow students to study the course material efficiently and incorporates the following features.

**OBJECTIVES** — are found at the beginning of each lesson and allow you to determine what you can expect to learn in the lesson.

**LESSON MATERIAL** — is logically organized and broken down into fundamental components by ordered headings to assist you to comprehend the subject.

**REFERENCING** — between lessons and within lessons allows you to integrate course material.

The last two digits of the page number identify the page and the digits preceding these identify the lesson number (eg., 107: Lesson 1, page 7 or 1227: Lesson 12, page 27).

Referencing:

> sections within the same lesson (eg., see OSMOSIS)

> sections in other lessons (eg., see Botany lesson, OSMOSIS)

> figures and tables (eg., see Figure 7-3)

**FIGURES AND TABLES** — are found in abundance throughout the lessons and are designed to convey useful information in an easy to understand form.

**SIDEBARS** — are those areas in the lesson which are boxed and toned. They present information supplementary to the core content of the lesson.

**PRACTICAL PROJECTS** — are integrated within the lesson material and are included to allow you to apply principles and practices.

**SELF-CHECK QUIZ** — is provided at the end of each lesson and allows you to test your comprehension of the lesson material. Answers to the questions and references to the sections dealing with the questions are provided in the answer section. You should review any questions that you are unable to answer.

**GLOSSARY** — is provided at the end of each lesson and alphabetically lists the definitions of key concepts and terms.

**RESOURCE MATERIALS** — are provided at the end of each lesson and comprise a list of recommended learning materials for further study of the subject. Also included are author's comments on the potential application of each publication.

**INDEX** — alphabetically lists useful topics and their location within the lesson.

1986 University of Alberta Faculty of Extension

**Written by: Rudi Kroon and Dr. Mohyuddin Mirza**

**ISBN 0-88864-852-9**
(Book 4, Lesson 15)

THE PRODUCTION TEAM

Managing Editor .................................................. Thom Shaw
Editor .............................................................. Frank Procter
Production Coordinator ............................ Kevin Hanson
Graphic Artists ........................... Melanie Eastley Harbourne
Lisa Marsh
Data Entry .............................................. Lois Hameister
Patricia McDonald

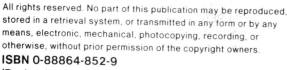

Published by the University of Alberta
Faculty of Extension, Corbett Hall
Edmonton, Alberta, T6G 2G4

# LEARNING OBJECTIVES

After completing this lesson, the student should be able to:

1. Determine the need for developing a comprehensive design and management plan for greenhouse construction and operation.

2. Identify the structural design elements and their interrelated purpose in greenhouse construction.

3. Recognize the importance of the greenhouse cover and select the most appropriate cover for the purpose it is to serve.

4. Identify the environmental elements that influence greenhouse design and select and use the most suitable environment controlling systems and devices.

5. Develop and implement a plan for establishing and maintaining selected plants in the greenhouse environment.

# TABLE OF CONTENTS

## LIST OF FIGURES AND TABLES

# INTRODUCTION

At one time or another, many home gardeners consider constructing a small hobby greenhouse. It is indeed possible for amateur gardeners to operate a small greenhouse structure in their backyard which can prove to be both enjoyable and practical as well, considering the price of young bedding plants, potted plants and certain vegetables. This lesson provides an insight into the various aspects of greenhouse design, so that you may understand what to look for in the optimum greenhouse whether you build it yourself or purchase it. It should, however, be pointed out that the optimum conditions may not always be obtainable. You may have to compromise often.

# GREENHOUSE DESIGN

## BRIEF HISTORY OF GREENHOUSE DESIGN

Romans in the Mediterranean area protected their medicinal and culinary herbs against cold weather by shielding them with 'Muscovy glass', a sheet of geological material (mica) which transmits a certain amount of light. Glass was first utilized as a greenhouse construction material in France around 1385. At that time, round panes were used since sheet glass was not yet produced. The history of greenhouse construction was very much affected by the ability to produce good quality sheet glass and, later, by the availability of good quality wood and by the ability to work this wood with great accuracy. There also had to be an incentive to grow plants during the winter months in protective structures.

With the colonializing activities of nations like England, France and Holland, more and more exotic plants were introduced to these countries, especially laurel (bay leaves), orange and lemon trees. The early colonial powers, including Portugal, Spain and various small Italian states did not have much trouble growing exotics due to their warmer south-European climates. The great wealth brought to the north-European countries during the 17th century colonializing era was responsible for the development of large estates with elaborate gardens. Initially, the imported tropical plants were grown in large wooden tubs and spent the summer outside in the gardens. With the onset of colder weather, they were carried into a special building. This building had tall, narrow doors to accommodate the trees being brought in. The doors had glass panes inlaid to allow light to enter, and wood-fired stoves kept the place warm. Such a building was known as an 'Orangery'. A number of them still remain in Europe, as in the Botanic Gardens in Amsterdam and Leiden, and on the large estates of Jardin Des Tuileries (Paris) and Versailles.

Many of the smaller estates in England and Holland surrounded their vegetable gardens and orchards with brick and masonry walls. It was observed that vines and trees (espaliers) grown against such sheltered, south-facing walls flowered and bore fruit much earlier than any other in the garden. Occasionally, however, late frosts would kill all the blossoms. To prevent this, window frames were placed in a leaning manner to protect trees such as apple, pear, peach and plum. This practice is generally considered to be the forerunner to the 'lean-to greenhouse'. It was soon realized that many other crops could also benefit from such covers.

Benjamin Franklin apparently erected the first small greenhouse in North America. Two other developments also had an influence on greenhouse construction. The first was the Industrial Revolution (in both Western Europe and North America) wherein large, rather poor, rural populations were drawn to the major industrial centers for employment. These people provided a ready market for vegetables and fruit, which were supplied by market gardeners around such centers. The realization that earlier crops fetched the best prices prompted the increased use of glass covers (mainly benches), often heated by means of horse manure dug into trenches next to the rows of plants. The fermentation of this fresh manure provided heat to the crops. The leaky nature of their construction must have prevented damage that would otherwise have been done by the high ammonia levels! Many of the main greenhouse centers in the world are remnants of this development, including Philadelphia, Amagar near Copenhagen, Aalsmeer near Amsterdam, the Westland between The Hague and Rotterdam, and the Venlo area near the Ruhr industrial district in Germany. Another important factor was the establishment of the Botanic Gardens and other display gardens with an entertainment value. Most of these have since disappeared, although some remnants remain. Examples include the Crystal Palace in London (1825-50) and the many palm gardens of Germany. Establishment of such gardens provided experience in construction and heating techniques.

The European greenhouse centers have steadily expanded and have had a strong influence on the technical and horticultural developments of most of the greenhouse industries worldwide. Canada's largest greenhouse designer company had its origins in 1854; in fact, Lord and Burnham are still going strong! The Alberta center of the greenhouse industry is in the Medicine Hat/Redcliff area and the supporting provincial research station in Brooks. All the major cities in Alberta have a number of larger greenhouse enterprises that concentrate on either vegetable or ornamental production. A few deal with both.

# TYPES OF GREENHOUSES

Greenhouses are traditionally built with a center ridge and sloping roof on either side. Why this method of construction was chosen is difficult to trace; it was most likely based on the conventional method of house construction. It is interesting to note, however, that greenhouse design has since been scientifically analyzed and it has become clear that this traditional method, in general, is a practical design. This can only be treated as a compliment to the observational abilities of the early horticulturists.

In connection with the optimum light transmittal factors, the ideal greenhouse is spherical. However, it is difficult to construct such a sphere with a minimum amount of shade factors, even with the advanced building techniques of today. A sphere is also the shape that produces the smallest surface area compared to its contents, but the ensuing floor area is not the most practical to utilize. Several attempts have been made to improve on the basic greenhouse design (see Figure 15-1). The only reasonably successful ones still resemble the traditional shape. An

**Figure 15-1**
TYPES OF GREENHOUSE STRUCTURES

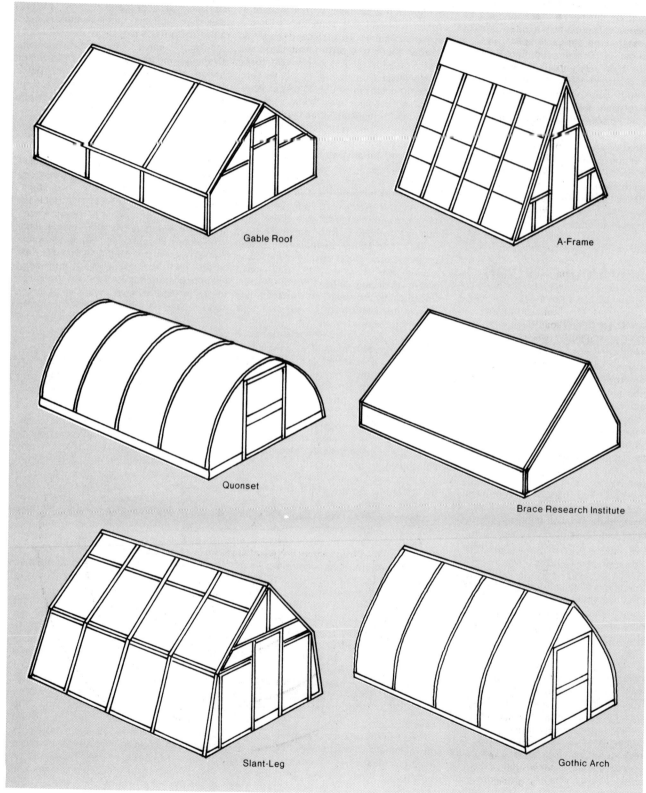

Gable Roof

A-Frame

Quonset

Brace Research Institute

Slant-Leg

Gothic Arch

exception is a greenhouse structure based on the Buckminster-Fuller principle of the geodetic dome. The amount of construction material required, however, still produces a lot of shade. Quonset type greenhouses are a practical variation and are widely adopted by commercial growers. Their use is restricted to plastic type coverings. This is also true of the Gothic Arch greenhouse which allows for the use of laminated spans. The Brace Research greenhouse (see STRUCTURAL VARIATIONS FOR MAXIMUM USE OF SOLAR ENERGY) is specifically designed for colder regions and is very original in that it has non-transparent, insulated north walls and roof. It also utilizes reflective material on the inside of the roof to distribute light evenly throughout the greenhouse in winter, when the sun is very low over the horizon. Semi-pit greenhouses are particularly useful on sloping sites and provide shelter from north winds. A-frames usually prove unsatisfactory. It is anticipated that you will consider the various design aspects before you decide which type best serves your purpose. The alternative to designing and building your own greenhouse is to purchase a pre-fabricated package greenhouse. In this case, it is also advantageous to understand design principles to help you make a choice.

## SITE SELECTION AND ORIENTATION

Two very important aspects of greenhouse design are site selection and orientation. There is often limited choice as to where the greenhouse can be situated. However, the site selected should provide adequate drainage of the surface, and the soil on which the greenhouse is built should also have sufficient drainage. It will definitely be to your advantage to build the greenhouse in a sheltered area. High winds have a tremendous cooling effect on the surface of a greenhouse. Most greenhouses also have numerous air leaks, which can play havoc with temperature control during periods of low temperature and high winds. We are well aware that throughout the seasons the sun not only rises and sets at different times, but that the position of the sun in the sky varies with each season. The ideal greenhouse should be a three-quarter sphere facing south. Lack of light in a greenhouse is

no problem in summer. In winter, however, both low sun angles and short periods affect the amount of light that reaches the greenhouse. This is a real problem! Should a greenhouse then be designed for this worst time of year, a situation which only lasts for about three months? The solar angle is so low and the photoperiod so short in winter that there is not enough light and heat from the sun during this time anyway. Therefore, the greenhouse should be designed for low light situations that occur twice during the growing season; the early spring and late fall periods.

Whatever the time of year, the sun during the middle of the day is in the southern hemisphere. A north to south axis is the best position during the summer, but if a greenhouse is built with its axis running north to south, the sloping roof sides will only be perpendicular (90°) to the sun during summer mornings and afternoons (see GLASS). However, summertime is not the

time we are concerned with in relation to obtaining maximum light intensity since growing conditions are such that we do not experience many problems at this time. The optimum orientation for this part of Canada is to run the axis east to west (see Figure 15-2).

## ROOF ANGLE AND LIGHT TRANSMISSION

The sun strikes the side of the greenhouse and a large part of the roof is close to perpendicular to the light source, providing that the roof slope is adjusted to the right angle. There is a method for calculating this angle accurately. The calculation is based on the fact that the earth's tilt is constant during its trip around the sun. This tilt is 23.5° out of the poles. The distance between the equator and the pole is also divided into 90°. Accordingly, knowing the latitude at your location allows you to calculate the angle of the sun for any day of the year. The latitudes of some of Alberta's major centres are:

Figure 15-2
INFLUENCE OF LIGHT PERIOD ON GREENHOUSE ILLUMINATION

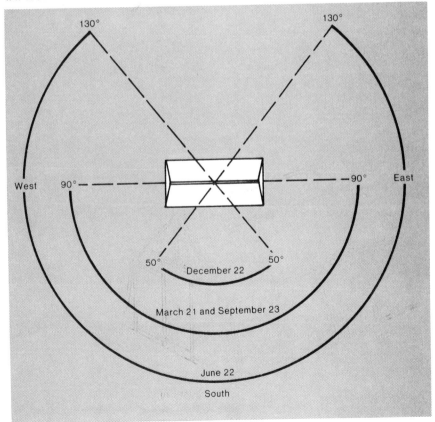

Fort McMurray 56.8° North
Peace River 56.4° North
Grande Prairie 55.1° North
Edmonton 53.5° North
Red Deer 52.4° North
Saskatoon 52.1° North
Calgary 51.1° North
Lethbridge 49.8° North
Regina 50.5° North
Medicine Hat 50.1° North
Winnipeg 49.9° North
Brandon 49.8° North

For example, there are 90° between the equator and the north pole. Edmonton is at 53.5° latitude and the earth is constantly tilted at 23.5°. Therefore, on December 22, the sun rises 90° - (53.5 + 23.5 = 77°) = 13° above the horizon at midday.

On June 21 then, the sun rises 90° - (53.5 - 23.5 = 30°) = 60° above the horizon at midday.

The difference between midwinter and midsummer is 60° - 13° = 47° over 182 days (half a year). This amounts to roughly 0.26° per day.

To determine the number of degrees the sun rises over the horizon 40 days after December 22, calculate: 13° + (40 x 0.26) = 23.4°

As previously discussed, adapt the roof slope to the light angle as it occurs around September 21 (late fall) and March 21 (early spring). Through calculation, a roof slope of about 26° is an acceptable angle. (The slope of the greenhouse roof should ideally be 64°, to transmit the maximum amount of light in the fall and spring. However, this is an unrealistic angle and would result in fairly high rooftops that are subject to winds and excessive cooling.) If the 26° slope is adopted, the north side roof slope is parallel to the direction of the incoming light (see Figure 15-3). It has been proven that such an angle also allows snow and ice to slide down easily. To utilize all possible benefits from the available light in winter, it is possible to have the sides extended higher than usual, and the wall placed at approximately a 13° angle. Modern European commercial greenhouses are increasingly constructed with sides approximately 50 per cent higher than their predecessors. The extra

## Figure 15-4
## OPTIMUM ROOF SLOPE

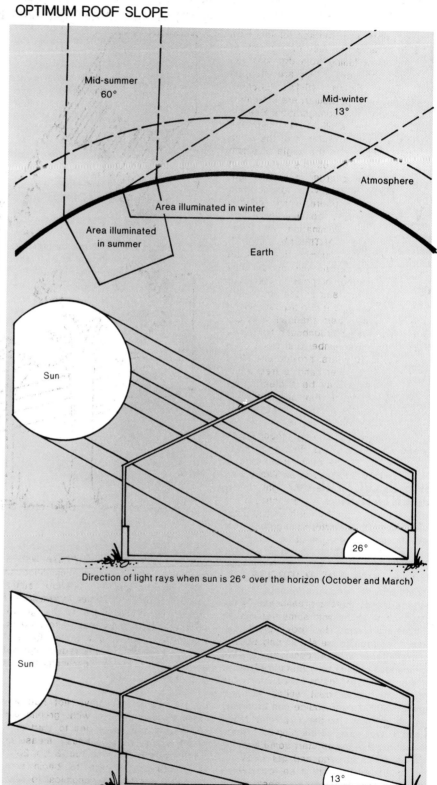

Direction of light rays when sun is 26° over the horizon (October and March)

Direction of light rays when sun is 13° over the horizon (December 21)

construction cost is apparently recovered by a saving in fuel costs.

One possible disadvantage for this type of side construction may be the risk of ice and snow falling from the roof and damaging the sides if they are 'stepped out' (see Figure 15-1). 'Lean-to' greenhouses, in particular, are extremely well suited to this configuration. Keep in mind that the sunlight reaching the earth's surface in winter is of the same intensity, but due to the angle at which this light strikes the earth's surface, it is distributed over a larger area. This light also travels a relatively longer path through the atmosphere, which reduces the initial intensity considerably. This results in an illumination of lower intensity (see ARTIFICIAL LIGHT). Knowing what the maximum height of the sun is during a certain time of year may also serve another purpose. If there are any buildings or trees on the south side of the selected site it, can be determined whether or not their shadows interfere with the available greenhouse light (see Figure 15-4). Remember that trees grow and may, in 10 years, provide unwanted shade. On the other hand, a tree which loses its leaves may be a blessing by providing shade in the summer while allowing sunlight to reach the greenhouse in winter. The initial situating of a greenhouse is only important in areas where the sky is clear and free of moisture, as is the case in Alberta. In high humidity areas, such as Vancouver, the atmosphere scatters the light. Nearly as much light enters the greenhouses in such an area from the north as any other direction. Such diffused light is not usually as intense as in Alberta.

## TYPE, SIZE AND PURPOSE

It is apparent that a greenhouse is not simply a structure with some transparent cover in which to grow plants. A practical greenhouse should only be built after a lot of careful consideration and planning. As previously discussed, there are a variety of design types to choose from. Which is best suited to your purpose? Before a choice can be made, you must determine the purpose of 'your' greenhouse. Are you planning to operate it seasonally, just to start some bedding plants for the spring and get tomatoes off to an early start? If so, consider a structure with removable panels or, at least, with removable sides which permits the entry of fresh air during the

### Figure 15-3
### SHADING AND SEASONAL ANGLE OF THE SUN

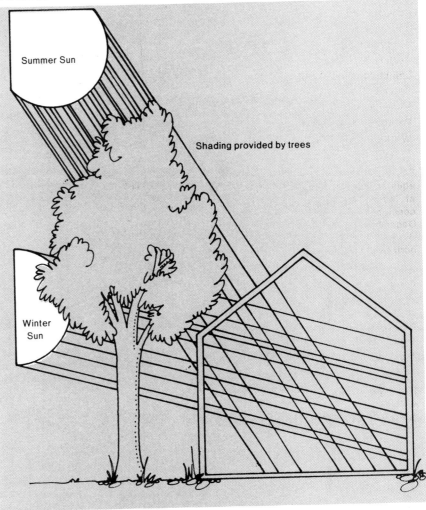

Summer Sun

Shading provided by trees

Winter Sun

growing season. A greenhouse with a reliable heating system, humidification and the means to provide ample ventilation in the summer is required if crops like orchids are to be grown. Another possible purpose is to produce fruits and vegetables in winter. Each of these different purposes require special features which make a particular type of greenhouse suitable.

In general, if you have not had any previous experience with greenhouse growing, it is a good idea to start on a small scale. A greenhouse measuring approximately 2.5 m x 6 m (8 ft x 20 ft) is a reasonable size to begin with. Smaller ones are uneconomical to heat, due to the ratio of contents to surface. Existing greenhouses can be extended if

provision for this is incorporated into the original planning and construction.

## STRUCTURAL DESIGN ELEMENTS

In the design (or selection) of the optimum greenhouse, consideration must be given to the structural components which are combined to produce a usable structure. The selection of these various components is based on the extent to which they satisfy the objectives of the greenhouse structure. The primary objectives of the greenhouse structure are:

- To allow the maximum amount of light to enter.

Figure 15-5
STRUCTURAL ELEMENTS IN GREENHOUSE DESIGN

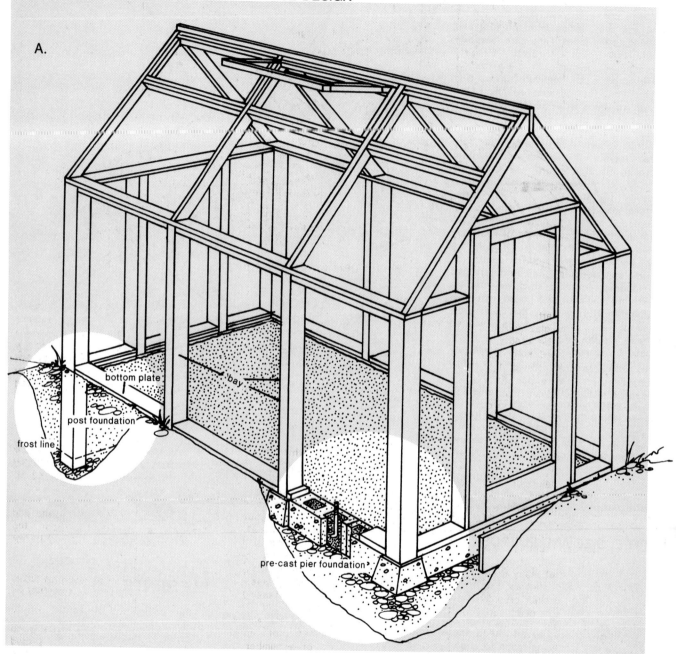

A.

bottom plate

bay

post foundation

frost line

pre-cast pier foundation

- To allow for the maintenance of a desired temperature with the aid of coolers or heaters in an economical manner.

- To last for a considerable amount of time with a minimum amount of maintenance.

There are a number of other objectives that could be added, but the ones listed are sufficient for our purposes. Note that the first and second points are somewhat contradictory in that most of the light transmitting covers used in greenhouses have a very low insulating ability. There are also contradictory

interests contained in the first and third points. In order to allow maximum light to enter, construction material must be reduced as much as possible without weakening the structural properties. Until about 30 years ago, there were not many construction material options available. In the early years, cast iron was used for

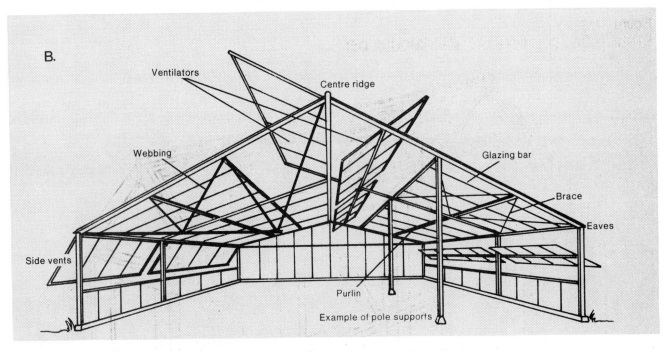

B.

Ventilators

Centre ridge

Webbing

Glazing bar

Brace

Eaves

Side vents

Purlin

Example of pole supports

the main structural parts in combination with wood for the glazing bars (see GLAZING BARS). In the 1940's, precast concrete and extruded steel was also used, but iron was found to be a problematic material, especially when it began to rust. Since rust has a larger volume than actual iron, rusting cracked the glass panes. For many years, wood has been the favored material for greenhouse builders. The best material to cover the greenhouse with, as far as durability and light transmittance is concerned, is still glass, although there are more and more lightweight materials competing for this distinction. The weight of glass is its major drawback in greenhouse construction (see GLASS). Additional weight factors, such as windforce, snow load, or rain, not to mention the fact that many greenhouse operators suspend shelves and other support material for their crop from the greenhouse frame, must also be considered in the design of a greenhouse (see SUPPORT). Also, the heating system is often hung from the rafters and purlins. All these factors may illustrate that it is not a simple task to build a greenhouse with the 'minimum amount of material' required. A discussion of glass greenhouse forms the standard from which other cover materials are adapted for use. The various structural elements as they pertain to the glass covered greenhouse follow (see Figure 15-5).

## FOUNDATIONS

Like any other building, three factors influence the foundation construction:

- The depth that frost penetrates the soil.

- The weight of the structure.

- The type of soil on which the greenhouse is built.

For greenhouses, the footing or foundation should extend below the frostline. If a post type of construction is considered, it could be argued that as the house is kept warm during the winter, the footing on which the poles are resting need not be all that deep. Unfortunately, a fair amount of glass or plastic may be lost due to the heaving of the footings, particularly if the greenhouse is not used in the winter. Usually, the foundation of most greenhouses consists of a number of columns which extend below the frostline. In most Alberta locations, footings or columns placed 1.2 m (about 4 ft) below ground level should be sufficient but speak to some local authorities to make sure. Holes for such columns can usually be dug with the aid of a post hole auger. Bridging between these foundation points can support the greenhouse. Obtain

information from local building experts for advice concerning the maximum recommended distance between foundation posts. In principle, divide the total weight of the greenhouse by the number of foundation points to determine how much weight each point is expected to carry.

For your guidance:

- The average (15 m² or 160 sq. ft) conventional glass greenhouse weighs approximately 25 kg/m² (about 5 lb./sq. ft).

- If a heating system with pipes and water is suspended from the greenhouse structure, add 10 kg/m² (2 lb./sq. ft).

- For occasional loads, such as snow, wind, and heavy rain, add another 25 kg/m² (about 5 lb./sq. ft).

- Crops suspended from the roof, such as cucumbers, tomatoes, or potted plants on shelves (including safety margin) add another 10 kg/m² (2 lb./sq. ft) to the overall weight.

The total weight of a glass greenhouse, then, is 70 kg/m² (14 lb./sq. ft). Greenhouses using plastic are considerably lighter, whereas greenhouses using double glass are considerably heavier. The calculations provided serve only as a guide in determining the weight of a greenhouse and identifying which factors play a key role. For foundation construction, engineers distinguish the following soils in our area:

Type 1 = 39000 kg/m² (55.5 lb./sq. in.)

Type 2 = 19500 kg/m² (27.7 lb./sq. in.)

Type 3 = 9750 kg/m² (13.8 lb./sq. in.)

*Example:*

A glass greenhouse 2.5 m wide and 6 m long (8 ft. x 20 ft) has an area of 2.5 x 6 = 15 m² (8 x 20 = 160 sq. ft). According to earlier calculations, the structure weighs 70 kg/m² (14 lb./sq. ft). The total weight of the structure is 70 x 15 = 1050 kg (160 x 14 = 2240 lb). The structure is to be supported by two rows of three foundation points; a total of six points. This means that each has to carry 1050 divided by 6 = 175 kg (2240 divided by 6 = 373 lb). If the greenhouse is built on a type 3 soil: 175 kg divided by 9750 kg/m² = 0.01795 m² or 179.5 cm² (373 lb. divided by 13.8 lb./sq. in. = 27 sq. in). Therefore, the surface area of each support footing must be about 180 cm² (27 sq. in). The shape of the footing does not matter as long as the area of support (the bottom) measures a minimum of 13.4 x 13.4 cm (5.2 x 5.2 in). The force produced by the weight of the greenhouse is not always entirely in a downward direction. In particular, foundations for the sidewalls experience a sideways thrust. Therefore, extra resistance is provided by the footing through a flat area on the outside of the footing. It is difficult for the uninitiated to calculate this force, but only in larger greenhouses is it necessary to construct such footings. In this case, the assistance of an engineer is required.

To prevent the loss of heat from the greenhouse by means of conductivity through the soil, insert styrofoam sheets along the foundations. This also protects the foundation from frost damage, as even the unused greenhouse (providing the windows and doors are kept closed) accumulates a fair amount of heat due to solar radiation.

## SUPPORT

In most small hobby greenhouses, the ridge, purlins and eaves rest on the end gables and, accordingly, no extra support is needed to hold the roof up. However, if the structure is longer than 3.6 m (12 ft) or wider than 5.5 m (18 ft), additional roof support must be provided. The simplest way of doing this is to erect a steel pole under the purlins or ridge beam, somewhere in the middle of the greenhouse. For many years even rather large greenhouses were supported this way. Such houses are called 'Post and Ridge' or 'Post and Purlin', depending on the system used. Commercially, this method was abandoned because:

- Poles settled at different rates, creating stress in the whole structure and resulting in excessive glass breakage.

- Poles often made it difficult to place beds, tables and walkways at their optimum or desired spacing.

In the 1940's, various truss and span frames replaced the poles as a means of support, and provided a large unobstructed area in the greenhouse. For hobby greenhouses, however, post supported greenhouses are the cheapest to build. Spans are expensive to manufacture unless they are made of laminated wood and gussetplates. There is a tendency in modern commercial greenhouses to use webbed trusses, as a well designed truss provides minimal shade relative to its strength. All non-post systems transfer the accumulated weight of the structure to the peripheral area of the greenhouse.

## RIDGE

The ridge is the backbone of any greenhouse structure and takes many forms, all dependent on the type of cover used. The ridge is usually the highest part of the structure and serves two main functions:

- To provide strength along the axis

- To support the upper end of the glazing bars

In 'lean-to' greenhouses, the ridge beam is bolted to the building, serving as support to the greenhouse. Due to the extensive and often elaborate joining work done to accommodate the glazing bars, the lumber used for a ridge beam should be of top quality heartwood. The top of the beam has a flat surface on which a wider plank is secured (to provide protection from rain). The ridge beam flares out at the line where the glass connects and maintains this width. The lower part of the glazing bar that is below the glass notch, is fitted into the wider part of the ridge.

## GLAZING BARS

Glazing bars are the parallel members on which the glass sheets are fixed They should be constructed of strong, flexible wood that is free of any blemishes or cracks. Larix wood is an excellent wood for use as glazing bars. An important aspect (to all parts of greenhouse construction) is the temperature difference between the outside and inside of the structure. Due to the relatively high rate of water usage inside the greenhouse, a large amount of condensation can form on the inside of the greenhouse. This ever present condensation has the tendency to penetrate any joining work of the wood, and gives rise to the possible occurrence of rot. In winter, this moisture can also cause considerable structural damage when it freezes and expands the joints. Therefore, the number of joints should be limited as much as possible, and all fittings should be made as sound as possible. Figure 15-6 shows a typical glazing bar. The rabbet is usually 12 mm (½ in) wide if typical size glass sheets are used (see GLASS). If larger panes are used (as is the trend), the rabbet may need to be slightly wider. Remember that glass, like all other materials, expands and contracts with changing temperatures. Therefore, glass should never be fitted tightly between the glazing bars. This is also the reason that the caulking on which glass sheets rest should be a non-hardening type. Excessive glass breakage may occur if these points are not observed. Sheets of glass also have to be secured on or in the glazing bar to prevent them from sliding down or lifting out. Triangular glazing nails are used in wooden glazing bars to accomplish this. Special clips are used with metal glazing bars. Before

## Figure 15-6
## GLAZING BARS

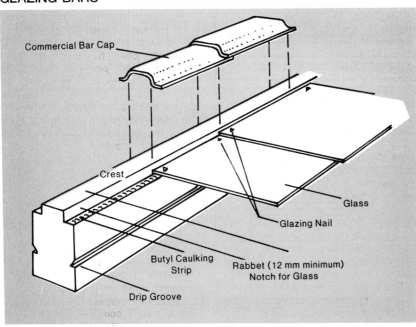

Commercial Bar Cap

Crest

Glass

Glazing Nail

Butyl Caulking Strip

Rabbet (12 mm minimum) Notch for Glass

Drip Groove

the introduction of barcaps (see Figure 15-6), a bead of caulking compound was used to provide a waterproof seal. Barcaps prevent water from entering and also serve to clamp the glass down and prevent sheets from sliding. Such caps are screwed into the wooden glazing bar with non-corrodable (brass) round-head screws. Metal glazing bars are fitted with a slot which accommodates self-tapping metal screws. The centre ridge (crest) of the glazing bar used to be made higher to accommodate extra caulking; those used with barcaps are (usually) only 12 mm (½ in) high.

A fair amount of condensed water forms on the inside of the glass pane. This water has a tendency to run towards the eaves, but usually forms large droplets which accumulate on the edges of window panes. When the droplets get large enough, they fall down inside the greenhouse. One has only to visit a not-so-well constructed greenhouse in spring to see the mess these falling droplets can make when they drip into pots and seed flats. Not only do they make ugly holes in the soil, but they also splatter soil onto surrounding plant material. In order to intercept a certain amount of this condensation, drainage strips are cut into the sides of glazing bars. Provided the grooves are kept clean and unobstructed, they evacuate a

fair amount of water. Glazing bars are supported in three main areas:

- On top by the ridge beam.

- The lower part by the eaves.

- In the course of the run by one or more purlins.

The fittings on both eaves and ridge should be accurately cut. Glazing bars should be well constructed; they are an important aspect!

## EAVES

Eaves intercept a great deal of light. The reason why they cannot be reduced beyond a certain minimum, is the fact that they accommodate the glazing bars forming the roof, as well as support the top part of the vertical bars forming the side wall. In the past, gutters were often attached to the eaves, and worsened the shadow problem. Today, the glazing bars of the roof and the last sheet of glass are often allowed to extend from 7-15 cm (3-6 in) beyond the wall, thereby leading any rain water away from the base and foundation of the greenhouse. In milder climates, a gap

can be left between the top of the eaves bar and the glass sheet to allow condensed water to escape. In our climate, however, the glass will crack as soon as the water freezes if it is allowed to accumulate between the top of the eaves and the glass. Lord and Burnham, a Canadian manufacturer, offers a type of greenhouse with a continuous curved glass sheet at the eaves. The vertical glass walls in such greenhouses are 'slant leg' (see Figure 15-1) which, as far as light entry is concerned, is an advantage. Problems may still be encountered with snow and ice sliding from the roof surface.

## BRACING

The greenhouse structure is subject to considerable forces. The weight of the greenhouse has been identified as a force that must be considered in design; windforce is another factor. Wind can apply pressure in practically any direction, even from the inside, and especially strong winds blowing against the side of the greenhouse can create areas of high and low pressure. Most glass greenhouses have high leakage rates. On a still day, glass greenhouses can have one complete air change per hour. On a windy day, this may increase to three complete air changes per hour. Air leakage allows a build up of air pressure inside the greenhouse. The standing glass and the roof directly facing the wind experience strong positive forces on the lee side (downwind) and extensive turbulation creates negative forces similar to the lift of an airfoil. Wooden or metal struts can be used to brace the greenhouse against external movement caused by wind or other forces (rain, snow, etc.).

## METAL GREENHOUSES

As previously discussed, early attempts to construct greenhouses from metal failed due to excessive rust problems. With the advancement of metal extrusion techniques, it became possible to produce many of the complicated structural parts required for greenhouses from corrosion-free aluminum. Greenhouses built from this material are lightweight, yet strong and durable. In addition, aluminum is a relatively maintenance-free building material.

Aluminum costs more than any other construction material, but the advantages of using it in greenhouse construction are well worth it. In search of a more economical alternative to aluminum, European manufacturers (Prinz Greenhouses) have produced a zinc coated steel greenhouse. This steel is rolled into the various configurations and dipped in a hot zinc solution. The resulting product has many of the same advantages as aluminum and has proven popular with commercial growers. Prinz Greenhouses offers packages in both wood and aluminum in Canada. The cross sections of metal greenhouse parts, serve the same principal functions as their wooden counterparts. The metal structures also include drip grooves, glass notches and caulking strips. Ornamental details are often present as well. They are actually included to provide additional rigidity to the metal member. Commercial greenhouse enterprises seem to have accepted the advantages of the more up-to-date metal design. There are also smaller home gardener type kits available in aluminum. Such kits have been around for several years and are popular with their owners.

## FLOORS, BEDS AND BENCHES IN GREENHOUSES

Crops are traditionally grown in the original soil of the greenhouse. However, it has been found that in winter, especially in colder regions like Alberta, the soil temperature often becomes too low to grow plants successfully in this manner. There are a number of other reasons why this system is not suitable. The eventual accumulation of soil borne pests and diseases, and the buildup of harmful levels of salts, can seriously hamper the growth of a crop. In order to overcome these drawbacks, plants are usually grown in raised benches where the soil is regularly renewed. Such benches may be constructed from any material at hand, as long as there is no risk of the material releasing damaging chemicals or fumes. This is often a problem when such beds are made out of wood, as there is a tendency by the users to treat the wood with a preservative. Many wood preservatives are harmful to the plant roots, so it is advisable to obtain information concerning the material to be used.

## Figure 15-7
## BENCH ARRANGEMENTS AND DESIGN

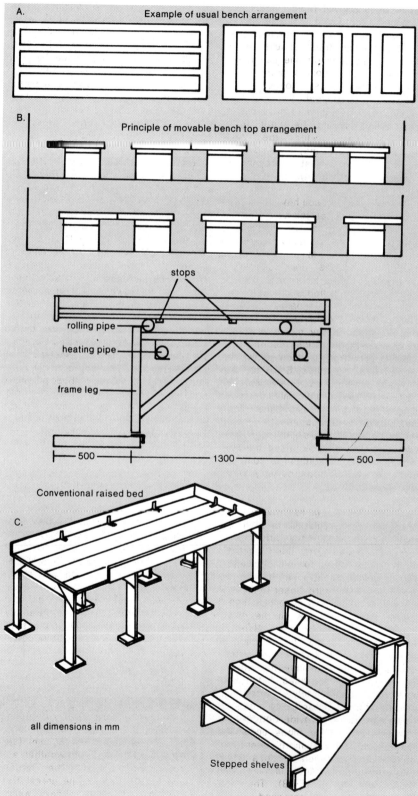

A. Example of usual bench arrangement

B. Principle of movable bench top arrangement

stops
rolling pipe
heating pipe
frame leg

500   1300   500

Conventional raised bed

C.

all dimensions in mm

Stepped shelves

Raised beds should be sufficiently deep to hold enough soil for optimum growth. Shallow beds dry out rapidly and crops may become rootbound. Make sure there is also allowance for drainage! In principle, planting beds should be no wider than the distance one can reach from either side (about 1 m or 3 ft). Walks between beds should be as narrow as is practical. Remember, a greenhouse is designed to grow plants; traffic areas should be kept to a minimum. Even under the best circumstances, walks may take up to 60 per cent of the available greenhouse space (see Figure 15-7A).

Raised benches with soil have to be well constructed and supported as the weight can be considerable. In commercial greenhouses, it may be advantageous to install solid floors. In certain cases, plastic greenhouses are constructed right on such floors. In order to prevent frost heaving, such floors should be laid on a thick bed of coarse drainage material. It is a good idea to provide rapid drainage of any moisture spilled during watering operations especially in a plastic greenhouse which allows far less moisture to escape. Black top and so-called sand-free concrete can be poured which have sufficient porosity to provide drainage through the floor. Container grown crops can be placed directly on such floors. Although it is often customary to use raised benches or tables for the production of container grown crops, this depends very much on the type grown.

It is usually desirable to provide some amount of air circulation through the bench top, although many potted plant crops are grown with flood systems which do not allow for air circulation. Raised benches have a number of advantages. Plants are closer to the roof and, therefore, receive more light and it is much easier to work on the plants without having to stoop down. Benches may be constructed from whatever material is most economical to obtain: wood, sheet metal or asbestos cement. Even plywood can be used, but it must be made completely waterproof! Concrete blocks can serve as a base. It is also possible to provide bottom heat by means of heating pipes under the bench. One of the more interesting modifications of raised benches which has been introduced lately is the roll-top bench (see Figure 15-7B). The total width of the bench is increased to such

an extent that the edges of benches touch each other, thereby eliminating the walkspace entirely. Such bench tops are placed on bench length pipes which allow the top of the bench to be rolled from one side to the other. This allows you to create working space between benches when required. The advantage is that the amount of space used for traffic can be reduced to only 10-20 per cent of the total greenhouse area, thereby increasing the production potential considerably. Before constructing such a bench, it may be advisable to obtain more information about the dimensions as there are certain proportions which should be observed. Bench tops can only extend a certain percentage of their total width without becoming unbalanced! There may be a real challenge for the home gardener with a small greenhouse to design his own movable bench. A tremendous increase in available bench space is the reward! A typical bench arrangement for the smaller greenhouse is the stepwise arrangement of shelves (see Figure 15-7C). This provides both a fair amount of shelf space and excellent air circulation. Often, shelves are supported by the roof of the greenhouse. This is an acceptable method, providing one is convinced that the roof can support this extra weight and that such shelves (with their plantload) do not take too much light away from the crop on the bench.

## THE GREENHOUSE COVER

Traditionally, glass was the only choice of covering for a greenhouse. With the development of plastics, the greenhouse industry is looking for an acceptable replacement for glass. Many replacements have been found, but none has proven completely satisfactory. Beginning with a discussion on glass, we will look at the various alternative covers available.

## GLASS

Glass material is transparent to most of the visual spectrum (390-780 nm) (see NATURAL LIGHT), does not weather, and is reasonably strong. The largest disadvantage it has for the greenhouse industry is its relatively heavy weight

and, consequently, the limit in size per sheet. Normal 'double diamond' glass weighs 7.32 kg/m² (24 oz/sq ft). Large sheets have a tendency to sag if not kept in an upright position. Glass deteriorates somewhat over many years of use, especially in industrial areas. This is due to the fact that various acids in the atmosphere etch the outer surface. The etching influences the light transmittance of glass. It has also been observed that older greenhouses accumulate more dust on the glass surface and need to be cleaned more often. Modern glass has a much smoother surface and is less subject to accumulation of dust and grime. In colder regions like ours, snow and ice adhere to glass and only when the temperature inside the greenhouse is raised does the additional heat melt the ice and allow it to slide down. Glass is reasonably flexible, particularly newer glass. Hail damage to greenhouses is not as common as many have come to believe. Common greenhouse glass sheet sizes are 50 x 50 cm (20 x 20 in) and 75 x 90 cm (30 x 36 in). Both these sizes are double diamond quality. With the introduction of Dutch designed greenhouses in North America, the 100 x 150 cm (39 x 59 in) and 60 x 174 cm (24 x 68.5 in) panes are becoming more common. Glazing panes are usually available pre-cut from most greenhouse suppliers. The fact that glass is applied in comparatively small panes and the method in which this is done is responsible for the leaky nature of glass greenhouses. Glass can be applied to the greenhouse in one of two ways: **butt-end construction** or the **lap method**. In butt-end construction, the sheets are applied edge to edge. This provides for a fair amount of air and water leakage, especially after a number of seasons and excessive amounts of splintering along the edges has occurred. This method is more commonly used for standing side walls, gables and interior partitions. Plastic 'H' shaped strips are fitted between the sheets of glass to reduce splintering. Butt-end construction is not recommended for glass roof installation.

The most common method of glass roof installation is the lap method, wherein the bottom edge of one pane overlaps the upper edge of the lower pane by about 12 mm (½ in) (see Figure 15-6). The advantage of overlapping is that condensed water, formed on the inside of the glass, can escape between the overlap and continue down the outside of the glass. As a result, there is often some moisture sitting between the overlaps and, because this is an attractive medium for algae, it can become quite messy. This is also responsible for a certain amount of shading in greenhouses. Well constructed 'glasshouses' can operate for over 50 years. This track record is not likely to be broken by any of the newer, cheaper and lighter plastic covers. If it is security you are after, glass is the answer!

Optimum light transmittance through glass (or any other cover) occurs if the source of light is at right angles (perpendicular) to the cover material. Clean, new greenhouse glass transmits 91 per cent of the available light, 8 per cent is reflected, and 1 per cent is absorbed as heat and UV radiation. Once glass becomes a number of years older and a film of dirt accumulates, this transmittance rate is reduced. Greenhouse roofs do not consist entirely of glass, but there is an additional loss of light due to glazing bars, glass overlap and other construction members. As a result, some greenhouses receive only 60 per cent of the available outside light. If the angle of incidence of the light is reduced to about 40°, the reflection increases to 11 per cent and the transmittance is reduced to 89 per cent

(see Figure 15-8). We may, therefore, draw the conclusion that we should always have as much of our greenhouse surface facing the sun at 90°.

## PLASTIC

Due to the comparatively lower weight of plastics used in greenhouse construction, the overall construction can be considerably lighter. Consequently, the dimensions of the foundation can also be greatly reduced (see FOUNDATIONS). Greenhouses covered with flexible sheet plastic utilize the frame entirely to keep a certain configuration, but are not usually used to attach the plastic to. In many cases, only a steel cable stretched across the frame keeps the sheet in place. Light braces keep these arches (which form the bays) in place. Due to the light weight of such structures, more attention must be given to anchoring the greenhouse to its foundation.

The adaptation of various types of plastics to greenhouse construction has had considerable influence on the industry. It allowed for the erection of less expensive greenhouses requiring less capital investment. Scientists were initially sceptical about the possibilities of using such plastics in greenhouse application because many of these

materials do not have the ability to reflect infrared (**IR**) radiation, and readily transmitted it. It is the IR reflecting ability of glass that gives rise to the 'greenhouse effect': the build up of heat due to re-radiation of IR radiation from surfaces in the greenhouse (less than 10 per cent transmitted). Many of the plastics, although unable to retain IR, do function reasonably well. This is due to the film of condensed water on the inside of the greenhouse. If such greenhouses are allowed to dry up, it is much more difficult to keep them warm. In the discussion of various plastics and their characteristics, their IR transmitting abilities are discussed.

Another important quality of greenhouse covers is that of ultraviolet (**UV**) radiation. Glass does not transmit UV readily but reflects most of it. UV transmittance is not of importance to plant growth, and UV reflectance is not something to worry about either! It is absorption of UV radiation which is responsible for the weathering and breakdown of plastics. Thus, if a certain plastic absorbs UV, recognize that it has a limited life span. Many of the flexible plastics also become brittle under low temperature conditions. The combination of low temperatures and high winds can reduce such a greenhouse cover to shreds within a matter of minutes. Relative light transmittance is another important consideration. Glass can transmit up to 91 per cent of the available light. Plastics are not able to improve on this, but this is often outweighed by the fact that less construction material is needed to support plastics. Many plastics become milky in color over the years and reduce light transmittance correspondingly. Crop production can be reduced considerably although this discoloration may take several years. There are two distinguishable types of plastic: flexible films and rigid sheets.

### FLEXIBLE FILMS
Polyethylene, often referred to as polythene, is the same plastic that is commonly used for bagging and wrapping of groceries. It is rather brittle in cold weather and deteriorates rapidly under the influence of UV light. It transmits 88 per cent of the IR and up to 86 per cent of the visible light. Polythene can develop rather high static charges, thereby attracting dust readily and potentially reducing light transmittance. It is also permeable to gases, especially

## Figure 15-8
## SOLAR ANGLE AND REFLECTANCE

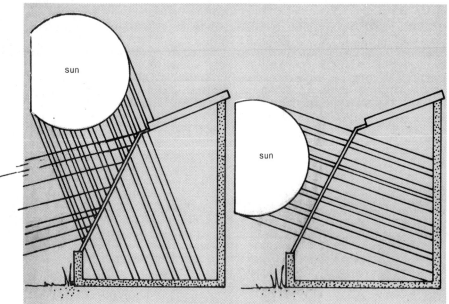

oxygen and carbon dioxide; therefore, there is no risk of plants growing in a structure covered by polythene depleting carbon dioxide. Accordingly, carbon dioxide enrichment in such a greenhouse should not be attempted. Polythene is not a good greenhouse cover but has application in greenhouses where temporary protection is required. For example, a second layer of plastic tacked to the inside of the greenhouse, either covered by a layer of plastic or glass, can reduce heat loss by up to 40 per cent. Polythene sheeting with a built-in reinforcement (Monarfol) was available for greenhouse use, but did not prove entirely satisfactory.

## POLYVINYL CHLORIDE

PVC, as polyvinyl chloride is commonly called, is better known in horticulture as a rigid sheet, but is also available in film. Light transmission is 88 per cent, IR transmission is only 12 per cent and UV transmittance is up to 20 per cent. Although this sounds like a good covering material, it discolors rapidly and may last up to 2 years. PVC film stays flexible at temperatures to -5 °C. The main drawback of film PVC is its susceptibility to fungal and bacterial growth in and on the film. For a while, certain PVC film was popular because it contained an internal, woven polyester reinforcement.

## POLYETHYLENE TEREPHTHALATE

Polyester film (tradename 'mylar') can last up to 4 years or more. Light transmittance is up to 88 per cent and IR transmittance is 25 per cent. Polyethylene copolymers are a newer breed of combined plastics which provide greater strength and better weatherability. Monsanto 602 is such a material.

## POLYVINYL FLUORIDE

DuPont markets polyvinyl fluoride film plastic under the tradename 'Tedlar'. This plastic is superior to most other film covers and can last up to 7 years. It is practically transparent to UV radiation. Light transmittance is up to 92 per cent (actually better than that of glass!) and IR transmittance is 33 per cent (which is not that impressive). This material is expensive. In fact, it is only slightly cheaper than glass.

## RIGID SHEET PLASTICS

There are presently three main types of rigid plastic sheets used in the greenhouse industry. The advantages of rigid sheets over flexible ones is their generally superior weathering abilities, higher impact strength and, consequently, their longer life span. They also do not require frequent replacement, as do the flexible ones.

## GLASS FIBRE REINFORCED POLYESTER

'Fibreglass', as this material is commonly called, consists of fibreglass strands sandwiched between layers of polyester resin. There are many brands available in varying qualities and prices. Hardware stores often offer sheets with color additives which should, of course, be avoided for greenhouse use. There are sheets available which contain 5 per cent acrylic additives. Although these are more expensive, such sheets have a considerably longer life span and are even available with a guarantee of 15 years ('Clear Lite Filon'). Fibreglass can be obtained as a flat sheet or with corrugations. Corrugated sheets (see Figure 15-9) have greater rigidity and require less support but it is rather difficult to use such sheets to cover 'round' greenhouses of the Quonset type, unless they are of considerable width. The Gothic Arch type greenhouses (see Figure 15-1) are often covered with corrugated fibreglass as the corrugated sheets can be bent to some extent, providing one starts off by firmly attaching one end before bending. In some cases, corrugated sheets have been used on Quonset greenhouses with the corrugation running along the axis of the structure. During the winter, these may intercept a fair amount of light during periods of low light angles but snow does not slide off this surface easily. Sheets come in 130 cm (51½ in) widths, and provide a 122 cm (48 in) coverage. Support should be provided across the corrugation every 90 cm (about 36 in). Special wooden corrugation strips and accessories are available from greenhouse suppliers. Fibreglass does not transmit any UV radiation. This is a disadvantage for certain specialized crops that need bees for pollination of their flowers, as bees rely entirely on UV light for their optical system and are unable to function beneath fibreglass. The initial light transmittance of fibreglass is 78 per cent but, as some of this material weathers and gathers dust, the transmittance is reduced. Greenhouses covered with this material should be cleaned each fall. There are coatings available to counteract the weathering process. Fibreglass should never be stored in damp conditions as it may absorb moisture and turn milky. For this same reason, the lower ends of fibreglass sheets should not extend below grade. As corrugated panels present a greater exposure surface for heat transmission (17 per cent), increasing heat costs should, therefore, be calculated against those of flat sheets.

## Figure 15-9
## CORRUGATED FIBREGLASS

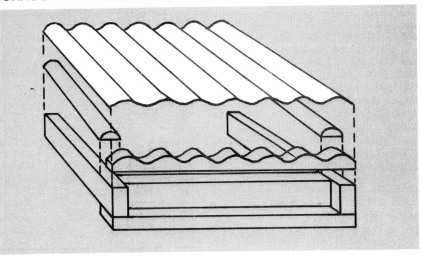

### RIGID PVC

PVC is available in both flat sheets and in corrugated form. It is not as rigid as fibreglass and needs more support. One of the drawbacks of PVC is its increasing 'opacity' with age; it weathers to a brown material. In combination with copolymer resins and polyethylene, interesting results are obtained in providing a cheaper and more durable rigid plastic sheet. Coroplast is such a copolymer resin sheet and its use is becoming popular (ethylene vinyl acolulc evu). This material comes in a flat, fluted sheet. Fluted sheets consist of two separate layers kept apart by upright ridges (see Figure 15-10). Although this reduces the light transmittance qualities, it is an excellent insulator for use as temporary protection on the exposed areas of greenhouses in winter. It is claimed that this sheet stays pliable at temperatures of -56°C! The light transmittance is 72 per cent.

## Figure 15-10
### FLUTED DOUBLE WALL PLASTIC

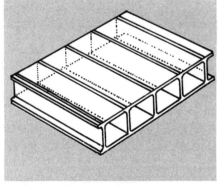

### POLYMETHYL METHACRYLATE (PMMA)

Polymethyl methacrylate is generally referred to in the trade as 'acrylic'. It is the material ideally suited for greenhouse covers, and may be the only real practical alternative to glass, except for its rather high price and certain technical installation problems. Single acrylic sheets transmit 90-95 per cent of available light and have about ten times the impact resitance with only half the weight of glass: 4.6 kg/m² (0.94 lb/sq ft). Rohm and Haas produces a double-fluted sheet of acrylic under the name SDP; the sheets are 122 cm (4 ft) wide and can be purchased in practically any length. As well, the sheets are nearly self supporting. Light

transmittance of double-fluted acrylic is as good as glass, but because of the reduced support material required, very high light levels can be achieved. Due to its fluted nature, the light inside SDP greenhouses is diffused, providing an even illumination throughout the greenhouse. SDP cannot be bent but can be curved by the manufacturer (on request). This material has a large expansion ratio; therefore, it cannot be fastened with screws or bolts. Rohm and Haas (Canadian rep.: Chemacryl, Montreal) has a wide range of special aluminum clamping devices designed to do this job. Price per square metre is rather high but, considering the savings obtainable through lighter construction, smaller foundations and increased light transmittance, this material is very attractive as a greenhouse cover. One of its major drawbacks is its flammability. Greenhouses near or attached to one's home, covered with this material may raise insurance premiums considerably.

### POLYCARBONATES

In many respects, polycarbonates are similar to acrylic, although their light transmittance is somewhat less and they do not support combustion. One type of polycarbonate sheet is identical to SDP and manufactured by the same company (Rohm and Haas). The other configuration looks much like coroplast (see RIGID PVC). It is called 'Qualex' and comes in a range of thicknesses from 3 to 7 mm (about ⅛ to ¼ in). Polycarbonates may eventually replace glass as a greenhouse cover. Tests done in Europe, where a number of greenhouses have been in operation with this material for several years, have provided very impressive results.

## SUMMARY OF PLASTIC AS A GREENHOUSE COVER

Sheet plastic finds a lot of application in the greenhouse industry. An interesting application is where a sheet of cheap plastic is applied over a glass roof and kept inflated by means of a small fan (see Figure 15-11). During the winter season, this provides savings in heating costs, although it reduces the amount of light transmitted. This same principle is also applied to greenhouses entirely covered with plastic. A double layer of plastic or glass can reduce heat loss by up to 40 per cent, providing the space

between the two layers is not larger than 7-10 cm (3-4 in). If the airspace is wide, convection flows reduce the initial savings. Often, there is not enough construction material available on the structure to provide this space. Conversely, if the two layers of plastic touch each other, condensed moisture will stick them together and nullify the objective. Small fans or complete kits are available from greenhouse suppliers.

Plastic sheets are available in rolls or in large widths. The ends are usually attached to the gables. The sides are often buried in the soil, stapled down with strips of wood, or attached with special clips available for this purpose (eg., polyzip, polylok, etc.). Plastic should be applied when it is warm and should be kept taut. Any wind movement on a cold plastic surface can damage it (especially in winter) and drastically reduce its usefulness. Before purchasing plastic material for a greenhouse cover, obtain sufficient information about the nature and chemical composition of the plastic. As is clear from the discussion, not every plastic can adequately do the job. If one has experience with a glass greenhouse, it may be found that general

## Figure 15-11
### DOUBLE LAYERED GREENHOUSE

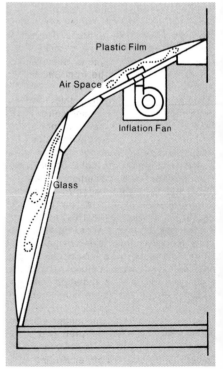

crop management in plastic greenhouses is somewhat different. Moisture has a tendency to build up rapidly in plastic greenhouses, so take care not to spill excessive amounts of water inside. This gives rise, especially in winter, to extraordinary amounts of condensation and troublesome drips on the plants.

## ENVIRONMENTAL DESIGN ELEMENTS

## LIGHT

Many of the greenhouse design criteria are based on the availability and behavior of natural light. Therefore, a discussion of the facts surrounding natural light, its qualities, quantities, duration, and how all these influence plant growth, is in order. If one obtains a good grasp of the various standards and their meaning, it also allows you to understand the use and manipulation of artificial light in greenhouses and other places where you may elect to grow plants.

### NATURAL LIGHT

Natural light (often referred to as white light) is a form of electromagnetic radiation plants receive from the sun. This electromagnetic radiation has specific vibration values. The wavelengths of these are expressed in different standards, often as multiples of the metre. Visible light is dealt with in wavelengths that range from 390 to 780 nm (nm = nanometre). Figure 2-2 in the Climate lesson identifies this range in millimicrons. The nanometre and millimicron are identical in magnitude. In normal circumstances, daylight does not display color to our eye and is often referred to as 'white light'. White light, however, is a combination of all the colors in the visible spectrum. Each of these colors has its own specific wavelength (see Figure 15-12). Although they don't have eyes, plants are photosensitive to a wider range of light than the human eye, especially in the 675 nm range. Certain insects and plants are receptive to the radiation found on either side of the visible light spectrum. On the short side, or blue end, is **ultra violet** (UV) and on the longer wave or red end is **infrared**. Infrared cannot be seen by the human eye, but we are often aware of it as a form of penetrating heat.

## Figure 15-12
## ELECTROMAGNETIC SPECTRUM

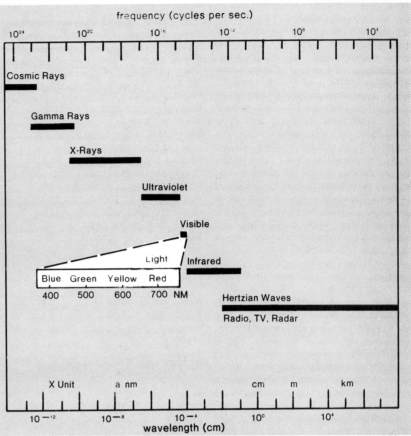

adapted from Withrow and Withrow, 1956

There are three main aspects of light that concern plant growth: quality, intensity and duration (photoperiod). The **quality** of light is important due to the specific sensitivity of plants to certain colors. Plants are also sensitive to the **intensity** of light they receive. This subject is a difficult one to deal with because different species of plants sometimes have very different and specific requirements concerning the amount (intensity) they require. The **duration** of light that a plant is subject to not only has an effect on its growth, but many growth processes (especially flowering) are strongly influenced by the length of exposure.

Plants are especially sensitive to two main radiation wave bands in the light spectrum: the blue (400-500 nm) and red (600-700 nm) wavelengths. Another problem, as far as natural light is concerned, is not only that the intensity during the winter season (Sept. to Feb.) is considerably reduced, but also that

the photoperiod is drastically shorter than in the summer. Compensation for short photoperiods can be achieved with practically any type of light of sufficient intensity.

**Quality** of light has an important influence on greenhouse design and operation. The fact that light consists of various colors, each with their own specific wavelength, is the principle behind the 'greenhouse effect'. Glass, the traditional greenhouse cover, does not transmit UV light, nor does it transmit IR radiation easily. As a consequence, plants grown in greenhouses are deprived of these types of radiation. However, it has not been proven that UV radiation is essential to the growth of plants. Far red and infrared radiation, due to their great intensity on certain days, can penetrate through the greenhouse cover and enter the greenhouse. Certain radiation is absorbed by the surface; the extent of absorption is determined by the type of cover (see GREENHOUSE COVER). Absorption of the IR radiation, in such cases, warms the area. The heat produced is a result of the absorbed IR radiation being re-radiated in the form of heat. Certain short wave radiation is re-radiated after absorption as long wave radiation. This phenomenon, combined with the fact that greenhouse glass does not transmit infrared radiation easily, is the reason why greenhouses get quite hot, even on rather dull days. It is the re-radiated infrared 'heat' that accumulates in the greenhouse and raises the temperature (greenhouse effect). The importance for knowing the level of absorption of IR radiation by certain greenhouse covering materials becomes apparent. Light shining on a greenhouse not only provides the plants inside with the required radiation, but that light also represents a free source of heat (see SOLAR HEATING).

**Intensity** is the term applied to the amount of actual energy received from the sun (natural light). Traditionally, horticulturists have accepted the footcandle (**fc**) as the standard for measuring intensity. This is a rather old-fashioned standard based on the amount of light (produced by one candle) reflected from a white 12 inch square piece of cardboard held 12 inches away from the candle. The amount of light reflected from full sunlight is 10,000 fc in midsummer. Although this standard does not take into account the quality of the light, most horticultural literature still uses it. The metric equivalent of the foot candle is lux (1 fc = 10.764 lx). Still other standards of light measurement are used for artificial light.

The Botany lesson deals with photosynthesis; what it does and how, and points out that photosynthesis increases with an increase in light intensity. The bothersome truth is that photosynthesis only increases up to a maximum intensity of about 4,000 fc. Any higher intensity does not increase the rate of photosynthesis. With that high light intensity there is also (usually) a large amount of heat produced on the surface of the leaves and inside the tissue of the plant, so much so that the plant uses a lot of energy to cool its surface. Less than half the available light is useful to the plant in midsummer! This is the reason why most greenhouses need some sort of shade on the glass in the summer. Duration varies with the seasons and the only

ways to control the period of illumination is either by shading the plants (see SHADING) or by providing additional artificial (electrical) light (see ARTIFICIAL LIGHT).

## ARTIFICIAL LIGHT
The natural light reaching the greenhouse during the winter months is especially lacking wavelengths in the red part of the spectrum. Therefore, the color compensation should (preferably) be in this wavelength. Until about 15 years ago, most of the artificial light used in greenhouses consisted of either fluorescent tubes (mainly blue radiation), or incandescent lamps (red light), or a combination of these two. Increasingly today, H.I.D. (high intensity discharge) lamps are being used in greenhouses and other plant growth facilities. Such lamps are available in two different types: mercury (blue) or high pressure sodium (red). Such lamps initially required extensive wiring and support work, which made making them rather expensive. Newer designs are more compact and cheaper, making them practical for the average hobby gardener. In order to provide a good insight into the advantages and disadvantages of the various types of lamps, each group is dealt with separately. At this point, it is useful to identify and understand the principle governing the relationship of intensities from a point source of light. The principle is referred to as the inverse square law. This law states: "Illumination from a point source is inversely proportional to the square of the distance between the

source and the subject". Simply stated, this means that if the distance between a lamp and the surface to be illuminated is doubled, the relative intensity is reduced four times (see Figure 15-13). Earlier it was stated that the footcandle is still the standard of light intensity used in horticulture. This is true when working with natural light but a different standard of intensity is used with artificial light because each lamp type has its own specific intensity output, and the typical spectrum (color quality) is also known. One of the standard units of energy used for artificial light is the watt (W). There is a close relationship between the energy potential of electrical power and the energy cycle in the plant. Therefore, the watt concept can be applied to a potential amount of plant growth.

All electrical lamps are identified by their wattage. Not all this energy can be transferred to visible light or even radiation visible by the plant. (There is a specific term one may encounter in horticultural literature indicating light to which plants are sensitive. The term is P.A.R. or **Photosynthetic Active Radiation**.) Some of the initial wattage is transferred into heat, some of it into sound and, often, there are energy losses in invisible light. For artificial lighting purposes, where the energy is lost is unimportant. Of consequence, however, is how much P.A.R. the lamp produces. As the electrical light is expressed in watts, it would be a bit confusing to express the P.A.R. output in watts as well. Therefore, the useful output (radiant flux) is expressed in

## Figure 15-13
## INVERSE SQUARE LAW

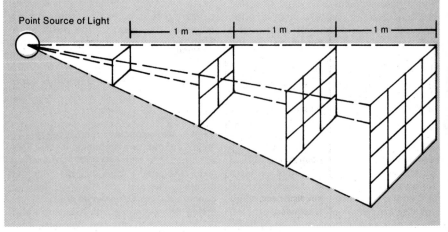

Point Source of Light

1 m    1 m    1 m

Table 15-1
## RECOMMENDATIONS FOR PLANT IRRADIATION

| Plant Species | | Required irradiance (mW/m²) | Annual Irradiance Period | Irradiance Time Per Day (including daylight) | Purpose and Method |
|---|---|---|---|---|---|
| **CUT FLOWERS AND POTPLANTS** | | | | | |
| Aster (Chinese aster) | young plants | 3000-5000 | Jan-March | 16 hr, followed by short days | improving vegetative growth and flower advancement. Short days after buds become visible. |
| Bedding plants | seedlings and young plants | 6000-10,000 | Jan-March | 16 hr | raising seedlings, improving vegetative growth and flower advancement in greenhouses and growing rooms. |
| Begonia | stockplants, cuttings and potplants | 7000-9000 300 | winter winter | 16 hr 16 hr | improving vegetative growth. preventing flower formation. |
| Bulbs: Tulipa Hyacinthus Narcissus (daffodil) Crocus | bulbs | 3000-5000 | Dec-Feb | 12 hr without daylight | flower forcing. |
| *Cactaceae* | seedlings and young plants | 14,000-18,000 | Sept-April | 16-18 hr | raising seedlings, improving vegetative growth, shorter culture time. |
| *Calceolaria* hybriden | potplants | 1000 | mid Nov-mid March | 16-24 hr | flower advancement. |
| *Chrysanthemum* | stockplants | 6000 | Sept-April | 18-20 hr (incl. photoperiodic lighting) | improving vegetative growth for good quality cuttings. |
| | cuttings | 6000-7000 | Sept-April | 18-20 hr (incl. photoperiod lighting) | improving vegetative growth for good quality cuttings. |
| | cut-flowers | 4000 | year round | 18-20 hr, later 12-14 hr (photoperiodic lighting) | improving vegetative growth, flower advancement, improving quality. |
| | potplants | 6000-7000 | Sept-April | 18-20 hr (incl. photoperiodic lighting) | improving vegetative growth, shorter culture time. |
| *Coleus* hybriden | potplants | 6000 | winter | 16 hr | improving vegetative growth. |
| *Cyclamen* persicum | seedlings and potplants | 6000 | Nov-Feb | 18 hr | raising seedlings and improving vegetative growth. |

| Plant Species | | Required Irradiance (mW / m²) | Annual Irradiance Period | Irradiance Time Per Day (including daylight) | Purpose and Method |
|---|---|---|---|---|---|
| *Dianthus* (carnation) | stockplants | 6000 | Sept-April | 16-18 hr | improving vegetative growth for good quality cuttings. |
| | cuttings | 6000 | Sept-April | 16-18 hr | improving vegetative growth and shorter culture time, rooting of cuttings. |
| | cut-flowers | 250-400 | Sept-April | 16-24 hr | flower advancement. |
| Forestry products | seedlings and cuttings | 9000 | Aug-March | 18-24 hr | raising seedlings and rooting of cuttings, speeding up growth. |
| (shrubs and trees) | young trees | 10,000-15,000 | Aug-March | 18-24 hr | prevention of dormancy, speeding up growth. |
| *Freesia* | cut-flowers | 3500-5500 | winter | 14 hr | improving vegetative growth, flower advancement, more and better quality flowers. |
| *Fuschia* hybrida | potplants | 1200 | Sept-Oct | 4 hr during night | flower advancement. |
| *Gladiolus* | cut-flowers | 8000-10,000 | Jan-March | 16 hr | flower advancement, improving vegetative growth. |
| *Kalanchoe* blossfeldiana | stockplants and cuttings, potplants | 4000 | Jan-March | 18-20 hr | deferring bud formation, improving vegetative growth, shorter culture time. |
| *Lilium* longiflorum | cut-flowers | 3000-5000 | winter | 16-24 hr | prevention of bud abscission, improving vegetative growth. |
| Lilium | cut-flowers | 8000-10,000 | after 6 wk, continuous lighting during | 24 hr during 4 wk | after bud formation, continuous flowering and vegetative growth are improved. Shorter culture time. |
| | cut-flowers | 300-500 | winter | 16 hr | flower advancement. |
| | cut-flowers | 5000-6000 | winter | 16-24 hr | improving vegetative growth, flower advancement, shorter culture time. |

| Plant Species | | Required Irradiance (mW/m²) | Annual Irradiance Period | Irradiance Time Per Day (including daylight) | Purpose and Method |
|---|---|---|---|---|---|
| *Orchis:* Cattleya Cymbidium Cyperidium Odontoglossum Paphiopedilum Phalaenopsis | seedlings and young plants | 7000-9000 | Sept-April | 16 hr | improving vegetative growth, flower advancement, high quality flowers. |
| Ornamental green plants | cuttings and young plants | 6000-9000 | winter | 16-18 hr | rooting of cuttings, improving vegetative growth. |
| *Pelargonium* | stockplants | 7000-9000 | winter | 16-18 hr | improving vegetative growth. |
| | cuttings | 9000 | winter | 16-18 hr | rooting of cuttings, better quality of young plants, shorter culture time. |
| *Rosa* hybrides | cut-flowers | 9000-14,000 | winter | 24 hr | high yields of good quality flowers. |
| *Saintpaulia* (African violet) | stockplants, cuttings and potplants | 5000-6000 | winter | 16-18 hr | improving vegetative growth for production of high quality cuttings, flower advancement, shorter culture time. |
| | potplants | 400 | 3 wk from mid Feb | 3-4 hr (night break) | flower advancement, 3-4 wk |
| *Sinningia* (gloxinia) | seedlings and young plants | 7000-9000 | Nov-Feb | 16 hr | raising seedlings, improving vegetative growth, flower advancement. |
| Succulents | seedlings and young plants | 9000-14,000 | winter | 16-18 hr | raising seedlings, improving vegetative growth. |
| **FRUIT AND VEGETABLES** | | | | | |
| Sweet peppers | seedlings | 20,000-40,000 | year round | 16-18 hr (without daylight) | seedling production in growing rooms. |
| | young plants | 6000 | winter | 14-16 hr | improving vegetative growth, harvest advancement. |
| Cucumbers | seedlings and young plants | 3500-6000 | Oct-March | 16 hr | improving vegetative growth, shorter culture time. |

| Plant Species | | Required Irradiance (mW/m²) | Annual Irradiance Period | Irradiance Time Per Day (including daylight) | Purpose and Method |
|---|---|---|---|---|---|
| Lettuce | seed production | 45,000-60,000 | winter | 16 hr | speeding up of culture time, 4-5 times. |
| | seedlings and young plants | 25,000 | winter | 24 hr (growing rooms) | improving vegetative growth, shorter culture time |
| | crop production | 7000-9000 | winter | 16 hr (greenhouses) | improving vegetative growth, shorter culture time. |
| Strawberries | fruit production | 200-350 | Jan-Feb | 15 min/hr (350 mW/m²) 8 hr/night continuously (200 mW/m²) | flower advancement, more and better fruit production. |
| Tomatoes | young plants | 6000 20,000 | Oct-Feb winter | 14 hr 14 hr (without daylight) | improving vegetative growth, shorter culture time (2 wk), more and better fruit production. |

milliwatts (one thousandth of a watt). It is also known how many milliwatts certain plants require to grow at their optimum rate (see Table 15-1). This amount of energy requirement is expressed as mW/m². The information in Table 15-1 is a compilation of information on the subject and should be used as a guide. Also, the information in Table 15-1 should not be considered in isolation as various environmental conditions, like temperature and humidity and the amount of available soil moisture and nutrition, can greatly influence the behavior of plants. Accordingly, if we have the mW output of a certain lamp, we can also calculate how many square metres such a lamp can illuminate to achieve a certain light intensity. Table 15-2 lists various lamp types and their radiant flux in mW.

## INCANDESCENT LAMPS

Through their extensive use for domestic purposes, incandescent lamps are familiar types of lightbulbs. They are one of the oldest electrical light sources. The principle of this light source is the fact that an electrical current is forced through a metal wire (tungsten). Internal resistance in the wire generates heat to such an extent that the light is emitted.

As a consequence, a tremendous amount of heat is also produced. Incandescent lamps are an excellent emitter of red light, although the intensity of the light is far from satisfactory for horticultural purposes. The amount of heat radiated by the bulb could cause injury to the plant if the bulb is brought closer to the plants (to improve the intensity). Incandescent lights have been used for a long time, mainly due to the fact that no other suitable sources of red radiation were available. They are far from satisfactory for our purposes! The life span of most incandescent bulbs is limited; if used on a 16 hour per day basis, they last usually no longer than 5-6 weeks. One type of incandescent lamp which may have applicaton in growth rooms is the quartz-iodine lamp. This tube-shaped lamp is available in 1000 W and higher capacity and can be, due to its high intensity, used some distance away from the plants and still provide enough light. The high wattage output can influence the air temperature of a small greenhouses. Under certain conditions, they can be combined with high pressure sodium lamps (see HIGH PRESSURE SODIUM LAMPS). Attempts have been made to produce combination lamps, with a normal screen base like that of incandescent bulbs, which also

contain a small mercury tube providing blue light. Such lamps are rather expensive and not generally satisfactory.

## FLUORESCENT LAMPS (TUBES)

Fluorescent lighting operates by a different principle than that of incandescent lamps. Fluorescent lamps consist of long, phosphor-coated glass tubes filled with low pressure mercury vapor. On either end of the tubes are metal electrodes. Initially, when starting the lamp, these electrodes are made to glow and start an electron current through the gas which radiates light in the 253 nm spectrum. This is invisible UV radiation. UV radiation activates the phosphorus coating, which starts to re-radiate in a different wavelength. It is this radiation that produces illumination. It may be of interest to note that this lamp is basically a short wave emitter (blue) and only by modification of the fluorescing phosphorus inside the tube can the radiation be shifted to a warmer (redder) light. Fluorescent lamps are, therefore, essentially a blue type of lighting with a shift into yellow and green light (550 nm). Various 'plant growth' tubes cannot provide enough red light to satisfy the plant requirements entirely.

Table 15-2

## RADIATION CHARACTERISTICS OF DIFFERENT TYPES OF LAMP IN THE WAVELENGTH BETWEEN 400 AND 700 nm

| Lamp Type and Denomination | | Approximate Power Consumption per Lamp, Ballast Included    W | Radiant Flux mW | Radiant Efficiency (of the total power consumed ballast losses included) mW/W |
|---|---|---|---|---|
| Incandescent | 60W | 60 | 3070 | 51 |
| | 100W | 100 | 5800 | 58 |
| | 150W | 150 | 9320 | 62 |
| | 200W | 200 | 13230 | 66 |
| | 500W | 500 | 34440 | 69 |
| Fluorescent | 40W | 51 | 6650 | 130 |
| (various types) | 40W | 51 | 8060 | 158 |
| | 40W | 51 | 7020 | 138 |
| | 40W | 51 | 9080 | 178 |
| | 40W | 51 | 7840 | 154 |
| | 40W | 51 | 6920 | 138 |
| | 40W | 51 | 7800 | 153 |
| | 40W | 51 | 9280 | 182 |
| Blended light | ML 250W | 250 | 18810 | 75 |
| (combination incand-fluor) | MLR 160W | 160 | 8400 | 53 |
| | MLR 250W | 250 | 13860 | 55 |
| High-pressure mercury | HPL-N 400W | 422 | 66700 | 158 |
| | HPLR 400W | 422 | 56000 | 133 |
| | HLRG 400W | 422 | 37800 | 90 |
| | HPI/T 400W | 425 | 91000 | 214 |
| High-pressure sodium | SON/T 400W | 436 | 110400 | 253 |
| | SON/H 330W | 352 | 69000 | 196 |

This type of lamp wastes less energy in the form of heat, and the tubes never get so hot that they cannot be touched. Accordingly, they can be brought very close to the plant without causing heat damage. They can be placed over plants on a window sill to provide an ideal source of supplemental light. One drawback of all discharge type lamps (like the fluorescent type) is that they are complicated electronic devices requiring a 'ballast'. The ballast consists of various circuits required for the starting procedure and to regulate the current. Discharge lamps without such control would burn brighter and brighter until they burnt up! Wiring and fitting fluorescent tubes, except when buying a complete unit, is complicated and, therefore, expensive. However, energy use is very economical as compared to incandescent lamps. One of the better aspects of fluorescent tubes is that they radiate light along the total length of the tube in all directions, thereby providing even illumination over a rectangular area, especially if reflectors (see REFLECTORS AND HOUSINGS) are used to concentrate lights below the light fixture (luminaire). In greenhouses, this is often not possible on account of the shadow factor of such luminaires. When comparing the amount of light produced by different types of lamps, keep in mind that the value of the radiant flux should be reduced by 50 per cent if no reflectors are used. Fluorescent tubes are available in several wattages; often two tubes are used per ballast (eg., 2 x 40 W). Fluorescent tubes are used to aid in crop production; in greenhouses, a solid bank of tubes is required to provide sufficient energy. Unfortunately, such banks can be a major shade factor and, since they are permanent fixtures suspended from steel cables, they cannot be removed when not in use. For many years, these were the most commonly used lights in greenhouses, but they were far from ideal.

## HIGH INTENSITY DISCHARGE (H.I.D.) LAMPS

H.I.D. lamps have been around for a long time and were primarily used for streetlights and illumination of large halls. Their application for horticultural purposes goes back only 25 years, and much of this was on an experimental basis. Serious commercial application is less than 15 years old. As explained previously, all discharge type lamps require ballasts; therefore, H.I.D. lamps are equipped with ballasts. There is a direct relationship between the wattage of the lamp and the size of the ballast. H.I.D. lamps used in greenhouses are usually of the 400 W type; the ballast for such a lamp is 15 cm x 15 cm and over 40 cm long (6 x 6 x 18 in) and weighs about 14 kg (30 lb). However, such 400 W lamps are only about 30 cm (12 in) long and, therefore, do not present much of a shade factor even when used with a reflector. Initially, H.I.D. lamps were fixed in the greenhouses and their ballasts

Figure 15-14
POWER DISTRIBUTION

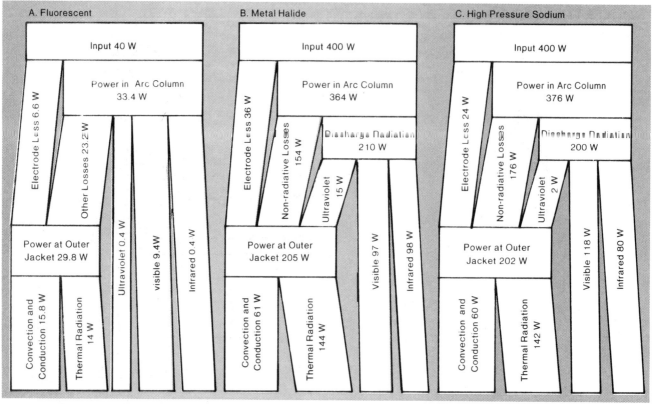

mounted out of the way. The ensuing wiring was expensive and required the services of an experienced electrician. Due to the high intensity of these lamps, it was often difficult to obtain even illumination on the plant bed, resulting in 'hot spots' and uneven crop production. Recent developments have removed most of the disadvantages mentioned. Therefore, H.I.D. lamps can now be considered one of the best light sources in greenhouses or other growth structures (see Figure 15-14). There are several types of H.I.D. lamps:

### HIGH PRESSURE MERCURY LAMPS (MERCURY FLUORESCENT)
High pressure mercury lamps were the first large (400 W) lamps used. In principle, they function very much like the fluorescent tubes, except that the entire lamp is not filled with mercury gas. Instead, they contain only a small, mercury gas filled quartz-glass bubble suspended in the centre of the lamp. This gas is under high pressure and, combined with the appropriate high voltage, produces a bright light. Most of this light, however, is in the UV range and, in order to turn this into a more useful radiation, the walls are coated with a fluorizing phosphor salt. The lamp, for technical reasons, must be used in an vertical position. Some of these lamps have silvered internal reflectors and do not need external reflectors. These lamps are usually ovoid in shape (see Figure 15-15).

### MERCURY HALIDE H.I.D. LAMPS
Mercury halide H.I.D. lamps are a logical development of the high pressure mercury type of lamp. The construction is very similar, but the small bulb in the centre contains not only mercury vapors, but also a halide which provides a shift in radiation towards the warmer (red) part of the spectrum. Accordingly, mercury halide lamps do not possess a fluorescent coating. Mercury halide lamps are available in the usual ovoid shape, but the tubular versions have become very popular due to their easier adaptation to reflector fitted luminaires (see Figure 15-15). These are the most widely used type of lamps where a blue type of light is required in horticulture.

### HIGH PRESSURE SODIUM LAMPS
For a source of red light radiation, high pressure sodium lamps are the best type to use. Their light discharge is not produced inside a quartz bulb, but inside a ceramic tube manufactured from polycrystalline alumina filled with a mixture of sodium, mercury and xenon. Sodium would corrode quartz glass. These lamps have a very high radiant flux and are useful for supplemental winter lighting in greenhouses. The starting current required is higher than that for mercury and mercury halide lamps, therefore the ballast required has to be larger. The emission from this lamp is in a very narrow spectral band (600 nm), with very little radiation in other color bands. Plants need a certain amount of far red and infrared radiation to complete certain biochemical processes (phytochrome). This red radiation is only required at the beginning and end of the photoperiod so

Figure 15-15
LAMP TYPES

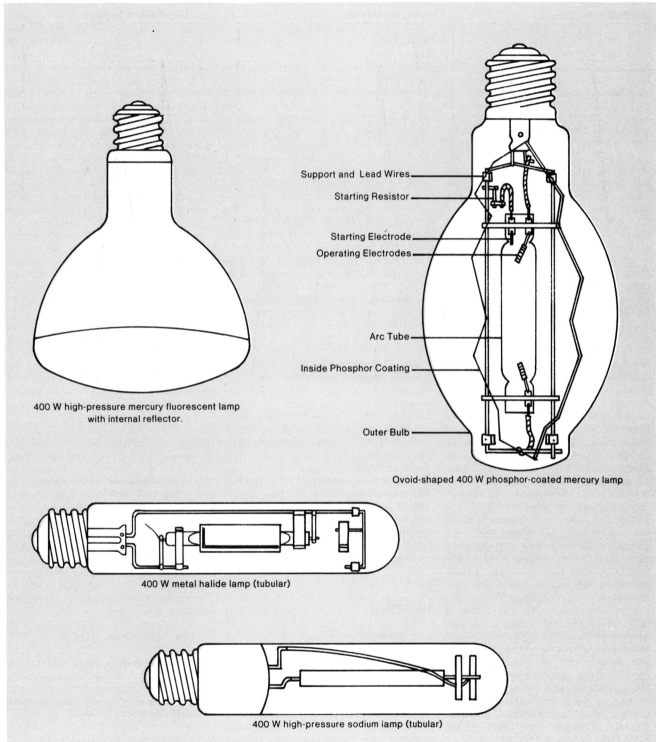

400 W high-pressure mercury fluorescent lamp
with internal reflector.

Support and Lead Wires

Starting Resistor

Starting Electrode

Operating Electrodes

Arc Tube

Inside Phosphor Coating

Outer Bulb

Ovoid-shaped 400 W phosphor-coated mercury lamp

400 W metal halide lamp (tubular)

400 W high-pressure sodium lamp (tubular)

if sodium-mercury halide combinations are used, it may be advisable to provide one short burst of light (10 minutes) from quartz-halogen lamps in the morning and another in the evening.

## REFLECTORS AND HOUSING

All the lamps so far described have not been exclusively designed for use in greenhouses and growth rooms. Most of the H.I.D. lamps have to be raised up to 4.5-6 m (15-20 ft) to provide an even distribution. Recently, a special reflector and luminaire has been developed for H.I.D. lamps. This reflector is in the shape of an internal Gothic arch and distributes light more sideways than down, resulting in an even distribution when hung about 2 m (6½ ft) above bench level. The luminaire contains the ballast and starter, allowing for a single plug-in installation. Units are light enough to be handled by one person, allowing for easy removal when not in use. These units are available in two models: mercury-halide or high pressure sodium. Called 'P.L. Lights', these units are also manufactured in Canada. Each unit costs about $250. This may seem expensive, but if one compares this with the cost of installing a comparable intensity of fluorescent-incandescent lamps, the latter would cost considerably more. Average life of H.I.D. lamps amounts to several years of use. The number of interrupting switches has a bearing on the expected life span. When installing or handling lamps, always make sure to wipe the surface with a dry cloth, as the oil from one's fingers may provide a different heat transmission rate thereby causing stress and, eventually, breakage of the lamp's surface. Another word of warning should be given about all mercury H.I.D. lamps. In cases where the outer surface of the lamp breaks, the lamp may still emit light, but anyone coming close to such a broken lamp may be subject to high doses of UV radiation and receive burns to the eyes or skin. It is expected that lower wattage mercury-halide and high pressure sodium lamps for horticultural purposes will soon become available. In fact, such lamps are presently available but are not housed in a suitable luminaire. The use of artificial light allows the year round usage of the greenhouse, providing adequate heating and cooling are available.

## CALCULATING ARTIFICIAL LIGHT REQUIREMENTS

The information concerning the various lamp types allows one to estimate the light intensity (more correctly called the 'irradiance'). Before this is possible, it is necessary to know what the requirements of plants are in mW/m² (see Table 15-1 and 15-2). Cucumber seedlings, for example, can be helped considerably if an irradiance of 45,000 mW/m² is provided for 24 hours during three days. In the period from November to February, vegetative growth of cucumbers can be improved by providing 14,000 to 22,000 mW/m² for the first 5-6 weeks (16 hours per day). Lettuce, growing under complete artificial light conditions or in greenhouses during the winter months, may require irradiances varying from 14,000 - 20,000 mW/m². Information concerning required light intensities is available in the commercial literature. There is, however, a lot of room for experimentation as practically every type of plant has its own requirements and differences can be expected even from one variety to another. Economy is also an important factor. Working out the investment versus the returns may cause one to reduce the amount of light to a point where it becomes profitable.

Example:

In a 2.5 m x 6 m (8 x 20 ft) = 15 m² (160 sq ft) we would like to grow lettuce during the winter under an irradiance of 12,000 mW/m². To provide enough light for the lettuce crop, we require 15 x 12,000 mW = 180,000 mW. 180,000 mW divided by 91,000 mW (the radiant flux of a 400 W high pressure mercury HPI/T from Table 15-2) = 1.98 lamps. Therefore, two 400 W high pressure HPI/T mercury lamps will produce the required amount of light.

# HEATING

If a greenhouse is a poorly insulated structure, it is difficult to heat in winter, cool in summer, and requires more heat than any other structure comparable in size. However, crops do require sufficient temperatures to maintain their rates of growth. Therefore, although the main purpose of a greenhouse is to gather light, providing the proper temperature regimes for plant growth is also a very important function.

At this point, you should identify what your requirements are. For example, you should have some idea of the types of plants you want to grow and whether or not you want to grow them year round. Plants have different temperature requirements (see GREENHOUSE PLANTS). For example, if seedless cucumbers are to be grown, then a 21°C night temperature must be maintained. Tomatoes can be grown at 17°C, while lettuce and Chinese vegetables require a 12°C night temperature. Similarly, bedding plants or potted plants (like geraniums or chrysanthemums) require a night temperature of 16°C. Thus, knowing the plants you want to grow and when you want to grow them helps you to select a suitable heating system. Most greenhouse plant growth problems under prairie climate conditions are related to inadequate heating systems. Large amounts of heat are required in winter. Thus, to maintain a uniform temperature throughout the greenhouse, the heating system needs to be carefully planned and designed.

Heating requirements can be calculated on an yearly, monthly or hourly basis. To accomplish this, inside desired temperatures, outside temperatures, the type of glazing material and surface area of the greenhouse should all be known. These factors determine the heating requirements.

Alberta Agriculture has a computer program available that calculates heat loss from a greenhouse. Through this program, information can be prepared on the heater size, monthly heating bills and on several other parameters. The program takes into consideration solar heat gain, maximum and minimum temperatures, wind velocity and several other relevant factors. To avail yourself of this service, contact your local district agriculturist or regional Alberta Agriculture engineer. Have information ready on:

- desired inside temperature

- type of glazing material for roof and side walls

- dimensions of greenhouse (height, width, length)

- orientation and location

- insulation

type of fuel available and cost per unit of fuel.

Other sources of assistance in planning heating systems are local greenhouse equipment suppliers and manufacturers, the local gas or electric company, and Alberta Agriculture's regional engineers and greenhouse specialists.

Regardless of the type of system used, the heat loss of the greenhouse has to be calculated in order to determine the size of heating unit needed. The following formula is used to determine the heat loss of a greenhouse:

$$Q = A \times B \times C \times W$$

$Q$ = heat loss in watts (W)

$A$ = the total exposed surface area (sidewalls and roof) of greenhouse in square metres (m²)

$B$ = the temperature differential between the coldest temperature outdoors during the period of greenhouse operation and the temperature desired inside the greenhouse (°C)

$C$ = the construction heat loss factor (W/m²°C)

```
single layer polyethylene 7.0
double layer polyethylene 4.0
old glass 8.5
new glass 7.0
rigid plastics 6.8
```

$W$ = The wind factor (average prevailing windspeed)

```
25 km/h    1.00
30 km/h    1.20
45 km/h    1.25
60 km/h    1.30
```

It is advisable to add 20-25 per cent to the calculated heat loss as a 'safety margin'.

To maintain a 35°C temperature differential, 350 W/m² are required for a glass greenhouse and 270 W/m² for a double polyethylene greenhouse. These recommendations are valid for most areas in southern Alberta, and are provided as guidelines against which comparisons can be made. Compare your calculations to these figures.

Since Canada has officially moved to adopt the metric system, the Btu is slowly disappearing. However, many of our heaters are manufactured in the USA or Britain where the Btu value is still very much in use. To convert W/m² to Btu per (square foot hour) divide W/m² by 3.155.

## TYPES OF HEATING SYSTEMS

There are several methods and systems available for heating or cooling a greenhouse, but before one can decide on a method and the type of equipment to purchase, performance requirements should be calculated. The type of heating system required depends on crops to be grown and glazing material used. Also, keep in mind that a large number of commercial greenhouse operations in Alberta began as hobby operations. So if you are considering a small greenhouse now and plan to expand it into a commercial greenhouse venture, then consider a good, expandable heating system right now.

### CENTRAL HEATING SYSTEM

Central heating, wherein heat is provided in the form of steam or hot water, is the system most commonly used in commercial greenhouses. The system consists of a central heater or boiler, a circulation pump, a heat exchanger (in the greenhouse to be heated) and controls. Typical heat exchangers are fin-tube convection pipes or unit heaters. Black iron pipe, used in many farm buildings, is not usually practical for a greenhouse.

Hot water heating systems are one of the most effective methods for heating large greenhouses but are not well adapted to small greenhouses because:

- they are very high cost systems

- small capacity boilers are not readily available

- most small greenhouses do not have room for enough fin-tube pipes and convectors (units heaters are cheaper and a better choice).

The exception is where the main residence is close and has hot water heating of adequate capacity. It can then be very practical to run another hot water circuit to a unit heater in the greenhouse.

If using hot water heating, select a heat distribution system in which the heat loss of the greenhouse corresponds to the heat output of the boiler or hot water heater. Heat output data for the heat exchanger, size of the heat exchanger, circulating pump capacity, expansion tank, valves, couplers, controls and installation details must all be considered. This requires competent design advice from an engineer or hot water system contractor.

Hot water heating systems can easily be adapted to provide bottom heat in the soil. Plastic or PVC pipes may be placed inside the soil and hot water run through them to keep the soil warm for plant growth.

### FORCED-AIR UNIT HEATER

Small oil- or natural gas-fired space heaters in the 5-20 kW range are ideal for heating small greenhouses (see Figure 15-16). Although the combustion efficiency of these unit heaters (65-75 per cent) may be lower than that of boilers, this system can be installed very economically. One major drawback is the lack of uniform heat distribution. A circulating fan hung over or behind the heater improves air circulation and heat distribution.

**Figure 15-16**
**NATURAL GAS HEATER**

Gas or oil heaters must be vented by an approved flue system outside the greenhouse. Provisions should also be made for fresh air to reach the burners. An opening of 10 cm² (1½ sq in) is needed for every 1000 W of burner capacity. Newer, sealed combustion units have provisions for fresh air at times of burning and are more energy efficient.

### INFRARED HEATERS

'Low intensity infrared heating' for greenhouses is a recent development. It is based on the principle that objects are primarily warmed by radiation emitted from a hot pipe rather than by convective heat transfer (see Figure 15-17). The heat radiated from the pipe is directed (by reflectors) toward the ground. Any object in its path is heated. The flue gases from the burners are exhausted outside the greenhouse.

Infrared heating systems are considerably more efficient than conventional boiler systems. (It should be noted that the existing burners can only burn natural gas or propane.) Uniformity of heat within the greenhouse is difficult to obtain and careful consideration to the layout of an infrared system is extremely important. Crops with a larger canopy, such as cucumbers and roses, may show signs of temperature stratification within the crop caused by interception of the radiation.

### Figure 15-17
### INFRARED NATURAL GAS HEATER

### KEROSENE HEATERS

In very small greenhouses or lean-to's, or where only a small amount of heat is required to keep out the frost, small kerosene heaters (which do not require a chimney) work satisfactorily and are fairly economical to operate. These heaters produce a certain quantity of fumes to which some plants are sensitive (eg., cucumbers, tomatoes, fuchsias and roses).

### ELECTRIC HEATERS

Electricity, although very convenient, is generally too expensive for heating. It can best be used in small, well built greenhouses (see Figure 15-18). Even in very small greenhouses, insulation, in the form of plastic stapled to the inside of the sashbars, should be used to reduce the heat loss. Electric heat supplied by soil-heating cables is the best way of providing bottom heat for a small propagating bed within the greenhouse.

### SOLAR HEATING

The sun is a ready source of heat that can be used in greenhouses. All greenhouses are 'solar heated' during the day in the sense that they trap energy from the sun, which is utilized to produce plants and to heat the air and objects inside the greenhouse. Solar heat gain is considered in the calculation for greenhouse heating requirements. Solar heat gain represents how much

### Figure 15-18
### SMALL ELECTRIC HEATER

heat is supplied through solar energy.

The greenhouse covering (glass or fibreglass), allows short wave visible radiation to enter the structure. Inside, light is absorbed by plants and other objects. It is later re-emitted as radiation of a longer wavelength (infrared), a large portion of which is low temperature thermal radiation or heat. Varying amounts of this infrared radiation (depending on the thermal transmission factor) remain trapped inside the greenhouse, heating the air and other objects. Even on a sunny winter day, a well-constructed, tightly sealed greenhouse can often capture enough heat to keep plants healthy during the day. At night, however, because a greenhouse (by itself) is a poor insulator, it rapidly loses the heat that it held during the day. Without supplemental heat, the temperature inside falls too low for plants to survive.

The goal for developers of solar heating, then, is to devise a system for capturing some of the excess heat during the day and storing it for use at night. This sounds simple in theory, but may be complicated in practice.

### PASSIVE AND ACTIVE SOLAR HEATING

There are two kinds of solar-heating systems - passive and active (see Figure 15-19). A **passive** system involves the uncontrolled storage of heat during the day and release of heat at night. An example of a passive system is installation of black-painted, water or stone-filled barrels in a greenhouse to collect and store heat. By definition, a passive system functions without the aid of external power devices, such as pumps or fans.

Figure 15-19
## PASSIVE AND ACTIVE SOLAR HEATING

Passive

heat storage (rocks)

solar collector

Active

STRUCTURAL VARIATIONS FOR MAXIMUM USE OF SOLAR ENERGY
Greenhouses can be made more efficient users of solar energy by varying some aspects of conventional greenhouse construction. Every possible effort should be made to reduce heat loss and to build the greenhouse to take maximum advantage of the solar energy available.

### Solar Heating Roof Angle
If the main concern is to maximize winter light, then a slope of 60° from the horizontal is recommended. This reduces the angle of incidence of winter light and increases light transmission. It also results in greater reflection of the hot, high-angled summer sunlight. However, in order to optomize light availability year round, an angle of 26° should be used (see ROOF ANGLE AND LIGHT TRANSMISSION).

### Solid North Wall
During the winter, much of the light comes from the south, especially at prairie latitudes. It is, therefore, possible to replace the heat-wasting north glazing with a well-insulated wall (see Figure 15-21). Lean-to styles are ideally suited to this purpose. To prevent the plants from straining towards the south wall (light source), the north wall should have a reflective inner surface (eg., aluminum foil, white plastic or paint) to bounce light onto the plants. This can increase the amount of light and solar energy in a greenhouse by 20-30 per cent on a sunny, midwinter day.

### Double Glazing
It is possible to reduce heat loss through the glazed surface of a greenhouse by using double acrylic or polycarbonate panels which contain a dead air insulating space (see SUMMARY OF PLASTIC AS A GREENHOUSE COVER). Avoid using two layers of fibreglass as the resulting heavy support frames necessary cause considerable shading. Also, consider using insulation at night, either on the inside or outside of the greenhouse.

Extra insulation can be provided at night (when heat requirements are greatest) by rolling insulatory blankets over the greenhouse, by snapping rigid styrofoam sheets on the inside of the structure, or by stretching a 'heat curtain' across the eaves to produce a flat 'fake' ceiling

**Active** heating systems involve collection of heat by a solar collector, transfer of heat to a storage device (rocks, water or chemicals) and release from storage into the greenhouse when needed through a distribution system. An active heating system is complicated and certainly more expensive than a passive heating system. It does, however, allow for better temperature control. True active systems require some form of power to transfer energy.

Many different 'solar' greenhouse designs have been tested and are 'technically feasible' (see Figure 15-20). On a commercial scale, it is not yet economical to have a greenhouse that is heated completely by solar energy. It will

be a while before such a solar heating system is designed and perfected for prairie climate conditions. Recent studies indicate that in milder climatic areas the point of a cost-effective system is being approached for at least some production systems. At present, however, unless a large and costly thermal storage system is designed, solar heating can only provide a percentage of the greenhouse heating requirements. To provide a partial supply of heat at night, a good rule of thumb is to plan for 50 L of water or 390 kg of rocks/m² (1 gal of water or 80 lb of rocks/sq ft) of glazed greenhouse surface. Ideas for some common active and passive solar-heated greenhouses are shown in Figure 15-20.

**Figure 15-20**

## SOLAR HEATED GREENHOUSE DESIGNS

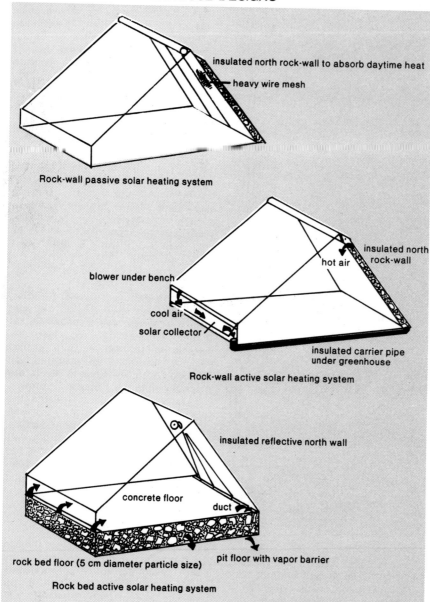

insulated north rock-wall to absorb daytime heat

heavy wire mesh

Rock-wall passive solar heating system

blower under bench

hot air

insulated north rock-wall

cool air

solar collector

insulated carrier pipe under greenhouse

Rock-wall active solar heating system

insulated reflective north wall

concrete floor

duct

rock bed floor (5 cm diameter particle size)

pit floor with vapor barrier

Rock bed active solar heating system

leaks between structural members or sheets of glazing materials which can allow heat to escape and cold air to enter (infiltration). Poorly constructed houses may allow two complete air changes per hour because of air gaps whereas, in a well-constructed unit, only half the air is changed per hour, resulting in a much lower heat loss.

If the greenhouse is to be operated during the winter, it is also recommended that the greenhouse be fitted with a double entrance, so that a resulting airlock buffers cold drafts when the greenhouse is entered.

**Brace Research Institute Greenhouse**
Figure 15-23 illustrates a greenhouse design developed by the Brace Research Institute at Macdonald College which incorporates all these structural variations for maximizing solar energy use (including roof angle at 35°).

In the experimental unit at Montreal, a reduction in heating requirements of 30-40 per cent has been found, compared with a standard gable, double-layered, plastic covered greenhouse. The University of Alberta's Devonian Botanic Garden utilizes a similar design.

## EMERGENCY HEATING
Unlike other buildings, a greenhouse cools very quickly at night when the heat is shut off. Since many of the plants grown in a greenhouse demand the maintenance of certain temperature levels, failure of the heating system could be dangerous. To reduce the danger of losing plants, consider installing an alarm system that is activated when heaters fail. Battery operated alarm systems should be checked regularly to ensure the batteries are working. If natural gas is being used for heating, install heating cables around the meter (if it is located outside). Water in the natural gas can freeze and stop the flow of the natural gas.

Having an adequate back-up system is a good idea. It may be a portable electric heater, a stand-by electric generator or a kerosene/propane burning unit. Because many other greenhouses may experience similar emergencies at the same time, it is better to own an emergency heater than to rely on obtaining a rental unit at critical times.

with a large, insulating air space above. Commercial heat curtains include a cotton-polyester blend or nylon with an aluminum facing to reflect the heat inward. Possibilities for preventing heat loss are only limited by imagination. Remember, during the daytime, allow maximum sunlight to come in.

### Heat Storage
Deep earth or rock floors (insulated beneath), raised planting beds and structural materials, such as rock, masonry and concrete, all store heat. Barrels painted black and filled with water are even more efficient (see Figure 15-22). The barrels can easily be arranged to support benches. To be most effective, incoming sunlight should strike all heat-storage materials directly.

### Sound Construction
A greenhouse should be well-constructed with few gaps or air

Figure 15-21
UNCOMMON, YET FUNCTIONAL SOLAR HEATED GREENHOUSE

Figure 15-22
STORING HEAT

Figure 15-23
SECTION VIEW OF BRACE EXPERIMENTAL GREENHOUSE

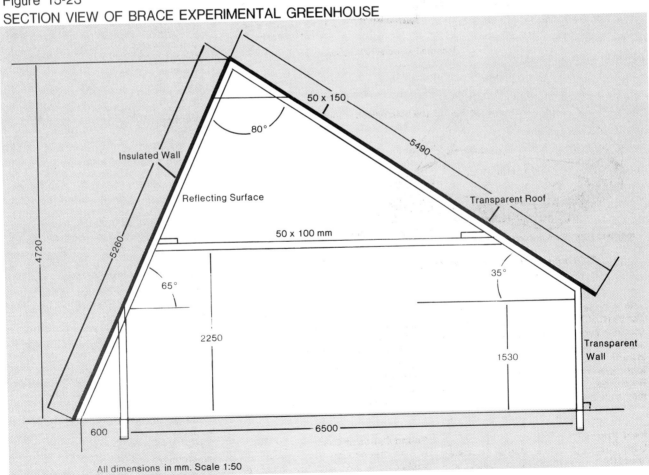

Burning newspaper inside the greenhouse to generate smoke can slow down the rate of drop in air temperature.

## COOLING AND VENTILATION

During periods of bright sunlight, air temperature in a greenhouse often rises above the outdoor ambient temperature due to the net influx of heat and the reduced air movement. Incoming radiation during summer months is approximately 17,000 kJ/m²/day (1500 Btu/sq ft/day) and is the primary cause of elevated temperatures. Plant temperature and that of the greenhouse air must often be lowered. This can be accomplished by both transpiration and mechanical means. Under optimum conditions, plant temperature can be regulated by the rate of transpiration. A full-grown crop can transpire up to 5 L of water/m²/day (16 fl oz/sq ft/day). This rate of evaporation provides about 12,500 kJ/m² (1100 Btu/sq ft) of cooling per day. The remainder of the heat load must be removed by mechanical means or excessively high temperatures will occur, thus reducing natural transpiration and plant growth.

Ventilation, the conventional method of lowering the temperature, is accomplished by drawing the cooler outside air into the greenhouse. Different methods of ventilation are available and vary primarily in their cooling capacity. When considering cooling for a greenhouse, it is important to appraise the different seasonal requirements. Ventilation must be considered a year round process. Generally, hobby growers install an inadequate ventilation capacity for extreme summer conditions. During the winter, however, a reduced capacity is needed to avoid excessive chilling. Winter ventilation is often used to reduce the relative humidity. There are three distinct systems whereby cool air is mixed with greenhouse air to reduce the temperature. Each system has its own characteristics and their selection depends on the final purpose.

### FORCED COOLING SYSTEMS

A forced cooling system, using electrical exhaust fans and inlet vents, is primarily used for cooling during periods of high temperatures. Ventilation is provided by electrical exhaust fans which are set in the side or end wall, and draw fresh air into the greenhouse from louvered or open ventilators on the opposite side or end wall (see Figure 15-24). To be adequate, the fan(s) must exchange the total volume of air in the greenhouse 1.5-2 times per minute. Since fans are rated by the volume of air they exchange per minute, determine fan size by calculating the greenhouse volume (cubic metres or cubic feet) and multiply by 1.5-2.0. The answer in cubic metres or cubic feet per minute is the fan capacity. Two speed or variable speed fans are preferred.

### Figure 15-24
### FORCED COOLING SYSTEM

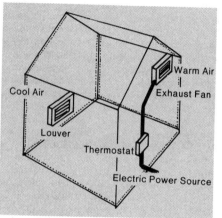

The exhaust fan system, similar in principle to a kitchen exhaust fan, draws out the heated air. Exhaust fans are installed high, near the roof line and above plant level to prevent drafts. A thermostat turns the exhaust fan on when a pre-set temperature is reached. A second vent - a louvered shutter - has movable horizontal flaps. When the exhaust fan starts, the flaps swing open because of the air pressure differential and cool air enters. This second vent is placed at a lower level, frequently below the benches. The cool air moving across the greenhouse mixes with the warmer air.

### CONVECTIVE COOLING

Convective cooling by roof and/or side ventilators utilizes the principle that warm air is lighter than cool air and, thus, warm air rises to the top of the greenhouse. An opening at the ridge of the greenhouse allows the warm air to

### Figure 15-25
### SIDE AND RIDGE VENTS

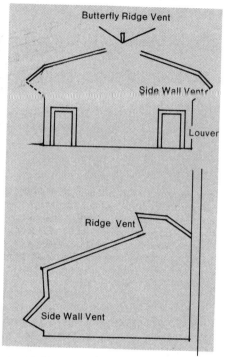

escape. The cold air is brought in through vents placed near the base of the greenhouse, either under or over the benches (Figure 15-25).

Ridge vents usually come with a notched handle and a prop, or a lever with a gearwheel to allow manual opening. By opening these vents, a warm-cool air exchange is established which provides fresh air for the plants. This air exchange creates air movement and circulation within the greenhouse. Since direct sunlight heats a small greenhouse very rapidly, a small greenhouse should have proportionately more ventilators than a large greenhouse.

A ridge vent system can be operated automatically by motor-run lifters triggered by a thermostat set to a desired temperature. Another automatic vent opener (called a 'heat motor') works without electricity or wiring. It consists of a tube filled with liquid that expands as the air temperature increases and contracts as it drops. The expanding liquid pushes a rod which opens the vent. With a dial, the device

## Figure 15-26
## PERFORATED TUBES

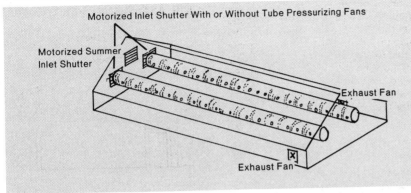

Motorized Inlet Shutter With or Without Tube Pressurizing Fans

Motorized Summer
Inlet Shutter

Exhaust Fan

Exhaust Fan

can be set to start opening at a desired temperature level. One advantage of automatic ventilators is that they keep the greenhouse from overheating during the day. When the greenhouse begins to cool off in the evening, they close and trap the remaining absorbed heat for use at night.

### FAN-JET SYSTEM
The fan-jet system consists of a tube-pressurizing fan, which is a perforated polyethylene tube and an air inlet shutter (Figure 15-26). The fan capacity should be about 0.4-0.6 m³ of air per square metre (1.3-2.0 cu ft/sq ft) of greenhouse floor area per minute.

The air inlet device consists of a spring-loaded shutter fastened to the exterior of the greenhouse and a tube housing fastened to the interior. The shutter device, which opens outward, may be motorized for automatic operation under thermostat and/or humidistat control. The shutters are always installed at the gable ends about gutter level. Usually, the shutters are opened at the first stage of cooling. A perforated polyethylene tube, 45 cm or more (about 18 in) in diameter, is fitted to the circular flange of the tube housing and suspended by wire the length of the house. The opposite end of the tube is tied off with twine.

Fans usually run 24 hours a day to provide air circulation within the greenhouse. The location of holes in the polyethylene tube determines the direction of the airflow. Air holes may have to be altered, depending on the

directional flow requirements. In larger, gutter-connected greenhouses, air flow should be directed just below the gutter, rather than against the greenhouse roof, to prevent excess heat loss during the winter. In gutter-connected greenhouses, fans may be positioned at alternating ends of adjacent greenhouses to provide better air circulation and temperature distribution.

### ALTERNATE COOLING SYSTEMS
Under prairie summer conditions, especially in June and July, greenhouse temperatures may rise above 30°C. Therefore, cooling is required (in addition to ventilation) in order to grow some plants. The following methods of cooling greenhouses are effective and commonly used.

### THERMAL CURTAINS
Greenhouses can be cooled by reducing the amount of incoming solar radiaton (see SHADING). Porous thermal curtains are excellent for reducing radiation influx. The main advantage to using a thermal curtain is the possibility of quick removal during occasional low light periods, often experienced in the spring and fall. Different shade cloths are available which reduce solar radiation by certain percentages. In summer, for example, a 50 per cent shade cloth is effective in reducing the temperature at the plant surface.

### EVAPORATIVE COOLERS
Evaporative coolers, usually called 'swamp coolers', are commonly used in Alberta. They require electricity to

operate. A fan, when activated by a thermostat, pulls air into the greenhouse through aspen fibre pads which are kept wet by water dripping from an overhead trough. Air moving through the water soaked pad is cooled as it absorbs some of the moisture. Not only does the evaporative cooling system cool the greenhouse, but it also provides some humidity. The aspen fibre pads must be washed down regularly to keep them from becoming clogged. Synthetic cooling pads are also available. Good quality water must be used with this system, otherwise the cooling pads can get clogged and reduce their efficiency. The pad and fan system can be purchased as separate components and mounted on opposite sides of the greenhouse (Figure 15-27), or as an integral unit called an 'Arctic cooler' (Figure 15-28).

If you plan to install separate pad and fan components, it is easy to determine the correct capacity needed. As described in the section on cooling, determine the fan size needed to provide two air changes per minute. One square metre of pad is needed for each 50 m³ (6 sq ft/1000 cu ft) per minute of fan capacity. Use 0.5 L of water per lineal metre (5.4 fl oz/lineal foot) of pad, regardless of pad height.

### Figure 15-27
### PAD AND FAN COOLING SYSTEM

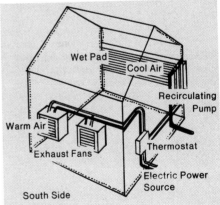

Wet Pad

Cool Air

Recirculating Pump

Warm Air

Thermostat

Exhaust Fans

Electric Power Source

South Side

### MISTING
A simple misting system can be set up to cool the greenhouse. Generally, a pressure of 500-1000 kPa (72-145 psi) is required to generate mist. The mist

## Figure 15-28
## ARCTIC COOLER

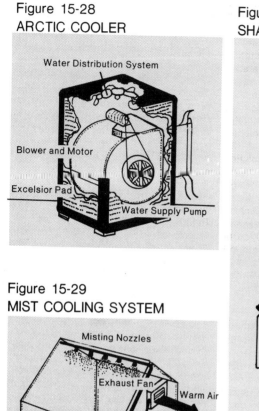

## Figure 15-29
## MIST COOLING SYSTEM

## Figure 15-30
## SHADING COVERS

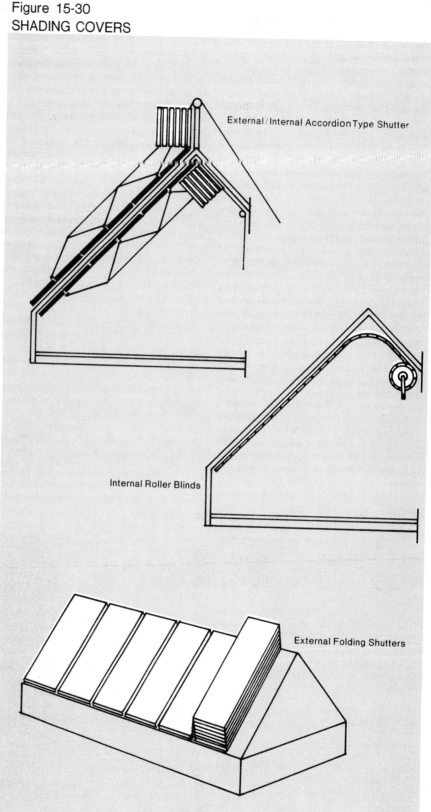

nozzles are specially made for this purpose and located at the ridge of the greenhouse (see Figure 15-29).

**HIGH PRESSURE FOGGING SYSTEMS**
High pressure fogging systems generate an extremely fine mist. The pump is able to generate pressures of 4000-8000 kPa (580-1160 psi) and is generally expensive. High pressure fogging systems are used mainly by commercial greenhouses, but a small system can be designed for hobby greenhouses.

## SHADING

Shading of greenhouses is necessary for cooling purposes. Shading helps to reduce the influx of light radiation and, thus, keep the air temperatures cooler. Besides cooling, shading helps to reduce sunlight intensity (see Figure 15-30). High light intensities are detrimental to plant growth. Shade should only be used between 10:00 a.m. and 3:00 p.m. in summer. However, larger greenhouses simply cannot afford the amount of labor required to manipulate the shades all day. Hobby greenhouse operators should, if possible, practice this. On a dark day, the shades should be left off all day. Certain plants are much quicker to photosaturate than others. The plant types adapted as house plants, in particular, are tolerant to low levels of light and are, therefore, also much sooner photosaturated. The need for elaborate equipment to obtain an idea of the point of photosaturation usually puts accurate determination out of reach of the hobby gardener. Careful observation, however, usually indicates if a certain method of shading is beneficial or not. The small home greenhouse, with a wide selection of plants, is much more difficult to manage in this respect than a greenhouse with a monotypic crop like chrysanthemums. To be on the safe side, start shading the greenhouse in the summer at about 9:00 a.m. and remove the shading at 5:00 p.m.

Glass houses frequently need shading more than greenhouses covered with rigid or film plastics. There are numerous ways of providing the needed shade, all equally satisfactory. Certain methods require more maintenance than others.

Whitewashing the greenhouse is perhaps the most widely used method of providing shade. During May, a white, paint-like solution is sprayed or brushed on the exterior of glass parts of the greenhouse. The whitewashing solution can be a commercial whitewash made for use on greenhouses, a white, cold-water paint, or a mixture of 1 kg of flour in 15 L of water (1 lb of flour / 1½ gal of water). A small sprayer can be used for this purpose. Whatever type of whitewash used, it gradually wears off as a result of rain and watering. If it hasn't all washed off by mid-October, scrape or scrub off any remaining paint. Sometimes, a good frost will remove it.

Besides whitewashing, several external or internal structures can provide shade: blinds made of wood strips, bamboo or aluminum slats; panels made of lath strips attached to the greenhouse (see Figure 15-31); shade cloth or saran cloth. Saran cloth is made from green or black plastic and comes in a variety of meshes, each providing a different degree of shade. Sometimes, only partial shading is required for a few plants. To accomplish this, the best method is to stretch pieces of shade cloth only over the plants that require shade.

## RELATIVE HUMIDITY

One of the most neglected factors in controlling the greenhouse environment is the regulation of relative humidity (RH). Relative humidity is the ratio of the actual amount of water vapor present in a given volume of air and the maximum amount which can be held in that volume of air at a given temperature.

Plants require a relative humidity of between 50-75 per cent for growth. Relative humidity above 75 per cent favors disease development; RH below 50 per cent causes stress on the plant and reduces its growth. For most greenhouse conditions, a rule of thumb is that for each °C increase in temperature, the RH drops about 6 per cent (the inverse is also true). These RH changes occur regularly in situations where different day and night time temperature regimes are established.

When moist air reaches its saturation point, condensation occurs on the cooler surfaces within the greenhouse. During daytime, leaves are usually warmer than the surrounding air but at night, the leaf temperature may drop 1-2°C below ambient air temperature. If the RH is near 95 per cent, condensation may easily take place on leaf surfaces. The presence of free water on leaves enables pathogenic spores to germinate and a disease problem may result. For example, a fungus called **Botrytis** (commonly called 'Grey Mold') attacks plants in the greenhouse when RH is above 90 per cent. The fungus can be controlled by increasing the night temperature 2-3°C so that the leaf surface is dried. Thus, increasing the temperature reduces the relative humidity and minimizes the chance of high RH related diseases.

Besides the direct effects of temperature on RH, there are other processes which have effects on the RH in the greenhouse. One of these processes is the evapotranspiration of the vegetated land surface, of which the transpiration from the plants is more important than the evaporation from the soil. Transpiration is important for the cooling of the plant and its surrounding air environment as heat is needed to

## Figure 15-31
## EXTERNAL SHADE ROLLERS

transfer water from the liquid to the vapor state. The rate of transpiration is highly dependent on the RH in the air. A lower RH creates a higher water vapor differential between the plant and the air and, thus, a higher transpiration rate. The same holds true for the soil.

The amount of water generated by evapotranspiration from a full crop of cucumbers, tomatoes, chrysanthemums and roses is considerable and under optimal conditions is estimated to be up to 5 L of water/m² (1 gal/10 sq ft) of greenhouse every 24 hours. **Optimal conditions are defined as a situation where there is an actively growing crop, sufficient moisture available to the plant, RH near 60-70 per cent and temperature about 20-25°C.** The transpiration rate is highest during daylight periods, although the amount at night can still be appreciable (5-20 per cent).

The natural exchange of air with the outside environment, especially during the winter, generally lowers the RH. The rate of air exchange depends on the air-tightness of the greenhouse and its exposure to wind. For single-layered glasshouses, 1.0-2.0 air exchanges per hour is normal and for double-skinned greenhouses (double polyethylene, double acrylic, etc.) 0.3-1.0 air exchanges per hour is normal.

Some water is lost due to natural air exchange and some due to condensation, but it is very easy to have greenhouse humidities near 100 per cent. High relative humidities are more common during the winter months. The normal procedure for the removal of excess moisture in greenhouses takes place by ventilation (which increases heating costs). Other methods, such as dehumidifiers or heat exchangers in fans, are currently cost prohibitive.

An excessively low relative humidity may occur when large amounts of dry air are allowed to enter the greenhouse. This may occur on a bright sunny day during the early part of the year. Too much ventilation can lower the RH too rapidly and burning of the tender foliage may result.

# GREENHOUSE MANAGEMENT

Greenhouse management involves:

- a maintenance program (electrical/mechanical/structural)

- sanitation and sterilization practices

- crop scheduling

- seedling health care

- transplanting

- nutrient/fertilizer preparation and application

- analysis of growing media at regular intervals

- crop maintenance - pollinating, pruning, training and harvesting

- pesticide scheduling/application

- timely trouble shooting.

For successful culture, a grower must understand the above mentioned management aspects. Timely trouble shooting is important. Assistance in diagnosing problems can be obtained by contacting the greenhouse crops specialists at the Alberta Horticultural Research Center at Brooks, Alberta Tree Nursery and Horticulture Center in Edmonton, or Regional Crops Laboratories located at Brooks, Olds, Vegreville and Fairview.

# GREENHOUSE SOIL

Most of the greenhouse crops in Alberta are grown in soil and, because of disease problems, many growers are switching to container growing. The main purpose of the soil is to provide a medium in which there is a proper balance between air, water and nutrients. When this balance exists, the roots can easily obtain their requirements of water and nutrients, and growth can be rapid. When the soil is in proper condition, it holds the optimum amount of air, water and nutrients, all at the same time.

A greenhouse soil should be a sandy loam with a high organic matter content (see Soils lesson, SOIL TEXTURE). A fine textured or heavy soil tends to

compact easily. It also stays wet during long periods of cloudy weather. In contrast, both air and water move freely and compaction is slight in a sandy soil, so roots are able to grow through the soil more easily.

By proper management, almost any soil can be made suitable for greenhouse production. Any soil, either in the greenhouse or in the field before being brought into the greenhouse, can be improved by the addition of organic matter. It should be kept in mind that the organic matter is primarily added as a soil conditioner, and not so much for its nutrient value. It takes several years to change the condition of a soil and the addition of organic matter to the soil should be a continuing process. Both light and heavy soils can be improved by organic matter. Heavy soil is opened up, that is, made more porous, and very light soil is better able to absorb and hold water and plant nutrients. The organic matter assists greatly in keeping the soil loose and holding water and nutrients in reserve for the plant.

## GREENHOUSE SOIL TESTING

Before planting greenhouse crops, it is advisable to have the soil tested in order that nutrient levels can be adjusted to the required levels. As only a small amount of soil is required for testing, it is important for the sample to truly represent the composition of all the soil in the area to be tested. To ensure this, take a number of samples from several areas of each greenhouse and bulk them. Then mix these sub-samples and take out the amount to be sent away. If the area is large and different soil textures are encountered, several samples should be sent. Samples should be taken at depths of 15-30 cm (6-12 in). It is preferable to dry them overnight before shipping. The final sample sent in for analysis should weigh from 200-500 g (7-17 oz) after drying.

A soil test should be done immediately after a crop is removed. The results of this test determine the nature and quantity of preplant fertilizers or manure to use. A second test should be done 2-3 weeks before planting and after soil sterilization (steam or chemicals) has been done (see SOIL STERILIZATION). In the case of fast growing crops like cucumber, weekly soil tests should be done for the first four weeks and monthly thereafter. Fertilizer schedules should be modified accordingly. A soil sample should also be taken whenever a fertility problem is suspected in a greenhouse.

When sent for testing, greenhouse soil samples receive priority and are analyzed in a different manner from field samples. It is very important, therefore, to identify them by filling in the greenhouse soil information sheet and labelling the containers as greenhouse soil samples as well, especially if they are sent under separate cover. Make sure that the requested information is Also provided. It will help you receive proper recommendations. A list of prairie soil testing laboratories is contained in the Soils lesson (see Soils Lesson, SOIL TESTING).

GREENHOUSE SOIL TEST RESULTS

Table 15-3 summarizes the accepted 'good' fertility levels for most greenhouse crops. Specific recommendations for balancing nutrients, correcting pH and improving soil texture are made for each soil sample sent. As different laboratories use different extraction procedures, it is therefore likely that recommended nutrient levels will differ between laboratories.

SOIL pH AND ITS CORRECTION

The term pH means the degree of acidity or alkalinity of the soil or growing media. It is measured on a scale of 0-14 with 7 being neutral (see Soils lesson, ADJUSTING SOIL pH, page 116). The

### Table 15-3
### RECOMMENDED FERTILITY LEVELS FOR A GROWING MEDIUM

| | |
|---|---|
| Ammonium nitrogen | 0-20 |
| Nitrate Nitrogen (ppm)* | 35-180 |
| Phosphorus (ppm) | 5-50 |
| Potassium (ppm) | 35-300 |
| Calcium (ppm) | 60-400 |
| Magnesium (ppm) | 30-200 |
| Sodium (ppm) | 0-30 |
| Sulfates -S, (ppm) | 30-60 |
| Nitrites (ppm) | nil |
| Chloride (ppm) | nil |
| Free Lime | trace |
| pH | 5.5-6.9 |
| Electrical Conductivity (mmhos/cm²) | 0.8-3.0 |

*Parts per million water extractable nutrients and salts in soil.

Courtesy of Alberta Agriculture

availability of many nutrients, especially micronutrients, is affected by the pH of the growing media. Cucumber, tomato and lettuce plants grow best at pH 6.0-7.0. In soilless mixes, the pH range is between 5.5 and 6.5.

The safest way to reduce pH is to incorporate acidic peat moss in growing beds prior to planting. Incorporate peat moss in the top 10-15 cm (4-6 in) of beds. Besides reducing pH, peat moss

application helps in the dilution of higher soluble salts.

Other precrop treatments to reduce alkaline pH are:

- finely ground sulfur    4 kg/100 m² (9 lb/1000 sq ft)
- aluminum sulfate    5 kg/100 m² (11 lb/1000 sq ft)
- iron sulfate  5 kg/100 m² (11 lb/1000 sq ft)

The application rates will reduce the pH by approximately one unit. Ground sulfur is the most commonly used. Its effect on pH becomes evident three to four months after application and generally lasts for one to two years.

When the growing medium is acidic (such as in prepared mixes), lime application is required. Use Table 15-4 as a guide for applying lime. The recommendations are made in terms of ground limestone, but dolomitic limestone may be substituted at par.

It is advisable for growers to conduct their own lime requirement test and allow for reaction time. Such a test can be conducted by analytical laboratories. Incorporating limestone into the soil does not immediately change the pH. The pH of some greenhouse soils may rise slowly for weeks after application. In some areas of the soil, the pH changes as soon as the limestone becomes moist. Hence, the root may pass through zones that differ widely in pH, absorbing the desired available nutrients from each zone.

### Table 15-4
### PREPLANT LIME APPLICATION FOR pH ADJUSTMENT TO 7.0 (NEUTRAL)

| Soil pH reading | SOIL TEXTURE | | | |
|---|---|---|---|---|
| | SANDS — | LOAMS — SILTY CLAY — LOAMS | CLAY — LOAMS — CLAY | ORGANIC |
| | kg of ground limestone per 100 m² | | | |
| 4.0 | — | — | — | 500 |
| 4.5 | — | — | — | 450 |
| 5.0 | — | — | — | 350 |
| 5.6 | 62.5 | 100 | 250 | 300 |
| 6.0 | 50.0 | 75 | 200 | 250 |
| 6.4 | 30.0 | 50 | 150 | 175 |
| 6.8 | 10.0 | 20 | 50 | 75 |

Generally, hydrated lime should not be used in greenhouse soil because it is much more reactive than limestone. Ammonium nitrogen is absorbed on the soil complex and hydrated lime may displace it in quantities sufficient to damage roots. Hydrated lime also increases soluble salts, often to dangerous levels. Furthermore, the rapid change in soil pH is seldom desirable. In the few instances where a crop is detected growing in an extremely acid medium, hydrated lime may be suspended in water at 1 kg/45 L (1 lb/4.5 gal) and applied at 200 L/100 m² (41 gal/1000 sq ft). This should be followed by an application of limestone to further correct the pH, assuming that the hydrated lime will have raised the pH 0.5 units.

Sphagnum peat moss is widely used in preparing various growing media. Its pH may vary from 3.0 to 4.5. As a general rule, 4 kg of dolomitic limestone/m³ of peat (as it comes from the bale) can be used (25 lb/10 cu ft). If the pH of the peat is below 4.0, increase limestone to 5-6 kg/m³ (3.1-3.7 lb/10 cu ft).

## SOIL STERILIZATION AND FUMIGATION

To prevent severe losses caused by soil borne diseases and nematodes, it is necessary to destroy as many of the causal organisms as possible by steaming or fumigating the soil between crops. Properly applied steam kills all living organisms in the soil and is still the most effective means of sterilization. With increasing fuel costs, however, chemical fumigation may appear more attractive.

The following rules must be followed to achieve satisfactory results:

- The soil temperature at 15 cm (6 in) depth must be 13°C or higher for successful treatment with chemicals.

- Soil must be in a loose condition so that penetration is complete. Sods, lumps and organic materials must be thoroughly broken up.

- If organic materials (compost, manure, etc.) are to be used, they must be incorporated before treatment so that recontamination does not occur.

- If straw is added, it must be well chopped and well decomposed before chemical fumigation.

- The soil must be moist, but not wet.

When soil is sterilized with steam or fumigated with chemicals, the number of soil micro-organisms is greatly reduced for the first few days. It then rises and eventually exceeds that of untreated soil. The first organisms to return after treatment meet no severe competition. Thus, if plant pathogens are among the first to recolonize the soil, they may develop rapidly and cause severe disease losses. It is important, therefore, that every effort be made to prevent disease organisms from gaining entrance to the soil. Pathogens can gain entrance to the soil by:

- splashing water

- infested cuttings

- soil in water hose

- infested containers, tools and equipment

- grower's hands and footwear

- placing containers on ground

- unsterilized covers

- infected plants or seeds

- spores in the air (*Fusarium oxysporum*).

## SOIL STEAMING

For soil steaming, use steam at a pressure of 48-83 kPa (7-12 psi). It is important to maintain a soil temperature of not less than 80°C (176°F) for 30 minutes throughout the soil or in ground beds to a depth of 36 cm (14 in). Use an accurate thermometer. Establishing this level of uniform temperature may require 4-8 hours, depending upon the soil texture. The most commonly used method of steaming is to cover the beds with a tarp and release steam inside. The penetration of steam by this method, however, is not very good. The best method is one in which steam is applied through a network of drain tiles. Such tiles should be laid approximately 60 cm (24 in) deep, at 60 cm (24 in) intervals

with a 5 cm (2 in) layer of gravel at the top. Steaming through drain tiles can achieve good penetration to control nematodes.

Particular care must be taken to adequately heat the soil adjacent to footings of walls, support poles and other underground structures. Escape of steam through blowholes in very loose, dry soil (eg., near heating pipes) should be prevented. Avoid oversteaming. Try to ensure that the temperature does not exceed 95°C (203°F) in any portion of the treated area.

Undesirable effects of oversteaming include:

- excessive ammonia release

- manganese toxicity

- increased total salts

- destruction of organic matter.

Leaching is usually required after steaming. Do not use ammonium fertilizers for at least two months after steaming because of the soil's lack of nitrifying bacteria which convert ammonium to nitrate nitrogen.

## SMALL SCALE SOIL PASTEURIZATION

Small quantities of soil can be pasteurized by baking soil in the oven:

1. Place 7-10 cm (3-4 in) of soil in a cake pan and moisten thoroughly (don't soak).

2. Cover with aluminum foil, insert a meat thermometer into the center of soil and place in the oven.

3. Set the oven at 93°C (200°F) and bake for one-half hour. Make sure the temperature in the soil mix does not go higher than 82°C (180°F) or beneficial bacteria will be killed.

4. Remove from oven and allow to cool.

For larger batches, small electric soil pasteurizers that heat 0.1 m³ (3.5 cu ft) at once can be used. Their operating cost is comparable to that of a home clothes dryer. Formaldehyde treatment is a simple and effective chemical soil treatment recommended for hobby greenhouses. Do not use in the greenhouse if plants are there or if there is a chance of fumes leaking into the house. Formaldehyde fumes are also harmful to humans, so it is advisable to work in a well-ventilated area and to wear a mask. Use 37-40 per cent formaldehyde as follows:

1. Dilute 14 mL in 1 L water (½ fl oz/qt).

2. Sprinkle the solution evenly over a layer of soil 2.5 cm (1 in) thick and 60 cm square (24 in square). Mix thoroughly (wear rubber gloves).

3. Place soil in a bucket that has been scrubbed with bleach.

4. Cover tightly with polyethylene and allow to stand for 24 hours.

5. Spread mix out and let stand until the odor of formaldehyde is completely gone. This may take two weeks.

## PRE-CROP APPLICATION OF STRAW, FERTILIZER AND MANURE

### APPLICATION OF STRAW
Straw is incorporated into soil to provide organic matter and to improve soil structure. Straw helps to loosen the soil and improve aeration. Wheat and barley straw are commonly used. Use 1 bale/10 m² (1 bale/108 sq ft). A bale is generally 18 kg (about 40 lb) in weight. Straw should be well chopped before incorporation. Straw can also be used as a mulch in growing beds to reduce weed development and diseases when, for instance, tomato crops are layered on the ground. Be sure that the straw is not contaminated with herbicide residues.

Decomposition of straw is a gradual process and extra nitrogen should be added to facilitate this process. If extra nitrogen is not added, the growing plants and decomposing straw compete for available nitrogen.

### APPLICATION OF FERTILIZERS
A soil test must be made before deciding on any precrop application of fertilizers. In general, less soluble fertilizers (such as superphosphate) should be incorporated (see Plant Nutrition lesson, APPLICATION OF FERTILIZERS). Nitrate and potassium are best applied at the time of planting (see Table 15-5).

### USE OF MANURE
Well rotted manure can be incorporated as an organic amendment and also as a source of potash and other nutrients. Manures are generally very high in salts like sodium and chloride. It is, therefore, very important that manure be analyzed **before application** and another soil test taken after incorporation. If sodium and potassium are above the recommended levels, leaching is recommended. **CAUTION**: If the growing medium is high in salts and the water is high in sodium, plant damage can occur as a consequence of the use of manure.

### STRAW BALE CULTURE
The use of straw bales often makes it possible to grow cucumber crops under conditions where cultivation might otherwise be very difficult, such as where the soil is cold or heavy, or is infested with pathogens. On the Prairies, straw bale culture has been used successfully to grow crops on nematode infested soils.

There are many advantages to straw bale culture. Straw bales provide a disease-free, well-aerated rooting medium and their use reduces the need for soil sterilization to control diseases. During fermentation of the straw, heat is produced directly under the plant roots and carbon dioxide is released. Both the extra heat and the carbon dioxide enhance plant growth (see PLANT NUTRIENT REQUIREMENTS).

Preparation of the bales involves the application of water and fertilizers to enhance fermentation of the straw. To initiate fermentation, greenhouse temperatures should be approximately 18°C. The schedule in Table 15-6 has proven successful for preparation of straw for use on cucumbers, tomatoes and lettuce.

The superphosphate and potassium nitrate may be omitted from the preparation treatment. However, the plants planted on those bales must be fed with readily available phosphate and potash much earlier than if these nutrients had been applied to the bales.

## Table 15-5
## SUGGESTED PRECROP FERTILIZERS

| Fertilizer | Major Nutrients Supplied | Effect on pH | Approximate Rate/100 m² |
|---|---|---|---|
| Superphosphate 0-20-0 | Phosphorus | no change | 25 kg |
| Gypsum | Calcium Sulfur | no change | 25 kg |
| Potassium Sulfate 0-0-50 | Calcium Sulfur Potassium | no change | 10 kg |
| Ground limestone | Sulfur Calcium | Alkaline | 25 kg |
| Dolomite limestone | Calcium Magnesium | Alkaline (slow acting) | 25 kg |

Use exact rates as determined by a soil test.

## Table 15-6
## BALE PREPARATION SCHEDULE

| FERTILIZERS | DAYS | | | | | | | | | | |
|---|---|---|---|---|---|---|---|---|---|---|---|
| | 1 | 2 | 3 | 4 | 5 | 6 | 7 | 8 | 9 | 10 | 11 |
| Ammonium Nitrate (34-0-0) | HEAVY | | | 140 g | water to soak bale | | 70 g | | | 70 g | |
| Superphosphate 0-20-0 | WATERING | | | 0 | | | 0 | water to soak bale | | 450 g | Water in, apply top-cap and plant |
| Potassium Nitrate 13-0-44 | DAILY | | | 0 | | | 0 | | | 370 g | |

For planting, a small amount of growing medium (called 'top-cap') is put on the bales just deep enough to take the ball of roots. This medium may be made of various materials, but the most suitable appears to be peat, thoroughly soaked and neutralized with limestone (about 9 kg or 20 lb of ground limestone per bale of peat). A mixture of equal parts sterilized soil, peat and sand has also proven successful. If the bales are set into a shallow trench, about 15-20 cm (6-8 in) deep, the soil dug out of the trench may be used as a top-cap, provided it is well structured and free from pests and pathogens. Some growers steam sterilize the soil top-cap and bale together.

The management of a crop growing on straw is more critical than for one growing in soil. More frequent watering and earlier and heavier feeding are required.

## SOILLESS MIXES

Soilless mixes consist of inert mineral particles, organic particles, and fertilizers, and are an alternative to soil. Soilless mixes are especially useful where significant deterrents to good production occur, such as inadequate drainage, unavailability of good soil or soil disease build up. Soilless mixes are pest-free (thus eliminating the need for pasteurization), lightweight, easy to handle and can be excellent for plant growth. However, since soilless mixes are inert (contain very little fertilizer and do not have the buffering capacity of soil), more attention must be given to the nutritional requirements of plants growing in a soilless mix.

The following materials are often used in soilless mixes: calcined clay, sand, perlite, vermiculite, peat moss, sawdust, bark, compost, viterra, charcoal and osmunda fiber. Fertilizer is either mixed in with these materials or added at watering time. A general purpose soilless mix formula is given in Table 15-7.

## Table 15-7
## A GENERAL PURPOSE SOILLESS MIX

| 1 cubic metre | |
|---|---|
| Peat (sphagnum) | 0.49 m³ |
| Horticultural Vermiculite | 0.49 m³ |
| Dolomite Limestone | 5.90 kg |
| Superphosphate 0-20-0 | 1.20 kg |
| Potassium Nitrate (13-0-44) | 0.90 kg |
| Chelated Iron | 37 g |
| Borax (Sodium Borate) | 37 g |
| Fritted Trace Elements | 110 g |

Fluff the baled peat before mixing. Mix very thoroughly. Calcite limestone can be used instead of dolomite, but then add magnesium sulfate at 3.0 kg per m³.

## PLANT NUTRIENT REQUIREMENTS

Plants need several nutrient elements to grow, flower and fruit properly. Those elements are: carbon, hydrogen, oxygen, nitrogen, phosphorus, potassium, calcium, magnesium, sulfur; iron, copper, zinc, manganese, boron, molybdenum and chlorine (see Plant Nutrition lesson, MAJOR AND MINOR PLANT NUTRIENT ELEMENTS and Table 4-2).

Carbon is provided by the carbon dioxide ($CO_2$) present in the air which contain about 300 ppm (parts per million) $CO_2$ (see FERTILIZER MANAGEMENT). In a greenhouse, carbon dioxide levels rise during the night, owing to release by the plants and by soil organic matter. If the greenhouse is kept closed during the day, carbon dioxide is rapidly depleted and may often be below 100 ppm on fairly bright days. This is the point at which the lack of $CO_2$ may become a limiting factor in plant growth. In hobby greenhouse situations, it may not be that serious unless artificial lights are used, wherein it may be difficult to size tomato and cucumber fruits. In commercial greenhouse situations, additional $CO_2$ must be provided to produce profitable crops. Research has shown that greenhouse crops will almost always be improved if $CO_2$ levels are raised to 1000-1500 ppm. The level to which the $CO_2$ concentration should be raised is dependent on the crop, light intensity, temperature and growth stage of the crop. $CO_2$ is taken up by the plant through pores in the leaves. These pores close if the plant is under water stress or if temperatures are excessive. Addition of $CO_2$ under either of these conditions is of no benefit. $CO_2$ should only be added when light is available. When ventilators are opened, it is not possible to maintain high $CO_2$ levels and $CO_2$ generators should be shut off when vents are open more than 20 per cent. Additional $CO_2$ can be obtained by burning natural gas, propane, or low sulfur containing kerosene. Pure $CO_2$ is available in cylinders. Addition of $CO_2$ should begin approximately one hour before sunrise and the system should be shut off one hour before sunset.

The rate of $CO_2$ supplementation is highly dependent on the rate of infiltration of outside air into the greenhouse. Assistance is available by contacting greenhouse specialists at the Alberta Horticultural Research Centre, Brooks or at the Alberta Tree Nursery and Horticulture Centre, Edmonton.

## FERTILIZATION

Most of the plant's nutrient requirements are provided through fertilizers, either pre-incorporated in the growing mix or through soluble fertilizers. Fertilizers can be classified as inorganic or organic. Organic nutrients are made up of natural plant and animal materials, such as manure, bones, ground fish, or dried blood. Inorganic fertilizers are chemical compounds, some of which are naturally mined materials while others are manufactured. Every fertilizer is described in terms of three nuumbers, for example, 10-52-10. These numbers represent the percentage of nitrogen (N), phosphorus ($P_2O_5$) and potassium ($K_2O$), the three nutrients used in largest quantities by plants. Products that contain at least these three nutrients are called complete fertilizers and are generally recommended for plant growth (see Plant Nutrition lesson, INORGANIC FERTILIZERS).

Fertilizer can be applied as dry granules, diluted liquids, dissolved crystals or slow-release pellets. Dry granules do not provide nutrients immediately because they must first become dissolved in the water around soil particles before they are available to the plant. Liquid feeding, such as by dilution of a fertilizer concentrate or crystals, allows for more frequent feeding than dry granules and,

thus, better control of plant growth. These types of fertilizer are also immediately available to the plant because they are already dissolved in water.

Another means of keeping nutrients constantly available for plant growth is through the use of controlled or slow-release fertilizers. This type of fertilizer is especially useful with soilless mixes that allow rapid drainage of water from the bed or pot and, thus, much fertilizer loss.

Organic fertilizers are much less concentrated and must be broken down by soil micro-organisms into a chemical form usable by plants. These two qualities make it difficult to overfertilize plants with organic fertilizers. Inorganic fertilizers are in the chemical form usable by plants and, as such, are much faster acting than organic fertilizers. Although some organic gardeners make a distinction between organic and inorganic nutrients, the plant is able to take up each nutrient in one chemical form only; the source is irrelevant to the plant. The fruit of plants grown with organic fertilizers are not necessarily of better quality or nutritional value than those grown with inorganic fertilizers.

### FERTILIZER MANAGEMENT

A growing medium nutrient analysis should be used as a guide for supplying fertilizers. If nutrient levels are low, apply enough to bring them to the acceptable range (see Soils lesson, SOIL TESTING). The management principles are as follows:

- High nitrogen - low potash fertilizers are used when vegetative growth of a plant is required under good light conditions. For example, fertilizers like 27-14-14, 20-10-10 (where nitrogen is two times more than potash) are used in summer when you want to grow plants. Such fertilizers should not be used in winter light conditions.

- Medium nitrogen - medium potash fertilizers are those where nitrogen-potash ratios are equal. For example, 20-20-20 and 10-10-10 type fertilizers are used to maintain growth. These types of fertilizers are commonly used in summer, early spring or fall.

- Low nitrogen - high potash fertilizers are those in which potash levels are 2-3 times higher than nitrogen. For example, 13-0-44 and 3-15-27 are high potash fertilizers used in winter and when the plant is flowering or fruiting.

- High phosphate fertilizers are used when root growth is desirable (eg., seedlings after transplanting). High phosphate fertilizers include 10-52-10, 15-30-15, and many others.

A commonly used measure in fertilizer management is parts per million (ppm). It is a measure of concentration of a chemical. There is a simple formula to calculate parts per million of a nutrient. Basically, one milligram of a chemical in a litre of water equals one ppm. Naturally, the purity of a chemical also affects the concentration, so milligram per litre is the same as grams per thousand litres. For example:

The results of a nutrient test in a growing mix indicated a nitrogen level of 50 ppm. To raise the levels to 150 ppm nitrogen, 100 ppm are required. To get this nitrogen from 20-10-20 fertilizer, use the following formula:

$$\text{grams of fertilizer} = \frac{\text{ppm desired} \times \text{litres of water}}{\text{grade of fertilizer} \times 10}$$

ppm desired = 100 nitrogen
litres of water = 100 L
grade of fertilizer = 20 per cent nitrogen

$$\text{grams of fertilizer} = \frac{100 \times 100}{20 \times 10} = 50$$

Thus, 50 grams of 20-10-20 fertilizer dissolved in 100 litres of water will supply 100 ppm of nitrogen.

The frequency of fertilizer application varies with the type of plant, growth stage, light conditions and many other factors. If a few plants are involved, use the label direction. In commercial production, a test should be taken and recommendations followed.

Regular application of fertilizers prevents nutrient deficiencies but it commonly results in sufficient build up of fertilizer salt in the medium to cause plant damage (especially in beds and containers without free drainage). The first symptom of excessive salt build up may be slow growth, yellowing of the

# CORNELL MIXES

From *Hobby Greenhouses in Alberta*
Agdex 731-5.

The Cornell Peat-Lite Mix* is formulated for growing tropical plants. The Foliage Plant Mix** and the Apiphytic Mix** formulas are adapted specifically for their respective plant types and are modifications of the original peat-lite mix.

Cornell has used Osmocote 14-14-14 and Peters 14-7-7 fertilizers with the tropical plant mixes with good results. Other fertilizers are omitted with the exception of dolomitic limestone and 20 per cent superphosphate which are added to adjust the pH and to maintain adequate phosphorus levels. A trace element mix is added to assure a balance of minor elements. Trace element mixes can be purchased from specialty gardening centers.

*"Cornell Tropical Plant Mixes" by Russell C. Mott
**L.H. Bailey Hortorium, Cornell University, Ithaca, New York

## CORNELL PEAT-LITE MIX

Mix ½ cubic metre each of sphagnum peat moss and perlite or vermiculite. Add 6 kg dolomitic limestone, 2.4 kg ammonium nitrate, 1.5 kg superphosphate, and 0.3 kg potassium chloride (omit if using vermiculite).

## SUGGESTED SOIL MIXES FOR VARIOUS PLANTS

| PLANT | SUGGESTED MIX |
|---|---|
| **African Violet** | 1/3 soil, 1/3 peat, 1/3 perlite or sand |
| **Azaleas** | peat |
| **Bedding Plants** | 1/3 soil, 1/3 peat, 1/3 perlite |
| **Begonias** | 1/2 soil, 1/2 peat |
| **Bonsai** | 1/3 soil, 1/3 sand, 1/3 peat |
| **Foliage Plants** | 1/2 peat, 1/4 vermiculite, 1/4 perlite |
| **Gardenias** | 1/2 soil, 1/2 acid peat (pH 4.5-5.0) |
| **Cattleyas** | 1/2 perlite, 1/2 firbark, osmunda or peat |
| **Cymbidiums** | 1/3 fir bark, 1/3 osmunda or redwood fiber, 1/3 perlite |
| **Seed Germination** | 1/2 fine sand, 1/2 peat |

## UNIVERSITY OF CALIFORNIA SOILLESS MIX (TO MAKE 1 CUBIC METRE)

| MIX | POTASSIUM NITRATE g | SINGLE SUPER-PHOSPHATE kg | DOLOMITIC LIME kg | CALCIUM CARBONATE LIME lb | GYPSUM kg | pH | FINE SAND cubic metre | PEAT MOSS cubic metre |
|---|---|---|---|---|---|---|---|---|
| **Rooting cuttings** | 300 | 1.5 | 0.9 | — | 1.5 | 7.0 | 1 | — |
| **Bedding Plants** | 220 | 1.5 | 2.7 | 0.7 | 0.7 | 6.8 | 3/4 | 1/4 |
| **Potting Plants** | 150 | 1.5 | 4.5 | 1.5 | — | 6.5 | 1/2 | 1/2 |
| **Transplanting, Seed Germination** | 150 | 1.2 | 3.0 | 2.4 | — | 6.0 | 3/4 | 1/4 |
| **Azaleas and other acid loving plants** | 20 | 0.6 | 1.5 | 3.0 | — | 5.7 | — | 1 |

*To each mix also add 1.5 lb. of blood meal or Hoof 'n Horn and 115 g of potassium sulphate.

## CORNELL FOLIAGE PLANT MIX

The Cornell Foliage Plant Mix was developed for those plants that need a growing medium with high moisture-retention characteristics. Plants having a fine root system or possessing many fine root hairs are included in this group.

| Material | 1 cubic metre |
|---|---|
| Sphagnum peat moss (screened ½" mesh) | 0.5 m³ |
| Horticultural vermiculite (No. 2) | 0.25 m³ |
| Perlite (medium grade) | 0.25 m³ |
| Ground dolomitic limestone | 4.9 kg |
| Superphosphate 20% (powdered) | 1.2 kg |
| Fertilizer (10-10-10) | 1.6 kg |
| Iron sulfate | 0.4 kg |
| Potassium nitrate (14-0-44) | 0.6 kg |
| Granular wetting agent | 0.9 kg |
| Trace element mix | according to label instructions |

## CORNELL EPIPHYTIC MIX

The Cornell Epiphytic Mix was developed for plants that require good drainage, aeration and have the ability to withstand drying between waterings. Plants having coarse, tuberous, or rhizomatous roots are in this category.

| Material | 1 cubic metre |
|---|---|
| Sphagnum peat moss (screened 2.5 cm mesh) | ⅓ m³ |
| Douglas fir or white fir bark* (about 0.5 cm size) | ⅓ m³ |
| Perlite (medium grade) | ⅓ m³ |
| Ground dolomitic limestone | 4.2 kg |
| Superphosphate 20% (powdered) | 2.7 kg |
| Fertilizer (10-10-10) | 1.5 kg |
| Iron sulphate | 0.3 kg |
| Potassium nitrate (14-0-44) | 0.5 kg |
| Granular wetting agent | 0.9 kg |
| Trace element mix | according to label instructions |

* Fir bark comes from Douglas fir, white or red fir, or redwood, ground and screened to a definite size. Finely ground bark (about 0.5 cm) has a dry weight of about 200 g per L³. Fresh bark has a pH of about 5.0. Upon weathering, it becomes slightly more alkaline. The bark contains some nutrients, but these will not meet the requirements of growing plants.

leaves, or wilting. As the salt concentration increases, symptoms can also include leaf scorch, leaf shed and plant collapse. Salts from the water supply can compound the problem. Excess salts can be removed by leaching the growth medium (see WATER QUALITY).

# WATER

## WATER QUALITY

Large quantities of water are used in a greenhouse for irrigation and fertilization. Have your water analyzed through your nearest district extension office. Ask for an analysis for irrigation purposes, along with an additional analysis for boron. Send a copy of the analysis to the greenhouse specialists at the Alberta Horticultural Research Center, Bag Service 200, Brooks, Alberta T0J 0J0 or Alberta Tree Nursery and Horticultural Center, R.R. 6, Edmonton, Alberta T5B 4K3, for interpretation of the results. The following broad guidelines can be used in the interpretation of water quality.

1. Electrical Conductivity (EC) of the water: For waters having a Sodium Absorption Ratio (SAR) of less than 6.0:

- Water with an EC of 0.8 mmhos/cm or less is considered suitable for irrigation of cucumber, tomatoes and lettuce, under normal use conditions.

- Water with an EC between 0.81 and 2.2 mmhos/cm is considered usable for irrigation, but only when accompanied by special management practices.

- Water with an EC above 2.2 is not recommended as the sole source of water for irrigation. Consider collecting rain water from the roof of your greenhouse to mix with such water.

2. Special Management Practices:

- Provide adequate drainage.

- Never allow the growing medium to become more than moderately dry. Maintain a higher moisture level in the rooting zone of plants than would be necessary with higher quality water. Reduce stress by designing a well drained mix.

- Analyze soil samples periodically to monitor the salt level.

- Leach periodically to remove excess salts from the medium. Use Table 15-8 as a guide.

## ACIDIFYING WATER SUPPLIES

Most of the water in prairie cities is alkaline and moderately hard - it contains moderate amounts of calcium and magnesium. However, most rural water supplies are soft in nature, that is, they contain moderate or large quantities of sodium. Soft water or chemically softened water is not suitable for growing plants.

Hard water can be used for growing plants but calcium can result in several problems, all of which can be alleviated by acidifying the water supply. Remember, water pH also affects the activity of chemical sprays. Many chemical sprays remain active longer in lower pH solutions than in high pH solutions.

The calcium in Alberta water supplies, for example, is largely in the form of calcium carbonate or bicarbonate which precipitates out as the familiar white deposit of calcium carbonate. The continued use of hard water for irrigation can lead to an accumulation of calcium in the growing media, unless it is leached out by heavy nitrogenous feeding. When hard water is used for misting purposes, it can leave white scales on leaf surfaces, thereby reducing photosynthesis.

Carbonates and bicarbonates interfere with the absorption of fertilizer as the amounts of these materials in the water become greater. Generally, there are few carbonates in water until the pH of the untreated water is above 8.3, but carbon dioxide in the air dissolves in water and makes bicarbonates with various minerals in solution. Acidification of the water with phosphoric or sulfuric or nitric acid is a means of overcoming the injurious effects of carbonates or bicarbonates by neutralization. Do not add acid to the fertilizer concentrate tank. Contact the greenhouse crops specialists at Brooks and at Edmonton, for calculating the exact amounts of acids needed. General guidelines are given in Figure 15-32. Figure 15-32 is a typical graph for a water sample containing 100 ppm of calcium. Here, 275 mL (9.7 fl oz) of concentrated nitric acid are required to bring the pH to 5.9.

## Table 15-8
## EFFECT OF EC ON WATER QUALITY

| EC OF WATER MMHOS/CM | PARTS PER MILLION SALTS (PPM) | LEACHING REQUIREMENTS % | RECOMMENDED LEACHING INTERVAL | INTERPRETATION OF WATER QUALITY |
|---|---|---|---|---|
| 0.35 | 245 | 5.0 | 12 weeks | excellent |
| 0.40 | 280 | 6.0 | 9 weeks | very good |
| 0.60 | 420 | 7.5 | 6 weeks | good |
| 1.00 | 700 | 12.5 | 4 weeks | fair |
| 1.40 | 980 | 17.5 | 3 weeks | permissible |
| 1.80 | 1280 | 22.5 | 2 weeks | permissible |
| 2.20 | 1540 | 27.5 | 1 week | excessive - too salty |

## Figure 15-32
## EFFECT OF ADDING ACID ON pH OF A WATER SAMPLE

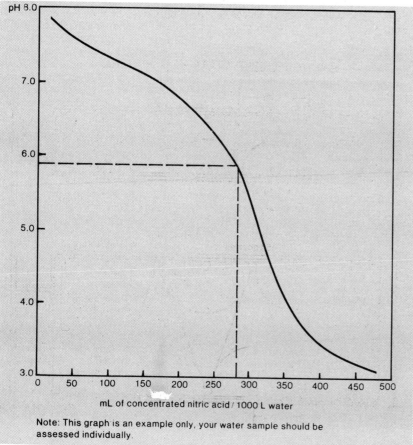

mL of concentrated nitric acid / 1000 L water

Note: This graph is an example only, your water sample should be assessed individually.

This also provides 60 ppm of nitrogen. The graph is only an example. Your water supply should be assessed individually.

PHOSPHORIC ACID
Phosphoric acid can be added through a fertilizer injector. An injector with two heads is suitable. Use injector heads meant for acids. An analysis of the water in terms of carbonate hardness is needed and can be obtained by subtracting noncarbonate hardness from total hardness. Generally in Alberta, 2-6 mL/100 L (0.03-0.09 fl oz/10 gal) of 85 per cent phosphoric acid is adequate for pH control.

NITRIC ACID
Concentrated nitric acid (70 per cent w/w) can also be used to acidify water. It also provides some nitrogen feed, helping to offset the cost of applying the acid. For each 1000 mL of concentrated nitric acid added to 1000 L of water, 220 ppm of nitrogen is supplied.

To accurately assess the amount of nitric acid required for your particular water supply, contact your local government or university extension office.

## SULFURIC ACID

Sulfuric acid can also be used to lower the pH of water. The amount has to be calculated based upon individual water quality. If sulfates are more than 100 ppm, then the use of sulfuric acid should be avoided.

## HYDROCHLORIC ACID

The use of hydrochloric acid should be avoided because of its chlorine content.

**Remember, concentrated acids are dangerous chemicals and must be handled with care. Always add acid to water, not water to acid. Acidified water is corrosive and may eat away the metallic components of your irrigation system.**

## CHLORINATION

Chlorination of city water to reduce the population of various micro-organisms is accomplished by dissolving chlorine gas (under pressure) in the water. The amount that goes into solution is relatively small and, although there may be a decided chlorine taste or smell, the water is safe for plants.

## FLUORIDATION

Fluoridation of water is common in many city water supplies and is included to minimize tooth decay in children. When water is fluoridated, sodium fluoride is added to provide about 3 ppm of fluoride in the water. The fluoride content is not harmful to cucumber plants.

## BORON

Boron is a fertilizer element which occasionally occurs in such quantities in Alberta water supplies as to be phytotoxic. When the level of boron is one or more ppm, the water is considered unsatisfactory for use. There is no inexpensive method for removing boron and an alternative source of water must be considered.

## SODIUM

Sodium is another element that is usually present in well water throughout much of Alberta. It is not required for plant growth and can reach levels that are toxic to plants. If sodium is above 100 ppm, reverse osmosis should be considered to remove it, or an alternate source of water found. Water with up to

100 ppm can be used if the potassium level is maintained above that and special management practices are followed (eg., regular leaching, good drainage, etc.).

## POLLUTANTS

Pollutants of various kinds, some of which are toxic to plants, may be found in certain water supplies. Such materials may have been discharged inadvertently into a stream or buried where it later infiltrated into the ground water. Long lasting herbicides, like Picloram (Tordon), can pollute water supplies and cause serious damage to crops. The best means of detection is to conduct a biological test with water intended for irrigation. Grow seeds of tomato and fababeans. Watch for any abnormal growth symptoms, such as crinkling of new leaves or abnormal spindly leaves. This can serve as a test of the suitability of your growth medium as well.

## WATERING SYSTEMS

In a small greenhouse, the traditional method of watering has been the watering can and garden hose. This is probably still the best method unless a large number of plants are being grown.

Be sure to use a water breaker to reduce the force of the water when using the watering can method.

If you have many plants or take frequent vacations, consider installing an automatic watering system such as spray nozzles, spaghetti tubes or a capillary mat (see Figure 15-33). A time clock wired to a solenoid valve automates the watering system.

A line strainer (to filter out sand and dirt) should be used with any watering system. Irrigation nozzles may also become plugged when using hard water. Acidification of the water with phosphoric or sulphuric acid is a means of overcoming this problem (see WATER QUALITY).

To warm the water before use, store it at room temperature for a day or install a hot water line and mixing valve. If large quantities of water are required, instant hot water natural gas heaters are also available.

## MIST NOZZLES

With a mist nozzle system, a polyethylene or PVC pipe is clamped on both sides of the bench. Nozzles that

## Figure 15-33
## AUTOMATIC SPRAY NOZZLE WATERING SYSTEM

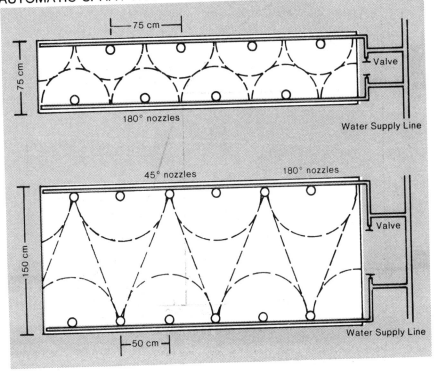

spray in a half circle (180°) are inserted every 75 cm (about 30 in) along the pipe. Benches wider than 75 cm (about 30 in) may need to alternate 180° nozzles and 45° nozzles, spaced 50 cm (about 20 in) apart to cover the bench area. Select nozzle size to suit your watering requirements. Spray nozzles are used for large scale watering purposes. Fine mist nozzles are used on propagation benches.

## SPAGHETTI TUBES

The spaghetti tube system conveniently waters potted plants or can be set up to water larger plants in ground beds. Small plastic tubes with weights on the end are inserted into the main polyethylene tube that runs down the center of the bench. Each weight holds a tube in a pot and helps spread water evenly (see Figure 15-34). Up to 400 pots can be watered from a 20 mm (¾ in) supply line. The system can be automated by using solenoid valves and time clocks.

## SUB-IRRIGATION SYSTEMS

Several sub-irrigation systems can be installed to water plants in a greenhouse. Sub-irrigation is a system used to flood benches for a certain period of time; let the water seep into pots and then let it drain out. Capillary mats are commonly used in this type of system. Installing a capillary watering system involves the layering of a fibreglass or matted-fibre mat that permits the movement of water from the mat to the plant through holes in the

bottom of the pot. The mat can be flooded or spaghetti tubes laid on the mat and the water turned on long enough to keep the mat moist. Careful attention must be given to the growth medium in the pot when using capillary matting. Heavy mixes do not drain properly. Algae and disease organisms may build up on the mats. Disinfectants, such as bleaches, may be used but should be hosed off after sitting for 5-10 minutes.

## WATER QUANTITY

Water is taken into plants through the roots and eventually lost (transpired) through the leaves in the form of water vapor. Physiologically, there should be a balance between the amount of water available in the soil and the amount transpired. If there is too much water, the roots cannot get oxygen and the plant drowns. If there is too little water, the plant wilts.

The amount of water a plant needs is dependent upon stage and rate of growth, the container used, environmental conditions and the growth medium. For example, germinating seeds and rapidly growing plants require a lot of water. Bright light and high temperatures increase transpiration and, thus, the need for water increases. A plant growing in very porous mix needs more water than a plant growing in a less porous one.

It is easy to identify when a plant is receiving too little water; however, it is difficult to tell when a plant is receiving

too much. The simultaneous presence of the following symptoms indicates overwatering: yellowing of leaves, leaf drop, sparse and weak root system, and soft or rotten large roots. Another sign of overwatering is oedema (see Plant Nutrition lesson, ABSORPTION). Oedema occurs when the plant takes up more water than it can transpire, causing water to accumulate in leaf cells until they burst. A brown corky-like growth often forms over the damaged cells. Oedema is more prevalent when the soil temperatures are warmer than the surrounding air temperatures.

To reduce the possibility of overwatering, use only pots with drainage holes. Water thoroughly until water drains from the pot and water again only when the top 2.5 cm (1 in) of soil becomes dry. Infrequent, thorough waterings are much better for most plants than frequent, light waterings.

## GREENHOUSE PLANTS

The biggest concern a hobby greenhouse grower must attend is deciding what NOT to grow. Consider the following points before making a decision:

- Different plants require different temperatures to grow well. For example, warm season crops (cucumbers, melons, tomatoes) prefer a temperature range of 20-27°C. Cool season crops, like lettuce, prefer a temperature range of 10-15°C. Whatever you decide to grow, identify the temperature requirements for germination, growth and flowering. Provision of proper growing conditions is very important to successful greenhouse gardening.

- Light is also an important environmental factor for plant growth. Different plants have different requirements for light. Do not try to raise shade-loving foliage plants along with plants which require high-light conditions (like tomatoes, roses, or carnations).

- To save on fuel costs, consider closing your greenhouse for part of the winter. For example, grow annual bedding plants and vegetable seedlings from February to June. Follow these crops with cucumbers,

## Figure 15-34
## SPAGHETTI TUBE WATER SYSTEM

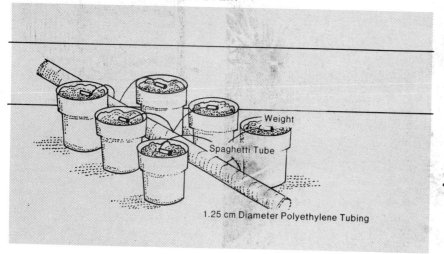

Weight

Spaghetti Tube

1.25 cm Diameter Polyethylene Tubing

tomatoes or peppers during the summer and, perhaps, move in potted chrysanthemums for late fall bloom. After this crop is finished, close the greenhouse.

Again, to reduce fuel costs, you can use your greenhouse in the winter only for carrying over dormant plants, such as fuchsias, geraniums, azaleas and chrysanthemums. Supply just enough heat to prevent freezing.

## ORNAMENTALS

### ANNUAL BEDDING PLANTS

Preparations for planting annual bedding plants must be started in late February; however, all bedding plants should not be seeded on the same date (see Vegetables lesson, Table 11-9). This is because each plant requires a different length of time from sowing to blooming. Adjustments may need to be made to suit the conditions of individual greenhouses. Sowing the seed too early is a common mistake made in handling annuals.

Plastic or clay flower pots (with drainage holes) or flats may be used. A 9 cm (3½ in) pot normally holds a sufficient number of seedlings of any one kind for most home gardens, but a 13 cm (5 in) pot may have to be used for large seeds. A

good soil mix contains one part pasteurized loam, one part peat moss and one part coarse sand. A soilless mix may also be used (see SOILLESS MIXES). Scatter the seeds thinly over the surface. Cover the seeds with growing mix to a depth twice the diameter of the seed. Very fine seeds need no cover.

After sowing, stand the containers in about 3 cm (about 1 in) of water and let the water soak up from below. Cover the flats with polyethylene, glass or newspaper to help maintain even moisture and temperature conditions and to protect them from direct sunlight. Remove the cover as soon as the seeds germinate.

Seeds of most annuals germinate readily at warm temperatures (18-22°C). Some plants, however, prefer slightly cooler or slightly warmer temperatures (see Figure 15-35).

These plants prefer cooler temperatures (7-10°C):

| | |
|---|---|
| Arctotis | Gypsophila |
| Centaurea | Iberis |
| Clarkia | Nemesia |
| Consolida | |

## PROPAGATION FROM CUTTINGS

from Hobby Greenhouses in Alberta
Agdex #731-5

Cuttings from most of your plants will root easily, provided they are given bottom heat and a moist temperature. A soil-heating cable is the most convenient way to provide heat. A single length of 250 watt heating cable is sufficient for about 2.3 m² of bed area. The cable should be first covered with 5 cm of sand. Ten cm of rooting medium should be placed over the sand and a tight-fitting glass or plastic cover placed over the cuttings with not more than 15 cm of air space between the surface of the rooting medium and the glass. Shade cuttings from direct sun. Cuttings will root more rapidly if dipped first in rooting hormone. If the area required for cuttings is very small, a light bulb placed in a flower pot or a tin can under the flats of cuttings will provide enough heat for a flat or two of cuttings.

### PROPAGATING CASE

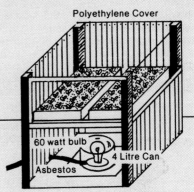

top of box is heavy tin, wood sides

Figure 15-35
BEDDING PLANTS

Courtesy of Alberta Agriculture

These plants require warm temperatures (21-27°C):

| | |
|---|---|
| Amaranthus | Gaillardia |
| Browallia | Helichrysum |
| Callistephus | Impatiens |
| Celosia | Lobelia |
| Cleome | Nierembergia |
| Cobaea | Petunia |
| Dahlia | Rudbeckia |

Transplant the tiny seedlings 5-8 cm (2-3 in) apart as soon as the first true leaves appear (the second visible set of leaves). Do not wait until these leaves have fully developed or the plants will be set back when they are moved. Drop the temperature to 13-15°C after transplanting to provide for optimum plant growth. As the weather becomes warmer, gradually expose the plants to cooler temperatures beginning three weeks before planting out in order to harden them off. Plants moved directly from the heat of a greenhouse to the garden are soft and are likely to wilt severely or die when set out.

### AFRICAN VIOLETS (Saintpaulia)
African violets are easy to propagate and grow. Use a soil mixture with a large amount of compost or peat moss, such as two parts peat moss to one part potting loam and one part sharp sand or perlite. A uniform moisture level is important during growth; however, keep them on the drier side after blooming. Avoid splashing cold water on the leaves. A night temperature of 18°C and a daytime range of 22-24°C are preferred. Although they need shade during most of the year, provide maximum light during the winter months to improve flowering. Fertilize regularly with a fertilizer higher in phosphorus than it is in nitrogen. Propagate well known (named) cultivars from leaf cuttings or crown divisions any time. Propagate new cultivars from seed (see Plant Propagation lesson, DIVISION CUTTINGS).

### BULBS (forced)
The two bulb groups are:

1. **tender tropical types**, including amaryllis, lachenalia, tuberous begonias, clivia, crinium, eucharis, tuber roses, gloriosas, haemanthus, neomarcia, freesia, oxalis, callas, achimenes and gloxinias. These bulbous plants can be grown indoors

all year round, although they go through a dormant period where the foliage dies down; and

2. **hardy bulbs**, including tulips, hyacinths, narcissus (or daffodil), and crocus. These plants are brought inside or bought in the fall and forced to bloom indoors during the winter months.

Select plump, sound bulbs free from blemishes; avoid very small ones. Bulbs are planted sometime in the fall, depending on when you want them to bloom. Store them dry in a cool, dark place until planting.

Bulbs require porous soil and do not thrive in a heavy, compacted medium. All bulbs do well in a good loam mixed with coarse builder's sand and peat moss or leaf-mold. Special bulb fiber (composed of peat, charcoal and oyster shell) may be used in place of potting soil. If fiber is used, place a 2.5 cm (1 in) layer of soil or sand in the bottom of the pot first.

Bulbs can be grown in any type of container. The roots are not long so the pot need not be deep. Pot diameter should be just large enough to hold all the bulbs without allowing them to touch each other or the sides of the pot. To pot, half-fill the container with sterile potting mixture or moist bulb fiber. Set the bulbs closely together on this layer but do not allow them to touch. The exception to this rule is with hyacinth, narcissus and amaryllis bulbs, whose necks should protrude through the soil level. The material around the bulbs should be firmed just enough to give them support.

After planting, water thoroughly and place in a cool (5-10°C), dark location. Keep the soil moist. When a strong root system is established and about 5 cm (2 in) of top growth is visible, move them into subdued light at 10-15°C for two or three weeks. When flower buds are well out of the necks and show some color, move them into full light at a temperature of about 18-20°C. The buds will then begin to open. Pay particular attention to water needs.

Daffodils, crocuses and muscari develop stronger, healthier stems and flowers if they are kept at cooler temperatures (near 15°C). After blooming, the flowers fade and should be removed. Continue to

water the plants while the foliage ripens. When the plant dies down completely, remove the bulbs and store them in a cool, dry place. Plant them outside in September (see Herbaceous Ornamentals lesson, TENDER BULBOUS ORNAMENTALS). It is not advisable to force bulbs a second year, but they will flower outside the following spring if properly ripened-off at the end of the forcing year.

### CACTI AND OTHER SUCCULENTS
Succulents (which include cacti) are plants which have thick, fleshy stems or leaves. They can survive in less than optimum growing conditions but maximum sunlight and warmth (21-24°C) are required for optimum growth.

Succulents should not be watered until the upper 1 cm (about ½ in) of soil feels completely dry, since they are very susceptible to stem rot as a result of overwatering. A moist, stuffy atmosphere may also cause this problem, so ventilation must be adequate.

A porous and well-drained soil mixture is needed for succulents. The best combination is one part loam, one part peat moss, and two parts coarse builder's sand.

Most succulents have a dormant period, usually during winter when light intensity is low. Careful observation is necessary to detect the signs of oncoming dormancy (growth slows and the plant may shrivel slightly). At the beginning of the resting period, gradually reduce water to about one light watering every one or two weeks, just enough to keep the soil from completely drying. Oedema (tissues swollen with water) is not an uncommon occurrence on cacti, particularly during the winter when light is low. To prevent this, avoid overwatering and do not allow soil temperature to rise above that of the surrounding air. When growth resumes, gradually increase watering again.

Succulents can be raised from seed but growth is slow. Bottom heat, shade, and an even moisture supply are needed for seed germination. Cuttings root well. Take cuttings with a clean, sharp knife and let them dry in a warm, dry place until a callus or skin has formed over the cut surface. Insert shallowly into a propagating mix, such as coarse sand or half peat and half sand. Transplant soon after rooting. Protect cuttings from direct sunlight, keep the soils lightly moist, and give them bottom warmth. Ventilation is essential to prevent basal decay. Many cacti produce plantlets that can be removed and inserted into the rooting medium.

Christmas cacti and forest-growing tropical cacti require quite different treatment from that described above. Most of the Christmas and tropical types require some shade during the hottest part of the year. They should not be allowed to dry out, although less water is required after completion of summer growth. A good potting mix for these types of cacti is one part loam, two parts peat and two parts coarse builder's sand.

### GERANIUMS
Geraniums require high light intensities to grow well. They can be grown from cuttings or seed anytime. Also, geraniums grown outdoors can be dug up and potted before winter and carried over in a cool greenhouse until spring. It is possible to take cuttings in late August to produce stock for planting indoors next spring. After rooting, pot in 10 cm (4 in) pots. Geraniums are very susceptible to viral, fungal and physiological disorders. If foliage becomes spotted or mottled, destroy the plants and start again with clean stock. Avoid overwatering.

Day temperatures for optimum growth should be 19-21°C and night temperatures should be 10-13°C. Use soluble fertilizers (such as 20-20-20) once every two weeks from March through October at a rate of 5 g in 1 L of water (0.8 oz/gal). Reduce fertilization in the winter.

### GLOXINIA
Gloxinias belong to the same plant Family as African violets and like the same environmental conditions. Plants grown from seeds take six months to flower, while tubers are much quicker.

For the growing medium, use two parts of soil, two parts of peat moss and one part of sand. Good commercial mixes are also available. After flowering, the plants should be kept drier and cooler to induce dormancy. The tops will die down and just enough moisture should be applied to prevent the tubers from

shrivelling. Tubers can either be allowed to rest where they are or stored out of the way in closed plastic bags filled with barely damp peat moss or vermiculite. Repot when new shoots start to appear (usually in 2-4 months). Propagate continuously blooming plants from leaf cuttings or from seeds anytime.

### ORCHIDS
Orchids are an interesting group of plants (see Plant Propagation lesson, ORCHIDS) which, in their natural habitat, grow on trees and absorb most of their nutrients from particles or organic matter carried to their large, fleshy roots by rain. The white, corky layer on the roots absorbs moisture readily. The leaves are usually thick and fleshy, helping to carry the plant through periods of drought.

Most orchids like a humid atmosphere, but temperature requirements vary. Some orchid types like a night temperature of 15°C, and 21°C in the daytime. The heat-loving types require a minimum night temperature of 21°C.

Most orchids are not grown in soil but are potted in ordinary clay pots, using chips of fir bark or osmunda fiber. Occasional feeding with a weak fertilizer solution may be required.

### TROPICAL FOLIAGE PLANTS
Tropical foliage plants require warm temperatures, shade and a moist atmosphere. The night temperature should not be below 16°C. There is an endless variety of tropical foliage plants that can be grown easily. Some of the commonly known types are the philodendrons, rex begonias, tropical ferns, many varieties of dracaena, and the green or variegated rubber plants.

Most require a well-drained soil mix containing plenty of peat moss. They can generally be propagated easily from cuttings and should be fertilized regularly with very dilute solutions of a complete fertilizer containing slightly more nitrogen than phosphorus.

## VEGETABLES AND FRUIT

### CUCUMBERS
Since cucumbers require fairly high light intensities, they are best started in spring so that they receive the bright

### Figure 15-36
### SEEDLESS CUCUMBERS

Courtesy of Alberta Agriculture

summer sunlight during the period of fruit production. If seed is started in February, placing the transplants into the greenhouse beds can begin in about three weeks and picking in about another six weeks. If you plan to grow cucumbers after bedding plants, sow about mid-May and transplant near June 7.

It is advisable to use your valuable greenhouse space to grow seedless long English cucumbers which do not grow well outside (see Figure 15-36). Recommended cultivars include Farbio, Corona, Pandex, Toska, and Sandra. Cucumbers have their sexual part separated into female and male flowers (see Figure 15-37).

The recommended cultivars produce mainly female flowers which can set fruit without pollination and, thus, the fruit is seedless. Any male flowers should be removed because if pollination does occur, seed will form and the fruit will

### Figure 15-37
### MALE AND FEMALE CUCUMBER FLOWERS

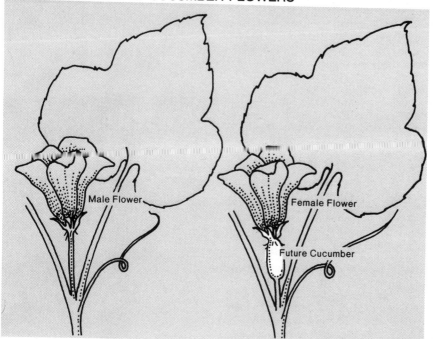

Male Flower

Female Flower

Future Cucumber

After transplanting, keep the temperature at 20°C during the night and 22-25°C during the day. When fruit begins to develop, add 12-0-44 or 15.5-0-0 at the rate of 1 kg/100 m² (2 lb/1000 sq ft).

Cucumbers need to be pruned for good fruit production. A good pruning method is outlined in the following steps (see Figure 15-39):

1. Remove the growing point of the first leaf above the wire.

2. Remove all sideshoots except for two near the top of the plant.

3. Train these two laterals over the wire and allow them to grow down. Remove growing tips 1 m (39 in) from the ground.

4. Do not allow fruit to develop on main stem up to 1 m (39 in) from the ground.

### Figure 15-38
### TRAINING CUCUMBERS

become misshapen and develop a bitter taste.

Seeds should be started in a porous mix at a temperature of 28°C. Transplanting in 10-12 cm (4-5 in) pots should be done when the seed leaves have fully expanded (about 4-5 days after germination). Since cucumbers are very susceptible to transplant shock, it is best to transplant into peat pots which do not have to be removed before transplanting.

Transplant into beds when plants are 15-20 cm (6-8 in) tall, allowing 0.7-0.8 m²/plant (7½-8½ sq ft/plant). Training the plants to grow upwards must begin when the plants are small. To do this, run two wires over the row, about 2.2 to 2.5 m (about 7-8 ft) above ground. Space the wires so that each wire is about 30-40 cm (12-16 in) to either side of the row. A string is then wound loosely around the stem of each plant and tied alternatively to the overhead wire so that the plants are inclined away from the row on each side (see Figure 15-38). This allows light to enter and the fruit to hang away from the stem.

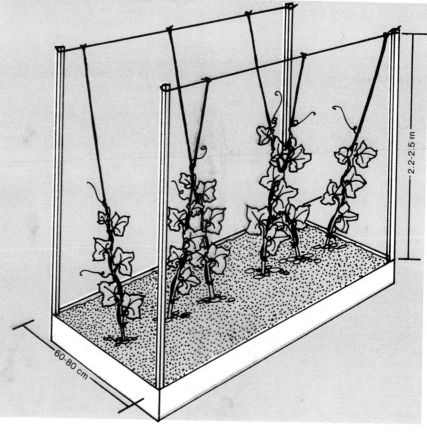

2.2-2.5 m

60-80 cm

## Figure 15-39
## PRUNING CUCUMBERS

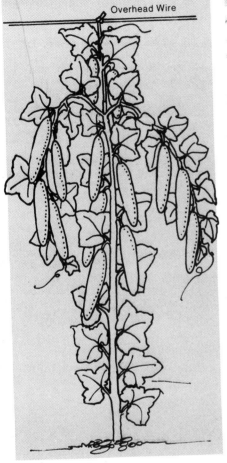

Overhead Wire

Harvest cucumbers frequently, as they develop quickly. The plants can be removed after one crop, or new laterals can be trained up from the main stem to replace the original laterals and extend production. Cucumbers are very susceptible to spider mite infestation.

### EGGPLANT
This much ignored plant can be easily grown in the home greenhouse in Alberta. It is naturally slow growing and, therefore, must be given an early start. It is very sensitive to low temperature. Plant growth is always checked and, often, permanently stunted if temperature falls below 10°C. The flower does not require pollination.

### LETTUCE
Leaf and buttercrunch lettuce are easily grown in the greenhouse year-round (see

## Figure 15-40
## GREENHOUSE LETTUCE

Courtesy of Alberta Agriculture
Figure 15-40). Lettuce prefers both cool soil and cool air temperatures and, therefore, does not always fit into the greenhouse program while other plants are being grown. If conditions are too warm, the lettuce will be bitter and go to seed quickly. Recommended leaf cultivars are Waldmans and Grand Rapids, and recommended butterhead cultivars are Ostinata, Deci Minor and White Boston. Many crisphead cultivars can also be grown.

Sow seeds in light, artificial mix in a tray or pot. After germination (1-2 weeks) transfer them to pots or flats with soil mix. Allow them to grow for another two weeks during the summer or another three weeks during the winter. Then transplant directly to soil or soilless mix at a spacing of about 20 cm x 20 cm (8 in x 8 in). Leaf lettuce requires a night temperature of 10-13°C and a day temperature of 13-21°C. Butterhead types require a night temperature of 18°C, a day temperature of 17-19°C on dull days, and 21-24°C on bright days.

The cultivars mentioned will be ready for harvest within 3-4 weeks if grown during the summer, or 5-6 weeks if grown during the winter. Crisphead cultivars take longer to reach a harvestable size.

Lettuce is a poor feeder, so a high level of nutrition must be maintained (see Vegetables lesson, Table 11-4). If a

good level of nutrition already exists, 1.5-2 kg of 20-20-20 per 100 m² (3-4 lb/1000 sq ft) worked into the soil before planting should be sufficient. If color of leaves is pale, 2 kg/100 m² (4 lb/1000 sq ft) of ammonium nitrate (34-0-0) should be used.

Botrytis grey mold is the most serious disease problem on lettuce. Avoid watering from the top or grow only leaf lettuce. Lettuce does not store well, so the best practice is to stagger small plantings over time so that all that is harvested can be used fresh.

### ONIONS
Onions are seldom considered a greenhouse crop, but they do respond well to greenhouse culture. Soil conditions are very important. Soil should be loose, well-drained, warm, highly retentive of moisture and well supplied with humus. Since onions are very shallow rooted, both moisture and fertilizer quickly drop below the root zone, unless replaced often at the soil surface. For this reason, a small amount of fertilizer applied frequently is much more effective than a larger amount mixed through all of the soil. Onions may be started from seeds or sets, but seed onions do not usually reach a size suitable for dry storage in the same year.

## PEPPERS

Peppers do best in well-drained, moist, light, warm soil containing large amounts of humus. Because the early culture of both peppers and tomatoes is the same, they can be grown together. Since peppers do not need as much fertilizer as tomatoes, it is wise to set all of the pepper plants in a group at one end of a bench or bed to avoid overfertilization. Peppers should be pollinated in the same manner as tomatoes (see TOMATOES). Since peppers are naturally determinate and, thus, do not form long vines, they are suited to bench culture. Peppers are relatively free of disease as long as there is a good ventilation and circulation around the plant.

## RADISHES

Radishes are normally a garden crop but a few rows can be planted between other crops in the greenhouse. Environmental conditions suitable for lettuce are also suitable for radishes (see LETTUCE).

## STRAWBERRIES

Strawberries are not commercially grown in prairie greenhouses for economic reasons. In hobby greenhouses, however, they are worthy of trial. Strawberries prefer a well-drained growth medium. Mixes containing slow release fertilizers should not be used as they are likely to cause foliar burn. Diluted concentrations of fertilizer should be applied 4-6 weeks after planting. Regular leachings should be done to prevent soluble salt build-up.

Strawberries require a great deal of water. Drought results in marginal burn. A night temperature of 17°C and a day temperature of 20-25°C are optimum. Hand pollination or shaking the inflorescence may be necessary to ensure pollination and, thus, fruit set.

No cultivars have been tested for greenhouse forcing under prairie conditions, but the following may be successful: June bearer (Protem. Senga, Sengana); Everbearer (Ogallala, Jubilee).

Powdery mildew and spider mites are the main pest problems. A preventative spray program for powdery mildew should be developed as it is extremely difficult to eradicate once it appears.

Figure 15-41
PRUNING AND TRAINING TOMATOES

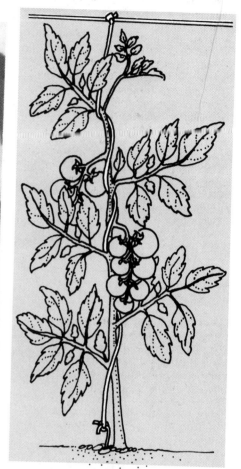

Courtesy of Alberta Agriculture

Courtesy of Alberta Agriculture

## TOMATOES

Tomatoes should be seeded and germinated in the same way as bedding plants. Tomatoes can be seeded as early as the beginning of January but may be delayed until May 1 if space is limited. Try using a greenhouse rather than a field cultivar, since they have been genetically selected for superior growth under greenhouse conditions. Greenhouse cultivars include Vendor, Tropic, Jumbo and Laura.

Once the first true leaves appear, transplant the seedlings into 7.5 cm (3 in) peat or plastic pots and grow on until they are ready to set out in ground beds or to transplant to larger pots. If seeding is done about May 1, the seedlings should be ready to transplant by June 1. When the plants are 15 cm (6 in) high they are ready to set out (allow 0.3-0.4 m² or 3-4 sq ft per plant). Temperatures of 21-24°C during the day and 16-18°C at night are desirable.

Greenhouse tomatoes are usually pruned to a single stem by removing lateral shoots from leaf axils before they are 2 cm (3/4 in) long (see Figure 15-41). Lateral shoots and fruit clusters alternate along the length of the stem. The plants can be supported by tying binder-twine loosely around the base of the plant and tying the other end to overhead supporting wires placed about 2-2.5 m (6½-8 ft) above ground. The plants are kept upright by twisting them loosely around the twine as they grow. The growing tip is usually broken off when it reaches the overhead wire and, after all fruit has been harvested, the plants are removed. If the growing tip is left, the plant will grow into a long vine.

Greenhouse tomatoes need to be artificially pollinated in order to set fruit. The supporting wire can be tapped lightly with a stick or individual flower clusters can be vibrated with an electric toothbrush to ensure the spread of pollen from flower to flower. By using a paintbrush or cotton swab, it is also possible to transfer pollen by hand. Pollination should be done about three times per week, between the hours of 11 a.m. and 2 p.m. Pollen is shed more abundantly on bright, sunny days when temperatures exceed 21°C.

Do not over-fertilize tomatoes. Establish good soil fertility conditions in the bed initially by applying 21-0-0 or 10-30-10 as needed (as determined by soil test).

Later on, when fruit is developing, add 15.5-0-0 at the rate of 1.25 kg/100 m² (2¾ lb/1000 sq ft). If soilless mixes are used, apply 21-10-30 at a rate of 200 g/200 L/100 m² (7 oz/44 gal/1000 sq ft) twice a week.

# PROBLEMS AND PREVENTION

## DISEASE CONTROL

Disease means a disturbance in function accompanied by the appearance of symptoms. The reaction of a plant to the cause of the disturbance produces the various symptoms by which disease can be recognized. Whether the disease is important depends on how seriously it affects the yield and quality of the product.

The alert greenhouse operator, hobbyist or commercial grower who can recognize plant diseases and knows how to deal with them can grow a more profitable crop. For the hobbyist, disease free plants provide a source of enjoyment and satisfaction. For the commercial grower, it is a matter of livelihood. The ability to recognize plant diseases and deal with them comes with experience, knowledge and sharing information with others.

Some diseases can be prevented if they are recognized early, or their impact can be reduced if appropriate control recommendations are followed. To understand the reasons for control recommendations, it helps to know about the diseases and the agents that cause them.

### CAUSES OF PLANT DISEASES

Diseases are caused either by unfavorable conditions in the environment (noninfectious disease) or by micro-organisms (infectious disease).

Some common causes of noninfectious diseases in greenhouse crops are:

- low temperature (eg., chilling injury)

- chemical injury (eg., improper application of a pesticide)

- lack of nutrients (eg., nitrogen deficiency)

- excess water (eg., 'wet feet' condition from lack of oxygen around the roots).

Four types of micro-organisms commonly cause infectious diseases on greenhouse crops: bacteria, fungus, virus and nematodes. For a complete discussion of plant diseases, their cause and treatment, refer to the Pest Control lesson, PLANT DISEASES and BACKYARD PEST MANAGEMENT.

### DIAGNOSING PLANT DISEASES

The first step in combatting a plant disease is to recognize that a problem exists. One must then identify the causal agent and determine whether the disease is noninfectious or infectious. This procedure is the art and science of diagnosis. The following are some important points to remember in diagnosing diseases of greenhouse crops:

1. An accurate diagnosis is essential before timely and appropriate control measures can be applied.

2. Examine all of the facts at hand. Like a detective, look for clues in cultural practices, unusual growing conditions, etc. Don't always assume that an infectious agent is the cause of the disease.

3. Know the crop. Many disease problems, especially noninfectious ones, can be prevented if one has a sound knowledge of the growth characteristics, nutritional requirements and optimal environmental conditions for good growth.

4. Learn to recognize the signs of insect and mite infestations. They can be easily confused with symptoms of certain diseases.

5. Close observation of symptoms with the naked eye should indicate the general type of disease (eg., leaf spot, wilt, root rot, etc.). Closer examination of the surfaces of spots or cankers (with a magnifying glass) often reveals the presence of spore-bearing bodies of fungi, bacterial exudates, insects, or mites. Diseased areas showing no evidence of surface growths could be young infections which may later develop structures, or they may be the result

of conditions causing noninfectious diseases.

6. Don't be afraid to consult a specialist for help. Alberta has regional plant diagnostic laboratories at Brooks, Olds, Vegreville and Fairview. Each laboratory is staffed with plant pathologists, entomologists, and weed scientists. These specialists can be contacted through district agriculture offices.

## CHEMICAL DISEASE CONTROL RECOMMENDATIONS

Before using any chemical, carefully read the manufacturer's instructions on the label. All pesticide products registered for use in Canada are licensed by Agriculture Canada. No disease control chemical should be used on any crop for which it is not registered. Such use may pose a threat to consumers of the treated produce and can result in seizure and destruction of the crop by federal inspectors.

Unless otherwise specified, all materials should be applied so as to obtain thorough coverage of the foliage. Applications can be repeated every 7-14 days, as long as there is a threat of disease spread. Over a period of time, disease organisms may become resistant or immune to certain pesticides. Therefore, it is advisable to make applications of alternate recommended chemicals where more than one is registered for use against a specific pathogen.

## INSECT CONTROL

### IDENTIFICATION AND CONTROL

Before an insect can be controlled, it must be identified so that the proper measures can be taken. Many greenhouse growers are turning to integrated pest management rather than relying totally on the use of chemicals for control. Integrated pest management involves combining cultural, biological and mechanical control methods with chemical control to reduce the problems associated with chemical use. This is an effective but complex control practice (see Pest Control lesson, INSECTS and BACKYARD PEST MANAGEMENT).

## BIOLOGICAL CONTROL

Biological control involves controlling insects with other organisms (predators or parasites) or with natural compounds. Natural compounds commonly used include organic plant extracts, such as nicotine, pyrethrum, and rotenone (derris dust). Predators currently available for use at home include lacewings, praying mantis, ladybugs, several species of wasps and predatory mice. Only one parasite (*Bacillus thuringensis*) is currently available for home use. This organism is a bacterium and is useful in controlling caterpillars (trade names - Dipel, Thuricide). Effective use of predators and parasites in an integrated pest management control program is complex.

## MECHANICAL AND PHYSICAL CONTROL

Mechanical control refers to the use of baits and traps. Baits formulated with metaldehyde are commonly used to control slugs. Traps using sticky substances to attract and hold insects are effective, especially if painted yellow. There are also light traps available that control insects by electrocution or by drowning them in soapy water. Physical control involves the removal of pests by hand; that is, physically picking out and destroying insect (or weed) pests.

## CHEMICAL CONTROL

In situations where an insect problem gets out of hand, biological, and mechanical or physical controls are not rapid or thorough enough and chemicals

## Table 15-9
## PEST CONTROL RECOMMENDATIONS

| Pest | Control[1] |
|------|-----------|
| Aphids | Malathion, diazinon[2], pyrethrum and pyrethroids (e.g., *tetramethrin* and *resmethrin*), rotenone, predators such as ladybug and wasp, insecticidal soaps, Pirimicarb, diatomaceous earth |
| Fungus Gnat | Diazinon soil drench, malathion |
| Mealy Bug | Malathion, diazinon[2], if only a few insects - touch insects with a Q-tip dipped in alcohol, insecticidal soap, diatomaceous earth |
| Scale | Malathion, diazinon[2] |
| Slugs | Metaldehyde (bait, dust, or spray) dishes of beer, sanitary greenhouse |
| Spider Mites | Dicofol (Kelthane), malathion, tetramethrin, predators (other mites), insecticidal soap |
| Thrips | Malathion, diazinon[2], tetramethrin, resmethrin |
| Whitefly | Tetramethrin, resmethrin, diazinon[2], (*Encarsia formosa* {wasp}), insecticidal soap |

[1] Ensure that the plant is not sensitive to the chemical chosen. Where applicable, some common trade names have been included in brackets.

[2] Registered for use indoors on noncommercial houseplants in the dust form only.

Courtesy of Alberta Agriculture.

must be used. Chemicals can be applied as fumigants, dusts, sprays, or as granules applied to the soil. Each formulation has advantages and disadvantages. Fumigants are very poisonous and, thus, are not registered for domestic use. Dusts are easy to apply and often contain a fungicide for added protection. They do, however, leave unsightly residues. Sprays provide very thorough coverage and control. Sprays can either be contact or systemic types. To be effective, contact sprays must hit the insect to be controlled. Systemics are taken up by the plant and transmitted internally, killing insects that feed on any part of the plant. The granular formations of insecticide applied to the soil are also systemic. In this case, however, the insecticide is taken up by the roots, not the leaves. Granular insecticides are easy to apply and provide longer term control than many sprays. Common insect pests found in the greenhouse and effective agents for their control are outlined in Table 15-9. Since most plants are sensitive to some chemicals, read insecticide labels for phytotoxicity information.

Plants in the greenhouse are more susceptible to injury from insecticides than are plants in the open, and sprays should usually be used at two-thirds or one-half the rate recommended for garden plants. If in doubt, treat one leaf before treating the entire plant.

Recommendations may change from year to year. Consult your greenhouse specialists for any changes. Label recommendations must be followed closely (see Figure 15-42). **If a plant name is not shown on the label, then that chemical should not be used**.

LABELLING OF PESTICIDES

Pesticides are labelled in accordance with Federal legislation and must provide the following information:

1. NAME AND ADDRESS OF THE CHEMICAL COMPANY

2. TRADE NAMES: These are almost always on the label in large print and may not be used in the 'active ingredient' section. Such names as sevin, cythion, or Dichlorvos are trades names.

3. LIST OF ALL ACTIVE INGREDIENTS

a. Official Common Name: a well-known name accepted by the Pesticide Registration Division. Laws require that officially approved common names, not the chemical name, appear in the 'active ingredient' section of the label. Not all pesticides have an official common name. Examples of common names are carbaryl, malathion, and DDVP.

b. Chemical Name: a scientific name telling the contents or chemical formula of the actual poison. When an accepted common name is not available, the chemical name must be used in the 'active ingredient' section of the label. However, if the chemical name is too long and complex, another name describing the poison is allowed.

4. TYPE OF PESTICIDE: insecticide, herbicide, fungicide, etc.

5. KIND OF FORMULATION: dusts, wettable powders, granules, sprays, baits, pressurized cans (bug bombs), emulsifiable concentrates.

Figure 15-42
PESTICIDE WARNING SYMBOLS

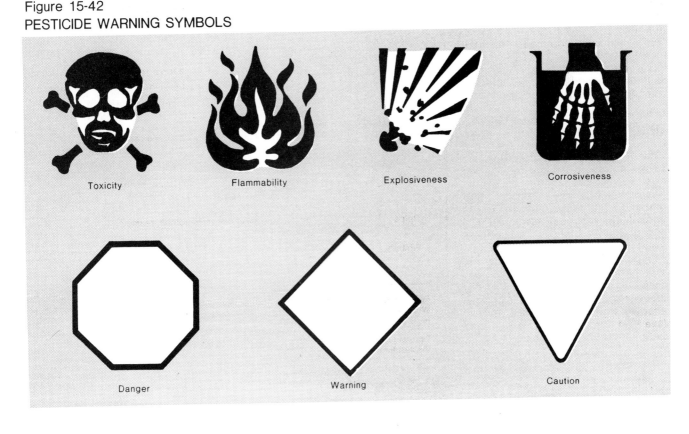

Toxicity    Flammability    Explosiveness    Corrosiveness

Danger    Warning    Caution

6. PCP ACT REGISTRATION NUMBER

7. STORAGE AND DISPOSAL PRECAUTIONS

8. HAZARD STATEMENTS: A pesticide should have on the label a statement 'keep out of reach of Children'. Pesticides have been grouped into categories according to their toxicity to animals, people and the environment. Special words and symbols on the label tell which group they are in (see Figure 15-42).

9. TOXICOLOGICAL INFORMATION, AND FIRST AID

10. DIRECTIONS FOR USE

   a. How to protect the crop

   b. How to mix the chemical

   c. Compatibility

11. NET CONTENTS

## CODE FOR THE SAFE HANDLING AND USE OF PESTICIDES

1. Always read the label before opening the container.

2. Use at recommended rates. Apply as directed.

3. Wear clean protective clothing as outlined on the label.

4. Do not inhale fumes, spray or dusts. Avoid skin contact. Wash immediately after accidental contact.

5. If pesticides are spilled on clothes, change immediately.

6. Do not eat, smoke or drink when mixing or applying or until after wash-up.

7. Follow 'days to harvest' on label.

8. Cover food and water containers when treating around livestock or pet areas. Do not contaminate water.

9. If any illness or abnormal condition occurs during or shortly after pesticide use, seek medical attention.

10. Wash equipment thoroughly after each pesticide application.

11. Shower or bath thoroughly after working with pesticides.

12. Use separate equipment for applying hormone type herbicides in order to avoid accidental injury to susceptible plants.

13. Always store pesticides in original containers and keep storage locked.

14. Keep ALL pesticides out of reach of children and animals.

15. Take precautions to reduce hazardous pesticide drift.

## DIAGNOSING NUTRIENT DISORDERS

A nutritional disorder is a malfunction in the physiological processes of a plant caused by either an excess or a lack of a mineral element or elements and resulting in abnormal growth. External and internal symptoms can be expressed. Distinct symptoms are caused by a deficiency or excess of each essential element which can be used to identify the disorder.

The grouping of essential elements for plant growth is based on their mobility in the plant. Although there is a general gradation of mobility of elements, they are generally classified as either **mobile** or **immobile** (see Plant Nutrition lesson, PLANT ANALYSES AND NUTRIENT INTERACTIONS).

Mobile elements are those which can be retranslocated. They do not move from their original site of deposition in older leaves to actively growing regions of the plant (such as younger leaves). As a result, the first symptoms appear on the older leaves on the lower portion of the plant. Examples of mobile elements are: nitrogen, potassium, phosphorus, magnesium and zinc.

Immobile elements are those which are not retranslocated to the growing region of the plant when need arises. They remain in the older leaves where they were originally deposited. Deficiency symptoms, therefore, first appear on the upper young leaves of the plant.

Immobile elements include: calcium, iron, boron, sulfur, copper and manganese. Excess of one element affects the uptake of another element. This phenomenon is called **antagonism**. Some common nutrient element antagonism is as listed in Table 15-10.

## Table 15-10 ANTAGONISM

| Element in Excess | Deficiency Caused |
|---|---|
| Nitrogen | Potassium |
| Phosphorus | Potassium, Iron |
| Potassium | Nitrogen, Calcium, Magnesium |
| Sodium | Potassium, Calcium, Magnesium |
| Zinc | Iron |
| Calcium | Potassium, Iron, Boron, Magnesium |
| Magnesium | Potassium, Calcium, Manganese |
| Iron | Manganese |
| Manganese | Iron, Zinc |
| Copper | Iron |

## OTHER TIPS FOR DIAGNOSIS

1. Grow an indicator plant along with the regular crop since the susceptibility of differrent plant Species to various nutritional disorders varies greatly. For example, if a crop of tomatoes is being grown, plant a few cucumbers. Cucumbers are very sensitive to boron and calcium deficiency. If such a deficiency occurs, the cucumbers will express symptoms from several days to a week before they appear in the tomatoes. Tomatoes will show a magnesium deficiency earlier than cucumbers.

2. Weaker plants of the same Species show nutrient deficiency symptoms before the more vigorous ones.

3. Every possible tactic must be employed to avoid a nutritional disorder in the main crop as some reduction in yield is inevitable once symptoms are expressed.

After the symptoms have been observed closely and described, it should be determined whether the disorder is caused by something other than a nutritional imbalance. The following list of other possible disorders should be checked:

- insect damage
- parasitic diseases
- pesticide damage
- pollution damage
- water stress
- light injury
- temperature injury.

Pesticide damage may cause burning if greater than recommended dosages are used on the plants. Also, the use of herbicides such as 2,4-D near a greenhouse may cause deformation of plant leaves, closely resembling the symptoms of tobacco mosaic virus (TMV). Pollution damage may cause burning or bleaching of leaf tissue or a stippled effect (pinpoint-sized chlorotic spots) on leaves. Water stress (lack or excess of water) causes wilting (loss of turgidity) of leaves. Excessive sunlight or temperature may burn and dry leaf tissue, particularly on the margins.

### GREENHOUSE SANITATION

Proper sanitation is very important in controlling various diseases and pests in a greenhouse. Remove crops promptly from the greenhouse at the end of the cropping season. If plants are left to decay, pest and disease levels may build up and survive until the next crop. If pests or diseases are at a high level, it may be advantageous to fumigate the greenhouse with the plants in place to prevent the dispersal of pests during their removal from the greenhouse.

Between successive crops, spray the greenhouse interior, walkways, training wires, gutters and tools with household bleach at a rate of 5 L/100 L (1 gal/22 gal) of water or with commercially available formaldehyde at a rate of 2.5 L/100 L (½ gal/22 gal) of water. Formaldehyde, when mixed with potassium permanganate can be used as soil and space fumigant as well. Be sure the formaldehyde is at room temperature. The formaldehyde is placed in heat resistant containers, (no more than 1 L to a 9 L container or 35 fl oz to a 2 gal container) add 188 g potassium permanganate to treat 56 m³ (3.3 oz/1000 cu ft) of greenhouse space.

Be careful when adding the permanganate as the reaction may be violent. A gas mask with a full face plate and a canister rated for organic vapors is recommended for use during the start of the procedure. Keep the greenhouse closed for 22-48 hours after completion of the fumigation procedure. Ventilate well before reentry.

Weeds (both in the greenhouse and in the surrounding area) are a continuous source of mite, aphid, whitefly and thrips. Use a contact weedkiller, such as Gramoxone (paraquat) to kill outside weeds. Proper sterilization of greenhouse soil should reduce or eliminate weed problems from the greenhouse. Remember - most of the soil sterilizing chemicals destroy germinating weed seeds only.

## CONCLUSION

Design and build a hobby greenhouse to suit your needs and time commitment. The greenhouse may be attached or could be free standing. Incorporate maximum passive solar aspects. Select a heating system which is most economical. A good cooling/ventilation system is required. Water quality is important. Pest and disease control must be practised in hobby greenhouses. Give a serious thought to biological control; it does work.

Select plants on the basis of what you like and also consider the temperature requirements of each plant. A hobby greenhouse can supply all of your fresh vegetable needs, if properly managed.

## SELF CHECK *QUIZ*

1. What information do I need to calculate the heater size for my greenhouse?

2. What is the best heating system and fuel for heating the greenhouse?

3. Is it possible to heat my greenhouse by solar energy alone?

4. What is the most important fact to remember about cooling?

5. Is it a good idea to set up an automatic watering system?

6. Does greenhouse growing differ from outside growing?

7. Is manure safe to use in greenhouse soils?

8. Do soilless mixes have advantages over soil?

9. How important is water quality for hobby growers?

10. What is the most important fact to remember when deciding to grow plants?

11. What is the most important design criterion of greenhouses?

12. In which direction is the axis of a greenhouse usually oriented on our latitude?

13. What do you consider the main advantages and disadvantages of flexible sheets of plastic?

14. Do you think that streetlights or a yard light may influence the growth of your plants in a nearby greenhouse?

15. Do you think that a plant collection containing many different species is easier to manage than a 'monotypic' crop like chrysanthemums, cucumbers or tomatoes?

*Lighting for Plant Growth*. Bickford and Dunn, Kent State University Press, 1972.

The best book on the subject.

*Artificial Light in Horticulture*. Philips Electronic Industries Ltd., 601 Milner Avenue, Scarborough, Ontario M1B 1M8. (36 pages)

A very good commerical source of information.

*Application of Growlight in Greenhouses*. J.A.B. Stolze and J. Poot.  P.L. Lightsystems Canada, Inc., St. Catharines, Ontario. (48 pages)

Commercial source of information.

*Greenhouse Management*. Hanam-Holley-Springer-Verlag, New York. 1978. (530 pages)

One of the more complete texts.

*The Greenhouse Environment*.  J.W. Mastalerz. 1977. John Wiley and Sons, Toronto (629 pages).

Essentially a horticulture text.

*Greenhouse Operation and Management*. P.V. Nelson. 1978. Reston Publishing Co. Inc., Reston, Virginia. (518 pages).

Hobby Greenhouses in Alberta. Alberta Agriculture - Agdex 731.5 (undated)

# SELF CHECK *ANSWERS*

1. You need to know inside desired temperature; outside temperatures; the type of glazing material; wind velocity; insulation type; and exposed greenhouse area (see HEATING, page 1524) .

2. Hot water heating systems gives the best heat distribution, but small boilers are not available. Natural gas heaters are most commonly used. Propane and kerosene heaters are also available (see HEATING, pages 1524-1530).

3. No, 100 per cent solar heat is not possible yet. Incorporate all possible passive solar heat designs to maximize the heat use (see SOLAR HEATING, page 1526).

4. Small greenhouses heat up easily, consequently they are difficult to cool. Make sure you have proper capacity ventilation fans (see COOLING AND VENTILATION, page 1530).

5. Yes, automatic watering systems are easy to set up and give you an opportunity to go away for a weekend as well (see WATERING SYSTEMS, page 1543).

6. Yes, because of good environment; vigorous growth of plants, fertilizer and water management is different. That is why you should start with a good, porous growing medium and fertilize on a regular basis. Remember analytical laboratories handle greenhouse soil analyses differently from a garden soil. Do specify that yours is a greenhouse sample (see GREENHOUSE MANAGEMENT, page 1534).

7. Yes, it is safe, if used in proper quantities. Manure may contain large quantities of sodium. Take a soil test to determine the needs (see USE OF MANURE, page 1537).

8. If your soil has poor drainage, or is disease infested or herbicide contaminated, then soilless mixes offer a good alternative. Soilless mixes require close watch on fertility and watering practices (see SOILLESS MIXES, page 1538).

9. Water quality is important for hobby growers. City water supplies are generally of good quality. Rural well water supplies may contain high quantities of sodium and thus are unfit for greenhouse use. Remember, soft water or chemically softened water is not suitable for plant growth (see WATER, page 1541).

10. Different temperature requirements for different plants must be kept in mind. For example, cucumbers require 20°C and above night temperature, while most houseplants require around 16°C night temperatures (see GREENHOUSE PLANTS, page 1544).

11. The availability of sufficient natural light throughout the seasons.

12. East-west; this intercepts the maximum amount of light in fall and spring (see SITE SELECTION AND ORIENTATION, page 1503).

13. Advantages:
    low in price
    light in weight
    allows the roof of greenhouses to be curved
    Disadvantages:
    usually limited lifespan
    has to be reapplied regularly (see FLEXIBLE FILMS, page 1512).

14. Yes, very much so, although the distance and therefore the intensity are important factors. The flowering of certain plants can be influenced by such light sources (see ARTIFICIAL LIGHT, page 1516).

15. Plant collections with many different plants have many different requirements and, therefore, are more difficult to manage (see GREENHOUSE PLANTS, page 1544).

bay - space between the upright wall supports of a greenhouse.

condensation - the reduction of a gas to a liquid.

convective cooling - based on the principle that warm air is lighter than cooler air. A top opening allows warm air to escape; openings at the base allow cool air to enter.

evapotranspiration - the total loss from the soil, including that by direct evaporation and that by transpiration from the surfaces of plants.

fumigant - a substance used to disinfect or kill vermin.

glazing bars - are the parallel members on which the glass sheets are fixed.

greenhouse effect - the retention of heat from sunlight at the earth's surface, caused by atmospheric carbon dioxide that admits shortwave radiation but absorbs the longwave radiation emitted by the earth.

infrared - invisible rays just beyond the red end of the visible spectrum; their waves are longer than those of the spectrum colors but shorter than radio waves, and have a penetrating heating effect: used in cooking, photography, etc.

irradiance - light intensity; the amount of light or other radiant energy striking a given area of a surface.

light intensity - amount of actual energy received from the sun (natural light).

photoperiod (duration) - length of exposure to solar radiation.

photosynthetic active radiation - P.A.R. - light to which plants are sensitive.

phytochrome - a bluish-green plant protein that, in response to variations in red light, regulates the growth of plants.

purlins - a horizontal timber supporting the common rafters of a roof.

radiant flux - the rate of flow of radiant energy.

ridge - highest part of the structure, providing strength along the axis and supporting the upper end of the glazing bars.

soilless mixes - consist of inert material particles, organic particles, and fertilizers, and are an alternative to soil.

solar heating - active - collection of heat by a solar collector, transfer of heat to a storage device and release from storage when needed.
        passive - the uncontrolled storage of heat during the day and release of heat at night.

ultraviolet - lying just beyond the violet end of the visible spectrum and having wavelengths shorter than approximately 4,000 angstroms.

visible light - wavelengths that range from 390-780 nm.

# HYDROPONICS

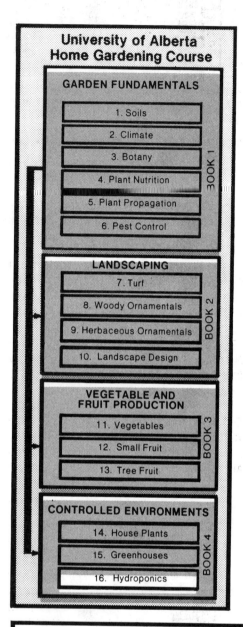

**University of Alberta Home Gardening Course**

**GARDEN FUNDAMENTALS**
1. Soils
2. Climate
3. Botany
4. Plant Nutrition
5. Plant Propagation
6. Pest Control
BOOK 1

**LANDSCAPING**
7. Turf
8. Woody Ornamentals
9. Herbaceous Ornamentals
10. Landscape Design
BOOK 2

**VEGETABLE AND FRUIT PRODUCTION**
11. Vegetables
12. Small Fruit
13. Tree Fruit
BOOK 3

**CONTROLLED ENVIRONMENTS**
14. House Plants
15. Greenhouses
16. Hydroponics
BOOK 4

# SELF-STUDY LESSON FEATURES

Self-study is an educational approach which allows you to study a subject when and when you want. The course is designed to allow students to study the cours material efficiently and incorporates the following features.

**OBJECTIVES** — are found at the beginning of each lesson and allow you to determine what you can expect to learn in the lesson.

**LESSON MATERIAL** — is logically organized and broken down into fundamental components by ordered headings to assist you to comprehend the subject.

**REFERENCING** — between lessons and within lessons allows you to integrate course material.

The last two digits of the page number identify the page and the digits preceding these identify the lesson number (eg., 107: Lesson 1, page 7 or 1227: Lesson 12, page 27).

Referencing:

sections within the same lesson (eg., see OSMOSIS)

sections in other lessons (eg., see Botany lesson, OSMOSIS)

figures and tables (eg., see Figure 7-3)

**FIGURES AND TABLES** — are found in abundance throughout the lessons and are designed to convey useful information in an easy to understar form.

**SIDEBARS** — are those areas in th lesson which are boxed and toned. The present information supplementary to th core content of the lesson.

**PRACTICAL PROJECTS** — ar integrated within the lesson material an are included to allow you to appl principles and practices.

**SELF-CHECK QUIZ** — is provided at th end of each lesson and allows you t test your comprehension of the lesso material. Answers to the questions an references to the sections dealing wit the questions are provided in the answe section. You should review an questions that you are unable to answer

**GLOSSARY** – is provided at the end o each lesson and alphabetically lists th definitions of key concepts and terms.

**RESOURCE MATERIALS** — ar provided at the end of each lesson an comprise a list of recommended learnin materials for further study of the subjec Also included are author's comments o the potential application of eac publication.

**INDEX** — alphabetically lists usef topics and their location within th lesson.

© 1986 University of Alberta Faculty of Extension

**Written by: Rudi Kroon**

Technical Reviewer: Dr. Mohyuddin Mirza

**ISBN 0-88864-852-9**
(Book 4, Lesson 16)

THE PRODUCTION TEAM

Managing Editor ................................................... Thom Shaw
Editor ............................................................ Frank Procter
Production Coordinator ............... Kevin Hanson
Graphic Artists ............................ Melanie Eastley Harbourne
Data Entry ................................................ Lois Hameister McDonald

Published by the University of Alberta Faculty of Extension Corbett Hall Edmonton, Alberta, T6G 2G4

After completing this lesson, the student should be able to:

1. appreciate the value of growing plants hydroponically to overcome problems of disease, buildup of salts, and lack of sufficient fresh water.

2. understand how plants function, and especially determine how hydroponic gardening complements such functions.

3. recognize the importance of water quality in hydroponic gardening.

4. identify the unique fertilizer and solution considerations and determine accurate formulations.

5. identify advantages and disadvantages of the media available for growing plants hydroponically and the methods to use these.

6. identify some of the special equipment needed by the hydroponic gardener.

## TABLE OF CONTENTS

# INTRODUCTION

The term hydroponics is loosely applied to a number of methods that are used to grow plants without soil. Other media are utilized that allow plants to anchor their roots but all these are 'inert media', and do not supply any nutrients to the plant. The word hydroponics was derived from the Greek **Hydro** meaning 'water', and **ponos** meaning 'work'. Water is indeed the main ingredient used to supply the plant with all it needs to grow. Hydroponics is really a catch-all name as it incorporates all the variations of growing plants without soil including: vermicuponics, water culture, sand culture, gravel culture, tank culture, airoponics, bag culture, NFT (Nutrient Film Technique), LFT (Liquid Film Technique), and sawdust culture. Due to increased (mainly misinformed) news coverage of hydroponics, there has been a marked increase in interest over the past 10 years. As a result, many sensational claims have been made regarding this 'new' method of growing plants. Some facts should be made clear before discussing hydroponics in detail:

- Hydroponics is not a new system of growing plants; it has been seriously practiced for at least 50 years.

- Hydroponics is by no means an easier or simpler way of growing plants; in fact, it is one of the more complicated and demanding forms of horticulture. If you cannot grow a decent tomato in your own backyard, forget about hydroponics!

- Due to the absence of soil as a growing media, fewer pests and diseases may be encountered. However, in hydroponics you will be confronted with more plant growth disorders than you may have ever believed existed.

Hydroponics brings together all of the latest developments in plant sciences, botany and modern technology to produce bigger and better horticultural crops. The aim in this lesson then, is to provide a solid introduction to the subject which allows the hobby gardener to start practicing hydroponics on a modest scale (see Figure 16-1).

# HISTORICAL BACKGROUND

Various authors claim that the history of hydroponics goes back to the hanging gardens of Babylon, the ancient Chinese, or other such ancestry. These claims, however, are highly speculative so our historical review must be limited to the documented history. In 1600, the Belgian, Jan van Helmond, grew some willow trees in measured amounts of water and soil. He came to the erroneous conclusion that water was the main ingredient required to grow plants because the amount of water used by the plant far exceeded the reduction of soil over a certain period of time. John Woodward, in 1699, grew plants in different mixtures of soil and water and found that the water with the largest amount of soil produced the best plants. He concluded that both water and soil are required for the growth of plants. In 1804, de Saussure of France maintained that plants consisted of various chemical elements obtained from water, soil and the atmosphere. Another French chemist named Boussinggault confirmed this in 1851 after growing plants in sand and feeding them with different chemical solutions. In about 1860 in Germany, the scientists Sachs and Knop, maintained plants in water cultures to which various chemicals in different concentrations were added. This led to the establishment of some standard recipes on which a series of researchers based further experiments.

In the period between 1861 and 1900, a long list of scientists contributed towards a better understanding of which nutritional factors influenced the growth of plants. During the late 1920's and early 1930's, the Californian plant physiologists Hoagland, Aron and Gerricke worked on the establishment of standard water culture recipes. These recipes produced excellent results and directly led to hydroponics as it is known today. Various Armed Forces used hydroponic cultures to produce fresh vegetables for their troops during the Second World War. As a result, hydroponics experienced an accelerated development due to the large investments made on technology to assist in the war effort. After the war, a large amount of commercial application took place which was not altogether successful. Those who would like to read more about the history of hydroponics should try to obtain a copy of the book 'Advanced Guide to Hydroponics' (see RESOURCE MATERIALS) which gives a detailed and very interesting account of its history.

## WHY HYDROPONICS?

Reasons for the development and application of hydroponics can be one or a combination of several circumstances.

### RESEARCH
By growing plants in hydroponic cultures, a good impression of the nutritional

## Figure 16-1
## SIMPLE HYDROPONIC GARDEN

Courtesy of Alberta Agriculture

requirements of a plant can be obtained by manipulating the solution in which these plants grow. Schools and universities use hydroponics regularly to illustrate certain phenomena in plant behavior and function. The beginning home gardener should start any hydroponic endeavor by growing a limited number of plants in a water culture to obtain experience and insight into the behavior of plants under certain circumstances.

## DISEASES

In the Netherlands in the late 1940's, efforts were made to grow carnations in gravel cultures to escape the devastating effects of a disease called Phytophthora. One of the reasons why vegetables for the occupational forces in Japan in 1945 were grown hydroponically was because the North Americans who ate produce grown in soil infected with bacteria and amoeba, resulting from the persistent use of human waste as manure, developed intestinal problems.

During the 1950's, it practically became impossible to grow tomatoes commercially on Vancouver Island due to a deterioration of soils, a buildup of soil-borne diseases, and the infestation of ne-nematodes (plant parasitising eelworms). This led to an intensified research program at the Federal Saanichton Research Station and eventual application of hydroponic techniques to grow crops in sawdust.

## BUILD UP OF SALTS

In order for plants to be able to grow well, high salt concentrations in the soil or water should be avoided. Hydroponic systems can be used as an alternative to the use of such salt laden soils. In greenhouses, particularly because of the lack of natural rain and the rather high rates of evaporation due to cooling and ventilation systems, salt levels in the top layers of the soil can reach high values and reduce crop production considerably. Leaching with copious amounts of water may provide a solution to the problem but, in those areas where salt content of the soil is high, the water used for leaching may also contain a fair amount of salt.

## LACK OF SUFFICIENT FRESH WATER

It is a well established fact that the lower the original salt content of the water, the faster the plant can take up that water. Unfortunately, the quality of our fresh water on a worldwide basis is not improving. Holland, which for centuries had the reputation of being a country with large amounts of fresh water, has found that the amount of pollution of groundwater makes it only marginally useful for use on plants. Taking into account that horticulture is a major industry in that country, one may understand the concern. There is an increasing amount of commercial hydroponics in Holland, and many of the new applications find their origin in that part of Europe. If a grower has spent a large amount of money removing these salts, he simply cannot let this expensive water run back into the soil. Such water is recycled over and over again through hydroponic benches. Israel has found that many of its desert soils are very fertile and, therefore, have a tremendous horticultural potential. Much of the required water is obtained from the Mediterranean Sea and partially purified. Here as well, more and more hydroponics are applied. A similar case occurs in Abu-Dhabi, one of the Persian Gulf states.

# PLANT ANATOMY AND PHYSIOLOGY

Before actual hydroponic issues are discussed, it must be clear what plants are about and how they function. However, only those aspects of direct interest and application to hydroponics need be detailed.

## CELLS AND TISSUES

The cells that make up a plant usually form groups of identical cells to form a tissue, and each tissue in the plant has a specific function (see Botany lesson, TISSUES). Two such tissues (three if you include the cambium) form the **vascular tissue**, which is responsible for the distribution of water and nutrients. The main components are **xylem** (the wood), which is responsible for the supply of water and nutrients from the roots to the rest of the plant. In the actively growing plants, this water and the nutrients are transported to the leaves to partake in the photosynthetic process. Under the influence of light, plants can produce sugar (carbohydrates) out of water and carbon dioxide. This sugar-containing solution is distributed throughout the plant to serve as a source of energy for other parts of the plant. A large amount can also be stored in the root system. The vascular tissue responsible for this return flow is the **phloem**. A practical hint to be given at this time is that when handling young plants, one should preferably not hold them at the stem, but rather at the leaves. If a leaf gets damaged, the plants can usually produce new ones soon enough. If, however, the stem is squeezed too hard, irreversible damage may occur to the vascular system and the functioning of the plant may become severely handicapped.

The vascular system is actually a solid core in the stem of a mature plant. This vascular system branches off at each side-shoot, as well as at each leaf. At each subsequent branching, the vascular bundle gets relatively thinner. However, it always consists of the two main types of tissues: phloem and xylem. Once it reaches the leaf, these bundles can actually be observed and are called veins. On both sides of the leaf are single layers of strong cells forming the epidermis (upper and lower). The pallisade parenchyme (Mesophyll), thus called on account of the resemblance to a row of pallisades, contains most of the chlorophyll, the pigment responsible for the photosynthetic process in the plant. In order to function to its full potential, it is located just beneath the upper epidermis. Each of these pallisade cells are long, tubular cells, and the chlorophyll is evenly distributed on the inner surface of the cell. It may be of interest to point out that leaves formed under conditions of strong light have a high density of chlorophyll, and leaves developed under low light conditions have fewer and are, as a consequence, lighter in color. Accordingly, if you move a plant from a locality of high light intensity to a low light level locality, the chlorophyll is unable to function to its full capacity as the density of the chlorophyll prevents the light from penetrating the full length of the cell. The vascular bundle is placed more or less in the middle of the leaf tissue. The lower section of the leaf is filled with another tissue known as the spongy mesophyll; as the name indicates, it is very loose in texture and contains many air spaces. This type is located near the underside of the leaf and is the reason why the lower sides of leaves are usually lighter in color. Due to the loose texture of this tissue, the combined surface area of all the cells is very large. The main objective of leaves is to photosynthesize; therefore, they are subject to solar radiation during the day. With the absorption of all this light, there is also a tremendous amount of heat absorbed. By evaporating water from the large surface of the spongy mesophyll, the leaf can keep its total structure cool. The water vapour can escape through small openings in the lower epidermis of the leaf called stomata. These openings can be controlled by two cells on either side of the stomata, depending on the amount of cooling required. During windy conditions the stomata closes.

Just as important (within the context of hydroponics) is the handling of the plant roots. Roots usually branch out from the main stem with the thicker roots situated near the stem of the plant. Roots have a tendency to spread out in a radial pattern from the plant and, besides anchoring the plant firmly in the soil, provide the plant with water and nutrition. Large trees have a root system which expands at least as far as the branches of the crown extend (dripline). Only the extreme tips of growing roots have the ability to take up water and nutrition. The older roots are soon covered with a layer of cork, to prevent the loss of any water to the surrounding soil. A large part of the older and thicker roots function as storage organs for carbohydrates produced by the leaves. Certain types of roots are specifically equipped to store such sugars (eg., carrots and beets). As previously mentioned, roots continually expand in order to obtain water and nutrition, as long as the plant is growing. Roots growing through the soil are subject to a great deal of friction at the extreme tip. This is why the tips of roots have an extra dense cap, the rootcap. This protective area is constantly renewed at the extreme tip, while a little further back, it simply deteriorates and disappears after having served its purpose. Around its outer surface, the young root has an epidermal layer very much like the one described for the leaf. This epidermis is only one cell layer thick. It is this single layer of cells that is entirely responsible for the intake of water. In order to have the maximum possible contact with the soil from which it takes the water, the area of these cells is greatly enlarged through the formation of hairlike structures, aptly named 'root hairs'. Root hairs start to develop just beyond the root tip, and are evident over an area usually no longer than 6 mm along the length of the root tip (approximately 20 - 200 mm). They have a relatively short life span, depending on the rate of growth of the roots. As soon as the root hairs disappear, subarization, which is the formation of cork, begins. The roots of bulbous plants, such as tulips and hyacinths, usually do not have root hairs. Plants grown hydroponically in water solutions often lack root hairs too. Once roots are covered with cork, hardly any water can enter that part of the root. The intake of water by the roots is, for the greatest part, due to a physical phenomenen called osmosis. Osmosis, as you recall, is the ability of water to move through a (semipermeable) membrane from a relatively weak solution to a stronger one and, as a consequence, the stronger solution is diluted. The greater the difference in concentration of the two solutions, the greater the force of this movement through the membranes. The speed and force of this water penetrating the membrane is called the osmotic potential. We should visualize the root and especially the root hairs of a plant as being surrounded by soil particles mixed with a large amount of water. Usually this water on the soil particles has a large number of soluble salts dissolved in it. Some of these salts are nutritious to the plant, but many are useless salts as far as plant nutrition is concerned. It should be obvious, then, that in order for the roots to be able to take up water from the soil by means of osmosis, there has to be a higher concentration of solution inside the plant to form an osmotic potential. The carbohydrate (sugar) solutions (the product of photosynthesis) stored inside the root forms an osmotic potential, and water travels mainly through the wall (membrane) of the cell towards the center of the root. Further transport of water is carried through the walls, between the cells to the inside of the root. Eventually, it reaches the xylem, where it is transported to other parts of the plant. Needless to say, this is a simplified explanation of the movement of water into the plant. There are a number of other forces that also play a role in this process. Diffusion is a force responsible for movement inside the plant (see Plant Nutrition lesson, ABSORPTION). It is interesting to note that the carbohydrates in the phloem, which form the osmotic potential, are not diluted by this water. The purer the water surrounding the roots, the greater the osmotic potential. This also explains the fact that too high a concentration of fertilizer may 'burn' plants. Such plants could be standing in water but are unable to take up any of it because the concentration of solution outside the root is higher than that inside the root.

## WATER QUALITY

It should become increasingly evident that water quality is of great importance to the hydroponic gardener. If water already contains a certain amount of solubles and, in order to feed the plants, more soluble salts (in the form of fertilizers) is added, it stands to reason that by lowering the osmotic potential, the rate at which growing plants can take up water, and consequently the amount of required nutrients, is influenced. One of the outstanding advantages of hydroponics is that the content of water can be completely controlled. For this reason, try to start with the cleanest water available. However, this represents a real problem for many considering hydroponic gardening. Much of the domestic drinking water, although fit for human consumption, contains a large amount of dissolved salts which considerably reduces the osmotic potential.

With regard to the quality of water, we should first try to establish the standards of salt content, its acidity and alkalinity (pH), and how to measure these qualities. Both salt content and water pH change seasonally in domestic or other water supplies (including hydroponic solutions). The salt content of water can be measured by making use of the physical fact that water containing dissolved salts has a greater electroconductivity, and that this conductivity is proportional to the salt concentration. Distilled water does not conduct. Thus, by having an electrical current directed through water, the amount (or lack of) conductivity can be measured. Conductivity is expressed as a lack of resistance (reciprocal ohms) and measured in a standard called mhos/cm. Since this is a rather large unit in terms of expressing harmful concentration to plant life, this unit is further divided into 1,000 smaller units called millimhos. The EC (electrical conductivity) may also be expressed in millisiemens (mS)/cm which is a more up to date standard but has the same value.

For those hydroponicists intending to obtain their own EC readings, it may be important to know that the conductivity of solutions increase by two per cent for each °C increase in temperature. EC meters are available in different price ranges. E587 Conductometer from Sybron/Brinkman in Calgary (403-263-2111) or Edmonton (403-426-1975) cost about $1300. This is a good EC meter and has a 14 cm long scale that provides great accuracy in reading. Then there is also the DP 50 soluble salt meter (Devon Products) with a dual scale, providing both ppm and micromhos (under $300). There are also a number of less expensive EC meters which simply indicate a 'safe' or 'danger' reading. Such meters (about $30.), although not very accurate, may be good enough to keep your mind at ease. Most hydroponic and horticulture/greenhouse supply houses are able to provide a choice of different meters. Another expression used in the laboratories to indicate salt content is the part per million (ppm). This cannot be directly measured, but can be calculated by multiplication of the EC readings in millimhos (mmhos) x 650 = ppm.
1ppm = 1 mg/L = 0.0001%.

**Acidity** and **alkalinity** of soils and solutions can also be measured. It is important to know the acidity levels of nutritional solutions as the roots are only able to take up certain nutrients within a certain range. The standard of acidity is pH. It is the measure of hydrogen ion acitivity (per Hydrogen = pH) in the solution. The pH scale runs from 0 to 14, by which 0 indicates extreme acidity and 14 extreme alkalinity. Accordingly, 7 indicates the neutral level between acidity and alkalinity. Under neutral conditions, there is a balance between H+ (hydrogen ions) and OH- (hydroxyl ions). H+ ions are part of acid molecules, eg. $H_2SO_4$ - HCl and $HNO_3$). OH- ions are part of hydroxides (eg. ammonium hydroxide, sodium hydroxide potassium hydroxide KOH). pH is measured with a pH meter, or by means of various color indicators. Remember that the pH scale is a logarithmic scale. This means that a pH of 4 is 10 times more acid than a reading of 5, and 100 times more acid than a pH of 6, and 1,000 times more acid than a pH of 7. Solutions can be adjusted to a lesser acidity by adding buffers (hydroxides) or made more acidic by adding acid. This has to be carried out very carefully, as an adjustment starts out very slowly,

then accelerates very suddenly past the mark. pH meters are available in a wide range. Top-of-the-line (digital meters) cost several thousands of dollars. However, the same sources mentioned in connection with EC meters have a whole range of less costly pH meters, starting at about $25 - $30. There are also pH test kits consisting of several rolls of indicating paper available. Such strips are dipped into a solution and the amount of discoloration on the strip indicates the solution's pH, which can be read from a standard strip ($8). No serious hydroponics can be attempted without some sort of EC or pH meter (see Figure 16-2).

It is not usually recommended that water with a total dissolved solids content larger than 300 ppm (EC = 0.47 mmhos) be used for hydroponics. When fertilizer is added to this water, the recommended total concentration for most crops should not exceed 1000 - 1500 ppm (1.5 - 3.5 mmhos). Later in the lesson, specific recipes for plant nutrition are given. It will be shown that in order to provide plants with sufficient nutrition, it is of great advantage to start with the purest water possible, as the total ppm of added soluble salts required will be high enough by itself. The purer the water, the more nutrients the plant can be provided. Where and how can clean

### Figure 16-2
### pH AND EC MONITORS

water be obtained? Very seldom is the water available in Alberta pure enough to be used without any pre-treatment. It is usually good enough to use in the garden, where natural precipitation in the form of rain and snow may leach excess salts to deeper layers. In greenhouses, where usually no more water than is required for the healthy production of the crop is provided, dangerous levels of salt may accumulate in the soil, especially when a fair deal of ventilation takes place. The large amounts of moisture that evaporate from the soils deposit high levels of dissolved mineral from groundwater in the top layer of the soil. Home gardeners may obtain a modest 'still' to produce distilled water for a reasonable price. Such stills have to be cleaned out regularly. Commercial operators may find stills rather expensive to obtain and operate. Revenue Canada also takes a great deal of interest in the operators of large stills, but you would not have to worry about them as long as you stick to distilling water! Commercial growers in Europe have, for the last ten years, made use of a relatively new process in water purification which is now becoming available in smaller and cheaper processing units (see Figure 16-3). The process is called reverse osmosis (see Agdex 716 - D36 in RESOURCE MATERIALS). It has very little to do with osmosis as outlined earlier, except that it uses an artificial membrane in the form of a long tube through which water is pumped at high pressure. Due to the nature of this membrane, only water and very small amounts of dissolved solids are able to pass through it. The process is called reverse osmosis because the water moves from a high salt concentration (with the aid of pumps) to a state of purity on the other side of the membrane. Up to 99% of some elements (aluminum - sulfate - phosphates) and as low as 60% (nitrate - silica) may be removed. Iron seems somewhat problematic with as low a removal as 30%. There are, however, different ways to remove iron (see Agdex #716-D12 and D11 in RESOURCE MATERIALS). Due to the nature of the equipment, it is advisable to have a series of filters on hand to remove eventual foreign particles or organic compounds. Larger reverse osmosis units may present problems due to the fact that the waste material flushed out of the membranes is a highly concentrated brine. Smaller units flush the concentrates into the sewer system (eg., Nimbus Water

## Figure 16-3
## REVERSE OSMOSIS UNIT

Systems). For more information contact the following companies:

Aqua-Cleer - Culligan's Representative in your area.

Alberta Softwater Co.

Big Lou Drilling Ltd.

If you consider obtaining any water purification equipment (water softeners are not of any help), remember that units with a low daily production can be used as only sufficient water to top off solutions is needed, plus an amount to store in case the solutions need to be renewed. Storage tank capacity should allow for approximately 1-2 L/plant.

## PLANT NUTRITION IN HYDROPONICS

Many of the basic principles concerning plant nutrition have sufficiently been dealt with in previous lessons (eg., Soils lesson, Plant Nutrition lesson). There is, therefore, no need to repeat this information. The fact that such elements have to be dissolved in the soil moisture is not difficult when plants are grown in inert material and provided with a solution containing these same elements. When this nutrition is needed in the garden or greenhouse soil, the necessary nutrients can be purchased in 50 kg bags and applied as required. The complete solubility or presence of any inert material does not necessarily

bother us. For hydroponic purposes, a slightly higher quality fertilizer which is completely water soluble and does not contain any ballast material is required. In gardens, the majority of the micronutrients are usually obtained from the soil and only on special occasions is it necessary to provide anything in addition to nitrogen, phosphorus, or potassium. In hydroponic gardening, the operators must provide all the required nutrients and elements in the right proportion at the right time, before any damage occurs. Organic fertilizers do not have much application for hydroponics as the contents and release of nutrition is usually irregular and there is seldom a reliable analysis for organic fertilizers. One of the most difficult aspects of hydroponic gardening is to be aware of the concentrations of nutrients to apply at any particular time, without unduly reducing the osmotic potential of the solution. It is, therefore, helpful to be able to calculate the total ppm of dissolved solids. It was mentioned earlier that water with an EC reading higher than 0.47 mmhos (300 ppm) is only marginally acceptable to water plants with. It is possible to accurately calculate the ppm concentration of your own mix of plant materials and, accordingly, determine the expected EC value. One also has to be aware of the purity of the water used. Most of the chemicals used for plant nutrition (fertilizers) are salts. Remember from

chemistry class that a base and an acid form salt + water.

Base + Acid = Salt + Water

Sodium Hydroxide + Hydrochloric Acid = Seasalt + Water

$(NaOH + HCl = NaCl + H_2O)$

As well as weak and strong bases, there are also weak and strong acids. Therefore, if a weak base is combined with a strong acid, an acid reaction salt is obtained. The opposite is also true: if a strong base is combined with a weak acid, the product is an alkaline reacting salt. In some cases, if the base and the acid of more or less equal strength are combined, a neutral reacting salt is obtained. The practical significance of this is that fertilizers used in hydroponic solutions influence the pH of that solution. Fertilizers produced with sulfuric acids are sulphates ($H_2SO_4$), chlorides ($HCl$), nitric acid ($HNO_3$), carbonates ($H_2CO_3$) and others. The contributing base provides the other part of the salt molecule: KOH (potassium hydroxide) + $H_2SO_4$ (sulfuric acid) produces a salt called potassium sulfate ($K_2SO_4$). The combination of one oxygen and one hydrogen atom is called an OH (hydroxyl group).

$2KOH + H_2SO_4 = K_2SO_4 + 2H_2O$.

To those of you who cannot remember much high school chemistry, don't panic! All the chemical names are used in combination with the formula. Each atom has its own specific weight. Accordingly, comparing the formula to the list of atomic weights allows you to calculate the ppm concentration of your fertilizer solution. It really isn't at all complicated! If it is not immediately clear, read it over a few times. It will be of great practical importance when you start preparing your own solutions.

If a concentration of 300 ppm of potassium is required for a solution (which is realistic), 300 mg of potassium/L is required. According to the calculations, there is 164.26 mg of potassium sulfate ($K_2SO_4$), 78.20 mg of which is potassium. Divide 300 by 78 (rounded off) = 3.84. Multiply this number by 164 mg to determine how many mg of $K_2SO_4$ is required. (164 mg x 3.84 = 629.76 or 630 mg of $K_2SO_4$.) This (630 mg) provides 300 ppm of potassium; don't however ignore the fact the total concentration of dissolved solids is increased to 629 ppm.

## Table 16-1
### ATOMIC WEIGHT OF ELEMENTS

| Name | Symbol | Atomic Weight |
|------|--------|---------------|
| Aluminum | Al | 26.98 |
| Boron | B | 10.81 |
| Calcium | Ca | 40.08 |
| Carbon | C | 12.011 |
| Chlorine | Cl | 35.453 |
| Copper | Cu | 63.54 |
| Hydrogen | H | 1.008 |
| Iron | Fe | 55.85 |
| Magnesium | Mg | 23.41 |
| Manganese | Mn | 54.94 |
| Molybdenum | Mo | 95.94 |
| Nitrogen | N | 14.01 |
| Oxygen | O | 16.00 |
| Phosphorus | P | 30.97 |
| Potassium | K | 39.10 |
| Selenium | Se | 78.96 |
| Silicon | Si | 28.09 |
| Sodium | Na | 22.99 |
| Sulfur | S | 32.06 |
| Zinc | Zn | 65.37 |

**Example** $K_2SO_4$ (Potassium Sulfate)

| | Atomic Weight | Molecular Weight |
|--|--|--|
| K = Potassium | $39.10 = 2 \times K$ | = 78.20 |
| S = Sulfur | $32.06 = S$ | = 32.06 |
| O = Oxygen | $16.00 = 4 \times O$ | = 164.26 |

## FERTILIZERS AND SOLUTIONS

Ready mixed fertilizers for hydroponic use are available from commercial sources. However, information about the exact nature of such mixes is difficult to obtain. To be of any benefit to the hydroponics gardener, an exact analysis of content must be determined to allow for calculation of total ppm concentrations of dissolved solids. Furthermore, it is very important to know how much of the contents are, for example, sulfates or nitrates. There should also be an analysis of the micronutrients. The statement 'contains micronutrients' is not sufficient. It may be of interest to note that most of the chemicals providing the essential elements contain small amounts of impurities which often contain traces of available micronutrients. Therefore, be sure to ask for a complete analysis. Each type of plant has its own specific nutrient requirements which changes during the growth of that particular plant. For this reason, ready mixes are also

inadequate. It would be much better if ready mixes were made available as base mixes, whereby the hydroponocist could modify a mix by adding the required fertilizers. This principle should be kept in mind, especially for use with the so-called 'water soluble fertilizers' (Tune Up, Peter's Plant Products) which are available in a wide range of concentrations and could be used for such a purpose. Detailed analysis for these brands is available upon request, and modified custom mixes may also be provided. For the home gardener, it may be advisable to start with your own mixture and, once you have a good idea what works for you, buy a large, commercially available supply. An excellent starter mixture for the beginner is the Hoagland solution, which dates back to the early 1930's and is still widely used for this purpose. When we start explaining how to set up a 'Nutrient Bank' we will also introduce the concept of 'stock solutions'. From the Hoagland Solution it becomes clear that the actual amount required per litre is very small. Each of the fertilizers are, therefore, prepared in a concentrated stock solution (see HOW TO MAKE ONE MOLAR STOCK SOLUTIONS) and small amounts of this are used to prepare the diluted solution. To prepare this solution, obtain the following:

Calcium Nitrate $Ca(NO_3)_2$ (formula weight) = 164.1
Magnesium Sulfate $MgSO_4 + 7H_2O$ FW = 246.5
Potassium Nitrate $KNO_3$ FW = 101.1
Potassium Phosphate $KH_2PO_4$ FW = 136.1

**four** dark brown one litre bottles with tight fitting caps
**six** litres distilled water
**one** weigh scale accurate to .00 mg or better
**one** measuring cylinder (1000 mL capacity)

### HOW TO MAKE ONE MOLAR STOCK SOLUTIONS

This system uses the molecular weight (MW) or the formula weight (FW) as the basis. This information is often found on the reagent quality chemicals obtained from chemical supply companies. If you obtain chemicals without this information, there is a list in this lesson containing the most widely used fertilizers and their formula weight (FW), although you should now be able with your knowledge of atomic weights to calculate these yourself! Calcium nitrate has a FW of 164.1.

## Table 16-2
### MODIFIED HOAGLAND SOLUTION

| Element | ppm | Stock | mL/L |
|---------|-----|-------|------|
| Ca++ | 200 | | |
| Mg++ | 48 | $Ca(NO_3)_2$ | 5 |
| K+ | 234 | $MgSO_4$ | 2 |
| NO3- | 210 | $KNO_3$ | 5 |
| PO4 | 31 | $KH_2PO_4$ | 1 |
| SO4 | 64 | | |
| FE++ | 0.6 | FeEDTA | 1 |
| Mn++ | 0.1 | | |
| Cu++ | 0.14 | | |
| Zn++ | 0.01 | A5 | 1 |
| B+++ | 0.1 | | |
| Mo+ | 0.016 | | |

FeEDTA = Fe Ethylene Diamine Tetra Acetic Acid (Fe++)
**or**
Ferric Citrate (Fe+++)
100 mg/100 mL $H_2O$
**or**
5 - 10 mg/L Sequestrene 330 (5-10 ppm)
A5 = micronutrient solution.

(Hoagland & Snyder 1938)

Weigh out 164.1 g of this fertilizer. Measure about 800 mL of the distilled water in the cylinder, add the calcium nitrate and stir with a glass or plastic rod until all of the fertilizer is completely dissolved. Then top up the container to 1000 mL (1 L). You now have one litre of one molar calcium nitrate. Don't forget to label the bottle! Store in a dark, cool place. Repeat this procedure for the other three fertilizers (magnesium sulfate, potassium nitrate, potassium phosphate). When making a nutrient solution, you have only to add the required number of millilitres of stock solution. This is not only an accurate but also a constant measure. The other two ingredients, iron and A5 require a slightly different approach to preparation. Once you have prepared them, they last a long time in comparison with the others, as you only use one mL/L of each solution. There are a number of different ways to provide iron (Fe) to plants. Iron intake is very much dependent on the pH of the solution. Therefore, we may have preference for a particular form of iron in our solution. Generally, iron becomes less available if the solution becomes more alkaline. For small operations, either 'Sequestrene 330 Fe Iron Ch elate', available from greenhouse

suppliers, or a solution of ferric citrate containing 100 mg/100 mL water (10 ppm) is recommended. A5 is a micronutrient solution, so accurate weighing equipment is required to prepare A5. It is a simple procedure. Start with about 800 mL of warm (70°C) water and measure out:
$H_3BO_4$ Boric Acid 2.86 g
$ZnSO_4 + 7H_2O$ Zinc Sulfate 0.222 g
$CuSO_4 + 5H_2O$ Cupric Sulfate 0.079 g
$MnCl + H_2O$ Manganese Chloride 1.81 g
$Na_2MoO_3$ Sodium Molybdolate 0.018 g
Add all the above and stir until dissolved. Then top off to 1000 mL. Store in the refrigerator. It was indicated that iron was best available at a certain level of solution acidity. This is a condition to which most elements in solutions are subject, although not always in such a dramatic manner as iron. By simply allowing the pH of the solution to drift, certain elements, although present in significant amounts, cannot be absorbed. For example, a drop in pH may release manganese at

such a rate that toxicity may occur. Plant roots continually exude weak acids which lower down the pH of the solution if not countered by the necessary buffers. It may also be worthwhile to point out that if certain stock solutions are mixed together in an undiluted state, they may react with each other. Therefore, have at least half the required amount of water ready to put the measured amounts of stock solution into, and then top off up to the desired total amount. When dissolving chemicals, it may sometimes be helpful to warm the water up to 90°C (195°F) if the chemical in question is slow to dissolve. This is especially true of the chemicals containing phosphorus (usually phosphates) because they are extremely difficult to dissolve. This is one reason why the commercial phosphate fertilizers like super phosphate, rock phosphate and bone meal cannot be used. Many of the ammonium phosphates are readily soluble. Monoammonium phosphate $NH_4H_2PO_4$ and diammonium phosphate

$(NH_4)_2H_2PO_4$ are two examples of such phosphates. They also contain a source of nitrogen in the form of ammonia ($NH_4$). Another source of phosphate, if you do not prefer or need the nitrogen source, is the calcium phosphate: monocalcium phosphate $Ca(H_2PO_4)_2$ or dicalcium phosphate $CaHPO_4$. The potassium phosphate ($KH_2PO_4$) used in the Hoagland Solution is a very good and soluble fertilizer, but is also very expensive. Other references contain many different recipes which can be used (see RESOURCE MATERIALS).

Much of the required background in plant nutrition can be obtained from the lesson on that subject. There is no difference in the basic intake of nutrients by plants in hydroponic cultures than those grown in soil. In hydroponic cultures, however, no slow release type fertilizers are used. Only those immediately available and soluble have applications. There is, however, in certain methods which use inert solids as media (sand and gravel),

## Table 16-3
## COMPOSITION OF A HYDROPONIC NUTRIENT SOLUTION

| SALT | FORMULA | STOCK SOLUTION g/L | DILUTION mL/L | CONCENTRATION (ppm) |
|---|---|---|---|---|
| Calcium Nitrate | $Ca(NO_3)_2\ 4H_2O$ | 787 | 1.25 | 117(N) 168 Ca |
| Potassium Nitrate | $KNO_3$ | 169 | 3.9 | 254 (K) 91 N |
| Potassium Phosphate | $KH_2PO_4$ | 91 | 3.0 | 62 (P) 78 K |
| Magnesium Sulphate | $MgSO_4\ 7H_2O$ | 329 | 1.5 | 49 (Mg) |
| Chelated Iron | FeNaEOTA | 12.3 | 3.0 | 5.6 (Fe) |
| Manganese Sulfate | $MnSO_4\ 4H_2O$ | 3.0 | 3.0 | 2.2 (Mn) |
| Boric Acid | $H_3BO_3$ | 1.23 | 1.5 | 0.32 (B) |
| Copper Sulfate | $CuSO_4\ 5H_2O$ | 0.17 | 1.5 | 0.064 (Cu) |
| Ammonium Molybdate | $(NH_4)_6MO_7O_{24}\ 4H_2O$ | 0.06 | 1.5 | 0.007 (Mo) |
| Phosphoric Acid | $H_3PO_3$ | — | 0.044 | 23 (P) |
| Zinc Sulfate | $ZnSO_4$ | 0.17 | 3.0 | 0.12 (Zn) |

an application of the information on soil colloids (see Soils lesson, SOIL COLLOIDS). The surface area of the medium used in hydroponics has a storage capacity for the dissolved fertilizers, but are also immediately available for the plant. Therefore, it is important to observe that such media are relatively free of colloidal dust. Gravel and sand should especially be tested for this type of dust. Usually a thorough washing with clean water, followed by treatment with a strong hydroxide and, thereafter, with acid will remove most of the colloidal dust. It may be surprising to find how much dust is removed with the acid rinse, even after the medium is thought to be clean. Washed gravel and washed mortar sand is available from building suppliers and has been washed to meet the standard of the building trade for use in the preparation of mortar and concrete. Such medium is not clean enough for hydroponic use. Sand available in 50 kg (110 lb) bags for sand-blasting purposes (SB-7) or (7 grade) is the cleanest sand available, but even this sand should be treated with mild acid to remove any traces of colloidal dust. After prolonged use, hydroponic media should be cleaned as well; no great clouds of dust are evident, but there is a large amount of accumulated material removed which, because of its chemical nature, attaches itself more strongly to the surface of medium particles than others (see Plant Nutrition lesson, ABSORPTION). Minerals are absorbed as either cations ($NH_4+$, $K+$, $Ca++$, $Na+$, $Mg++$) (univalent $+$ cations are taken up easier than divalent $++$) or as anions ($NO_3-$, $H_2PO_4=$, $SO_4=$, $Cl-$).

## MEDIA

As has been indicated earlier, there is a choice of media in which to grow plants hydroponically. Any compound will serve the purpose as long as it is inert, not too fine a texture, and easy to obtain. For this reason, it can be expected that new (different) media will appear on the market from time to time.

## WATER CULTURES

The original hydroponics use water as the only medium. For experimental, short-term purposes, this is an adequate method. However, it should be realized that most plants do not normally grow with their roots submerged. Recall, also, that roots can absorb gases. Therefore, plants grow much better if there is allowance for a regular period of aeration in the medium. This can be produced by draining the container for short intervals. Aerating the solution does not put extra air into a solution, but provides circulation which helps the gas exchange of the solution (allows the escape of excess $CO_2$ gas). Another drawback is that plant roots are unable to perform one of their functions in water; that is, to anchor plants. Furthermore, water cultures have a reputation for getting infected with bacteria and algae if in use for any length of time. In larger systems, the amount of solution to renew is excessive. In order to overcome some of these drawbacks for water cultures, inert media are used in combination with water. Such media should not influence the culture by either permanently absorbing or supplying nutritional or other substances. The most commonly used inert media are sand, gravel, vermiculite, perlite, clay-base aggregate and peat moss. One can, in fact, use anything as a medium for this purpose, as long as it is inert and fulfils a number of other requirements (discussed later in the lesson). Price is also (naturally) a very important factor.

## SAND

Providing that the warning stated earlier concerning colloidal dust is heeded and the sand is cleaned appropriately, it makes a reasonably good medium. The size of the grain is an important aspect as the rate of percolation (the downward movement of water, drainage) is strongly influenced by grain size. If the sand is too fine, drainage is very slow and may allow plant roots to deplete most of the nutrients from the water before the excess has drained out. As previously stated, it is also advisable to allow fresh air to have access to the roots. A medium that does not have the ability to drain rapidly and completely is undesirable. Another consequence of grain size is the cooling effect on constantly wet media. Evaporation from a wet surface can cool that surface considerably. The combined surface area of all the sand grains on the surface is very large. The rate of relative evaporation increases when the air becomes drier. Although roots should normally be kept at cooler temperatures than the air temperature ($\pm 5°C$ difference), excessive cooling can seriously slow down the growing process. With the use of coarser media, temperature compensation can be provided by feeding with warmer solutions (here is a potential use of waste heat!). Application of fresh solution to a coarser medium prevents depletion of nutrients; the faster rate of drainage and the larger spaces between particles allows more fresh air to enter the media. Fine textured aggregate media like sand also have a tendency to compact. Algae growth on the surface of such a texture can effectively seal off the surface and prevent sufficient gas exchange. It is difficult to clean sand of organic debris, like old roots, etc. after repeated use. Sand, then, especially the finer grades, should usually be avoided for hydroponic cultures.

## GRAVEL

Much of what has been discussed about sand is applicable to gravel as well. However, after a thorough cleansing, gravel can be used indefinitely and is one of the better mediums. Especially useful is 'pea gravel' with an average diameter of 1 cm (3/8 in). This is available in 50 kg (110 lb) bags from sand and gravel suppliers. Rinsing after an initial flush with clean water with a 1/10 diluted solution of either hydrochloric or acetic acid removes most collodial dust. When diluting acid, remember to put the acid in the water and not the other way around! This type of treatment should be carried out in the open to avoid the accumulation of toxic vapors. Drainage is rapid and the large spaces between the gravel provides excellent aeration. Cleaning after repeated use is not difficult; submerging the gravel in water and stirring it around brings any dead roots and other organic particles to the surface. Algae are not a major problem on the surface of gravel, especially as it is not difficult to keep the upper surface of the plant bed drier. Some of the initial commercial applications were, in fact, gravel cultures. Extensive carnation production in Holland during the late 1940's used gravel as a medium. Especially with recirculating systems, it is much easier to keep gravel out of the pumps and return lines than, for example, sand

and/or vermiculite. Most of the local gravel, which has its origin in riverbeds, is acceptable. In certain cases, crushed granite can be used (try to avoid the finer grade). There can be a certain amount of dust, which is usually easy to remove with plain water. Marble chips should be avoided as they are not inert! On contact with even mild acids, they release calcium and related chemical compounds.

## VERMICULITE

Vermiculite is a useful medium which is inert as long as it is not subject to low pH. At lower pH levels, it releases toxic amounts of manganese. It does release small amounts of magnesium and potash. Some problems may be encountered with drainage, especially when the vermiculite gets older as it has a tendency to remain wet for longer periods. Vermiculite actually deteriorates in structure after some time. It should never be reused, but rather displaced with fresh material. Vermiculite is available in plastic bags and is relatively inexpensive. Vermiculite is increasingly used in combination with sphagnum peat moss in bag culture (see PEAT MOSS AND BAG CULTURES).

## PERLITE

This is in many ways similar to vermiculite; however, it does not deteriorate in structure as rapidly as vermiculite. It also has applications in mixtures with sphagnum peat moss and is inert. As a result of rough handling, there may sometimes be a rather large amount of dust in the bags. One serious drawback of perlite in general is its color — white. When absorbing nutrient solution and being exposed to light, perlite becomes an attractive medium for algae to grow on. Algae compete with the plants for nutrition, especially phosphates, and can become an unsightly nuisance. Perlite is often mixed with sphagnum peat moss to provide a better structure, especially in 'bag cultures'. In situations where light is kept away from the medium, there is an application for perlite.

## FIRED-SHALE AGGREGATE

Fired-shale aggregate consists of small pellets about 12 mm (½ in) in diameter

with many pores. This is a byproduct of the cement industry. Small quantities are expensive to purchase when required in bulk (25 kg = 1.5 cu ft = $12); from the source, it can be an economic material. Due to its structure, over time it accumulates a rather large amount of organic debris which is difficult to remove. This material finds a lot of application in various forms of hydroponics. Especially in Holland, many of the Bromeliads grown in pots use this medium in combination with a flood type irrigation system. Certain difficulties are sometimes experienced after prolonged use with an excess accumulation of nutrients. This medium is also used in hydroponic planters (like the Luwasa system) as the aggregate does provide an attractive texture and, even if some algae are present, does not become unsightly.

## SAWDUST

Sawdust is an organic medium that is not entirely inert. During the slow deterioration process, certain elements become available and the organic breakdown process also requires certain nutrients. As long as this is understood, compensation can be made and the crop grown in it will not be disadvantaged. Not all sawdust is suitable and some is toxic (cedar). It may be advisable to sterilize the sawdust before using it. Needless to say, it is not practical to clean it after prolonged use; it should be discarded and replaced with fresh sawdust. Sawdust, as a medium in hydroponics, is a typical western Canadian method and is especially useful in 'bag systems'.

## PEAT MOSS

Sphagnum peat moss is the partially decomposed remainder of years and years of growth of a bog or marsh moss called *Sphagnum*. It has a high water absorption capability (10 times its own weight), is relatively sterile and inert, and is (usually) rather low in pH (acid). There are also other types of peat which originate from other plant remains (sedge). They are, however, usually coarser in texture, very fibrous and are often alkaline. Traditionally, peat moss has widespread application in the horticultural trade (horticultural peat moss) for soil mixtures, as a substrate for pot plants, and as a general soil conditioner in nursing beds. It also has

wide application in 'soilless' mixtures where, with the addition of perlite and/or vermiculite, it serves as an excellent short-term soil mix. After its use in hydroponics, peat still has application as a soil conditioner in the nursery or garden.

## METHODS

Historically, the first methods applied in water cultures were rather simplistic: a container with the solution and some means of suspending the plant with its roots into that medium. Experimental and educational short-term cultures still apply the same principle. It is not difficult to set up or maintain and, for beginners, it may be the method to try on a small scale. For the more advanced hydroponocist, it may be a good idea to try out a new nutrient solution or a different crop. There is also a use for hydroponics to demonstrate aspects of plant nutrition. The definition for deficiency suggests that a deficiency is a symptom caused by the lack of a certain element, and that such a symptom disappears if that element is provided. With these solutions you can try to promote the appearance of such symptoms. However, certain deficiencies (like calcium) are so devastating that the plant is unable to recover. Figure 16-4 demonstrates the set up to experiment with the role of nutrients in plants. Seedling plants are raised in a seedbed or container with vermiculite, and transferred to the water culture as soon as they are large enough and their roots long enough to be suspended into the water. A word of warning about the deficiency experiment: if you try to have plants develop deficiency symptoms, and these plants have rather large seeds (like beans and corn), remove the remaining seeds at transplanting. The endosperm in these seeds may provide the seedling with deficient elements for some time to come and delay the appearance of symptoms. Handle young seedlings by one of their leaves, not the stem, as it is easily damaged and will delay, if not prevent, the plants from growing. Any plastic pail of about 2 L capacity (about 1/2 gal) with a snap-on lid makes an excellent water culture container. If the container is translucent, it may need to be wrapped in aluminum foil or painted with a dark paint. Algae can start to grow in the solution if this precaution is not taken. Always keep any nutrient solution in the dark as much as

## Figure 16-4
## NUTRIENT DEFICIENCY EQUIPMENT

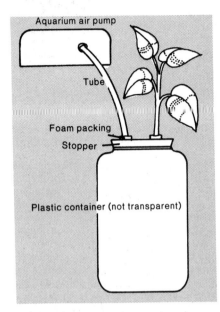

possible. The lid should have two holes cut in it; one small hole to put an airline and airstone into, and a larger hole to accommodate the plant. Obtain some soft foam plastic and cut it into long ribbons. Wrap or roll strips around the stem of the young plants until they fit (with some friction) into the large hole. One can also make a round foam cork to fit the hole and, with a razor blade, make a cut or wedge in which the young plant is clamped. It is also possible to make a long, narrow 'U-shaped' cut from the edge of the lid towards the centre and slide the plant, clamped between the strip of foam plastic, toward the center. In this case, it is not necessary to make two holes as the aeration tube can usually be accommodated in the same hole (Figure 16-4). Aeration into water cultures is advisable. The name is a bit misleading as no extra air can be made to dissolve in the nutrient solution. However, the constant agitation will allow other undesirable gases to escape and fresh air to enter. An experiment for those of you who are not easily convinced would be to grow two treatments side by side, one aerated, the other non-aerated. Closely monitor the pH. Certain plants, through excretion from the root system, may gradually reduce the pH. As it is advisable to renew the solution once a week, buffering is normally not required. Another application of water culture connects a series of containers with

plastic hose and allows fresh nutrients to irrigate the container. This usually requires pumps or other methods to force the nutrient solution to circulate. Water culture systems using forced circulation do not need aeration, as there is sufficient agitation created by the pumps. There has been a rapid development in the commercial use of water cultures through the use of a gutter system or flood bench. The latter is simply a bench able to hold potted plants. It has rather high sides and a waterproofed liner (see Figure 16-5). Nutrients are pumped into the bench from a holding tank and, after a certain period of time, allowed to drain back. (This concept is illustrated in Figure 16-6.) Needless to say, algae are numerous in such systems. The larger systems use one holding tank which, through an array of timers and valves, irrigate each bench in turn from the same holding tank.

Another application of a constant flow system is the gutter system which has many variations. Long plastic gutters placed on a gentle gradient slope receive a constant flow of nutrient solution through them. This solution is allowed to flow out on the lower end and can, with the aid of a pump, be brought back to the original point and recirculated (see Figure 16-7). Often, a cover with holes to accommodate the plants rests on top of the gutter. Plastic

## Figure 16-5
## FLOOD BENCH

pipe 5 cm (about 2 in) in diameter can also be used, with holes drilled into the top surface of pipe to accommodate plants. Plants grown in this way develop a rather reduced root system. Nutrient solutions in large enterprises can be controlled by computers that continually monitor the pH and E.C. values, and automatically readjusts the solution to keep it in optimum condition. Many such computer systems also measure temperature in the greenhouse and the available light to compensate for the increase and decrease of the growth rate of the plants. Once such a program exists for gutter systems, it can be supported in many ways. In Holland and Germany, blocks of foam plastic are used, very much like the material known here as 'oasis' and used in floral design. Such blocks have a hole in the centre where a cutting can be rooted in, or a young plant can be inserted. These blocks clamp firmly enough between the sides of the gutter to support the plant. Jiffy-7 pellets are also used in a similar manner. This system is also based on the same principle as the 'living lettuce' concept. Lettuce is not only grown in a block of inert material, but harvested with the roots attached. These root blocks are placed into a plastic container when marketed and allow the retailer and consumer to keep the lettuce fresh for longer periods of time. Such living lettuce enterprises are in operation in Ontario and the Vancouver area. A consequential development has been that of nutrient film techniques (NFT). The father of this concept is Dr. Allan Cooper who started and developed this system in the Glasshouse Crops Research Institute in Littlehampton, England (1965). NFT now finds wide application in a range of vegetable and cutflower crops. This system is very much like the gutter system, but uses a black plastic film folded in such a manner as to form a closed gutter in which holes are cut to accommodate plants (see Figure 16-8). Some adaptations start with a flat strip of sheet plastic and the edges brought together and stapled at the top. Seedlings are often started on Jiffy blocks and placed on the plastic sheet, then enclosed by folding over the edges to form a long channel. Quite often, a taut wire is suspended along the centre of this channel and the centre of the channel is supported by this wire (see Figure 16-9). Imagination is the only limit to the application of such systems. The obvious simplicity of this system has been attractive for many growers as well

## Figure 16-6
## SIMPLE HYDROPONICS SYSTEM

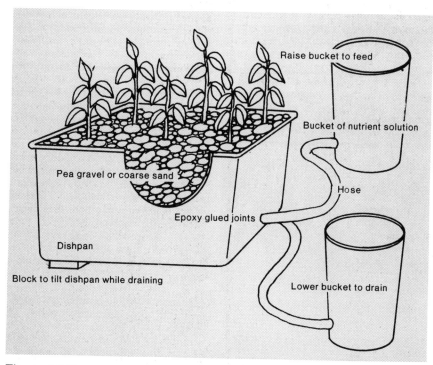

Raise bucket to feed

Bucket of nutrient solution

Pea gravel or coarse sand

Hose

Epoxy glued joints

Dishpan

Block to tilt dishpan while draining

Lower bucket to drain

as its widespread potential application. A firm underground, preferably with a slight slope, is important. The ends of the channel connect in a central channel which collects the solution for recirculation. Besides the rather low cost, other advantages to the system are that light can be kept out and evaporation can be drastically reduced. A number of variations have been produced, some with special extended plastic canals. Such modifications are usually considerably more expensive. Tomatoes, cucumbers, lettuce, chrysanthemums, peppers, eggplants and many other crops have been commercially grown in such systems (see Figure 16-10). Another interesting development in energy savings has been obtained by using waste heat of relatively low temperatures (too low to be of use in heating greenhouse air) to warm the nutrient solution. Black plastic pipe to conduct the warm water is, in such instances, incorporated in the LFT channel and provides heat to the solution and the root system. It has been found that crops can then be successfully grown with relatively lower greenhouse temperatures.

## Figure 16-7
## NUTRIENT FILM TECHNIQUE (AUTOMATIC HYDROPONICS)

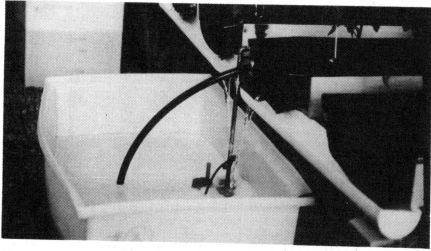

# AEROPONICS

Rather than suspending the roots into solution, aeroponics uses atomizers to blow a fine mist of nutrient solution into the root system. The 'Ein-Gedi System (EGS)', developed in Israel, is such a system and is still, more or less, an experimental method. Plants have to grow considerably better and the method produce considerable advantages before it is likely to find wide application. The control and implications are rather elaborate and, therefore, too much of a financial investment to be attractive to even the commercial grower.

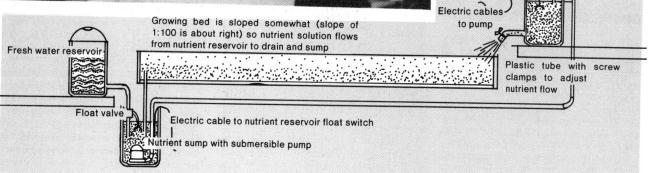

Growing bed is sloped somewhat (slope of 1:100 is about right) so nutrient solution flows from nutrient reservoir to drain and sump

Cable to electric outlet

Electric cables to pump

Fresh water reservoir

Plastic tube with screw clamps to adjust nutrient flow

Float valve

Electric cable to nutrient reservoir float switch

Nutrient sump with submersible pump

## Figure 16-8
## ROSES ON NFT

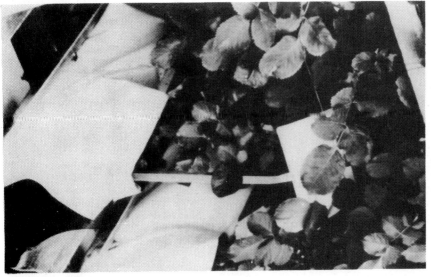

## Figure 16-9
## PLASTIC GULLY

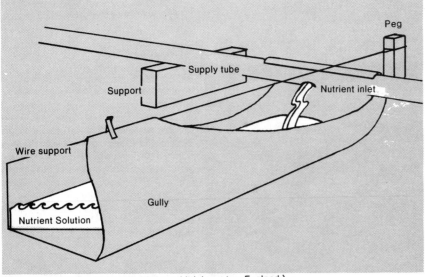

(Glasshouse Crops Research Institute, Littlehampton, England.)

## GRAVEL CULTURES

Most gravel systems are combined with irrigation systems which either pump constant or interrupted flows of nutrients through the gravel bed. For commercial applications, gravel cultures have seen their best days, but for the home gardener, small flow-through systems with gravel are still an attractive system. Where rapid filling and draining is an item of the system design, gravel can hardly be beaten. One such system is a cascading or terrace system. Here nutrient solutions are pumped only into the highest bed and allowed, through gravitational pull, to find their way to successively lower levels until arriving at the last bed. From here it is pumped back to the highest bed (see Figure 16-11). A well developed system only pumps the return flow a certain number of times per day, thereby providing an economic base of operation. Gravel beds are also attractive in long construction, where a reasonable rate of flow can be maintained without the nutrient being entirely removed by the time the solution reaches the end of the bench. This principle also applies to those systems which use the flood method. The rapid return allows the supply from one storage basin to several beds, which represents a reduction in the investment of pumps and other control equipment. Gravel is also less likely to damage pumps and valves as a number of screens can assure that the gravel stays in the beds. There is practically no grit developed due to deterioration. A major disadvantage of gravel cultures is due to the weight of gravel. Gravel beds have to be very strong, which also makes them very expensive. Clay pellets are lighter in weight and behave very much like gravel, except that they disintegrate slightly over a period of use.

## SAND CULTURES

Sand cultures find most of their application in those areas where sand is abundant. For a number of reasons (see SAND), sand is not an 'easy' medium. For home gardeners, it is only appropriate if a real coarse and clean sand is available. Not withstanding its shortcomings as a hydroponic medium, some of the largest commercial hydroponic enterprises in the middle East use sand. These systems are called 'open systems', which means that

## GRASS GROWING SYSTEMS

This system may be of a limited application to the home gardener, but for anyone involved with livestock, it is worth mentioning the production of greenfeed for cattle through hydroponics. Grains like corn, barley, wheat, soybean and rye are pre-soaked and then germinated under artificial light. When a 12-15 cm (5-6 in) swath has grown, this whole 'cake' is fed to the animals. Only water has to be provided as most of the nutritional requirements are found in the endosperm of the seeds. Several tests apparently showed a gain in milk production of dairy cattle. With the long winters in this part of the world, there may be a great potential for this application of hydroponics.

## Figure 16-10
## NFT CANAL SYSTEM

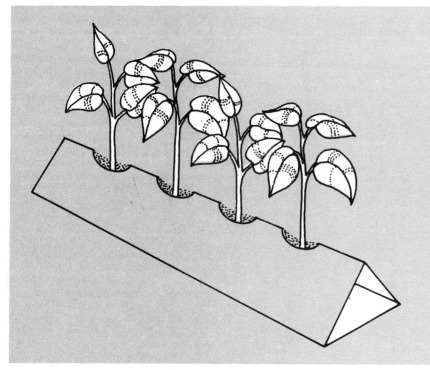

application in circumstances where water conservation is the main reason for hydroponics.

## VERMICULITE AND PERLITE

Although attempts have been made in the past to have larger hydroponic systems utilize vermiculite and perlite, they have never been completely successful. These materials are practically inert, but their nature produces problems for recirculating systems.

## PEAT MIXES AND BAG CULTURES

More and more horticulturists use the commercially prepared 'soilless mixes' or produce a mix of their own manufacturing. The reasons for this are many: difficulties in obtaining good black loam, herbicide residue in loam, or, simply, the price. Many of the soilless mixes are based on peat moss, vermiculite and/or perlite mixed with limestone, trace elements, and slow release fertilizers. Such mixes lend

there is no attempt to catch and recycle the used water. Sand culture has many disadvantages and is no longer a method home gardeners should employ.

## SAWDUST CULTURE

Most sawdust cultures use wooden raised beds, made waterproof with a polyethylene liner. The center of the bench is normally the lowest point and it is here that a perforated drainpipe is placed. Supply is by means of a trickle system or intermittent dosage from larger lines. One of the reasons for the development of this method in B.C. was the occurrence of certain soil–borne diseases and pests. Tomatoes, especially, grow very well in this medium. Most of this application is in greenhouses. Nutrients can be supplied through irrigation water. It is also possible, however, to pre-mix slow release fertilizers through the sawdust before planting. Sawdust is discarded after use and replaced with fresh material. 'Old' sawdust can be used to improve the structure of garden soil. Sawdust cultures are usually open systems and, therefore, do not have

## Figure 16-11
## TERRACE OR CASCADE SYSTEM

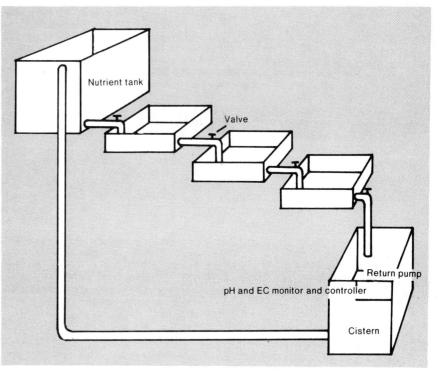

Table 16-4
## RECIPE FOR HARROW PEAT BAG MIXTURE

A) 3   6 cu ft bags (170 L) Canadian Sphagnum Peatmoss
       (approx. 47% of total volume)

    3   4 cu ft bags (113 L) Medium Hort. Vermiculite
       (approx. 31% of total volume)

    2   4 cu ft bags (113 L) Medium Hort. Perlite
       (approx. 21% of total volume)

| B) | | |
|---|---|---|
| 5 kg of limestone powder 97% Calcium Carbonate | (11 lbs) | |
| 4 kg of Dolomitic limestone (ground) | (8 lb 8 oz) | |
| 1.5 kg of Super Phosphate (20% P) | (3 lb 3 oz) | |
| 1 kg of Potassium Sulfate | (2 lbs 2 oz) | |
| 150 g of Fritted Trace Elements (FTE 302) (Plant Products) | (5 oz) | |

C) 2 kg of 18-6-12 (9 months Osmocote)         (4 lbs 4 oz)

| D) Dissolve into 20 L of water | (4.4 gal) |
|---|---|
| 2 kg of Potassium Nitrate | (4 lbs 4 oz) |
| 0.3 kg of Magnesium Sulfate | (11 oz) |
| 35 g Borax (15% B) | (2 oz) |
| 35 g of Chilated Iron | (2 oz) |
| 0.1 L of wetting agent | (3½ fl oz) |

Mix all the dry ingredients thoroughly and moisten with the 20 L solution. Pay attention to the mixing process; the total mass should be turned over at least six times. This mixture provides enough material to fill at least 32 bags (0.35 m x 1.0 m). The amount of ingredients can be mixed proportionally for smaller or larger quantities. All ingredients are obtainable from local greenhouse suppliers. It is possible to use this mix in many other systems besides peat bags; however, it has been specifically designed for a crop lasting 9 months. The osmocote mentioned is also available with shorter release periods and a different formula; inquire at your supply company.

themselves very well to open hydroponic systems. Water is the only additional requirement. Plant beds or containers filled with such a mix are often irrigated by trickle systems.

A logical development has been the introduction of bag cultures. Long plastic bags are filled with peat mix and sealed on either end. Pre-filled bags are available in many countries and the dimensions differ between suppliers. The bags are lined out in rows in the greenhouse and small holes cut in the top surface of the bag where the plants are to be grown. Often, young plants are established in peat blocks or Jiffy-7 pellets and placed on top of the newly cut holes. They soon root into the peat mix. Watering is by trickle irrigation. Not much evaporation takes place from the bag and, accordingly, no excess cooling

of the medium results. As many modern greenhouses use forced air heating and cooling, this is a decided advantage. However, care must be taken to ensure that there is no overwatering, as drainage from the bag is minimal. A special peat/vermiculite/perlite mix has been developed by the Agriculture Canada Research Station at Harrow, Ontario (see Table 16-4). The mixture is specially formulated for the production of greenhouse tomatoes but, with experience, the mix can be modified for many other fast growing crops.

## IRRIGATION TECHNIQUES AND EQUIPMENT

There are two basic irrigation methods used in hydroponics:

1. those that use plain water to irrigate the crop, and
2. those that have nutrients dissolved in the water.

The plain water systems can use normal plumbing equipment, such as valves made out of brass or other metals. Any system in the second classification should incorporate plastic components, as the dissolved salts in the solutions can interact with any metal parts and not only corrode them, but also give rise to toxic levels of certain metals (such as copper and zinc) in the solutions. There is a general tendency in the plumbing trade to use various plastic components, so obtaining plastic components is much easier than a few years ago. There is also transparent plastic tubing on the market which is nice to work with, but keep in mind the facts about algae that were mentioned previously (see METHODS). If you plan on working with such tubing, wrap it in foil or anything else that keeps out the light. If you have a choice of plastic water lines, always choose the darkest color available. Even the white plastic tubing used in the plumbing trade transmits enough light to support algae growth. There is a gray type of tubing available that is more suitable for hydroponic plumbing. Such pipe and the various fittings are easy to work with as they can be glued to make a perfect waterproof joint. It may be worthy to note that there are sterilizers available that will, with the aid of ultra violet light, kill bacteria, viruses and algae present in the water. These are

## Figure 16-12
## DRIP STICK IRRIGATION

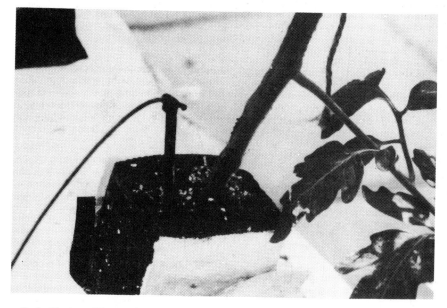

called 'Trojan Water Sterilizers' and operate on a flow-through principle. Storage tanks (especially) should also be kept dark. After long periods of use, algae build up in a recirculating system anyways. Don't forget that we operate with two opposing interests; on one hand we try to provide our plants with the optimum amount of light but, on the other hand, we have to keep light away from the nutrient solution. Each time a crop is terminated, the whole system could be thoroughly cleaned. Household bleach does a good job, and scrubbing with water and household salt is also useful. However, rinse everything thoroughly with water to remove all traces of salt and bleach before starting the system up again.

Presently, there is a wide range of automatic watering equipment available. Many of these are designed for use in gardens and parks, but some also have possible application in hydroponic set-ups. The various automatic drip systems designed for greenhouses are excellent for adaptation to a hydroponic system. Most of such systems consist of a supply line with lateral lines into which holes are punched. The holes accommodate thin tubes known as 'spaghetti tubes'. These 'drip lines' are able to provide water to pot plants, bag cultures, or to individual plants in benches (see Figure 16-12). Familiarize yourself with the various types of

equipment available to determine where and how they can be used in a hydroponics set-up. Rainbird, Toro, Buckner, Spot-Systems, and Irri-Troll are only a few of the manufacturers. There are many stores, particularly in the larger centers, that specialize in hydroponic supplies. Many offer ready-made systems.

Once the system and the pipes have been selected, it is time to decide what provides the flow of liquid through the system. In a **open system**, water can either be dispensed on a medium that already contains the required nutrients (like the bag system), or the required nutrition can be injected into the water flow with the aid of an injector or liquid-feed metering system (see Figure 16-13) . Such devices vary in price according to their size (capacity) and accuracy. The 'Hozon Siphon Mixer', which sucks up 1 part of concentrated solution for every 16 parts of water, is one inexpensive type. Variations in flow and pressure influence the ratio considerably. The 'Cameron Bucket Diluter' is calibrated against a constant pressure and flow, and provides a wide range of ratios with the aid of different nozzles. Fluctuations in pressure and flow influence the performance of injectors. The 'Smith-Measure Mix' works by hydraulic piston movement. This accurate unit is available in different ratios and flow rates. Other brands include 'Anderson', 'HPA-GEWA' and 'Rossel'. Rossel is especially designed for commercial NFT systems. Open systems are not that difficult to design because they utilize the available water flow and pressure from the domestic water supply. A drawback is that if the

## Figure 16-13
## NUTRIENT PROPORTIONER

E.C. value of that water is relatively high, only small concentrations can be injected. If higher concentrations are used in such cases, the optimum osmotic potential value will be exceeded.

**Closed systems** rely on a flow and pressure created by some pumping device. Small cascading systems could use a flow of air bubbles to pump the water to the top tank. A small aquarium pump will usually do the job (see Figure 16-11). Another pumping system that makes use of compressed air is the air cushion system. This requires a closed container into which compressed air is blown. The ensuing pressure forces the liquid out of the tank through the supply line. Pressure for such systems usually comes from a larger air compressor. It also requires a series of solenoid valves to open and close certain lines (see SOLENOID AND OTHER ELECTRICAL CONTROL VALVES). Air pressure systems are an efficient means of directing solution flows, as they reduce the use of electrical power and wiring. In most cases, airlines are also simpler to connect. Larger units usually require electrically driven pumps. For smaller hydroponic systems, there are a number of small pumps available from the 'Little Giant Company'; dealers are located in Edmonton and Calgary. There are basically two of these pump types available: sump pumps and submersible pumps. Sump pumps stand in the liquid and precautions must be taken with them to ensure that the electrical part does not get submerged. These are small pumps with a maximum pumping height of about 1 m (3-4 ft). Their flow rate is also limited. For smaller systems, however, they are adequate. Submersible pumps are available in various capacities. They are filled with a non-conductive oil and can be submerged into the solution. They are also constructed from non-corrosive materials. Due to their electrical nature, they do generate a small amount of heat which can be utilized to keep the solution warm. For small recirculating systems, this is one of the better types of pumps to use. Larger commercial units use strong pumps. In order to overcome the corrosive effects of the solution, they are often constructed of rubber and stainless steel. When shopping around for a suitable pump, always try to get one that is corrosive resistant.

## SOLENOID AND OTHER ELECTRICAL CONTROL VALVES

In order to make a system automatic, a valve that can be electrically opened and closed is required. The simplest form of this is the solenoid valve. The solenoid valve is an electromagnetic valve which can be obtained in the normally open or the normally closed mode. The normally closed valve stays shut when there is no electrical current running through the electromagnet. The valve opens when current is applied. The other type, the normally open valve, operates exactly opposite. Solenoids are available with nylon bodies and a choice of voltages (120 V or 24 V). The 24 V version is used with a reducing transformer, making it less expensive to wire if the wire has to be strung over any great distance, and also less hazardous when used in combination with solutions and the general plant growing environment. One drawback of solenoid valves is that their action is rapid and may give rise to leakage and breakage of lines. Solenoids are usually controlled by a timing device like a timeclock. The diameter of the line in which the solenoid is used has a major influence on the price of the valve. Large diameter solenoid valves can be very expensive. There are also valves available that are driven by a small (usually 24 V) electrical motor. Their advantage is that they close or open gradually, thereby avoiding the water-hammer effect. Such valves can also be made to operate proportionally (i.e., they can be made to open or close only partially). With the incorporation of micro-processors, this can be of interest to the home gardener who is 'into' this kind of approach. Small diameter solenoid valves can be used to control air flow and pressure in those systems that operate with this technology. For example, a 6 mm (¼ in) solution line would severely restrict the flow of a solution, but for air pressure, this is more than enough to either let air pressure build up or reduce.

## TIMERS

The switching of solenoids and pumps can be made completely automatic with the aid of timeclocks. There are essentially two types of timeclocks available for hydroponic purposes. One is the 24 Hour Clock, which rotates on a 24 hour basis, and functions through the use of trippers. The minimum time between on and off actions is usually one hour. There are also plug-in timers available with a plastic housing and a series of lugs for programming. For continuous hydroponic use, the commercial types (Tork or G.E.) are recommended. Tork also produces an electronic digital timeclock with a memory and battery back-up. This option is, of course, more expensive but allows a wider scope as far as minimum interval is concerned. The 24 hour clocks are used for the on and off switching of an entire system or to control lights.

### 30 AND 60 MINUTE TIMECLOCKS
These types of timeclocks make one full revolution every hour (Paragon and Tork produce both options). The switching lugs are permanently mounted on their dials. The 60 minute dial allows one switch per minute, whereas the 30 minute version has two switches per minute. With the aid of such clocks, one can program a series of actions to take place and have them repeated for as long as the master (24 hour clock) keeps the system activated. Commercially, there are ready made watering computers available (Irri-Trol).

## THE USE OF LIGHT IN HYDROPONICS

To make up for the lack of photoperiod (daylight) and the lack of light intensity in our climate, it is often necessary to introduce some type of supplemental light source to the hydroponic garden. Traditionally, a combination of fluorescent and incandescent lights have been used. For small hydroponic systems, a number of 40 W fluorescent tubes may suffice, although the spectrum provided by such tubes is not really the type of light required (see Greenhouse Gardening lesson, ARTIFICIAL LIGHT). Many home gardeners practise hydroponics in basements or garages, where no natural light is available. In such cases, fluorescent-incandescent combinations can be used. If the hydroponic system is 10 m² (108 sq ft) or larger, consider the use of H.I.D. (high intensity discharge) lamps. Such lamps are available in two types: mercury halide and sodium. If they are to operate in a structure without natural light, a ratio of 6:4 (60% mercury halide and 40% sodium) should be used. For winter illumination in greenhouses, use only sodium lamps. These units cost approximately $250 each, use 400 W of electricity (3 per 15 amp circuit can be used) and are the most economical light source for horticultural use. The price of such units may seem somewhat prohibitive, but if a bank of fluorescent lights were installed to produce the same intensity, the cost of materials and consumed power would be appreciably more. There are a number of manufacturers supplying such lamps (Sylvania, PL, Philips). All units are of the plug-in type; ballast and starter are an integrated part of the luminaries. The PL type is somewhat superior in design than the other units. They all use the same lamps, but the difference is in the reflectors and suspension systems. Timeclocks can be used to control the period of illumination. If the right combination of lamps are used and the correct intensity obtained, crop production can be as rapid (or better) as under summer conditions. The merging of hydroponics and artificial light is already showing promise for the future. A complete discussion of plant illumination requirements and artificial lighting is contained in the Greenhouse Gardening lesson.

## CONCLUSION

This lesson is intended to provide an introduction to the concept of hydroponics. Certain topics are discussed in more detail than others, however, it is the author's opinion that an excess of information is usually more useful than a shortage. Hopefully, this lesson is of sufficient interest to have you try some of the principles. If not, perhaps you have gained a general insight into how plant growth can be influenced. The literature included in RESOURCE MATERIALS is by no means comprehensive of the topic, but includes some of the most recent and accurate material available.

## SELF CHECK *QUIZ*

1. Do you think that John Woodward's experiment was a true hydroponic application?

2. Which of the three reasons for hydroponic culture (diseases, build-up of salts, or lack of sufficient fresh water) do you think would apply to certain parts of Alberta?

3. a. Calculate the molecular weight of calcium nitrate $Ca(NO_3)_2$.
   Note: Observe that this nitrate indicates that there are two of these nitrate groups in this molecule. Therefore,

there are:
1 - Ca
2 - N
6 - O

b. Assuming that you need 250 ppm of Ca in a solution, how many mg of $Ca(NO_3)_2$ do you need per litre?

c. What is the total ppm concentration, assuming you use water with an EC value of 0.47 mmhos?

d. How large is the ppm concentration of nitrogen in the solution?

airstone - a porous stone through which air is forced and filtered.

bag culture - long plastic bags filled with peat mix and sealed on either end are placed in rows in the greenhouse and small holes cut in the top surface of the bag where the plants are grown

ballast material - heavy material to secure stability.

colloidal dust - particles small enough to stay suspended in water with a high surface area per unit of mass.

diffusion - a force responsible for movement inside the plant.

electrical conductivity (E.C.) - the extent to which water conducts a current. Measured in mhos/cm.

flooded bench system - a growing system consisting of a bench able to hold potted plants and having high sides and a waterproof liner. Nutrients are pumped into the bench from a holding tank and, after a certain period of time, allowed to drain back.

gutter system - a system wherein long plastic gutters placed on a gentle gradient slope have a constant flow of nutrient solution running through them.

inert - without active chemical or other properties.

leach - percolate through some material.

nutrient film techniques (NFT) - a growing system that uses a black plastic film folded in such a manner as to form a closed gutter in which holes are cut to accommodate plants.

osmosis - the ability of water to move through a semipermeable membrane from a relatively weak solution to a stronger and, as a consequence, diluting this strong solution.

osmotic potential - during osmosis, the speed and force of the water penetrating the membrane.

reverse osmosis - water moves from a high salt concentration, with the aid of pumps, to a state of purity on the other side of the membrane.

solenoid valve - a valve that can be electrically opened and closed.

subarization - formation of cork.

substrate - nutrient medium for bacteria culture.

## SELF-CHECK *ANSWERS*

1. No, the soil he used was not an inert medium (see HISTORICAL BACKGROUND, page 1601).

2. High salt concentration is a problem in many parts of Alberta. Also, major rivers are becoming polluted (see WHY HYDROPONICS, page 1601).

3. a. From Table 16-1
   Ca = 40.08
   N = 14.01
   O = 16.00
   1xCa = 40.08
   2xN = 28.02
   6xO = 96.00
   $Ca(NO_3)_2$ = 164.10

   b. 250 divided by 40.08 = 6.24. Thus you used 6.24 x 164.1 = 1024 mg/L $Ca(NO_3)_2$

   c. 6.24 x 164.1 = 1024 ppm
   EC value 0.47 mmhos = 300 ppm for a total value of 1324 ppm.

   d. There is 28.02 mg of N/L (28 ppm). However, 6.24 times the original molecular weight is needed. Therefore, you will also have 6.24 x 28.02 = 174.8 ppm of nitrogen/L (see PLANT NUTRITION HYDROPONICS, page 1605 and Table 16-1, page 1606).

Beardsley, P.C., Jones, Rev. L. *Home Hydroponics and How To Do It!* Ward Ritchie Press, Pasadena, California, 1977.

Bridwell, R. *Hydroponic Gardening.* Woodbridge Press Publ. Co., 1974.

Dickerman, Collins A. *Discovering Hydroponic Gardening.* Woodbridge Press Publ. Co., 1975.

Cooper, Dr. Alan. *The A.B.C. of N.F.T.* Grower Books, London, Reprinted 1985.
(the best available on this subject)

*Commercial Commercial Application of N.F.T.* 1982. Grower Books, London
(very good)

Douglas, James Sholto. *Advanced Guide to Hydroponics.* Pelham Books, London, England, 1976.
(excellent book for the advanced hobbyist)

Douglas, James Sholto.
*Beginners Guide to Hydroponics.* General Publishing Co. Ltd., Don Mills, Ontario, 1976.
(recommended)

*Grower Guide #15 - Cucumbers.* Grower Books, London
(very good)

*Grower Guide #21 - Lettuce Under Glass.* Grower Books, London
(very good)

Harris, D. *Hydroponics - Growing Plants Without Soil!* Coles Publishing Co. Ltd., Toronto, 1975.
(handy book, recommended)

Nicholls, R.E. *Beginning Hydroponics.* Running Press, Philadelphia, 1977.

Penningsfield, F. & Kurzmann, P. *Hydrokultuk und Torfkultur (German)* Verlag. Eugen Ulmer, Stuttgart, Germany 1966.
(in German; very good, professional book)

Resh, Howard M. *Hydroponic Food Production.* 384 pages. Woodbridge Press Publ. Co. 3rd Ed. 1985.
(good book for advanced hobbyist and commercial grower).

State of the Art in Soilless Crop Production. *Hydroponics Worldwide.* Editor: A.J. Savage
F.A. & International Centre for Spec. Studies
Honolulu, Hawaii, 1985.
(advanced literature)

Schwartz, Meier. *Guide to Commercial Hydroponics*
Israel University Press, New York, 1968
(classical, professional literature)

Alberta Agriculture. *Reverse Osmosis.* 1979. Agdex 716 (036).
Alberta Agriculture. *Exchanging Filter Media* 1979. Agdex 716 (D40)

Alberta Agriculture. *Bacterial Analysis of Farm Water Supplies.* 1979. Agdex 716 (D03).
Alberta Agriculture. *Chemical Analysis of Farm Water Supplies.* 1979. Agdex 716 (004).
Alberta Agriculture. *Alternatives for Iron Removal.* 1979. Agdex 716 (011).
Alberta Agriculture. *Choosing a Water Pump.* 1980. Agdex 716 (C10).
Alberta Agriculture. *Chemical Injection in Irrigation Systems.* 1979. - Agdex 753-2 Sept. 1979.
Alberta Agriculture. *Dissolved Gases in Wellwater.* 1980. Agdex 716 (D18).
Alberta Agriculture. *Diagnosis and Prevention of Salinity in Commercial Greenhouse Soils.* 1981. Agdex 518-7.
Alberta Agriculture. *High Salt Content in Garden Soil.* 1980. Agdex 518-6.
Alberta Agriculture. *Shock Chlorination and Control of Iron Bacteria.* 1983. Agdex 716 (D12).
Alberta Agriculture. *Iron Deficiency in Plants.* 1979. Agdex 532.
Alberta Agriculture. *Micronutrient Requirements of Crops in Alta.* 1983. Agdex 531-1.
Alberta Agriculture. *Soilless Culture of Commercial Greenhouse Tomatoes.* Revised 1978. Agriculture Canada - Publication 1460
(good, commercial publication)

AHRC (pamphlet) *Hydroponics: A Guide to Soilless Culture Systems.* 82-19.

## INDEX